CODE OF ALABAMA

1975

———

With Provision for Subsequent Pocket Parts

———

Prepared Under the Supervision of

The Code Revision Subcommittee of
The Legislative Council

Robert H. Harris, Chairman

by

The Editorial Staff of the Publisher

Under the Direction of

D. P. Harriman, S. C. Willard, W. L. Jackson
and S. S. West

———

VOLUME 22

1982 Replacement Volume

———

*Including Acts of the 1982 Regular Session and 1982 First Extra
Session and annotations taken through Southern Reporter,
Second Series, Volume 410, Page 1336*

———

THE MICHIE COMPANY
Law Publishers
Charlottesville, Virginia
1982

Table of Titles

TABLE OF TITLES

In Addition, This Publication Contains

Table of Contents

VOLUME 22

Title 41.

State Government.

Title 42.

United States.

Title 43.

Wills and Decedents' Estates.

Title 44.

Youth Services.

TITLE 41.

STATE GOVERNMENT.

CHAPTER 1.

GENERAL PROVISIONS.

Cross references. — As to state symbols and honors generally, see § 1-2-1 et seq. As to fiscal year of the state, see § 1-3-4. As to state aeronautics department, see § 4-2-30 et seq. As to state banking department generally, see § 5-2-1 et seq. As to establishment or

1

restoration of lost, mislaid, destroyed or mutilated records of the state or of any department, agency or instrumentality thereof, see § 12-20-50. As to state department of education, see § 16-2-1 et seq. As to department of adult blind and deaf at Alabama Institute for Deaf and Blind, see § 21-1-15. As to department of mental health, see § 22-50-2 et seq. As to highway department, see § 23-1-20 et seq. As to department of industrial relations, see § 25-2-1 et seq. As to department of labor, see § 25-3-1 et seq. As to department of insurance, see § 27-2-1 et seq. As to state department of veterans' affairs, see § 31-5-1 et seq. As to state civil defense agency, see § 31-9-4. As to department of public safety, see § 32-2-1 et seq. As to state docks department, see § 33-1-2. As to conveyances, etc., of real estate by governor or state agencies or institutions, see § 35-4-380 et seq. As to public officers and employees generally, see § 36-1-1 et seq. As to state personnel department, see § 36-26-4. As to state department of pensions and security, see § 38-2-1. As to department of revenue, see § 40-2-1 et seq. As to cession of land to United States by state of Alabama, see § 42-3-1 et seq. As to department of youth services, see § 44-1-20 et seq.

§ 41-1-1. Sovereignty and jurisdiction of state.

The sovereignty and jurisdiction of the state extend to all places within the boundaries thereof, but the extent of such jurisdiction over places that have been or may be ceded to the United States is qualified by the terms of such cession. (Code 1852, § 18; Code 1867, § 19; Code 1876, § 15; Code 1886, § 15; Code 1896, § 3749; Code 1907, § 2056; Code 1923, § 2993; Code 1940, T. 55, § 10.)

Cited in State v. Blair, 238 Ala. 377, 191 So. 237 (1939).
Collateral references. — 81 C.J.S., States, §§ 2-5.

72 Am. Jur. 2d, States, Territories & Dependencies, § 18.

§ 41-1-2. Maintenance and defense of state authority and jurisdiction.

It is the duty of the governor and of all the subordinate officers of the state to maintain and defend its authority and jurisdiction. (Code 1852, § 19; Code 1867, § 20; Code 1876, § 16; Code 1886, § 16; Code 1896, § 3750; Code 1907, § 2057; Code 1923, § 2994; Code 1940, T. 55, § 11.)

§ 41-1-3. Compromise of claims in favor of state.

The governor, attorney general and auditor have authority to adjust, compromise and settle, on such terms as to them may seem just and reasonable, any doubtful claim of the state against any person or corporation, or any public officer, or his sureties, or because of the negligence or default in the safekeeping, collection or disbursement of the public moneys, funds or property by any officer having charge or custody of either. Such settlement or compromise being made, the governor must file a statement thereof in the office of the treasurer, showing the nature and character of the claim, the terms of the settlement or compromise and the reasons for the making thereof. (Code 1886, §§ 70, 71; Code 1896, §§ 3753, 3754; Code 1907, §§ 2441, 2442; Code 1923, §§ 5645, 5646; Code 1940, T. 55, §§ 12, 13.)

Constitution. — For constitutional provisions authorizing legislature to provide for compromise of doubtful claims, see Const., § 100.

Cross references. — As to immunity of state from tort liability for acts done in construction, operation, etc., of airports and other air navigation facilities, see § 4-2-4. As to duty of state department of education to purchase and furnish textbooks to schools operated by the above institutions, see § 16-36-25.

History of section. — See Opinion of Justices, 251 Ala. 96, 36 So. 2d 480 (1948).

Board of compromise is administrative body with quasi-judicial powers. It is obviously a board of special and limited jurisdiction, and therefore its records must affirmatively show every fact which is necessary to confer jurisdiction. State v. Brooks, 255 Ala. 689, 53 So. 2d 329 (1951).

Adoption of Constitution 1901, § 100 had effect of amending this section and must be read into it. It should be considered as dealing with "doubtful claims" only. Opinion of Justices, 251 Ala. 96, 36 So. 2d 480 (1948).

Section provides for settlement of state claims only. It makes no provision for the settlement or compromise of claims of any political subdivision of the state. Opinion of Justices, 251 Ala. 96, 36 So. 2d 480 (1948).

"Claims" referred to in section necessarily mean claims for debts or money demands owing or claimed by the state, and not to controversies such as whether or not a corporation is a foreign or domestic one, notwithstanding this fact may have some bearing upon the amount of the claim. Atlantic Coast Line Ry. v. State, 204 Ala. 80, 85 So. 424 (1920).

Section includes claims arising under revenue laws. State v. Brooks, 255 Ala. 689, 53 So. 2d 329 (1951).

Final tax assessment made by the department of revenue against a solvent taxpayer, after legal and proper notice to the taxpayer, which tax is authorized by statute to be assessed by the department of revenue, no appeal having been taken to the circuit court from such final assessment, is not a doubtful claim within the purview of Constitution 1901, § 100 and cannot be released, diminished or compromised. Opinion of Justices, 251 Ala. 96, 36 So. 2d 480 (1948). See also State v. Brooks, 255 Ala. 689, 53 So. 2d 329 (1951).

A final assessment cannot be compromised or settled for an amount less than that as finally fixed, by reason of the inhibition of Constitution 1901, § 100, unless the claim is doubtful of collection and then only by authority of the board of compromise. State ex rel. Carmichael v. Jones, 252 Ala. 479, 41 So. 2d 280 (1949).

The board of compromise has the authority to compromise a final tax assessment against an insolvent taxpayer where the assessment thereof is doubtful of collection. Opinion of Justices, 251 Ala. 96, 36 So. 2d 480 (1948).

Board of compromise would not have authority to compromise a final tax assessment if the taxpayer is insolvent but has assets subject to the tax lien sufficient to discharge it. Its collection could not be doubtful. Opinion of Justices, 251 Ala. 96, 36 So. 2d 480 (1948).

If there is doubt as to collectibility by reason of the financial condition of the taxpayer or his lack of assets sufficient to discharge the lien of the state, the claim can be compromised; but if the doubt lies in the ability of the state to establish its claim because of meritorious defenses which the taxpayer may have against the claim, then the claim cannot be compromised, released or diminished. State v. Brooks, 255 Ala. 689, 53 So. 2d 329 (1951).

Cited in State v. Overby, 265 Ala. 39, 89 So. 2d 525 (1956).

Collateral references. — 81 C.J.S., States, § 211.

§ 41-1-4. When bonds of state payable.

Any bonds which may be issued by the governor of Alabama for the purpose of renewing or funding the bonded debt of this state shall be made payable and subject to redemption at any time not exceeding 50 years from the date of issue of said bonds. (Code 1907, § 82; Code 1923, § 84; Code 1940, T. 55, § 14.)

Collateral references. — 81 C.J.S., States, §§ 182, 189.

§ 41-1-5. Nepotism in state service prohibited.

No officer or employee of the state or of any state department, board, bureau, committee, commission, institution, corporation, authority or other agency of the state shall appoint any person related to him within the fourth degree of affinity or consanguinity to any job, position or office of profit with the state or with any of its agencies. Any person related to the appointing authority within the prohibited degree shall be ineligible to serve in any capacity with the state under authority of such an appointment, and any appointment so attempted shall be void. Whoever violates this section is guilty of a misdemeanor and shall be punished by a fine not to exceed $500.00 or by imprisonment not to exceed one year, or both. This section shall not apply, however, in the case of an appointment of a person to a position in the classified service of the state made from the register of persons eligible\ as certified by the state director of personnel.

The provisions of this section shall not apply to any individual or individuals employed as of September 16, 1963, in any branch, department or bureau of the state or the reappointment of any individuals employed on September 16, 1963. (Acts 1963, No. 588, p. 1285.)

Intent of section is to prohibit the appointment or employment by the appointing authority of persons related to him who will serve in subordinate jobs, positions or offices of profit in the state government. Opinion of Justices, 291 Ala. 581, 285 So. 2d 87 (1973).

It does not apply to gubernatorial appointment of circuit judge, and if the proposed appointee meets the constitutional qualifications for that office, he may be appointed to it. Opinion of Justices, 291 Ala. 581, 285 So. 2d 87 (1973).

Because a circuit judge is a member of the judicial branch of the government, which is separate and equal from other branches, he is not subordinate to the executive or the legislative, and hence, this section is inapplicable. Opinion of Justices, 291 Ala. 581, 285 So. 2d 87 (1973).

Collateral references. — 66 C.J.S., Nepotism, p. 6.

Validity, construction, and effect of state constitutional or statutory provision regarding nepotism in the public service. 11 ALR4th 826.

§ 41-1-6. Inventory of nonconsumable personal property by departments and agencies.

The property manager of each department or agency of the state shall, every six months, make a full and complete inventory of all nonconsumable personal property, except books, of the value of $100.00 or more hereafter acquired or used by said department or agency. (Acts 1973, No. 1283, p. 2196.)

CHAPTER 2.

BOUNDARIES OF STATE.

Constitution. — For constitutional provisions as to boundaries of state, see Const., § 37.

Collateral references. — 81 C.J.S., States, §§ 14, 18.

72 Am. Jur. 2d, States, Territories & Dependencies, §§ 24-34.

§ 41-2-1. General description.

The boundaries of this state are established and declared to be as follows: Beginning at the point where the thirty-first degree of north latitude crosses the Perdido river; thence east to the western boundary line of the state of Georgia; thence along said line, to the southern boundary line of the state of Tennessee; thence west along the southern boundary line of the state of Tennessee, crossing the Tennessee river, and on to the second intersection of said river by said line; thence up said river to the mouth of Big Bear creek; thence by a direct line to the northwest corner of Washington county, in this state, as originally formed; thence southerly along the line of the state of Mississippi to the Gulf of Mexico; thence eastwardly, including all islands within six leagues of the shore, to the Perdido river; and thence up the said river to the beginning. (Code 1852, § 15; Code 1867, § 16; Code 1876, § 12; Code 1886, § 12; Code 1896, § 623; Code 1907, § 83; Code 1923, § 85; Code 1940, T. 55, § 16.)

Cited in Bosarge v. State, 23 Ala. App. 18, 121 So. 427 (1928).

§ 41-2-2. Boundary between Alabama and Georgia.

The boundary line between Alabama and Georgia commences on the west side of the Chattahoochee river, at the point where it enters the state of Florida; from thence up the river, along the western bank thereof, to the point on Miller's Bend, next above the place where the Uchee creek empties into such river; thence in a direct line to the Nickajack. (Code 1852, § 16; Code 1867, § 17; Code 1876, § 13; Code 1886, § 13; Code 1896, § 624; Code 1907, § 84; Code 1923, § 86; Code 1940, T. 55, § 17.)

§ 41-2-3. Boundary between Alabama and Florida — Generally.

The boundary line between Alabama and Florida is the line commonly known as the "mound line," or "Ellicott's line," as distinguished from a blazed line known as the "upper" or "Coffee line," commencing at a point on the Chattahoochee river, near a place known as "Irwin's Mills"; and from thence to the Perdido river, marked the whole distance by blazes on the trees and by mounds of earth, at distances of about one mile. (Code 1852, § 17; Code 1867, § 18; Code 1876, § 14; Code 1886, § 14; Code 1896, § 625; Code 1907, § 85; Code 1923, § 87; Code 1940, T. 55, § 18.)

§ 41-2-4. Same — Precise location at mouth of Perdido river and adjacent thereto.

(a) The state of Alabama hereby ratifies, confirms and adopts the recommendations of the joint committee heretofore appointed by the governor of Florida and the governor of Alabama to locate and mark the boundary line between the said states at the mouth of the Perdido river and adjacent thereto. Said committee consists of Honorable Richard W. Ervin, Honorable Richard H. Simpson, Honorable Philip D. Beall and Honorable F. C. Elliot, all on the part of the state of Florida, and Honorable Earl M. McGowin, Honorable W. C. Pruett and Honorable William N. McQueen, all on the part of the state of Alabama.

(b) In accordance with the recommendations of the said joint committee, the boundary at the location referred to in subsection (a) of this section shall be as follows:

(1) The middle of the Perdido river at its mouth, as defined by the constitutions of the states of Alabama and Florida, is at latitude 30° 16′ 53″ north and longitude 87° 31′ 06″ west as the control point;

(2) That the boundary line at the mouth of Perdido river is fixed, as nearly as may be, in the axis of the mouth of said river, passing through the control point and running north and south and having as its northern terminus a point of latitude 30° 17′ 02″ north and longitude 87° 31′ 06″ west, and as its southern terminus a point 1,000 feet due south of the control point;

(3) That from the northern terminus of the boundary line at the mouth of the river, the boundary up the lower portion of said river be a straight line to a point at latitude 30° 18′ 00″ north, longitude 87° 27′ 08″ west, thence by a straight line to a point in the center line of the Intracoastal Canal at longitude 87° 27′ 00″ west;

(4) That the seaward boundary between Florida and Alabama extends from the south end of the boundary line at the mouth of Perdido river, thence south 0° 01′ 00″ west to the seaward limit of each respective state;

(5) And shall be deemed, taken and declared, and is hereby deemed, taken and declared, to be the boundary line between the states of Florida and Alabama, at the mouth of the Perdido river and adjacent thereto, and shall be deemed and taken as such by the authorities and people of this state.

(c) Nothing contained in this section, nor any operations of the provisions of this section, shall prejudice the rights or claims of private individuals to any of the lands herein involved. (Acts 1953, No. 440, p. 547, §§ 1, 2, 5.)

Code commissioner's note. — Following ratification by the state of Florida, the governor of Alabama, by proclamation dated September 23, 1953, declared the boundary described in subsection (b) of this section to be the true and only boundary between Alabama and Florida at the mouth of the Perdido river and adjacent thereto. (Book 1, page 3, on file in office of secretary of state.)

CHAPTER 3.

ABORIGINAL MOUNDS, EARTHWORKS AND OTHER ANTIQUITIES.

§ 41-3-1. Reservation of exclusive right and privilege of state to explore, excavate or survey aboriginal mounds, earthworks, burial sites, etc.; state ownership of objects found or located therein declared.

The state of Alabama reserves to itself the exclusive right and privilege of exploring, excavating or surveying, through its authorized officers, agents or employees, all aboriginal mounds and other antiquities, earthworks, ancient or historical forts and burial sites within the state of Alabama, subject to the rights of the owner of the land upon which such antiquities are situated, for agricultural, domestic or industrial purposes, and the ownership of the state is hereby expressly declared in any and all objects whatsoever which may be found or located therein. (Acts 1915, No. 669, p. 728; Code 1923, § 1418; Code 1940, T. 55, § 272.)

§ 41-3-2. Nonresidents not to explore or excavate remains or carry away, etc., from state objects discovered therein, etc.

No person not a resident of the state of Alabama, either by himself personally or through any agent or employee or anyone else acting for such person, shall explore or excavate any of the remains described in section 41-3-1 or carry or send away from the state any objects which may be discovered therein or which may be taken therefrom or found in the vicinity thereof. (Acts 1915, No. 669, p. 728; Code 1923, § 1419; Code 1940, T. 55, § 273.)

§ 41-3-3. Explorations or excavations of remains not to be done without consent of owner of land and not to injure crops, houses, etc., thereon.

No explorations or excavations shall be made in any of such remains without the consent of the owner of the land first had and obtained and unless such work is done in such way as not to injure any crops, houses or improvements on the land adjacent to or forming a part of such remains. (Acts 1915, No. 669, p. 728; Code 1923, § 1420; Code 1940, T. 55, § 274.)

§ 41-3-4. Explorations or excavations not to destroy, deface, etc., remains; restoration of remains after explorations or excavations.

No explorations or excavations shall be made which will destroy, deface or permanently injure such remains; and, after any such explorations or excavations, they shall be restored to the same or like condition as before such explorations or excavations were made. (Acts 1915, No. 669, p. 728; Code 1923, § 1421; Code 1940, T. 55, § 275.)

§ 41-3-5. Disposition of objects taken from remains.

No objects taken from such remains shall be sold or disposed of out of the state, but when removed therefrom the objects so gathered shall be retained in state custody and either placed in the collection of the department of archives and history or in the museums or in the libraries of the educational or other institutions of the state or they may be exchanged for similar or other objects from other states, museums, libraries or individuals. (Acts 1915, No. 669, p. 728; Code 1923, § 1422; Code 1940, T. 55, § 276.)

§ 41-3-6. Exploration or excavation of aboriginal mounds, earthworks, etc., contrary to law.

Any person who shall explore or excavate any of the aboriginal mounds, earthworks or other antiquities of this state contrary to the laws of this state shall be guilty of a misdemeanor and, upon conviction, shall be fined not more than $1,000.00 for each offense. (Acts 1915, No. 669, p. 728; Code 1923, § 4453; Code 1940, T. 55, § 277; Acts 1980, No. 80-777, p. 1612.)

CHAPTER 4.

DEPARTMENT OF FINANCE.

ARTICLE 1.

GENERAL PROVISIONS.

Cross references. — As to state treasurer, see § 36-17-1 et seq. As to department of revenue, see § 40-2-1 et seq.

Collateral references. — 81 C.J.S., States, §§ 154-167.

§ 41-4-1. Definitions.

The words "state and the departments, boards, bureaus, commissions, agencies, offices and institutions thereof," and the words "departments, boards, bureaus, commissions, agencies, offices and institutions of the state," wherever they appear in this chapter, shall not be construed to include counties, municipal corporations, political subdivisions, county and city boards of education, district boards of education of independent school districts and other local public bodies. (Acts 1939, No. 112, p. 144; Code 1940, T. 55, § 60.)

§ 41-4-2. General purpose of department; seal.

There shall be a department of finance, which shall be an executive and administrative department and which shall have general supervision of all matters pertaining to the finances of the state and the departments, boards, bureaus, commissions, agencies, offices and institutions thereof and, to the extent herein indicated, over the finances of the counties, municipal corporations, political subdivisions and local public bodies in the state, and to furnish the physical facilities, equipment and supplies and, to the extent herein indicated, the personnel, for the operation of the state and such departments, boards, bureaus, commissions, agencies, offices and institutions thereof. The department of finance shall have a seal, which shall be affixed to official acts. (Acts 1939, No. 112, p. 144; Code 1940, T. 55, § 61.)

§ 41-4-3. Duties of department generally.

It shall be the duty of the department of finance:

(1) To manage, supervise and control all matters pertaining to the fiscal affairs and fiscal procedure of the state, except such as may, by the Constitution or statute, be specifically required to be performed by the auditor, the treasurer or the department of revenue, and to keep all records, accounts and data relating thereto.

(2) To manage, supervise and control the insurance of all state property, wherever located.

(3) To operate, manage and administer the state insurance fund.

(4) To make the annual financial report of the state, as soon as possible after the close of each fiscal year, in accordance with approved public accounting practice, and in such form and such detail as may be necessary to present an accurate description of the financial condition of the state during the preceding fiscal year. The reports of the auditor and the treasurer shall be bound with, and printed as a part of, such report.

(5) To conduct such studies, to secure such information and data, to make such reports and to furnish such information as may be required by the governor or the legislature. (Acts 1939, No. 112, p. 144; Code 1940, T. 55, § 62.)

Cross references. — As to duty of department to maintain White House of the Confederacy, see § 41-12-2. As to duty of department to administer state insurance fund, see § 41-15-2. As to purchase, maintenance, etc., of state-owned vehicles, see § 41-17-1 et seq.

Department of finance succeeded to powers and authority of former public works board of Alabama. Landstreet v. City of Fort Payne, 238 Ala. 212, 190 So. 420 (1939); Alabama Power Co. v. City of Scottsboro, 238 Ala. 230, 190 So. 412 (1939).

§ 41-4-4. Certain appropriations to be expended by department.

All appropriations heretofore or hereafter made for the purchase, acquisition or use of furniture, fixtures, supplies, materials, equipment or other personal property, appropriations for printing and binding and the distribution of printed matter, appropriations for the maintenance, repair, improvement, lighting, heating and cleaning of the state Capitol and other property owned or leased by the state in the city of Montgomery, and appropriations for postage and telephone expenses for any department, board, bureau, commission, agency or office of the state located and operating in the city of Montgomery shall be used for the purpose and, if so made, for the department, board, bureau, commission, agency, office or institution for which made. Such appropriations shall be expended by and on the order of the department of finance for such purposes. (Acts 1939, No. 112, p. 144; Code 1940, T. 55, § 63.)

§ 41-4-5. Appointment of employees; officers and employees subject to merit system.

The director of finance shall, subject to the provisions of the merit system, have the right to appoint any employee in the department. All employees and officers of the department of finance, including the chiefs of divisions, shall be subject to the merit system. (Acts 1939, No. 112, p. 144; Code 1940, T. 55, § 72.)

§ 41-4-6. Oath of office and full-time service of officers and chiefs of divisions.

Before entering upon the discharge of their duties, the comptroller, the budget officer, the purchasing agent, the chief of the division of service, the chief of the division of local finance and the chief of any other division established by the director of finance shall take the constitutional oath of office. Each of such officers shall devote his full time to his official duties and shall hold no other lucrative position while serving as such. (Acts 1939, No. 112, p. 144; Code 1940, T. 55, § 71.)

Cited in Alabama Elec. Coop. v. Alabama Power Co., 251 Ala. 190, 36 So. 2d 523 (1948).

§ 41-4-7. Bonds of comptroller, purchasing agent, chiefs of divisions of department, etc.

Before entering upon the duties of their respective offices, the comptroller, the purchasing agent, the chief of the division of service, the chief of the division of finance, the chief of any other division established by the director of finance and such other officers or employees of the department of finance as are permitted to handle any money or to draw any warrants shall execute to the state of Alabama a bond, to be approved by the governor, in amounts to be fixed by the director of finance, but, in the case of any officer or employee authorized to draw any warrants upon the treasurer, not less than $25,000.00, for the faithful performance of their duties. (Acts 1943, No. 122, p. 123; Acts 1961, Ex. Sess., No. 208, p. 2190.)

§ 41-4-8. Powers and duties of department as to educational and eleemosynary institutions.

(a) With respect to all state educational or eleemosynary institutions which are governed by a board of trustees or other similar governing body, the department of finance shall have the following powers and duties only:

(1) To make all budget allotments to such institutions.

(2) To require the furnishing of all information concerning such institutions insofar as necessary in the preparation of the general revenue bill.

(3) To maintain perpetual inventories of all furniture, fixtures, supplies, materials, equipment and other similar personal property on hand, or as may have been or as may be assigned to such institutions, and to make such periodic examinations of such property as may be necessary.

(4) To examine and audit, as provided by law, the records and accounts of all such institutions.

(5) To perform all functions and duties prescribed in sections 41-4-36, 41-4-50 and 41-4-80 insofar as the provisions thereof are applicable to such institutions.

(6) To perform, unless otherwise provided by law, all the functions provided in division 1 of article 5 of this chapter with respect to purchases, contracts and leases for the use of, or acquisition for, such institutions of any personal property, with the exception of mortgages, bonds, choses in action or any other forms of personal property purchased for investment, resale or exchange, or perishable goods, or medical or surgical equipment and supplies.

(7) To maintain records as to prices and sources of supply of such personal property.

(b) None of the provisions of this chapter shall apply to any purchase of $50.00 or less, made by any such institutions. (Acts 1939, No. 112, p. 144; Code 1940, T. 55, § 73.)

Cross references. — As to competitive bidding on certain contracts of educational institutions, see § 41-16-50 et seq.

§ 41-4-9. Grants received from the federal government.

Nothing in this chapter shall be deemed to authorize or require the allotment, handling or expenditure of any moneys received as grants from the federal department of health, education and welfare or any other agency of the federal government, or the use or disposition of any properties purchased therewith, in a manner contrary to any condition or limitation attached to any such grant. (Acts 1939, No. 112, p. 144; Code 1940, T. 55, § 74.)

§ 41-4-10. Use of funds in sinking fund — Purchase and holding in trust of state bonds.

With the consent of the governor, the funds in the sinking fund for retiring old bonded debt may be used from time to time by the department of finance for the purpose of purchasing and holding in trust in said fund bonds of the state of Alabama. It shall be the duty of the department of finance to see that the funds coming into any sinking fund are applied in satisfaction of the bonds against which said sinking fund was created. (Acts 1935, No. 311, p. 743; Acts 1939, No. 112, p. 144; Code 1940, T. 55, § 75.)

Cited in Keller v. State Board of Educ., 236 Ala. 400, 183 So. 268 (1938).

Collateral references. — 81 C.J.S., States, § 188.

§ 41-4-11. Same — Sale of bonds; reinvestment of funds; cancellation of paid bonds.

With the consent of the governor, said bonds so purchased and held in trust may be sold from time to time by the department of finance, if it is deemed for the best interest of the sinking fund that said transactions be had, and the proceeds held or reinvested from time to time, provided always said fund be kept intact and be used at the maturity of the said bonds for the retirement of the same. Bonds in said sinking fund on maturity dates shall be cancelled and destroyed as other bond obligations of the state are handled when paid at maturity. (Acts 1935, No. 311, p. 743; Acts 1939, No. 112, p. 144; Code 1940, T. 55, § 76.)

Cited in Keller v. State Board of Educ., 236 Ala. 400, 183 So. 268 (1938).

Collateral references. — 81 C.J.S., States, § 184.

64 Am. Jur. 2d, Public Securities & Obligations, § 218 et seq.

Right of purchaser of stolen bonds. 1 ALR 717, 85 ALR 357, 102 ALR 28.

Assignment and transfer of state bond. 22 ALR 775.

Statutes in relation to the issuance of duplicate or mutilated, lost, or destroyed bonds. 39 ALR 1246, 63 ALR 388.

Power of state to issue bonds for relief of distress due to unemployment or other unusual conditions. 73 ALR 699, 87 ALR 371.

Sale of state bonds at less than par or face value. 91 ALR 7, 162 ALR 396.

Constitutionality of statutory plan for financing, or refinancing bonds of smaller political units by larger political units. 106 ALR 608.

Undelivered bonds, authorized prior to adoption or effective date of constitutional or statutory provision limiting state indebtedness or taxation or regulating issuance of bonds, as affected by such provision. 109 ALR 961.

Revenue bonds or other bonds or instruments creating indebtedness as within constitutional or statutory requirement of prior approval by electors of issuance of bonds by state. 146 ALR 604.

Validity of bond issue in excess of amount permitted by law, within authorized debt, tax, or voted limit. 175 ALR 823.

§ 41-4-12. Same — Purchase of state bonds in lieu of use of sinking fund; cancellation and destruction of bonds purchased.

Instead of, or in lieu of, using sinking funds, as is provided for in this article, the director of finance, by and with the advice and consent of the governor, may purchase, upon the best terms obtainable, state bonds or obligations for the payment of which the sinking fund was created, and when such bonds or obligations are so purchased they may be cancelled and retired by the treasurer, with the advice and consent of the governor, but no bond or obligation so purchased shall be cancelled or destroyed unless it was purchased by and with the sinking funds which were created for the ultimate payment of such bond or obligation so purchased and cancelled. Such bonds or obligations, when so cancelled and retired, shall be cancelled and destroyed by the treasurer in the presence of the governor and the attorney general, and entry thereof shall be made on the books of the treasurer as to the number, amount, character and denomination of the bonds or obligations so cancelled and destroyed, and the treasurer, governor and attorney general shall certify to the correctness of the entries so made upon the books of the treasurer. (Acts 1923, No. 436, p. 585; Code 1923, § 846; Acts 1939, No. 112, p. 144; Code 1940, T. 55, § 77.)

Collateral references. — 64 Am. Jur. 2d, Public Securities & Obligations, § 250 et seq.

Funding or refunding obligations as subject to conditions respecting approval by voters. 97 ALR 442.

Mandatory or permissive character of legislation in relation to payment of state bond. 103 ALR 813.

Calling of state bonds in advance of maturity. 109 ALR 988.

Power of state to issue bonds as implying power to refund them. 1 ALR2d 134.

§ 41-4-13. Same — Deposit of funds in savings banks.

If any state sinking funds or any part thereof cannot be invested profitably in any of the other modes provided for in this article, the director of finance, by and with the advice and consent of the governor, may direct the treasurer to deposit any sinking fund or part thereof in a reputable and solvent savings bank on the best terms obtainable. (Acts 1923, No. 436, p. 585; Code 1923, § 847; Acts 1939, No. 112, p. 144; Code 1940, T. 55, § 78.)

§ 41-4-14. Same — Books to be kept showing full entries as to sinking fund.

The director of finance shall keep a separate book in which separate and full entries shall be made as to all deposits of sinking funds, which entries shall show with what bank deposited, or from whom bonds or other obligations are purchased and the terms of the deposit or the purchase. In the event any sinking fund is used for the purchase of any interest-bearing bonds or other obligations of the state, the book entries shall show the amount of the funds so used and from whom the bonds or obligations were purchased. In the event any sinking fund or part thereof is used for the purchase of any bond or obligation under section 41-4-12, for which the particular sinking fund so used was intended and created, which is authorized to be cancelled and retired when so purchased, the book entries shall show the particular fund so used, the amount thereof and the time, character and denomination of the bond, coupon or other obligation so purchased, which is authorized to be cancelled, destroyed and retired, together with the necessary and proper entry as is hereinbefore provided, showing when such bonds, coupons or obligations were cancelled, destroyed or retired. (Acts 1923, No. 436, p. 585; Code 1923, § 848; Acts 1939, No. 112, p. 144; Code 1940, T. 55, § 79.)

§ 41-4-15. Same — Sinking fund not to be diverted from its object.

This article is not intended and shall not be executed, enforced or construed so as to allow any diversion or conversion of any particular sinking funds, or part thereof, from the object and purpose for which such particular fund or part thereof was created, but they shall be executed and enforced so as to enhance and increase the value of all sinking funds and to apply each particular fund and the increased value or interest accruing therefrom to the prompt and faithful payment of the particular indebtedness or obligation for which the fund was created, and no sinking funds or any part thereof shall be devoted to any other use or purpose than that for which it was created and provided. (Acts 1923, No. 436, p. 585; Code 1923, § 849; Acts 1939, No. 112, p. 144; Code 1940, T. 55, § 80.)

Collateral references. — 81 C.J.S., States, § 188.

§ 41-4-16. Consent of department prerequisite to issuance of securities by state commissions, authorities, etc.; exception as to municipalities.

No bonds or other evidences of indebtedness of any commission or authority created to construct or reconstruct highway bridges, approaches and appurtenances thereto, any housing authority, any state rural electrification authority, any electric membership corporation, any power district or any improvement authority shall be issued or sold until the consent to the issuance and sale thereof shall have been given by the department of finance, to be evidenced by the written approval of the director of finance. Such consent shall be granted only after a public hearing and after a petition requesting such consent has been duly filed by the corporation, authority, district, commission or other body seeking such consent with the department more than five days before such public hearing. Such petition shall specify the plan or program of the body seeking such consent and the uses to which it is proposed to put the proceeds of such issue and such other matters as are necessary to fully advise such department of the nature of the proposed project, and said petition shall include such other information as may be required by the rules of the department. The department of finance shall grant such consent only after it finds that such issue or sale serves some public need and is in the public interest. It shall be unlawful for the body seeking such consent or anyone to use the proceeds of any such issue or sale contrary to the plan and purposes presented to the department in obtaining its consent thereto. The provisions of this section shall not apply to any bonds or other evidence of indebtedness issued by any municipality, or any agencies, bureaus or commissions thereof. (Acts 1935, No. 65, p. 151; Code 1940, T. 55, § 155; Acts 1951, No. 191, p. 454.)

Intervention by electric power companies. — Electric power companies had the right to intervene and be heard in a proceeding before the director of finance involving a petition brought by an electric cooperative seeking consent of the finance department for the issuance of bonds to construct a generating plant and transmission lines. Alabama Elec. Coop. v. Alabama Power Co., 278 Ala. 123, 176 So. 2d 483 (1964).

Evidence sustaining bond issue. — See Alabama Elec. Coop. v. Alabama Power Co., 278 Ala. 123, 176 So. 2d 483 (1964).

§ 41-4-17. Rent charged for use of state buildings in Capitol complex; fund for operation, maintenance, etc.

(a) The department of finance shall charge reasonable rent for the use and occupancy of any building owned by the state, with the exception of the state Capitol building, located in the Capitol complex and maintained by the department of finance or any other building maintained by the department of finance now or in the future. The director of finance shall establish such rent at rates which shall not be more than an amount sufficient to pay the reasonable costs of operation, maintenance, repair, renovation and any other necessary expenses.

(b) All rents collected, and income earned from such rents, under the provisions of this section shall be deposited into a revolving fund in the state treasury designated as the Capitol complex maintenance and repair fund, and the director of finance is authorized to make deposits and expenditures from time to time from such fund for said purposes. (Acts 1979, No. 79-456, p. 745.)

ARTICLE 2.

DIRECTOR OF FINANCE.

§ 41-4-30. Head of department; chief financial officer of state; advisor to governor and legislature; appointment; term of office; filling of vacancies; oath of office; full-time position; conflicts of interest.

The department of finance shall be headed by, and shall be under the direction, supervision and control of, an officer who shall be known and designated as the director of finance. The director of finance shall be the chief financial officer of the state and the advisor of the governor and of the legislature in financial matters, and he shall at all times be charged with protecting the financial interests of the state. He shall be responsible to the governor for the administration of the department of finance. The director of finance shall be appointed and hold office at the pleasure of the governor. Vacancies for any reason shall be filled in the same manner as original appointments are made. Before entering upon the discharge of his duties, the director of finance shall take the constitutional oath of office. The director of finance shall devote full time to his office and shall not hold another office under the government of the United States, or under any other state, or of this state or any political subdivision thereof, during his incumbency in such office, and he shall not hold any position of trust or profit or engage in any occupation or business, the conduct of which shall interfere or be inconsistent with the performance of his duties as director of finance. (Acts 1939, No. 112, p. 144; Code 1940, T. 55, § 64; Acts 1951, Ex. Sess., No. 8, p. 174.)

Director has general administrative supervision. — This section and § 41-4-32 vest in the director of finance the general supervision and control over the department, but this is as regards executive and administrative matters and the right to supervise the proper functioning of the various divisions. Alabama Elec. Coop. v. Alabama Power Co., 251 Ala. 190, 36 So. 2d 523 (1948).

Duties of the state finance director include informing the public of the results of statutorily prescribed investigations of state departments and agencies, this activity being within the penumbra of his official duties. Fulton v. Advertiser Co., 388 So. 2d 533 (Ala. 1980), cert. denied, 449 U.S. 1125, 101 S. Ct. 942, 67 L. Ed. 2d 111, 449 U.S. 1131, 101 S. Ct. 954, 67 L. Ed. 2d 119 (1981).

§ 41-4-31. Bond.

Before entering the duties of his office, the director of finance shall execute to the state of Alabama a bond, to be approved by the governor, in an amount to be fixed by the governor, but not less than $150,000.00, for the faithful performance of his duties. (Acts 1943, No. 122, p. 123; Acts 1961, Ex. Sess., No. 208, p. 2190.)

Cross references. — As to authority of governor to require additional bond, see § 36-5-40.

§ 41-4-32. Exercise of functions and duties of department of finance.

All functions and duties of the department of finance shall be exercised by the director of finance, acting by and through such administrative divisions or such officers as he may designate. He shall have all power and authority necessary or convenient to carry out the functions and duties of the department of finance. (Acts 1939, No. 112, p. 144; Code 1940, T. 55, § 65.)

Duties of the state finance director include informing the public of the results of statutorily prescribed investigations of state departments and agencies, this activity being within the penumbra of his official duties. Fulton v. Advertiser Co., 388 So. 2d 533 (Ala. 1980), cert. denied, 449 U.S. 1125, 101 S. Ct. 942, 67 L. Ed. 2d 111, 449 U.S. 1131, 101 S. Ct. 954, 67 L. Ed. 2d 119 (1981).

Cited in Landstreet v. City of Fort Payne, 238 Ala. 212, 190 So. 420 (1939).

§ 41-4-33. Sale of certain surplus lands.

As to all lands owned or claimed by the state and not presently used for governmental purposes, where no other department of the state is vested with the power and authority to obtain or negotiate a sale of such lands, the director of finance, with the approval of the governor, if satisfied that said sale is to the best interests of the state of Alabama, may offer the same for sale at public auction by advertising for and receiving sealed bids or by private sale. (Code 1940, T. 55, § 66.)

Cross references. — As to sale of certain state personal property or standing timber, see § 41-16-100 et seq.

§ 41-4-33.1. State owned surplus property transferred to volunteer fire departments; determination by forestry commission; approval by department; penalty for unauthorized use; final disposition of property.

(a) All surplus property owned by the state to be disposed of by sale at auction by the finance department shall first be screened by the forestry commission to determine if such property may be of use by volunteer fire departments for specific use in fire suppression activities. If the forestry commission finds such property to be useful for such purposes, then, with the approval of the state finance director, such property shall be transferred to the forestry commission. All such property shall be loaned to the volunteer fire departments.

(b) Any property transferred to a volunteer fire department under the provisions of this section shall be used exclusively for fire protection purposes. The use of any such property other than on the business of the volunteer fire department is expressly prohibited. Any violation of the provision of this section shall be a Class A misdemeanor punishable as provided under Title 13A.

(c) Final disposition of all properties loaned by the forestry commission as a result of this section shall rest with the finance department of the state. (Acts 1980, No. 80-364, p. 483.)

Cross references. — As to state, county, municipality or district donating money, property, etc., to voluntary fire departments, see § 9-3-18.

Collateral references. — 73 C.J.S., Public Lands, §§ 235-253.

63 Am. Jur. 2d, Public Lands, §§ 108-112.

§ 41-4-34. Duty as to offices and rooms in Capitol and other locations in Montgomery.

The director of finance must assign rooms in the Capitol to the secretary of state, auditor, treasurer, the department of revenue and such other officers as may be designated by law, or which, in the discretion of the governor, should have such offices, and, in the absence of any legislative provision, designate the purposes to which other rooms are to be applied. The director may supply offices or quarters for state officers or departments of the state outside of the state Capitol, within the city of Montgomery, when, in the discretion of the governor, the public interest and welfare will be subserved or promoted thereby. (Code 1852, § 50; Code 1867, § 58; Code 1876, § 56; Code 1886, § 57; Code 1896, § 1956; Code 1907, § 553; Code 1923, § 756; Code 1940, T. 55, § 67.)

Cross references. — For provision authorizing the department of finance to charge rent on state buildings, with the exception of the state Capitol building, see § 41-4-17.

§ 41-4-35. Promulgation and effect of rules and regulations; enforcement and amendment of rules and regulations.

The director of finance shall, with the approval of the governor, establish and promulgate rules and regulations with respect to the manner of performance of all functions and duties of the department of finance, the execution of the business of the department and its relations to and business with the other departments, boards, bureaus, commissions, agencies, offices and institutions of the state, the officers and employees thereof, the counties, municipal corporations, political subdivisions and local public bodies in the state, the officers and employees thereof, and the public, which rules and regulations shall be reasonably calculated to effect the expeditious and efficient performance of such functions and duties and shall not be in conflict with applicable statutes. When approved by the governor, such rules and regulations shall have the effect of law and shall govern all departments, boards, bureaus, commissions, agencies, offices and institutions of the state and the officers and employees thereof, the counties, municipal corporations, political subdivisions and local public bodies in the state, the officers and employees thereof, and the public, in their respective relations to and business with the department of finance. Compliance with any such rules or regulations may be compelled by mandamus. Such rules and regulations may be amended from time to time, with the approval of the governor. Anything herein to the contrary notwithstanding, the department of finance shall have no power to adopt any rule which shall impose any mandatory duties upon counties, municipal corporations, political subdivisions and local public bodies, including county and city boards of education and district boards of education of independent school districts, other than such mandatory duties as may be imposed upon them by law. (Acts 1939, No. 112, p. 144; Code 1940, T. 55, § 68.)

§ 41-4-36. Inspection and production of books, records, accounts, etc.; examination of witnesses.

The director of finance and any authorized officer or employee of the department of finance shall, in the performance of his official duties, for the purpose of examination, have access to, and the right to copy from, any book, record, account, document, receipt or paper of any of the departments, boards, bureaus, commissions, agencies, offices or institutions of the state or of any of the counties, municipal corporations, political subdivisions or public bodies in the state or of the officers or employees thereof, in such manner as may be reasonable and at reasonable times. The director of finance or any officer or employee of the department of finance designated by the director, in the performance of his official duties, shall have the power to administer oaths, certify to official acts, take and cause to be taken depositions of witnesses, issue subpoenas, compel the attendance of witnesses and the production of accounts, documents, receipts, papers and testimony, and all witnesses regularly summoned as herein provided shall be paid $.05 per mile each way for the distance traveled plus $3.00 per diem for each day consumed in the hearing and in the traveling to and from the place of hearing. In the event of the failure of any person to comply with any subpoena lawfully issued, or on the refusal of any witness to produce evidence or to testify as to any matter regarding which he may be lawfully interrogated, it shall be the duty of any court of competent jurisdiction or the judge thereof, upon the application of the director of finance or any officer of the department of finance designated by the director, to compel obedience by attachment proceedings for contempt, as in the case of disobedience of the requirements of a subpoena issued for such court or a refusal to testify therein. A wilfully false material statement in any examination herein provided for shall constitute perjury and be punishable as such. (Acts 1939, No. 112, p. 144; Code 1940, T. 55, § 69.)

§ 41-4-37. Creation of additional divisions in department; assignment of functions and duties of divisions.

With the approval of the governor, the director of finance may create and establish such additional divisions as may be determined to be necessary or convenient in the efficient and expeditious performance of the functions and duties of the department of finance and assign functions and duties for such divisions, and he may, with the approval of the governor, reassign functions and duties as between existing divisions. Chiefs of such new divisions shall be appointed by the director of finance, with the approval of the governor, subject to the provisions of the merit system. (Acts 1939, No. 112, p. 144; Code 1940, T. 55, § 70.)

ARTICLE 3.

DIVISION OF CONTROL AND ACCOUNTS.

Collateral references. — 81 C.J.S., States, § 66(b).   72 Am. Jur. 2d, States, Territories & Dependencies, § 75 et seq.

§ 41-4-50. Established; functions and duties.

There shall be in the department of finance the division of control and accounts. The functions and duties of the division of control and accounts shall be as follows:

(1) To keep all books, records and accounts relating to the finances of the state government (including the budget accounts) which are authorized or required to be kept by the department of finance, in accordance with recognized standards of public accounting and in such a manner as at all times to reveal the true financial status of the state government and of each special fund and account in the state treasury.

(2) To control and make records of all payments into and out of the state treasury and each special fund and account therein.

(3) To audit currently all receipts and receivables.

(4) To preaudit and determine the correctness and legality of every claim and account submitted for the issuance of a warrant and to determine that

funds have been appropriated and allotted and are then available in the state treasury for the payment of such claim or account before any warrant on the state treasury shall be issued; except, that the preaudit of claims for unemployment compensation or confederate widows' pensions or public assistance or child welfare shall be performed by the department or departments having charge of the other functions and duties relating to unemployment compensation, confederate widows' pensions or public assistance, or child welfare, subject to the general supervision of the division of control and accounts.

(5) To draw every warrant authorized to be drawn upon the state treasury and any fund therein, whether a special or earmarked fund or not.

(6) To secure such information and data, to prepare or make such studies and reports and to perform such other functions and duties of the department of finance as may from time to time be assigned by the director of finance. (Acts 1939, No. 112, p. 144; Code 1940, T. 55, § 81.)

§ 41-4-51. Comptroller — Head of division; appointment.

The division of control and accounts shall be headed by and be under the direction, supervision and control of an officer who shall be designated the comptroller. The comptroller shall be appointed by the director of finance, with the approval of the governor. (Acts 1939, No. 112, p. 144; Code 1940, T. 55, § 81.)

§ 41-4-52. Same — Restrictions on receipt of revenue.

The comptroller has no authority in any civil action or proceeding commenced or directed by him, or in any other case, unless such authority is expressly given, to receive any of the state revenue. (Code 1852, § 368; Code 1867, § 420; Code 1876, § 97; Code 1886, § 108; Code 1896, § 2007; Code 1907, § 611; Code 1923, § 818; Acts 1939, No. 112, p. 144; Code 1940, T. 55, § 82.)

§ 41-4-53. Same — Restrictions on drawing warrants in favor of defaulters.

The comptroller must not give any public defaulter any warrant for moneys due him from the state, except the balance which is due after the application of the amount due from the state to the extinguishment of the debt, interest and damages, if any are given by law, due from such defaulter. (Code 1852, § 367; Code 1867, § 419; Code 1876, § 96; Code 1886, § 107; Code 1896, § 2006; Code 1907, § 610; Code 1923, § 817; Acts 1939, No. 112, p. 144; Code 1940, T. 55, § 83.)

Section is limited to officer charged with handling state funds who becomes defaulter, guilty of breach of trust imposed by law. Hall v. Blan, 227 Ala. 64, 148 So. 601 (1933).

And its purpose is to give state right to retain moneys due such officer. — The purpose of this section is to give the state an unqualified right to retain moneys in the public treasury, appropriated by law to a person who is indebted to the state, in satisfaction of such indebtedness, when such indebtedness arises from the breach of duty while occupying a public office. State v. Brewer, 62 Ala. 215 (1878).

Ascertainment of default by action is unnecessary; the auditor (now comptroller) acts merely on the information furnished by the books and records of his department. State v. Brewer, 62 Ala. 215 (1878).

Withholding warrant not conclusive of fact or amount of default. — The action of the auditor (now comptroller) in withholding the warrant is not conclusive of the fact or amount of default. It has no more force than has the refusal by an individual to answer a demand against him because he has a setoff. State v. Brewer, 62 Ala. 215 (1878), holding that the remedy against the auditor was mandamus.

Collateral references. — 81 C.J.S., States, § 169.

§ 41-4-54. Accounts against state to be itemized.

All accounts against the state must be accurately and fully itemized. (Code 1852, § 369; Code 1867, § 421; Code 1876, § 98; Code 1886, § 109; Code 1896, § 2008; Code 1907, § 612; Code 1923, § 819; Code 1940, T. 55, § 84; Acts 1969, No. 272, p. 603.)

Claim for taxes paid by mistake need not be verified or itemized, as this section has reference to special claims against the state in the form of open accounts. White v. Smith, 117 Ala. 232, 23 So. 525 (1898).

§ 41-4-55. Method of indicating governor's approval of vouchers or accounts where required.

On all vouchers or accounts for payment of state funds by warrant of the state comptroller which, by general or special law, require the approval of the governor, such approval may be indicated thereon by method of certification by the director or executive officer duly designated for the department requesting payment that the governor's approval has been obtained.

Certification executed pursuant to this section shall constitute prima facie evidence of the governor's approval for such payment. (Acts 1969, No. 224, p. 544.)

§ 41-4-56. Evidence required for payment from contingent funds.

No money shall be paid out of any contingent fund, except upon account stated, setting forth the items upon which payment is claimed, signed by the proper person, with such authentication as the governor may require of the correctness of the same. (Code 1867, § 416; Code 1876, § 94; Code 1886, § 105; Code 1896, § 2004; Code 1907, § 608; Code 1923, § 815; Code 1940, T. 55, § 85.)

§ 41-4-57. Statement of expenses of state officers and employees to be filed with comptroller before warrant issued.

All officers and employees who travel at the expense of the state or any of its departments, agencies, boards, bureaus or commissions shall file with the comptroller an itemized statement of all expenses incurred, including those for transportation, in connection with such travel at the expense of the state, agency, institution, board, bureau, or commission, verified by affidavit, before any warrant shall issue for such expenses. (Acts 1919, No. 151, p. 145; Code 1923, § 820; Acts 1939, No. 112, p. 144; Code 1940, T. 55, § 86; Acts 1943, No. 160, p. 153.)

Collateral references. — 81 C.J.S., States, §§ 91, 92.

Mileage incidental to duty of office but which represented no actual expense or outlay by officer, officer's rights and duties in respect of. 81 ALR 493.

Mileage of traveling expense, allowance for, to officer as affected by use of his own vehicle for transportation. 112 ALR 172.

Accepting excessive mileage allowance as punishable offense. 134 ALR 1258.

Constitutional provision fixing or limiting salary of public officer as precluding allowance for mileage or traveling expenses. 5 ALR2d 1182.

§ 41-4-58. Issuance of duplicate warrants when originals lost.

The comptroller must issue duplicate warrants upon the treasury whenever he is satisfied that the original warrant has been destroyed or lost. The party holding the duplicate shall have the same right as if he held the original, and the treasurer is authorized to pay the same. (Code 1876, § 100; Code 1886, § 111; Code 1896, § 2010; Code 1907, § 613; Code 1923, § 821; Acts 1939, No. 112, p. 144; Code 1940, T. 55, § 87.)

§ 41-4-59. When warrant deemed duly executed.

Every warrant authorized to be drawn upon the state treasury by the state comptroller shall be deemed to have been duly executed if it is signed by the comptroller himself or if it bears a facsimile of the comptroller's signature placed thereon by the comptroller or a duly authorized employee of the division of control and accounts in the department of finance, with the intent to execute such warrant. (Acts 1956, 1st Ex. Sess., No. 120, p. 176.)

§ 41-4-60. When warrants void and claims based thereon barred.

(a) Any warrant heretofore or hereafter drawn by the state comptroller on any fund in the state treasury which has not been presented for payment and is, or was, outstanding and unpaid at the close of the fiscal year next following the fiscal year in which it was issued shall be void and payment of the warrant shall be stopped by the state treasurer. Any claim on which any such voided warrant was based shall be forever barred after the expiration of six years from the date on which the warrant was issued. If at any time during such six-year period, the claimant makes satisfactory proof to the department, board, institution or other agency on whose account the warrant was issued that the warrant issued in his behalf has been voided and that his claim is unsettled, a new warrant shall be issued to the claimant in lieu of the voided warrant, and such new warrant shall be refunded out of the state general fund.

(b) Upon the expiration of the period of time provided herein for the voiding of warrants, the state treasurer shall draw his check in the amount of the voided warrant payable to the state general fund.

(c) Duplicate warrants issued to replace warrants which have been lost, mutilated or destroyed shall be deemed to be original warrants for the purposes of this section. (Acts 1969, No. 226, p. 545.)

§ 41-4-61. Comptroller may require proof of correctness of claim.

The comptroller has authority to require information on oath, to be administered by him, from any person, touching any claim or account he is required to audit. (Code 1852, § 366; Code 1867, § 418; Code 1876, § 93; Code 1886, § 104; Code 1896, § 2003; Code 1907, § 607; Code 1923, § 814; Acts 1939, No. 112, p. 144; Code 1940, T. 55, § 88.)

§ 41-4-62. Refund of money paid for invalid or unissued bonds, etc. — Authorized; interest.

In cases where any person, firm or corporation has purchased or may hereafter purchase from the state, or of its officers acting under authority or under color of authority purporting to be conferred by an act or resolution of the legislature of this state, bonds or securities issued or proposed to be issued in consideration of funds or money which such person, firm or corporation has actually paid or caused to be paid into the treasury of the state, and where for any reason such bonds or securities have not been paid or cannot be issued and delivered or, if issued and delivered, have been declared invalid by the supreme court, such person, firm or corporation may have the funds or money so paid into the treasury of the state refunded, together with interest thereon at the rate of interest said bonds or securities proposed to bear from the date of the payment of said funds or money into the treasury, on complying with the provisions and requirements of section 41-4-63. (Acts 1921, Ex. Sess., No. 10, p. 8; Code 1923, § 824; Code 1940, T. 55, § 90.)

§ 41-4-63. Same — Application to comptroller; proceedings.

Any person, firm or corporation entitled to the benefit of section 41-4-62 and desiring to obtain relief hereunder may file an application with the comptroller of the state, stating the facts upon which relief is sought, verified by his affidavit or that of a duly authorized agent or representative having knowledge of the facts, and when such an application is filed, the comptroller shall ascertain from the records of the treasurer of Alabama and other records whether the facts are correctly set forth in the application, and if it is made to appear to the satisfaction of the comptroller that the state has actually received the funds or money of the applicant under the circumstances named in section 41-4-62, upon the approval of the governor and the treasurer, the comptroller shall draw a warrant on the treasurer for the payment to such person, firm or corporation of the amount of such funds or money, together with interest thereon at the rate said bonds or securities proposed to bear from the time said funds or money was paid into the treasury. (Acts 1921, Ex. Sess., No. 10, p. 8; Code 1923, § 825; Acts 1939, No. 112, p. 144; Code 1940, T. 55, § 91.)

§ 41-4-64. Comptroller may close out certain inactive funds and transfer balance to general fund.

The state comptroller is authorized to transfer to the state general fund all sums carried in special funds on the books and daily balance sheets of the comptroller but which have become inactive because all claims against them have been paid or when requests for payments from such funds have not been made or for any other reasons and a reasonable time for making such claims has been allowed. When the comptroller transfers the balance in any special fund into the general fund, he shall close out such special fund. (Acts 1969, No. 166, p. 451.)

ARTICLE 4.

DIVISION OF THE BUDGET.

§ 41-4-80. Established; functions and duties.

There shall be in the department of finance a division of the budget. The functions and duties of the division of the budget shall be as follows:

(1) To prepare and administer the budget, and direct the execution thereof.

(2) To prepare a detailed tentative budget for every department, board, bureau, commission, agency, office and institution of the state, including those which employ special or earmarked funds, and all earmarked and special funds shall be included in the regular budget of each such department, board, bureau, commission, agency, office or institution.

(3) To make all budget allotments.

(4) To administer, enforce and supervise the execution of the budget, including the enforcement of penalties for the violation of any law, rule or regulation with respect thereto.

(5) To perform all acts and duties required with respect to the budget by the provisions of this article.

(6) To furnish all information for and assist in the preparation of the general revenue bill and all appropriation bills.

(7) To prepare or make such comparisons, studies and reports as may be helpful in the preparation or execution of the budget or the making of budget allotments or as may be required from time to time by the director of finance or the governor.

(8) To secure such information and data from any department, board, bureau, commission, agency, office or institution of the state or any officer or employee thereof as may be needed or considered helpful in the preparation of the budget or any report, study, comparison or other assignment of the division of the budget.

(9) To perform such other functions and duties of the department of finance as may from time to time be assigned by the director of finance. (Acts 1939, No. 112, p. 144; Acts 1939, No. 144, p. 190; Code 1940, T. 55, § 92.)

§ 41-4-81. Budget officer.

The division of the budget shall be headed by and under the direction, supervision and control of an officer who shall be designated the budget officer. The budget officer shall be appointed by the director of finance, with the approval of the governor. (Acts 1939, No. 112, p. 144; Acts 1939, No. 144, p. 190; Code 1940, T. 55, § 92.)

Cited in In re Opinion of Justices, 227 Ala. 289, 149 So. 775 (1933); In re Opinion of Justices, 229 Ala. 98, 155 So. 699 (1934); Southern Indus. Inst. v. Lee, 234 Ala. 404, 175 So. 365 (1937).

§ 41-4-82. Transmission of budget to legislature.

Within five days after the convening of each regular business session of the legislature, the governor shall transmit to the legislature a document to be known as a budget, setting forth his financial program for each of the fiscal years which will have begun before the next succeeding regular session of the legislature (hereinafter referred to as "budget years," regardless of the number thereof) and having the character and scope hereinafter set forth. (Acts 1932, Ex. Sess., No. 37, p. 35; Acts 1939, No. 144, p. 190; Code 1940, T. 55, § 93.)

§ 41-4-83. Form and contents of budget.

The budget shall consist of three parts, the nature and contents of which shall be as follows:

(1) Part I shall consist of the governor's budget message, in which he shall set forth:

a. His program for meeting all the expenditure needs of the government for each of the budget years, indicating the fund, general or special, from which such expenditures are to be made and the means through which such expenditures are to be financed.

b. Financial statements giving in summary form:

1. The condition of the treasury at the end of the last completed fiscal year, the estimated condition of the treasury at the end of the fiscal year in progress and the estimated condition of the treasury at the end of each of the budget years if his budget proposals are to be put into effect.

2. Statements showing the bonded indebtedness of the government, debt authorized and unissued, debt redemption and interest requirements and the condition of the sinking funds, if any.

3. A summary of appropriations recommended for each of the budget years for each department, board, bureau, commission, agency, office and institution of the state and for the government as a whole, in comparison with the actual expenditures for each of the completed fiscal years covered by the last preceding budget and the estimated expenditures for the fiscal year in progress.

4. A summary of the revenue, classified according to sources, estimated to be received by the government during each of the budget years,

in comparison with the actual revenue received by the government during each of the completed fiscal years covered by the last preceding budget and the estimated income for the fiscal year in progress.

c. Such other financial statements, data and comments as in his opinion are necessary or desirable in order to make known in all practicable detail the financial condition and operation of the government and the effect that the budget as proposed by him will have on such condition and operation.

d. If the estimated revenues for the budget years plus the estimated amounts in the treasury at the close of the fiscal year in progress are less than the aggregate appropriations recommended for the budget years, the governor shall make recommendation to the legislature with respect to the manner in which such deficit shall be met, whether by the imposition of new taxes, increased rates in existing taxes or otherwise. If the revenues are more than the aggregate appropriations recommended, he shall make such recommendations with respect to the application of such surplus to the reduction of debt, to reductions in taxation or to such other action as in his opinion is in the public interest.

(2) Part II shall present in detail for each of the budget years his recommendations for appropriations to meet the expenditure needs of the government from each fund, general or special, in comparison with the actual expenditures for each of said purposes during the completed fiscal years covered by the last preceding budget and the estimated expenditures for the fiscal year in progress, classified by departments, boards, bureaus, commissions, agencies, officers and institutions of the state and indicating for each the appropriations recommended for meeting the cost of salaries, travel and per diem expenses, administration, operation and maintenance. Each item of expenditure, actual or estimated, and appropriations recommended shall be supported by detailed statements showing the actual and estimated expenditures and appropriations classified according to a standard scheme of classification to be prescribed by the department of finance and the purchase of land, public improvements and other capital outlays in connection therewith.

(3) Part III shall embrace a proposed appropriation bill and a proposed revenue bill or bills for the purpose of proposing in statutory form the recommendations made in Parts I and II. Such appropriation bill or bills shall indicate the funds, general or special, from which such appropriations shall be made, but such appropriations need not be in greater detail than to indicate the total appropriation to be made for each department, board, bureau, commission, agency, office and institution of the state for each budget year for salaries, travel and per diem expenses, administration, operation and maintenance and the cost of land, public improvements and other capital outlays, itemized by specific projects or classes of projects of the same general character. (Acts 1932, Ex. Sess., No. 37, p. 35; Acts 1939, No. 144, p. 190; Code 1940, T. 55, § 94.)

Collateral references. — 81 C.J.S., States, § 94.

§ 41-4-84. Estimates of appropriations to be submitted to department of finance.

On or before the first day of the third month next preceding each regular business session of the legislature, each department, board, bureau, commission, agency, office and institution of the state shall transmit to the department of finance, on blanks to be furnished it, estimates of their expenditure requirements for each budget year, classified so as to distinguish between expenditures estimated for salaries, travel and per diem expenses, administration, operation and maintenance and the cost of each project involving the purchase of land or the making of a public improvement or a capital outlay of a permanent character, together with such supporting data and explanations as may be called for by the department of finance. In case of the failure of any department, board, bureau, commission, agency, office or institution of the state to submit such estimate within the time above specified, the governor shall cause to be prepared such estimates for such department, board, bureau, commission, agency, office or institution of the state as in his opinion are reasonable and proper. (Acts 1932, Ex. Sess., No. 37, p. 35; Acts 1939, No. 144, p. 190; Code 1940, T. 55, § 95.)

§ 41-4-85. Estimates of income to be prepared by department of finance.

On or before the first day of the third month next preceding each regular business session of the legislature, the department of finance shall prepare an estimate of the total income of the government for each budget year, in which the several items of income shall be listed and classified according to source or character and by departments, boards, bureaus, commissions, agencies, officers and institutions of the state producing such funds and in which such items shall be compared with the income actually received during the completed fiscal years covered by the next preceding budget and the estimated income to be received during the fiscal year then in progress. (Acts 1932, Ex. Sess., No. 37, p. 35; Acts 1939, No. 144, p. 190; Code 1940, T. 55, § 96.)

§ 41-4-86. Tentative budget — Preparation.

Upon the receipt of the estimates of expenditure requirements called for by section 41-4-84 and the preparation of the estimates of income called for by section 41-4-85, and not later than the first day of the second month preceding each regular business session of the legislature, the department of finance shall prepare a tentative budget conforming as to scope, contents and character to the requirements of section 41-4-83, and containing the estimates of expenditure and revenue called for by sections 41-4-84 and 41-4-85, which tentative budget shall be transmitted to the governor. All facts relating to past receipts and expenditures shall be certified as correct and accurate by the comptroller in the department of finance. (Acts 1932, Ex. Sess., No. 37, p. 35; Acts 1939, No. 144, p. 190; Code 1940, T. 55, § 97.)

§ 41-4-87. Same — Hearings.

The governor shall, upon receipt by him of the tentative budget provided for by section 41-4-86, make provision for public hearings thereon not later than two weeks prior to the convening of the next ensuing regular business session of the legislature. To any such public hearings on the tentative budget, the governor shall extend invitations to and may require the attendance of the heads of all departments, boards, bureaus, commissions, agencies, offices and institutions of the state and other persons receiving or requesting state funds and the giving by them of such explanations and suggestions as they may be called upon to give or as they may desire to offer with respect to the items of requested appropriations in which they are interested. He shall also extend invitations and may require the attendance of the budget officer and the comptroller and the giving by them of any information or data pertinent to the proposed budget. The governor shall also extend invitations to the chairman of the ways and means committee of the house and the chairman of the finance and taxation committee of the senate of the legislature which is then in office to be present at such hearings and to participate in such hearings through the asking of questions or the expression of opinions with regard to the items of the tentative budget. The governor shall also extend a like invitation to the governor-elect if such there be. The chairmen of said committees, while sitting at such hearings, shall hold the offices of budget advisors, and shall receive a per diem of $10.00 for each day in attendance at such hearings. If either chairman shall be unable to attend, the next ranking member of his committee shall act in his place. (Acts 1932, Ex. Sess., No. 37, p. 35; Acts 1939, No. 144, p. 190; Code 1940, T. 55, § 98.)

§ 41-4-88. Formulation of final budget.

After such public hearings, the governor shall proceed to the formulation of the budget provided for in sections 41-4-82 and 41-4-83. In doing so, he shall give such weight to the estimates of income prepared by the department of finance, to the estimates of expenditure requirements submitted by the departments, boards, bureaus, commissions, agencies, offices and institutions of the state, to the tentative budget prepared by the department of finance and to the testimony elicited at the hearing thereon as he deems proper, but the proposals contained in the budget shall represent his judgment and recommendations with respect to the provisions to be made for meeting the revenue and expenditure needs of the government for each of the budget years. (Acts 1932, Ex. Sess., No. 37, p. 35; Acts 1939, No. 144, p. 190; Code 1940, T. 55, § 99.)

§ 41-4-89. Supplemental estimates for additional appropriations.

The governor shall transmit to the legislature supplemental estimates for such appropriations as in his judgment may be necessary on account of laws enacted after the transmission of the budget, or as he deems otherwise in the public interest. He shall accompany such estimates with a statement of the reasons therefor, including the reasons for their omission from the budget.

Whenever such supplemental estimates amount to an aggregate which, if they had been contained in the budget would have required the governor to make a recommendation for the raising of additional revenue, he shall make such recommendation. (Acts 1932, Ex. Sess., No. 37, p. 35; Code 1940, T. 55, § 100.)

§ 41-4-90. Availability and effect of appropriations; restriction of allotments by governor.

No appropriations made by the legislature shall be available for expenditures until allotted as provided for in section 41-4-91. All appropriations, except per capita appropriations now in force or hereafter made to eleemosynary and correctional institutions and the Alabama School for the Deaf and Blind, located at Talladega, Alabama, which appropriations shall remain in full force and effect and be payable and disbursed as now provided by law, are hereby declared to be maximum, conditional and proportionate appropriations, the purpose being to make appropriations payable in full in the amounts named only in the event that the estimated budget resources during each budget year of the period are sufficient to pay all of the appropriations for such year in full. The governor shall restrict allotments to prevent an overdraft or deficit in any fiscal year for which appropriations are made by prorating without discrimination against any department, board, bureau, commission, agency, office or institution of the state, the available revenues among the various departments, boards, bureaus, commissions, agencies, offices and institutions of the state. In other words, said appropriations shall be payable in such proportion as the total sum of all appropriations bears to the total revenues estimated by the department of finance as available in each of said fiscal years. The purpose of this provision is to insure that there shall be no overdraft or deficit in the several funds of the state at the end of any fiscal year, and the governor is directed and required so to administer this article to prevent any such overdraft or deficit. (Acts 1932, Ex. Sess., No. 37, p. 35; Acts 1939, No. 144, p. 190; Code 1940, T. 55, § 101.)

Purpose of Budget Act was to make state operate within income. Southern Indus. Inst. v. Lee, 234 Ala. 404, 175 So. 365 (1937).

Act is held restricted to appropriations required to be allotted, which are appropriations for administration, operation and maintenance of any department, institution, bureau, board, commission or other state agency upon quarter requisitions for amount estimated to be necessary for succeeding quarter. Abramson v. Hard, 229 Ala. 2, 155 So. 590 (1934).

And it is not applicable to fixed salaries, etc. — To fixed salaries and to other fixed expenses, such as the per diem allowed to officers for traveling expenses, both of which are appropriations to the officers to whom they are due rather than to any department, institution, bureau, board, commission or other state agency, the proration provisions of the Budget Act have no application. Abramson v. Hard, 229 Ala. 2, 155 So. 590 (1934).

Laws not affected by act. — Statute appropriating money to pay for realty purchased by state held not affected by the Budget Act. In re Opinion of Justices, 234 Ala. 555, 176 So. 367 (1937).

"Permanent" and "unpaid" appropriations. — See Southern Indus. Inst. v. Lee, 234 Ala. 404, 175 So. 365 (1937).

Cited in Baker v. Singleton, 237 Ala. 394, 187 So. 478 (1939).

Collateral references. — 81 C.J.S., States, §§ 160-167.

§ 41-4-91. Requisition, duration, approval and modification of allotments of appropriations.

Before an appropriation for any purpose to any department, board, bureau, commission, agency, office or institution of the state shall become available, there shall be submitted to the department of finance, not less than 20 days before the expiration of the last period for which an allotment has been or shall have been made, a requisition for an allotment of the amount estimated to be necessary to carry on its work during the period for which allotments are made. Allotments shall be made for such length of time as may be determined to be appropriate and convenient by the department of finance, with the approval of the governor, but no allotment (except for the acquisition of land, permanent improvements or other capital projects) shall, in any event, be for a period of longer than three months. Such requisition for an allotment shall contain such information and data and be in such detail as may be required by the department of finance. The department of finance shall examine such requisition and, with the approval of the governor, shall make such allotment, or modification thereof, as may be deemed necessary, but the total amount of annual appropriations to any department, board, bureau, commission, agency, office or institution of the state shall not be reduced except proportionately as provided for in section 41-4-90. The department of finance shall submit copies of each allotment thus approved to the head of the department, board, bureau, commission, agency, office or institution of the state for which such allotment shall have been made. The comptroller in the department of finance shall set up such allotment on his book and be governed accordingly in his control of expenditures. Allotments of appropriations made for the acquisition of land, permanent improvements and other capital projects may, however, be allotted in one amount by major classes or projects for which they are expendable without regard to allotment periods. Any allotments may be subsequently modified by the department of finance, with the approval of the governor, either upon the written request of the head of the department, board, bureau, commission, agency, office or institution of the state concerned or upon the initiative of the department of finance or the governor, and notice of such modification shall be given and such modification shall be set upon the books of said comptroller in the same way as in the case of original allotments. (Acts 1932, Ex. Sess., No. 37, p. 35; Acts 1939, No. 144, p. 190; Code 1940, T. 55, § 102.)

§ 41-4-92. Disposition of departmental and institutional fees, receipts, etc.

All fees, receipts and income collected or received by any department, board, bureau, commission, agency or office or institution of the state shall be paid into the state treasury or deposited in an approved state depository to the credit of the general fund of the state of Alabama or to the credit of a special fund if the latter is required by law. No such payment or deposit shall be subject to withdrawal by any such department, board, bureau, commission, agency, office or institution, and all appropriations made to any such department, board, bureau, commission, agency, office or institution shall be specified amounts and shall be subject to allotment as provided in this article. Anything herein to the contrary notwithstanding, however, this article shall not apply to the fees, receipts and income (other than appropriations) of the department of conservation and natural resources, the department of agriculture and industries or any educational, correctional or eleemosynary institution, or to any endowment or trust fund or gifts to any such institutions, or to the income from such endowments or trust funds, or to private funds belonging to students or inmates of such institutions, nor shall such funds be subject to any allotment under this article or be taken into consideration in making any allotment or prorating of appropriations under this article, and all appropriations made to any such institutions are hereby declared to be in addition to such fees, receipts and other income, and all allotments from such appropriations shall be paid over to such institution, and when such allotments are received by such institutions, the same shall be deposited in any bank or banks in the state of Alabama, which have been duly designated and qualified as state depositories, for the use and benefit of such institution, and such funds shall be available only on the check of such institution depositing them, which is hereby authorized to withdraw such funds at its discretion. (Acts 1932, Ex. Sess., No. 37, p. 35; Acts 1939, No. 144, p. 190; Code 1940, T. 55, § 103.)

§ 41-4-93. Lapsing of appropriations.

All unencumbered balances of all appropriations shall revert to the state treasury at the end of each fiscal year and to the credit of the general fund or the special fund from which the appropriation or appropriations were made. Appropriations for the purchase of land or the erection of buildings or new constructions or for highway department maintenance of roads and bridges on the state highway system shall continue in force until the attainment of the object or the completion of the work for which such appropriations are made. (Acts 1932, Ex. Sess., No. 37, p. 35; Acts 1939, No. 144, p. 190; Code 1940, T. 55, § 104; Acts 1979, No. 79-744, p. 1320.)

Cited in Baker v. Singleton, 237 Ala. 394, 187 So. 478 (1939).

§ 41-4-94. Emergency appropriations.

To the end that all expenses of the state may be brought and kept within the budget, the budget appropriation bills shall contain a specific sum or sums as an emergency appropriation or appropriations. Such sum shall not, however, exceed two percent of the total amount appropriated by such bill. The manner of allotment of such emergency appropriation shall be as follows: Any department, board, bureau, commission, agency, office or institution of the state or any person or persons in charge of any activity in which the state is interested, desiring an allotment out of such appropriation, shall present such request in writing to the department of finance with such information as it may require, and, such request shall be handled and allotments may be made pursuant thereto as in the case of regular allotments. Such allotments shall be made only for any purpose authorized by law for which no specific appropriation has been made or for which inadvertently an insufficient appropriation has been made. (Acts 1932, Ex. Sess., No. 37, p. 35; Acts 1939, No. 144, p. 190; Code 1940, T. 55, § 105.)

Cited in Eagerton v. Graves, 252 Ala. 326, 40 So. 2d 417 (1949).

§ 41-4-95. Appropriations wrongfully expended.

It shall be unlawful for any trustee, commissioner, director, manager, building committee or other officer or person connected with any department, institution, bureau, board, commission or other state agency to which an appropriation is made to expend any appropriation for any purpose other than that for which the money was appropriated, budgeted and allotted, or to consent thereto. If the governor shall ascertain that any department, institution, bureau, board, commission or other state agency has used any of the moneys appropriated to it for any purpose other than that for which the money was appropriated, budgeted and allotted and not in strict accordance with the provisions of law, the governor shall have the power and he is hereby authorized to suspend all appropriations and allotments to such department, institution, bureau, board, commission or other state agency until and after such amounts diverted or wrongfully expended have been replaced. (Acts 1932, Ex. Sess., No. 37, p. 35; Code 1940, T. 55, § 106.)

§ 41-4-96. Penalties for violations of article.

A wilful and knowing refusal to perform any of the requirements of this article or a wilful and knowing refusal to perform any rule or requirement or request of the governor, director of finance or the budget officer made pursuant to or under authority of this article by any trustee, commissioner, director, manager, building committee or other officer or person connected with any department, board, bureau, commission, agency, office or institution of the state shall subject the offender to a penalty of $250.00, to be recovered in an action instituted in the circuit court of Montgomery county by the attorney general for the use of the state of Alabama and shall also constitute a misdemeanor, punishable by fine or imprisonment or both, in the discretion of the court, and shall subject such offender to dismissal from office by the person, department, board, bureau, commission, agency, office or institution of the state under which such offender holds office or appointment in accordance with the provisions of the merit system. If such offender is an officer elected by vote of the people, such offense shall be sufficient cause to subject the offender to impeachment. A refusal to perform any requirement of this article or an improper or illegal performance of any requirement of this article shall subject the budget officer or the director of finance to a penalty of $500.00, to be recovered in an action instituted in the circuit court of Montgomery county by the attorney general for the use of the state of Alabama, and it shall also constitute a felony. A refusal to perform any of the requirements of this article or an improper or illegal performance of any requirement of this article by the governor shall make him subject to impeachment. (Acts 1932, Ex. Sess., No. 37, p. 35; Acts 1939, No. 144, p. 190; Code 1940, T. 55, § 107.)

ARTICLE 5.

DIVISION OF PURCHASES AND STORES.

Division 1.

General Provisions.

Cross references. — As to public contracts generally, see § 41-16-1 et seq.

§ 41-4-110. Established; functions and duties; contracts for stationery, printing, paper and fuel.

(a) There shall be in the department of finance the division of purchases and stores. The functions and duties of the division of purchases and stores shall be as follows:

(1) To purchase all personal property, except alcoholic beverages, which shall be purchased by the alcoholic beverage control board and except as otherwise provided by law, for the state and each department, board, bureau, commission, agency, office and institution thereof.

(2) To make and supervise the execution of all contracts and leases for the use or acquisition of any personal property unless otherwise provided by law.

(3) To distribute all furniture, fixtures, supplies, materials, equipment and other personal property purchased or acquired for the use of the state or any of its departments, boards, bureaus, commissions, agencies, offices or institutions unless otherwise provided by law, and to maintain a storeroom or storerooms for the safekeeping and distribution thereof. No such property shall be distributed or delivered to any such department, board, bureau, commission, agency, office or institution of the state unless affirmatively required by law or unless provided for on a requisition previously approved as within an allotment previously made therefor by the division of the budget and unless an authorized officer or employee of such department, board, bureau, commission, agency, office or institution shall have given his receipt therefor.

(4) To maintain a perpetual inventory of all furniture, fixtures, supplies, materials, equipment and other personal property on hand by its order and undistributed.

(5) To fix standards of quality and quantity and to develop standard specifications for all personal property required by the state or any department, board, bureau, commission, agency, office or institution thereof.

(6) To maintain records as to prices and sources of supply of such personal property, such records to be open to the inspection of any state, county,

municipal or other public officer or employee charged with the duty of acquiring any such property or article for his department, board, bureau, commission, agency, office, institution, county, municipal corporation or local public body.

(7) To manage, supervise and control all printing and binding for the state and for each department, board, bureau, commission, agency, office and institution thereof and the distribution of all printed matter and to make and supervise the execution of all contracts with respect thereto, unless otherwise provided by law.

(8) To require the periodic reporting of all purchases of furniture, fixtures, supplies, material, equipment and other personal property, except printing, and all contracts and leases for the use or acquisition thereof by or for counties, the purchase, contract or lease price of which is $100.00 or more, and to require information in connection therewith, to prescribe forms and fix the time for submitting such reports, and, when requested by any county, municipal corporation and other local public body (including any board of education) to make such purchases, contracts or leases for it. It shall be the duty of every county to make such report on forms furnished by the department of finance, whenever requested so to do, but not more than once every 30 days.

(9) To perform such other functions and duties of the department of finance as may from time to time be assigned by the director of finance.

(b) As long as the Constitution so requires, all stationery, printing, paper and fuel used in the legislative and other departments of the government shall be furnished, and the printing, binding and distribution of the laws, journals, departmental reports and all other printing, binding and repairing and furnishing the halls and rooms used for the meetings of the legislature and its committees shall be performed under contract, to be given to the lowest responsible bidder below a maximum price, under such regulations as have been or may be prescribed by law and as may be promulgated by the director of finance. No member or officer of any department of the government shall be in any way interested in such contracts, and all such contracts shall be subject to the approval of the governor, the auditor and the treasurer. All contracts not required to be approved by a named officer or officers by the Constitution shall be subject to the approval of the director of finance, who may, however, provide for the automatic approval thereof by compliance with the general rules or regulations promulgated by him. (Acts 1939, No. 112, p. 144; Code 1940, T. 55, § 108.)

Constitution. — For constitutional provisions requiring stationery, printing, paper and fuel used by legislative and other departments to be purchased by contract awarded to lowest responsible bidder below a maximum price, see Const., § 69.

§ 41-4-111. Purchasing agent.

The division of purchases and stores shall be headed by and be under the direction, supervision and control of an officer who shall be designated the purchasing agent. The purchasing agent shall be appointed by the director of finance with the approval of the governor. (Acts 1939, No. 112, p. 144; Code 1940, T. 55, § 108.)

§ 41-4-112. When vendor's affidavit not necessary before payment of invoices for state purchases.

In all cases where the state purchasing agent has issued a purchase order for the purchase of any supplies, material, equipment or other personal property, no affidavit of the vendor shall be required before payment of the invoice if the account is accurately and fully itemized. (Acts 1945, No. 213, p. 339.)

§ 41-4-113. Procedure for obtaining supplies or materials for departments or institutions.

Unless otherwise provided by law, when the head of any department of the state shall desire any office supplies or materials or other articles of use or necessity, written application shall be made therefor to the division of purchases and stores, sworn to and stating by items the articles desired and needed, showing out of what fund they are to be paid, that the articles are necessary, that the amount of the requisition is not excessive, and that no part of the same will be used except in conducting the public business. Such application shall be kept on file in the office of the division of purchases and stores. (Acts 1923, No. 85, p. 67; Code 1923, § 43; Acts 1939, No. 112, p. 144; Code 1940, T. 55, § 109.)

§ 41-4-114. Purchase of property from United States or its agencies.

(a) Whenever it appears advantageous to the state or any department, division, bureau, commission, board or other agency thereof to purchase or otherwise acquire any equipment, supplies, material or other property which may be offered for sale by the United States of America or any agency thereof, the state purchasing agent may, with the approval of the governor and the director of finance, enter into a contract for such purchase with the federal government or with any federal agency charged with the sale or disposition of such equipment, supplies, material or other property, and, subject to the aforesaid approval, said state purchasing agent is hereby authorized to execute such contract or contracts.

(b) Subject to the approval of the governor and the director of finance, the state purchasing agent may enter a bid or bids in behalf of any department, division, bureau, commission, board or other agency of the state at any sale of any equipment, supplies, material or other property offered for sale through written proposals by the United States of America or any agency thereof when it appears that it is to the interest of the state to do so.

(c) Should the regulations of the federal government, or any agency thereof handling the disposition and sale of any equipment, supplies, material or other property which it would be advantageous to the state to purchase, require that partial or full payment be made at the time sale is effected and before the equipment, supplies, material or other property will be delivered, or where such equipment, supplies, material or other property is sold under bids and the federal agency in charge of such sale requires a deposit in support of bids, the state comptroller, upon requisition by the state purchasing agent, shall, with the approval of the governor and the director of finance, draw a state warrant against the funds of such department or agency payable to the United States of America or its proper agency in such amount as may be necessary to meet the terms and conditions of sale without requiring a certificate showing that the equipment, supplies, material or other property has actually been delivered to the state department or other agency in whose behalf the purchase is being negotiated. (Acts 1945, No. 88, p. 87.)

§ 41-4-115. State departments and agencies authorized to enter into lease-sale contracts for procurement of equipment, etc.

All departments and agencies of the state of Alabama may, subject to the provisions of this chapter and articles 2 and 3 of chapter 16 of this title, execute and enter into lease-sale contracts for the procurement of materials, machinery and other equipment which are necessary to enable such state department or agency to carry out the obligations imposed by law upon such agency or department of the state of Alabama and which is in the best interest of the state of Alabama. All contracts under this section must be approved in writing by the governor or by the director of finance when so authorized by the governor. (Acts 1969, No. 225, p. 545.)

Collateral references. — 81 C.J.S., States, §§ 112-114.

Division 2.

Public Printing and Binding.

Constitution. — For constitutional provisions requiring contracts for public printing to be awarded to lowest responsible bidder below a maximum price, see Const., § 69.

§ 41-4-130. Public printing and binding to be done under contract.

The acts and journals of the legislature, the revenue laws of each session of the legislature, in separate pamphlets, the reports of the decisions of the supreme court, the reports of the decisions of the court of civil appeals and the court of criminal appeals, the annual or biennial reports of all officials, boards, commissions, bureaus, departments and institutions, which are required by law to make such reports, and all handbooks, pamphlets, blanks, bulletins, circulars, notices, reports, messages and forms used, published or required by all such officials, boards, commissions, bureaus, departments and institutions, and also by the clerk of the supreme court, the clerk of the court of civil appeals, the clerk of the court of criminal appeals, and all bills, papers, documents and reports ordered by and for the use of the legislature or either house thereof, shall be printed, or printed and bound, as the case may be, and the records of the supreme court, the court of civil appeals and the court of criminal appeals shall be bound as ordered by the clerks of said courts, under contract as provided in this division. No printing or binding for the state shall be done under contracts made in pursuance of the provisions of this division other than such as are covered and provided for in this division. This division shall not apply, however, to printing and binding required by any college, vocational-technical school or trade school subject to the jurisdiction and control of the state board of education; such printing and binding shall be performed or furnished under contracts let on a competitive bidding basis by the purchasing agent or chief executive officer of the institution affected. (Code 1896, § 3385; Code 1907, § 1647; Code 1923, § 2895; Acts 1939, No. 112, p. 144; Code 1940, T. 55, § 110; Acts 1967, No. 223, p. 592.)

Cited in Stewart v. Wilson Printing Co., 210 Ala. 624, 99 So. 92 (1924).

Collateral references. — 72 C.J.S., Print, pp. 845, 846.

§ 41-4-131. Classification of public printing and binding.

The printing and binding authorized in section 41-4-130, for the purposes of the contracts provided in this division, shall be divided into classes, each class to be let in a separate contract:

Class 1. The reports of the decisions of the supreme court, the court of civil appeals and the court of criminal appeals.

Class 2(a). The acts passed by the legislature.

Class 2(b). The journals of the house and senate.

Class 3. Annual or biennial reports of all officials, boards, commissions, bureaus, departments and institutions which are required by law, and all handbooks, pamphlets or bulletins which the commissioner of agriculture and industries is or may be authorized by law to publish, and all other pamphlets or documents of a public nature, the publication of which is ordered by the governor in pursuance of law.

Class 4. All messages of the governor to the legislature, all bills, documents and reports ordered by and for the use of the legislature or either house thereof while in session; all blanks, circulars, notices and forms used in the office of or ordered by the governor, or by any other state official, board, commission, bureau or department, or by the clerks of the supreme court, the court of civil appeals and the court of criminal appeals; and all blanks and forms ordered by and for the use of the secretary of the senate and clerk of the house of representatives, and binding the original records and opinions of the supreme court, the court of civil appeals and the court of criminal appeals. (Code 1896, § 3386; Code 1907, § 1648; Code 1923, § 2896; Acts 1939, No. 112, p. 144; Code 1940, T. 55, § 111; Acts 1949, No. 28, p. 42.)

Cited in Stewart v. Wilson Printing Co., 210
Ala. 624, 99 So. 92 (1924).

§ 41-4-132. Biennial advertisements for bids for printing.

It shall be the duty of the director of finance to advertise biennially for 10 days in not less than two nor more than four daily newspapers published in the state for proposals to do the printing and binding for the state for the term of two years, commencing on October 1 next thereafter. (Code 1896, § 3387; Code 1907, § 1649; Code 1923, § 2897; Acts 1939, No. 112, p. 144; Code 1940, T. 55, § 112.)

§ 41-4-133. Proposals to be in writing; bonds.

All proposals for the printing and binding for the state must be in writing, signed by the person, firm or corporation making the proposal and must be accompanied by a bond in some guaranty company authorized to do business in the state of Alabama in such penalty for each class as the director of finance may determine, to be approved by the governor, auditor and treasurer, payable in every instance to the state of Alabama and conditioned for the faithful performance of the contract made on the acceptance of the proposal. The proposals with the bonds must be sealed, endorsed "proposals for class . . . . (specifying the class the proposal is for) of public printing and binding" and delivered to the director of finance, by mail or otherwise, on or before the twentieth day of the month in which the advertisement is made. The proposals for each class of public printing and binding must be delivered in separate envelopes addressed as above. (Code 1896, § 3388; Code 1907, § 1650; Acts 1911, No. 397, p. 559; Code 1923, § 2898; Acts 1939, No. 112, p. 144; Code 1940, T. 55, § 113.)

§ 41-4-134. Opening of bids; acceptance of bids; rejection and readvertisement of bids.

The director of finance must, after the twentieth and before the thirtieth day of the month in which bids are received, open the same in the presence of the governor, auditor and treasurer, or any two of them, and the director of finance, by and with the approval of the governor, auditor and treasurer, any two concurring, shall select the lowest responsible bidder, either for the classes separately or for the classes combined, as may be to the best interest of the state, but no bid unaccompanied by a bond as required in this division shall be considered. If, in the judgment of a majority of the said officers present, the public interest can be served best thereby, all the proposals, or all for either class, may be rejected, whereupon the director of finance shall advertise again in all respects as in the first instance for proposals to do the public printing or binding, or that class of it, the bids for which were rejected, and, upon the coming in of the new bids, they shall be considered, passed on and accepted or rejected, and in the last event, advertisement made again as provided in this division with respect to the proposals first made. (Code 1896, § 3390; Code

1907, § 1652; Code 1923, § 2899; Acts 1939, No. 112, p. 144; Code 1940, T. 55, § 114.)

§ 41-4-135. Entering into contract; failure of bidder to enter into contract within 10 days of acceptance.

When any proposal has been accepted, the director of finance must endorse the fact and the date of its acceptance therein and give notice thereof to the person, firm or corporation whose proposal has been accepted. Thereupon, the director of finance, in the name of the state, and such person, firm or corporation shall enter into contract in writing for the printing and binding covered by the accepted proposal for the time and in the manner prescribed by law on the terms expressed in the proposal. If such person, firm or corporation fails for 10 days to enter into the contract, the officers named in section 41-4-134 may select the next lowest bidder for the printing and binding as to which the failure has occurred, and the person, firm or corporation failing and the sureties on his bond shall be jointly and severally liable to the state for all damages that may result from such failure, including the increased cost of the printing and binding, or either, for the term under any contract afterwards made and the expenses incident to the making of any subsequent contract. (Code 1896, § 3391; Code 1907, § 1653; Code 1923, § 2900; Acts 1939, No. 112, p. 144; Code 1940, T. 55, § 115.)

§ 41-4-136. Contract and bond to be approved by governor, auditor and treasurer; filing of bonds.

All contracts for public printing and binding and all bonds to secure the faithful performance of the same shall be approved by the governor, auditor and treasurer, and a new or additional bond may be required whenever they deem it necessary; but the giving of such new or additional bond shall in no way affect the liability of the sureties on the original or any existing bond. All such bonds must be filed and recorded in the office of the secretary of state. (Code 1896, § 3392; Code 1907, § 1654; Code 1923, § 2901; Code 1940, T. 55, § 116.)

§ 41-4-137. Forfeiture of contract for cause; new contract.

Any contract made under the provisions of this division may be declared forfeited by a majority of the officers therein named for the failure or neglect of the contractor to execute the same faithfully, promptly and skillfully, and, upon such forfeiture, the printing and binding embraced in said contract shall be relet after advertisement in all respects as in the original contract, and the sureties on his bond shall be jointly and severally liable to the state for all damages which result from such failure. In case the contract is declared forfeited as herein provided, such damages shall include the increased cost of the printing and binding, or either, under any subsequent contract for the term covered by the original contract, and all expenses incident to reletting. (Code 1896, § 3393; Code 1907, § 1655; Code 1923, § 2902; Code 1940, T. 55, § 117.)

§ 41-4-138. Venue of actions on contracts.

Actions against contractors for public printing and binding and the sureties on their bonds, either or both, may be prosecuted in the courts of Montgomery county, without regard to the residence of the defendants. (Code 1896, § 3394; Code 1907, § 1656; Code 1923, § 2903; Code 1940, T. 55, § 118.)

§ 41-4-139. Where printing to be done.

The printing and binding in class 4 must be done in the city of Montgomery. All other printing and binding enumerated in 1, 2 and 3 may be done wherever the best work at the lowest bid can be had. (Code 1896, § 3395; Code 1907, § 1657; Code 1923, § 2906; Code 1940, T. 55, § 119.)

§ 41-4-140. Paper and parchment for blanks.

The parchment for blanks, when it may be necessary to use that material, shall be furnished by the state. All blanks provided for by this division shall be printed on good paper, except where parchment is used, of such size and with such type as the officer ordering the same may direct. (Code 1896, § 3397; Code 1907, § 1658; Code 1923, § 2907; Code 1940, T. 55, § 120.)

§ 41-4-141. Time for making reports by departments, officers, boards, etc.; printing of same.

All reports of departments, officers, commissioners, boards and bureaus, authorized to be printed by this division, shall be made to the governor on or before October 10, annually or biennially as may be required by law, for the annual or biennial period ending September 30 theretofore. The governor shall have them, or such parts thereof as he may deem necessary, printed in such numbers as the public interest may, in his judgment, require. One half of the edition in each instance shall be reserved for the use of the legislature, and the remainder for distribution as prescribed by law. The governor shall have 25 copies of each of the reports provided for in this division bound in durable binding for distribution among the several executive officers of the state and the state library. (Code 1896, § 3398; Code 1907, § 1659; Code 1923, § 2908; Code 1940, T. 55, § 121.)

§ 41-4-142. Preparation of acts and joint resolutions for printing.

In addition to other duties imposed by law, the secretary of the senate and the clerk of the house of representatives must, during and after each session of the legislature, prepare for publication correct copies of the bills and joint resolutions passed by the legislature. The number of the bill or resolution passed by the two houses of the legislature, as the same is placed thereon by the secretary or clerk, the name of the author and the number of the act shall be printed on the act and be published in the bound volume of the session laws. (Acts 1949, No. 27, p. 39, § 1.)

§ 41-4-143. Number, size and contents of volumes of acts; delivery of material to printer.

The acts of the legislature shall be printed and bound in one volume, unless they require more than 1,200 pages, in which event they shall be printed and bound in two or more volumes of approximately equal size. In addition to the acts, the bound volume shall contain the messages of the governor, the names and post-office addresses of the heads of all state agencies and the names and post-office addresses of the members and officers of the legislature. The secretary of state shall compile and deliver to the printer all material to be inserted in the bound volume within 10 days after adjournment of the legislature. (Acts 1949, No. 27, p. 39, § 2.)

§ 41-4-144. Volumes of acts to be certified.

The title page of each volume of the acts shall have printed thereon the following certificate, to be executed by the secretary of state: "The undersigned, as Secretary of State of the State of Alabama, does hereby certify that this book contains bills and joint resolutions enacted at the (   ) session of the Legislature of Alabama and is the official publication of such acts." (Acts 1949, No. 27, p. 39, § 3.)

§ 41-4-145. Preparation of journals.

The journals must be prepared with a title page and index and must be substantially half-bound and lettered. (Code 1852, § 76; Code 1867, § 112; Code 1876, § 124; Code 1886, § 216; Code 1896, § 3405; Code 1907, § 1666; Code 1923, § 2915; Code 1940, T. 55, § 128.)

§ 41-4-146. Delivery and certification of acts and joint resolutions to printer.

The secretary of the senate or the clerk of the house of representatives shall furnish the printer a copy of each bill and joint resolution within three working days after the enrolled act is deposited in the office of the secretary of state, together with a certificate that such copy has been compared with the enrolled act and is a correct copy of the original. (Acts 1949, No. 27, p. 39, § 4.)

§ 41-4-147. Penalty for not delivering copies of acts to printer.

For each day's delay of the secretary of the senate, clerk of the house, secretary of state, director of the legislative reference service or other officer in furnishing the printer the copy required in printing the acts and journals at the time prescribed for delivery, such officer shall forfeit the sum of $20.00, to be deducted by the comptroller from salary first accruing thereafter. The comptroller must not pay to such officer any salary accruing next after the period when such copy should have been by law delivered to the printer without first having received and filed in his office, as a voucher, the certificate of such officer that copy for the acts or journals, as the case may be, has been delivered by him to the printer within the time prescribed by law. (Acts 1949, No. 27, p. 39, § 13.)

§ 41-4-148. Style of printing and quality of paper of acts and journals; index.

(a) The acts and the journals of the legislature shall be printed on paper of the same weight and quality as that required for the supreme court's reports, in 10-point type solid, 26 pica ems wide and not less than 44 lines on the page. The pages must be sewed to two strong tapes and be bound in the best quality American buckram. The titles of acts, affidavits required to be printed in the journals, messages, reports and inserted matter shall be printed in eight-point type solid. Votes shall be printed in four columns solid, with the words "Yeas" and "Nays" printed in italics.

(b) The journal of each house, if not more than 1,200 pages in length, shall be bound in one volume; and if more than 1,200 pages, it shall be bound in two or more volumes.

(c) Each journal shall be provided with an index, which shall be prepared by the secretary of the senate or the clerk of the house, as the case may be, within 30 days from receipt of a paged copy from the printer.

(d) The acts shall be provided with an index, which shall be prepared by the legislative reference service within 10 days after receipt of a paged copy of the acts from the printer. (Acts 1949, No. 27, p. 39, § 5.)

§ 41-4-149. Revenue laws to be printed separately.

The revenue laws passed at each session are not only to be printed in the acts and joint resolutions, but must be separately prepared for publication, and 500 copies printed on the same paper, of the same size and with the same type as the acts. (Code 1852, § 79; Code 1867, § 116; Code 1876, § 128; Code 1886, § 220; Code 1896, § 3409; Code 1907, § 1670; Code 1923, § 2919; Code 1940, T. 55, § 132.)

§ 41-4-150. When acts and journals must be printed and delivered by printer.

(a) The printer must, within 90 days after being furnished a copy of the last act, print, as herein provided, package or box in complete sets and distribute pursuant to an address list furnished by the secretary of state, 2,000 copies of the bound acts, which copies shall be indexed, stitched, half-bound and lettered.

(b) Within 180 days after receipt of the copy from the secretary of the senate and clerk of the house of representatives, which period shall include the 30 days mentioned in subsection (c) of section 41-4-148, the printer must distribute in packaged or boxed sets pursuant to an address list furnished by the secretary of state, 550 copies of the journal of each house, which copies shall also be indexed, stitched, half-bound and lettered. (Acts 1949, No. 27, p. 39, § 6; Acts 1959, No. 403, p. 1035; Acts 1975, No. 1161, § 1.)

§ 41-4-151. Payment for printing — Generally.

For all printing done by order of either house of the legislature, or for the executive or state officers, the public printer must procure a certified copy of such order from the secretary of the senate, clerk of the house or from the officer ordering the work, upon the presentation of which to the comptroller and the production of a copy of the work ordered, he must issue his warrant for the payment of the same according to the prices specified in the contract. (Code 1852, § 91; Code 1867, § 130; Code 1876, § 135; Code 1886, § 227; Code 1896, § 3412; Code 1907, § 1673; Code 1923, § 2922; Acts 1939, No. 112, p. 144; Code 1940, T. 55, § 135.)

§ 41-4-152. Same — Laws and journals.

Upon the delivery of the requisite number of the laws and journals, within the time prescribed and executed in all respects as herein provided, the secretary of state must give his receipt for the same, upon which the comptroller must issue his warrant for payment. (Code 1852, § 92; Code 1867, § 131; Code 1876, § 136; Code 1886, § 228; Code 1896, § 3413; Code 1907, § 1674; Code 1923, § 2923; Acts 1939, No. 112, p. 144; Code 1940, T. 55, § 136.)

§ 41-4-153. Same — Revenue laws.

Upon the delivery of the requisite number of the revenue laws, printed as herein provided, the comptroller must issue his warrant for payment. (Code 1852, § 93; Code 1867, § 132; Code 1876, § 137; Code 1886, § 229; Code 1896, § 3414; Code 1907, § 1675; Code 1923, § 2924; Acts 1939, No. 112, p. 144; Code 1940, T. 55, § 137.)

§ 41-4-154. Same — Source of funds.

Payments for all printing done for or on account of the department of agriculture and industries shall be made out of the funds of that department in the same manner as other expenses of that department are paid. Payment for printing for the public service commission shall be made out of the funds arising from the inspection and supervision fees collected from transportation companies and public utilities for the support of that commission, on the certificate of the president of the commission to the secretary of state that the work has been done on his order, or the order of the governor if it be the annual report, and the certificate of the secretary of state to the comptroller setting forth the amount due for the work under the contract. Payment for all other printing authorized by this division shall be made out of the general annual appropriation for that purpose. (Code 1896, § 3415; Code 1907, § 1676; Code 1923, § 2925; Acts 1939, No. 112, p. 144; Code 1940, T. 55, § 138.)

§ 41-4-155. Charge for matters ordered to be printed by both houses.

When any matter is ordered to be printed by both houses, charge must be made for the same in all respects as though ordered by one house only, except in cases where 10 days intervene between the times of the respective orders. (Code 1867, § 134; Code 1876, § 139; Code 1886, § 231; Code 1896, § 3416; Code 1907, § 1677; Code 1923, § 2926; Code 1940, T. 55, § 139.)

§ 41-4-156. Printing of acts and resolutions in pamphlet form — Distribution to certain officers, departments, etc.; certain officers to keep pamphlets in books until acts published in permanent form.

(a) Within three working days after an enrolled bill or joint resolution has been delivered to and filed in the office of the secretary of state, it shall be numbered, in the order in which it is received, and a copy of each local or general act shall be placed in the hands of the printer by the secretary of the senate or clerk of the house, as the case may be. The printer must immediately print 1,200 copies in slip or pamphlet form in accordance with section 41-4-158, which the printer must distribute as follows: two copies for every member and officer of the legislature, which copies shall be delivered to the secretary of the senate and the clerk of the house of representatives, 25 copies to the supreme court library, 15 copies to the legislative reference service, 20 copies to the law library at the University of Alabama, 50 copies to the department of archives and history, one copy to every judge of a court of record, circuit court clerk, register of the circuit court, district court clerk, district attorney, deputy district attorney, and sheriff, and the remainder shall be delivered to the secretary of state.

(b) Each probate judge, circuit court clerk, register of the circuit court, district court clerk and sheriff shall preserve in his office, in a book kept for that purpose, each pamphlet furnished him until the acts are published in permanent form. Pamphlet acts shall be open to public inspection during regular business hours. (Acts 1949, No. 27, p. 39, § 7; Acts 1975, No. 1161, § 1; Acts 1981, No. 81-347, p. 503.)

The 1981 amendment, effective April 29, 1981, inserted "local or" preceding "general act" in the first sentence and added "15 copies to the legislative reference service" following "25 copies to the supreme court library" in subsection (a).

§ 41-4-157. Same — Paper; type size; size of pages.

The pamphlet acts shall be printed on good white paper, of octavo form, 26 ems measure in width, in 10-point type solid, with not less than 44 lines to the page. (Acts 1949, No. 27, p. 39, § 8.)

§ 41-4-158. Same — Order of printing acts; size of pamphlets; required heading.

(a) The acts shall be printed in slip or pamphlet form in the order in which they are numbered, and each pamphlet or slip must be complete within itself. If there are more than four pages, the pamphlet must be stitched, stapled or pasted on the side, to make a pamphlet of not less than six by nine inches in size.

(b) At the top of the front page of every slip or pamphlet the following words shall be printed in bold type: "Each probate judge, sheriff, district court clerk and the clerk and register of the circuit court is required by law to preserve this slip or pamphlet in a book kept in his office until the act is published in permanent form." Following such heading, the act number shall be printed on the left and the bill number, with the name of the author of the law or resolution, on the right. (Acts 1949, No. 27, p. 39, § 9.)

§ 41-4-159. Same — Pamphlet acts to be delivered in 10 days; new contract upon failure of printer to deliver.

In addition to other duties imposed by law, the secretary of the senate and the clerk of the house shall see to it that the printer prints and delivers the acts promptly. If, for any cause, the printer cannot print and deliver pamphlet acts within 10 calendar days after receiving the copy, exclusive of the time allowed the secretary of state for proofreading, which shall not exceed three working days, the secretary of the senate and clerk of the house shall, with the approval of the governor, state auditor and state treasurer, forthwith contract for this printing with some person who will print and deliver the acts as herein required. (Acts 1949, No. 27, p. 39, § 10.)

§ 41-4-160. Bond of printer of acts and journals; deductions from contract price for failure to perform within time.

(a) In making the contracts for publication of the acts and journals, the state purchasing agent shall require the printer to give bond, in such sum as he may direct, conditioned that the acts and journals shall be printed as herein provided and be delivered as herein required.

(b) In the event the printer fails to perform his contract within the time prescribed for performance, the comptroller must cause to be deducted from the contract price, as liquidated damages, $100.00 for each day's delay; except that the printer shall be allowed one day for each day his performance is delayed by reason of the neglect of duty by a state official or by strike or vis major. (Acts 1949, No. 27, p. 39, § 11.)

§ 41-4-161. Printing of acts when recess taken by legislature.

If a recess is taken by the legislature for a longer time than 30 days, all of the acts passed before the recess may, in the discretion of the secretary of the senate and clerk of the house, be ordered printed and bound immediately. (Acts 1949, No. 27, p. 39, § 12.)

ARTICLE 6.

DIVISION OF SERVICE.

§ 41-4-180. Established; duties generally.

There shall be in the department of finance the division of service. The functions and duties of the division of service shall be as follows:

(1) To provide for the stamping and mailing for each state department, board, bureau, commission, agency and office located and operating in the city of Montgomery and to operate a central mailing room or rooms and service for said departments, boards, bureaus, commissions, agencies and offices. The director of finance shall direct the delivery of mail to such mailing room or rooms by such of said departments, boards, bureaus, commissions, agencies and officers as he may see fit, ready to be delivered to the United States post office, except that it shall not be stamped with postage stamps or by means of a postage meter. Every piece of mail, when so delivered, shall bear the name of the department, board, bureau, commission, agency or office of the state sending it, and all mail received in a mailing room shall be properly stamped with postage stamps or passed through an authorized postage meter and then delivered to the United States post office. The chief of the division of service shall cause an accurate account to be kept of all pieces of mail from and the postage used on account of each department, board, bureau, commission, agency and office of the state, and the cost of such postage shall be charged by the comptroller against its appropriation for such purpose. Such central mailing rooms shall be conveniently located and shall be kept open for business as long as may be necessary to dispose of all outgoing mail daily. The expenditure of any state funds for postage by any department, board, bureau, commission, agency or office of the state required to deliver its mail to a central mailing room (other than the department of finance) shall be unlawful. This section shall not, however, prevent the stamping or metering of envelopes for the transmittal of unemployment compensation warrants and warrants for the payment of any public assistance benefits in, or the mailing of such envelopes from, the department or departments having charge of the other functions and duties relating to unemployment compensation and public assistance.

(2) To provide exclusively for all telephone service for each state department, board, bureau, commission, agency and office located and operating in the city of Montgomery and make all contracts and agreements in relation to the telephone service to each of the departments, boards, bureaus, commissions, agencies and offices of the state located and operating in the city of Montgomery. Insofar as practicable, all telephones shall be connected through a central switchboard or switchboards, into which there may be as many trunk lines as the business of the state justifies. The telephone expense of each such department, board, bureau, commission, agency or office of the state shall be charged by the comptroller against its appropriation for such purpose.

(3) To provide exclusively for all clerical and stenographic services to all state departments, boards, bureaus, commissions, agencies and offices located in the city of Montgomery for part-time or emergency needs, and to operate and maintain a central clerical and stenographic pool for the purpose of providing each department, board, bureau, commission, agency and office of the state located and operating in the city of Montgomery with all part-time and emergency employees.

(4) To manage, supervise, maintain, repair, improve, light, heat and clean the Capitol and all buildings and property owned or leased by the state in the city of Montgomery, including monuments and historical sites. In any case in which an appropriation has been or shall be made for such purposes to any department, board, bureau, commission, agency or office of the state for such purpose, the expenses of such services for buildings or property used by it shall be charged by the comptroller to such department, board, bureau, commission, agency or office.

(5) With the approval of the governor, to allocate space in the Capitol and in all buildings owned or leased by the state in the city of Montgomery for the use of the departments, boards, bureaus, commissions, agencies and offices of the state.

(6) To provide a guard, watchman and police service for the Capitol and the other buildings and property owned or leased by the state and located in the city of Montgomery.

(7) With the approval of the governor, to transfer between departments, boards, bureaus, commissions, agencies, offices and institutions of the state any furniture, fixtures, supplies, material, equipment or other personal property.

(8) To sell, exchange or otherwise dispose of any personal property of the state determined by the director of finance not to be needed for public use or to have become unsuited for such use.

(9) To perform such other functions and duties of the department of finance as may from time to time be assigned, by the director of finance. (Acts 1939, No. 112, p. 144; Code 1940, T. 55, § 145.)

Cross references. — As to the chief of service of the division of service working in cooperation with the legislature regarding the control and usage of streets and parking lots in or near the state Capitol complex, see § 29-1-19.1.

§ 41-4-181. Chief of service.

The division of service shall be headed by and be under the direction, supervision and control of an officer who shall be designated the chief of service. The chief of service shall be appointed by the director of finance, with the approval of the governor. (Acts 1939, No. 112, p. 144; Code 1940, T. 55, § 145.)

§ 41-4-182. Employment of police officers at Capitol and other state buildings; authority to prescribe duties and type and color of uniforms; minimum standards for such officers.

The director of finance shall employ the necessary state Capitol police officers, subject to the state merit system laws, to preserve order, prevent crime, and protect and save from injury persons and property at the Capitol and all state buildings and buildings occupied by state departments and agencies within the state of Alabama, and he shall prescribe their duties and the type and color of uniform they shall wear. Said officers shall be required to meet the minimum standards of law enforcement officers, as provided by the peace officers' standards and training commission, prior to being granted permanent employment status. (Code 1896, § 1967; Code 1907, § 564; Acts 1923, No. 600, p. 789; Code 1923, § 767; Acts 1933, Ex. Sess., No. 138, p. 124; Acts 1939, No. 112, p. 144; Code 1940, T. 55, § 146; Acts 1953, No. 891, p. 1198; Acts 1981, No. 81-356, p. 521, § 1.)

The 1981 amendment, effective April 29, 1981, rewrote this section.

§ 41-4-183. Employment of landscape gardener for Capitol grounds.

The director of finance shall employ a landscape gardener whose duty it shall be to look after the grounds, etc., of the Capitol. (Acts 1923, No. 600, p. 789; Code 1923, § 768; Acts 1933, Ex. Sess., No. 138, p. 124; Acts 1939, No. 112, p. 144; Code 1940, T. 55, § 147; Acts 1981, No. 81-356, p. 521, § 2.)

The 1981 amendment, effective April 29, 1981, deleted "in addition to the watchmen mentioned in section 41-4-182, the," inserted "The" preceding "director" and inserted "of finance" following "director."

§ 41-4-184. Color of uniform to be worn by state Capitol police officers; powers of such officers.

(a) State Capitol police officers shall be required to wear a gray uniform.

(b) State Capitol police officers, when duly appointed, shall have the powers of peace officers in this state and may exercise such powers anywhere within the state. (Code 1896, § 1968; Code 1907, §§ 565, 566; Code 1923, §§ 769, 770; Code 1940, T. 55, §§ 148, 149; Acts 1981, No. 81-356, p. 521, § 3.)

The 1981 amendment, effective April 29, 1981, rewrote this section.

§ 41-4-185. Uniforms and necessary equipment for state Capitol police officers to be furnished; authority to insure such officers against injury or death caused by accident or violence while discharging duties; limits as to amount of insurance; payment for such insurance.

(a) All state Capitol police officers shall be furnished with uniforms, firearms, ammunition, flashlights and all other equipment necessary for the effective performance of their duties.

(b) The state department of finance is authorized, subject to approval by the governor, to insure state Capitol police officers in some insurance company or companies authorized to do business in the state of Alabama against personal injury or death caused by accident or violence while discharging their duties as such state Capitol police officers; provided, the amount of insurance to be procured as to any such state Capitol police officer shall not exceed the amount which would be payable to such state Capitol police officer under the workmen's compensation laws of the state of Alabama if such state Capitol police officer were privately employed; except, that such policy may provide additional benefits not to exceed $10,000 per state Capitol police officer for the payment of hospital and medical expenses. The cost of such insurance shall be paid by the state department of finance out of any funds appropriated to its use, in the manner provided by law. (Acts 1971, No. 2401, p. 3831; Acts 1981, No. 81-356, p. 521, § 4.)

The **1981 amendment,** effective April 29, 1981, inserted "state" preceding "Capitol," substituted "police" for "security," deleted "patrolmen, nightwatchmen and guards" following "officers," and inserted "uniforms" preceding "firearms" in subsection (a), and added subsection (b).

§ 41-4-186. Montgomery city council authorized to adopt ordinances to protect Capitol grounds.

The city council of Montgomery may, with the approval of the governor, pass such ordinances as may be necessary for the protection of the grass, trees and other public property on the Capitol grounds, but no ordinance or bylaw of the city council of Montgomery shall be operative within the Capitol building or grounds without the consent of the governor. (Code 1896, § 1969; Code 1907, § 567; Code 1923, § 771; Code 1940, T. 55, § 150.)

ARTICLE 7.

LEGAL DIVISION.

§ 41-4-200. Established.

There shall be in the department of finance a legal division. (Acts 1953, No. 448, p. 552, § 1.)

§ 41-4-201. Chief of legal division — Head of division; vacancies in office.

The legal division shall be headed by and be under the direction, supervision and control of the chief of said division. Any vacancy in this office shall, subject to the provisions of the state merit system law, be filled by appointment by the director of finance, with the approval of the attorney general. (Acts 1953, No. 448, p. 552, § 1.)

§ 41-4-202. Same — Chief designated assistant attorney general; oath; duties.

The chief of the legal division shall be an assistant attorney general, shall take the oath required of other assistant attorneys general, shall be commissioned as an assistant attorney general, and shall, in addition to the duties and functions herein provided for, have the duties and functions of an assistant attorney general; except, that his entire time shall be devoted to the department of finance. (Acts 1953, No. 448, p. 552, § 2.)

§ 41-4-203. Same — Advice and opinions; appearance in financial litigation.

The chief of the legal division shall confer with and advise the director of finance and any and all of the subordinate officers and employees of the department of finance on all legal matters pertaining to said department. He shall furnish either verbal or written opinions, when requested by the director of finance, on legal questions pertaining to said department, but such opinions shall not have the force and effect of official opinions of the attorney general unless approved by the attorney general. He shall appear for the state in all litigation, both civil and criminal, affecting the department of finance, when authorized to do so by the director of finance and the attorney general. (Acts 1953, No. 448, p. 552, § 3.)

§ 41-4-204. Same — Representation of state board of adjustment.

The chief of the legal division shall represent the state board of adjustment in all legal matters, and the legal division shall do and perform all clerical duties and functions prescribed by the board. He shall attend all hearings of the board and advise with the members, when requested, on any legal questions arising from claims filed against the state or any of its agencies or institutions. (Acts 1953, No. 448, p. 552, § 4.)

Cross references. — As to board of adjustment generally, see § 41-9-60 et seq.

ARTICLE 8.

DIVISION OF DATA SYSTEMS MANAGEMENT.

§ 41-4-220. Created.

There shall be in the department of finance a division of data systems management. (Acts 1973, No. 1299, p. 2214, § 1.)

§ 41-4-221. Duties generally.

The functions, powers and duties of the division of data systems management shall be as follows:

(1) To plan, control and coordinate state data processing activities in such manner to insure the most economical use of state resources.

(2) To develop and maintain a master plan for the state's data processing activities.

(3) To establish and supervise the administration of such data processing centers deemed necessary to best serve the data processing needs of all agencies.

(4) To provide for the centralization, consolidation and shared use of equipment and services deemed necessary to obtain maximum utilization and efficiency in data processing operations.

(5) To transfer to any data processing center the data processing activities of any agency.

(6) To provide systems design and programming services to all state agencies.

(7) To select and procure by purchase or by lease any and all data processing systems and associated software deemed necessary to best serve the data processing needs of the state.

(8) To conduct data processing studies as deemed necessary and to enter contracts with other agencies, organizations, corporations or individuals to make such studies as are deemed to be necessary.

(9) To prepare contract specifications for equipment and services.

(10) To adopt such rules and regulations deemed necessary to carry out the duties and responsibilities imposed by this article. (Acts 1973, No. 1299, p. 2214, § 2.)

§ 41-4-222. Director.

The division of data systems management shall be headed by and under the direction, supervision and control of an officer who shall be designated as director of such division, to be appointed by the director of finance with the approval of the governor. (Acts 1973, No. 1299, p. 2214, § 1.)

§ 41-4-223. Employees.

The director of finance may employ, subject to the state Merit System Act, such additional employees as are deemed necessary to enable the division to perform its duties and responsibilities set out in this article. Their compensation shall be fixed in accordance with the state merit system pay plan. (Acts 1973, No. 1299, p. 2214, § 3.)

§ 41-4-224. Advisory committee.

There is hereby created an advisory committee to meet on the call of the director of the data systems management division and to advise him on such matters as he deems necessary. The advisory committee shall be composed of the head of each data processing unit in state service. (Acts 1973, No. 1299, p. 2214, § 4.)

ARTICLE 9.

MANAGER OF PRINTING AND PUBLICATIONS.

§ 41-4-240. Office created; under direction of director of finance; subject to state merit system; compensation.

There shall be in the department of finance an officer who will be responsible for coordination and control of all printing and publication performed by all agencies of the state of Alabama. This officer shall serve under the direction and control of and be appointed by the director of the department of finance, with the approval of the governor, subject to the state merit system law, and his compensation shall be fixed in accordance with the state merit system pay plan. (Acts 1973, No. 1286, p. 2198, § 1.)

Cited in Associated Indus. of Ala., Inc. v. Britton, 371 So. 2d 904 (Ala. 1979).

§ 41-4-241. Functions, powers and duties.

The functions, duties and powers of such officer are as follows:

(1) To make investigations, studies and inventories relative to all printing and publication activities performed by state agencies.

(2) To make recommendations to the director of finance and with his approval to consolidate and centralize the present printing facilities of the state and to specify the number and location of such facilities.

(3) To approve and to consolidate all purchases of printing equipment and supplies, equipment locations and printing schedules in the Capitol complex.

(4) To centralize printing order schedules to enable such work to be performed at the lowest possible cost.

(5) To establish a formal cost and billing system.

(6) To review all work done by vendors for the state in an effort to determine how much of such work could be performed by state printing facilities.

(7) To consolidate and authorize all purchase of photographic equipment and supplies.

(8) To promulgate such rules and regulations as he may deem necessary to carry out the provisions of this article. (Acts 1973, No. 1286, p. 2198, § 2.)

Cited in Associated Indus. of Ala., Inc. v. Britton, 371 So. 2d 904 (Ala. 1979).

§ 41-4-242. Additional employees.

Such additional employees as may be needed shall be employed subject to the provisions of the state Merit System Act. Their compensation shall be fixed in accordance with the merit system pay plan. (Acts 1973, No. 1286, p. 2198, § 3.)

Cross references. — As to merit system, see
§ 36-26-1 et seq.

§ 41-4-243. Exemption from sections 41-4-240 through 41-4-242 for departments and agencies whose printing costs are borne from certain federal grants.

Any department or agency of this state whose cost of printing and publishing, including the cost of the equipment, machines, supplies or any other item of inventory, documents, publications, reports, forms, regulations, instruction or other printed matter for use in the administration of the employment security program in the state, is borne from federal grants under authority of Title IX of the Social Security Act of 1935, as amended, shall be exempt from the requirements of sections 41-4-240 through 41-4-242. (Acts 1981, No. 81-799, p. 1407.)

Effective date. — The act which added the
section became effective May 27, 1981.

ARTICLE 10.

OFFICE OF SPACE MANAGEMENT.

§ 41-4-260. Established.

There shall be in the department of finance an office of space management. (Acts 1973, No. 1294, p. 2206, § 1.)

§ 41-4-261. Duties generally.

The functions, powers and duties of the office of space management shall be as follows:

(1) To formulate a statewide space management program.

(2) To establish long range plans in regard to state space needs.

(3) To make studies, surveys, investigations and inventories of all buildings owned or leased by the state and to require all agencies to assist in such activities.

(4) To promulgate uniform standards for allocation of facilities owned or leased by the state.

(5) To investigate all requests for additional facilities needed by all state agencies and to make recommendations concerning the need for and the best method of allocating or acquiring such facilities.

(6) To contract with other agencies, corporations or individuals to make studies, surveys, investigations, inventories and recommendations relative to the most economic and feasible methods of acquiring new space and utilization of present space.

(7) To assist and advise the director of finance in allocating available space and in acquiring new space.

(8) To make recommendations and reports to the legislature relative to the proper utilization of and acquisition of space by state agencies.

(9) To make rules and regulations necessary to implement the provisions of this article. (Acts 1973, No. 1294, p. 2206, § 2.)

§ 41-4-262. Director.

The office of space management shall be headed by and under the supervision, direction and control of an officer who shall be designated director of space management. He shall be appointed, subject to the provisions of the state merit system law, by the director of finance, with the approval of the governor. The compensation of such officer shall be fixed in accordance with the pay plan of the state merit system. (Acts 1973, No. 1294, p. 2206, § 1.)

§ 41-4-263. Additional employees.

The director of finance may employ, subject to the provisions of the state merit system, such additional employees as may be needed and fix their compensation in accordance with the state merit system pay plan. (Acts 1973, No. 1294, p. 2206, § 3.)

Cross references. — As to merit system, see § 36-26-1 et seq.

CHAPTER 5.

DEPARTMENT OF EXAMINERS OF PUBLIC ACCOUNTS.

§ 41-5-1. Created; divisions.

There is created a department of examiners of public accounts, composed of such divisions as the chief examiner determines to be necessary. (Acts 1947, No. 351, p. 231, § 2.)

§ 41-5-2. Offices.

The offices of the department of examiners of public accounts shall be located at the seat of government, but the department may conduct examinations and audits at the seat of government or elsewhere. The chief examiner shall keep his offices open at all reasonable times for the transaction of public business. (Acts 1947, No. 351, p. 231, § 6.)

§ 41-5-3. Chief examiner — Head of department; appointment; term of office; succession; filling of vacancies; confirmation of appointment by senate; removal from office.

(a) The affairs of the department shall be administered by a chief examiner, whose actions shall be supervised and controlled by a legislative committee on public accounts. The chief examiner shall be selected and appointed by the legislative committee on public accounts to serve for a term of seven years and until his successor is appointed and qualified. The first of such terms shall commence on October 1, 1947, and such officer shall be eligible for reappointment to such office for such subsequent term of like duration as shall be deemed appropriate by the legislative committee on public accounts.

Vacancies in the office of chief examiner arising from any cause shall be filled by the legislative committee on public accounts, the person so appointed to hold office for the unexpired term of his predecessor. Every appointment of the chief examiner shall be subject to confirmation by the senate at the first regular or special session of the legislature held thereafter; provided, however, that this shall not affect the right or authority of the chief examiner to act pending senatorial confirmation or rejection.

(b) The chief examiner may be removed from office through impeachment proceedings instituted before the supreme court by the legislative committee on public accounts, the governor or by charges preferred by not less than 15 members of the legislature for any of the causes enumerated in section 173 of the Constitution of Alabama 1901, such proceedings to be conducted in accordance with the provisions of sections 36-11-7 through 36-11-12. (Acts 1947, No. 351, p. 231, § 3; Acts 1961, No. 85, p. 100.)

§ 41-5-4. Same — Qualifications; not eligible for appointment or election to other office during term; political affiliation during term.

(a) The chief examiner shall be selected with special reference to his training, experience, capacity and fitness for the duties as executive and administrative head of the department of examiners of public accounts. He shall not be less than 35 years of age, a resident citizen of the state of Alabama and a qualified elector of the state of Alabama at the time of his appointment.

(b) The chief examiner shall not be eligible for appointment or election to any state, county or municipal office, nor shall he be a member of a committee of any political party during the term for which he is appointed. Violation of this provision shall automatically vacate the office of chief examiner. (Acts 1947, No. 351, p. 231, § 4.)

Collateral references. — 81 C.J.S., States, § 67.

Age requirement for state public officer. 90 ALR3d 900.

§ 41-5-5. Same — Oath of office; bond.

The chief examiner, before entering upon the duties of his office, shall take and subscribe to the oath prescribed by article XVI, section 279 of the Constitution, and shall give bond for the faithful performance of his duties in the penal sum of $25,000.00. The oath and the bond, which must be approved by the legislative committee on public accounts and paid for from funds available to the department of examiners of public accounts, shall be filed with the secretary of state. The chief examiner shall be a commissioned officer of the state. (Acts 1947, No. 351, p. 231, § 5.)

§ 41-5-6. Same — Powers and duties generally.

The chief examiner shall be the executive and administrative head of the department and shall have the power and duty to:

(1) Exercise general supervision of and make regulations for the government of the department;

(2) Prescribe uniform rules pertaining to investigations, examinations, audits and departmental hearings;

(3) Supervise the fiscal affairs and responsibilities of the department;

(4) Appoint and remove the officers and employees of the department, subject to the provisions of the Merit System Act and the rules and regulations issued pursuant thereto;

(5) Keep an accurate and complete record of all departmental proceedings, record and file all bonds, reports and other documents and assume responsibility for the custody and preservation of all papers and documents of the department;

(6) Make recommendations and an annual report to the governor and to the legislative committee on public accounts concerning the condition, operation, functioning and findings of the department;

(7) Invoke any legal, equitable or special remedy for the enforcement of orders or the provisions of this chapter;

(8) Exercise any other power necessary to expedite the making of thorough and accurate audits of the accounts of all persons receiving or disbursing public funds;

(9) Examine and audit the books, accounts and records of all state and county offices, officers, bureaus, boards, commissions, corporations, departments and agencies;

(10) Prepare, except with respect to county boards of education, such bookkeeping, accounting and reporting systems, procedures, records and forms as may be necessary to install a uniform system of accounting and reporting in the various state and county offices;

(11) Report to the legislative committee on public accounts and the governor every expenditure or contract found to have been made in violation of law;

(12) Prepare, for use by the county boards of education, such bookkeeping, accounting and reporting systems, procedures, records and forms as may be necessary to the installation of a uniform system of accounting and reporting by the several county boards of education, install such bookkeeping, accounting and reporting systems in and for such county boards of education and exercise and maintain continuing supervision thereof; and

(13) Prepare and furnish to the chairmen of the county commissions of the several counties of the state a fiscal statement of each county, as of the end of each fiscal year, said statement showing receipts, disbursements, outstanding indebtedness and securities owned of and by each of the several counties. (Acts 1947, No. 351, p. 231, § 8; Acts 1951, No. 353, p. 640, § 1.)

Cited in Rogers v. Alabama Bd. of Educ., 392 So. 2d 235 (Ala. Civ. App. 1980).

Collateral references. — 81 C.J.S., States, § 203.

§ 41-5-7. Same — Delegation of power.

All powers and duties vested in the chief examiner may be delegated by him to his appointed assistants, deputies and employees, but the chief examiner shall be responsible for their acts. (Acts 1947, No. 351, p. 231, § 10.)

§ 41-5-8. Assistant chief examiner.

The chief examiner of public accounts may, with the approval of the legislative committee on public accounts, appoint an assistant chief examiner, who shall exercise such authority and perform such duties as the chief examiner may prescribe. The assistant chief examiner shall be selected because of his fitness and capacity. He must be some person who is eligible for appointment to, or holds the position of, public accounts examiner II in the classified service of the state; and he must have had not less than eight years, actual experience as an examiner of public accounts; provided, however, that the chief examiner may, at his discretion, have the employee so appointed revert to the classification previously held by him under the classified service and appoint some other employee, qualified under the provisions of this section, as assistant chief examiner. The assistant chief examiner shall be in the unclassified service of the state as defined in the Merit System Act. (Acts 1953, No. 791, p. 1085, §§ 1, 2.)

Cross references. — As to merit system, see § 36-26-1 et seq.

§ 41-5-9. Salaries of chief examiner and assistant chief examiner.

(a) The salary of the chief examiner of public accounts shall be fixed from time to time by the legislative committee on public accounts.

(b) The salary of the assistant chief examiner shall be fixed by the chief examiner at an amount not to exceed $1,000.00 less than the amount fixed by the legislative committee on public accounts as the salary for the chief examiner.

(c) The compensation for the chief examiner and the assistant chief examiner shall be paid out of funds appropriated to the department of examiners of public accounts and in the same manner as salaries of other officers and employees are paid. (Acts 1969, No. 777, p. 1393; Acts 1980, No. 80-704, p. 1422.)

§ 41-5-10. Assistants and employees.

(a) Upon a nonpartisan merit basis and subject to the Merit System Act, the chief examiner shall appoint division and unit heads and such assistants, deputies and employees as may be necessary to the efficient operation of the department. Assistant and deputy examiners shall be required to give bond for the faithful performance of their duties in the penal sum of $3,000.00.

(b) Subject to the Merit System Act, the chief examiner shall establish regulations governing dismissals, terminations, layoffs and suspensions. Severance of an employee's relationship with the department shall be in accordance with these regulations. All severances shall be for good cause. Failure to maintain technical or professional qualifications shall be good cause for severance. (Acts 1947, No. 351, p. 231, § 9.)

Cross references. — As to merit system, see § 36-26-1 et seq.

§ 41-5-11. Legal assistance by attorney general and district attorneys.

(a) The attorney general and his assistants and the district attorneys of the several circuits shall render to the chief examiner, without additional compensation, such legal services as he may request.

(b) Whenever the legality of any payment or shortage is involved in an examination, the chief examiner shall submit the facts in writing to the attorney general and request his opinion as to the law applying. A copy of every opinion of the attorney general affecting any state or county officer in the collection or disbursement of public funds shall be furnished to the officer affected, to the chief examiner and to the governor by the attorney general immediately upon release. (Acts 1947, No. 351, p. 231, § 11.)

§ 41-5-12. Legal counsel for department.

(a) The chief examiner of public accounts, with the approval of the attorney general, shall be authorized, subject to the provisions of the state merit system law, to appoint a legal counsel for the department of examiners of public accounts.

(b) The legal counsel for the department of examiners of public accounts must be at least 30 years of age, of good character, learned in the law and be qualified by training and experience to perform the duties of his office. He shall be commissioned as an assistant attorney general and shall have the authority and duties of an assistant attorney general, but he shall devote his entire time to the business of the department of examiners of public accounts.

(c) The compensation for the said legal counsel shall be paid out of the funds appropriated to the department of examiners of public accounts and in the same manner as the salaries of other employees are paid. (Acts 1950, 5th Ex. Sess., No. 62, p. 124; Acts 1951, No. 917, p. 1568.)

Cross references. — As to merit system, see § 36-26-1 et seq.

§ 41-5-13. Assistant legal counsels.

(a) The chief examiner of public accounts, with the approval of the attorney general, shall be authorized, subject to the provisions of the state merit system, to appoint not more than two assistant legal counsels for the department of examiners of public accounts. Each such assistant legal counsel shall be at least 22 years of age, of good character and learned in the law. Each such assistant legal counsel shall be commissioned as an assistant attorney general and have the authority and duties of an assistant attorney general, but he shall devote his entire time to the business of the department of examiners of public accounts and shall be subject to the supervision and control of the legal counsel of the department of examiners of public accounts.

(b) The compensation for the assistant legal counsels shall be paid out of the funds appropriated to the department of examiners of public accounts and in the same manner as the salaries of other employees are paid. (Acts 1969, No. 778, p. 1394.)

Cross references. — As to merit system, see § 36-26-1 et seq.

§ 41-5-14. Periodic examinations and audits of state and county offices, departments, boards, etc.

(a) The books, records, vouchers and accounts of every state and county office, officer, bureau, board, commission, corporation, institution, department and agency shall be examined and audited at least once in every period of two years and more frequently or continuously if that is deemed necessary or desirable by the chief examiner. The books, records, vouchers and accounts of municipal boards of education may be examined and audited upon request.

(b) Examinations and audits shall be made at the expense of the state. (Acts 1947, No. 351, p. 231, § 1.)

§ 41-5-15. Authority to administer oaths, take depositions and certify official acts.

The chief examiner and his assistant and deputy examiner shall have the power to administer oaths, take depositions and certify official acts. (Acts 1947, No. 351, p. 231, § 12.)

§ 41-5-16. Subpoenas.

The chief examiner or his specially authorized representatives shall have the power to issue subpoenas to compel the attendance of witnesses and production of papers necessary as evidence in connection with a dispute, claim, examination, audit or the administration of this chapter. In case a person refuses to obey such subpoena, the chief examiner or his representatives may invoke the aid of any circuit court in order that the testimony or evidence be produced. Upon proper showing, such court shall issue a subpoena or order requiring such person to appear before the chief examiner or his representative and produce all evidence and give all testimony relating to the matter in issue. A person failing to obey such order may be punished by the court as for contempt. (Acts 1947, No. 351, p. 231, § 13.)

§ 41-5-17. Publication of rules, regulations, etc.

The chief examiner shall compile and print for distribution:

(1) The rules and regulations of the department; and

(2) Such other material as the chief examiner deems relevant and suitable for the more effective administration of this chapter. (Acts 1947, No. 351, p. 231, § 14.)

§ 41-5-18. Legislative committee on public accounts — Established; supervisory agency; membership; chairman and vice-chairman; election and terms of members; filling of vacancies.

There shall be a legislative committee on public accounts to exercise general supervision and control over the actions of the chief examiner and the department of examiners of public accounts. The legislative committee on public accounts shall have 12 members. Five members shall be elected by the house of representatives from its membership and five members shall be elected by the senate from its membership. The president of the senate shall be a member of the committee and the chairman thereof. The speaker of the house of representatives shall be a member of the committee and the vice-chairman thereof. Members of the committee shall be elected at the first regular session of each legislature and shall hold office, as long as they remain legislators, until their successors are elected at the next regular session. Vacancies shall be filled by the remaining members of the committee from members of the house of representatives or the senate, depending upon in which representation the vacancy occurs, until the next session of the legislature, organizational, regular or special, at which time they shall be filled by the proper house. (Acts 1947, No. 351, p. 231, § 15.)

§ 41-5-19. Same — Meetings; compensation and expenses of members.

The legislative committee on public accounts shall meet annually at the capital, at a time which it shall set by resolution, for the purpose of receiving the report and recommendations of the chief examiner. The chief examiner shall attend such meetings and give such evidence, make such reports and perform such duties as the committee may direct. Annual meetings of the committee shall not be held for longer than 10 days. Special meetings not exceeding 10 days in total during any year may be called by the chairman and must be called by him within 10 days after receipt of a written request by the chief examiner, a majority of the committee or the governor. The members of the committee shall not receive any compensation for their attendance at meetings, but each shall be reimbursed for his expenses in accordance with article 2 of chapter 7 of Title 36 of this Code. Such expenses shall be paid from funds available to the department of examiners of public accounts. (Acts 1947, No. 351, p. 231, § 16.)

§ 41-5-20. Same — Reports.

The legislative committee on public accounts shall report its findings and recommendations and concerning the work of the department of examiners of public accounts to the senate and house of representatives at each session of the legislature and to the governor. (Acts 1947, No. 351, p. 231, § 17.)

§ 41-5-21. Examiners to make sworn reports of audits.

The examiners shall make a sworn report of their findings within a reasonable time after an audit is completed. The chief examiner shall certify one copy of each report to the circuit judge of the county in which the office examined is located. The judge shall refer to the report in his next oral charge to the grand jury. The report shall be entered in full upon the minutes of the court. Such reports shall be public records and prima facie evidence of what they charge. One copy of each report shall be certified to the governor. (Acts 1947, No. 351, p. 231, § 18.)

Report as evidence. — A report showing items of sheriff's fees collected by a clerk is sufficient as evidence if it shows that all the items were collected during the clerk's incumbency covered by the official bond upon which an action is brought, it being immaterial that the date of each collection is not contained therein. Hurst v. Kirby, 213 Ala. 640, 105 So. 872 (1925).

In prosecution of court clerk for embezzlement of public funds, the court did not err in allowing the state to introduce a copy of a report of an audit made by the examiners of public accounts of the state of Alabama. Chambers v. State, 352 So. 2d 21 (Ala. Crim. App.), cert. denied, 352 So. 2d 25 (Ala. 1977).

§ 41-5-22. Settlement of charges.

The chief examiner shall keep a docket in which shall be entered, in favor of the state, county or municipality, as the case may be, cases against persons who have not properly and lawfully accounted for all sums of money coming into their hands as public officers, agents or employees. If an amount found to be due the state, county or other governmental unit or agency as a result of an examination or audit is not settled upon demand by the examiner, the chief examiner shall immediately thereafter issue notice to the person in default and require him to appear on a day certain and show cause why the amount due should not be paid. If the defaulting officer fails to settle or to show just cause why the amount due should not be collected, the chief examiner shall certify such facts and the amount due the state to the attorney general, and the attorney general shall bring a civil action in the name of the state of Alabama against said officer and his bondsmen. If the amount due by said officer is in favor of the county or municipality, then the chief examiner shall certify to the district attorney of the circuit the amount or amounts so due, and such district attorney shall proceed to collect the same by a civil action against the officer and his bondsmen. (Acts 1947, No. 351, p. 231, § 19.)

Cited in State ex rel. Russell County v. Fourth Nat'l Bank, 270 Ala. 135, 117 So. 2d 145 (1959).

§ 41-5-23. Officers to keep uniform accounts.

Every state and county officer shall keep the books, records and accounts and make the reports of his office in accordance with such systems, procedures and forms as may be prescribed by the chief examiner pursuant to this chapter. Any officer who fails or refuses willfully to do so and the surety on his official bond shall be liable for a penalty of $50.00 for each week such failure or refusal continues. Penalties imposed and collected under this section shall be paid into the general fund of the state treasury. (Acts 1947, No. 351, p. 231, § 20.)

§ 41-5-24. Disposition of money received by department.

All moneys or funds received or collected by the department of examiners of public accounts in the form of fees, receipts or income as a result of services rendered in connection with municipal audits shall be covered by said department into the treasury of the state of Alabama to the credit of the general fund of the state of Alabama. All moneys or funds received or collected by the department of examiners of public accounts from the federal government shall be deposited into a special fund in the state treasury and these moneys and funds are hereby appropriated or reappropriated as necessary for the sole use of the department of examiners of public accounts.

No special, general or local law shall be repealed by this section, and the provisions of section 41-4-92 remain fully effective as to the department of examiners of public accounts. (Acts 1951, No. 285, p. 570; Acts 1980, No. 80-768, p. 1598.)

Collateral references. — 81A C.J.S., States, §§ 223, 224.

63 Am. Jur. 2d, Public Funds, §§ 1, 2.

CHAPTER 6.

DEPARTMENT OF ARCHIVES AND HISTORY.

ARTICLE 1.

GENERAL PROVISIONS.

Cross references. — As to establishment or restoration of any lost, mislaid, destroyed or mutilated records of the state, county or municipality, or of any department, agency or instrumentality thereof, see § 12-20-50. As to aboriginal mounds, earthworks and other antiquities, see § 41-3-1 et seq. As to historical commissions, see § 41-9-240 et seq.

§ 41-6-1. Establishment; location.

There shall be a department of archives and history, to be located at Montgomery. (Code 1907, § 793; Code 1923, § 1398; Code 1940, T. 55, § 255.)

§ 41-6-2. Objects and purposes.

(a) The objects and purposes of the department are:

(1) The care and custody of official archives;

(2) The collection of materials bearing upon the history of the state and of the territory included therein from the earliest times;

(3) The completion and publication of the state's official records and other historical materials;

(4) The diffusion of knowledge in reference to the history and resources of the state;

(5) The encouragement of historical work and research;

(6) The encouragement of and assistance in the establishment of public school libraries and in the improvement and strengthening of those already in existence; and

(7) The provision of advice and assistance to libraries and library workers in library administration, methods and economy.

(b) The department shall bring together and arrange for ready consultation a reference collection of materials for the use of members of the legislature, state officers and others on all subjects which may, from time to time, be deemed of public interest and importance to the people of the state.

(c) The department shall perform such other acts and requirements as may be enjoined by law. (Code 1907, § 794; Code 1923, § 1399; Code 1940, T. 55, § 256.)

§ 41-6-3. Board of trustees of department — Composition.

Said department shall be under the control of a board of trustees, one from each congressional district. (Code 1907, § 795; Acts 1923, No. 40, p. 23; Code 1923, § 1401; Code 1940, T. 55, § 258.)

§ 41-6-4. Same — Vacancies; terms of office; meetings; officers; compensation; powers and duties generally.

The said board shall fill all vacancies occurring therein, whether by expiration of term of service or by death or resignation, but the names of all newly elected members shall be communicated to the next ensuing regular session of the state senate for confirmation; and, in case it shall reject any of the said newly elected trustees, it shall proceed forthwith to fill the vacancy or vacancies by an election.

All trustees appointed to succeed the present members or their successors, whose terms shall have fully expired, shall serve for a term of six years, and appointees to fill vacancies by death or resignation shall only serve out the unexpired terms of their predecessors.

The board shall hold at the state Capitol at least one regular meeting during every year and as many special meetings as may be necessary, and at said meeting a majority of the trustees shall constitute a quorum. The governor of the state shall be a member of said board, and he shall, as far as possible, lend every encouragement to the success and upbuilding thereof. The director shall be the secretary of the board. The trustees shall receive no compensation for their services.

The board may adopt rules for its own government and also for the government of the department, may elect a director and may provide for the selection or appointment of other officials or employees as may be authorized, may provide for the publication of historical material pertaining to the state under the supervision of the director, may have the direction and control of the marking of historical sites or houses and the exploration of prehistoric and Indian mounds and other remains existing in the state, may control and expend such appropriations as may be made for the maintenance of the department and may do and perform such other acts and things as may be necessary to carry out the true intent and purposes of this article. (Code 1907, § 796; Code 1923, § 1402; Code 1940, T. 55, § 259.)

§ 41-6-5. Director — Election; term of office.

The department shall be under the immediate management and control of a director, to be elected by the board of trustees, whose term of office shall be six years and until his successor is elected and qualified. (Code 1907, § 797; Code 1923, § 1403; Code 1940, T. 55, § 260.)

§ 41-6-6. Same — Oath of office; director to be commissioned.

The director shall take an oath of office as other public officials and shall be commissioned in like manner. (Code 1907, § 798; Code 1923, § 1404; Code 1940, T. 55, § 261.)

§ 41-6-7. Same — Salary.

The director shall receive an annual salary to be fixed in accordance with the provisions of section 36-6-6, which shall be payable as the salaries of other state officers are paid. (Code 1907, § 804; Acts 1923, No. 600, p. 789; Code 1923, § 1411; Acts 1933, Ex. Sess., No. 138, p. 124; Acts 1935, No. 373, p. 792; Acts 1939, No. 435, p. 582; Code 1940, T. 55, § 268; Acts 1943, No. 396, p. 364; Acts 1953, No. 594, p. 846.)

§ 41-6-8. Same — Powers, functions and duties generally.

The powers, functions and duties of the director of the department of archives and history shall be as follows:

(1) To control and direct the work and operations of the department of archives and history;

(2) To administer the state official archives;

(3) To prepare the Alabama official and statistical register;

(4) To diffuse knowledge in reference to the history and resources of the state;

(5) To administer all military records for historical purposes;

(6) To administer the state's historical library and to collect and administer historical portraits and museums;

70

(7) To collect, organize and preserve noncurrent county records for historical purposes;

(8) To edit the Alabama Historical Quarterly and other historical publications;

(9) To distribute state official reports;

(10) To designate and describe historic spots in Alabama for monumental purposes;

(11) To have custody and supervision, under the direction of the director of finance, of the Alabama memorial building; and

(12) To perform any and all other powers, functions and duties as may now or hereafter be placed upon the director of the department of archives and history. (Code 1907, § 799; Code 1923, § 1405; Acts 1939, No. 435, p. 582; Code 1940, T. 55, § 262.)

§ 41-6-9. Clerical assistants in department.

Subject to the provisions of the state merit system, there may be employed in the department of archives and history such number of curators, clerks, librarians, stenographers, statisticians and other employees as are necessary to carry out the functions and duties of the department. (Code 1907, § 809; Acts 1923, No. 600, p. 789; Code 1923, § 1417; Acts 1933, Ex. Sess., No. 138, p. 124; Acts 1939, No. 58, p. 68; Code 1940, T. 55, § 270.)

Cross references. — As to merit system, see § 36-26-1 et seq.

§ 41-6-10. Surrender by state, county, etc., officials of books, records, etc., not in current use to department for permanent preservation.

Any state, county or other official may, in his discretion, turn over to the department for permanent preservation therein any official books, records, documents, original papers, newspaper files and printed books not in current use in his offices. (Code 1907, § 800; Code 1923, § 1406; Code 1940, T. 55, § 263.)

§ 41-6-11. Provision of certified copies of books, records, etc., surrendered to department.

When books, records, documents, original papers and newspaper files have been surrendered in accordance with section 41-6-10, copies therefrom shall be made and certified by the director upon the application of any person interested, which certificate shall have all the force and effect as if made by the officer originally in the custody of them and for which the same fees shall be charged, to be collected in advance. (Code 1907, § 801; Code 1923, § 1407; Code 1940, T. 55, § 264.)

§ 41-6-12. Provision of official publications, etc., of commissions, bureaus, boards, etc., to department; disposition of same by department.

In addition to the number of copies of any report or other official publication of any executive office, department, commission, bureau, board and state institution now or which may hereafter be authorized by law, except the reports of the supreme court, the court of civil appeals, the court of criminal appeals and the acts and journals of the legislature, the state printer or other person printing such report or document shall print 250 additional copies for the use of the department of archives and history, to be held for free distribution and exchange with state libraries, public libraries, institutions and individuals in Alabama and elsewhere. (Acts 1915, No. 679, p. 738; Code 1923, § 1408; Code 1940, T. 55, § 265.)

§ 41-6-13. Collection, etc., of data as to Alabama soldiers in war between states.

The department shall make special effort to collect data in reference to soldiers from Alabama in the war between the states, both from the department of defense and also from private individuals, and to cause the same to be prepared for publication as speedily as possible. (Code 1907, § 803; Code 1923, § 1410; Code 1940, T. 55, § 267.)

§ 41-6-14. Statistical register.

(a) An official and statistical register of the state of Alabama shall be compiled every two years by the director to contain:
   (1) Brief sketches of the several state officials, the members of congress from Alabama, the supreme court judges and the members of the senate and house of representatives of the state of Alabama;
   (2) Rosters of all state and county officials;
   (3) Lists of all state institutions with officials;
   (4) State and county population and election statistics; and
   (5) Miscellaneous statistics.
(b) Said register shall be published in an edition of 1,000 copies for free distribution, the printing and binding to be paid for as other printing and binding. (Code 1907, § 802; Code 1923, § 1409; Code 1940, T. 55, § 266.)

§ 41-6-15. Historical quarterly.

One thousand copies of the Alabama Historical Quarterly shall be published each quarter. The said quarterly shall be edited by the director of the department of archives and history and shall be supplied gratis to public officials, public and high school libraries and, upon call, to any responsible person in the interest of propagating facts about the history of the state. (Acts 1939, No. 583, p. 953; Code 1940, T. 55, § 271.)

ARTICLE 2.

ENDOWMENT FUND.

§ 41-6-30. Gifts or donations of money to department of archives and history to be deposited in state treasury to credit of department.

Unless otherwise provided, in accordance with section 41-6-50, whenever any gift or donation of money from any source is made to the department of archives and history of this state, the same must be deposited in the state treasury for the use of said department as provided in this article. (Acts 1943, No. 454, p. 416, § 1.)

§ 41-6-31. Endowment fund established; composition; expenditure; investment of fund.

The principal amount of such gift or donation shall be set aside by the state treasurer in a special fund designated: "endowment fund — department of archives and history," and moneys so deposited shall constitute an endowment fund for said department. In no event shall more than 10 percent of the amount remaining in said fund be expended in any one fiscal year. The director of finance shall invest or reinvest from time to time, at his discretion and with the approval of the governor, all or any part or portion of said fund in such bonds as are authorized by the laws of Alabama governing investments in bonds by domestic life insurance companies, and the interest thereon shall be paid to said department by the state treasurer upon a requisition signed by the director of said department and approved by the governor. (Acts 1943, No. 454, p. 416, § 2.)

§ 41-6-32. Interest accruing, earned or paid from investment of fund appropriated to department; expenditure thereof.

The interest accrued, earned or paid as the result of investment of said endowment fund is hereby appropriated to said department of archives and history and shall be used by said department only for such purposes as its trustees may specify and the governor approve; provided, however, that no expenditure of such funds may be made or approved by said board of trustees unless it is for the purpose of acquiring rare and valuable articles, property or materials or acquiring, marking and preserving or maintaining historical locations or spots within the state of Alabama. (Acts 1943, No. 454, p. 416, § 3.)

§ 41-6-33. Lease, sale, etc., of gifts or donations of real property authorized; disposition of proceeds from sale or rent.

Should any gift or donation to said department be in the form of real property, it may be leased, rented or sold in the discretion of said board of trustees, but the sum received as rent or the amount received as the purchase price, in the event of sale, must be deposited to the credit of said endowment fund, and such sum shall remain intact as a part of the principal amount of such endowment fund, and the interest received from the investment thereof shall be paid in the same manner as provided in this article for the payment of interest on other moneys deposited to the credit of said endowment fund. (Acts 1943, No. 454, p. 416, § 4.)

§ 41-6-34. Perpetuation or memorialization of names of certain donors.

Should any gift or donation by any person amount in value to as much as $5,000.00, said board of trustees is hereby authorized to perpetuate or memorialize the name of the persons making such gift or donation by designating any property or project or material or program acquired or carried on by proceeds derived from said endowment fund with appropriate nomenclature. (Acts 1943, No. 454, p. 416, § 5.)

ARTICLE 3.

MEMORIAL FUND.

§ 41-6-50. Establishment; certain gifts or donations of money to be deposited in state treasury in said fund.

Whenever any gift or donation of money to the department of archives and history is in an amount not exceeding $100.00 or whenever the donor thereof, regardless of the amount of the gift, requests that such gift be used for a specified purpose and such purpose is a purpose approved by the board of trustees of such department and whenever the donor designates the gift as a memorial gift, such money shall be deposited in the state treasury in a special fund designated "memorial fund — department of archives and history," which fund is hereby established. (Acts 1967, No. 522, p. 1252, § 1.)

§ 41-6-51. Disposition and expenditure of fund.

Such part of the fund as is derived from gifts for a designated purpose shall be used and expended by the director of the department of archives and history in accordance with the terms of the gift. The remainder of the fund shall be used and expended by the director in accordance with such policies as may be established by the board of trustees, and, at each regular meeting of the board of trustees, the director shall report all such expenditures made since the next preceding regular meeting. (Acts 1967, No. 522, p. 1252, § 2.)

§ 41-6-52. Identification of item or purpose for which gift expended where gift designated in memory of specified person.

When a gift is designated as a gift in memory of a specified person, then the item or purpose for which such gift is expended shall be identified as a memorial to such designated person. (Acts 1967, No. 522, p. 1252, § 3.)

§ 41-6-53. Gifts deemed gifts to state; deduction of amount of gift for income tax purposes.

Every gift to the department of archives and history payable into the fund, whether or not the use thereof is prescribed by the donor or the gift is designated as a memorial to a specified person, shall be deemed a gift to the state of Alabama. The donor in computing his net income for state income tax purposes for the year in which he makes the gift may deduct the amount of the gift from his gross income as authorized in section 40-18-15. (Acts 1967, No. 522, p. 1252, § 4.)

CHAPTER 6A.

DEPARTMENT OF ENERGY.

Collateral references. — 38 C.J.S., Gas,
§ 3. 81A C.J.S., States, §§ 141, 142.
1 Am. Jur. 2d, Administrative Law, §§ 23,
36-38.
38 Am. Jur. 2d, Gas and Oil, §§ 145-148.

§ 41-6A-1. Short title.

This chapter shall be known and may be cited as the "Alabama Energy
Management and Conservation Act of 1980." (Acts 1980, No. 80-449, p. 696,
§ 1.)

§ 41-6A-2. Legislative intent.

The legislature finds that the development, management and efficient use of
energy resources and the conservation of energy is of prime importance in an
era of rising costs, foreign dependence and uncertain supplies. At the same
time it is also important to protect the economic, social and environmental
values of the citizens of the state. Such responsibilities require a comprehensive, coordinated capacity on the part of the state to respond to the needs
and demands of her citizens. It is therefore the intent of the legislature:

(1) To ensure the wise development and efficient use of traditional energy
sources;

(2) To encourage and assist the development, the use of renewable energy
resources, demonstration, and placement in the marketplace of viable, alternative energy sources, more efficient uses of energy sources and other appropriate technology;

(3) To encourage the conservation and efficient use of all energy resources
and to provide a governmental environment which will encourage and promote private investment and initiative in the development of new energy
resources and more efficient use of all energy resources;

(4) To provide information to the public relating to energy saving uses, designs and construction methods and techniques for all new and existing buildings;

(5) To increase the ability of state government to respond in an efficient, comprehensive and coordinated manner to energy problems which may arise;

(6) To assure, as far as practicable, an energy supply adequate to protect the economic, social and environmental values the state's citizens now enjoy;

(7) To promote the identification of specifically designed energy management technologies;

(8) To disseminate information about such technologies;

(9) To promote the acceptance and adoption of such technologies by all energy-consuming sectors of the state's economy; and

(10) That the state shall not enter into the production or distribution of energy in any form. (Acts 1980, No. 80-449, p. 696, § 2.)

§ 41-6A-3. Department created; organization; duties of officers; director; employees.

(a) There is hereby created and established the Alabama department of energy. For the purposes of this chapter, the term "department" or "ADE" means the "Alabama department of energy."

(b) The programs and activities of the department shall be administered by a director with the assistance of such other officers, agents and employees as are necessary to carry out the functions of the agency. The director shall propose priorities and funding required to ensure that the programs and activities as provided in this chapter are effectively and efficiently carried out and that the intent of the legislature is fully implemented. The director shall organize and employ the staff of the department.

(c) The director of the department shall be appointed by, and serve at the pleasure of the governor. The pay of the director shall be set by the governor without regard to any other limitation set by law. Division chiefs shall be appointed by, and serve at the pleasure of, the director. The director shall be exempt from the provisions of article 1 of chapter 26 of Title 36, and the division chiefs shall serve as unclassified personnel under the provisions of article 1 of chapter 26 of Title 36. All except the director shall be members of the Alabama state employees retirement system. The director may, however, at his option, become a member of such system. All other employees of the department except as provided in this subsection shall be classified personnel and shall be members of the state merit system. (Acts 1980, No. 80-449, p. 696, § 3; Acts 1981, No. 81-866, p. 1658.)

The 1981 amendment, effective May 28, 1981, in subsection (c), inserted "except the director" following "All," deleted "state of" preceding "Alabama" and inserted "state employees" preceding "retirement" in the fifth sentence, added the sixth sentence and inserted "except as herein above provided" in the seventh sentence.

§ 41-6A-4. Departmental functions; clearinghouse for energy data.

The programs and activities of the department shall include, but are not limited to, the following:

(1) To develop and promulgate a state energy policy;

(2) To report regularly to the governor and annually to the legislature on the programs and activities of the department and to recommend needed changes in law or administrative practice;

(3) To periodically assess state energy requirements, and to coordinate with the state geologists, the state oil and gas board, and other parties and with appropriate governmental agencies in their determination of available energy supplies and their capacities and their development;

(4) To formulate and update annually a comprehensive state energy management program which shall identify alternative ways in which projected demands for all forms of energy may be met;

(5) To formulate and update annually a contingency plan to provide for adequate energy supplies during any energy shortages which may occur;

(6) To monitor existing programs relating to curtailment, allocation, conservation, planning, regulation and management of all forms of energy and energy sources; and to administer all other programs that are not otherwise provided by law;

(7) To serve as the state's clearinghouse for energy data. The clearinghouse shall be developed with the coordination and cooperation of other governmental data collection and record keeping systems to provide for an inventory, and the cataloging, and dissemination of energy-related information. Upon the request of the director of the department, other governmental agencies, boards and commissions shall, to the fullest extent possible, exchange records, reports, material and other energy-related information in an effort to avoid unnecessary duplication. If the amount of data requested by the department places an unreasonable burden on another agency's manpower or moneys, then the department shall monetarily reimburse such agency for its efforts;

(8) To ensure that all information of a proprietary nature shall remain confidential;

(9) To develop, conduct and disseminate educational and training programs as provided in section 41-6A-5;

(10) To review and study energy usage by state government agencies in order to determine the potential for energy conservation, and to recommend to the appropriate agency and the governor any administrative or legislative changes necessary to promote energy conservation;

(11) To assist and encourage the various state agencies and universities when applying for energy-related contracts with federal or regional agencies or other groups. This shall be accomplished in such a manner to support and encourage the individual entrepreneurship of the universities in obtaining separately sponsored research;

(12) To review with appropriate energy related agencies regulatory or revenue-producing practices for their impact on energy production and

consumption, and to recommend appropriate changes or modifications which may improve the state's energy position without harming its economic status;

(13) To constitute the responsible agency for administering and coordinating federal energy programs delegated to the state subsequent to the enactment of this chapter. Excluded are those programs currently delegated to other agencies, and those programs having objectives consistent with the jurisdiction of other agencies;

(14) To encourage, and coordinate research, development and demonstration activities in the energy areas;

(15) To apply for, when appropriate, and receive and administer federal and private grant funds which contribute to the programs and activities as set forth in this chapter;

(16) To enter into interstate agreements and contracts, when appropriate, to accomplish jointly with other states and the federal government energy research or planning which contribute to the purposes of the department; and

(17) To perform any other function necessary for implementation and enforcement of this chapter. (Acts 1980, No. 80-449, p. 696, § 4.)

§ 41-6A-5. Public awareness and education programs; objectives.

The department shall conduct and administer public awareness and education programs which shall inform the public and state and local government policymakers of at least the following:

(1) The energy prospects for the state;

(2) The alternative futures in economic and environmental terms under different energy policies;

(3) The manpower needs of alternative energy policies;

(4) The probable impact of existing and proposed actions of state and federal government;

(5) The potential of research and development programs; and

(6) The importance of, and the technologies and methods necessary to achieve, energy conservation goals in all consuming sectors of the state's economy. (Acts 1980, No. 80-449, p. 696, § 5.)

§ 41-6A-6. Rulemaking power; scope of rules.

The department may, after appropriate notice and public hearing, upon request, promulgate reasonable rules consistent with the laws of this state, for the following purposes:

(1) To ensure the department will, for the purpose of planning and policy formulation, be able to obtain all necessary information from state agencies, and information from energy producers, suppliers and consumers that is not required to be submitted to other state government agencies;

(2) To ensure that energy conservation measures shall be practiced by state government; and

(3) To establish such advisory groups that from time to time may be beneficial to the department. (Acts 1980, No. 80-449, p. 696, § 6.)

§ 41-6A-7. Administration of chapter; contracts with other agencies, departments, etc.; other agencies, departments, etc., affecting chapter to report to department; abstracts of proposals sent to department.

The department is solely responsible for the administration of this chapter; however, the department may enter into a contractual agreement with state agencies or departments, educational institutions and such other organizations and individuals necessary to fulfill its responsibilities. Any agency, department, educational institution or organization of the state which affects the administration or implementation of this chapter is required to communicate such activities to the department. Abstracts of proposals for energy-related grants shall be sent to the department for informational and coordination purposes. Such abstracts shall remain confidential. (Acts 1980, No. 80-449, p. 696, § 7.)

§ 41-6A-8. Advisory council created; membership; officers; meetings; compensation; term.

(a) There is hereby created and established the energy advisory council. For the purposes of this chapter the term "council" means the "energy advisory council." The council shall be composed of the following:

(1) Two members of the state senate designated by the president of the senate;

(2) Two members of the state house of representatives designated by the speaker of the house of representatives;

(3) Four representatives from state institutions of higher learning designated by the governor, provided, however, that no two representatives shall be from the same institution, and provided, further, that one representative shall be from an historically black institution;

(4) Three representatives of the citizens of the state, one designated by the governor, one by the president of the senate and one by the speaker of the house of representatives;

All other members will be appointed by the governor from nominations submitted as follows:

(5) One representative of the oil and gas board designated by the board;

(6) One representative of the public service commission designated by the commission;

(7) One representative of the natural gas industry; designated by the governor;

(8) One representative of the petroleum industry, designated by the governor;

(9) One representative from the private investor-owned electric utility industry and one representative from the rural electric cooperatives;

(10) One representative of the coal industry, designated by the governor;

(11) One representative of agriculture to be designated by the commissioner of agriculture and industries and one representative of private, nonindustrial forestry to be designated by the Alabama forestry commission;

(12) One representative of the manufacturing industry, designated by the Associated Industries of Alabama;

(13) One representative of city government to be designated by the Alabama League of Municipalities;

(14) One representative of county government to be designated by the Association of County Commissioners of Alabama;

(15) One representative of registered professional engineers nominated by the Joint Engineers Council of Alabama, Inc.;

(16) One representative of the Alabama Homebuilders Association to be nominated by the association;

(17) One representative from an Alabama technical college which offers a coal mine technology program; and

(18) One representative of the state department of education.

(b) The advisory committee shall set up such subcommittees as it deems necessary.

(c) The director of the department shall serve ex officio as secretary to the council. The council shall meet as soon as practicable after May 19, 1980, and shall choose from among its members a chairman and a vice-chairman. The council shall meet at least twice annually, at the call of the chairman, or when at least seven members of the council officially and in writing request the secretary of the council to call a meeting.

(d) Members of the council shall serve without compensation.

(e) Members of the council shall serve at the pleasure of the official responsible for designating them members, but in no case shall the term of any member exceed four years unless such member is redesignated in accordance with subsection (a) of this section. (Acts 1980, No. 80-449, p. 696, § 8.)

§ 41-6A-9. Council duties and functions.

The duties and functions of the council shall include, but are not limited to, the following:

(1) To evaluate and assess state energy policy and its impact upon the economy and the environment, and to report to the director of the department on its findings;

(2) To facilitate and encourage the cooperation of federal, state and local government in the promotion and attainment of the purposes of this chapter;

(3) To enlist the cooperation of all appropriate private, public, civic and community organizations and groups in implementing the purposes of this chapter;

(4) To advise the director of the department on matters relating to energy resource policy, development and management and the programs and activities of the department; and

(5) To recommend to the director of the department additional legislation to further enhance the state's capabilities in energy matters. (Acts 1980, No. 80-449, p. 696, § 9.)

§ 41-6A-10. Funding and assumption of contracts.

The legislature shall appropriate moneys from the general fund for operation of the department; provided, however, that any appropriations or grants from any source whatsoever made to the Alabama energy management board prior to May 19, 1980, shall continue in full force and effect and shall be managed by the department. Any contracts or grants established by the energy management board prior to May 19, 1980, shall remain in effect and shall be assumed by the department. (Acts 1980, No. 80-449, p. 696, § 10.)

Collateral references. — 81A C.J.S., States, § 226.
63 Am. Jur. 2d, Public Funds, § 45.

§ 41-6A-11. Proprietary information; confidentiality.

No departmental employee or independent contractor shall divulge or make known in any manner any proprietary information acquired under the provisions of this chapter except in accordance with the order of a court of competent jurisdiction, as otherwise provided by law or in the publication of statistical information compiled by methods which do not disclose the source of the information or the identity of individual companies. Nothing in this section shall be construed to prevent inspection of reports by the attorney general, members of the legislature or other state agencies, provided, however, that such agencies and their employees and members are bound by the requirements set forth in this section. (Acts 1980, No. 80-449, p. 696, § 11.)

CHAPTER 7.

BUREAU OF PUBLICITY AND INFORMATION.

§ 41-7-1. Created; composition; powers and duties.

(a) There is created hereby a state bureau of publicity and information, hereinafter referred to as the bureau, composed of a division of records and reports and such other divisions as the director determines to be necessary.

(b) The bureau shall, with the advice and assistance of the advisory board provided for in section 41-7-3, have exclusive power and authority to plan and conduct all state programs of information and publicity designed to attract tourists to the state of Alabama. It shall be the duty of the principal administrator of each state department, board, commission, institution, agency and office, upon request, to assist the director of publicity in preparing news items of general interest relating to tourism. (Acts 1943, No. 253, p. 223, §§ 2, 4; Acts 1951, No. 712, p. 1250, § 1.)

§ 41-7-2. Director of publicity; division and unit heads; assistants and employees; welcome center workers; Capitol hostesses.

The bureau shall be in charge of a director of publicity. The director shall be appointed by and serve at the pleasure of the governor. The governor shall fix his compensation in accordance with the provisions of section 36-6-6. The director shall appoint division and unit heads and such assistants and employees as may be necessary to the efficient operation of the bureau. All employees of the bureau shall be subject to the provisions of the Merit System Act. It is further provided, however, that all persons employed by the bureau for positions in state welcoming centers as of June 22, 1979, shall retain their employment positions with the bureau. All such persons so retained by the bureau shall immediately receive all benefits and privileges of the state merit system law in the same manner and to the same extent as other merit system employees of the state. All persons employed by the bureau after June 22, 1979, shall be employed subject to the provisions of the state merit system law and such other state and federal laws, including state and federal court requirements and mandates, as may be applicable. It is further provided that any person, who is now serving as a Capitol hostess, and has been so employed for a period of 12 months immediately preceding June 22, 1979, without merit system status, shall become an employee of the bureau with automatic classification under the state merit system as a welcome center worker. The duties of such person shall include assignment to the Capitol building as a hostess. (Acts 1951, No. 712, p. 1250, § 2; Acts 1979, No. 79-252, p. 383.)

Code commissioner's note. — Acts 1979, No. 79-743, p. 1319, effective August 8, 1979, provides that in Acts 1979, No. 79-252, p. 383, it was the legislative intent that Capitol hostesses now assigned as "welcome center workers" and assigned to the Capitol for the preceding 12 months prior to the enactment of Act No. 79-252, p. 383, continue to perform their duties in the Capitol building and be paid at the same rate as other Capitol hostesses and that such persons not be required to travel. The act further provides that the director of the state bureau of publicity and information, the personnel department and any other person responsible under Act No. 79-252, p. 383, shall proceed to see that the provisions of that act are implemented and any salary which should have been paid shall be paid retroactively to the effective date of Act No. 79-252, p. 383.

Cross references. — As to the Merit System Act, see § 36-26-1, et seq. As to cooperation with state industrial development board, see § 41-9-188.

§ 41-7-3. Advisory board.

There is hereby created a board to advise and assist the director. The board shall be composed of the governor, the director of public safety, the highway director, the commissioner of conservation and natural resources and 12 members appointed by the governor for terms to run concurrently with the term of the governor. Ten members shall be selected as representatives of the following organizations: Alabama state chamber of commerce, Alabama hotel and motel association, Alabama motel association, Alabama petroleum council, Alabama broadcasters association, Alabama press association, Alabama restaurant association, outdoor advertising association of Alabama, public relations council of Alabama and Alabama travel council. Two members representing attractions shall be selected from the state at large. All members of the board shall serve without compensation. (Acts 1951, No. 712, p. 1250, § 3; Acts 1957, No. 562, p. 780; Acts 1967, No. 267, p. 764.)

§ 41-7-4. Use of appropriations generally.

The bureau may, with the approval of the governor, expend any funds appropriated to the bureau for advertising and promotions and for other purposes that support tourism in Alabama; provided, that no part of any appropriation made to the bureau by the legislature shall be used to purchase any advertising within the state of Alabama; provided further, that the bureau may procure the printing of pamphlets, circulars, maps, leaflets and similar material in the state of Alabama to be circulated by the bureau for tourist advertising and promotion purposes.

§ 41-7-5. Director may contract with and spend funds in support of southern travel directors council.

The director of the bureau of publicity and information may, with the approval of the governor, enter into contracts and agreements with the organization known as the southern travel directors council, a regional travel advertising and promotion agency, for the purpose of expanding and extending the state's tourist advertising program. The director may, with the governor's approval, spend a sum not exceeding $15,000.00 per annum for the support of the council, such expenditures to be made from legislative appropriations for tourist advertising. (Acts 1967, No. 269, p. 775.)

CHAPTER 8.

ALABAMA PUBLIC LIBRARY SERVICE.

Cross references. — As to free public libraries in counties and municipalities, see § 11-90-1 et seq.

ARTICLE 1.

GENERAL PROVISIONS.

§ 41-8-1. Creation; chief objective.

In order to aid in the development of higher ideals of citizenship and the enlargement of opportunity for culture and recreation and in order to afford an additional means for the further upbuilding of the educational facilities of the state, there shall be a public library service, which shall be known as the Alabama public library service and shall have as its chief objective the development of a cooperative system of providing books and library service for the various municipalities and counties of the state. (Acts 1939, No. 171, p. 297; Code 1940, T. 55, § 278; Acts 1959, No. 600, p. 1488.)

Cited in James v. Wallace, 533 F.2d 963 (5th Cir. 1976).

§ 41-8-2. Executive board generally.

The executive board of the Alabama public library service shall consist of five members appointed by the governor. Such members shall be qualified electors of the state and shall have resided in the state for five years next preceding their appointment. Appointments shall be for five years, and all vacancies, including expired and unexpired terms, shall be filled by the governor by appointment. Members of the executive board shall be allowed $10.00 per day, not to exceed 20 days per year, plus travel expenses pursuant to article 2 of chapter 7 of Title 36 of this Code. It shall be the duty and power of the executive board to conduct the affairs of the public library service, to administer the funds received from the treasury that are allocated to the public library service and to be responsible for the program and for such other activities as would naturally be administered by such an executive board. (Acts 1939, No. 171, p. 297; Code 1940, T. 55, § 279; Acts 1959, No. 600, p. 1488.)

§ 41-8-3. Election of officers of executive board; director of public library service and assistants.

The members of the executive board shall elect from its membership a chairman and vice-chairman.

The board shall appoint a director. The director shall be a graduate of an accredited library school who shall have had a minimum of three years of library experience in an administrative capacity or shall be a college graduate with a master's degree with a major in library science who shall have had a minimum of five years of library experience in an administrative capacity. The director shall not be a member of the executive board and shall serve at the pleasure of the board. All other members of the staff of the service shall be appointed by the executive board on the nomination of the director and shall be subject to the provisions of the state merit system law. The director shall keep a record of the proceedings of the board, shall keep accurate accounts of all financial transactions of the service, shall have charge of its work in organizing new libraries and improving those already established and in general perform such duties as may from time to time be assigned by the executive board. (Acts 1939, No. 171, p. 297; Code 1940, T. 55, § 281; Acts 1959, No. 600, p. 1488.)

§ 41-8-4. Annual report of executive board to governor.

The executive board shall make an annual report to the governor. The report shall show public library conditions and progress in Alabama and a statement of the expenses and activities of the public library service. These annual reports shall be printed as other annual reports of the state departments and shall be distributed by the board or the director thereof. (Acts 1939, No. 171, p. 297; Code 1940, T. 55, § 282; Acts 1959, No. 600, p. 1488.)

§ 41-8-5. Powers and duties of public library service generally.

(a) The Alabama public library service shall give advice to all free public, regional, municipal and county libraries and to all communities in the state which may propose to establish public libraries, in the manner provided in this article, as to the best means of establishing and administering such public library service, selecting and cataloging books and other details of library management and may send any of its staff to aid in organizing such libraries or to assist in the improvement of those already established. The service may advise as to the proper qualifications of librarians of free public, regional, municipal and county libraries and shall perform such other services consistent with and in furtherance of the purpose of this article as shall from time to time appear feasible. Moreover, the service shall advise as to arrangements as provided in section 11-90-4, by which local governmental agencies may combine in the establishment of joint units of library service. The service may receive and shall administer all funds, books or other property from whatever source, under such conditions as may be deemed necessary in order to carry out the purpose of this article; and, by the use of such means and methods as circumstances warrant, the service may acquire and operate traveling libraries, and circulate or loan such books and libraries among communities, libraries, library associations, social and civic clubs and organizations and other public agencies and institutions under such conditions and rules as the board deems necessary in order to protect the interests of the state and to increase the efficiency and promote the extension of public library service throughout the state.

(b) The Alabama public library service, through its board, shall have the authority to make exceptions in their criteria for receiving state aid as they relate to educational requirements and hours of operation. (Acts 1939, No. 171, p. 297; Code 1940, T. 55, § 280; Acts 1959, No. 600, p. 1488; Acts 1982, No. 82-154, § 4.)

The 1982 amendment, effective March 30, 1982, designated the first paragraph of this section as subsection (a) and added subsection (b).

§ 41-8-6. Scholarships and grants in field of library service.

The executive board of the Alabama public library service may, upon such terms and conditions as it may fix, award scholarships or grants in the field of library science on the graduate or undergraduate level to persons of high integrity whom it may select to the extent that funds are available therefor from funds not otherwise obligated which are available to the Alabama public library service in accordance with the state plan provided for by United States Public Law 597, approved June 19, 1965, the "Library Services Act," as now exists or is hereafter amended or replaced. (Acts 1961, No. 812, p. 1188, § 1.)

§ 41-8-7. Service to obtain reports from public libraries.

The Alabama public library service shall each year obtain from all free public libraries in the state of Alabama reports showing the conditions, growth, development and conduct of said libraries. This provision shall not apply to the libraries of the supreme court of Alabama, the department of archives and history or school libraries aided and supervised by the department of education and the libraries of institutions of higher learning. (Acts 1915, No. 693, p. 745; Code 1923, § 1400; Acts 1939, No. 171, p. 297; Code 1940, T. 55, §§ 257, 283; Acts 1959, No. 600, p. 1488; Acts 1982, No. 82-154, § 4.)

The 1982 amendment, effective March 30, 1982 deleted "(a)" at the beginning of the section and deleted former subsection (b), relating to reports to the Alabama public library service by the libraries in this state.

§ 41-8-8. Applicability and effect of article.

This article shall in no way affect the administration and supervision of public school libraries which have been or may hereafter be established by aid through the department of education, except by agreement, nor shall this article affect in any way the administration and supervision of public school libraries under the control of any city or county board of education, except by agreement; nor shall it, except by agreement, affect or apply to libraries of institutions of higher learning nor to free public libraries in counties where a city having a population of not less than 65,000 already maintains a free public library. (Acts 1939, No. 171, p. 297; Code 1940, T. 55, § 284.)

ARTICLE 2.

INTERSTATE LIBRARY COMPACT.

§ 41-8-20. "State library agency" defined.

As used in the compact, "state library agency" with reference to this state means the Alabama public library service. (Acts 1973, No. 1121, p. 1884, § 3.)

§ 41-8-21. Enactment of compact; form.

The Interstate Library Compact is hereby enacted into law and entered into by this state with all states legally joining therein in the form substantially as follows:

INTERSTATE LIBRARY COMPACT.

Article I. Policy and Purpose.

Because the desire for the services provided by libraries transcends governmental boundaries and can most effectively be satisfied by giving such services to communities and people regardless of jurisdictional lines, it is the policy of the states party to this compact to cooperate and share their responsibilities; to authorize cooperation and sharing with respect to those types of library facilities and services which can be more economically or efficiently developed and maintained on a cooperative basis and to authorize cooperation and sharing among localities, states and others in providing joint or cooperative library services in areas where the distribution of population or of existing and potential library resources makes the provision of library service on an interstate basis the most effective way of providing adequate and efficient service.

Article II. Definitions.

As used in this compact:

(a) "Public library agency" means any unit or agency of local or state government operating or having power to operate a library.

(b) "Private library agency" means any nongovernmental entity which operates or assumes a legal obligation to operate a library.

(c) "Library agreement" means a contract establishing an interstate library district pursuant to this compact or providing for the joint or cooperative furnishing of library services.

Article III. Interstate Library Districts.

(a) Any one or more public library agencies in a party state in cooperation with any public library agency or agencies in one or more other party states may establish and maintain an interstate library district. Subject to the provisions of this compact and any other laws of the party states which pursuant hereto remain applicable, such district may establish, maintain and operate some or all of the library facilities and services for the area concerned in accordance with the terms of a library agreement therefor. Any private library agency or agencies within an interstate library district may cooperate therewith, assume duties, responsibilities and obligations thereto and receive benefits therefrom as provided in any library agreement to which such agency or agencies become party.

(b) Within an interstate library district and as provided by a library agreement, the performance of library functions may be undertaken on a joint or cooperative basis or may be undertaken by means of one or more arrangements between or among public or private library agencies for the extension of library privileges to the use of facilities or services operated or rendered by one or more of the individual library agencies.

(c) If a library agreement provides for joint establishment, maintenance or operation of library facilities or services by an interstate library district, such district shall have power to do any one or more of the following in accordance with such library agreement:

1. Undertake, administer and participate in programs or arrangements for securing, lending or servicing of books and other publications, any other materials suitable to be kept or made available by libraries and library equipment or for the dissemination of information about libraries, the value and significance of particular items therein and the use thereof.

2. Accept for any of its purposes under this compact any and all donations and grants of money, equipment, supplies, materials and services (conditional or otherwise) from any state or the United States or any subdivision or agency thereof, or interstate agency, or from any institution, person, firm or corporation, and receive, utilize and dispose of the same.

3. Operate mobile library units or equipment for the purpose of rendering bookmobile service within the district.

4. Employ professional, technical, clerical and other personnel and fix terms of employment, compensation and other appropriate benefits and, where desirable, provide for the in-service training of such personnel.

5. Acquire, hold and dispose of any real or personal property or any interest or interests therein as may be appropriate to the rendering of library service.

6. Construct, maintain and operate a library, including any appropriate branches thereof.

7. Do such other things as may be incidental to or appropriate for the carrying out of any of the foregoing powers.

Article IV. Interstate Library Districts, Governing Board.

(a) An interstate library district which establishes, maintains or operates any facilities or services in its own right shall have a governing board which shall direct the affairs of the district and act for it in all matters relating to its business. Each participating public library agency in the district shall be represented on the governing board, which shall be organized and conduct its business in accordance with provisions therefor in the library agreement. But in no event shall a governing board meet less often than twice a year.

(b) Any private library agency or agencies party to a library agreement establishing an interstate library district may be represented on or advise with the governing board of the district in such manner as the library agreement may provide.

Article V. State Library Agency Cooperation.

Any two or more state library agencies of two or more of the party states may undertake and conduct joint or cooperative library programs, render joint or cooperative library services and enter into and perform arrangements for the cooperative or joint acquisition, use, housing and disposition of items or collections of materials which, by reason of expense, rarity, specialized nature or infrequency of demand therefor would be appropriate for central collection and shared use. Any such programs, services or arrangements may include provision for the exercise on a cooperative or joint basis of any power exercisable by an interstate library district and an agreement embodying any such program, service or arrangement shall contain provisions covering the subjects detailed in Article VI of this compact for interstate library agreements.

Article VI. Library Agreement.

(a) In order to provide for any joint or cooperative undertaking pursuant to this compact, public and private library agencies may enter into library agreements. Any agreement executed pursuant to the provisions of this compact shall, as among the parties to the agreement:

(1) Detail the specific nature of the services, programs, facilities, arrangements or properties to which it is applicable.

(2) Provide for the allocation of costs and other financial responsibilities.

(3) Specify the respective rights, duties, obligations and liabilities of the parties.

(4) Set forth the terms and conditions for duration, renewal, termination, abrogation, disposal of joint or common property, if any, and all other matters which may be appropriate to the proper effectuation and performance of the agreement.

(b) No public or private library agency shall undertake to exercise itself, or jointly with any other library agency, by means of a library agreement any power prohibited to such agency by the constitution or statutes of its state.

(c) No library agreement shall become effective until filed with the compact administrator of each state involved and approved in accordance with Article VII of this compact.

Article VII. Approval of Library Agreements.

(a) Every library agreement made pursuant to this compact shall, prior to and as a condition precedent to its entry into force, be submitted to the attorney general of each state in which a public library agency party thereto is situated, who shall determine whether the agreement is in proper form and compatible with the laws of his state. The attorneys general shall approve any agreement submitted to them unless they shall find that it does not meet the conditions set forth herein and shall detail in writing addressed to the governing bodies of the public library agencies concerned the specific respects in which the proposed agreement fails to meet the requirements of law. Failure to disapprove an agreement submitted hereunder within 90 days of its submission shall constitute approval thereof.

(b) In the event that a library agreement made pursuant to this compact shall deal in whole or in part with the provision of services or facilities with regard to which an officer or agency of the state government has constitutional or statutory powers of control, the agreement shall, as a condition precedent to its entry into force, be submitted to the state officer or agency having such power of control and shall be approved or disapproved by him or it as to all matters within his or its jurisdiction in the same manner subject to the same requirements governing the action of the attorneys general pursuant to paragraph (a) of this article. This requirement of submission and approval shall be in addition to and not in substitution for the requirement of submission to and approval by the attorneys general.

Article VIII. Other Laws Applicable.

Nothing in this compact or in any library agreement shall be construed to supersede, alter or otherwise impair any obligation imposed on any library by otherwise applicable law, nor to authorize the transfer or disposition of any property held in trust by a library agency in a manner contrary to the terms of such trust.

Article IX. Appropriations and Aid.

(a) Any public library agency party to a library agreement may appropriate funds to the interstate library district established thereby in the same manner and to the same extent as to a library wholly maintained by it and, subject to the laws of the state in which such public library agency is situated, may pledge its credit in support of an interstate library district established by the agreement.

(b) Subject to the provisions of the library agreement pursuant to which it functions and the laws of the states in which such district is situated, an interstate library district may claim and receive any state and federal aid which may be available to library agencies.

Article X. Compact Administrator.

Each state shall designate a compact administrator with whom copies of all library agreements to which this state or any public library agency thereof is party shall be filed. The administrator shall have such other powers as may be conferred upon him by the laws of his state and may consult and cooperate with the compact administrators of other party states and take such steps as may effectuate the purposes of this compact. If the laws of a party state so provide, such state may designate one or more deputy compact administrators in addition to its compact administrator.

Article XI. Entry Into Force and Withdrawal.

(a) This compact shall enter into force and effect immediately upon its enactment into law by any two states. Thereafter, it shall enter into force and effect as to any other state upon the enactment thereof by such state.

(b) This compact shall continue in force with respect to a party state and remain binding upon such state until six months after such state has given notice to each other party state of the repeal thereof. Such withdrawal shall not be construed to relieve any party to a library agreement entered into pursuant to this compact from any obligation of that agreement prior to the end of its duration as provided therein.

Article XII. Construction and Severability.

This compact shall be liberally construed so as to effectuate the purposes thereof. The provisions of this compact shall be severable; and, if any phrase, clause, sentence or provision of this compact is declared to be contrary to the constitution of any party state or of the United States or the applicability thereof to any government, agency, person or circumstance is held invalid, the validity of the remainder of this compact and the applicability thereof to any government, agency, person or circumstance shall not be affected thereby. If this compact shall be held contrary to the constitution of any state party thereto, the compact shall remain in full force and effect as to the remaining states and in full force and effect as to the state affected as to all severable matters. (Acts 1973, No. 1121, p. 1884, § 1.)

§ 41-8-22. Compact administrator; deputy compact administrators.

The director of the Alabama public library service shall be the compact administrator pursuant to Article X of the compact. The director of the Alabama public library service may appoint one or more deputy compact administrators pursuant to said article. (Acts 1973, No. 1121, p. 1884, § 5.)

§ 41-8-23. Restrictions as to entry into library agreements for construction or maintenance of libraries, etc., by counties, municipalities, etc.

No county, municipality or other political subdivision of this state shall be party to a library agreement which provides for the construction or maintenance of a library pursuant to Article III, subdivision (c) 7 of the compact nor pledge its credit in support of such a library or contribute to the capital financing thereof, except after compliance with any laws applicable to such counties, municipalities or other political subdivisions relating to or governing capital outlays and the pledging of credit. (Acts 1973, No. 1121, p. 1884, § 2.)

§ 41-8-24. State aid to interstate library districts lying partly within state; application for and receipt of federal aid by such districts.

(a) An interstate library district lying partly within this state may claim and be entitled to receive state aid in support of any of its functions to the same extent and in the same manner as such functions are eligible for support when carried on by entities wholly within this state. For the purposes of computing and apportioning state aid to an interstate library district, this state will consider that portion of the area which lies within this state as an independent entity for the performance of the aided function or functions and compute and apportion the aid accordingly.

(b) Subject to any applicable laws of this state, such a district also may apply for and be entitled to receive any federal aid for which it may be eligible. (Acts 1973, No. 1121, p. 1884, § 4.)

§ 41-8-25. Sending and receipt of notices required in event of withdrawal from compact.

In the event of withdrawal from the compact the governor shall send and receive any notices required by Article XI (b) of the compact. (Acts 1973, No. 1121, p. 1884, § 6.)

CHAPTER 8A.

ALABAMA LAW ENFORCEMENT PLANNING AGENCY.

Collateral references. — 81A C.J.S., States, §§ 141, 142.

72 Am. Jur. 2d, States, Territories and Dependencies, § 41.

§ 41-8A-1. Definitions.

(a) The following words, when used in this chapter, shall have the meanings ascribed to them below, unless the context clearly indicates a different meaning:

(1) LAW ENFORCEMENT AND CRIMINAL JUSTICE. Any activity pertaining to crime prevention, control or reduction or enforcement of the criminal law, including, but not limited to, police efforts to prevent, control or reduce crime or to apprehend criminals, activities of courts having criminal jurisdiction and related agencies (including prosecutorial and defender services), activities of corrections, probation or parole authorities and programs relating to the prevention, control or reduction of juvenile delinquency or alcoholism, narcotic and drug addiction.

(2) STATE. The state of Alabama and all political subdivisions thereof.

(3) UNIT OF GENERAL LOCAL GOVERNMENT OR UNIT OF LOCAL GOVERNMENT. Any city, county, township, town, borough, village or other general purpose political subdivision of the state of Alabama which performs law enforcement functions as determined by the United States secretary of the interior, or as may be otherwise defined by the Alabama law enforcement planning agency.

(4) COMBINATION. Such term, as applied to state agencies or departments or units of local government, means any grouping or joining together of such state agencies, departments or units for the purpose of preparing, developing or implementing a law enforcement plan.

(5) METROPOLITAN AREA. A standard metropolitan statistical area as established by the bureau of the budget of the United States, subject, however, to such modifications and extensions as the law enforcement assistance administration may determine to be appropriate from time to time.

(6) PUBLIC AGENCY. Any state agency or state department or unit of local government, combination of such state agencies, departments or units or any department, agency or instrumentality of any of the foregoing described state agencies, units or departments within the state of Alabama.

(7) JUVENILE CORRECTIONAL INSTITUTION OR FACILITY. Any place for the confinement or rehabilitation of juvenile offenders or individuals charged with or convicted of criminal offenses.

(8) COMPREHENSIVE. The plan must be a total and integrated analysis of the problems regarding the law enforcement and criminal justice system within the state of Alabama; goals, priorities and standards must be established in the plan and the plan must address methods, organization and operation performance, physical and human resources necessary to accomplish crime prevention, identification, detection and apprehension of suspects, adjudication, custodial treatment of suspects and offenders and institutional and noninstitutional rehabilitative measures.

(9) TREATMENT. Such term includes, but is not limited to, medical, educational, social, psychological and vocational services, corrective and preventive guidance and training and other rehabilitative services designed to protect the public and benefit the addict or other user by eliminating his dependence on addicting or other drugs or by controlling his dependence, his susceptibility to addiction or use.

(10) ACRONYMS. The acronyms as used herein are as follows:

    a. ALEPA. The Alabama law enforcement planning agency.

    b. LEAA. The law enforcement assistance administration.

    c. RPU. Regional planning unit.

(11) STATE BOARD. The Alabama law enforcement planning agency's state supervisory board.

(12) REGIONAL BOARDS. The regional advisory planning boards and the high crime commission's advisory board.

(13) SAFE STREETS ACT. The Omnibus Crime Control and Safe Streets Act of 1968, as amended.

(14) CENTRAL OFFICE. The ALEPA office in Montgomery, Alabama. (Acts 1978, No. 820, p. 1195, § 1-101.)

§ 41-8A-2. Creation; composition; director generally.

(a) There is hereby established within the executive department of the state of Alabama, under the general authority, policy direction and general control of the chief executive, the governor of the state of Alabama, and Alabama law enforcement planning agency (hereinafter referred to as the agency or ALEPA or the administrative agency) composed of a staff which shall carry out the planning and administrative functions of said agency.

(b) Central responsibility for the development, maintenance, operation and administration of the Alabama law enforcement planning agency shall be vested with the director of ALEPA under the general overview of the ALEPA state supervisory board.

(c) The director shall maintain the necessary staff along with support services necessary to enable the effective and efficient performance of the duties and responsibilities ascribed to ALEPA herein. (Acts 1978, No. 820, p. 1195, § 1-102.)

§ 41-8A-3. Staff.

The ALEPA staff of the central office, the staff of the regional units and the high crime commission as presently employed by the authority of an executive order of the governor and personnel presently under the supervision and direction of ALEPA which are employed under planning grants to other agencies shall be encompassed within this chapter, and shall, by virtue of this chapter, be considered to meet the requirements of the agency in terms of education, training and experience, and shall automatically be placed within the state merit system with all the rights and privileges thereof and shall enjoy the same employment and retirement privileges and rights as the legislature may determine from time to time or as may be otherwise determined by law or administrative rule or regulation according to the rules and regulations of the personnel department of the state of Alabama which shall be consistent with the Omnibus Crime Control and Safe Streets Act of 1968, as amended. All new future employees of ALEPA shall be required to meet the requirements of the state merit system.

All present employees of ALEPA shall remain in their respective positions and continue to enjoy employment conditions, including, but not limited to, salary range and advancement at a level no less than those enjoyed prior to the enactment of this chapter. However, nothing herein shall be construed to prevent or preclude the removal of an employee for cause in the manner provided by law. (Acts 1978, No. 820, p. 1195, § 1-103.)

§ 41-8A-4. Powers and duties of director.

(a) The ALEPA director shall:

(1) Supervise and be responsible for the administration of the policies established by the state supervisory board in accordance with the Safe Streets Act and LEAA regulations and guidelines.

(2) Establish, consolidate or abolish any administrative subdivision within the Alabama law enforcement planning agency and appoint and remove for cause the heads thereof, and delegate appropriate powers and duties to them.

(3) Establish and administer programs and projects for the operation of ALEPA.

(4) Appoint and remove employees of ALEPA as provided by law and delegate appropriate powers and duties.

(5) Make rules and regulations for the management and the administration of policies of ALEPA and the conduct of employees under his jurisdiction.

(6) Collect, develop and maintain statistical information, records and reports as the state supervisory board may determine relevant to the functions of ALEPA.

(7) Execute and carry out the provisions of all contracts, leases and agreements authorized by the state supervisory board with agencies of federal, state or local governments, corporations or persons.

(8) Perform such additional duties as may be assigned to him by the state supervisory board, the chairperson of the board, the governor or by law.

(b) The ALEPA director is authorized to accept block grants, discretionary grants or any other funds from the federal government or state government as pertains to law enforcement and the criminal justice system, including juvenile justice and juvenile delinquency prevention, or any other federal grant designated by the governor.

(c) The ALEPA director shall have the authority to administratively reject any subgrant application which is not in compliance with the state comprehensive plan, the state supervisory board policy directives, the Safe Streets Act or LEAA requirements or is incorrect in regard to fiscal computations, and if no funds are available under the program area for which applied. (Acts 1978, No. 820, p. 1195, § 1-111.)

§ 41-8A-5. State supervisory board — Creation; composition; qualifications, appointment, terms of office and compensation of members generally; filling of vacancies; officers; executive committee generally; appointment of director.

(a) There is hereby established a state supervisory board of the Alabama law enforcement planning agency, hereinafter called "the state board," which shall be subject to the jurisdiction of the governor of the state of Alabama.

(b) (1) There is hereby created within the executive branch the Alabama law enforcement planning agency (ALEPA), the state supervisory board and the executive committee, which shall be under the jurisdiction of the governor. The state supervisory board shall consist of not more than 45 members appointed by the governor. The members shall be selected from among residents of the state who are representative of the criminal justice system, including, but not limited to, police agencies, the judiciary, prosecutorial and defense council, adult correctional and rehabilitative agencies and juvenile justice agencies; state and general local government; public and private agencies related to the criminal justice system; and private citizens. The board must be of representative character in accordance with LEAA guidelines.

(2) The executive committee shall consist of not more than 30 members appointed by the governor. The members shall be selected from the state

supervisory board membership and must be of representative character in accordance with the LEAA guidelines.

(3) Of the members first appointed by the governor after May 4, 1978, one third shall serve for a term of two years, one third shall serve for a term of four years and one third shall serve for a term of six years; provided, that a member appointed to succeed another member whose term has not expired shall be appointed for a period of the unexpired term. Should any member cease to be an officer or employee of the unit or agency he is appointed to represent, his membership on the state supervisory board and/or executive committee shall terminate immediately and a new member shall be appointed in the same manner as his predecessor to fill the unexpired term. Other vacancies occurring, except those by the expiration of a term, shall be filled for the balance of the unexpired term in the same manner as the original appointment within 90 days of the vacancy.

(4) Members of the state supervisory board and executive committee shall serve without compensation, except payment of their expenses may be paid in accordance with the applicable state travel regulations.

(5) The governor shall appoint a chairperson for the state supervisory board and executive committee. A vice-chairperson shall be selected by the state supervisory board and executive committee from among its members and shall serve as chairperson in the event of the chairperson's absence.

(6) The executive committee shall appoint a director who shall be responsible for the administration of the Alabama law enforcement planning agency (ALEPA) as required by the terms of this chapter and the federal criminal justice programs as directed by the governor.

The qualifications of the director shall be established by the executive committee in coordination with the state personnel department under its rules and regulations for establishing the position under the state merit system. (Acts 1978, No. 820, p. 1195, § 1-104.)

§ 41-8A-6. Same — Powers and duties of board generally; powers as to law enforcement and criminal justice plans and applications.

(a) The state supervisory board shall have authority to:

(1) Adopt bylaws governing the organization and operation of the state board;

(2) Adopt internal management rules and regulations governing the exercise of its powers and the fulfillment of its purposes under this chapter and the Safe Streets Act of 1968, as amended;

(3) Delegate to one or more of its members such powers and duties as it may deem proper;

(4) Coordinate and jointly pursue its activities with the central state planning and administrative office;

(5) Appoint and abolish such advisory committees as may be necessary for the performance of its functions and delegate appropriate powers and duties to them;

(6) Conduct research and stimulate research by public and private agencies which shall be designed to improve the administration of criminal justice;

(7) Accept and administer loans, grants and donations from the federal government, its agencies, the state of Alabama, its agencies and from other sources, public and private, for carrying out any of its functions;

(8) Enter into, as applicable under Alabama state laws, contracts, leases and agreements necessary, convenient or desirable for carrying out its purposes and the powers granted under this chapter with agencies of state and local government, corporations or persons;

(9) Acquire, hold and dispose of personal property in the exercise of its powers;

(10) Delegate any duty, responsibility or power to the director of ALEPA as it may deem proper; and

(11) Do all things necessary to carry out its purposes and for the exercise of the powers granted in this chapter and the Safe Streets Act of 1968, as amended.

(b) (1) The Alabama law enforcement planning agency and its state supervisory board shall have the power and authority to review, approve or disapprove all plans and all applications for subgrants which pertain to law enforcement and the criminal justice system, including juvenile delinquency and prevention. ALEPA will serve as the state clearinghouse for all criminal justice plans and subgrant applications;

(2) Should any part of this chapter be construed to be in conflict with Executive Order Number 23 pursuant to sections 11-85-50 through 11-85-56 and section 11-85-58, which established state planning and development districts, then to the extent that said sections 11-85-50 through 11-85-56 and section 11-85-58 apply to law enforcement and criminal justice, including juvenile justice, and the state boards and regional boards and as to boundaries, powers and authority of said boards, and to that extent only, shall be repealed by this chapter, otherwise to remain in full force and effect.

(3) The state comprehensive plan, the part B planning grant plan and any other block grant plans shall be submitted to the Alabama development office for review and approval in regard to environmental impact in accordance with the National Environmental Policy Act;

(4) All discretionary grants shall be submitted to the Alabama development office and to the respective regional development district for an environmental evaluation;

(5) Any subgrant application submitted to ALEPA which proposes construction or major renovation, or any other purpose specified in the National Environmental Policy Act, 28 C.F.R., 19.6 and 19.7 shall be submitted to the Alabama development office and the respective regional development district for an environmental evaluation. (Acts 1978, No. 820, p. 1195, § 1-105.)

§ 41-8A-7. Same — Powers and duties of executive committee of board.

(a) The executive committee of the state supervisory board shall have the authority to review, approve or disapprove all applications for subgrants presented to it by the ALEPA staff, either in whole or in part; provided, that an applicant may appeal the action of the executive committee to the state supervisory board in accordance with rules and regulations established by the state supervisory board.

(b) The executive committee shall have the authority to appoint the director of ALEPA as provided for within this chapter. (Acts 1978, No. 820, p. 1195, § 1-106.)

§ 41-8A-8. Regional advisory boards and planning units — Establishment; composition; purpose; membership; officers and staff generally.

(a) The regional planning units (RPUs), with boundaries as established April 22, 1969, shall be continued and established by virtue of this chapter. The regional planning units, as designated below, shall be and are hereby officially established for the purpose of regional planning, accepting and review of applications pertaining to law enforcement and the criminal justice system, including juvenile justice and delinquency prevention within their respective regions, and to assist the ALEPA central office in planning, coordination and implementation of plans.

The county lines shall be the boundaries of the regions, and the regions shall include the counties as indicated below:

Region One: Lauderdale, Colbert, Franklin, Limestone, Lawrence, Madison, Morgan, Jackson, Marshall, DeKalb and Cullman.

Region Two: Marion, Lamar, Fayette, Pickens, Tuscaloosa, Greene, Hale, Bibb, Sumter and Marengo.

Region Three: Winston, Walker, Blount, St. Clair, Shelby and Chilton.

Metro 1 — High Crime Commission: Jefferson.

Region Four: Cherokee, Etowah, Calhoun, Talladega, Cleburne, Clay, Randolph, Coosa, Tallapoosa and Chambers.

Region Five: Perry, Dallas, Autauga, Elmore, Wilcox, Lowndes, Montgomery, Macon, Lee, Russell, Bullock, Butler, Crenshaw and Pike.

Region Six: Choctaw, Clarke, Washington, Monroe, Conecuh, Mobile, Baldwin and Escambia.

Region Seven: Barbour, Henry, Dale, Coffee, Covington, Geneva and Houston.

(b) (1) The composition of the regional planning advisory boards shall incorporate the general representative character elements prescribed for the state supervisory board in section 41-8A-5 and shall not consist of more than 30 members. In addition, regional boards shall be comprised of a majority of local elected officials.

(2) The members of the regional planning advisory boards shall be appointed by the governor and the governor shall appoint the chairperson of

said regional boards. The membership of each board shall select a vice-chairperson and fiscal officer.

(3) The staff of each regional planning unit shall consist of a planning coordinator and staff necessary to carry out the duties of the regional unit.

(4) The ALEPA director shall have complete supervision of the regional planning unit staff.

(5) The ALEPA director shall have the authority to increase or decrease the staff in all regional planning units as necessary due to workloads and/or funds available. The ALEPA director shall have the authority to temporarily assign any personnel within any of the regional planning units to other duties outside his/her RPU if the need arises.

(6) The ALEPA director shall have the power to consolidate regions if feasible and desirable, depending upon workloads and funds available. (Acts 1978, No. 820, p. 1195, § 1-107.)

§ 41-8A-9. Same — Powers and duties; compensation of members.

(a) The regional advisory board shall have authority to:

(1) Adopt bylaws governing the organization and operation of the board and the regional planning units in accordance with ALEPA bylaws.

(2) Adopt internal management rules and regulations.

(3) Accept, administer and account for allocation of funds for the operation of the board and the planning units.

(4) Enter into, as applicable under Alabama state laws, contracts, leases and agreements necessary, convenient and desirable for carrying out its purposes under this chapter and the Safe Streets Act; provided, that any such contract, lease or agreement must have prior approval of the ALEPA director and must be countersigned by the director.

(5) Review all subgrant applications at the local level from within its region which pertain to law enforcement or criminal justice, including juvenile justice and delinquency prevention; provided, that the regional advisory board only has the authority to recommend approval/disapproval to the state supervisory board.

(b) The requirements in regard to the National Environmental Act set out in subdivisions (4) and (5) of subsection (b) of section 41-8A-6 shall also apply to the regional advisory boards and RPUs.

(c) The regional planning units shall submit a regional plan each year to the ALEPA central office in accordance with instructions and guidelines from the central office.

(d) The regional advisory boards shall be responsible for the RPU's operations being in compliance with policy directives of the state supervisory board, requirements of the Safe Streets Act and LEAA regulations.

(e) The members of the regional advisory boards shall serve without compensation.

(f) The members of the regional advisory board shall be entitled to receive reimbursement for any reasonable actual expense incurred as necessary and incident to such services. Applicable state regulations in regard to travel and per diem shall apply. (Acts 1978, No. 820, p. 1195, § 1-108.)

§ 41-8A-10. Same — Budgetary and other financial procedures.

(a) The regional planning units shall prepare and submit budgets each year to the ALEPA central office for the operational expenses, equipment, salaries and other maintenance costs of the regional advisory board and the regional planning units. Funds for the operation of these RPUs shall be allocated to each RPU by the central office of ALEPA. Also planning funds may be allocated to individual units of government or agencies by the state supervisory board. The minimum amount of such funds shall be governed by the requirements established in the Safe Streets Act and/or LEAA regulations under the requirements known as "pass-through" funds to local units of government or combinations thereof for planning purposes.

(b) The salaries and travel expenses of the regional planning units, even though they may be paid through the state office for accounting purposes, are chargeable to and become a part of the regional budgets. Any equipment purchased by the central ALEPA office, for procurement reasons, or any other expense paid·by the central ALEPA office for the use of or benefit of the RPUs shall be charged to each respective RPU and shall become a part of the regional budget. (Acts 1978, No. 820, p. 1195, § 1-109.)

§ 41-8A-11. Service by same individual on state supervisory board and regional advisory board; representation of more than one element or interest by board member.

An individual may serve as a member of the state supervisory board and as a member of the regional advisory board simultaneously. It is possible for one board member to represent more than one element or interest. (Acts 1978, No. 820, p. 1195, § 1-110.)

§ 41-8A-12. Submission to governor of annual budget and request for funds; request for funds by governor in appropriation bill.

Annually, the Alabama law enforcement planning agency shall present to the governor a request for funds based on projected needs of the agency, together with a budget showing proposed expenditures, and the governor may include in his appropriation bill a request for funds to meet the financial needs of the agency. (Acts 1978, No. 820, p. 1195, § 2-201.)

§ 41-8A-13. Construction of chapter; effect of chapter in event provisions thereof found in conflict with Omnibus Crime Control and Safe Streets Act of 1968.

(a) The provisions of this chapter are cumulative and shall not be construed to repeal or supersede any laws not inconsistent herewith.

(b) Should any provision of this chapter be found to be in conflict with the Omnibus Crime Control and Safe Streets Act of 1968, as amended, then, and in that event only, the Safe Streets Act shall be deemed to prevail, and to such limited extent this chapter is abridged and is subject to the provisions of the Safe Streets Act. (Acts 1978, No. 820, p. 1195, § 3-302.)

CHAPTER 9.

BOARDS AND COMMISSIONS.

Collateral references. — 81A C.J.S., States,
§§ 141, 142.

1 Am. Jur. 2d, Administrative Law, §§ 23,
36-38, 69-74.

ARTICLE 1.

GENERAL PROVISIONS.

Cross references. — As to board of agriculture and industries, see § 2-3-1 et seq. As to
agricultural center board, see § 2-6-1 et seq. As
to agricultural and industrial exhibit commission, see § 2-7-1 et seq. As to Alabama Dairy
commission, see § 2-13-40 et seq. As to state

aeronautics commission, see § 4-2-30 et seq. As
to state banking board, see § 5-2A-40 et seq. As
to state savings and loan board, see § 5-2A-63.
As to state credit union board, see § 5-2A-120
et seq. As to securities commission, see § 8-6-50
et seq. As to advisory board of conservation and

natural resources, see § 9-2-14 et seq. As to state forestry commission, see § 9-3-1 et seq. As to minerals resource management committee, see § 9-5-1 et seq. As to coastal area board, see § 9-7-14 et seq. As to surface mining reclamation commission, see § 9-16-73 et seq. As to oil and gas board, see § 9-17-3 et seq. As to liquefied petroleum gas board, see § 9-17-101 et seq. As to public park and recreation boards in counties, see § 11-22-1 et seq. As to industrial development boards in municipalities, see § 11-54-80 et seq. As to board of corrections, see § 14-1-15 et seq. As to board of pardons and paroles, see § 15-22-20 et seq. As to state board of education, see § 16-3-1 et seq. As to Alabama commission of higher education, see § 16-5-1 et seq. As to Alabama education study commission, see § 16-6-1 et seq. As to Alabama educational television commission, see § 16-7-1 et seq. As to state tenure commission for teachers, see § 16-24-30. As to governor's committee on employment of the handicapped, see § 21-5-1 et seq. As to state board of health, see § 22-2-1 et seq. As to state committee of public health, see § 22-2-4 et seq. As to state commission on physical fitness, see § 22-5-1 et seq. As to state water improvement commission, see § 22-22-1 et seq. As to the department of environmental management, see § 22-22A-4 et seq. As to mental health board, see § 22-50-4 et seq. As to alcoholic beverage control board, see § 28-3-40 et seq. As to military advisory board, see § 31-2-64 et seq. As to armory commission of Alabama, see § 31-4-1 et seq. As to state board of veterans' affairs, see § 31-5-3. As to state pilotage commission, see § 33-4-1 et seq. As to Ameraport offshore harbor and terminal commission, see § 33-10-1 et seq. As to Elk River development agency, see § 33-12-1 et seq. As to Alabama port authority, see § 33-13-1 et seq. As to Bear Creek development authority, see § 33-15-1 et seq. As to Coosa Valley development authority, see § 33-16-1 et seq. As to Tombigbee Valley development authority, see § 33-17-1 et seq. As to state board of public accountancy, see § 34-1-3. As to state board for registration of architects, see § 34-2-38 et seq. As to board of examiners of state bar, see § 34-3-2. As to board of commissioners of state bar, see § 34-3-40 et seq. As to board of trustees of state bar building foundation, see § 34-3-103. As to state board of auctioneers, see § 34-4-50 et seq. As to state board of barber examiners, see § 34-5-13. As to

state board of cosmetology, see § 34-7-40 et seq. As to state licensing board for general contractors, see § 34-8-20 et seq. As to state board of dental examiners, see § 34-9-40 et seq. As to board of registration for professional engineers and land surveyors, see § 34-11-30 et seq. As to state board of registration for foresters, see § 34-12-30 et seq. As to state board of funeral service, see § 34-13-20 et seq. As to state board of hearing aid dealers, see § 34-14-30 et seq. As to state board of examiners of landscape architects, see § 34-17-2 et seq. As to state board of medical technicians examiners, see § 34-18-40 et seq. As to state board of examiners of nursing home administrators, see § 34-20-4 et seq. As to state board of nursing, see § 34-21-2. As to state board of optometry, see § 34-22-40 et seq. As to state board of pharmacy, see § 34-23-90 et seq. As to medical licensure commission, see § 34-24-310 et seq. As to state board of medical examiners, see § 34-24-53 et seq. As to state board of chiropractic examiners, see § 34-24-140 et seq. As to state board of physical therapy, see § 34-24-192 et seq. As to state board of podiatry, see § 34-24-250 et seq. As to state polygraph examiners' board, see § 34-25-4. As to state board of examiners in psychology, see § 34-26-20 et seq. As to state real estate commission, see § 34-27-7 et seq. As to state board of examiners for speech pathology and audiology, see § 34-28A-40 et seq. As to state board of veterinary medical examiners, see § 34-29-20 et seq. As to peace officers' standards and training commission, see § 36-21-40 et seq. As to board of commissioners of Alabama peace officers' annuity and benefit fund, see § 36-21-61 et seq. As to state ethics commission, see § 36-25-3 et seq. As to state personnel board, see § 36-26-5 et seq. As to board of control of state employees' retirement system, see § 36-27-23. As to state employees' insurance board, see § 36-29-2. As to board of social work examiners, see § 34-30-50 et seq. As to fire fighters' personnel standards and education commission, see § 36-32-1 et seq. As to public service commission, see § 37-1-1 et seq. As to state board of pensions and security, see § 38-2-2. As to commission on the aging, see § 38-3-1 et seq. As to board of trustees of department of archives and history, see § 41-6-3 et seq. As to executive board of Alabama public library service, see § 41-8-2 et seq. As to youth services board, see § 44-1-50 et seq.

§ 41-9-1. Reserved.

ARTICLE 2.

ART COMMISSION.

Cross references. — As to council on the
arts and humanities, see § 41-9-40 et seq.

§ 41-9-20. Creation.

There shall be a commission to be known as the art commission. (Acts 1919,
No. 636, p. 880; Code 1923, § 79; Code 1940, T. 55, § 328.)

§ 41-9-21. Composition; qualifications, appointment, term of office and compensation of members.

The commission shall consist of the governor, the superintendent of education, the state highway director, the director of the department of archives and
history, all ex officio members and six other members to be appointed by the
governor, which said appointive members shall be qualified by training, previous experience, profession or occupation in the fine and useful arts. The commissioners shall be appointed for a term of six years; and, on the resignation
or death of a member, his successor shall be appointed by the governor to serve
out the unexpired term. The members of the commission shall serve without
compensation. (Acts 1919, No. 636, p. 880; Code 1923, § 80; Code 1940, T. 55,
§ 329.)

Cross references. — As to travel expenses,
see § 36-7-20 et seq.

§ 41-9-22. Officers and employees; meetings; offices, books, etc.; powers and duties generally.

(a) The commission may receive donations and contributions to carry on its
work. It may establish and maintain permanent offices and rooms. It may elect
an executive officer, employ other officers and employees and fix their compensation. It shall hold an annual meeting and as many special meetings as
may be necessary to conduct its business. Its books shall be subject to examination by the department of examiners of public accounts. It shall have power to
adopt such rules and regulations, not inconsistent with the provisions of this
chapter, as may be necessary for the execution of the powers and duties herein
conferred.

(b) The commission shall encourage the study of the fine and useful arts and
art teaching, shall make investigations and surveys, shall adopt standards and
shall do and perform such other things as will promote an interest in art in all
of its relations. When called upon by state, county or municipal officials or by
the trustees or other officials of state or private institutions or by individuals,
it shall advise in determining plans, designs and models for buildings, parks,
statues, fountains and public monuments or in the making of additions or
alterations in existing buildings. It may maintain permanent or temporary

exhibitions and a library of art and allied subjects. (Acts 1919, No. 636, p. 880; Code 1923, §§ 81, 83; Code 1940, T. 55, §§ 330, 332.)

§ 41-9-23. Annual report to governor; issuance, etc., of publications.

The commission may make an annual report to the governor and may issue such other publications as are necessary to better develop its activities, all to be printed and distributed as other state documents. (Acts 1919, No. 636, p. 880; Code 1923, § 82; Code 1940, T. 55, § 331.)

ARTICLE 3.

COUNCIL ON THE ARTS AND HUMANITIES.

Cross references. — As to art commission, see § 41-9-20 et seq.

§ 41-9-40. Legislative findings; declaration of public policy.

(a) It is hereby found that many of our citizens lack the opportunity to view, enjoy or participate in living theatrical performances, musical concerts, operas, dance and ballet recitals, art exhibits, examples of fine architecture and the performing and fine arts generally. It is hereby further found that, with increasing leisure time, the practice and enjoyment of the arts are of increasing importance and that the general welfare of the people of the state will be promoted by giving further recognition to the arts as a vital aspect of our culture and heritage and as a valued means of expanding the scope of our educational programs.

(b) It is hereby declared to be the policy of the state to join with private patrons and with institutions and professional organizations concerned with the arts to insure that the role of the arts in the life of our communities will continue to grow and will play an ever more significant part in the welfare and educational experience of our citizens. (Acts 1967, No. 551, p. 1300, § 1.)

§ 41-9-41. Establishment; composition; qualifications and appointment of members.

There is hereby established a state commission to be known as the Alabama state council on the arts and humanities, to consist of 15 members, broadly representative of all fields of the performing and fine arts, to be appointed by the governor from among citizens of Alabama who are widely known for their competence and experience in connection with the performing and fine arts. In making such appointments, due consideration shall be given to the recommendations made by representative civic, educational and professional associations and groups concerned with or engaged in the production or presentation of the performing and fine arts generally. (Acts 1967, No. 551, p. 1300, § 2; Acts 1969, No. 1065, p. 1986, § 1.)

§ 41-9-42. Terms of office of members; officers generally; filling of vacancies; compensation of members.

The term of office of each member shall be six years; provided, however, that of the members first appointed, five shall be appointed for terms of two years, five for terms of four years and five for terms of six years. The council shall elect a chairman and a vice-chairman from the members of the council to serve at the pleasure of the council. The chairman and vice-chairman shall be the executive officers of the council. The council itself shall nominate three persons from the same geographical area to replace each of the members whose term of service is expiring, not less than six months prior to expiration of a regular term of service and promptly upon other occurrences of a vacancy. Vacancies shall be filled by appointment by the governor from such nominees. The members of the council shall not receive any compensation for their services. (Acts 1967, No. 551, p. 1300, § 3; Acts 1976, No. 689, p. 952.)

Cross references. — As to travel expenses, see § 36-7-20 et seq.

§ 41-9-43. Executive director, consultants, advisors, etc.

The chairman, with the approval of the council, may employ an executive director and such additional personnel as may be necessary to accomplish the purpose of this article. The executive director, consultants, advisors, and any such additional personnel as may be necessary shall serve at the pleasure of the council and shall be paid such compensation as may be specified by the council. Except for the executive director and employees paid by federal funds such additional personnel shall be subject to the provisions of the state Merit System Act receiving the same salaries for the position each employee holds as of August 21, 1981 unless such salary is less than the minimum set by the merit system and in that instance such salary shall be raised to the minimum; and shall be eligible for participation in the state health insurance plan and benefits for state employees as provided in sections 36-29-1 through 36-29-12 and they shall not be eligible for participation in the state employees' retirement system. (Acts 1967, No. 551, p. 1300, § 4; Acts 1969, No. 1065, p. 1986, § 2; Acts 1981, 1st Ex. Sess., No. 81-982, § 1.)

The 1981 amendment, effective August 21, 1981, rewrote the last sentence.

§ 41-9-44. Powers of council generally; liability upon debts or obligations incurred by council.

(a) The council is hereby authorized and empowered:

(1) To hold public and private hearings;

(2) To enter into contracts, within the limits of funds available therefor, with individuals, organizations and institutions, for services furthering the educational objectives of the council's program;

(3) To enter into contracts, within the limit of funds available therefor, with local and regional associations, for cooperative endeavors furthering the educational objectives of the council's programs;

(4) To accept public or private gifts, grants, donations or bequests of unrestricted funds;

(5) To acquire real property by lease or gift but not by purchase;

(6) To renovate, furnish and maintain such real property and to lease or sublease the same;

(7) To allocate and expend funds from all donations, income and revenue from any source whatsoever coming into the treasury, for the fulfillment and accomplishment of the objectives for which the council was created;

(8) To make and sign any agreements and to do and perform any acts that may be necessary to carry out the purposes of this article.

(b) All debts or obligations incurred by the council shall be solely and exclusively obligations of the council and shall not create an obligation of the state of Alabama or of any county or municipality. (Acts 1967, No. 551, p. 1300, § 6; Acts 1969, No. 1065, p. 1986, § 3.)

§ 41-9-45. Duties of council generally.

The duties of the council shall be:

(1) To stimulate and encourage throughout the state the study and presentation of the performing and fine arts and public interest and participation therein;

(2) To make such surveys as may be deemed advisable of public and private institutions engaged within the state in artistic and cultural activities, including, but not limited to, music, theatre, dance, painting, sculpture, architecture and allied arts and crafts and to make recommendations concerning appropriate methods to encourage participation in and appreciation of the arts to meet the legitimate needs and aspirations of persons in all parts of the state;

(3) To take such steps as may be necessary and appropriate to encourage public interest in the cultural heritage of our state and to expand the state's cultural resources; and

(4) To encourage and assist freedom of artistic expression essential for the well-being of the arts. (Acts 1967, No. 551, p. 1300, § 5.)

§ 41-9-46. Council designated official agency to receive and disburse funds from national foundation on the arts and humanities; request and receipt of assistance and data from departments, agencies, etc., of state.

(a) The council shall be the official agency of this state to receive and disburse any funds made available by the national foundation on the arts and humanities.

(b) The council may request and shall receive from any department, division, board, bureau, commission or agency of the state such assistance and data as may be reasonably consistent with the facilities, personnel and duties of the organization to which the request is made so as to enable the council properly to carry out its powers and duties under this article. (Acts 1967, No. 551, p. 1300, § 7; Acts 1969, No. 1065, p. 1986, § 4.)

§ 41-9-47. Reports to governor and legislature.

The council shall make an interim report to the governor and the legislature not later than the thirtieth legislative day of the 1967 regular session of the legislature and from time to time thereafter. (Acts 1967, No. 551, p. 1300, § 9.)

ARTICLE 4.

BOARD OF ADJUSTMENT.

Legislature in article recognizes that there is sometimes a moral obligation which justifies it under the Constitution to appropriate money for certain claims when there is no legal obligation to pay them, but there is a duty to do so in the interest of the general public. Hawkins v. State Bd. of Adjustment, 242 Ala. 547, 548, 7 So. 2d 775 (1942).

Article is to be strictly construed, since it did not create a right but granted a privilege in the exact terms employed. State ex rel. McQueen v. Brandon, 244 Ala. 62, 12 So. 2d 319 (1943).

Board gives relief where state not legally liable. — The purpose for which the state board of adjustment was created was to afford a means of extending a measure of compensation or relief to citizens entitled thereto, who unfortunately suffered injury occasioned by the state or some of its agencies, commissions, boards or institutions or departments, while engaged in the performance of the sovereign functions or duties of the state, and for which the rule of sovereign immunity exempts the state and its respective agencies, commissions, boards, institutions or departments from any other duly recognized form of legal action to compensate for such unlawful act and proximate injury. State ex rel. McQueen v. Brandon, 244 Ala. 62, 12 So. 2d 319 (1943).

And it has power to review and revoke order denying claim. — If a just and proper claim has been denied, the state board of adjustment necessarily has the power to revoke its order and make the award because the appropriation stands ready and awaiting the claimant who is entitled to it in "law, justice or good morals." The power to review on proper charges of newly discovered evidence while the fund is still under its administrative control is of the essence of the authority granted the state board of adjustment under the statutes. State ex rel. Carmichael v. State Bd. of Adjustment, 249 Ala. 542, 32 So. 2d 216 (1947).

Board acts as quasi-judicial body. — The state board of adjustment acts as a fact-finding body for the legislature and in so acting is proceeding as a quasi-judicial body for the state, its agencies, commissions, boards, institutions or departments, within the provisions of this article. State ex rel. McQueen v. Brandon, 244 Ala. 62, 12 So. 2d 319 (1943).

Legislature, when it deems necessary, can pass relief bills to compensate individuals who have been harmed. Therefore, a claimant is not completely without some recourse if he suffers injury because of the action of state officials in carrying out their duties. Hutchinson v. Board of Trustees of Univ. of Ala., 288 Ala. 20, 256 So. 2d 281 (1971).

Cited in Employers Ins. Co. v. Harrison, 250 Ala. 116, 33 So. 2d 264 (1947); Stone v. State ex rel. Horn, 251 Ala. 240, 37 So. 2d 111 (1948).

Division 1.

General Provisions.

§ 41-9-60. Purpose of division.

The purpose of this division is to provide a method of payment by the state of Alabama or any of its agencies, commissions, boards, institutions or departments to persons for injuries to person or property or for death occasioned by the state of Alabama or any of its agencies, commissions, boards, institutions or departments where in law, justice or good morals the same should be paid. (Acts 1935, No. 546, p. 1164; Code 1940, T. 55, § 344.)

§ 41-9-61. Creation; composition; officers; attorney general to attend meetings of board, etc.; quarters, etc.; quorum; board may take views, conduct interviews, etc.; board to supervise, etc., preparation, etc., of records of cases.

There shall be a board of adjustment to be composed of the director of finance, the state treasurer, the secretary of state and the state auditor. The chairman of said board shall be selected by the board from its members. The secretary of state shall also be the secretary of said board and shall perform all the duties, powers and functions required of the secretary by the board. The attorney general shall attend the meetings of the board and represent the state of Alabama in all proceedings before the board.

The board of adjustment shall be furnished with necessary quarters, stationery and postage in the same manner as the same are furnished to other state officers, agencies, commissions, boards, institutions or departments.

Any three of said board members shall constitute a quorum to transact business and discharge the functions of said board; provided, however, that in case there is an equal division of opinion on any decision or claim that the board is authorized to hear, the chairman of the board shall determine the decision in such instance.

The board of adjustment shall have the power, if, in its opinion the situation warrants it, to visit any scene of any injury or accident and make a view thereof and take said facts in consideration and personally interview such persons as may have knowledge or information as to the subject matter of the claim under consideration by said board and may take such views and information into consideration in reaching its conclusion and making awards on claims.

The board of adjustment shall supervise and direct the secretary of the board as to making a record as provided in section 41-9-71 and shall aid and direct said secretary in making up a report of all cases heard and determined by said board, stating the substance of the claim and the disposition made of the case, and shall cause said cases to be classified under said board's direction in accordance with the types and kinds of cases coming before said board. (Acts 1935, No. 546, p. 1164; Acts 1939, No. 449, p. 602; Code 1940, T. 55, § 333; Acts 1943, No. 421, p. 386.)

Cross references. — As to duty of chief of legal division of department of finance to represent board of adjustment, see § 41-4-204.

§ 41-9-62. Claims within jurisdiction of board generally; employees of municipalities, counties, etc., not within jurisdiction of board, etc.

(a) The board of adjustment shall have the power and jurisdiction and it shall be its duty to hear and consider:

(1) All claims for damages to the person or property growing out of any injury done to either the person or property by the state of Alabama or any of its agencies, commissions, boards, institutions or departments;

(2) All claims for personal injuries to or the death of any employee of the state of Alabama or any of its agencies, commissions, boards, institutions or departments arising out of the course of his employment or sustained while engaged in the business of the state of Alabama or any of its agencies, commissions, boards, institutions or departments;

(3) All claims for personal injuries to or the death of any convict;

(4) All claims of members of the public at large or of officers of the law arising out of injuries sustained while attempting to recapture escaped convicts, which convicts have escaped after they have been placed in the actual custody of the board of corrections;

(5) All claims against the state of Alabama or any of its agencies, commissions, boards, institutions or departments arising out of any contract, express or implied, to which the state of Alabama or any of its agencies, commissions, boards, institutions or departments are parties, where there is claimed a legal or moral obligation resting on the state;

(6) All claims for money overpaid on obligations to the state of Alabama or any of its agencies, commissions, boards, institutions or departments;

(7) All claims for money voluntarily paid to the state of Alabama or any of its agencies, commissions, boards, institutions or departments, where no legal liability existed to make such payment;

(8) All claims for underpayment by the state of Alabama or any of its agencies, commissions, boards, institutions or departments to parties having dealings with the state of Alabama or any of its agencies, commissions, boards, institutions or departments;

(9) All claims for money or property alleged to have wrongfully escheated to the state of Alabama; and

(10) All claims for injury or death of any student duly enrolled in any of the public schools of this state resulting from an accident sustained while being transported to or from school or in connection with any school activity in any bus or any motor vehicle operated directly by any school board or agency of the state or through contract with another. Awards payable to any such student for injuries sustained in such accident shall be equal to the maximum benefits payable to employees as provided in chapter 5 of Title 25 for injuries, loss of time or medical attendance; and, where death results from such injuries, the amount payable to the parent or parents of such student shall be equal to the maximum amount payable to a totally dependent parent or parents as provided by chapter 5 of Title 25; provided, however, that no payment for death of such student shall be made to any parent or parents

unless they were actually supporting such student at the time of the accident causing the injuries and death. The fact that such student has no earning capacity or earns an average wage of less than the amount which would entitle him to maximum benefits under chapter 5 of Title 25 shall in no way limit an award to him, his parent or parents. Awards for such injuries or death shall constitute a prior and preferred claim against moneys appropriated for the minimum program fund, and no part of any such award shall be charged against any funds allotted to the school board of the county or city or the district board of education of the independent school district where said accident occurred. If it should appear to the board of adjustment after investigation that the accident causing the injury or death of such student was caused under circumstances also creating a legal liability for damages on the part of any party and it should further appear to the board of adjustment that claim may be made against such party by such student, his parent or legal representative to recover damages, then, in that event, any payment otherwise due under this subdivision may be withheld by the board of adjustment pending final settlement of such claim and, if said student or his parent or legal representative recovers damages against said party, any sum so recovered and collected may be offset against payments due under this subdivision, and the balance due, if any, shall thereafter be promptly paid by the board of adjustment. The provisions of this subdivision shall apply to all claims relating to injuries to school children filed with said board within one year of the date of an accident. Minor students shall have, for the purpose of this subdivision, the same power to contract, make elections of remedy, make settlements and receive compensation as adults would have subject to the power of the board of adjustment in its discretion at any time to require the appointment of a guardian to receive moneys or awards and payments of awards made to such minor students or their guardian shall exclude any further compensation either to the minor students or to their parents for loss of service or otherwise.

(b) The jurisdiction of the board of adjustment is specifically limited to the consideration of the claims enumerated in subsection (a) of this section and no others; provided, that nothing contained in this division shall confer upon the board of adjustment any jurisdiction now conferred by law upon the state board of compromise provided for in sections 41-1-3 and 41-1-4, and nothing contained in this division shall be construed to confer jurisdiction upon the board of adjustment to settle or adjust any matter or claim of which the courts of this state have or had jurisdiction; provided further, that the board of adjustment shall have no jurisdiction over claims growing out of forfeitures or of contracts with any state agency, commission, board, institution or department where, by law or contract, said state agency, commission, board, institution or department is made the final arbiter of any disagreement growing out of forfeitures or of contracts of said state agency, commission, board, institution or department, and, particularly, the board of adjustment shall have no jurisdiction of disagreements arising out of contracts entered into by the highway department.

(c) Employees of municipalities and counties are not to be considered employees of the state of Alabama or of any of its agencies, commissions, boards, institutions or departments within the jurisdiction of this board and within the meaning of the word "employee" as used in this section. (Acts 1935, No. 546, p. 1164; Acts 1936-37, Ex. Sess., No. 173, p. 205; Code 1940, T. 55, § 334; Acts 1953, No. 540, p. 755.)

Duty of board under this and the following sections is to ascertain the persons who should be included in an appropriation, which the legislature has made, to reimburse persons injured by the negligence, etc., of state agencies. By so doing the legislature is relieved of the burden of relief bills and a moral or legal duty claimed to rest on the state is fulfilled. State ex rel. Carmichael v. State Bd. of Adjustment, 249 Ala. 542, 32 So. 2d 216 (1947).

Board does not sit as court nor legislate. — The authority of the board of adjustment is to act for the legislature on facts found by the board within defined limits, when no court has jurisdiction, but when one of the state agencies has so acted as to create a moral obligation which should be discharged as a public duty. The board does not sit as a court and does not legislate. But the legislature makes the appropriation and imposes the duty on the board to find facts and draw deductions within defined limitations. The legislative act then operates upon that finding. Hawkins v. State Bd. of Adjustment, 242 Ala. 547, 7 So. 2d 775 (1942).

Section grants privilege of filing claims in exact terms stated. — Prior to the enactment of this section creating the state board to hear claims against the state, the right or privilege of filing a claim against the state for injury caused by its agencies did not exist. This section did not create a right, but granted a privilege in the exact terms stated. Turner v. Lumbermens Mut. Ins. Co., 235 Ala. 632, 180 So. 300 (1938).

And is to be strictly construed. — This section creating the state board of adjustment to hear claims against the state is to be strictly construed. Turner v. Lumbermens Mut. Ins. Co., 235 Ala. 632, 180 So. 300 (1938).

Insurance companies which had paid insured for fire losses allegedly caused by negligence of the state were not entitled by way of subrogation to maintain a claim against the state before the state board of adjustment where statute contained no specific provision for right of subrogation. Turner v. Lumbermens Mut. Ins. Co., 235 Ala. 632, 180 So. 300 (1938).

This section must be strictly construed; its purpose is to confer a privilege rather than create a right. Hawkins v. State Bd. of Adjustment, 30 Ala. App. 450, 7 So. 2d 773 (1942).

Jurisdiction of board predicated on legislative right to delegate power respecting details. — The jurisdiction of state board of adjustment to hear and consider all claims for damages done by state agencies, commissions or boards is predicated on legislature's right to confer on administrative commission or board power to act respecting details as to which it is not convenient for legislature to act in session. John E. Ballenger Constr. Co. v. State Bd. of Adjustment, 234 Ala. 377, 175 So. 387 (1937).

And it may exercise only jurisdiction and powers conferred. — The state board of adjustment is of limited jurisdiction and powers and may exercise only the jurisdiction and powers conferred by statute. Turner v. Lumbermens Mut. Ins. Co., 235 Ala. 632, 180 So. 300 (1938); State ex rel. McQueen v. Brandon, 244 Ala. 62, 12 So. 2d 319 (1943).

And has no jurisdiction of claims for damages caused by county employees. — This section means that the board of adjustment does not have jurisdiction of claims for damages caused by county employees as well as claims for damages caused to such employees. State Bd. of Adjustment v. Lacks, 247 Ala. 72, 22 So. 2d 377 (1945).

Second feature of section is apparently in nature of workmen's compensation law for state employees and is limited by the last sentence so as not to include employees of municipalities, counties and governmental relief agencies, and so that the term "employee" used in this section shall not relate to them. State Bd. of Adjustment v. Lacks, 247 Ala. 72, 22 So. 2d 377 (1945).

Board cannot be vested with jurisdiction over claims analogous to action. — The state board of adjustment is created at state's option and cannot be vested with jurisdiction over claims analogous to action against state. Dunn Constr. Co. v. State Bd. of Adjustment, 234 Ala. 372, 175 So. 383 (1937).

And claims cognizable by courts excluded from board's jurisdiction. — The legislative purpose disclosed in this section was to confer on the board of adjustment jurisdiction over claims against the state, colorable legally and morally well grounded, not justiciable in the courts, because of the state's constitutional immunity from being made a defendant (Constitution 1901, § 14), and to exclude from its jurisdiction claims well grounded in law, cognizable by the courts. Lee v. Cunningham, 234 Ala. 639, 176 So. 477 (1937).

The clause excluding "any matter or claim of which the courts of the state have jurisdiction" excepts from this section claims for money which state is obligated by law or contract to pay through public officers, on whom is imposed official duty, performance of which may be compelled by mandamus, to make payment from funds appropriated therefor. Dunn Constr. Co. v. State Bd. of Adjustment, 234 Ala. 372, 175 So. 383 (1937).

A claim for refund of a ship broker's license tax on the ground that claimant was engaged exclusively in interstate and foreign commerce, being cognizable by the courts, the board of adjustment had no jurisdiction of the claim and its order and decree in respect thereto has no legal force. Lee v. Cunningham, 234 Ala. 639, 176 So. 477 (1937).

The authority of the board of adjustment is prescribed in this section. It does not include any matter of which courts have jurisdiction and its authority extends to claims for damages to a person, growing out of an injury done to him "by the state of Alabama or any of its agencies, commissions, boards, institutions or departments." Hawkins v. State Bd. of Adjustment, 242 Ala. 547, 7 So. 2d 775 (1942). See also State Bd. of Adjustment v. Lacks, 247 Ala. 72, 22 So. 2d 377 (1945).

Section does not conflict with court's power to require officer to perform legal duty. — This section conferring on state board of adjustment power and duty to hear and consider all claims for damages done by state agencies, commissions or boards does not conflict with court's power to require officer to perform clear legal duty, though it be to pay money of state as required by law, such board not being in nature of court with power to settle unliquidated disputes between citizens and state as to whether latter must discharge its obligations as courts require citizens to do. John E. Ballenger Constr. Co. v. State Bd. of Adjustment, 234 Ala. 377, 175 So. 387 (1937).

Claim by county for wrongful payment to state of expenses incurred in examination of accounts of county superintendent of education and custodian of public funds, where there was no liability for such payment, was within this section giving the board of adjustment jurisdiction to hear claims "for money overpaid on obligations due state" or "for money voluntarily paid to state where no legal liability existed to make such payment." Calhoun County v. Brandon, 237 Ala. 537, 187 So. 868 (1939).

Provision depriving board of jurisdiction over claims under certain class of contracts with state agencies is valid. Dunn Constr. Co. v. State Bd. of Adjustment, 234 Ala. 372, 175 So. 383 (1937); John E. Ballenger Constr. Co. v. State Bd. of Adjustment, 234 Ala. 377, 175 So. 387 (1937).

City board of education is within purview of section. — A city board of education is an "agency, commission, board, institution, or department of the state" within purview of this section, and hence, board properly entertained claim of one who was injured because of the negligent operation of a truck belonging to city board of education. State ex rel. McQueen v. Brandon, 244 Ala. 62, 12 So. 2d 319 (1943).

Claim for negligence of servant of county board of education. — The legislature extended the jurisdiction of the board of adjustment under this section to all state agencies, whether immediate or more remote, while they are engaged in governmental functions, so as to be immune from action on claims of the sort there enumerated; hence, the board had jurisdiction of a claim for the negligence of a servant of a county board of education in causing his death. Hawkins v. State Bd. of Adjustment, 242 Ala. 547, 7 So. 2d 775 (1942).

Claim for rent improperly paid to state land commissioner. — Where land was sold to state to satisfy a tax lien and the tax sale was void because of irregularities, remedy, if any, of occupant of the land paying rent to agents of the state land commissioner was required to be pursued before the board of adjustment. Clifton v. Curry, 30 Ala. App. 584, 10 So. 2d 51 (1942).

Action of board subject to prerogative writ. — The action of the state board of adjustment may be subject to a prerogative writ in a proper case by a higher court having the power of supervision. State ex rel. McQueen v. Brandon, 244 Ala. 62, 12 So. 2d 319 (1943).

Precludes mandamus requiring hearing of such claims. — Mandamus cannot issue to require state board of adjustment to hear and adjust state highway contractor's claim for damages because of state highway commission's failure to provide proper engineering services and delay in securing part of right-of-way, in view of provision withdrawing from such board jurisdiction over claims under certain class of contracts with state agencies, and particularly of disagreements arising out of contracts with state highway department. Dunn Constr. Co. v. State Bd. of Adjustment, 234 Ala. 372, 175 So. 383 (1937).

But county may bring mandamus to compel hearing of proper claims. — A "county" being a "person" within statute creating the state board of adjustment to hear claims of "persons" against the state was entitled to bring mandamus to compel the board to hear claim for wrongful payment to state of expenses incurred in examination of accounts of superintendent of education and custodian of public funds where there was no liability for such payment. Calhoun County v. Brandon, 237 Ala. 537, 187 So. 868 (1939).

Proceeding on claim before state board of adjustment is not an action on existing cause of action within constitutional provision that legislature cannot take away cause of action after commencement of an action thereon, in view of provision that state shall never be made defendant in any court. Dunn Constr. Co. v. State Bd. of Adjustment, 234 Ala. 372, 175 So. 383 (1937).

Status of claimant ascertained by board of adjustment to be included in appropriations made by statutes to meet moral and legal obligations specified by legislature is as though legislature had passed act appropriating

amount to be paid him out of treasury. State v. Inman, 239 Ala. 348, 195 So. 448 (1940).

Board's decision binding as to liability and amount of the award. — One claiming damages for personal injuries incurred on account of negligence is bound by the board's decision both as to liability and the amount of the award. Higgins v. Nationwide Mut. Ins. Co., 291 Ala. 462, 282 So. 2d 301 (1973).

Cited in Employers Ins. Co. v. Harrison, 250 Ala. 116, 33 So. 2d 264 (1947); Stone v. State ex rel. Horn, 251 Ala. 240, 37 So. 2d 111 (1948); Rainer v. Tillett Bros. Constr. Co., 381 So. 2d 36 (Ala. 1980).

§ 41-9-63. Claimant may prosecute claim in person or by counsel or agent.

A claimant shall have the right to file and prosecute his claim before the board in person or by counsel or agent of his own choice, whether such agent be licensed to practice law or not. (Acts 1935, No. 546, p. 1164; Code 1940, T. 55, § 344; Acts 1963, No. 307, p. 786, § 2.)

§ 41-9-64. Claims for death to be made by personal representative; distribution of proceeds of claim.

Claims for death shall be made by the personal representative, who shall distribute the proceeds of the claim in the same manner as is provided by law with respect to damages awarded for death by wrongful act. (Acts 1935, No. 546, p. 1164; Acts 1936-37, Ex. Sess., No. 173, p. 205; Code 1940, T. 55, § 339.)

Collateral references. — Effect of death of beneficiary upon right of action under death statute. 13 ALR4th 1060.

§ 41-9-65. Limitation periods for presentation of claims.

(a) Unless otherwise provided in this section, all claims must be presented to the board of adjustment within one year after the cause of action accrues.

(b) Claims for injury to the person resulting in death must be presented to the board of adjustment within two years after the cause of action accrues, unless the same is first carried into the courts of the state, in which event the statute of limitations shall not begin to run until the date on which a final judgment in the same, holding the claimant not entitled to relief through the courts of the state, is entered.

(c) In the matter of escheats to the state of Alabama, any such claim must be filed with the board of adjustment within 10 years from the time of the escheat to the state of Alabama; except, that such claims of minors may be considered by the board of adjustment if the same are filed within three years after such minor has reached the age of 19 years.

(d) The board of adjustment is prohibited from hearing or considering any claim not filed within the time specified and the limitations provided in this section shall apply both to claims which have already accrued and to those which accrue after July 10, 1943. (Acts 1935, No. 546, p. 1164; Acts 1936-37, Ex. Sess., No. 173, p. 205; Code 1940, T. 55, § 335; Acts 1943, No. 583, p. 585.)

Reconsideration of claim more than one year after cause accrued. — This section providing that "all claims must be presented to the board of adjustment within one year after the cause of action accrues" presents no defense to the allowance of claims by the board when these claims were presented within the required time and reopened more than one year after the cause accrued. Their reconsideration after denial does not change the situation. State ex rel. Carmichael v. State Bd. of Adjustment, 249 Ala. 542, 32 So. 2d 216 (1947).

Collateral references. — 81 C.J.S., States, § 199.

§ 41-9-66. Board may prescribe forms and adopt rules of evidence and procedure.

The board of adjustment may prescribe such forms and adopt such rules of evidence and procedure as it may deem necessary or proper, not inconsistent with the provisions of this division. (Acts 1935, No. 546, p. 1164; Code 1940, T. 55, § 337.)

Cited in State ex rel. Carmichael v. State Bd. of Adjustment, 249 Ala. 542, 32 So. 2d 216 (1947).

Collateral references. — Admissibility of opinion evidence as to employability on the issue of disability in insurance and workmen's compensation cases. 89 ALR3d 783.

§ 41-9-67. Powers, etc., of board as to requirement of production of documents, etc., generally; employment of clerical, etc., help for investigation of claims, etc.

(a) The board of adjustment shall have the power and it shall be its duty when any claim or claims for damages provided for in this division are presented to it to require any employee, agency, commission, board, institution or department of the state of Alabama to furnish any documents or information deemed necessary by the board of adjustment and to require the presence of any person or the production of any documents in the same manner as in circuit court trials with the same rights as the circuit courts to punish for contempt.

(b) With the approval of the governor and subject to the provisions of the merit system, the board of adjustment may employ such necessary clerical or other help in ascertaining the facts incident to or growing out of claims presented to it and to make such investigations and to interview such witnesses as in the opinion of the board of adjustment are essential to ascertain the true facts upon which to base their findings and awards. (Acts 1935, No. 546, p. 1164; Code 1940, T. 55, § 338.)

§ 41-9-68. Determination of amount of injury or damage and entry of award for payment of damages generally.

(a) When claims are properly prepared and presented to the board of adjustment and, after ascertaining the facts in the case, it is directed to determine the amount of the injury, death or disability or other injury or damage arising from contract or business and to fix the damages, using as its guide, when applicable, the ordinary rules of negligence and workmen's compensation laid down by the courts and the moral obligation of the state of Alabama, and to award and find the person entitled to payment and the amount, if any, which should be paid and any other facts necessary for a proper adjustment of claims. The ordinary rules of negligence as to liability are to be followed in claims by parties not employees of the state of Alabama or any of its agencies, commissions, boards, institutions or departments. The rules of chapter 5 of Title 25 as to liability are to be followed in claims for personal injury or death of employees of the state of Alabama or of any of its agencies, commissions, boards, institutions or departments and also in claims for the injury or death of convicts.

(b) Whenever the provisions of this division authorize ascertainment of the amount of damages and provide for payment of the judgment, finding or award of the board of adjustment, they shall be construed to include also claims arising from contract or business dealings as well as for personal injury, property damage, death and disability. (Acts 1935, No. 546, p. 1164; Acts 1936-37, Ex. Sess., No. 173, p. 205; Code 1940, T. 55, § 339.)

Measure of an injured person's rights under section is not equivalent to that afforded by a common-law action. Higgins v. Nationwide Mut. Ins. Co., 291 Ala. 462, 282 So. 2d 301 (1973).

Section does not require board to set amount of its awards of compensation in strict accordance with compensation schedules of Workmen's Compensation Act; the amount of compensation to be awarded, if any, is a matter within the discretion of the board. This section merely directs that the board, in exercising that discretion, consider the facts of each case in light of the rules of workmen's compensation and the moral obligation of the state. Moody v. University of Ala., 405 So. 2d 714 (Ala. Civ. App.), cert. denied, 405 So. 2d 717 (Ala. 1981).

§ 41-9-69. Determination of agency, commission, etc., of state inflicting injury or damage and entry of award for payment of damages out of funds appropriated thereto.

The board of adjustment in its findings of facts and its findings and awards as to the amount of payment may also find the agency, commission, board, institution or department of the state of Alabama which inflicted the injury or damage complained of, if it finds there is injury or damage done to persons or property, and may adjudge and find that said damage shall be paid out of the appropriation made to the agency, commission, board, institution or department of the state of Alabama whose employees, servants, agents or instrumentalities inflicted the damages and injuries complained of; provided, that the board of adjustment may order the payment of any claim out of any fund or funds appropriated for the purposes of this division. (Acts 1935, No. 546, p. 1164; Code 1940, T. 55, § 340.)

§ 41-9-70. Limitation on amount of award for personal injury or death.

The board of adjustment shall not fix a greater amount to be paid on any claim for death or personal injuries than the limits fixed in chapter 5 of Title 25 for injuries, loss of time, medical attendance or death; provided, that convicts shall be considered as receiving the minimum wages mentioned in chapter 5 of Title 25. (Acts 1935, No. 546, p. 1164; Code 1940, T. 55, § 336.)

Benefits payable under section are to equal maximums payable under workmen's compensation law. Higgins v. Nationwide Mut. Ins. Co., 291 Ala. 462, 282 So. 2d 301 (1973).

§ 41-9-71. Secretary of board to prepare, etc., history of cases, etc., and deliver to comptroller certified copy of findings and awards of board; comptroller to draw warrant in favor of persons, etc., found entitled to damages, etc.

The secretary of the board of adjustment shall make a record of and file in the office of the secretary of state a history of the case, together with the findings and awards of the board of adjustment, and shall deliver to the comptroller of the state of Alabama a certified copy of its findings and awards.

Upon receipt of such a copy of the findings and awards of the board of adjustment, the comptroller of the state of Alabama is authorized and directed to draw his warrant in favor of the person or persons, association or corporation found by the board of adjustment to be entitled to the damages in the amount of the damages so certified, and he shall charge the same to the appropriation as directed in said findings or awards. (Acts 1935, No. 546, p. 1164; Code 1940, T. 55, § 341.)

General funds of state not available to pay certain claims for damages. — There is nothing in this section indicative of an intention on the part of the legislature to make the general funds of the state available for the payment of a claim for damages based on the negligence of an employee of a county board of education. Hawkins v. State Bd. of Adjustment, 30 Ala. App. 450, 7 So. 2d 773, rev'd on other grounds, 242 Ala. 547, 7 So. 2d 775 (1942).

§ 41-9-72. Payment by treasurer of warrants drawn pursuant to findings and awards of board.

The treasurer of the state of Alabama is authorized and directed to pay the warrants of the comptroller, drawn pursuant to the findings and awards of the board of adjustment out of any money in the treasury of the state of Alabama as directed by such findings and awards. (Acts 1935, No. 546, p. 1164; Code 1940, T. 55, § 342.)

Collateral references. — 81 C.J.S., States, § 212.

§ 41-9-73. Appropriations for payment of awards, etc.

There is hereby appropriated annually out of the general fund of the state of Alabama, the state insurance fund, the fund of the department of corrections, the special educational trust fund, the special mental health fund or any other fund of the state, to be determined by the board of adjustment, an amount, not exceeding $750,000.00 for each fiscal year, as may be necessary to pay the claims ordered paid by the board of adjustment and its expenses. There is also hereby appropriated, for each fiscal year, an additional amount, not exceeding $175,000.00, from funds of the state highway department to pay the claims chargeable against the highway department which are ordered paid by the board of adjustment and its expenses. There is also appropriated, in addition to the foregoing appropriations, from the state general fund to the state board of adjustment, the sum of $200,000.00 for each fiscal year for the purpose of paying death benefits covered under the provisions of article 1 of chapter 30 of Title 36. (Acts 1935, No. 546, p. 1164; Code 1940, T. 55, § 343; Acts 1951, No. 943, p. 1609; Acts 1963, No. 307, p. 786, § 1; Acts 1965, 1st Ex. Sess., No. 218, p. 286; Acts 1977, No. 675, p. 1166; Acts 1982, No. 82-576, § 1.)

The 1982 amendment, effective May 4, 1982, in the first sentence substituted "department of corrections" for "board of corrections" and "$750,000.00" for "$350,000.00" and in the last sentence substituted "$200,000.00" for "$150,000.00."

State debt not created. — The legislative appropriation of state's money to meet moral and legal obligations of state to pay for damages done by state agencies, commissions or boards, as by act creating state board of adjustment to ascertain persons entitled thereto, nature of their claims and amount thereof, is not state debt, though legal duty is imposed on executive officers to pay amount thereof out of moneys in treasury subject to its payment, appropriation being subject to repeal until paid. John E. Ballenger Constr. Co. v. State Bd. of Adjustment, 234 Ala. 377, 175 So. 387 (1937).

Section no bar to allowance of claims previously denied. — The appropriation of $50,000.00 (now $200,000.00) a year for payment of awards is no impediment to the allowance of claims previously denied. When the award is made, its amount will be included in the appropriation made for the year during which it is allowed. State ex rel. Carmichael v. State Bd. of Adjustment, 249 Ala. 542, 32 So. 2d 216 (1947).

§ 41-9-74. Board to pay judgments against board of corrections officials; limitations, exceptions, etc.

(a) As part of the consideration of the employment or appointment of the commissioner of the board of corrections, deputy commissioners of the board of corrections, members of the board of corrections and other officers, employees and agents of the board of corrections, whether part-time or full-time, the board of adjustment shall pay all final judgments awarded in courts of competent jurisdiction against the aforesaid commissioner, deputy commissioners, members of the board of corrections, officers, employees and agents, for acts arising out of and performed in connection with their official duties in behalf of the state of Alabama, except to the extent that such coverage may be provided by an insurance carrier.

(b) Payment shall be limited to a maximum of $100,000.00 for all claims arising out of the same act.

(c) No part of this section shall be admissible evidence in any court of law wherein any of the officers or persons indemnified herein are parties. Nothing in this section shall be deemed to waive the sovereign immunity of the state with respect to a claim covered under this section or to authorize the payment by the state of any judgment or settlement against the aforesaid commissioner, deputy commissioners, members of the board of corrections, officers, employees and agents, to the extent that the same exceeds the sum of $100,000.00.

(d) The provisions of this section shall not apply to the commissioner, any deputy commissioner, any member of the board of corrections and any other officer, employee and agent of the board of corrections who is found guilty of gross negligence or intentional or knowingly unlawful behavior. (Acts 1979, No. 79-670, p. 1179.)

Code commissioner's notes. — Acts 1979, No. 79-670, p. 1179, § 7, effective July 30, 1979, provides that this act shall also apply to all applicable lawsuits filed in court on its effective date.

Acts 1979, No. 79-426, p. 667, effective October 1, 1979, abolished the board of correc-

tions and vested all its rights, duties, power, property, etc., in the governor, and authorized him to exercise such functions and duties himself or through designated administrators. See §§ 14-1-15 through 14-1-17, and also Acts 1979, No. 79-154, p. 253.

Division 2.

Escrow Accounts for Benefit
of Crime Victims.

§ 41-9-80. Entity contracting with convicted felon to pay money to board; felony upon failure to pay; escrow account for crime victim who recovers judgment against felon.

Every person, firm, corporation, partnership, association or other legal entity contracting with any person or the representative or assignee of any person, indicted or convicted of a felony in this state, with respect to the reenactment of such crime, by way of a movie, book, magazine article, radio or television presentation, live entertainment of any kind, or from the expression of such person's thoughts, feelings, opinions or emotions regarding such crime, shall pay over to the board of adjustment any moneys which would otherwise, by terms of such contract, be owing to the person so convicted or his representatives. Any person, firm, corporation, partnership, association or other legal entity who fails to pay said moneys to the board of adjustment shall be guilty of a felony punishable by imprisonment for not less than one nor more than 10 years and by a fine equal to the net proceeds earned as a result of the reenactment of the crime. The board of adjustment shall deposit such moneys in an escrow account for the benefit of and payable to any victim of crimes committed by such person, provided that such person is eventually convicted of the crime and provided further that such victim, within five years of the date of the crime, brings a civil action in a court of competent jurisdiction and recovers a money judgment against such person or his representatives. (Acts 1979, No. 79-600, p. 1063, § 1.)

§ 41-9-81. List of criminals to probate judge; board to notify victims of escrow money.

The board of adjustment shall maintain a list of criminals for whom money is being held in escrow. Said board of adjustment shall, once a year, send such list to each judge of probate of the state to be kept as a public record, open for inspection by the public.

The board of adjustment shall notify all known victims or their families, as determined by the criminal's record, that such escrow moneys are available to satisfy money judgments pursuant to this division. The cost of publication of the list of criminals and for the notification of victims as required by this section shall be paid out of the escrow account. (Acts 1979, No. 79-600, p. 1063, § 2.)

§ 41-9-82. Escrow money to revert to state after five years.

If, five years after the establishment of the escrow account, neither the victim nor any of his heirs, as described above, have applied for the escrow moneys, such moneys shall revert to the state. (Acts 1979, No. 79-600, p. 1063, § 3.)

§ 41-9-83. Limitation begins running when escrow account established.

Notwithstanding any inconsistent provision of the civil practice law and rules with respect to the timely bringing of an action, the five year period provided for in section 41-9-80 shall not begin to run until an escrow account has been established. (Acts 1979, No. 79-600, p. 1063, § 4.)

§ 41-9-84. Action to defeat division purpose null and void.

Any action taken by any person convicted of a crime, whether by way of execution of a power of attorney, creation of corporate entities or otherwise, to defeat the purpose of this division shall be null and void as against the public policy of this state. (Acts 1979, No. 79-600, p. 1063, § 5.)

ARTICLE 5.

STATE ATHLETIC COMMISSION.

Athletic commission constitutional. — The legislature by enacting Act No. 80-121 sought to restructure the commission regulating boxing, sparring and wrestling through the establishment of a state athletic commission. The establishment of a new commission was well within the power of the legislature and is constitutional. The court should not contravene the clear intent of the legislature, which is to regulate boxing, sparring and wrestling. Eagerton v. Gulas Wrestling Enters., Inc., 406 So. 2d 366 (Ala. 1981).

The legislature has the authority to regulate wrestling, sparring and boxing in the manner prescribed in Act No. 80-121 and the legislation has a rational basis and is not arbitrary. Eagerton v. Gulas Wrestling Enters., Inc., 406 So. 2d 366 (Ala. 1981).

The state has the authority to regulate boxing, sparring and wrestling regardless of the absence of, or the existence of, lesser regulations imposed on other sporting events in the state. Eagerton v. Gulas Wrestling Enters., Inc., 406 So. 2d 366 (Ala. 1981).

Classifying and fixing the measure of regulatory tax are legislative and not judicial functions. The legislature may decide the amount of money to be charged for permits, licenses and taxes and to distribute such funds in accord with its determination. Eagerton v.

Gulas Wrestling Enters., Inc., 406 So. 2d 366 (Ala. 1981).

Collateral references. — 72 C.J.S., Prize Fighting, §§ 1-7.

4 Am. Jur. 2d, Amusements & Exhibitions, § 26.

Division 1.

General Provisions.

§ **41-9-90.** Repealed by Acts 1980, No. 80-121, p. 171, § 3, effective May 24, 1980.

§ **41-9-90.1. Creation of commission; composition; appointment and terms of members; officers; vacancies; mileage and per diem allowance; certain charges and interests unlawful for members and employees; penalty; meetings; quorum; function and purpose; rules and regulations; powers; revenue department to furnish clerical help; joint promulgation of administrative rules.**

(a) A state athletic commission is hereby created. The commission shall be composed of seven members who shall be appointed by the governor, one from each of the seven U.S. congressional districts, with the advice and consent of the senate, for terms of four years each, provided that of the members initially appointed, three shall serve for two years and four shall serve for four years, as the governor may direct. The members of the commission shall select a chairman and vice-chairman from among their members. Vacancies on the board during a term shall be filled for the unexpired portion of the term in the same manner as the member whose place is being filled.

(b) Members of the commission shall receive the same mileage and per diem allowance as paid to state employees. All such expenses shall be paid from the funds of the commission. It shall be unlawful for any member of the commission or any employee thereof to charge, receive or obtain, either directly or indirectly, any fee, commission, retainer or brokerage out of the funds of the commission, and no member of the commission or officer or employee thereof shall have any interest in any materials or contracts sold to or made or negotiated with the commission, or with any member or employee thereof acting in his capacity as a member of such commission. Violation of any provision of this section shall be a misdemeanor and upon conviction shall be punishable by removal from membership or employment and by a fine of not less than $100.00 or by imprisonment not to exceed six months or both.

(c) The meetings shall be at the call of the chairman at least on a quarterly basis, not to exceed 20 meetings per year. A majority of the members shall constitute a quorum for the transaction of business. The members of the commission shall determine the times and places within the state for their meetings as may be necessary, desirable or convenient. In the event of the absence or incapacity of the chairman, meetings may be on the call of the vice-chairman, or on the call of any five members of the commission. The commission shall determine and establish its own organization and procedures necessary to accomplish its purpose and function.

(d) It shall be the function and main purpose of the commission to encourage and attract more professional athletic, sporting and promotional events to the state, and develop the publicity and promotional programs for the support of these events. It is specifically provided that all rules and regulations promulgated by the boxing and wrestling commission created by section 41-9-90, are in full force and effect. The state athletic commission shall be required to enforce such rules and regulations and the state athletic commission is hereby granted power to alter, amend or promulgate new rules and regulations governing boxing and/or wrestling events. In addition to the general powers, the commission's powers shall include those incidental or necessary to the discharge of its said powers and duties.

(e) The state revenue department shall furnish the commission with necessary secretarial and clerical help. The commission and the revenue department shall jointly promulgate all necessary administrative rules and regulations regarding the keeping and transfer of records, forms, licenses and other material. (Acts 1980, No. 80-121, p. 171, § 6.)

Code commissioner's note. — Section 41-9-90, referred to in subsection (d) was repealed by Acts 1980, No. 80-121, p. 171, § 3, effective May 24, 1980.

Cross References. — As to travel expenses, see § 36-7-20 et seq.

Collateral references. — 81A C.J.S., States, § 239.

§ **41-9-91.** Repealed by Acts 1980, No. 80-121, p. 171, § 3, effective May 24, 1980.

Code commissioner's note. — Acts 1980, No. 80-121, p. 171, § 3, amended this section, retroactive to October 31, 1977, to read as follows: The chairman and each member of the commission shall serve as such without salary, but shall receive his actual expenses while engaged in the performance of his duties, and a per diem of $10.00 per day. The chairman of the commission shall be ex officio the recorder of permits and licenses and for such service one-half of all moneys collected shall be paid to the American Legion, department of Alabama, to be used in their programs. The act further provided that any actions taken or payments made in accordance with this section since October 31, 1977, are ratified, validated and confirmed; and also, that the legislature waives all debts incurred by the American Legion to the state regarding funds collected by the boxing and wrestling commission since October 31, 1977 and May 24, 1980.

§§ **41-9-92 through 41-9-95.** Repealed by Acts 1980, No. 80-121, p. 171, § 3, effective May 24, 1980.

§ **41-9-96. Collection of boxing, sparring and wrestling license and permit fees or taxes by commissioner of revenue department; distribution of proceeds.**

(a) The commissioner of the revenue department, hereinafter called "commissioner," shall have full power and authority and it shall be his duty, to collect:

(1) A fee of $1.00 for every permit or license to hold a boxing, sparring or wrestling match or exhibition;

(2) A reasonable fee, to be fixed by the commissioner, not to exceed $500.00 for each annual license or permit issued to a promoter;

(3) One hundred and fifty dollars for each annual license or permit issued to a matchmaker;

(4) Twenty dollars for each annual license or permit issued to a wrestler, manager or boxer; and

(5) Five dollars for each annual license or permit issued to a referee, judge, ticket seller, announcer, trainer, second, medical examiner, ticket taker, director or timekeeper.

(b) Nothing in this section shall be construed as permitting, authorizing or enjoining the commissioner, or his authorized agent, to collect any license, permit fee or tax for any amateur boxing, sparring or wrestling matches or exhibitions held under the auspices of educational institutions when the proceeds of such are to be used to foster, aid or abet programs of education in the state of Alabama, or when the same are held under the auspices, rules and regulations of any national amateur athletic association or union, but no exemption from license, permit fee, tax or charges shall be granted to any person, group of persons or organization for such amateur boxing, sparring or wrestling matches or exhibitions when the proceeds or any part thereof are for personal or private gain.

(c) After first paying all operating expenses incurred in the collection of such fees, licenses and taxes, and all operational expenses of the state athletic commission, the commissioner shall distribute, on or before January 15 of each year, all proceeds and moneys received therefrom as follows:

(1) One-half to the state general fund; and

(2) One-half to the American Legion, department of Alabama, for use in their programs in service to the people of the state of Alabama. (Acts 1939, No. 489, p. 703; Code 1940, T. 55, § 348; Acts 1965, 2nd Ex. Sess., No. 128, p. 180; Acts 1973, No. 1241, p. 2088, § 2; Acts 1980, p. 171, No. 80-121, § 4; Acts 1982, No. 82-558, § 1.)

The 1982 amendment, effective May 4, 1982, in subsection (a) deleted former subdivisions (2) and (3) and redesignated former subdivisions (4) through (7) as present subdivisions (2) through (5), deleted former subsection (c), and redesignated former subsection (d) as present subsection (c).

Distribution of moneys to American Legion improper where no two-thirds vote. — While the legislature has the power to regulate wrestling, sparring and boxing, the distribution, by the legislature, of one-half the moneys to the American Legion was improper and violates Ala. Const., article IV, § 73, in that the evidence shows that the vote in the house on the bill enacted as Act No. 80-121 was not a two-thirds vote. Eagerton v. Gulas Wrestling Enters., Inc., 406 So. 2d 366 (Ala. 1981).

Collateral references. — 53 C.J.S., Licenses, §§ 6-9.

4 Am. Jur. 2d, Amusement & Exhibitions, §§ 29-34.

§§ 41-9-97 through 41-9-103. Repealed by Acts 1980, No. 80-121, p. 171, § 3, effective May 24, 1980.

Division 2.

Regulation of Boxing, Sparring and Wrestling Matches and Exhibitions.

§§ 41-9-120 through 41-9-126. Repealed by Acts 1980, No. 80-121, p. 171, § 3, effective May 24, 1980.

ARTICLE 6.

BUILDING COMMISSION AND BUILDING CODE.

Collateral references. — 81 C.J.S., States, §§ 103-105.

Division 1.

Building Commission.

§ 41-9-140. Creation; composition; election and filling of vacancies of legislative members; officers; compensation and expenses of members; meetings generally.

There is hereby created a building commission, to be known as the building commission, the membership of which shall consist of the governor, the state health officer, the director of finance, the state superintendent of education, four members from the senate to be elected by that body at each regular session of the legislature and four members from the house of representatives to be elected by that body at each regular session of the legislature. In the event of a vacancy on the commission caused by the death or resignation of a member elected by the senate, such vacancy shall be filled by election by the commission at the next regular meeting, such member to be elected from the membership of the senate. In the event of a vacancy on the commission caused by the death or resignation of a member elected by the house of representatives, such vacancy shall be filled by election by the commission at its next regular meeting, such member to be elected from the membership of the house.

The governor shall be chairman of the commission, and the budget officer of the state department of finance shall be the secretary thereof, but he shall not be a member. The secretary shall be custodian of its books, records and papers which he shall keep at the office of the commission to be provided at the seat of government.

All members of said commission shall serve without compensation. The legislative members shall receive reimbursement for their expenses when actively engaged on the commission's business, such expenses to be paid in accordance with article 2 of chapter 7 of Title 36 of this Code.

Said commission shall convene upon the call of the governor or at such other time or times as the commission shall designate by a resolution spread upon its minutes. (Acts 1945, No. 128, p. 116, § 1; Acts 1951, No. 356, p. 644, § 1.)

Effect of listing certain projects as "deferrable". — The legislature, in listing certain projects as "deferrable" in the capital improvement program set out in § 5 of the Building Commission Act, did not thereby intend to abrogate its prerogative to deal with those projects later and to make appropriations accordingly. Norton v. Lusk, 248 Ala. 110, 26 So. 2d 849 (1946).

Cited in In re Opinion of Justices, 256 Ala. 170, 54 So. 2d 68 (1951).

§ 41-9-141. Powers and duties generally; appointment, etc., of officers, employees and agents; adoption of rules, regulations and plans; approval and allocation of funds; notice of meetings required.

(a) The commission shall have full power and authority for and on behalf of the state of Alabama:

(1) To acquire lands by purchase, condemnation or otherwise;

(2) To plan buildings and designate the location thereof;

(3) To plan and provide for the improvement of all property now owned or hereafter acquired by the state or any institution or agency thereof;

(4) To construct, repair, equip, remodel, enlarge, renovate, furnish, refurnish, improve and locate such buildings, structures and facilities for the use of the state of Alabama or any of its institutions or agencies as in its judgment shall be necessary for state, institutional or agency purposes;

(5) To enter into contract to perform any of the functions provided for in this subsection;

(6) To receive any moneys, land or equipment donated, appropriated or otherwise acquired by it for the purposes provided for in this subsection; and

(7) To take such steps, generally, as may be necessary to accomplish the purposes provided for in this subsection.

(b) The commission is authorized and empowered to use the services, facilities or employees of the Alabama development office in furthering the objects of this article when its request so to do is approved by the governor.

(c) The commission may appoint and dismiss such officers, employees and agents including competent architectural and technical employees as may be necessary to effectuate the purposes of this article. All employees of said commission shall be subject to the provisions of the merit system. The commission is authorized to fix by contract the fees or compensation of all architectural and technical employees without regard to the Merit System Act.

(d) The commission is authorized and empowered to make and adopt all necessary rules, regulations and plans for its own guidance and for the proper conduct of the duties imposed upon it.

(e) The decisions of the commission with respect to approval and allocations of funds shall be final.

(f) No meeting of the commission shall be held on less than three days' actual notice to the members thereof. (Acts 1945, No. 128, p. 116, § 2.)

Cross references. — As to authority of department of conservation and natural resources to prepare plans and specifications for construction or modification of buildings and facilities within jurisdiction of said department and enter into contracts for construction and modification of said facilities, see § 9-2-40 et seq. As to duty of technical staff of commission to approve, inspect and supervise armory construction, see § 31-4-13.

Power does not include requiring minimum wage. — The power to designate the quality of workmanship does not carry with it the power to require that a minimum hourly wage shall be paid to all employees of the same class performing the work. Wallace v. Board of Educ., 280 Ala. 635, 197 So. 2d 428 (1967).

Nor specified minimum price. — The power to designate the quality of material to be used does not carry with it the power to require that the contractor must pay a specified minimum price to the seller for each unit of material used. Wallace v. Board of Educ., 280 Ala. 635, 197 So. 2d 428 (1967).

But does include power to designate quality of work and materials. — The powers delegated to the commission authorize it to designate the quality and nature of material to be used and the quality of the work to be required. Wallace v. Board of Educ., 280 Ala. 635, 197 So. 2d 428 (1967).

Cited in Wyatt v. Bronner, 500 F. Supp. 817 (M.D. Ala. 1980).

Division 2.

Minimum Building Standards Code.

§ 41-9-160. Definitions.

When used in this division, the following words and phrases shall have the following meanings, respectively, unless the context clearly indicates otherwise:

(1) STATE BUILDING AND CONSTRUCTION. All buildings and other structures erected or acquired by or in behalf of the state of Alabama or any of its agencies or instrumentalities.

(2) SCHOOLHOUSE. Any building or other structure erected or acquired by the public schools of Alabama and also shall mean any private building in which 25 or more persons are congregated regularly for the purpose of instruction in any branch of knowledge.

(3) HOTEL. Any public inn or lodging house of 15 or more bedrooms, in which transient guests are lodged for pay.

(4) MOVING PICTURE THEATRE. Any building in which moving pictures are featured regularly for charge of admission. (Acts 1945, No. 290, p. 480, § 2.)

§ 41-9-161. Promulgation, distribution and enforcement of code of minimum building standards by commission generally.

For the further protection of the people of Alabama, the building commission is authorized and directed hereby to promulgate and to enforce a code of minimum building standards. The code adopted by the building commission under the provisions of this section, after having been recorded in the office of secretary of state for 60 days, shall become effective.

The building commission shall have the code printed suitably immediately subsequent to its filing and shall distribute promptly the printed copies thereof in the same manner as acts of the legislature are distributed; provided, however, that no charge may be collected by the building commission for copies of the code and that any person shall be furnished a copy upon request. (Acts 1945, No. 290, p. 480, § 1.)

§ 41-9-162. Applicability of building code.

(a) The code of minimum building standards promulgated and enforced by the building commission shall be applicable only to all state buildings and construction, schoolhouses, hotels and moving picture theatres in Alabama.

(b) The effect of the building code shall be limited, in the cases of state building and construction and public schoolhouses, to buildings and structures erected or acquired after the operative date thereof. As to private schoolhouses, hotels and moving picture theatres, the code shall apply to the place of conduct of each such business activity not employed or in the process of erection for that purpose prior to the effective date thereof. (Acts 1945, No. 290, p. 480, §§ 2, 3.)

Collateral references. — Liability of hotel or motel operator for injury or death of guest or privy resulting from condition in plumbing or bathroom of room or suite. 93 ALR3d 253.

§ 41-9-163. Requirements of building code; erection or acquisition of state building or construction or public schoolhouse not conforming to code; operation of private school, hotel, etc., not conforming to code.

(a) The requirements of the building code shall be such that the safety, health, general welfare and morals of the people of Alabama thereby will be protected.

(b) It shall be unlawful for any state building or construction or any public schoolhouse which does not conform to the requirements of the building code to be erected or acquired.

(c) It shall be unlawful for any person to operate a private school, hotel or moving picture theatre which does not meet fully the requirements of the building code unless such building was used for that purpose prior to the effective date of the code. (Acts 1945, No. 290, p. 480, § 3.)

Cross references. — As to accessibility to and use of public buildings and facilities by physically handicapped persons, see § 21-4-1 et seq. As to construction of public buildings with radioactive fallout protection, see § 39-6-1 et seq.

Collateral references. — Liability of hotel or motel operator for injury or death of guest or privy resulting from condition in plumbing or bathroom of room or suite. 93 ALR3d 253.

Coverage under builder's risk insurance. 97 ALR3d 1270.

§ 41-9-164. Changes in building code.

The building commission is authorized and directed to make such changes in the code from time to time as seem advisable in the best interest of the people of Alabama. Changes in the code shall take effect and shall be printed and distributed in the same manner as the original code was made effective, printed and distributed. (Acts 1945, No. 290, p. 480, § 4.)

§ 41-9-165. Enforcement of building code.

The building commission is empowered to provide adequate inspection service to insure compliance with the building code. Other agencies and instrumentalities of the state government are directed hereby to cooperate, as requested by the commission, in the enforcement of the building code. The commission may appoint, subject to the merit system, such persons, including architectural and technical employees, as are necessary for the duties hereby imposed. (Acts 1945, No. 290, p. 480, § 6.)

§ 41-9-166. Adoption, etc., of building code by municipalities and counties.

Any municipality in the state of Alabama is empowered hereby to adopt the provisions of the building code as a municipal ordinance, enlarging the applicability thereof to include private buildings and structures other than private schoolhouses, hotels and moving picture houses as it deems necessary and to prescribe penalties for violations thereof in the same manner in which other ordinances and related penalty provisions are adopted and prescribed.

Any county commission similarly may adopt and enlarge the applicability of the building code for the county, prescribing penalties for violations thereof, by resolution duly recorded in its minutes and, after notice of four weeks, by publication once weekly in some county newspaper, if there is one published in the county, and by posted notices at the door of each courthouse in the county.

Changes in the provisions of the building code effected by the building commission may be adopted similarly by counties and municipalities.

No county or municipality shall so apply the provisions of the building code to state buildings and construction of public schoolhouses.

Nothing contained in this section shall be construed as requiring the advertising or posting of the code itself. The provisions of this section shall be satisfied by giving of notice that it is proposed to adopt a code. (Acts 1945, No. 290, p. 480, § 5.)

Division 3.

Energy Conservation Building Code.

§ 41-9-170. Definitions.

When used in this division, the following words and phrases shall have the following meanings, respectively, unless the context clearly indicates otherwise:

(1) COMMISSION. The state building commission.

(2) DIRECTOR. The director of the technical staff of the state building commission.

(3) CODE. The state building code to be adopted by the state building commission. (Acts 1978, No. 766, p. 1105, § 1.)

§ 41-9-171. Promulgation, distribution and enforcement of code of minimum building standards for buildings constructed or remodeled with state funds by building commission generally.

For the health and welfare of the people of Alabama, the building commission of the state of Alabama, which was created in 1945 by the legislature, is authorized and hereby directed to adopt, promulgate and enforce a state building code. The code adopted by the commission under the provisions of this division, after having been recorded in the office of secretary of state for 60 days, shall become effective. The code shall be applicable to all buildings constructed or remodeled after May 2, 1978, with state appropriated funds or funds from any other instrumentality of the state. It shall include a minimal energy conservation section which controls those items affecting heat loss in the exterior envelopment of buildings and affecting climatic control and illumination of buildings. (Acts 1978, No. 766, p. 1105, § 2.)

Collateral references. — 13 Am. Jur. 2d, Building and Construction Contracts, §§ 130, 131; 13 Am. Jur. 2d, Buildings, §§ 1-4, 13.

§ 41-9-172. Powers and duties of director of technical staff of commission as to promulgation, adoption and modification of code; standards to be included in code.

The director of the technical staff of the commission shall have the responsibility for developing said code and presenting it to the commission for adoption and, in fulfillment of such responsibility, may, as it becomes necessary, contract for the consultant services of architects, engineers and other technicians with a portion of the funds provided. It shall be the further responsibility of the director to keep the code updated and consistent with acceptable engineering and architectural practices by from time to time presenting the commission with recommended changes and modifications for adoption. The director shall, at the earliest possible date after the passage of this division, submit a state building code for any building or construction utilizing state funds to the commission for adoption. Said code shall contain provisions for an energy conservation code which regulates the thermal efficiency of the exterior of buildings and the efficiency of lighting design and climatic control in buildings.

The director shall include in the said code thermal and lighting efficiency standards which will meet the following criteria:

(1) Be applicable to all new and renovated buildings; and

(2) Be no less stringent than the appendix J of the standard building code. (Acts 1978, No. 766, p. 1105, § 3.)

Collateral references. — 13 Am. Jur. 2d, Buildings, § 5.

§ 41-9-173. Preparation and offering by director of training and assistance in implementing provisions of division, etc.

The director shall prepare and offer such training and assistance as the state building commission deems necessary in implementing the provisions of this division and the standards herein established. (Acts 1978, No. 766, p. 1105, § 3.)

§ 41-9-174. Formulation by director of thermal and lighting efficiency guidelines applicable to all new and renovated buildings.

The commission also shall cause the director to formulate guidelines for thermal and lighting efficiency applicable to all new and renovated buildings, whether such buildings are state funded or not, and the manner of implementation therefor. (Acts 1978, No. 766, p. 1105, § 3.)

ARTICLE 7.

STATE INDUSTRIAL DEVELOPMENT BOARD.

Code commissioner's note. — Sections 41-9-180 through 41-9-183 were impliedly repealed by Acts 1980, No. 80-736, p. 1498, codified as article 7A of this chapter, which creates the Alabama industrial development advisory board.

Acts 1980, No. 80-735, p. 1491, § 6, provides that all functions, powers, etc., relative to a planning program for human, economic, etc., development vested by former §§ 41-9-181 through 41-9-183 in the Alabama development office as they relate to federal programs, grants, etc., are transferred to and vested in the office of state planning and federal programs. See § 41-9-211.

§§ 41-9-180 through 41-9-183. Repealed.

§ 41-9-184. Transferred.

Code commissioner's note. — This section has been transferred to article 7A and has been renumbered § 41-9-188, in order to effect the changes brought about by Acts 1980, No. 80-736, p. 1498.

ARTICLE 7A.

ALABAMA INDUSTRIAL DEVELOPMENT
ADVISORY BOARD.

Collateral references. — 81A C.J.S., States, §§ 141, 142.

1 Am. Jur. 2d, Administrative Law, §§ 23, 36-38, 69-74.

§ 41-9-185. Board established; officers; members; appointment; term; oath; removal; expenses; seal; meetings; quorum; rules and regulations.

(a) There is hereby created and established the Alabama industrial development advisory board. The Alabama industrial development advisory board shall consist of nine members at-large who shall be appointed by the governor for terms of two years each and the governor, as chairman of the board. When appointing members of the board, the governor shall select citizens who are outstanding in the fields of manufacture and processing, business and commercial enterprise, engineering and industrial development, natural resources, electric and gas utilities, industrial real estate and industrial property management, banking and finance, labor relations and mass communications.

The initial terms of the appointees shall be as follows: four members for one year and five members for two years. Subsequent appointments shall be for two-year terms, and appointments to fill vacancies shall be for the unexpired terms. Provided, however, that members may be appointed for successive terms at the discretion of the chairman.

Before entering upon the discharge of their duties, the members of the board shall take the oath of office prescribed for other state officers. The members of the board shall hold office only during the tenure of the governor making the appointment and until their successors are appointed and qualified. The governor may remove any member of the board who fails to attend its meetings regularly or to perform properly his duties as a member of the board, by notifying the member in writing of his removal.

(b) Each member shall be paid the actual and necessary expenses incurred in the performance of his duties as a member of the board when approved by the chairman. Ex officio members of the board shall receive no additional compensation for their services as members of the board.

The board may have an appropriate seal with such words and emblem as it may prescribe.

A majority of the board shall constitute a quorum for the transaction of business. The secretary shall notify each member in writing of all meetings of the board in such manner and under such rules and regulations as the board may prescribe. The board shall adopt rules and regulations for the transaction of its business, and the secretary shall keep a record of all its proceedings and, upon request, furnish a copy thereof to each member of the board. (Acts 1980, No. 80-736, p. 1498, § 1.)

§ 41-9-186. Duties.

It shall be the duty of the said board to consult with the governor and the director of the Alabama development office, to advise the governor of the industrial possibilities of the state and to furnish him with such information and studies as it deems desirable to accomplish a comprehensive program for the promotion of the commercial and industrial development of the state and the counties and municipalities thereof, and as the governor may request. It shall also consult and advise in the facilitation of foreign investment and foreign industry location within the state, as the governor may request. (Acts 1980, No. 80-736, p. 1498, § 2.)

§ 41-9-187. Transfer of powers, functions, etc., of industrial development board.

On May 28, 1980, all powers, duties, functions and authority invested in the state industrial development board, including those in section 41-9-183, shall be continued, transferred to and shall be vested in the Alabama industrial development advisory board, except those powers, duties and functions prescribed for the office of state planning and federal programs by article 8A of this chapter. All books, records, supplies, funds, equipment, personnel, assets and property of whatsoever nature, had, exercised, used or employed by the state industrial development board are transferred to the Alabama industrial development advisory board and all laws or parts of laws relating to the state industrial development board shall be repealed and the said state industrial development board shall be abolished. (Acts 1980, No. 80-736, p. 1498, § 3.)

Code commissioner's note. — As to implied repeal of § 41-9-183, referred to in this section, see code commissioner's note under article 7 of this chapter.

§ 41-9-188. Cooperation of director of state bureau of publicity and information.

The authority of the state bureau of publicity and information to plan and conduct all state programs of information and publicity designed to attract tourists to the state of Alabama is hereby confirmed and continued; provided, however, that the director of the state bureau of publicity and information shall cooperate to the fullest possible extent with the Alabama industrial development advisory board and the director of the Alabama development office, toward the end that an integrated program of economic expansion and promotion may be pursued by the public agencies of this state. (Acts 1955, No. 342, p. 765, § 3(b); Code 1975, § 41-9-184; Acts 1980, No. 80-736, p. 1498, § 4.)

ARTICLE 8.

STATE DEVELOPMENT OFFICE.

Code commissioner's note. — Acts 1980, No. 80-735, p. 1491, § 6, provides that all functions, powers, etc., relative to a planning program for human, economic, etc., development vested by §§ 41-9-200 through 41-9-204 in the Alabama development office as they relate to federal programs, grants, etc., are transferred to and vested in the office of state planning and federal programs. See § 41-9-211.

Acts 1981, No. 81-705, p. 1182, §§ 1 and 2, provided that the modular housing division of the Alabama development office is abolished and all funds, appropriations, papers, documents, etc., of the modular housing division shall become the property of the office of the state fire marshall and that all of the duties, responsibilities, functions and powers heretofore exercised or held by the director of the modular housing division shall pass to and be the responsibility of and performed by the state fire marshall.

Cross references. — As to the fire marshal, see § 36-19-1, et seq. As to authority of state, counties and municipalities to remit taxes on certain factories, industries and plants for a limited number of years, see § 40-9-40 et seq. As to Alabama industrial development advisory board, see § 41-9-185 et seq. As to industrial development authority, see § 41-10-20 et seq.

§ 41-9-200. Legislative findings; purpose of article.

(a) The legislature finds and declares that:

(1) The people of this state have a fundamental interest in the orderly development of the state and its regions;

(2) The state has a positive interest in the preparation and maintenance of long-term, comprehensive plans for the economic, physical and human resource development of the whole state and of each of its regions, which plans can serve as a guide for local governmental units and state departments and agencies;

(3) The continued growth of the state, particularly in urban areas, and the readjustment of the people to the changed economy of the state present problems which can best be solved by overall state planning guidance for their solution;

(4) Local governmental planning and program implementation can be strengthened when done in relation to and coordinated with the planning efforts and program implementation of the state and of the regions of the state; and

(5) Orderly and harmonious coordination of state and local plans and programs with those of the federal government, state and regional planning and programming requires direct leadership by the governor.

(b) It is the purpose of this article to promote the development of the state's human, economic and physical resources and to promote the health, safety and general welfare of its citizens by creating, within the executive branch, an agency for comprehensive statewide planning and economic development. The agency shall act as an advisory, consulting and coordinating agency to harmonize activities at all levels of government, render planning assistance to governmental units and stimulate public interest and participation in the human resource, economic and physical development of the state. (Acts 1969, No. 657, p. 1187, § 1.)

§ 41-9-201. Creation; composition; encouragement by governor of comprehensive and coordinated planning and programming of state governmental affairs; furnishing of personnel, equipment, etc., to office by departments or agencies.

(a) There is hereby created the Alabama development office within the office of the governor and directly under his supervision and control. The Alabama development office shall consist of the governor as the state planning and development officer and a chief administrative officer to be designated as director of development, who shall be appointed by the governor and serve at his pleasure at a salary to be set in the same manner and with the same limitations as otherwise provided by law for executive department heads. All other employees necessary to carry out the duties and functions of the Alabama development office shall be employed subject to the provisions of the merit system law.

(b) The governor, through the Alabama development office, shall encourage comprehensive and coordinated planning and programming of the affairs of state government.

(c) The governor may direct any state department or other agency of state government directly under his control and supervision to furnish the Alabama development office with such personnel, equipment and services as are necessary to enable it to carry out its responsibilities and duties and prescribe the terms thereof, including reimbursement of costs thereof. (Acts 1969, No. 657, p. 1187, § 2.)

§ 41-9-202. Powers, duties and functions of development office generally.

(a) The Alabama development office shall be the principal staff agency of the executive branch to plan with the other departments of state government and with other governmental units for the comprehensive development of the state's human, economic and physical resources and their relevance for programs administered by the state and the governmental structure required to put such programs into effect. It shall provide information, assistance and staff support by all appropriate means. The Alabama development office shall perform all the duties and exercise all the powers and authority relative to state regional and local planning and industrial development heretofore vested in the state planning and industrial development board. All the functions, powers, authority and duties relative to carrying on a planning program for the promotion of the commercial and industrial development of the state and the counties and the municipalities thereof, including the preparation of a state master plan, as well as the authority to provide an assistance program to regions, counties and municipalities in the preparation of comprehensive physical plans for such regions, counties and municipalities vested by sections 41-9-180 through 41-9-184 in the state planning and industrial development board, are confirmed, continued, transferred to and hereafter shall be vested in the Alabama development office. All books, records, supplies, funds, equipment and personnel of the state planning and industrial development board are also hereby transferred to the Alabama development office.

(b) All of the powers and authority heretofore vested in the Alabama program development office, created by executive order of the governor number 2, dated July 17, 1968, are confirmed, continued, transferred to and hereafter shall be vested in the Alabama development office created by this article. All books, records, supplies, funds, equipment and personnel of the Alabama program development office heretofore created by executive order of the governor are hereby transferred to the Alabama development office.

(c) Without in any way limiting the foregoing general powers and duties, the Alabama development office shall have the following additional powers and duties:

(1) To formulate a long-range state comprehensive plan, to be submitted by the governor to the legislature for its consideration;

(2) To formulate, for approval by the governor and the legislature, long-range plans and policies for the orderly and coordinated growth of the state, including, but not limited to, functional plans;

(3) To prepare special reports and make available the results of the agency's research, studies and other activities through publications, memoranda, briefings and expert testimony;

(4) To analyze the quality and quantity of services required for the continued orderly and long-range growth of the state, taking into consideration the relationship of activities, capabilities and future plans of local units of government, area commissions, development districts, private enterprise and the state and federal governments;

(5) To encourage the coordination of the planning and programming activities of all state departments, agencies and institutions, local levels of government and other public and private bodies within the state;

(6) To advise and consult with regional, county and local planning and development agencies;

(7) To work with the state budget agency and other state departments, agencies and institutions to study and review plans, programs and federal aid applications filed with the federal government;

(8) To survey, review and appraise the accomplishments of state government in achieving its goals and objectives at the direction of the governor and in cooperation with the state budget agency;

(9) To apply for and accept advances, loans, grants, contributions and any other form of assistance from the federal government, the state or other public body or from any sources, public or private, for the purposes of this article and to enter into and carry out contracts or agreements in connection therewith and to include in any contract for financial assistance with the federal government such conditions imposed pursuant to federal laws as it may deem reasonable and appropriate and which are not inconsistent with the purposes of this article;

(10) To review and comment on all local and areawide applications for federal planning assistance or to delegate such authority to a regional planning and development commission; and

(11) To exercise all other powers necessary and proper for the discharge of its duties, including the promulgation of reasonable rules and regulations.

(d) The Alabama development office is hereby authorized to make grants from appropriations to regional planning and development commissions which are certified to receive such grants by the governor under the provisions of sections 11-85-50 through 11-85-55. (Acts 1969, No. 657, p. 1187, § 5.)

Code commissioner's note. — Sections 41-9-180 through 41-9-183, referred to in this section, were repealed by Acts 1980, No. 80-736, p. 1498. Section 41-9-184 was transferred and renumbered as § 41-9-188.

Cross references. — As to duties of office relative to development, etc., of coastal areas, see § 9-7-14. As to authority to perform comprehensive advisory planning and research and other activities related thereto for urban areas and regions or areas where rapid urbanization has occurred or is expected to occur, see § 11-85-40.

§ 41-9-203. Advisory committees or councils.

The governor, in carrying out his responsibilities under this article, may establish advisory committees or councils and appoint the members thereof, who shall serve at his pleasure. Members shall serve without compensation. The governor shall designate the chairmen and such other officers as he may deem necessary for each advisory committee or council. Advisory committees or councils established pursuant to this section shall meet at the call of their chairmen or of the director of development. (Acts 1969, No. 657, p. 1187, § 4.)

Cross references. — As to travel expenses, see § 36-7-20 et seq.

§ 41-9-204. Consolidation and transfer to development office of certain appropriations.

All appropriations heretofore or hereafter made to the industrial development board, the planning and industrial development board (community planning) and the Alabama program development office heretofore established by executive order of the governor are hereby consolidated and transferred to the Alabama development office. (Acts 1969, No. 657, p. 1187, § 6.)

ARTICLE 8A.

OFFICE OF STATE PLANNING AND FEDERAL PROGRAMS.

Collateral references. — 81A C.J.S., States, §§ 141, 142.　　1 Am. Jur. 2d, Administrative Law, §§ 23, 36-38, 69-74.

§ 41-9-205. Definitions.

As used in this article, the following terms shall have the following meanings, respectively, unless the context clearly indicates otherwise:

(1) A-95. The process of evaluation, review and coordination of federal and federally assisted programs and projects;

(2) A-102. The process of establishing uniform administrative requirements for programs that provide financial assistance through grant or contractual arrangements;

(3) GOVERNING BODY. The chief legislative body of a governmental unit;

(4) GOVERNMENTAL UNIT. Counties and municipalities;

(5) MUNICIPALITY. Cities, towns, villages and other incorporated jurisdictions;

(6) REGION. All the geographical area contained within the aggregate territorial limits of all governmental units participating in regional planning and development commission as stipulated in sections 41-9-181 through 41-9-183 and 41-9-200 through 41-9-201;

(7) REVIEW AND COMMENT. Review and comment of the office of state planning and federal programs as directly related to those federal programs covered under currently effective office of management and budget (OMB) circular A-95, A-102, and other appropriate OMB circulars. (Acts 1980, No. 80-735, p. 1491, § 1.)

Code commissioner's note. — As to implied repeal of §§ 41-9-181 through 41-9-183, referred to in this section, see code commissioner's note under article 7 of this chapter.

§ 41-9-206. Powers, duties, etc., of state development office retained except as to federal programs, etc.

It specifically is the legislative intent to maintain and retain all of the powers, duties, responsibilities, personnel, property and assets of whatsoever nature, not involved in federal programs and federal grants and federal assistance, in the Alabama development office and in the director of the Alabama development office, as the case may be, and that the Alabama development office shall retain all of its authority, powers, duties, responsibilities and functions for industrial development. (Acts 1980, No. 80-735, p. 1491, § 2.)

§ 41-9-207. Legislative findings and declarations; purpose of article; agencies; duties and goals.

(a) The legislature finds and declares that:

(1) The people of this state have a fundamental interest in the orderly development of the state and its regions;

(2) The state has a positive interest in the preparation and maintenance of long-term, comprehensive plans for the economic, physical and human resource development of the whole state and of each of its regions which plans can serve as guides for local governmental units and state departments and agencies;

(3) The continued growth of the state and the readjustment of the people to the changing economy of the state, present problems which can best be solved by overall state planning guidance for their solution;

(4) Local governmental planning and program implementation can be strengthened when done in relation to and coordinated with the planning efforts and program implementation of the state and of the regions of the state;

(5) Orderly and harmonious coordination of state and local plans and programs with those of the federal government, state and regional planning and programming requires direct leadership by the governor;

(6) The state has a positive interest in assisting the various local governmental units, and state departments, agencies and institutions, in the procurement of various forms of assistance from the federal government for the benefit of the people of the state and to meet critical state needs;

(7) Orderly and efficient administration of state finances and programs, and improved state assistance to local governmental units and state departments, agencies, political subdivisions and institutions in the procurement

of federal assistance can most effectively be accomplished if the state can monitor the types, amounts and purposes of advances, loans, grants, contributions and any other form of assistance from the federal government which is applied for and/or accepted by departments, agencies, institutions and political subdivisions of the state.

(b) It is the purpose of this article to promote the development of the state's human, economic and physical resources, and to promote the health, safety and general welfare of its citizens, by creating within the executive branch, an agency for comprehensive statewide planning and federal assistance oversight. The agency shall act as an advisory, consulting, monitoring and coordinating agency to harmonize activities at all levels of government, render technical assistance to governmental units and political subdivisions of this state and stimulate public interest and participation in the human resource, economic and physical development of the state as these relate to federal programs, federal grants and federal assistance. (Acts 1980, No. 80-735, p. 1491, § 3.)

§ 41-9-208. Office created; director; salary; comprehensive planning encouraged; other agencies to aid office.

(a) There is hereby created the office of state planning and federal programs within the office of the governor and directly under his supervision and control. The office of state planning and federal programs shall consist of the governor as the state planning and federal programs officer, a chief administrative officer to be designated as director of the office of state planning and federal programs, who shall be appointed by the governor, and serve at his pleasure, at a salary to be set in the same manner and with the same limitations as otherwise provided by law for executive department heads. The director of the office of state planning and federal programs shall be a member of such boards and commissions, as they relate to his authority under the provisions of this article, and as required and currently authorized under the various federal programs for the director of the Alabama development office, and as approved by the governor. All other employees necessary to carry out the duties and functions of the office of state planning and federal programs shall be employed subject to the provisions of the state merit system laws and shall be entitled to the same rights and benefits thereunder. Salaries set for employees shall not exceed the salary set by law for executive department heads.

(b) The governor, through the office of state planning and federal programs, shall encourage comprehensive and coordinated planning and programming of the affairs of state government.

(c) The governor may direct any state department or other agency of state government, directly under his control and supervision, to furnish the office of state planning and federal programs with such personnel, equipment and services as are necessary to enable it to carry out its responsibilities and duties, and he may prescribe the terms thereof, including reimbursement of costs therefor. (Acts 1980, No. 80-735, p. 1491, § 4.)

§ 41-9-209. Advisory committees or councils authorized; membership; expenses; chairman; meetings.

The governor, in carrying out his responsibilities under this article, may establish advisory committees or councils and appoint the members thereto, which members shall serve at his pleasure. Members shall serve without compensation, but shall be reimbursed for the necessary and actual expenses incurred in the performance of their duties. The governor shall designate the chairman and such other officers as he may deem necessary for each advisory committee or council. Advisory committees or councils, established pursuant to this section, shall meet at the call of their chairman, or of the director of the office of state planning and federal programs. (Acts 1980, No. 80-735, p. 1491, § 5.)

§ 41-9-210. Office to succeed to state development office as federal programs; purpose, responsibilities, etc.

The office of state planning and federal programs shall be the principal staff agency of the executive branch to plan with the other departments of state government, and with other governmental units, for the comprehensive development of the state's human, economic and physical resources and their relevance for programs administered by the state and the governmental structure required to put such programs into effect. The purpose of such planning shall be to insure that the maximum benefit will accrue to the state from the advances, loans, grants and other forms of assistance made available to local governmental units and state departments, agencies and institutions by the federal government, or any agency, or any political subdivision thereof. It shall provide information, assistance and staff support by all appropriate means available. The office of state planning and federal programs shall perform all duties and exercise all the powers and authority relative to state, regional and local planning, and to the study and review of plans, programs and federal aid applications filed with the federal government vested in the Alabama development office prior to May 28, 1980. All the functions, powers, authority and duties relative to carrying on a planning program for the human, economic and physical development of the state and the counties and municipalities thereof, including the preparation of a state master plan as well as the authority to provide an assistance program to regions, counties and municipalities in the preparation of comprehensive physical plans for such regions, counties and municipalities vested by sections 41-9-181 through 41-9-183, and 41-9-200 through 41-9-204 in the Alabama development office and as they relate to federal programs, federal grants or federal assistance, are confirmed, continued, transferred to and shall be vested in the office of state planning and federal programs. All books, records, supplies, funds, equipment, personnel and assets and property of whatsoever nature, had, exercised, used or employed by the Alabama development office in the pursuit of the functions herein delineated are also hereby transferred to the office of state planning and federal programs. (Acts 1980, No. 80-735, p. 1491, § 6.)

Code commissioner's note. — As to
implied repeal of §§ 41-9-181 through 41-9-183,
referred to in this section, see code commissioner's note under article 7 of this chapter.

§ 41-9-211. Powers and duties of office.

(a) The powers and duties of the office of state planning and federal programs shall be as follows:

(1) To develop a comprehensive state plan, and yearly updates to the plan,
to be submitted by the governor to the legislature for its consideration;

(2) To develop, for approval by the governor and the legislature,
long-range plans and policies for the orderly and coordinated growth of the
state, including but not limited to, functional plans;

(3) To prepare special reports and make available the results of the
research, studies and other activities, through publications, memoranda,
briefings and expert testimony;

(4) To analyze the quality and quantity of services required for the continued orderly and long-range growth of the state, taking into consideration
the relationship of activities, capabilities and future plans of local units of
government, area commissions, development districts, private enterprise
and the state and federal government;

(5) To encourage the coordination of the planning and programming
activities of all state departments, agencies and institutions, local levels of
government, and other public and private bodies with the state;

(6) To advise and consult with regional, county and local units of government and planning and development agencies on matters of planning;

(7) At the direction of the governor, and in cooperation with the state
budget division of the finance department, survey, review and appraise the
accomplishments of state government in achieving its goals and objectives;

(8) To apply for, accept and disburse advances, loans, grants,
contributions and any other form of assistance from the federal government,
the state or other public body, or from any sources, public or private, for the
purposes of this article, and enter into and carry out contracts or agreements
in connection therewith, and include in any contract for financial assistance
with the federal government such conditions imposed pursuant to federal
laws as it may deem reasonable and appropriate and which are not
inconsistent with the purposes of this article;

(9) To make grants from said appropriations to regional planning and
development commissions which are certified to receive such grants by the
governor, under the provisions of law heretofore or hereafter enacted
providing for the delineation and designation of state planning and
development districts and authorizing the governing bodies of counties and
municipalities to establish regional planning and development commissions,
in sections 11-85-50 through 11-85-56 and 11-85-58;

(10) To advise and consult with state agencies, departments and institutions, political subdivisions and local units of government for the purpose of
increasing their capacity to identify and obtain all forms of federal assistance;

(11) To review and comment on all local and areawide applications for federal planning assistance, or delegate such authority to a regional planning and development commission;

(12) To review and comment upon prior to their submission, as required by OMB A-95 regulations, plans, programs and federal assistance applications filed with the federal government or any instrumentality of the federal government by state departments, agencies and institutions;

(13) To maintain a record of and periodically analyze all action taken by any federal agency concerning plans, programs and federal assistance applications submitted to the federal government or any instrumentality of the federal government by state departments, agencies and institutions, local governmental units, and political subdivisions of the state;

(14) To monitor and analyze the sources, types, amounts and purposes of federal assistance received by state agencies, departments and institutions, local governmental units, and political subdivisions;

(15) To provide information and recommendations to the governor and legislature with respect to federal programs of state interest or programs pending congressional or federal administrative action which may affect or be of interest to the state or any of its agencies or political subdivisions;

(16) To promote the development and coordination of the federal assistance activities of all state departments, agencies and institutions, local levels of government and other public and private bodies within the state to meet state needs;

(17) To insure that data used by the federal government and its agencies and instrumentalities for calculating the state's share of formula-based federal assistance are accurate;

(18) To represent the governor, and serve as an official liaison for the state in respect to federal assistance programs available to the state and its agencies and political subdivisions and be responsible for the establishment of responsible representation to assist in securing maximum benefits of the many forms of federal assistance; and

(19) To exercise all other powers necessary and proper for the discharge of its duties, including the promulgation of reasonable rules and regulations and to perform such other functions and duties of the office of state planning and federal programs as may from time to time be assigned by the director of the office of state planning and federal programs. All state agencies, departments, institutions and political subdivisions are hereby empowered and authorized to make available to the office of state planning and federal programs such reasonable assistance and information as the office may request in carrying out the intentions and purposes of this article.

(b) It is the intent of this article that all reference herein to the duties and functions regarding review and comment of the office of state planning and federal programs be directly related to those federal programs covered under currently effective office of management and budget circulars A-95, A-102 and other appropriate office of management and budget circulars. (Acts 1980, No. 80-735, p. 1491, § 7.)

§ 41-9-212. Transfer of appropriations.

All parts of the state appropriation and any funds from federal sources made prior to May 28, 1980, to the Alabama development office for the planning office functions are hereby transferred to the office of state planning and federal programs. (Acts 1980, No. 80-735, p. 1491, § 8.)

§ 41-9-213. Director to employ one unclassified employee; employees of community services administration placed in classified service; limitation upon employees' salaries.

The director of the office of state planning and federal programs is authorized to employ one person in the unclassified service; without participation in the state merit system; provided, however, that such person shall be entitled to the same rights, privileges and benefits as provided for classified employees within the state merit system. All employees of the state community services administration shall be placed in a classified position within the state merit system and under state planning and federal programs. Salaries set for employees shall not exceed the salary set by law for executive department heads. (Acts 1980, No. 80-735, p. 1491, § 9.)

Collateral references. — 73 C.J.S., Public Administrative Bodies and Procedure, § 16.   63 Am. Jur. 2d, Public Officers and Employees, § 93.

§ 41-9-214. Article not to apply to law enforcement planning agency or criminal justice information center.

The provisions of this article shall not apply to the Alabama law enforcement planning agency and the Alabama criminal justice information center. (Acts 1980, No. 80-735, p. 1491, § 10.)

ARTICLE 9.

MEMORIAL BOARDS.

§ 41-9-220. Gorgas memorial board.

(a) The people of Alabama desire to honor and commemorate the memory of General Josiah Gorgas, former president of the University of Alabama, and Amelia Gayle Gorgas, daughter of Governor John Gayle, for many years in charge of the student hospital and library of the university, and William Crawford Gorgas, whose fight against yellow fever and tropical diseases made possible the building of the Panama Canal. To that end, there is hereby created a board, to be known as the "Gorgas memorial board," to consist of the governor, the president of the University of Alabama, the dean of women of the university, the president of the Alabama Federation of Women's Clubs and three members appointed by the governor; provided, that no two appointed members of said board shall be residents of the same congressional district. The members shall be appointed for terms of six years, and at the expiration of said terms, their successors shall be appointed for terms of six years. The membership of the Gorgas memorial board, with the exception of the members appointed by the governor, shall change as the persons holding the offices change. The governor shall be chairman of the Gorgas memorial board, the president of the university shall be vice-chairman and the president of the Alabama Federation of Women's Clubs shall be secretary. Four members shall constitute a quorum to transact business. No member of the Gorgas memorial board shall receive any pay or emolument for his services as a member of such board.

(b) The Gorgas memorial board, with the consent of the board of trustees of the University of Alabama, shall take charge of the Gorgas home on the campus of the university and maintain and arrange the same for the safe and convenient storing and exhibiting the objects of art, relics and antiques connected with the Gorgas family. They shall provide a custodian for the building and contents and shall provide for the compensation, if necessary, of such custodian. They shall have power to do whatever may be necessary or proper in their judgment to carry out the purpose of this section; provided, that their expenditures shall not be in excess of the appropriations made and to be made for that purpose; provided further, that their several acts shall at all times be subject to the approval of the board of trustees of the University of Alabama.

(c) For the purpose of this section, the sum of $2,500.00 per annum is hereby appropriated out of the state treasury to be paid to the Gorgas memorial board in warrants by the comptroller as other public funds are disbursed.

(d) The Gorgas memorial board may receive and administer any other gifts or appropriations made by persons, partnerships, corporations, clubs or state institutions for the purpose of this section. (Acts 1943, No. 417, p. 383.)

§ **41-9-221.** Repealed by Acts 1980, No. 80-208, p. 289, § 4, effective April 15, 1980.

§ **41-9-222. Hobson memorial board abolished; powers, etc., transferred to historical commission.**

The Richmond Pearson Hobson memorial board as established in section 41-9-221 is abolished. All property, real and personal, under the management and control of the memorial board, including but not limited to "Magnolia Grove," the Richmond Pearson Hobson home and lands located in Greensboro, Alabama, and all powers, authority and jurisdiction over such property, are hereby transferred to the Alabama historical commission; and any right, title or interest which the state has in the above described property is also transferred to the Alabama historical commission. The Alabama historical commission shall have full authority to develop, renovate, restore, preserve, maintain, operate, exhibit and publicize such property in accordance with the powers and responsibilities of the Alabama historical commission. (Acts 1980, No. 80-208, p. 289, § 1.)

Code commissioner's note. — Section 41-9-221, referred to in this section, was repealed by Acts 1980, No. 80-208, p. 289, § 4, effective April 15, 1980.

ARTICLE 10.

HISTORICAL COMMISSIONS.

Cross references. — As to department of archives and history, see § 41-6-1 et seq. As to USS Alabama Battleship commission, see § 41-9-340 et seq. As to state capitol preservation commission, see § 41-9-510 et seq.

Division 1.

Alabama Historical Commission.

§ 41-9-240. Legislative findings; purpose of division; creation of commission.

The historical heritage of the state of Alabama is among its most valued and important·assets, and the preservation of historic sites, buildings and objects within the state is of great concern to Alabama and its people. It is of special value to the youth of Alabama as a constant reminder of the circumstances under which our state was born and nurtured and under which our great nation has developed. To further foster the understanding and preservation of our heritage, there is hereby created and established an agency of the state of Alabama to be known as the Alabama historical commission. (Acts 1966, Ex. Sess., No. 168, p. 190, § 1.)

Cited in Floyd v. Alabama Historical Comm'n, 388 So. 2d 182 (Ala. 1980).

§ 41-9-241. Commission a public body corporate.

The commission, as an agency of the state of Alabama, constitutes a public body corporate and shall have, in addition to those set forth specifically in this division, all powers necessary or convenient to effect the purposes for which it has been established under and by the terms of this division, together with all powers incidental thereto or necessary to the discharge of its powers and duties. (Acts 1966, Ex. Sess., No. 168, p. 190, § 8.)

§ 41-9-242. Purpose of commission.

The purpose of the Alabama historical commission, hereinafter referred to as the commission, shall be to acquire in its own name or in the name of the state of Alabama by purchase, devise, lease, assignment, license, condemnation, gift, bequest, transfer or otherwise buildings, objects and sites deemed worthy of being preserved, improved, protected and maintained for or on account of their particular historic, archaeological or architectural significance, including adjacent properties deemed necessary for the proper setting, use and administration of same, and said buildings, objects and sites shall include, but shall not be limited to, the following:

(1) Buildings in which events of great significance to Alabama's or the nation's history have taken place and the sites surrounding them;

(2) Birthplaces or residences of outstanding personages and the sites surrounding them;

(3) The sites of historic or significant events in Alabama or United States history, including military engagements, Indian treaties and massacres;

(4) Buildings of significant or outstanding architectural value;

(5) Buildings, sites, objects or monuments of special significance to our cultural, military, social, economic, religious or commercial heritage, including post roads, traces, ruins, railroads, plantations, wharfs, missions, places of treaties, cemeteries, fortifications and places of worship; and

(6) Archaeological sites for excavational, salvage, protective and interpretative purposes. (Acts 1966, Ex. Sess., No. 168, p. 190, § 2; Acts 1971, No. 500, p. 1213, § 1.)

Review of commission's actions. — If, where fraud is not evident, the court sets itself up as a reviewing authority of purchases by the Alabama historical commission, litigation could result seeking the court's supervision and revision of activity that rightfully is the responsibility and prerogative of the governmental agencies and bodies concerned. This the courts are without constitutional authority to do and will not undertake to do. State ex rel. Baxley v. Givhan, 292 Ala. 533, 297 So. 2d 357 (1974).

§ 41-9-243. Composition of commission; qualifications, appointment, terms of office and removal of members; vacancies.

The commission shall consist of 20 members, one of whom shall be the governor, one of whom shall be the lieutenant governor, one of whom shall be the speaker of the house of representatives, one of whom shall be the director of the department of archives and history, one of whom shall be the director of the state bureau of publicity and information, one of whom shall be the commissioner of conservation and natural resources, one of whom shall be the director of the technical staff of the Alabama building commission and 13 other persons to be appointed by the governor, one of whom shall be selected from a list of three nominees submitted by the Alabama council of the American institute of architects, one from a list of three nominees submitted by the Alabama historical association, one from a list of three nominees submitted by the Alabama state chamber of commerce, one from a list of three nominees submitted by the Alabama farm bureau federation, one from a list of three nominees submitted by the president of the University of Alabama, one from a list of three nominees submitted by the president of Auburn University, one from a list of three nominees submitted by the president of the University of South Alabama, one from a list of three nominees submitted by the president of Troy State University, one from a list of three nominees submitted by the president of the University of Montevallo, one from a list of three qualified archaeologists nominated by the Alabama archaeological society and three from the state-at-large.

Said nominees and appointees shall be persons who have demonstrated interest in and concern about the preservation of his state's rich history and traditions and who are conversant with the history of the state and who are qualified to direct and supervise the work of the commission.

The members appointed by the governor shall serve for terms of six years each; except, that the terms of the members of the first commission shall be three years for one half of the members appointed by the governor and six years for the remaining members. After the expiration of the term of the initial members, all members appointed by the governor shall be appointed for terms of six years each.

Any member of the commission may be removed by the governor for cause, and vacancies in the commission shall be filled by the governor by the appointment of a competent and qualified person for the unexpired term, from a list of three nominees submitted to him by the organization which originally nominated the member being replaced.

The chairman of the restructured historic Chattahoochee commission shall serve as an ex officio policymaking member of the commission. (Acts 1966, Ex. Sess., No. 168, p. 190, § 13; Acts 1969, No. 768, p. 1366, § 1; Acts 1971, No. 500, p. 1213, § 9; Acts 1973, No. 1077, p. 1831.)

Code commissioner's note. — The last paragraph of this section was added by the code commissioner in order to conform the provisions of this section with the provisions of former § 41-9-304, as amended.

§ 41-9-244. Members to serve without pay; expenses.

No member of the commission shall receive any pay or emolument other than his expenses incurred in the discharge of his duties as a member of the commission which expenses shall be paid in the amounts provided for in article 2 of chapter 7 of Title 36 of this Code. All such expenses are to be paid from the funds of the commission. (Acts 1966, Ex. Sess., No. 168, p. 190, § 14.)

§ 41-9-245. Meetings generally; quorum; organization and procedure; officers.

The commission shall hold an annual meeting at the capitol building in Montgomery, and eight members of the commission shall constitute a quorum for the transaction of business. Additional meetings will be held at such times and places within the state of Alabama as may be considered necessary, desirable or convenient upon call of the chairman or, in the case of his absence or incapacity, of the vice-chairman. However, by four-fifths vote of the commission, such meetings may be held outside the state of Alabama. The commission shall determine and establish its own organization and procedures in accordance with the provisions of this division and the general law. The commission shall elect a chairman, a vice-chairman, a secretary and a treasurer, and such officers shall hold office for a period of one year and until successors are elected. (Acts 1966, Ex. Sess., No. 168, p. 190, § 15; Acts 1969, No. 768, p. 1366, § 2.)

§ 41-9-246. Board of advisors.

(a) There is hereby established a board of advisors to the Alabama historical commission. Said board of advisors shall consist of no less than 15 persons. Each of the below listed societies, organizations, individuals, commissions and institutions shall have the authority to name one member of said board and shall submit the name of said person to the chairman of the commission prior to the annual meeting of the commission:

(1) The Alabama Division, United Daughters of the Confederacy;

(2) The Alabama Society of the Daughters of the American Revolution;

(3) The Alabama Society of the Daughters of the American Colonists;

(4) The Mobile Historic Development Commission;

(5) The National Society of the Colonial Dames of America in the State of Alabama;

(6) The Huntsville Historic Preservation Commission;

(7) The Alabama Department of the Sons of Confederate Veterans;

(8) The Gorgas Memorial Board;

(9) The Hobson Memorial Board;

(10) The Cahaba Advisory Committee;

(11) The LaGrange Historical Commission;

(12) The Fort Morgan Historical Commission;

(13) The USS Alabama Battleship Commission;

(14) The Tennessee Valley Historical Society;

(15) The Montgomery Antiquarian Society;

(16) The Helen Keller Property Board;

(17) The Birmingham Historical Society;

(18) The board of trustees of the Mobile Museum Board;

(19) The board of trustees of the Montgomery Museum Board;

(20) The head of the department of history and the head of the department of archaeology of each accredited, four year, degree granting university and college located within the state of Alabama;

(21) The John H. Forney Historical Society;

(22) The Tuscaloosa County Preservation Society;

(23) The Blount County Historical Society;

(24) The Chattahoochee Valley Historical Society;

(25) The Dale County Historical Society;

(26) The Etowah Historical Society;

(27) The Hale County Historical Society;

(28) The Huntsville Historical Society;

(29) The North Alabama Historical Society;

(30) The Old South Historical Society;

(31) The Pike County Historical Society;

(32) The Society of Pioneers of Montgomery;

(33) The Eufaula Heritage Association;

(34) The Marengo Historical Society;

(35) The Historic Mobile Preservation Society;

(36) The Alabama Society, Sons of the American Revolution;

(37) The Alabama Society, Southern Dames of America;

(38) The Huguenot Society in Alabama;

(39) The Alabama Society of the Colonial Dames of the 17th Century;

(40) The Coweta Memorial Association; and

(41) Any other local or regional historical society duly recognized by the commission which may exist or which may be created subsequent to August 19, 1966.

(b) Said advisory board shall meet annually at a place to be designated by the commission and shall serve without compensation. The board shall advise the commission on matters relating to the historic and architectural assets of the state of Alabama and assist the commission in compiling and maintaining an inventory of such assets and in carrying out all of its various duties.

(c) There may further be added to the advisory board by the commission such other civic, charitable and patriotic organizations as it may from time to time deem to be to the best interest of the commission. (Acts 1966, Ex. Sess., No. 168, p. 190, § 16; Acts 1969, No. 768, p. 1366, § 3.)

Code commissioner's note. — The Fort Morgan Historical Commission, referred to in subdivision (12) of subsection (a) of this section, was abolished and all properties, powers, funds, etc., thereof transferred to the Alabama historical commission by Acts 1976, No. 628, p. 865.

The LaGrange Historical Commission, referred to in subdivision (11) of subsection (a) of this section, has been redesignated the LaGrange Advisory Committee, by Acts 1979, No. 614, p. 1084, § 3.

The Richmond Pearson Hobson memorial board, referred to in subdivision (9) of subsection (a) of this section, was abolished and all properties, powers, funds, etc., thereof were transferred to the Alabama historical commission by Acts 1980, No. 80-208, p. 289, § 1. See § 41-9-222.

Cross references. — As to Fort Tombeckbee historical advisory board, see § 41-9-262.

§ 41-9-247. Executive director.

The commission may employ an executive director, who shall serve at the pleasure of the commission and who shall be responsible directly to the commission for the general supervision and execution of the work of the commission. The commission shall fix his compensation, with the approval of the governor and the state personnel board, the same to be paid from the funds of the commission, and shall further designate his duties and authority. (Acts 1966, Ex. Sess., No. 168, p. 190, § 6.)

Function of commission and executive director. — It is apparent from this statute that the function of the commission and the executive director is to achieve the objects and purposes for which the commission was created. Floyd v. Alabama Historical Comm'n, 388 So. 2d 182 (Ala. 1980).

§ 41-9-248. Employees.

The commission may employ either on a part-time or full-time basis such advisors, archaeologists, architects, engineers, attorneys, real estate appraisers, laborers, artisans, historians, caretakers, guides, peace officers, technicians, superintendents, stenographers and administrative employees and supervisory and professional personnel as may be necessary or advisable for carrying out in the most efficient and beneficial manner the purposes and provisions of this division, and all permanent full-time employees other than the executive director, the state officer of archaeology and projects supervisor shall be subject to the state merit system. (Acts 1966, Ex. Sess., No. 168, p. 190, § 5; Acts 1971, No. 500, p. 1213, § 4; Acts 1975, No. 1173, § 1.)

Cross references. — As to merit system, see § 36-26-1 et seq.

§ 41-9-249. Powers and duties of commission generally.

The commission shall have the following duties and powers:

(1) To promote and increase knowledge and understanding of the history of this state from the earliest time to the present, including the archaeological, Indian, Spanish, British, French, colonial, Confederate and American eras, by adopting and executing general plans, methods and policies for permanently preserving and marking objects, sites, structures and ruins as defined in section 41-9-242;

(2) To promote and assist in the publicizing of the historic resources of the state by preparing and furnishing information to public mass media and to governmental agencies charged with publicity and to coordinate any of its objectives, efforts or functions with any agency or agencies of the federal government, of the state of Alabama and of other states or local governments having objectives similar or related to those of the commission;

(3) To accept for renovation, maintenance, restoration, preservation or management and operation any building or site within the state of Alabama owned by the United States, the state of Alabama or any agency or subdivision thereof or by the national trust for historic preservation or by natural or corporate persons, public or private, upon such terms and conditions as to the commission shall be deemed in the best interest of the state of Alabama in conformity with the purposes of this division;

(4) To acquire, by exercise of the power of eminent domain, historic structures of paramount or exceptional importance, such as those Alabama landmarks eligible for nomination to or recorded in the national register of historic places; provided, that at least two thirds of the members of the commission shall vote to acquire such structures by the exercise of this measure;

(5) To charge admissions at the various buildings and sites under the control of the commission throughout the state and to sell booklets, pamphlets and souvenirs at said locations and to retain and use the proceeds of said sales and admissions for the furtherance of the purposes of the commission as defined by this division;

(6) To adopt a seal for the commission and to use the same on its brochures, stationery and other official publications and upon its historic site markers;

(7) To maintain an office in a location in the state to be selected by the commission for the use of the executive director, the employees and the commission and to acquire the necessary furniture and equipment therefor;

(8) To prepare, create, purchase and distribute pamphlets and brochures describing the various historic buildings and sites under the jurisdiction of the state of Alabama or any of its agencies;

(9) To make and publish a survey of the buildings, ruins and sites of historic, architectural or archaeological significance within the state of Alabama and to make available such survey to individuals, institutions and governmental bodies desiring copies of same;

(10) To determine from such survey the buildings, ruins and sites listed therein which are considered worthy of permanent preservation, to certify same as being worthy and to publish said list;

(11) To establish criteria for the certification, selection and acquisition of historic properties for state ownership and for state aid to local historic site projects;

(12) To nominate selected landmarks with historic, architectural and archaeological significance to the national register of historic places using priorities established by the commission;

(13) To establish and maintain an Alabama state historic preservation depository into which may be deposited antiques, relics, artifacts, mementos, paintings and other objects contributed to or acquired by the state or the commission. The commission shall have the authority to restore these objects and to use them for the furnishing of its own historic buildings and other selected landmarks in Alabama;

(14) To rent or lease any of its acquisitions to public or private agencies;

(15) To publish an informational newsletter which shall periodically report on and promote local, regional and state historic preservation activities;

(16) To produce and publish technical ("how to") manuals on historic preservation;

(17) To publish and present citations and distinguished service awards to selected private and public organizations and individuals for outstanding achievements in preserving the heritage of Alabama;

(18) To purchase, produce, sell and distribute historic souvenir items;

(19) To improve, restore, preserve, renovate, maintain, exhibit, repair, rebuild, recreate and reconstruct its acquisitions, and the commission shall have jurisdiction over the same and the exhibits located thereon;

(20) To purchase or otherwise acquire and to erect and maintain "historic markers" on such buildings, roads, trails, routes and sites as it shall designate and to cooperate with and assist local, regional and state historical groups in selecting and erecting such markers; and

(21) To accept the gift of money and real and personal property from any and all public and private sources. Such gifts shall be deductible from Alabama state income tax by the donor. (Acts 1966, Ex. Sess., No. 168, p. 190, §§ 3, 7, 10, 11; Acts 1971, No. 500, p. 1213, §§ 2, 5, 6, 7.)

Cross references. — As to eminent domain generally, see § 18-1-1 et seq.

§ 41-9-250. Preservation, operation, etc., of certain historical properties and sites by commission.

(a) The following historic properties and sites shall be under the jurisdiction and control of the Alabama historical commission:

(1) Fort Mims, Stockton, Baldwin county;

(2) Fort Toulouse, Wetumpka, Elmore county;

(3) Gaineswood, Demopolis, Marengo county; and

(4) Confederate Memorial Cemetery, Mountain Creek, Chilton county.

(b) The Alabama historical commission shall have full authority to develop, renovate, restore, preserve, maintain, operate, exhibit and publicize such properties in accordance with the powers and responsibilities of the said commission. (Acts 1971, No. 665, p. 1374.)

Code commissioner's note. — Acts 1980, No. 80-208, p. 289, § 1, transfers to the Alabama historical commission all property under the management and control of the Richmond Pearson Hobson memorial board, which was abolished, with full authority to develop, renovate, restore, preserve, maintain, operate, exhibit and publicize such property. See § 41-9-222.

§ 41-9-251. Cahaba historical site — Preservation, operation, etc., by commission generally.

The Cahaba historical site, a property on the national register of historic places, Dallas county, Alabama, shall be under the jurisdiction and control of the Alabama historical commission, which shall have full authority to develop, renovate, preserve, maintain, operate, exhibit and publicize the Cahaba historical site in accordance with the powers and responsibilities of said commission. (Acts 1975, 3rd Ex. Sess., No. 155, § 1.)

§ 41-9-252. Same — Advisory committee.

There is hereby established an advisory committee to be known as the Cahaba advisory committee. The committee shall be composed of 16 members, 15 of whom shall be appointed by the governor. The probate judge of Dallas county shall be the sixteenth member but shall be a member ex officio and shall not be entitled to a vote on the advisory committee. The trustees shall serve for terms of four years each, and the probate judge shall serve throughout his term of office. Members of the advisory committee shall be appointed so that each congressional district shall be represented by one appointed member on the advisory committee; except, that the congressional district in which Cahaba is situated shall be represented by eight appointed members, five of whom shall be residents of Dallas county and three of whom shall be from some other county in such congressional district. The advisory committee shall select one of its members who is a resident of Dallas county as secretary of the committee. The offices of the Selma and Dallas county chambers of commerce shall be designated as the official office of the committee, and all records, reports and files of the commission shall be maintained therein, except financial records which shall be maintained as hereinafter provided. Members of the advisory committee shall serve without compensation other than payment of a per diem allowance and travel expenses incurred in attending meetings of the advisory committee or in performing any actual service under the direction of the advisory committee, such expenses to be paid in accordance with article 2 of chapter 7 of Title 36, after the account for such expense has been approved by the judge of probate of Dallas county. All remaining funds appropriated for 1981-82 to the Cahaba historical commission shall be transferred quarterly to the judge of probate, Dallas county, by the state comptroller. All expense reimbursements and any other payments shall be made promptly by the judge of probate of Dallas county on behalf of the Cahaba advisory committee. He shall keep all financial records. The judge of probate is authorized to establish and maintain a bank account on behalf of said committee and to draw warrants for any lawful expenditures therefrom. The advisory committee shall advise the Alabama historical commission regarding the restoration and the development of the site. All future appropriations for the Cahaba historical resources management program shall be made to the Cahaba advisory committee and disbursed in accordance with this section. (Acts 1943, No. 486, p. 449; Acts 1959, No. 387, p. 1012; Acts 1961, No. 815, p. 1191; Acts 1975, 3rd Ex. Sess., No. 155, § 3; Acts 1981, 1st Ex. Sess., No. 81-944, § 1; Acts 1982, No. 82-368.)

The **1981 amendment,** effective August 19, 1981, in the fifth sentence substituted "the congressional district in which Cahaba is situated" for "the fourth congressional district" and "such congressional district" for "the fourth congressional district," at the end of the seventh sentence added "except financial records which shall be maintained as hereinafter provided," in the former ninth sentence substituted "judge of probate of Dallas county" for "historical commission," and added the present tenth and eleventh sentences.

The **1982 amendment,** effective April 26, 1982, combined the eighth sentence with the former ninth sentence, substituting "after the account for such expense has been approved by the judge of probate of Dallas county" for the former provision that expenses be paid out of appropriations made for the Alabama historical commission upon warrant of the comptroller after approval by the judge of probate of Dallas county and the governor, added the present ninth sentence, rewrote the tenth sentence, and added the twelfth and fourteenth (last) sentences.

§ 41-9-253. Same — Powers of commission; payment of expenses.

The Alabama historical commission, within its discretion, may acquire title, possession or control of such properties and also of objects of historic interest at the Cahaba historical site as it may deem necessary or proper to be maintained, preserved and protected on behalf of the state of Alabama and may acquire, by purchase, construction, lease, gift, condemnation or otherwise, lands and rights in land, including leaseholds and easements, and water rights in the rivers and lands adjacent to or in the immediate vicinity of Cahaba. The commission's power of eminent domain may be exercised under Title 18 of this Code and any amendments thereto, or pursuant to any other general statutory provision enacted for the exercise of the power of eminent domain. The commission may mark in suitable manner the places or locations of historic interest at such point and prepare and publish for distribution pamphlets or other printed matter with respect thereto. The expenses incurred for such purposes by the historical commission shall be paid out of any appropriation made to the commission, upon warrant drawn by the comptroller, supported by an itemized account thereof approved by the board of trustees and by the governor. (Acts 1943, No. 486, p. 449; Acts 1959, No. 387, p. 1012; Acts 1961, No. 815, p. 1191; Acts 1969, No. 854, p. 1560; Acts 1975, 3rd Ex. Sess., No. 155, § 1.)

§ 41-9-254. Acquisition, operation, etc., of libraries or museums by commission; commission not to engage in publishing or printing of historical quarterlies.

The commission shall not accept, acquire, operate or maintain libraries or museums, except when the same are an integral part of one of the properties owned or managed by the commission, nor shall the commission engage in the publishing or printing of historical quarterlies. (Acts 1966, Ex. Sess., No. 168, p. 190, § 12; Acts 1971, No. 500, p. 1213, § 8.)

§ 41-9-255. Alabama state historic preservation fund.

There is hereby established in the state treasury a fund to be known as the "Alabama state historic preservation fund" into which shall be deposited all moneys received by the commission from admissions, inspection fees, gifts, donations, grants, leases, rentals, bequests, loans, governmental appropriations or any other sources, either public or private. Such funds shall be used by the commission to pay the costs of the maintenance, acquisitions, preservation and operation of its acquisitions and for carrying out any and all of the purposes of this division, including the payment of the salaries of any employees of said commission and any expenses of said commission. Money contributed to or deposited in this fund for capital outlay projects and from any source other than state appropriations for operations shall not revert to the general fund of the state, but shall remain in the preservation fund until expended by the commission. (Acts 1966, Ex. Sess., No. 168, p. 190, § 4; Acts 1971, No. 500, p. 1213, § 3.)

§ 41-9-256. Exemption from taxation of commission and properties, income, etc., thereof.

The commission, as an agency of the state of Alabama, shall constitute a nonprofit governmental agency and shall have a tax-exempt status, and the properties of the commission and the income therefrom, all lease agreements and contracts made by it shall be forever exempt from any and all taxation by the state of Alabama and any political subdivision thereof, including, but not limited to, income, admission, amusement, excise, sales, use and ad valorem taxes. (Acts 1966, Ex. Sess., No. 168, p. 190, § 9.)

161

§ 41-9-257. Council on historic pilgrimages — Created; purpose.

There is hereby created the Alabama council on historic pilgrimages, the same to be established under the auspices of the Alabama historical commission, said council having the purpose of coordinating the efforts of each of the existing and proposed historic pilgrimages in the state of Alabama, whether publicly or privately sponsored. (Acts 1975, 4th Ex. Sess., No. 67.)

§ 41-9-258. Same — Composition.

The council on historic pilgrimages shall consist of seven individual members, one being appointed from each of the six districts of the state as the same shall be established by the Alabama historical commission and one being a representative of the Alabama historical commission. Additionally, there shall be two ex officio individual members, one representing the Alabama travel council and one representing the state bureau of publicity and information. (Acts 1975, 4th Ex. Sess., No. 67.)

§ 41-9-259. Same — Appointment and terms of members; duties.

(a) The individual members of the council on historic pilgrimages who represent the six above described districts shall each be appointed, initially, by the Alabama historical commission, and three of the initially appointed members shall serve for terms of one year, with the other three serving for terms of two years each. Subsequent to the initial appointment, future individual members of the council shall be named for terms of two years each, and such future members of the council shall be named by the member historic pilgrimage organizations within the district represented by such council member.

(b) The council on historic pilgrimages shall have the authority to establish such policies as it deems necessary for the carrying out of its purposes and to admit as general nonvoting members of the council such organizations in the state of Alabama engaged in the business of historic pilgrimages as it may, in its discretion, determine.

(c) The council shall have among its duties the duty to work closely with the Alabama travel council and the state bureau of publicity and information, and such organizations shall, themselves, provide assistance and advice to the council on historic pilgrimages. (Acts 1975, 4th Ex. Sess., No. 67.)

§ 41-9-260. Transfer to commission of certain parts of Fort Morgan Military Reservation, etc.; development, restoration, etc., thereof by commission; operation of portion of reservation retained by department of conservation and natural resources.

All of that part of the Fort Morgan Military Reservation lying within the Fort Morgan Military Reservation conveyed from the United States of America to the state of Alabama by quitclaim deed executed May 26, 1927, and on which Fort Morgan itself is located, and also a certain part of the Fort Morgan Military Reservation conveyed by the United States of America to the state of

Alabama by deed executed December 16, 1946, including all that area south of the outer south face of the east-west sea wall and west of the north-south sea wall, is hereby transferred to the Alabama historical commission. All other property, both real and personal, including structures and objects located on either of said tracts of land, owned by the Fort Morgan historical commission and all of its powers, authority and jurisdiction over said property are also hereby transferred to the Alabama historical commission, and any right, title or interest which the state department of conservation and natural resources has in the above described property is also hereby transferred to the Alabama historical commission.

Such commission shall have full authority to develop, renovate, restore, preserve, maintain, operate, exhibit and publicize the above described properties in accordance with the powers and responsibilities of said Alabama historical commission.

Any right, title or interest of the department of conservation and natural resources in all that part of the Fort Morgan Military Reservation not hereinabove transferred to the Alabama historical commission shall continue to be held by the state department of conservation and natural resources, and all such property may be used as a public park for recreation, such as camping, boating, fishing and any other purposes for which the department of conservation and natural resources is authorized to maintain and operate a public park. The paved road that runs south at the sea wall shall, however, be open for use by vehicles for ingress and egress to the beach, and the department of conservation and natural resources shall not prohibit camping on any part of the reservation under their jurisdiction and control. (Acts 1976, No. 628, p. 865.)

§ 41-9-261. Designation of commission as agency responsible for restoration and preservation of state Capitol; powers and duties.

(a) The primary restoration, planning and preservation responsibility for the state Capitol of Alabama and its contiguous historic grounds, designated by the United States government as a national historic landmark, is hereby delegated to the Alabama historical commission.

(b) The Alabama historical commission is instructed to protect the historic and architectural integrity of this historic Greek revival masterpiece which served as the first Capitol of the Confederacy in 1861 and has served as the Capitol of Alabama for more than 120 years.

(c) The agencies of the state of Alabama charged with architectural, engineering, maintenance and alteration responsibilities for the state Capitol shall submit plans and specifications to the Alabama historical commission which shall review them for the retention of the historic merit and architectural integrity of the landmark prior to any adaptive or construction activities.

(d) The commission shall be authorized and empowered to promote and preserve the historic character and architectural purity of the Capitol building and grounds and, to that end, it shall exercise its authority, control and general supervisory jurisdiction over the Capitol grounds, including walkways and driveways, and over all public areas within the Capitol building, including the outer office of the executive suite. Such authority shall specifically include, but not be limited to, the corridors, rotundas, lobbies, entranceways, stairways, restrooms, porticos, steps and elevators. The commission shall have no jurisdiction over the areas used for private office space, except as to structural modifications, but shall have jurisdiction over all areas specified in this section, and any and all changes contemplated, whether they be architectural in nature or merely the moving or replacement of furniture and furnishings, shall first require the approval of the commission.

With respect to the legislative chambers, legislative lounges and legislative meeting rooms, the commission shall be authorized and empowered to advise and consult with the clerk of the house and the secretary of the senate and the presiding officer, respectively, and to suggest and recommend changes and renovations within such spaces that would be appropriate and in keeping with the preservation of the historic value and architectural purity therein; provided, however, that no changes or renovations to the said chambers, lounges or meeting rooms shall be undertaken or initiated without the approval of the clerk of the house or the secretary of the senate and the presiding officer, respectively; provided further, that no changes or renovations to the Capitol building and grounds as defined in this section, other than the legislative chambers, legislative lounges and legislative meeting rooms provided for in the preceding provisions of this sentence, shall be undertaken or initiated without the approval of the governor.

(e) Nothing in this section shall be construed as to supersede any authority of the state building commission and, if so, that portion is expressly repealed. (Acts 1969, No. 1148, p. 2153, § 2; Acts 1976, No. 634, p. 881.)

Code commissioner's note. — The provisions of subsection (d) of this section were formerly codified as former § 41-9-512. For reasons for transfer, see code commissioner's note to former § 41-9-512.

Cross references. — As to state Capitol advisory committee generally, see § 41-9-510 et seq. As to state building commission generally, see § 41-9-140 et seq.

§ 41-9-262. Fort Tombeckbee historical advisory board.

(a) An advisory board to be known as the Fort Tombeckbee historical advisory board is hereby authorized to be appointed by the governor for the purpose of advising the Alabama historical commission on the acquisition, maintenance and protection of certain properties and objects of historical interest at Fort Tombeckbee in Sumter county. Said board shall be composed of three members, and the first appointees shall be appointed to serve for terms of two, four and six years, respectively, and subsequent appointees shall serve for terms of four years. Such members shall serve without compensation.

(b) Said board shall advise the Alabama historical commission: To acquire title, possession or control of such properties and also of objects of historic interest at Fort Tombeckbee as it may deem necessary or proper, to be maintained, preserved and protected on behalf of the state of Alabama; to mark in suitable manner the places or locations of historic interest at such point; and to prepare and publish for distribution pamphlets or other printed matter with respect thereto. The Alabama historical commission may, in its complete discretion, act upon any suggestions or advice of the advisory board. Any expenses incurred by the board shall be paid out of any money appropriated by the legislature or by any gift, bequest or grant from whatever source. (Acts 1978, No. 516, p. 571.)

Cross references. — As to board of advisors of commission generally, see § 41-9-246.

Collateral references. — 62 C.J.S., Municipal Corporations, § 225.

Division 2.

LaGrange Historical Commission.

Code commissioner's note. — The LaGrange historical site, owned by the LaGrange historical commission, has been transferred to the Alabama historical commission, which has been given full authority to develop, renovate, preserve, maintain, operate, exhibit and publicize the LaGrange historical site in accordance with the powers and responsibilities of said commission, and the LaGrange historical commission has been redesignated the LaGrange advisory committee with the function of advising the Alabama historical commission regarding the restoration and development of the site, by Acts 1979, No. 614, p. 1084, effective October 1, 1979. See § 41-9-271.

§ 41-9-270. LaGrange historical commission.

(a) A board of trustees, to be known as LaGrange historical commission, is hereby authorized to be appointed by the governor for the purpose of acquiring, maintaining and protecting certain properties and objects of historical interest at LaGrange, in Colbert county, the site of the first chartered college in Alabama. Said board shall be composed of three members, and the first appointees shall be appointed to serve for terms of two, four and six years, respectively, and subsequent appointees shall serve for terms of four years. Such trustees shall serve without compensation other than payment of a per diem allowance and travel expenses in attending meetings of the board or in performing any actual service under the direction of the board, such expenses to be paid in accordance with article 2 of chapter 7 of Title 36 of this Code. Such expenses shall be payable out of the appropriation made by subsection (c) of this section, upon warrant of the comptroller, after the account for such expenses has been approved by the board of trustees and by the governor.

(b) Said board of trustees, within its discretion, may acquire title, possession or control of such properties and also of objects of historic interest at LaGrange as it may deem necessary or proper to be maintained, preserved and protected on behalf of the state of Alabama, mark in suitable manner the places or locations of historic interest at such point and prepare and publish for distribution pamphlets or other printed matter with respect thereto. The expenses incurred for such purposes by the board of trustees shall be paid out of the appropriation made by subsection (c) of this section, upon warrant drawn by the comptroller, supported by an itemized account thereof approved by the board of trustees and by the governor.

(c) For the purposes provided by this section, the sum of $500.00 is hereby appropriated annually payable out of any funds in the treasury, not otherwise appropriated, all of which shall be released on order of the governor. (Acts 1943, No. 551, p. 540.)

§ 41-9-271. LaGrange historical site transferred to state commission.

The LaGrange historical site, Colbert county, Alabama, owned by the LaGrange historical commission is hereby transferred to the Alabama historical commission which shall have full authority to develop, renovate, preserve, maintain, operate, exhibit and publicize the LaGrange historical site in accordance with the powers and responsibilities of said commission. The LaGrange historical commission board of trustees shall cause an appropriate deed or conveyance to be executed in accordance with the provisions of this section. (Acts 1979, No. 79-614, p. 1084.)

Code commissioner's note. — Acts 1979, No. 79-614, p. 1084, § 5, provides that the act shall become effective October 1, 1977. However, it appears that the date should be October 1, 1979, since the governor signed the act on July 30, 1979.

Division 3.

Fort Morgan Historical Commission.

Code commissioner's note. — Certain parts of the Fort Morgan Military Reservation and all powers, authority, etc., of the Fort Morgan historical commission with respect thereto were transferred to the Alabama historical commission by § 41-9-260.

§§ 41-9-280 through 41-9-287. Repealed by Acts 1976, No. 628, p. 865, § 4, effective January 15, 1977.

Division 4.

Historic Chattahoochee Commission.

§§ 41-9-300 through 41-9-310. Repealed by Acts 1978, No. 545, p. 609, § 3.

Code commissioner's note. — Acts 1978, No. 545, p. 609, § 3, provides that §§ 41-9-300 through 41-9-310 are repealed immediately upon the ratification by the state of Georgia of the Historic Chattahoochee Compact, set out in § 41-9-311, and by consent of congress thereto. The state of Georgia ratified the compact in Ga. L. 1978, No. 1254, p. 1497, approved April 3, 1978. Congress consented to the compact in Pub. L. No. 95-462, 92 Stat. 1271, approved October 14, 1978. Section 2 of Pub. L. No. 95-462, 92 Stat. 1271, provides that the consent is subject to the understanding that nothing contained therein shall be construed to confer upon the historic Chattahoochee commission, or upon any other person, the right of eminent domain. Sections 41-9-300 through 41-9-310 are therefore treated as repealed.

§ 41-9-311. Historic Chattahoochee compact.

The governor on behalf of this state is hereby authorized to execute a compact, in substantially the following form, with the state of Georgia, and the legislature hereby signifies in advance its approval and ratification of such compact, which compact is as follows:

HISTORIC CHATTAHOOCHEE COMPACT

Article I.

The purpose of this compact is to promote the cooperative development of the Chattahoochee valley's full potential for historic preservation and tourism and to establish a joint interstate authority to assist in these efforts.

Article II.

This compact shall become effective immediately as to the states ratifying it whenever the states of Alabama and Georgia have ratified it and congress has given consent thereto.

Article III.

The states which are parties to this compact (hereinafter referred to as "party states") do hereby establish and create a joint agency which shall be known as the Historic Chattahoochee Commission (hereinafter referred to as the "commission"). The commission shall consist of 28 members who shall be appointed by the historical commission or organization or similar historical body or other designated authority in each of the counties represented by the commission who shall be bona fide residents and qualified voters of the party states. In Alabama, two shall be residents of Barbour county, two shall be residents of Russell county, two shall be residents of Henry county, two shall be residents of Chambers county, two shall be residents of Lee county, two shall be residents of Houston county and two shall be residents of Dale county. If there are two historical organizations in any of said counties, then one commission member shall be selected from each organization; if there are more than two organizations in any such county, then the organization shall meet and decide on the designation of members which will represent their respective county. In Georgia, one shall be a resident of Troup county, one shall be a resident of Harris county, one shall be a resident of Muscogee county, one shall be a resident of Chattahoochee county, one shall be a resident of Stewart county, one shall be a resident of Randolph county, one shall be a resident of Clay county, one shall be a resident of Quitman county, one shall be a resident of Early county, one shall be a resident of Seminole county and one shall be a resident of Decatur county. In addition, these 11 Georgia members shall choose three at large members who shall be selected from any three of the Georgia member counties listed above. The commission at its discretion may appoint as many advisory members as it deems necessary from any Georgia or Alabama county which is located in the Chattahoochee valley area. The contribution of each party state shall be in equal amounts. If the party states fail to appropriate equal amounts to the commission during any given fiscal year, voting membership on the commission board shall be determined as follows: The state making the larger appropriation shall be entitled to full voting membership. The total number of members from the other state shall be divided into the amount of the larger appropriation and the resulting quotient shall be divided into the amount of the smaller appropriation. The then resulting quotient, rounded to the next lowest whole number, shall be the number of voting members from the state making the smaller contribution. The members of the commission from the state making the larger contribution shall decide which of the members from the other state shall serve as voting members, based upon the level of tourism, renovation and promotional activity and general support of the commission's activities by and in the county of residence of each of the members of the state making the smaller appropriation. Such determination shall be made at the next meeting of the commission following September 30 of each year. Members of the commission shall serve for terms of office as follows: Of the 14 Alabama voting members, one from each of said counties shall serve for two years and the remaining member of each county shall serve for four years. The member appointed by the older organization of each county shall serve for the four-year term for the initial term of this compact. Upon the expiration of the original terms of office of Alabama members, all successor Alabama voting members shall be appointed for four-year terms of office, with seven vacancies in the Alabama voting membership occurring every two years. Of the 14 Georgia voting members, seven shall serve four-year terms and seven two-year terms for the initial term of this compact. The terms of the individual Georgia voting members shall be determined by their place in the alphabet by alternating the four and two year terms beginning with Chattahoochee county, four years, Clay county, two years, Decatur county, four years, etc. Upon the expiration of the original terms of office of Georgia members, all successor Georgia voting members shall be appointed for four-year terms of office, with seven vacancies in the Georgia voting membership occurring every two years. Of the three Georgia at large board members, one shall serve a four-year term and two shall serve two-year terms.

All board members shall serve until their successors are appointed and qualified. Vacancies shall be filled by the members of the commission. The first chairman of the commission created by this compact shall be elected by the board of directors from among its voting membership. Annually thereafter, each succeeding chairman shall be selected by the members of the commission. The chairmanship shall rotate each year among the party states in order of their acceptance of this compact. Members of the commission shall serve without compensation but shall be entitled to reimbursement for actual expenses incurred in the performance of the duties of the commission.

Article IV.

The headquarters of the commission shall be selected by the commission and shall be centrally located in the Chattahoochee valley area. Such headquarters shall be consistent with the legitimate need of the commission. The commission shall hold an annual meeting at the commission headquarters and one-half of the then members of the commission shall constitute a quorum for the transaction of business. Additional meetings may be held at such times and places as may be considered necessary, desirable or convenient, upon call of the chairman, or, in the case of his absence or incapacity, of the vice-chairman, or, on call of any three members of the commission. The commission shall determine and establish its own organization and procedure in accordance with the provisions of this compact and shall have an official seal. The commission shall elect its chairman, its vice-chairman, its secretary and its treasurer, and such officers shall hold office for a period of one year or until a successor is elected. Neither the secretary nor the treasurer need be members of the commission. The commission may require that the treasurer thereof be bonded in an amount to be determined by the commission.

Article V.

The commission shall have the right to adopt such rules and regulations as may be necessary to carry out the intent and purposes of this compact, and shall be authorized to provide for an executive committee of not fewer than five of its members to whom it may delegate such powers and authority as the commission may deem to be advisable.

Article VI.

No member of the commission shall receive any pay or emolument other than his actual expenses incurred in the discharge of his duties as a member of the commission. All such expenses are to be paid from the funds of the commission. Further, it shall be unlawful for any member of the commission or any employee thereof to charge, receive or obtain, either directly or indirectly, any fee, commission, retainer or brokerage out of the funds of the commission, and no member of the commission or officer or employee thereof shall have any interest in any land, materials or contracts sold to or made or negotiated with the commission, or with any member or employee thereof acting in his capacity as a member of such commission. Violation of any provisions of this section shall be a misdemeanor and upon conviction shall be punishable by removal from membership or employment and by a fine of not less than $100.00 or by imprisonment not to exceed six months or both.

Article VII.

The commission shall establish and maintain at such lawful depository or depositories as it shall select, a "historic Chattahoochee fund" composed of the money or moneys which may come into its hands from admissions, inspection fees, gifts, donations, grants, bequests, loans, bond issues, governmental appropriations or other sources, either public or private. Such funds shall be used by the commission to pay for the purposes herein set forth, and the servicing, retirement or amortization of any bonds or other evidences of indebtedness issued by the commission.

Article VIII.

The commission shall be authorized:

1. To investigate and select available sites for housing historic exhibits, including the surrounding grounds, with such state, federal or local agencies and governments and private individuals, corporations, associations or other organizations as may be involved, taking into consideration all pertinent factors affecting the suitability of such sites; to acquire, transport, renovate, maintain and exhibit appropriate and suitable military, or historic units, articles, exhibits and attractions; to have full, complete and exclusive jurisdiction over the sites and any related exhibits;

2. To promote tourism throughout the Chattahoochee valley by attending travel shows; issuing news releases, calendars of events and news letters; publishing brochures and pamphlets; constructing mobile travel exhibits; producing films and other visual presentations as may be necessary; and advertising in magazines and/or newspapers;

3. To acquire by rent or lease agreement or otherwise the necessary housing facilities; and to establish, improve and enlarge available facilities, including providing them with necessary equipment, furnishings, landscaping and related facilities, including parking areas and ramps, roadways, sewers, curbs and gutters;

4. To enter into such contracts and cooperative agreements with the local, state and federal governments, with agencies of such governments, with private individuals, corporations, associations and other organizations as the commission may deem necessary or convenient to carry out the purposes of this compact, with such contracts and agreements to include leases to private industry;

5. To borrow money from private sources, the state emergency fund or such other source as may be acceptable to the commission under such terms and conditions as may be provided by law, and, in order to provide security for the repayment of any such private loans, the commission shall have the authority to pledge such future revenues from admissions and any other sources as may from time to time, be necessary or desirable;

6. To issue and sell at any time and from time to time its revenue bonds for the purpose of providing funds to acquire, enlarge, improve, equip and maintain its property, and for the payment of obligations incurred for such

170

purposes. The principal and interest on any such revenue bonds shall be payable solely out of the revenues derived from the project;

7. To make such contracts in the issuance of its bonds as may seem necessary or desirable to assure their marketability and to provide for their retirement by a pledge of all or any revenue which may come to the commission from the investment of the proceeds of the sale of such bonds or from any other source whatsoever;

8. To accept public or private gifts, grants and donations;

9. To acquire property by purchase, lease, gift or license; and to dispose of any property of the commission when, in the opinion of the commission, such disposition is deemed expedient;

10. To allocate and expend funds from all donations, income and revenue from any source whatsoever coming into its treasury for the fulfillment and accomplishment of its duties and responsibilities in such manner as may be necessary and appropriate for the perfection of the purposes of this compact;

11. To sell, convey, transfer, lease or donate any property, franchise, grant, easement, license or lease or interest therein which it may own, and to transfer, assign, sell, convey or donate any right, title or interest which it may have in any lease, contract, agreement, license or property;

12. To hire such laborers, artisans, caretakers, technicians, stenographers and administrative employees and supervisory and professional personnel as may be necessary or advisable for the carrying out in the most efficient and beneficial manner of the purposes and provisions of this compact;

13. To employ an executive director who shall serve at the pleasure of the commission, who shall be responsible directly to the commission, whose compensation shall be fixed by the commission, whose duties and authority shall be designated by the commission and who shall be paid from funds of the commission;

14. To make such rules and regulations as the commission may deem necessary and desirable to provide for the operation, management and control of its facilities; and

15. To perform such other acts necessary or incidental to the accomplishment of the purposes of this compact, whether or not specifically authorized in this section, and not otherwise prohibited by law.

Article IX.

The commission shall constitute a public body corporate and shall have, in addition to those set forth specifically in this compact, all powers necessary or convenient to effect the purposes for which it has been established under and by the terms of this compact, together with all powers incidental thereto or necessary to the discharge of its said powers and duties.

Article X.

The commission, its property and income and all bonds issued by the commission, the income from such bonds or from the investment of such income and all conveyances, leases, mortgages and deeds of trust by or to the commission shall be exempt from all taxation in the state of Alabama and the state of Georgia.

Article XI.

All obligations incurred by the commission and all bonds issued by it shall be solely and exclusively an obligation of the commission and shall not create an obligation or debt of the state of Alabama or the state of Georgia or any county or municipality of either.

Article XII.

The commission shall maintain at all times accurate records and books of account covering revenues and expenditures. Such records and books shall be available for audit at any time by the department of examiners of public accounts, and shall be audited at least every two years in the same manner as audits are made of other state agencies and departments. (Acts 1978, No. 545, p. 609, § 1.)

Code commissioner's note. — Acts 1978, No. 545, p. 609, § 3, provides that §§ 41-9-300 through 41-9-310 are repealed immediately upon the ratification by the state of Georgia of the Historic Chattahoochee Compact, set out in § 41-9-311, and by consent of Congress thereto. The state of Georgia ratified the compact in Ga. L. 1978, No. 1254, p. 1497, approved April 3, 1978. Congress consented to the compact in Pub. L. No. 95-462, 92 Stat. 1271, approved October 14, 1978. Section 2 of Pub. L. No. 95-462, 92 Stat. 1271, provides that the consent is subject to the understanding that nothing contained therein shall be construed to confer upon the historic Chattahoochee commission, or upon any other person, the right of eminent domain. Sections 41-9-300 through 41-9-310 are therefore treated as repealed.

Collateral references. — 81A C.J.S., States, § 31.

Division 5.

Tannehill Furnace and Foundry Commission.

§ 41-9-320. Creation; purpose.

(a) There is hereby created the Tannehill furnace and foundry commission to establish, operate and maintain as a state park or historic site the land and buildings in the county of Tuscaloosa where one of the state's early ironworks, known as the Tannehill furnace and foundry, was located.

(b) The purpose of the commission shall be to preserve, restore, maintain and promote as a state park or historic site the land and relics of the Tannehill furnace and, in recognition of the important part played by the iron and steel industry in the development of this state, to exhibit this old furnace as an example of the process of making iron in this state's early days. (Acts 1969, No. 994, p. 1760, § 1.)

§ 41-9-321. Composition; appointment and terms of office of members; vacancies.

The commission shall be composed of 16 members, one of whom shall be appointed by the board of trustees of the University of Alabama, and one of whom shall be a member of the Alabama historical commission, chosen by such commission in the manner prescribed by it. The remaining 14 members shall be appointed by the governor. Four of the first members appointed by the governor shall be appointed for eight-year terms, four shall be appointed for six-year terms, four shall be appointed for four-year terms, and two shall be appointed for two-year terms. The first member appointed by the board of trustees of the university and the first member representative of the Alabama historical commission shall be appointed for two-year terms. Successors to these first members shall all be appointed for eight-year terms.

Vacancies on the board during a term shall be filled for the unexpired portion of the term in the same manner and by the same appointing authority as the member whose place is being filled. (Acts 1969, No. 994, p. 1760, § 4.)

§ 41-9-322. Members not to receive pay, etc.; payment of expenses of members; conflicts of interest of members or employees of commission.

No member of the commission shall receive any pay or emolument other than his expenses incurred in the discharge of his duties as a member of the commission, which expenses shall be paid in the amounts provided for in article 2 of chapter 7 of Title 36 of this Code. All such expenses shall be paid from the funds of the commission.

It shall be unlawful for any member of the commission or any employee thereof to charge, receive or obtain, either directly or indirectly, any fee, commission, retainer or brokerage out of the funds of the commission, and no member of the commission or officer or employee thereof shall have any interest in any land, materials or contracts sold to or made or negotiated with the commission or with any member or employee thereof acting in his capacity as a member or employee of such commission. Violation of any provision of this section shall be a misdemeanor and, upon conviction, shall be punishable by removal from membership or employment and by a fine of not less than $100.00 or by imprisonment not to exceed six months, or both. (Acts 1969, No. 994, p. 1760, § 5.)

§ 41-9-323. Meetings generally; quorum; organization and procedure; seal; officers; requirement of bond from treasurer.

The commission shall hold an annual meeting in the city of Tuscaloosa. Eight members shall constitute a quorum for the transaction of business. Additional meetings may be held at such times and places within the state as may be necessary, desirable or convenient upon call of the chairman or, in the case of his absence or incapacity, of the vice-chairman or on the call of any three members of the commission. The commission shall determine and establish its own organization and procedure in accordance with the provisions of this division, and shall have an official seal. The commission shall elect its chairman, its vice-chairman, its secretary and its treasurer, and such officers shall hold office for a period of one year or until a successor is elected. Neither the secretary nor the treasurer need be members of the commission. The commission may require that the treasurer thereof be bonded in an amount to be determined by the commission. (Acts 1969, No. 994, p. 1760, § 7.)

§ 41-9-324. Commission a body corporate.

The commission shall constitute a body corporate and shall have, in addition to those set forth specifically in this division, all powers necessary or convenient to effect the purposes for which it has been established under and by the terms of this division, together with all powers incidental thereto or necessary to the discharge of its said powers and duties. (Acts 1969, No. 994, p. 1760, § 8.)

§ 41-9-325. Commission a state agency; commission to have exclusive control over Tannehill furnace and foundry; rule making and police power.

The commission shall be a state agency and shall have exclusive control over the Tannehill furnace and foundry and the area appurtenant thereto, the memorial park established under this division, all improvements and exhibits located thereon and any additions constructed, created, leased, acquired or erected in connection therewith. The commission shall have the power and authority to establish and promulgate and from time to time alter, amend or repeal rules and regulations concerning the preservation, protection and use of the Tannehill furnace and foundry and the memorial park and to preserve the peace therein. Any person who violates any rule or regulation so established and promulgated shall be guilty of a misdemeanor and shall be punished by a fine of not more than $1,000.00 or imprisonment for not more than one year, or both, and may be adjudged to pay all costs of the proceedings. The commissioners shall have and are hereby vested with full police power to prefer charges against and to make arrests of any person or persons violating any such rule or regulation. The commission shall have full authority to designate any employee or employees of the commission as deputy police officers, who shall have full authority to prefer charges against or to make arrests of any person or persons violating any rule or regulation established and promulgated by the commission as provided hereunder. (Acts 1969, No. 994, p. 1760, § 6; Acts 1979, No. 79-606, p. 1074.)

§ 41-9-326. Acquisition of property; borrowing of money and issuance of revenue bonds.

(a) The commission is authorized to take possession under a lease or a deed of the land and other property in the county of Tuscaloosa, known as "old Tannehill furnace," which is now owned by the University of Alabama, and the board of trustees of the University of Alabama is hereby authorized, in its discretion, to lease or to deed in fee simple such lands and appurtenances thereto to the commission. Such board of trustees may also sell, give or lend any other relics of old-style iron making or other items appropriate for display along with or as a part of a display or exhibit of iron making. The commission is further authorized to lease, accept as a gift or loan or otherwise acquire any other property, real or personal, including gifts or bequests of money or other things of value to be used in fulfilling the purpose for which it is established or for any auxiliary purpose incidental or appropriate thereto.

(b) The commission is also authorized to borrow money and issue revenue bonds in evidence thereof, but no such bonds shall be general obligations of the state of Alabama or any agency or any political subdivision thereof. Nor shall such commission pledge to the payment of any such loans the land, buildings, exhibits or other appurtenances thereto. It may, however, pledge to the repayment thereof the proceeds derived from admission fees or charges or other fees or charges made in connection with such park or historical site. (Acts 1969, No. 994, p. 1760, § 2.)

§ 41-9-327. Operation, etc., of park or historic site; entry into agreements with civic organizations, etc.; acceptance of gratuitous services and employment of hostesses, guards, etc.

(a) The commission shall operate or provide for the operation of the park or historic site hereby provided for and any appurtenances thereto in such manner as to facilitate its exhibition to the public either with or without a charge. If the commission, in its discretion, decides that a charge is appropriate, then the commission shall fix and provide for the collection of such charge or charges as it deems appropriate for admission to the park and for the use, viewing of or other enjoyment of exhibits and other facilities appurtenant to the park.

(b) The commission may enter into agreements with any civic organization, lay group or industrial, professional or governmental organization relative to the general management of the park or historic site.

(c) The commission is also specifically authorized to accept gratuitous services from individuals and organizations and to employ such hostesses, guards, superintendents and other employees as, in its opinion, are needed for the operation and exhibition of such park or historic site. (Acts 1969, No. 994, p. 1760, § 3.)

§ 41-9-328. Appropriations by counties and municipalities.

The county commission of any county or governing body of any municipality in this state shall be authorized, by resolution duly adopted and recorded, to appropriate any available public funds not otherwise pledged to the use of any such commission. (Acts 1969, No. 994, p. 1760, § 10.)

§ 41-9-329. Exemption from taxation of commission and income, properties, etc., thereof.

This commission shall have a tax-exempt status, and the properties of the commission and the income therefrom, all lease agreements and contracts made by it, all bonds issued by it and the coupons applicable thereto and the income therefrom and all indentures executed with respect thereto shall be forever exempt from any and all taxation by the state of Alabama and any political subdivision thereof, including, but not limited to, income, admission, amusement, excise and ad valorem taxes. (Acts 1969, No. 994, p. 1760, § 9.)

§ 41-9-330. Insurance programs for employees.

(a) All full-time employees of the Tannehill furnace and foundry commission shall be treated as state employees for the purpose of participating in any insurance programs provided for state employees.

(b) The Tannehill furnace and foundry commission is hereby authorized and empowered to pay the employer's contributions to any such programs out of any funds appropriated to them or available to them for any purpose whatsoever, and it may deduct the employees' contributions for such programs by means of payroll deductions or otherwise from any salary or compensation paid said employees. (Acts 1975, No. 1245, §§ 1, 2.)

ARTICLE 11.

USS ALABAMA BATTLESHIP COMMISSION.

§ 41-9-340. Creation; composition; qualifications, appointment, terms of office and removal of members; vacancies.

There is hereby created a state commission to be known as the "USS Alabama battleship commission," the membership of which shall consist of 18 competent and qualified citizens of Alabama. The members shall be appointed by the governor, with at least three of said members being residents of Mobile county and at least one being a resident of Baldwin county. The remaining members shall be appointed from throughout the state in such a manner as to provide general statewide representation of the commission.

The terms of the members of the first commission shall be four years for one half of the members appointed by the governor and eight years for the remaining members. After the expiration of the terms of the initial members, all members shall be appointed for terms of eight years each.

Any member of the commission may be removed by the governor for cause, and vacancies in the commission shall be filled by the governor by appointment of a competent and qualified person for the unexpired term. (Acts 1963, No. 481, p. 1028, § 2.)

§ 41-9-341. Members not to receive pay, etc.; payment of expenses of members; conflicts of interest of members or employees of commission.

No member of the commission shall receive any pay or emolument other than his expenses incurred in the discharge of his duties as a member of the commission, which expenses shall be paid in the amounts provided for in article 2 of chapter 7 of Title 36 of this Code. All such expenses are to be paid from the funds of the commission.

It shall be unlawful for any member of the commission or any employee thereof to charge, receive or obtain, either directly or indirectly, any fee, commission, retainer or brokerage out of the funds of the commission, and no member of the commission or officer or employee thereof shall have any interest in any land, materials or contracts sold to or made or negotiated with the commission or with any member or employee thereof acting in his capacity as a member or employee of such commission. Violation of any provision of this section shall be a misdemeanor and, upon conviction, shall be punishable by removal from membership or employment and by a fine of not less than $100.00 or by imprisonment not to exceed six months or both. (Acts 1963, No. 481, p. 1028, § 3.)

§ 41-9-342. Meetings generally; quorum; organization and procedure; seal; officers; requirement of bond from treasurer.

The commission shall hold an annual meeting at the site of the park whenever the same has been selected, and one half of the then members of the commission shall constitute a quorum for the transaction of business. Additional meetings may be held at such times and places within the state of Alabama as may be considered necessary, desirable or convenient upon call of the chairman or, in the case of his absence or incapacity, of the vice-chairman or on call of any three members of the commission. However, by four-fifths vote of the commission, such meetings may be held outside the state of Alabama. The commission shall determine and establish its own organization and procedure in accordance with the provisions of this article and shall have an official seal. The commission shall elect its chairman, its vice-chairman, its secretary and its treasurer, and such officers shall hold office for a period of one year or until a successor is elected. Neither the secretary nor the treasurer need be members of the commission. The commission may require that the treasurer thereof be bonded in an amount to be determined by the commission. (Acts 1963, No. 481, p. 1028, § 5.)

Cross references. — As to special motor vehicle license plates for chairman of USS Alabama Battleship commission, see § 32-6-55.

§ 41-9-343. Executive committee.

The commission may, at its discretion, create and provide for an executive committee of not fewer than five members and delegate to such committee such powers and authority as are deemed advisable by the commission; except, that the executive committee may not be empowered to issue revenue or any other bonds or execute any lease or contract for a period in excess of one year or execute any contract for an amount in excess of $10,000.00. (Acts 1963, No. 481, p. 1028, § 6.)

§ 41-9-344. Executive director.

The commission may employ an executive director, who shall serve at the pleasure of the commission and who shall be responsible directly to the commission for the general supervision, promotion and development of the battleship and of the state memorial park. The commission shall fix his compensation, the same to be paid from the funds of the commission and shall further designate his duties and authority. (Acts 1963, No. 481, p. 1028, § 11.)

Cross references. — As to travel expenses, see § 36-7-20 et seq.

§ 41-9-345. Employees.

The commission may hire such laborers, artisans, caretakers, technicians, stenographers and administrative employees and supervisory and professional personnel as may be necessary or advisable for the carrying out in the most efficient and beneficial manner of the purposes and provisions of this article. (Acts 1963, No. 481, p. 1028, § 10.)

§ 41-9-346. Commission a public body corporate.

The commission shall constitute a public body corporate and shall have, in addition to those set forth specifically in this article, all powers necessary or convenient to effect the purposes for which it has been established under and by the terms of this article, together with all powers incidental thereto or necessary to the discharge of its said powers and duties. (Acts 1963, No. 481, p. 1028, § 12.)

§ 41-9-347. Commission to establish, operate, etc., memorial park and acquire, exhibit, etc., battleship USS Alabama.

The commission created under this article shall itself establish, operate and maintain a state memorial park to honor the Alabamians who participated so valiantly in World War II and the Korean campaign, which shall be under the exclusive management and control of the commission as a separate agency of the state government as provided for in this article, the principal purpose and function of which shall be to acquire, transport, berth, renovate, equip, maintain and exhibit the battleship USS Alabama as a permanent public memorial. (Acts 1963, No. 481, p. 1028, § 1.)

§ 41-9-348. Commission to be state agency; commission to have exclusive control over battleship, park, etc.

The commission shall be a state agency and shall have exclusive control over the battleship USS Alabama, the memorial park established under this article, any and all improvements and exhibits located thereon and any additions constructed, created, leased, acquired or erected in connection therewith. (Acts 1963, No. 481, p. 1028, § 4.)

§ 41-9-349. Powers and duties of commission generally.

The commission shall have the duty and authority to acquire the battleship USS Alabama (BB60) and to select and improve appropriate sites for the permanent or temporary berthing of said vessel, taking into consideration factors, including, but not limited to, the accessibility of same, the location of nearby roads and highways, scenic attractions, esthetic value, cost, cooperation with federal, state, county, municipal and other governmental authorities, protection from the hazards of weather, fire and sea and any other factors which may affect the suitability of such site for the establishment of the ship as a temporary or permanent memorial and exhibit.

The commission may accept public or private gifts, grants and donations for the purposes of this article, may make and enter into contracts with other governmental departments, agencies and boards, either federal, state or municipal, and with private persons and corporations, may transport the ship to and berth the same at temporary and permanent park sites, ready the ship for visitation by the public, establish and provide for a proper charge for admission to the ship and otherwise renovate, maintain and operate the ship as a permanent memorial and exhibit.

The commission shall have full, complete and exclusive jurisdiction over the vessel, the sites and the related exhibits and shall have the power and authority to allocate funds from its treasury for the fulfillment and accomplishment of its duties and responsibilities in such manner as may be necessary and appropriate for the perfection of the purposes of this article, including the authority to pledge revenues from its income from long term leases, future revenues from admissions and any other sources as may from time to time be necessary or desirable. (Acts 1963, No. 481, p. 1028, § 7; Acts 1965, 1st Ex. Sess., No. 169, p. 220, § 1.)

§ 41-9-350. Maintenance and audits of records and books of account; establishment, etc., of reserve fund for special contingencies and emergencies.

(a) The commission shall maintain books of account covering revenues derived by it from all sources whatsoever, together with accounts of all expenses incurred in connection with the carrying out by the commission of its purposes as established by and under the terms of this article. Such records and books shall be available for audit at any time by the department of examiners of public accounts and shall be audited at least every two years in the same manner as audits are made of other state agencies and departments.

(b) The commission shall establish a reserve fund for special contingencies and emergencies over and beyond those occurring in the normal course of routine maintenance and operation and may authorize the deposit of this reserve fund in any lawful depository or depositories. (Acts 1963, No. 481, p. 1028, § 9.)

§ 41-9-351. Commission may provide for insurance for properties and employees.

The commission may provide insurance covering loss or damage to its properties or any properties of others in its custody, care or control or any properties as to which it has any insurable interest caused by fire or other casualty and may likewise provide insurance for the payment of damages on account of the injury to or death of persons and the loss of or destruction of properties of others, and may pay the premiums thereon out of the revenues of the commission. Nothing in this section shall be construed to authorize or permit the institution of any civil action or proceeding in any court against the commission for or on account of any matter referred to in this section; provided, that any contracts of insurance authorized by this section may, in the discretion of the chairman of the commission, provide for a direct right of action against the insurance carrier for the enforcement of any such claims or causes of action.

The liability under any such policy or contract of insurance, arising out of such facts and circumstances as would bring such claim or cause of action within the provisions of chapter 5 of Title 25 if the commission were subject to the provisions of said law shall be governed by the provisions of said law; provided, however, that the chairman of the commission may increase the hospital and medical liability coverage if in his opinion he deems such increase of such liability coverage to be in the best interests of the commission. The liability in all other cases from any such policy or contract of insurance, except to the extent expressly stated to the contrary therein, shall be the same as that imposed by law upon private persons, firms or corporations in like circumstances.

The commission may, with the approval of the governor, enter into contract by bond or policy with an insurance company authorized to do business in this state covering a certain amount to be paid to the employees of the commission who may be killed or injured in the line and scope of their employment; provided, that the amount paid to such employee on account of death or injury shall not exceed the amount or amounts as provided by chapter 5 of Title 25; provided further, that such bond or policy may provide additional benefits not to exceed $10,000.00 per employee for the payment of hospital and medical expenses. The premium upon such bond or policy shall be paid out of the revenues of the commission. (Acts 1965, 2nd Ex. Sess., No. 95, p. 129.)

§ 41-9-352. Authority for issuance and sale of revenue bonds; form, terms, denomination, etc., generally; sale; redemption; payment of principal and interest on bonds and security therefor.

The commission shall have the power and authority to issue and sell at any time and from time to time its revenue bonds for the purpose of providing funds to acquire, transport, outfit, renovate, maintain, improve and berth the battleship USS Alabama and to construct, improve, enlarge, complete, maintain, operate and equip the memorial park established in this article and for the payment of obligations incurred for such purpose or purposes; provided, however, that the first proceeds from the first revenue bonds issued under this section shall be used to repay the loan received from the Alabama state docks department.

The principal of and interest on any such bonds shall be payable solely out of the revenues derived from the project. All bond service payments shall be subordinate to the acquisition, establishment and maintenance of a reasonable maintenance and operating fund.

Any bonds of the commission may be delivered by it at any time and from time to time, shall be in such form and denominations and of such tenor and maturities, shall bear such rate or rates of interest, payable and evidenced in such manner, may contain provisions for redemption prior to maturity and may contain other provisions not inconsistent with this section, all as provided by duly adopted resolutions of the commission whereunder such bonds are authorized to be issued; provided, however, that no bond of the commission shall have a specified maturity date later than 30 years after its date. Each bond of the commission having a specified maturity date more than 10 years after its date shall be made subject to redemption at the option of the authority of the commission at the end of the tenth year after its date and on any interest payment date thereafter under such terms and conditions as may be provided in the resolution under which such bond is authorized to be issued.

Bonds of the commission may be sold at either public or private sale in such manner and at such time or times as may be determined by the commission to be most advantageous to it.

Bonds issued by the commission shall not be obligations of the state of Alabama but shall be payable solely out of the revenue derived from the park project in respect of which such bonds are issued. The principal of and the interest on the bonds shall be secured by a pledge of the revenues out of which the bonds shall be payable and by a pledge of the rentals or leases from any concessions granted by the commission and may be secured by nonforeclosable indenture covering the park project. (Acts 1963, No. 481, p. 1028, § 13.)

§ 41-9-353. Bonds and other obligations to be exclusively obligations of commission; bonds and coupons to be negotiable instruments and to constitute legal investments for banks, insurance companies and fiduciaries; effect of recital as to issuance in resolution authorizing bonds.

All obligations incurred by the commission and all bonds issued by it shall be solely and exclusively an obligation of the commission and shall not create an obligation or debt of the state of Alabama or any county or municipality therein.

All bonds issued by the commission, while not registered, shall be construed to be negotiable instruments even though they are payable from a limited source. All coupons applicable to any bonds issued by the commission, while the applicable bonds are not registered as to both principal and interest, shall likewise be construed to be negotiable instruments although payable from a limited source. Such bonds shall constitute legal investments for savings banks and insurance companies organized under the laws of the state; and, unless otherwise directed by the court having jurisdiction thereof or the document that is the source of authority, a trustee, executor, administrator, guardian or one acting in any other fiduciary capacity may, in addition to any other investment powers conferred by law and with the exercise of reasonable prudence, invest trust funds in the bonds of the commission.

Any resolution authorizing any bonds under this article shall contain a recital that they are issued pursuant to this article, which shall be conclusive evidence that said bonds have been duly authorized, notwithstanding the provisions of any other law now in force or hereafter enacted or amended. (Acts 1963, No. 481, p. 1028, § 15.)

§ 41-9-354. Borrowing of money from private sources, etc., authorized generally; pledge of future revenues from admissions, etc., as security for repayment of such loans.

The commission shall have the authority to borrow money from private sources, the state emergency fund or such other sources as may be acceptable to the commission under such terms and conditions as may be provided by law. In order to provide security for the repayment of any such private or public loans, the commission shall have the authority to pledge such future revenues from admissions and any other sources as may, from time to time, be necessary or desirable. (Acts 1963, No. 481, p. 1028, § 16; Acts 1965, 1st Ex. Sess., No. 169, p. 220, § 2.)

§ 41-9-355. Loan from state docks department; commission may borrow from banks pending such loan and pledge loan as security.

At such time as existing revenue bond covenants of the Alabama state docks department are satisfied as a result of any refunding of revenue bond issues of the Alabama state docks department that are outstanding as of August 1, 1963, the Alabama state docks department shall loan $50,000.00 to the USS Alabama battleship commission from the trust fund that will be released to the Alabama state docks department as a result of said refunding. This loan shall be repaid to the Alabama state docks department from the proceeds of the first revenue issue authorized under this article.

Pending said loan from the Alabama state docks department from the released trust fund, the USS Alabama battleship commission is hereby authorized to borrow from any bank or banks in the state of Alabama such sums up to $50,000.00 as are needed to carry out the purposes of this article. The USS Alabama battleship commission may pledge as collateral for this loan or loans the above described loan that will be received from the Alabama state docks department. (Acts 1963, No. 481, p. 1028, § 17.)

§ 41-9-356. Appropriations by counties and municipalities.

The county commissions of the several counties of the state and the city commissions, the city councils and other like governing bodies of the cities and towns of the state are hereby authorized to make appropriations to the commission for the purposes enumerated in this article. (Acts 1964, 1st Ex. Sess., No. 146, p. 213; Acts 1965, 1st Ex. Sess., No. 169, p. 220.)

§ 41-9-357. Battleship fund.

The commission shall establish and maintain at such lawful depository or depositories in the state of Alabama as it shall select a "battleship fund," composed of the money or moneys which may come into its hands from admissions, inspection fees, gifts, donations, grants, bequests, loans, bond issues, governmental appropriations or other sources, either public or private. Such funds shall be used by the commission to pay the costs of outfitting, transporting, operating, renovating and berthing said battleship, the costs of creating, establishing, enlarging, maintaining and operating the state memorial park for the purposes set forth in this article and the servicing, retirement or amortization of any bonds or other evidences of indebtedness issued by the commission. (Acts 1963, No. 481, p. 1028, § 8.)

§ 41-9-358. Exemption from taxation of commission and income, properties, etc., thereof.

The commission shall have a tax exempt status, and the properties of the commission and the income therefrom, all lease agreements and contracts made by it, all bonds issued by it and the coupons applicable thereto and the income therefrom and all indentures executed with respect thereto shall be forever exempt from any and all taxation by the state of Alabama and any political subdivision thereof, including, but not limited to, income, admission, amusement, excise and ad valorem taxes. (Acts 1963, No. 481, p. 1028, § 14.)

ARTICLE 12.

COMMISSION ON UNIFORM STATE LAWS.

§ 41-9-370. Creation; composition; appointment and terms of office of members.

A commission is hereby created to be known as the commission on uniform state laws which shall consist of three recognized members of the bar who shall be appointed by the governor for terms of four years each or until their successors are appointed and, in addition thereto, any residents of this state who because of long service in the cause of the uniformity of state legislation shall have been elected life members of the national conference of commissioners on uniform state laws. (Acts 1951, No. 926, p. 1575, § 1.)

§ 41-9-371. Vacancies.

Upon the death, resignation, failure or refusal to serve of any appointed commissioner, his office shall become vacant, and the governor shall make an appointment to fill the vacancy, such appointment to be for the unexpired term of the former appointee. (Acts 1951, No. 926, p. 1575, § 2.)

§ 41-9-372. Meetings and organization.

The commissioners shall meet at least once in two years and shall organize by the election of one of their number as chairman and another as secretary, who shall hold their respective offices for a term of two years and until their successors are elected. (Acts 1951, No. 926, p. 1575, § 3.)

§ 41-9-373. Duties of commission generally; reports to legislature.

Each commissioner shall attend the meeting of the national conference of commissioners on uniform state laws and, both in and out of such national conference, shall do all in his power to promote uniformity in state laws upon all subjects where uniformity may be deemed desirable and practicable. The commission shall report to the legislature at each regular session and from time to time thereafter as said commission may deem proper an account of its transactions and its advice and recommendations for legislation. It shall also be the duty of said commission to bring about as far as practicable the uniform judicial interpretation of all uniform laws. (Acts 1951, No. 926, p. 1575, § 4.)

§ 41-9-374. Appropriation; payment of expenses and contributions.

There is hereby appropriated out of state funds not otherwise appropriated a sum sufficient to reimburse appointed members of the commission on uniform state laws for their necessary expenses in performing the duties of their offices, to defray the cost of printing the commission's reports and to make a contribution on behalf of this state to the national conference of commissioners on uniform state laws in a sum not to exceed $1,500.00 per annum. The amount of such expenses and contributions shall be certified to the finance director by the chairman of the commission, and the finance director is hereby authorized to draw warrants and the treasurer of the state to pay same for these purposes. (Acts 1951, No. 926, p. 1575, § 5.)

ARTICLE 13.

COMMISSION ON INTERGOVERNMENTAL COOPERATION.

§§ 41-9-390 through 41-9-395. Repealed by Acts 1977, No. 117, p. 147, effective March 10, 1977.

ARTICLE 14.

CONTINUING WOMEN'S COMMISSION.

§ 41-9-410. Creation; composition; qualifications, appointment and terms of office of members; vacancies; compensation and expenses of members.

There is hereby created and established a continuing women's commission, hereinafter referred to as the commission, which shall be composed of three members of the house of representatives appointed by the speaker of the house, two members of the senate appointed by the president pro tem of the senate and 10 members appointed by the governor. Of those members appointed by the governor, one member shall be appointed from each congressional district as the same are established on September 20, 1971, and two members shall be appointed from the state-at-large. At least seven of the members appointed by the governor shall be women. The five members representing the legislature shall be appointed for terms of two years, and their successors shall be appointed for terms of two years. Of those members appointed by the governor, five members shall be appointed for terms of five years, and five members shall be appointed for terms of three years, and the successors to such 10 appointees shall serve for terms of three years.

Vacancies on the commission shall be filled by appointment in the same manner provided for the appointment of the initial members.

Members of the commission shall receive no compensation for their services. (Acts 1971, No. 1937, p. 3127, § 1.)

Cross references. — As to travel expenses, see § 36-7-20 et seq.

§ 41-9-411. Selection of chairman and other officers; adoption of procedures and rules; appointment of committees and task forces; office space and equipment; engagement of employees and consultants, holding of public hearings, etc.

The commission shall hold an organizational session at which time the commission shall select a chairman and such other officers from its membership as it deems necessary. The commission shall at its organizational session adopt such procedures and rules that will enable the implementation of the purposes of the commission. It shall have the responsibility of appointing such committees and task forces as they deem necessary. Members of such committees shall serve without compensation. It shall be provided with office space and necessary office equipment. It may engage employees and consultants, hold public hearings and generate other activities as may be needed to realize the purposes of the commission. (Acts 1971, No. 1937, p. 3127, § 2.)

§ 41-9-412. Meetings.

The commission shall meet at least three times a year. (Acts 1971, No. 1937, p. 3127, § 4.)

§ 41-9-413. Functions of commission generally.

The commission shall be a continuing vehicle for the determination of effective policy and legislation in the areas which will affect Alabama's women. It shall study the status of women in this state and make recommendations to the governor and legislature for constructive action in the following areas:

(1) Public and private employment policies and practices;

(2) Labor laws dealing with hours, wages and working conditions;

(3) Legal rights and responsibilities;

(4) Policies and practices with regard to education, counseling and job training;

(5) Citizen volunteers; and

(6) Home and community. (Acts 1971, No. 1937, p. 3127, § 3.)

§ 41-9-414. Annual report to governor and legislature.

The commission shall submit an annual report to the governor and the legislature of its activities and findings and any suggested legislation which would aid in accomplishing its objectives. (Acts 1971, No. 1937, p. 3127, § 5.)

ARTICLE 15.

SPACE SCIENCE EXHIBIT COMMISSION.

§ 41-9-430. Creation; commission a public body corporate; commission to provide, etc., facilities for exhibits of national aeronautics and space administration, department of army, etc.

There is hereby created and established a state agency to be known as the Alabama space science exhibit commission, which shall be a public body corporate with all the powers and privileges of a corporation, for the purpose of providing for and participating in the management and control of facilities to house and display such visual exhibits of space exploration and hardware used therefor as may be made available by the national aeronautics and space administration. Such facility shall constitute a permanent housing for the national aeronautics and space administration exhibit, which shall be open to the general public and shall be located at a place to be designated and made available in Madison county for a nominal cost through the cooperation of the department of the army or at such other locations as the commission may deem appropriate.

The commission is further empowered to provide such facilities as will be mutually agreed upon between the commission and department of the army for the housing and display of army weaponry and mementos of national defense.

The commission is further empowered to establish an energy information and exhibit center in order to provide information to the public on research and development in the field of energy as developed by the national aeronautics and space administration, the department of the army, the energy research and development administration, other federal and state agencies, including universities and colleges, and other public and private sectors engaged in energy related activities. (Acts 1965, No. 863, p. 1605, § 1; Acts 1966, Ex. Sess., No. 408, p. 553; Acts 1976, No. 587, p. 799.)

§ 41-9-431. Composition; qualifications, appointment, terms of office and removal of members; vacancies; chairman; compensation of members; meetings generally; quorum; executive committee.

The commission created by section 41-9-430 shall consist of 18 members, to be appointed by the governor, who shall be bona fide residents and qualified voters of this state, at least three of whom shall be residents of Madison county. The remaining members of the commission shall be appointed from throughout the state in such manner as to provide general statewide representation on the commission, but all members shall be qualified persons of unquestioned loyalty to this country who are knowledgeable and interested in national defense and space exploration and in the promotion of interest in such fields. Nine of the original members shall be appointed for terms of four years, and nine members shall be appointed for terms of eight years. Thereafter, all members shall serve for terms of eight years. All members shall serve until their successors are appointed and qualified, but any member may be removed by the governor for just cause. Vacancies shall be filled in the same manner as original appointments are made.

The first chairman of the commission shall be appointed by the governor from among the original appointees. Thereafter, each succeeding chairman shall be selected by the other members of the commission.

Members of the commission shall serve without compensation.

The commission shall hold at least one annual meeting at the site of the exhibit, and one half of the members shall constitute a quorum for the transaction of any business which may properly come before the commission at any such meeting.

The commission shall be authorized to provide for an executive committee of not fewer than five of its members to whom it may delegate such powers and authority as the commission may deem to be advisable. (Acts 1965, No. 863, p. 1605, § 2.)

Cross references. — As to travel expenses, see § 36-7-20 et seq.

§ 41-9-432. Powers generally.

The commission shall be authorized:

(1) To investigate and select an available site for housing the exhibits, including the surrounding grounds, in cooperation with the department of the army and the community, taking into consideration all pertinent factors affecting the suitability of such site;

(2) To acquire by rent or lease agreement or otherwise the necessary housing facilities and to establish, improve and enlarge the available facility, including providing it with necessary equipment, furnishings, landscaping and related facilities, including parking areas and ramps, roadways, sewers, curbs and gutters;

(3) To enter into such contracts and cooperative agreements with the local, state and federal governments, with agencies of such governments, including the department of the army and the national aeronautics and space administration, with private individuals, corporations, associations and other organizations as the commission may deem necessary or convenient to carry out the purpose of this article, such contracts and agreements to include leases to private industry;

(4) To borrow money from private sources or such other source as may be acceptable to the commission under such terms and conditions as may be provided by law and, in order to provide security for the repayment of any such private loans, to pledge such future revenues from admissions and any other sources as may from time to time be necessary or desirable;

(5) To issue and sell, subject to the approval of the governor, interest-bearing general obligation bonds not in excess of $1,900,000.00 in principal amount as authorized by constitutional amendment. Such bonds shall be general obligations of the state of Alabama with full faith and credit and taxing power of the state to be pledged to the prompt and faithful payment of the principal of the bonds and the interest thereon. The proceeds from the sale of such bonds shall be used exclusively for the purpose of paying the expenses incurred in the sale and issuance thereof and for the construction, establishment, improvement or enlargement and equipment of building facilities and related grounds, including the renewal or replacement of structural parts of such facility, but not including the purchase of the site for such facility;

(6) To issue and sell at any time and from time to time its revenue bonds for the purpose of providing funds to acquire, enlarge, improve, equip and maintain a facility and for the payment of obligations incurred for such purposes. The principal and interest on any such revenue bonds shall be payable solely out of the revenues derived from the project;

(7) To make such contracts in the issuance of its bonds as may seem necessary or desirable to assure their marketability and to provide for their retirement by a pledge of all or any revenue which may come to the commis-

sion from the investment of the proceeds of the sale of such bonds or from any other source whatsoever;

(8) To accept public or private gifts, grants and donations;

(9) To acquire property by purchase, lease, gift or license, such power not to include the purchase of a site for the facility;

(10) To allocate and expend funds from all donations, income and revenue from any source whatsoever coming into its treasury for the fulfillment and accomplishment of its duties and responsibilities in such manner as may be necessary and appropriate for the perfection of the purposes of this article;

(11) To sell, convey, transfer, lease or donate any property, franchise, grant, easement, license or lease or interest therein which it may own and to transfer, assign, sell, convey or donate any right, title or interest which it may have in any lease, contract, agreement, license or property;

(12) To employ an executive director and such additional personnel as may be necessary to accomplish the purposes of this article. The executive director and such additional personnel as may be employed by the commission will serve at the pleasure of the commission. The commission shall fix the compensation of the executive director, and such additional personnel and such compensation shall be paid from the funds of the commission. The commission shall designate the duties and authority of the executive director and such additional personnel. The executive director and such additional personnel shall not be subject to the provisions of the state Merit System Act; provided, however, that they shall be eligible for participation in the state health insurance plan and benefits as provided in sections 36-29-1 through 36-29-12, and they shall be eligible for participation in the state employees' retirement system under the provisions of section 36-27-6 governing counties, cities, towns and other quasi-public organizations of the state;

(13) To make such rules and regulations as the commission may deem necessary and desirable to provide for the operation, management and control of the facility in cooperation with the department of the army and with the national aeronautics and space administration; and

(14) To perform such other acts necessary or incidental to the accomplishment of the purposes of this article, whether or not specifically authorized in this section, and not otherwise prohibited by law. (Acts 1965, No. 863, p. 1605, § 3; Acts 1969, No. 280, p. 611, § 1; Acts 1971, No. 2339, p. 3772.)

Constitution. — For constitutional provision pertaining to issuance of bonds for purpose of providing and equipping permanent facilities in Madison county for display of exhibits of national aeronautics and space administration and department of army, see Const., Amendment No. 224.

§ 41-9-433. Form, terms, denominations, etc., of bonds; sale; redemption; execution of bonds and coupons.

All bonds shall be issued, subject to the approval of the governor, in such forms, denominations, series and numbers, may be of such tenor and maturities, may bear such date or dates, may be in registered or bearer form either as to principal or interest or both with rights of conversion into another form, may be payable in such installments and at such place or places, may bear interest at such rate or rates payable and evidenced in such manner and may contain provisions for redemption at the option of the state, to be exercised by said commission at such date or dates prior to their maturity and upon payment of such redemption price or prices, as shall be provided by said commission in the resolution or resolutions whereunder the bonds are authorized to be issued. The principal of each series of bonds shall mature in annual installments in such amounts as shall be specified in the resolution or resolutions of the said commission under which they are issued, the first of which installments shall mature not later than one year after the date of the bonds of such series, and the last of which installments shall mature not later than 20 years after the date of the bonds of the same series. When each series of bonds is issued, the maturities of the bonds of that series shall, to such extent as may be practicable, be so arranged that during each then succeeding fiscal year of the state government the aggregate installments of principal and interest that will mature on all bonds that will be outstanding under this article immediately following the issuance of the bonds of that series will be substantially equal; provided, that the determination by the said commission that the requirements of this sentence have been complied with shall be conclusive of such compliance and the purchasers of the bonds with respect to such determination is made and all subsequent holders thereof shall be fully protected thereby.

None of the bonds shall be sold for less than face value plus accrued interest thereon to the date of delivery. All of the bonds shall be sold only at public sale or sales, either on sealed bids or at public auction, after such advertisement as may be prescribed by said commission, to the bidder whose bid reflects the lowest net interest cost to the state computed to the respective maturities of the bonds sold; provided, that if no bid deemed acceptable by the said commission is received, all bids may be rejected.

The bonds shall be signed in the name of the state by the governor and countersigned by the chairman of the commission and the great seal of the state of Alabama or a facsimile thereof shall be impressed, printed or otherwise reproduced thereon and shall be attested by the signature of the secretary of state; provided, that facsimile signatures of any one or any two but not all of said officers may be reproduced on such bonds in lieu of their manually signing the same. Coupons attached to the bonds and representing installments of interest thereon shall be signed with the facsimile signature of the state treasurer, which facsimile signature is hereby adopted as due and sufficient authentication of said coupons. (Acts 1965, No. 863, p. 1605, § 4.)

§ 41-9-434. Pledge of revenues and income of commission for security and payment of general obligation bonds.

Any general obligation bonds shall also be payable from and secured by a pledge of the revenues and income of the commission remaining after the payment of the reasonable and necessary expenses of operating and maintaining the facilities to be constructed by the commission. (Acts 1965, No. 863, p. 1605, § 6a.)

§ 41-9-435. Liability upon revenue bonds issued by commission.

All revenue bonds issued by the commission shall be solely and exclusively the obligations of the commission and shall not create an obligation or debt of the state or of any county or of any municipality within the state. (Acts 1965, No. 863, p. 1605, § 6.)

§ 41-9-436. Promotion and advertising of exhibits and facilities by commission; purchase and acquisition of tangible personal property; operation or leasing of concessions in or on grounds and facilities of commission.

In view of the unique character and complexity of the duties and responsibilities imposed on the commission by this article, it is hereby specifically provided that the commission shall have, in addition to the power and authority enumerated in section 41-9-432, the right, power and authority to:

(1) Develop and institute a program of promotion and advertising of the exhibits and facilities provided for by this article, said program of promotion and advertising to be conducted by the commission both within and without the state in such manner and to such extent as may be deemed economically advisable and appropriate by the commission;

(2) Purchase and acquire items of tangible personal property on a competitive bid basis in the manner prescribed by law for the purchase of such items by state trade schools, state junior colleges and state colleges and universities under the supervision and control of the state board of education, the city and county boards of education, the district boards of education of independent school districts, the county commissions and the governing bodies of the municipalities of the state and the governing boards of instrumentalities of counties and municipalities under sections 41-16-50, 41-16-51 and 41-16-53 through 41-16-63; and

(3) Operate itself or, in its discretion enter into lease agreement with a person or agency of its choosing to operate, all concessions located in or on the grounds and facilities operated by the commission, any such lease agreement to be so designated as to provide maximum services and convenience to the patrons of the exhibit center and to provide reasonable revenue return to the commission. (Acts 1965, No. 863, p. 1605, § 8; Acts 1969, No. 280, p. 611, § 2.)

§ 41-9-437. Maintenance and audit of records and books of account.

It shall be the duty of the commission to maintain at all times accurate records and books of account covering revenues and expenditures which shall be subject to the audit of the department of examiners of public accounts. (Acts 1965, No. 863, p. 1605, § 7.)

§ 41-9-438. Exemption from taxation of commission and properties, income, etc., thereof.

The commission, its property and income and all bonds issued by the commission, the income from such bonds or from the investment of such income and all conveyances, leases, mortgages and deeds of trust by or to the commission shall be exempt from all taxation in the state of Alabama. (Acts 1965, No. 863, p. 1605, § 5.)

§ 41-9-439. Construction of article.

The provisions of this article shall be construed liberally, it being the purpose to provide in this state appropriate housing facilities for displaying to the general public exhibits of the department of the army and of the national aeronautics and space administration and for providing for the management and control of that portion of the display furnished and supplied by the national aeronautics and space administration by such means as may be feasible and agreed upon. (Acts 1965, No. 863, p. 1605, § 8; Acts 1969, No. 280, p. 611, § 2.)

ARTICLE 16.

SPORTS HALL OF FAME BOARD.

§ 41-9-450. Creation; composition; appointment and terms of office of members; officers; compensation and expenses of members; meetings generally; quorum.

There shall be created and established as provided in this article a board to be designated and known as the Alabama sports hall of fame board. The board shall be composed of 10 members, eight of whom shall be appointed by the governor of Alabama for terms of six years each; provided, that of the first members appointed, two shall serve for two years, and three shall serve for four years as the governor may direct. One board member shall be appointed for each congressional district in the state. The ninth member of the board shall be the chairman or president of the Jefferson county civic center board by virtue of his office. The tenth member shall be appointed by the governor of Alabama from the state at-large for a term of six years.

The members of the board shall select a chairman and vice-chairman from among their own number. Members of the board shall not be compensated for their services, but each member shall be entitled to reimbursement for expenses incurred in attending board meetings. The board shall meet quarterly and at such other times as its rules and bylaws may prescribe. A majority of the members shall constitute a quorum for transaction of business. (Acts 1967, No. 225, p. 594, § 1; Acts 1980, No. 80-447, p. 694.)

Cross references. — As to travel expenses, see § 36-7-20 et seq.
Administrative Bodies and Procedure, § 7. 81A C.J.S., States, §§ 141, 142.
Collateral references. — 73 C.J.S., Public

1 Am. Jur. 2d, Administrative Law, §§ 23, 36-38, 69-74.

§ 41-9-451. Quarters, etc.; executive secretary or director; staff; display of busts, exhibits, etc., in Jefferson county civic center.

The board shall be domiciled at the Jefferson county civic center, where it shall maintain such halls, rooms or quarters as may be considered suitable and appropriate for conducting its affairs. The board may appoint an executive secretary or director and such staff as may be necessary for performance of its duties and functions. The director of the Jefferson county civic center shall cause to be set apart at the center a section thereof to be used by the board for display of busts, statues, plaques, books, papers, pictures and other exhibits relating to sports, athletics and athletes. (Acts 1967, No. 225, p. 594, § 2.)

§ 41-9-452. Purpose of board; adoption of rules, regulations and bylaws; conduct of annual function to honor sports dignitaries; conduct of surveys and polls; appointment of committees and representatives.

It shall be the function and main purpose of the board to honor those, living or dead, who by achievement or service have made outstanding and lasting contributions to sports in Alabama or elsewhere. The board may adopt such rules, regulations and bylaws as may be needed to carry out its functions. The board may honor Alabama sports dignitaries at an annual function and may pay the actual expenses of celebrities and/or guest speakers who are invited to participate in the ceremonies. It may also conduct surveys and polls and may appoint such committees and representatives as it may determine necessary or desirable. (Acts 1967, No. 225, p. 594, § 3; Acts 1978, No. 667, p. 961.)

§ 41-9-453. Solicitation and acceptance of donations, contributions, etc.; exemption from taxation of property, income, etc., of board and gifts thereto.

The board may solicit and accept donations, contributions and gifts of money and property, and all gifts made to the board shall be exempt from all taxation in Alabama. All property, money, income, resources and activities of the board shall likewise be exempt from taxation. (Acts 1967, No. 225, p. 594, § 4.)

§ 41-9-454. Expenditure of appropriations and other funds.

The board may spend all legislative appropriations made for the use of the board and may expend funds donated or contributed for its support. (Acts 1967, No. 225, p. 594, § 5.)

ARTICLE 17.

MOTOR SPORTS HALL OF FAME COMMISSION.

§ 41-9-470. Created; purpose; location of exhibition facility.

There is hereby created and established a state agency to be known as the motor sports hall of fame commission for the purpose of providing for and participating in the management and control of facilities to house and display such visual exhibits relating to the automobile racing industry and the automobile industry as may be made available by the automobile racing industry, the automobile industry or any other individual, corporation or legal entity. Such facility shall constitute a permanent housing for the exhibit, which shall be open to the general public and shall be located at a place to be designated and made available in Talladega county. (Acts 1975, No. 1137, § 1.)

§ 41-9-471. Composition; appointment, qualifications, terms, compensation and removal of members; filling of vacancies; chairman; annual meetings; quorum; executive committee; adoption of rules and regulations.

The commission created herein shall consist of 18 members, to be appointed by the governor, who shall be bona fide residents and qualified voters of this state, at least six of whom shall be residents of Talladega county. The remaining members of the commission shall be appointed from throughout the state in such manner as to provide general statewide representation on the commission. All members shall be knowledgeable and interested in the automobile racing industry and the automobile industry and in the promotion of interest in such fields. Nine of the original members shall be appointed for terms of four years, and nine members shall be appointed for terms of eight years. All members shall serve until their successors are appointed and qualified, but any member may be removed by the governor for just cause. Vacancies shall be filled in the same manner as original appointments are made. The first chairman of the commission shall be appointed by the governor from among the original appointees. Thereafter, each succeeding chairman shall be selected by the other members of the commission. Members of the commission shall serve without compensation, but shall be entitled to reimbursement for expenses incurred in the performance of the duties of the commission in the amounts provided by law. The commission shall hold at least one annual meeting at the site of the exhibit, and one half of the members shall constitute a quorum for the transaction of any business which may properly come before the commission at any such meeting. The commission shall have the right to adopt such rules and regulations as may be necessary to carry out the effect and purposes of this article and shall be authorized to provide for an executive committee of not fewer than five of its members to whom it may delegate such powers and authority as the commission may deem to be advisable. (Acts 1975, No. 1137, § 2.)

§ 41-9-472. Powers and duties.

The commission shall be authorized:

(1) To investigate and select an available site for housing the exhibits, including the surrounding grounds, in cooperation with the community, taking into consideration all pertinent factors affecting the suitability of such site;

(2) To acquire by rent or lease agreement or otherwise the necessary housing facilities; and to establish, improve and enlarge the available facility, including providing it with necessary equipment, furnishings, landscaping and related facilities, including parking areas and ramps, roadways, sewers, curbs, and gutters;

(3) To enter into such contracts and cooperative agreements with local, state and federal governments, with agencies of such governments, with private individuals, corporations, associations and other organizations as the commission may deem necessary or convenient to carry out the purpose of this article, with such contracts and agreements to include leases to private industry;

(4) To borrow money from private sources or such other source as may be acceptable to the commission under such terms and conditions as may be provided by law; and, in order to provide security for the repayment of any such private loans, the commission shall have the authority to pledge such future revenues from admissions and any other sources as from time to time, be necessary or desirable;

(5) To issue and sell, subject to the approval of the governor, interest-bearing general obligation bonds not in excess of $3,000,000.00 in principal amount, as authorized by constitutional amendment; such bonds shall be general obligations of the state of Alabama, with full faith and credit and taxing power of the state to be pledged to the prompt and faithful payment of the principal of the bonds and the interest thereon. The proceeds from the sale of such bonds shall be used exclusively for the purpose of paying the expenses incurred in the sale and issuance thereof and for the construction, establishment, improvement or enlargement and equipment of building facilities and related grounds including the renewal or replacement of structural parts of such facility, but not including the purchase of the site for such facility;

(6) To issue and sell at any time and from time to time its revenue bonds for the purpose of providing funds to acquire, enlarge, improve, equip and maintain a facility and for the payment of obligations incurred for such purposes. The principal and interest on any such revenue bonds shall be payable solely out of the revenues derived from the project;

(7) To make such contracts in the issuance of its bonds as may seem necessary or desirable to assure their marketability and to provide for their retirement by a pledge of all or any revenue which may come to the commission from the investment of the proceeds of the sale of such bonds or from any other source whatsoever;

(8) To accept public or private gifts, grants and donations;

(9) To acquire property by purchase, lease, gift or license, but not to include the purchase of a site for the facility;

(10) To allocate and expend funds from all donations, income and revenue from any source whatsoever coming into its treasury, for the fulfillment and accomplishment of its duties and responsibilities in such manner as may be necessary and appropriate for the perfection of the purposes of this article;

(11) To sell, convey, transfer, lease or donate any property, franchise, grant, easement, license or lease or interest therein which it may own and to transfer, assign, sell, convey or donate any right, title or interest which it may have in any lease, contract, agreement or license of property;

(12) To employ an executive director and such additional personnel as may be necessary to accomplish the purposes of this article. The executive director and such additional personnel as may be employed by the commission will serve at the pleasure of the commission. The commission shall fix the compensation of the executive director and such additional personnel, and such compensation shall be paid from the funds of the commission. The commission shall designate the duties and authority of the executive director and such additional personnel. The executive director and such additional personnel shall not be subject to the provisions of the state Merit System Act; however, they shall be eligible for participation in the state health insurance plan and benefits as provided in chapter 29 of Title 36 of this Code, and they shall be eligible for participation in the state employees' retirement system law governing counties, cities, towns and other quasi-public organizations of the state; and

(13) To make such rules and regulations as the commission may deem necessary and desirable to provide for the operation, management and control of the facility. (Acts 1975, No. 1137, § 3.)

§ 41-9-473. Form, maturity, sale, etc., of bonds.

All bonds shall be issued, subject to the approval of the governor, in such forms, denominations, series and numbers, may be of such tenor and maturities, may bear such date or dates, may be in registered or bearer form either as to principal or interest or both with rights of conversion into another form, may be payable in such installments and at such place or places, may bear interest at such rate or rates payable and evidenced in such manner and may contain provisions for redemption at the option of the state to be exercised by said commission at such date or dates prior to their maturity and upon payment of such redemption price or prices, all as shall be provided by said commission in the resolution or resolutions whereunder the bonds are authorized to be issued. The principal of each series of bonds shall mature in annual installments in such amounts as shall be specified in the resolution or resolutions of the said commission under which they are issued, the first of which installments shall mature not later than one year after the date of the bonds of such series, and the last of which installments shall mature not later than 20 years after the date of the bonds of the same series. When each series of bonds is issued, the maturities of the bonds of that series shall, to such extent as may be practicable, be so arranged that during each then succeeding fiscal year of the state the aggregate installments of principal and interest that will mature on all bonds that will be outstanding under this article, immediately following the issuance of the bonds of that series, will be substantially equal; provided, that the determination by the said commission that the requirements of this sentence have been complied with shall be conclusive of such compliance, and the purchasers of the bonds with respect to such determination is made and all subsequent holders thereof shall be fully protected thereby. None of the bonds shall be sold for less than face value plus accrued interest thereon to the date of delivery. All of the bonds shall be sold only at public sale or sales, either on sealed bids or at public auction, after such advertisement as may be prescribed by said commission, to the bidder whose bid reflects the lowest net interest cost to the state computed to the respective maturities of the bonds sold; provided, that if no bid deemed acceptable by said commission is received, all bids may be rejected. The bonds shall be signed in the name of the state by the governor and countersigned by the chairman of the commission, and the great seal of the state of Alabama or a facsimile thereof shall be impressed, printed or otherwise reproduced thereon and shall be attested by the signature of the secretary of state; provided, that facsimile signatures of any one or any two, but not all, of said officers may be reproduced on such bonds in lieu of their manually signing the same. Coupons attached to the bonds and representing installments of interest thereon shall be signed by the facsimile signature of the state treasurer, which facsimile signature is hereby adopted as due and sufficient authentication of said coupons. (Acts 1975, No. 1137, § 4.)

§ 41-9-474. Exemptions from taxation.

The commission, its property and income and all bonds issued by the commission, the income from such bonds or from the investment of such income, and all conveyances, leases, mortgages and deeds of trust by or to the commission shall be exempt from all taxation in the state of Alabama. (Acts 1975, No. 1137, § 5.)

§ 41-9-475. Bonds not obligation of state, counties or municipalities.

All revenue bonds issued by the commission shall be solely and exclusively the obligations of the commission and shall not create an obligation or debt of the state or any county or of any municipality within the state. (Acts 1975, No. 1137, § 6.)

§ 41-9-476. Pledge of revenues for payment of bonds.

Any general obligation bonds shall also be payable from and secured by a pledge of the revenues and income of the commission remaining after the payment of the reasonable and necessary expenses of operating and maintaining the facilities to be constructed by the commission. (Acts 1975, No. 1137, § 7.)

§ 41-9-477. Books and records; audits.

It shall be the duty of the commission to maintain at all times accurate records and books of account covering revenues and expenditures, which shall be subject to the audit of the department of examiners of public accounts. (Acts 1975, No. 1137, § 8.)

§ 41-9-478. Liberal construction of article; additional powers.

(a) The provisions of this article shall be construed liberally, it being the purpose to provide in this state appropriate housing facilities for displaying to the general public exhibits relating to the automobile racing industry and the automobile industry and providing for the management and control of the displays by such means as may be feasible and agreed upon.

(b) In view of the unique character and complexity of the duties and responsibilities imposed on the commission by this article, it is hereby specifically provided that the commission shall have, in addition to the power and authority enumerated in section 41-9-472, the right, power and authority to:

(1) Develop and institute a program of promotion and advertising of the exhibits and facilities provided for by this article, said program of promotion and advertising to be conducted by the commission both within and without the state in such manner and to such extent as may be deemed economically advisable and appropriate by the commission;

(2) Purchase and acquire items of tangible personal property on a competitive bid basis in the manner prescribed by law for the purchase of such items by state trade schools, state junior colleges, state colleges and universities under the supervision and control of the state board of education, the city and county boards of education, and the county boards of revenue or other similar county governing bodies and the governing bodies of the municipalities of the state and the governing boards of instrumentalities of counties and municipalities under article 3 of chapter 16 of this title; and

(3) Itself operate, or in its discretion enter into lease agreement with a person or agency of its choosing to operate, all concessions located in or on the grounds and facilities operated by the commission, any such lease agreement to be so designated as to provide maximum services and convenience to the patrons of the exhibit center and to provide reasonable revenue to the commission. (Acts 1975, No. 1137, § 9.)

ARTICLE 18.

BEAUTIFICATION BOARD.

§ 41-9-490. Creation; composition.

There is hereby created and established in the state of Alabama a board to be known as the beautification board of the state of Alabama, hereinafter referred to as the board, to be composed of 25 members. (Acts 1969, No. 1115, p. 2050, § 1.)

§ 41-9-491. Appointment, terms of office and qualifications generally of members.

Members of the board shall be appointed by the governor to serve as follows:

(1) Eight members initially appointed shall be designated to serve until October 1, 1969, and until their successors are elected and qualified. The members appointed under this subdivision shall be one from each congressional district of the state of Alabama. No member shall be eligible to serve under this subdivision at any time he or she ceases to be a resident citizen of the congressional district for which he or she was initially appointed.

(2) Nine members with the qualifications described in this subdivision shall be appointed by the governor to serve until October 1, 1970, and until their successors are elected and qualified. One member appointed under this subdivision shall be a person primarily engaged in the practice of architecture in the state of Alabama, who shall hold a state registration for the practice of architecture within the state. One member appointed under this subdivision shall be a person primarily engaged in the wholesale or retail nursery business within the state of Alabama, either as owner or employee. One member appointed under this subdivision shall be a person primarily engaged within the state of Alabama in the practice of law. One member appointed under this subdivision shall be a person primarily engaged either as owner or manager in the home-building trade. One member appointed under this subdivision shall be a person primarily engaged as owner or manager of a large commercial contractor's firm holding a commercial contractor's license from the state of Alabama. One member appointed under this subdivision shall be a person primarily engaged either as owner or manager within the state of Alabama in the business of constructing streets and highways and holding a qualified contractor's license within the state of Alabama for that purpose. One member appointed under this subdivision shall be a person primarily engaged within the state of Alabama as a landscape architect. One member appointed under this subdivision shall be a person primarily engaged as a municipal planner within the state of Alabama.

(3) Eight members initially appointed shall be designated by the governor to serve until October 1, 1971, and until their successors are elected and qualified. At least one of the persons appointed by the governor under this subdivision shall be a person who at the time of his or her appointment is active as an officer or committee chairman in a civic organization engaged in the promotion of beautification projects throughout the state. At least one of the members serving under this subdivision shall be a person who at the time of his or her appointment is actively engaged as an officer or committee member of a civic organization within the state having a continuing project promoting beautification in rural and agricultural areas of the state. The remainder of members serving under this subdivision shall be appointed by the governor without further qualifications, except that all shall be resident citizens of the state of Alabama.

(4) Thereafter all members shall be appointed by the governor to serve for a term of three years. (Acts 1969, No. 1115, p. 2050, § 2.)

§ 41-9-492. Members to be resident citizens of state.

No person shall be eligible to serve on the board who is not a bona fide resident citizen of the state of Alabama. (Acts 1969, No. 1115, p. 2050, § 3.)

§ 41-9-493. Vacancies.

Vacancies on the board shall be filled by appointment in the same manner and on the same conditions provided for initial members. Appointments to fill vacancies shall be for the unexpired terms. An appointee shall cease to be a member upon resignation to the governor, upon ceasing to be a resident of the state of Alabama and, if serving from a geographical area, upon ceasing to be a resident of the geographical area from which he or she was appointed or upon ceasing to be engaged in the activity, business or profession where the same is made a qualification for membership or upon two-thirds vote of the board for failure to attend meetings. (Acts 1969, No. 1115, p. 2050, § 4.)

§ 41-9-494. Meetings generally; officers; quorum; maintenance and examination of record of proceedings of board; meetings of board to be open to public.

The board shall hold regular meetings at such time and place within the state of Alabama as it may from time to time determine; provided, however, that the board shall hold at least one regular or one special meeting every 90 days.

At the first meeting of the board, the members thereof shall elect one of their number as chairman and one of their number as secretary. Thereafter, the committee shall annually elect from among its number a chairman and secretary and such other officers as it may from time to time determine necessary and appropriate for the conduct of board proceedings. Vacancies in the office of chairman and secretary and in other offices as provided in this section shall be filled by the board from among the membership of the board for the unexpired term. The chairman of the board or any eight members of the board may call a meeting at any time he or they consider that business demands that a meeting should be held. The chairman and any 12 members of the board shall constitute a quorum for the conduct of business at all regular or special meetings.

A thorough record of all meetings of the board shall be kept by the secretary. On the call of any member, the vote upon any pending question shall be taken by ayes and nays, and the same shall be entered on the record. A record of the proceedings of the board shall be open to the governor and to the public at all reasonable times. All meetings of the board shall be open to the public. (Acts 1969, No. 1115, p. 2050, § 5.)

§ 41-9-495. Compensation and expenses of members.

The members of the board shall serve without compensation but may be reimbursed for the expenses incurred in the performance of their duty, which expenses shall be paid in the amounts provided for in article 2 of chapter 7 of Title 36 of this Code; provided, that such members' expenses shall be limited to such amount as may be appropriated for that purpose. (Acts 1969, No. 1115, p. 2050, § 6.)

§ 41-9-496. Powers and duties of board generally.

The board shall have the following powers and duties:

(1) To study the cause of unsightly and unsanitary conditions within the state of Alabama and within any county or municipality thereof. Such studies shall include, but shall not be limited to, the following: litter and other unsanitary conditions over and along public streets and highways within the state of Alabama; unsanitary and unsightly conditions existing or which may hereafter exist in and around public buildings, public parks and other public places within the state of Alabama; unsightly and unsanitary conditions in and around public alleys and easements of the state or of any subdivision thereof; and rubbish, trash and waste material on and around private premises within the state of Alabama;

(2) To study the laws of the state of Alabama, the ordinances of the various municipal corporations of the state of Alabama and the rules and regulations of the various boards and agencies of the state of Alabama as the same pertains to litter, rubbish, waste and other unsightly and unsanitary conditions;

(3) To conduct or cause to be conducted surveys, routine observations and inspections for the purpose of finding and identifying the causes and sources of unsightly and unsanitary conditions within the state;

(4) To study and report from time to time all such matters and things as may be referred to them by the governor, the legislature or any other board, agency or political subdivision of the state;

(5) To encourage through mass media and through the various departments and agencies of the state of Alabama and through the various civic and governmental organizations of the state of Alabama the initiation and execution by governmental agencies, civic clubs and associations, merchants and property owners' associations of programs to enhance the cleanliness and beautification of the state of Alabama and its environs;

(6) To counsel with governmental agencies and private individuals when requested to do so on matters and things concerning the cleanliness and beautification of the state of Alabama and its environs;

(7) To counsel with nurseries, garden shops, landscaping establishments, garden clubs and private developers on a voluntary basis for the purpose of encouraging a comprehensive, coordinated program for beautification of private and public premises within the state of Alabama;

(8) To sponsor contests, offer prizes and confer awards to individuals and institutions for outstanding contributions to beautification in the state of Alabama; and

(9) To perform such other and additional duties as the legislature and the governor may from time to time direct. (Acts 1969, No. 1115, p. 2050, § 8.)

§ 41-9-497. Boards, commissions, etc., of state and political subdivisions to cooperate with board; board to make recommendations, criticisms and reports to governor and to boards, commissions, etc.

(a) Every board, commission and department of the state of Alabama, or any political subdivision thereof, is hereby authorized and directed to cooperate with the beautification board of the state of Alabama in promoting the orderly and attractive operation of premises and facilities under its jurisdiction and control and in providing for the beautification of the state as a whole.

(b) The beautification board shall have the right and it shall be its duty to make recommendations, criticisms and reports to the governor and to boards, commissions and agencies affected concerning beautification within the state. (Acts 1969, No. 1115, p. 2050, § 9.)

§ 41-9-498. Appropriations.

The legislature shall appropriate such funds from the general funds of the state of Alabama which they may deem necessary for the reasonable and necessary expenses of the board. (Acts 1969, No. 1115, p. 2050, § 7.)

ARTICLE 19.

STATE CAPITOL ADVISORY COMMITTEE.

§ 41-9-510. Creation; composition; qualifications, appointment, terms of office, compensation, etc., of members.

There is hereby created and established a committee to be known as the state Capitol advisory committee. Such committee shall be composed of eight members, including two ex officio members, who shall be the director of the technical staff of the Alabama building commission and the director of the department of archives and history, one member shall be appointed by the Mobile historic development commission, one shall be appointed by the Montgomery historic development commission, and one member shall be appointed by the Huntsville historic preservation commission. The governor shall appoint three members from the state at large to serve for terms of two, three and four years respectively. Such members shall reside in divergent areas of the state and in some other area other than those areas in which the other appointed members reside. The three members representative of the historical commissions in the cities of Mobile, Montgomery and Huntsville shall draw lots to determine which of such members shall serve for terms of two, three or four years. Thereafter all appointed members of the committee shall serve for terms of four years each, and the ex officio members shall serve throughout their terms of office. Members of the committee shall serve without compensation for their services and without reimbursement for expenses incurred. (Acts 1969, No. 1148, p. 2153, § 1; Acts 1976, No. 634, p. 881, § 4.)

Code commissioner's note. — As Acts 1976, No. 634, p. 881, § 4 redesignated the state Capitol preservation commission as the state Capitol advisory committee, "state Capitol advisory committee" and "committee" have been substituted for "state Capitol preservation commission" and "commission" wherever such terms appear in this section.

§ 41-9-511. Meetings; officers.

The committee shall meet at the state Capitol building at least twice each year, one of which said meetings shall be designated as the annual meeting. The committee at its organizational meeting shall elect a chairman and secretary. Said officers shall serve terms of one year each and until their successors are elected and take office. (Acts 1969, No. 1148, p. 2153, § 3; Acts 1976, No. 634, p. 881, § 4.)

Code commissioner's note. — As Acts 1976, No. 634, p. 881, § 4 redesignated the state Capitol preservation commission as the state Capitol advisory committee, "committee" has been substituted for "commission" wherever such term appears in this section.

§ 41-9-512. Transferred.

Code commissioner's note. — As Acts 1976, No. 634, p. 881, redesignated the state Capitol preservation commission as the state Capitol advisory committee and provided that it should advise the Alabama historical commission, which was designated as the agency responsible for the restoration and preservation of the state Capitol, as to such restoration and preservation, the powers granted by this section to the former state Capitol preservation commission with respect to the Capitol and building and grounds are deemed to now be vested in the Alabama historical commission. Therefore, the provisions of this section have been transferred and incorporated in § 41-9-261, which provides for the powers and duties of the Alabama historical commission with respect to the restoration and preservation of the state Capitol.

§ 41-9-513. Duties.

The committee shall advise the Alabama historical commission regarding the restoration and preservation of the state Capitol. (Acts 1976, No. 634, p. 881, § 4.)

ARTICLE 20.

GOVERNOR'S MANSION ADVISORY BOARD.

§ 41-9-530. Creation; composition; appointment and terms of office of members; election of chairman and secretary; members to serve without compensation.

There is hereby created the governor's mansion advisory board consisting of eight members, four of whom, the wife of the governor, the director of the technical staff of the Alabama building commission, the executive director of the Alabama historical commission and the director of the department of archives and history shall be ex officio members. One member shall be appointed by the speaker of the house of representatives; one member shall be appointed by the lieutenant governor, and two members shall be appointed by the governor, one for two years and one for four years. Thereafter each member appointed by the governor shall serve for four years. The term of each member appointed by the governor shall commence on July 1 of the year in which he is appointed, and each shall serve until his successor is appointed and qualified. The members appointed by the speaker of the house of representatives and the lieutenant governor shall be appointed after October 1, 1971, and thereafter at each organizational session of the legislature. The advisory board shall elect a chairman and a secretary. All members of the advisory board shall serve without compensation. (Acts 1971, No. 2329, p. 3756, § 1.)

§ 41-9-531. Purpose of board.

The purpose of the advisory board shall be:

(1) To supervise the maintenance of the governor's mansion and surrounding grounds;

(2) To approve alterations in the existing structure;

(3) To insure that the private quarters of the governor are in good condition;

(4) To acquire and maintain suitable furnishings for the reception rooms;

(5) To improve the furnishings of the governor's mansion by acquiring gifts of furniture, objets d'art and articles which may have historical value relating to the governors of Alabama and by purchasing the same;

(6) To receive and expend appropriations from the legislature in carrying out the purposes of this article; and

(7) To keep a complete list of all gifts and articles received. (Acts 1971, No. 2329, p. 3756, § 2.)

§ 41-9-532. Receipt of gifts, contributions, etc., by board and vesting of title thereto; expenditure of funds; maintenance of account of receipts and expenditures and inventory of gifts.

The advisory board is hereby empowered on behalf of the state of Alabama to receive appropriations, gifts, contributions of money and objets d'art consistent with the purpose for which the advisory board is created. Title to all gifts, articles and moneys received by the advisory board shall be vested in the state of Alabama and shall remain in the custody and control of the advisory board. The advisory board is authorized to accept loans of furniture and other objects as in its discretion it deems suitable.

The advisory board shall be empowered to expend such funds as it may receive under this article in such manner as it deems appropriate and consistent with the purposes set forth herein.

The advisory board shall keep an account of all receipts and expenditures as well as an inventory of gifts. (Acts 1971, No. 2329, p. 3756, § 3.)

ARTICLE 21.

WOMEN'S HALL OF FAME.

§ 41-9-550. Creation; composition; appointment; qualifications of members; meetings; quorum; compensation; expenses; terms of office; chairman and executive secretary of board; vacancies on board.

There shall be created and established as herein provided a board to be designated and known as the Alabama women's hall of fame. The board shall be composed of 11 members with at least one member chosen from each of the following fields: politics, art, education, business, law, community service, medicine, religion and science. The initial members of the board shall be appointed by the governor. In addition, the governor of the state of Alabama and the president of Judson College shall serve as voting members of the board. The executive secretary, shall serve as a nonvoting member of the board. The board shall meet semiannually and at such other times as its rules and bylaws may prescribe. A quorum of seven members of the board must be present for business to be conducted. The members of the board shall not be compensated for their services, but each member shall be entitled to reimbursement for expenses incurred in attending board meetings. Members of the board shall serve for terms of three years. The board will fill vacancies as they occur and shall have full and final right of choosing succeeding members. The chairman shall be elected annually. The executive secretary shall serve at the pleasure of the board. (Acts 1975, No. 1061, § 1.)

Cross references. — As to travel expenses, see § 36-7-20 et seq.

§ 41-9-551. Location and offices of board and hall of fame.

The board shall be domiciled at Judson College, Marion, Perry county, where it shall maintain such halls, rooms or quarters as may be considered suitable and appropriate for conducting its affairs. Judson College shall cause to be set apart a section thereof to be used by the board for display of plaques, busts, books, papers, pictures and other memorabilia relating to women of achievement. (Acts 1975, No. 1061, § 2.)

§ 41-9-552. Functions and purposes of board; election and installation of members of hall.

It shall be the function and main purpose of the board to honor those women of Alabama who have rendered outstanding services or have won fame on account of their achievements. It shall elect to the Alabama women's hall of fame such women who are nominated for election and who receive a unanimous vote of the board of directors with at least a quorum of the board present and voting unanimously. The installation of each elected member of the Alabama women's hall of fame may occur on a separate occasion so as to focus attention on the individual contribution of each honoree. No more than two new members of the hall shall be selected each year, and these new members must be deceased at the time of their selection. Nominations shall be received from the public. (Acts 1975, No. 1061, § 3.)

§ 41-9-553. Appropriations to board.

The board shall receive an annual appropriation not to exceed $6,000.00, which shall be fixed by the legislature during each regular session thereof. The appropriation provided shall be used by the board to pay for stationery, plaques, display cases, installation programs, administrative functions and such other necessary or appropriate expenses incurred in carrying out the purposes of the board. (Acts 1975, No. 1061, § 4.)

§ 41-9-554. Donations, gifts, etc.

The board may solicit and accept donations, contributions and gifts of money and property, and all gifts made to the board shall be exempt from taxation in Alabama. All property, money, income, resources and activities of the board shall likewise be exempt from taxation. (Acts 1975, No. 1061, § 6.)

ARTICLE 22.

CRIMINAL JUSTICE ADVISORY COMMISSION.

§ 41-9-570. Created; composition.

There is hereby created the Alabama criminal justice advisory commission, hereinafter referred to as the commission, to be composed of the following members: The commissioner of the board of corrections; the chairman of the board of pardons and paroles; the commissioner of mental health; the director of the department of public safety; the attorney general; the chief justice of the Alabama supreme court; the head of the Alabama law enforcement planning agency; the superintendent of education; the president of the fraternal order of police; the director of the Alabama law institute; the chairman of the Alabama bar association committee on correctional institutions and procedures; the finance director of the state of Alabama; the governor; the lieutenant governor; the speaker of the house of representatives; the director of the department of youth services; the chairmen of the judiciary committees of the house of representatives and senate of the state of Alabama; or a designated representative of each of the above. In addition, the president of the Alabama district attorneys' association shall be a member of the commission. In addition, the members of any joint interim committee of the legislature created by Act 12, S.J.R. 9, Organizational Session 1975 to study the criminal justice system shall be members of the commission until January 1, 1979. Thereafter, the members of any joint interim committee of the legislature created to study the criminal justice system shall be members of the commission. (Acts 1975, No. 1201, § 1.)

Code commissioner's note. — Acts 1979, No. 79-426, p. 667, effective October 1, 1979, abolished the board of corrections and vested all its rights, duties, power, property, etc., in the governor, and authorized him to exercise such functions and duties himself or through designated administrators. See §§ 14-1-15 through 14-1-17, and also Acts 1979, No. 79-154, p. 253.

§ 41-9-571. Meetings; officers.

The commission shall meet in the Capitol on the call of the governor and shall elect one of its members as chairman and one of its members as vice-chairman and thereafter shall meet from time to time on call of the chairman; except, that the commission shall meet at least twice yearly for the conduct of its business. (Acts 1975, No. 1201, § 2.)

§ 41-9-572. Function.

It shall be the function of the commission to encourage cooperation among its members in order to improve the operations of the criminal justice system. (Acts 1975, No. 1201, § 3.)

§ 41-9-573. Reports.

The commission shall report to the governor and to the legislature within 15 days after the convening of each regular session of the legislature and at such other times as it deems appropriate. (Acts 1975, No. 1201, § 4.)

§ 41-9-574. Expenses.

Members of the commission shall be reimbursed for actual expenses for mileage, meals and lodging while attending meetings of the commission. (Acts 1975, No. 1201, § 5.)

ARTICLE 23.

CRIMINAL JUSTICE INFORMATION
CENTER COMMISSION.

Division 1.

General Provisions.

§ 41-9-590. Definitions.

When used in this article, the following terms shall have the following meanings, respectively, unless the context clearly indicates a different meaning:

(1) CRIMINAL JUSTICE AGENCIES. Such term shall include those public agencies at all levels of government which perform as their principal function activities or planning for such activities relating to the identification, apprehension, prosecution, adjudication or rehabilitation of civil, traffic and criminal offenders.

(2) OFFENSE. Any act which is a felony or is a misdemeanor as described in section 41-9-622.

(3) CRIMINAL JUSTICE INFORMATION SYSTEM and SYSTEM. Such terms shall include that portion of those public agencies, procedures, mechanisms, media and criminal justice information center forms as well as the information itself involved in the origination, transmittal, storage, retrieval, analysis and dissemination of information related to reported offenses, offenders and actions related to such events or persons required to be reported to and received by, as well as stored, analyzed and disseminated by the Alabama criminal justice information center commission through the center.

(4) COMMISSION. The Alabama criminal justice information center commission.

(5) ACJICC. The Alabama criminal justice information center commission.

(6) ACJIC. The Alabama criminal justice information center.

(7) CENTER. The Alabama criminal justice information center.

(8) DIRECTOR. The director of the Alabama criminal justice information center. (Acts 1975, No. 872, § 1.)

§ 41-9-591. Creation; functions generally; responsibility for development, administration, etc., of Alabama criminal justice information center.

There is hereby created and established an Alabama criminal justice information center commission, which shall establish, develop and continue to operate a center and system for the interstate and intrastate accumulation, storage, retrieval, analysis and dissemination of vital information relating to certain crimes, criminals and criminal activity to be known as the Alabama criminal justice information center.

Central responsibility for the development, maintenance, operation and administration of the Alabama criminal justice information center shall be vested with the director of the ACJIC under the supervision of the Alabama criminal justice information center commission. (Acts 1975, No. 872, § 2.)

§ 41-9-592. Composition of commission; terms of service of members of commission.

The commission shall be composed of two sections.

The voting section will include: the attorney general, the chairman of the board of pardons and paroles, the commissioner of the board of corrections, the president of the Alabama sheriffs' association, the director of the department of public safety, the president of the Alabama association of chiefs of police, the director of the Alabama law enforcement planning agency, the president of the district attorney's association, the president of the circuit clerks' association, the chief justice of the Alabama supreme court, the president of the Alabama association of intermediate court judges, the president of the circuit judges' association, the governor's coordinator of Alabama highway and traffic safety and the director of the data systems management division of the Alabama department of finance.

The advisory section will include: the presiding officer of the Alabama senate, the speaker of the Alabama house of representatives, the president of the association of county commissions of Alabama, the president of the Alabama league of municipalities, the administrative director of the courts and a citizen of the state of Alabama, to be appointed by the governor. The member shall have authority to select a designee based upon qualifications and with a view of continuity of representation and attendance at the commission meetings.

No person or individual shall continue to serve on the commission when he no longer officially represents the function or serves in the capacity enumerated in this section as a member to which he was elected or appointed. (Acts 1975, No. 872, § 3.)

Code commissioner's note. — Acts 1979, No. 79-426, p. 667, effective October 1, 1979, abolished the board of corrections and vested all its rights, duties, power, property, etc., in the governor, and authorized him to exercise such functions and duties himself or through designated administrators. See §§ 14-1-15 through 14-1-17, and also Acts 1979, No. 79-154.

§ 41-9-593. Chairman and vice-chairman; meetings; quorum; record of transactions discussed or voted upon; compensation of members of commission.

The commission shall, upon its first meeting, elect from its membership a chairman and a vice-chairman who shall serve for a period of one year. The vice-chairman shall act in the place of the chairman in his absence or disability.

The commission shall meet at such times as designated by the commission or by the chairman at the state capital or at other places as is deemed necessary or convenient, but the chairman of the commission must call a meeting four times a year at the state capital or main location of the ACJIC in the months of January, April, July and October. The chairman of the commission may also call a special meeting of the commission at any time he deems it advisable or necessary. A quorum shall be a simple majority of the voting commission membership or their designees and all matters coming before the commission shall be voted on by the commission.

The commission will keep or cause to be kept a record of all transactions discussed or voted on by the commission.

Members of the commission and their designees shall serve without compensation; except, that payment of their expenses may be paid in accordance with the applicable state travel regulations. (Acts 1975, No. 872, § 4.)

Cross references. — As to travel expenses, see § 36-7-20 et seq.

§ 41-9-594. Establishment of rules, regulations and policies by commission generally; establishment of policies, safeguards, etc., as to collection, use, dissemination, etc., of criminal justice information; establishment, etc., of privacy and security committee.

The commission shall establish its own rules, regulations and policies for the performance of the responsibilities charged to it in this article.

The commission shall ensure that the information obtained under authority of this article shall be restricted to the items germane to the implementation of this article and shall ensure that the Alabama criminal justice information center is administered so as not to accumulate any information or distribute any information that is not required by this article. The commission shall ensure that adequate safeguards are incorporated so that data available through this system is used only by properly authorized persons and agencies.

The commission shall appoint a privacy and security committee from the membership of the commission who are elected officials, consisting of a chairman and three members, to study the privacy and security implications of criminal justice information and to formulate policy recommendations for consideration by the commission concerning the collection, storage, dissemination or usage of criminal justice information. The commission may establish other policies and promulgate such regulations that provide for the efficient and effective use and operation of the Alabama criminal justice information center under the limitations imposed by the terms of this article. (Acts 1975, No. 872, § 5.)

§ 41-9-595. Director and deputy director of criminal justice information center.

The commission shall appoint a director and a deputy director for the Alabama criminal justice information center who shall be responsible for the development, maintenance and operation of the ACJIC as required by the terms of this article and the implementation and operation of policies, programs and procedures established by the commission under the limitations of this article. The qualifications of the director and deputy director shall be determined by the state personnel department. (Acts 1975, No. 872, § 6.)

§ 41-9-596. Maintenance of staff and support services for center.

The director shall maintain the necessary staff along with support services necessary to enable the effective and efficient performance of the duties and responsibilities ascribed to the ACJIC in this article under the supervision of the commission. (Acts 1975, No. 872, § 7.)

§ 41-9-597. Applicability of rules and regulations of state personnel merit system to staff and personnel employed by commission; employment conditions, etc., of employees of agencies or institutions transferred to center or commission.

The staff and personnel employed by the commission for the development and operation of the center and system shall be governed by the personnel merit system rules and regulations of the state personnel department.

Employees of agencies or institutions which are transferred to the center or commission under the provisions of this article shall remain in their respective employments and shall be considered to meet the requirements of the department in terms of training and experience, but nothing in this section shall be construed to prevent or preclude the removal of an employee for cause in the manner provided by law. Such employees shall continue to enjoy employment conditions, including, but not limited to, salary range and advancement at a level no less than those enjoyed prior to transfer to the center or commission. All time accumulated while engaged in such prior employment shall be credited toward all privileges enjoyed under state merit employment. (Acts 1975, No. 872, § 8.)

§ 41-9-598. Appeals from rules and regulations promulgated by commission.

The process for appeals by an individual or governmental body of any rules and regulations promulgated by the commission shall first be to the commission proper. The appellant may present his argument at a regular meeting of the commission requesting the alteration or suggesting the nonapplicability of a particular rule and/or regulation. If the appellant is not satisfied by the action of the commission, then an appeal may be made to the circuit court in Montgomery county. (Acts 1975, No. 872, § 42.)

§ 41-9-599. Annual request for funds and budget; appropriations.

Annually the commission shall present to the governor a request for funds based on projected needs for criminal justice information systems in the state, together with a budget showing proposed expenditures, and the governor may include in his appropriation bill a request for funds to meet the financial needs of the commission. (Acts 1975, No. 872, § 43.)

§ 41-9-600. Failure of officer or official to make report or do act required by article.

Any officer or official mentioned in this article who neglects or refuses to make any report or to do any act required in this article shall be subject to prosecution for a misdemeanor and, if found guilty, may be fined not less than $100.00 nor more than $10,000.00 and may be confined in a county jail for not more than one year. He shall also be subject to prosecution for nonfeasance and, if found guilty, shall be subject to removal from office therefor. (Acts 1975, No. 872, § 37.)

§ 41-9-601. Obtaining, etc., of criminal offender record information under false pretenses, falsification of information, etc.

Any person who willfully requests, obtains or seeks to obtain criminal offender record information under false pretenses or who willfully communicates or seeks to communicate criminal offender record information to any agency or person except in accordance with this article, or any member, officer, employee or agent of the ACJICC, the ACJIC or any participating agency who willfully falsifies criminal offender record information or any records relating thereto shall, for each offense, be fined not less than $5,000.00 nor more than $10,000.00 or imprisoned in the state penitentiary for not more than five years or both. (Acts 1975, No. 872, § 35.)

§ 41-9-602. Communication, etc., of criminal offender record information in violation of article.

Any person who knowingly communicates or seeks to communicate criminal offender record information, except in accordance with this article, shall, upon conviction, be guilty of a misdemeanor and, for each such offense, may be fined not less than $500.00 nor more than $10,000.00 or imprisoned for not less than 30 days nor more than one year or both. (Acts 1975, No. 872, § 36.)

§ 41-9-603. Effect of article upon other provisions of law, etc.

(a) In the event of conflict, this article shall, to the extent of the conflict, supersede all conflicting parts of existing statutes which regulate, control or otherwise relate, directly or by implication, to the collection, storage and dissemination or usage of fingerprint identification, offender criminal history, uniform crime reporting and criminal justice activity data records or any conflicting parts of existing statutes which relate, directly or by implication, to any other provisions of this article.

(b) The provisions of this article shall not alter, amend or supersede the statutes and rules of law governing the collection, storage, dissemination or usage of records concerning individual juvenile offenders in which they are individually identified by name or other means until such time as the Alabama legislature provides legislation permitting the collection, storage, dissemination or usage of records concerning individual juvenile offenders.

(c) All laws or parts of laws which conflict with this article are hereby repealed. No part of this article shall violate provisions of article 8 of chapter 4 of Title 41 of this Code, Article VI of the Constitution of Alabama of 1901 or chapter 1 of Title 44 of this Code. (Acts 1975, No. 872, §§ 38, 39, 41.)

Division 2.

Collection, Dissemination, etc., of Criminal Data.

Cross references. — For provisions authorizing corporations which operate, construct or maintain nuclear powered electric generating facilities to conduct inquiries into the criminal records of any employees, see §§ 22-14-30 through 22-14-35.

§ 41-9-620. Commission to provide for uniform crime reporting system.

The commission shall provide for a uniform crime reporting system for the periodic collection and analysis of crimes reported to any and all criminal justice agencies within the state. The collection of said data and the time for submission of said data shall be subject to the commission's regulation-making authority. (Acts 1975, No. 872, § 9.)

§ 41-9-621. Powers and duties of commission as to collection, dissemination, etc., of crime and offender data, etc., generally.

The commission, acting through the director of the Alabama criminal justice information center, shall:

(1) Develop, operate and maintain an information system which will support the collection, storage, retrieval, analysis and dissemination of all crime and offender data described in this article consistent with those principles of scope, security and responsiveness prescribed by this article;

(2) Cooperate with all criminal justice agencies within the state in providing those forms, procedures, standards and related training assistance necessary for the uniform operation of the statewide ACJIC crime reporting and criminal justice information system;

(3) Offer assistance and, when practicable, instruction to all criminal justice agencies in establishing efficient systems for information management;

(4) Compile statistics on the nature and extent of crime in Alabama and compile data for planning and operating criminal justice agencies; provided, that such statistics shall not identify persons. The commission shall make available all such statistical information obtained to the governor, the legislature, the judiciary and any such other governmental agencies whose primary responsibilities include the planning, development or execution of crime reduction programs. Access to such information by such governmental agencies shall be on an individual written request basis or in accordance

with the approved operational procedure, wherein must be demonstrated a need to know, the intent of any analyses and dissemination of such analyses, and shall be subject to any security provisions deemed necessary by the commission;

(5) Periodically publish statistics, no less frequently than annually, that do not identify persons and report such information to the chief executive officers of the agencies and branches of government concerned; such information shall accurately reflect the level and nature of crime in this state and the general operation of the agencies within the criminal justice system;

(6) Make available, upon request, to all criminal justice agencies in this state, to all federal criminal justice and criminal identification agencies and to state criminal justice and criminal identification agencies in other states any information in the files of the ACJIC which will aid these agencies in crime fighting; for this purpose the ACJIC shall operate 24 hours per day, seven days per week;

(7) Cooperate with other agencies of this state, the crime information agencies of other states and the uniform crime reports and national crime information center systems of the federal bureau of investigation or any entity designated by the federal government as the central clearinghouse for criminal justice information systems in developing and conducting an interstate, national and international system of criminal identification, records and statistics;

(8) Provide the administrative mechanisms and procedures necessary to respond to those individuals who file requests to view their own records as provided for elsewhere in this article and to cooperate in the correction of the central ACJIC records and those of contributing agencies when their accuracy has been successfully challenged either through the related contributing agencies or by court order issued on behalf of the individual; and

(9) Institute the necessary measures in the design, implementation and continued operation of the criminal justice information system to ensure the privacy and security of the system. Such security measures must meet standards to be set by the commission as well as those set by the nationally operated systems for interstate sharing of such information. (Acts 1975, No. 872, § 10.)

§ 41-9-622. Report, collection, dissemination, etc., of data pertaining to persons arrested or convicted of felonies or certain misdemeanors generally.

The commission is authorized to obtain, compare, file, analyze and disseminate, and all state, county and municipal criminal justice agencies are required to report fingerprints, descriptions, photographs and any other pertinent identifying and historical criminal data on persons who have been or are hereafter arrested or convicted in this state or any state for an offense which is a felony or an offense which is a misdemeanor escalating to a felony involving, but not limited to: possession of burglary tools or unlawful entry; engaging in unlawful commercial gambling; dealing in gambling; dealing in gambling devices; contributing to the delinquency of a child; robbery, larceny or dealing in stolen property; possession of controlled substances and illegal drugs, including marijuana; firearms; dangerous weapons; explosives; pandering; prostitution; rape; sex offenses, where minors or adults are victims; misrepresentation; fraud; and worthless checks. (Acts 1975, No. 872, § 11.)

§ 41-9-623. Submission to department of public safety by criminal justice agencies of fingerprints, photographs, etc., of persons arrested for felonies and misdemeanors described in section 41-9-622; duty of sheriffs, parole and probation officers, etc., to furnish other data to center.

All criminal justice agencies within the state shall submit to the ACJIC, by forwarding to the Alabama department of public safety, fingerprints, descriptions, photographs, when specifically requested, and other identifying data on persons who have been lawfully arrested in this state for all felonies and certain misdemeanors described in section 41-9-622.

It shall be the duty of all chiefs of police, sheriffs, prosecuting attorneys, parole and probation officers, wardens or other persons in charge of correctional or detention institutions in this state to furnish the ACJIC with any other data deemed necessary by the commission to carry out its responsibilities under this article. (Acts 1975, No. 872, § 12.)

§ 41-9-624. Determination by commission as to criminal record of person arrested and notification of requesting agency or arresting officer.

The commission is authorized to compare all fingerprints and other identifying data received with information already on file, to ascertain whether or not a criminal record is found for that person and at once to inform the requesting agency or arresting officer of such facts. (Acts 1975, No. 872, § 15.)

§ 41-9-625. Obtaining by law enforcement and correction agencies of fingerprints, photographs, etc., of persons arrested as fugitives from justice, unidentified human corpses, etc.; procedure where persons arrested released without charge or cleared of offense.

All persons in this state in charge of law enforcement and correction agencies shall obtain or cause to be obtained the fingerprints according to the fingerprint system of identification established by the commission, full face and profile photographs, if photo equipment is available, and other identifying data of each person arrested for an offense of a type designated in section 41-9-622, of all persons arrested or taken into custody as fugitives from justice and of all unidentified human corpses in their jurisdictions, but photographs need not be taken if it is known that photographs of the type listed taken within the previous year are on file. Fingerprints and other identifying data of persons arrested for offenses other than those designated in this article may be taken at the discretion of the agency concerned.

If any person arrested or taken into custody is subsequently released without charge or cleared of the offense through criminal justice proceedings, such disposition shall be reported by all state, county and municipal criminal justice agencies to ACJIC within 30 days of such action, and all such information shall be eliminated and removed. (Acts 1975, No. 872, § 19.)

Collateral references. — Right of exoner-   or other criminal identification or arrest
ated arrestee to have fingerprints, photographs,   records expunged or restricted. 46 ALR3d 900.

§ 41-9-626. Forwarding of fingerprints, photographs, etc.

Fingerprints and other identifying data required to be taken by this article shall be forwarded within 24 hours after taking for filing and classification, but the period of 24 hours may be extended to cover any intervening holiday or weekend. Photographs taken shall be forwarded at the discretion of the agency concerned; but, if not forwarded, the fingerprint record shall be marked "photo available," and the photographs shall be forwarded subsequently if the commission so requests. (Acts 1975, No. 872, § 20.)

§ 41-9-627. Forwarding to department of public safety of descriptions of arrest warrants which cannot be served; notice where warrant subsequently served or withdrawn; annual, etc., confirmation of warrants remaining outstanding.

All persons in this state in charge of criminal justice agencies shall submit to the ACJIC by forwarding to the Alabama department of public safety detailed descriptions of arrest warrants and related identifying data immediately upon determination of the fact that the warrant cannot be served for the reasons stated.

If the warrant is subsequently served or withdrawn, the criminal justice agency concerned must immediately notify the ACJIC of such service or withdrawal.

The agency concerned also must annually, no later than January 31 of each year and at other times if requested by the commission, confirm to the ACJIC all arrest warrants of this type which continue to be outstanding. (Acts 1975, No. 872, § 21.)

§ 41-9-628. Obtaining and forwarding to department of public safety by penal and correctional institutions of fingerprints, photographs, etc., of persons committed thereto; procedure upon release of such persons.

All persons in charge of state penal and correctional institutions shall obtain fingerprints, according to the fingerprint system of identification established by the commission, and full face and profile photographs of all persons received on commitment to these institutions. The prints so taken shall be forwarded to the ACJIC by forwarding to the Alabama department of public safety together with any other identifying data requested within 10 days after the arrival at the institution of the person committed.

At the time of release, the institution will again obtain fingerprints as before and forward them to ACJIC within 10 days along with any other related information requested by the commission. Immediately upon release, the institution shall notify ACJIC of the release of such person. (Acts 1975, No. 872, § 22.)

§ 41-9-629. Forwarding of data to criminal justice information center by department of public safety.

The Alabama department of public safety shall forward to ACJIC within a reasonable period, not to exceed 72 hours, all data collected pursuant to sections 41-9-623, 41-9-627 and 41-9-628. (Acts 1975, No. 872, § 23.)

§ 41-9-630. Furnishing of other identifying data to center by criminal justice agencies generally; furnishing of information in criminal identification files.

All persons in charge of criminal justice agencies in this state shall furnish the ACJIC with any other identifying data required in accordance with guidelines established by the ACJIC.

All criminal justice agencies in this state having criminal identification files shall cooperate in providing to ACJIC information in such files as will aid in establishing the nucleus of the state criminal identification file. (Acts 1975, No. 872, § 24.)

§ 41-9-631. Submission by criminal justice agencies of uniform crime reports; contents thereof.

All criminal justice agencies within the state shall submit to the ACJIC periodically, at a time and in such a form as prescribed by the commission, information regarding only the cases within its jurisdiction. Said report shall be known as the "Alabama uniform crime report" and shall include crimes reported and otherwise processed during the reporting period.

Said report shall contain the number and nature of offenses committed, the disposition of such offenses and such other information as the commission shall specify relating to the method, frequency, cause and prevention of crime. (Acts 1975, No. 872, § 25.)

§ 41-9-632. Submission of uniform crime reports by other governmental agencies; use of information contained therein.

Any governmental agency which is not included within the description of those departments and agencies required to submit the uniform crime report which desires to submit such a report shall be furnished with the proper forms by the ACJIC. When a report is received by ACJIC from a governmental agency not required to make such a report, the information contained therein shall be included within the periodic compilation provided for in this article. (Acts 1975, No. 872, § 30.)

§ 41-9-633. Reporting by criminal justice agencies of persons wanted and vehicles and property stolen.

All criminal justice agencies within the state shall report to the ACJIC, in a time and manner prescribed by the commission, all persons wanted by and all vehicles and property stolen from their jurisdictions. The reports shall be made as soon as is practical after the investigating department or agency either ascertains that a vehicle or identifiable property has been stolen or obtains a warrant for an individual's arrest or determines that there are reasonable grounds to believe that the individual has committed the crime. In no event shall this time exceed 12 hours after the reporting department or agency determines that it has grounds to believe that a vehicle or property was stolen or that the wanted person should be arrested. The commission shall have authority to institute any and all procedures necessary to trace and complete the investigative cycles of stolen vehicles or wanted persons. (Acts 1975, No. 872, § 26.)

§ 41-9-634. Notification of center, etc., of apprehension of person or recovery of property.

If it is determined by the reporting agency that a person is no longer wanted due to his apprehension or any other factor, or when a vehicle or property reported stolen is recovered, the determining agency shall notify immediately the Alabama criminal justice information center. Furthermore, if the agency making such apprehension or recovery is other than the one which made the original wanted or stolen report, then it shall notify immediately the originating agency of the full particulars relating to such apprehension or recovery. (Acts 1975, No. 872, § 27.)

§ 41-9-635. Supplying of information on delinquent parolees by probation and parole officers.

All probation and parole officers shall supply the ACJIC with the information on delinquent parolees required by this article in a time and manner prescribed by the commission. (Acts 1975, No. 872, § 29.)

§ 41-9-636. Limitations upon provision of information generally.

Provision of information under this article shall be limited by all constitutional provisions, limitations and guarantees, including, but not limited to, due process, the right of privacy and the tripartite form of Alabama's state government. (Acts 1975, No. 872, § 41.)

§ 41-9-637. Obtaining and dissemination of identifying data and criminal histories generally — Persons convicted of offenses described in section 41-9-622 and confined to jails, workhouses, etc.

Pertinent identifying data and historical criminal information may be obtained and disseminated on any person confined to any workhouse, jail, reformatory, prison, penitentiary or other penal institution having been convicted of an offense described in section 41-9-622. (Acts 1975, No. 872, § 13.)

§ 41-9-638. Same — Unidentified human corpses found in state.

Pertinent identifying data and historical criminal information may be obtained and disseminated on any unidentified human corpse found in this state. (Acts 1975, No. 872, § 14.)

§ 41-9-639. Information which may be included in criminal histories.

Information in a criminal history, other than physical and identifying data, shall be limited to those offenses in which a conviction was obtained or to data relating to the current cycle of criminal justice administration if the subject has not yet completed that cycle. (Acts 1975, No. 872, § 16.)

§ 41-9-640. Log of disseminations of criminal histories.

A log shall be maintained of all disseminations made of each criminal history, including the date of information request and the recipient of said information. (Acts 1975, No. 872, § 17.)

§ 41-9-641. Dissemination of information to criminal justice agencies outside state.

The ACJIC shall not disseminate any information concerning any person to any criminal justice agencies outside of the state of Alabama unless said information pertains to a conviction of the person. (Acts 1975, No. 872, § 6.)

§ 41-9-642. Unconstitutional, etc., invasions of privacy of citizens not authorized by article; disclosure of criminal histories, etc., which might lead to identification of individuals to whom information pertains not to be made to persons, agencies, etc., not having "need to know" or "right to know."

Nothing in this article shall be construed to give authority to any person, agency or corporation or other legal entity to invade the privacy of any citizen as defined by the Constitution, the legislature or the courts other than to the extent provided in this article.

Disclosure of criminal histories or other information that may directly or otherwise lead to the identification of the individual to whom such information pertains may not be made to any person, agency, corporation or other legal entity that has neither the "need to know" nor the "right to know" as deter-

219

mined by the commission pursuant to section 41-9-594. (Acts 1975, No. 872, § 31.)

§ 41-9-643. Inspection of criminal records by persons to whom records pertain or attorneys thereof; establishment of procedures, etc., pertaining thereto by commission generally.

The center shall make a person's criminal records available for inspection to him or his attorney upon written application to the commission. Forms, procedures, identification and other related aspects pertinent to such access may be prescribed by the commission in providing access to such records and information. (Acts 1975, No. 872, § 32.)

§ 41-9-644. Establishment of procedures, fees, etc., by agencies for inspection of criminal offender records; disposition of fees collected.

Agencies, including ACJIC, at which criminal offender records are sought to be inspected may prescribe reasonable hours and places of inspection and may impose such additional procedures, fees (not to exceed $5.00) or restrictions, including fingerprinting, as are reasonably necessary to assure the records' security, to verify the identities of those who seek to inspect them and to maintain an orderly and efficient mechanism for such accesses.

All fees collected are to be forwarded to the state general fund for disposition. (Acts 1975, No. 872, § 35.)

§ 41-9-645. Purging, modification or supplementation of criminal records — Applications to agencies by individuals; appeals to circuit courts upon refusal of agencies to act, etc.; costs.

If an individual believes such information to be inaccurate or incomplete, he may request the original agency having custody or control of the detail records to purge, modify or supplement them and to so notify the ACJIC of such changes.

Should the agency decline to so act or should the individual believe the agency's decision to be otherwise unsatisfactory, the individual or his attorney may within 30 days of such decision enter an appeal to the circuit court of the county of his residence or to the circuit court in the county where such agency exists, with notice to the agency, pursuant to acquiring an order by such court that the subject information be expunged, modified or supplemented by the agency of record. The court in each such case shall conduct a de novo hearing and may order such relief as it finds to be required by law. Such appeals shall be entered in the same manner as appeals are entered from the court of probate; except, that the appellant shall not be required to post bond nor pay the costs in advance. If the aggrieved person desires, the appeal may be heard by the judge at the first term or in chambers. A notice sent by registered or certified mail shall be sufficient service on the agency of disputed record that such appeal has been entered.

The party found to be in error shall assume all costs involved. (Acts 1975, No. 872, § 33.)

§ 41-9-646. Same — Entry of court order for purging, modification or supplementation of record and compliance therewith by agencies, etc.; notification of agencies, individual, etc., of deletions, amendments, etc., in records.

Should the record in question be found to be inaccurate, incomplete or misleading, the court shall order it to be appropriately purged, modified or supplemented by an explanatory notation. Each agency or individual in the state with custody, possession or control of any such record shall promptly cause each and every copy thereof in his custody, possession or control to be altered in accordance with a court order. Notification of each such deletion, amendment and supplementary notation shall be promptly disseminated to any individuals or agencies to which the records in question have been communicated, including the ACJIC, as well as to the individual whose records have been ordered so altered. (Acts 1975, No. 872, § 34.)

Collateral references. — Judicial expunction of criminal record of convicted adult. 11 ALR4th 956.

§ 41-9-647. Establishment of guidelines for action and institution of actions for violations as to data reporting or dissemination.

The commission shall establish guidelines for appropriate measures to be taken in the instance of any violation of data reporting or dissemination and shall initiate and pursue appropriate action for violations of rules, regulations, laws and constitutional provisions pertaining thereto. (Acts 1975, No. 872, § 18.)

§ 41-9-648. Compilation of information and statistics pertaining to disposition of criminal cases.

The administrator of the department of court management or the chief administrative officer of any other entity that is charged with the compilation of information and statistics pertaining to the disposition of criminal cases shall report such disposition to the ACJIC within a reasonable time after formal rendition of judgment as prescribed by the commission. (Acts 1975, No. 872, § 28.)

ARTICLE 24.

FOREIGN TRADE AND RELATIONS
COMMISSION.

§ 41-9-660. Creation; composition; qualifications, appointment and terms of office of members; filling of vacancies; quorum.

There is hereby created a commission called the foreign trade and relation commission of Alabama which shall be composed of five members, each of whom shall be a citizen of the United States and a resident of the state of Alabama.

The members of the commission shall be appointed by the governor with the advice and consent of the senate. One of such members shall be appointed for a term of two years from August 23, 1976, two shall be appointed for terms of four years from August 23, 1976 and two for terms of six years from such date. Each two years after August 23, 1976, the governor shall appoint one or two members of the commission, as the case may be, to fill any vacancy or vacancies, and such appointment shall be for a term of six years.

Vacancies in the membership of the commission shall be filled, as in the first instance, for the unexpired term.

Three members of the commission shall constitute a quorum for the transaction of business. (Acts 1976, No. 682, p. 936, § 1.)

§ 41-9-661. Powers and duties generally.

(a) It shall be the duty of the commission to devise and put into effect methods by which inter-American understanding and good will may be promoted and inter-American relations advanced without resort to tentative measures or the application of civil or criminal sanctions.

(b) The commission shall have power:

(1) To elect from its members a chairman and such other officers as it may deem desirable; provided, that the first chairman of the commission shall be named by the governor and shall call the first meeting of the commission and serve as such president until his successor shall be elected by the commission. All officers of the commission shall serve as such only during the pleasure of the commission.

(2) To hold such meetings, at such places within or without the state of Alabama and at such times as the commission may designate.

(3) To conduct such research, investigations and inquiries as may be necessary to inform the commission as to matters concerning inter-American relations.

(4) To appoint committees from its membership and prescribe their duties.

(5) To appoint consultants to the commission.

(6) To make rules and regulations for the government of the commission, its officers and committees and to prescribe the duties of its officers, consultants and employees.

(7) To employ an executive secretary and such other clerical employees as it may think necessary and to fix the pay and compensation of such employees within the limits of funds available to it for such purposes.

(8) To receive, hold and expend any funds granted, donated or given to it. Any funds derived from a gift for a designated purpose shall be used and expended by the commission in accordance with the terms of the gift, but any funds received by the commission which are not limited to specified uses by the donor may be used and expended for the payment of salaries and expenses of the commission and its employees and for any other purpose incident to or which will promote the purposes of this article. Such funds when received by the commission shall be deposited with the state treasury and shall be placed to the credit of a special account to be known as "the foreign trade and relations commission of Alabama fund." (Acts 1976, No. 682, p. 936, § 2.)

§ 41-9-662. Annual report to governor and legislature; compensation of members, officers and consultants.

(a) On or before April 1 of each year, the commission shall make in writing a complete and detailed report to the governor and to the presiding officer of each house of the legislature of its activity.

(b) No member, consultant or officer of the commission shall receive any compensation for his services in acting in such capacity, but shall be paid his traveling and other necessary expenses incurred in attending the meetings of the commission and in the discharge of his duties as a member, consultant or officer, upon verified and itemized accounts approved by the chairman of the commission, in accordance with the provisions of article 2 of chapter 7 of Title 36 of this Code. (Acts 1976, No. 682, p. 936, § 3.)

§ 41-9-663. Payment of clerical expenses, etc.; cooperation and assistance of officers, departments and agencies of state.

(a) The necessary clerical and other expenses of the commission shall be paid in the same manner as provided in section 41-9-662 for the payment of expenses of members, consultants or officers of the commission.

(b) All officers, departments and agencies of the state government shall cooperate with the commission and, when requested by the commission, render to it such assistance as the officer, department or agency can without interfering with the discharge of its other regular duties. (Acts 1976, No. 682, p. 936, § 4.)

§ 41-9-664. Gifts to commission deemed gifts to state; taxation thereof.

Every gift to the foreign trade and relations commission, whether or not the use thereof is prescribed by the donor, shall be deemed a gift to the state of Alabama.

The donor in computing his net income for state income tax purposes for the year in which he makes his gift may deduct the amount of the gift from his gross income as authorized in section 40-18-15. (Acts 1976, No. 682, p. 936, § 5.)

ARTICLE 25.

MUSIC HALL OF FAME BOARD.

§ 41-9-680. Creation; membership; appointment, qualifications, terms and compensation of members; officers; meetings; quorum.

There shall be created and established as herein provided a board to be designated and known as the Alabama music hall of fame board. The board shall be composed of seven members, who shall be appointed by the governor of Alabama for terms of six years each; provided, that of the first members appointed under any restructured board, two shall serve for two years and two shall serve for four years, as the governor may direct. Four board members shall be appointed from the membership of the Muscle Shoals Music Association and three board members shall be appointed from the state at large and shall not be employed in the music business. The members of the board shall select a chairman and vice-chairman from among their own number. Members of the board shall not be compensated for their services, but each member shall be entitled to reimbursement for expenses incurred in attending board meetings. The board shall meet quarterly and at such other times as its rules and bylaws may prescribe. A majority of the members shall constitute a quorum for transaction of business. (Acts 1977, No. 645, p. 1093, § 1; Acts 1982, No. 82-403.)

The 1982 amendment, effective April 26, 1982, in the second sentence inserted "under any restructured board," and rewrote the third sentence, which formerly provided for one board member from each congressional district in the state.

§ 41-9-681. Domicile of board; halls, quarters, etc.; executive secretary or director; staff.

The board shall be domiciled within Colbert county, Alabama, where it shall maintain such halls, rooms or quarters as may be considered suitable and appropriate for conducting its affairs. The board may appoint an executive secretary or director and such staff as may be necessary for the performance of its duties and functions. (Acts 1977, No. 645, p. 1093, § 2.)

§ 41-9-682. Function and powers generally.

It shall be the function and main purpose of the board to honor those, living or dead, who, by achievement or service, have made outstanding and lasting contributions to music in Alabama or elsewhere. The board may adopt such rules, regulations and bylaws as may be needed to carry out its functions. Also, it may conduct surveys and polls and may appoint such committees and representatives as it may determine necessary or desirable. The board may acquire suitable quarters to be used by the board for the display of busts, statues, plaques, books, papers, pictures and other exhibits relating to music and musicians. (Acts 1977, No. 645, p. 1093, § 3.)

§ 41-9-683. Solicitation and acceptance of gifts, etc.; exemption from taxation.

The board may solicit and accept donations, contributions and gifts of money and property. All gifts made to the board shall be exempt from all taxation in Alabama. All property, money, income, resources and activities of the board shall likewise be exempt from taxation. (Acts 1977, No. 645, p. 1093, § 4.)

§ 41-9-684. Expenditures and appropriations.

(a) The board may spend all legislative appropriations made for the use of the board and may expend funds donated or contributed for its support.

(b) There are no state funds appropriated for the expenses and implementation of this article. (Acts 1977, No. 645, p. 1093, §§ 5, 6.)

ARTICLE 26.

SOUTHWEST ALABAMA INDIAN AFFAIRS COMMISSION.

§ 41-9-700. Creation.

There is hereby created and established a commission to be known as the southwest Alabama Indian affairs commission. (Acts 1978, No. 677, p. 976, § 1.)

§ 41-9-701. Purpose.

The purpose of this commission shall be to deal fairly and effectively with Indian affairs; to bring local, state and federal resources into focus for the implementation or continuation of meaningful programs for Indian citizens of the state of Alabama; to provide aid and protection for the Indians as needs are demonstrated; to prevent undue hardships; to assist Indian communities in social and economic development; and to promote recognition of the right of Indians to pursue cultural and religious traditions considered by them to be sacred and meaningful to native Americans. (Acts 1978, No. 677, p. 976, § 2.)

§ 41-9-702. Powers and duties generally.

It shall be the duty of the commission to study, consider, accumulate, compile, assemble and disseminate information on any aspect of Indian affairs; to investigate relief needs of Indians of Alabama and to provide technical assistance in the preparation of plans for the alleviation of such needs; to confer with appropriate officials of local, state and federal governments and agencies of those concerned with Indian affairs to encourage and implement coordination of applicable resources to meet the needs of Indians in Alabama; to cooperate with and secure the assistance of the local, state and federal governments or any agencies thereof in formulating any such programs; and to coordinate such programs with any program regarding Indian affairs adopted or planned by the federal government to the end that the southwest Alabama Indian affairs commission secure the full benefit of such programs, provided, however, that such commission is hereby authorized to directly seek and receive from the federal government any grants, funds or other benefits which may be available for Indians; to review all proposed or pending legislation and amendments to existing state legislation affecting Indians in Alabama; to conduct public hearings on matters relating to Indian affairs and to subpoena any information or documents deemed necessary by the commission; to study the existing status of recognition of all Indian groups, tribes and communities presently existing in the state of Alabama; to establish appropriate procedures to provide for legal recognition by the state and to initiate procedures for their recognition by the federal government; to employ and fix the compensation of an executive director of the commission and such supporting staff as may be required to carry out the responsibility of the commission; to expend funds in compliance with state regulations; to make legislative recommendations; and, to make and publish reports of findings and recommendations. (Acts 1978, No. 677, p. 976, § 3.)

Collateral references. — 42 C.J.S., Indians, § 42.
41 Am. Jur. 2d, Indians, §§ 63, 64.

§ 41-9-703. Composition; qualifications, appointment, terms of office and compensation of members; filling of vacancies; officers.

(a) The southwest Alabama Indian affairs commission shall be composed of those members of the council of the Creek Indians east of the Mississippi who reside in Alabama; provided, however, that said commission may appoint any person of non-Indian descent to serve on said commission and may prescribe the disposition of the term of such member.

(b) Members serving by virtue of their seats on said council shall serve so long as they hold such seats. All members of said commission shall hold their offices until their successors are appointed and qualified. Any vacancy occurring on the commission shall be filled with temporary appointment by the governor until the vacant seat on said council is filled. The governor shall appoint a chairman of the commission from among the members of the commission, subject to ratification by the full commission. The commission shall elect its own secretary.

(c) Recognition of presently unrecognized tribes or groups of Indians shall be at the discretion of the southwest Alabama Indian affairs commission.

(d) All commission members shall be compensated at the same rate as other statutory commission members and pursuant to prevailing state regulations. Travel reimbursement shall be in accord with state regulations. (Acts 1978, No. 677, p. 976, § 4.)

§ 41-9-704. Employment of executive director, staff and consultants.

The commission may, subject to legislative or other funds that would accrue to the commission, employ an executive director and, also subject to legislative or other funds that would accrue to the commission, may hire additional staff and consultants to assist in the discharge of members' responsibilities, as determined by the commission. The executive director shall not be a member of the commission, and shall be of Indian extraction. (Acts 1978, No. 677, p. 976, § 5.)

§ 41-9-705. Meetings generally; quorum; voting.

(a) The commission shall meet quarterly, and at any other such time that it shall deem necessary. Meetings may be called by the chairman or by a petition signed by a majority of the members of the commission. Ten days' notice shall be given in writing prior to the meeting date.

(b) Five members of the commission must be present to constitute a quorum.

(c) Proxy vote shall not be permitted. (Acts 1978, No. 677, p. 976, § 6.)

§ 41-9-706. Preparation and disposition of annual report.

The commission shall prepare a written annual report giving an account of its proceedings, transactions, findings and recommendations. This report shall be submitted to the governor, the legislature and the secretary of the Creek Nation East of the Mississippi, Inc. The report will become a matter of public record and will be maintained in the state department of archives and history. It may also be furnished to such other persons or agencies as the commission may deem proper. (Acts 1978, No. 677, p. 976, § 7.)

§ 41-9-707. Maintenance and audit of fiscal records; disposition of audit report; requirement of bonds for certain commission members and employees.

(a) Fiscal records shall be kept by the executive director or his designee, if applicable, otherwise by the commission chairman, and will be subject to annual audit by the state examiner of public accounts. The audit report will become a part of the annual report and will be submitted in accordance with the regulations governing preparation and submission of the annual report.

(b) Commission members or employees of the commission who are responsible for receiving and disbursing commission funds shall be bonded in an amount satisfactory to the commission, but not less than $50,000.00. (Acts 1978, No. 677, p. 976, § 8.)

ARTICLE 27.

AVIATION HALL OF FAME BOARD.

§ 41-9-720. Board created; purpose, function, etc.

There is hereby created and established a public agency of the state to be known as the Alabama aviation hall of fame board which shall be permanently located in the Southern Museum of Flight Building in Birmingham, Alabama. The purpose and function of the board shall be to promote and encourage the growth and public support of aviation, especially general aviation within the state by providing official and public recognition and honor to individuals, living or dead, who by extraordinary achievement and service have made outstanding and substantial contributions to aviation in Alabama. Persons to receive such recognition may be residents of the state who receive national recognition for aviation achievements elsewhere, or nonresidents who contributed directly to aviation in this state. (Acts 1979, No. 79-663, p. 1162, § 1; Acts 1981, 2nd Ex. Sess., No. 81-1074, § 1.)

The 1981 amendment, effective October 27, 1981, inserted "which shall be permanently located in the Southern Museum of Flight Building in Birmingham, Alabama" at the end of the first sentence.

§ 41-9-721. Meetings; composition; appointment, terms, etc., of members; expenses; organization.

The board shall meet annually by the first day of March each year and at such other times as called either by the chairman or upon petition for such meeting submitted by three or more members. The board shall be composed of seven Alabama residents, who shall serve for terms as herein prescribed until a successor is named or they are reappointed. Two members shall be appointed by the governor of Alabama for terms of four years and six years, one shall be appointed by the trustees of the Southern Museum of Flight for a term of six years, and one each by the mayors or chief executives of Mobile, Montgomery, Huntsville and Birmingham. The first members appointed by the governor shall serve for a term of four years, and the first members appointed by the mayors of Montgomery, Huntsville, Birmingham and Mobile shall serve for four years. Members of the board shall not be compensated for their services, but may be reimbursed for expenses in attending meetings of the board. The board shall elect a chairman from its members, and shall adopt bylaws to govern its organization and procedures. (Acts 1979, No. 79-663, p. 1162, § 2; Acts 1981, 2nd Ex. Sess., No. 81-1074, § 1.)

The 1981 amendment, effective October 27, 1981, rewrote this section.

§ 41-9-722. Legislative appropriations, contributions, etc.; exempt from taxation.

The board may receive and expend legislative appropriations as provided by law, and may submit, receive and expend contributions of money and property. All gifts to, and property, funds, income and activities of the board shall be exempt from taxation. (Acts 1979, No. 79-663, p. 1162, § 3.)

CHAPTER 10.

AUTHORITIES.

ARTICLE 1.

GENERAL PROVISIONS.

Cross references. — As to farmers' market authority, see § 2-5-1 et seq. As to airport authorities, see § 4-3-1 et seq. As to environmental improvement authorities, see § 9-6-1 et seq. As to Alabama Corrections Institution Finance Authority, see § 14-2-1 et seq. As to Alabama education authority, see § 16-15-1 et seq. As to Alabama public school and college authority, see § 16-16-1 et seq. As to educational building authorities, see § 16-17-1 et seq. As to public educational building authorities, see § 16-18-1 et seq. As to pollution control finance authority, see § 22-29-1 et seq. As to Alabama highway authority, see § 23-1-150 et seq. As to Alabama Highway Finance Corporation, see § 23-1-170 et seq. As to Alabama Toll Road, Bridge and Tunnel Authority, see § 23-2-140 et seq. As to housing authorities, see § 24-1-1 et seq.

§ 41-10-1. Alabama building authority.

To the extent that such have not been heretofore exercised or discharged, all rights, powers, duties and liabilities of the Alabama building authority created by Act No. 205 of the 1955 Legislature, page 501, Acts of 1951, approved August 3, 1955, are hereby continued in full force and effect until such have been fully exercised and discharged. At such time as all of the rights, powers, duties and liabilities of the said Alabama building authority have been exercised or discharged, including specifically the payment or discharge of all bonds or other securities issued by such authority, the said authority shall perform the acts of dissolution prescribed by section 18 of said Act, and thereupon the said authority shall cease to exist.

§ 41-10-2. Alabama building finance authority.

To the extent that such have not been heretofore exercised or discharged, all rights, powers, duties and liabilities of the Alabama building finance authority created by Act No. 658 of the 1961 Legislature, page 807, Acts of 1961, approved September 6, 1961, are hereby continued in full force and effect until such have been fully exercised and discharged. At such time as all of the rights, powers, duties and liabilities of the said Alabama building finance authority have been exercised or discharged, including specifically the payment or discharge of all bonds or other securities issued by such authority, the said authority shall perform the acts of dissolution prescribed by section 25 of said Act, and thereupon the said authority shall cease to exist.

§ 41-10-3. Alabama building corporation.

To the extent that such have not been heretofore exercised or discharged, all rights, powers, duties and liabilities of the Alabama building corporation created by Act No. 477 of the 1951 Legislature, page 845, Acts of 1951, approved August 17, 1951, are hereby continued in full force and effect until such have been fully exercised and discharged. At such time as all of the rights, powers, duties and liabilities of the said Alabama building corporation have been exercised or discharged, including specifically the payment or discharge of all bonds or other securities issued by such corporation, the said corporation shall perform the acts of dissolution prescribed by section 18 of said Act, and thereupon the said corporation shall cease to exist.

ARTICLE 2.

INDUSTRIAL DEVELOPMENT AUTHORITY.

Cross references. — As to state industrial development board, see § 41-9-185 et seq. As to state development office, see § 41-9-200 et seq.

Constitutionality. — This article is not contrary to the prohibition in Constitution 1901, § 93, against lending money in aid of works of internal improvement. There is nothing in this article which suggests that there is any violation of this constitutional prohibition. Edmonson v. State Indus. Dev. Auth., 279 Ala. 206, 184 So. 2d 115 (1966).

Article does not authorize the state to borrow any money or incur any indebtedness. — The bonds issued by the authority do not create an obligation or debt of the state. The bonds are payable out of the receipts of a new special tax, §§ 40-25-60 through 40-25-62; and there is no assurance that there will ever be sufficient funds to pay the bonds; and the state has not pledged its faith and credit. The article does not contravene this part of Constitution 1901, § 93. Edmonson v. State Indus. Dev. Auth., 279 Ala. 206, 184 So. 2d 115 (1966).

Sale of bonds of authority does not create state debt. — The sale and issuance of the bonds by the state industrial development authority, or the appropriation and pledge made in this article for servicing the bonds, does not create a new debt of the state and thereby contravene Constitution 1901, § 213. Edmonson v. State Indus. Dev. Auth., 279 Ala. 206, 184 So. 2d 115 (1966).

Article does not authorize state to engage in any private enterprise, nor does it authorize the state industrial development authority so to do. The authority uses the proceeds from the sale and issuance of its bonds to make grants to local public bodies. Edmonson v. State Indus. Dev. Auth., 279 Ala. 206, 184 So. 2d 115 (1966).

Nor in internal improvement works. — This article does not authorize the state to engage in works of internal improvement in violation of Constitution 1901, § 93. Edmonson v. State Indus. Dev. Auth., 279 Ala. 206, 184 So. 2d 115 (1966).

It limits authority's power to make surveys and grants. — This article does not authorize either the state or the state industrial development authority to engage in works of internal improvement. Instead, the authority's functions are to conduct certain surveys and make grants of money to local public bodies. The local public bodies may, if they so choose, use the grants for preparation of industrial sites or for the other purposes specified in this article. If the local public bodies choose to use the grants in whole or in part for a work of internal improvement, it is they — and not the state or the authority — that have made the choice. Edmonson v. State Indus. Dev. Auth., 279 Ala. 206, 184 So. 2d 115 (1966).

Article does not authorize lending to private parties. — This article does not authorize or contemplate that the state or the state industrial development authority will lend either its money or its credit to private parties and has adequate safeguards to insure that public funds of the authority are not so used. Edmonson v. State Indus. Dev. Auth., 279 Ala. 206, 184 So. 2d 115 (1966).

And has adequate safeguards. — This article contains adequate safeguards to insure that none of the grants made by the authority will become the property of any private individ-

ual, association or corporation without fair consideration. Edmonson v. State Indus. Dev. Auth., 279 Ala. 206, 184 So. 2d 115 (1966).

§ 41-10-20. Definitions.

When used in this article, the following terms shall have the following meanings, respectively, unless the context clearly indicates otherwise:

(1) AUTHORITY. The public corporation organized pursuant to the provisions of this article.

(2) BOARD OF DIRECTORS. The board of directors of the authority.

(3) BONDS. The bonds issued under the provisions of this article.

(4) GRANTEE. A county, municipality or local industrial development board organized as a public corporation in this state, or an airport authority organized as a public corporation in this state pursuant to chapter 3 of Title 4, or whether created by general, special or local laws, or general acts of local application, if such authority governs an airport operated by a county and at least one municipality therein jointly, to which a grant of money is made as provided in section 41-10-26.

(5) INDUSTRIAL SITES. Land owned by a grantee or potential grantee on which industrial facilities have been or will be constructed for sale or lease to an individual, private association or private corporation.

(6) NOMINAL TRANSFEREE. Any person to whom a grantee transfers one or more industrial sites or any part of any thereof for less than fair market value and any person who derives title to such industrial sites or any part of any thereof through such a transferee.

(7) PERSON. Unless limited to a natural person by the context in which it is used, such term includes a private firm, a private association, a public or private corporation, a municipality, a county or an agency, department or instrumentality of the state or of a county or municipality.

(8) PREPARATION OF INDUSTRIAL SITES. The grading and draining of industrial sites and the means of access thereto.

(9) STATE. The state of Alabama. (Acts 1965, No. 662, p. 1187, § 2; Acts 1980, No. 80-437, p. 662, § 1; Acts 1981, No. 81-289, p. 370, § 1.)

The 1981 amendment, effective April 20, 1981, added the language beginning "of the Code" and ending "municipality therein jointly" in subdivision (4).

§ 41-10-21. Legislative findings of fact and declaration of intent; construction of article.

The legislature hereby makes the following findings of fact and declares its intent to be as follows: In recent years changes have taken place in the economy of this state which have had a far-reaching effect on the welfare of its citizens. The agrarian economy which once prevailed in this state and provided the principal means of livelihood for most of the citizens of the state has proven inadequate to provide employment for the state's growing population. The advent of mechanized and scientific farming methods has reduced greatly the number of persons required to obtain increased yields of agricultural products from land under cultivation. There has been a correspondingly greater dependence upon industrial development as the bulwark of the economy of this state. It is appropriate and necessary that measures be taken to secure to the citizens of this state the benefits of a strengthened economy resulting from increased industrial development. Among these benefits are diversification of available job opportunities, higher salaries, better working conditions, lower consumer prices for industrial products, conservation and efficient use of natural resources and maximum utilization of technical skills possessed by the citizens of this state. The police power of the state casts upon the legislature the peculiar function of ascertaining and determining when the welfare of the people needs its exercise. The public interest lies in the promotion of industry, and the welfare of the people is so inextricably tied up with industry and industrial development as to make its well-being a matter of governmental concern.

It is the intention of the legislature by the passage of this article to exercise its police power to authorize the formation of an independent public corporation which shall have as its general purpose the promotion of industrial development in this state and which shall have power to issue bonds payable solely from the proceeds of a special state tax set aside by this article for the purpose of retiring the said bonds. It is the further intention of the legislature that the public corporation authorized by this article shall have discretion as to the manner of expending funds at its disposal for the purpose of promoting industrial development in this state, subject to the limitations more particularly detailed in this article.

This article shall be liberally construed in accordance with the foregoing findings of fact and declaration of intent. (Acts 1965, No. 662, p. 1187, § 1.)

§ 41-10-22. Authorization and procedure for incorporation generally.

The director of the state industrial development board, the commissioner of revenue and the director of finance may become a public corporation with the powers provided for in this article by proceeding according to the provisions of section 41-10-23. (Acts 1965, No. 662, p. 1187, § 3; Acts 1965, 3rd Ex. Sess., No. 2, p. 208, § 1.)

§ 41-10-23. Filing of application for incorporation with secretary of state; contents and execution thereof; filing and recordation of application by secretary of state.

(a) To become the public corporation authorized by this article, the director of the state industrial development board, the commissioner of revenue and the director of finance shall present to the secretary of state of Alabama an application signed by them which shall set forth:

(1) The name, official designation and official residence of each of the applicants, together with a certified copy of the commission evidencing each applicant's right to office;

(2) The date on which each applicant was inducted into office and the term of office of each applicant;

(3) The name of the proposed public corporation, which shall be the state industrial development authority; and

(4) The location of the principal office of the proposed corporation. The applicants may also include in the said application any other matters which are not inconsistent with this article or with any of the other laws of the state.

(b) The application shall be subscribed and sworn to by each of the applicants before an officer authorized by the laws of this state to take acknowledgments to deeds.

(c) The secretary of state shall examine the application and, if he finds that it substantially complies with the requirements of this section, he shall receive and file it and record it in an appropriate book of records in his office. (Acts 1965, No. 662, p. 1187, § 4; Acts 1965, 3rd Ex. Sess., No. 2, p. 208, § 2.)

§ 41-10-24. Issuance and recordation of certificate of incorporation by secretary of state; secretary of state to receive no fees in connection with incorporation, dissolution, etc., of authority.

(a) When the application has been made, filed and recorded as provided in this article, the applicants shall constitute a corporation under the name proposed in the application, and the secretary of state shall make and issue to the applicants a certificate of incorporation pursuant to this article, under the great seal of the state, and shall record the certificate with the application.

(b) There shall be no fees paid to the secretary of state for any service rendered or work performed in connection with the authority, its incorporation, dissolution or records. (Acts 1965, No. 662, p. 1187, § 5.)

§ 41-10-25. Members, officers and directors of association; reduction to writing, recordation and filing of proceedings of board of directors; admissibility in evidence of proceedings of board.

(a) The applicants named in the application and their respective successors in office shall constitute the members of the authority. The director of the state industrial development board shall be the president of the authority, the commissioner of revenue shall be the vice-president thereof, and the director of finance shall be the secretary thereof. The state treasurer shall be treasurer of the authority, shall act as custodian of its funds and shall pay the principal of and interest on the bonds of the authority out of the funds provided for in this article. The members of the authority shall constitute all the members of the board of directors of the authority, and any two members of the said board of directors shall constitute a quorum for the transaction of business. Should any person holding any state office named in this section cease to hold such office by reason of death, resignation, expiration of his term of office or for any other reason, then his successor in office shall take his place as an officer and member of the board of directors of the authority. No officer or member of the board of directors of the authority shall draw any salary in addition to that now authorized by law for any service he may render or for any duty he may perform in connection with the authority.

(b) All proceedings had and done by the board of directors shall be reduced to writing by the secretary of the authority, shall be signed by at least two members of the authority present at the proceedings and shall be recorded in a substantially bound book and filed in the office of the secretary of state. Copies of such proceedings, when certified by the secretary of the authority under the seal of the authority, shall be received in all courts as prima facie evidence of the matters and things therein certified. (Acts 1965, No. 662, p. 1187, § 6; Acts 1965, 3rd Ex. Sess., No. 2, p. 208, § 3.)

§ 41-10-26. Powers of authority generally.

The authority shall have the following powers:

(1) To have succession by its corporate name until dissolved as provided in this article;

(2) To institute and defend legal proceedings in any court of competent jurisdiction and proper venue; provided, that the authority may not be sued in any trial court other than the courts of the county in which is located the principal office of the authority; provided further, that the officers, directors, agents and employees of the authority may not be sued for actions in behalf of the authority in any trial court other than the courts of the county in which is located the principal office of the authority;

(3) To have and to use a corporate seal and to alter the seal at pleasure;

(4) To establish a fiscal year;

(5) To anticipate by the issuance of its bonds the receipt of the revenues appropriated and pledged in this article;

(6) To pledge the proceeds of the appropriations and pledges provided for in this article as security for the payment of the principal of and interest on its bonds;

(7) To make surveys to determine suitable locations in the state for prospective industries;

(8) To make surveys to determine the availability of labor in various parts of the state and to classify such labor in terms of skills and educational levels;

(9) To assist counties, municipalities, local industrial development boards organized as public corporations in the state, or airport authorities organized as public corporations in this state pursuant to chapter 3 of Title 4, or whether created by general, special or local law, or general acts of local application, if such authority governs an airport operated by a county and at least one municipality therein jointly, in the survey and analysis of their industrial resources and needs;

(10) To make grants of money to counties, municipalities and local industrial development boards organized as public corporations in the state, or airport authorities organized as public corporations in this state pursuant to

chapter 3 of Title 4, or whether created by general, special or local law, or general acts of local application if such authority governs an airport operated by a county and at least one municipality therein jointly, for the purposes and subject to the terms and conditions set forth in section 41-10-27; and

(11) To appoint and employ such attorneys and agents as the authority may require for the carrying out of its corporate purposes and the exercise of the foregoing powers. (Acts 1965, No. 662, p. 1187, § 7; Acts 1980, No. 80-437, p. 662, § 2; Acts 1981, No. 81-289, p. 370, § 2.)

The 1981 amendment, effective April 20, 1981, added the language beginning "of the Code" and ending "municipality therein jointly" in subdivisions (9) and (10).

Collateral references. — 73 C.J.S., Public Administrative Bodies and Procedure, §§ 48-77.

1 Am. Jur. 2d, Administrative Law, §§ 158-173.

§ 41-10-27. Issuance and sale of bonds for purpose of making grants for certain purposes authorized; terms and conditions of grants.

(a) The authority is hereby authorized from time to time to sell and issue its bonds, not exceeding $2,600,000.00 in aggregate principal amount, for the purpose of making the grants of money authorized in section 41-10-26. The grantees may use the said grants authorized in the said section for the following purposes:

(1) The making of surveys to determine the location of suitable industrial sites in the locality of the grantee;

(2) The making of surveys to determine the availability of labor in the locality of the grantee and to classify such labor in terms of skills and educational level;

(3) The preparation of industrial sites; or

(4) Any combination of any of the foregoing which the grantees consider appropriate and necessary for the promotion of industrial development in their respective localities.

(b) Every grant of money made by the authority pursuant to section 41-10-26 shall be made subject to the following terms and conditions, which are hereby declared to be legally enforceable in any court of competent jurisdiction:

(1) No part of any such grant or grants shall be used with respect to the preparation of industrial sites in excess of one and one-half percent of the amount that it is anticipated will be spent for the construction and equipment of the facilities that will occupy the said industrial sites as such anticipated amount shall be certified to the authority by the architect or engineer for the facilities to be constructed and equipped or by the chief executive officer of the grantee;

(2) No part of any such grant or grants shall be used with respect to the preparation of industrial sites in any case where any individual, private association or private corporation has received or is to receive an option to purchase such industrial sites or any part of any thereof from the grantee or any nominal transferee of the grantee for less than the fair market value of such industrial sites;

(3) The authority shall have power to audit the disbursements by the grantee from such grant or grants; and

(4) Any other appropriate terms and conditions to facilitate the enforcement of the foregoing provisions of this subsection. (Acts 1965, No. 662, p. 1187, § 8.)

Code commissioner's note. — The legislature has, by the acts listed below, authorized the industrial development authority to issue additional bonds, for the purpose of making grants, in the amounts indicated below:

(1) Acts 1967, No. 231, p. 600, § 2, $5,000,000.00.

(2) Acts 1969, No. 169, p. 454, § 2, $3,000,000.00.

(3) Acts 1971, No. 1420, p. 2423, § 2, $3,000,000.00.

(4) Acts 1973, No. 1039, p. 1621, § 2, $2,000,000.00.

(5) Acts 1975, No. 1217, p. 2533, § 2, $3,000,000.00.

(6) Acts 1978, 2nd Ex. Sess., No. 99, p. 1806, § 2, $3,000,000.00.

(7) Acts 1981, No. 81-843, § 2, $3,000,000.00.

Acts 1981, 2nd Ex. Sess., No. 81-1051, effective October 27, 1981, amends Acts 1981, No. 81-843, to provide that the authority be exempt from the laws of this state governing usury or prescribing or limiting interest rates, including, without limitation, the provisions of chapter 8 of Title 8.

§ 41-10-28. Execution of bonds and interest coupons; form, terms, denominations, etc., of bonds; sale; refunding bonds; liability upon bonds; pledges of certain funds as security for payment of principal and interest on bonds generally; bonds to be deemed negotiable instruments; bonds and income therefrom exempt from taxation; use of bonds as security for deposits of funds of state, etc.; investment of certain state funds and private trust funds in bonds; public hearing or consent of department of finance, etc., not a prerequisite to issuance of bonds.

The bonds of the authority shall be signed by its president and attested by its secretary, and the seal of the authority shall be affixed thereto, and any interest coupons applicable to such bonds shall be signed by the president; provided, that a facsimile of the signature of one, but not both, of said officers may be printed or otherwise reproduced on any such bonds in lieu of being manually subscribed thereon, a facsimile of the seal of the authority may be printed or otherwise reproduced on any such bonds in lieu of being manually affixed thereto, and a facsimile of the president's signature may be printed or otherwise reproduced on any such interest coupons in lieu of being manually subscribed thereon.

Any bonds of the authority may be executed and delivered by it at any time and from time to time and shall be in such form and denominations and of such tenor and maturities, shall bear such rate or rates of interest, not exceeding five percent per annum, shall be payable at such times and evidenced in such manner and may contain such other provisions not inconsistent with this article as may be provided by the resolution of the board of directors of the authority under which such bonds are authorized to be issued; provided, that no bond of the authority shall have a specified maturity date later than 20 years after its date. Any bond of the authority may be made subject to redemption at the option of the authority at such times and after such notice and on such conditions and at such redemption price or prices as may be provided in the resolution under which it is authorized to be issued; provided, that those bonds of the authority having specified maturity dates more than 10 years after their date shall be made subject to redemption at the option of the authority not later than the end of the tenth year after their date and on any interest payment date thereafter, under such terms and conditions and at such redemption price or prices as may be provided in the resolution under which such bonds are authorized to be issued.

Bonds of the authority may be sold from time to time as the board of directors of the authority may consider advantageous, but bonds of the authority must be sold only at public sale, either on sealed bids or at public auction, to the bidder whose bid reflects the lowest net interest cost to the authority for the bonds being sold, computed from their date to their respective maturities; provided, that if no bid acceptable to the authority is received, it may reject all bids. Notice of each such sale shall be given by publication in either a financial journal or a financial newspaper published in the city of New York, New York, and also by publication in a daily newspaper published in the state of Alabama not less than five days during each calendar week, each of which notices must be published at least one time not less than 10 days before the date fixed for the sale. The board of directors of the authority may fix the terms and conditions under which such sale may be held; provided, that none of the bonds may be sold for a price less than the face value thereof; provided further, that such terms and conditions shall not conflict with any of the requirements of this article.

Subject to the provisions and limitations contained in this article, the authority may from time to time sell and issue refunding bonds for the purpose of refunding any matured or unmatured bonds of the authority then outstanding. Such refunding bonds shall be subrogated and entitled to all priorities, rights and pledges to which the bonds refunded thereby were entitled.

Approval by the president of the authority of the terms and conditions under which any bonds of the authority may be issued shall be requisite to their validity. Such approval shall be entered on the minutes of the meetings of the board of directors at which the bonds are authorized and shall be signed by the president of the authority.

The authority may pay out of the proceeds of the sale of its bonds attorneys' fees and the expenses of issuance which the said board of directors may deem necessary and advantageous in connection with the issuance of such bonds. No fiscal agents' fees shall be paid in connection with the issuance or sale of any bonds.

Bonds issued by the authority shall not be general obligations of the authority but shall be payable solely out of the funds appropriated and pledged therefor in section 41-10-30.

As security for the payment of the principal of and interest on the bonds issued by it, the authority is hereby authorized and empowered to pledge for payment of such principal and interest the funds that are appropriated and pledged in section 41-10-30 for payment of such principal and interest. All such pledges made by the authority shall take precedence in the order of the adoption of the resolutions containing such pledges; provided, that each pledge for the benefit of refunding bonds shall have the same priority as the pledge for the benefit of the bonds refunded thereby.

All contracts made and all bonds issued by the authority pursuant to the provisions of this article shall be solely and exclusively obligations of the authority and shall not constitute or create an obligation or debt of the state of Alabama.

Bonds issued by the authority shall be construed to be negotiable instruments, although payable solely from a specified source as provided in this article.

All bonds issued by the authority and the income therefrom shall be exempt from all taxation in the state.

Any bonds issued by the authority may be used by the holder thereof as security for any funds belonging to the state or to any political subdivision, instrumentality or agency of the state in any instance where security for such deposits may be required by law.

Unless otherwise directed by the court having jurisdiction thereof or the document that is the source of authority, a trustee, executor, administrator, guardian or one acting in any other fiduciary capacity may, in addition to any other investment powers conferred by law and with the exercise of reasonable business prudence, invest trust funds in bonds of the authority.

Neither a public hearing nor consent of the state department of finance or any other department or agency shall be a prerequisite to the issuance of bonds by the authority. The bonds issued under the provisions of this article shall be legal investments for funds of the teachers' retirement system of Alabama, the employees' retirement system of Alabama and the state insurance fund. (Acts 1965, No. 662, p. 1187, § 9.)

General funds of state may not be used to service or pay bonds. — A new tax (§§ 40-25-60 through 40-25-62) has been levied and appropriated to pay, at their respective maturities, the principal of, and interest on, bonds issued by the authority. No part of the taxes presently paid into the general fund of the state will or can be used to service the bonds authorized to be issued by the authority. Furthermore, this section expressly provides that the bonds do not create a debt of the state, and the general faith and credit of the state are not pledged to service the bonds. The bonds are required to be retired solely from the receipts of the special tax levied for that purpose. Edmonson v. State Indus. Dev. Auth., 279 Ala. 206, 184 So. 2d 115 (1966).

§ 41-10-29. Disposition of proceeds from sale of bonds and refunding bonds.

The proceeds of all bonds, other than refunding bonds, issued by the authority remaining after paying expenses of their issuance shall be deposited in the state treasury and shall be carried in the state treasury in a special or separate account. Such funds shall be subject to be drawn upon by the authority with the approval of the president of the authority, but any funds so withdrawn shall be used solely for the purposes for which the bonds were issued as authorized in this article.

The state treasurer, with the approval of the president of the authority, shall invest funds not needed immediately or within the ensuing 30 days for any purpose for which they are held, which investments shall be made in the manner authorized and provided for in section 36-17-18.

The proceeds from the sale of any refunding bonds issued under this article remaining after paying the expenses of their issuance shall be used only for the purpose of refunding the principal of outstanding bonds of the authority and of paying any premium that may be necessary to be paid in order to redeem or retire the bonds to be refunded. (Acts 1965, No. 662, p. 1187, § 10.)

§ 41-10-30. Pledge and appropriation of certain tax receipts for sinking fund for payment of principal and interest on bonds.

For the purpose of providing funds to enable the authority to pay, at their respective maturities, the principal of and interest on any bonds issued by it under the provisions of this article and to accomplish the objects of this article, there is hereby irrevocably pledged to such purpose and there is hereby appropriated so much as may be necessary for such purpose of the receipts from the tax levied by sections 40-25-2 and 40-25-41 and distributed in accordance with subparagraph (1) b. 1. i. of section 40-25-23. All moneys hereby appropriated and pledged shall constitute a sinking fund for the purpose of paying the principal of and the interest on the bonds authorized by this article. (Acts 1965, No. 662, p. 1187, § 11.)

§ 41-10-31. Payment of principal and interest on bonds and maintenance of records pertaining thereto by state treasurer.

Out of the revenues appropriated and pledged in section 41-10-30, the state treasurer is hereby authorized and directed to pay the principal of and interest on the bonds issued by the authority under the provisions of this article, as said principal and interest shall respectively mature, and the state treasurer is further authorized and directed to set up and maintain appropriate records pertaining thereto. (Acts 1965, No. 662, p. 1187, § 12.)

§ 41-10-32. Dissolution of authority; title to property of authority to vest in state upon dissolution of authority.

At any time when no bonds of the authority are outstanding, the authority may be dissolved upon the filing with the secretary of state of an application for dissolution, which shall be subscribed by each of the members of the authority and sworn to by each such member before an officer authorized to take acknowledgments to deeds. Upon the filing of such application for dissolution, the authority shall cease to exist. The secretary of state shall file and record the application for dissolution in an appropriate book of record in his office and shall make and issue, under the great seal of the state, a certificate that the authority is dissolved and shall record such certificate with the application for dissolution.

Title to all property held in the name of the authority shall be vested in the state upon dissolution of the authority. (Acts 1965, No. 662, p. 1187, § 13.)

ARTICLE 3.

SOUTHERN PRODUCTS MART AUTHORITY.

§ 41-10-50. Short title.

This article shall be known as and may be cited as the Southern Products Mart Authority Act. (Acts 1973, No. 1210, p. 2032, § 21.)

§ 41-10-51. Definitions.

When used in this article, the following terms shall have the following meanings, respectively, unless the context clearly indicates otherwise:

(1) STATE. The state of Alabama.

(2) COUNTY. Jefferson county in this state.

(3) AUTHORITY. The southern products mart authority authorized to be incorporated under the provisions of this article.

(4) BOARD or BOARD OF DIRECTORS. The board of directors of the authority.

(5) DIRECTOR OF FINANCE. The director of finance of the state.

(6) DIRECTOR OF THE ALABAMA DEVELOPMENT OFFICE. The director of the Alabama development office of the state.

(7) EXECUTIVE SECRETARY TO THE GOVERNOR. The executive secretary to the governor of the state.

(8) STATE TREASURER. The treasurer of the state.

(9) STATE TREASURY. The treasury of the state.

(10) BOND. Any bond authorized to be issued pursuant to the provisions of this article, including a refunding bond as hereinafter authorized.

(11) COUPON. Any interest coupon evidencing an installment of interest payable with respect to a bond.

(12) PERSON. Any individual, firm, partnership, corporation, company, association, joint-stock association, the state or any political subdivision thereof, any agency or board of the state, any municipality or body politic and includes any trustee, receiver, assignee or other similar representative thereof. (Acts 1973, No. 1210, p. 2032, § 2.)

§ 41-10-52. Purpose of article; construction of article.

It is the intention of the legislature by the passage of this article to authorize the incorporation of the director of finance, the director of the Alabama development office, the state treasurer and the executive secretary to the governor for the purpose of acquiring land for and erecting, constructing, maintaining and operating thereon a products market, exhibition halls, buildings and other related structures and facilities in Jefferson county, Alabama, where products and goods may be displayed to encourage the buying and selling of such products and goods, to encourage the expansion of existing industries in

Alabama, to encourage the location of new industries in Alabama and to foster and encourage the growth of the general economy of Alabama, through a corporation to be composed of said officials whose incorporation is hereby authorized and to vest such corporation with all powers, authorities, rights, privileges and titles that may be necessary to enable it to accomplish such purpose.

This article shall be liberally construed in order to effect the said purpose. (Acts 1973, No. 1210, p. 2032, § 1.)

§ 41-10-53. Authority and procedure for incorporation of authority; members, officers and directors of authority; reduction to writing, recordation and admissibility in evidence of proceedings of board of directors.

(a) The director of finance, the director of the Alabama development office, the state treasurer and the executive secretary to the governor are hereby authorized to become a corporation, with the powers and authorities provided for in this article, by proceeding according to the provisions hereinafter outlined in this article. To become a corporation, the director of finance, the director of the Alabama development office, the state treasurer and the executive secretary to the governor shall present to the secretary of state of Alabama an application signed by them which shall set forth:

(1) The name, official designation and official residence of each of the applicants, together with a certified copy of the commission evidencing each applicant's right to office;

(2) The date on which each applicant was inducted into office and the term of office of each of the applicants;

(3) The name of the proposed corporation, which shall be "southern products mart authority";

(4) The location of the principal office of the proposed corporation; and

(5) Any other matter relating to the proposed corporation which the applicants may choose to insert and which shall not be inconsistent with this article or the laws of the state.

The application shall be subscribed and sworn to by each of the applicants before an officer authorized by the laws of the state to take acknowledgments to deeds. The secretary of state of Alabama shall examine the application; and, if he finds it to be in substantial compliance with the provisions of this article, he shall receive and file it and record it in an appropriate book of record in his office. The secretary of state of Alabama shall then make and issue to the applicants a certificate of incorporation, under the great seal of the state, reciting the fact of the incorporation of the authority and shall record a counterpart of said certificate of incorporation with the application. There shall be no fees paid to the secretary of state of Alabama for any work in connection with the incorporation of the authority or in connection with the dissolution of the authority. Upon the issuance of said certificate of incorporation, the authority shall constitute a body corporate having corporate succession under the name proposed in the application.

(b) The applicants named in the application and their respective successors in office shall constitute the members of the authority. The director of the Alabama development office shall be the president of the authority, the executive secretary to the governor shall be the vice-president of the authority, the director of finance shall be the secretary of the authority, and the state treasurer shall be the treasurer of the authority and shall act as custodian of its funds. The members of the authority shall constitute all the members of the board of directors of the authority, and any three members of said board of directors shall constitute a quorum for the transaction of business. The concurrence of three members of the board of directors shall be necessary for any action taken by the authority. Should any of said officials of the state die or should his term of office (as director of finance, director of the Alabama development office, state treasurer or executive secretary to the governor, as the case may be) expire or should he resign therefrom, his successor in office shall take his place as a member, officer and director of the authority. No member, officer or director of the authority shall draw any salary, in addition to that now authorized by law, for any service he may render or any duty he may perform in connection with the authority.

(c) All proceedings had and done by the board of directors shall be reduced to writing by the secretary of the authority and recorded in a substantially bound book. Copies of such proceedings, when certified by the secretary of the authority under the seal of the authority, shall be received in all courts as prima facie evidence of the matters and things therein certified. (Acts 1973, No. 1210, p. 2032, § 3.)

§ 41-10-54. Powers of authority generally; acquisition by eminent domain of real property or rights owned by railroads or utilities not authorized.

(a) The authority shall have the following powers:

　(1) To have succession by its corporate name until it is dissolved;

　(2) To adopt bylaws for the regulation of its affairs and the conduct of its business;

　(3) To adopt and use an official seal and alter the same at pleasure;

　(4) To maintain a principal office in Jefferson county, Alabama, and suboffices at such places within the state as it may designate;

　(5) To sue and be sued and to prosecute and defend civil actions in any court having jurisdiction of the subject matter and of the parties;

　(6) To acquire by purchase, gift, condemnation or any other lawful means any real, personal or mixed property necessary or convenient in connection with the purpose for which the authority is formed and to hold title to such property, together with all rights incidental to its estate in such property;

　(7) To establish in Jefferson county, Alabama, a products market to be known as the southern products mart authority and, in connection therewith, to acquire, erect, construct, insure, maintain, manage, operate and lease all real and personal property, facilities, buildings, warehouses, storage facilities, exhibition halls, parking areas and other structures and

appurtenances of every kind and character used or useful in promoting the buying and selling of products and goods or used or useful in promoting the expansion of existing industries in the state or used or useful in promoting the location of new industries in the state or used or useful in fostering and encouraging the growth of the general economy of the state, together with all the rights incidental to such acquiring, erecting, constructing, insuring, maintaining, managing, operating and leasing;

(8) To exercise the right of eminent domain to acquire property used or useful for the purpose for which the authority is formed as freely and completely as and in the same manner that the state of Alabama is empowered to exercise such rights;

(9) To lease all or any part of the facilities or property of the authority to any person and to fix, revise from time to time, charge and collect rentals under such leases;

(10) To establish rules and regulations for the use of any of the facilities or property of the authority;

(11) To make and enter into contracts, leases and agreements with any person necessary for or incidental to the execution of the powers of the authority under this article, including contracts and agreements for professional services deemed necessary for such purpose by the authority;

(12) To appoint and employ such managers, employees, agents, fiscal advisors and attorneys as the business of the authority may require for efficient accomplishment of the purpose of this article;

(13) To appoint an advisory committee consisting of any number of persons not in excess of nine to advise the authority on its affairs;

(14) To borrow money for its corporate purposes and, in evidence of such borrowing, to sell and issue bonds of the authority and to refund any thereof by the issuance of refunding bonds, such bonds to be payable as to both principal and interest solely from the revenues of the authority and proceeds from the sale of such bonds as provided in this article and, as security for payment of the principal of and the interest on its bonds, to pledge the revenues and anticipated revenues of the authority as provided in this article. No bonds issued under the provisions of this article shall constitute a debt or liability of the state or any political subdivision thereof other than the authority or a pledge of the faith and credit of the state or of any political subdivision thereof, but such bonds shall be payable solely from the revenues and anticipated revenues pledged or available for that payment as authorized in this article. All such bonds shall contain on the face thereof a statement to the effect that the authority is obligated to pay the principal thereof and interest thereon only from its revenues and the proceeds from the sale of such bonds, that neither the state nor any political subdivision thereof other than the authority is obligated to pay such principal or interest and that neither the faith and credit nor the taxing power of the state or of any political subdivision thereof is pledged to the payment of such principal or interests;

(15) To anticipate by the issuance of its bonds, as limited in this article, the receipt of the revenues from its facilities and, as security for the payment of the principal of and interest on its bonds, to enter into any lawful covenant and to pledge the revenues from its facilities;

(16) To invest as provided in this article the proceeds from the sale of its bonds pending need therefor;

(17) To establish a fiscal year; and

(18) To do all other acts and things necessary or convenient to carry out the powers granted in this article.

(b) Notwithstanding any provision to the contrary, nothing in this article shall be construed to authorize the acquisition by eminent domain of any real property or right owned or held by railroads or utilities, both public and private. (Acts 1973, No. 1210, p. 2032, § 4.)

Cross reference. — As to eminent domain generally, see § 18-1-1 et seq.

§ 41-10-55. Issuance and sale of bonds authorized generally; form, terms, denominations, etc., thereof; bonds to be deemed negotiable instruments; redemption.

Bonds of the authority may be sold from time to time as the board of directors may deem advantageous; provided, that the aggregate principal amount of bonds of the authority which may be issued under this article shall be limited to $20,000,000.00, but the said limitation shall not apply to refunding bonds which may be issued under this article and also shall not apply to bonds of the authority which may be issued under any other act which may at any time hereafter be enacted.

The bonds shall be in such forms and denominations and of such tenor and maturities, shall bear such rate or rates of interest payable and evidenced in such manner and may contain other provisions not inconsistent with this article as may be provided in the resolution or resolutions of the board of directors of the authority wherein the bonds are authorized to be issued; provided, that none of the bonds shall have a specified maturity date later than 30 years after its date. Such bonds may be in bearer form with interest coupons or registered as to principal and interest or may be registered as to principal only and, upon surrender and endorsement or assignment, may be exchanged for a like bearer or registered security for a reasonable fee and upon such signature guarantees and other assurances as the authority may prudently require.

The bonds and coupons shall be construed to be negotiable instruments although payable from a specified source as provided in this article, and such bonds and coupons shall have and are hereby declared to have all the qualities and incidents of negotiable instruments under the negotiable instruments law of the state.

The authority may at its election retain in the resolution or resolutions under which any of the bonds are issued an option to redeem all or any thereof and at such redemption price or prices and after such notice or notices and on such terms and conditions as may be set forth in said resolution or resolutions and as may be briefly recited on the face of the bonds with respect to which such option of redemption is retained. With respect to those of the bonds having stated maturities more than 10 years after the date thereof, the authority shall retain in the resolution or resolutions authorizing their issuance an option to redeem at the expiration of the tenth year following the date thereof and on any interest payment date thereafter all or any of the bonds having stated maturities after the expiration of the tenth year following their date, at such redemption price or prices and after such redemption notice or notices and on such terms and conditions as may be set forth in said resolution or resolutions and briefly recited on the face of the bonds. (Acts 1973, No. 1210, p. 2032, § 5.)

§ 41-10-56. Resolution authorizing issuance of bonds to contain recital as to authority for issuance; notice of passage of resolution; limitation period and venue for actions to contest validity of resolutions, bonds, etc.

(a) Any resolution authorizing any bonds under this article shall contain a recital that they are issued pursuant to the provisions of this article, which recital shall be conclusive evidence that said bonds have been duly authorized pursuant to the provisions of this article, notwithstanding the provisions of any other law now in force or hereafter enacted or amended.

(b) Upon the adoption by the board of directors of any resolution providing for the issuance of bonds under the provisions of this article, the authority may in its discretion cause to be published once a week for two consecutive weeks, in a newspaper published and having general circulation in Jefferson county, Alabama, a notice in substantially the following form (the blanks being properly filled in): "Southern Products Mart Authority, an agency of the State of Alabama, on the . . . . . . day of . . . ., adopted a resolution providing for the issuance of $. . . . . principal amount of bonds of the said Authority for purposes authorized in the act of the Legislature of Alabama under which the said Authority was organized. Any civil action or proceeding questioning the validity of said resolution or said bonds or the pledge and agreements made in said resolution for the benefit thereof or the proceedings authorizing the same must be commenced within 20 days after the first publication of this notice. Southern Products Mart Authority, by: . . . ., its president."

(c) Any civil action or proceeding in any court seeking to set aside or invalidate a resolution providing for the issuance of bonds under the provisions of this article or to contest the validity of any such bonds or the validity of the pledge or agreement made therefor must be commenced within 20 days after the first publication of such notice. After the expiration of the said 20-day period, no right of action or defense founded upon the validity of the resolution or other proceedings, if any, or of the said bonds, or the said pledge or agreement shall be asserted. In the event of such publication, the validity of the said resolution, proceedings, bonds, pledge or agreement shall not be open to question in any court on any ground whatever, except in a civil action or proceeding commenced within such period. Any such civil action and any civil action to protect or enforce any rights under the provisions of this article shall be brought in the circuit court of Jefferson county. (Acts 1973, No. 1210, p. 2032, § 15.)

§ 41-10-57. Execution and delivery of bonds and interest coupons.

The bonds shall be signed by the president of the authority and attested by its secretary, and all interest coupons applicable to the bonds shall be signed by the president of the authority; provided, that a facsimile of the signature of one, but not of both, of said officers may be printed or otherwise reproduced on any of the bonds in lieu of their being manually signed, and a facsimile of the president's signature may be printed or otherwise reproduced on any of the interest coupons in lieu of their being manually signed. The seal of the authority shall be impressed on the bonds; provided, that a facsimile of said seal may be printed or otherwise reproduced on any of the bonds in lieu of being manually impressed thereon. If any officer duly authorized thereunto, after signing any of such bonds or the interest coupons thereunto appertaining, manually or by facsimile, shall for any reason vacate said office, the said bonds and interest coupons may nevertheless be delivered at any time thereafter as the act and deed of the authority. (Acts 1973, No. 1210, p. 2032, § 6.)

§ 41-10-58. Sale of bonds; public hearing or consent of department of finance, etc., not a prerequisite to issuance of bonds.

(a) Any of the bonds may be sold at any time and from time to time as said board of directors may deem advantageous. The bonds must be sold only at public sale, either on sealed bids or at public auction, to the bidder whose bid reflects the lowest net interest cost to the authority for the bonds being sold, computed from the date of those at the time being sold to their respective maturities; provided, that if no bid acceptable to the authority is received, it may reject all bids. Notice of each such sale must be given by publication in either a financial journal or a financial newspaper published in the city of New York, New York, and also by publication in a newspaper published in this state which is customarily published not less often than six days during each calendar week, each of which notices must be published at least one time not less than 10 days prior to the date fixed for the sale. The board of directors may fix the terms and conditions under which each such sale may be held; provided, that none of the bonds may be sold for a price less than the face value thereof; provided further, that such terms and conditions shall not conflict with any of the requirements of this article.

(b) Neither a public hearing nor consent of the state department of finance or any other department or agency shall be a prerequisite to the issuance of any of the bonds. (Acts 1973, No. 1210, p. 2032, § 7.)

§ 41-10-59. Refunding bonds.

Subject to the provisions contained in this article, the authority may from time to time sell and issue refunding bonds for the purpose of refunding any matured or unmatured bonds of the authority issued under this article and then outstanding, together with any premium that may be necessary to be paid in order to redeem or retire the bonds proposed to be refunded. The limitations provided for in section 41-10-56 on the amount of bonds authorized in this article shall not apply to the said refunding bonds. (Acts 1973, No. 1210, p. 2032, § 8.)

§ 41-10-60. Disposition of proceeds from sale of bonds and refunding bonds.

(a) The authority shall pay out of the proceeds from the sale of any of the bonds all expenses, including fees of agents and attorneys and other charges, which said board of directors may deem necessary or advantageous in connection with the issuance of the bonds. The proceeds of the bonds, other than refunding bonds, remaining after paying the expenses of their issuance shall be turned over to the state treasurer and shall be carried by him in a special account to the credit of the authority and shall be subject to be drawn on by the authority solely for the purposes of acquiring real estate suitable for the purpose of the authority in Jefferson county, Alabama, including all expenses reasonably necessary in connection with such acquisition, and erecting, constructing and equipping on such real estate exhibition halls, buildings, warehouses, storage facilities, parking areas and other structures and appurtenances of every kind and character used or useful in connection with the purpose for which the authority is created and all reasonable and necessary expenses incidental thereto and to the issuance of said bonds, including payment of principal of those bonds which shall mature during the construction of said facilities and for a period not exceeding six months thereafter and including payment of interest which shall accrue on said bonds during the construction of said facilities and for a period not exceeding six months thereafter.

Any portion of the principal proceeds derived from the sale of the bonds which the board of directors of the authority may determine is not then needed for any of the purposes for which the bonds are authorized to be issued shall, on order of the authority, be invested by the state treasurer in any securities that are direct general obligations of the United States of America or the principal of and interest on which are unconditionally and irrevocably guaranteed by the United States of America. Any such securities may, at any time and from time to time on order of the authority, be sold or otherwise converted by the state treasurer into cash. The income derived from any such investments shall be disbursed on order of the authority for any purpose for which it may lawfully expend funds.

Any balance in said account shall, upon completion of the facilities above described and the payment of all costs, be transferred to the reserve fund account of the authority provided for in this article.

(b) The proceeds from the sale of all refunding bonds issued by the authority under this article remaining after paying the expenses of their issuance shall be turned over to the state treasurer and used only for the purpose of refunding the principal of bonds of the authority theretofore issued under this article and then outstanding and paying any premium that may be necessary to be paid in order to redeem or retire the bonds to be refunded. (Acts 1973, No. 1210, p. 2032, § 11.)

§ 41-10-61. Exemption from taxation of bonds, properties, income, etc., of authority; use of bonds as security for deposits of state funds; investment of trust funds in bonds.

(a) The properties of the authority and the income therefrom and all lease agreements made by the authority and income therefrom shall be forever exempt from any and all taxation in the state of Alabama. The bonds of the authority and the income therefrom shall be forever exempt from any and all taxation in the state of Alabama.

(b) Any of the bonds may be used by the holder thereof as security for the deposit of any funds belonging to the state or to any instrumentality or agency of the state in any instance where security for such deposits may be required by law.

(c) Unless otherwise directed by the court having jurisdiction thereof or by the document that is the source of authority, a trustee, executor, administrator, guardian or one acting in any other fiduciary capacity may, in addition to any other investment powers conferred by law and with the exercise of reasonable business prudence, invest trust funds in any of the bonds. (Acts 1973, No. 1210, p. 2032, § 9.)

§ 41-10-62. Liability upon bonds, debts, agreements, etc., of authority.

All debts assumed or created by the authority and all bonds issued by it shall be solely and exclusively obligations of the authority and shall not be obligations or debts of the state of Alabama. All contracts and agreements made by the authority pursuant to the provisions of this article shall be solely and exclusively obligations of the authority and shall not be obligations of the state of Alabama. (Acts 1973, No. 1210, p. 2032, § 10.)

§ 41-10-63. Authority and procedure for pledge of revenues of authority and creation of statutory lien upon facilities and properties thereof for payment of principal and interest on bonds; remedies upon default in payment of principal or interest on bonds.

(a) In the proceedings authorizing the issuance of any of its bonds, the authority is hereby authorized and empowered to pledge for the payment of the principal of and interest on such bonds, as the said principal and interest shall respectively mature, and to agree to use solely for such purpose all the revenues which under the provisions of section 41-10-65 are provided for the payment of the said principal and interest. All such pledges made by the authority shall take precedence in the order of the resolutions containing such pledge.

(b) In said proceedings the authority may further provide and create a statutory lien upon the facilities and properties of the authority as security for the payment of said principal and interest. Such statutory lien shall not be subject to foreclosure.

(c) Upon the issuance of any bonds pursuant to this article, the authority shall file in the office of the judge of probate of Jefferson county, Alabama, an instrument reciting the issuance of such bonds and the pledge of said revenues and the creation of said statutory lien as security therefor, and the filing of such instrument shall constitute constructive notice of said pledge and lien. Such instrument shall be received and recorded by said judge of probate upon payment of the fee for the recording of mortgages, but no tax shall be payable with respect thereto.

(d) If there be any default in the payment of the principal of or interest on any bonds issued under this article, then the holders of any of the bonds and any of the interest coupons applicable thereto or any one or more of them shall be limited to the following remedies:

(1) They may by civil action, mandamus or other proceeding compel performance of all duties of the officers and directors of the authority and of the state treasurer with respect to the use of funds for the payment of the bonds and for the performance of the agreements of the authority contained in the proceedings under which they were issued; and

(2) They shall be entitled, regardless of the sufficiency of the security for the bonds in default and as a matter of right, to the appointment of a receiver to administer and operate the facilities and other properties of the authority out of the revenues from which the bonds issued with respect thereto are payable, with power to make leases and fix and collect rents sufficient to provide for the payment of the principal of and interest on the bonds and any other obligations outstanding against the facilities and other properties of the authority or the revenues therefrom and for the payment of the expenses of operating and maintaining such facilities and properties and with power to apply the income therefrom in accordance with the provisions of the proceedings under which the bonds were authorized to be issued; provided, that said receiver shall have no power to sell any of the property or facilities of the authority. (Acts 1973, No. 1210, p. 2032, § 13.)

§ 41-10-64. Special and continuing trust fund for payment of principal and interest on bonds of authority and maintenance, etc., of facilities thereof.

For the purpose of providing funds for the payment of the costs and expenses necessary to accomplish the purpose of this authority and for the payment of the principal of and interest on any bonds issued by the authority under the provisions of this article, there is hereby created and irrevocably pledged to the payment of such obligations a special and continuing trust fund which shall consist of all revenues, receipts and income from rents contracted for and received by the authority and all revenues, receipts and income received by the authority from any other source whatsoever.

There shall be created within said special and continuing trust fund a reserve fund account of said authority in the state treasury, in which shall be placed as a trust fund and held separate and apart from all other moneys of the state or of the authority, any moneys left over after the completion of the acquisition, erection and construction of the facilities of the authority and the payment of all costs in connection therewith and in connection with the issuance of the bonds and all excess rentals and other surplus income after the payment of all annual charges and expenses of operation in each fiscal year, including principal and interest. Said reserve fund shall be held by the state treasurer in trust for the authority and the holders of its bonds and may be ihvested only in securities which are either direct obligations of the United States of America or fully guaranteed as to principal and interest by the United States of America. Said reserve fund shall be used by the state treasurer to pay, when due and payable, any installment of principal and interest or both on the outstanding bonds of the authority for which said fund was created which cannot be paid out of current revenues or other moneys of the authority. Said funds shall not be diverted or used for any other purpose.

There shall be created in said special and continuing trust fund an account thereof in which shall be deposited, segregated and held only the amounts reasonably estimated to be necessary for the maintenance, operation and upkeep of the facilities of the authority, with all excess moneys at the end of each fiscal year being transferred to the reserve fund, and the authority is authorized and is hereby directed to pay out of such account in the special and continuing trust fund all reasonable expenses of the maintenance, operation and upkeep of the facilities of the authority. (Acts 1973, No. 1210, p. 2032, § 12.)

§ 41-10-65. Payment of principal and interest on bonds and maintenance of records pertaining thereto by state treasurer.

Out of the revenues referred to in section 41-10-64, the state treasurer is authorized and directed to pay the principal of and interest on the bonds issued by the authority under the provisions of this chapter as such principal and interest shall respectively mature, and he is further authorized and directed to set up and maintain appropriate records pertaining thereto. (Acts 1973, No. 1210, p. 2032, § 14.)

§ 41-10-66. Annual audit of books and accounts of authority; disposition of reports thereof.

At least once every 12 months subsequent to the formation of the authority, the authority shall appoint and employ a certified public accountant who shall make an examination in detail of all books and accounts of the authority since the preceding examination and make a full report thereof in writing to be submitted to the authority and spread upon its minute book at the first meeting of the board after the receipt of said report. A copy of each such report shall be retained in the principal office of the authority and made available at reasonable hours to any holder of any bond of the authority upon request. A copy of each such report shall also be delivered by the authority to the state treasurer within 30 days after its receipt by the authority. (Acts 1973, No. 1210, p. 2032, § 16.)

§ 41-10-67. Awarding, etc., of contracts for construction of facilities, buildings and structures; supervision, etc., of construction; payments to contractors; agreement of authority and building commission as to construction cost estimate.

All facilities, buildings and structures constructed by the authority shall be constructed according to plans and specifications of architects or engineers selected by the authority. Such construction shall be done under the supervision and direction of the Alabama building commission or any agency designated by the legislature as its successor following award for each part of the work to the lowest responsible bidder after advertising for receipt and public opening of sealed bids; provided, that the invitations for bids and the bidding documents shall be so arranged that any alternates from the base bid shall constitute cumulative deductions from the base bid; and, in determining the lowest bidder, if funds are insufficient to construct the facilities, buildings and structures on the lowest base bid, then the commission may proceed to consider the bids upon the basis of the base bids of all bidders minus the respective reductions stated for the first alternate and, if the lowest bid so determined is not then within the funds available, the commission shall proceed to consider the base bid minus the first and second alternates together to determine the lowest bid and in like manner throughout all alternates, if need be, so that in no event shall there be any discretion as to which alternate or alternates will be used in determining the lowest responsible bidder. All such contracts shall be lump sum contracts. All contracts for the entire work shall be awarded at the same time, but notice to proceed may be withheld until prior work under another contract has progressed to a point where the joint or following work can best be coordinated for the earliest completion of the entire project in a sound and workmanlike manner. The contracts shall be executed by the authority upon the determination of the commission as to the lowest bidders, respectively.

Payments made by the authority under the construction contracts shall be upon the contractor's written sworn request only if endorsed as approved by the commission or in any lesser amount the commission shall endorse as having been then earned on said contract.

The authority and the commission shall agree to a construction cost estimate including reimbursement to the commission of its reasonable direct cost in having plans, specifications and contract documents prepared and in supervising and inspecting the work. After the contracts have been awarded, such construction cost estimates shall be revised, and all extras on the contracts may be awarded within the funds available. (Acts 1973, No. 1210, p. 2032, § 17.)

§ 41-10-68. Leasing of buildings, facilities and structures.

The authority and any person are hereby authorized to enter into a lease or leases for the use and occupancy of any or all property of the authority or for the use and occupancy of any space in or all of any buildings or facilities constructed by the authority under the provisions of this article; provided, that the proposed use by any such lessee or lessees shall be in furtherance of the purpose for which the authority is created; provided further, that an adequate rental is established in said lease or leases. Any executive head of any agency, board, commission, public corporation, bureau or department of the state is hereby separately authorized to enter into any said lease with the authority.

No free space shall be available to any person on any of the property or in any of the buildings, facilities and structures of the authority so long as the principal of or interest on any bonds, including refunding bonds, issued by the authority remains unpaid. If at any time there is or is about to be vacant space on the property or in the buildings, facilities or structures constructed by the authority and there is no person available to rent such space for the purpose for which the authority is created, then, but only in such event, in order to prevent default in its bonds, the authority is hereby authorized to enter into leases with any person for any lawful purposes pursuant to and subject to such rules and regulations as to such occupancy as may be adopted by the authority; provided, that the use of such facilities by such tenants shall not interfere with the use of the premises by other tenants who are occupying same in furtherance of the purpose for which the authority is created; provided further, that any such leases shall be based upon a rental rate, established by the authority, commensurate with the then current commercial rates for similar facilities and space of like character in the city of Birmingham, Jefferson county, Alabama. Any such lease shall not be for the purpose of competing with private enterprise or for lending public credit, but shall be solely for the use and benefit of the holders of the authority's bonds to avoid default thereon and to insure the prompt payment of the principal thereof and interest thereon when due. (Acts 1973, No. 1210, p. 2032, § 18.)

§ 41-10-69. Conveyance of lands, buildings, properties, etc., of authority to state upon payment in full of bonds, etc.; dissolution of authority.

(a) When all bonds issued by the authority and all obligations assumed by it under the provisions of this article shall have been paid in full, the president of the authority shall thereupon execute and deliver in the name of and in behalf of the authority an appropriate deed or deeds, to which the seal of the authority shall be affixed and attested by the secretary of the authority, whereby there shall be conveyed to the state all the lands, buildings, fixtures, properties and other assets then owned by the authority.

(b) The then officers and directors of the authority shall at such time file with the secretary of state a written statement, subscribed and sworn to by each of them, reciting the payment in full of all bonds theretofore issued by the authority and the execution and delivery of such deed or deeds to the state, which statement shall be filed by the secretary of state and recorded with the certificate of incorporation of the authority, whereupon the authority shall stand dissolved. (Acts 1973, No. 1210, p. 2032, § 19.)

ARTICLE 4.

STATE PRODUCTS MART AND COLISEUM AUTHORITIES.

§ 41-10-80. Short title.

This article shall be known and may be cited as the State Products Mart and Coliseum Authority Act. (Acts 1965, 1st Ex. Sess., No. 174, p. 224, § 1.)

§ 41-10-81. Definitions.

When used in this article, the following terms shall have the following meanings, respectively, unless the context clearly indicates otherwise:

(1) CORPORATION. A corporation organized pursuant to the provisions of this article.

(2) BOARD. The board of directors of the corporation.

(3) STATE. The state of Alabama.

(4) COUNTY. That county in the state which authorized the organization of the corporation.

(5) MUNICIPALITY. The incorporated cities or towns located in the county which authorized the organization of the corporation.

(6) PUBLIC CORPORATION. Any public corporation now or hereafter organized or created in the state pursuant to the authorization or determination by the municipality or by the municipality and any one or more other cities and towns in the state or by the county or by the county and any one or more counties in the state.

(7) STATE AGENCY. Any public corporation now or hereafter organized or created in the state pursuant to the authorization or determination of the legislature of the state or any of its boards or agencies which are separate corporate entities from the state and from any of the counties or municipalities in the state and the debts of which are not debts of the state or any county or any municipality within the meaning of sections 213, 224 or 225 of the Constitution of the state.

(8) GOVERNING BODY. The county commission in which jurisdiction over the affairs of the county is vested by law.

(9) PROJECT. Any buildings and other improvements and facilities located or to be located within the municipality or within its police jurisdiction and designed for use as a products market, exhibition hall or coliseum where products and goods may be displayed to encourage the buying or selling thereof or where exhibits, contests and sporting events may be conducted, together with any lands deemed by the board to be desirable in connection therewith.

257

(10) Bond. Any bond authorized to be issued pursuant to the provisions of this article, including refunding bonds.

(11) Coupon. Any interest coupon evidencing an installment of interest payable with respect to a bond.

(12) Indenture. A mortgage, an indenture of mortgage, deed of trust, trust agreement or trust indenture executed by the corporation as security for any bonds. (Acts 1965, 1st Ex. Sess., No. 174, p. 224, § 3.)

§ 41-10-82. Purpose of article; construction of article generally.

It is the intention of the legislature by the passage of this chapter to empower each county in the state to authorize the incorporation of one or more public corporations as political subdivisions of the state for the purpose of providing products markets, exhibition halls, coliseums and buildings and related structures where products and goods may be displayed and exhibits, contests and sporting events conducted in order to encourage the buying and selling of products and goods, to encourage the expansion of existing industries in Alabama, to encourage the location of new industries in Alabama and to encourage public interest in sports and amusements and thus to promote commerce and goodwill in the state of Alabama and to invest each corporation organized hereunder with such powers as may be necessary or desirable to enable it to accomplish such purposes.

This article shall be liberally construed in conformity with such intent. (Acts 1965, 1st Ex. Sess., No. 174, p. 224, § 2.)

§ 41-10-83. Application for authority to incorporate; adoption by governing body of resolution authorizing formation of corporation.

In the event that any number of natural persons, not less than three, shall file with the governing body an application in writing for authority to incorporate a public corporation under the provisions of this article, and it shall be made to appear to the governing body that each of said persons is a duly qualified elector of and owner of property in the municipality and the governing body shall duly adopt a resolution declaring that it will be wise, expedient and necessary or advisable that such corporation be formed and that the persons filing such application shall be authorized to proceed to form such corporation, then the said persons shall become the incorporators of and shall proceed to incorporate the corporation in the manner provided in this article. No corporation shall be formed under this article unless the application provided for in this section shall be made and unless the resolution provided for in this section shall be adopted. (Acts 1965, 1st Ex. Sess., No. 174, p. 224, § 4.)

§ 41-10-84. Contents of certificate of incorporation generally; adoption of resolution by governing body approving form and contents of certificate of incorporation.

(a) The certificate of incorporation of the corporation shall state:

(1) The names of the persons forming the corporation, together with the residence of each thereof and a statement that each of them is a duly qualified elector of and owner of property in the municipality;

(2) The name of the corporation (which shall be "the state products mart (coliseum) authority located in . . . . county" or some other name of similar import which is available for use);

(3) The location of its principal office, which shall be in the municipality;

(4) The purposes for which the corporation is proposed to be organized;

(5) The number of directors, which shall be not less than three nor more than five, subject, however, to mandatory increase as provided in this article; and

(6) Any other matter relating to the corporation which the incorporators may choose to insert and which is not inconsistent with this chapter or with the laws of the state.

(b) The form and contents of the certificate of incorporation must be submitted to the governing body for its approval. Any approval of such certificate by the governing body shall be evidenced by resolution duly entered upon the minutes of the governing body. (Acts 1965, 1st Ex. Sess., No. 174, p. 224, § 5.)

§ 41-10-85. Execution of certificate of incorporation; filing of certificate of incorporation, resolution of governing body, etc., with probate judge and recordation thereof by probate judge.

(a) The certificate of incorporation shall be signed and acknowledged by the incorporators before an officer authorized by the laws of the state to take acknowledgments of deeds and shall have attached thereto a certified copy of the resolution provided for in section 41-10-84 and a certificate by the secretary of state of the state that the name proposed by the corporation is not identical with that of any other corporation in the state or so nearly similar thereto as to lead to confusion or uncertainty.

(b) The certificate of incorporation, together with the documents required by section 41-10-84 to be attached thereto, shall be filed in the office of the judge of probate of the county, who shall forthwith receive and record the same.

(c) When such certificate of incorporation and attached documents have been so filed, the corporation shall come into existence and shall constitute a body corporate and politic and a political subdivision of the state under the name set forth in such certificate of incorporation, whereupon the corporation shall be vested with the rights and powers granted in this article. (Acts 1965, 1st Ex. Sess., No. 174, p. 224, § 6.)

§ 41-10-86. Amendment of certificate of incorporation.

The certificate of incorporation may at any time and from time to time be amended so as to make any change therein and add any provision thereto which might have been included in the certificate of incorporation in the first instance.

Any such amendment shall be effected in the following manner: The members of the board of directors of the corporation shall file with the governing body an application in writing seeking permission to amend the certificate of incorporation, specifying in such application the amendment proposed to be made. Such governing body shall consider such application and, if it shall by appropriate resolution duly find and determine that it is wise, expedient, necessary or advisable that the proposed amendment be made and shall authorize the same to be made and shall approve the form of the proposed amendment, then the persons making such application shall execute an instrument embodying the amendment specified in such application and shall file the same with the judge of probate of the county in which the certificate of incorporation was originally filed. The proposed amendment shall be subscribed and acknowledged by each member of the board before an officer authorized by the laws of Alabama to take acknowledgments to deeds. Such judge of probate shall thereupon examine the proposed amendment and, if he finds that the requirements of this section have been complied with and that the proposed amendment is within the scope of what might properly be included in an original certificate of incorporation, he shall approve the amendment and record it in an appropriate book in his office. When such amendment has been so made, filed and approved, it shall thereupon become effective, and the certificate of incorporation shall thereupon be amended as provided in the amendment.

No certificate of incorporation shall be amended except in the manner provided in this section. (Acts 1965, 1st Ex. Sess., No. 174, p. 224, § 7.)

§ 41-10-87. Board of directors of corporation — Composition; qualifications, reelection, etc., of members; vacancies; quorum; compensation and expenses of members; reduction to writing, recordation and admissibility in evidence of proceedings of board.

The corporation shall have a board of directors composed of the number of directors provided for in the certificate of incorporation and as otherwise provided in this article. All powers of the corporation shall be exercised by its board or pursuant to its authorization. All directors shall be residents of the county. No director shall be an officer of the state or of the county. If any director resigns, dies, becomes incapable of acting as director or ceases to reside in the county, the governing body shall elect a director to serve for the unexpired term of any director elected by it, and the governor shall appoint a successor to serve the unexpired term of any director appointed by him. Directors shall be eligible for reelection or reappointment to succeed themselves in office. A majority of the qualified and voting members of the board shall constitute a quorum for the transaction of business. No vacancy in the membership of the board shall impair the right of a quorum to exercise the powers and duties of the corporation. The members of the board and the officers of the corporation shall serve without compensation, except that they may be reimbursed for actual expenses incurred in and about the performance of their duties. All proceedings of the board shall be reduced to writing by the secretary of the corporation and recorded in a well-bound book. Copies of such proceedings, when certified by the secretary of the corporation under its seal, shall be received in all courts as evidence of the matters and things therein certified. (Acts 1965, 1st Ex. Sess., No. 174, p. 224, § 8.)

§ 41-10-88. Same — Election and terms of office of members generally.

The governing body shall elect the number of directors provided in the certificate of incorporation of the corporation for staggered terms of office. At the time of the election of the first board, the governing body shall divide the directors into three groups containing as nearly equal whole numbers as may be possible. The first term of the directors included in the first group shall be two years; the first term of the directors included in the second group shall be four years; the first term of the directors included in the third group shall be six years; and, thereafter, the terms of all directors shall be six years; provided, that if at the expiration of any term of office of any director a successor shall not have been elected, then the director whose term of office shall have expired shall continue to hold office until his successor shall be so elected. (Acts 1965, 1st Ex. Sess., No. 174, p. 224, § 9.)

§ 41-10-89. Same — Appointment of additional members to board by governor; terms of office, etc., of additional members.

In the event that there shall be provided to the corporation either by legislative appropriation or by executive allocation from funds of the state either moneys sufficient to pay the cost of necessary preliminary surveys and engineering, architectural or feasibility studies or reports or, in the alternative, one fourth or more of the total cost of constructing the project, then and in either of such events, the number of directors provided for in this article and in the certificate of incorporation of the corporation shall be doubled, and all the additional directors shall be appointed by the governor for staggered terms of office terminating on the same respective dates as the terms of office of the directors elected by the governing body. The governor shall likewise appoint the successors to such additional directors.

In all other respects, directors appointed by the governor and the board, with such directors as members, shall be subject to the other provisions of this chapter respecting the individual directors and the board. (Acts 1965, 1st Ex. Sess., No. 174, p. 224, § 10.)

§ 41-10-90. Officers of corporation.

The officers of the corporation shall consist of a chairman, a vice-chairman, a secretary, a treasurer and such other officers as the board shall deem necessary to accomplish the purposes for which the corporation was organized. The offices of secretary and treasurer may but need not be held by the same person. The chairman and vice-chairman of the corporation shall be elected by the board from its membership. The secretary, the treasurer and any other officers of the corporation who may but need not be members of the board, shall also be elected by the board. Before he shall receive any moneys or securities of the corporation, the treasurer shall make appropriate bond in such amount as the board shall determine. (Acts 1965, 1st Ex. Sess., No. 174, p. 224, § 11.)

§ 41-10-91. Powers of corporation — Generally.

The corporation shall have the following powers, together with all powers incidental thereto or necessary to the discharge thereof in corporate form:

(1) To have succession by its corporate name until dissolved as provided in this article;

(2) To sue and be sued, to prosecute and defend civil actions in any court having jurisdiction of the subject matter and the parties;

(3) To make use of a corporate seal and to alter the same at pleasure;

(4) To adopt and alter bylaws for the regulation and conduct of its affairs and business;

(5) To acquire, whether by purchase, gift, lease, devise, exercise of the power of eminent domain or otherwise, property of every description which the board may deem necessary to the acquisition, construction, improvement, enlargement, operation or maintenance of one or more projects and to hold title thereto or a leasehold interest therein;

(6) To borrow money for any of its corporate purposes and to sell and issue, in evidence of such borrowing, its interest-bearing revenue bonds;

(7) To sell and issue refunding revenue bonds;

(8) To secure any of its bonds by indenture as provided in this article;

(9) To appoint, employ and compensate such agents, architects, engineers and attorneys as the business of the corporation may require;

(10) To provide for such insurance as the board may deem advisable;

(11) To invest in obligations which are direct and general obligations of the United States of America or which are unconditionally guaranteed as to both principal and interest by the United States of America any of its funds that the board may determine are not presently needed for its corporate purposes;

(12) To contract, lease and make lease agreements respecting its properties or any thereof; and

(13) To sell and convey any of its properties that may have become obsolete or worn out or that may no longer be needed or useful in connection with the operation of any project; provided, that it shall not have the power to sell or convey any project substantially as a whole except as provided in this article. (Acts 1965, 1st Ex. Sess., No. 174, p. 224, § 12.)

§ 41-10-92. Same — Eminent domain.

The corporation shall have the same powers of eminent domain as are vested by law in the county, which powers shall be exercised in the same manner and under the same conditions as are provided by law for the exercise of the power of eminent domain by the county. (Acts 1965, 1st Ex. Sess., No. 174, p. 224, § 14.)

Cross references. — As to eminent domain generally, see § 18-1-1 et seq.

§ 41-10-93. Authority for issuance of bonds by corporation; liability upon bonds; form, terms, denominations, etc.; redemption; sale; payment of expenses in connection with authorization, sale and issuance; bonds to contain recital as to authority for issuance; bonds to be deemed negotiable instruments.

The corporation is authorized at any time and from time to time to issue its interest-bearing revenue bonds for the purpose of acquiring, constructing, improving, enlarging, completing and equipping one or more projects. The principal of and interest on any such bonds shall be payable solely out of the rent, revenues and income derived from the project with respect to which such bonds are issued. None of the bonds of the corporation shall ever constitute an obligation or debt of the state, the county or the municipality or a charge against the credit or taxing power of the state, the county or municipality.

The bonds of the corporation may be in such form and denomination, may be of such tenor, may be coupon bonds and may be payable to bearer or be registrable as to principal only or as to both principal and interest, may mature at such time or times, not exceeding 30 years from their date, may be payable at such place or places, whether within or without the state and, may bear interest at such rate or rates, payable and evidenced in such manner as shall not be inconsistent with the provisions of this article and as may be provided in the proceedings of the board wherein the bonds shall be authorized to be issued.

Any bond having a specified maturity of more than 10 years after its date shall be made subject to prior redemption at the option of the corporation at a time not later than the expiration of 10 years from its date and on any interest payment date thereafter, at such price or prices, not exceeding the par value thereof plus accrued interest thereon to the redemption date plus a premium which shall not exceed 12 months interest thereon, computed at the rate which such bond would bear on the redemption date as specified therein, if such option had not been exercised, and after such notice or notices and on such terms and in such manner as may be provided in the indenture or the proceedings of the board wherein such bond is authorized to be issued.

The bonds of the corporation shall be sold at public sale, on sealed bids or at auction, as the board may determine to be most advantageous and on such prior published notice as the board shall determine.

The corporation may pay all expenses, premiums and commissions which the board may determine to be necessary or advantageous in connection with the authorization, sale and issuance of its bonds.

All bonds shall contain a recital that they are issued pursuant to the provisions of this article, which recital shall be conclusive that they have been duly authorized pursuant to the provisions of this article.

All bonds issued under the provisions of this article shall be and they hereby are declared to be negotiable instruments under the laws of the state, despite the fact that they are payable from a limited source. (Acts 1965, 1st Ex. Sess., No. 174, p. 224, § 18.)

§ 41-10-94. Notice of resolution authorizing issuance of bonds; limitation period for actions contesting validity of bonds, etc.

(a) Upon the adoption by the board of any resolution providing for the issuance of bonds, the corporation may, in its discretion, cause to be published once a week for two consecutive weeks in a newspaper published in the county a notice in substantially the following form (the blanks being properly filled in) at the end of which shall be printed the name and title of either the chairman or secretary of the corporation: "Notice of proposed issuance of revenue bonds of . . . . (name of corporation). The above named public corporation which is a political subdivision of the state of Alabama on the . . . . day of . . . ., adopted a resolution authorizing the issuance of $. . . . . . . principal amount of the revenue bonds of said corporation for . . . ., which is a project authorized and permitted by the act of the legislature of Alabama under which said corporation was organized. Any civil action or proceeding questioning the validity of the said bonds or pledge of any rent, revenues or income to the payment thereof or the indenture under which said bonds will be issued or the proceedings authorizing the same must be commenced within 20 days after the first publication of this notice."

(b) Any civil action or proceeding in any court to set aside, contest or question the legality of the bonds referred to in said notice or the proceedings authorizing the issuance of such bonds or the validity of the pledges made therefor or the indenture under which they are to be issued must be commenced within 20 days after the first publication of such notice. After the expiration of said period, no right of action or defense questioning or attacking the validity of said proceedings or the said bonds or the said pledges or indenture shall be asserted nor shall the validity of the said proceedings, bonds, pledges or indenture be open to question in any court on any grounds whatsoever except in a civil action commenced within such period. (Acts 1965, 1st Ex. Sess., No. 174, p. 224, § 26.)

§ 41-10-95. Execution and delivery of bonds and interest coupons.

All bonds shall be signed by the chairman or vice-chairman of the corporation, and the seal of the corporation shall be affixed thereto and attested by its secretary. A facsimile of the seal of the corporation and of the signature of either of said officers, but not both of them, may be impressed on the bonds in lieu of their manually signing the same.

Coupons shall be signed by the chairman or vice-chairman of the corporation, but a facsimile of the signature of such chairman or such vice-chairman may be impressed on any such coupons in lieu of his manually signing the same. Bonds so executed shall be valid and may be delivered, notwithstanding any changes in the officers or the seal of the corporation after the signing and sealing of the bonds. (Acts 1965, 1st Ex. Sess., No. 174, p. 224, § 19.)

§ 41-10-96. Security for payment of principal and interest on bonds.

The principal of and interest on the bonds shall be secured by a pledge of the rent, revenues and income out of which the bonds shall be made payable and by a pledge of any lease agreements covering the project or any part thereof from which the rent, revenues and income so pledged shall be derived and may be secured by an indenture covering such project. The trustee under an indenture may be a trust company or bank having trust powers, whether located within or without the state. The indenture may contain any agreements and provisions customarily contained in instruments securing evidences of indebtedness, including, without limiting the generality of the foregoing, provisions respecting the collection, segregation and application of the rent, revenues and income from any project covered by such indenture, the terms to be incorporated in the lease agreements respecting such project or any part thereof, the maintenance and insurance of such project, the creation and maintenance of special funds from the rent, revenues and income of such project and the rights and remedies available in the event of default to the holders of the bonds or the trustee under the indenture as the board shall deem advisable and as shall not be in conflict with the provisions of this article. (Acts 1965, 1st Ex. Sess., No. 174, p. 224, § 20.)

§ 41-10-97. Disposition of proceeds from sale of bonds generally.

The proceeds derived from the sale of any bonds, other than refunding bonds, may be used only to pay the cost of acquiring, constructing, improving, enlarging and equipping the project with respect to which they were issued, as may be specified in the indenture or the proceedings in which the bonds are authorized to be issued. Such cost shall be deemed to include the following: the cost of acquiring any interest in the land forming a part of the project; the cost of the labor, materials and supplies used in any such construction, improvement or enlargement, including architect's and engineer's fees and the cost of preparing contract documents and advertising for bids; the purchase price of and the cost of installing equipment for the project, the cost of landscaping the land forming a part of the project and of constructing and installing roads, sidewalks, curbs, gutters, utilities and parking places in connection therewith; legal fees and recording fees and expenses incurred in connection with the authorization, sale and issuance of the bonds issued in connection with such project and interest on the said bonds for a reasonable period prior to and during the time required for such construction and equipment and for not more than one year thereafter.

If any of the proceeds derived from the sale of the bonds remains undisbursed upon completion of such work and payment of all the costs and expenses thereof, such balance shall be used for the retirement of the principal of the bonds of the same issue. (Acts 1965, 1st Ex. Sess., No. 174, p. 224, § 21.)

§ 41-10-98. Proceeds of bonds not to be used for payment of fees, commissions, etc., for services in sale, issuance, execution, etc., of bonds; maximum amount payable to attorneys for services rendered.

No part of any of the proceeds of the bonds provided for herein shall be used for the payment of fees, commission, expense, salary or other remuneration to any fiscal agent, person, firm or corporation for services in the sale, issuance, execution or refunding of the bonds provided for in this article, and the total attorneys' fees which may be paid for services rendered to the authority shall not exceed one half of one percent of the face amount of the bonds issued under the provisions of this article. (Acts 1965, 1st Ex. Sess., No. 174, p. 224, § 29.)

§ 41-10-99. Refunding bonds.

The corporation may at any time and from time to time issue refunding bonds for the purpose of refunding the principal of and interest on any bonds of the corporation theretofore issued under this article and then outstanding, whether or not such principal and interest shall have matured at the time of such refunding, and for the payment of any expenses incurred in connection with such refunding and such premium as is necessary to be paid in order to redeem or retire the bonds to be refunded. The proceeds derived from the sale of any refunding bonds shall be used only for the purposes for which the refunding bonds were authorized to be issued. Any such refunding may be effected either by sale of the refunding bonds, in the manner provided for in this article with respect to bonds, the application of the proceeds thereof or by exchange of the refunding bonds for the bonds or interest coupons to be refunded thereby; provided, that the holders of any bonds or coupons so to be refunded shall not be compelled without their consent to surrender their bonds or coupons for payment or exchange prior to the date on which they may be paid or redeemed by the corporation under their respective provisions. Any refunding bonds of the corporation shall be payable solely from the revenues out of which the bonds or coupons to be refunded thereby were payable. All provisions of this article pertaining to bonds of the corporation that are not inconsistent with the provisions of this section shall also apply to refunding bonds issued by the corporation. (Acts 1965, 1st Ex. Sess., No. 174, p. 224, § 22.)

§ 41-10-100. Investment of surplus, etc., county funds in bonds of corporation.

The governing body is authorized in its discretion to invest in bonds of the corporation any idle or surplus money held in the treasury of the county which is not otherwise earmarked or pledged. (Acts 1965, 1st Ex. Sess., No. 174, p. 224, § 24.)

§ 41-10-101. Investment in bonds of corporation by savings banks, insurance companies, trustees, etc.

Bonds issued under the provisions of this article are hereby made legal investments for executors, administrators, trustees and other fiduciaries and for savings banks and insurance companies organized under the laws of the state. (Acts 1965, 1st Ex. Sess., No. 174, p. 224, § 25.)

§ 41-10-102. Remedies upon default on bonds, etc.

(a) *Remedies upon default on bonds or indenture.* — If there shall be any default in the payment of the principal of or interest on any of the bonds issued under this article, or in the performance of any provisions of the indenture or proceedings authorizing the issuance of such bonds, then the holder of any of the bonds and the interest coupons applicable thereto and the trustee under such indenture or any one or more of them shall have and may exercise any one or more of the following remedies:

(1) They may by civil action, mandamus, injunction or other proceeding compel the performance of all duties of the officers and directors of the corporation with respect to the use of funds for the payment of the bonds and for the performance of the bonds and the agreements of the corporation contained in the bonds, the indenture or in the proceedings under which they were issued;

(2) They may institute a civil action and shall be entitled to a judgment against the corporation for the principal of and interest on the bonds so in default;

(3) They shall be entitled, regardless of the sufficiency of the security for the bonds in default and as a matter of right, to the appointment of a receiver to operate, administer and maintain the project out of the rent, revenues and income from which the bonds so in default are payable, with power to lease the project and the various parts thereof and to fix and collect rents therefor and to fix and collect charges and fees for exhibitions and contests conducted therein sufficient to provide for the payment of the principal of and interest on the bonds and any other obligations outstanding against the project or the revenues therefrom and for the payment of the expense of operating and maintaining the project and to apply the rent, revenues and income so collected to the court costs and expenses of the receivership and as provided in the indenture;

(4) They may foreclose any mortgage, conditional sale or lien upon the project or any part thereof provided in the indenture under which such bonds were issued and cause the project to be sold, either with or without court proceedings, either by the trustee or by the creditors or by their attorneys, or, if foreclosure is by court proceedings, by such official as the court may designate. The trustee or any holder of any of the bonds or coupons or any creditor may become a purchaser at any such foreclosure sale; and

(5) They may exercise any right or remedy, including the possession, operation and leasing of the project by the trustee under the indenture, as may be provided in the indenture.

(b) *Remedies upon default in lease agreement.* — If there be any default by the municipality, county, state or any public corporation or state agency in the payment of any installment of rent or the performance of any agreement required to be made or performed by them under the provisions of any lease agreement, the corporation and the trustee under any indenture or either of them shall have and may exercise any one or more of the following remedies:

(1) They may by mandamus, injunction or other proceedings, compel performance by the officials of such lessee of their duties respecting payment of the rentals required to be paid and the performance of the agreements on the part of such lessee required to be performed under any such lease agreement;

(2) They shall be entitled to a judgment against such lessee for all monetary payments required to be made by such lessee under the provisions of such lease agreement with respect to which the lessee is then in default;

(3) They may terminate the lease and take possession of the project or part thereof leased to such lessee; and

(4) They may exercise any other remedy provided for in such lease.

(c) *Remedies provided by section cumulative.* — The remedies specified in this section shall be cumulative to all other remedies which may otherwise be available to or for the benefit of the holders of the bonds and the coupons applicable thereto or the corporation as lessor of a project or any part thereof. (Acts 1965, 1st Ex. Sess., No. 174, p. 224, § 23.)

§ 41-10-103. Leasing of projects.

(a) *Leases to municipality, county or state.* — The corporation, the municipality, the county and the state are hereby respectively authorized to enter into with each other one or more lease agreements whereunder a project or any part thereof shall be leased by the corporation to such other party for a term not longer than the then current fiscal year of such lessee, but any such lease agreement may contain a grant to such lessee of successive options of renewing said lease agreement on the term specified therein for any subsequent fiscal year or years of such lessee. The rental for each fiscal year during which said lease agreement shall be in effect shall be due in advance on the first day of the fiscal year, and the said rental for said fiscal year shall be payable and any such covenant to pay rent on the part of such municipality or county or the state shall be performed solely out of its current revenues for such fiscal year. The rental payable and the covenants to be performed by the municipality or the county or the state under the provisions of said lease agreement shall not be such as to create an indebtedness within the meaning of sections 213, 224 or 225 of the Constitution.

(b) *Leases to public corporations or state agencies.* — The corporation and any public corporation or state agency are hereby respectively authorized to enter into with each other one or more lease agreements whereunder a project or any part thereof shall be leased by the corporation to said public corporation or state agency for a term not longer than 30 years. Neither the state, the county nor any municipality in the county shall in any manner be liable for the performance of any obligation or agreement contained in any lease agreement between the corporation and a public corporation or state agency. The rental payable and the covenants to be performed by a public corporation or state agency under the provisions of any such lease agreement shall never create a debt of the state, the county or any municipality therein within the meaning of sections 213, 224 or 225 of the Constitution.

(c) *Leases to others.* — The corporation is hereby authorized to lease a project or any part thereof to any person, firm or corporation for such period of time and on such terms and conditions as may be mutually agreed on by the parties to the agreement under which such lease shall be made. (Acts 1965, 1st Ex. Sess., No. 174, p. 224, § 16.)

§ 41-10-104. Conduct of sporting events, exhibits, etc., in projects.

The corporation or any lessee of the project or a part thereof shall have the right to conduct such exhibits, contests and sporting events in a project or any part thereof as in the judgment of the board may be in the public interest or as may tend to promote and develop trade, industry or commerce in the state or to provide public recreation and enjoyment or to create goodwill for the state, with or without fees or charges for admission thereto. (Acts 1965, 1st Ex. Sess., No. 174, p. 224, § 17.)

§ 41-10-105. Conveyances of property to corporation by municipality, county or state authorized.

The municipality, the county and the state are hereby respectively authorized to convey to the corporation, with or without the payment of monetary or other consideration therefor, any property that may be owned by the municipality, the county or the state, whether or not such property is necessary to the conduct of the governmental or other public functions of the municipality, the county or the state. (Acts 1965, 1st Ex. Sess., No. 174, p. 224, § 13.)

§ 41-10-106. Appropriations to corporation by municipality or county authorized; limitations.

The municipality and the county are hereby each respectively authorized to appropriate and pay over to or for the use of the corporation such sums as they consider desirable either to provide funds to pay for preliminary surveys, engineering and architectural studies to determine the feasibility of a project and reports of such studies or to pay all or any part of the cost of any project. Neither the municipality nor the county shall be obligated to make any such appropriation nor shall they do so in such manner as to constitute the revenue bonds of the corporation an indebtedness of the municipality or the county within the meaning of section 224 or 225 of the Constitution of the state or bonds within the meaning of section 222 thereof. (Acts 1965, 1st Ex. Sess., No. 174, p. 224, § 15.)

§ 41-10-107. Exemption from taxation of bonds, income, projects, etc., of corporation.

Each project and the income from all leases made with respect thereto, the bonds issued by the corporation and the income therefrom and all lease agreements and indentures made pursuant to the provisions of this article shall be exempt from all taxation in the state. (Acts 1965, 1st Ex. Sess., No. 174, p. 224, § 27.)

§ 41-10-108. Dissolution of corporation and vesting of title to properties thereof upon dissolution; vesting of title to projects upon payment in full of bonds pertaining thereto; formation of corporation not to prevent subsequent formation of other corporations by same county.

(a) At any time when the corporation does not have any bonds outstanding, the board may adopt a resolution, which shall be duly entered upon its minutes, declaring that the corporation shall be dissolved. Upon the filing for record of a certified copy of said resolution in the office of the judge of probate of the county, the corporation shall thereupon stand dissolved and, in the event that it owns any property at the time of its dissolution, the title to all its property shall thereupon vest in the county.

(b) In the event that the corporation shall at any time have outstanding bonds issued under this article payable out of the revenues from different projects, then as and when the principal of and interest on all bonds payable, in whole or in part, from the revenues derived from any project shall have been paid in full, title to the project with respect to which the bonds so paid in full have been paid shall thereupon vest in the county, but such vesting of title in the county shall not affect the title of the corporation to any other project the rent, revenues or income from which are pledged to the payment of any other bonds then outstanding.

(c) The formation of one or more corporations under the provisions of this article shall not prevent the subsequent formation under this article of other corporations pursuant to the authorization by the same county. (Acts 1965, 1st Ex. Sess., No. 174, p. 224, § 28.)

§ 41-10-109. Construction of article.

This article shall not be construed as a restriction or limitation upon any power, right or remedy which any county or any corporation now in existence or hereafter formed may have in the absence thereof and shall be construed as cumulative and independent thereof. (Acts 1965, 1st Ex. Sess., No. 174, p. 224, § 30.)

ARTICLE 5.

HISTORICAL PRESERVATION AUTHORITIES.

§§ 41-10-120 through 41-10-134. Repealed by Acts 1979, No. 79-441, p. 710, § 18, effective July 19, 1979.

Cross references. — For provision recognizing continuing validity of authorities organized under former §§ 41-10-120 through 41-10-134 prior to July 19, 1979, and authorizing reincorporation under §§ 41-10-135 through 41-10-151, see § 41-10-151.

§ 41-10-135. Short title.

This article shall be known and cited as the Historical Preservation Authorities Act of 1979. (Acts 1979, No. 79-441, p. 710, § 1.)

§ 41-10-136. Definitions.

The following words and phrases used in this article and others evidently intended as the equivalent thereof shall, in the absence of clear implication in this article otherwise, be given the following respective interpretations:

(1) APPLICANT. A natural person who files a written application with the governor in accordance with the provisions of section 41-10-138.

(2) AREA OF OPERATION. The area specified in the certificate of incorporation of an authority, within which the authority is empowered to carry on its business and activities under this article.

(3) AUTHORITY. A public corporation organized pursuant to the provisions of this article.

(4) BOARD. The board of directors of an authority.

(5) BONDS. Includes bonds, notes, debentures and certificates representing an obligation to pay money.

(6) COMMISSION. The Alabama historical commission, an agency of the state established under section 41-9-240.

(7) COUNTY. Any county in this state.

(8) DIRECTOR. A member of the board of directors of an authority.

(9) INCORPORATORS. The persons who form an authority pursuant to this article.

(10) MUNICIPALITY. Any incorporated city or town in this state.

(11) NATIONAL REGISTER OF HISTORIC PLACES. The national register of districts, sites, buildings, structures and objects significant in American history, architecture, archaeology and culture maintained by the secretary of the interior pursuant to the laws of the United States of America, including particularly the National Historic Preservation Act of 1966, as amended.

(12) PERSON. Unless limited to a natural person by the context in which it is used, such term includes a public or private corporation, a partnership, an association, a municipality, a county or an agency, department or instrumentality of this state or of a county or municipality.

(13) PROPERTY. Includes real, personal and mixed property and interests therein.

(14) STATE. The state of Alabama.

(15) VICINITY IMPROVEMENTS. Buildings, facilities and improvements for the accommodation of visitors to any facility owned by an authority which is registered in the National Register of Historic Places including, without limitation, motels, restaurants, coffee shops, stores to provide gifts and souvenir items, picnic areas, camp sites, trailer sites, cabins, lodges, parking lots, museums, exhibition and lecture rooms and areas, comfort stations, meeting halls, pavilions, centers for cultural entertainment, exhibitions and exhibits and administrative or office buildings; provided that nothing contained in this article is intended to authorize any authority itself to operate as a commercial enterprise any such motel, restaurant, shop or store; and provided further that all such buildings, facilities and improvements are located within one-fourth of one mile of the facility registered in the National Register of Historic Places which is owned or operated or controlled by an authority, and within the area of operation of such authority. (Acts 1979, No. 79-441, p. 710, § 2.)

§ 41-10-137. Purposes for which authorities may be formed.

Public corporations may be formed under the provisions of this article as agencies or instrumentalities of this state for any one or more or all of the following purposes:

(1) To undertake and to make or cause to be made engineering, architectural, technical, financial, legal and other appropriate studies and surveys with respect to restoring, renovating, preserving, improving, protecting or maintaining any public or private property within the state that has been listed in the National Register of Historic Places, or providing vicinity improvements.

(2) To restore, construct, acquire, own and operate, singly or in conjunction with others, lease, sell and otherwise dispose of land, buildings, houses or other structures, facilities or property within the state that have been listed in the National Register of Historic Places, and any vicinity improvements.

(3) To cooperate with and lend financial assistance and other aid to persons in any matters and undertakings having to do with or the end purpose of which is to restore, renovate, preserve, improve, protect or maintain any public or private property that has been listed in the National Register of Historic Places, or to provide vicinity improvements. (Acts 1979, No. 79-441, p. 710, § 3.)

§ 41-10-138. Application for authority to incorporate; contents; review of application and issuance of executive order by governor.

(a) In order to form a public corporation under the provisions of this article, any number of natural persons, not less than three, shall first file a written application with the governor. Such application shall:

(1) Contain a statement that such public corporation proposes to undertake and carry out one or more or all of the purposes defined in section 41-10-137 with respect to public corporations formed under this article;

(2) Contain a description by county name or otherwise of the area of operation in which the public corporation proposes to carry on its activities;

(3) State that land, buildings, houses or other structures, facilities or property located in the area of operation of the public corporation and listed in the National Register of Historic Places are in need of restoration, renovation, preservation, improvement, protection or maintenance;

(4) State that the proposed activities of the public corporation within the area of operation will promote the preservation of and interest in property listed in the National Register of Historic Places;

(5) State that each of the applicants is a person of good moral character and is a duly qualified elector of the state who resides in the proposed area of operation; and

(6) Request that the governor issue an executive order declaring that he has reviewed the contents of the application and has found the statements of fact contained therein to be true and authorizing the persons filing the application to proceed to form such public corporation. Every such application shall be accompanied by such supporting documents or evidence as the applicants may deem appropriate.

(b) As promptly as is practicable after the application is filed as provided in this section, the governor shall review the contents of the application and shall find and determine whether the statements of fact contained in the application are true. If the governor finds and determines that any of the statements of fact contained in the application are not true, the governor shall forthwith issue an executive order denying the application; but, if the governor finds and determines that the statements of fact contained in the application are true, the governor shall forthwith issue an executive order declaring that he has reviewed the contents of the application and has found and determined that the statements of fact contained in the application are true, declaring that the proposed activities of such public corporation in the area of operation described will promote the restoration, renovation, preservation, improvement, protection or maintenance of, and public interest in, land, buildings, houses or other structures, facilities or property listed in the National Register of Historic Places and that, for such reason, it is wise, expedient and necessary that such public corporation be formed and authorizing the persons filing the application to proceed to form such public corporation.

In finding and determining whether the statements of fact contained in the application are true, the governor may, without investigation or further consideration, assume that the statements made pursuant to subdivisions (1) and (2) of subsection (a) of this section are true and, upon such assumption, so find and determine. It shall be sufficient to establish the truth of the statement made pursuant to subdivision (3) of subsection (a) of this section if there accompanies the application a resolution by the commission that land, buildings, houses or other structures, facilities or property located in the proposed area of operation of the public corporation and listed in the National Register of Historic Places are in need of restoration, renovation, preservation, improvement, protection or maintenance; provided, however, that such means of establishing the truth of said statements are not to be taken as being exclusive. If the statement of fact made pursuant to subdivision (3) of subsection (a) of this section is found and determined to be true, then the governor may without investigation or further consideration assume that the statement of fact made pursuant to subdivision (4) of subsection (a) of this section is true and, upon such assumption, so find and determine.

Notwithstanding the preceding provisions of this subsection, the governor shall notify the respective county governing bodies of any requests to form an authority in an area comprising two or more counties. Such notice must precede any executive order relating to the request by 20 days. (Acts 1979, No. 79-441, p. 710, § 4; Acts 1980, No. 80-366, p. 485.)

Collateral references. — 18 C.J.S., Corporations, § 23 et seq.
18 Am. Jur. 2d, Corporations, § 24 et seq.

§ 41-10-139. Filing certificate of incorporation with secretary of state; contents, execution, recordation, etc.

(a) After the date of issuance by the governor of his executive order authorizing the applicants to proceed to form a public corporation, as provided in section 41-10-138, the applicants or not less than three of the applicants shall proceed to incorporate a public corporation by filing of record in the office of the secretary of state a certificate of incorporation which shall comply in form and substance with the requirements of this section and be executed in the manner provided in this section.

(b) The certificate of incorporation of the authority shall state:

(1) The names of the persons incorporating the authority, together with their post office addresses and a statement that each of them is a qualified elector of the state;

(2) The name of the authority (which shall include the words "historical preservation authority");

(3) The location of the principal office of the authority, which shall be within the area of operation;

(4) A description, by county name or otherwise, of the area of operation;

(5) The objects for which the authority is incorporated;

(6) The period for the duration of the authority (which may be perpetual if so stated); and

(7) Any other matters relating to the authority not contrary to law which the incorporators choose to insert.

(c) The certificate of incorporation shall be signed by each of the incorporators and shall be acknowledged before an officer authorized by the laws of this state to take acknowledgments to deeds. When the certificate of incorporation is filed for record there shall be attached to it a copy of the executive order of the governor authorizing the incorporation of the authority. When the certificate of incorporation is filed in his office, the secretary of state shall forthwith receive and record the same, and thereupon the authority shall be in existence under the name stated in the certificate of incorporation and shall constitute and be a public corporation and instrumentality of the state. (Acts 1979, No. 79-441, p. 710, § 5.)

§ 41-10-140. Board of directors; appointment, terms, vacancies, reappointment, expenses, removal, etc.

Each authority shall be governed by a board of directors consisting of three directors, all of whom shall be persons of good moral character, duly qualified electors of the state and residents of the area of operation of the authority. All powers of an authority shall be exercised by the board or pursuant to its authorization. If the area of operation of an authority shall be wholly within the corporate limits of any municipality, the directors of that authority shall be appointed by the governing body of that municipality. If the area of operation of an authority shall be wholly within a single county, the directors of that authority shall be appointed by the governing body of that county. If the area of operation of an authority shall be larger than any single county, the directors of that authority shall be appointed by the governor. Whenever the appointment of directors of such an authority is required, the governor shall notify the respective county governing bodies in writing of the authority and the number of directors to be appointed. The governor may appoint as a director of the authority any person qualified to serve as such under the provisions of this article; provided, however, that the governor shall notify the respective county governing bodies, in writing, 20 days prior to the appointment. The terms of the directors shall be staggered, the first term of one director being for two years from and after the date of his appointment, the first term of another director being for four years from and after the date of his appointment, and the first term of the remaining director being for six years from and after the date of his appointment; thereafter, the term of office of each director shall be for six years. Each director shall serve during his term of office, and until his successor is appointed and qualified. Vacancies on the board shall be filled by appointment by the governing body or the governor having the power to make the appointment for the full term. Appointments to fill vacancies which occur during a regular term shall be for the unexpired term. Directors shall be eligible for reappointment. If the certificate of incorporation shall so provide, each director may be reimbursed by the authority for actual expenses incurred by him in and about the performance of his duties. Any director of an authority may be impeached and removed from office in the same manner and on the same grounds provided by section 175 of the Constitution of Alabama and the general laws of the state for impeachment and removal from office of the officers mentioned in said section 175. (Acts 1979, No. 79-441, p. 710, § 6; Acts 1980, No. 80-366, p. 485.)

§ 41-10-141. Powers and duties of authority generally.

An authority shall have the following powers, together with all powers incidental thereto or necessary to the discharge thereof in corporate form:

(1) To have succession by its corporate name for the duration of time (which may be in perpetuity) specified in its certificate of incorporation;

(2) To maintain civil actions and have civil actions maintained against it in its corporate name, except as otherwise provided in this article, and to defend civil actions against it;

(3) To adopt and make use of a corporate seal and to alter the same at pleasure;

(4) To amend its certificate of incorporation by filing in the office of the secretary of state a certificate signed by all of the directors of the authority setting forth the details of the amendment, such certificate to be acknowledged in the same manner as the certificate of incorporation;

(5) To adopt and alter bylaws for the regulation and conduct of its affairs and business;

(6) To acquire, receive and take title to, by purchase, gift, lease, devise or otherwise, to hold, keep and develop and to transfer, convey, lease, assign or otherwise dispose of property of every kind and character, real, personal and mixed, and any and every interest therein, located within the area of operation of the authority, to any person;

(7) To undertake and to make or cause to be made, either singly or in conjunction and cooperation with others, appropriate studies, surveys, arrangements, undertakings and construction designs and plans and supervision having to do, directly or indirectly, with the restoration, renovation, preservation, improvement, protection or maintenance of, or interest in, any public or private property that has been listed in the National Register of Historic Places or acquisition or construction of any vicinity improvements; provided, however, that the authority shall not pay out any of its funds by way of any form of remuneration or compensation to any persons engaged in the making of any such studies, surveys, arrangements, undertakings and construction designs, plans and supervision other than to persons who are directly employed in that connection by the authority;

(8) To make available and give, subject to the provisions of subdivision (7) of this section, to any person, financial and technical assistance and aid of every kind and character which will directly or indirectly promote, encourage or effect the restoration, renovation, preservation, improvement, protection or maintenance of, or interest in, any public or private property that has been listed in the National Register of Historic Places or acquisition or construction of any vicinity improvements;

(9) To make, enter into and execute such contracts, agreements, leases and other legal arrangements and to take such other steps and actions as may be necessary or convenient in the furtherance of any purpose or the exercise of any power provided or granted to it by law;

(10) To borrow money for any corporate purpose, function or use and to issue in evidence of the borrowing, interest-bearing bonds payable solely

from the revenues derived from the operation or leasing or sale of any of its property;

(11) To pledge for the payment of any bonds issued or obligations assumed by the authority any revenues from which those bonds or obligations are made payable and to execute and deliver, as security for such bonds and obligations, mortgages, deeds of trust, trust indentures and pledge indentures as provided for hereinafter;

(12) To carry out all of its functions, exercise all of its powers and conduct all of its business and affairs without regard to the provisions of sections 41-16-50 through 41-16-63, or any similar law respecting competitive bidding, that might otherwise be applicable;

(13) To provide for such insurance as the authority may deem advisable;

(14) To invest any of its funds deemed by the authority to be not presently needed in the operation of its properties and undertakings in bonds, bills or notes of the United States of America, bonds of the state, bonds of any county or municipality within the state and interest-bearing deposits in banks and savings and loan institutions or any thereof; and

(15) To cooperate with the United States of America and any agency or instrumentality thereof, any state and its agencies and instrumentalities, any county or municipality or other political subdivision of a state and any other person, and to make and enter into contracts and all manner of legal arrangements with them or any of them and to obtain money by way of loans, grants or payments from them or any of them or property or other forms of assistance as the authority may deem advisable to accomplish the purposes for which the authority was created. (Acts 1979, No. 79-441, p. 710, § 7.)

§ 41-10-142. Bonds — Issuance; form, terms, denominations, etc.; sale; refunding bonds; negotiable; security for payment.

All bonds issued by an authority may be executed by such officers of the authority and in such manner as shall be provided in the proceedings of the board whereunder the bonds shall be authorized to be issued. Any such bonds may be executed and delivered by an authority at any time and from time to time, shall be in such form and denominations and of such tenor and maturities, shall contain such provisions not inconsistent with the provisions of this article and shall bear such rate or rates of interest, payable and evidenced in such manner as may be provided by resolution of its board. Bonds of an authority may be sold at either public or private sale in such manner and at such price or prices and at such time or times as may be determined by the board to be most advantageous. The principal of or interest on any bonds issued or obligations assumed by an authority may thereafter at any time (whether before, at or after maturity of any such principal and whether at, after or not exceeding six months prior to the maturity of any such interest) and from time to time be refunded by the issuance of refunding bonds of the authority, which may be sold by the authority at public or private sale at such price or prices as may be determined by its board to be most advantageous or which may be exchanged for the bonds or other obligations to be refunded. An authority may pay all expenses, premiums and commissions which its board may deem necessary and advantageous in connection with any financing done by it. All bonds issued by an authority, unless registered as to principal, shall be construed to be negotiable instruments though payable from a specified source. All obligations created or assumed by an authority shall be solely and exclusively an obligation of the authority and shall not create an obligation or debt of any county or municipality or of the state; provided, that this sentence shall not be construed to release the original obligor from liability on any bond or other obligation assumed by an authority. Any bonds issued by an authority shall be limited or special obligations of the authority payable solely out of the revenues of the authority specified in the proceedings authorizing those bonds. Any such proceedings may provide that the bonds therein authorized shall be payable solely out of the revenues derived from the operation or leasing or sale of all property and facilities owned or operated by the authority or solely out of the revenues from the operation or leasing or sale of any one or more of such property and facilities, or parts thereof, regardless of the fact that those bonds may have been issued with respect to or for the benefit of only certain property and facilities of the authority. An authority may pledge for the payment of any of its bonds issued or obligations assumed the revenues from which such bonds or obligations are payable and may execute and deliver a trust indenture evidencing any such pledge or a mortgage and deed of trust conveying as security for such bonds or obligations the property and facilities, or any part of any thereof, the revenues or any part of the revenues from which are so pledged. Any mortgage and deed of trust or trust indenture made by an authority may contain such agreements as the board may deem advisable respecting the operation, leasing and maintenance of the property and the use of the revenues subject to such mortgage and deed of trust or affected by such trust indenture and respecting the rights, duties and remedies of the parties to any such instrument and the parties for the benefit of whom such instrument is made; provided, that no such instrument shall be subject to foreclosure unless the person to whom the property or facilities are leased by the authority operates for profit, in which event any such mortgage may be subject to foreclosure. (Acts 1979, No. 79-441, p. 710, § 8.)

§ 41-10-143. Same — Contracts to secure payment of principal and interest.

As security for payment of the principal and interest on bonds issued or obligations assumed by it, an authority may enter into a contract or contracts binding itself for the proper application of the proceeds of bonds and other funds, for the continued operation, leasing and maintenance of any property and facilities owned or controlled and operated by it or under its authority or any part or parts thereof, for the imposition and collection of reasonable rates and rentals for and the promulgation of reasonable regulations respecting the use of property and facilities of the authority and any service furnished therefrom, for the disposition and application of its gross revenues or any part thereof and for any other act or series of acts not inconsistent with the provisions of this article for the protection of the bonds and other obligations being secured and the assurance that revenues from such property and facilities will be sufficient to cover the cost of all direct operation of such property and facilities by the authority and the maintenance in good condition of such property and facilities owned and controlled by the authority, the payment of the principal of and interest on any bonds payable from such revenues and the maintenance of such reserves as may be deemed appropriate for the protection of the bonds, the efficient operation of such property and facilities, and the making of replacements thereof and capital improvements thereto. Any contract pursuant to the provisions of this section may be set forth in any resolution of the board authorizing the issuance of bonds or the assumption of obligations or in any mortgage and deed of trust and trust indenture made by an authority under this article. (Acts 1979, No. 79-441, p. 710, § 9.)

§ 41-10-144. Same — Statutory mortgage lien to secure payment of principal and interest; recording notice.

Any resolution of the board or trust indenture under which bonds may be issued pursuant to the provisions of this article may contain provisions creating a statutory mortgage lien in favor of the holders of such bonds and of the interest coupons applicable thereto on the property and facilities, or any part thereof (including any after-acquired property) out of the revenues from which such bonds are made payable. The said resolution of the board or the said trust indenture may provide for the filing for record in the office of the judge of probate of each county in which any property and facilities, or any part thereof, may be located of a notice containing a brief description of such bonds and a declaration that the said statutory mortgage lien has been created for the benefit of the holders of such bonds and the interest coupons applicable thereto upon such property and facilities, or any thereof, including additions thereto and extensions thereof. Each judge of probate shall receive and record and index under the name of the authority any such notice filed for record in his office. The recording of such notice, as provided in this section, shall operate as constructive notice of the contents thereof. (Acts 1979, No. 79-441, p. 710, § 10.)

§ 41-10-145. Same — Use of proceeds from sale.

All moneys derived from the sale of any bonds issued by an authority shall be used solely for the purpose or purposes for which the same are authorized and any costs and expenses incidental thereto. Such costs and expenses may include, but shall not be limited to:

　　(1) The fiscal, engineering, architectural, legal and other expenses incurred in connection with the issuance and sale of the bonds;

　　(2) In the case of bonds issued to pay costs of construction, building, acquisition, restoration, renovation or improvement of property of the authority, interest on such bonds (or, if a part only of bonds of any series is issued for such purposes, interest on that portion of the bonds of that series that is issued to pay such costs) prior to and during such construction, building,

acquisition, restoration, renovation or improvement of property of the authority; and

(3) In the case of bonds issued for the purpose of refunding principal and interest or either with respect to bonds issued or obligations assumed by the authority, any premium that it may be necessary to pay in order to redeem or retire the bonds or other obligations to be refunded. (Acts 1979, No. 79-441, p. 710, § 11.)

§ 41-10-146. Loans, sales, grants, etc., of money, property, etc., to authority by counties, municipalities, etc.

For the purpose of effecting the restoration, renovation, preservation, improvement, protection or maintenance of, or interest in, any public or private property that has been listed in the National Register of Historic Places, any county, municipality or other political subdivision, public corporation, agency or instrumentality of this state may, upon such terms and with or without consideration, as it may determine:

(1) Lend or donate money to or perform services for the benefit of an authority;

(2) Donate, sell, convey, transfer, lease or grant to an authority, without the necessity of authorization at any election of qualified voters, any property of any kind, any interest therein and any franchise; and

(3) Do any and all things, whether or not specifically authorized in this article and not otherwise prohibited by law, that are necessary or convenient in connection with aiding and cooperating with an authority in its efforts to restore, renovate, preserve, improve, protect, maintain or promote interest in any public or private property that has been listed in the National Register of Historic Places. (Acts 1979, No. 79-441, p. 710, § 12.)

§ 41-10-147. Exemption from taxation, fees and costs.

Each authority formed under this article, the property and income of the authority, all bonds issued by the authority, the income from such bonds or from any other sources, the interest and other profits from such bonds enuring to and received by the holders thereof, conveyances by and to the authority and leases, mortgages and deeds of trust by and to the authority shall be exempt from all taxation in the state. An authority shall not be obligated to pay or allow the payment of any fees, taxes or costs to the secretary of state in connection with its incorporation or with any amendment to its certificate of incorporation or otherwise or to any judge of probate of any county in connection with the recording by it of any document or otherwise, each authority being hereby exempted from the payment of any such fees, taxes and costs. No license or excise tax may be imposed by any authority with respect to the privilege of engaging in any of the activities authorized by this article. (Acts 1979, No. 79-441, p. 710, § 13.)

§ 41-10-148. Reports by authority to governor.

Each authority shall submit to the governor a detailed report of its activities during the previous year and of its financial condition. Such annual report shall be submitted as of October 1 of each year. The governor may also require special interim reports by an authority of its activities and its financial condition; provided, that such interim reports may not be required more often than once each calendar quarter year. (Acts 1979, No. 79-441, p. 710, § 14.)

§ 41-10-149. Construction of article generally; certain provisions exclusive.

This article is intended to aid the state in the execution of its duties by providing appropriate and independent instrumentalities of the state with full and adequate powers to fulfill their functions. The foregoing sections of this article shall be deemed to provide additional and alternative methods for the doing of the things authorized thereby and shall be regarded as supplemental and additional to and not in derogation of any powers conferred upon corporations created by municipalities within this state or upon any other agencies of the state or the municipalities thereof which are concerned with the restoration, renovation, preservation, improvement, protection or maintenance of or interest in any public or private property that has been listed in the National Register of Historic Places.

Neither this article nor any provision contained in this article shall be construed as a restriction or limitation upon any power, right or remedy which any corporation organized under this article may have in the absence thereof, but shall be construed as cumulative and independent of any such power, right or remedy. No proceedings, notice or approval shall be required for the incorporation of such corporation or the amendment of its certificate of incorporation, the acquisition of any property or facilities, the making of any loans or the borrowing of money or assumption of obligations or the issuance of bonds or other instruments in evidence thereof or as security therefor except as prescribed in this article, any other law to the contrary notwithstanding. (Acts 1979, No. 79-441, p. 710, § 15.)

§ 41-10-150. Dissolution of authority; title to property vests in state.

At any time when no bonds or obligations assumed by an authority are outstanding, the board of directors of an authority may adopt a resolution, which shall be entered upon its minutes, declaring that the authority shall be dissolved. Upon the filing for record of a certified copy of the said resolution in the office of the secretary of state, the authority shall thereupon stand dissolved and, in the event it owned any property at the time of its dissolution, the title to all of its properties shall thereupon pass to and vest in the state. (Acts 1979, No. 79-441, p. 710, § 16.)

§ 41-10-151. Authority organized under former law valid; reincorporation under this article.

Any authority organized under Acts 1978, No. 822, p. 1213 prior to July 19, 1979 shall continue to be valid and shall be governed by said act, and any authority organized under said act may reincorporate under sections 41-10-135 through 41-10-150 by action of its board of directors and by the filing of documents required to be filed in forming a new authority under sections 41-10-135 through 41-10-150. (Acts 1979, No. 79-441, p. 710, § 18.)

Code commissioner's note. — Acts 1978, No. 822, p. 1213, was codified as §§ 41-10-120 through 41-10-134.

§ 41-10-152. Historical preservation authorities — To be nonprofit corporations; distribution of net earnings.

Each authority heretofore or hereafter organized pursuant to sections 41-10-135 through 41-10-151, shall be a nonprofit corporation, and no part of its net earnings remaining after payment of its expenses shall inure to the benefit of any private individual, firm or corporation; except that in the event the governing body of any such authority shall determine that sufficient provision has been made for the full payment of the expenses, bonds and other obligations of such authority, then any net earnings thereafter accruing to such authority may be paid to the state of Alabama. (Acts 1980, No. 80-659, p. 1337, § 1.)

§ 41-10-153. Same — Exempt from usury or other interest limiting laws.

Each such authority is and shall be exempt from the laws of the state of Alabama governing usury or prescribing or limiting interest rates, including, without limitation, the provisions of chapter 8 of Title 8. (Acts 1980, No. 80-659, p. 1337, § 2.)

§ 41-10-154. Application of sections 41-10-152 through 41-10-154; provisions not retrospectively validating.

The provisions of sections 41-10-152 through 41-10-154 shall apply both prospectively and retrospectively, except that sections 41-10-152 through 41-10-154 shall not apply retrospectively so as to validate, cure or remedy any act taken by an authority where such action has, prior to May 28, 1980, been held invalid by a court of competent jurisdiction and the period for appeal therefrom has expired or where such action is alleged to be invalid in an appropriate suit or proceeding pending in any court of competent jurisdiction on May 28, 1980. (Acts 1980, No. 80-659, p. 1337, § 3.)

ARTICLE 6.

HISTORIC BLAKELEY AUTHORITY.

Effective date. — The act which added this article became effective May 27, 1981.

Collateral references. — 82 Am. Jur. 2d, Zoning and Planning, § 40.

§ 41-10-170. Creation and purposes.

There is hereby created the Historic Blakeley Authority:

(1) To establish, develop, operate, promote, protect, preserve, and maintain as a state historic park the lands in Baldwin county, Alabama listed on the National Register of Historic Places as the Blakeley site along with reconstructed buildings and all other present and future improvements within said sites, including, but not limited to:

a. The specific sites of Old Town Blakeley, Civil War battlegrounds, breastworks, batteries and encampments;

b. Early American military encampments;

c. Sites of Indian villages and encampments;

d. Period French plantations;

e. Early American residences, farms, homes, businesses and commercial sites and buildings;

f. Civilian and military roads and turnpikes; and

g. Significant natural plant and animal life and its habitat and specifically threatened or endangered plant and animal species;

(2) To protect and preserve bays, bayous, streams, marshlands, swamps and shorelines of rivers, bays and streams within the National Register site, including bottomlands of all rivers and streams within or along the Blakeley site;

(3) To preserve and protect archaeological sites;

(4) To establish, develop, promote and maintain educational and cultural programs and facilities consistent with the role and influence of Blakeley in Alabama history;

(5) To develop, build, manage, operate, promote and maintain any and all types of public and private facilities consistent with the reconstruction of historic Old Town Blakeley and the development of an historic and recreational park and cultural center. (Acts 1981, No. 81-792, p. 1390, § 1.)

§ 41-10-171. Composition; appointment, terms, vacancies, etc.

The authority shall be composed of 21 members as follows:

(1) Two representatives of education, one to be appointed by the president of the University of South Alabama for a two-year term and one to be appointed by the Baldwin county board of education from among school board members, who are residents of the geographic area that is now Baldwin county commission district no. 2 for a two-year term;

(2) Four elected public officials or their representatives, who shall be

a. The chairman of the Baldwin county commission or a member of the Baldwin county commission to be chosen by the commission to serve during that commissioner's term of office;

b. The sheriff of Baldwin county during his term of office;

c. The Alabama house of representatives district 95 member during his term of office; and

d. The governor of the state of Alabama or a representative appointed by him to serve during the governor's term of office;

(3) Three representatives of historic organizations as follows:

a. The president of the Baldwin County Historic Society or a person designated by the president for a two-year term;

b. A representative of the Fort Bowyer Chapter, Daughters of the American Revolution to be chosen by the chapter for a two-year term; and

c. The president of descendants of Blakeley residents or a person designated by the president for a six-year term;

(4) Three representatives of public service and civic organizations as follows:

a. A representative of the Eastern Shore chamber of commerce to be selected by the organization for a two-year term;

b. The chairman of the board of directors of the Tallulah Bankhead Center for the performing arts for a four-year term; and

c. The chairman of the Blakeley courthouse museum board for a term of four years; and

(5) Nine at-large members to be appointed by the governor from nominations submitted by the Historic Blakeley Foundation according to the following:

a. Places 1-4 for six-year terms commencing with their appointment by the governor;

b. Places 5-7 for four-year terms commencing with the appointment by the governor; and

c. Places 8-9 for two-year terms commencing with their appointment by the governor. Upon completion of the initial staggered terms all subsequent appointments of authority members in category 5 shall be by the same method, except they shall be for terms of four years.

Vacancies on the board during a term shall be filled for the unexpired portion of the term in the same manner and by the same appointing authority as the member whose place is being filled. (Acts 1981, No. 81-792, p. 1390, § 2.)

§ 41-10-172. Pay, emoluments, and expenses of members of the authority.

No member of the authority shall receive any pay or emolument other than his expenses incurred in the discharge of his duties as a member of the authority, which expenses shall be paid in the amounts provided for by the Code of Alabama 1975. All such expenses shall be paid from the funds of the authority. (Acts 1981, No. 81-792, p. 1390, § 3.)

§ 41-10-173. Charging, receiving, or obtaining of fees, etc., from the authority by members, employees, etc.; interests held by members, employees, etc., in land, materials, or contracts sold to, made with, etc., the authority.

It shall be unlawful for any member of the authority or any employee thereof to charge, receive or obtain, either directly or indirectly, any fee, commission, retainer or brokerage out of the funds of the authority, and no member of the authority or officer or employee thereof shall have any interest in any land, materials or contracts sold to or made or negotiated with the authority or with any member or employee thereof acting in his capacity as a member or employee of such authority. Violation of any provision of this section shall be a misdemeanor and, upon conviction, shall be punishable by removal from membership or employment and by a fine of not less than $100.00 or by imprisonment not to exceed six months, or both. (Acts 1981, No. 81-792, p. 1390, § 4.)

§ 41-10-174. Meetings; quorum; organization and procedure of the authority; official seal; election and terms of office of chairman, vice-chairman, secretary and treasurer; bonding requirements for treasurer.

(a) The authority shall hold an annual meeting at Blakeley each September on a day designated by the chairman. Eleven members shall constitute a quorum for the transaction of business. Additional meetings may be held at such times and places within the state as may be necessary, desirable or convenient, upon call of the chairman or, in the case of his absence or incapacity, of the vice-chairman or on the call of any 12 members of the authority.

(b) The authority shall determine and establish its own organization and procedure in accordance with the provisions of this article, and shall have an official seal.

(c) The authority shall elect its chairman, its vice-chairman, its secretary and its treasurer, and such officers shall hold office for a period of two years or until a successor is elected. Neither the secretary nor the treasurer need be members of the authority. The authority may require that the treasurer thereof be bonded in an amount to be determined by the authority. (Acts 1981, No. 81-792, p. 1390, § 5.)

§ 41-10-175. Powers and duties of authority generally.

The authority shall constitute a body corporate and shall have, in addition to those set forth specifically in this article, all powers necessary or convenient to effect the purposes for which it has been established under and by the terms of this article, together with all powers incidental thereto or necessary to the discharge of its said powers and duties, together with all powers and duties set forth in sections 41-10-141 through 41-10-147. (Acts 1981, No. 81-792, p. 1390, § 6.)

§ 41-10-176. Power to take possession under lease, etc., of property within the Blakeley national register site; power to lease, purchase, etc., any property in order to fulfill the purposes of the authority, power to borrow money, issue revenue bonds, and pledge security.

(a) The authority is authorized to take possession under a lease or a deed or other instrument granting use or easement property in Baldwin county, Alabama within the Blakeley national register site which is now owned by the Historic Blakeley Foundation or others. The authority is further authorized to lease, purchase, accept as a gift or loan or otherwise acquire any other property, real or personal, including gifts or bequests of money or other things of value to be used in fulfilling the purpose for which it is established or for any auxiliary purpose incidental or appropriate thereto.

(b) The authority is also authorized to borrow money and issue revenue bonds in evidence thereof, but no such bonds shall be general obligations of the state of Alabama or any agency or any political subdivision thereof nor shall such authority pledge to the payment of any such loans the land. It may, however, pledge to the repayment thereof buildings, exhibits, utilities, docks, roads, walks or other appurtenances; or improvements made by the authority and it may pledge to the repayment thereof the proceeds derived from admission fees or charges or other fees or charges made in connection with such park or historical site. (Acts 1981, No. 81-792, p. 1390, § 7.)

§ 41-10-177. Duty to facilitate exhibition of park and historic site to the public; admission charges; agreements with other groups or organizations relative to management of the park and historic site; authority to accept gratuitous services.

(a) The authority shall operate or provide for the operation of the park or historic site hereby provided for and any appurtenances thereto in such manner as to facilitate its exhibition to the public, either with or without a charge. If the authority, in its discretion, decides that a charge is appropriate, then the authority shall fix and provide for the collection of such charge or charges as it deems appropriate for admission to the park and for the use, viewing of or other enjoyment of exhibits and other facilities appurtenant to the park.

(b) The authority may enter into agreements with any civic organization, lay group or industrial, professional, educational or governmental organization relative to the general management of the park or historic site.

(c) The authority is also specifically authorized to accept gratuitous services from individuals and organizations and to employ such rangers, guides, maintenance people, guards, superintendents and professional staff and other employees as, in its opinion, are needed for the operation and exhibition of such park or historic site. (Acts 1981, No. 81-792, p. 1390, § 8.)

§ 41-10-178. Appropriation of public funds and construction and maintenance of roads and other public facilities, etc., for the authority by counties and municipalities.

The county commission of any county or governing body of any municipality in this state shall be authorized, by resolution duly adopted and recorded, to appropriate any available public funds not otherwise pledged to the use of the authority and shall be authorized to construct and maintain roads and bridges and other public facilities and improvements on authority owned or controlled land. (Acts 1981, No. 81-792, p. 1390, § 9.)

§ 41-10-179. Taxation of income, property, leases, bonds, etc., of the authority.

The authority shall have a tax-exempt status, and the properties of the authority and the income therefrom, all lease agreements and contracts made by it, all bonds issued by it and the coupons applicable thereto and the income therefrom and all indentures executed with respect thereto shall be forever exempt from any and all taxation by the state of Alabama and any political subdivision thereof, including, but not limited to, income, admission, amusement, excise, and ad valorem taxes. (Acts 1981, No. 81-792, p. 1390, § 10.)

§ 41-10-180. Participation of employees of the authority in insurance programs provided for state employees; payment of contributions for such insurance.

(a) All full-time employees of the authority shall be treated as state employees for the purpose of participating in any insurance programs provided for state employees.

(b) The authority is hereby authorized and empowered to pay the employer's contributions to any such programs out of any funds appropriated them or available to them for any purpose whatsoever, and it may deduct the employees' contributions for such programs by means of payroll deductions or otherwise from any salary or compensation paid said employees. (Acts 1981, No. 81-792, p. 1390, § 11.)

§ 41-10-181. Authority as state agency; control over Blakeley site, historic park, etc.; promulgation, alteration, etc., of rules and regulations concerning preservation, etc., of Blakeley historic site; penalty for violation of rules or regulations; police powers of authority members; designation of deputy police officers.

(a) The authority shall be a state agency, and shall have exclusive control over the Blakeley site, the historic park, recreational areas, all improvements and exhibits located thereon, and any additions constructed, created, leased, acquired or erected in connection therewith.

287

(b) The authority shall have the power and authority to establish and promulgate and from time to time alter, amend, or repeal rules and regulations concerning the preservation, protection, and use of the Blakeley historic site and to preserve the peace therein. Any person who violates any rule or regulation so established and promulgated shall be guilty of a misdemeanor and shall be punished by a fine of not more than $1,000.00 or imprisonment for not more than one year, or both, and may be adjudged to pay all costs of the proceedings.

(c) The authority members shall have and are hereby vested with full police power to prefer charges against and to make arrests of any person or persons violating any such rule or regulation. The authority shall have full authority to designate any employee or employees of the authority as deputy police officers, who shall have full authority to prefer charges against or to make arrests of any person or persons violating any rule or regulation established and promulgated by the authority, as provided in this section. (Acts 1981, No. 81-792, p. 1390, § 12.)

§ 41-10-182. Reaffirmation of charter of town of Blakeley; recognition as municipality; boundaries; persons recognized as citizens for purposes of electing town officials and conducting town business; authority as governing body of town of Blakeley.

The original charter of the town of Blakeley by act of the Alabama legislature in 1818 strengthened by an act of the Alabama state legislature in 1820 and never revoked following demise of the town is hereby reaffirmed, and the town of Blakeley is recognized as a municipality of the state of Alabama whose boundaries are hereby established as those of the national register site. Members of the authority and any other persons over the age of 21 whom the authority may designate, their place or places of residence in Alabama notwithstanding, shall be recognized as citizens of the town of Blakeley for the purpose of conducting elections of town officials and other town business decided by referendum, until such time as citizens shall elect to come within the general provisions of the Code of Alabama 1975 as to government of municipalities. Until such time as the town of Blakeley citizens decide on an alternative form of government, the authority shall be recognized as the governing body of the town of Blakeley and is hereby empowered to elect from Blakeley citizens a mayor and members of town council to serve according to terms of office to be set by the authority. (Acts 1981, No. 81-792, p. 1390, § 13.)

CHAPTER 11.

ALABAMA ACADEMY OF HONOR.

§ 41-11-1. Creation; purpose.

There is hereby created and established an organization which shall be known as the "Alabama academy of honor," hereinafter referred to as "the academy." The purpose of the academy shall be to bestow honor and recognition upon living Alabamians for their outstanding accomplishments and service. (Acts 1965, 3rd Ex. Sess., No. 15, p. 219, § 1.)

§ 41-11-2. Composition; qualifications and election of members generally.

The academy shall be composed of not more than 100 living members, and no more than 10 of such members shall be elected to membership in any calendar year. Each person elected for membership shall be a distinguished citizen of Alabama who shall be chosen for accomplishment or service greatly benefiting the state or for accomplishment or service reflecting great credit on the state. Each living governor or former governor of Alabama shall be a member of the academy but shall not be counted in the total maximum membership nor in the 10 members who may be elected annually. No more than 25 percent of the elected members at any time shall be from the political field. (Acts 1965, 3rd Ex. Sess., No. 15, p. 219, § 2.)

§ 41-11-3. Election of members; nominations for new members.

(a) The initial 10 members of the academy shall be elected by a committee appointed for such purpose by the governor.

New members, not to exceed 10 in any calendar year, shall be elected by the existing members of the academy. A majority vote of the existing members shall be necessary for the election of each new member, and new members shall be chosen in order of the highest number of votes received.

(b) Nominations for new members shall be made by the academy and in writing by citizens of the state. (Acts 1965, 3rd Ex. Sess., No. 15, p. 219, § 3.)

§ 41-11-4. Chairman; secretary; clerical assistance.

The members of the academy shall elect among themselves a chairman and shall fix his term of office. The chairman shall preside over meetings, direct the business of the academy and perform such other duties as may be prescribed or delegated to him by the academy. The members shall appoint one of their number as secretary, who shall keep minutes of each meeting. The governor's office shall provide such clerical assistance as may be needed by the academy. (Acts 1965, 3rd Ex. Sess., No. 15, p. 219, § 5.)

§ 41-11-5. Meetings generally; quorum; adoption of rules and regulations.

The academy shall meet at least once annually to award new memberships and shall hold such other meetings as necessary to carry out its purpose. The time and place of meetings shall be designated by the members. A majority of the members shall constitute a quorum for conducting business. The academy may make rules and regulations necessary to carry out its purposes and functions as prescribed in this chapter. (Acts 1965, 3rd Ex. Sess., No. 15, p. 219, § 4.)

§ 41-11-6. Maximum amount and use of annual appropriation.

The academy shall receive an annual appropriation not to exceed $2,000.00, which shall be fixed by the legislature during each regular session thereof. The appropriation provided shall be used by the academy to pay for stationery, membership certificates, membership pins or plaques or the like, an annual banquet for members and such other necessary or appropriate expenses incurred in carrying out the purposes of the academy. (Acts 1965, 3rd Ex. Sess., No. 15, p. 219, § 6.)

CHAPTER 12.

WHITE HOUSE OF THE CONFEDERACY.

§ 41-12-1. Designation as memorial; purposes for which memorial may be used.

The building and grounds known as the first White House of the Confederacy, opposite the Capitol and now the property of the state, shall be preserved and held inviolate as a perpetual memorial to Jefferson Davis and the men and women associated with him in the organization of the Confederate government and as a reminder to all future generations that this great historical event, one of the most memorable in the annals of time, occurred in the city of Montgomery and state of Alabama.

To this end its use shall be confined to a display of what is known as the Jefferson Davis relics and such other relics of the Confederacy as may be gathered from time to time; provided, that vacant space not so in use may be occupied by such state officials as the governor may from time to time direct. (Acts 1923, No. 244, p. 248; Code 1923, § 3180; Code 1940, T. 55, § 290.)

§ 41-12-2. Department of finance to maintain building; payment of expenses thereof.

The care and upkeep of the building as a building shall be a part of the duties of the department of finance, and the expenses for such care and upkeep shall be payable from the funds annually appropriated therefor by the legislature. (Acts 1923, No. 244, p. 248; Code 1923, § 3181; Code 1940, T. 55, § 291; Acts 1951, No. 917, p. 1568.)

§ 41-12-3. White House association to manage building.

The management of the first White House of the Confederacy as an institution for the cultivation of Confederate history, the preservation of Confederate relics and as a reminder for all time of how pure and great were southern statesmen and southern valor is confided to the organization known as the White House association, through its duly accredited officers, this association having begun the work of acquiring the building and having carried it to a successful conclusion. Their several acts shall at all times be subject to the approval of the governor. (Acts 1923, No. 244, p. 248; Code 1923, § 3182; Code 1940, T. 55, § 292.)

CHAPTER 13.

PUBLIC RECORDS.

ARTICLE 1.

GENERAL PROVISIONS.

Cross references. — As to destruction of public records of municipalities, see § 11-47-150 et seq.

§ 41-13-1. Public records defined.

As used in this article, the term "public records" shall include all written, typed or printed books, papers, letters, documents and maps made or received in pursuance of law by the public officers of the state, counties, municipalities and other subdivisions of government in the transactions of public business and shall also include any record authorized to be made by any law of this state belonging or pertaining to any court of record or any other public record authorized by law or any paper, pleading, exhibit or other writing filed with, in or by any such court, office or officer. (Acts 1945, No. 293, p. 486, § 1.)

Cited in Stone v. Consolidated Publishing Co., 404 So. 2d 678 (Ala. 1981).

§§ 41-13-2, 41-13-3. Repealed by Acts 1977, No. 607, p. 812, § 9901, as amended, effective January 1, 1980.

§ 41-13-4. Assistance of public officials in preserving, filing, etc., of public records by department of archives and history.

The department of archives and history may examine into the condition of public records and shall at the request of the custodian thereof give advice and assistance to any public official in the solution of his problems of preserving, filing and making available the public records in his custody. (Acts 1945, No. 293, p. 486, § 5.)

§ 41-13-5. Destruction, etc., of public records having no significance, importance or value.

Any public records, books, papers, newspapers, files, printed books, manuscripts or other public records which have no significance, importance or value may, upon the advice and recommendation of the custodian thereof and upon the further advice, recommendation and consent of the state or county records commission be destroyed or otherwise disposed of. The state and county records commissions are hereby authorized and empowered to make such orders, rules, and regulations as may be necessary or proper to carry the provisions of this section into effect. (Acts 1945, No. 293, p. 486, § 3.)

ARTICLE 2.

STATE AND COUNTY RECORDS COMMISSIONS.

§ 41-13-20. State records commission created; composition; certain members subject to removal; compensation of members generally; meetings.

There is hereby created a state records commission consisting of seven members as follows: the director of the department of archives and history, who shall be chairman of the commission; the chief examiner of the department of examiners of public accounts; the attorney general; the secretary of state; the commissioner of the department of revenue; one member from the University of Alabama, to be designated by the head of the department of history and one member from Auburn University, to be designated by the head of the department of history. The representatives of the University of Alabama and Auburn University may be removed at any time. No salary or compensation shall be allowed any member of the commission except expenses incurred in the performance of their duties, which expenses shall be paid pursuant to article 2 of chapter 7 of Title 36 of this Code. The commission shall hold regular quarterly meetings in January, April, July and October of each year and at other times upon the call of the chairman. (Acts 1955, No. 565, p. 1226, § 5.)

§ 41-13-21. State records commission to make determination as to state records to be preserved or destroyed, etc., after or without microfilming; classification of records; state officers, etc., not to cause destruction, etc., of records without prior approval of commission; supreme court to determine disposition of court records.

The state records commission shall be charged with the responsibility of determining which state records shall be permanently preserved because of historical value, which state records may be destroyed or otherwise disposed of after they have been microfilmed and which state records may be destroyed or otherwise disposed of without microfilming. The commission may classify the different types of records accordingly.

No state officer or agency head shall cause any state record to be destroyed or otherwise disposed of without first obtaining approval of the state records commission; provided, however, that records of the courts within the unified judicial system may be disposed of in the manner and in accordance with such procedures as may be prescribed by rule of the supreme court, after consultation with the state records commission. Any such retention schedule prescribed by rule of the supreme court pertaining to records of the unified judicial system shall be deemed sufficient authorization for disposal and shall supersede any prior retention schedule with respect to such records, other provisions of the law to the contrary notwithstanding. (Acts 1955, No. 565, p. 1226, § 6; Acts 1967, No. 425, p. 1095; Acts 1980, No. 80-636, p. 1202.)

§ 41-13-22. County records commission created; composition; certain members subject to removal; compensation of members generally; meetings.

There is hereby created a county records commission consisting of 11 members as follows: the director of the department of archives and history, who shall be the chairman of the commission; the chief examiner of the department of examiners of public accounts; the attorney general; one member from the University of Alabama, to be designated by the head of the department of history; one member from Auburn University, to be designated by the head of the department of history; two probate judges; two county tax assessors, one register and one circuit clerk, to be appointed by the governor. The representatives of the University of Alabama and Auburn University, the probate judges, the tax assessors, the register and the circuit clerk may be removed at any time. No salary or compensation shall be allowed any member of the commission except expenses incurred in the performance of their duties, which expenses shall be paid pursuant to article 2 of chapter 7 of Title 36 of this Code. The commission shall hold regular quarterly meetings in January, April, July and October of each year and at other times upon the call of the chairman. (Acts 1955, No. 565, p. 1226, § 7.)

§ 41-13-23. County commission to make determination as to county records to be preserved or destroyed, etc., after microfilming; classification of records; county officials not to cause destruction, etc., of records without prior approval of commission.

The county records commission shall be charged with the responsibility of determining which county records shall be permanently preserved because of historical value and which county records may be destroyed or otherwise disposed of after they have been microfilmed. The commission may classify the different types of records accordingly.

No county official shall cause any county record to be destroyed or otherwise disposed of without first obtaining the approval of the county records commission. (Acts 1955, No. 565, p. 1226, § 8.)

§ 41-13-24. Conduct of surveys by state and county records commissions authorized; issuance, etc., by commissions of regulations classifying public records, etc.

(a) Both the state records commission and the county records commission are hereby empowered to conduct surveys of public records in carrying out the provisions of this chapter.

(b) Both commissions shall from time to time issue regulations classifying all public records and shall prescribe the period for which records of each class shall be retained. Such records may be permanent or for a lesser number of years. Such regulations may from time to time be amended or repealed. Prior to issuing such regulations, both the state records commission and the county records commission shall consider the following factors:

(1) Actions at law and administrative proceedings in which the production of public records might be necessary or desirable;

(2) State and federal statutes of limitation applicable to such actions or proceedings;

(3) The availability of information contained in public records from other sources;

(4) The actual or potential historical value of certain public records; and

(5) Such other matters as the commissions shall deem pertinent in order that public records be retained for as short a period as is commensurate with the interests of the public. (Acts 1955, No. 565, p. 1226, § 10.)

§ 41-13-25. Payment of expenses of certain members of state and county records commissions.

The expenses allowed by law for the county officials who are members of the county records commission shall be paid by their respective counties. The expenses allowed by law for the representatives of the University of Alabama and Auburn University who are members of either the state records commission or the county records commission shall be paid by their respective institutions. (Acts 1955, No. 565, p. 1226, § 11.)

ARTICLE 3.

PHOTOGRAPHING OR MICROPHOTOGRAPHING OF
RECORDS.

§ 41-13-40. Photographing or microphotographing of records, books, files, etc.; admissibility in evidence, etc., of photographs, microfilms, etc.

The head of any office, court, commission, board, institution, department or agency of the state or of any political subdivision thereof may cause any record, document, plat, court file, book, map, paper, or writing made, acquired or received as required by law to be photographed or microphotographed on plate or film. Such photographs, microfilms or prints made therefrom, when duly authenticated by the custodian thereof, shall have the same force and effect at law as the original record or of a record made by any other legally authorized means and may be offered in like manner and shall be received in evidence in any court where such original record or record made by other legally authorized means could have been so introduced and received; provided, that the provisions of this article shall not apply to the state department of pensions and security, the state health department, the state board of health, the state department of industrial relations or to any other office, court, commission, board, institution, department or agency of the state which is otherwise authorized by law to provide for the photographing or microphotographing of its records. (Acts 1955, No. 565, p. 1226, § 1.)

Collateral references. — 76 C.J.S., Records, §§ 12, 35.   Admissibility of photographs of stolen property. 94 ALR3d 357.

§ 41-13-41. Photographing or microphotographing of state records centralized in department of archives and history; charges for photographing or microphotographing.

The photographing or microphotographing of public records, except the public records of counties, municipalities and other political subdivisions of the state of Alabama, shall be centralized in the department of archives and history. The department of archives and history is authorized to charge any office, court, commission, board, institution, department or agency of the state for the photographing or microphotographing of public records belonging to that office, court, commission, board, institution, department or agency. Such charge shall be on a cost basis. (Acts 1955, No. 565, p. 1226, § 2.)

§ 41-13-42. Purchase or lease of photographic or microphotographic equipment and supplies by department of archives and history authorized; appropriation of funds therefor.

The department of archives and history is hereby authorized to purchase or lease photographic or microphotographic equipment and supplies necessary to carry out the duties prescribed in this article.

There is hereby appropriated out of the general fund of the state an amount sufficient to cover the cost of purchase or lease of such equipment and supplies, such appropriation to be released only upon the approval of the governor. (Acts 1955, No. 565, p. 1226, § 4.)

§ 41-13-43. Appropriation of funds by counties or municipalities for photographing or microphotographing of public records authorized.

The county commission of any county or municipality may appropriate an amount sufficient to cover the cost of photographing or microphotographing the public records belonging to that county or municipality. (Acts 1955, No. 565, p. 1226, § 3.)

§ 41-13-44. State and county officials, etc., not to destroy, etc., public records until microfilmed copies processed and checked for accuracy.

No state or county official or employee shall destroy, dispose of or cause to be destroyed or disposed of any public record that has been microfilmed under the provisions of this article until the microfilm copy has been processed and checked with the original for accuracy. (Acts 1955, No. 565, p. 1226, § 9.)

CHAPTER 14.

STATE FUNDS GENERALLY.

Collateral references. — 81 C.J.S., States, §
155.

63 Am. Jur. 2d, Public Funds, §§ 9-41.

ARTICLE 1.

STATE DEPOSITARIES.

Cross references. — As to county
depositories, see § 11-1-7.

§ 41-14-1. Governor may designate banks or trust companies as state depositaries.

The governor may designate any bank or trust company incorporated under
the laws of this state or of the United States and actually doing business in this
state as a state depositary as provided in this article. (Code 1907, § 641; Code
1923, § 891; Code 1940, T. 55, § 379.)

State's claim preferred on liquidation of
depositary. — State held entitled to receive
out of assets of bank in liquidation amount by
which deposit of state's money exceeded security. Green v. City of Homewood, 222 Ala. 225,
131 So. 897 (1931).

Collateral references. — 63 Am. Jur. 2d,
Public Funds, §§ 17, 18.

Custom or usage as affecting officer's deposit
of public money in manner other than that
required by statute. 65 ALR 814.

Deposit of public funds in bank as violation of
constitutional or statutory provision against
loan of public credit or money. 87 ALR 168.

Power of boards or officials to depart from
literal requirements in respect of deposits or
loans of public funds under their control. 104
ALR 623.

Constitutionality, construction, and application of statute for prevention or equalizing of
loss to governmental or political units as result
of insolvency or failure of depositories of public
funds. 104 ALR 1372.

§ 41-14-2. Application for designation as state depositary to be filed with state treasurer, etc.; verified statement as to assets and liabilities, capital stock, etc., and deposit of bonds or securities to accompany application.

Before any bank or trust company shall be designated as a state depositary,
it shall file with the state treasurer an application in writing to be designated
as a state depositary under the terms of this article.

Such bank or trust company shall accompany such application with a
statement, verified by the affidavit of its president or other executive head,
setting forth the amount of its paid-in capital stock, the amount of its surplus
and undivided profits, its principal place of business, the length of time it has
been engaged in business and its assets and liabilities at the time of making
application.

Such bank or trust company shall also accompany the application with a deposit of bonds or securities in an amount not less than $10,000.00 par or face value or with federal reserve bank receipts evidencing the fact that bonds or securities in an amount not less than $10,000.00 par or face value are being held by a federal reserve bank as security for the deposit of state funds, such bonds or securities to be released only to the lawful holder of such receipts upon presentation of the receipts. A copy of such application and statement shall be filed with the director of finance.

The only bonds or securities which can be accepted as security or for which receipts can be accepted as security for the deposit of state funds are the direct obligations of the state of Alabama or the direct obligations of the United States government, the bonds and other securities issued by the Alabama highway finance corporation, the bonds and other securities issued by the Alabama public schools corporation and the bonds to secure the payment of which any rentals or revenues of the state docks department have been pledged prior to January 1, 1948. At least 60 percent of the first $10,000.00 principal amount of any securities so deposited or receipts for which are so deposited must consist of the direct obligations of the state of Alabama, but the bank or trust company shall have the privilege of making the balance of its deposit in any of the other bonds or securities hereinabove set forth or in receipts representing any of the bonds or securities hereinabove set forth. All securities so deposited or receipts for which so deposited, whether direct obligations of the state of Alabama or otherwise, must be accepted at face or par value. Such securities shall be registered in the name of the bank or trust company depositing the same or receipts therefor, and the securities or receipts therefor shall be kept and held by the treasurer, and it shall be so stated in said application, as a security to the state for the faithful performance of the duties of such bank or trust company as a state depositary and that the bank or trust company will well and truly account for and pay over any moneys or funds of the state upon the check or order of the treasurer. (Code 1907, § 642; Code 1923, § 892; Acts 1939, No. 195, p. 349; Code 1940, T. 55, § 380; Acts 1943, No. 14, p. 17, § 1; Acts 1947, No. 411, p. 301, § 1.)

Cited in Madison County v. Williams, 236 Ala. 470, 183 So. 452 (1938).

Collateral references. — 63 Am. Jur. 2d, Public Funds, § 21 et seq.

Waiver of right of government to preference by taking securities. 24 ALR 1495, 83 ALR 1119.

Constitutionality of statute relating to preference of public funds on insolvency of bank. 31 ALR 790, 79 ALR 582, 83 ALR 1080.

Waiver of state's priority, by deposits on interest. 42 ALR 1296.

Right, in absence of statute, to preference in respect of public funds in insolvent bank. 51 ALR 1336, 65 ALR 690, 103 ALR 621.

Prerogative right of state to preference at common law. 51 ALR 1355, 65 ALR 1331, 90 ALR 184, 167 ALR 640.

Trust or preference in respect of public money deposited in bank by court, or pursuant to its order, or by officer of court. 86 ALR 209.

Constitutionality, construction, and application of statute for prevention or equalizing of loss to governmental or political units as result of insolvency or failure of depositories of public funds. 104 ALR 1372.

§ 41-14-3. Certification to governor of filing of application and deposit of bonds or securities by bank or trust company; promulgation of order by governor declaring bank or trust company a state depositary.

Upon the filing of such application with the state treasurer and the deposit of bonds or other securities or receipts therefor with the treasurer as provided in section 41-14-2, the treasurer shall certify to the governor the fact of such application and the sworn statement accompanying the same, and thereupon the governor may designate the applicant as a state depositary.

In the event the application is granted by the governor, he shall promulgate an order declaring that the applicant is a state depositary until its authority is revoked and that as such it may receive or have at any time state funds in an amount equal to the par value of the bonds and other securities deposited or receipts for which are deposited by it with the treasurer as provided in section 41-14-2. (Code 1907, § 643; Code 1923, § 893; Code 1940, T. 55, § 381; Acts 1943, No. 14, p. 17; Acts 1947, No. 411, p. 301, § 2.)

Cited in Madison County v. Williams, 236 Ala. 470, 183 So. 452 (1938).

Collateral references. — 63 Am. Jur. 2d, Public Funds, § 23 et seq.

Waiver of right of government to preference by taking securities. 24 ALR 1495, 83 ALR 1119.

Constitutionality of statute relating to preference of public funds on insolvency of bank. 31 ALR 790, 79 ALR 582, 83 ALR 1080.

Waiver of state's priority, by deposits on interest. 42 ALR 1296.

Right, in absence of statute, to preference in respect of public funds in insolvent bank. 51 ALR 1336, 65 ALR 690, 103 ALR 621.

Prerogative right of state to preference at common law. 51 ALR 1355, 65 ALR 1331, 90 ALR 184, 167 ALR 640.

Trust or preference in respect of public money deposited in bank by court, or pursuant to its order, or by officer of court. 86 ALR 209.

Constitutionality, construction, and application of statutes for prevention or equalizing of loss to governmental or political units as result of insolvency or failure of depositories of public funds. 104 ALR 1372.

§ 41-14-4. Designation of depositaries and transfer or removal of state funds to or from same to be without cost, expense or risk to state.

The designation of state depositaries and the transfer or removal of funds to or from any state depositary shall be without any cost or expense to the state, and when any funds or moneys are transmitted or transferred by any state depositary upon the order of the treasurer, the same shall be and continue at the risk of such depositary until it shall have reached the destination contemplated by the order. (Code 1907, § 652; Code 1923, § 902; Code 1940, T. 55, § 390.)

§ 41-14-5. State or county officers may deposit state funds in depositaries; maximum amount of state funds which depositaries may receive, etc.

Any state or county officer in this state having in his possession or under his control funds or moneys belonging to the state may place the same in a state depositary to the credit of the state treasurer and subject to the check or order of the treasurer. No state depositary shall receive or have at any time an amount of paid money or funds in excess of the face value of bonds and other securities deposited or for which receipts have been deposited by it with the treasurer. (Code 1907, § 644; Code 1923, § 894; Code 1940, T. 55, § 382; Acts 1943, No. 14, p. 17; Acts 1947, No. 411, p. 301, § 3; Acts 1949, No. 223, p. 332.)

Cross references. — See note to § 41-14-1.

Deposit in bank not a depositary is conversion of fund. — Tax collector receiving money for state taxes is its bailee and must use money collected as directed by law. Where county tax collector deposited state tax money to own account in a bank not a state depositary this constituted a conversion of the fund, making collector liable to state as for debt. Wadsworth v. State, 225 Ala. 118, 142 So. 529 (1932).

§ 41-14-6. Depositaries to remit to treasurer state funds received, etc., in excess of authorized amount; withdrawal of state funds from and revocation of authority to act as state depositary of bank or trust company failing to remit surplus state funds to treasurer.

If any bank or trust company designated as a state depositary shall receive, or have on hand at the close of any day's business, state funds or moneys in excess of the amount it is authorized in this article to receive or have at any time, such depositary shall at once remit such surplus direct to the treasurer; and, on failing to do so, the governor, upon the fact being certified to him by the treasurer or otherwise coming to his knowledge, shall forthwith direct the withdrawal by the treasurer from such bank or trust company of said funds or moneys; and, the same being withdrawn, he shall forthwith revoke the authority of such bank or trust company to be or continue [as] a state depositary. (Code 1907, § 645; Code 1923, § 895; Code 1940, T. 55, § 383.)

§ 41-14-7. Depositaries to give receipts to officers making deposits; disposition of copies of receipts, etc.

Each state depositary shall give to the officer placing funds or moneys therein to the credit of the treasurer a receipt therefor in duplicate, and such officers shall immediately mail to the department of finance a duplicate of the said receipt. The department of finance shall, upon receiving the same, pass the amount therein mentioned to the credit of said officer and transmit the duplicate receipt to the treasurer, who shall mail to the said officer a receipt for the same. (Code 1907, § 646; Code 1923, § 896; Code 1940, T. 55, § 384.)

§ 41-14-8. Depositaries to report daily deposits to treasurer; monthly statements of balance in depositaries to be made to treasurer, governor, etc.

Each state depositary shall report in writing at the close of each business day to the treasurer the total amount of all sums placed therein for his account on that day, by whom made and for what purpose made.

At the end of each calendar month, a statement of the balance to the credit of the treasurer in such depositary shall be made by it to the governor, department of finance and treasurer. (Code 1907, § 647; Code 1923, § 897; Code 1940, T. 55, § 385.)

§ 41-14-9. Sale of bonds, etc., deposited as security upon failure of depositary to pay check, etc., of treasurer or account for state funds generally.

The funds or moneys so placed in every state depositary shall be held by it subject to the check or order of the state treasurer; and, if any state depositary having funds or moneys to the credit of the treasurer shall fail to pay any check drawn or order made by the treasurer or shall fail to account faithfully for all the state funds or moneys that may have come into its possession, the treasurer shall forthwith sell the bonds or securities deposited by it under the terms of this article or a sufficient amount thereof to pay off and discharge any sum or sums which are in such state depositary to the credit of the treasurer and which are unpaid, together with the cost and expense of advertising a sale of the bonds or securities. The treasurer shall advertise the proposed sale of such bonds or securities for 10 days in a daily newspaper published in Montgomery, Mobile and Birmingham, and the sale shall be made in front of the Capitol and at public outcry for cash. In case receipts are deposited with the treasurer by such a defaulting depositary, the treasurer shall present receipts to the federal reserve bank for a sufficient amount of the bonds or securities represented thereby and shall receive the bonds or securities for sale as above provided. (Code 1907, § 648; Code 1923, § 898; Code 1940, T. 55, § 386; Acts 1947, No. 411, p. 301, § 4.)

§ 41-14-10. Sale passes title to bonds to purchaser; registration of bonds in name of purchaser.

Any sale of said bonds or part thereof authorized by this article to be made by the treasurer shall, when the sale is made and the purchase price paid, have the effect of transferring to and vesting in the purchaser at such sale title to the said bonds so purchased, and the purchaser shall thereby be authorized to have the bonds so purchased by him registered in his own name. (Code 1907, § 649; Code 1923, § 899; Code 1940, T. 55, § 387.)

§ 41-14-11. Notice to governor, treasurer, etc., by bank or trust company surrendering designation as state depositary.

Before any voluntary surrender of its designation, such bank or trust company shall give at least 30 days' notice to the governor, department of finance and treasurer of its purpose to cease acting as a state depositary. (Code 1907, § 651; Code 1923, § 901; Code 1940, T. 55, § 389.)

§ 41-14-12. Withdrawal of bonds, securities, etc., by bank or trust company ceasing, etc., to act as state depositary.

When any bank or trust company acting as a state depositary ceases or desires to cease acting as such, it shall, after making a full account of its transactions as state depositary and discharging all the obligations and liabilities imposed by this article, and paying into the state treasury any and all sums it may be liable for to the treasurer or to the state, be entitled to withdraw the bonds, securities or receipts deposited by it, and thereupon its right to act as a state depositary shall cease and determine. (Code 1907, § 650; Code 1923, § 900; Code 1940, T. 55, § 388; Acts 1947, No. 411, p. 301, § 5.)

§ 41-14-13. Deposit of state funds in depositaries by state or county officers not required by article.

Nothing in this article shall be construed as requiring county or state officers to place state funds in state depositaries, and they may pay such funds into the state treasury as now provided by law. (Code 1907, § 654; Code 1923, § 904; Code 1940, T. 55, § 392.)

§ 41-14-14. Treasurer may deposit funds received from state or county officers in state depositaries.

The treasurer, by and with the approval of the governor, may place all funds or any part thereof paid to him by county or state officers or any other funds that he may have at any time on hand in any one or more of the state depositaries under the same rules and regulations governing other deposits made under this article. (Code 1907, § 655; Code 1923, § 905; Code 1940, T. 55, § 393.)

§ 41-14-15. Governor, treasurer, etc., to establish regulations and collection methods for transaction of business with state depositaries.

The governor, the department of finance and the treasurer are authorized to establish such regulations and collection methods not inconsistent with the provisions of this article as they may deem necessary for the convenient transaction of business with state depositaries. (Code 1907, § 653; Code 1923, § 903; Code 1940, T. 55, § 391.)

§ 41-14-16. Penalties for violations of provisions of article.

Any state or county officer, or state depositary or agent thereof, who shall violate any of the provisions of this article shall be guilty of a misdemeanor and may, on conviction, be fined not more than $2,500.00; and, in addition to the fine, such state or county officer may be removed from office. (Code 1907, § 7453; Code 1923, § 5045; Code 1940, T. 41, § 220.)

ARTICLE 2.

DEPOSIT OF STATE FUNDS.

§ 41-14-30. General authority of state treasurer to deposit funds in state depositaries; when funds may be invested in notes, bonds, etc., of United States or federal agencies.

The state treasurer may deposit the money of the state in any bank or trust company designated as a state depositary according to law, so long as said bank or trust company agrees to pay interest on a portion of said money as provided in this article. Where the amount to be deposited on time deposits exceeds the amount which all banking institutions in the state are willing to accept on the terms specified in this section, the state treasurer may invest so much of said funds as he may deem appropriate in bonds, notes or treasury bills of the United States, federal land bank bonds, federal home loan bank notes and bonds, federal national mortgage association notes and debentures, federal intermediate credit bank debentures, banks for cooperative debentures or any of its other agencies or obligations guaranteed as to principal and interest by the United States maturing or becoming payable not more than one year from the date of purchase. Funds may also be invested in such obligations of the United States or its agencies under a repurchase agreement for a shorter time than the maturity date of the security itself. (Acts 1967, No. 3, p. 336, § 1; Acts 1977, 1st Ex. Sess., No. 45, p. 1460.)

Collateral references. — 81A C.J.S., States, § 225.

§ 41-14-31. Moneys for current operational expenses to be maintained in treasury in cash or in demand deposits in state depositaries; apportionment of demand deposits among state depositaries.

As much money as may be needed for current operational purposes of the state government, as determined by the state treasurer in accordance with procedures prescribed by section 41-14-32 and with the approval of the governor, shall be maintained at all times in the state treasury in cash or in demand deposits with state depositary banks.

The state treasurer shall apportion such demand deposits among state depositaries, giving due consideration to the activities of the various banking accounts maintained therein, the reasonable value of the banking services rendered or to be rendered the state by depositary banks and to the value and importance of such deposits to the economy of the communities and the various areas of the state to be affected thereby, as indicated by the loan to deposit ratio. (Acts 1967, No. 3, p. 336, § 2; Acts 1971, 1st Ex. Sess., No. 62, p. 99.)

§ 41-14-32. Determination of income from time deposits, open account; determination of funds needed for projected monthly expenditures and payments; depositaries of funds needed for projected daily expenditures; excess funds to be deposited in time deposits, open account, in state depositaries; investment of funds which will be in treasury 30 days or less.

(a) The commissioner of revenue shall, at least 30 days prior to the effective date of contracts with state depositaries covering time deposits, open account, determine the income payable into the state treasury on a monthly basis for the next succeeding three calendar months of the interest period of such contracts.

(b) The director of finance shall, at least 30 days prior to the effective date of contracts with the state depositaries covering time deposits, open account, determine the amount of funds estimated to be needed for all expenditures and payments out of the state treasury, computed on a monthly basis for the next succeeding three calendar months of the interest period of such contracts.

(c) The commissioner of revenue and the director of finance are authorized to require such information and reports from all state departments, boards, commissions and agencies as may be necessary to carry out their respective functions under this section.

(d) The director of finance shall transmit this information to the state treasurer, who shall determine and compute the net minimum balance estimated to be available at any time during the period covered under such contracts for time deposits, open account, and shall report such determination and computation to the director of finance.

(e) The state treasurer shall continuously study the cash flow of the state treasury, including all receipts and disbursements therefrom, and shall make projections of the amount of funds required to meet the daily demands or expenditures for the state government for the next succeeding three calendar months and shall report such projected amount to the director of finance. The state treasurer shall place such projected amount in demand deposits in banks designated as state depositaries. All funds in excess of this amount shall be deposited in banks designated as state depositaries in time deposits, open account, as authorized in section 41-14-33, or shall invest all or any part thereof as authorized in section 41-14-30. The amount placed in time deposits, open account, shall be as great as operational obligations permit.

(f) At any time the state treasurer determines that certain cash receipts will be in the treasury for 30 days or less, the state treasurer is hereby authorized to invest such sums in obligations of the United States Treasury Department, investments with commercial banks in the state or in repurchase agreements on United States treasury obligations, whichever yields the highest interest income to the state. (Acts 1967, No. 3, p. 336, § 3; Acts 1971, 1st Ex. Sess., No. 62, p. 99; Acts 1975, 1st Ex. Sess., No. 1, p. 57, § 1; Acts 1977, 1st Ex. Sess., No. 45, p. 1460.)

Collateral references. — 81A C.J.S., States, § 226.

§ 41-14-33. Execution by state treasurer of contracts with state depositaries covering time deposits, open account; annual rate of interest on time deposits, open account, generally.

(a) The state treasurer is authorized to execute contracts with the state depositaries covering time deposits, open account; provided, that no funds may be withdrawn from said account except upon 30 days' notice in writing or for the minimum period of time prescribed by applicable banking regulations then in force and effect.

(b) The annual rate of interest on time deposits, open account, shall be the average for the most recent four weeks of the prices of the 91-day United States treasury bill auction; provided, that the rate shall not exceed the maximum permitted by applicable banking regulations. (Acts 1967, No. 3, p. 336, § 4; Acts 1971, 1st Ex. Sess., No. 62, p. 99; Acts 1975, 1st Ex. Sess., No. 1, § 2.)

§ 41-14-34. How interest on time deposits, open account, calculated and paid; emergency withdrawal of funds on time deposit, open account.

(a) Interest shall be calculated on the basis of the contracts existing with respect to time deposits, open account, and shall be payable quarterly to the state treasurer and by that officer paid into the state treasury to the credit of the general fund of the state.

(b) In the event of an emergency, the treasurer is authorized to comply with applicable banking regulations in order to receive all or any portion of the funds placed on time deposits, open account, on shorter notice than the agreement provides and to forfeit such amount of accrued and unpaid interest as may be required by such regulations. (Acts 1967, No. 3, p. 336, § 5.)

§ 41-14-35. Security for state money deposited in state depositaries in demand deposits and time deposits, open account.

(a) All state money deposited in state depositaries in demand accounts and time deposits, open account, shall be secured as required by section 5-1-14 and article 1 of this chapter; provided, however, that for amounts deposited in time deposits, open account, and in demand accounts there may also be accepted as security for said deposits bonds and other securities issued by any agency or instrumentality of the United States of America, any general obligation bonds or securities of any of the various states of the continental United States or any of their instrumentalities which have a rating of "A" or better by Moody's Investors Rating Services, Inc., New York City, or any successor firm to that corporation, any general obligation bonds or warrants of any county or any municipality of the state of Alabama, warrants or securities of any county secured by a pledge of the special road, bridge and public building tax authorized by article XI, section 215 of the Constitution, bonds or warrants of any

307

county or city board of education secured by a pledge of taxes levied under the authority of constitutional amendment 3 or any other constitutional amendment authorizing the levying of special ad valorem taxes for schools or secured by a pledge of county or city sales taxes, any gasoline tax anticipation warrants secured by a pledge of gasoline tax revenues derived from the gasoline excise tax levied by the state and distributed to counties under section 40-17-74 or any successor statute, and electric, natural gas, sewer and water revenue bonds issued by any municipality of the state of Alabama or any board created by or with the consent of any such municipality.

(b) To be eligible to secure state deposits, revenue or limited obligation bonds or warrants must have a current average annual debt service coverage of at least two times.

(c) No security shall be required for the amount of any deposit or account to the extent said deposit or account is insured by the Federal Deposit Insurance Corporation.

(d) The state treasurer is authorized to disapprove any security offered or pledged as collateral. (Acts 1967, No. 3, p. 336, § 6.)

Code commissioner's note. — Section 5-1-14, referred to in this section, was repealed by Acts 1980, No. 80-658, § 5-13-3, effective May 28, 1980. See § 5-5A-28.

§ 41-14-36. Receipt, etc., of fee, compensation, etc., for placement, etc., of state moneys in time deposits, open account, demand deposits, etc.

Any person who knowingly demands or receives any fee, compensation or reward or who demands or accepts directly or indirectly as payment or gift or otherwise any sum of money or other thing of value as an inducement or in return for the placement of any funds or for assistance either directly or indirectly in securing the placement of any moneys of the state of Alabama in time deposits, open account, demand accounts or otherwise shall be guilty of a felony and, upon conviction, shall be imprisoned for not more than three years or fined not more than $3,000.00 or both; and, in the event the person convicted is an officer, agent or employee of the state of Alabama, he shall be dismissed from office or discharged from employment. (Acts 1967, No. 3, p. 336, § 7.)

§ 41-14-37. Section 36-17-18 not affected by provisions of article.

Nothing contained in this article shall be construed to modify, amend or repeal the provisions of section 36-17-18, as now existing or hereafter amended, relating to investment in direct obligations of the United States of America registered in the name of the state treasurer. (Acts 1967, No. 3, p. 336, § 8; Acts 1971, 1st Ex. Sess., No. 62, p. 99; Acts 1975, 1st Ex. Sess., No. 1, § 3.)

§ 41-14-38. Applicability of provisions of article.

The provisions of this article shall not apply to funds subject to withdrawal by a state official, state department or state agency other than the state treasurer. (Acts 1967, No. 3, p. 336, § 9.)

CHAPTER 15.

STATE INSURANCE FUND.

§ 41-15-1. Creation; purpose.

There shall be a fund, to be known as the state insurance fund, carried by the state treasurer for the purpose of insuring loss by fire, lightning, windstorm and hail or fire and all the perils included under extended coverage on buildings in which title in whole or in part is vested in the state of Alabama or any of its agencies or institutions or in which funds provided by the state have been used for the purchase of the land, construction of the building, purchase or maintenance of any equipment, furniture, fixtures or supplies in such buildings and public school buildings together with the contents of all such buildings; provided, that this section shall neither repeal nor in any manner affect the provisions of any local act of the legislature or any general act of local application authorizing city or county boards of education or district boards of education of independent school districts to insure school buildings and property either in the state insurance fund or in an insurance company, whichever in the opinion of such board provides the best coverage for such school buildings and property. (Acts 1923, No. 593, p. 769; Code 1923, § 8539; Code 1940, T. 28, § 317; Acts 1949, No. 675, p. 1045, § 1; Acts 1957, No. 596, p. 833, § 1.)

Collateral references. — 67 C.J.S., Officers, § 54(1).

§ 41-15-2. Department of finance to administer chapter; administrator of state insurance fund.

The department of finance is hereby constituted and designated as the agency through which this chapter shall be administered, and the director of said department is empowered with such authority as may be necessary to carry out its purposes.

The director of said department, with the approval of the governor, may appoint an actuary as administrator of the state insurance fund, who is familiar with insurance custom and practices and is otherwise qualified by actual experience in the underwriting of risks and adjustment of losses, to assist the director of said department in carrying out the purpose of this chapter. The said actuary shall install and keep an accurate system of accounting and statistical records and shall adjust losses, make appraisals of state-owned properties for insurance purposes, when necessary, and shall handle or supervise the handling of all other details incident to carrying out the provisions of this chapter. The actuary shall furnish to the department of finance each month a statement showing in detail the accumulated income and disbursements during the fiscal year, together with a financial statement showing assets and liabilities of the state insurance fund. At the close of each fiscal year the actuary shall furnish to the said department an annual statement of the affairs of the state insurance fund. The unearned net premium computed on a pro rata basis shall be considered as a liability and carried as a reserve. Said actuary shall file with the said department a bond in the penal sum of $10,000.00, executed by a surety company authorized to do business in this state, conditioned upon faithful performance of his duties, payable to the state of Alabama. (Acts 1923, No. 593, p. 769; Code 1923, § 8540; Acts 1936-37, Ex. Sess., No. 219, p. 260; Acts 1939, No. 112, p. 144; Code 1940, T. 28, § 318; Acts 1949, No. 675, p. 1045, § 2.)

Collateral references. — 67 C.J.S., Officers, § 92.

§ 41-15-3. Inspection and appraisal of property.

The director of finance shall make or cause to be made an inspection and appraisal of all property, the value of which has not already been satisfactorily established, for the purpose of determining the amount of insurance necessary to be carried on the several properties and to classify all property and give it the current rating of commercial fire and casualty insurance companies. (Acts 1923, No. 593, p. 769; Code 1923, § 8541; Acts 1939, No. 112, p. 144; Code 1940, T. 28, § 319.)

§ 41-15-4. Value for which state property to be insured; annual certification to department of finance of description and value of buildings and equipment; insuring of county school buildings; inspection of public property and distribution of copies of reports thereof.

(a) All state property shall be insured for 75 percent of its actual value, and any property except rural schoolhouses and equipment may, at the option of the director, be insured up to 100 percent of its value.

(b) The officer or person having charge by law of insuring any public building shall annually certify to the department of finance the description and the value of all buildings and equipment under his supervision or control on forms prescribed by the department for the purpose of showing the character of the risk and determining the rate of premium. No coverage shall be issued unless such certificate is on file in the office of the department of finance or the director has waived, in writing, the filing of the same.

(c) Buildings owned by any county and used for school purposes under control of the county board of education may be insured under the provisions of this chapter.

(d) The department of finance shall cause to be inspected, annually if practicable, all public property coming within the provisions of this chapter, to ascertain to what extent any hazard has been increased or reduced, and the officer or person in charge of the public property shall receive a copy of such inspection report. (Acts 1923, No. 593, p. 769; Code 1923, § 8542; Acts 1936-37, Ex. Sess., No. 219, p. 260; Acts 1939, No. 112, p. 144; Code 1940, T. 28, § 320; Acts 1949, No. 675, p. 1045, § 3.)

Cited in Waggoner v. Whatley, 282 Ala. 84, 209 So. 2d 370 (1968).

§ 41-15-5. Basis upon which premiums charged generally; reinsurance.

The net premium charged shall be based on the current commercial rate, less 40 percent discount, except on such risks as may be listed in the underwriting schedule showing amounts reinsured over and above amounts retained by the state insurance fund. No discount shall be allowed on or with respect to the amounts reinsured either with insurance companies or under a contingent reinsurance account which may be carried by the state insurance fund. The director of finance may, with the approval of the governor, purchase such reinsurance as may in the opinion of the director of finance be necessary for the proper distribution of the risk. The director of finance shall collect such reinsurance upon any loss sustained and pay the same into the state insurance fund. When the director of finance purchases reinsurance as provided in this section, he or his duly authorized representative shall be considered the agent of the insurer for the receipt of the agent's commission on insurance so obtained, and when such commissions are collected or received by him they shall be paid into the state treasury and deposited to the credit of the state general fund. (Acts 1923, No. 593, p. 769; Code 1923, § 8543; Acts 1936-37, Ex. Sess., No. 219, p. 260; Acts 1939, No. 112, p. 144; Code 1940, T. 28, § 321; Acts 1949, No. 675, p. 1045, § 4; Acts 1967, No. 435, p. 1104.)

§ 41-15-6. Payment of premiums generally.

All of such premiums shall be paid to the department of finance, not later than 60 days from the effective date of such insurance or renewal thereof, by the treasurer or executive officer of the agency affected. Such funds shall be promptly transmitted to the state treasurer, who shall place the same to the credit of the state insurance fund. Upon failure or refusal of any officer to comply with the provisions of this section with regard to the payment of premiums, the state comptroller shall, when requested by the director of the department of finance, deduct from any funds due or which may become due the delinquent amount of unpaid premiums and pay the same to the state insurance fund. (Acts 1923, No. 593, p. 769; Code 1923, § 8544; Acts 1936-37, Ex. Sess., No. 219, p. 260; Acts 1939, No. 112, p. 144; Code 1940, T. 28, § 322; Acts 1949, No. 675, p. 1045, § 5.)

§ 41-15-7. Pro rata premiums.

In case of the expiration of any policy before October 1 of any year, then, in such event, the director of finance shall assume the risk and assess the premium for that year in that proportion of an annual premium as the number of unexpired days before the next October 1 bears to a year. In the case of all such pro rata premiums, the same shall be due and payable on or before the fifteenth day of the next succeeding month and, if not paid, shall be subject to the penalty prescribed in section 41-15-6. (Acts 1923, No. 593, p. 769; Code 1923, § 8554; Code 1940, T. 28, § 328.)

§ 41-15-8. Resolution of disagreements between department of finance and person in charge of state property as to value of property, premium rates, etc.

In the event a disagreement arises between the department of finance and any person or persons in charge of any state property as to its true value or the amount payable under the claim for loss or the proper premium rate or rates, the matter in disagreement shall be determined by a third person to be agreed upon by the director of finance on the one hand and the person or persons disagreeing with him on the other. In case of inability to agree on such third person, the governor shall appoint a third person to determine the question, and his decision thereon shall be binding on all parties concerned. (Acts 1923, No. 593, p. 769; Code 1923, § 8552; Acts 1936-37, Ex. Sess., No. 219, p. 260; Acts 1939, No. 112, p. 144; Code 1940, T. 28, § 326.)

§ 41-15-9. Director of finance may prescribe forms of policies, etc., and make rules and regulations for administration of chapter.

The director of finance is authorized to prescribe forms of policies, proofs of losses and other forms and to make such rules and regulations as may be necessary or expedient for the proper administration of the provisions of this chapter. (Acts 1923, No. 593, p. 769; Code 1923, § 8553; Acts 1936-37, Ex. Sess., No. 219, p. 260; Code 1940, T. 28, § 327; Acts 1949, No. 675, p. 1045, § 8.)

§ 41-15-10. Premiums and collected earnings to constitute trust fund; surplus may be invested in bonds, stocks, mutual funds, etc.; limitations and conditions; requisition for payment of losses, expenses, etc.

All premiums and earnings collected under the provisions of this chapter shall constitute a trust fund to be applied as authorized in this chapter.

With the approval of the governor, any surplus in the fund over a necessary working capital, which shall be determined by the director of finance, at not less than $400,000.00, may be invested in the bonds or other obligations of the United States, of the state of Alabama or of any agency, institution or instrumentality of the state of Alabama. The director of finance shall also have the authority to invest and reinvest said state insurance trust funds in such classes of bonds, mortgages, common and preferred stocks, shares of investment companies or mutual funds or other investments as the finance director with the consent of the governor may approve, subject to all the terms, conditions, limitations and restrictions imposed by the laws of Alabama upon domestic life insurance companies in the making of their investments. Subject to like terms, conditions, limitations and restrictions, the finance director shall have full power to hold, purchase, sell, assign, transfer and dispose of any such investments, as well as the proceeds of said investments. The necessary working capital may also be invested and reinvested by the finance director in securities deemed to be cash equivalents. Any and all funds derived from operations under this chapter shall be subject to requisition by the director of finance, approved by the governor, for the payment of losses, necessary expenses of administering this chapter and for investment. (Acts 1923, No. 593, p. 769; Code 1923, § 8545; Acts 1936-37, Ex. Sess., No. 219, p. 260; Acts 1939, No. 112, p. 144; Code 1940, T. 28, § 323; Acts 1949, No. 675, p. 1045, § 6; Acts 1979, No. 79-704, p. 1252.)

§ 41-15-10.1. Transfer of funds to state general fund for medicaid purposes; transfer back to state insurance fund; interest.

Provided there is no monetary loss in the liquidation of securities held by the state insurance fund on short term securities based on their purchase price, and no monetary loss on bonds sold based on their book value as of March 10, 1980, there is hereby transferred from the state insurance fund, as provided for in this chapter, the sum, to be determined by the governor, of up to $25,000,000.00, to the credit of the state general fund, and such sum is hereby appropriated and shall be used only for medicaid purposes. Such amounts as transferred to the state general fund as provided herein, or any part thereof, may be transferred back from the state general fund to the state insurance fund, with interest at eight percent per annum, whenever the state finance director, with the approval of the governor, determines that there are sufficient funds in the state general fund. (Acts 1980, No. 80-90, p. 119.)

§ 41-15-11. Limitations upon expenditure of funds; employees subject to merit system.

No part of the funds provided for in section 41-15-10 shall be used to increase the salary of any state employee. Only the salary of the designated administrator, stenographic secretary, inspector, clerical force and such other expense as may be necessary for the efficient administration of the provisions of this chapter shall be paid from these funds. Such expenditures shall be limited to that amount appropriated by the legislature, and all such expenditures shall be limited to six percent of the amount of premiums written in each year or so much thereof as may be required.

All employees as provided in this section shall be subject to the Merit System Act. (Acts 1923, No. 593, p. 769; Code 1923, § 8550; Acts 1936-37, Ex. Sess., No. 219, p. 260; Code 1940, T. 28, § 325; Acts 1949, No. 675, p. 1045, § 7; Acts 1957, No. 596, p. 833, § 2.)

§ 41-15-12. Appropriation for payment of excess fire or tornado losses; reimbursement.

There is hereby appropriated from the treasury the sum of $100,000.00 to be available only in case the loss by fire or tornado in any year shall exceed the premiums collected under the provisions of this chapter, and then only in such amount as may be required in addition to the amount of funds on deposit in the state insurance fund at the time of said loss for the payment thereof, less the amounts set aside in this chapter for the purpose of administration of the provisions of this chapter.

The first surplus next thereafter accruing to such fund shall be used to reimburse the treasury for any amount which may have been drawn therefrom under this appropriation. (Acts 1923, No. 593, p. 769; Code 1923, § 8546; Acts 1936-37, Ex. Sess., No. 219, p. 260; Code 1940, T. 28, § 324.)

§ 41-15-13. Appropriation of funds received in payment for loss to property by fire, etc.

There is hereby appropriated in addition to all other appropriations and for capital outlay purposes only any and all funds received by the state of Alabama or any department, board, bureau, agency or institution of the state in payment for any loss to property suffered by reason of fire, lightning, windstorm or hail. (Acts 1951, No. 1000, p. 1671.)

CHAPTER 16.

PUBLIC CONTRACTS.

ARTICLE 1.

GENERAL PROVISIONS.

§ 41-16-1. Withdrawal by contractor of amounts retained from payments under contract.

(a) Under any contract for public improvements awarded by the state or by any department, agency, board, commission, authority or political subdivision thereof, including any municipality, county and any board, commission or agency of such municipality or county, the contractor may, from time to time, withdraw the whole or any part of the amounts retained from payments due the contractor under the terms and conditions of such contract by depositing with the state treasurer of the state of Alabama or the treasurer or comptroller of any municipality or county holding funds belonging to the contractor, the following security or any combination thereof in an amount at least equal to the amount so withdrawn, said security to be accepted at the time of deposit at market value but not in excess of par value:

(1) U.S. treasury bonds, U.S. treasury notes, U.S. treasury certificates of indebtedness or U.S. treasury bills;

(2) Bonds or notes of the state of Alabama;

(3) Bonds of any political subdivision of the state of Alabama;

(4) Certificates of deposit issued by the Federal Deposit Insurance Corporation insured banks located in the state of Alabama; provided, that such certificates are negotiable and only in an amount not in excess of the maximum dollar amount of coverage by the Federal Deposit Insurance Corporation; or

(5) Certificates of deposit issued by savings and loan associations located in the state of Alabama, the accounts of which are insured by the Federal Savings and Loan Insurance Corporation or whose accounts are insured by a company approved by the state board savings and loan associations; provided, that such certificate is made payable with accrued interest on demand; and, further provided, that any such certificate from any of the savings and loan associations referred to in this subdivision shall not be for an amount in excess of the maximum dollar amount of coverage of the Federal Savings and Loan Insurance Corporation.

All securities listed above shall be readily negotiable.

(b) The agency or department of the state having jurisdiction over any public improvement contract shall notify the state treasurer of the amount of the deposit required and shall also notify the state treasurer when to release the deposit.

(c) The engineer representing any municipality or county or the chairman of any board, commission or agency of any such municipality or county shall notify the municipality or county treasurer or comptroller of the amount of deposit required and shall also notify the said municipal or county treasurer or comptroller when to release the deposit.

(d) At the time of deposit of any security the same shall be endorsed, if necessary, and shall be accompanied by a conditional assignment to the public body designated as owner in the contract document, which assignment will empower the treasurer of the state of Alabama or the treasurer or comptroller of any municipality or county to negotiate the said security at any time to the extent necessary to cause the contract to be fulfilled.

(e) Any interest or income due on any security so deposited shall be paid to the contractor. If the deposit is in the form of coupon bonds, the coupons as they respectively become due shall be delivered to the contractor.

(f) In the event the contractor shall default in the performance of the contract or any portion thereof, the securities deposited by the contractor in lieu of retainage and all interest, income and coupons accruing on said securities, after default, may be sold by the state or any agency or department thereof or by any municipality or county or any board, commission or agency of such municipality or county as the case may be and the proceeds of said sale used as if such proceeds represented the retainage provided for under the contract. (Acts 1975, No. 950, § 1.)

§ 41-16-2. Limitation on prosecutions for violations of competitive bid laws.

A prosecution for any offense in violation of the competitive bid laws of articles 2 and 3 of this chapter must be commenced within six years after the commission of the offense. (Acts 1981, No. 81-350; Acts 1981, No. 81-851, p. 1529.)

Effective date. — The act which added this section became effective May 27, 1981.

Code commissioner's note. — Acts 1981, No. 81-350, p. 506, § 1, effective April 29, 1981, enacted this section. Acts 1981, No. 81-851, p. 1529, § 1, effective May 27, 1981, also enacted this section. The section is set out above as enacted by Acts 1981, No. 81-851, p. 1529, being the last signed by the governor.

Collateral references. — 53 C.J.S., Limitations of Actions, §§ 6, 13.

51 Am. Jur. 2d, Limitation of Action, §§ 9, 12, 62.

ARTICLE 2.

COMPETITIVE BIDDING ON PUBLIC CONTRACTS GENERALLY.

The Competitive Bid Law does not require that the lowest bid be accepted. International Telecommunications Systems v. State, 359 So. 2d 364 (Ala. 1978).

The single most important requirement of the Competitive Bid Law is the good faith of the officials charged in executing the requirements of the law. A bad motive, fraud or a gross abuse of discretion will vitiate an award whether made with specifications which are quite general or very precise. International Telecommunications Systems v. State, 359 So. 2d 364 (Ala. 1978).

Collateral references. — 81 C.J.S., States, § 116.

Right of bidder for state or municipal contract to rescind bid on ground that bid was based upon his own mistake or that of his employee. 2 ALR4th 991.

§ 41-16-20. Contracts for which competitive bidding required generally.

All contracts of whatever nature for labor, services or work or for the purchase or lease of materials, equipment, supplies or other personal property, involving $2,000.00 or more made or on behalf of any state department, board, bureau, commission, committee, institution, corporation, authority or office shall, except as otherwise provided in this article, be let by free and open competitive bidding, on sealed bids, to the lowest responsible bidder. (Acts 1957, No. 343, p. 452, § 1; Acts 1961, No. 870, p. 1365; Acts 1976, No. 751, p. 1032, § 1.)

The legislative intent in passing the Competitive Bid Law was to get the best quality equipment at the lowest possible price, and the executive authorities should carry out this intent. Arrington v. Associated Gen. Contractors of Am., 403 So. 2d 893 (Ala. 1981).

It is of no consequence that a municipal ordinance contravenes the competitive bidding statute if the ordinance provisions are required by the United States Constitution. The dispositive issue is whether a municipal affirmative action program is constitutionally required or whether the program is merely constitutionally permissible. Arrington v. Associated Gen. Contractors of Am., 403 So. 2d 893 (Ala. 1981).

Intrusive specifications inhibit fair and open competition. — While bid specifications are permissible where their purpose is reasonably related to contract requirements or the quality of the product or service in question, intrusive specifications wholly unrelated to contract requirements or to product suitability or quality unduly inhibit fair and open competition. Arrington v. Associated Gen. Contractors of Am., 403 So. 2d 893 (Ala. 1981).

Cited in Jefferson County Pharmaceutical Ass'n v. Abbott Labs., 656 F.2d 92 (5th Cir. 1981).

Collateral references. — Requirement that public contract be awarded on competitive bidding as applicable to contract for public utility. 81 ALR3d 979.

§ 41-16-21. Contracts for which competitive bidding not required generally; certain institutions, state agencies, etc., exempt from provisions of article relating to powers, duties, etc., of department of finance; said institutions, etc., to establish and maintain facilities necessary for competitive bidding in operation and management thereof; contracts entered into in violation of article declared void.

(a) Competitive bids shall not be required for utility services where no competition exists or where rates are fixed by law or ordinance, and the competitive bidding requirements of this article shall not apply to: the purchase of insurance by the state; contracts for the securing of services of attorneys, physicians, architects, teachers, superintendents of construction, artists, appraisers, engineers or other individuals possessing a high degree of professional skill where the personality of the individual plays a decisive part; contracts of employment in the regular civil service of the state; tourist advertising by the state bureau of publicity and information authorized under section 41-7-4; purchases of alcoholic beverages only by the alcoholic beverage control board; purchases by the state highway department of local materials from any property owners in the vicinity of a project on which such local materials shall be used or purchases and contracts for repair of equipment used in the construction and maintenance of highways by the state highway department; purchases of products made or manufactured by the blind or visually handicapped under the direction or supervision of the Alabama Institute for Deaf and Blind in accordance with sections 21-2-1 through 21-2-4; purchases of maps or photographs purchased from any federal agency; purchases of manuscripts, maps, books, pamphlets or periodicals purchased for the use of any state library or any other library in the state supported in whole or in part by state funds; contractual services and purchases of commodities for which there is only one vendor or supplier; contractual services and purchases of personal property, which by their very nature are impossible of award by competitive bidding; barter transactions by the board of corrections; and purchases, contracts or repairs by the state docks department when it is deemed by the director of state docks and the secretary-treasurer of the state docks department that such purchases, contracts or repairs are impractical of award by competitive bidding due to the exigencies of time or interference with the flow of commerce; provided, that the director of state docks and the secretary-treasurer of the state docks department shall place a sworn statement in writing in the permanent file or records setting out the emergency relied upon and the necessity for negotiation instead of proceeding by competitive bidding in said instance, and such sworn statement shall be open to public inspection. A copy of such sworn statement shall be furnished forthwith to the chief examiner of public accounts.

(b) All educational and eleemosynary institutions governed by a board of trustees or other similar governing body and the state docks department shall be exempt from the provisions of this article which relate to the powers, duties, authority, restrictions and limitations conferred or imposed upon the department of finance, division of purchases and stores; provided, however, that the said educational and eleemosynary institutions, the state docks department and the other state agencies exempted from the provisions of this article or any part hereof shall let by free and open competitive bidding on sealed bids to the lowest responsible bidder all contracts of whatever nature for labor, services or work or for the purchase or lease of materials, equipment, supplies or other personal property involving $2,000.00 or more. The said institutions, departments and agencies shall establish and maintain such purchasing facilities as may be necessary to carry out the intent and purpose of this article by complying with the requirements for competitive bidding in the operation and management of each such institution, department or agency.

(c) Contracts entered into in violation of this article shall be void.

(d) Nothing in this section shall be construed as repealing sections 9-2-106 and 9-2-107. (Acts 1957, No. 343, p. 452, § 2; Acts 1961, No. 870, p. 1365; Acts 1969, No. 1053, p. 1973, §§ 1, 2; Acts 1976, No. 751, p. 1032, § 2.)

Cited in Jefferson County Pharmaceutical Ass'n v. Abbott Labs., 656 F.2d 92 (5th Cir. 1981).

§ 41-16-21.1. Joint purchasing agreements.

The governing authorities of two or more agencies within the same county or adjoining counties, whose contracts are required under this article to be let by competitive bidding, may provide by joint agreement for the purchase of labor, services or work or for the purchase or lease of materials, equipment, supplies or other personal property for use by their respective agencies. Such agreement shall be entered into by similar executive orders or resolutions issued or adopted by each of the participating governing authorities which shall set forth the categories of labor, services or work or the materials, equipment, supplies or other personal property to be purchased or leased, the manner of advertising for bids and of awarding of contracts, the method of payment by each participating contracting agency, and other matters deemed necessary to carry out the purposes of the agreement. Each contracting agency's share of expenditures for purchases under any such agreement shall be appropriated and paid in the manner set forth in the agreement and in the same manner as for other expenses of the contracting agency. The contracting agencies entering into a joint agreement, as permitted by this section, may designate a joint purchasing agent and such agent shall have the responsibility to comply with the provisions of this article. Purchases, contracts or agreements made pursuant to a joint purchasing agreement shall be subject to all of the terms and conditions of this article. (Acts 1976, No. 751, p. 1032, § 3.)

Code commissioner's note. — The words "or leased" have been inserted following "purchased" near the middle of the second sentence in order to clarify the obvious intent of the legislature.

Collateral references. — 20 C.J.S., Counties, §§ 236, 238.

§ 41-16-21.2. Exemption of certain departments or agencies whose principal business is honorariums from competitive bid laws.

All laws to the contrary notwithstanding, any state department or agency whose principal business is honorariums and whose annual appropriation, from the legislature is less than $75,000.00 is hereby exempted from the provisions of the state competitive bid laws on purchases and contracts for services made by such department or agency. (Acts 1982, No. 82-565.)

Effective date. — The act which added this section became effective May 4, 1982.

§ 41-16-22. Competitive bidding not required on purchases from federal government.

The state may without advertisement or receiving competitive bids purchase materials, equipment, supplies or other personal property from the United

States government or any agency, division or instrumentality thereof when such purchase is deemed by the state purchasing agent to be in the best interest of the state of Alabama. (Acts 1973, No. 1288, p. 2200.)

§ 41-16-23. Letting of contracts without public advertisement authorized in case of emergencies affecting public health, safety, etc.

In case of emergency affecting public health, safety or convenience, so declared in writing by the head of the institution or state agency involved, setting forth the nature of the danger to public health, safety or convenience involved in delay, contracts may be let to the extent necessary to meet the emergency without public advertisement. Such action and the reasons therefor shall immediately be made public by the awarding authority. (Acts 1957, No. 343, p. 452, § 7.)

§ 41-16-24. Advertisement for and solicitation of bids; bids to be sealed; opening of bids; bids, etc., to be retained and to be open to public inspection; contracts not to be split to avoid requirements of article; certain partial contracts declared void.

(a) The purchasing agent shall advertise for sealed bids on all purchases in excess of $2,000.00 by posting notice thereof on a bulletin board maintained outside his office door or by publication of notice thereof one time in a newspaper published in Montgomery county, Alabama or in any other manner and for such lengths of time as he may determine; provided, however, that the purchasing agent shall also solicit sealed bids by sending notice by mail to all persons, firms or corporations who have filed a request in writing that they be listed for solicitation on bids for such particular items as are set forth in such request. If any person, firm or corporation whose name is listed fails to respond to any solicitation for bids after the receipt of three such solicitations, such listing may be cancelled by the purchasing agent, at his discretion.

(b) All bids shall be sealed when received, shall be opened in public at the hour stated in the notice, and all original bids together with all documents pertaining to the award of the contract shall be retained and made a part of a permanent file or records and shall be open to public inspection.

(c) If the purchase or contract will involve an amount of $2,000.00 or less, the purchasing agent may make such purchases or contracts either upon the basis of sealed bids or in the open market, in his discretion.

(d) No purchase or contract involving an amount in excess of $2,000.00 shall be divided into parts involving amounts of $2,000.00 or less for the purpose of avoiding the requirements of this article. All such partial contracts involving $2,000.00 or less shall be void. (Acts 1957, No. 343, p. 452, § 6; Acts 1961, No. 870, p. 1365; Acts 1976, No. 751, p. 1032, § 4.)

§ 41-16-25. Effect of agreements or collusion among bidders in restraint of competition; sworn statements as to agreements to accompany bids.

Any agreement or collusion among bidders or prospective bidders in restraint of freedom of competition by agreement to bid at a fixed price or to refrain from bidding or otherwise shall render the bids of such bidders void. Each bidder' shall accompany his bid with a sworn statement that he has not been a party to such an agreement. (Acts 1957, No. 343, p. 452, § 4.)

State policy may not require that lower prices be given to governmental purchasers than to private purchasers, but only that the governmental purchaser buy at the lowest price offered; it is perhaps of significance that the state bid laws contain exceptions for sales made in violation of the Sherman Anti-Trust Law but not for those contrary to the Robinson-Patman Act. Jefferson County Pharmaceutical Ass'n v. Abbott Labs., 656 F.2d 92 (5th Cir. 1981).

§ 41-16-26. Effect of advance disclosure of terms of bid.

Any disclosure in advance of the terms of a bid submitted in response to an advertisement for bids shall render the proceedings void and require advertisement and award anew. (Acts 1957, No. 343, p. 452, § 5.)

§ 41-16-27. Manner of awarding contracts generally; award of negotiated contracts; records as to awarding of contracts to be open to public inspection; preference to be given to Alabama commodities, firms, etc., in contracts for purchase of personal property or contractual services; maximum duration of contracts for purchase of personal property or contractual services; awarding of medicaid contracts.

(a) When purchases are required to be made through competitive bidding, award shall, except as provided in subsection (e), be made to the lowest responsible bidder taking into consideration the qualities of the commodities proposed to be supplied, their conformity with specifications, the purposes for which required, the terms of delivery, transportation charges and the dates of delivery provided, that the awarding authority may at any time within five days after the bids are opened negotiate and award the contract to anyone, provided he secures a price at least five percent under the low acceptable bid. The award of such a negotiated contract shall be subject to approval by the director of finance and the governor. The awarding authority or requisitioning agency shall have the right to reject any bid if the price is deemed excessive or quality of product inferior.

(b) Each bid, with the name of the bidder, shall be entered on a record. Each record, with the successful bid indicated thereon and with the reasons for the award if not awarded to the lowest bidder shall, after award of the order or contract, be open to public inspection.

(c) The purchasing agent in the purchase of or contract for personal property or contractual services shall give preference, provided there is no sacrifice or loss in price or quality, to commodities produced in Alabama or sold by Alabama persons, firms or corporations.

(d) Contracts for the purchase of personal property or contractual services shall be let for periods not greater than one year.

(e) Contracts for the purchase of services for receiving, processing, and paying claims for services rendered recipients of the Alabama medicaid program authorized under section 22-6-7 which are required to be competitively bid may be awarded to the bidder whose proposal is most advantageous to the state, taking into consideration cost factors, program suitability factors (technical factors) including understanding of program requirements, management plan, excellence of program design, key personnel, corporate or company resources and designated location, and other factors including financial condition and capability of the bidder, corporate experience and past performance and priority of the business to insure the contract awarded is the best for the purposes required. Each of these criteria shall be given relative weight value as designated in the invitation to bid, with price retaining the most significant weight. Responsiveness to the bid shall be scored for each designated criteria. If, for reasons cited above, the bid selected is not from the lowest bidding contractor, the Alabama medicaid agency shall present its reasons for not recommending award to the low bidder to the medicaid interim committee. The committee shall evaluate the findings of the Alabama medicaid agency and must, by resolution, approve the action of the awarding authority before final awarding of any such contract. The committee shall also hear any valid appeals against the recommendation of the Alabama medicaid agency from the low bid contractor(s) whose bid was not selected. (Acts 1957, No. 343, p. 452, § 9; Acts 1961, No. 870, p. 1365; Acts 1976, No. 751, p. 1032, § 5; Acts 1982, No. 82-353.)

The 1982 amendment, effective April 26, 1982, added subsection (e).

Legislative intent in passing the Competitive Bid Law was to get the best quality equipment at the lowest possible price, and the executive authorities should carry out this intent of the legislature. White v. McDonald Ford Tractor Co., 287 Ala. 77, 248 So. 2d 121 (1971).

Award made to lowest responsible bidder. — The legislature did not direct that the award must be made to the lowest bidder, but to the lowest responsible bidder, and specifically provided that in making the award to the lowest responsible bidder consideration could be given to the quality of the commodity proposed to be supplied, its conformity to specifications, the purposes for which required, the terms of delivery, transportation charges and the dates of delivery. White v. McDonald Ford Tractor Co., 287 Ala. 77, 248 So. 2d 121 (1971).

Reasons must be stated where award not made to lowest bidder. — The Competitive Bid Law specifically provides that if the award is not made to the lowest bidder, the reasons must be stated why the award was not made to the lowest bidder, and these records must be open to public inspection. White v. McDonald Ford Tractor Co., 287 Ala. 77, 248 So. 2d 121 (1971).

State authorities should have discretion in determining who is lowest responsible bidder, and this discretion should not be interfered with by any court unless it is exercised arbitrarily or capriciously, or unless it is based upon a misconception of the law or upon ignorance through lack of inquiry or in violation of law or is the result of improper influence. White v. McDonald Ford Tractor Co., 287 Ala. 77, 248 So. 2d 121 (1971).

Single most important requirement of Competitive Bid Law is good faith of officials charged in executing the requirements of the law, because a bad motive, fraud or a gross abuse of discretion will vitiate an award whether made with specifications which are quite general or very precise. White v. McDonald Ford Tractor Co., 287 Ala. 77, 248 So. 2d 121 (1971).

§ 41-16-28. Bond for faithful performance of contract to be required.

Bond in a responsible sum for faithful performance of the contract, with adequate surety, shall be required in an amount specified in the advertisement for bids. (Acts 1957, No. 343, p. 452, § 8.)

Collateral references. — 81 C.J.S., States, §§ 117-119.

§ 41-16-29. Assignment of contracts.

No contract awarded to the lowest responsible bidder shall be assignable by the successful bidder without written consent of the awarding authority and requisitioning agency, and in no event shall a contract be assigned to an unsuccessful bidder whose bid was rejected because he was not a responsible bidder. (Acts 1957, No. 343, p. 452, § 11.)

Collateral references. — 81 C.J.S., States, § 121.

§ 41-16-30. Conflicts of interest of purchasing agents, assistants, etc., generally; making of purchases or awarding of contracts in violation of article.

Neither the purchasing agent nor any assistant or employee of his shall be financially interested or have any personal beneficial interest, either directly or indirectly, in the purchase of or contract for any personal property or contractual service, nor in any firm, partnership, association or corporation furnishing any such personal property or contractual services to the state government or to any of its departments, agencies or institutions. Neither the purchasing agent nor any assistant or employee of his shall accept or receive, directly or indirectly, from any person, firm, association or corporation to whom any contract may be awarded, by rebate, gifts or otherwise, any money or thing of value whatsoever or any promise, obligation or contract for future reward or compensation, nor shall any person willfully make any purchase or award any contract in violation of the provisions of this article.

Any violation of this section shall be deemed a misdemeanor, and any person who violates this section shall, upon conviction, be imprisoned for not more than 12 months or fined not more than $500.00 or both. Upon conviction thereof, any such purchasing agent, assistant or employee of his or any person who willfully makes any purchase or awards any contract in violation of the provisions of this article shall be removed from office. (Acts 1957, No. 343, p. 452, § 3.)

Collateral references. — Validity of state statute prohibiting award of government contract to person or business entity previously convicted of bribery or attempting to bribe state public employee. 7 ALR4th 1202.

§ 41-16-31. Institution of actions to enjoin execution of contracts entered into in violation of article.

Any taxpayer of the area within the jurisdiction of the awarding authority and any bona fide unsuccessful bidder on a particular contract shall be empowered to bring a civil action in the appropriate court to enjoin execution of any contract entered into in violation of the provisions of this article. (Acts 1957, No. 343, p. 452, § 10.)

Cross references. — As to statute of limitations on prosecution of infractions of this chapter, see § 41-16-2.

§ 41-16-32. Provisions of article cumulative; repeal of other provisions of law.

This article shall be cumulative in its nature.

All conflicting provisions of law are hereby expressly repealed; however, this article shall in no manner repeal any of the provisions of chapter 36 of Title 16 of this Code or chapters 2 and 5 of Title 39 of this Code or article 5 of chapter 4 of this title. (Acts 1957, No. 343, p. 452, § 12.)

ARTICLE 3.

COMPETITIVE BIDDING ON CONTRACTS OF CERTAIN STATE AND LOCAL AGENCIES, ETC.

Cross references. — As to exemption of historical preservation authorities from the provisions of this article, see § 41-10-141.

Cited in Jefferson County Pharmaceutical Ass'n v. Abbott Labs., 656 F.2d 92 (5th Cir. 1981).

§ 41-16-50. Contracts for which competitive bidding required; manner of awarding contracts generally; award of contracts to resident bidders; negotiation of contracts; joint contracts.

(a) (1) All expenditure of funds of whatever nature for labor, services or work, or for the purchase or lease of materials, equipment, supplies or other personal property involving $2,000.00 or more, made by or on behalf of any state trade school, state junior college, state college or university under the supervision and control of the state board of education, the city and county boards of education, the district boards of education of independent school districts, the county commissions and the governing bodies of the municipalities of the state and the governing boards of instrumentalities of counties and municipalities, including waterworks boards, sewer boards, gas boards and other like utility boards and commissions, except as hereinafter provided, shall be made under contractual agreement entered into by free and open competitive bidding, on sealed bids, to the lowest responsible bidder; provided, that in the event a bid is received for an item of personal property to be purchased or contracted for from a person, firm or corporation deemed to be a responsible bidder, having a place of business within the county, where the awarding authority is the county or instrumentality thereof, or within the municipality, where the municipality or an instrumentality thereof is the awarding authority, which such bid is no more than three percent greater than the bid of the lowest responsible bidder, the awarding authority may award the contract to such resident responsible bidder. In the event only one bidder responds to the invitation to bid, the awarding authority may reject the bid and negotiate the purchase or contract, providing the negotiated price is lower than the bid price.

(2) a. Provided, however, all expenditures of funds for whatever nature for, including all service, concessions, goods, and/or rental contracts, of $75,000.00 or more made by or on behalf of any governing boards, commissions, committees or like governing bodies of instrumentalities of counties and municipalities, including, but not limited to, waterworks boards, sewer boards, gas boards, park boards, the Alabama state fair authority, and library boards shall be made under contractual agreement entered into by free and open competitive bid on sealed bids, to the lowest responsible bidder. When a definite monetary sum is not determinable prior to contracting, prior contracts by that body or a similar body for similar type service or rental contracts shall be used as criteria for ascertaining whether competitive bids should be let.

b. Whenever any said governing board, committee, commission or like body shall contract with a person or business entity whose cumulative service, concessions, goods, or rental contracts, including the contract in question, with any said board, committee, commission or like body under the domain of the same governing municipality or county, shall total $200,000.00 or more, then said contract with said individual shall be null and void ab initio and said body shall submit the contract to competitive bid, as provided in this section.

Provided, however, the provisions of paragraphs a. and b. of this subdivision shall not apply to radio or television sales by institutions of higher education nor to the exemptions prescribed in section 41-16-51.

c. For the purposes of paragraphs a. and b. of this subdivision the term "instrumentalities of counties and municipalities" shall not include the county commission or municipal council, or municipal commission of the counties or municipalities of this state and the provisions of paragraphs a. and b. of this subdivision shall have no application whatsoever to the expenditure of funds or contracts entered into by said county or municipal governing bodies.

(b) The governing bodies of two or more contracting agencies, as hereinabove enumerated within the same county or adjoining counties, may provide by joint agreement for the purchase of labor, services or work, or for the purchase or lease of materials, equipment, supplies or other personal property for use by their respective agencies. Such agreement shall be entered into by similar ordinances, in the case of municipalities, or resolutions, in the case of other contracting agencies, adopted by each of the participating governing bodies, which shall set forth the categories of labor, services or work, or for the purchase or lease of materials, equipment, supplies or other personal property to be purchased, the manner of advertising for bids and of awarding of contracts, the method of payment by each participating contracting agency and other matters deemed necessary to carry out the purposes of the agreement. Each contracting agency's share of expenditures for purchases under any such agreement shall be appropriated and paid in the manner set forth in the agreement and in the same manner as for other expenses of the contracting agency. The contracting agencies entering into a joint agreement, as herein permitted, may designate a joint purchasing agent, and such agent shall have the responsibility to comply with the provisions of this article. It is provided further that purchases, contracts or agreements made pursuant to a joint purchasing agreement shall be subject to all of the terms and conditions of this article.

(c) It is further provided that all bidders must furnish a bid bond on any contract exceeding $10,000.00; provided, that bonding is available for such services, equipment or materials. (Acts 1967, Ex. Sess., No. 217, p. 259, § 1; Acts 1975, No. 1136, p. 2234, § 1; Acts 1979, No. 79-452, p. 732; Acts 1979, No. 79-662, p. 1160; Acts 1980, No. 80-429, p. 598; Acts 1981, No. 81-434, p. 679, § 1.)

The 1981 amendment, effective May 6, 1981, redesignated former subsection (a) as subdivision (a) (1) and added subdivision (2) in subsection (a), and added subsection (c).

Code commissioner's note. — Acts 1979, No. 79-452, p. 732, § 2, provides that the amendatory act shall have retroactive effect to May 1, 1979.

The legislative intent in passing the competitive bid law was to get the best quality equipment at the lowest possible price, and the executive authorities should carry out this intent. Arrington v. Associated Gen. Contractors of Am., 403 So. 2d 893 (Ala. 1981).

It is of no consequence that a municipal ordinance contravenes the competitive bidding statute if the ordinance provisions are required by the United States Constitution. The dispositive issue is whether a municipal affirmative action program is constitutionally required or whether the program is merely constitutionally permissible. Arrington v. Associated Gen. Contractors of Am., 403 So. 2d 893 (Ala. 1981).

Intrusive specifications inhibit fair and open competition. — While bid specifications are permissible where their purpose is reasonably related to contract requirements or the quality of the product or service in question, intrusive specifications wholly unrelated to contract requirements or to product suitability or quality unduly inhibit fair and open competition. Arrington v. Associated Gen. Contractors of Am., 403 So. 2d 893 (Ala. 1981).

§ 41-16-51. Contracts for which competitive bidding not required generally; governing bodies or instrumentalities of counties, municipalities and certain state and local institutions to establish and maintain purchasing facilities and procedures for competitive bidding in operation and management of institutions, facilities, etc., under supervision and control thereof; contracts entered into in violation of article void.

(a) Competitive bids shall not be required for utility services, the rates for which are fixed by law, regulation or ordinance, and the competitive bidding requirements of this article shall not apply to:

(1) The purchase of insurance;

(2) The purchase of ballots and supplies for conducting any primary, general, special or municipal election;

(3) Contracts for the securing of services of attorneys, physicians, architects, teachers, superintendents of construction, artists, appraisers, engineers, consultants, certified public accountants, public accountants or other individuals possessing a high degree of professional skill where the personality of the individual plays a decisive part;

(4) Contracts of employment in the regular civil service;

(5) Contracts for furnishing of fiscal or financial advice or services;

(6) Purchases of products made or manufactured by the blind or visually handicapped under the direction or supervision of the Alabama Institute for Deaf and Blind in accordance with sections 21-2-1 through 21-2-4;

(7) Purchases of maps or photographs from any federal agency;

(8) Purchases of manuscripts, books, maps, pamphlets or periodicals;

(9) The selection of paying agents and trustees for any security issued by a public body;

(10) Existing contracts up for renewal for sanitation or solid waste collection and disposal between municipalities and those providing the service; nor

(11) Contractual services and purchases of commodities for which there is only one vendor or supplier and contractual services and purchases of personal property which by their very nature are impossible of award by competitive bidding.

(b) This article shall not apply to:

(1) Any purchases of products where the price of such products is already regulated and established by state law;

(2) Purchases made by individual schools of the county or municipal public school systems from moneys other than those raised by taxation or received through appropriations from state or county sources;

(3) The purchase, lease, sale, construction, installation, acquisition, improvement, enlargement or expansion of any building or structure or other facility designed or intended for lease or sale by a medical clinic board organized under the provisions of sections 11-58-1 through 11-58-14;

(4) The purchase, lease or other acquisition of machinery, equipment, supplies and other personal property or services by a medical clinic board organized under the provisions of sections 11-58-1 through 11-58-14;

(5) Purchases for public hospitals and nursing homes operated by the governing boards of instrumentalities of the state, counties and municipalities;

(6) Contracts for the purchase, lease, sale, construction, installation, acquisition, improvement, enlargement or extension of any plant, building, structure or other facility or any machinery, equipment, furniture or furnishings therefor designed or intended for lease or sale for industrial development, other than public utilities, under the provisions of sections 11-54-80 through 11-54-99 or sections 11-54-20 through 11-54-28 or any other statute or amendment to the Constitution of Alabama heretofore or

hereafter enacted or adopted authorizing the construction of plants or other facilities for industrial development or for the construction and equipment of buildings for public building authorities under the provisions of sections 11-56-1 through 11-56-22;

(7) The purchase of equipment, supplies or materials needed, used and consumed in the normal and routine operation of any waterworks system, sanitary sewer system, gas system or electric system, or any two or more thereof, that are owned by municipalities, counties or public corporations, boards or authorities that are agencies, departments or instrumentalities of municipalities or counties and no part of the operating expenses of which system or systems have, during the then current fiscal year, been paid from revenues derived from taxes or from appropriations of the state, a county or a municipality; nor

(8) Purchases made by local housing authorities, organized and existing under chapter 1, Title 24, from moneys other than those raised by state, county or city taxation or received through appropriations from state, county or city sources.

(c) The said state trade schools, state junior colleges, state colleges and universities under the supervision and control of the state board of education, the city and county boards of education, the district boards of education of independent school districts, the county commissions and the governing bodies of the municipalities of the state shall establish and maintain such purchasing facilities and procedures as may be necessary to carry out the intent and purpose of this article by complying with the requirements for competitive bidding in the operation and management of each such state trade school, state junior college, state college or university under the supervision and control of the state board of education, the city and county boards of education, the district boards of education of independent school districts, the county commissions and the governing bodies of the municipalities of the state and the governing boards of instrumentalities of counties and municipalities, including waterworks boards, sewer boards, gas boards, and other like utility boards and commissions.

(d) Contracts entered into in violation of this article shall be void. (Acts 1967, Ex. Sess., No. 217, p. 259, § 2; Acts 1967, No. 209, p. 573; Acts 1967, No. 769, p. 1625; Acts 1969, No. 763, p. 1352; Acts 1980, No. 80-463, p. 723; Acts 1982, No. 82-425, § 1; Acts 1982, No. 82-508, § 1.)

The 1982 amendments. — The first 1982 amendment, effective May 4, 1982, added subdivision (8) of subsection (b). The second 1982 amendment, also effective May 4, 1982, in subsection (a) deleted "nor" at the end of subdivision (9), inserted present subdivision (10), and redesignated former subdivision (10) as present subdivision (11).

§ 41-16-52. Expenditures for repair or lease of heavy duty off-highway construction equipment may be made without regard to provisions of article.

(a) All expenditure of funds of whatever nature for repair parts and repair of heavy duty off-highway construction equipment, including machinery used for grading, drainage, road construction and compaction for the exclusive use of county and municipal, highway, street and sanitation departments, involving not more than $6,000.00 made by or on behalf of any county commissions and the governing bodies of the municipalities of the state, and the governing boards of instrumentalities, including waterworks boards, sewer boards, gas boards and other like utility boards and commissions, shall be made, at the option of said governing boards, bodies, instrumentalities and commissions, without regard to the provisions of this article.

(b) The option provided by subsection (a) of this section may be exercised by said governing boards, bodies, instrumentalities and commissions by specific reference to this section on any and all purchase orders and purchase commitments executed by said governing boards, bodies, instrumentalities and commissions.

(c) All expenditures of funds of whatever nature for the leasing of heavy duty off-highway construction equipment, including machinery for grading, drainage, road construction and compaction for the exclusive use of county and municipalities, highway, street and sanitation departments, involving a monthly rental of not more than $3,000.00 per month made by or on behalf of any county commissions and the governing boards of municipalities of the state and the governing bodies of instrumentalities, including waterworks boards, sewer boards, gas boards and other like utility boards and commissions shall be made, at the option of the said governing boards, bodies, instrumentalities and commissions, without regard to the provisions of this article. (Acts 1969, No. 493, p. 952; Acts 1971, No. 2338, p. 3771; Acts 1981, No. 81-626, p. 1042.)

The **1981 amendment,** effective May 17, 1981, substituted "$6,000.00" for "$1,500.00" in subsection (a) and "$3,000.00" for "$1,500.00" in subsection (c).

§ 41-16-53. Letting of contracts without public advertisement authorized in case of emergencies affecting public health, safety, etc.

In case of emergency affecting public health, safety or convenience, so declared in writing by the awarding authority, setting forth the nature of the danger to public health, safety or convenience involved in delay, contracts may be let to the extent necessary to meet the emergency without public advertisement. Such action and the reasons therefor shall immediately be made public by the awarding authority. (Acts 1967, Ex. Sess., No. 217, p. 259, § 7.)

§ 41-16-54. Advertisement for and solicitation of bids; bids to be sealed; opening of bids; bids, etc., to be retained and to be open to public inspection; when purchases or contracts may be made in open market; contracts not to be split to avoid requirements of article; certain partial contracts declared void.

(a) All proposed purchases in excess of $2,000.00 shall be advertised by posting notice thereof on a bulletin board maintained outside the purchasing office and in any other manner and for such lengths of time as may be determined; provided, however, that sealed bids shall also be solicited by sending notice by mail to all persons, firms or corporations who have filed a request in writing that they be listed for solicitation on bids for such particular items as are set forth in such request. If any person, firm or corporation whose name is listed fails to respond to any solicitation for bids after the receipt of three such solicitations, such listing may be cancelled.

(b) All bids shall be sealed when received, shall be opened in public at the hour stated in the notice, and all original bids together with all documents pertaining to the award of the contract shall be retained and made a part of a permanent file or records and shall be open to public inspection.

(c) If the purchase or contract will involve an amount of $2,000.00 or less, the purchases or contracts may be made upon the basis of sealed bids or in the open market.

(d) No purchase or contract involving an amount in excess of $2,000.00 shall be divided into parts involving amounts of $2,000.00 or less for the purpose of avoiding the requirements of this article. All such partial contracts involving $2,000.00 or less shall be void. (Acts 1967, Ex. Sess., No. 217, p. 259, § 6; Acts 1975, No. 1136, § 2.)

§ 41-16-55. Effect of agreements or collusion among bidders in restraint of competition; knowing participation in collusive agreement.

Any agreement or collusion among bidders or prospective bidders in restraint of freedom of competition, by agreement to bid at a fixed price or to refrain from bidding or otherwise shall render the bids of such bidders void and shall cause such bidders to be disqualified from submitting further bids to the awarding authority on future purchases.

Whoever knowingly participates in a collusive agreement in violation of this section shall be guilty of a misdemeanor and, upon conviction, shall be fined not more than $500.00 and may also be imprisoned in the county jail or sentenced to hard labor for the county for not more than six months. (Acts 1967, Ex. Sess., No. 217, p. 259, § 4.)

State policy may not require that lower prices be given to governmental purchasers than to private purchasers, but only that the governmental purchaser buy at the lowest price offered; it is, perhaps of significance that the state bid laws contain exceptions for sales made in violation of the Sherman Anti-Trust Law but not for those contrary to the

Robinson-Patman Act. Jefferson County Pharmaceutical Ass'n v. Abbott Labs., 656 F.2d 92
(5th Cir. 1981).

§ 41-16-56. Effect of advance disclosure of terms of bid.

Any disclosure in advance of the terms of a bid submitted in response to an advertisement for bids shall render the proceedings void and require advertisement and award anew. (Acts 1967, Ex. Sess., No. 217, p. 259, § 5.)

§ 41-16-57. Awarding of contracts generally; preference to be given to Alabama commodities, firms, etc., in contracts for purchase of personal property or contractual services; rejection of bids; records as to awarding of contract to be open to public inspection; maximum duration of contracts for purchase of personal property or contractual services.

(a) When purchases are required to be made through competitive bidding, awards shall be made to the lowest responsible bidder taking into consideration the qualities of the commodities proposed to be supplied, their conformity with specifications, the purposes for which required, the terms of delivery, transportation charges and the dates of delivery.

(b) The awarding authority in the purchase of or contract for personal property or contractual services shall give preference, provided there is no sacrifice or loss in price or quality, to commodities produced in Alabama or sold by Alabama persons, firms or corporations.

(c) The awarding authority or requisitioning agency shall have the right to reject any bid if the price is deemed excessive or quality of product inferior.

(d) Each record, with the successful bid indicated thereon, and with the reasons for the award if not awarded to the lowest bidder, shall, after award of the order or contract, be open to public inspection.

(e) Contracts for the purchase of personal property shall be let for periods not greater than one year, and contracts for the purchase of contractual services shall be let for periods of not greater than three years. (Acts 1967, Ex. Sess., No. 217, p. 259, § 9; Acts 1975, No. 1136, § 3.)

Collateral references. — Right of public authorities to reject all bids for public work or contract. 31 ALR2d 469.

Determination of amount involved in contract within statutory provision requiring public contracts involving sums exceeding spec-

ified amount to be let to lowest bidder. 53 ALR2d 498.

Revocation, prior to execution of formal written contract, of vote or decision of public body awarding contract to bidder. 3 ALR3d 864.

§ 41-16-58. Bond for faithful performance of contract may be required.

Bond in a responsible sum for faithful performance of the contract, with adequate surety, may be required in an amount specified in the advertisement for bids. (Acts 1967, Ex. Sess., No. 217, p. 259, § 8.)

§ 41-16-59. Assignment of contracts.

No contract awarded to the lowest responsible bidder shall be assignable by the successful bidder without written consent of the awarding authority, and in no event shall a contract be assigned to an unsuccessful bidder whose bid was rejected because he was not a responsible bidder. (Acts 1967, Ex. Sess., No. 217, p. 259, § 11.)

§ 41-16-60. Conflicts of interest of members or officers of governing bodies or instrumentalities of counties, municipalities and certain state and local institutions generally; making of purchases or awarding of contracts in violation of article.

No member or officer of the said state trade schools, state junior colleges, state colleges and universities under the supervision and control of the state board of education, the city and county boards of education, the district boards of education of independent school districts, the county commissions and the governing bodies of the municipalities of the state and the governing boards of instrumentalities of counties and municipalities, including waterworks boards, sewer boards, gas boards and other like utility boards and commissions, shall be financially interested or have any personal beneficial interest, either directly or indirectly, in the purchase of or contract for any personal property or contractual service, nor shall any person willfully make any purchase or award any contract in violation of the provisions of this article.

Any violation of this section shall be deemed a misdemeanor, and any person who violates this section shall, upon conviction, be imprisoned for not more than 12 months or fined not more than $500.00 or both. Upon conviction thereof, any person who willfully makes any purchase or awards any contract in violation of the provisions of this article shall be removed from office. (Acts 1967, Ex. Sess., No. 217, p. 259, § 3.)

Intent of legislature was to prevent a conflict of interests so that no member of a governing board would endeavor to give favorable treatment to businesses in which he would be financially or beneficially interested in connection with purchases of personal property or a contractual service. City of Montgomery v. Brendle Fire Equip., Inc., 291 Ala. 216, 279 So. 2d 480 (1973).

Sensible construction should be given to section. City of Montgomery v. Brendle Fire Equip., Inc., 291 Ala. 216, 279 So. 2d 480 (1973).

Any general terms appearing in it should be limited in their application so as not to lead to absurd consequences. City of Montgomery v. Brendle Fire Equip., Inc., 291 Ala. 216, 279 So. 2d 480 (1973).

Section silent as to applicability. — This section is silent as to whether a member or officer of any of the listed governmental entities or instrumentalities is prohibited from having such an interest in all or any group of the listed governmental entities and instrumentalities, or whether the prohibition applies only to the entity or instrumentality of which such person is a member or officer. City of Montgomery v. Brendle Fire Equip., Inc., 291 Ala. 216, 279 So. 2d 480 (1973).

§ 41-16-61. Institution of actions to enjoin execution of contracts entered into in violation of article.

Any taxpayer of the area within the jurisdiction of the awarding authority and any bona fide unsuccessful bidder on a particular contract shall be empowered to bring a civil action in the appropriate court to enjoin execution of any contract entered into in violation of the provisions of this article. (Acts 1967, Ex. Sess., No. 217, p. 259, § 10.)

Cross references. — As to statute of limitations on prosecution of infractions of this chapter, see § 41-16-2.

Language of section is unambiguous. City of Montgomery v. Brendle Fire Equip., Inc., 291 Ala. 216, 279 So. 2d 480 (1973).

It does not authorize injunctive relief with respect to the formation of future contracts. City of Montgomery v. Brendle Fire

Equip., Inc., 291 Ala. 216, 279 So. 2d 480 (1973).

A court should not grant an injunction to prevent in the future that which in good faith has been discontinued and where there is no evidence that the offense is likely to be repeated in the future. City of Montgomery v. Brendle Fire Equip., Inc., 291 Ala. 216, 279 So. 2d 480 (1973).

§ 41-16-62. Provisions of article not applicable to certain municipal contracts.

The provisions of this article shall not be applicable to any contracts made by a municipality pursuant to the provisions of Act No. 4 adopted at the 1956 second special session of the legislature of Alabama, as amended, which relates to the promotion of trade by inducing commercial enterprises to locate in the state and which confers on municipalities having a population not exceeding 100,000 inhabitants, according to the last or any subsequent federal census, powers with respect to the acquisition, leasing and financing of projects suitable for use by certain commercial enterprises. (Acts 1971, No. 1880, p. 3062.)

§ 41-16-63. Provisions of article cumulative.

This article shall be cumulative in its nature. (Acts 1967, Ex. Sess., No. 217, p. 259, § 12.)

ARTICLE 4.

SURETY BONDS OR INSURANCE UNDER PUBLIC BUILDING
OR CONSTRUCTION CONTRACTS.

§ 41-16-80. Officers or employees, etc., of state, public corporations, etc., not to require procurement of surety bond or insurance contract from particular surety company, insurance company, agent, etc., or negotiate, obtain, etc., surety bond or insurance contract which can be obtained or procured by bidder, contractor, etc.

No officer or employee of this state or any public corporation or of any public agency or authority and no person acting or purporting to act on behalf of such officer, employee or public agency or authority, except a public agency or authority created pursuant to agreement or compact with another state, shall, with respect to any public building or construction contract, require the bidder to obtain or procure any surety bond or contract of insurance specified in connection with such contract or specified by any law, ordinance or regulation from a particular surety company, insurance company, bonding company, agent or broker. No officer, employee, person, firm or corporation acting or purporting to act on behalf of any officer or employee of this state, public corporation or public agency or authority shall negotiate, make application, obtain or procure any surety bond or contract of insurance, except contracts of insurance for builder's risk or owner's protective liability, which can be obtained or procured by the bidder, contractor or subcontractor. (Acts 1969, No. 314, p. 650, § 1.)

§ 41-16-81. Approval of form; sufficiency or manner of execution of surety bonds or insurance contracts furnished by surety company, insurance company, etc., selected by bidder.

The provisions of section 41-16-80 shall not prevent the exercise by an officer or employee on behalf of the state, public agency, political subdivision or public authority from exercising the right to approve the form, sufficiency or manner of execution of the surety bonds or contracts of insurance furnished by the surety company, insurance company or bonding company selected by the bidder to underwrite bonds or contracts of insurance. The insurance company, bonding company or surety company shall meet all requirements for such companies otherwise provided for by law. (Acts 1969, No. 314, p. 650, § 2.)

§ 41-16-82. Provisions in invitations for bids and contract documents in conflict with article declared void and unenforceable.

All provisions in any invitation for bids or in any of the contract documents in conflict with this article are hereby declared to be void and unenforceable as contrary to the public policy of this state. (Acts 1969, No. 314, p. 650, § 3.)

ARTICLE 5.

CONTRACTS FOR SALE OF CERTAIN STATE PROPERTY.

§ 41-16-100. Contracts for the sale or disposal of certain state property to be let by public auction or sealed bids; notice of sale and advertisement for bids; furnishing of description of articles to be sold, etc.; acceptance and opening of bids; awarding of contract; bids to be placed on file open to public inspection.

(a) All contracts made by, or on behalf of, the state of Alabama, or any department, board, bureau, commission, institution, corporation or agency thereof, of whatever nature for the sale or disposal of tangible personal property or standing timber owned by the state of Alabama, other than (1) alcoholic beverages, (2) products of the Alabama Institute for Deaf and Blind, (3) barter arrangements of the state prison system, (4) books, (5) school supplies, (6) food, (7) property used in vocational projects, (8) property owned by any state college or university not under the control of the board of education of the state of Alabama, which has trade-in value which may be credited against the cost of

337

replacement property purchased in accordance with the Alabama competitive bid laws, and (9) types of property, the disposal of which is otherwise provided for by law or which, by nature, are incapable of sale by auction or bid, shall be let by free and open competitive public auction or sealed bids.

(b) Every proposal to make a sale covered by this article shall be advertised for at least two weeks in advance of the date fixed for receiving bids. Such advertisement shall appear at least once a week for two consecutive weeks in a newspaper of general circulation in the county where the sale is to be made, and a copy of such proposal shall simultaneously be posted on a readily accessible public bulletin board at the main office of the state finance director. Advertisements for bids shall state the item or items to be sold, by class and description, where the property is located and the dates, time and place the property may be inspected. The advertisements shall further state the date, time and place of auction or opening of sealed bids, and no bid shall be received at any time after the time advertised.

(c) The bids shall be publicly taken or opened, in case of sealed bids, by the state finance director or his authorized representative, and all bidders shall be entitled to be present in person or by representative.

(d) The award of the contract shall be made to the successful bidder within 72 hours after taking of the bids, unless the awarding authority, by formal action, provides for a reasonable extension of that period.

(e) The bid of the successful bidder so marked, as well as the bids of the unsuccessful bidders in the case of sealed bids, shall be placed on file open to public inspection and shall become matters of public record.

(f) Upon written request, the state finance director shall furnish to any person a description of the article or articles to be sold together with a statement as to the terms of the proposed sale and, in addition if the request specifies, the director shall furnish the same information to such person making such request with respect to all future sales of articles of the same class. (Acts 1969, No. 473, p. 927, § 1; Acts 1979, No. 79-227, p. 348.)

§ 41-16-101. Items may be sold by lot or individually; procedure where all bids received below estimated market value of property.

(a) The finance director may sell all items by lot or by individual item, whichever method, in his opinion, will bring the highest return for the items so advertised.

(b) In the event all bids received are less than the estimated market value of the property, the finance director may reject all bids and readvertise or sell by negotiated sale; provided, that in the event the property is sold by negotiated sale under the provisions of this section, the value received must be more than the highest bid or bids received. (Acts 1969, No. 473, p. 927, § 2.)

§ 41-16-102. Property to be available for inspection prior to sale.

All property advertised under the provisions of this article shall be available for inspection during the normal state office hours and at whatever place advertised for at least 48 hours prior to sale. (Acts 1969, No. 473, p. 927, § 5.)

§ 41-16-103. Payment for and removal of property by purchaser.

All property sold under the provisions of this article shall be paid for by the purchaser or his representative at the time of removal, and said removal shall be not later than seven days after the awarding of the contract unless extended in writing by the finance department director; provided, however, that the time limit of seven days shall not be applicable to sales of standing timber. (Acts 1969, No. 473, p. 927, § 7.)

§ 41-16-104. Disposition of proceeds from sale.

All proceeds from sales made under the provisions of this article shall be paid into the state treasury or other legally authorized depositary to be credited to the fund from which originally purchased. (Acts 1969, No. 473, p. 927, § 6.)

§ 41-16-105. State officers or employees not to act as agents for bidders; bidding upon or purchase of property by state officers or employees.

No officer or employee of the state of Alabama or any of its departments, boards, bureaus, commissions, institutions, corporations or agencies shall act as agent for any bidder; provided, however, that such officers or employees shall not be excluded from bidding on or purchasing state property under this article. (Acts 1969, No. 473, p. 927, § 4.)

§ 41-16-106. Sales in violation of article declared null and void; recovery of penalty from persons, etc., responsible for sales in violation of article.

Any sale of tangible personal property or standing timber of the state made in violation of the terms of this article shall be null and void, and the person or persons responsible for the transaction and his bondsman shall be subject to a penalty of not less than $100.00 nor more than $1,000.00, which may be recovered for the state of Alabama by the attorney general by civil action in the circuit court of Montgomery county. (Acts 1969, No. 473, p. 927, § 8.)

Cross references. — As to statute of limitations on prosecution of infractions of this chapter, see § 41-16-2.

§ 41-16-107. Sale of diseased, storm or fire-damaged timber and timber cut on rights-of-way or easements; sale or disposal of tangible personal property by state highway department.

(a) The provisions of this article shall not apply to the sale of diseased, storm or fire-damaged timber, nor shall it apply to timber cut on rights-of-way or easements. Such timber may be sold in such manner as the commissioner of conservation and natural resources deems in the best interest of the state; provided, that no sale of diseased timber shall be made until the state forester shall certify that such timber is diseased, and such certification shall be in written form and filed with the director of finance.

(b) The provisions of this article shall not apply to the sale or disposal of tangible personal property by the state highway department when the purchaser or recipient of such property is a county governing body or municipal governing body of this state. Such tangible personal property may be sold or released to any such governing body in such manner and on such terms as the state highway director deems in the best interest of the state; provided, that all proceeds from any sale under the provisions of this subsection shall be paid into the state treasury to the credit of the public road and bridge fund for the use of the state highway department; provided, that the county or municipal governing body shall certify to the highway director that the property will be retained for use for a period of at least two years by the government making the purchase and it cannot be sold or traded for a period of two years. (Acts 1969, No. 473, p. 927, § 11; Acts 1981, No. 81-434, p. 679, § 1.)

The 1981 amendment, effective May 6, 1981, added subsection (b).

§ 41-16-108. Applicability of provisions of article to educational and eleemosynary institutions and certain state departments.

All educational and eleemosynary institutions governed by a board of trustees or other similar governing body, the department of mental health and state docks department shall be governed by the provisions of this article, with the exception that the director or such other official designated by the governing body or by the governor in the case of the state docks shall be the substitute for the state finance director for the purposes of this article. (Acts 1969, No. 473, p. 927, § 3.)

§ 41-16-109. Violations of provisions of article deemed misdemeanors.

Violation of any of the provisions of this article shall constitute a misdemeanor. (Acts 1969, No. 473, p. 927, § 9.)

Cross references. — As to statute of limitations on prosecution of infractions of this chapter, see § 41-16-2.

CHAPTER 17.

STATE-OWNED MOTOR VEHICLES.

§ 41-17-1. Standards.

After July 19, 1976, all passenger automobiles bought wholly or partially with state funds for use of state officers, officials or employees on official business, including those bought by or for state colleges or universities, shall be standard two-door or four-door sedans purchased from authorized General Motors, Ford, Chrysler or American Motors dealerships, the wheel base to be no longer than 118.0 inches and the engine to be no larger than the smallest eight cyclinder engine available on the particular model sought to be purchased. Such automobiles shall otherwise be equipped as the finance director may direct. Such limitations shall not apply to the limousine bought for the use of the governor, any constitutional officer or members of the governor's cabinet, nor to automobiles purchased for the department of public safety, the alcoholic beverage control board, the department of conservation and natural resources or the department of agriculture and industries for use in high speed law enforcement work only by the patrolmen, policemen or investigators assigned to such departments. All such automobiles may be specifically equipped for the purposes for which they are to be used. Also excluded from the provisions of this chapter shall be vehicles used or operated by presidents of colleges, technical institutes and universities, emergency vehicles, vehicles purchased for use in transporting drugs, plants, animals or for hospital and health use and vehicles deemed necessary by the board of trustees of the four-year colleges and universities to be incident to the operation of such college or university. (Acts 1969, No. 471, p. 914, § 1; Acts 1975, 4th Ex. Sess., No. 92, p. 2770, § 1; Acts 1976, No. 135, p. 129.)

§ 41-17-2. Purchase for or assignment to state officers or employees of passenger automobiles.

No passenger automobile shall be purchased for or assigned to any officer or employee of any state agency (which term as used in this chapter shall include state boards, commissions, committees, corporations, departments and offices) except the head or chief executive officer of the agency and such employees of the agency whose duties require the assignment of an automobile, as determined by the head or chief executive officer of the agency and approved by the state finance director; provided, that no such redetermination and approval shall be required for any officer or employee referred to in section 41-17-1. (Acts 1969, No. 471, p. 914, § 2.)

§ 41-17-3. Maintenance and operation of transportation pool in city of Montgomery by department of finance generally; establishment of mileage fees and charges for use of pool cars.

A transportation pool shall be maintained at a convenient location in the city of Montgomery by the state department of finance, division of service, for the purpose of providing necessary motor vehicle transportation for state officers and employees who do not have automobiles regularly assigned to them. It shall be the duty of the chief of the division of service to see that all pool cars are maintained in a clean, safe and efficiently operable condition. The chief of the division of service shall appoint a pool dispatcher and such other personnel as may be necessary to effectively operate the pool, who shall, upon request of a state agency head, provide the agency with the automobile as requested. Such pool car shall be loaned to an agency only for a single trip and shall not be assigned to any officer, employee or other person or agency on any basis other than a trip basis. The pool dispatcher shall keep the necessary maintenance and mileage records for each pool car, and the division of service shall charge state agencies a mileage fee for the use of pool cars.

Subject to approval by the director of finance, the chief of the division of service shall fix the mileage fee at an amount sufficient to pay only the cost of salaries of motor pool employees, operating expenses and maintaining and replacing pool cars. Based upon monthly mileage reports submitted by the pool dispatcher, the division of service shall render mileage fee bills monthly to state agencies for their use of pool cars. The mileage fee and charges collected shall be deposited to the credit of the revolving fund provided for in section 41-17-5. (Acts 1969, No. 471, p. 914, § 3.)

§ 41-17-4. Number, etc., of automobiles to be kept in pool.

As many automobiles as needed, maintained in a clean, safe and efficient operable condition, shall be kept in the transportation pool at all times for the use of state officers and employees who need transportation on official business. (Acts 1969, No. 471, p. 914, § 4.)

§ 41-17-5. Establishment of transportation revolving fund; disposition of fees collected for use of pool cars; transportation pool to be self-supporting.

(a) To finance the operation of the transportation pool and the repair, maintenance and replacement of pool cars, there is hereby established a transportation revolving fund for the use of the department of finance.

(b) All fees collected from state agencies for the use of pool cars shall be paid to the finance department to the credit of the transportation revolving fund for the necessary maintenance and replacement of pool cars.

(c) It is the intention of the legislature that the transportation pool be made financially self-supporting from the fees charged the various state agencies for pool services. (Acts 1969, No. 471, p. 914, § 5.)

§ 41-17-6. Establishment, operation, etc., of area transportation pools.

All state agencies having their main office or branch offices in an area or areas beyond the serviceable limits of the transportation pool in Montgomery shall pool their automobiles in the area or areas in which they are located if their total assignment of automobiles is more than one. Such pools shall be operated and maintained, insofar as is feasible, under the same rules and regulations as are provided for the operation of the transportation pool in Montgomery. (Acts 1969, No. 471, p. 914, § 6.)

§ 41-17-7. Promulgation of rules and regulations for provision of parking and storage for pool, etc., by director of finance.

The director of finance is hereby empowered to promulgate such reasonable rules and regulations as may be necessary from time to time to administer the provisions of this article and to provide adequate parking and storage for the pool within the vicinity of the Capitol. (Acts 1969, No. 471, p. 914, § 8.)

§ 41-17-8. Maintenance and repair of state-owned automobiles.

All state automobiles shall be maintained and repaired at cost by the bureau of equipment of the state highway department or by the public safety department, and all gasoline, lubrication jobs, grease jobs, oil changes, tires and car washes for state automobiles shall be obtained at the facilities of such departments, except in cases which constitute emergencies or whenever such departments are unable to handle the work load or when it is adjudged to be more economical by reason of time or distance to obtain such services elsewhere. The director of finance may, however, promulgate reasonable regulations permitting services to be obtained for state automobiles from other sources under such circumstances or conditions as may be necessary or expeditious. (Acts 1969, No. 471, p. 914, § 9.)

§ 41-17-9. Unauthorized use, etc., of state-owned automobile; alteration, etc., of license plate affixed to state vehicle.

It shall be a misdemeanor for any person to use or permit any other person to use any state-owned automobile for any purpose other than official state business; provided, that driving from his home to his office or place of employment or from his office or place of employment to his home by an officer or employee to whom an automobile is permanently assigned or by an employee to whom a pool car is assigned, if hours of departure or return are inconsistent with normal working hours, shall be deemed to be an authorized use of the automobile for the purposes of this chapter.

It shall be a misdemeanor for any state employee to obliterate, alter, cover or conceal all or any portion of a license plate affixed to a state vehicle.

The director of the state department of public safety shall be responsible for the enforcement of the provisions concerning the use of state-owned automobiles.

Any unauthorized or improper use of a state automobile by a merit system employee shall constitute grounds for his dismissal or suspension. (Acts 1969, No. 471, p. 914, § 7.)

CHAPTER 18.

SOUTHERN GROWTH POLICIES AGREEMENT.

§ 41-18-1. Text.

Article I. Findings and Purposes.

(a) The party states find that the South has a sense of community based on common social, cultural and economic needs and fostered by a regional tradition. There are vast potentialities for mutual improvement of each state in the region by cooperative planning for the development, conservation and efficient utilization of human and natural resources in a geographic area large enough to afford a high degree of flexibility in identifying and taking maximum advantage of opportunities for healthy and beneficial growth. The independence of each state and the special needs of subregions are recognized and are to be safeguarded. Accordingly, the cooperation resulting from this agreement is intended to assist the states in meeting their own problems by enhancing their abilities to recognize and analyze regional opportunities and take account of regional influences in planning and implementing their public policies.

(b) The purposes of this agreement are to provide:

(1) Improved facilities and procedures for study, analysis and planning of governmental policies, programs and activities of regional significance;

(2) Assistance in the prevention of interstate conflicts and the promotion of regional cooperation;

(3) Mechanisms for the coordination of state and local interests on a regional basis; and

(4) An agency to assist the states in accomplishing the foregoing.

Article II. The Board.

(a) There is hereby created the southern growth policies board, hereinafter called "the board."

(b) The board shall consist of five members from each party state, as follows:

(1) The governor,

(2) Two members of the state legislature, one appointed by the presiding officer of each house of the legislature or in such other manner as the legislature may provide, and

(3) Two residents of the state who shall be appointed by the governor to serve at his pleasure.

(c) In making appointments pursuant to paragraph (b)(3), a governor shall, to the greatest extent practicable, select persons who, along with the other members serving pursuant to paragraph (b), will make the state's representation on the board broadly representative of the several socio-economic elements within his state.

(d) (1) A governor may be represented by an alternate with power to act in his place and stead, if notice of the designation of such alternate is given to the board in such manner as its bylaws may provide.

(2) A legislative member of the board may be represented by an alternate with power to act in his place and stead, unless the laws of his state prohibit such representation, and if notice of the designation of such alternate is given to the board in such manner as its bylaws may provide. An alternate for a legislative member of the board shall be selected by the member from among the members of the legislative house in which he serves.

(3) A member of the board serving pursuant to paragraph (b)(3), of this article may be represented by another resident of his state who may participate in his place and stead, except that he shall not vote; provided, that notice of the identity and designation of the representative selected by the member is given to the board in such manner as its bylaws may provide.

Article III. Powers.

(a) The board shall prepare and keep current a statement of regional objectives, including recommended approaches to regional problems. The statement may also identify projects deemed by the board to be of regional significance. The statement shall be available in its initial form two years from the effective date of this agreement and shall be amended or revised no less frequently than once every six years. The statement shall be in such detail as the board may prescribe. Amendments, revisions, supplements or evaluations may be transmitted at any time. An annual commentary on the statement shall be submitted at a regular time to be determined by the board.

(b) In addition to powers conferred on the board elsewhere in this agreement, the board shall have the power to make or commission studies, investigations and recommendations with respect to:

(1) The planning and programming of projects of interstate or regional significance;

(2) Planning and scheduling of governmental services and programs which would be of assistance to the orderly growth and prosperity of the region and to the well-being of its population;

(3) Effective utilization of such federal assistance as may be available on a regional basis or as may have an interstate or regional impact;

(4) Measures for influencing population distribution, land use, development of new communities and redevelopment of existing ones;

(5) Transportation patterns and systems of interstate and regional significance;

(6) Improved utilization of human and natural resources for the advancement of the region as a whole; and

(7) Any other matters of a planning, data collection or informational character that the board may determine to be of value to the party states.

Article IV. Avoidance of Duplication.

(a) To avoid duplication of effort and in the interest of economy, the board shall make use of existing studies, surveys, plans and data and other materials in the possession of the governmental agencies of the party states and their respective subdivisions or in the possession of other interstate agencies. Each such agency, within available appropriations and if not expressly prevented or limited by law, is hereby authorized to make such materials available to the board and to otherwise assist it in the performance of its functions. At the request of the board, each such agency is further authorized to provide information regarding plans and programs affecting the region, or any subarea thereof, so that the board may have available to it current information with respect thereto.

(b) The board shall use qualified public and private agencies to make investigations and conduct research, but if it is unable to secure the undertaking of such investigations or original research by a qualified public or private agency, it shall have the power to make its own investigations and conduct its own research. The board may make contracts with any public or private agencies or private persons or entities for the undertaking of such investigations or original research within its purview.

(c) In general, the policy of paragraph (b) of this article shall apply to the activities of the board relating to its statement of regional objectives, but nothing herein shall be construed to require the board to rely on the services of other persons or agencies in developing the statement of regional objectives or any amendment, supplement or revision thereof.

Article V. Advisory Committees.

The board shall establish a local governments advisory committee. In addition, the board may establish advisory committees representative of subregions of the South, civic and community interests, industry, agriculture, labor or other categories or any combinations thereof. Unless the laws of a party state contain a contrary requirement, any public official of the party state or a subdivision thereof may serve on an advisory committee established pursuant hereto, and such service may be considered as a duty of his regular office or employment.

Article VI. Internal Management of the Board.

(a) The members of the board shall be entitled to one vote each. No action of the board shall be binding unless taken at a meeting at which a majority of the total number of votes on the board are cast in favor thereof. Action of the board shall be only at a meeting at which a majority of the members or their alternates are present. The board shall meet at least once a year. In its bylaws, and subject to such directions and limitations as may be contained therein, the board may delegate the exercise of any of its powers relating to internal administration and management to an executive committee or the executive director. In no event shall any such delegation include final approval of:

(1) A budget or appropriation request,

(2) The statement of regional objectives or any amendment, supplement or revision thereof,

(3) Official comments on or recommendations with respect to projects of interstate or regional significance, or

(4) The annual report.

(b) To assist in the expeditious conduct of its business when the full board is not meeting, the board shall elect an executive committee of not to exceed 17 members, including at least one member from each party state. The executive committee, subject to the provisions of this agreement and consistent with the policies of the board, shall be constituted and function as provided in the bylaws of the board. One half of the membership of the executive committee shall consist of governors, and the remainder shall consist of other members of the board, except that at any time when there is an odd number of members on the executive committee the number of governors shall be one less than half of the total membership. The members of the executive committee shall serve for terms of two years, except that members elected to the first executive committee shall be elected as follows: one less than half of the membership for two years and the remainder for one year. The chairman, chairman-elect, vice-chairman and treasurer of the board shall be members of the executive committee and, anything in this paragraph to the contrary notwithstanding, shall serve during their continuance in these offices. Vacancies in the executive committee shall not affect its authority to act, but the board at its next regularly ensuing meeting following the occurrence of any vacancy shall fill it for the unexpired term.

(c) The board shall have a seal.

(d) The board shall elect from among its members a chairman, a chairman-elect, a vice-chairman and a treasurer. Elections shall be annual. The chairman-elect shall succeed to the office of chairman for the year following his service as chairman-elect. For purposes of the election and service of officers of the board, the year shall be deemed to commence at the conclusion of the annual meeting of the board and terminate at the conclusion of the next annual meeting thereof. The board shall provide for the appointment of an executive director. Such executive director shall serve at the pleasure of the board and, together with the treasurer and such other personnel as the board may deem appropriate, shall be bonded in such amounts as the board shall determine. The executive director shall be secretary.

(e) The executive director, subject to the policy set forth in this agreement and any applicable directions given by the board, may make contracts on behalf of the board.

(f) Irrespective of the civil service, personnel or other merit system laws of any of the party states, the executive director, subject to the approval of the board, shall appoint, remove or discharge such personnel as may be necessary for the performance of the functions of the board and shall fix the duties and compensation of such personnel. The board in its bylaws shall provide for the personnel policies and programs of the board.

(g) The board may borrow, accept or contract for the services of personnel from any party jurisdiction, the United States or any subdivision or agency of the aforementioned governments, or from any agency of two or more of the party jurisdictions or their subdivisions.

(h) The board may accept for any of its purposes and functions under this agreement any and all donations and grants of money, equipment, supplies, materials and services, conditional or otherwise, from any state, the United States, or any other governmental agency or from any person, firm, association, foundation, or corporation, and may receive, utilize and dispose of the same. Any donation or grant accepted by the board pursuant to this paragraph or services borrowed pursuant to paragraph (g) of this article shall be reported in the annual report of the board. Such report shall include the nature, amount and conditions if any, of the donation, grant or services borrowed and the identity of the donor or lender.

(i) The board may establish and maintain such facilities as may be necessary for the transacting of its business. The board may acquire, hold and convey real and personal property and any interest therein.

(j) The board shall adopt bylaws for the conduct of its business and shall have the power to amend and rescind these bylaws. The board shall publish its bylaws in convenient form and shall file a copy thereof and a copy of any amendment thereto with the appropriate agency or officer in each of the party states.

(k) The board annually shall make to the governor and legislature of each party state a report covering the activities of the board for the preceding year. The board at any time may make such additional reports and transmit such studies as it may deem desirable.

(l) The board may do any other or additional things appropriate to implement powers conferred upon it by this agreement.

Article VII. Finance.

(a) The board shall advise the governor or designated officer or officers of each party state of its budget of estimated expenditures for such period as may be required by the laws of that party state. Each of the board's budgets of estimated expenditures shall contain specific recommendations of the amount or amounts to be appropriated by each of the party states.

(b) The total amount of appropriation requests under any budget shall be apportioned among the party states. Such apportionment shall be in accordance with the following formula:

(1) One third in equal shares,

(2) One third in the proportion that the population of a party state bears to the population of all party states, and

(3) One third in the proportion that the per capita income in a party state bears to the per capita income in all party states.

In implementing this formula, the board shall employ the most recent authoritative sources of information and shall specify the sources used.

(c) The board shall not pledge the credit of any party state. The board may meet any of its obligations in whole or in part with funds available to it pursuant to article VI (h) of this agreement, provided that the board takes specific action setting aside such funds prior to incurring an obligation to be met in whole or in part in such manner. Except where the board makes use of funds available to it pursuant to article VI (h), or borrows pursuant to this paragraph, the board shall not incur any obligation prior to the allotment of funds by the party states adequate to meet the same. The board may borrow against anticipated revenues for terms not to exceed two years, but in any such event the credit pledged shall be that of the board and not of a party state.

(d) The board shall keep accurate accounts of all receipts and disbursements. The receipts and disbursements of the board shall be subject to the audit and accounting procedures established by its bylaws. However, all receipts and disbursements of funds handled by the board shall be audited yearly by a certified or licensed public accountant, and the report of the audit shall be included in and become part of the annual report of the board.

(e) The accounts of the board shall be open at any reasonable time for inspection by duly constituted officers of the party states and by any persons authorized by the board.

(f) Nothing contained herein shall be construed to prevent board compliance with laws relating to audit or inspection of accounts by or on behalf of any government contributing to the support of the board.

Article VIII. Cooperation With the Federal Government and Other Governmental Entities.

Each party state is hereby authorized to participate in cooperative or joint planning undertakings with the federal government, and any appropriate agency or agencies thereof, or with any interstate agency or agencies. Such participation shall be at the instance of the governor or in such manner as state law may provide or authorize. The board may facilitate the work of state representatives in any joint interstate or cooperative federal-state undertaking authorized by this article, and each such state shall keep the board advised of its activities in respect of such undertakings, to the extent that they have interstate or regional significance.

Article IX. Subregional Activities.

The board may undertake studies or investigations centering on the problems of one or more selected subareas within the region; provided, that in its judgment such studies or investigations will have value as demonstrations for similar or other areas within the region. If a study or investigation that would be of primary benefit to a given state, unit of local government, or intrastate or interstate area is proposed, and if the board finds that it is not justified in undertaking the work for its regional value as a demonstration, the board may undertake the study or investigation as a special project. In any such event, it shall be a condition precedent that satisfactory financing and personnel arrangements be concluded to assure that the party or parties benefited bear all costs which the board determines that it would be inequitable for it to assume. Prior to undertaking any study or investigation pursuant to this article as a special project, the board shall make reasonable efforts to secure the undertaking of the work by another responsible public or private entity in accordance with the policy set forth in article IV (b).

Article X. Comprehensive Land Use Planning.

If any two or more contiguous party states desire to prepare a single or consolidated comprehensive land use plan or a land use plan for any interstate area lying partly within each such state, the governors of the states involved may designate the board as their joint agency for the purpose. The board shall accept such designation and carry out such responsibility; provided, that the states involved make arrangements satisfactory to the board to reimburse it or otherwise provide the resources with which the land use plan is to be prepared. Nothing contained in this article shall be construed to deny the availability for use in the preparation of any such plan of data and information already in the possession of the board or to require payment on account of the use thereof in addition to payments otherwise required to be made pursuant to other provisions of this agreement.

Article XI. Compacts and Agencies Unaffected.

Nothing in this agreement shall be construed to:

(1) Affect the powers or jurisdiction of any agency of a party state or any subdivision thereof;

(2) Affect the rights or obligations of any governmental units, agencies or officials, or of any private persons or entities conferred or imposed by any interstate or interstate-federal compacts to which any one or more states participating herein are parties; or

(3) Impinge on the jurisdiction of any existing interstate-federal mechanism for regional planning or development.

Article XII. Eligible Parties; Entry Into and Withdrawal.

(a) This agreement shall have as eligible parties the states of Alabama, Arkansas, Delaware, Florida, Georgia, Kentucky, Louisiana, Maryland, Mississippi, Missouri, North Carolina, Oklahoma, South Carolina, Tennessee, Texas, Virginia and West Virginia.

(b) Any eligible state may enter into this agreement, and it shall become binding thereon when it has adopted the same; provided, that in order to enter into initial effect, adoption by at least five states shall be required.

(c) Adoption of the agreement may be either by enactment thereof or by adherence thereto by the governor; provided, that in the absence of enactment, adherence by the governor shall be sufficient to make his state a party only until December 31, 1977. During any period when a state is participating in this agreement through gubernatorial action, the governor may provide to the board an equitable share of the financial support of the board from any source available to him. Nothing in this paragraph shall be construed to require a governor to take action contrary to the Constitution or laws of his state.

(d) Except for a withdrawal effective on December 31, 1977, in accordance with paragraph (c) of this article, any party state may withdraw from this agreement by enacting a statute repealing the same, but no such withdrawal shall take effect until one year after the governor of the withdrawing state has given notice in writing of the withdrawal to the governors of all other party states. No withdrawal shall affect any liability already incurred by or chargeable to a party state prior to the time of such withdrawal.

Article XIII. Construction and Severability.

This agreement shall be liberally construed so as to effectuate the purposes thereof. The provisions of this agreement shall be severable, and if any phrase, clause, sentence or provision of this agreement is declared to be contrary to the Constitution of any state or of the United States, or the application thereof to any government, agency, person or circumstance is held invalid, the validity of the remainder of this agreement and the applicability thereof to any government, agency, person or circumstance shall not be affected thereby. If this agreement shall be held contrary to the Constitution of any state participating therein, the agreement shall remain in full force and effect as to the state affected as to all severable matters. (Acts 1975, No. 1206, § 1.)

§ 41-18-2. Copies of bylaws and amendments.

Copies of bylaws and amendments to be filed pursuant to article VI (j) of the agreement shall be filed with the secretary of state. (Acts 1975, No. 1206, § 2.)

§ 41-18-3. Effect of adoption.

Nothing contained in the southern growth policies agreement, as enacted by this chapter, shall in any event be construed to terminate the participation of this state with any state which adopted the southern growth policies agreement prior to October 10, 1975; except, that the provisions of article XII (c) shall govern with respect to the continuance of states as parties thereto after December 31, 1977.

No section, article or provision contained in this chapter shall be construed so as to prohibit, restrict or restrain the actions of any individual member state or the actions of any county or municipal government within the boundaries of any individual member state, nor shall any delegate from the state of Alabama be authorized by this legislature to cast any vote that would in any manner restrict the sovereign rights presently granted to or retained by this state under the United States Constitution, or the rights of any local governments granted by the Constitution of the state of Alabama or by statutory acts of the legislature. (Acts 1975, No. 1206, §§ 3, 4.)

CHAPTER 19.

BUDGET MANAGEMENT.

Cross references. — As to preparation, etc., of budget generally, see § 41-4-82 et seq.

§ 41-19-1. Short title.

This chapter may be cited as The Budget Management Act. (Acts 1976, No. 494, p. 614, § 1.)

§ 41-19-2. "Agency/department" defined.

For the purposes of this chapter, the term "agency/department" shall include state agencies, departments, boards, bureaus, the legislature and institutions of the state. (Acts 1976, No. 494, p. 614, § 2.)

§ 41-19-3. Purpose of chapter.

It is the purpose of this chapter to establish a comprehensive system for budgeting and financial management which furthers the capacity of the governor and the legislature to plan and finance the services which they determine the state will provide for citizens. The system shall include procedures for:

(1) The orderly establishment, continuing review and periodic revision of the program and financial goals and policies of the state;

(2) The development, coordination and review of long range program and financial plans that will implement established state goals and policies;

(3) The preparation, coordination, analysis and enactment of a budget, organized to focus on state services and their costs, that authorizes the implementation of policies and plans in the succeeding budget period;

(4) The evaluation of alternatives to existing policies, plans and procedures that offer potential for more efficient or effective state services; and

(5) The regular appraisal and reporting of program performance. (Acts 1976, No. 494, p. 614, § 2.)

§ 41-19-4. Responsibilities of governor as to preparation and adminis- tration of state budget, etc., generally.

The governor is responsible for the preparation and administration of the state budget and the evaluation of the long range program plans, requested budgets and alternatives to state agency/department policies and programs and formulation and recommendation for consideration by the legislature of a proposed comprehensive program and financial plan which shall cover all estimated receipts and expenditures of the state government, including all grants, loans and moneys received from the federal government. Proposed expenditures shall not exceed estimated revenues and resources. (Acts 1976, No. 494, p. 614, § 3.)

§ 41-19-5. Responsibilities of department of finance as to preparation of budget, etc., generally.

The department of finance shall:

(1) Assist the governor in the preparation and explanation of the proposed comprehensive program and financial plan, including the coordination and analysis of state agency/department program goals and objectives, program plans and program budget requests;

(2) Develop procedures to produce the information needed for effective decision making;

(3) Assist agencies/departments in preparing their statement of goals and objectives, program plans, program budget requests and reporting of program performance;

(4) Administer its responsibilities under the program execution provisions of this chapter so that the policy decisions and budget determination of the governor and the legislature are implemented to the fullest extent possible within the concepts of proper management;

(5) Provide the legislature with budget information; and

(6) Assist agencies/departments in the preparation of their proposals under section 41-19-6. This assistance shall include organization of mate- rials, provision of centrally collected accounting, budgeting and personnel information, standards and guidelines formulation, provision of population and other required data, and any other assistance that will help the state

agencies/departments produce the information necessary for efficient agency/department management and effective decision making by the governor and the legislature. (Acts 1976, No. 494, p. 614, § 5.)

Cross references. — As to department of finance generally, see § 41-4-1 et seq. As to budget officer generally, see § 41-4-81.

Collateral references. — 81A C.J.S., States, § 232.

§ 41-19-6. Program and financial information to be submitted to department of finance by agencies/departments; preparation of information by department of finance upon failure of agencies/departments to transmit same; compilation and submission to governor of summary of information.

(a) Each state agency/department, on the date and in the form and content prescribed by the department of finance, shall prepare and forward to the budget officer the following program and financial information:

(1) The goals and objectives of the agency/department programs, together with proposed supplements, deletions and revisions to such programs;

(2) Its proposed plans to implement the goals and objectives, including estimates of future service needs, planned methods of administration, proposed modification of existing program services and establishment of new program services, and the estimated resources needed to carry out the proposed plan;

(3) The budget requested to carry out its proposed plans in the succeeding fiscal year. The budget request information shall include the expenditures during the last fiscal year, those estimated for the current fiscal year, those proposed for the succeeding fiscal year and any other information requested by the department of finance;

(4) A report of the revenues during the last fiscal year, an estimate of the revenues during the current fiscal year and an estimate for the succeeding fiscal year;

(5) A statement of legislation required to implement the proposed programs and financial plans; and

(6) An evaluation of the advantages and disadvantages of specific alternatives to existing or proposed program policies or administrative methods.

(b) The state agency/department proposals prepared under subsection (a) of this section shall describe the relationships of their programs services to those of other state agencies/departments and other branches of state government.

(c) If any state agency/department fails to transmit the program and financial information required under subsection (a) of this section on the specified date, the department of finance may prepare such information.

(d) The department of finance shall compile and submit to the governor or the governor-elect for any year when a new governor has been elected, not later than November 20, a summary of the program and financial information prepared by state agencies/departments. (Acts 1976, No. 494, p. 614, § 6.)

§ 41-19-7. Formulation and presentation to legislature and agencies/departments of governor's proposed program and financial plan.

(a) The governor shall formulate the program and financial plan to be recommended to the legislature after considering each state agency's proposed program and financial plan. The governor's plan shall include his recommended goals and policies, recommended plans to implement the goals and policies, recommended budget for the succeeding fiscal year and recommended revenue measures to balance the budget.

(b) The proposed comprehensive program and financial plan shall be presented by the governor in a message to a joint session of the legislature on or before the fifth legislative day of each regular session of the legislature. The message shall be accompanied by an explanatory report which summarizes recommended goals, plans and appropriations. The explanatory report shall be furnished each member of the legislature and each state agency/department on or before the fifth legislative day of the regular session of the legislature. The report shall contain the following information:

(1) The coordinate program goals and objectives that the governor recommends to guide the decisions on the proposed program plans and budget appropriations;

(2) The program and budget recommendations of the governor for the succeeding fiscal year;

(3) A summary of state revenues in the last fiscal year, a revised estimate for the current fiscal year and an estimate for the succeeding fiscal year;

(4) A summary of expenditures during the last fiscal year, those estimated for the current fiscal year and those recommended by the governor for the succeeding fiscal year; and

(5) Any additional information which will facilitate understanding of the governor's proposed program and financial plan by the legislature and the public. (Acts 1976, No. 494, p. 614, § 7.)

Collateral references. — 63 Am. Jur. 2d,
Public Funds, § 47.

§ 41-19-8. Responsibilities of legislature as to consideration and adoption of program and financial plan, etc. — Generally.

The legislature shall:

(1) Consider the program and financial plan recommended by the governor, including proposed goals and policies, tax rate and other revenue changes and long range program plans;

(2) Adopt programs and alternatives to the plan recommended by the governor which it deems appropriate;

(3) Adopt legislation to authorize the implementation of a comprehensive program and financial plan; and

(4) Provide for a post audit of financial transactions, program accomplishments and execution of legislative policy direction. (Acts 1976, No. 494, p. 614, § 4.)

§ 41-19-9. Same — Balancing of authorized expenditures and estimated revenues and resources.

The legislature shall consider the governor's proposed comprehensive program and financial plan, evaluate alternatives to the governor's recommendations and determine the comprehensive program and financial plan to support the services to be provided the citizens of the state; provided, however, that in such determination authorized expenditures shall not exceed estimated revenues and resources. (Acts 1976, No. 494, p. 614, § 8.)

Collateral references. — 81A C.J.S., States, § 204.

§ 41-19-10. Authority of agencies/departments as to administration of programs and appropriations generally; preparation, review, approval, etc., of annual plans for operation of programs; granting of salary increases, etc., by agencies/departments; transfers or changes of appropriations; quarterly reports by department of finance as to operations of agencies/departments.

(a) Except as limited by policy decisions of the governor, appropriations by the legislature and other provisions of law, the several state agencies/departments shall have full authority for administering their program assignments and appropriations and shall be responsible for their proper management.

(b) Each state agency/department shall prepare an annual plan for the operation of each of its assigned programs. The operations plan shall be prepared in the form and content and be transmitted on the date prescribed to the department of finance.

(c) The department of finance shall:

(1) Review each operations plan to determine that it is consistent with the policy decisions of the governor and appropriations by the legislature, that it reflects proper planning and efficient management methods and that appropriations have been made for the planned purpose and will not be exhausted before the end of the fiscal year;

(2) Approve the operations plan if satisfied that it meets the requirements under subdivision (1) of this subsection; otherwise, the department of finance shall require revision of the operations plan in whole or in part; and

(3) Modify or withhold the planned expenditures at any time during the appropriation period if the department of finance finds that such expenditures are greater than those necessary to execute the programs at the level authorized by the governor and the legislature or that the revenues and resources will be insufficient to meet the authorized expenditure levels.

(d) No state agency/department may increase salaries of its employees, employ additional employees or expend money or incur any obligations except in accordance with law and with a properly approved operations plan by the director of finance.

(e) Appropriation transfers or changes as between objects of expenditures within a program may be made only by the director of finance. Appropriation transfers or changes between programs within an agency/department may be made only by the governor and shall be reported to the legislature quarterly. No transfers shall be made between agencies/departments except pursuant to interagency agreements executed for purposes of accomplishing objectives for which the funds involved were appropriated.

(f) The department of finance shall report quarterly to the governor and the legislature on the operations of each state agency/department, relating actual accomplishments to those planned and modifying, if necessary, the operations plan of any agency/department for the balance of the fiscal year. (Acts 1976, No. 494, p. 614, § 9.)

Collateral references. — 81A C.J.S., States, § 232.

§ 41-19-11. Submission of performance reports to department of finance by agencies/departments; form and contents thereof; preparation and forwarding to members of legislature of summary of reports.

(a) Each state agency/department, shall submit a performance report to the department of finance on or before November 1 for the preceding fiscal year. These reports shall be in the form prescribed by the budget officer and shall include statements concerning:

(1) The work accomplished and the services provided in the preceding fiscal year or other meaningful work period, relating actual accomplishments to those planned under subsection (b) of section 41-19-10;

(2) The relationship of accomplishments and services to the policy decisions and budget determinations of the governor and the legislature;

(3) The costs of accomplishing the work and providing the services, to the extent feasible, citing meaningful measures of program effectiveness and costs; and

(4) The administrative improvements made in the preceding year, potential improvements in future years and suggested changes in legislation or administrative procedures to make further improvements.

(b) The finance department shall summarize the performance reports and forward copies to each member of the legislature annually. (Acts 1976, No. 494, p. 614, § 10.)

§ 41-19-12. Preparation for presentation or presentation to legislative committee of false budget or fiscal information.

(a) Any person in state government, including elected or appointed officials, who prepares false budget or fiscal information to be presented to any legislative committee or who presents false budget or fiscal information to any legislative committee, knowing such budget or fiscal information to be false, shall be guilty of a misdemeanor and, on conviction, shall be imprisoned in the county jail for not more than one year and may also be fined not more than $1,000.00.

(b) In the event of a second conviction under this section, such person shall be forever ineligible to hold any position with the state of Alabama. (Acts 1976, No. 389, p. 495.)

CHAPTER 20.

CONTINUATION OR TERMINATION OF STATE AGENCIES.

Cited in Opinion of Justices, 396 So. 2d 81 (Ala. 1981); Eagerton v. Gulas Wrestling Enters., Inc., 406 So. 2d 366 (Ala. 1981).

§ 41-20-1. Short title.

This chapter shall be known as the Alabama Sunset Law of 1981. (Acts 1976, No. 512, p. 641, § 1; Acts 1981, No. 81-61, p. 74, § 1.)

The 1981 amendment, effective February 25, 1981, substituted "1981" for "1976."

Cited in Opinion of Justices, 381 So. 2d 183 (Ala. 1980).

§ 41-20-2. Definitions.

As used in this chapter, unless the context requires a different meaning, the following words shall be defined as follows:

(1) ENUMERATED AGENCY. All departments, councils, boards, commissions, divisions, bureaus or like governmental units or subunits of the state of Alabama which are enumerated herein.

(2) NONENUMERATED AGENCY. All departments, councils, boards, commissions, divisions, bureaus or like governmental units of the state of Alabama which are not enumerated herein.

(3) CONTINUANCE. Such term, or any derivative thereof shall mean continuance as presently in existence or as modified or reestablished by recommended legislation.

(4) PERFORMANCE AUDIT. The same as operational audit.

(5) SUNSET BILL. Any bill introduced pursuant to subsection (d) of section 41-20-4 of this act.

(6) TERMINATION. The end, abolishment or annulment of any agency or the act of causing the existence to cease. (Acts 1976, No. 512, p. 641, § 2; Acts 1979, No. 79-542, p. 976; Acts 1981, No. 81-61, p. 74, § 1.)

The 1981 amendment, effective February 25, 1981, in subdivision (1), added "enumerated" preceding "agency," and substituted "enumerated herein" for "regulatory in nature" at the end; redesignated former subdivisions (2), (3), and (4), as (3), (4) and (6), respectively, and added subdivisions (2) and (5).

§ 41-20-3. Specification of termination dates for certain agencies; date and procedure generally for termination of agencies not designated; committee's right to review and make recommendations.

(a) The following agencies shall automatically terminate on the dates specified, unless a bill is passed that they be continued, modified or reestablished:

(1) October 1, 1981 shall be the termination date for:

a. State board of auctioneers — created by section 34-4-50.

b. Alabama board of cosmetology — created by section 34-7-40.

c. Boxing and wrestling commission — created by section 41-9-90.

d. Examining board for professional entomologists, horticulturists, plant pathologists, floriculturists and tree surgeons — created by section 2-28-2.

e. Alabama board of funeral service — created by section 34-13-20.

f. State pilotage commission — created by section 33-4-1.

g. Polygraphic examiners board — created by section 34-25-4.

h. Alabama board of examiners for speech pathology and audiology — created by section 34-28A-40.

i. State board of veterinary medical examiners — created by section 34-29-20.

j. Alabama real estate commission — created by section 34-27-7.

k. Board of bar examiners — created by section 34-3-2.

l. Board of registration for sanitarians — created by section 34-28-20.

m. Board of examiners of mine personnel — created by section 25-9-9.

n. Alabama board of social work examiners — created by section 34-30-50.

o. State agency for social security and state social security advisory board — created by section 36-28-3.

(2) October 1, 1982, shall be the termination date for:

a. Alabama board of barber examiners — created by section 34-5-13.

b. State board for registration of architects — created by section 34-2-38.

c. Alabama board of examiners of landscape architects — created by section 34-17-2.

d. Alabama state board of public accountancy — created by section 34-1-3.

e. State board of registration for foresters — created by section 34-12-30.

f. State board for registration of professional engineers and land surveyors — created by section 34-11-30.

g. State licensing board for general contractors — created by section 34-8-20.

h. State board of chiropractic examiners — created by section 34-24-140.

i. Alabama firefighters' personnel standards and education commission — created by section 36-32-2.

j. Board of hearing aid dealers — created by section 34-14-30.

k. Alabama board of optometry — created by section 34-22-40.

l. Alabama peace officers' standards and training commission — created by section 36-21-41.

m. Board of physical therapy — created by section 34-24-192.

n. Board of plumbing examiners — created by section 40-12-145.

o. Alabama board of examiners in psychology — created by section 34-26-20.

p. State board of heating, air conditioning, roofing and sheet metal contractors — created by section 34-31-2.

q. Alabama dairy commission — created by section 2-13-42.

r. Board of medical technicians examiners — created by section 34-18-40.

s. Board of dental examiners of Alabama — created by section 34-9-40.

t. Board of nursing — created by section 34-21-2.

u. State board of examiners of nursing home administrators — created by section 34-20-4.

v. State board of pharmacy — created by section 34-23-90.

w. State board of podiatry — created by section 34-24-250.

x. State athletic commission — created by section 41-9-90.1.

(3) October 1, 1983 and every fourth year thereafter shall be the termination date for:

a. Board for registration of architects — created by section 34-2-38.

b. Alabama board of examiners of landscape architects — created by section 34-17-2.

c. State licensing board for general contractors — created by section 34-8-20.

d. State board of registration for professional engineers and land surveyors — created by section 34-11-30.

363

e. Alabama coastal area board — created by section 9-7-14.

f. Board of bar examiners — created by section 34-3-2.

g. Polygraphic examiners board — created by section 34-25-4.

(4) October 1, 1984 and every fourth year thereafter shall be the termination date for:

a. Alabama state board of social work examiners — created by section 34-30-50.

b. Alabama board of examiners in psychology — created by section 34-26-20.

c. Alabama state board of public accountancy — created by section 34-1-3.

d. Alabama board of cosmetology — created by section 34-7-40.

e. Alabama board of funeral service — created by section 34-13-20.

f. Alabama real estate commission — created by section 34-27-7.

g. Alcoholic beverage control board — created by section 28-3-40.

h. Department of insurance — created by section 27-2-1.

i. Alabama securities commission — created by section 8-6-50.

j. State pilotage commission — created by section 33-4-1.

k. Public service commission — created by section 37-1-1.

l. Examining board for professional entomologists, horticulturists, plant pathologists, floriculturists and tree surgeons — created by section 2-28-2.

m. State board of heating, air conditioning, roofing and sheet metal contractors — created by section 34-31-2.

n. Board of examiners of mine personnel — created by section 25-9-9.

o. Plumbing examiners board — created by section 40-12-145.

p. Alabama liquified petroleum gas board — created by section 9-17-101.

q. State board of auctioneers — created by section 34-4-50.

(5) October 1, 1985 and every fourth year thereafter shall be the termination date for:

a. Alabama board of examiners for speech pathology and audiology — created by section 34-28A-40.

b. Board of nursing — created by section 34-21-2.

c. State board of chiropractic examiners — created by section 34-24-140.

d. State board of veterinary medical examiners — created by section 34-29-20.

e. Board of examiners of nursing home administrators — created by section 34-20-4.

f. Board of physical therapy — created by section 34-24-192.

g. State licensing board for the healing arts — created by section 34-24-1.

h. Board of hearing aid dealers — created by section 34-14-30.

i. Alabama board of examiners for speech pathology and audiology — created by section 34-28A-40.

j. Board of dental examiners in Alabama — created by section 34-9-40.

k. State board of medical examiners — created by section 34-24-53.

l. Board of medical technicians examiners — created by section 34-18-40.

m. Alabama board of optometry — created by section 34-22-40.

n. State board of pharmacy — created by section 34-23-90.

o. State board of podiatry — created by section 34-24-250.

(6) October 1, 1986 and every fourth year thereafter shall be the termination date for:

a. Alabama water well standards board — created by section 22-24-3.

b. Board of certification for water and waste water systems personnel — created by section 22-25-3.

c. Board of registration for sanitarians — created by section 34-28-20.

d. Alabama surface mining reclamation commission — created by section 9-16-33.

e. State oil and gas board — created by section 9-17-3.

f. State board of registration of foresters — created by section 34-12-30.

g. Alabama dairy commission — created by section 2-13-42.

h. State radiation control agency — created by section 22-14-4.

i. Water improvement commission — created by section 22-22-3.

j. Air pollution control commission — created by section 22-28-5.

(b) Any law to the contrary notwithstanding, nothing in this chapter shall be construed to limit the joint committee's right to call any enumerated agency for review at a date earlier than specified in this section; nor shall the committee be limited to making recommendations for termination only or continuance only.

(c) The sunset committee shall have the authority to review any enumerated or nonenumerated agency and shall make recommendations for continuance, termination or modification. Any nonenumerated agency reviewed shall continue unless a bill is passed and becomes law to terminate or modify the agency.

(d) Either house may pass a resolution instructing the sunset committee to review an enumerated or nonenumerated agency. After passage of said resolution, the sunset committee shall review such agency and report its findings as provided for in subsection (d) of section 41-20-4. (Acts 1976, No. 512, p. 641, § 3; Acts 1979, No. 79-542, p. 976; Acts 1981, No. 81-61, p. 74, § 1.)

The 1981 amendment, effective February 25, 1981, rewrote subsections (a) and (b), and added subsections (c) and (d).

Code commissioner's notes. — The board of plumbing examiners, referred to in paragraph n. of subdivision (2) of subsection (a) of this section, does not appear to be created by § 40-12-145 or any other section in the Code of Alabama 1975.

Acts 1979, No. 153, p. 252, effective May 29, 1979, pursuant to the terms of the "Alabama Sunset Law of 1976," Act No. 512, 1976 Regular Session, p. 640, terminates the Civil Defense Advisory Council.

Acts 1979, No. 154, p. 253, effective May 29, 1979, pursuant to the terms of the "Alabama Sunset Law of 1976," Act No. 512, 1976 Regular Session, p. 640, terminates the board of corrections.

Acts 1980, No. 80-121, p. 142, § 3, repeals § 41-9-90, which created the boxing and wrestling commission, referred to in paragraph

c. of subdivision (1) of subsection (a) of this section. A state athletic commission is created by § 41-9-90.1.

Acts 1981, No. 81-195, p. 230, continues the Board of Bar Examiners pursuant to the Sunset Act.

Acts 1981, No. 81-196, p. 231, continues the Board of Dental Scholarship Awards pursuant to the Sunset Act.

Acts 1981, No. 81-197, p. 232, continues the Board of Medical Scholarship Awards pursuant to the Sunset Act.

Acts 1981, No. 81-198, p. 233, continues the State Pilotage Commission pursuant to the Sunset Act.

Acts 1981, No. 81-199, p. 234, continues the State Real Estate Commission pursuant to the Sunset Act.

Acts 1981, No. 81-200, p. 234, continues the Board of Funeral Services pursuant to the Sunset Act.

Acts 1981, No. 81-201, p. 242, continues the Board of Examiners of Mine Personnel.

Acts 1981, No. 81-208, p. 249, continues the Examining Board for Professional Entomologists, Horticulturists, Floriculturists and Tree Surgeons pursuant to the Sunset Act.

Acts 1981, No. 81-209, p. 250, continues the Board of Speech Pathology and Audiology pursuant to the Sunset Act.

Acts 1981, No. 81-217, p. 271, abolishes the state licensing board for the healing arts, referred to in paragraph g. of subdivision (5) of subsection (a) of this section, and transfers its functions relating to the practice of chiropractic to the state board of chiropractic examiners and its property, assets, etc., between the state board of medical examiners for the use of the medical licensure commission and the state board of chiropractic examiners.

Acts 1981, No. 81-220, p. 290, § 1, effective April 9, 1981, provides that pursuant to the Alabama Sunset Law the State Board of Registration of Sanitarians (§ 34-28-20), referred to in paragraph l. of subdivision (1) of subsection (a) of this section, is terminated and the board transfers any funds or moneys it now holds to the State Board of Health which shall be used by the latter exclusively for training and orientation of environmentalists of the department.

Acts 1981, No. 81-221, p. 291, provides that the Board of Social Work Examiners is continued. Section 5 of such act provides that such board shall be reviewed by the Sunset Committee for the legislative year 1982.

Acts 1981, No. 81-222, p. 293, provides that the Board of Polygraph Examiners is continued.

Acts 1981, No. 81-256, p. 339, § 3 continues the Board of Veterinary Medical Examiners pursuant to the Sunset Act.

Acts 1981, No. 81-378, p. 555, § 3 continues the Board of Auctioneers pursuant to the Sunset Act.

Acts 1981, No. 81-435, p. 682, continues the Alabama surface mining reclamation commission, referred to in paragraph d. of subdivision (6) of subsection (a) of this section, under the name of the Alabama surface mining commission. Sections 9-16-30 through 9-16-53 were repealed by said act. See article 3 of chapter 16 of Title 9.

Acts 1981, No. 81-762, p. 1288, continues the Board of Cosmetology pursuant to the Sunset Act.

Acts 1982, No. 82-134 continues the state board of podiatry, pursuant to the Sunset Act.

Acts 1982, No. 82-135 continues the board of registration for professional engineers and land surveyors pursuant to the Sunset Act.

Acts 1982, No. 82-136 continues the board of registration of foresters, pursuant to the Sunset Act.

Acts 1982, No. 82-137 continues the board of optometry, pursuant to the Sunset Act.

Acts 1982, No. 82-138 continues the Alabama firefighters personnel standards and education commission, pursuant to the Sunset Act.

Acts 1982, No. 82-139 continues the peace officers standards and training commission pursuant to the Sunset Act.

Acts 1982, No. 82-140, continues the board of dental examiners, pursuant to the Sunset Act.

Acts 1982, No. 82-141 continues the state board of pharmacy, pursuant to the Sunset Act.

Acts 1982, No. 82-142 continues the board of chiropractic examiners, pursuant to the Sunset Act.

Acts 1982, No. 82-143, continues the state board of public accountancy, pursuant to the Sunset Act.

Acts 1982, No. 82-144 continues the state athletic commission, pursuant to the Sunset Act.

Acts 1982, No. 82-145 continues the board of examiners of nursing home administrators, pursuant to the Sunset Act.

Acts 1982, No. 82-146 continues the board of hearing aid dealers, pursuant to the Sunset Act.

Acts 1982, No. 82-147 continues the board of registration of architects, pursuant to the Sunset Act.

Acts 1982, No. 82-148 provides for the continuance of the Alabama dairy commission, pursuant to the Sunset Act. The act further provides, however, that if on or prior to December 1, 1982, the secretary of agriculture of the United States Department of Agriculture approves, issues and implements a proposed Alabama-West Florida milk marketing order, the dairy commission shall be phased out, and that §§ 2-13-40 through 2-13-66 shall be repealed six months following implementation of said order. The federal milk marketing order in question was promulgated and became effective on May 1, 1982. See 47 Fed. Reg. 11495 (1982) (to be codified in 7 C.F.R. pt. 1093).

Acts 1982, No. 82-149 continues the board of nursing, pursuant to the Sunset Act, but provides that the board shall automatically terminate on October 1, 1984, unless a bill is passed that it be continued, modified or reestablished.

Acts 1982, No. 82-152 continues the Alabama board of examiners in psychology, pursuant to the Sunset Act.

Acts 1982, No. 82-153 continues the board of pardons and paroles, pursuant to the Sunset Act.

Acts 1982, No. 82-154 continues the Alabama Public Library Service, pursuant to the Sunset Act.

Acts 1982, No. 82-189 continues the board of physical therapy, pursuant to the Sunset Act.

Acts 1982, No. 82-345 continues the board of examiners of landscape architects, pursuant to the Sunset Act.

Acts 1982, No. 82-400 continues the licensing board for general contractors, pursuant to the Sunset Act.

Section 34-31-2, which created the state board of heating, air conditioning, roofing and sheet metal contractors, referred to in paragraph p. of subdivision (2) of this section, was repealed by Acts 1982, No. 82-547, § 3. A board of heating and air conditioning contractors is created by § 34-31-20.

Collateral references. — 73 C.J.S., Public Administrative Bodies and Procedure, § 23; 81A C.J.S., States, § 41.

§ 41-20-4. Creation of select joint committee for review and evaluation of agencies; composition; selection of members; chairman; duties generally; submission of data and report of recommendations as to continuation or termination of agencies; voting upon committee recommendations by legislature generally; compensation of members of committee.

(a) A select joint committee, known as the sunset committee, shall be constituted as follows:

(b) Three members of the house and three members of the senate shall be elected in the same manner as the elected members of the legislative council by the respective houses: two from the Alabama senate and two from the Alabama house of representatives shall be appointed by the presiding officer of said elected bodies; and the president pro tempore of the senate and the speaker pro tem of the house of representatives. The chairman shall be elected from among the members of the committee, alternating annually between a house member and a senate member. Any vacancy in the sunset committee shall be filled through appointment by the presiding officer of the elected body having the vacancy.

(c) Said select joint committee shall be charged with the duty of assisting in the implementation of the procedures of this chapter and shall be charged with the duty of establishing administrative procedures which shall facilitate the review and the evaluation procedure as provided for in this chapter.

(d) The committee shall submit its report and any accompanying legislation to the offices of the speaker and the president for distribution to legislators and the governor on or before the first legislative day of the ensuing regular legislative session.

(e) The committee members shall be entitled to their usual legislative per diem and expenses for attending meetings of the committee, which shall be paid from funds appropriated for the payment of the expenses of the legislature.

There shall be no limitation upon the number of days the committee or any subcommittee thereof shall meet; provided, however, the members shall be entitled to payment only for the days they are actually engaged in committee business. (Acts 1976, No. 512, p. 641, § 10; Acts 1979, No. 79-542, p. 976; Acts 1981, No. 81-61, p. 74, § 1.)

The 1981 amendment, effective February 25, 1981, in subsection (a), substituted "known" for "know" following "committee," in subsection (b), added the language beginning "Any vacancy in the sunset committee . . ." as the last sentence; in subsection (d), inserted "and any accompanying legislation" following "report," and deleted the last six sentences of the subsection which provided for submission of data and report of committee recommendations as to continuation or termination of agencies and voting upon said recommendations by the legislature.

§ 41-20-5. Procedure for review and evaluation of agencies — Commencement and conclusion.

Legislative committee review of the enumerated agencies shall begin in the year prior to the scheduled regular legislative session next preceding the date upon which the enumerated agencies are scheduled to terminate pursuant to section 41-20-3, and shall conclude with a recommendation for continuation, modification or termination on or before the first legislative day immediately following said review. (Acts 1976, No. 512, p. 641, § 4; Acts 1979, No. 79-542, p. 976; Acts 1981, No. 81-61, p. 74, § 1.)

The 1981 amendment, effective February 25, 1981, inserted "enumerated" preceding "agencies," inserted "modification" following "continuation" and deleted the last sentence which authorized the committee to call other agencies for review with no less than 30 days notice in writing to the director or head of such agency.

§ 41-20-6. Same — Public hearings and receipt of testimony generally; burden of establishing public need for continuation of agencies; information to be provided by agencies under review.

(a) The sunset committee reviewing enumerated or nonenumerated agencies, shall hold public hearings and receive testimony from the public and all interested parties.

(b) All enumerated or nonenumerated agencies shall bear the burden of establishing that sufficient public need is present which justifies their continued existence.

(c) All enumerated or nonenumerated agencies shall provide the reviewing and evaluating committee with the following information:

(1) The identity of all agencies under the direct or advisory control of the agency under review;

(2) All powers, duties and functions currently performed by the agency under review;

(3) All constitutional, statutory or other authority under which said powers, duties and functions of the agency are carried out;

(4) Any powers, duties or functions which, in the opinion of the agency under review, are being performed and duplicated by another agency within the state, including the manner in which and the extent to which this duplication of efforts is occurring and any recommendations as to eliminating the duplication;

(5) Any powers, duties or functions which, in the opinion of the agency under review, are inconsistent with current and projected public needs and which should be terminated or altered; and

(6) Any other information which the reviewing committee, in its discretion, feels is necessary and proper in carrying out its review and evaluative duties. (Acts 1976, No. 512, p. 641, § 7; Acts 1981, No. 81-61, p. 74, § 1.)

The **1981 amendment,** effective February 25, 1981, in subsection (a), substituted "The sunset committee" for "Pursuant to the language of section 41-20-5, the legislative," and substituted "enumerated or nonenumerated" for "such" and inserted "enumerated or nonenumerated" preceding "agencies" in subsections (b) and (c).

Collateral references. — 73 C.J.S., Public Administrative Bodies & Procedure, § 23.

§ 41-20-7. Same — Factors to be considered in determining public need for continuation of agencies generally.

In said public hearings, the determination as to whether a sufficient public need for continuance is present shall take into consideration the following factors concerning the enumerated or nonenumerated agency under review and evaluation:

(1) The extent to which any information required to be furnished to the reviewing committee pursuant to section 41-20-6 has been omitted, misstated or refused and the extent to which conclusions reasonably drawn from said information is adverse to the legislative intent inherent in the powers, duties and functions as established in the enabling legislation creating said agency or is inconsistent with present or projected public demands or needs;

(2) The extent to which statutory changes have been recommended which would benefit the public in general as opposed to benefitting the agency;

(3) The extent to which operation has been efficient and responsive to public needs;

(4) The extent to which it has been encouraged that persons regulated, report to the agency concerning the impact of rules and decisions regarding improved service, economy of service or availability of service to the public;

(5) The extent to which the public has been encouraged to participate in rule and decision making as opposed to participation solely by persons regulated;

(6) The extent to which complaints have been expeditiously processed to completion in the public interest;

(7) The extent to which the division, agency or board has permitted qualified applicants to serve the public;

(8) The extent to which affirmative action requirements of state and federal statutes and constitutions have been complied with by the agency or the industry it regulates; and

(9) Any other relevant criteria which the reviewing committee, in its discretion, deems necessary and proper in reviewing and evaluating the sufficient public need for continuance of the respective agency. (Acts 1976, No. 512, p. 641, § 8; Acts 1981, No. 81-61, p. 74, § 1.)

The 1981 amendment, effective February 25, 1981, inserted "enumerated or nonenu-merated" preceding "agency" in the introductory paragraph.

§ 41-20-8. Same — Zero-based review and evaluation.

(a) In conjunction with the criteria enumerated in section 41-20-7, one criterion which may be used in determining sufficient public need in such public hearings shall be a "zero-based review and evaluation." A "zero-based review and evaluation" shall be a comprehensive review and evaluation to determine if the merits of the agency support continuation rather than termination and a finding as to what amounts of funding, if any, shall be authorized to produce correspondingly greater or lesser levels of responsibility and service output. Such a procedure shall necessitate the review and evaluation of all powers, duties and functions which currently are exercised by the agency as well as any request for additions to said powers, duties or functions when reviewing the sufficient public need of the agency.

(b) Said "zero-based review and evaluation" shall include, but not be limited to, the following factors:

(1) An identification of other agencies having the same or similar objective, along with a comparison of the cost and effectiveness of said agencies, and any duplication of the agency under review;

(2) An identification of any agency which has not received and expended state tax dollar revenues within a period of two years prior to said hearings;

(3) An examination of the extent to which the objectives of the agency have been achieved in comparison with the objectives as initially set forth in the enabling legislation and an analysis of any significant variance between projected and actual performance;

(4) A specification, to the extent feasible, in quantitative terms of the objectives of said agency for the next four years; and

(5) An examination of the impact of said agency on the economy of the state. (Acts 1976, No. 512, p. 641, § 9; Acts 1981, No. 81-61, p. 74, § 1.)

The 1981 amendment, effective February 25, 1981, in subsection (a), substituted "may" for "shall" following "one criterion which" in the first sentence.

§ 41-20-9. Same — Furnishing of information by department of examiners of public accounts; legislative reference service; and legislative fiscal office.

The department of examiners of public accounts, the legislative reference service and the legislative fiscal office of the state shall furnish, upon request of the reviewing and evaluating committee, any relevant information, including the results of prior audits and reviews of any agency under review. (Acts 1976, No. 512, p. 641, § 12; Acts 1981, No. 81-61, p. 74, § 1.)

The 1981 amendment, effective February 25, 1981, inserted "the legislative reference service" following "the department of examiners of public accounts."

Cross references. — As to department of examiners of public accounts generally, see § 41-5-1 et seq.

§ 41-20-10. Debate and voting upon recommendations as to continuance or termination of agencies.

(a) On the tenth legislative day of the regular session, one hour after the convening of the house of which the chairman of the select joint committee of the sunset committee is a member, voting in that house on sunset bills not previously considered during this regular session shall commence and thereafter continue as the first order of business, from day to day, until voting on all the bills with respect to each enumerated or nonenumerated agency is completed.

(b) On the fifth legislative day after passage of bills passed pursuant to subsection (a) of this section, one hour after convening of the house of which the chairman of the select joint committee of the sunset committee is not a member, voting in that house on said sunset bills not previously considered during this regular session shall commence and thereafter continue as the first order of business, from day to day, until voting on said bills is completed. Provided, however, that either house may, by a three-fifths vote of those members present and voting, consider other business before that house.

(c) (1) If a committee considering sunset legislation recommending modification shall fail to report a sunset bill within the time prescribed in subsection (a) or (b) of this section, then a substitute bill specifying only continuance concerning the status of the state agency shall be referred to the considering legislative body as a committee of the whole on the legislative day preceding the legislative day of prescribed reporting, there to be acted on by the legislature as a committee of the whole.

(2) Debate on a sunset bill being acted upon by the legislature as a committee of the whole shall be limited to one hour and must be continuous and uninterrupted. Thereafter a recorded vote must be taken at the expiration of said debate.

(3) An additional one hour of debate, beyond the time permitted in subdivision (2) of this subsection, may be permitted by a vote of two-thirds of those voting. Such additional period of debate may not be allowed more than one time per bill and must be continuous and uninterrupted. Thereafter a recorded vote must be taken at the expiration of said debate.

(d) Debate on the termination or continuance of any enumerated or nonenumerated agency shall not continue beyond the period of one hour from the start of the debate on each bill and a recorded vote must be taken at the expiration of said debate. "Debate" as used in this section shall mean one hour total time allocated for discussion on each agency considered. At the end of this one hour period of time allocated, which shall be continuous and uninterrupted, it shall be mandatory for the presiding officer of the house considering the bill to call for a recorded vote with respect to the agency in question.

(e) An additional one hour for debate on termination or continuation of said agency, beyond the time permitted in subsection (d) of this section, may be permitted by a vote of two-thirds of those voting. Such additional period of debate may not be allowed more than one time per bill and must be continuous and uninterrupted. Thereafter a recorded vote must be taken at the expiration of said debate.

(f) A sunset bill which terminates or continues an agency and is passed by the originating house, amended by the second house and returned to the originating house shall be allowed one hour of debate upon return to the originating house. Such debate must be continuous and uninterrupted. Thereafter a recorded vote must be taken at the expiration of said debate.

(g) An additional one hour for debate on termination or continuation of said agency, beyond the time permitted in subsection (f) of this section, may be permitted by a vote of two-thirds of those voting. Such additional period of debate may not be allowed more than one time per bill and must be continuous and uninterrupted. Thereafter a recorded vote must be taken at the expiration of said debate.

(h) The debate limitations established under this section relate only to those bills that either continue or terminate an agency. (Acts 1976, No. 512, p. 641, § 11; Acts 1979, No. 79-542, p. 976; Acts 1981, No. 81-61, p. 74, § 1.)

The 1981 amendment, effective February 25, 1981, rewrote this section.

Cross references. — As to voting upon recommendations of select joint committee as to continuation or termination of agencies generally, see § 41-20-4.

Cited in Opinion of the Justices, 356 So. 2d 617 (Ala. 1978); Gafford v. Pemberton, 409 So. 2d 1367 (Ala. 1982).

§ 41-20-11. Requirement as to bill continuing, modifying or reestablishing agencies.

No more than one enumerated or nonenumerated agency shall be continued, modified or reestablished in any one bill for an act, as provided for in section 41-20-4, and such agency shall be mentioned in title as provided by law. (Acts 1976, No. 512, p. 641, § 14; Acts 1979, No. 79-542, p. 976; Acts 1981, No. 81-61, p. 74, § 1.)

The 1981 amendment, effective February 25, 1981, inserted "enumerated or nonenumerated" following "no more than one."

§ 41-20-12. Cessation of affairs of agencies terminated; abolition of personnel positions and reversion to state of unexpended funds; expiration of licenses; penalties unenforceable.

Any enumerated agency which is terminated shall cease its affairs on the date specified in section 41-20-3. Any nonenumerated agency shall cease its affairs on the date specified in the bill terminating said agency. From the date of sine die of the regular legislative session, immediately preceding the date of termination, any enumerated agency terminated pursuant to section 41-20-3 shall exercise no functions or powers except to administratively wind up its affairs. Any nonenumerated agency which has been terminated shall exercise no functions or powers, except to administratively wind up its affairs, after the date provided for in the bill terminating such agency. Upon the termination date such enumerated or nonenumerated agency, its personnel position shall be abolished with all unexpended funds reverting back to the state fund from which its appropriation was made, unless otherwise provided by law. Any license issued by any agency, which has an expiration date after the agency's date of termination, shall expire on the effective date of the agency's abolishment. Any penalties for engaging in any profession or activity without being licensed therefor shall not be enforceable with respect to activities occurring after an enumerated or nonenumerated agency has ceased its functions pursuant to this chapter. (Acts 1976, No. 512, p. 641, § 5; Acts 1979, No. 79-542, p. 976; Acts 1981, No. 81-61, p. 74, § 1.)

The 1981 amendment, effective February 25, 1981, inserted "enumerated" preceding "agency," and deleted "specified" following "agency" in the first sentence; added the second sentence; in the third sentence, inserted "enumerated" preceding "agency," deleted "automatically" following "agency," inserted "pursuant to section 41-20-3" following "terminated," and deleted "because of the legislature not continuing, modifying or reestablishing it"; added the fourth sentence, inserted "enumerated or nonenumerated" preceding "agency," deleted "and" following "agency," and deleted "unless otherwise provided by law" at the end of the fifth sentence; in the sixth sentence, substituted "any" for "such" preceding "agency" and in the seventh sentence, deleted "the" following "occurring after" and inserted "an enumerated or nonenumerated" preceding "agency."

§ 41-20-13. Repealed by Acts 1981, No. 81-61, p. 74, § 1, effective February 25, 1981.

§ 41-20-14. Effect of termination of agency upon claims or rights against said agency; payment of unsettled accounts.

(a) This chapter shall not cause the dismissal of any claim or right of any citizen which is subject to administrative hearing or litigation against any state agency terminated pursuant to the provisions of this chapter.

(b) The state comptroller is authorized to draw warrants on the state treasury for any outstanding accounts which are legally owed but unsettled by any agency which has ceased functioning pursuant to this chapter. Such claims must be presented and paid in the same manner as required by law for any claim for the payment of state funds. (Acts 1976, No. 512, p. 641, § 15; Acts 1979, No. 79-542, p. 976; Acts 1981, No. 81-61, p. 74, § 1.)

Code commissioner's note. — Acts 1981, No. 81-61, p. 74, § 1, reenacted this section without change.

§ 41-20-15. Utilization of principles of zero-based review and evaluation by governor in preparation of budget.

The governor is urged to utilize the principles of "zero-based review and evaluation" for each state agency in his preparation of the budget for each fiscal year and to include such analysis, together with his recommendations, in his transmission of the budget to the legislature. (Acts 1976, No. 512, p. 641, § 13; Acts 1981, No. 81-61, p. 74, § 1.)

Code commissioner's note. — Acts 1981, No. 81-61, p. 74, § 1, reenacted this section without change.

Cross references. — As to preparation, etc., of budget generally, see § 41-4-82 et seq. As to responsibilities of governor in preparation and management of budget generally, see § 41-19-1 et seq.

§ 41-20-16. Construction of chapter.

Nothing in this chapter shall be construed to abrogate any powers, duties or functions of any agency established by the people of Alabama in the Constitution of 1901. (Acts 1976, No. 512, p. 641, § 16; Acts 1981, No. 81-61, p. 74, § 1.)

Code commissioner's note. — Acts 1981, No. 81-61, p. 74, § 1, reenacted this section without change.

CHAPTER 21.

STATE CODE DISTRIBUTION.

§ 41-21-1. Distribution of sets of state code to agencies, departments, etc., by secretary of state generally.

It shall be the duty of the secretary of state, on publication and delivery to the state, to transmit sets of the 1975 Code of Alabama, and supplements or replacement volumes thereof, to the following agencies, departments, institutions, bureaus, boards, commissions and offices:

(1) One set to the law library of congress;

(2) One set to the custodian of the law library of the court of last resort of every state and territory for exchange upon the approval of the state law librarian of the request therefor;

(3) One set to the library of the University of Alabama and one set to the land commissioner of the University of Alabama;

(4) Two sets to each member of the legislature, including the lieutenant governor, for each legislative term, and to the clerk of the house and to the secretary of the senate;

(5) One set to the library of each junior college, trade school, technical college and public institution of higher education;

(6) Ten sets to the librarian of the supreme court and state law library for the use of the library;

(7) Two sets to the department of archives and history;

(8) Four sets to the governor's office;

(9) Fifty-five sets to the attorney general's office;

(10) Eleven sets to the legislative reference service;

(11) Four sets to the department of court management;

(12) Three sets to the state superintendent of education;

(13) Seven sets to the department of mental health;

(14) Ten sets to the department of public safety;

(15) Two sets to the department of agriculture and industries;

(16) Three sets to the alcoholic beverage control board;

(17) Three sets to the banking department;

(18) Two sets to the state military department;

(19) Three sets to the state department of insurance;

(20) Five sets to the board of corrections;

(21) Five sets to the health department;

(22) Four sets to the department of industrial relations;

(23) Two sets to the retirement systems of Alabama;

(24) Six sets to the finance department;

(25) Four sets to the pardons and paroles board;

(26) Four sets to the conservation and natural resources department;

(27) Five sets to the highway department;

(28) Three sets to the department of labor;

(29) Five sets to the public service commission;

(30) Five sets to the department of pensions and security;

(31) Ten sets to the department of revenue;

(32) Five sets to the state toxicologist;

(33) One set to each functioning agency, department, institution, bureau, board and commission of state government not otherwise provided for by this chapter, upon application therefor to the secretary of state;

(34) One set each to every congressman and representative from the state of Alabama in the congress of the United States;

(35) One set each to every sheriff;

(36) One set to the commission of each county for use of said county commission and for use of the tax assessor, tax collector and other county officers to whom distribution is not otherwise provided;

(37) One set to the circuit court of each county and, in counties having two courthouses, one set for the office of the circuit clerk maintained in each of said courthouses;

(38) One set to the register of the circuit court in every county and, in counties having two courthouses, one set to the office of the register maintained in each of said courthouses; provided, however, that in counties where the offices of circuit clerk and of register are held by the same person, only one set shall be provided;

(39) One set to the clerk of the district court and juvenile court in counties where clerks offices for these courts are maintained;

(40) One set to the probate judge of each county;

(41) One set to every justice of the supreme court and every judge of the court of criminal appeals and court of civil appeals and one set to each law clerk or research assistant thereof;

(42) One set each to the clerk of the supreme court, court of criminal appeals, court of civil appeals and reporter of decisions;

(43) One set to every judge of the circuit and district courts;

(44) One set to every district attorney and deputy district attorney;

(45) One set to the office of the secretary of the senate for the use of the senate and one set to the office of the clerk of the house of representatives for the use of the house of representatives;

(46) One set to the mayor or other executive or presiding officer of each municipality for use of such municipality;

(47) Two sets to the Alabama state bar association; and

(48) Five sets to the clerk of the house and five sets to the secretary of the senate. (Acts 1977, No. 352, p. 470, § 1; Acts 1979, Ex. Sess., No. 79-28, p. 38.)

Cross references. — As to county law libraries being on the distribution list to receive state codes, see § 11-25-10.

§ 41-21-2. Storage of additional sets of code; distribution thereof.

The secretary of state shall set aside in the place provided for the storage of the sets of said annotated code 200 thereof, which may be distributed to any public agency or officer applying therefor upon the approval of the governor of said application. (Acts 1977, No. 352, p. 470, § 2.)

§ 41-21-3. Furnishing of duplicate copies to replace lost or destroyed sets of code.

Duplicate sets of said annotated code, to replace sets lost or destroyed without fault of the custodian, may be furnished to any officer entitled thereto upon application to the secretary of state, provided said application is approved by the governor. (Acts 1977, No. 352, p. 470, § 3.)

§ 41-21-4. Sale of code by publisher.

The publisher of the 1975 Code of Alabama is hereby authorized to sell said annotated code to any person, firm or corporation within or without the state, so long as the same are available for sale at prices as may be determined and fixed by said publisher and the governor. (Acts 1977, No. 352, p. 470, § 4.)

§ 41-21-5. Vesting of title to sets of code; duty of officers, employees, etc., of state as to disposition of sets of code in custody thereof upon severance of connection with offices, etc.; effect of failure to dispose of code in manner prescribed by section.

Except those sets of codes distributed to members of the legislature and the lieutenant governor, the title to all of the sets of the annotated code, the distribution of which to officers and offices of the state and the several counties and municipalities thereof is provided for in this chapter, shall forever remain in the state of Alabama and said sets shall never become the personal property of any person or corporation, however long they shall have had possession thereof. Officers, employees and agents of the state and of the several counties thereof to whom a set of said annotated code is transmitted by the secretary of state under the provisions of this chapter, upon the severance of their connection with their offices, employments or agencies, shall deliver over to their successors, if any, and, if there are no successors, to the secretary of state, sets of the annotated code in their custody. Upon the failure of any officer, employee or agent to comply with the provisions of this section relative to the return of sets of annotated code in their custody, they and the sureties upon their official bonds, if any, shall be liable for the value of the sets or volumes thereof not returned as required by this section, to be recovered by action in the name of the state, commenced and prosecuted by the district attorney of the county of their respective residences in any court having jurisdiction of said action. (Acts 1977, No. 352, p. 470, § 5.)

§ 41-21-6. Taking of receipts from officers, etc., to whom sets of code distributed; maintenance by secretary of state of record book as to distribution of sets of code.

It shall be the duty of the secretary of state to take receipts from each public official of the state and of the several counties to whom he distributes sets of said annotated code. And, in the event that the secretary of state shall transmit sets for the use of all of the officers of a county to one officer of the county for distribution to the several officers in said county entitled thereto, the officer making such distribution shall take receipts from the officers, agents or employees in said county to whom he distributes said sets, showing the number of sets distributed and the date of distribution, which said receipts must be witnessed by the officer distributing the same, and said receipts shall forthwith be sent by registered mail to the office of the secretary of state.

The secretary of state shall register in a well-bound book, which shall be a permanent record in his office, the name, official title and address of every public official, employee or agent of the state and of the several counties thereof to whom has been distributed sets of said annotated code under the provisions of this chapter, and who has signed a receipt therefor and shall record the date of said distribution and the number of sets distributed to each such officer, agent or employee. Upon the return of any sets by officers, agents and employees of the state or of any county thereof, as provided in this chapter, the secretary of state shall note in said record book the date of said return and the number of sets or volumes returned. (Acts 1977, No. 352, p. 470, § 6.)

§ 41-21-7. Preparation and publication of compilations or abridgments of code provisions relating to specific agencies, departments, etc.

The governor of the state of Alabama shall be and he is hereby authorized to contract for the preparation and publication of a compilation or abridgment of those sections of the Code of Alabama relating to a specific agency, department, institution, bureau, board or commission which, in the opinion of the governor, is essential to the effective performance of the duties of said agency, department, institution, bureau, board or commission. Such contract for the publication of such compilation or abridgment may be entered into only after funds have been appropriated or is otherwise available to such agency, department, institution, bureau, board or commission for such publication. Such compilation shall be completely indexed and may include the annotations to the sections of the code included in the compilation. (Acts 1977, No. 352, p. 470, § 7.)

§ 41-21-8. Appropriation.

There is hereby appropriated, out of the moneys in the state treasury not otherwise appropriated, such amounts of money as are, or may be, necessary to carry out the provisions of this chapter relating to the distribution of the sets of said code to the several state and county officers, agents and employees. (Acts 1977, No. 352, p. 470, § 8.)

CHAPTER 22.

ADMINISTRATIVE PROCEDURE.

Effective date. — The act which added this chapter was approved by the governor on May 27, 1981. As to specific effective dates for various provisions, see § 41-22-27.

§ 41-22-1. Short title.

This chapter shall be known as and may be cited as the "Alabama Administrative Procedure Act." (Acts 1981, No. 81-855, p. 1534, § 1.)

Commentary

The Revised Model State Administrative Procedure Act does not have a short title section, but one is included here for convenient reference.

§ 41-22-2. Legislative intent and purpose; effect on substantive rights; applicability; authority to prescribe rules and regulations required in connection with this chapter.

(a) This chapter is intended to provide a minimum procedural code for the operation of all state agencies when they take action affecting the rights and duties of the public. Nothing in this chapter is meant to discourage agencies from adopting procedures conferring additional rights upon the public; and, save for express provisions of this act to the contrary, nothing in this chapter is meant to abrogate in whole or in part any statute prescribing procedural duties for an agency which are in addition to those provided herein.

(b) The purposes of the Alabama Administrative Procedure Act are:

(1) To provide legislative oversight of powers and duties delegated to administrative agencies;

(2) To increase public accountability of administrative agencies;

(3) To simplify government by assuring a uniform minimum procedure to which all agencies will be held in the conduct of their most important functions;

(4) To increase public access to governmental information;

(5) To increase public participation in the formulation of administrative rules;

(6) To increase the fairness of agencies in their conduct of contested case proceedings; and

(7) To simplify the process of judicial review of agency action as well as increase its ease and availability.

In accomplishing its objectives, the intention of this chapter is to strike a fair balance between these purposes and the need for efficient, economical and effective government administration.

(c) This chapter is not meant to alter the substantive rights of any person or agency. Its impact is limited to procedural rights with the expectation that better substantive results will be achieved in the everyday conduct of state government by improving the process by which those results are attained.

(d) Every state agency having express statutory authority to promulgate rules and regulations shall be governed by the provisions of this chapter and any additional provisions required by statute, and shall also have the authority to amend or repeal rules and regulations, and to prescribe methods and procedures required in connection therewith. Nothing in this chapter shall be construed as granting to any agency the authority to adopt or promulgate rules and regulations.

(e) All agencies whose rules or administrative decisions are subject to approval by the supreme court of Alabama and the department of insurance of the state of Alabama are exempted from the provisions of this chapter. (Acts 1981, No. 81-855, p. 1534, § 2.)

Collateral references. — 73 C.J.S., Public Administrative Bodies and Procedure, § 2.
1 Am. Jur. 2d, Administrative Law, § 2.

Commentary

The first two paragraphs of this section are adopted from Iowa Code § 17A.1 (1976 Cum. Supp.). The last two paragraphs are an adoption of the suggestions of the Alabama state bar administrative law committee.

This section is generally self-explanatory as a statement of purpose for the Alabama Administrative Procedure Act, both in the expression of what is and is not intended, as set out in the first and third clauses, and in the enumeration of its specific purposes in the second clause.

This section and section 41-22-25, together, provide the key to understanding the Alabama Administrative Procedure Act. These two sections provide a minimum procedural code creating rights in parties and imposing requirements upon agencies that are additional to those created or imposed by other statutes, including their individual enabling acts. The act, of course, applies only to procedural rights, not the substantive rights, involved in agency actions. Substantive rights and duties are the subject of the individual acts establishing the agencies, as well as their own particular rules and regulations. See 1 Am. Jur. 2d 809, Administrative Law, § 6 (1962). It is not intended to encourage agencies to reduce any procedural duties which may be greater than those herein imposed, nor to discourage them from providing greater procedural rights than herein provided.

Section 41-22-25 provides that the act "shall be construed broadly to effectuate its purposes", which are enumerated in this section. Thus, it is the intent of this act that the specific purposes enumerated in this section shall be applied to the actions of all agencies not specifically exempted from the provisions of this act, and to the courts, in interpreting any ambiguity in the language of this act for the purpose of giving effect to the requirements of its sections.

As stated in this section, "the intention of this act is to strike a fair balance between these purposes [enumerated in this section] and the need for efficient, economical, and effective government administration", as well as to make uniform the law of administrative rulemaking and adjudication. See generally 1 K. Davis, Administrative Law Treatise § 8.02, at 515-20 (1958).

The preceding paragraph excludes agencies whose rules or administrative decisions are subject to the approval of the supreme court. This excludes the Alabama state bar association. This section also purports to exclude the Alabama insurance department.

§ 41-22-3. Definitions.

The following words and phrases when used in this chapter shall, for the purpose of this chapter, have meanings respectively ascribed to them in this section, except when the context otherwise requires:

(1) AGENCY. Every board, bureau, commission, department, officer, or other administrative office or unit of the state, other than the legislature and its agencies, the water improvement commission, the air pollution control commission, the division of solid and hazardous wastes of the Alabama department of public health and Alabama state docks, the courts or the Alabama public service commission or the state banking department, whose administrative procedures are governed by sections 5-2A-8 and 5-2A-9. The term shall not include boards of trustees of postsecondary institutions, counties, municipalities, or any agencies of such local governmental units, unless they are expressly made subject to this act by general or special law.

(2) COMMITTEE. The joint committee on administrative regulation review shall be the members of the legislative council.

(3) CONTESTED CASE. A proceeding, including but not restricted to ratemaking, price fixing, and licensing, in which the legal rights, duties, or privileges of a party are required by law to be determined by an agency after an opportunity for hearing; provided, however, that the term shall not include intra-agency personnel actions.

(4) LICENSE. The whole or part of any agency franchise, permit, certificate, approval, registration, charter or similar form of permission required by law, but not a license required solely for revenue purposes when issuance of the license is merely a ministerial act.

(5) LICENSING. The agency process respecting the grant, denial, renewal, revocation, suspension, annulment, withdrawal, or amendment of a license or imposition of terms for the exercise of a license.

(6) PARTY. Each person or agency named or admitted as a party or properly seeking and entitled as a matter of right (whether established by constitution, statute or agency regulation or otherwise) to be admitted as a party, or admitted as an intervenor under section 41-22-14. An agency may by rule authorize limited forms of participation in agency proceedings for persons who are not eligible to become parties.

(7) PERSON. Any individual, partnership, corporation, association, governmental subdivision, or public or private organization of any character other than an agency.

(8) QUORUM. No less than a majority of the members of a multimember agency shall constitute a quorum authorized to act in the name of the agency, unless provided otherwise by statute.

(9) RULE. Each agency regulation, standard or statement of general applicability that implements, interprets, or prescribes law or policy, or that describes the organization, procedure, or practice requirements of any agency and includes any form which imposes any requirement or solicits any information not specifically required by statute or by an existing rule. The term includes the amendment or repeal of all existing rules but does not include the following:

a. Statements concerning only the internal management of an agency and not affecting private rights or procedures available to the public;

b. Declaratory rulings issued pursuant to section 41-22-11;

c. Intergovernmental, interagency, and intra-agency memoranda, directives, manuals or other communications which do not substantially affect the legal rights of, or procedures available to, the public or any segment thereof;

d. Determinations, decisions, orders, statements of policy and interpretations that are made in contested cases;

e. An order which is directed to a specifically named person or to a group of specifically named persons which does not constitute a general class, and the order is served on the person or persons to whom it is directed by the appropriate means applicable thereto. The fact that the named person who is being regulated serves a group of unnamed persons who will be affected does not make such order a rule;

f. An order which applies to a specifically described tract of real estate; or

g. Any rules or actions relating to:

1. The conduct of inmates of public institutions;

2. The curriculum of public educational institutions or the admission, conduct, discipline, or graduation of students of such institutions; provided, however, that this exception shall not extend to rules or actions of the state department of education;

3. Opinions issued by the attorney general of the state of Alabama;

4. The conduct of commissioned officers, warrant officers and enlisted persons in the military service; or

5. Advisory opinions issued by Alabama ethics commission. (Acts 1981, No. 81-855, p. 1534, § 3.)

Collateral references. — 73 C.J.S., Public Administrative Bodies and Procedure, § 21.
1 Am. Jur. 2d, Administrative Law, § 196.

Commentary

(1) By operation of sections 41-22-2 and 41-22-25, this act applies to all of the entities encompassed within this definition of "agency" except those specifically exempted (i.e., water improvement commission, the air pollution control commission, the division of solid waste of Alabama department of public health, Alabama state docks, state banking department, public service commission, and any legislative agency). This act encompasses state agencies and has no application to schools, counties, cities or their agencies. Agencies whose rules are subject to approval by the Alabama supreme court are excluded under section 41-22-2. Section 41-22-2 also purports to exclude the Alabama insurance department. In his treatise, Davis points out that nothing of substance hinges on the name applied to an agency; an agency by any other name is still an agency. K. Davis, Administrative Law Text § 1.01, at 1 (3d ed. 1972).

The first sentence of the definition of "agency" is adapted from the first sentence of Iowa Code § 17A.2(1) (1976 Cum. Supp.), with the exclusion of the courts and the legislature adopted from the second sentence of that Iowa subsection. The inclusion of every "bureau" in the definition is adopted from Ga. Code § 3A-102(a) (1975). The second sentence, excluding counties, municipalities, and local governments except as provided by other law, is an adaptation of Fla. Stat. § 120.52(1)(c) (1977).

(2) The membership of the legislative council is determined by section 29-6-2. Authority of the "committee" is found in sections 41-22-22 and 41-22-23.

(3) The first sentence of the definition of "contested case" is taken from section 1(2) of the Revised Model State Administrative Procedure Act promulgated by the National Conference of Commissioners on Uniform State Laws in 1961. The second sentence reinforces the definition that interagency personnel actions are not included within the definition of contested cases.

(4) The definition of "license" is adapted from the Revised Model State Administrative Procedure Act § 1(3) (1961), except that the word "franchise" and the last part of the definition, dealing with licenses issued for revenue purposes, are adopted from Fla. Stat. § 120.52(7) (1977).

The definition of a "license" is intended to include any form of permission required by law for which there are substantive requirements to be met, but to exclude forms of permission requiring payment of a fee but nothing substantive. For an example applicable to individuals, a person might obtain a motor vehicle operator's permit, or "driver's license," for which there are substantive requirements and which consequently is a license under this definition, and also a hunting license, for which there are no substantive requirements, but for which there is a fee required, and which, consequently, is not a license under this definition. As with the definition of "agency," here also the name applied is not important. It is the function of the required permission that determines whether this definition is applicable or inapplicable.

(5) The definition of "licensing" is adopted verbatim from the Revised Model State Administrative Procedure Act § 1(4) (1961) with the addition of the language "or imposition of terms for the exercise of a license," which is taken from Fla. Stat. § 120.52(8) (1977). The definition of "licensing" is intended to encompass every agency process or proceeding that in any way affects one's application for a license or renewal thereof, or one's ability to exercise the privileges conferred by license, or in any other way restricts or reduces such privileges.

(6) The first sentence of the definition of "party" is taken from the Revised Model State Administrative Procedure Act § 1(5) (1961), except for the parenthetical,

taken from Fla. Stat. § 120.52(10)(b) (1977). The final sentence of the definition, allowing the agency to authorize by rule the limited participation of persons not parties is a verbatim adoption of the second sentence of Fla. Stat. § 120.52(10)(c) (1977). Thus, this definition is intended to permit persons or agencies able to demonstrate a substantial interest in the outcome access to agency proceedings, either as parties or as limited participants. See also section 41-22-14.

(7) This definition of "person" is adopted verbatim from the Revised Model State Administrative Procedure Act § 1(6) (1961). It is intended to encompass any individual or entity other than an agency.

(8) The definition of "quorum" means a simple majority of current members of an agency.

(9) The general definition of "rule," up to the provision regarding forms is adopted from the Revised Model State Administrative Procedure Act § 1(7) (1961). The provision regarding forms is taken from Fla. Stat. § 120.52(14) (1977). The second sentence and exclusion clauses (a) and (b) are adopted from the Revised Model Act. Exclusion clause (c) is adopted from Iowa Code § 17A.2(7)(c) (1976 Cum. Supp.). Exclusion clause (d) is derived from Iowa Stat. § 17A.2(7)(d) (1976 Cum. Supp.) and Ga. Code § 3A-102(f)(4) (1975). Exclusion clauses (e) and [(g)(i)-(ii)] are included at the suggestion of the administrative law section of the Alabama state bar. Exclusion clause (f) removes orders of the state oil and gas board which pertain to specifically described tracts of land or areas which are less than statewide application from the definition of a rule. Rules of statewide application of the oil and gas board are within the coverage of this definition. Exclusion clause (g) has been included to emphasize that rules or actions relating to bodies listed in subparagraphs (9)(g)(1) through (9)(g)(5) are not rules within this section.

The importance in having a careful and precise definition of "rule" is to distinguish the regulatory activity that resembles legislation, applicable to all persons or a relatively large segment of the population outside the context of any specific controversy, from administrative activity that has a more judicial character and which, therefore, ought to be subject to judicial review. See generally, K. Davis, Administrative Law Text § 5.06, at 137-38 (3d ed. 1972).

§ 41-22-4. Adoption by agencies of rules governing organization, practice, etc.; public access to rules, orders, etc.; effect of rules, orders, etc., not made available to public.

(a) In addition to the other rulemaking requirements imposed by law, each agency shall:

(1) Adopt as a rule a description of its organization, stating the general course and method of its operations and the methods whereby the public may obtain information or make submissions or requests;

(2) Adopt rules of practice setting forth the nature and requirements of all formal and informal procedures available, including a description of all forms and instructions used by the agency;

(3) Make available for public inspection and copying, at cost, all rules and all other written statements of policy or interpretations formulated, adopted or used by the agency in the discharge of its functions;

(4) Make available for public inspection and copying, at cost, and index by name and subject all final orders, decisions, and opinions which are issued after October 1, 1982, except those expressly made confidential or privileged by statute or order of court.

(b) No agency rule, order, or decision shall be valid or effective against any person or party nor may it be invoked by the agency for any purpose until it has been made available for public inspection and indexed as required by this section and the agency has given all notices required by section 41-22-5. This provision is not applicable in favor of any person or party who has actual knowledge thereof, and the burden of proving such knowledge shall be on the agency. (Acts 1981, No. 81-855, p. 1534, § 4.)

Collateral references. — 73 C.J.S., Public Administrative Bodies and Procedure, §§ 2, 130-132.

Commentary

This section is adapted from Revised Model State Administrative Procedure Act § 2 (1961) with certain modifications taken from various other state acts. Subsections (1)(a) and (1)(b) are taken directly from the Revised Model Act. Subsection (1)(c) includes the language "at cost" which is similar to "and copying, at no more than cost," which is taken from Fla. Stat. § 120.53(2) (1977). Subsection (1)(d) is from Ga. Code § 3A-103(a)(4) (1975), except for the language "and index by name and subject," which is from Iowa Code § 17A.3(1)(d) (1976 Cum. Supp.). Subsection (2) is taken from Ga. Code § 3A-103(b) (1975) with modifications, derived from Iowa Code § 17A.3(2) (1976 Cum. Supp.), to encompass the indexing requirement and to place the burden of proof of the person's actual knowledge upon the agency.

The requirement that no agency rule be effective until all required notice has been given is included at the suggestion of the administrative law section of the Alabama state bar.

This section is intended to insure the public of fair notice of all agency law, fair notice being one of the essentials of due process. See Mullane v. Central Hanover Bank & Trust Co., 339 U.S. 306 (1950); L. Tribe, American Constitutional Law 544 (1978). Agencies will be required to educate the public as to the nature of their rights and how to exercise them.

Adoption of rules describing the internal organization of an agency and the actual procedures and policies of a state agency will enable the public to hold agencies to the standards to which it is intended they be held.

The indexing requirement will enable the public to determine whether there have been rulings, and what such rulings were, in areas of agency responsibility of interest to them. By having agency decisions published and available, there will be no need for case-by-case determination of agency policies of organization and procedure. Departure from procedural rules will be readily apparent, and the public will have available the means to get relief from such departure. Thus, the public will derive the benefit of consistency in agency procedure.

§ 41-22-5. Notice of intent to adopt, amend, or repeal rules; submission of data, views, etc., by interested persons; procedure for adoption of emergency rules; effect of this section on other procedural requirements; validity of rules in substantial compliance with this section; limitation of proceedings to contest rules.

(a) Prior to the adoption, amendment, or repeal of any rule, the agency shall:

(1) Give at least 35 days' notice of its intended action. Date of publication in the Alabama Administrative Monthly shall constitute the date of notice. The notice shall include a statement of either the terms or substance of the intended action or a description of the subjects and issues involved, and the time when, the place where, and the manner in which interested persons may present their views thereon. The notice shall be given to the chairman of the legislative committee, as provided in section 41-22-23, and mailed to all persons who pay the cost of such mailing and who have made timely request of the agency for advance notice of its rulemaking proceedings and shall be published, prior to any action thereon, in the Alabama Administrative Monthly. A complete copy of the proposed rule shall be filed with the secretary of the agency and the legislative reference service.

(2) Afford all interested persons reasonable opportunity to submit data, views, or arguments, orally or in writing. The agency shall consider fully all written and oral submissions respecting the proposed rule. Upon adoption of a rule, the agency, if conflicting views are submitted on the proposed rule, shall issue a concise statement of the principal reasons for and against its adoption, incorporating therein its reasons for overruling any considerations urged against its adoption.

(b) Notwithstanding any other provision of this chapter to the contrary, if an agency finds that an immediate danger to the public health, safety, or welfare requires adoption of a rule upon fewer than 35 days' notice or that action is required by or to comply with a federal statute or regulation which requires adoption of a rule upon fewer than 35 days' notice and states in writing its reasons for that finding, it may proceed without prior notice or hearing or upon any abbreviated notice and hearing that it finds practicable, to adopt an emergency rule. The rule shall become effective immediately, unless otherwise stated therein, upon the filing of the rule and a copy of the written statement of the reasons therefor with the legislative reference service and the secretary of the agency. The rule may be effective for a period of not longer than 120 days and shall not be renewable. An agency shall not adopt the same or a substantially similar emergency rule within one calendar year from its first adoption unless the agency clearly establishes it could not reasonably be foreseen during the initial 120-day period that such emergency would continue or would likely reoccur during the next nine months. The adoption of the same or a substantially similar rule by normal rule making procedures is not precluded.

(c) It is the intent of this section to establish basic minimum procedural requirements for the adoption, amendment or repeal of administrative rules. Except for emergency rules which are provided for in subsection (b) of this section, the provisions of this section are applicable to the exercise of any rulemaking authority conferred by any statute, but nothing in this section repeals or diminishes additional requirements imposed by law or diminishes or repeals any summary power granted by law to the state or any agency thereof.

(d) No rule adopted after October 1, 1982, is valid unless adopted in substantial compliance with this section. A proceeding to contest any rule on the ground of noncompliance with the procedural requirements of this section must be commenced within two years from the effective date of the rule; provided, however, that a proceeding to contest a rule based on failure to provide notice as herein required may be commenced at any time. (Acts 1981, No. 81-855, p. 1534, § 5.)

Collateral references. — 73 C.J.S., Public Administrative Bodies and Procedure, §§ 60, 130.

1 Am. Jur. 2d, Administrative Law, §§ 92, 189, 230.

Commentary

Subsection (a) of this section is adopted from the Revised Model State Administrative Procedure Act, § 3 (1961), except that the Model Act requires 20 days' notice of agency action while this section requires 35, as does the Iowa statute, Iowa Stat. 17A.4(1)(a) (1976 Cum. Supp.). This section also requires publication of notice in the Alabama Administrative Monthly and notice mailed to those who request it, increasing the likelihood that interested parties will gain actual notice. All proposed rules and amendments must be filed in three places: (1) secretary of the agency, (2) legislative reference service, and (3) joint committee on administrative regulative review. The 35-day notice requirement commences with the date of publication of the Alabama Administrative Monthly and not the date of filing with the legislative reference service. The complete rule must be filed but the publishing of the "terms or substance" of the rule is all that is required under the notice provisions.

Subsection (b) of this section is an amalgamation of the Revised Model State Administrative Procedure Act § 4(b)(2) and portions of statutes of several other states. The language from the beginning through the comma after "contrary", is adopted from the Tenn. Code Ann. § 4-5-104(g)(1) (1979 Replacement). The provision for the immediate effectiveness of emergency rules upon filing is also derived from the same Tennessee statute. The remainder of subsection (b) of this section is also from Tenn. Code Ann. § 4-5-104(g)(1) (1979 Replacement) except that the wording "and shall not be renewable" is adopted from Fla. Stat. § 120.54(9)(c) (1977). The provision that allows rule adoption in less than 35 days when required by federal statute or regulation was added by the legislature to accommodate occasions when the industrial relations board and others must make immediate rule changes. This provision is only applicable for 120 days and is treated as any other emergency rule.

Subsection (c) of this section is adopted directly from Ga. Code § 3A-104(2)(c) (1975). This act does not grant any agency rulemaking authority nor does it expand or diminish the rulemaking authority granted the agency by statute. Subsection (d) of this section is a direct adoption of § 3(c) of the Revised Model State Administrative Procedure Act, except that the provision allowing for commencement of a proceeding to contest a rule based on failure to provide required notice at any time was adopted upon the suggestion of the administrative law section of Alabama state bar.

As stated in subsection (c) of this section, this section is intended to establish minimum procedural requirements for the adoption, amendment, or repeal of administrative rules, and applies to any rulemaking authority, but is not intended to lessen any requirements imposed upon such authority which are greater than or additional to those requirements established by this section.

The notice requirement is established for the purpose of creating an informed public. Thirty-five days' notice is required in order that such notice will have time to appear in the Alabama Administrative Monthly, and in order to give all interested persons reasonable opportunity to air their views. An agency is required to provide information regarding the adoption of a rule within 30 days of a request for such, as another means of assuring the public of the availability of information within a reasonable time frame.

The use of the phrase "interested persons" in subdivision (2) of subsection (a) of this section is intended to be interpreted broadly. It is not to be construed to confine interested persons to those who might be defined in terms of the constitutional doctrine of standing to sue. Nor is the phrase to be construed as narrowly as the similar phrase in Rule 17(a) of the Alabama Rules of Civil Procedure. Thus "interested persons" may be construed to include those with a genuine and deeply felt interest even if that interest is not an economic one.

Subsection (b) of this section is intended to enable an agency to exercise its rulemaking powers without the constraints of normal procedure as provided by this act when protection of the public health, safety, or welfare requires immediate action or when immediate implementation is required by federal statute or rule. Such action may include, but is not limited to summary processes such as quarantines, contrabands, seizures and the like authorized by law without notice. Limitations of time are placed upon any rule so adopted and the power to adopt a substantially similar rule to insure that this provision in no case becomes a method of circumventing other requirements of this act. One hundred twenty days is provided as a reasonable time for such an emergency to have subsided or for normal rulemaking measures within the scope of this act to have been taken.

It is provided that no rule adopted without compliance with this rule is valid, but there is a two-year limitation imposed on challenges to the rule, except where the challenges are based on failure to give notice.

§ 41-22-6. Designation of agency secretary; filing of copies of rules with secretary; information as to authorship of rules; filing of copies of rules with legislative reference service; maintenance of and public access to permanent registers of rules; effective dates of rules.

(a) Each agency shall have an officer designated as its secretary and shall file in the office of the secretary of the agency a certified copy of each rule adopted by it, including all rules, as defined in this chapter, existing on the effective date of this act. Each rule or regulation promulgated, whether the original or a revision, and all copies thereof, shall have the name or names of the author or authors, respectively, on its face. The secretary of the agency shall keep a permanent register of the rules open to public inspection.

(b) The secretary of each agency shall file in the office of the legislative reference service, no later than 15 days after the filing with the secretary of the agency, in a form and manner prescribed by the legislative reference service, a certified copy of each rule adopted by it, including all rules, as defined in this chapter, existing on the effective date of this act. The legislative reference service shall keep a permanent register of the rules open to public inspection.

(c) Each rule hereafter adopted is effective 35 days after filing with the legislative reference service, except that:

(1) If a later date is required by statute or specified in the rule, the later date is the effective date;

(2) Subject to applicable constitutional or statutory provisions, a rule becomes effective immediately upon filing with the legislative reference service, or at a subsequent stated date prior to indexing and publication, or at a stated date less than 35 days after filing, if the agency finds:

a. That a statute so provides; or

b. That this effective date is necessary because of immediate danger to the public health, safety or welfare. In any subsequent action contesting the effective date of a rule promulgated under this paragraph, the burden of proof shall be on the agency to justify its finding. The agency's finding and a brief statement of the reasons therefor shall be filed with and made a part of the rule. Prior to indexing and publication, the agency shall make reasonable efforts to apprise the persons who may be affected by its rules of the adoption of rules made effective under the terms of this paragraph. (Acts 1981, No. 81-855, p. 1534, § 6.)

Cross references. — As to the effective date of this act generally and the effective date of subsections (a) and (b) of this section, see § 41-22-27.

Collateral references. — 73 C.J.S., Public Administrative Bodies and Procedure, § 22.

Commentary

This section is substantially an adoption of Iowa Code § 17A.5 (1976 Cum. Supp.), except for such substitutions and deletions as are necessary to render this section consistent with this act.

This section insures that the public has reasonable opportunity to be informed of all agency rules, both those existing at the time of passage of this act and those later promulgated, and has permanent access to all such rules. At least 35 days is required to lapse between filing and the effective date of a rule, which is consistent with the requirement for published notice, as discussed in the commentary to section 41-22-5. Section 41-22-5 provides 35 days notice and "notice" begins on the date of publication of the administrative monthly. The exceptions allowed to the 35-day filing requirement are intended to give the rights of the public greater protection; this end is accomplished both in specifying that a later date, if required by statute or within the rule itself, shall take precedence over the 35-day requirement, and in allowing a rule to become effective sooner than the passing of the 35 days if statutorily permitted only if further notice requirements are met.

The emergency rule exception, which allows an earlier effective date, is intended to provide protection to the public health, safety, and welfare or where implementation with less than 35 days' notice is required by federal law; this section still requires an agency reasonably to attempt to inform those persons most affected by the rule of its impending effect upon them, and that an agency be prepared to prove the necessity of circumventing the normal rulemaking and filing requirements under this act should its actions be contested. Thus, the intent of this section is to protect the public right and access to information regarding agency rules, and provide the agency with the flexibility required to both keep the public informed and carry out its function in the public interest. In his commentary on the emergency rule provision, Professor Bonfield has written helpful interpretative commentary. Bonfield, The Iowa Administrative Procedure Act: Background, Construction, Applicability, Public Access to Agency Law, The Rulemaking Process, 60 Iowa L. Rev. 731, 887-91 (1975). The exemption from the normal time requirement can be used only where, in the language of this act, there is an "immediate danger to the public health, safety or welfare." Commenting on the closely similar language of the Iowa Act: "peril to the public health, safety, or welfare", he states:

> This means that the agency must pinpoint the precise nature of that peril in its finding. The terms "health, safety, and welfare" should be construed narrowly in accordance with the notion that a principal reason for the enactment of the [Procedure Act] was to secure as much standardization of administrative procedure as possible. The exception should also be construed narrowly to maximize the fulfillment of the very important objectives sought to be achieved by the major provision from which the exception operates — the objectives of providing the public with fair notice of a rule's existence and with a chance to adjust to its prescriptions. Id. at 887.

§ 41-22-7. Contents, publication, and availability of agency administrative codes, Alabama Administrative Code, and Alabama Administrative Monthly; filing of rules, amendments and repealers with legislative reference service; uniform system for numbering rules; omission from publications of rules which are applicable to only one county; cost to agencies for use of Alabama Administrative Monthly.

(a) The secretary of the agency shall establish and maintain an official register of regulations which shall be compiled, indexed, published in loose-leaf form, and kept up to date by the secretary of the agency. This register of regulations shall be known as "The (name of the agency) Administrative Code," and it shall be made available, upon request, at cost to all persons for copying and inspection and to those persons who subscribe thereto. Supplementation shall be made as often as is practicable, but at least once every year. The secretary of the agency shall number and renumber rules to conform with a uniform numbering system devised by the legislative reference service.

(b) The secretary of the agency may omit from its administrative code rules that are general in form but are applicable to only one county or a part thereof. Rules so omitted shall be filed with the secretary of the agency, and exclusion from publication shall not affect their validity or effectiveness. The secretary of the agency shall publish a compilation of and index to all rules so omitted at least annually.

(c) The secretary of the agency shall make copies of the agency's administrative code available on an annual subscription basis, at cost.

(d) The secretary of the agency shall file with the legislative reference service, not later than 15 days after filing with the secretary of the agency, all rules or amendments or repeal of rules promulgated by the agency. In addition, the secretary of the Alabama public service commission, the water improvement commission, the air pollution control commission, the division of solid and hazardous wastes of the Alabama department of public health and the Alabama state docks shall file with the legislative reference service, not later than 15 days after filing with the secretary of the commission, all rules or amendments or repeal of rules promulgated by that commission.

(e) The legislative reference service shall establish and maintain an official register of regulations which shall be so compiled, indexed, published in loose-leaf form and kept up to date by the legislative reference service. The register of regulations shall be known as the "Alabama Administrative Code," and shall be made available at cost, upon request, to all persons for inspection and copying or who subscribe thereto. Supplementation shall be made as often as is practicable, but at least once every year. The legislative reference service shall devise a uniform numbering system for rules and may renumber rules before publication to conform with the system.

(f) The legislative reference service shall publish a monthly bulletin entitled the "Alabama Administrative Monthly," which shall contain a statement of either the terms or substance of all rules filed during the preceding month, excluding rules in effect on October 1, 1982, together with other material required by law and such other material the agency or committee determines to be of general interest.

(g) The legislative reference service may omit from the Alabama Administrative Monthly and the Alabama Administrative Code rules that are general in form but are applicable to only one county or a part thereof. Rules so omitted shall be filed with the legislative reference service, and exclusion from publication shall not affect their validity or effectiveness. The legislative reference service shall publish a compilation of, and index to, all rules so omitted at least annually.

(h) The legislative reference service shall make copies of the Alabama Administrative Code and copies of the Alabama Administrative Monthly available at cost on an annual subscription basis.

(i) The legislative reference service shall charge each agency using the Alabama Administrative Monthly a space rate computed to cover all publishing or printing costs related to the Alabama Administrative Monthly. (Acts 1981, No. 81-855, p. 1534, § 7.)

Cross references. — As to the effective date of this act generally and the effective date of subsections (a) through (e) of this section, see § 41-22-27.

Collateral references. — 73 C.J.S., Public Administrative Bodies and Procedure, § 101.

Commentary

The first sentence of subsection (a) of this section is from Va. Code § 9-6.19 (1975 Cum. Supp.), except for the specifications that the material be compiled and published in loose-leaf form, which is derived from Iowa Code § 17A.6(1) (1976 Cum. Supp.). The second sentence is derived from Iowa Code § 17A.6(3) (1976 Cum. Supp.). The requirement that supplementation be as often as practicable comes from Fla. Stat. § 120.55(1)(b) (1977) although Florida requires a minimum of monthly supplementation, while this section requires it annually.

Subsection (d) of this section provides that although several agencies have been excluded in section 41-22-2 and subdivision (1) of section 41-22-3 from coverage of the act, all will file their rules with the legislative reference service. An excluded agency's failure to file a rule does not affect its validity since this section is intended to place in one convenient place all agency rules.

Subsections (b) and (g) of this section provide that local rules are filed with the secretary of the agency and the legislative reference service but are not published. An index is maintained by the agency secretary and the legislative reference service.

Subsection (f) of this section is an adoption of Revised Administrative Procedure Act § 5(b) (1961) and also contains provisions for the naming of the monthly bulletin, and for the inclusion of other materials which are material to the promulgation of the rules under scrutiny.

Subsection (g) of this section is adopted from the last three sentences of Fla. Stat. § 120.55(1)(b) (1977). Subsection (h) of this section is adopted from Fla. Stat. § 120.55(1)(g) (1977). Subsection (i) of this section is adopted from Fla. Stat. § 120.55(1)(h) (1977).

This section, requiring the legislative reference service to maintain, in a uniform manner, a master register of all rules of all agencies, and to publish these rules, both in supplemented code form and also to publish a monthly compilation of all new rules, is intended to provide the public and all legislators, judges, attorneys-at-law, the state agencies and their members, and other governmental officers, full and free access to all of the rules of administrative agencies in the state. The information, via these publications, is to be available from the legislative reference service at the cost of publication, in order to provide as free access to this body of law as economically feasible. Rules applicable to only one county are omitted from the publication requirement, except in the annual supplement, to reduce the volume of material and the cost of publication, and, consequently, reduce the cost to the public of obtaining these publications.

This section is based upon the premise that there can be no openness in government, indeed no due process of law, without publication of, and full public access to, the rules by which the government governs. For further discussion on this point see the Preface. See also Fletcher v. Peck, 10 U.S. (6 Cranch) 87 (1810) and the very theoretical discussion in L. Tribe, American Constitutional Law 456-563 (1978), especially at 465-67 (contract impairment clause) and 499-501 (applying bill of attainder doctrine to administrative and executive action).

§ 41-22-8. Form for petition for adoption, amendment or repeal of rules; procedure upon submission of petition.

Each agency shall prescribe by rule the form for petition requesting the adoption, amendment or repeal of a rule and the procedure for submission, consideration, and disposition thereof. Within 60 days after submission of a petition, the agency either shall deny the petition in writing on the merits, stating its reasons for the denial, or initiate rulemaking proceedings in accordance with section 41-22-5. (Acts 1981, No. 81-855, p. 1534, § 8.)

Commentary

This section is adopted from Iowa Code § 17A.7 (1976 Cum. Supp.).

This section is intended to provide the members of the public with a mechanism for affecting the content of an agency's rules but leaves to each agency to determine the form and procedure of petitioning the particular agency. The section is mandatory in that such a procedure "shall" be prescribed by individual agency rule.

By imposing a time limit of 60 days upon the agency action, it is also intended that agencies be constrained to taking timely action upon each petition, so that the public can derive the benefit of a decision within a reasonable time. If the petition is denied, the agency is required to state its reasons for such denial for the public's information, a requirement consistent with the purposes of this act as reflected in such other sections as sections 41-22-7 and 41-22-11.

§ 41-22-9. Adoption by reference of codes, standards, and regulations of other agencies of this state or the United States or of other approved organizations; form of reference; availability from agency of information as to rules, etc., adopted by reference.

An agency may adopt, by reference in its rules and without publishing the adopted matter in full, all or any part of a code, standard or regulation which has been adopted by any other agency of this state or any agency of the United States or by a generally recognized organization or association approved by the joint committee administrative regulation review. The reference shall fully identify the adopted matter by date and otherwise. The agency shall have available copies of the adopted matter for inspection and the rules shall state where copies of the adopted matter can be obtained and any charge therefor as of the time the rule is adopted. (Acts 1981, No. 81-855, p. 1534, § 9.)

Commentary

This section is a direct adoption of N.C. Gen. Stat. § 150A-14 (1976 Interim Supp.). There is no corresponding section in the Model State Administrative Procedure Act.

This section is intended to ease the difficulty in the adoption of rules, and lessen the volume of material published and the cost of publication thereof, by allowing adoption by reference as described. This is consistent with section 41-22-7 by providing that the public have free access to the information, either by inspection thereof at the agency, or by obtaining the material from a source and at a cost specified within the rule adopting the matter. The legitimacy of the matter adopted is insured by restricting the original adopting source to other state agencies, U.S. government agencies, rules of a generally recognized organization or association, or by a generally recognized organization or association approved by the joint committee on administrative regulation review, as well as by the requirement that the adopted matter be fully identified. The rule adopting the referenced material is intended to be filed, indexed, and published just as any other agency rule is, thus putting the public on notice of what the adopted material is and where public access to it may be gained. This allows the department of pensions and securities to adopt by reference rules of health and human resources and other agencies, the adoption of the Southern Building Code, and like standards.

The practice of incorporation by reference, while said to be rare in administrative procedure codes, see Daye, North Carolina's New Administrative Procedure Act: An Interpretive Analysis, 53 N.C.L. Rev. 833, 864 (1975), is fully consistent with practice in civil actions in the courts of Alabama. See Ala. R. Civ. P. 9(d) & 10(c). Moreover, incorporation by reference has been used in this state in other legislation including a general provision assuming that incorporation is a valid legislative technique. Ala. Code § 1-1-15(b) (1975), as well as the statute incorporating the common law of England. Ala. Code § 1-3-1 (1975). The advantages of such incorporation by reference have been described as follows:

An agency dealing with a subject upon which there has been promulgated, for example, a national code may wish to adopt such a code without publishing the code itself. This process, if pursued, would constitute an adoption by reference, and is permitted by [this] section. . . .

It is clear that the adoption-by-reference provision is not intended to permit dispensing with either the prior notice requirement (including a statement of the terms or substance of the proposed rule) or the procedural opportunity to participate through the submission of data, views, and arguments required by subdivision (2) of subsection (a) of section 41-22-5. For example, the intent to adopt some standardized code by reference would [itself] seem to be a matter upon which views might be submitted in the course of a rulemaking proceeding. Daye, supra at 864.

§ 41-22-10. Action for declaratory judgment as to validity or applicability of rule; stay of enforcement of rule by injunction.

The validity or applicability of a rule may be determined in an action for a declaratory judgment or its enforcement stayed by injunctive relief in the circuit court of Montgomery county, unless otherwise specifically provided by statute, if the court finds that the rule, or its threatened application, interferes with or impairs, or threatens to interfere with or impair, the legal rights or privileges of the plaintiff. The agency shall be made a party to the action. In passing on such rules the court shall declare the rule invalid only if it finds that it violates constitutional provisions or exceeds the statutory authority of the agency or was adopted without substantial compliance with rulemaking procedures provided for in this chapter. (Acts 1981, No. 81-855, p. 1534, § 10.)

Collateral references. — 73 C.J.S., Public Administrative Bodies and Procedure, §§ 44, 45.

Commentary

This section is an adoption of Tenn. Code Ann. § 4-5-106 (1979 Replacement) except that the word "plaintiff" is substituted for "complainant", and "action" is substituted for "suit", which is the language used in section 41-22-7 of the Revised Model State Administrative Procedure Act, and is consonant with practice under the Alabama Rules of Civil Procedure.

This section also allows for injunctive relief, for which provision was made at the suggestion of the administrative law section of the Alabama state bar.

Requiring the plaintiff to request the agency to pass on the question before proceeding to the circuit court for a declaratory judgment thereon could have the effect of reducing the burden upon the plaintiff, the agency, and the court, in time, costs, and in other ways, if the agency makes a decision on the question that makes a court judgment unnecessary. The procedure in the circuit court would, of course, be governed by the Alabama Uniform Declaratory Judgements Act, Ala. Code §§ 6-6-220 through 6-6-232 (1975). Declaratory relief might be available even in the absence of this section of the Administrative Procedure Act. Nevertheless, this section appears to make the matter clear and to require that the petitioner exhaust his administrative remedies before seeking judicial declaratory or injunctive relief.

It is interesting to note a general reluctance on the part of state courts in the absence of a section such as this one, to grant declaratory or injunctive relief. As Professor Kenneth Culp Davis has noted:

> The state courts often have been either unable or unwilling to copy from the federal courts what is especially splendid about the use of injunction and declaratory judgment, usually in combination, as general utility remedies for nonstatutory review of administrative action. The two remedies have been so successful in the federal courts that any informed observer would expect alert state judges to strive to copy the federal system, which has been achieved almost entirely through judicial action. See generally, K. Davis, Administrative Law Text § 24.05, at 461 (3d ed. 1972).

§ 41-22-11. Petition for declaratory ruling as to validity of rule, as to applicability of any rule or statute enforceable by an agency, or as to meaning and scope of agency order; form and contents; binding effect of agency ruling; effect of failure to issue ruling; judicial review.

(a) On the petition of any person substantially affected by a rule, an agency may issue a declaratory ruling with respect to the validity of the rule or with respect to the applicability to any person, property or state of facts of any rule or statute enforceable by it or with respect to the meaning and scope of any order of the agency. The petition seeking an administrative determination under this section shall be in writing and shall state with particularity facts sufficient to show the person seeking relief is substantially affected by the rule. Each agency shall prescribe by rule the form of such petitions and the procedure for their submission, consideration and disposition, and shall prescribe in its rules the circumstances in which rulings shall or shall not be issued.

(b) A declaratory ruling is binding on the agency and the person requesting it unless it is altered or set aside by a court in a proper proceeding. Such rulings are subject to review in the circuit court of Montgomery county, unless otherwise specifically provided by the statute, in the manner provided in section 41-22-12 for the review of decisions in contested cases. Failure of the agency to issue a declaratory ruling on the merits within 45 days of the request for such ruling shall constitute a denial of the request as well as a denial of the merits of the request and shall be subject to judicial review. (Acts 1981, No. 81-855, p. 1534, § 11.)

Commentary

The first sentence is adopted from Tenn. Code Ann. § 4-5-107 (1979 Replacement), except that the language "any person substantially affected by a rule" is taken from Fla. Stat. § 120.56(1) (1977). The second sentence is adopted from Fla. Stat. § 120.56(2) (1977). The first part of the third sentence, requiring the agency to prescribe by rule the form of the petition, is an adoption of the last sentence of Tenn. Code Ann. § 4-513 (1976 Cum. Supp.) while the last part is adapted from N.C. Gen. Stat. § 150A-17 (1975 Cum. Supp.). The fourth sentence, stating that a declaratory ruling is binding on the requesting party and the agency, is also adopted from N.C. Gen. Stat. § 150A-17 (1975 Cum. Supp.). The fifth sentence, dealing with review of such hearing, is adopted from Tenn. Code Ann. § 4-5-107 (1979 Replacement). The last sentence, limiting the agency to 45 days to act on the request, is adopted from N.C. Gen. Stat. § 150A-17 (1975 Cum. Supp.), except that the North Carolina statute provides for 60 days.

This section is intended to protect the rights of members of the public by providing a declaratory ruling mechanism by which an agency may, upon petition to the agency, pass on the applicability of an agency rule or of a statute enforceable by the agency or on the meaning and scope of an order of the agency, with respect to the situation or property of the petitioner or petitioners. Consistent with other sections of this act, this section requires that each agency adopt rules setting forth fully the form of petition required, the procedures involved, and the circumstances required to elicit a ruling, so that the public is fully informed in advance of what action is available to them from the agency. Both the agency and the public interest are protected from the issuance of unwarranted declaratory rulings by the requirement that the petition document the substantial interest of the petitioner. The requirement that a ruling is binding upon both the petitioner and the agency is intended to give the ruling the force of law to the petitioner, and yet protect the petitioner from inconsistencies caused by a shift in the agency's policy stance or other reasons. Any such ruling is judicially reviewable, and the petitioner is further protected by the provision that failure of the agency to rule pursuant to the petition within 45 days constitutes a reviewable denial of the request.

This section of the act may be considered as the administrative analogue of the Alabama Uniform Declaratory Judgments Act, Ala. Code §§ 6-6-204 through 6-6-232 (1975). Many of the provisions of this act find counterparts in the general declaratory statute. Thus, this section of this act read in connection with the section on construction, section 41-22-25 (the act "shall be construed broadly to effectuate its purposes") finds a counterpart in a section of the Declaratory Judgments Act that provides that it "is to be liberally construed and administered." Ala. Code § 6-6-221 (1975). This section should also be read in light of Ala. R. Civ. P., Rule 57, which provides, inter alia: "The existence of another adequate remedy does not preclude a judgment for declaratory relief in cases where it is appropriate." On the other hand, when parties have sought relief under this section and feel that the declaratory ruling was erroneous, their proper and only recourse is by appeal and not by commencing another proceeding under the Declaratory Judgments Act. See Alabama Pub. Serv. Comm'n v. AAA Motor Lines, Inc., 272 Ala. 362, 369, 131 So. 2d 172, 177 (1961).

§ 41-22-12. Notice and opportunity for hearing in contested cases; contents of notice; procedure upon failure of notified party to appear; presentation of evidence and argument; right to counsel; disposition by stipulation, settlement, etc.; contents of record; public attendance at oral proceedings; recordings and transcripts of oral proceedings.

(a) In a contested case, all parties shall be afforded an opportunity for hearing after reasonable notice in writing delivered either by personal service as in civil actions or by certified mail, return receipt requested. However, an agency may provide by rule for the delivery of such notice by other means. Delivery of the notice referred to in this subsection shall constitute commencement of the contested case proceeding.

(b) The notice shall include:

(1) A statement of the time, place and nature of the hearing;

(2) A statement of the legal authority and jurisdiction under which the hearing is to be held;

(3) A reference to the particular sections of the statutes and rules involved; and

(4) A short and plain statement of the matters asserted. If the agency or other party is unable to state the matters in detail at the time the notice is served, the initial notice may be limited to a statement of the issues involved. Thereafter, upon application, a more definite and detailed statement shall be furnished.

(c) If a party fails to appear in a contested case proceeding after proper service of notice, the presiding officer may, if no adjournment is granted, proceed with the hearing and make a decision in the absence of the party.

(d) Opportunity shall be afforded all parties to respond and present evidence and argument on all material issues involved and to be represented by counsel at their own expense.

(e) Unless precluded by statute, informal dispositions may be made of any contested case by stipulation, agreed settlement, consent order or default or by another method agreed upon by the parties in writing.

(f) The record in a contested case shall include:

(1) All pleadings, motions, and intermediate rulings;

(2) All evidence received or considered and all other submissions; provided, in the event that evidence in any proceeding may contain proprietary and confidential information, steps shall be taken to prevent public disclosure of that information;

(3) A statement of all matters officially noticed;

(4) All questions and offers of proof, objections and rulings thereon;

(5) All proposed findings and exceptions;

(6) Any decision, opinion or report by the hearing officer at the hearing; and

(7) All staff memoranda or data submitted to the hearing officer or members of the agency in connection with their consideration of the case unless such memoranda or data is protected as confidential or privileged; provided, if such memoranda or data contains information of a proprietary and confidential nature, it shall be protected by the agency from public disclosure.

(g) Oral proceedings shall be open to the public, unless private hearings are otherwise authorized by law. Oral proceedings shall be recorded either by mechanized means or by qualified shorthand reporters. Oral proceedings or any part thereof shall be transcribed at the request of any party with the expense of the transcription charged to the requesting party. The recording or stenographic notes of oral proceedings or the transcription thereof shall be filed with and maintained by the agency for at least five years from the date of decision and shall be made available for inspection by the public, except in those cases where private hearings are authorized by law, or where the proceedings shall be ordered sealed by order of court, or are required to be sealed by statute.

(h) Findings of fact shall be based solely on the evidence in the record and on matters officially noticed in the record. (Acts 1981, No. 81-855, p. 1534, § 12.)

Collateral references. — 73 C.J.S., Public Administrative Bodies and Procedure, §§ 87, 88, 130, 133-138, 153.

1 Am. Jur. 2d, Administrative Law, §§ 78, 88, 232, 287, 315, 328, 397-426.

Commentary

This section is an adoption of Iowa Code § 17A.12 (1976 Cum. Supp.) except that subdivision (7) of subsection (f) of this section is adapted from § 9(e)(1) of the Revised Model State Administrative Procedure Act (1961).

Administrative agencies make law by issuing general statements of policy and by resolving specific disputes on a case-by-case basis. See Bonfield, The Iowa Administrative Procedure Act: Background, Construction, Applicability, Public Access to Agency Law, The Rulemaking Process, 60 Iowa L. Rev. 731, 924-28 (1975). These methods of conflict resolution are delegated preemptions of the legislative and judicial functions respectively. This section focuses on the latter situation in which an action contemplated or executed by the agency is being contested by an affected party and the procedure by which such conflict may approach resolution within the agency itself without forcing the parties to resort to the more costly and lengthy proceedings of the traditional judicial forum.

There are several immediate problems inherent in such a scheme: the agency is required to police itself and so is presented with a conflict of interest when it demands a continual reevaluation of its policies and its statutory purpose. This section and those that follow attempt to delineate procedures consonant with the flexibility of administrative decisionmaking processes as well as preparing a record upon which formal judicial action may be taken if the conflict cannot be resolved within the agency structure. Thus, the procedures coincide with the Alabama Rules of Civil Procedure with minor variations.

400

Subsection (a) of this section provides for a hearing with delivery of notice commencing the proceeding, rather than the filing of the claim as provided for civil actions under Ala. R. Civ. P., Rule 3. The service requirements of the first sentence of subsection (a) of this section are currently acceptable under Ala. R. Civ. P., Rule 4. The second sentence provides that an agency may provide by rule a mode of delivery other than by personal service or certified mail.

Subsection (b) of this section delineates the substance of the notice and is comparable to the requirements of brevity and clarity intrinsic to rule pleading under Ala. R. Civ. P., Rule 8(e) as well as an allegation of jurisdictional (statutory) authority analogous to Fed. R. Civ. P. 8(a)(1).

Subsection (c) of this section is consistent with Ala. R. Civ. P., Rule 55 on default judgments by discouraging nonappearance to avoid resolution of the controversy.

Subsection (d) of this section conforms to due process requirements by allowing each interested party to present favorable evidence and by providing the opportunity to attack adverse evidence, as well as providing for legal representation at the expense of the client.

Subsection (e) of this section is consistent with Alabama's statutory requirement that the judiciary encourage informal settlement of disputes, section 6-6-1, as well as the intent of Ala. R. Civ. P., Rule 16 to discourage judicial proceedings if resolution may be reached in a more informal manner.

Subsection (f) of this section describes the items to be included in the record. The addition of subdivision (7) of subsection (f) of this section, not included in the Iowa statute, is pertinent to the information required for an informed judicial review of the agency decision. Protected from disclosure are memoranda that contain data of a proprietary and confidential nature.

Subsection (g) of this section provides for public proceedings unless otherwise mandated by statute. The record of the proceeding must be kept by the agency for a stated period of time as such adjudications represent precedents for future agency determinations and therefore must be available to the public absent strong policy reasons against disclosure either recognized by statute or by a court of competent jurisdiction.

§ 41-22-13. Rules of evidence in contested cases.

(a) In contested cases, the rules of evidence as applied in nonjury civil cases in the circuit courts of this state shall be followed. When necessary to ascertain facts not reasonably susceptible of proof under those rules, evidence not admissible thereunder may be admitted (except where precluded by statute) if it is of a type commonly relied upon by reasonably prudent persons in the conduct of their affairs. Agencies shall give effect to the rules of privilege recognized by law. Objections to evidentiary offers may be made and shall be noted in the record. Whenever any evidence is excluded as inadmissible, all such evidence existing in written form shall remain a part of the record as an offer of proof. The party seeking the admission of oral testimony may make an offer of proof by means of a brief statement on the record describing the testimony excluded. All rulings on the admissibility of evidence shall be final and shall appear in the record. Subject to these requirements, when a hearing will be expedited and the interests of the parties will not be prejudiced substantially, any part of the evidence may be received or may be required to be submitted in verified form;

provided, the adversary party shall not be denied the right of cross-examination of the witness. The testimony of parties and witnesses shall be made under oath.

(b) Documentary evidence otherwise admissible may be received in the form of copies or excerpts, or by incorporation by reference to material already on file with the agency. Upon request, parties shall be given an opportunity to compare the copy with the original.

(c) A party may conduct cross-examination required for a full and true disclosure of the facts, except as may otherwise be limited by law.

(d) Official notice may be taken of all facts of which judicial notice may be taken and of other scientific and technical facts within the specialized knowledge of the agency. Parties shall be notified at the earliest practicable time, either before or during the hearing, or by reference in preliminary reports, preliminary decisions or otherwise, of the facts proposed to be noticed and their source, including any staff memoranda or data, and the parties shall be afforded an opportunity to contest such facts before the decision is announced unless the agency determines as part of the record or decision that fairness to the parties does not require an opportunity to contest such facts.

(e) The experience, technical competence, and specialized knowledge of the agency may be utilized in the evaluation of the evidence. (Acts 1981, No. 81-855, p. 1534, § 13.)

Collateral references. — 73 C.J.S., Public Administrative Bodies and Procedure, §§ 85, 122-126. 1 Am. Jur. 2d, Administrative Law, §§ 376-396.

Commentary

This section is an amalgamation of corresponding sections from the statutes of several states.

The first sentence of subsection (a) of this section, providing for the following of rules of evidence from nonjury civil cases is adopted from the first sentence of Mich. Comp. Laws § 24.275 (1970). The rules of evidence are found in the case law and are treated generally in Ala. R. Civ. P., Rule 43. See commentary for subsection (c) of this section.

The second sentence adopts the first sentence of Fla. Stat. § 120.58(1)(a) (1977) and allows more evidentiary latitude than in a civil action with the provision for judicial review if a resolution cannot be reached by administrative procedures. See section 41-22-12.

The first part of the third sentence, giving effect to the rules of privilege, is adopted from Iowa Code § 17A.14(1) (1976 Cum. Supp.). Alabama currently in civil actions recognizes a number of privileges, including a privilege for confidential communications between spouses, Gordon, Rankin & Co. v. Tweedy, 71 Ala. 202, 210 (1881), a licensed psychiatrist or psychologist-parent privilege, Ala. Code § 34-26-2 (1975), the privilege against self-incrimination, Murphy v. Waterfront Commission of New York, 378 U.S. 52 (1964), and the attorney-client privilege, Ala. Code § 12-21-161 (1975). See also Ala. Code § 12-21-142 (1975) (privilege of news reporters not to disclose sources). Decisions, opinions, etc., of review committee of physicians are privileged under section 34-24-58.

The fourth sentence, allowing objection to evidentiary offers, and the fifth sentence, regarding submission of evidence in verified form, are substantial adoptions of the last two sentences of Iowa Code § 17A.14(1) (1976 Cum. Supp.). The former is consistent with Ala. R. Civ. P., Rules 12 and 32(b). The latter appears to be a best evidence rule subject to the convenience of the agency and parties involved and is comparable to the provisions of Ala. R. Civ. P., Rule 44. See subsection (b) of this section.

The fifth and sixth sentences relate to the offer of proof of written evidence and oral testimony, respectively.

The last sentence of subsection (a) of this section, requiring testimony to be under oath, is adapted from Fla. Stat. § 120.58(1)(a) (1977). The oath is considered to be, if not a guarantee of veracity, notice of the seriousness of the proceeding and the attendant consequences, although used here in a quasi-judicial setting.

Subsection (b) of this section is substantially adopted from Tenn. Code Ann. § 4-5-109(5) (1979 Replacement) and is consistent with the liberality and simplicity of Ala. R. Civ. P., Rule 44. Incorporation by reference to agency files is analogous to the provisions of Ala. R. Civ. P., Rule 10(c) concerning incorporation by reference to the pleadings and is simply a convenient shorthand to expedite resolution.

Subsection (c) of this section on cross-examination allows cross-examination of all witnesses, phrased even more liberally than the comparable provision in Ala. R. Civ. P., Rule 43(b): "any matter material to any issue." Problems thereby caused may be rectified at a judicial proceeding, if necessary.

Subsection (d) of this section is adopted from Iowa Code § 17A.14(4) (1976 Cum. Supp.) except that the limitation of official notice of facts within the specialized knowledge of the agency to "scientific and technical" facts is added. This limitation appears in several other states' statutes, including Ga. Code § 3A-116(d) (1975) and Tenn. Code Ann. § 4-5-109(7) (1979 Replacement). Official notice is the technical analogue of judicial notice; however, because of the specialized knowledge of the agency, official notice may be taken of facts which a court would not consider appropriately handled by this method. The opportunity to contest facts officially noticed is not automatic but if denied the agency must, as a part of the record, state reasons for denying such contest. Nothing in this subsection precludes judicial review of facts officially noticed.

Subsection (e) of this section is adopted from Iowa Code § 17A.14(5) (1976 Cum. Supp.) and seeks to take advantage of the specialized skills of the agency in assessing the evidence within its expertise.

§ 41-22-14. Intervention in contested cases.

In contested cases, upon timely application, any person shall be permitted to intervene when a statute confers an unconditional right to intervene, or when the applicant has an individual interest in the outcome of the case as distinguished from a public interest and the representation of the interest of the applicant is inadequate. (Acts 1981, No. 81-855, p. 1534, § 14.)

Commentary

This section is based upon but varies somewhat from Rule 24 of the Alabama Rules of Civil Procedure and has no counterpart in the Revised Model State Administrative Procedure Act.

Intervention as a matter of right is mandated if (1) provided by statute or (2) the applicant has an individual interest in the case as distinguished from a public interest which is not adequately represented. The former category is finite and self-explanatory, but the latter presents some problems which have not been resolved in litigation concerning the corresponding subsections of Ala. R. Civ. P., Rule 24(a) and Fed. R. Civ. P., Rule 24(a), the most perplexing aspect of which concerns what will be deemed adequate representation. See Cascade Natural Gas Corp. v. El Paso Natural Gas Co., 386 U.S. 129 (1967); see generally Hoff, Joinder of Claims and Parties Under the Alabama Rules of Civil Procedure, 25 Ala. L. Rev. 667, 694-96 (1973).

§ 41-22-15. Majority requirement for adoption of final decision in contested cases; use of proposed orders in cases where any official is unfamiliar with the case; finality of proposed orders.

In a contested case, a majority of the officials of the agency who are to render the final order must be in accord for the decision of the agency to be a final decision. If any official of the agency who is to participate in the final decision has not heard the case or read the record and his vote would affect the final decision, the final decision shall not be made until a proposed order is prepared and an opportunity is afforded to each party adversely affected by the proposed order to file exceptions and present briefs and oral argument to the official not having heard the case or read the record. The proposed order shall contain a statement of the reasons therefor and of each issue of fact or law necessary to the proposed decision prepared by the person who conducted the hearing or one who read the record. The proposed order shall become the final decision of the agency without further proceedings, unless there are exceptions filed or an appeal to the agency within the time provided by rule. The parties by written stipulation may waive compliance with this section. (Acts 1981, No. 81-855, p. 1534, § 15.)

Collateral references. — 1 Am. Jur. 2d, Administrative Law, §§ 196, 434-505.

Commentary

This section is based on the Florida and Iowa statutes, in combination, with some modifications. The first sentence is based on Iowa Code § 17A.15(1) (1976 Cum. Supp.) except that where the Iowa statute refers to "the agency" presiding, this section requires "a majority of the officials of the agency who are to render the final order", and this section requires a majority of the members who are to make the decision to be in accord, rather than merely to have heard the case or read the record; if the latter were the case, fewer than a majority of the members of the agency who would render the order could conceivably decide what the order is to be. The second sentence is adapted from the first sentence of Fla. Stat. § 120.58(1)(e) (1977) and from Iowa Code § 17A.15(3) (1976 Cum. Supp.). The provisions dealing with preparation and content of the proposed order, are adapted from Fla. Stat. § 120.58(1)(e) (1977). The provision that a proposed order can become a final decision without further proceedings is adapted from Iowa Code § 17A.15(3) (1976 Cum. Supp.). The final sentence in this section, allowing the parties to waive compliance with this section by written stipulation, is adopted from Fla. Stat. § 120.58(1)(e) (1977).

In terms of the constitutional requirement of due process, the section represents a codification of the opinion rendered in Morgan v. United States, 298 U.S. 468 (1936). That case arose from the imposition of a rate order of the secretary of agriculture under the Packers and Stockyards Act. The order was contested on the grounds that the official authorized to make the decision had delegated the power to conduct the administrative hearing to an assistant but had made the final decision himself. The plaintiffs sought to restrain the enforcement of the rate order in the United States district court for the Western District of Missouri, but that court dismissed the bills of complaint. On a direct appeal to the Supreme Court of the United States the district court's dismissal was reversed and the case remanded. The court's opinion was written by Chief Justice Hughes, who said:

[T]o give the substance of a hearing, which is for the purpose of making determinations upon evidence, the officer who makes the determination must consider and appraise the evidence which justifies them. 298 U.S. at 481-82.

That duty cannot be performed by one who has not considered evidence or argument. It is not an impersonal obligation. It is a duty akin to that of a judge. The one who decides must hear.

This necessary rule does not preclude practical administrative procedure in obtaining the aid of assistants in the department. Assistants may prosecute inquiries. Evidence may be taken by an examiner. . . . The requirements are not technical. But there must be a hearing in a substantial sense. 298 U.S. at 481 (emphasis supplied). See also Alabama Elec. Coop. v. Ala. Power Co., 251 Ala. 190, 36 So. 2d 523 (1948); National Nutr. Foods Ass'n v. Food & Drug Admin., 491 F.2d 1141 (2d Cir. 1974).

It must be emphasized that this section is designed to apply to agency's judicial rather than its legislative function, in which the standards are less strict. In United States v. Fla. East Coast Ry., 410 U.S. 224 (1973), the court, distinguishing between an agency's legislative and its adjudicative functions, determined that the facts there which involved an ICC rate promulgation presented a situation in which the agency was creating a generally applicable rule rather than adjudicating a factual dispute. Therefor, the court concluded that under the pertinent cases the Constitution had never required exhaustive judicial-like hearings in cases like the one before it.

§ 41-22-16. Form and content of final order; when final order to be rendered; service of notice and copies of final order.

(a) The final order in a proceeding which affects substantial interests shall be in writing and made a part of the record and include findings of fact and conclusions of law separately stated, and it shall be rendered within 30 days:

(1) After the hearing is concluded, if conducted by the agency;

(2) After a recommended order, or findings and conclusions are submitted to the agency and mailed to all parties, if the hearing is conducted by a hearing officer; or

(3) After the agency has received the written and oral material it has authorized to be submitted, if there has been no hearing.

The 30-day period may be waived or extended with the consent of all parties and may be extended by law with reference to specific agencies.

(b) Findings of fact, if set forth in a manner which is no more than mere tracking of the statutory language, shall be accompanied by a concise and explicit statement of the underlying facts of record which support the findings. If, in accordance with agency rules, a party submitted proposed findings of fact or filed any written application or other request in connection with the proceeding, the order shall include a ruling upon each proposed finding and a brief statement of the grounds for denying the application or request.

(c) If an agency head finds that an immediate danger to the public health, safety, or welfare requires an immediate final order, it shall recite with particularity the facts underlying such findings in the final order, which shall be appealable or enjoinable from the date rendered.

(d) Parties shall be notified either personally or by certified mail return receipt requested of any order and, unless waived, a copy of the final order shall be so delivered or mailed to each party or to his attorney of record. (Acts 1981, No. 81-855, p. 1534, § 16.)

Commentary

This section is adapted from Fla. Stat. § 120.59 (1977). This section requires that a final order in a contested case include as a part of the record separate statements of the findings of fact and findings of law. Requiring a statement of these underlying bases for administrative orders obviously facilitates judicial review of such orders. The requirement that such statements appear in the record may also help protect against careless or arbitrary action; the possibility of review of the order or findings may evoke special care from those who bear the responsibility of making and filing such findings.

Additionally, such findings give the losing party knowledge of the reasons why the case was lost, which can aid in the preparation of cases for rehearing or for review. Also, should the order stand, notice is provided to the public. See subdivision (4) of subsection (a) of section 41-22-4. This can be the starting point for what has been termed "administrative stare decisis". Levinson, The Florida Administrative Procedure Act, 29 U. Miami L. Rev. 617, 650 (1975).

The time requirement imposed in subsection (a) of this section is intended to insure that orders and decisions are speedily rendered, which is to the advantage of all parties to the contested case. Final orders must be rendered within 30 days unless all parties consent to delay.

§ 41-22-17. Filing of application for rehearing in contested cases; form and content; effect of application on final order; grounds for rehearing; service of application on parties of record; agency decision on application.

(a) Any party to a contested case who deems himself aggrieved by a final order and who desires to have the same modified or set aside may, within 15 days after entry of said order, file an application for rehearing, which shall specify in detail the grounds for the relief sought therein and authorities in support thereof.

(b) The filing of such an application for rehearing shall not extend, modify, suspend or delay the effective date of the order, and said order shall take effect on the date fixed by the agency and shall continue in effect unless and until said application shall be granted or until said order shall be superseded, modified, or set aside in a manner provided by law. .

(c) Such application for rehearing will lie only if the final order is:

(1) In violation of constitutional or statutory provisions;

(2) In excess of the statutory authority of the agency;

(3) In violation of an agency rule;

(4) Made upon unlawful procedure;

(5) Affected by other error of law;

(6) Clearly erroneous in view of the reliable, probative, and substantial evidence on the whole record; or

(7) Unreasonable, arbitrary or capricious or characterized by an abuse of discretion or a clearly unwarranted exercise of discretion.

(d) Copies of such application for rehearing shall be served on all parties of record, who may file replies thereto.

(e) Within 30 days from the filing of an application the agency may in its discretion enter an order:

(1) Setting a hearing on the application for a rehearing which shall be heard as soon as practicable; or

(2) With reference to the application without a hearing; or

(3) Granting or denying the application.

If the agency enters no order whatsoever regarding the application within the 30-day period, the application shall be deemed to have been denied as of the expiration of the 30-day period. (Acts 1981, No. 81-855, p. 1534, § 17.)

Collateral references. — 1 Am. Jur. 2d, Administrative Law, §§ 520-552.

Commentary

This section is an adaptation of Tenn. Code Ann. § 4-5-114 (1979 Replacement). Where the Tennessee statute requires the filing of a "written petition" for rehearing, the language of this section calls for "an application" for rehearing. The grounds provided for in subsection (c) of this section are adopted from Iowa Code § 17A.19(8) (1976 Cum. Supp.), except for subdivision (6) of subsection (c) of this section, which was adopted at the suggestion of the administrative law section of the Alabama state bar. Subsection (f) of the Tennessee section is deleted, but the first sentence of that subsection, requiring that upon granting of a rehearing, such rehearing be set for as soon a time as practicable, is included as subsection (e) of this section.

There is no corresponding section in the Model State Administrative Procedure Act.

This section sets forth a mechanism by which a party to a contested case can, through timely application, request a rehearing of the case, and a mechanism by which parties to the original case can become parties to the rehearing. The maximum amount of time which would be permitted to elapse between the time of the rendering of the order appealed from in the original contested case and the time of the disposition of the application for rehearing would be 45 days. That includes 15 days to file the application and 30 days for the agency to: (a) set a hearing on the application; (b) enter an order without a hearing; or (c) grant or deny such application. If such application were granted, the agency would have to set the matter for rehearing as soon as practicable; in meting out justice, speed is of the essence and this is particularly true under this section where the application for rehearing does not stay the action of the order from which relief is being sought.

An application for rehearing will lie only if the order upon which the application is based is within the scope of the criteria listed in subsection (c). These criteria are the same criteria to be applied by a court under subsection (k) of section 41-22-20 in an action for review of an agency action when deciding whether such agency action should be affirmed, remanded, reversed, or modified, or whether some other appropriate relief from the action should be granted.

§ 41-22-18. Disqualification from participation in proposed order or final decision based upon conflict of interest or personal bias.

(a) No individual who participates in the making of any proposed order or final decision in a contested case shall have prosecuted or represented a party in connection with that case, the specific controversy underlying that case, or another pending factually related contested case, or pending factually related controversy that may culminate in a contested case involving the same parties. Nor shall any such individual be subject to the authority, direction or discretion of any person who has prosecuted or advocated in connection with that contested case, the specific controversy underlying that contested case, or a pending factually related contested case or controversy, involving the same parties.

(b) A party to a contested case proceeding may file a timely and sufficient affidavit asserting disqualification according to the provisions of subsection (a) or asserting personal bias of an individual participating in the making of any proposed order or final decision in that case. The agency shall determine the matter as part of the record in the case. When an agency in these circumstances makes such a determination with respect to an agency member, that determination shall be subject to de novo judicial review in any subsequent review proceeding of the case. (Acts 1981, No. 81-855, p. 1534, § 18.)

Commentary

This section is a direct adoption of the separation of functions section of Iowa Code § 17A.17 (1976 Cum. Supp.), except that where the phrase "proposed or final decision" appears in the Iowa section, this section includes the word "order" after "proposed", thus making it "proposed order or final decision", in order to keep this section consistent with the language of other sections of this act. Also, in subsection (a) of this section, where the Iowa act refers to having "advocated" in connection with a case, this draft substitutes the language "represented a party".

This section addresses itself to a problem of procedural due process of law; specifically the problem of ensuring internal separation of functions within an agency. Under this section, the functions and duties of a prosecutor and a judge cannot be embodied in the same person or persons. This is accomplished by utilizing different individuals in these distinct positions, and then by establishing a communications barrier between the two as regards the matter in dispute. If ex parte communications were not banned, there is a possibility that the adjudicative process in a case would be contaminated through contacts of deciding officers with persons prosecuting, advocating, or investigating. See generally K. Davis, Administrative Law Text § 13.07, at 267-70 (3d ed. 1972).

This section also seeks to ensure the fairness of a hearing in a contested case by providing a description of what might constitute a disqualifying condition in an agency member to judge and by providing for the exclusion of individuals who may be biased under these criteria from the judging function. Subsection (b) of this section provides a mechanism by which a party may petition for the removal from the judging function of an agency member who should be removed under subsection (a) of this section or for other personal bias, and provides that this is a determination that shall be subject to review in any subsequent judicial review.

§ 41-22-19. Grant, denial, renewal, etc. of licenses.

(a) The provisions of this chapter concerning contested cases shall apply to the grant, denial, revocation, suspension, or renewal of a license.

(b) When a licensee has made timely and sufficient application for the renewal of a license or a new license with reference to any activity of a continuing nature, the existing license does not expire until the application has been finally determined by the agency, and, in case the application is denied or the terms of the new license limited, until the last day for seeking review of the agency order or a later date fixed by order of the reviewing court.

(c) No revocation, suspension, or withdrawal of any license is lawful unless, prior to the institution of agency proceedings, the agency gave notice by certified mail to the licensee of facts or conduct which warrant the intended action, and the licensee was given an opportunity to show compliance with all lawful requirements for the retention of the license.

(d) If the agency finds that danger to the public health, safety, or welfare requires emergency suspension of a license and states in writing its reasons for that finding, it may proceed without hearing or upon any abbreviated hearing that it finds practicable to suspend the license. The suspension shall become effective immediately, unless otherwise stated therein. The suspension may be effective for a period of not longer than 120 days and shall not be renewable. An agency shall not suspend the same license for the same or a substantially similar emergency within one calendar year from its first suspension unless the agency clearly establishes that it could not reasonably be foreseen during the initial 120-day period that such emergency would continue or would likely reoccur during the next nine months. When such summary suspension is ordered, a formal suspension or revocation proceeding under subsection (c) of this section shall also be promptly instituted and acted upon. (Acts 1981, No. 81-855, p. 1534, § 19.)

Collateral references. — 53 C.J.S., Licenses, §§ 6, 7, 9, 37, 38, 44. 73 C.J.S., Public Administrative Bodies and Procedure, § 71.

Commentary

Subsection (a) of this section is adopted at the suggestion of the administrative law section of the Alabama State Bar Association. Subsection (b) of this section is an adoption of Revised Model State Administrative Procedure Act § 14(b) (1961). Subsection (c) of this section is an adoption of Fla. Stat. § 120.60(4) (1977). Subsection (d) of this section is adapted from Fla. Stat. § 120.60(5) (1977), including an adaption of the language of subsection (b) of section 41-22-5, detailing the procedures to be followed in the event of emergency suspension of a license.

The terms "license" and "licensing" have precise meanings ascribed to them by subdivisions (4) and (5) of section 41-22-3, which must be read in conjunction with this section.

This section requires that there must be an opportunity for a hearing regarding any action taken against any licensee's license, except in cases where such action is taken for emergency purposes. This section also requires notice to the licensee of intended agency actions against his license and the reasons therefor, and an opportunity for said licensee to defend against such action. These provisions are intended to ensure that no action is taken against the licensee without due process of law. Although a license may be regarded as a privilege rather than something to which the licensee has a right, the licensee does have a right to due process of law in the application of licensing provisions. See generally Note, Due Process Limitations on Occupational Licensing, 59 Va. L. Rev. 1097 (1973):

> The due process clause imposes three essential requirements on occupational licensing schemes: specificity, rationality, and fairness. Specificity focuses on the standards and guidelines that a licensing board uses in granting, denying, suspending, renewing, or revoking a license and demands that they be intelligible. Rationality requires that the standards bear a reasonable relation to effective practice of the regulated occupation. Fairness concerns the makeup of the licensing board, the procedures it follows, and the necessity and timing of judicial review. Id. at 1103-04. See also 1 F. Cooper, State Administrative Law 147-51 (1965).

This conclusion is supported by numerous determinations of the Supreme Court of the United States, including one in which the court, using typical language, said:

> A state cannot exclude a person from the practice of law or from any other occupation in a manner or for reasons that contravene the due process or equal protection clause of the fourteenth amendment.

Schware v. Board of Bar Examiners, 353 U.S. 232, 238-39 (1957). And in a footnote the court commented on the right-privilege distinction:

> We need not enter into a discussion whether the practice of law is a 'right' or 'privilege.' Regardless of how the state's grant of permission to engage in this occupation is characterized, it is sufficient to say that a person cannot be prevented from practicing except for valid reasons. Certainly the practice of law is not a matter of the state's grace. Id. at 239, n.5.

For a discussion of the provisions of subsection (a) of this section see the Commentary to section 41-22-12.

For a discussion of the provisions of subsection (c) of this section see the Commentary to section 41-22-5 regarding adoption of emergency rules.

§ 41-22-20. Judicial review of preliminary, procedural, etc., actions or rulings and final decisions in contested cases.

(a) A person who has exhausted all administrative remedies available within the agency (other than rehearing) and who is aggrieved by a final decision in a contested case is entitled to judicial review under this chapter. A preliminary, procedural, or intermediate agency action or ruling is immediately reviewable if review of the final agency decision would not provide an adequate remedy.

(b) Except in matters for which judicial review is otherwise provided for by law, all proceedings for review shall be instituted by filing of notice of appeal or review and, where required by statute, a cost bond, with the agency. A petition shall be filed in the circuit court of the county in which the agency maintains its headquarters, or unless otherwise specifically provided by statute, where a party (other than an intervenor) resides or if a party (other than an intervenor), is a corporation, domestic or foreign, having a registered office or business office in this state, then in the county of such registered office or principal place of business within this state.

(c) The filing of the notice of appeal or the petition does not itself stay enforcement of the agency decision. If the agency decision has the effect of suspending or revoking a license, a stay or supersedeas shall be granted as a matter of right upon such conditions as are reasonable, unless the reviewing court, upon petition of the agency, determines that a stay or supersedeas would constitute a probable danger to the public health, safety, or welfare. In all other cases, the agency may grant, or the reviewing court may order, a stay upon appropriate terms, but, in any event, the order shall specify the conditions upon which the stay or supersedeas is granted; provided, however, if the appeal or proceedings for review to any reviewing court are from an order of the agency increasing or reducing or refusing to increase rates, fares or charges, or any of them, or any schedule or parts of any schedule of such rates, fares or charges, the reviewing court shall not direct or order a supersedeas or stay of the action or order to be reviewed without requiring, as a condition precedent to the granting of such supersedeas, that the party applying for supersedeas or stay shall execute and file with the clerk of said court a bond as provided for and required by statute or law. If the circuit court shall fail or refuse to grant supersedeas or stay, the party seeking such relief may petition the court of civil appeals or the supreme court to order a supersedeas or stay of the action or order of the agency from which review is sought. After the required bond shall have been filed and approved by the clerk, such agency order shall be stayed and superseded, and it shall be lawful to charge the rates, fares or charges which have been reduced, refused or denied by said agency order, until the final disposition of the cause. The provisions of this subsection shall apply when applicable, anything in Rule 60 of the Alabama Rules of Civil Procedure restricting the provisions of this subsection to the contrary notwithstanding.

(d) The notice of appeal or review shall be filed within 30 days after the receipt of the notice of or other service of the final decision of the agency upon the petitioner or, if a rehearing is requested under section 41-22-17, within 30 days after the decision thereon. The petition for judicial review in the circuit court shall be filed within 30 days after the filing of the notice of appeal or review. Copies of the petition shall be served upon the agency and all parties of record after the petition is filed with the court. Any party to the agency proceeding may become a party to the review proceedings by notifying the court within 30 days after receipt of the copy of the petition. Any person aggrieved may petition to become a party by filing a motion to intervene as provided in section 41-22-14. Failure to file such petition within the time stated shall operate as a waiver of the right of such person to review under this chapter, except that for good cause shown, the judge of the reviewing court may extend the time for filing, not to exceed an additional 30 days, or, within four months after the issuance of the agency order, issue an order permitting a review of the agency decision under this chapter notwithstanding such waiver.

(e) If there has been no hearing prior to agency action and the reviewing court finds that the validity of the action depends upon disputed facts, the court shall order the agency to conduct a prompt fact-finding proceeding under this chapter after having a reasonable opportunity to reconsider its determination on the record of the proceedings.

(f) Unreasonable delay on the part of an agency in reaching a final decision shall be justification for any person whose rights, duties, or privileges are adversely affected by such delay to seek a court order compelling action by the agency.

(g) Within 30 days after receipt of the notice of appeal or within such additional time as the court may allow, the agency shall transmit to the reviewing court the original or a certified copy of the entire record and transcript of the proceedings under review. With the permission of the court, the record of the proceedings under review may be shortened by stipulation of all parties to the review proceedings. Any party found by the reviewing court to have unreasonably refused to stipulate to limit the record may be taxed by the court for such additional costs as may be occasioned by the refusal. The court may require or permit subsequent corrections or additions to the record when deemed desirable.

(h) The petition for review shall name the agency as respondent and shall contain a concise statement of:

(1) The nature of the agency action which is the subject of the petition;

(2) The particular agency action appealed from;

(3) The facts and law on which jurisdiction and venue are based;

(4) The grounds on which relief is sought; and

(5) The relief sought.

(i) In proceedings for judicial review of agency action in a contested case, however, a reviewing court shall not itself hear or accept any further evidence with respect to those issues of fact whose determination was entrusted by law to the agency in that contested case proceeding; provided, however, that evidence may be introduced in the reviewing court as to fraud or misconduct of some person engaged in the administration of the agency or procedural irregularities before the agency not shown in the record and the affecting order, ruling or award from which review is sought, and proof thereon may be taken in the reviewing court. If, before the date set for hearing a petition for judicial review of agency action in a contested case, it is shown to the satisfaction of the court that additional evidence is material and that there were good reasons for failure to present it in the contested case proceeding before the agency, the court may remand to the agency and order that the additional evidence be taken before the agency upon conditions determined by the court. The agency may modify its findings and decision in the case by reason of the additional evidence and shall file that evidence and any modification, new findings, or decision with the reviewing court and mail copies of the new findings or decision to all parties.

(j) The review shall be conducted by the court without a jury and shall in the review of contested cases be confined to the record and such additions thereto as may be made under subsection (i) of this section. The court, upon request, shall hear oral argument and receive written briefs.

(k) The agency order shall be taken as prima facie just and reasonable and the court shall not substitute its judgment for that of the agency as to the weight of the evidence on questions of fact, except where otherwise authorized by statute. The court may affirm the agency action or remand the case to the agency for taking additional testimony and evidence or for further proceedings. The court may reverse or modify the decision or grant other appropriate relief from the agency action, equitable or legal, including declaratory relief, if the court finds that the agency action is due to be set aside or modified under standards set forth in appeal or review statutes applicable to that agency, or where no such statutory standards for judicial review are applicable to the agency, if substantial rights of the petitioner have been prejudiced because the agency action is:

(1) In violation of constitutional or statutory provisions;

(2) In excess of the statutory authority of the agency;

(3) In violation of any pertinent agency rule;

(4) Made upon unlawful procedure;

(5) Affected by other error of law;

(6) Clearly erroneous in view of the reliable, probative, and substantial evidence on the whole record; or

(7) Unreasonable, arbitrary or capricious or characterized by an abuse of discretion or a clearly unwarranted exercise of discretion.

(l) Unless the court affirms the decision of the agency, the court shall set out in writing, which writing shall become a part of the record, the reasons for its decision. (Acts 1981, No. 81-855, p. 1534, § 20.)

Collateral references. — 73 C.J.S., Public Administrative Bodies and Procedure, §§ 41, 160.

Commentary

Subsection (a) of this section is an adoption of the first and third sentences of the Revised Model State Administrative Procedure Act § 15(a) (1961). Subsection (b) of this section is an adaption of Fla. Stat. § 120.68(2) (1977), together with provisions suggested by the administrative law section of the Alabama state bar. Subsection (c) of this section is adopted from Fla. Stat. § 120.68(3) (1977), except that where the Florida act provides for "a supersedeas as a matter of right," this section provides for "a stay of supersedeas . . .". A court order must specify the conditions upon which a stay is granted. Where the appeal order involves a rate change the reviewing court may require a bond to be posted. This subsection also adds a final sentence which renders Rule 60 of the Alabama Rules of Civil Procedure inapplicable to actions under this subsection.

The first sentence of subsection (d) of this section, providing for the time of filing a petition for review, is based on the Revised Model State Administrative Procedure Act § 15(b) (1961). The remainder of this subsection, except for time extension is based on provisions of N.C. Gen. Stat. §§ 150A-45 through 46 (1975 Cum. Supp.).

Subsection (e) of this section is an adoption of Fla. Stat. § 120.68(6) (1977). Subsection (f) of this section is an adoption of N.C. Gen. Stat. § 150A-44 (1975 Cum. Supp.). Subsection (g) of this section is an adoption of N.C. Gen. Stat. § 150A-47 (1975 Cum. Supp.), except that in the second sentence this section uses the language "the record of the proceedings under review may be shortened" instead of just "the record may be shortened." Subsection (h) of this section is a direct adoption of Iowa Code § 17A.19(4) (1976 Cum. Supp.) except the jurisdiction requirement has been added as subsection (c) of this section.

Subsection (i) of this section is an adoption of Iowa Code § 17A.19(7) (1976 Cum. Supp.) with modifications. Where the Iowa statute uses the language "was entrusted by constitution or statute to the agency" this section substitutes "was entrusted by law to the agency." The provision allowing proof to be taken in court on alleged irregularities in procedure before the agency is adopted from the Revised Model State Administrative Procedure Act § 15(f). Subsection (j) of this section adopts the remaining parts of the Revised Model State Administrative Procedure Act § 15(f) (1961), but modifies it by providing that the review is confined to the record "in the review of contested cases", and by allowing additions to the record as permissible under subsection (i) of this section.

The first sentence of subsection (k) of this section is an adoption of the first sentence of the Revised Model State Administrative Procedure Act § 15(g) (1961), with the addition of a provision allowing the court to weigh additional evidence heard pursuant to subsection (i) of this section and that the agency order shall be taken as "prima facie" just and reasonable. The remainder of subsection (k) of this section relating to standards on review where not otherwise provided by statute applicable to a particular agency is a direct adoption of Iowa Code § 17A.19(8) (1976 Cum. Supp.), except subdivision (6) of subsection (k) of this section, which is adopted at the suggestion of the administrative law section of the Alabama state bar and the addition of "pertinent" to subdivision (3) of subsection (k) of this section.

Subsection (l) of this section is an adoption of the last sentence of N.C. Gen. Stat. § 150A-51 (1975 Cum. Supp.), together with language providing that an explanatory writing must become a part of the record whenever any appropriate relief is granted, not just a reversal or modification of the agency decision as provided for in the North Carolina statute.

In interpreting this section, it must be remembered that it has broad application because of the very broad definition of "contested case" in section 3(3): "A proceeding, including but not restricted to ratemaking, price fixing, and licensing, in which the legal rights, duties, or privileges of a party are required by law to be determined by an agency after an opportunity for hearing."

Since the adjudicative process to some extent involves the agencies' engaging in adjudicative functions, to that extent parties affected by administrative action must have access to review by the judicial branch of government. Indeed, Professor Gellhorn has recently stated:

Despite the fact that the federal constitutional theory of separation of powers does not apply to the states [this, of course, would not preclude the states' own separation of powers of nondelegation doctrines], their courts are more restrictive and have frequently disapproved the delegation of lawmaking powers to state agencies if the enabling legislation lacks "standards." Judicial disapproval in the states occurs most frequently where the delegated power involves the regulation of a profession (from plumbers to doctors) or the private use of real property (specifically, zoning).

E. Gellhorn, Administrative Law and Process In A Nutshell 21 (1972). Since, as Gellhorn suggests, judicial review will frequently be invoked in licensing determinations, a specific focus on such cases is in order. As one commentator has put it:

The courts have come to recognize the need to focus increased attention on the administration of state occupational licensing laws. Since states typically grant licensing boards broadly defined powers, in essence the judicial problem is control of administrative discretion. The task is complicated by the fact that, unlike other administrative tribunals, the occupational licensing board's membership is usually drawn from the ranks of the regulated occupation. The danger of bias apparently warrants an active judicial role to insure impartial decisionmaking.

Note, Due Process Limitations on Occupational Licensing, 59 Va. L. Rev. 1097, 1099-1100 (1973). At a later point the commentator makes the broader statement pertinent to this entire section:

The dominant view today is that judicial review is a necessary component of due process in an administrative law setting, "unless review is specifically precluded by statute" or "a special reason for nonreviewability exists."

Id. at 1128, quoting E. Gellhorn, supra at 245, and noting that "The presumption of reviewability is most clearly articulated in Abbott Laboratories v. Gardner, 387 U.S. 136 (1967)." Id. at 1128, n. 160.

§ 41-22-21. Appeal of final judgment of circuit court under section 41-22-20.

An aggrieved party may obtain a review of any final judgment of the circuit court under section 41-22-20 by appeal to the court of civil appeals, except as provided by statute which authorizes an appeal to the supreme court. The appeal shall be taken as in other civil cases, although the appeal may be taken regardless of the amount involved. (Acts 1981, No. 81-855, p. 1534, § 21.)

Collateral references. — 73 C.J.S., Public Administrative Bodies and Procedure, § 242.

Commentary

The first sentence of this section is adapted from the first sentence of the Revised Model State Administrative Procedure Act § 16, with the appropriate courts provided for, and with exceptions for appeal to the supreme court as provided by separate statutes. The second sentence is a verbatim adoption of the second sentence of Iowa Code § 17A.20 (1976 Cum. Supp.).

This section provides for appeals from decisions of reviewing courts rendered pursuant to section 41-22-20. The procedure on appeal will, of course, be pursuant to the Alabama Rules of Appellate Procedure. Ala. R. App. P., Rule 1. The last clause of the final sentence is fully consistent with the present statutory provision regarding the appellate jurisdiction of the court of civil appeals, section 12-3-10, except that it is now made explicitly clear that original review comes in the circuit court and not in the court of civil appeals. As provided in subsection (b) of section 41-22-20 and in the present version of section 12-3-10, appeals from the public service commission will continue to be heard in the first instance by the circuit court of Montgomery county, section 37-1-120, with a direct right of further appeal from that court to the supreme court of Alabama, section 37-1-132.

This section is also consistent with section 12-3-10, in not making jurisdictional amount a consideration in the exercise of the appellate jurisdiction of the court of civil appeals, even though under this act, that court will become clearly the second reviewing court and not the reviewing court in the first instance, as a literal reading of section 12-3-10 might seem to suggest.

§ 41-22-22. Creation of joint committee on administrative regulation review; composition, chairman, meetings, compensation and expenses, etc.; functions of the committee.

(a) There shall be a joint standing legislative committee known as the joint committee on administrative regulation review, to review all agency rules. The committee shall consist of the members of the legislative council and shall meet on the call of the chairman. The chairman shall be authorized to name subcommittees to meet and review agency rules and report to the full committee. Members of the committee shall receive the same compensation, expenses and transportation allowances for meetings as they receive for attendance at meetings of the legislative council. All such compensation and expenses authorized by the provisions of this section shall be paid from funds appropriated to the use of the legislative council.

(b) The committee shall:

(1) Maintain a continuous review of the statutory authority on which each administrative rule is based, and whenever such authority is eliminated or significantly changed by repeal, amendment, or other factor, advise the agency concerned of the fact;

(2) Review administrative rules and advise the agencies concerned of its findings;

(3) Have the further duties prescribed in section 41-22-23; and

(4) The committee shall determine and report annually to the legislature the total cost to the state allocated to the implementation of this chapter. (Acts 1981, No. 81-855, p. 1534, § 22.)

Cross references. — As to the effective date of this act generally and the effective date of this section, see § 41-22-27.

Commentary

There is no corresponding provision in the Revised Model State Administrative Procedure Act. Thirty-eight states however have adopted a legislative review procedure. There are four general categories into which the powers of legislatures to review rules may be placed. The first is advisory review power, under which a legislature may comment and object to a rule but no action to suspend or nullify the rule. Twenty states use this system. The legislature has the inherent power to modify or repeal a rule by legislature and the second power category is repeal of an objectionable regulation by the legislature through the passage of either a bill or a resolution, which is usually done on the recommendation of the reviewing committee. Fourteen states use this method and repeal by joint or concurrent resolution or passage of a statute. Eight states have adopted a third legislative oversight system under which the reviewing committee has the power to suspend a rule for a period of time, during which the suspension must be ratified by the full legislature in order for the regulation to be permanently nullified. This is the scheme Alabama has chosen. The last category of the legislative power is suspension of a regulation by the committee which is considered to be permanent unless the legislature reverses the committee's action. Four states use this method. Several states which allow use of the advisory category of review provides for repeal of the rule by the legislature through the legislature's inherent power to regulate agency powers, thus several states may be classified in more than one category.

Subsection (a) of this section provides for an oversight committee which shall consist of the legislative council. The membership of the legislative council is found in section 29-6-2. The first sentence is a combined adoption of Conn. Gen. Stat. § 4-170(a) (1977 Cum. Supp.) and Fla. Stat. § 11.60(1) (1977).

Subsection (b) of this section is based on Fla. Stat. § 11.60(2) (1977) except for subdivision (4) of subsection (b) of this section which was added by the legislature to apprise itself of the cost of implementation of this act.

§ 41-22-23. Submission of proposed rules by agency to the joint committee on administrative regulation review; approval, disapproval, or amendment by committee; criteria for review of rules.

(a) The notice required by subdivision (1) of subsection (a) of section 41-22-5 shall be given, in addition to the persons therein named, to the chairman of the legislative committee. The agency shall furnish the committee with ten copies of the proposed rule or rules, and no rule, except an emergency rule issued pursuant to subsection (b) of section 41-22-5 shall be effective until these copies are so furnished. Any member of the senate or house of representatives who requests a copy of proposed agency rules from the chairman of the joint committee on administrative regulation review shall be provided a copy and the agency proposing rules shall furnish additional copies of the proposed rule or rules immediately. The form of the proposed rule presented to the committee shall be as follows: New language shall be underlined and language to be deleted shall be typed and lined through.

(b) The committee shall study all proposed rules and, in its discretion, may hold public hearings thereon. In the event the committee fails to give notice to the agency of either its approval or disapproval of the proposed rule within 60 days after its presentation to the committee, the committee shall be deemed to have approved the proposed regulation for the purposes of this section. In the event the committee disapproves a proposed rule or any part thereof, it shall give notice of such disapproval to the agency. Any disapproved rule shall be suspended until the adjournment of the next regular session of the legislature following the date of disapproval and suspension of committee or until the legislature shall, by joint resolution, revoke the suspension of the committee. The rule shall be reinstated on the adjournment of said legislative session in the event the legislature by joint resolution, fails to sustain the disapproval and suspension of the committee.

(c) The committee may propose an amendment to any proposed rule and may disapprove the proposed rule and return it to the agency with the suggested amendment. In the event the agency accepts the rule as amended, the agency may resubmit the rule as amended to the committee. In the event the agency does not accept the amendment, the proposed amended rule shall be submitted to the legislature as disapproved, as provided in section 41-22-24.

(d) An agency may withdraw a proposed rule by leave of the committee. An agency may resubmit a rule so withdrawn or returned under this section with minor modification. Such a rule is a new filing and subject to this section but is not subject to further notice as provided in subsection (a) of section 41-22-5.

(e) The committee is authorized to review and approve or disapprove any rule adopted prior to October 1, 1982.

(f) In determining whether to approve or disapprove proposed rules, the committee shall consider the following criteria:

(1) Would the absence of the rule or rules significantly harm or endanger the public health, safety, or welfare?

(2) Is there a reasonable relationship between the state's police power and the protection of the public health, safety, or welfare?

(3) Is there another, less restrictive method of regulation available that could adequately protect the public?

(4) Does the rule or do the rules have the effect of directly or indirectly increasing the costs of any goods or services involved and, if so, to what degree?

(5) Is the increase in cost, if any, more harmful to the public than the harm that might result from the absence of the rule or rules?

(6) Are all facets of the rulemaking process designed solely for the purpose of, and so they have, as their primary effect, the protection of the public?

(7) Any other criteria the committee may deem appropriate. (Acts 1981, No. 81-855, p. 1534, § 23.)

Collateral references. — 1 Am. Jur. 2d,
Administrative Law, §§ 289, 557-609.

Commentary

Subsection (a) of this section is based on Conn. Gen. Stat. § 4-170(b) (1977 Cum. Supp.) with some differences. This section and subdivision (1) of subsection (a) of section 41-22-5(a)(1) require notice to the committee as well as copies of proposed rules to be furnished the committee; the Connecticut statute makes no mention of a notice requirement as well as copies of proposed rules. Forms of rules submitted to the committee are same as bills submitted to the legislature. The committee may hold hearings on proposed rules but are not required to do so. In the event the committee takes no action on a rule within 60 days from the day it is presented to them the rule is deemed approved.

The committee may disapprove the rule and its implementation suspended until the adjournment of the next regular session of the legislature. Tennessee has a similar veto provision, Tenn. Code Ann. § 4-5-129, as well as Michigan, 24.245 Mich. Code. The Alabama act allows rule suspension but the suspension is temporary and expires unless the full legislature sustains the suspension by joint resolution.

Subsection (b) of this section is similar to a provision found in the West Virginia Code § 29A-3-11.

Subsection (c) of this section which allows for agency withdrawal of a rule is adopted from 24.245(6) Michigan Code.

Subsection (d) of this section is adopted from Conn. Gen. Stat. § 4-170(a) (1977 Cum. Supp.).

Subdivisions (1) through (6) of subsection (f) of this section are an adaptation of Fla. Stat. § 11.61(4) (1977) except when that statute uses the word "regulation", this section substitutes the word "rule". Subdivision (7) of subsection (f) of this section was added to allow the committee broad authority in determining approval or disapproval of rules.

§ 41-22-24. Reconsideration of disapproved rules by the legislature.

On the first day of each regular session of the Alabama legislature the chairman of the committee shall submit copies of all proposed regulations that have been disapproved by the committee under section 41-22-23 to each member of both houses of the legislature for their study. Such rules shall be referred by the speaker of the house or the lieutenant governor or both to an appropriate committee or committees, other than the joint committee on administrative regulation review, for consideration and such committee or committees shall schedule hearings thereon, if requested by an affected party or the submitting agency. The legislature may, by joint resolution, sustain the disapproval of the committee under section 41-22-23. In the event the legislature fails to sustain such committee disapproval by the adjournment of the next regular session of the legislature, the rule shall be reinstated. (Acts 1981, No. 81-855, p. 1534, § 24.)

Commentary

This section is adopted from Conn. Gen. Stat. § 4-171 (1977 Cum. Supp.), with such modification as was necessary to keep it consistent with this act. The Alabama act differs from the other acts insofar as the legislature must vote by joint resolution to agree with the suspension and disapprove a rule. Failure to rescind the rule either through inaction of the legislature or failure to vote on the joint resolution will result in the reinstatement of the rule. There is no provision in this act similar to "sunset" legislation that requires a vote on each pending piece of legislation submitted by the committee.

§ 41-22-25. Construction and applicability of chapter.

(a) This chapter shall be construed broadly to effectuate its purposes. Except as expressly provided otherwise by this chapter or by another statute referring to this chapter by name, the rights created and the requirements imposed by this chapter shall be in addition to those created or imposed by every other statute in existence on the date of the passage of this chapter or thereafter enacted. If any other statute in existence on the date of the passage of this chapter or thereafter enacted diminishes any right conferred upon a person by this chapter or diminishes any requirement imposed upon an agency by this chapter, this chapter shall take precedence unless the other statute expressly provides that it shall take precedence over all or some specified portion of this named chapter.

(b) Except as to proceedings in process on that date which shall be October 1, 1983, this chapter shall be construed to apply to all covered agency proceedings and all agency action not expressly exempted by this chapter or by another statute specifically referring to this chapter by name. (Acts 1981, No. 81-855, p. 1534, § 25.)

Cross references. — As to the effective date of this act generally and the effective date of certain sections, see § 41-22-27.

Commentary

This section is based on Iowa Code § 17A.23 (1976 Cum. Supp.). There is no corresponding section in the Revised Model State Administrative Procedure Act.

As has already been noted, this section must be read together with section 4-22-2. See Commentary to section 41-22-2. The following comments on the Iowa counterpart to this section will be helpful:

The reason for the use of this particular linguistic technique . . . is relatively simple. The [Act] is viewed as an embodiment of the fundamental minimum elements of fairness regardless of circumstance, or agency, or time. It is true that what is fair usually varies with the circumstances. But this act, like the Revised Model Act which is its progenitor, does not address itself to details or minutia. Rather, it limits itself in almost all cases to general principles of fairness and justice; and it seeks to implement the proposition quoted earlier from the commissioners on uniform state laws that there are some minimum general precepts that can and should prevail universally in the administrative process — at all times, at all places, and in all circumstances. Therefore, the burden should be on those seeking an exemption from the general principles embodied in the [Act] to demonstrate clearly the necessity for an exemption, and to have their claim for any such exception embodied in unmistakable statutory language indicating that the legislature has actually considered the question of an exemption and determined that it is warranted.

Bonfield, The Iowa Administrative Procedure Act: Background, Construction, Applicability, Public Access to Agency Law, the Rulemaking Process, 60 Iowa L. Rev. 731, 756 (1975).

§ 41-22-26. Repeal of inconsistent laws.

It is the express intent of the legislature to replace all provisions in statutes of this state relating to rulemaking, agency orders, administrative adjudication, or judicial review thereof that are inconsistent with the provisions of this chapter. Therefore, all laws or parts of laws that conflict with this chapter are hereby repealed on October 1, 1982; provided, however, nothing contained in this section shall be construed to repeal or modify sections 22-22-1, 22-22-4, 22-22-8 through 22-22-10, 22-22-12 and 22-22-14, authorizing the water improvement commission as the state water pollution control agency to issue one stop permits for the state for all purposes of the federal Water Pollution Control Act, as amended. (Acts 1981, No. 81-855, p. 1534, § 26.)

Code commissioner's note. — Sections 22-22-4, 22-22-8, 22-22-10 and 22-22-12, referred to in this section, were repealed by Acts 1982, No. 82-612, § 14(a)(2), effective October 1, 1982.

U.S. Code. — The federal Water Pollution Control Act, referred to in this section, is codified at 33 U.S.C.A. § 1251 et seq.

Commentary

As emphasized in the preceding section, this act is designed merely as a minimum procedural safeguard, and provisions in other statutes conferring other or greater rights than expressed herein are not to be regarded as inconsistent with this act. Inasmuch as Alabama had no general Administrative Procedure Act, there will be little with which this act would conflict.

§ 41-22-27. Effective date of this chapter; validity, review, etc., of existing rules; disposition of adjudicative proceedings commenced prior to October 1, 1983.

(a) This chapter shall take effect at 12:01 A.M., October 1, 1982; provided, however, that section 41-22-22 shall take effect October 1, 1981. In order that the legislative reference service may appoint and hire an aid to receive the rules and in order to promulgate the Alabama Administrative Code and the Alabama Administrative Monthly as soon as possible, subsections (a) and (b) of section 41-22-6 and subsections (a) through (e) of section 41-22-7 shall also become effective October 1, 1981. It shall be the duty of all agencies in existence on the passage of this chapter and all agencies created thereafter to cooperate with the office of the legislative reference service in compiling the

Alabama Administratice Code and the Alabama Administrative Monthly by submitting to the committee all rules now and hereafter in effect, and all proposed rules.

(b) All existing rules shall be indexed by October 1, 1983, and the administrative code of each agency shall be completed and up-to-date at that time and the Alabama Administrative Code shall be completed and up-to-date by November 15, 1983.

(c) Any rule in effect before 12:01 A.M., October 1, 1983, except those adopted following a public hearing that was required by statute, shall forthwith be reviewed by the agency concerned on the written request of a person substantially affected by the rule involved. The agency concerned shall initiate the rulemaking procedures provided by this chapter within 90 days after receiving such written request. If the agency concerned fails to initiate the rulemaking procedures within 90 days, the operation of the rule shall be suspended. The right of review established by this subsection shall be exercisable no earlier than October 1, 1983.

(d) All rules in effect on the passage of this chapter and in effect October 1, 1983, shall be valid if validly adopted under procedures prior to those provided by this chapter; and such rules shall be indexed and published in the administrative code of each agency; provided, however, that in the case of rules not adopted following a public hearing expressly required or permitted by statute, such rules shall be invalid and of no effect on October 1, 1983, unless the agency shall have adopted or readopted said rules pursuant to the requirements of this chapter.

(e) All contested cases and other adjudicative proceedings conducted pursuant to any provision of the statutes of this state that were begun prior to October 1, 1983, shall be continued to a conclusion, including judicial review, under the provisions of such statutes, except that contested cases and other adjudicative proceedings that have not progressed to the stage of a hearing may, with the consent of all parties and the agency conducting the proceedings, be conducted in accordance with the provisions of this chapter as nearly as feasible. (Acts 1981, No. 81-855, p. 1534, § 27.)

Effective date. — The act which added this chapter was approved by the governor on May 27, 1981.

Commentary

This section provides two separate effective dates, October 1, 1982, as the effective date for the general provisions of this act, and October 1, 1981, as the effective date for those sections which contain the requirements for filing with the legislative reference service (subsection (b) of section 41-22-6), for publication of rules (section 41-22-7), and for the creation of the joint committee on administrative regulation review (section 41-22-22). It is necessary to provide the one-year lapse between the effective dates of these provisions to ensure that the mechanisms necessary to effectuate the purposes of this act are functioning by the time the rulemaking requirements go into effect.

This will provide agencies sufficient time to review their rules and submit them to the legislative reference service, and to provide the legislative reference service sufficient time to compile, index and publish such rules and make them available to the public. This revision will also provide sufficient time for the legislative council to be acquainted with their review procedure, hire its staff, and begin to perform its functions. In short, the one-year period is necessary as preparatory time before the remaining provisions of this act become effective.

The October 1 date was chosen to coincide with the fiscal year, so that funds can be allotted in the budget to cover the costs of implementing the provisions of this act.

This section also provides for the review of rules adopted prior to the effective date of this statute, except for those adopted after a public hearing required or permitted by statute, upon request following the effective date of this act, or within one year of the effective date of this act if there is no such request. In other words, it is the intention of this section that all rules previously adopted without public hearing shall be either readopted by October 1, 1983, under the requirements of this act, or shall become invalid.

It is not intended that any proceedings of an adjudicative nature that are in progress on the effective date of this act be terminated and reinstituted to comply with the provisions of the applicable sections of this act; however, it is provided in this section that adjudicative procedures in a prehearing stage may be conducted in accordance with the provisions of this act, with the consent of the agency and all parties to the action, in order that the procedural protections intended to be provided by this act may be fully taken advantage of at the earliest opportunity.

TITLE 42.

UNITED STATES.

Constitution. — For provision of federal Constitution, see Const., article I, § 8, paragraph 17.

Action under federal Employees Compensation Act, see Webb v. White Eng'r Corp., 204 Ala. 429, 85 So. 729 (1920).

Cited in City of Birmingham v. Thompson, 200 F.2d 505 (5th Cir. 1952).

CHAPTER 1.

GENERAL PROVISIONS.

Sec.
42-1-1. United States may acquire lands.
42-1-2. Consent to acquisition of lands needed for consolidation and administration of national forests.

Cross references. — As to post-office projects in municipalities, see § 11-55-1 et seq. As to election of United States senators, see § 17-2-11. As to presidential and vice-presidential electors, see § 17-19-1 et seq. As to congressional districts and elections for seats in United States House of Representatives, see § 17-20-1 et seq. As to lien for United States taxes, see § 35-11-40 et seq. As to disposition of unclaimed property held by federal courts, officers, authorities or agencies, see § 35-12-28. As to prohibition against person holding office of profit under the United States holding office of profit under this state at same time, see § 36-2-1. As to taxation of property and activities of United States and its agencies not constitutionally exempt from taxation, see § 40-11-2. As to taxation of federal property where immunity waived, see § 40-11-3.

Collateral references. — 91 C.J.S., United States, § 71.

§ 42-1-1. United States may acquire lands.

The United States may acquire and hold lands within the limits of this state as sites for forts, magazines, arsenals, dockyards and other needful buildings, or either of them, as contemplated and provided by the Constitution of the United States, which purchase may be made by contract with the owners or as otherwise provided in this title. In like manner, the United States may acquire and hold lands, rights-of-way and material needed in maintaining, operating or prosecuting works for the improvement of rivers and harbors within this state. (Code 1852, § 24; Code 1867, § 22; Code 1876, § 19; Code 1886, § 19; Code 1896, § 626; Code 1907, § 2413; Code 1923, § 3147; Code 1940, T. 59, § 1.)

Cross references. — As to nonconsent of the state of Alabama to the acquisition by the United States of property for the use of depositing or dumping spent nuclear fuel generated outside of Alabama, see § 22-14-16.

§ 42-1-2. Consent to acquisition of lands needed for consolidation and administration of national forests.

The consent of the state of Alabama is hereby given to the United States to acquire by purchase, condemnation or gift, for forest purposes, such lands, within the exterior national forest boundaries or within the watershed or drainage areas of the Tennessee river in Alabama, as have heretofore or may hereafter be approved by the department of conservation and natural resources and as, in the opinion of the administrative executives of the United States, may be or are needed for the consolidation, extension and administration of national forests. In all condemnation proceedings for the acquisition of lands, the rights of the United States shall be limited to the specific object set by the laws of the United States regarding national forests. (Acts 1931, No. 88, p. 165; Acts 1933, Ex. Sess., No. 120, p. 113; Code 1940, T. 59, § 2.)

Collateral references. — 91 C.J.S., United States, §§ 7, 74.

CHAPTER 2.

CONDEMNATION OF LAND OR RIGHTS-OF-WAY.

Ascertaining value of land in condemnation proceedings. — In a proceeding to condemn land for a nitrate plant under this chapter landowners were entitled to have the enhanced value of the land, due to the prior location nearby of another nitrate plant by the government, considered on the question of damage; the location of the second plant being unexpected, and not a part of the general scheme when the first plant was designated. United States v. Goodloe, 204 Ala. 484, 86 So. 546 (1920).

In such proceedings opinion evidence is not binding on jury. — In a proceeding under this chapter to condemn land, opinion evidence as to value of the land was not binding on the jury, although the evidence was confined solely to opinion testimony dealing entirely with the valuation of the property, since it related to a matter as to which the members of the jury are presumed to have some general knowledge. United States v. Goodloe, 204 Ala. 484, 86 So. 546 (1920).

§ 42-2-1. When authorized; jurisdiction of probate court.

If the agent of the United States and the owner of the lands or right-of-way to be condemned cannot agree as to the terms of the sale and purchase thereof, the probate court of the county in which such lands or any part thereof may lie may, on the application of the agent of the United States, proceed to condemn such lands to such uses as may be provided for. (Code 1852, § 22; Code 1867, § 23; Code 1876, § 20; Code 1886, § 20; Code 1896, § 627; Code 1907, § 2414; Code 1923, § 3148; Code 1940, T. 59, § 4.)

Collateral references. — 91 C.J.S., United States, §§ 7, 71.

§ 42-2-2. Application.

The application of the United States or its agent must be in writing, verified by the oath of an agent or attorney, and must state with certainty the uses or purposes for which the land is to be taken or the interest or easement therein to be acquired, and must state the name and residence of the owner if known or, if unknown, must show that reasonable diligence has been used to ascertain the same. (Code 1907, § 2415; Code 1923, § 3149; Code 1940, T. 59, § 5.)

§ 42-2-3. Order appointing day of hearing; publication and service of notice of hearing.

On the filing of the application, the court must make and enter an order appointing the day for the hearing thereof. If the owner of the land resides within the state, the court must issue notice to him of the application and of the day of the hearing thereof, which must be served by the sheriff or other legal officer at least 10 days before the day appointed for the hearing. If the owner is unknown or if he resides without the state or has been absent from the state or beyond the jurisdiction of the court in which the application is made for six months next before the time of the filing of the application in said court, notice may be given by advertisement in any newspaper published in the county or, if there be no newspaper published in the county, by posting notice at the courthouse and three other public places for at least three weeks before the day appointed for the hearing. If the owner is an infant or of unsound mind, notice must be served on his guardian, if any he have, resident in the state, but if he resides in the state and has no such guardian, then the person who may have him in charge or with whom he may reside. If the owner is dead and the lands are in the possession or under the control of his personal representative, notice must be served on such representative and on the heirs at law of the decedent. (Code 1907, § 2416; Code 1923, § 3150; Code 1940, T. 59, § 6.)

§ 42-2-4. Appointment of guardian ad litem and counsel for infants and persons of unsound mind.

If the owner of the lands is an infant or is of unsound mind, the court, on the day appointed for the hearing, must appoint a guardian ad litem to represent him, and the guardian so appointed must file a written acceptance of the appointment, must appear and protect the rights and interests of such infant or person of unsound mind and, if he deems it necessary, may employ counsel to assist him. The compensation of such guardian and of his counsel must be ascertained by the court and taxed as costs of the proceedings. (Code 1907, § 2417; Code 1923, § 3151; Code 1940, T. 59, § 7.)

§ 42-2-5. Failure of owner to appear at hearing.

If the owner does not appear on the hearing of the application, the court must hear the same and, if the application is granted, must appoint commissioners as herein provided for, and thereafter the same proceedings shall be had as if such owner had appeared. (Code 1907, § 2418; Code 1923, § 3152; Code 1940, T. 59, § 8.)

§ 42-2-6. Conduct of hearing; order granting or refusing application; appeal from grant or refusal of application.

On the day appointed or any other day to which the hearing may be continued, the court must hear the allegations of the application and any objections which may be filed to the granting thereof and any legal evidence touching the same, and shall make an order granting or refusing the application.

The hearing herein provided for must in all respects be conducted and evidence taken as in civil cases, and either party may, by bill of exception, reserve any opinion or decision of the court. Either party is entitled to an appeal to the supreme court from the order of the court granting or refusing the application within 42 days from the making thereof. (Code 1907, §§ 2419, 2420; Code 1923, §§ 3153, 3154; Code 1940, T. 59, §§ 9, 10.)

§ 42-2-7. Commissioners for assessment of damages and compensation — Appointment; notice to commissioners; duties.

If the application is granted, the judge of probate must appoint three citizens of the county in which the lands sought to be condemned are situated, who shall possess the qualifications of jurors, who shall be disinterested and who shall be required to file a certificate along with their award that neither of them had ever been consulted, advised with or approached by any person in reference to the value of the lands or the proceedings to condemn the same, prior to the assessment of the damages, and that they knew nothing of the same before their appointment. The judge of probate is authorized to fill any vacancy occasioned by the death, resignation, failure to act or any disqualification of any such commissioners from interest, prior knowledge of the subject matter or by being consulted, advised with or approached in reference to the condemnation of such lands prior to appointment or to the assessment of damages. When the court shall have appointed the commissioners as herein provided, it shall at once issue a notice of such appointment to the sheriff, whose duty it shall be to serve such notice upon the person therein designated within five days of the receipt thereof, and the sheriff shall receive the same compensation for serving such notice as allowed for summoning jurors. It shall be the duty of the commissioners, or a majority of them, thus appointed by the judge of probate to assess the damages and compensation to which the owner of the land is entitled, and they shall be sworn as jurors are sworn. The commissioners may view the lands to be subjected and must receive all legal evidence that may be offered by either party touching the amount of the damages the owner of the lands will sustain and the amount of compensation he is entitled to receive. The amount of compensation to which the owner is entitled must not be reduced or diminished because of any incidental benefits which may accrue to him or to his remaining lands in consequence of the uses to which the lands proposed to be taken or in which an easement is proposed to be acquired will be appropriated. Nothing in this section shall be construed to prevent any applicant for the condemnation of land or any landowner whose land is sought to be condemned from being present in person or by attorney at any of the proceedings or trials provided for in this chapter. (Code 1907, § 2421; Code 1923, § 3155; Code 1940, T. 59, § 11.)

§ 42-2-8. Same — Report.

The commissioners must, within 10 days from their appointment, report in writing to the court the amount of damages and compensation ascertained and assessed by them, and thereupon the court must order the same to be recorded and must make an order of condemnation in pursuance thereof upon payment of the damages and compensation so assessed and reported or the deposit of the same in court. (Code 1907, § 2422; Code 1923, § 3156; Code 1940, T. 59, § 12.)

Cited in American Sur. Co. v. Moran, 75 F.2d 646 (D.C. Cir. 1935).

§ 42-2-9. Appeal from assessment of damages.

Either party may appeal from the assessment of damages and compensation by the commissioners to the circuit court of the county within 30 days after the making of the order of condemnation, upon the report of the commissioners, by filing in the court rendering the judgment a written notice of appeal, a copy of which shall be served on the opposite party, and on such appeal the trial shall be de novo. No appeal shall suspend the judgment if the applicant shall pay into court in money the amount of damages assessed and give bond in double the amount so assessed, with good and sufficient surety, to be approved by the judge of probate, to pay such damages as the owner may sustain. (Code 1907, § 2423; Code 1923, § 3157; Code 1940, T. 59, § 13.)

§ 42-2-10. Order of condemnation vests title; right of entry on land pending appeal.

The order of condemnation, upon the payment of the sum ascertained and assessed by the verdict of the jury, or the deposit thereof in the court for the defendant, shall vest in the United States the title in fee simple to the lands to be acquired for the uses and purposes stated in the application. But if an appeal shall be taken by either party, then the United States or its agents, upon the deposit in the court for the party whose land is sought to be condemned of the amount of damages and compensation so assessed, together with the cost of the proceeding, and giving a bond in double the amount of damages assessed, shall be entitled to enter upon the land so condemned and survey, construct and operate on the same for the uses, and purposes stated in the application, but such easement shall not vest absolutely in the United States until the final determination of the cause and payment or deposit in court of such damages and compensation as shall then be adjudged. (Code 1907, § 2424; Code 1923, § 3158; Code 1940, T. 59, § 14.)

§ 42-2-11. When damages to be paid; failure to pay damages.

The applicant may pay the damages and compensation assessed at any time within six months after the assessment thereof or, in case an appeal is taken, within six months after the appeal is determined. If the applicant fails to pay the same within such time, such assessment shall cease to be binding on the owner of the lands, and the rights of the United States thereunder shall be terminated. (Code 1907, § 2425; Code 1923, § 3159; Code 1940, T. 59, § 15.)

§ 42-2-12. Appointment of commissioner to execute conveyance.

If the application is granted and the lands condemned, as provided in this chapter, and no appeal is taken therefrom, or, if appeal is taken and the lands described are condemned on appeal, the probate court in which the application is filed shall at once appoint a commissioner to execute the conveyance of the title to the lands so condemned and shall convey thereby all such title as the owners had therein to the United States, free from the claims of all persons whomsoever. (Code 1907, § 2426; Code 1923, § 3160; Code 1940, T. 59, § 16.)

CHAPTER 3.

CESSION OF LAND BY STATE.

Sec.

§ 42-3-1. Authority of governor to cede jurisdiction.

The governor, upon application made to him in writing on behalf of the United States for that purpose, accompanied by the proper evidence of title in the United States describing the lands, is authorized on the part of the state, by patent to be recorded in the office of the secretary of state, to cede to the United States such jurisdiction as he may deem wise over such lands, to hold, to use and occupy the same for the purposes of the cession and none other. (Code 1852, § 23; Code 1867, § 24; Code 1876, § 21; Code 1886, § 21; Code 1896, § 628; Code 1907, § 2427; Code 1923, § 3161; Code 1940, T. 59, § 18.)

Instrument of cession or patent should be recorded in the office of secretary of state of Alabama. Graham v. Brewer, 295 F. Supp. 1140 (N.D. Ala. 1968).

Cited in City of Birmingham v. Thompson, 200 F.2d 505 (5th Cir. 1952); Alabama-Tennessee Natural Gas Co. v. City of Huntsville, 275 Ala. 184, 153 So. 2d 619 (1963).

§ 42-3-2. Cession of sites covered by navigable waters.

Whenever the United States desires to acquire title to land belonging to this state, covered by the navigable waters of the United States and within the limits of this state for the site of a lighthouse, beacon or other aid to navigation, and application is made therefor by a duly authorized agent of the United States, describing the site required for one of the purposes aforesaid, then the governor of the state may convey the title to the United States and may also cede to the United States such jurisdiction over the same as may be necessary for the purposes of the United States. Upon like application, the governor may convey to the United States the title to any land belonging to this state and covered by the navigable waters of the United States upon which any lighthouse or other aid to navigation has heretofore been erected, and may also cede to the United States such jurisdiction over the same as may be necessary for the purposes of the United States. No single tract shall contain more than 10 acres. (Code 1876, § 22; Code 1886, § 22; Code 1896, § 629; Code 1907, § 2428; Code 1923, § 3162; Code 1940, T. 59, § 3.)

§ 42-3-3. Reservation of rights, etc., by state.

The jurisdiction heretofore ceded to the United States over any lands acquired by it within the state of Alabama, with the consent of the state, shall be subject to such reservations, restrictions and conditions as provided in the act or instrument of cession relating to such acquisition and shall be subject to the exercise by the state of such jurisdiction, rights, privileges or powers as may now or hereafter be ceded by the United States to the state. The jurisdiction ceded to the United States over any lands hereafter acquired by it within the state of Alabama, with the consent of the state, pursuant to the provisions of this title or any other law of the state, unless otherwise expressly provided in the act or instrument of cession, shall be subject to the following reservations, restrictions or conditions:

(1) The jurisdiction so ceded shall not prevent the execution upon such lands of any process, civil or criminal, issued under the authority of this state, except as such process might affect the property of the United States thereon.

(2) The state expressly reserves the right to tax all persons, firms, corporations or associations now or hereafter residing or located upon such lands.

(3) The state expressly reserves the right to tax the exercise by any person, firm, corporation or association of any and all rights, privileges and franchises upon said lands, and to tax property of all persons, firms, corporations or associations situated upon such lands.

(4) The jurisdiction ceded to the United States shall be for the purposes of the cession and none other and shall continue during the time the United States shall be or remain the owner thereof and shall use such lands for the purpose of the cession.

(5) The state expressly reserves the right to exercise over or upon any such lands any and all rights, privileges, powers or jurisdiction which may now or hereafter be released or receded by the United States to the state. (Code 1923, § 3166; Code 1940, T. 59, § 19.)

Jurisdiction is in state when property only rented to United States. — If a post office building is rented to the postmaster and has not been ceded to the United States no question can arise as to jurisdiction of the state court to try offenses committed therein as jurisdiction has not been ceded to the United States. Brooke v. State, 155 Ala. 78, 46 So. 491 (1908).

Nonresident subcontractor not "doing business" in state. — Where it appeared that nonresident subcontractor, accepting subcontract outside state, was constructing certain features of veterans' hospital on government land, that subcontractor used streets outside the government reservation in transporting shipments, that materials were purchased within state, that checks were cashed at local bank, that foreman and employee lived outside the reservation, but that offices of subcontractor were maintained in reservation, the subcontractor was held not subject to state license tax, since subcontractor was not "doing business" in state. O'Pry Heating & Plumbing Co. v. State, 241 Ala. 507, 3 So. 2d 316 (1941).

Ceded land not subject to local building code. — The University of Alabama conveyed

land in Birmingham to the United States, and pursuant to § 42-3-1 and this section the governor ceded to the government jurisdiction of said land which was to be used as the site of a veterans' administration hospital. The contractors constructing the hospital paid to the city, under protest, the building permit fee imposed pursuant to its building code. It was held that, as the state did not reserve the right to regulate the construction of buildings on hospital site lands a fortiori, no such right was vested in the city and the enforcement of the ordinance involved a permit for and control of the construction of the building on government lands, matters beyond the jurisdiction of the city. The ordinance was not saved by the fact that a proper ordinance could have required payment of a business license fee or of compensation for the substantial benefits furnished by the city. City of Birmingham v. Thompson, 200 F.2d 505 (5th Cir. 1952).

Section reserves particulars in which state law prevails. — Alabama laws do not prevail in federal enclaves, such as Redstone arsenal and military reservations, except in certain particulars reserved in this section. Alabama-Tennessee Natural Gas Co. v. City of

Huntsville, 275 Ala. 184, 153 So. 2d 619 (1963).

Effect of cession on contract describing exclusive sales territory. — The ceding of territory to the federal government by the state did not change either state or county boundaries, and the territory over which the federal government acquired jurisdiction still remained in the area described in a contract which gave one of the parties the exclusive right to sell gas in that territory. Alabama-Tennessee Natural Gas Co. v. City of Huntsville, 275 Ala. 184, 153 So. 2d 619 (1963).

Cited in Alabama Gas Co. v. City of Montgomery, 249 Ala. 257, 30 So. 2d 651 (1947); Graham v. Brewer, 295 F. Supp. 1140 (N.D. Ala. 1968).

Collateral references. — 91 C.J.S., United States, § 7.

TITLE 43.

WILLS AND DECEDENTS' ESTATES.

CHAPTER 1.

TRANSFERRED AND REPEALED.

ARTICLE 1.

GENERAL PROVISIONS.

§§ 43-1-1 through 43-1-13. Repealed by Acts 1982, No. 82-399, § 8-102, effective January 1, 1983.

§ 43-1-14. Transferred.

Code commissioner's note. — Section 43-1-14, as set out in the original 1975 Code, has been renumbered as § 43-8-254.

§§ 43-1-15 through 43-1-17. Repealed by Acts 1982, No. 82-399, § 8-102, effective January 1, 1983.

§ 43-1-18. Transferred.

Code commissioner's note. — Section 43-1-18, as set out in the original 1975 Code, has been renumbered as § 43-8-255.

§ 43-1-19. Transferred.

Code commissioner's note. — Section 43-1-19, as set out in the original 1975 Code, has been renumbered as § 43-8-256.

ARTICLE 2.

EXECUTION AND PROBATE OF WILLS.

§ 43-1-30. Repealed by Acts 1982, No. 82-399, § 8-102, effective January 1, 1983.

§ 43-1-30.1. Transferred.

Code commissioner's note. — Section 43-1-30.1, as set out in the 1975 Code, as amended, has been renumbered as § 43-8-132.

§§ 43-1-31 through 43-1-35. Repealed by Acts 1982, No. 82-399, § 8-102, effective January 1, 1983.

§ 43-1-36. Transferred.

Code commissioner's note. — Section 43-1-36, as set out in the original 1975 Code, has been renumbered as § 43-8-160.

§ 43-1-37. Transferred.

Code commissioner's note. — Section 43-1-37, as set out in the original 1975 Code, has been renumbered as § 43-8-161.

§ 43-1-38. Transferred.

Code commissioner's note. — Section 43-1-38, as set out in the original 1975 Code, has been renumbered as § 43-8-162.

§ 43-1-39. Transferred.

Code commissioner's note. — Section 43-1-39, as set out in the original 1975 Code, has been renumbered as § 43-8-163.

§ 43-1-40. Repealed by Acts 1982, No. 82-399, § 8-102, effective January 1, 1983.

§ 43-1-41. Transferred.

Code commissioner's note. — Section 43-1-41, as set out in the original 1975 Code, has been renumbered as § 43-8-164.

§ 43-1-42. Transferred.

Code commissioner's note. — Section 43-1-42, as set out in the original 1975 Code, has been renumbered as § 43-8-165.

§ 43-1-43. Transferred.

Code commissioner's note. — Section 43-1-43, as set out in the original 1975 Code, has been renumbered as § 43-8-166.

§ 43-1-44. Transferred.

Code commissioner's note. — Section 43-1-44, as set out in the original 1975 Code, has been renumbered as § 43-8-167.

§ 43-1-45. Transferred.

Code commissioner's note. — Section 43-1-45, as set out in the original 1975 Code, has been renumbered as § 43-8-168.

§ 43-1-46. Transferred.

Code commissioner's note. — Section 43-1-46, as set out in the original 1975 Code, has been renumbered as § 43-8-169.

§ 43-1-47. Transferred.

Code commissioner's note. — Section 43-1-47, as set out in the original 1975 Code, has been renumbered as § 43-8-170.

§ 43-1-48. Transferred.

Code commissioner's note. — Section 43-1-48, as set out in the original 1975 Code, has been renumbered as § 43-8-171.

§ 43-1-49. Transferred.

Code commissioner's note. — Section 43-1-49, as set out in the original 1975 Code, has been renumbered as § 43-8-172.

§ 43-1-50. Transferred.

Code commissioner's note. — Section 43-1-50, as set out in the original 1975 Code, has been renumbered as § 43-8-173.

§ 43-1-51. Transferred.

Code commissioner's note. — Section 43-1-51, as set out in the original 1975 Code, has been renumbered as § 43-8-174.

§ 43-1-52. Transferred.

Code commissioner's note. — Section 43-1-52, as set out in the original 1975 Code, has been renumbered as § 43-8-175.

ARTICLE 3.

CONTESTING VALIDITY OF WILLS.

§ 43-1-70. Transferred.

Code commissioner's note. — Section 43-1-70, as set out in the original 1975 Code, has been renumbered as § 43-8-190.

§ 43-1-71. Transferred.

Code commissioner's note. — Section 43-1-71, as set out in the original 1975 Code, has been renumbered as § 43-8-191.

§ 43-1-72. Transferred.

Code commissioner's note. — Section 43-1-72, as set out in the original 1975 Code, has been renumbered as § 43-8-192.

§ 43-1-73. Transferred.

Code commissioner's note. — Section 43-1-73, as set out in the original 1975 Code, has been renumbered as § 43-8-193.

§ 43-1-74. Transferred.

Code commissioner's note. — Section 43-1-74, as set out in the original 1975 Code, has been renumbered as § 43-8-194.

§ 43-1-75. Transferred.

Code commissioner's note. — Section 43-1-75, as set out in the original 1975 Code, has been renumbered as § 43-8-195.

§ 43-1-76. Transferred.

Code commissioner's note. — Section 43-1-76, as set out in the original 1975 Code, has been renumbered as § 43-8-196.

§ 43-1-77. Transferred.

Code commissioner's note. — Section 43-1-77, as set out in the original 1975 Code, has been renumbered as § 43-8-197.

§ 43-1-78. Transferred.

Code commissioner's note. — Section 43-1-78, as set out in the original 1975 Code, has been renumbered as § 43-8-198.

§ 43-1-79. Transferred.

Code commissioner's note. — Section 43-1-79, as set out in the original 1975 Code, has been renumbered as § 43-8-199.

§ 43-1-80. Transferred.

Code commissioner's note. — Section 43-1-80, as set out in the original 1975 Code, has been renumbered as § 43-8-200.

§ 43-1-81. Transferred.

Code commissioner's note. — Section 43-1-81, as set out in the original 1975 Code, has been renumbered as § 43-8-201.

§ 43-1-82. Transferred.

Code commissioner's note. — Section 43-1-82, as set out in the original 1975 Code, has been renumbered as § 43-8-202.

CHAPTER 2.
ADMINISTRATION OF ESTATES.

441

Article 1.

General Provisions.

Cross references. — As to disposition of small bank deposits of deceased persons, see §§ 5-5A-38, 5-5A-39. As to disposition of bank deposit in trust for another upon death of trustee, see § 5-5A-40. As to disposition of bank deposits made in names of two persons upon death of one, see § 5-5A-41. As to ownership of bank deposits made in names of two persons upon death of one person, see § 5-5A-41. As to common trust funds administered by banks and trust companies, see § 5-12A-1 et seq. As to title to and payment of savings and loan accounts in names of two persons upon death of one, see §§ 5-16-44, 5-16-45. As to disposition of small savings and loan accounts of deceased persons, see § 5-16-46. As to disposition of credit union accounts in names of two persons upon death of one, see § 5-17-15. As to disposition of small credit union accounts upon death of depositor, see § 5-17-16. As to proceedings on administration of estates in circuit court, see § 12-11-40. As to removal of administration of estates from probate court to circuit court, see § 12-11-41. As to estate and inheritance tax, see § 40-15-1 et seq.

§ 43-2-1. Recordation of letters and bonds; transcripts as evidence.

All letters testamentary and of administration, general or special, and the bonds given by executors and administrators must be recorded by the judge of probate. Transcripts thereof, duly certified, are evidence in all the courts of this state to the same extent as if the originals were produced. (Code 1852, § 1695; Code 1867, § 2016; Code 1876, § 2378; Code 1886, § 2036; Code 1896, § 79; Code 1907, § 2546; Code 1923, § 5768; Code 1940, T. 61, § 102.)

Article 2.

Grant of Letters Testamentary and of Administration.

Division 1.

Grant of Letters Testamentary.

Cross references. — As to tolling of statute of limitations between death of a person and grant of letters testamentary or of administration, see § 6-2-14.

§ 43-2-20. Generally.

Whenever a will has been admitted to probate in this state, the judge of the court in which the will was probated may issue letters testamentary, according to the provisions of this article, to the persons named as the executors in such will, if they are fit persons to serve as such. (Code 1852, § 1657; Code 1867, § 1975; Code 1876, § 2339; Code 1886, § 2003; Code 1896, § 45; Code 1907, § 2507; Code 1923, § 5729; Code 1940, T. 61, § 68.)

Jurisdiction of probate court is original, general and unlimited. — In the grant of administrations, the jurisdiction of the probate court is derived from constitutional provisions, and is original, general and unlimited. Gray v. Cruise, 36 Ala. 559 (1860); Barclift v. Treece, 77 Ala. 528 (1884).

Under this section probate court has exclusive jurisdiction to grant letters testamentary. Ex parte Lunsford, 117 Ala. 221, 23 So. 528 (1898).

Court first acquiring jurisdiction has exclusive power. — A probate court of one county, on determining that testatrix is an inhabitant thereof, and that the paper propounded for probate is her last will, has the exclusive power to issue letters testamentary. In other words, it is almost a matter of absolute necessity for the application of the rule that the court first assuming jurisdiction must be allowed to pursue its jurisdiction to the exclusion of other coordinate tribunals, since any other rule would bring about two administrations of one estate, and the resulting legal impossibilities flowing therefrom. McDonnell v. Farrow, 132 Ala. 227, 31 So. 475 (1902).

"Executors" and "will" defined. — The testamentary executors referred to in this section are such only as are named by a will executed in accordance with former § 43-1-30. And a will in this connection is defined as an instrument by which a person makes disposition of his property to become effective after his death and is in its own nature ambulatory and revocable during the life of the testator. Blacksher Co. v. Northrup, 176 Ala. 190, 57 So. 743 (1911).

Probate of will prerequisite to granting of letters. — Letters may not be granted to executors until after the will has been admitted to probate. Blacksher Co. v. Northrup, 176 Ala. 190, 57 So. 743 (1911).

Duty of court to appoint person named in will. — See Thomas v. Field, 210 Ala. 502, 98 So. 474 (1923). See also Kidd v. Bates, 120 Ala. 79, 23 So. 735 (1898).

Naming executor through agent is valid. — By virtue of the provisions of the statute of wills, a testator may name the person who shall be the executor of his will. Not only is this right of a decedent now universally recognized, but in many jurisdictions it is within the power of a testator, not only to appoint personally, but to project his power of appointment into the future, and exercise it after death through an agent selected by him. Such agent may be pointed out by name, or by his office or other method of certain identification. A testator may even authorize the court of another state to name a suitable person as executor. Thomas v. Field, 210 Ala. 502, 98 So. 474 (1923), giving effect to testatrix's intent to have daughter name executor upon a failure of her brothers to act.

And agent's authority does not terminate until estate is divided. — The extent to which the court will go in giving effect to testator's desire to have an agent point out the executor is illustrated by the holding that the right of the agent (daughters) to select an executor does not terminate upon the selection of one who failed to act and resigned, but continued while the estate remained undetermined and undivided. Thomas v. Field, 210 Ala. 502, 98 So. 474 (1923).

Cited in Brown v. Hay, 1 Stew. & Port. 102 (1831); Bryant v. Ingraham, 16 Ala. 116 (1849); Kirby v. Anders, 26 Ala. 466 (1855); Ikelheimer v. Chapman, 32 Ala. 676 (1858); Ward v. Oates, 43 Ala. 515 (1869); Bryant v. State, 46 Ala. 302 (1871); Whitaker v. Kennamer, 229 Ala. 80, 155 So. 855 (1934); Moore v. Strickland, 246 Ala. 624, 21 So. 2d 665 (1945); Smith v. Rice, 265 Ala. 236, 90 So. 2d 262 (1956).

Collateral references. — 33 C.J.S., Executors & Administrators, § 69. 95 C.J.S., Wills, §§ 317, 526.

Relation back of letters testamentary or of administration. 26 ALR 1359.

Extrinsic evidence to identify person whom testator intended to name as executor. 94 ALR 127.

Court's power to refuse letters testamentary to one named in will as executor, absent specific statutory disqualification. 95 ALR 828.

Judgment or order in connection with appointment of executor or administrator as res judicata, as law of the case, or as evidence, on question other than the validity of the appointment. 110 ALR 594.

Services as executor or administrator or in connection with administration of estate is practice of law. 111 ALR 42, 125 ALR 1173, 151 ALR 781.

Delegation by will of power to nominate executor. 11 ALR2d 1284.

Loss of right to be appointed executor by delay in presenting will for probate or in seeking letters testamentary. 45 ALR2d 916.

Relation back of letters testamentary or of administration as validating prior sales of decedent's property. 2 ALR3d 1105.

§ 43-2-21. Form.

Letters testamentary may be substantially in the following form:

The State of Alabama, }　　　　　　　　　　　　Court of Probate.
. . . . County. }

The will of . . . ., having been duly admitted to record in said county, letters testamentary are hereby granted to . . . ., the executor named in said will, who has complied with the requisitions of the law and is authorized to take upon himself the execution of such will.

Witness my hand and dated this . . . . . . day of . . . . . ., 19. . . .

. . . .
Judge of Probate.

(Code 1852, § 1687; Code 1867, § 2007; Code 1876, § 2369; Code 1886, § 2005; Code 1896, § 47; Code 1907, § 2509; Code 1923, § 5731; Code 1940, T. 61, § 70.)

§ 43-2-22. Disqualification of certain persons to serve as executor or administrator.

(a) No person must be deemed a fit person to serve as executor who is under the age of 19 years, or who has been convicted of an infamous crime, or who, from intemperance, improvidence or want of understanding, is incompetent to discharge the duties of the trust. Nor shall any nonresident of the state be appointed as administrator unless he is at the time executor or administrator of the same estate in some other state or territory or jurisdiction, duly qualified under the laws of that jurisdiction.

(b) If the person named in the will as sole executor is or if all the persons named therein as executors are, from any of the causes enumerated in subsection (a), unfit to serve as executor or executors, letters of administration, with the will annexed, may be granted on the testator's estate, under the provisions of section 43-2-27. (Code 1852, §§ 1658, 1659; Code 1867, §§ 1976, 1977; Code 1876, §§ 2340, 2341; Code 1886, §§ 2004, 2006; Code 1896, §§ 46, 48; Code 1907, §§ 2508, 2510; Code 1923, §§ 5730, 5732; Code 1940, T. 61, §§ 69, 71.)

Cross references. — As to removal of executors or administrators, see § 43-2-290 et seq.

Common-law rule. — The rule of the common law was that all persons might be appointed executors who were capable of making a will. Neither infancy, nonresidence, coverture, intemperance, improvidence, ignorance, vice, dishonesty nor any degree of moral guilt or delinquency disqualified one for the office. Idiots and lunatics were practically the only classes disqualified. Kidd v. Bates, 120 Ala. 79, 23 So. 735 (1898).

Origin of section. — This section is a substantial copy of the New York statute, and is very similar to that of California. Kidd v. Bates, 120 Ala. 79, 23 So. 735 (1898).

Purpose. — The purpose of this section was not to declare, except indirectly, by the process of exclusion, who were fit and competent persons to discharge the duties of the trust, since the common law declared all persons competent except idiots and lunatics, but to enumerate the causes which should render persons incompetent. Kidd v. Bates, 120 Ala. 79, 23 So. 735 (1898).

When section comes into operation. — This section comes into operation only where there exists one or more of the causes enumerated in this section or in the event of the death of the executor or his renunciation of the right to act, as provided for in §§ 43-2-25 and 43-2-28. Kidd v. Bates, 120 Ala. 79, 23 So. 735 (1898).

It is applicable to administrators. — This section is applicable in the determination of the disqualification of administrators although the term executor only is mentioned in reference to some of the causes. Crommelin v. Raoul, 169 Ala. 413, 53 So. 745 (1910), following the early case of Williams v. McConico, 27 Ala. 572 (1855).

The prescriptions as to the qualifications of executors pertain also to administrators. Griffin v. Irwin, 246 Ala. 631, 21 So. 2d 668 (1945); Burnett v. Garrison, 261 Ala. 622, 75 So. 2d 144 (1954).

The fitness of an executor named in a will is controlled by this section. Riley v. Wilkinson, 247 Ala. 231, 23 So. 2d 582 (1945); Smith v. Rice, 265 Ala. 236, 90 So. 2d 262 (1956).

Enumerated causes in section limit the power of the court. — As indicated in Kidd v. Bates, 120 Ala. 79, 23 So. 735 (1898), the phrase in § 43-2-20 "if they are fit persons to serve as such," if standing alone, would place in the court a broad discretionary power. But this power of the court is greatly limited by the provisions of the instant section which define (negatively) the meaning of the phrase. And as already pointed out, the court can deny the application of a person otherwise entitled to administer only for causes herein enumerated.

Hence, a father cannot be denied the right to administer the estate of his infant child though he had no peculiar fitness for the office, and had abandoned his family, and although it was inferable that his desire to administer was for the purpose of using the situation for his own advantage. And no account may be taken of the general moral unfitness of the statutory preferred person. Nichols v. Smith, 186 Ala. 587, 65 So. 30 (1914).

And an allegation that the interests of the person named are already adverse to the estate and antagonistic to the legatees and devisees and others interested therein shows no legal disability of such person. Kidd v. Bates, 120 Ala. 79, 23 So. 735 (1898). See also Crommerlin v. Raoul, 169 Ala. 413, 53 So. 745 (1910).

Thus, its discretionary power may only be exercised to determine the existence of such causes. — Construing this section with § 43-2-20 (the two being in pari materia), it is held that the only discretion intended to be conferred is that to be exercised in the determination of the existence of those particular causes of disability enumerated. Kidd v. Bates, 120 Ala. 79, 23 So. 735 (1898).

And the court must appoint the applicant where there existed no disqualifying causes herein named. Bell v. Fulgham, 202 Ala. 217, 80 So. 39 (1918).

It sets out exclusive grounds of unfitness. — The statutory grounds of unfitness to serve as an administrator are exclusive and disqualification of an applicant to administer an estate who is otherwise entitled to preference not based on one of statutory grounds is not authorized. Griffin v. Irwin, 246 Ala. 631, 21 So. 2d 668 (1945); Burnett v. Garrison, 261 Ala. 622, 75 So. 2d 144 (1954).

A probate court is not authorized to refuse appointment of executor named in will on the ground that if appointed the court would have to remove him for alleged fraud under § 43-2-290. Smith v. Rice, 265 Ala. 236, 90 So. 2d 262 (1956).

Where decedent's next of kin are all nonresidents of Alabama, they not only occupy no preferential position, but are themselves disqualified from serving as administrators. Burnett v. Garrison, 261 Ala. 622, 75 So. 2d 144 (1954).

Meaning of "improvidence". — Within the meaning of this section, improvidence denotes a lack of care and foresight, thrift or business capacity, as would endanger the assets of the estate, but a capacity for care and foresight need not be evidenced by the accumulation of any considerable estate. Nichols v. Smith, 186 Ala. 587, 65 So. 30 (1914); Griffin v. Irwin, 246 Ala. 631, 21 So. 2d 668 (1945).

That applicant for letters of administration might because of her physical ailment and expressed intention resort to assistance of relatives in proper execution of duties did not establish applicant's "improvidence" as basis for disqualification, since improvidence connotes a trait of character already established. Griffin v. Irwin, 246 Ala. 631, 21 So. 2d 668 (1945).

Evidence including showing that intestate's sister was afflicted with arthritis, that she seldom was away from her home, that she could make trips if necessary and that entire administration would be concluded within a year did not show sister's disqualification on ground of "improvidence." Griffin v. Irwin, 246 Ala. 631, 21 So. 2d 668 (1945).

Executor could not be denied an appointment because of "improvidence" based on charges of fraudulent misconduct. Smith v. Rice, 265 Ala. 236, 90 So. 2d 262 (1956).

Generally, old age and bodily infirmities do not disqualify an applicant for letters of administration unless there is such physical disability as to indicate lack of intelligent capacity to execute duties of trust. Griffin v. Irwin, 246 Ala. 631, 21 So. 2d 668 (1945).

Statutory preferential right not lost. — The statutory preferential right to administer, as declared by § 43-2-42, is not lost because a person not in the same preferred class is found by the probate court to be better qualified, unless the person who is preferred is disqualified under this section. Calvert v. Beck, 240 Ala. 442, 199 So. 846 (1941).

Incompetence must be established by clear and convincing evidence to defeat the right to letters of administration. Griffin v. Irwin, 246 Ala. 631, 21 So. 2d 668 (1945).

Cited in Curtis v. Williams, 33 Ala. 570 (1859); Bingham v. Crenshaw, 34 Ala. 683 (1859); Broughton v. Bradley, 34 Ala. 694 (1859); Stallworth v. Farnham, 64 Ala. 259 (1879); Brown v. Brown, 204 Ala. 157, 85 So. 439 (1920); Marcus v. McKee, 227 Ala. 577, 151 So. 456 (1933); Johnston v. Pierson, 229 Ala. 85, 155 So. 695 (1934); Moore v. Strickland, 246 Ala. 624, 21 So. 2d 665 (1945); Hollis v. Crittenden, 251 Ala. 320, 37 So. 2d 193 (1948); Binford v. Penney, 255 Ala. 20, 49 So. 2d 665 (1950).

Collateral references. — 33 C.J.S., Executors & Administrators, §§ 3, 28, 31, 46.

Removal of executor or administrator because of disqualification. 8 ALR 181.

Status and acts of one appointed executor or administrator who was ineligible. 14 ALR 619.

Special or temporary administrator: personal interest, conduct, or attitude as affecting question of whom to appoint. 136 ALR 606.

Executor de son tort, propriety of refusal to appoint as executor or administrator. 157 ALR 237.

Governing law as to existence of character of offense for which one has been convicted in federal court or court of another state, as bearing upon disqualification as executor or administrator. 175 ALR 806.

Effect of divorce, separation, desertion, unfaithfulness, and the like, upon right to administer upon estate of spouse. 34 ALR2d 876.

Power of public administrator to contest appointment of administrator. 56 ALR2d 1194.

Construction and effect of statutory provision that no person is competent to act as executor or administrator whom court finds incompetent by reason of want of integrity. 73 ALR2d 458.

Physical condition as affecting competency to act as executor or administrator. 71 ALR3d 675.

Adverse interest or position as disqualification for appointment as personal representative. 11 ALR4th 638.

Adverse interest or position as disqualification for appointment of administrator, executor, or other personal representative. 11 ALR4th 638.

§ 43-2-23. Issuance of letters to married woman.

It shall not be necessary, in order for letters testamentary to issue to a married woman, for her husband to consent thereto; and the husband shall not be responsible for her acts. (Code 1852, § 1660; Code 1867, § 1978; Code 1876, § 2342; Code 1886, § 2007; Code 1896, § 49; Code 1907, § 2511; Code 1923, § 5733; Code 1940, T. 61, § 72.)

Section changes prior law. — The laws relating to grant of letters testamentary to married women have been altered by this section to the end that married women, as in many other phases of the law, have been given the powers to act as if they were femme sole, thus rendering obsolete cases holding that during coverture administratrix is incapable of valid act. Pistole v. Street, 5 Port. 64 (1837); Hopper v. Steel, 18 Ala. 828 (1851); Rambo v. Wyatt, 32 Ala. 363 (1858).

Upon marriage of administratrix, husband acquires right of administration for joint lives. Pistole v. Street, 5 Port. 64 (1837); Kavanaugh v. Thompson, 16 Ala. 817 (1849); Carlisle v. Tuttle, 30 Ala. 613 (1857); Dowty v. Hall, 83 Ala. 165, 3 So. 315 (1887).

Collateral references. — 33 C.J.S., Executors & Administrators, § 28.

Effect of divorce, separation, desertion, unfaithfulness, and the like, upon right to administer upon estate of spouse. 34 ALR2d 876.

§ 43-2-24. Supplemental letters for minors and married women upon removal of disability.

If the disability of a person under age or of a married woman named as executor in any will is removed before the administration of such will is completed, such person is entitled to supplementary letters testamentary, to be issued in the same manner as original letters, and shall thereupon be authorized to join in the execution of such will with the persons previously appointed. (Code 1852, § 1661; Code 1867, § 1979; Code 1876, § 2343; Code 1886, § 2008; Code 1896, § 50; Code 1907, § 2512; Code 1923, § 5734; Code 1940, T. 61, § 73.)

Letters to a minor cannot be revoked where he ratifies appointment after attaining majority. Davis v. Miller, 106 Ala. 154, 17 So. 323 (1895).

§ 43-2-25. Procedure for renouncing appointment.

Any person named as executor in a will may renounce such appointment by appearing before the judge of probate and declaring such renunciation, which must be entered of record; or such person may renounce his appointment by an instrument in writing executed by him and acknowledged before an officer authorized to take and certify acknowledgments to conveyances, whether within or beyond the state; and such instrument must be filed and recorded in the office of the judge of probate of the county in which the will is probated. (Code 1852, § 1662; Code 1867, § 1980; Code 1876, § 2344; Code 1886, § 2009; Code 1896, § 51; Code 1907, § 2513; Code 1923, § 5735; Code 1940, T. 61, § 74.)

Cited in Curtis v. Williams, 33 Ala. 570 (1859); Sowell v. Sowell, 41 Ala. 359 (1867).

Collateral references. — 33 C.J.S., Executors & Administrators, § 29.

§ 43-2-26. Issuance of letters to others named in will upon renunciation or failure to apply by one named.

If any person named as executor in the will renounces his appointment or fails to apply for letters testamentary within 30 days after probate and any other persons named therein as executors make application for such letters and are fit persons to discharge the trust, letters testamentary must issue to them if they comply with the other requisitions of the law. (Code 1852, § 1663; Code 1867, § 1981; Code 1876, § 2345; Code 1886, § 2010; Code 1896, § 52; Code 1907, § 2514; Code 1923, § 5736; Code 1940, T. 61, § 75.)

Purpose of section. — The manifest purpose of this section is to avoid a vacuum of indefinite continuance in the administration of the estate, and to quicken the diligence of the person having the right to qualify as executor, in its exercise. Keith v. Proctor, 114 Ala. 676, 21 So. 502 (1897).

Failure of timely application. — The failure of one of several executors to apply for letters within 30 days after probate vests the exclusive right to administration in the executors who apply within such period. Pruett v. Pruett, 131 Ala. 578, 32 So. 638 (1902).

And such failure is a surrender and renunciation of all preference which the statute confers. (See § 43-2-42 and notes thereto.) Wheat v. Fuller, 82 Ala. 572, 2 So. 628 (1887).

And the renunciation is as effectual, in legal contemplation, as a renunciation in writing, filed in the court from which the letters must issue. Keith v. Proctor, 114 Ala. 676, 21 So. 502 (1897).

No hard and fast rule for computing time for ancillary probate. — It seems that no hard and fast rule, applicable to every case, can be laid down. Each case must be considered and determined in the light of its own facts and circumstances. It is held that the time within which the application for letters (for ancillary administration) must be made is not computed from the original or domiciliary probate, nor can it correctly be said to be computed from the ancillary probate although this is the general rule. Keith v. Proctor, 114 Ala. 676, 21 So. 502 (1897). In this case there was a lapse of a year between the original probate and the ancillary probate and this was held to be a renunciation of the executory trust.

Cited in Kirby v. Anders, 26 Ala. 466 (1855); Underwood v. School Township, 34 Ala. 29 (1859); Robertson v. United States, 199 F. Supp. 78 (N.D. Ala. 1961).

Collateral references. — 33 C.J.S., Executors & Administrators, § 47.

Brevity of period after death of decedent as affecting propriety of grant of letters testamentary or of administration. 133 ALR 1483.

§ 43-2-27. Letters of administration granted in stated order on failure of executor to apply, etc.

If no person is named in the will as executor, or if named executors, one or more, all renounce or fail to apply within 30 days after probate or are unfit persons to serve, the residuary legatee, or if he fails to apply within such time, refuses to accept or is unfit to serve, then the principal legatee, is entitled to letters of administration, with the will annexed; and, if both residuary and principal legatees fail to apply within such time, refuse to accept or are unfit to serve, then such letters may be granted to the same persons and in the same order as letters of administration are granted in cases of intestacy. (Code 1852, §§ 1664, 1665; Code 1867, §§ 1982, 1983; Code 1876, §§ 2346, 2347; Code 1886, § 2011; Code 1896, § 53; Code 1907, § 2515; Code 1923, § 5737; Code 1940, T. 61, § 76.)

Cross references. — See notes to § 43-2-26.

Court has no discretion in appointing principal legatee. — Probate court has no discretion as regards appointment of administrator under this section providing that principal legatee shall be appointed if those appointed are disqualified, unless legatee is within § 43-2-22 prohibiting certain persons to act as administrator. Marcus v. McKee, 227 Ala. 577, 151 So. 456 (1933).

Principal legatee held not disqualified to act as administratrix with will annexed because she claimed that bank account of testator belonged to her and instituted proceedings therefor. Marcus v. McKee, 227 Ala. 577, 151 So. 456 (1933).

Right of principal legatee to act as administrator with will annexed where named executor died held not lost because heir of estate was better qualified than legatee. Marcus v. McKee, 227 Ala. 577, 151 So. 456 (1933).

Cited in Hitchcock v. United States Bank, 7 Ala. 386 (1845); Erwin v. Branch Bank, 14 Ala. 307 (1848); Randall v. Shrader, 17 Ala. 333 (1850); Montgomery, etc., R. Co. v. Varner, 19 Ala. 185 (1851); Pettit v. Pettit, 32 Ala. 288 (1858); Broughton v. Bradley, 34 Ala. 694 (1859); Ward v. Oates, 43 Ala. 515 (1869).

Collateral references. — Brevity of period after death of decedent as affecting propriety of grant of letters testamentary or of administration. 133 ALR 1483.

§ 43-2-28. Death of sole or surviving executor.

No executor of an executor can, as such, administer on the estate of the first testator; but on the death of a sole or surviving executor, letters of administration with the will annexed may be granted to the persons entitled thereto, as in any case in which a sole executor has renounced his appointment. (Code 1852, § 1666; Code 1867, § 1984; Code 1876, § 2348; Code 1886, § 2012; Code 1896, § 54; Code 1907, § 2516; Code 1923, § 5738; Code 1940, T. 61, § 77.)

§ 43-2-29. Grant of letters testamentary after revocation of letters of administration.

(a) If, after letters of administration have been granted as in case of intestacy, any will is proved and the executor therein named appears, claims letters testamentary and complies with the requisition of the law, the probate court having jurisdiction must revoke the letters of administration and grant letters testamentary to such executor.

(b) If, in the case provided for by subsection (a), the sole executor or some of the executors, within five days after the proof of such will, do not appear and take out letters testamentary thereon, a copy of the will must be annexed to the letters of administration and must be executed by the administrator. (Code 1852, §§ 1722, 1723; Code 1867, §§ 2045, 2046; Code 1876, §§ 2414, 2415; Code 1886, §§ 2066, 2067; Code 1896, §§ 113, 114; Code 1907, §§ 2517, 2518; Code 1923, §§ 5739, 5740; Code 1940, T. 61, §§ 78, 79.)

Court must revoke letters of administration where will proved within five years. — Under statute dictating that if after letters of administration have been granted, will is proved and executor appears and complies with requisite requirements, probate court must revoke letters of administration and grant letters testamentary to executor, a will located within five years of the death of the testator should not be denied probate solely because the estate has been fully administered and settled in accordance with the laws of intestacy of Alabama. Gross v. Slye, 360 So. 2d 333 (Ala. 1978).

Rule of Civil Procedure was inapplicable to bar attack on final settlement decree. — Probate court, which after administration of estate and distribution of assets according to intestacy laws entered decree of final settlement and then subsequently denied petition for probate of wife's will which had allegedly been located by husband, was not exercising "equity jurisdiction" within the meaning of Rules of Civil Procedure and thus provision of rule providing for relief from final judgment order or proceeding was inapplicable to, and thus did not bar, husband's "direct" attack on final settlement decree. Gross v. Slye, 360 So. 2d 333 (Ala. 1978).

Petition for probate of will constituted direct attack on final settlement. — Petition for probate of will of deceased wife, filed after administration of estate and distribution of assets in accordance with laws of intestacy and entry of decree of final settlement, was provided for by law and thus constituted "direct" attack rather than a collateral one of decree of final judgment. Gross v. Slye, 360 So. 2d 333 (Ala. 1978).

Administration issued as in case of intestacy, when deceased left a will which is afterwards produced and probated, is voidable and not void. This results because a failure to appear authorizes a copy of the will to be annexed to the letters of administration, by the provisions of subsection (b) of this section. Sands v. Hickey, 135 Ala. 322, 33 So. 827 (1903).

Cited in Broughton v. Bradley, 34 Ala. 694 (1859); Watson v. Glover, 77 Ala. 323 (1884); Fields v. Baker, 259 Ala. 336, 67 So. 2d 10 (1953).

Collateral references. — 33 C.J.S., Executors & Administrators, §§ 84-88.

Probate of will subsequently discovered or annulment of will as affecting removal of administrator. 8 ALR 177.

Division 2.

Grant of Letters of Administration.

Cited in Woodward v. Harbin, 1 Ala. 104 (1840); Sale v. Branch Bank, 1 Ala. 425 (1840); Hammett v. Smith, 5 Ala. 156 (1843); Bryant v. Ingraham, 16 Ala. 116 (1849); Ikelheimer v. Chapman, 32 Ala. 676 (1858); Watson v. Collins, 37 Ala. 587 (1861); Hatchett v. Berney, 65 Ala. 39 (1880); Masterson v. Pullen, 62 Ala. 145 (1878); Bishop v. Lalouette, 67 Ala. 197 (1880); Barclift v. Treece, 77 Ala. 528 (1884); Winter v. London, 99 Ala. 263, 12 So. 438 (1893); Carr v. Illinois Cent. R.R., 180 Ala. 159, 60 So. 277 (1912); Terry v. Gresham, 254 Ala. 349, 48 So. 2d 437 (1950).

Collateral references. — Necessity and sufficiency of assets to justify appointment of administrator at domicile of decedent. 59 ALR 87.

Situs of corporate stock for purpose of probate jurisdiction and administration. 72 ALR 179.

Adverse adjudications of courts of different states as to domicile of decedent. 121 ALR 1200.

What constitutes "estate" of nonresident decedent within statute providing for local ancillary administration where decedent died leaving an estate in jurisdiction. 34 ALR2d 1270.

Potential liability of indemnity or liability insurer or other person to the estate, dependent upon establishment of claim against estate, as justifying grant of administration. 67 ALR2d 936.

Relation back of letters testamentary or of administration as validating prior sales of decedent's property. 2 ALR3d 1105.

§ 43-2-40. Generally.

Courts of probate, within their respective counties, have authority to grant letters of administration on the estates of persons dying intestate, as follows:

(1) Where the intestate, at the time of his death, was an inhabitant of the county.

(2) Where the intestate, not being an inhabitant of the state, dies in the county, leaving assets therein.

(3) Where the intestate, not being an inhabitant of the state, dies out of the county, leaving assets therein.

(4) Where the intestate, not being an inhabitant of the state, dies, leaving no assets therein, and assets are afterwards brought into the county.

(5) Where the intestate, being an inhabitant of the state, dies, leaving no assets subject to administration in the county of his residence, and no administration has been granted in such county within three months after the death of the intestate, then administration may be granted in any county where the intestate leaves assets. (Code 1852, § 1667; Code 1867, § 1985; Code 1876, § 2349; Code 1886, § 2013; Code 1896, § 55; Code 1907, § 2519; Code 1923, § 5741; Code 1940, T. 61, § 80.)

Cross references. — As to requirement that letters of administration be recorded, see § 43-2-1. As to letters of administration for estates of persons presumed dead, see § 43-2-230 et seq.

Jurisdiction of probate court is original, unlimited and general. — The jurisdiction of probate courts of the grant of administration is original, unlimited and general. And their decrees, orders, etc., granting administration are entitled to the same presumptions, when collaterally assailed as other courts of general jurisdiction. Beasley v. Howell, 117 Ala. 499, 22 So. 989 (1898).

The probate court first granting letters under this section still retains exclusive jurisdiction after the resignation of the administrator. And the action of another court appointing an administrator is absolutely void. Beasley v. Howell, 117 Ala. 499, 22 So. 989 (1898).

Element of "inhabitancy". — Where the fact of inhabitancy does not exist, the grant of administration is not void but voidable by direct proceeding. Holmes v. Holmes, 212 Ala. 597, 103 So. 884 (1925), containing a good discussion of the principles concerning domicile and residence.

Where the fact of inhabitancy of intestate does not exist, the grant of administration is not void, but may be avoided by direct proceeding for that purpose. City of Bessemer v. Clowdus, 258 Ala. 378, 63 So. 2d 355 (1953).

Thus, letters of administrator appointed in another county may be revoked, in a direct proceeding for that purpose, by administratrix appointed in county where intestate died and left assets. Tubbs v. Barnard, 225 Ala. 435, 143 So. 448 (1932).

Revocation where appointment is void. — If the appointment of an administrator is void for want of jurisdiction of the subject matter as distinguishable from the venue in which the appointment was made, such void appointment may be revoked by anyone interested in the estate of the decedent or by the court ex mero motu or upon the suggestion of some person amicus curiae. City of Bessemer v. Clowdus, 258 Ala. 378, 63 So. 2d 355 (1953).

Right to revoke because appointment was not justified by this section does not depend upon the fact that the petitioner has or has not applied for letters to himself. This power to revoke because its issuance is not so authorized is said to be an exercise of the inherent power of the court. Clark v. Glenn, 249 Ala. 342, 31 So. 2d 507 (1947).

Insufficient interest to support petition to revoke. — Where administratrix of estate of deceased entered action against city claiming damages for wrongful death of deceased, city had no such interest in the estate of deceased as would support its petition to revoke letters of administration granted to administratrix. City of Bessemer v. Clowdus, 258 Ala. 378, 63 So. 2d 355 (1953).

Section is inapplicable in removal proceedings. — This section is applicable to the issuance of letters of administration, and not to the removal of the administration from the probate to the circuit court. Colquitt v. Gill, 147 Ala. 554, 41 So. 784 (1906).

It does not affect appointment of special administrator. — The mere fact that a person is entitled to letters under this section does not entitle him to preference in the appointment of a special administrator under § 43-2-47, this on the ground that such officer has nothing to do with the administration of the estate as contemplated by this section. Arendale v. Johnson, 206 Ala. 245, 89 So. 603 (1921).

A deceased insured's potential right of exoneration under an insurance policy constitutes sufficient "assets," "property" or "estate" of a nonresident decedent to justify a grant of an administration of his estate in the state in which he dies. Campbell v. Davis, 274 Ala. 187, 145 So. 2d 725 (1962).

The right of exoneration and indemnity of a nonresident insured under an automobile insurance policy issued by a company doing business in the county in which the administrator is appointed constitutes an asset authorizing the grant of an administration of his estate in the county in which he died. Campbell v. Davis, 274 Ala. 187, 145 So. 2d 725 (1962).

While the right of the decedent's personal representative to the benefits of the indemnity clause contained in the policy of insurance will not mature until action is brought against him, nevertheless, it has a present value to the estate. Campbell v. Davis, 274 Ala. 187, 145 So. 2d 725 (1962).

Challenge of grant of letters. — Where the material fact of inhabitancy does not exist, the grant of letters upon false information is not void and may be avoided only by a direct proceeding for that purpose. But where a direct proceeding is instigated through a petition to revoke letters of administration by a party in interest and addressed to the court which granted the letters, that court's subject matter jurisdiction may be attacked and the letters revoked. Meriwether v. Reynolds, 289 Ala. 361, 267 So. 2d 434 (1972).

Cited in Piel v. Brown, 361 So. 2d 90 (Ala. 1978).

Collateral references. — 33 C.J.S., Executors & Administrators, §§ 13-21.

§ 43-2-41. Form.

Letters of administration may be substantially in the following form:

The State of Alabama, ⎱
 . . . . County. ⎰   Court of Probate.

Letters of administration on the estate of . . . . (or letters of administration on the annexed will of . . . ., as the case may be) are hereby granted to . . . ., who has duly qualified and given bond as such administrator, and is authorized to administer such estate (or to execute such will, as the case may be).

Witness my hand and dated this . . . . day of . . . ., 19. . . . .

                . . . .
                     Judge of Probate.

(Code 1852, § 1688; Code 1867, § 2008; Code 1876, § 2370; Code 1886, § 2015; Code 1896, § 57; Code 1907, § 2521; Code 1923, § 5743; Code 1940, T. 61, § 82.)

Cited in Dent v. Foy, 206 Ala. 454, 90 So. 317 (1921).

§ 43-2-42. Order of grant of administration.

(a) Administration of an intestate's estate must be granted to some one of the persons herein named if willing to accept and satisfactory to serve in the following order:

(1) The husband or widow.

(2) The next of kin entitled to share in the distribution of the estate.

(3) The largest creditor of the estate residing in this state.

(4) Such other person as the judge of probate may appoint.

(b) Notwithstanding the provisions of subsection (a) of this section, in all counties having a population of 400,000 or more, according to the last or any subsequent federal census, administration of an intestate's estate must be granted to some one of the persons hereinafter named, if willing to accept and satisfactory to serve, in the following order:

(1) The husband or widow.

(2) The next of kin entitled to share in the distribution of the estate.

(3) The largest creditor of the estate residing in this state.

(4) The county or general administrator.

(5) Such other person as the judge of probate may appoint. (Code 1852, § 1668; Code 1867, § 1986; Code 1876, § 2350; Code 1886, § 2014; Code 1896, § 56; Code 1907, § 2520; Code 1923, § 5742; Acts 1931, No. 551, p. 649; Acts 1936, Ex. Sess., No. 52, p. 29; Code 1940, T. 61, § 81; Acts 1945, No. 356, p. 574; Acts 1951, No. 635, p. 1091; Acts 1956, 1st Ex. Sess., No. 128, p. 190.)

I. GENERAL CONSIDERATION.

Editor's note. — Section 43-2-43 serves to qualify the preference given by this section by prescribing the time within which the right must be exercised. The two sections should therefore be read together. And inasmuch as the two are nearly always construed together the notes found under both sections should be considered.

Some of the cases placed in this note have already been touched upon in the treatment given to § 43-2-22, but where repetition occurs it is for the purpose of emphasizing the importance of referring to the kindred section and the notes thereto.

Historical policy. — Historically, it has been the policy of the law to award administration of estates of decedents to those having the greatest interest therein, the reason being that such persons would be most likely to exercise the greatest care in its management. Griffin v. Irwin, 246 Ala. 631, 21 So. 2d 668 (1945).

Proceedings under this section are in personam. — The proceedings determining the right to the grant of letter, including priority, or inclusion within one of the classes herein defined are in personam. White v. Hill, 176 Ala. 480, 58 So. 444 (1912).

But the grant of letters are, in many important aspects, proceedings in rem. Nelson v. Boynton, 54 Ala. 368 (1875), cited in the White case, supra, which contains a review of the cases on this point.

Probate court has no discretion in enforcing preferential right. — In respect to enforcing the preferential right to administer, as declared by this section, the probate court has no discretion. It may not weigh the relative qualifications of two applicants and choose between them when one has a statutory preference. Calvert v. Beck, 240 Ala. 442, 199 So. 846 (1941); Burnett v. Garrison, 261 Ala. 622, 75 So. 2d 144 (1954); Smith v. Rice, 265 Ala. 236, 90 So. 2d 262 (1956).

It is well understood that in the enforcement of preferential right of administration there is left with the probate court no discretion if the person seeking such preferential right is a fit person. Loeb v. Callaway, 250 Ala. 524, 35 So. 2d 198 (1948); Hollis v. Crittenden, 251 Ala. 320, 37 So. 2d 193 (1948).

Probate court must grant letters of administration to one having statutory preference in absence of his disqualification. Johnston v. Pierson, 229 Ala. 85, 155 So. 695 (1934).

The right is not lost because one not in the same preferred class may be found by the court to be better qualified, unless the one who is preferred is disqualified under § 43-2-22. Griffin v. Irwin, 246 Ala. 631, 21 So. 2d 668 (1945).

The 1936 amendment by substituting word "satisfactory" for word "fit" worked no change in meaning of this section as previously construed, and hence probate court was without discretion to consider any other disqualifications than those set down in § 43-2-22. Moore v. Strickland, 246 Ala. 624, 21 So. 2d 665 (1945); Burnett v. Garrison, 261 Ala. 622, 75 So. 2d 144 (1954).

Delegation of preferential status. — One occupying a preferential status cannot delegate his preferential status to another, except in certain situations authorized by § 43-2-44. Burnett v. Garrison, 261 Ala. 622, 75 So. 2d 144 (1954).

The right to appointment regarding administrator cannot be delegated to another to the exclusion of the person upon whom this section next casts the right. Bivin v. Millsap, 238 Ala. 136, 189 So. 770 (1939).

Adjudication as to relationship is conclusive. — Where the right to letters of administration depends upon the relationship of the applicant to the intestate, an adjudication as to the relationship of decedent to the parties in that proceeding is conclusive, and not subject to a collateral attack. White v. Hill, 176 Ala. 480, 58 So. 444 (1912).

Letters improperly granted may be recalled. — Letters of administration improperly or improvidently granted may be recalled by the court granting them, or having jurisdiction of the administration of the estate, either ex mero motu or on application of any person in interest. Brown v. Brown, 204 Ala. 157, 85 So. 439 (1920).

While probate court has inherent right to revoke letters of administration, it can be done only when some other person has prior right either under a will or the law, and has not waived that right and is seeking to enforce it, or when person appointed is unfit or disqualified. Starlin v. Love, 237 Ala. 38, 185 So. 380 (1938).

Illiteracy is not a cause of disqualification of an applicant under this section since it is not named in § 43-2-22 and the causes therein mentioned are exclusive of all others. Bell v. Fulgham, 202 Ala. 217, 80 So. 39 (1918). See § 43-2-22 and the treatment there given.

Nor is insolvency of estate. — See Johnston v. Pierson, 229 Ala. 85, 155 So. 695 (1934).

Facts considered in making appointments. — The fact that an applicant is largely indebted to the estate, that he claimed unfounded credits, and was friendly to other debtors are proper considerations for the probate judge in selecting an appointee (though, of course, these are not grounds for disqualification). McFry v. Casey, 211 Ala. 649, 101 So. 449 (1924).

A petition to appoint another as waiver of appointees' right. — A petition to appoint another as administrator can operate as a waiver of the claims of those making the petition of a prior right of appointment, if they have one. Bivin v. Millsap, 238 Ala. 136, 189 So. 770 (1939).

Grandniece was "party interested" by whom court's power to revoke letters of administration could be invoked on ground that neither of administrators theretofore appointed was next of kin to intestate. Clark v. Whorton, 239 Ala. 238, 194 So. 661 (1940).

Where testimony sustained averments of petition by grandniece for revocation of letters of administration theretofore issued, that one of appointees was merely a friend of intestate and that the other had married a niece of intestate but that niece died before death of intestate, the letters were properly revoked. Clark v. Whorton, 239 Ala. 238, 194 So. 661 (1940).

A "temporary administrator," or an administrator ad colligendum, is the mere agent or officer of the court to collect and preserve decedent's goods until someone is clothed with authority to administer them, and other than the preliminary duty of collection and preservation, he has nothing to do with administration of the estate. Little v. Gavin, 244 Ala. 156, 12 So. 2d 549 (1943).

Cited in Williams v. McConico, 27 Ala. 572 (1855); Dunham v. Roberts, 27 Ala. 701 (1855); Curtis v. Williams, 33 Ala. 570 (1859); Curtis v. Burt, 34 Ala. 729 (1859); Coate v. Coate, 37 Ala. 695 (1861); Ward v. Oates, 43 Ala. 515 (1869); Davis v. Swearingen, 56 Ala. 31 (1876); Davis v. Swearingen, 56 Ala. 539 (1876); Cunningham v. Thomas, 59 Ala. 158 (1877); Nichols v. State, 186 Ala. 587, 65 So. 30 (1914); Awbrey v. Estes, 216 Ala. 66, 112 So. 529 (1927); Missouri State Life Ins. Co. v. Robertson Banking Co., 223 Ala. 177, 134 So. 800 (1931); Terry v. Gresham, 254 Ala. 349, 48 So. 2d 437 (1950); In re Estate of Dawson, 346 So. 2d 386 (Ala. 1977); Tighe v. Bagwell, 379 So. 2d 1261 (Ala. 1980).

II. HUSBAND OR WIDOW.

The wife may waive or relinquish her preferential right given by this section. Brown v. Brown, 204 Ala. 157, 85 So. 439 (1920). See also Wheat v. Fuller, 82 Ala. 572, 2 So. 628 (1887).

And it is waived by failure to apply for letters within the 40-day period prescribed by § 43-2-43. Stanley v. Stanley, 202 Ala. 661, 81 So. 617 (1919).

Where a widow failed to apply for letters of administration within the 40-day period after the death of the intestate prescribed by § 43-2-43, she waived her preferential right to be issued letters of administration. McCord v. Stephens, 295 Ala. 162, 325 So. 2d 155 (1975).

But notwithstanding a preferred person's loss, through delay, of his preferential right, he is nevertheless to be preferred over an applicant who has never been in the same or a prior preferred class, provided he is fit to serve, under subdivision (4) of subsection (a) of this section. McFry v. Casey, 211 Ala. 649, 101 So. 449 (1924).

This right is not lost even though she has an adverse interest in the estate. — The widow does not lose her preference over others in the administration of the husband's estate even though she has an adverse interest in the estate, or claims to a right superior or antagonistic to decedent's next of kin. And this preferential right is not taken away though the wife has abandoned her husband. Willoughby v. Willoughby, 203 Ala. 138, 82 So. 168 (1919), followed in Brown v. Brown, 204 Ala. 157, 85 So. 439 (1920).

When she has waived her rights she cannot object to a premature appointment. — A widow who has waived her preferential right to letters by not timely applying therefor cannot complain of mere prematurity of issuance thereof to another. Garrett v. Harrison, 201 Ala. 186, 77 So. 712 (1918); Castleberry v. Hollingsworth, 215 Ala. 445, 111 So. 35 (1927). See also Markland v. Albes, 81 Ala. 433, 2 So. 123 (1887).

Petitioner may testify to fact of marriage with deceased. — In proceeding in which letters of administration were revoked and it was ordered that petitioner serve as administratrix of estate, it was not error to permit petitioner to testify that she and decedent were married at time of his death. It is well established in this state that a widow may testify to the fact of marriage between herself and her deceased husband. Piel v. Brown, 361 So. 2d 90 (Ala. 1978).

III. NEXT OF KIN.

"Next of kin" is. — The next of kin entitled to a preference in the administration of an estate is that person in the nearest degree of kinship to the intestate as determined by the rules of civil law. Worley v. Worley, 361 So. 2d 1067 (Ala. 1978).

The right under this section of the next of kin to administer on such an estate is not to be determined by the character of assets comprising it or whether there will be assets available for distribution on final settlement, but by whether or not such a next of kin designated under the second classification is one of those of that preferred class who under the law would inherit from the decedent if there should be assets discovered and distributable. Loeb v. Callaway, 250 Ala. 524, 35 So. 2d 198 (1948).

"Nephew" and "niece" mean only relationship by consanguinity. — The terms "nephew" and "niece" in their primary sense, and within meaning of this section conferring on "next of kin entitled to share in distribution of an estate," include only relationship by consanguinity. Clark v. Whorton, 239 Ala. 238, 194 So. 661 (1940).

Brother of whole blood preferred over husband of niece. — A brother of the whole blood of deceased was in the second "degree of kindred," and a husband of niece of deceased was in the third "degree of kindred," and hence brother had preferential right to administer estate of deceased and was entitled, as against husband of niece, to grant of letters of administration, where brother was not disqualified. Calvert v. Beck, 240 Ala. 442, 199 So. 846 (1941).

Under this subsection the father of deceased is entitled to preference over a half-brother. Bell v. Fulgham, 202 Ala. 217, 80 So. 39 (1918).

And uncle is preferred to husband of cousin. — Uncle of intestate who died without widow, descendants or parents, and who was not disqualified, was entitled to letters of administration as against husband of intestate's first cousin. Johnston v. Pierson, 229 Ala. 85, 155 So. 695 (1934).

Son preferred to granddaughter. — Son of decedent, being the first degree of kinship, is entitled to a preference as administrator over the granddaughter of decedent, who is in the second degree of kinship. Worley v. Worley, 361 So. 2d 1067 (Ala. 1978).

A nonresident first cousin of deceased was not in the preferred class in the order of grant of administration, since his nonresidency wholly disqualified him to be appointed as administrator. Starlin v. Love, 237 Ala. 38, 185 So. 380 (1938).

But he could have unfit appointee's rights revoked. — A first cousin of deceased, being interested person in the estate, would have right to have letters of administration revoked if they were issued to unfit or disqualified person, though he was disqualified from being appointed administrator himself by reason of his nonresidence. Starlin v. Love, 237 Ala. 38, 185 So. 380 (1938).

IV. OTHER PERSON.

Diligence required under subdivision (a)(4). — Grantee was not excused from exercising option within the seven-year period, because grantor had died and no administrator had been appointed until after expiration of the period, where he failed to exercise diligence under subdivision (a)(4) of this section to have administrator appointed in default of those first entitled to administer. W.T. Smith Lumber Co. v. Waller, 218 Ala. 546, 119 So. 663 (1929).

Court has large discretionary powers in making appointments under this subdivision. — When the probate judge appoints under subdivision (a)(4) of this section, he is clothed with "large discretionary powers." Phillips v. Peteet, 35 Ala. 696 (1860). See also Davis v. Swearingen, 56 Ala. 539 (1876); McFry v. Casey, 211 Ala. 649, 101 So. 449 (1924); Burnett v. Garrison, 261 Ala. 622, 75 So. 2d 144 (1954).

Where there is no applicant entitled to preference. — Where there is no applicant for letters of administration within any of the classes entitled to a preference by this section, the court may appoint any qualified person. Burnett v. Garrison, 261 Ala. 622, 75 So. 2d 144 (1954).

By failing to apply for letters of administration within 40 days after the death of intestate, persons entitled to the administration according to the first three subdivisions of subsection (a) of this section waived all rights of preference to the issuance of letters of administration, and the appointment of a creditor as administrator was justified under subdivision (a)(4) of this section. Gilmore v. Roberson, 273 Ala. 230, 139 So. 2d 604 (1962).

Premature appointment is voidable. — The appointment of one coming within subdivision (a)(4) (all those in the first three subdivisions are allowed 40 days in which to establish their preference by subsection (b) of § 43-2-43) before the expiration of 40 days is not void but voidable upon reasonable objection by the preferred person. Childs v. Davis, 172 Ala. 266, 55 So. 540 (1911); Bivin v. Millsap, 238 Ala. 136, 189 So. 770 (1939).

Collateral references. — 33 C.J.S., Executors & Administrators, §§ 22, 31-46.

Selection of administrator from among members of class equally entitled. 1 ALR 1245.

Residence contemplated by statute or rule making residence within state qualification of executor or administrator. 18 ALR 581.

Separation agreement as affecting right of husband or wife to administer deceased spouse's estate. 35 ALR 1511, 34 ALR2d 1020.

Eligibility of foreign corporation to appointment as executor or administrator. 65 ALR 1267.

Deferred class of next of kin named in statutes, but not beneficially interested in particular estate, preference respecting appointment in favor of person in. 70 ALR 1466.

Right to pass over eligible person interested in estate and appoint stranger. 80 ALR 824.

Choice and appointment of administrator as between nominee of one in higher order of statutory preference and one in lower order of preference. 113 ALR 780.

Grantees of, or successors to, interest of one eligible because of specified relationship to deceased, who are within statute making such person eligible to appointment. 114 ALR 275.

Appointment as administrator of one not a member, nor nominee of a member, of the class of persons designated by statute as eligible to appointment, where no one in better right has applied. 119 ALR 143.

Right of guardian of infant or incompetent to appointment as executor or administrator as representative or substitute for infant or incompetent. 135 ALR 585.

Preference in appointment of special or temporary administrator pending will contest. 136 ALR 606.

Scope and effect of waiver or renunciation of right to administer decedent's estate. 153 ALR 220.

Executor de son tort, propriety of appointment as executor or administrator. 157 ALR 237.

Effect of divorce, separation, desertion, unfaithfulness, and the like, upon right to name appointee for administration of estate of spouse. 34 ALR2d 876.

Creditor of estate as having adverse interest or position disqualifying him for appointment as personal representative. 11 ALR4th 638.

§ 43-2-43. Renunciation or relinquishment of right to administration.

(a) Any person entitled to administration may relinquish his right thereto in the same manner as executors are authorized to renounce their appointment.

(b) If no person entitled to the administration of the estate, according to the first three subdivisions of subsections (a) or (b) of section 43-2-42, applies for letters within 40 days after the death of the intestate is known, the persons so entitled must be held to have relinquished their right to the administration. (Code 1852, §§ 1669, 1674; Code 1867, §§ 1987, 1992; Code 1876, §§ 2351, 2356; Code 1886, §§ 2016, 2018; Code 1896, §§ 58, 60; Code 1907, §§ 2522, 2524; Code 1923, §§ 5744, 5746; Code 1940, T. 61, §§ 83, 85.)

Editor's note. — Inasmuch as this section and § 43-2-42 are nearly always construed together the notes found under both these sections should be considered.

Cross reference. — Renunciation is treated in the notes to § 43-2-26.

Priority of appointment under section 43-2-42 must be preserved within time limit. — A relative with priority of right to appointment as administrator cannot cause to be revoked letters of administration which were issued within the 40-day period of priority unless within that time he took the necessary steps to preserve his priority. Curtis v. Burt, 34 Ala. 729 (1859); Ward v. Cameron, 37 Ala. 691 (1861); Sowell v. Sowell, 41 Ala. 359 (1867); Markland v. Albes, 81 Ala. 433, 2 So. 123 (1887); Childs v. Davis, 172 Ala. 266, 55 So. 540 (1911); Garrett v. Harrison, 201 Ala. 186, 77 So. 712 (1918); Castleberry v. Hollingsworth, 215 Ala. 445, 111 So. 35 (1927); Starlin v. Love, 237 Ala. 38, 185 So. 380 (1938).

Anyone having prior right may take the steps. — The probate court will revoke letters of administration issued within 40 days after death of deceased was known to one not in the right of priority only when one with such right has within that time sought to make it available and to have appointment of himself made instead of the one prematurely appointed. Starlin v. Love, 237 Ala. 38, 185 So. 380 (1938).

Thus, letters of administration issued within 40 days after death of deceased was known, to a second cousin of deceased not in the right of priority, were not revocable on petition of a first cousin of deceased who was disqualified from serving as administrator because of nonresidency, though petition was filed within 40-day period and there were other first cousins with right of priority qualified to serve as administrators, since failure of probate court to enforce priorities in appointment of administrator would be cause for revocation only at instance seasonably presented by one in prior right and not disqualified. Starlin v. Love, 237 Ala. 38, 185 So. 380 (1938).

Until steps are taken other appointment is merely voidable. — The appointment as administrator within 40 days after death of deceased was known, of a second cousin of deceased who was not in the right of priority, was not void, but only revocable at action of one in priority pursued within the 40 days. Starlin v. Love, 237 Ala. 38, 185 So. 380 (1938).

Cited in Dunham v. Roberts, 27 Ala. 701 (1855); Curtis v. Williams, 33 Ala. 570 (1859); Sowell v. Sowell, 41 Ala. 359 (1867); Cunningham v. Thomas, 59 Ala. 158 (1877); Mitchell v. Duncan, 94 Ala. 192, 10 So. 331 (1891); Alabama Co. v. Brown, 207 Ala. 18, 92 So. 490 (1921); Murphy v. Freeman, 220 Ala. 634, 127 So. 199 (1930); Terry v. Gresham, 254 Ala. 349, 48 So. 2d 437 (1950).

Collateral references. — 33 C.J.S., Executors & Administrators, § 47.

Brevity of period after death of decedent as affecting propriety of grant of letters testamentary or of administration. 133 ALR 1483.

Resignation of public administrator. 56 ALR2d 1187.

§ 43-2-44. Grant of administration when more than one person entitled thereto; preference of whole blood over half blood.

If several persons of the same degree of kindred to the intestate, computed by the rules of the civil law, are entitled to the administration, and when several persons are equally entitled thereto, the court may, in its discretion, grant letters to one or more of them; except, that the whole blood shall be preferred to the half blood. When a married woman is entitled to the administration, it may be granted to her husband in her right. (Code 1852, §§ 1670-1673; Code 1867, §§ 1988-1991; Code 1876, §§ 2352-2355; Code 1886, § 2017; Code 1896, § 59; Code 1907, § 2523; Code 1923, § 5745; Code 1940, T. 61, § 84.)

Delegation of preferential status. — One occupying a preferential status cannot delegate his preferential status to another, except in certain situations authorized by this section. Burnett v. Garrison, 261 Ala. 622, 75 So. 2d 144 (1954).

Cited in English v. McNair, 34 Ala. 40 (1859); Bingham v. Crenshaw, 34 Ala. 683 (1859); Davis v. Swearingen, 56 Ala. 539 (1876); Turnipseed v. Fitzpatrick, 75 Ala. 297 (1884); Keith v. Proctor, 114 Ala. 676, 21 So. 502 (1897); Loeb v. Callaway, 250 Ala. 524, 35 So. 2d 198 (1948); McCord v. Stephens, 295 Ala. 162, 325 So. 2d 155 (1975).

Collateral references. —. Selection of administrator from among members of class equally entitled. 1 ALR 1245.

§ 43-2-45. Letters not granted until five days after intestate's death; examination of applicants and witnesses.

No letters of administration must be granted until the expiration of five days after the death of the intestate is known; and the court may, in all cases, examine the persons applying therefor, on oath, touching the time and place of the death of the intestate and as to whether or not he left any will and other matters necessary to give the court jurisdiction; and may also examine any other witnesses as to the same facts and may compel their attendance for that purpose by subpoena and attachment. (Code 1852, § 1675; Code 1867, § 1993; Code 1876, § 2357; Code 1886, § 2019; Code 1896, § 61; Code 1907, § 2525; Code 1923, § 5747; Code 1940, T. 61, § 86.)

Premature granting of letters of administration did not render sale of lands on administratrix' petition for payment of estate's debts void, but was mere irregularity which could not affect validity of sale on collateral attack. Peek v. Haardt, 235 Ala. 145, 177 So. 634 (1937).

Cited in Kirby v. Anders, 26 Ala. 466 (1855); McNeill v. McNeill, 35 Ala. 30 (1859); Curtis v. Williams, 33 Ala. 570 (1859); Hatchett v. Curbow, 59 Ala. 516 (1877); Nelson v. Murfee, 69 Ala. 598 (1881); Espalla v. Gottschalk, 95 Ala. 254, 10 So. 755 (1892); Sharp v. Shannon, 218 Ala. 170, 118 So. 173 (1928); Hollis v. Crittenden, 251 Ala. 320, 37 So. 2d 193 (1948); Hunnicutt v. City of Tuscaloosa, 337 So. 2d 346 (Ala. 1976).

Collateral references. — 33 C.J.S., Executors & Administrators, § 52.

Brevity of period after death of decedent as affecting propriety of grant of letters testamentary or of administration. 133 ALR 1483.

§ 43-2-46. Postponing issuance of letters during time for appeal.

When there are contesting applicants for letters testamentary or of administration, no letters must issue until the time for taking an appeal from the judgment thereon has passed; and, if such appeal is taken, no letters in chief must be granted until the appeal is finally disposed of; but a special administrator may be appointed if necessary. (Code 1852, § 1694; Code 1867, § 2015; Code 1876, § 2377; Code 1886, § 2035; Code 1896, § 78; Code 1907, § 2531; Code 1923, § 5753; Code 1940, T. 61, § 88.)

Cited in Alexander v. Nelson, 42 Ala. 462 (1868); Briarfield Iron Works Co. v. Foster, 54 Ala. 622 (1875); Ex parte Garrison, 260 Ala. 379, 71 So. 2d 33 (1954).

Collateral references. — 33 C.J.S., Executors & Administrators, § 64.

§ 43-2-47. Special administrator ad colligendum.

(a) The judge of probate may, in any contest respecting the validity of a will, or for the purpose of collecting the goods of a deceased, or in any other case in which it is necessary, appoint a special administrator, authorizing the collection and preservation by him of the goods of the deceased until letters testamentary or of administration have been duly issued.

(b) Every such special administrator has authority to collect the goods and chattels of the estate and debts of the deceased, to give receipts for moneys collected, to satisfy liens and mortgages paid to him and to secure and preserve such goods and chattels at such expense as may be deemed reasonable by the probate court; and for such purposes, he may maintain civil actions as administrator.

(c) Such special administrator may also, under the direction of the probate court, sell such goods as are perishable or wasting, after the same have been appraised, upon such notice as the judge of probate may prescribe.

(d) Upon the grant of letters testamentary or of administration, the authority of such special administrator ceases, and on demand he must deliver to the rightful executor or administrator all the assets of the deceased which may be in his hands and render an account on oath of all his proceedings to the probate court. (Code 1852, §§ 1676-1679; Code 1867, §§ 1994-1997; Code 1876, §§ 2358-2361; Code 1886, §§ 2020-2023; Code 1896, §§ 62-65; Code 1907, §§ 2526-2529; Code 1923, §§ 5748-5751; Code 1940, T. 61, §§ 89-92.)

A temporary administrator, or an administrator ad colligendum, as he is usually called, "is the mere agent, or officer of the court, to collect and preserve the goods of the deceased, until someone is clothed with authority to administer them." Flora v. Mennice, 12 Ala. 836 (1848).

Power is limited. — Where no special equity is averred, the powers of a special administrator are defined by this section and limited to the personal assets. Little v. Gavin, 244 Ala. 156, 12 So. 2d 549 (1943).

The court, in acting under this section, is a court of general jurisdiction, its authority being traceable to the Constitution. Breeding v. Breeding, 128 Ala. 412, 30 So. 881 (1900).

Court's power of appointment is limited. — The authority of the probate court, in the appointment of a special administrator, is fixed and limited by this section. It is only that the appointment is for special administrator for the collection and preservation of the goods of the deceased, and not for the purpose of the administration of the estate. Little v. Gavin, 244 Ala. 156, 12 So. 2d 549 (1943).

Petition for appointment is not essential. — A petition is not a necessary prerequisite to the validity of an appointment. Breeding v. Breeding, 128 Ala. 412, 30 So. 881 (1900).

However, it is a desirable practice. Davis v. Swearingen, 56 Ala. 31 (1876).

Special administration is granted at any time after intestate's death. Espalla v. Gottschalk, 95 Ala. 254, 10 So. 755 (1892).

And may be revoked at any time. — An administrator ad colligendum is a mere agent of the court and may be removed at any time. Flora v. Mennice, 12 Ala. 836 (1848).

The validity of the appointment is subject to direct attack only. — The validity of the appointment of a special administrator cannot be collaterally assailed or questioned otherwise than in a direct proceeding. Breeding v. Breeding, 128 Ala. 412, 30 So. 881 (1900).

Allowance of compensation to a special administrator is a matter of judicial discretion. Hale v. Cox, 240 Ala. 622, 200 So. 772 (1941).

Appointment during will contest. — When a will is propounded for probate and a contest is filed, it is not unusual to appoint an administrator ad colligendum, as authorized by this section. When the contest is successful, and an administrator with full authority is appointed, the temporary administrator must file his accounts and make settlement as such. Hale v. Cox, 240 Ala. 622, 200 So. 772 (1941).

Authority generally. — Other than the collection and preservation, the special administrator has nothing to do with administration as contemplated by §§ 43-2-40 and 43-2-42. Arendale v. Johnson, 206 Ala. 245, 89 So. 603 (1921).

Other than this preliminary duty of collection and preservation, he has nothing to do with the administration of the estate. Little v. Gavin, 244 Ala. 156, 12 So. 2d 549 (1943).

Authority fixed by this section. — The authority of the special administrator, being fixed by this section, the same can neither be restricted nor enlarged by the court appointing him. Underhill v. Mobile Fire Dept. Ins. Co., 67 Ala. 45 (1880).

The law fixes the duty of the special administrator after the appointment and not the judge who makes the appointment. Wolffe v. Eberlein, 74 Ala. 99 (1883); Little v. Gavin, 244 Ala. 156, 12 So. 2d 549 (1943).

Regular appointment terminates special administrator's authority. — The regular appointment of an administrator in chief terminates the authority of special administrator. Briarfield Iron Works Co. v. Foster, 54 Ala. 622 (1875). See also Espalla v. Gottschalk, 95 Ala. 254, 10 So. 755 (1892).

He is an officer of probate court. — Administrator ad colligendum is officer or agent of probate court and must find his authority in law which governs his situation and in orders of probate court. Mitchell v. Parker, 227 Ala. 676, 151 So. 842 (1933); Little v. Gavin, 244 Ala. 156, 12 So. 2d 549 (1943); Arnold v. Garrison, 255 Ala. 11, 49 So. 2d 787 (1950).

His allowance for credits and claims governed by equitable principles. — Probate court is governed by equitable principles in determining allowance for credits and claims to special administrator. Mitchell v. Parker, 227 Ala. 676, 151 So. 842 (1933).

Administrator ad colligendum held entitled to attorney's and stenographer's fees in attempting to probate will and prosecute appeal from denial of probate in absence of showing of bad faith and that fees were improper. Mitchell v. Parker, 227 Ala. 676, 151 So. 842 (1933).

Where named executor acts in good faith in propounding will for probate, though contest is filed, and though he is unsuccessful in his effort to probate, he may be allowed reasonable expense unless court in its discretion finds it inequitable to allow expense out of estate. Mitchell v. Parker, 227 Ala. 676, 151 So. 842 (1933).

Probate court may authorize administrator's commission, etc. — The probate court had jurisdiction of the parties and the subject matter and was authorized to make an allowance to the special administrator for his commissions and for such fees to his attorney as were reasonable. Arnold v. Garrison, 255 Ala. 11, 49 So. 2d 787 (1950).

Which commission is prior claim on assets. — Though part of the judgment attempted to enter a money judgment in a case against the administrator ad colligendum and was of no effect, the judgment was nonetheless an allowance of commissions due the outgoing administrator ad colligendum and attorney's fee to his attorney and a fixation of the amounts, and these commissions constitute a prior claim on the assets of the estate. Arnold v. Garrison, 255 Ala. 11, 49 So. 2d 787 (1950).

Special administrator may make final settlement, etc. — Special administrator has duty to make final settlement and pay reasonable fees to attorneys in collection of deceased's goods, chattels and debts and their preservation and other reasonable expenditures, including his own commission. Mitchell v. Parker, 227 Ala. 676, 151 So. 842 (1933).

And may maintain adversary civil actions for recovery of assets of estate. Dobson v. Neighbors, 228 Ala. 407, 153 So. 861 (1934).

This section was held to apply to a complaint by special administrator to reclaim an estate for administration, which estate consisted of realty and personalty, and to recover as assets certain items of such property and for instructions, where complaint was filed after administration was removed to circuit court. Little v. Gavin, 244 Ala. 156, 12 So. 2d 549 (1943).

But he cannot pay debts or receive presentation of claims. Mitchell v. Parker, 227 Ala. 676, 151 So. 842 (1933). See also Erwin v. Branch Bank, 14 Ala. 307 (1848); Little v. Gavin, 244 Ala. 156, 12 So. 2d 549 (1943).

A special administrator cannot pay debts of the estate and is not liable to civil action on a contract of the decedent. Little v. Gavin, 244 Ala. 156, 12 So. 2d 549 (1943).

An administrator ad colligendum has no authority to pay the debts of the estate of the decedent or to administer such an estate. He is but the mere agent or officer of the court to collect and preserve the estate of the deceased until someone is clothed with authority to administer the estate. Little v. Gavin, 244 Ala. 156, 12 So. 2d 549 (1943); Ex parte Garrison, 260 Ala. 379, 71 So. 2d 33 (1954).

Nor take steps with regard to realty. — Under this section a special administrator is not authorized to take any steps with regard to decedent's interest in realty. Little v. Gavin, 244 Ala. 156, 12 So. 2d 549 (1943).

Probate court cannot render money judgment against special administrator. — There was no authority to render a money judgment against a special administrator. If he has no authority to pay debts and cannot be made liable for debts, no judgment for any debt can be rendered against him. Arnold v. Garrison, 255 Ala. 11, 49 So. 2d 787 (1950).

A special administrator may file complaint for a receiver. Briarfield Iron Works Co. v. Foster, 54 Ala. 622 (1875).

Allowance of reasonable expenses. — When administrator ad colligendum is the person named in the contested will as executor, and the one who propounded the will for probate, on settlement of his accounts if he has acted in good faith, the court may allow him his reasonable expenses in such contest unless the court in its sound judicial discretion finds that it would be inequitable and unjust to allow it out of the estate. Hale v. Cox, 240 Ala. 622, 200 So. 772 (1941).

Cited in Randall v. Shrader, 17 Ala. 333 (1850); Whitworth v. Hart, 22 Ala. 343 (1853); Farrow v. Bragg, 30 Ala. 261 (1857); Curtis v. Williams, 33 Ala. 570 (1859); Broughton v. Bradley, 34 Ala. 694 (1859); Clemens v.

Walker, 40 Ala. 189 (1866); Brock v. Frank, 51 Ala. 85 (1874); Cochran v. Miller, 74 Ala. 50 (1883); McDonnell v. Farrow, 132 Ala. 227, 31 So. 475 (1902); Alabama Co. v. Brown, 207 Ala. 18, 92 So. 490 (1921); Turley v. Hazelwood, 234 Ala. 186, 174 So. 616 (1937); Ex parte Pettus, 245 Ala. 349, 17 So. 2d 409 (1944).

Collateral references. — 34 C.J.S., Executors & Administrators, §§ 1035-1040.

Termination of authority of administrator pendente lite by termination of litigation. 8 ALR 180.

Person to be appointed as special or temporary administrator pending will contest. 136 ALR 604.

Authority of special or temporary administrator, or administrator pendente lite, to dispose of, distribute, lease, or encumber property of estate. 148 ALR 275.

§ 43-2-48. Conclusiveness of letters.

Letters testamentary or of administration and letters to a special administrator or to any general administrator, sheriff or coroner, granted by any court having jurisdiction, are conclusive evidence of the authority of the person to whom the same are granted, from the date thereof until the same are revoked; and, when granted, such letters exclude the probate court of every other county from the jurisdiction thereof and extend to all the property of the deceased in the state. (Code 1852, § 1693; Code 1867, § 2014; Code 1876, § 2376; Code 1886, § 2034; Code 1896, § 77; Code 1907, § 2530; Code 1923, § 5752; Code 1940, T. 61, § 87.)

Allegation of fraudulent appointment. — This section prevents a party who is sued from alleging that the appointment of one having letters is voidable for fraud. Carr v. Illinois Cent. R.R., 180 Ala. 159, 60 So. 277 (1912). As to necessity of direct attack on validity of appointment, see notes to § 43-2-47.

Conclusiveness of letters illustrated. — Under this section, the letters of an executrix are conclusive evidence of her authority to collect and receive assets of her testator in this state, though they show testator to have been a resident of another state. And this is true though the letters fail to show proper antecedent proceedings necessary to authorize the issuance of letters. Johnson v. Kyser, 127 Ala. 309, 27 So. 784 (1900).

The entertainment of administratrix' petition for sale of land for payment of debts containing recital of jurisdictional facts, rendition of decree of sale and further orders in such proceedings involved a judicial determination of fact that petitioner was administratrix, and sale could not be impeached in collateral proceeding on ground that petitioner was not administratrix or that grant of administration

was invalid, if there was an estate to be administered within court's jurisdiction. Peek v. Haardt, 235 Ala. 145, 177 So. 634 (1937).

Letters testamentary were prima facie evidence of right to act thereunder, and after six months to close administration where warranted by facts. Whitaker v. Kennamer, 229 Ala. 80, 155 So. 855 (1934).

Cited in Sims v. Boynton, 32 Ala. 353 (1858); Broughton v. Bradley, 34 Ala. 694 (1859); Stoudenmire v. Brown, 48 Ala. 699 (1872); Nelson v. Boynton, 54 Ala. 368 (1875); Lee v. Winston, 68 Ala. 402 (1880); Landford v. Dunklin, 71 Ala. 594 (1882); Barclift v. Treece, 77 Ala. 528 (1884); Alabama Co. v. Brown, 207 Ala. 18, 92 So. 490 (1921); Clark v. Glenn, 249 Ala. 342, 31 So. 2d 507 (1947); Tighe v. Bagwell, 379 So. 2d 1261 (Ala. 1980).

Collateral references. — 33 C.J.S., Executors & Administrators, §§ 63, 74.

Ineligibility of one appointed executor or administrator as affecting validity of his acts. 14 ALR 619.

Premature grant of letters of administration or letters testamentary as affecting acts or proceedings thereunder. 113 ALR 1398.

Creditor's or debtor's right to attack issuance
of letters of administration. 123 ALR 1225.

ARTICLE 3.

NOTICE OF APPOINTMENT OF EXECUTORS OR ADMINISTRATORS.

Collateral references. — 33 C.J.S., Executors & Administrators, § 70.

§ 43-2-60. Generally.

Executors and administrators must, within one month from the grant of
letters, give notice of their appointment, stating the name of the deceased, the
day on which letters were granted, by what court, stating the county and
notifying all persons having claims against the estate to present the same
within the time allowed by law or that the same will be barred. (Code 1852, §
1734; Code 1867, § 2057; Code 1876, § 2426; Code 1886, § 2075; Code 1896, §
122; Code 1907, § 2586; Code 1923, § 5811; Code 1940, T. 61, § 93.)

**No compensation when administrator
fails to give notice of appointment.** — The
evidence authorized the conclusion that appellant did not give notice of his appointment as
executor as required by this section, and under
the mandatory provisions of § 43-2-62 that "any
executor or administrator failing to make the
same [that is publication of his appointment]
must not be allowed any compensation as such"
executor or administrator, the court did not err
in refusing to allow the appellant commissions
and compensation for his services as such executor. Grist v. Carswell, 231 Ala. 442, 165 So.
102 (1935).

**Failure to give notice does not prevent
statute of limitations from running.** — The
failure to give notice as herein prescribed does
not prevent the statute of limitations from
beginning to run against claims under
§ 43-2-350. Johnson v. Bain, 17 Ala. App. 71,
81 So. 849 (1919).

Cited in McCaskle v. Amarine, 12 Ala. 17
(1847); Bank of Montgomery v. Plannett, 37
Ala. 222 (1861); Barrett v. Fondren, 262 Ala.
537, 80 So. 2d 243 (1955).

Collateral references. — Consul's right to
be notified of his national's death or institution
of administration upon his estate. 157 ALR 107.

§ 43-2-61. Manner of giving notice.

Such notice must be given in a newspaper published in the county in which
the letters were granted or, if none is published in such county, in the one
published nearest to the courthouse thereof or in an adjoining county; and it
must be published once a week for three successive weeks. (Code 1852, § 1735;
Code 1867, § 2058; Code 1876, § 2427; Code 1886, § 2076; Code 1896, § 123;
Code 1907, § 2587; Code 1923, § 5812; Code 1940, T. 61, § 94.)

Cited in Thompson v. Acree, 69 Ala. 178
(1881); Barrett v. Fondren, 262 Ala. 537, 80 So.
2d 243 (1955).

§ 43-2-62. Penalty for failure to give notice.

It is the duty of the judge of probate to see that such publication is duly made; and any executor or administrator failing to make the same must not be allowed any compensation as such; and he and his sureties are liable, on proof that such notice has not been given, to any creditor for the amount which he would have been entitled to out of the assets of the estate had his claim been duly presented. (Code 1852, § 1736; Code 1867, § 2059; Code 1876, § 2428; Code 1886, § 2077; Code 1896, § 124; Code 1907, § 2588; Code 1923, § 5813; Code 1940, T. 61, § 95.)

Cross references. — See notes to § 43-2-60. As to limits of liability of executors and administrators generally, see § 43-2-110.

Creditor's knowledge of lack of notice. — The absence of the creditor's knowledge of the grant of letters testamentary or administration is not an element of the burden of proof prescribed as requisite to liability of the executor or administrator and his sureties, although such knowledge on the part of the creditor within the statutory period may be shown as a matter of defense. Johnson v. Bain, 17 Ala. App. 71, 81 So. 849 (1919).

An averment in the complaint negativing the knowledge of the creditor of the grant of letters is not essential to the statement of a cause of action. Johnson v. Bain, 17 Ala. App. 71, 81 So. 849 (1919).

Action of debt should be brought to recover penalties. — The action of debt is the appropriate remedy for the recovery of the penalties referred to in this section. Johnson v. Bain, 17 Ala. App. 71, 81 So. 849 (1919).

Cited in Brake v. Graham, 214 Ala. 10, 106 So. 188 (1925); Barrett v. Fondren, 262 Ala. 537, 80 So. 2d 243 (1955).

Collateral references. — Failure of personal representative to file proof of publication of notice of appointment or notice to creditors within specified time as tolling statute of nonclaim. 42 ALR2d 1218.

ARTICLE 4.

BONDS OF EXECUTORS AND ADMINISTRATORS.

Cross references. — As to actions on official bonds of executors and administrators, see § 6-5-30 et seq. As to bonds of foreign executors and administrators, see § 43-2-210 et seq.

Cited in Hitchcock v. United States Bank, 7 Ala. 386 (1845); Clements v. Moore, 11 Ala. 35 (1847); Petty v. Wafford, 11 Ala. 143 (1847); Howell v. Reynolds, 12 Ala. 128 (1847); Amason v. Nash, 24 Ala. 279 (1854); Hamner v. Mason, 24 Ala. 480 (1854); Cooper v. Machlin, 25 Ala. 298 (1854); Dunham v. Hatcher, 31 Ala. 483 (1858); English v. McNair, 34 Ala. 40 (1859); Harrison v. Harrison, 39 Ala. 489 (1864); Mobile v. Dargan, 45 Ala. 310 (1871); Charles v. Stickney, 50 Ala. 86 (1873); Morrow v. Wood, 56 Ala. 1 (1876); Steele v. Tutwiler, 68 Ala. 107 (1880); Landford v. Dunklin, 71 Ala. 594 (1882); Griffith v. Rudisill, 141 Ala. 200, 37 So. 83 (1904); Evans v. Evans, 200 Ala. 329, 76 So. 95 (1917); Alabama Co. v. Brown, 207 Ala. 18, 92 So. 490 (1921); Terry v. Gresham, 254 Ala. 349, 48 So. 2d 437 (1950).

Collateral references. — 33 C.J.S., Executors & Administrators, § 67.

Public officer administering estate or his bond as liable for faults and misfeasance of his deputy. 1 ALR 241, 116 ALR 1064, 71 ALR2d 1140.

Leave of court as prerequisite to action on bond. 2 ALR 563.

Bond of executor or administrator as covering debt due from principal to decedent. 8 ALR 84.

Fraud of administratrix in securing her appointment by misrepresenting the decedent's identity or her relationship to him as affecting liability of sureties on her bond. 9 ALR 1138.

Responsibility of executor or administrator or his bond for default of guardian of minor beneficiary of estate. 54 ALR 1274.

Liability of bond for loss of money deposited in bank by executor or administrator in his representative capacity. 60 ALR 488.

Liability for depreciation in value of corporate stock or other corporation's securities held by estate because of executor's or administrator's conduct, for which he is directly responsible to the corporation. 62 ALR 563.

Acts or omissions in respect of cause of action for death, or the funds received on that account, as within coverage of bond. 68 ALR 1543.

Rights and liabilities between sureties on successive bonds. 76 ALR 904.

Right of surety to take advantage of noncompliance with statutory requirements as to approval of bond. 7 ALR 1482.

Liability on bond of public officer administering estate for acts or defaults after termination of office. 81 ALR 63.

Liabilities of sureties on bond for defalcation or deficit occurring before bond was given. 82 ALR 585.

Delay of executor or administrator in completing administration as affecting liability on bond. 85 ALR 440.

Liability of bondsman for interest on account of preferential payment to distributee before payment of other distributees. 91 ALR 705.

Sale of real property directed or authorized by will, liability of sureties on bond of executor or administrator c.t.a. in respect of proceeds of. 91 ALR 943.

Liability for loss of funds after final order for distribution. 100 ALR 1126.

Liabilities of surety in respect of property or funds not assets of estate coming into hands of principal. 104 ALR 180.

Liability on bond in respect of sale of property of estate which is invalid. 106 ALR 429.

Liability for losses incurred in carrying on business pursuant to direction or permission of will. 109 ALR 639.

Liability of sureties as affected by actual, constructive, or asserted transfer of property or funds by fiduciary acting in one capacity to himself acting in another capacity. 111 ALR 267.

Invalidity of appointment of administrator as

affecting liability of surety on his bond. 113 ALR 411.

Right of surety to terminate liability as regards future defaults of principal. 118 ALR 1261, 150 ALR 485.

Accounting as necessary condition of action on bond. 119 ALR 103.

Discretion or power of court, after bond of executor or administrator has been given, to dispense with, discontinue, or modify bond. 121 ALR 951.

Payment or delivery of legacy or distributive share before decree of distribution as defense to action by legatee or distributee on bond of personal representative. 121 ALR 1069.

Official bond as covering appeal taken by executor or administrator. 132 ALR 1280.

Subrogation of surety of executor or administrator to claim of estate against third person who knew or was chargeable with notice that personal representative's transaction with him involved breach of latter's obligation. 134 ALR 999.

Liability of surety for failure of executor or administrator to require securities from life tenant. 138 ALR 443.

Nature of bond as affecting coexecutor's or coadministrator's liability for defaults or wrongful acts of fiduciary in handling estate. 65 ALR2d 1054.

Liability for loss caused to estate by acts or defaults of agent or attorney appointed by executor or administrator. 28 ALR3d 1191.

What funds, not part of the estate, are received under color of office so as to render liable surety on executor's or administrator's bond. 82 ALR3d 869.

§ 43-2-80. Persons required to give bond; amount; sureties required; approval by probate judge.

Every person appointed executor, administrator or special administrator, except in cases otherwise provided for in this article, must give bond, with at least two sufficient sureties or a sufficient guaranty or surety company, payable to and to be approved by the judge of probate of the county having jurisdiction of the estate, in a penalty prescribed by him, which must be a sum not less than double the estimated value of the personal property and double the estimated value of the rent of the real estate of the decedent for a term of three years, or at the discretion of the judge of probate, in a sum not less than double the estimated value of the real and personal property of the estate and conditioned to perform all the duties which are or may be required of him as such executor or administrator. But an executor or administrator, other than the general administrator, or the sheriff or an executor relieved from giving bond, who has not given bond in double the estimated value of the estate, real and personal, of the decedent, must not obtain an order for the sale of lands of the decedent and must not, under any authority or power, make sale of any lands of the decedent, until he has given bond in double the estimated value of such lands. (Code 1852, §§ 1683, 1684; Code 1867, §§ 2003, 2004; Code 1876, §§ 2365, 2366; Code 1886, § 2024; Code 1896, § 66; Code 1907, § 2540; Code 1923, § 5762; Code 1940, T. 61, § 96.)

Conditions contained in court orders. — The legal effect of an order requiring an executor to give bond to "keep and perform and pay all decrees which may be rendered against him in a cause" is no more than that flowing from the statutory conditions herein prescribed. No greater obligations are placed upon the executor by the conditions used. Hence, the use of such conditions does not render invalid the orders of the court (appointment of receiver in this case) issued upon a failure to give the required bond. Hurt v. Hurt, 157 Ala. 126, 47 So. 260 (1908).

Sale not subject to collateral attack when section not followed. — Failure of administratrix to give bond in double value of realty and personalty before sale of land for payment of estate's debt did not invalidate sale or render it void on collateral attack. Peek v. Haardt, 235 Ala. 145, 177 So. 634 (1937).

Sureties cannot deny validity of administrator's appointment. — Sureties on a bond of an administrator who qualified and obtained possession of the assets of an estate cannot, when called to account for his breaches of duty, deny the validity of his appointment. Plowman v. Henderson, 59 Ala. 559 (1877).

Their liability extends only to liability of principal in representative capacity; sureties cannot be bound for anything for which the administrator cannot be bound in his official capacity. Campbell v. American Bonding Co., 172 Ala. 458, 55 So. 306 (1911).

This liability is not discharged by administrator's death. — The liability of a surety on an administrator's bond is not discharged by his death, although the default occurred afterwards. Hightower v. Moore, 46 Ala. 387 (1871).

The liability of a surety continues on an administrator's bond if the final decree is set aside. Fidelity & Deposit Co. v. Hendrix, 215 Ala. 555, 112 So. 117 (1927); Maryland Cas. Co. v. Owens, 261 Ala. 446, 74 So. 2d 608 (1954).

Collateral references. — 34 C.J.S., Executors & Administrators, § 944.

§ 43-2-81. Exemption of executor by express provision in will.

(a) Any testator may, by express provision in his will to that effect, exempt an executor from giving bond; and when such provision is made, such bond must not be required except in the following cases:

(1) When any executor, heir, legatee or other person interested in the estate makes affidavit, showing his interest and alleging that such interest is, or will be, endangered for want of security; or

(2) When, in the opinion of the judge of probate, the estate is likely to be wasted, to the prejudice of any person interested therein.

(b) In the cases provided for by subsection (a), upon application for the executor to give bond, he may show cause against such application and must have such notice as the judge may deem reasonable; but if he is not in the state, the application may be heard and determined without notice. (Code 1852, §§ 1685, 1686; Code 1867, §§ 2005, 2006; Code 1876, §§ 2367, 2368; Code 1886, §§ 2025, 2026; Code 1896, §§ 67, 68; Code 1907, §§ 2541, 2542; Code 1923, §§ 5763, 5764; Code 1940, T. 61, §§ 97, 98.)

In general. — The requirement of bond of an executor under this section is only a judicial finding that the estate is likely to be wasted to the prejudice of some person interested therein. Naugher v. Hinson, 211 Ala. 278, 100 So. 221 (1924).

The right is applicable in circuit court. — The right to exact a bond of executor given by this section obtains where the administration is removed from the probate into the circuit court. Cronk v. Cronk, 148 Ala. 337, 42 So. 450 (1906).

The obvious purpose of subsection (b) is to give an executor, who has been relieved by the will of giving bond, an opportunity to controvert the allegation of the affidavit (or sworn application) for bond that the interest of the affiant (applicant) in the estate is "endangered for want of security." Ex parte Griffin, 274 Ala. 391, 150 So. 2d 216 (1963).

Court has inherent power to protect from waste. — Where executors and trustees are permitted by will to act without giving bonds securing faithful performance of duties, an imperiled trust estate may be protected from waste by action taken pursuant to statutes and inherent powers of court. Rudulph v. Hodo, 228 Ala. 170, 153 So. 238 (1934).

Named exemption exclusive. — This section does not permit a testator to exempt an executor from filing an inventory under article 13 of this chapter. Hence a provision in a will so exempting an executor is ineffective, although this is probably a good excuse in avoiding removal under § 43-2-290 for not filing an inventory until an application filed by legatee under this section. Parker v. Robertson, 205 Ala. 434, 88 So. 418 (1921), decided prior to enactment of § 43-2-311.

This section does not exempt an executor who was granted letters testamentary without bond as provided in testator's will, from bond for ancillary executorship. Keith v. Proctor, 114 Ala. 676, 21 So. 502 (1897).

Similarity between exceptions in section 43-2-311, validating wills exempting executors from filing inventory or making settlement, and exceptions in this section suggests similarity of construction. Wright v. Menefee, 226 Ala. 55, 145 So. 315 (1932).

Section 43-2-311 is practically the same as this section, and should have a construction similar to that given this section. Ex parte Griffin, 274 Ala. 391, 150 So. 2d 216 (1963).

Compensation for services in requiring executrix to give bond, though she was exempted from giving bond by testator who was indebted to client, must be sought from client and not from estate, if services did not inure to benefit of other creditors of estate. Whether such services inured to benefit of other creditors held for probate court. Keith v. Forsythe, 227 Ala. 555, 151 So. 60 (1933).

Amount of distributive share immaterial. — In hearing on a complaint pursuant to this section, seeking to have an executor bonded, no inquiry is made as to the quantum of the distributee's share on final settlement, but it is sufficient that he is a distributee entitled to share in whatever may remain after debt payments. Farmers' Bank & Trust Co. v. Borroughs, 217 Ala. 97, 114 So. 909 (1927).

Whether the interest of a beneficiary under a will is "endangered" because the executor is not under bond, since the will exempted him from giving bond, is answered under this section, by determining whether the estate is likely to be wasted to the prejudice of persons interested unless the executor is required to give security. Farmers' Bank & Trust Co. v. Borroughs, 217 Ala. 97, 114 So. 909 (1927).

Denying relief under one application is not prejudicial to another. — In bank's action for declaratory judgment to determine rights to deposit of testatrix, wherein trial court found that deposit did not belong to estate of testatrix because duly transferred to a joint account, and no other estate was disclosed in the record, reviewing court would not impute error to trial court in denying legatee's motion to require executors to give bond, but would make the judgment without prejudice to rights of any party in interest to make an application to require bond. Bowie v. Phenix-Girard Bank, 237 Ala. 44, 185 So. 363 (1938).

Interested person illustrated. — Petitions have been filed under this section by the following persons: legatee, Allen v. Draper, 98 Ala. 590, 13 So. 529 (1893); widow of testator, Johnson v. Clements, 14 So. 14 (Ala. 1893); devisees, Cronk v. Cronk, 148 Ala. 337, 42 So. 450 (1906).

Sufficiency of petition. — See Allen v. Draper, 98 Ala. 590, 13 So. 529 (1893); Johnson v. Clements, 14 So. 14 (Ala. 1893); Cronk v. Cronk, 148 Ala. 337, 42 So. 450 (1906); Farmers' Bank & Trust Co. v. Borroughs, 217 Ala. 97, 114 So. 909 (1927).

The executor has the first burden of showing that there is no necessity for a bond, in an action under this section. Farmers' Bank & Trust Co. v. Borroughs, 217 Ala. 97, 114 So. 909 (1927); Bowie v. Phenix-Girard Bank, 237 Ala. 44, 185 So. 363 (1938).

Upon the filing of a sufficient affidavit (or sworn application) under this section, the executor then has the burden of showing no necessity for a bond, that is, that affiant's (applicant's) interest in the estate is not "endangered for want of security." Ex parte Griffin, 274 Ala. 391, 150 So. 2d 216 (1963).

Sufficiency of answer. — As will be seen from the provisions of subsection (b) of this section, it rests upon the executor to show cause why the petition should not be granted. The following facts were held to be an insufficient answer: An allegation that defendant (executor) is a merchant, that he furnishes testator's widow (petitioner) and children with supplies at cost, for which reason it would not be to petitioner's interest to have him removed. Such allegations were held to be entirely irrelevant. Johnson v. Clements, 14 So. 14 (Ala. 1893).

An answer alleging that the estate will be exhausted in paying debts, and that, therefore, petitioner has no interest, sets up no defense. In such case it is improper to determine whether the person will realize anything from the legacy, it being sufficient that she is a named "legatee." Allen v. Draper, 98 Ala. 590, 13 So. 529 (1893).

Sufficient facts to make prima facie case to compel giving of bond. — In bank's action for declaratory judgment to determine rights to bank deposit of a testatrix, legatee's sworn petition claiming the deposit under the will, and also as a creditor, showing that such legatee's interest was or would be in danger for want of security, presented a prima facie case under this section. Bowie v. Phenix-Girard Bank, 237 Ala. 44, 185 So. 363 (1938).

Where will relieved executors of giving bond, filing inventory or reporting to the courts, failure to file inventory was not a dereliction material to legatee's application to require executors to give bond. Bowie v. Phenix-Girard Bank, 237 Ala. 44, 185 So. 363 (1938).

Bond requirement rests on judicial finding, not affidavit. — This section and § 43-2-311 do not require the court to order the giving of a bond or the filing of an inventory simply because there is an appropriate affidavit (or sworn application) to that end. Requiring a bond or inventory rests upon a judicial finding that affiant's (applicant's) interest in the estate "is, or will be, endangered for want of security." Ex parte Griffin, 274 Ala. 391, 150 So. 2d 216 (1963).

Likelihood of waste is addressed to court's discretion. — A finding that the estate is likely to be wasted to the prejudice of some person interested therein necessarily is based on the particular facts and circumstances before the court, and is a matter which is addressed to the court's discretion. Ex parte Griffin, 274 Ala. 391, 150 So. 2d 216 (1963).

Cited in Matthews v. Hobbs, 51 Ala. 210 (1874); Smith v. Phillips, 54 Ala. 8 (1875); Phillips v. Smith, 62 Ala. 575 (1878); Walker v. Johnson, 82 Ala. 347, 2 So. 744 (1887); Tillman v. Tillman, 271 Ala. 373, 124 So. 2d 80 (1960).

§ 43-2-82. Liability of judge in taking bond.

The judge of probate is liable for any neglect or omission in not taking bond or for taking an insufficient bond from any executor or administrator; and any person injured thereby may maintain an action against such judge and his sureties and recover according to the injury proved. (Code 1852, § 1692; Code 1867, § 2013; Code 1876, § 2375; Code 1886, § 2033; Code 1896, § 76; Code 1907, § 2545; Code 1923, § 5767; Code 1940, T. 61, § 101.)

In general. — Both the protection of all who may have interests involved and his official oath demand the performance by the judge of the duty of requiring the bond. And he cannot forego this duty without imperiling himself and his sureties. Keith v. Proctor, 114 Ala. 676, 21 So. 502 (1897).

Letters granted without taking bond are voidable. — Letters testamentary or letters of administration, granted without the taking of bond, are not esteemed void, when the validity is collaterally questioned; they are irregular, voidable and subject to revocation on the application of any party interested. Keith v. Proctor, 114 Ala. 676, 21 So. 502 (1897).

Cited in Cunningham v. Lindsay, 77 Ala. 510 (1884).

§ 43-2-83. Discharge of surety; new bond.

(a) Upon the application in writing of any surety or sureties upon the bond of an executor or administrator requesting to be discharged from any future liability as such surety or sureties, or upon the application in writing of the personal representative or of an heir or devisee of a deceased surety upon such bond requesting that the estate of such deceased surety be discharged from future liability by reason of such suretyship, the court shall give to such executor or administrator notice of such application and require him, within 15 days after the service of the notice, to make a new bond; and upon the failure to make such bond, such executor or administrator shall be removed and his letters revoked; and upon such removal he shall make settlement of his administration. Any number of persons having the right to make application under this section may join in the application.

(b) When a new bond is given under subsection (a) of this section, the surety on whose application or the estate of the deceased surety on whose behalf the application was made, as the case may be, is discharged as to all breaches subsequent to the execution and approval of the new bond. (Code 1876, § 2385; Code 1886, § 2044; Code 1896, §§ 90, 91; Code 1907, §§ 2547, 2548; Code 1923, §§ 5769, 5770; Code 1940, T. 61, §§ 103, 104.)

Cited in Ashurst v. Union Bank & Trust Co., 200 Ala. 559, 76 So. 917 (1917).

Collateral references. — 34 C.J.S., Executors & Administrators, § 959.

Rights and liabilities between sureties on successive bond. 76 ALR 904.

Liability of surety on bond for defalcations or deficit occurring before bond was given. 82 ALR 585.

§ 43-2-84. Bond of applicant when administration committed to general administrator or sheriff.

(a) When administration is committed to the general administrator or sheriff, on the application of a third person, such letters must not be granted unless such person enters into bond, with surety, to be approved by the judge, to pay the fees and allowances made by the court on such administration, if the property of the estate is insufficient therefor.

(b) If, upon the settlement of an administrator appointed under subsection (a), it appears that sufficient assets of his intestate have not come to his hands to pay the costs and expenses legally incurred in his administration, the probate court having jurisdiction of such administration may enter a judgment and thereon issue execution against the obligors in the bond mentioned in subsection (a), for any excess due above the assets in the hands of such administrator. (Code 1852, § 1691; Code 1867, §§ 2011, 2012; Code 1876, §§ 2373, 2374; Code 1886, §§ 2031, 2032; Code 1896, §§ 74, 75; Code 1907, §§ 2543, 2544; Code 1923, §§ 5765, 5766; Code 1940, T. 61, §§ 99, 100.)

Collateral references. — 34 C.J.S., Executors & Administrators, § 969.

Public officer administering estate or his bond as liable for defaults and misfeasance of his deputy. 1 ALR 241, 116 ALR 1064, 71 ALR2d 1140.

Liability on bond of public officer administering estate for acts or defaults after termination of office. 81 ALR 63.

§ 43-2-85. Bond of general administrator.

The general administrator of a county must give bond, with at least two sufficient sureties or a sufficient guaranty or surety company, in an amount to be prescribed by the judge of probate sufficient to secure all persons interested, payable to the judge of probate and conditioned faithfully to administer all estates which may come to his charge as such general administrator, which bond must be approved by such judge. (Code 1852, § 1689; Code 1867, § 2009;

Code 1876, § 2371; Code 1886, § 2028; Code 1896, § 70; Code 1907, § 2536; Code 1923, § 5758; Code 1940, T. 61, § 135.)

Cited in Mitchell v. Nelson, 49 Ala. 88 (1873); May v. Marks, 74 Ala. 249 (1883); Daly v. Mallory, 123 Ala. 170, 26 So. 217 (1899).

§ 43-2-86. Additional bond of general administrator.

An additional bond may also be required of the general administrator, whenever the judge of probate deems it necessary to secure the interests of the estate confided to his charge or the sureties may be unwilling to remain longer bound; and, if he fails to give such bond within the time prescribed by the court, he must be removed and his letters revoked; and when any person interested in an estate committed to the general administrator shall give notice in writing to the judge of probate that the interest of the estate requires that the general administrator should give an additional bond, such judge must require him to give such bond; and if, in such case, the judge of probate fails or omits to require such bond and loss thereby results to anyone interested, he and the sureties on his official bond shall be responsible therefor. (Code 1852, § 1711; Code 1867, § 2032; Code 1876, § 2401; Code 1886, § 2055; Code 1896, § 102; Code 1907, § 2549; Code 1923, § 5771; Code 1940, T. 61, § 105.)

§ 43-2-87. Additional bond of sheriff.

When the administration of any estate is committed to the sheriff, the judge of probate, at such time or at any time thereafter, while the administration is in the hands of such officer, may require of him an additional bond if, in his opinion, the official bond of such officer is not sufficient security for the protection of the estate; and if he fails to give such additional bond for 10 days after notice that the same is required, he vacates his office, and the judge of probate must certify the vacancy to the appointing power. (Code 1852, § 1712; Code 1867, § 2033; Code 1876, § 2402; Code 1886, § 2056; Code 1896, § 103; Code 1907, § 2550; Code 1923, § 5772; Code 1940, T. 61, § 106.)

Cited in Harbin v. Knox, 7 Ala. 675 (1845); Croft v. Terrell, 15 Ala. 652 (1849); Montgomery, etc., R. Co. v. Varner, 19 Ala. 185 (1851); Hanna v. Price, 23 Ala. 826 (1853); Strong v. Catlin, 35 Ala. 607 (1860); Ryall v. Maix & Co., 48 Ala. 537 (1872); Burnett v. Nesmith, 62 Ala. 261 (1878).

§ 43-2-88. When sureties discharged by additional bond.

When an additional bond is given on the application of the surety of an executor or administrator, such surety is discharged as to all breaches subsequent to the execution and approval of the additional bond. (Code 1852, § 1715; Code 1867, § 2036; Code 1876, § 2405; Code 1886, § 2057; Code 1896, § 104; Code 1907, § 2551; Code 1923, § 5773; Code 1940, T. 61, § 107.)

Cited in Rives v. Flinn, 47 Ala. 481 (1872);
Jones v. Ritter, 56 Ala. 270 (1876); Buckley v.
McQuire, 58 Ala. 226 (1877).

§ 43-2-89. Force and obligations of former bonds continued.

When the additional bond is not given on the application of a surety, the former bonds are not discharged, but each remains of the same force and obligation as if such additional bond had not been given; and any person aggrieved, for a breach of the last bond, may proceed on either or all of the bonds, in the same or in separate proceedings. (Code 1852, § 1716; Code 1867, § 2037; Code 1876, § 2406; Code 1886, § 2058; Code 1896, § 105; Code 1907, § 2552; Code 1923, § 5774; Code 1940, T. 61, § 108.)

Application by surety is necessary to effect a discharge of former bonds. Jones v. Ritter, 56 Ala. 270 (1876).

Cited in Cochran v. Adler, 121 Ala. 442, 25 So. 761 (1899).

Collateral references. — 34 C.J.S., Executors & Administrators, § 946.

Discretion or power of court, after bond of executor and administrator has been given, to dispense with, discontinue, or modify bond. 121 ALR 951.

§ 43-2-90. Rights of sureties among themselves.

The sureties in either bond, who have been compelled to make any payment thereon for the principal obligor, on a breach subsequent to the execution of the last bond, have the same remedies against the sureties on the remaining bonds as cosureties have against each other and may recover against such sureties such an amount as shall be in the same proportion to the sum paid by the plaintiff as the aggregate penalty of the two bonds bears to the penalty of the bond of the defendant, apportioning the same among the solvent sureties. (Code 1852, § 1717; Code 1867, § 2038; Code 1876, § 2407; Code 1886, § 2059; Code 1896, § 106; Code 1907, § 2553; Code 1923, § 5775; Code 1940, T. 61, § 109.)

Collateral references. — Rights and liabilities between sureties on successive bond. 76 ALR 904.

§ 43-2-91. Bonds valid and operative as statutory bonds.

The bond of the general administrator of the county or of any executor or administrator is valid and operative as a statutory bond and is of the same obligation, force and effect as a statutory bond, though it may not be approved, or in the penalty, or payable or with the condition required by law. (Code 1852, § 1714; Code 1867, § 2035; Code 1876, § 2404; Code 1886, § 2273; Code 1896, § 342; Code 1907, § 2554; Code 1923, § 5776; Code 1940, T. 61, § 110.)

Cited in Steele v. Tutwiler, 68 Ala. 107 (1880).

§ 43-2-92. Conditional execution or delivery of bond.

A surety on the bond of the general administrator of the county or on the bond of any executor or administrator cannot avoid liability thereon on the ground that he signed or delivered it on condition that it should not be delivered to the judge of probate or should not become perfect, unless it was executed by some other person who does not execute it. (Code 1886, § 2274; Code 1896, § 343; Code 1907, § 2555; Code 1923, § 5777; Code 1940, T. 61, § 111.)

§ 43-2-93. Reducing amount of bond.

Upon the filing of any partial settlement by the executor under a will, or the administrator of the estate of a deceased person, in the court in which such estate is pending, such executor or administrator may pray for a reduction in the amount of his or her bond as a fiduciary, and thereupon the court must set a day for the hearing of such partial settlement and must cause notices to be issued to all parties in interest as is now provided by law for final settlements of such estates. And on the day set for hearing the court may fix the amount to which the bond shall be reduced, which shall be determined as now provided by law for such bonds. (Acts 1939, No. 560, p. 883; Code 1940, T. 61, § 112.)

ARTICLE 5.

LIABILITY OF EXECUTORS AND ADMINISTRATORS.

§ 43-2-110. Limits of liability generally.

No executor or administrator is liable, except in the case provided by section 43-2-62, beyond the amount of assets which have come to his hands or which have been lost, destroyed, wasted, injured, depreciated or not collected by want of diligence on his part or an abuse of his trust. (Code 1852, § 1919; Code 1867, § 2278; Code 1876, § 2616; Code 1886, § 2269; Code 1896, § 337; Code 1907, § 2798; Code 1923, § 6037; Code 1940, T. 61, § 114.)

In general. — The liability of an administrator as to the money of an estate in his hands is that of an ordinary bailee for hire. He is not an insurer and is not liable where it is shown that he acted in good faith and diligence usual with good businessmen under similar circumstances. Lehman v. Robertson, 84 Ala. 489, 4 So. 728 (1888).

But he is liable when he fails to act in this manner. Dean v. Rathbone, 15 Ala. 328 (1849).

Personal liability for judgment. — In Dangaix v. Lunsford, 112 Ala. 403, 20 So. 639 (1896), cited in Boyte v. Perkins, 211 Ala. 130, 99 So. 652 (1924), it was held that, unless the administrator protects himself by insolvency proceedings, the return of no property found belonging to the estate is conclusive of a devastavit on his part, and he becomes personally liable for the judgment.

Cited in Holley v. Acre, 23 Ala. 603 (1853); Amason v. Nash, 24 Ala. 279 (1854); Grace v. Martin, 47 Ala. 135 (1872).

Collateral references. — 33 C.J.S., Executors & Administrators, §§ 142, 184, 196, 242-249.

31 Am. Jur. 2d, Executors & Administrators, §§ 186-192.

Liability of personal representative for injury to person in street by fall of part of structure of completed building. 7 ALR 212, 138 ALR 1078.

Individual liability of executor or administrator for injury to person or property of third person due to negligence, or violation of statute or ordinance, in management of estate. 7 ALR 408, 123 ALR 458.

Liability of executor or administrator to account for receipts before letters were granted. 26 ALR 1367.

Liability of personal representative for injury to one in street by object falling from window. 29 ALR 85, 53 ALR 462.

Right of one whose estate is administered as that of absentee presumed to be dead to hold administrator personally liable. 37 ALR 826.

Responsibility of personal representative for loss of funds deposited in bank in his own name or other form not indicating fiduciary character. 43 ALR 600.

Estate's liability for torts of executor or administrator. 44 ALR 637, 127 ALR 687.

Delegation of power as affecting liability of executor or administrator. 50 ALR 214.

Responsibility of executor or administrator for default of guardian of minor beneficiary. 54 ALR 1274.

Liability of executor or administrator for loss of money deposited in bank in his representative capacity. 60 ALR 488.

Stockholder's statutory added liability, personal liability for, of his executor or administrator. 79 ALR 1556, 96 ALR 1466.

Partner who is also executor of deceased partner's estate, accountability of, for profits earned subsequently to death. 80 ALR 23, 54, 55 ALR2d 1391.

Court order authorizing investment as affecting liability of executor or administrator for loss of funds invested. 88 ALR 325.

Liability for loss by depreciation in value because of retaining or deferring sale of securities. 92 ALR 436.

Loss of funds after final order for distribution, liability of executor or administrator for. 100 ALR 1126.

Purchase from or sale to corporation of which he is officer or stockholder by executor or administrator as voidable or ground for surcharging his account. 105 ALR 449.

Liability of fiduciary for loss on investment as affected by fact that it was taken in his own name without indication of fiduciary capacity. 106 ALR 271, 150 ALR 805.

Order or decree of distribution of decedent's estate as protection of executor or administrator against claims of one not named therein who is entitled to a share of the estate. 106 ALR 817.

Protection or preservation of property of estate pending appointment of executor or administrator, personal liability of representative for services rendered or supplies furnished for purpose of. 108 ALR 388.

Losses incurred in carrying on business pursuant to direction or permission of will, liability of executor or his sureties for. 109 ALR 639.

Liability of executor in case of depreciation in assets of estate after partial distribution. 114 ALR 461.

Liability in absence of mandatory statute of executor or administrator for loss of funds as affected by failure to obtain court order authorizing investment. 116 ALR 437.

Surchargeability of executor or administrator in respect of mortgage investment as affected by matters relating to value of property. 117 ALR 871.

Duty and liability in respect to specifically bequeathed personal property not needed for payment of debts, duty and liability in respect to, of executor or administrator with will annexed. 127 ALR 1071.

Liability for failure to require security from life tenant. 138 ALR 443.

Personal liability of executor or administrator as affected by terms of contract or form of signature. 138 ALR 155.

Amount of attorney's compensation for services rendered in administration of decedent's estate. 143 ALR 735, 56 ALR2d 13.

Right of attorney whose selection is directed or suggested by will, against estate or personal representative. 166 ALR 491.

Liability for depreciation in value of securities as affected by appreciation of other securities. 171 ALR 1422.

Duty of personal representative with respect to completion of improvements contracted for by decedent. 5 ALR2d 1250.

Liability of executor as affected by will authorizing or directing executor to retain investments received under will. 47 ALR2d 273.

Compensation of attorney for executor or administrator as affected by representation of heir or other beneficiary in controversy with other heirs or beneficiaries. 47 ALR2d 1104.

Liability of personal representative for losses incurred in carrying on, without testamentary authorization, decedent's nonpartnership mercantile or manufacturing business. 58 ALR2d 365.

Power and responsibility of executor or administrator to compromise claim against estate. 72 ALR2d 243.

Duty and liability of executor to locate and notify legatee or devisee. 10 ALR3d 547.

Liability of executor or administrator for loss caused to estate by acts or default of agent or attorney employed by him. 28 ALR3d 1191.

Liability of executor, administrator, trustee, or his counsel, for interest, penalty, or extra taxes assessed against estate because of tax law violations. 47 ALR3d 507.

§ 43-2-111. Liability for damages recovered under sections 6-5-391, 6-5-410 or 25-6-3.

The personal representative and the sureties on his bond are liable to the parties in interest for the due and legal distribution of all damages recovered by such representative under sections 6-5-391, 6-5-410 or 25-6-3, and are subject to all remedies which may be pursued against such representative and sureties for the due administration of personal assets. (Code 1886, § 2593; Code 1896, § 338; Code 1907, § 2799; Code 1923, § 6038; Code 1940, T. 61, § 115.)

Code commissioner's note. — The sections mentioned in this section pertain to the following subjects: § 6-5-391, right of personal representative to commence an action for injuries causing death of minor child; § 6-5-410, action for death by wrongful act; § 25-6-3, action by personal representative of servant or employee for latter's death.

§ 43-2-112. Executor or administrator of decedent who wasted or converted another decedent's assets.

The executor or administrator of any decedent who, as executor, administrator or otherwise, has wasted or converted to his own use any assets of any other decedent is liable in the same manner as his testator or intestate would have been if living. (Code 1852, § 1928; Code 1867, § 2287; Code 1876, § 2631; Code 1886, § 2268; Code 1896, § 336; Code 1907, § 2797; Code 1923, § 6036; Code 1940, T. 61, § 113.)

Investment of funds. — The mere fact that a tenant told executor not to invest funds gave him no right to convert same to his own use. Collins v. Clements, 199 Ala. 618, 75 So. 165 (1917).

Cited in Nelson v. Goree, 34 Ala. 565 (1859); Harrison v. Harrison, 39 Ala. 489 (1864).

Collateral references. — 34 C.J.S., Executors & Administrators, §§ 942, 944.

§ 43-2-113. Executor de son tort.

No person is liable to an action, as executor of his own wrong, for having taken, received or interfered with the property of a deceased person but is liable to the executor or administrator for the value of all the property so taken or received and for all damages caused by his act to the estate of the deceased; but the provisions of this section must not be construed so as to prevent any creditor from maintaining a civil action against anyone in possession of property fraudulently transferred by such deceased person. (Code 1852, § 1933; Code 1867, § 2292; Code 1876, § 2636; Code 1886, § 2271; Code 1896, § 340; Code 1907, § 2801; Code 1923, § 6040; Code 1940, T. 61, § 117.)

An executor de son tort is a person who without authority intermeddles with the estate of decedent and does such acts as properly belong to the office of an executor or administrator. He becomes an executor of his own wrong. Johnston v. Johnston, 256 Ala. 485, 55 So. 2d 838 (1951).

To be an executor de son tort or trustee in invitum, the person must be in the attitude of one acting without authority. McInnis v. Sutton, 260 Ala. 432, 70 So. 2d 625 (1953).

Creditors. — This section precludes a creditor of a decedent from subjecting funds in the hands of an executor de son tort to the payment of a note on which decedent was liable as surety. Winfrey v. Clarke, 107 Ala. 355, 18 So. 141 (1895).

Cited in Grace v. Martin, 47 Ala. 135 (1872); Abernathy v. Bankhead, 71 Ala. 190 (1881); Ex parte Johnston, 258 Ala. 545, 64 So. 2d 67 (1953).

Collateral references. — 34 C.J.S., Executors & Administrators, §§ 1063-1068.

§ 43-2-114. Resignation as defense.

No executor or administrator can allege his resignation in defense to any action or proceeding without an averment that he has settled his administration and delivered over the assets of the estate as required by law. (Code 1852, § 1920; Code 1867, § 2279; Code 1876, § 2617; Code 1886, § 2270; Code 1896, § 339; Code 1907, § 2800; Code 1923, § 6039; Code 1940, T. 61, § 116.)

Cross references. — As to resignation, etc., of executors or administrators generally, see § 43-2-270 et seq.

Cited in Ex parte State, 247 Ala. 207, 23 So. 2d 545 (1945).

Collateral references. — 33 C.J.S., Executors & Administrators, § 82.

ARTICLE 6.

ACTIONS BY AND AGAINST EXECUTORS AND ADMINISTRATORS.

Division 1.

General Provisions.

Cited in First Nat'l Bank v. Chichester, 352 So. 2d 1371 (Ala. Civ. App. 1977).

§ 43-2-130. Venue; service of process.

Civil actions may be brought against executors or administrators in their representative character, in all cases, in the county in which letters were granted. Service of process may be made on them in any county in the state. (Code 1852, § 1918; Code 1867, § 2277; Code 1876, § 2615; Code 1886, § 2262; Code 1896, § 330; Code 1907, § 2802; Code 1923, § 6041; Code 1940, T. 61, § 118.)

Cross references. — As to rules of supreme court as to service of process, see A.R.C.P., Rule 4 et seq.

Cited in Erwin v. Branch Bank, 14 Ala. 307 (1848); Ikelheimer v. Chapman, 32 Ala. 676 (1858).

Collateral references. — 34 C.J.S., Executors & Administrators, § 727.

§ 43-2-131. Limitation on actions against executor or administrator.

No civil action must be commenced against an executor or administrator, as such, until six months after the grant of letters testamentary or of administration, unless the executor or administrator has given notice of the disallowance of the claim. (Code 1852, § 1917; Code 1867, § 2276; Code 1876, § 2614; Code 1886, § 2263; Code 1896, § 331; Code 1907, § 2803; Code 1923, § 6042; Acts 1931, No. 725, p. 841; Code 1940, T. 61, § 119.)

Cross references. — As to exception regarding actions to enforce liens for improvements on public streets, etc., see § 35-11-415.

History of section. — See Barrett v. Fondren, 262 Ala. 537, 80 So. 2d 243 (1955).

The manifest purpose of this section is to protect the estate and to prevent claims being established against it by judicial proceedings until the personal representative has had ample opportunity to ascertain the condition of the estate and the true status of the claims against it. Consolidated Mercantile Co. v. Warren, 15 Ala. App. 623, 74 So. 738 (1917). See also Smith v. Alabama G.S.R.R., 212 Ala. 166, 102 So. 118 (1924).

Section applicable only to actions against administrator "as such". — This section applies only to actions against the executor or administrator purely in his representative capacity, and an action against decedent to recover land, which, on his death, was immediately revived against his administrator, was properly at issue after such revival, and could properly proceed to judgment, since, if decedent had no title to the land, the holding thereof by the administrator was his personal tort. Torrey v. Bishop, 104 Ala. 548, 16 So. 422 (1894).

And does not apply to actions by the personal representative to recover the assets of an estate. Consolidated Mercantile Co. v. Warren, 15 Ala. App. 623, 74 So. 738 (1917).

Nor to action by distributee. — The inhibition of this section only applies where there is an action against the administrator as such which seeks to fasten or establish a liability against the estate. Baker v. Mitchell, 109 Ala. 490, 20 So. 40 (1896), holding the section inapplicable to an action by distributee for removal of administration. See also St. John v. St. John, 150 Ala. 237, 43 So. 580 (1907); Hardwick v. Hardwick, 164 Ala. 390, 51 So. 389 (1909); Manfredo v. Manfredo, 182 Ala. 247, 62 So. 522 (1913).

Nor to actions to subject to the debts of decedent property fraudulently conveyed by him, because the conveyance is valid as against the grantor and the property cannot become assets of the estate. Freeman v. Pullen, 119 Ala. 235, 24 So. 57 (1898).

Nor to action to enforce testamentary trust. — This section has no application to a complaint against executor filed for the purpose of enforcing a testamentary trust. Smith v. Cain, 187 Ala. 174, 65 So. 367 (1914).

And action against administrator of deceased partner is prohibited. — This section prohibits an action against the surviving partner and administrator of his deceased partner for settlement of the partnership accounts, brought within the time limitation

herein contained. Word v. Word, 90 Ala. 81, 7 So. 412 (1890).

Computing time limitation. — In computing the three-year limitation in an action against an administrator for services rendered his intestate, the six months in which, under this section, no action can be brought against an administrator, must be excluded. Hood v. League, 102 Ala. 228, 14 So. 572 (1894). As to exclusion of time between death of person and grant of letters, not exceeding six months, see § 6-2-14, and notes thereto.

In open account claims for services rendered a deceased, compensation can be recovered only for those services rendered within three years before the beginning of the action, excluding the six months in which no action can be brought against the administrator. Norton v. Liddell, 280 Ala. 353, 194 So. 2d 514 (1967).

Premature payment of claims. — This section avoids all reason and necessity for the distribution of the assets of the estate by the payment of claims until the lapse of the period for presentation of claims, and if an administrator prematurely pays the claims he does so at his risk. His remedy in such case is by subrogation to the rights of the creditor whose claim he has paid. Pryor v. Davis, 109 Ala. 117, 19 So. 440 (1896). As to distribution before final settlement, and the order thereon not being a defense to an action brought against administrator as such, see § 43-2-640. See also Walker v. Johnson, 82 Ala. 347, 2 So. 744 (1887).

Where it does not appear on face of complaint that action against administrator was prematurely brought, such question cannot be raised by demurrer (now motion to dismiss). American-Traders' Nat'l Bank v. Henderson, 222 Ala. 426, 133 So. 36 (1931).

The benefit of this section may be available by demurrer (now motion to dismiss) if the complaint shows on its face that it is violated. Barrett v. Fondren, 262 Ala. 537, 80 So. 2d 243 (1955).

Action against administrator of beneficiary of life policy to establish constructive trust in policy and proceeds held not within this section prohibiting actions against administrator for six months after appointment. American-Traders' Nat'l Bank v. Henderson, 222 Ala. 426, 133 So. 36 (1931).

Cited in Taylor v. Perry, 48 Ala. 240 (1872); Fretwell v. McLemore, 52 Ala. 124 (1875); Steele v. Steele, 64 Ala. 438 (1879); Espy v. Comer, 76 Ala. 501 (1884); Alabama State Bank v. Glass, 82 Ala. 278, 2 So. 641 (1887); Goldsmith v. Eichold, 94 Ala. 116, 10 So. 80 (1891); Whaley v. Rothschild & Co., 176 Ala. 69, 57 So. 707 (1912).

Collateral references. — 34 C.J.S., Executors & Administrators, § 729.

Constitutionality, construction and application of statute forbidding suit against representative of estate until expiration of prescribed period. 104 ALR 892.

§ 43-2-132. Actions begun by special administrator not abated.

Civil actions commenced by a special administrator do not abate by the appointment of an executor or administrator in chief, but may be prosecuted by such executor or administrator. (Code 1852, § 1924; Code 1867, § 2283; Code 1876, § 2621; Code 1886, § 2264; Code 1896, § 332; Code 1907, § 2804; Code 1923, § 6043; Code 1940, T. 61, § 120.)

Cited in Farrow v. Bragg, 30 Ala. 261 (1857); Morrow v. Taggart, 45 Ala. 292 (1871); Gibbs v. Hodge, 65 Ala. 366 (1880); Little v. Gavin, 244 Ala. 156, 12 So. 2d 549 (1943).

§ 43-2-133. Succeeding executor or administrator to be made party to civil actions.

When any civil action has been commenced by or against the personal representative of a decedent, the same may be prosecuted by or against any succeeding executor or administrator, who may, on motion, be made a party. (Code 1852, § 1925; Code 1867, § 2284; Code 1876, § 2622; Code 1886, § 2265; Code 1896, § 333; Code 1907, § 2805; Code 1923, § 6044; Code 1940, T. 61, § 121.)

Application. — This section applies according to its own language only to actions "commenced by or against the personal representative of a decedent." Ex parte State, 247 Ala. 207, 23 So. 2d 545 (1945).

Cited in Doe v. Collins, 7 Ala. 480 (1845); Skinner v. Frierson, 8 Ala. 915 (1846); Holman v. Bank of Norfolk, 12 Ala. 369 (1847); Wilkins v. Judge, 14 Ala. 135 (1848); Erwin v. Branch Bank, 14 Ala. 307 (1848); Varner v. Bevil, 17 Ala. 286 (1850); Townsend v. Jeffries, 24 Ala. 329 (1854); Robinson v. Tipton, 31 Ala. 595 (1858); Russell v. Erwin, 41 Ala. 292 (1867); Morrow v. Taggart, 45 Ala. 293 (1871); Whitfield v. Woolf, 51 Ala. 202 (1874); White v. Smith, 51 Ala. 405 (1874); Brown v. Tutwiler, 61 Ala. 372 (1878); Wells v. Elliott, 68 Ala. 183 (1880).

Collateral references. — 34 C.J.S., Executors & Administrators, §§ 1048, 1049.

Statute dealing with existing intestate administration, upon discovery of will, as affecting competency of later executor or administrator cum testamento annexo to defend a suit against the estate. 65 ALR2d 1201.

§ 43-2-134. Judgments against administrators in chief revived against administrators de bonis non.

In all cases where judgment has been rendered against an administrator in chief of any estate, and such administrator in chief dies, resigns or is removed before the satisfaction of such judgment, such judgment may be revived in favor of the owners of such judgment, or their personal representative, against the administrator de bonis non of such estate on 10 days' notice to such administrator de bonis non; but such liabilities shall only bind the administrator de bonis non to the extent of the assets of the estate which have come into his possession. (Code 1907, § 2806; Code 1923, § 6045; Code 1940, T. 61, § 122.)

Rule under prior law. — Prior to this section a judgment or decree against an administrator in chief was not binding upon, and furnished no cause of action against, a succeeding administrator de bonis non. Hence it could not be revived against him. Brothers v. Gunnels, 110 Ala. 436, 18 So. 3 (1895). See also Bobo v. Gunnels, 92 Ala. 601, 8 So. 797 (1891).

Effect of revival. — The revival of the judgment is, in effect, an adjudication that the decree is still unsatisfied, protects the administrator de bonis non in its payment and imposes the same duty of payment from assets in his hands as was imposed upon the administrator in chief. Cowan v. Perkins, 214 Ala. 158, 107 So. 66 (1926).

§ 43-2-135. Actions against survivor of two or more executors or administrators.

If any one of two or more executors or administrators, against whom a civil action is pending, die during the pendency of the action, it does not abate but may be continued against the survivor or survivors, on a suggestion of such death on the record. (Code 1852, § 1927; Code 1867, § 2286; Code 1876, § 2624; Code 1886, § 2266; Code 1896, § 334; Code 1907, § 2807; Code 1923, § 6046; Code 1940, T. 61, § 123.)

§ 43-2-136. Survival of actions for damages to realty.

All proceedings to ascertain damages done to real property survive to the executors or administrators. (Code 1852, § 1929; Code 1867, § 2288; Code 1876, § 2632; Code 1886, § 2267; Code 1896, § 335; Code 1907, § 2808; Code 1923, § 6047; Code 1940, T. 61, § 124.)

This section provides only for the survival of "all proceedings." McDowell v. Henderson Mining Co., 276 Ala. 202, 160 So. 2d 486 (1963).

And the term "proceedings" does not include "causes of action." McDowell v. Henderson Mining Co., 276 Ala. 202, 160 So. 2d 486 (1963).

"Actions" and "causes of action" distinguished. — There is a distinction between "actions" and "causes of action." An "action" is a proceeding pending in court to determine the parties' rights and liabilities with respect to a legal wrong or cause of action. A "cause of action" is a legal wrong for which an "action" may be, but has not been, brought in court. McDowell v. Henderson Mining Co., 276 Ala. 202, 160 So. 2d 486 (1963).

Statutes intended to aid the survival of "actions" are remedial, and are to be liberally construed, while those in aid of survival of "causes of action" are in derogation of the common law, and are to be strictly construed. McDowell v. Henderson Mining Co., 276 Ala. 202, 160 So. 2d 486 (1963).

The term "proceedings" clearly imports that some measure, step or act must have been taken in some legal forum prior to the landowner's death for the purpose of ascertaining the damages to his realty. McDowell v. Henderson Mining Co., 276 Ala. 202, 160 So. 2d 486 (1963).

Filing notice of foreclosure allowed administrator to bring action for slander of title. — Action for slander of title could be maintained by administrator of property owner despite contention that such a cause of action does not survive the death of the property owner and though allegedly forged mortgage was filed for record during the lifetime of owner and no action for slander of title was filed by owner during her lifetime since more than three years after the death of owner the defendant caused to be published the notice of foreclosure on the property described in the forged mortgage, and the act of filing the foreclosure notice constituted a separate and distinct slander for title for which the defendant may be held answerable in damages. Proctor v. Gissendaner, 579 F.2d 876 (5th Cir. 1978).

§ 43-2-137. Action on bond.

Civil actions may be brought or proceedings had on any bond given by an executor or administrator, as such, in the name of the party aggrieved until the whole penalty is exhausted. (Code 1852, § 1713; Code 1867, § 2034; Code 1876, § 2403; Code 1886, § 2272; Code 1896, § 341; Code 1907, § 2809; Code 1923, § 6048; Code 1940, T. 61, § 125.)

Cross references. — As to bonds of executors and administrators generally, see § 43-2-80 et seq.

§ 43-2-138. Action by legatee to recover legacy.

Any legatee, after six months from the grant of letters testamentary or of administration, with the will annexed, may bring a civil action and recover his legacy, upon proof that the executor assented to the same. (Code 1852, § 1931; Code 1867, § 2290; Code 1876, § 2634; Code 1886, § 2275; Code 1896, § 344; Code 1907, § 2810; Code 1923, § 6049; Acts 1931, No. 725, p. 841; Code 1940, T. 61, § 126.)

Cited in Bonner v. Young, 68 Ala. 35 (1880); Walker v. Johnson, 82 Ala. 347, 2 So. 744 (1887); Eastburn v. Canias, 193 Ala. 574, 69 So. 459 (1915).

§ 43-2-139. Inventory as evidence.

In an action against an executor or administrator, in which the fact of his having administered the estate of his testator or intestate, or any part thereof, comes in issue, and the inventory of the property of the deceased, filed by him, is given in evidence, the effect of the same may be repelled by evidence:

(1) That any property has been omitted in such inventory, or was not returned therein at its full value, or since the filing thereof has increased in value; or

(2) That such property has perished, or been lost without the fault of such executor or administrator, or that it has been fairly sold, according to law, at a less price than the value so returned, or that, since the return of the inventory, such property has deteriorated or decreased in value; and in such action the defendant cannot be charged for anything in action specified in the inventory, unless it appears that it was, or might have been, collected by the exercise of due diligence. (Code 1852, § 1932; Code 1867, § 2291; Code 1876, § 2635; Code 1886, § 2282; Code 1896, § 351; Code 1907, § 2811; Code 1923, § 6050; Code 1940, T. 61, § 127.)

Division 2.

Execution and Garnishment to Enforce Judgments and Decrees Against Personal Representatives.

§ 43-2-150. Enforcement of judgments, etc., of probate court against representatives — Generally.

All judgments, orders, and decrees of the probate court against an executor or administrator for the payment of money may be enforced by execution or by process of garnishment, which may issue in like cases and manner as it may issue on judgments in circuit courts, and may, in like manner, be prosecuted to judgment against the garnishee; for the delivery of personal property, by attachment or a special order to the sheriff, requiring him to take such property and deliver the same according to the judgment, order or decree; for the possession of land, by a writ to the sheriff against the executor or administrator, requiring him to put the heir or devisee in possession of the same. (Code 1852, § 1921; Code 1867, § 2280; Code 1876, § 2618; Code 1886, § 2276; Code 1896, § 345; Code 1907, § 2812; Code 1923, § 6051; Code 1940, T. 61, § 128.)

Cross references. — See notes to § 43-2-151.

Cited in Gibbs v. Hodge, 65 Ala. 366 (1880); Boyte v. Perkins, 211 Ala. 130, 99 So. 652 (1924).

Collateral references. — 34 C.J.S., Executors & Administrators, § 806.

Garnishment against executor or administrator by creditor of heir, legatee, distributee, or creditor of estate. 59 ALR 768.

Right of creditors to reach commissions of debtor as executor or administrator. 143 ALR 190.

§ 43-2-151. Same — Liability of sureties.

When an execution against an executor or administrator, issued from the probate court on any judgment, order or decree for money is returned to any regular term of such court "no property" by the sheriff of the county, such judgment, order or decree may be enforced against the executor or administrator and his sureties, by execution or by process of garnishment, which may issue in like cases and manner as it may issue on judgment in circuit courts and may, in like manner, be prosecuted to judgment against the garnishee. (Code 1852, § 1922; Code 1867, § 2281; Code 1876, § 2619; Code 1886, § 2277; Code 1896, § 346; Code 1907, § 2813; Code 1923, § 6052; Code 1940, T. 61, § 129.)

Cross references. — As to bonds of executors and administrators generally, see § 43-2-80 et seq.

When decree against representative of deceased administrator is improper. — On a settlement by a personal representative of a deceased administrator, under § 43-2-550, where no maladministration by such personal representative, a decree directing execution against him and his sureties under this section is improper. Boyte v. Perkins, 211 Ala. 130, 99 So. 652 (1924).

Return of "no property" is indispensable. — It is indispensable that execution should have been issued against personal representative and returned no property found. Poacher v. Weisinger, 20 Ala. 102 (1852).

Cited in Kirby v. Anders, 26 Ala. 466 (1855); Jewett v. Hoogland, 30 Ala. 716 (1857); Henderson v. Simmons, 33 Ala. 291 (1858);

Harrison v. Harrison, 39 Ala. 489 (1864); Tyson v. Sanderson, 45 Ala. 364 (1871); Ryall v. Maix & Co., 48 Ala. 537 (1872); Smith v. Jackson, 56 Ala. 25 (1876); — v. —, 58 Ala. 107 (1877); Garrett v. Garrett, 64 Ala. 263 (1879); Hudson v. Modawell, 64 Ala. 481 (1879); Steele v. Graves, 68 Ala. 17 (1880); Berry v. Perry, 81 Ala. 103, 1 So. 118 (1886); National Sur. Co. v. Rudder, 225 Ala. 549, 144 So. 21 (1932).

§ 43-2-152. Enforcement of judgment rendered against decedent before his death.

When a judgment has been entered against a decedent before his death, no execution can issue thereon against his personal representative, except in the case provided for in section 6-9-62; but such judgment may be revived against his personal representative by appropriate action or motion after the lapse of six months from the grant of letters; and sections 43-2-709 and 43-2-810 through 43-2-812 are applicable to such proceeding. (Code 1852, § 1930; Code 1867, § 2289; Code 1876, § 2633; Code 1886, § 2280; Code 1896, § 349; Code 1907, § 2816; Code 1923, § 6055; Code 1940, T. 61, § 132.)

Prior rule as to revivor. — A judgment against an administrator in chief could not be revived against an administrator de bonis non. Bobo v. Gunnels, 92 Ala. 601, 8 So. 797 (1891). See now § 43-2-134.

Motion or action to revive judgment is without warrant if there has been no administration. — If there has been no administration on the estate of the deceased debtor, and hence no personal representative has been appointed, the proceeding of scire facias (now motion or appropriate action to revive judgment) is without warrant. Carr v. Cowan, 261 Ala. 23, 72 So. 2d 726 (1954).

Judgment against debtor not revived against his heirs by motion or action to revive judgment. — There is no provision in this section which authorizes the revival of a judgment recovered against a deceased debtor to be revived against the heirs at law of such debtor by scire facias (now motion or appropriate action to revive judgment). Ranier v. Moseley, 255 Ala. 253, 51 So. 2d 244 (1951); Carr v. Cowan, 261 Ala. 23, 72 So. 2d 726 (1954).

Cited in Kirby v. Anders, 26 Ala. 466 (1855); McPherson v. State, 54 Ala. 221 (1875); Phillips v. Ash, 63 Ala. 414 (1879); Brown v. Newman, 66 Ala. 275 (1880); May v. Parham, 68 Ala. 253 (1880); Keel v. Larkin, 72 Ala. 493 (1882); Reynolds v. Crook, 95 Ala. 570, 11 So. 412 (1892); Enslen v. Wheeler, 98 Ala. 200, 13 So. 473 (1893).

§ 43-2-153. Enforcement of judgment of circuit court against representative.

When any judgment is entered in the circuit court against any executor or administrator, as such, and an execution thereon has been returned "no property" by the sheriff or other officer of the county in which such judgment was entered, an execution may issue against the executor or administrator personally, to be levied on his goods and chattels, lands and tenements. (Code 1852, § 1923; Code 1867, § 2282; Code 1876, § 2620; Code 1886, § 2278; Code 1896, § 347; Code 1907, § 2814; Code 1923, § 6053; Code 1940, T. 61, § 130.)

Proceedings are substitute for an action for devastavit against personal representatives when execution de bonis intestati has been returned "no property." Smith v. Alabama G.S.R.R., 212 Ala. 166, 102 So. 118 (1924); Moebes v. Kay, 241 Ala. 294, 2 So. 2d 754 (1941).

When judgment conclusive. — A judgment against a personal representative, as such, at the action of a creditor of the estate which he represents, whether the estate be solvent or insolvent, if allowed to stand, and execution thereon returned "no property," is conclusive on the personal representative of the amount due and owing by him as representative, and that he has in his hands sufficient assets for its payment. Moebes v. Kay, 241 Ala. 294, 2 So. 2d 754 (1941).

Cited in Grace v. Martin, 47 Ala. 135 (1872); McGehee v. Lomax, 49 Ala. 131 (1873); Lyon v. Robertson, 50 Ala. 74 (1873); Boykin v. Cook, 61 Ala. 472 (1878); Martin v. Ellerbe, 70 Ala. 326 (1881); Allen v. Allen, 80 Ala. 154 (1885); Whetstone v. McQueen, 137 Ala. 301, 34 So. 229 (1903); Merchants Nat'l Bank v. Cotnam, 250 Ala. 316, 34 So. 2d 122 (1948).

Collateral references. — 34 C.J.S., Executors & Administrators, § 1068.

§ 43-2-154. Purchase of property sold under execution.

The executor or administrator of any decedent may purchase for the estate property sold under any judgment of the circuit court or under any execution in his favor as such executor or administrator. (Code 1886, § 2281; Code 1896, § 350; Code 1907, § 2817; Code 1923, § 6056; Code 1940, T. 61, § 133.)

§ 43-2-155. Right of succeeding representative to execution.

Any subsequent administrator, or administrator with the will annexed, may have execution on any judgment recovered by any person who preceded him in the administration of the same estate, without reviving the same or without proceeding to notify the defendant in such judgment. (Code 1852, § 1926; Code 1867, § 2285; Code 1876, § 2623; Code 1886, § 2279; Code 1896, § 348; Code 1907, § 2815; Code 1923, § 6054; Code 1940, T. 61, § 131.)

ARTICLE 7.

COUNTY OR GENERAL ADMINISTRATORS.

Collateral references. — 34 C.J.S., Executors & Administrators, §§ 1050-1053.

§ 43-2-170. Appointment and duties generally; term of office.

Each judge of probate must appoint a suitable person as a general administrator within his county, who must take charge of the estates of deceased persons or act as special administrator, in those cases in which no other persons entitled thereto will administer and no other person is appointed by the court. His office shall expire with the expiration of the term of the judge who appointed him. (Code 1852, § 1680; Code 1867, § 2000; Code 1876, § 2362; Code 1886, § 2027; Code 1896, § 69; Code 1907, § 2535; Code 1923, § 5757; Code 1940, T. 61, § 134.)

History of section. — See Daly v. Mallory, 123 Ala. 170, 26 So. 217 (1899).

Cited in Clemens v. Walker, 40 Ala. 189 (1866); Russell v. Erwin, 41 Ala. 292 (1867); Mitchell v. Nelson, 49 Ala. 88 (1873); — v. —, 51 Ala. 94 (1874); Landford v. Dunklin, 71 Ala. 594 (1882); Pickett v. Doe, 74 Ala. 122 (1883); May v. Marks, 74 Ala. 249 (1883); Eubank v. Clark, 78 Ala. 73 (1884).

Collateral references. — Powers and duties of public administrator. 56 ALR2d 1183.

Priority, as regards right to appointment, as between public administrators and others. 99 ALR2d 1063.

§ 43-2-171. Time delay for committing administration of estate.

The administration of an estate must not be committed to the general administrator or to the sheriff, except as special administrator, until the death of the decedent has been known 40 days, nor until one month after the death, resignation or removal of an executor or administrator previously appointed. (Code 1852, § 1682; Code 1867, § 2002; Code 1876, § 2364; Code 1886, § 2030; Code 1896, § 73; Code 1907, § 2539; Code 1923, § 5761; Code 1940, T. 61, § 138.)

Largest creditor may apply for revocation of letters. — The largest creditor of an estate may make application to revoke letters prematurely granted to another, under this section and § 43-2-43, but to do so must make his own application for letters within the 40-day period. Clark v. Glenn, 249 Ala. 342, 31 So. 2d 507 (1947).

Cited in Martin v. Hill, 8 Ala. 43 (1845); Boring v. Williams, 17 Ala. 510 (1850); Curtis v. Williams, 33 Ala. 570 (1859); May v. Marks, 74 Ala. 249 (1883).

§ 43-2-172. Commitment of administration to sheriff.

In case there is no general administrator and no other fit person will administer, the court may commit administration to the sheriff of the county; when so committed, the administration attaches to the office, and the official oath and bond of such office are the security for his faithful administration. (Code 1852, §§ 1681, 1690; Code 1867, §§ 2001, 2010; Code 1876, §§ 2363, 2372; Code 1886, § 2029; Code 1896, § 72; Code 1907, § 2538; Code 1923, § 5760; Code 1940, T. 61, § 137.)

Cited in Walker v. Driver, 7 Ala. 679 (1845); Croft v. Terrell, 15 Ala. 652 (1849); Montgomery, etc., R. Co. v. Varner, 19 Ala. 185 (1851); Hanna v. Price, 23 Ala. 826 (1853); Ragland v. Calhoun, 36 Ala. 606 (1860); Ryall v. Maix & Co., 48 Ala. 537 (1872); Burnett v. Nesmith, 62 Ala. 261 (1878); Burke v. Mutch, 66 Ala. 568 (1880); Landford v. Dunklin, 71 Ala. 594 (1882); Pickett v. Doe, 74 Ala. 122 (1883); May v. Marks, 74 Ala. 249 (1883).

§ 43-2-173. Resignation and removal — Generally.

(a) The general administrator may be removed for the same causes as other administrators. Such removal may be made by the judge of probate without notice, but the grounds thereof must be entered on the minutes of the court.

(b) The resignation of the office of general administrator shall not operate to discharge the incumbent from the administration of any estate previously committed to his charge as such general administrator; but he may proceed, notwithstanding such resignation, to administer and finally settle the same, as if he had not resigned such office; and the sureties on his bond as general administrator shall be liable for every act of maladministration on such estate committed after his resignation, to the same extent as if he had not resigned; but he may be removed from the administration of such estate for any of the causes prescribed by law, or he may resign his administration thereon by leave of the probate court of his county. (Code 1852, § 1710; Code 1867, §§ 2031, 2041; Code 1876, §§ 2400, 2410; Code 1886, §§ 2054, 2062; Code 1896, §§ 101, 109; Code 1907, §§ 2575, 2578; Code 1923, §§ 5798, 5801; Code 1940, T. 61, §§ 174, 188.)

Cross references. — As to resignation and removal of executors or administrators generally, see § 43-2-270 et seq.

Cited in Mitchell v. Nelson, 49 Ala. 88 (1873).

Collateral references. — 34 C.J.S., Executors & Administrators, § 1051.

§ 43-2-174. Same — Appointment of successor.

Upon the resignation or removal of a general administrator from office, the judge of the probate court of the proper county must proceed to appoint some other suitable person general administrator for such county, who shall give bond as required by law, and administer on such estates as may be committed to his charge by the probate court of his county. (Code 1867, § 2042; Code 1876, § 2411; Code 1886, § 2063; Code 1896, § 110; Code 1907, § 2532; Code 1923, § 5754; Code 1940, T. 61, § 139.)

Cross references. — As to bonds of executors and administrators generally, see § 43-2-80 et seq.

§ 43-2-175. Record of official acts.

The general administrator must, from time to time, enter, in a well-bound book to be supplied by the court of county commissioners, a full and complete record of his official acts concerning each estate in his charge. Such book shall be kept in the office of the judge of probate and free to the examination of all persons when not in use. (Code 1896, § 71; Code 1907, § 2537; Code 1923, § 5759; Code 1940, T. 61, § 136.)

ARTICLE 8.

NONRESIDENTS AS EXECUTORS AND ADMINISTRATORS.

Cross references. — As to foreign executors and administrators, see § 43-2-210 et seq.

§ 43-2-190. Applications for letters testamentary or of administration.

The application filed by a nonresident for letters testamentary or of administration must set forth his name and post-office address; but the address so given may, at any time, be changed by such nonresident executor or administrator, such change to be shown by a written statement setting forth his present post-office address, signed by such executor or administrator, or his attorney and filed and recorded in the court granting the letters. (Code 1896, § 83; Code 1907, § 2559; Code 1923, § 5782; Code 1940, T. 61, § 144.)

§ 43-2-191. Appointment of nonresident executor — Generally.

Judges of probate are authorized to issue letters testamentary to persons named as executors in wills regularly probated who are nonresidents of this state, upon like bond and surety and upon the same terms, conditions and requirements as are required by law of citizens of this state. (Code 1876, § 2379; Code 1886, § 2037; Code 1896, § 80; Code 1907, § 2556; Code 1923, § 5778; Code 1940, T. 61, § 140.)

Purpose of section. — It appears that the primary and controlling legislative intent was the removal of inhabitancy or residence within the state as an essential qualification of an executor. Keith v. Proctor, 114 Ala. 676, 21 So. 502 (1897).

Residents and nonresidents are on same footing. — The right of the nonresident does not vary from, but is coextensive and coequal with, the right of the citizen. Whatever are the requirements or conditions upon which the right of the citizen may depend affect the right of the nonresident, and he is bound to their observance. Keith v. Proctor, 114 Ala. 676, 21 So. 502 (1897).

Attack on original appointment. — Where the sufficiency of the certificate of the judge of a foreign state in granting letters testamentary is attacked for noncompliance of statutory conditions in such state, then the law of the sister state, applicable thereto, must be introduced in evidence. And even if the grant of letters in the foreign state is irregular, the subsequent appointment in Alabama is valid until set aside in a direct proceeding. Leatherwood v. Sullivan, 81 Ala. 458, 1 So. 718 (1887), followed in Blacksher Co. v. Northrup, 176 Ala. 190, 57 So. 743 (1911).

Bond may be waived by will. — A bond is not a prerequisite to taking out letters in this state by a nonresident executor where the will dispenses with this requirement. Leatherwood v. Sullivan, 81 Ala. 458, 1 So. 718 (1887). See notes to § 43-2-81.

Bond for ancillary executorship is essential. — This section and § 43-2-192 do not exempt an executor who has given bond for his principal executorship from another bond for his ancillary executorship. Keith v. Proctor, 114 Ala. 676, 21 So. 502 (1897). As to requisites of bond, see § 43-2-80 and notes thereto.

Time of applying for letters. — See Keith v. Proctor, 114 Ala. 676, 21 So. 502 (1897).

Cited in Daniel v. Sorrells, 9 Ala. 436 (1846); Blacksher Co. v. Northrup, 176 Ala. 190, 57 So. 743 (1911); Fields v. Baker, 259 Ala. 336, 67 So. 2d 10 (1953).

Collateral references. — 33 C.J.S., Executors & Administrators, § 22.

Eligibility of foreign corporation to appointment as executor or administrator. 65 ALR 1237.

Nonresident's loss of right to be appointed executor by delay in presenting will for probate or in seeking letters testamentary. 45 ALR2d 928.

Who is resident within meaning of statute prohibiting appointment of nonresident executor or administrator. 9 ALR4th 1223.

§ 43-2-192. Same — Filing of copies of will and letters testamentary; bond and surety.

When the will has been probated in another state or territory, before issuing letters testamentary thereon to a nonresident executor, the judge of probate must require him to file in court a copy of the will under which he is appointed, together with a certificate of the judge of the court in which the will was probated, that such will was regularly proved and established and that letters testamentary were issued to him thereon, in accordance with the laws of the state or territory in which such original letters were granted, and also to give bond and surety upon the same terms, conditions and requirements as are required by law of citizens of this state. But if it shall appear from the will that the testator, by an express provision therein, has exempted the applicant from giving bond as executor, such bond must not be required, except in the cases specified in section 43-2-81. The certified copy of the foreign letters must be filed and recorded. (Code 1876, § 2380; Code 1886, § 2038; Code 1896, § 81; Code 1907, § 2557; Code 1923, § 5780; Code 1940, T. 61, § 142.)

Editor's note. — This section is usually considered by the courts in connection with § 43-2-191. The practitioner is referred to the notes to § 43-2-191, and the citations there given.

Cross references. — As to bonds of executors and administrators generally, see § 43-2-80 et seq.

There is no interdependence between this section and § 43-8-175. The one provides how a will proved in another state may be probated in this state. The other provides for issue of letters testamentary to an executor named in a will probated in another state. That there is a distinction between the filing of a copy of such a will in this state and the probating of such will in this state appears from the terms of the two sections. Certainly it could not be contended that a foreign will could be probated in this state by proceeding under this section, else there would have been no purpose in the enactment of § 43-8-175. That the two sections

were intended to accomplish different purposes is apparent. Having resorted to one seeking only such benefits as may be derived therefrom, as in §§ 43-2-190 through 43-2-200 and 43-2-275, appellants cannot be said to be bound to observe the requirements of the other from which greater benefits may be derived. Fields v. Baker, 259 Ala. 336, 67 So. 2d 10 (1953).

Cited in McBrayer v. Cariker, 64 Ala. 50 (1879); Wright v. Lang, 66 Ala. 389 (1880).

Collateral references. — 34 C.J.S., Executors & Administrators, §§ 989-996.

Transmission of funds from ancillary to domiciliary jurisdiction, or liability of sureties on bond given in the latter jurisdiction, as affecting liability of sureties on bond given in the former jurisdiction. 78 ALR 575.

Right of nonresident surviving spouse or minor children to allowance of property exempt from administration or to family allowance from local estate of nonresident decedent. 51 ALR2d 1026.

§ 43-2-193. Appointment of nonresident administrator.

When any nonresident dies, leaving assets in this state, if no application for letters of administration is made by a relative or creditor entitled thereto, an administrator of his estate, appointed by the competent authority of the state or territory of his domicile, shall be entitled to letters of administration on such estate in this state, upon the production of the letters granted to him by the state or territory of his intestate's domicile, duly certified as required by law, in preference to any other person, upon his giving like bond and surety and upon the same terms, conditions and requirements as are required by law of citizens of this state. The certified copy of his foreign letters shall be filed and recorded in the office of the judge of probate issuing letters in this state. (Code 1886, § 2039; Code 1896, § 82; Code 1907, § 2558; Code 1923, § 5781; Code 1940, T. 61, § 143.)

A foreign administrator can bring a wrongful death action in this state without first going through the ancillary procedures set out in this section and § 43-2-196. Hatas v. Partin, 278 Ala. 65, 175 So. 2d 759 (1965).

Collateral references. — 33 C.J.S., Executors & Administrators, § 46(f).

Eligibility of foreign corporation to appointment as executor, administrator, or testamentary trustee. 26 ALR3d 1019.

§ 43-2-194. Manner of administering and settling estate.

When letters are granted to a nonresident executor or administrator, the assets of the estate upon which such letters are granted, which may be within this state at the date of such letters, shall in all respects be administered and settled as if such letters had been issued to a resident executor or administrator. (Code 1876, § 2381; Code 1886, § 2040; Code 1896, § 84; Code 1907, § 2560; Code 1923, § 5783; Code 1940, T. 61, § 145.)

§ 43-2-195. Collection of debts and deposits by nonresident personal representative.

The personal representative of a deceased person, by appointment of a court having jurisdiction in any state other than the state of Alabama, may receive and collect any indebtedness or bank deposit owing to the deceased by any person who is a resident of Alabama, and such personal representative may execute a release, discharge and satisfaction of such indebtedness. Such personal representative, at the time of or before making such collection and satisfaction, release or discharge, shall file for record in the probate office of the county wherein the debtor resides a certified copy of the letters testamentary or of administration issued to such personal representative, certified in accordance with 28 U.S.C.A., § 1738, but no such collection shall be made until the lapse of 60 days from the date of the death of the deceased, and no such collection shall be made if proceedings are pending for the grant of letters testamentary or of administration in or have been issued by any court having jurisdiction in Alabama. (Acts 1919, No. 731, p. 1082; Code 1923, § 5779; Code 1940, T. 61, § 141.)

Effect of failure to record letters. — A foreclosure sale made by a foreign executor who had not given bond and had his letters recorded in the county where action was brought, as required by this section and § 43-2-211, was void. Dowling v. Murray, 263 Ala. 113, 81 So. 2d 588 (1955).

Collateral references. — 34 C.J.S., Executors & Administrators, §§ 1000, 1008.

§ 43-2-196. Right to maintain actions.

Nonresident executors or administrators appointed under the provisions of this article may, by giving security for costs as required by law of nonresidents, bring and maintain civil actions in the courts of this state in all respects as may be done by resident executors and administrators. (Code 1896, § 85; Code 1907, § 2561; Code 1923, § 5784; Code 1940, T. 61, § 146.)

Cross references. — As to actions by and against executors and administrators generally, see § 43-2-130 et seq. See notes to § 43-2-193.

§ 43-2-197. Liability to actions; venue.

Civil actions may be brought against nonresident executors and administrators in their representative character, in all cases, in the county in which letters were granted. (Code 1896, § 86; Code 1907, § 2562; Code 1923, § 5785; Code 1940, T. 61, § 147.)

Cross references. — As to actions by and against executors and administrators, see § 43-2-130 et seq.

Collateral references. — 34 C.J.S., Executors & Administrators, §§ 1012, 1013.

§ 43-2-198. Service of process — Generally.

Service of summons or other process may be made upon nonresident executors and administrators personally if found within the state. Such service may be made in any case by personal service upon them if found within the state, or by filing in the probate court granting letters a copy of the summons or other process and by sending a copy thereof through the mail to such executor or administrator and serving a copy thereof upon a resident surety, if there be one, as provided in section 43-2-199. (Code 1896, § 86; Code 1907, § 2562; Code 1923, § 5785; Code 1940, T. 61, § 147.)

Cross references. — As to rules of supreme court relative to service of process, see A.R.C.P., Rule 4 et seq.

§ 43-2-199. Same — Citations or notices, etc.; return of process.

Citations to make settlements and other citations or notices to such nonresident executors and administrators, and all writs or legal process, including executions on decrees and judgments, may be served by depositing a copy in a sealed envelope, postage prepaid, in a post office at or near the court or office issuing such process, such envelope to be plainly addressed and directed to such nonresident executor or administrator at the place and by the name furnished by him upon the filing of his application for letters, or thereafter as provided in section 43-2-190 and, when the sureties, or either of them, reside in the state, and their place of residence is known, by the service of a copy of such writ or process upon one of such sureties. When service is had by depositing a copy of the writ or process in the post office only and not accompanied by service upon a surety, such service shall not take effect until the expiration of 10 days from the date of mailing such copy. If the post-office address of such nonresident executor or administrator is not furnished as required by section 43-2-190, service on one of his sureties is sufficient. If such post-office address is not so furnished and if there be no resident surety, notice of such writ or process may be given by publication in a newspaper published in the county wherein the proceedings are had for two consecutive weeks, and a copy thereof must be sent by mail to such nonresident executor or administrator, if his post-office address can be ascertained; and, if in such case there be no newspaper published in the county, the notice may be given by posting a copy thereof at the door of the courthouse for 15 days. The sheriff or other officer executing the writ or process must make return thereof according to the facts. (Code 1876, § 2382; Code 1886, § 2041; Code 1896, § 87; Code 1907, § 2563; Code 1923, § 5786; Code 1940, T. 61, § 148.)

§ 43-2-200. Liability of sureties to execution.

Upon the return of an execution as provided in section 43-2-199 and, further, that no property of such executor or administrator, or property not sufficient to satisfy the same, is found in the county in which the execution is issued, the sureties on his bond shall be liable in all respects as in cases of a return of no property found on executions issued against resident executors or administrators. (Code 1876, § 2383; Code 1886, § 2042; Code 1896, § 88; Code 1907, § 2564; Code 1923, § 5787; Code 1940, T. 61, § 149.)

ARTICLE 9.

FOREIGN EXECUTORS AND ADMINISTRATORS.

Cross references. — As to nonresidents as executors and administrators, see § 43-2-190 et seq.

Collateral references. — Discharge or assignment of debt by foreign executor or administrator. 10 ALR 276.

Power to impound assets of nonresident decedent in state. 44 ALR 801.

Situs of corporate stock for purposes of probate jurisdiction and administration. 72 ALR 179.

Sale of land located in state other than domicile, for payment of decedent's debts, rights and remedies in respect to, and proceeds thereof. 81 ALR 665.

Payment of negotiable paper to personal representative of owner appointed to one state as affected by appointment of another representative in another state. 114 ALR 1461, 149 ALR 1083.

Capacity of local or foreign personal representative to maintain action for death under foreign statute providing for action by personal representative. 52 ALR2d 1016.

Applications of rule permitting courts to exercise jurisdiction over equity actions against foreign personal representatives to actions for accounting where there are assets within forum. 53 ALR2d 331.

§ 43-2-210. Bond.

The judge of probate, in determining the amount of the bond which such executor or administrator should give, may examine him on oath; and such bond, when given, stands as security, on its condition being broken, for any person thereby injured. (Code 1852, § 1936; Code 1867, § 2295; Code 1876, § 2639; Code 1886, § 2293; Code 1896, § 362; Code 1907, § 2828; Code 1923, § 6067; Code 1940, T. 61, § 154.)

Cross references. — As to bonds of executors and administrators generally, see § 43-2-80 et seq.

Collateral references. — 34 C.J.S., Executors & Administrators, § 995.

§ 43-2-211. Right to maintain actions and recover or receive property in state.

Any executor or administrator who has obtained letters testamentary or of administration on the estate of a person who was not, at the time of his death, an inhabitant of this state, in any other of the United States, and who has not obtained letters of administration thereon in this state, as authorized by article 8 of chapter 2 of this title, may maintain civil actions and recover or receive property in this state:

(1) By recording, at any time before judgment or the receipt of the property, a copy of his letters, duly authenticated according to the laws of the United States, in the office of the judge of probate of the county in which such civil action is brought or property received; or

(2) By giving bond, with at least two good and sufficient sureties, payable to and approved by such judge of probate, in such amount as he may prescribe, to be determined with reference to the value of the property to be recovered or received and conditioned to faithfully administer such recovery or property according to law. (Code 1852, § 1934; Code 1867, § 2293; Code 1876, § 2637; Code 1886, § 2290; Code 1896, § 359; Code 1907, § 2825; Code 1923, § 6064; Code 1940, T. 61, § 151.)

Cross references. — See notes to § 43-2-212.

It is unnecessary that the letters be recorded before the action, but is sufficient if recorded before judgment. Campbell v. Hughes, 155 Ala. 591, 47 So. 45 (1907).

Proof of recordation of letters. — Under this section recordation of the letters may be shown by a certified copy thereof, or by the record book, or probably by a copy of the letters, with the probate judge's certificate attached, showing that it was recorded in a certain book in his office on a certain date. Campbell v. Hughes, 155 Ala. 591, 47 So. 45 (1907).

Authentication according to federal law essential. — A copy of the letters of a foreign administrator not authenticated according to the federal laws is without effect. Campbell v. Hughes, 155 Ala. 591, 47 So. 45 (1907).

Effect of noncompliance. — A foreclosure sale made by a foreign executor who had not given bond and had his letters recorded in the county where the action was brought, as required by this section and § 43-2-195, was void. Dowling v. Murray, 263 Ala. 113, 81 So. 2d 588 (1955).

Under the common law, letters of administration having no extraterritorial force, a foreign administrator could only commence an action and collect assets in another jurisdiction through legislative permission. Campbell v. Hughes, 155 Ala. 591, 47 So. 45 (1907).

At common law no action could be maintained by an administrator in his official capacity except within the limits of the state from which he derived his authority. Hatas v. Partin, 278 Ala. 65, 175 So. 2d 759 (1965).

This section is not only permissive, but it is also prohibitory; permissive, upon the compliance with its conditions; prohibitory, in the absence of such compliance. Hatas v. Partin, 278 Ala. 65, 175 So. 2d 759 (1965).

It is not limited to property. — The supreme court found no limitation or suggestion that this section applies only to property. Hatas v. Partin, 278 Ala. 65, 175 So. 2d 759 (1965).

It permits a foreign executor or administrator to maintain an action, prior to qualifying in this state, in the courts of Alabama. Hatas v. Partin, 278 Ala. 65, 175 So. 2d 759 (1965).

And it has been construed as conferring the right to maintain any action in the courts of this state. Hatas v. Partin, 278 Ala. 65, 175 So. 2d 759 (1965).

Including action for wrongful death. — A foreign administrator can bring a wrongful death action in this state without first going through the ancillary procedures set out in this section and § 43-2-193. Hatas v. Partin, 278 Ala. 65, 175 So. 2d 759 (1965).

The mere fact that there was no statutory action for wrongful death prior to 1911 does not mean that this section should not apply if such a cause of action was created. Hatas v. Partin, 278 Ala. 65, 175 So. 2d 759 (1965).

Cited in Kennedy v. Kennedy, 8 Ala. 391 (1845); Hudson v. Daily, 13 Ala. 722 (1848); Harrison v. Mahorner, 14 Ala. 829 (1848); Varner v. Bevil, 17 Ala. 286 (1850); Ex parte Walker, 25 Ala. 81 (1854); Broughton v. Bradley, 34 Ala. 694 (1859); Manly v. Turnipseed, 37 Ala. 522 (1861); Grace v. Martin, 47 Ala. 135 (1872); Erwin v. Hill, 51 Ala. 580 (1874); Hatchet v. Berney, 65 Ala. 39 (1880); Sloan v. Frothingham, 65 Ala. 593 (1880); Harris v. Moore, 72 Ala. 507 (1882); Sloan v. Frothingham, 72 Ala. 589 (1882); Barclift v. Treece, 77 Ala. 528 (1884); International Bhd. of Teamsters v. Hatas, 287 Ala. 344, 252 So. 2d 7 (1971).

Collateral references. — 34 C.J.S., Executors & Administrators, §§ 1001, 1007, 1008.

§ 43-2-212. Action not affected by grant of letters of administration in state; right of intervention.

No civil action brought by any foreign executor or administrator, under the provisions of section 43-2-211, must be abated, barred or affected by the grant of letters of administration in this state, either prior or subsequent to the institution of such action; but, in such case, the administrator appointed in this state may, if necessary for the protection of creditors, distributees, or legatees, resident in this state, intervene in such action and shall be entitled to the recovery therein. (Code 1867, § 2293; Code 1876, § 2637; Code 1886, § 2291; Code 1896, § 360; Code 1907, § 2826; Code 1923, § 6065; Code 1940, T. 61, § 152.)

Foreign administrator may now commence action to foreclose mortgage on land. — Under this section and § 43-2-211, a foreign administrator upon compliance with the foregoing requirements may commence an action to foreclose a mortgage on land in Alabama after the appointment of an administrator there. Campbell v. Hughes, 144 Ala. 393, 42 So. 42 (1905).

But formerly grant of letters in Alabama good defense to such action. — But prior to the adoption of this section it was held that, to an action commenced by a foreign administrator who had complied with § 43-2-211, a pleading puis darrein continuance, setting up the grant of letters of administration to the defendant, after the commencement of the action, by a probate court of this state which had jurisdiction of the subject matter, presented a good defense to the further maintenance of the action. Broughton v. Bradley, 34 Ala. 694 (1859); Campbell v. Hughes, 144 Ala. 393, 42 So. 42 (1905).

§ 43-2-213. Plaintiff required to prove compliance with section 43-2-211.

Before a judgment is rendered in a civil action brought by such foreign executor or administrator, the plaintiff must prove that he has complied in all respects with the provisions of section 43-2-211, and, failing to do so, he cannot recover. (Code 1852, § 1935; Code 1867, § 2294; Code 1876, § 2638; Code 1886, § 2292; Code 1896, § 361; Code 1907, § 2827; Code 1923, § 6066; Code 1940, T. 61, § 153.)

Cross references. — See notes to §§ 43-2-211 and 43-2-212.

Necessity of plea of "ne unques administrator". — It has been held that the proof under this section need not be made in the absence of a pleading of "ne unques administrator." Berlin v. Sheffield Coal & Iron Co., 124 Ala. 322, 26 So. 933 (1899). But in Campbell v. Hughes, 155 Ala. 591, 47 So. 45 (1907), it is held that while the denials of the answers may not amount to a technical pleading of "ne unques," they must be held to operate to require proof of the filing of the copy of the letters, duly authenticated, before judgment.

Circuit clerk's labeling of certificate of judge of probate not held failure of proof. — It would be altogether unrealistic to hold that there was a failure of proof within the meaning of this section, because of the manner in which the circuit clerk labeled the certificate of the judge of probate. International Bhd. of Teamsters v. Hatas, 287 Ala. 344, 252 So. 2d 7 (1971).

Cited in Kennedy v. Kennedy, 8 Ala. 391 (1845); Hudson v. Daily, 13 Ala. 722 (1848); Harrison v. Mahorner, 14 Ala. 829 (1848); Varner v. Bevil, 17 Ala. 286 (1850); Ex parte Walker, 25 Ala. 81 (1854); Manly v. Turnipseed, 37 Ala. 522 (1861); Rainey v. Smith, 250 Ala. 690, 36 So. 2d 78 (1948).

§ 43-2-214. Protection afforded by delivery of property or recovery of judgment.

A delivery of property or the recovery of judgment, under the provisions of section 43-2-211, is a protection to the defendant or to the person delivering the property, to the extent of such judgment or the value of such property. (Code 1852, § 1937; Code 1867, § 2296; Code 1876, § 2640; Code 1886, § 2294; Code 1896, § 363; Code 1907, § 2829; Code 1923, § 6068; Code 1940, T. 61, § 155.)

ARTICLE 10.

ADMINISTRATION OF ESTATES OF PERSONS PRESUMED DEAD.

Rule on presumption of death unchanged. — This article deals with the appointment of administrators of persons presumed to be dead. It does not change the well-established rule that a person absent for seven years from the place of his last domicile without word from him, or about him, to members of his family, is presumed dead at the end of such seven years of absence. Quicksey v. Hall, 260 Ala. 162, 69 So. 2d 698 (1954).

Collateral references. — 33 C.J.S., Executors & Administrators, § 16.

Right of one whose estate is administered as that of absentee presumed to be dead to hold administrator personally liable. 37 ALR 826.

§ 43-2-230. Applications for letters of administration.

Whenever letters of administration on the estate of any person presumed to be dead on account of absence for seven or more years from the place of his last domicile within this state shall be applied for, it shall be the duty of the judge of probate to whom the application shall be made to accept and file the same and to thereupon take the testimony with respect to whether the petitioner is entitled to such letters; and, if the court is satisfied by the testimony that the applicant would be entitled thereto were the supposed decedent in fact dead, the court shall cause to be advertised in a newspaper published in the county, once a week for four consecutive weeks, the fact of said application, together with notice that on a day certain which shall be at least two weeks after the last of said advertisements, the court will hear evidence concerning the alleged absence of the supposed decedent, and the circumstances and duration thereof. (Acts 1939, No. 46, p. 53; Code 1940, T. 61, § 157.)

Cross references. — As to grant of letters of administration generally, see § 43-2-40 et seq.

§ 43-2-231. Appointment of administrators.

It shall be lawful for the respective probate courts of this state to appoint administrators of the estates of persons who are presumed to be dead on account of absence for five or more years from the place of their last domicile within this state as provided in this article. (Acts 1939, No. 46, p. 53; Code 1940, T. 61, § 156; Acts 1982, No. 82-399, § 8-102.)

The 1982 amendment, effective January 1, 1983, substituted "five" for "seven."

Proof of death of person missing less than seven (now five) years. — The legislature has adopted the common law of England which appears to have allowed proof of death in less than seven (now five) years; therefore, upon proper proof, a person missing less than seven (now five) years may be proven dead. In re Estate of Dawson, 346 So. 2d 386 (Ala. 1977).

§ 43-2-232. Hearing.

At the hearing, the probate court shall take such legal evidence as shall then be offered for the purpose of ascertaining whether the presumption of death is established, and no person shall be disqualified to testify by reason of his or her relationship as husband or wife to the supposed decedent or of his or her interest in the estate of the person supposed to be dead. (Acts 1939, No. 46, p. 53; Code 1940, T. 61, § 158.)

§ 43-2-233. Publication of notice of presumption of death.

If satisfied upon the hearing that the legal presumption of death is made out, the court shall so decree and shall forthwith cause notice thereof to be inserted for two successive weeks in a newspaper published in the county and also, when practicable, in a newspaper published at, or near, the place shown in the commonwealth, where, when last heard from, the supposed decedent had his residence. The said notice shall require the supposed decedent, if alive, or any other person for him to produce to the court, within 12 weeks from the date of its last insertion, satisfactory evidence of his continuance in life. (Acts 1939, No. 46, p. 53; Code 1940, T. 61, § 159.)

§ 43-2-234. Issuance of letters of administration.

If, within the period of said 12 weeks, evidence satisfactory to the probate court of the continuance in life of the said decedent shall not be forthcoming, it shall be the duty of the court to issue the letters of administration to the party thereto entitled, and the said letters, until revoked, and all acts done in pursuance thereof, and in reliance thereupon, shall be as valid as if the supposed decedent were actually dead. (Acts 1939, No. 46, p. 53; Code 1940, T. 61, § 160.)

§ 43-2-235. Revocation of letters upon proof that supposed decedent is alive — Distribution of assets.

The probate court may revoke the said letters at any time on due and satisfactory proof that the supposed decedent is in fact alive, after which revocation all the powers of the administrator shall cease, but all receipts, disbursements of assets and other acts previously done by him shall remain as valid as if the said letters were unrevoked. The administrator shall settle an account of his administration, down to the time of such revocation, and shall transfer all assets remaining in his hands to the person as whose administrator he had acted or to his duly authorized agent or attorney. Nothing in this article shall validate the title of any person to any property or money received as widow, next of kin or heir of such supposed decedent, but the same may be recovered from such person, provided such supposed decedent shall make due and sufficient legal proof to the court having jurisdiction of said estate, within one year after the petition for letters of said administration was filed, that he is alive; provided further, that if such proof is not furnished as provided in this article, the court having jurisdiction of said estate is authorized and directed to direct the administrator of said estate to disburse such funds or money as he may have belonging to said estate to the persons entitled to receive the same under the law. (Acts 1939, No. 46, p. 53; Code 1940, T. 61, § 161; Acts 1945, No. 509, p. 732.)

Collateral references. — 33 C.J.S., Executors & Administrators, §§ 84, 85, 87. Right of one whose estate is administered as that of absentee presumed to be dead to hold administrator personally liable. 37 ALR 826.

§ 43-2-236. Same — Substitution of parties; reopening judgments.

After revocation of the letters, the person erroneously supposed to be dead, may, on suggestion filed of record of the proper fact, be substituted as plaintiff in all actions brought by the administrator, whether prosecuted to judgment or otherwise. He may in all actions previously brought against his administrator be substituted as defendant on proper suggestion filed by him, or by the plaintiff therein, but shall not be compelled to go to trial in less than three months from the time of such suggestion filed. Judgments recovered against the administrator before revocation, as aforesaid, of the letters may be reopened on application by the supposed decedent made within three months from the said revocation and supported by affidavit denying specifically on the knowledge of the affiant the cause of action or specifically alleging the existence of facts which would be a valid defense; but, if within the said three months, such application shall not be made or, being made, the facts exhibited shall be adjudged an insufficient defense, the judgment shall be conclusive to all intents, saving the defendant's right to have it reviewed, as in other cases, by certiorari, or writ of error or by appeal, whichever is applicable under the practice then prevailing in this state with respect thereto. (Acts 1939, No. 46, p. 53; Code 1940, T. 61, § 162.)

§ 43-2-237. Costs.

The costs attending the issue of letters, or their revocation, shall be paid out of the estate of the supposed decedent. Costs arising upon an application for letters which shall not be granted shall be paid by the applicant. (Acts 1939, No. 46, p. 53; Code 1940, T. 61, § 163.)

§ 43-2-238. Applicability of other laws relating to administration of decedents' estates.

All laws in this state with respect to procedure in the administration of estates of deceased persons which are not in conflict with the provisions of this article are made applicable to proceedings under this article. (Acts 1939, No. 46, p. 53; Code 1940, T. 61, § 164.)

Cited in Quicksey v. Hall, 260 Ala. 162, 69 So. 2d 698 (1954).

ARTICLE 11.

ADMINISTRATORS AD LITEM.

§ 43-2-250. Appointment.

When, in any proceeding in any court, the estate of a deceased person must be represented, and there is no executor or administrator of such estate, or he is interested adversely thereto, it shall be the duty of the court to appoint an administrator ad litem of such estate for the particular proceeding, without bond, whenever the facts rendering such appointment necessary shall appear in the record of such case or shall be made known to the court by the affidavit of any person interested therein. (Code 1876, § 2625; Code 1886, § 2283; Code 1896, § 352; Code 1907, § 2818; Code 1923, § 6057; Code 1940, T. 61, § 165.)

Prior to the enactment of this section an administrator ad litem was unknown to our law and the appointment of such an administrator was void. Ex parte Riley, 247 Ala. 242, 23 So. 2d 592 (1945).

Purpose of provision for appointment of administrator ad litem where administrator is interested adversely is to confer jurisdiction on probate court to make settlements when the administrator is interested adversely and to obviate the necessity of a resort to another court. Faulk v. Money, 236 Ala. 69, 181 So. 256 (1938); Smith v. Smith, 248 Ala. 49, 26 So. 2d 571 (1946).

Under this section three things must concur to justify the appointment of an administrator ad litem: (1) The estate of the deceased person "must be represented," which means that the interests of the estate require representation. (2) "There is no executor or administrator of such estate, or he is interested adversely thereto." (3) "The facts rendering such appointment necessary shall appear in the record of such case, or shall be made known to the court by the affidavit of any person interested therein." Ex parte Riley, 247 Ala. 242, 23 So. 2d 592 (1945).

Record warranting appointment of administrator ad litem. — Recital in decree appointing administrator ad litem for cross-claimant that it had been made known to court that cross-claimant had died and that no administrator had been appointed to represent his estate sufficiently showed that facts appeared in the record warranting appointment of administrator ad litem as required by this section. Griffin v. Proctor, 244 Ala. 537, 14 So. 2d 116 (1943).

No appointment where all interested parties are before court. — An administrator ad litem will not be appointed under this section where all the parties interested in the final settlement of the estate are before the court. Ex parte Baker, 118 Ala. 185, 23 So. 996 (1898), discussing origin of the section. See also Gayle v. Johnston, 72 Ala. 254 (1882).

An administrator ad litem would not be appointed to represent an estate in action for settlement of an administration and for an accounting of proceeds of deceased's life policies paid by administrator to deceased's creditors, notwithstanding that administrator was interested adversely, where all parties in interest were before the court. Faulk v. Money, 236 Ala. 69, 181 So. 256 (1938).

Appointee as representative of estate. — Where an administrator ad litem has been appointed under this section and is made a party to the petition in ancillary proceeding for distribution of funds in hands of trustees, no one can complain that the administratrix was not a party, since the estate is properly represented. Cannon v. Birmingham Trust & Sav. Co., 212 Ala. 316, 102 So. 453 (1924).

Claim of dower by administratrix. — A widow, who is also administratrix of an estate, who commences an action in both capacities to enforce an equitable conversion, which would increase the assets of the estate and which in turn would be beneficial to her, does not represent an antagonistic interest, but if she goes further and asks for dower out of the proceeds then there is an antagonistic feature justifying appointment of administrator ad litem under this section. Flomerfelt v. Siglin, 155 Ala. 633, 47 So. 106 (1908).

Where there is conflict of interest between the heirs of two estates, the same person acting as administrator of the two, then this is insufficient ground for removing such administrator under the authority of § 43-2-290, but any anticipated difficulty of settlement is answered by this section authorizing the appointment of an administrator ad litem. Castleberry v. Hollingsworth, 215 Ala. 445, 111 So. 35 (1927); Binford v. Penney, 255 Ala. 20, 49 So. 2d 665 (1950).

In an action for partition by a cotenant, the personal representative of the estate of a deceased cotenant should be made a party, or an administrator ad litem appointed under this section. Winsett v. Winsett, 203 Ala. 373, 83 So. 117 (1919).

In action to amend or annul prior divorce judgment. — Where controversy is between the two wives each desiring to establish her position as the lawful widow of husband so that she may claim the rights of a widow in any estate left by the husband and the right to social security benefits as his widow, and the estate of the husband will not be increased or diminished in any event by a decision establishing either wife as the lawful widow, the second wife is said to be "the proper one to represent" the husband's interest in an action to amend the prior divorce judgment, and the estate of the husband is not a necessary party to the action. Turner v. Hargrove, 293 Ala. 166, 300 So. 2d 828 (1974).

The personal representative of a deceased husband, or an administrator ad litem appointed under this section, is not a necessary party to an action brought by the first wife, after the husband's death, against the second wife to annul a divorce judgment entered in an action by the husband against the first wife during his life, the purpose of the annulment action being to establish that the first wife and not the second is his widow. Turner v. Hargrove, 293 Ala. 166, 300 So. 2d 828 (1974).

In action for settlement and distribution of intestate's estate where administrator is deceased, ordinarily, administrator de bonis non or ad litem is necessary party. Cook v. Castleberry, 233 Ala. 650, 173 So. 1 (1937).

In action to set aside alleged fraudulent conveyance by deceased, his estate need not be represented by an administrator ad litem if the legal title was conveyed, but, if legal title did not pass, estate of deceased must be represented, and, if there is no administrator, estate may be represented by an administrator ad litem. Trotter v. Brown, 232 Ala. 147, 167 So. 310 (1936).

Administrator was not required to have been appointed prior to institution of creditor's action to set aside an alleged fraudulent conveyance by deceased as court could appoint an administrator ad litem if necessary. Trotter v. Brown, 232 Ala. 147, 167 So. 310 (1936).

Cited in Teague v. Corbitt, 57 Ala. 529 (1877); Ex parte Lyon, 60 Ala. 650 (1877); Malone v. Hill, 68 Ala. 225 (1880); Alexander v. Alexander, 70 Ala. 212 (1881); Clark v. Knox, 70 Ala. 607 (1881); Gayle v. Johnston, 72 Ala. 254 (1882); Cochran v. Miller, 74 Ala. 50 (1883); Clark v. Head, 75 Ala. 373 (1883); Ballard v. Johns, 80 Ala. 32 (1885); Marcy v. Howard, 91 Ala. 133, 8 So. 566 (1890); Paige v. Bartlett, 101 Ala. 193, 13 So. 768 (1893); Martin v. Atkinson, 108 Ala. 314, 18 So. 888 (1896); Keith v. McCord, 140 Ala. 402, 37 So. 267 (1904); Eastis v. Mountain Terrace Land Co., 214 Ala. 638, 108 So. 740 (1926); Young v. Powell, 179 F.2d 147 (5th Cir. 1950); Garrison v. Kelley, 257 Ala. 105, 57 So. 2d 345 (1952); Vaughan v. Vaughan, 258 Ala. 336, 62 So. 2d 466 (1952); Merrill v. Zera, 265 Ala. 390, 91 So. 2d 472 (1956).

Collateral references. — 34 C.J.S., Executors & Administrators, § 1035.

Propriety of court's appointment, as administrator of decedent's estate, of stranger rather than person having statutory preference. 84 ALR3d 707.

§ 43-2-251. Decree in favor of administrator ad litem.

When, in such proceedings, the estate represented by the administrator ad litem is entitled to a decree or judgment for the recovery of money or for the possession of real or personal property, such decree or judgment shall be rendered in favor of the administrator ad litem for the use of the estate. (Code 1876, § 2626; Code 1886, § 2284; Code 1896, § 353; Code 1907, § 2819; Code 1923, § 6058; Code 1940, T. 61, § 166.)

Section is mandatory. — Where the moneyed decree purports to be in favor of "the present administrator de bonis non," instead of the administrator ad litem appointed under § 43-2-250, such decree is void on its face.

Martin v. Atkinson, 108 Ala. 314, 18 So. 888 (1896).

Cited in Ex parte Lyon, 60 Ala. 650 (1877); Smith v. Smith, 248 Ala. 49, 26 So. 2d 571 (1946).

Collateral references. — 34 C.J.S., Executors & Administrators, § 1040.

§ 43-2-252. Execution on money decree or judgment.

When such decree or judgment is for the recovery of money and the estate has no executor or administrator, execution shall issue thereon in favor of the administrator ad litem for the use of the estate, and the money, when collected, shall be paid by the officer to the judge of the probate court, or to the clerk or register of the circuit or other court having jurisdiction, from which the execution issued. The party against whom such decree or judgment is rendered may pay the same to such judge, clerk or register, before the issue of execution, whose receipt to him therefor shall be a full discharge of such decree or judgment. (Code 1876, § 2626; Code 1886, § 2285; Code 1896, § 354; Code 1907, § 2820; Code 1923, § 6059; Code 1940, T. 61, § 167.)

§ 43-2-253. Enforcement of decree or judgment for recovery of property.

When such decree or judgment is for the recovery of real or personal property and the estate has no executor or administrator, no writ of possession or other writ for the enforcement of such decree or judgment shall issue thereon until there shall be some person duly authorized under the laws of this state to receive the possession of such property, and then such writ shall issue in favor of such person. (Code 1876, § 2627; Code 1886, § 2286; Code 1896, § 355; Code 1907, § 2821; Code 1923, § 6060; Code 1940, T. 61, § 168.)

§ 43-2-254. Enforcement of decree or judgment when administrator adversely interested.

When such administrator ad litem is appointed on account of the adverse interest of the executor or administrator, and the decree or judgment is rendered against such executor or administrator, no execution, writ of possession or other writ for the enforcement of the decree or judgment shall issue thereon, but in such decree or judgment the court shall require the executor or administrator to charge himself, as executor or administrator of the estate represented by the administrator ad litem, with the money or property recovered of him by the administrator ad litem; but when the decree or judgment is not against the executor or administrator, execution, writ of possession, or other writ for the enforcement of the judgment or decree, shall issue thereon in favor of such executor or administrator. (Code 1876, § 2628; Code 1886, § 2287; Code 1896, § 356; Code 1907, § 2822; Code 1923, § 6061; Code 1940, T. 61, § 169.)

Cited in Copeland v. Loeb, 269 Ala. 295, 112 So. 2d 475 (1959).

§ 43-2-255. Duty of judge, clerk or register to make payment; penalty.

It shall be the duty of the judge of probate, clerk or register receiving the money to pay over the same, less one half of one percent thereon, to the person entitled thereto, on demand; and for failure to do so, he incurs a penalty in favor of such person of 10 percent thereon, which, together with the money received and interest thereon, may be recovered by suit on his bond. (Code 1876, § 2629; Code 1886, § 2288; Code 1896, § 357; Code 1907, § 2823; Code 1923, § 6062; Code 1940, T. 61, § 170.)

§ 43-2-256. Compensation of administrator ad litem.

Such administrator ad litem must be allowed for his services such compensation as the judge of probate or judge of the circuit court appointing him may direct, to be taxed and collected as part of the costs of the proceedings, either out of the estate represented by him, or out of the general fund administered therein or out of any party to the action who may be taxed therewith, as the court may direct. (Code 1876, § 2630; Code 1886, § 2289; Code 1896, § 358; Code 1907, § 2824; Code 1923, § 6063; Code 1940, T. 61, § 171.)

Cited in Clark v. Knox, 70 Ala. 607 (1881).

ARTICLE 12.

RESIGNATION, REMOVAL, ETC., OF EXECUTORS OR ADMINISTRATORS.

Division 1.

General Provisions.

Collateral references. — Resignation as affecting revocation or termination of authority. 8 ALR 175.

Right of executor or administrator to resign. 91 ALR 712.

Statutory exemption of representative from suit until expiration of prescribed period as affected by resignation of original administrator and appointment of a new one. 104 ALR 909.

Resignation of public administrator. 56 ALR2d 1187.

§ 43-2-270. Filing and recordation of resignation.

An executor or administrator may, by a writing subscribed by him, resign; and his resignation must be filed and entered of record in the court having jurisdiction of the administration. (Code 1852, § 1718; Code 1867, § 2039; Code 1876, § 2408; Code 1886, § 2060; Code 1896, § 107; Code 1907, § 2576; Code 1923, § 5799; Code 1940, T. 61, § 172.)

Cross references. — As to resignation as a defense in actions or proceedings against executors or administrators, see § 43-2-114.

Resignation is filed in court granting letters. — Though the proceedings have been removed to circuit court, the resignation under this section is filed in the probate court which granted the letters. Lunsford v. Lunsford, 122 Ala. 242, 25 So. 171 (1899), holding that the removal of such proceedings in nowise impairs the right of resigning.

Cited in Skinner v. Frierson, 8 Ala. 915 (1846); Huckabee v. May, 14 Ala. 263 (1848); Rambo v. Wyatt, 32 Ala. 363 (1858); Whitworth

v. Oliver, 39 Ala. 286 (1864); Whitfield v. Woolf, 51 Ala. 202 (1874).

Collateral references. — 33 C.J.S., Executors & Administrators, § 82.

§ 43-2-271. Liability for assets upon resignation.

In case of resignation, the executor or administrator and his sureties are bound for all the assets not administered, which have not been delivered over to his successor. (Code 1852, § 1719; Code 1867, § 2040; Code 1876, § 2409; Code 1886, § 2061; Code 1896, § 108; Code 1907, § 2577; Code 1923, § 5800; Code 1940, T. 61, § 173.)

Cited in Kyle v. Gray, 11 Ala. 233 (1847); Hendricks v. Thornton, 45 Ala. 299 (1871).

§ 43-2-272. Duty of probate court to grant letters of administration upon vacancy.

(a) If the sole executor or all the executors die, resign or are removed, the probate court having jurisdiction of the estate must grant letters of administration, with will annexed, to the person entitled thereto under section 43-2-27.

(b) If an administrator dies, resigns or is removed, the probate court having jurisdiction of the estate must grant letters of administration of the goods and chattels, rights and credits, unadministered, to the person entitled thereto, as in cases of intestacy. (Code 1852, § 1720; Code 1867, § 2043; Code 1876, § 2412; Code 1886, § 2064; Code 1896, § 111; Code 1907, § 2533; Code 1923, § 5755; Code 1940, T. 61, § 175.)

Section is imperative. — The section being imperative, the court cannot refuse to appoint on proper application. Ex parte Jordan, 145 Ala. 658, 39 So. 618 (1905).

Jurisdiction of court appointing administrator in chief is exclusive. — The words "the probate court having jurisdiction of the estate" can have reference only to the court which had appointed the administrator in chief. And the jurisdiction of this court is exclusive of all others, and the appointment under this section by any other court is absolutely void. Beasley v. Howell, 117 Ala. 499, 22 So. 989 (1898).

When estate is finally settled and administrator is discharged there is no authority to appoint under this section, since it is not within the letter of this section to disturb the title of the heirs in such a case. Hickey v. Stallworth, 143 Ala. 535, 39 So. 267 (1905).

Appointment under this section should in terms be restricted to character of administrator de bonis non, but an appointment without this restriction does not render the second appointment void in toto. Sands v. Hickey, 135 Ala. 322, 33 So. 827 (1903).

Termination of first grant of letters and vacancy in administration is essential. — It is essential that before a second grant of letters can be made, the first must have terminated. And a second grant, in absence of a vacancy, would be a mere nullity. Sands v. Hickey, 135 Ala. 322, 33 So. 827 (1903). See also Hickey v. Stallworth, 143 Ala. 535, 39 So. 267 (1905).

A grant of letters of administration de bonis non, when there is no vacancy in the administration, is a mere nullity, and may be attacked in a collateral proceeding. Sims v. Waters, 65 Ala. 442 (1880); Allen v. Kellam, 69 Ala. 442 (1881); Bean v. Chapman, 73 Ala. 140 (1882).

Appointment under this section is prima facie evidence that there was a vacancy in the administration, and will be held conclusive until it is clearly and explicitly disproved. Smith v. Alexander, 148 Ala. 554, 42 So. 29 (1906). See also Sands v. Hickey, 135 Ala. 322, 33 So. 827 (1903).

While a grant of administration de bonis non when there is no vacancy is void, yet the rule is well settled that, on collateral attack, it will be presumed, from the exercise by the probate court of the power to appoint an administrator de bonis non, that a vacancy did exist, unless the contrary affirmatively appears. Sims v. Waters, 65 Ala. 442 (1880); Morgan v. Casey, 73 Ala. 222 (1882).

Hence, though it be alleged that the proceedings leading up to the removal were not in conformity to the statutes, the appointment will nevertheless be upheld unless it plainly appears that the court had no jurisdiction. Smith v. Alexander, 148 Ala. 554, 42 So. 29 (1906).

The strict application of these principles is well illustrated by the facts of Smith v. Alexander, 148 Ala. 554, 42 So. 29 (1906), wherein it affirmatively appeared that no citation was served as required by § 43-2-294 in the proceedings for removal nor publication made, yet the jurisdiction over the person to whom the citation was to issue was still presumed. And even though it may appear that this person was beyond the borders of the state, it must still affirmatively appear that he was not represented by counsel, and that citation or publication was not waived, and that the judgment order of removal was not entered by consent.

Instance of vacancy. — The administration of an administratrix and that of her husband by virtue of their marriage terminates upon her death, and as to any unadministered property of deceased the administration is vacant. Sands v. Hickey, 135 Ala. 322, 33 So. 827 (1903).

Acts under void appointment are null. — The acts of an administrator de bonis non are null if the appointment is void. Hooper v. Scarborough, 57 Ala. 510 (1877).

Cited in Watson v. Collins, 37 Ala. 587 (1861); Waring v. Lewis, 53 Ala. 615 (1875); Winslow v. Bracken, 57 Ala. 368 (1876); Patterson v. First Nat'l Bank, 261 Ala. 601, 75 So. 2d 471 (1954).

Collateral references. — 34 C.J.S., Executors & Administrators, §§ 1016, 1030.

31 Am. Jur. 2d, Executors & Administrators, §§ 603-623.

Construction and application of statutes relating specifically to preferences in appointment as administrator with will annexed. 164 ALR 844.

§ 43-2-273. When survivor continues to act.

When an executor or administrator dies, resigns or is removed, and there is any other executor or administrator, no other must be appointed; but such administrator or executor must complete the administration, unless the testator has provided by his will for the nomination or appointment of a substitute or successor, when the person nominated, in accordance with the provisions of the will, shall be permitted to qualify as executor. (Code 1852, § 1721; Code 1867, § 2044; Code 1876, § 2413; Code 1886, § 2065; Code 1896, § 112; Code 1907, § 2534; Code 1923, § 5756; Code 1940, T. 61, § 176.)

In absence of provision in will for substitution of another executor. — Proof that executrix' acts were in willful disregard of her duties under will, authorizes her removal from control of property and as executrix, whereupon her coexecutor, named in will, must complete administration and perform trust duties imposed by will, in absence of provision therein for substitution of another executor. Amos v. Toolen, 232 Ala. 587, 168 So. 687 (1936). See also Alabama Home Bldg. & Loan Ass'n v. Amos, 233 Ala. 367, 172 So. 102 (1937).

Cited in Elrod v. Simmons, 40 Ala. 274 (1866); Hendricks v. Thornton, 45 Ala. 299 (1871); Hooper v. Scarborough, 57 Ala. 510 (1877); Miller v. Irby, 63 Ala. 477 (1879); Humphrey v. Boschung, 47 Ala. App. 310, 253 So. 2d 760 (1970).

§ 43-2-274. Appointment of administrator after final settlement.

After a final settlement, there being personalty not administered which requires an administrator for the proper disposition thereof, the judge of probate of the proper county must proceed to appoint a suitable person as administrator who shall give bond as required by law and administer the personal estate of the decedent not already administered. (Code 1940, T. 61, § 177.)

§ 43-2-275. Removal of resident executor from state.

The removal of any resident executor from this state to any other state or territory of the United States shall not be cause for his removal from the office of executor; but, on and after his removal, he shall in all respects be regarded and treated as a nonresident executor, and the provisions of article 8 of this chapter shall be applicable to him. Upon such removal, his sureties may require him to resign and make final settlement of his accounts or give a new bond as such executor. (Code 1876, § 2384; Code 1886, § 2043; Code 1896, § 89; Code 1907, § 2565; Code 1923, § 5788; Code 1940, T. 61, § 150.)

Cross references. — As to nonresident executors and administrators generally, see § 43-2-190 et seq.

Division 2.

Removal and Proceedings to Require New or Additional Bond.

Cross references. — As to irregularity in proceedings hereunder as affecting "vacancy" justifying appointment of administrator de bonis non, see notes to § 43-2-272.

Collateral references. — 31 Am. Jur. 2d, Executors & Administrators, §§ 109-118.

Probate of will subsequently discovered or annulment of will as affecting removal of administrator. 8 ALR 177.

Changes in corporate organization as affecting status of the executor or administrator. 61 ALR 994, 131 ALR 753.

Dilatoriness of executor or administrator in filing inventory, or making report, as ground for removal. 72 ALR 596.

Appeal from order appointing or removing executor or administrator, or proceeding to supplant him, as affecting rights of persons who dealt with him pending such appeal or proceeding. 99 ALR 862.

Statutory exemption of representative from suit until expiration of prescribed period as affected by removal or death of original representative and appointment of a new one. 104 ALR 909.

Appeal without bond by executor or administrator from order, decree, or judgment removing him, or holding letters of administration to have them improperly issued. 104 ALR 1197.

Personal interest of executor or administrator adverse to or conflicting with those of other persons interested in estate as ground for revocation of letters or removal. 119 ALR 306.

Removal of executor because of delay in exercising power of sale under will. 132 ALR 1479.

Requisites of notice and hearing in court proceedings for removal of personal representative. 47 ALR2d 307.

Power and responsibility of executor or administrator to compromise claim against estate. 72 ALR2d 243.

Who may waive privilege of confidential communication to physician by person since deceased. 97 ALR2d 393.

§ 43-2-290. Causes of removal generally.

An administrator may be removed, and his letters revoked for his removal from the state; and an administrator or executor may be removed and his letters revoked for any of the following causes:

(1) Imbecility of mind; intemperance; continued sickness, rendering him incapable of the discharge of his duties; or when from his conduct or character there is reason to believe that he is not a suitable person to have the charge and control of the estate.

(2) Failure to make and return inventories or accounts of sale; failure to make settlements as required by law; or the failure to do any act as such

executor or administrator, when lawfully required by the judge of probate.

(3) The wasting, embezzlement or any other maladministration of the estate.

(4) The using of any of the funds of the estate for his own benefit.

(5) A sentence of imprisonment in the penitentiary, county jail or for hard labor for the county for a term of 12 months or more. (Code 1852, § 1696; Code 1867, § 2017; Code 1876, § 2386; Code 1886, § 2045; Code 1896, § 92; Code 1907, § 2566; Acts 1919, No. 37, p. 40; Code 1923, § 5789; Code 1940, T. 61, § 178.)

Comparison of section with section 43-2-22. — See Brown v. Brown, 204 Ala. 157, 85 So. 439 (1920); McFry v. Casey, 211 Ala. 649, 101 So. 449 (1924).

Enumerated causes are exclusive. — Grounds for removal of administrator, specified in this section are exclusive, so far as court of probate is concerned. Castleberry v. Hollingsworth, 215 Ala. 445, 111 So. 35 (1927); Binford v. Penney, 255 Ala. 20, 49 So. 2d 665 (1950).

Failure to return inventory. — Under this section the failure of administratrix to file an inventory within the prescribed time is not ground for removal where there is no loss to the estate, and her failure is due to inadvertence. Willoughby v. Willoughby, 203 Ala. 138, 82 So. 168 (1919). See also Oglesby v. Howard, 43 Ala. 144 (1869), wherein the facts merited the removal of the administrator.

As regards executor's duty to return inventory, executor following testator's directions was not put in default in absence of demand or order for inventory, even in absence of statute. Black v. Morgan, 227 Ala. 327, 149 So. 845 (1933).

Conflict of interest between heirs of two estates, over which the same person is acting as administrator, is not ground for removal under this section. Castleberry v. Hollingsworth, 215 Ala. 445, 111 So. 35 (1927); Binford v. Penney, 255 Ala. 20, 49 So. 2d 665 (1950).

Not bad faith for executor to contest as beneficiary. — It is not sound to charge the executor with bad faith or the commission of waste merely because without subterfuge or deceit he asserts as the beneficiary of the estate the right to contest a codicil. Binford v. Penney, 255 Ala. 20, 49 So. 2d 665 (1950).

Conspiracy to defraud. — Evidence that will of deceased, purporting to devise and bequeath entire estate to administratrix, was forgery concocted by administratrix and executed under her advice and direction, after alleged testator's death, and imposed on probate court by means of conspiracy to defraud petitioner's ward and another of their heritable interest in estate, authorized removal of administratrix. Kelen v. Brewer, 220 Ala. 175, 124 So. 247 (1929).

Routine general deposit of estate funds in solvent executor bank does not render executor liable for interest or subject to removal. First Nat'l Bank v. Weaver, 225 Ala. 160, 142 So. 420 (1932).

Protection of beneficiaries of trust. — Where continuing express trusts are created by the will, and the jurisdiction of a court is properly invoked to effectuate their due execution, the court has the power to remove the trustee-executor, if need be, in protecting the beneficiaries of the trust. Woods v. Chrissinger, 230 Ala. 678, 163 So. 318 (1935).

Where property rights of administrator involved. — This section, providing for removal of administrator when there is reason to believe he is not suitable person to have control of estate, should not be denied statutory and necessary operation in case where, from nature of case, evidence sustaining charge that administrator is not suitable person happens also to have bearing on disputed question as to his property rights. Kelen v. Brewer, 220 Ala. 175, 124 So. 247 (1929).

Order to quash and vacate ends all matters of administration in probate court. — The probate court after quashing and annulling all proceedings was without authority to retain the matter of administration in the probate court to compel the appellant to make final settlement of said administration, there being no such administration after such quashing and vacating order was entered. Terry v. Gresham, 254 Ala. 349, 48 So. 2d 437 (1950).

Order of removal at special term. — Order of probate court, removing executor, made at a special term to which the cause was not adjourned or appointed, was void. Boynton v. Nelson, 46 Ala. 501 (1871).

Judgment removing executor held not res judicata of question of his liability to estate, notwithstanding same line of evidence may be presented, but hearing on liability will be de novo. Lindsey v. Lindsey, 226 Ala. 489, 147 So. 425 (1933).

Evidence. — On application for removal of executor, testator's declarations made subsequent to date of check payable to executor, indicating that he still had fund in bank and that he wanted his children to share it alike, held admissible on issues of forgery and undue influence as against objection of hearsay. Lindsey v. Lindsey, 226 Ala. 489, 147 So. 425 (1933).

That evidence that executor forged testator's check or obtained it by undue influence indirectly proves executor liable in assumpsit or chargeable with money on settlement after removal, held no ground for its exclusion on hearing of application for removal. Lindsey v. Lindsey, 226 Ala. 489, 147 So. 425 (1933).

Cited in Hunter v. O'Neil, 12 Ala. 37 (1847); Schaefer v. Adler, 14 Ala. 723 (1848); Lay v. Lawson, 23 Ala. 377 (1853); Harris v. Dillard, 31 Ala. 191 (1857); Curtis v. Williams, 33 Ala.

570 (1859); Broughton v. Bradley, 34 Ala. 694 (1859); Forrester v. Forrester, 37 Ala. 398 (1861); Oglesby v. Howard, 43 Ala. 144 (1869); Lawson v. Moore, 45 Ala. 519 (1871); Godwin v. Hooper, 45 Ala. 613 (1871); Bryant v. State, 46 Ala. 302 (1871); Fretwell v. McLemore, 52 Ala. 124 (1875); Watson v. Glover, 77 Ala. 323 (1884); Keith v. Proctor, 114 Ala. 676, 21 So. 502 (1897); Griffin v. Irwin, 246 Ala. 631, 21 So. 2d 668 (1945); Riley v. Wilkinson, 247 Ala. 231, 23 So. 2d 582 (1945); Brewer v. Brewer, 250 Ala. 658, 35 So. 2d 557 (1948); Smith v. Rice, 265 Ala. 236, 90 So. 2d 262 (1956); Brooks v. Brooks, 272 Ala. 614, 133 So. 2d 259 (1961).

Collateral references. — 33 C.J.S., Executors & Administrators, § 90.

Physical condition as affecting competency to act as executor or administrator. 71 ALR3d 675.

§ 43-2-291. Rights terminated by sentence of imprisonment.

A sentence of imprisonment in the penitentiary, imprisonment in the county jail or hard labor for the county, for a term of 12 months or more, terminates the right of the convict to execute the office of executor or administrator, in the same manner as if he had been removed from office and extinguishes all private trusts not susceptible of delegation by him. (Code 1852, § 263; Code 1867, § 3811; Code 1876, § 4511; Code 1886, § 4505; Code 1896, § 5427; Code 1907, § 7636; Code 1923, § 5292; Code 1940, T. 61, § 179.)

Cited in Bibb v. State, 83 Ala. 84, 3 So. 711 (1888).

§ 43-2-292. Additional bond may be required; removal for default.

An executor or administrator may also be required to give additional bond and, in default thereof, may be removed and his letters revoked, in the following cases:

(1) When it is shown to the court by his sureties, or either of them, that he has become, or is likely to become, insolvent, and that they have sustained, or probably will sustain, loss thereby.

(2) When his letters have been granted on insufficient security, or the security has become insufficient since the grant, or any of his sureties have died or have removed from the state.

(3) When the penalty of the bond is not sufficient to secure the due performance of the trusts committed to him. (Code 1852, § 1697; Code 1867, § 2018; Code 1876, § 2387; Code 1886, § 2046; Code 1896, § 93; Code 1907, § 2567; Code 1923, § 5790; Code 1940, T. 61, § 180.)

Cross references. — As to bonds generally, see § 43-2-80 et seq.

No appeal from order requiring additional bond. — No appeal can be taken from an order requiring additional bond. But if the order both requires bond and orders a removal for bond not given, then it might support an appeal. Betts v. Cobb, 121 Ala. 154, 25 So. 692 (1899). See also Boynton v. Nelson, 46 Ala. 501 (1871).

Collateral references. — 33 C.J.S., Executors & Administrators, § 67.

§ 43-2-293. Application for removal or additional bond.

Application for the removal of any executor or administrator, or for an additional bond, must be in writing, verified by oath, must specify the grounds of complaint and must be made to the court from which letters issued, or in which the administration is pending; and may be made by any creditor, legatee, devisee, heir or distributee, or by any coexecutor, coadministrator or the sureties, or any of them. (Code 1852, §§ 1698, 1699; Code 1867, §§ 2019, 2020; Code 1876, §§ 2388, 2389; Code 1886, § 2047; Code 1896, § 94; Code 1907, § 2568; Code 1923, § 5791; Code 1940, T. 61, § 181.)

Coexecutors can join in residuary legatees' application for removal of executor, either as legatees or executors, or both. Lindsey v. Lindsey, 226 Ala. 489, 147 So. 425 (1933).

Cited in Blackman v. Davis, 42 Ala. 184 (1868); Crawford v. Tyson, 46 Ala. 299 (1871); Rives v. Flinn, 47 Ala. 481 (1872); Smith v. Alexander, 148 Ala. 554, 42 So. 29 (1907); Riley v. Wilkinson, 247 Ala. 231, 23 So. 2d 582 (1945).

§ 43-2-294. Service of citation.

A citation to such executor or administrator to appear and answer the application on a day specified therein must be served on him five days before the hearing of the complaint. (Code 1852, § 1700; Code 1867, § 2021; Code 1876, § 2390; Code 1886, § 2048; Code 1896, § 95; Code 1907, § 2569; Code 1923, § 5792; Code 1940, T. 61, § 182.)

Cited in Crawford v. Tyson, 46 Ala. 299 (1871); Myers v. Parker, 349 So. 2d 1136 (Ala. 1977).

§ 43-2-295. Notice by publication.

If such executor or administrator is not an inhabitant of the state, or is absent therefrom, upon such fact being shown by proof satisfactory to the judge, he must direct notice of such application to be given by publication for three successive weeks in some newspaper published in the county, or if none is published therein in the newspaper published nearest to the courthouse thereof; and the applicant must pay the expense of such publication, which may be taxed as costs. (Code 1852, §§ 1701, 1702; Code 1867, §§ 2022, 2023; Code 1876, §§ 2391, 2392; Code 1886, § 2049; Code 1896, § 96; Code 1907, § 2570; Code 1923, § 5793; Code 1940, T. 61, § 183.)

Cited in Crawford v. Tyson, 46 Ala. 299 (1871).

§ 43-2-296. Trial.

On the day specified in the citation, or after publication as required, or on any day thereafter to which the hearing may be continued, the court must proceed to hear the evidence, and may, in its discretion, examine the parties; and when the application charges embezzlement, waste or any other maladministration of the estate, either party is entitled to a trial by jury. (Code 1852, §§ 1703, 1704; Code 1867, §§ 2024, 2025; Code 1876, §§ 2393, 2394; Code 1886, § 2050; Code 1896, § 97; Code 1907, § 2571; Code 1923, § 5794; Code 1940, T. 61, § 184.)

Cited in Boynton v. Nelson, 46 Ala. 501 (1871).

§ 43-2-297. Costs.

If the application is determined against the applicant, he, otherwise the executor or administrator, must be taxed with the costs, for which execution may be issued. (Code 1852, § 1705; Code 1867, § 2026; Code 1876, § 2395; Code 1886, § 2051; Code 1896, § 98; Code 1907, § 2572; Code 1923, § 5795; Code 1940, T. 61, § 185.)

§ 43-2-298. Order to give additional bond.

If an additional bond is required by the court, an order must be made to that effect, allowing such time to give the same as the court may think reasonable; and if such order is not complied with within the time prescribed, the executor or administrator must be removed and his letters revoked. (Code 1852, §§ 1706, 1707; Code 1867, §§ 2027, 2028; Code 1876, §§ 2396, 2397; Code 1886, § 2052; Code 1896, § 99; Code 1907, § 2573; Code 1923, § 5796; Code 1940, T. 61, § 186.)

Cited in Boynton v. Nelson, 46 Ala. 501 (1871).

§ 43-2-299. Removal or additional bond on motion of court.

Whenever the judge of probate has reason to believe that any just ground or cause of removal exists, or that an additional bond should be required of an executor, or administrator, he may cause a citation to be served on such executor or administrator, requiring him to appear on a day therein named, five days after service thereof, and show cause why he should not be removed, or give an additional bond, as the case may be; and if no sufficient cause is shown, the court may remove such executor or administrator, or require him to give an additional bond; and, if an additional bond is required, on failure to give the same within the time prescribed the court may remove him. (Code 1852, §§ 1708, 1709; Code 1867, §§ 2029, 2030; Code 1876, §§ 2398, 2399; Code 1886, § 2053; Code 1896, § 100; Code 1907, § 2574; Code 1923, § 5797; Code 1940, T. 61, § 187.)

Cited in Crawford v. Tyson, 46 Ala. 299 (1871).

ARTICLE 13.

COLLECTION, INVENTORY AND APPRAISEMENT OF PERSONAL PROPERTY.

Collateral references. — 33 C.J.S., Executors & Administrators, §§ 129-140, 167-183.

31 Am. Jur. 2d, Executors & Administrators, §§ 209, 215.

Dilatoriness of executor or administrator in filing inventory, or making reports, as ground for removal. 72 ALR 956.

Right to commissions as affected by failure to file, or improper filing of, inventory or account. 83 ALR 732.

§ 43-2-310. Duty of executor or administrator to collect property and make inventory.

It is the duty of every executor or administrator, immediately after taking out letters, to collect and take into his possession the goods and chattels, money, books, papers and evidences of debt of the decedent, except the personal property specifically exempted from administration under section 6-10-63 and to make a full inventory of the same. (Code 1852, § 1724; Code 1867, § 2047; Code 1876, § 2416; Code 1886, § 2068; Code 1896, § 115; Code 1907, § 2579; Code 1923, § 5802; Code 1940, T. 61, § 189.)

Code commissioner's note. — Section 6-10-63, referred to in this section, was repealed by Acts 1982, No. 82-399, § 8-102, effective January 1, 1983.

Section is not mandate for bringing action. — This section is not a mandate to executors and administrators to bring civil action for the possession of personal property, or for the recovery of money, belonging to or due to the estates of their decedents. The fact that the duty herein imposed is to be performed "immediately after taking out letters" clearly and conclusively distinguishes this duty of physical collection and possession from the general common-law duty to recover all debts due the estate, by civil action or otherwise. Phillips v. First Nat'l Bank, 208 Ala. 589, 94 So. 801 (1922).

Grant of letters of administration vests representative with legal title to personal assets. Butler v. Gazzam, 81 Ala. 491, 1 So. 16 (1886).

Presumption of payment of note arising from maker's possession has no application where the maker is appointed the payee's administrator, since this section entitled an administrator to take possession of his intestate's evidence of debt. In such case the burden is on the administrator to establish that the notes were not binding, subsisting obligations upon him at the date of his intestate's death. Arnold v. Arnold, 124 Ala. 550, 27 So. 465 (1900).

Cited in Spivey v. State, 26 Ala. 90 (1855); Oglesby v. Howard, 43 Ala. 144 (1869); Avery v. Avery, 47 Ala. 505 (1872); Ramsey v. McMillan, 214 Ala. 185, 106 So. 848 (1925); Rainey v. Smith, 250 Ala. 690, 36 So. 2d 78 (1948).

Collateral references. — 33 C.J.S., Executors & Administrators, § 167.

§ 43-2-311. Testator may exempt executor from filing inventory or making report or final settlement.

Any testator may, by express provision in his will to that effect, exempt an executor from filing an inventory or making any report or final settlement, and when such provision is made, such inventory, report or final settlement shall not be required except in the following cases:

(1) When any executor, heir, legatee or other person interested in the estate makes affidavit showing his interest, and alleging that such interest is or will be endangered for want of security.

(2) When, in the opinion of the judge of the court having jurisdiction of the estate, the estate is likely to be wasted, to the prejudice of any person interested therein. (Code 1923, § 5803; Code 1940, T. 61, § 190.)

Formerly testator could not exempt executor from filing inventory required in § 43-2-310. Parker v. Robertson, 205 Ala. 434, 88 So. 418 (1921).

This section is practically the same as § 43-2-81 and should have a construction similar to that given that section. Ex parte Griffin, 274 Ala. 391, 150 So. 2d 216 (1963).

Executor's obligation faithfully to execute will is not lessened by this section. Wright v. Menefee, 226 Ala. 55, 145 So. 315 (1932).

Bond requirement rests on judicial finding not affidavit. — This section and § 43-2-81 do not require the court to order the giving of a bond or the filing of an inventory simply because there is an appropriate affidavit (or sworn application) to that end. Requiring a bond or inventory rests upon a judicial finding that affiant's (applicant's) interest in the estate "is, or will be, endangered for want of security." Ex parte Griffin, 274 Ala. 391, 150 So. 2d 216 (1963).

Cited in Rudulph v. Hodo, 228 Ala. 170, 153 So. 238 (1934); Oxford v. Estes, 229 Ala. 606, 158 So. 534 (1934); Pinckard v. Ledyard, 251 Ala. 648, 38 So. 2d 580 (1949).

Collateral references. — 33 C.J.S., Executors & Administrators, § 139.

§ 43-2-312. Contents of inventory.

The inventory must set forth the goods and chattels, enumerating each article separately, all debts or demands due or accruing to the decedent, the time such debts or demands are due, the amount of the same and how evidenced, with the credits, if any, and the name of the debtor and the amount of money. (Code 1852, § 1725; Code 1867, § 2048; Code 1876, § 2417; Code 1886, § 2069; Code 1896, § 116; Code 1907, § 2580; Code 1923, § 5804; Code 1940, T. 61, § 191.)

Cited in Dobbs v. Cockerham, 2 Port. 328 (1835); Branch Bank v. Wade, 13 Ala. 427 (1848); Parker v. Robertson, 205 Ala. 434, 88 So. 418 (1921); Hinson v. Naugher, 207 Ala. 592, 93 So. 560 (1922).

Collateral references. — 33 C.J.S., Executors & Administrators, § 133.

§ 43-2-313. Oath upon return of inventory.

On the return of the inventory, the executor or administrator must take and subscribe an oath, to be administered by the judge of probate, or any justice of the peace or notary public of the county, that such inventory is full and complete, as to the goods, chattels, debts and money of the decedent, which have come to his knowledge or possession. (Code 1852, § 1726; Code 1867, § 2049; Code 1876, § 2418; Code 1886, § 2070; Code 1896, § 117; Code 1907, § 2581; Code 1923, § 5805; Code 1940, T. 61, § 192.)

§ 43-2-314. Appointment, duties, oath and compensation of appraisers.

At the time of the filing of the inventory, the court must appoint three appraisers in each county in which it is necessary to make an appraisement of the estate of the decedent, who must appraise each article specified in the inventory made by the executor or administrator at its true value and set down opposite to such articles, respectively, the values thereof in dollars and cents, in figures. The appraisement must be subscribed and sworn to by them, and the executor or administrator is authorized to administer the oath. Such appraisers, for such service, shall each be entitled to receive $2.00 per day while actually engaged in making the appraisement. (Code 1852, §§ 1727, 1728, 1729; Code 1867, §§ 2050, 2051, 2052; Code 1876, §§ 2419, 2420, 2421; Code 1886, § 2071; Code 1896, § 118; Code 1907, § 2582; Code 1923, § 5806; Code 1940, T. 61, § 193.)

Cited in Gray v. Weatherford, 227 Ala. 324, 149 So. 819 (1933).

Collateral references. — 33 C.J.S., Executors & Administrators, § 135.

31 Am. Jur. 2d, Executors & Administrators, § 215.

§ 43-2-315. Time for returning inventory and appraisement.

The inventory and appraisement must be returned within two months after the grant of letters. (Code 1852, § 1730; Code 1867, § 2053; Code 1876, § 2422; Code 1886, §·2072; Code 1896, § 119; Code 1907, § 2583; Code 1923, § 5807; Code 1940, T. 61, § 194.)

Cited in Willoughby v. Willoughby, 203 Ala. 138, 82 So. 168 (1918); Parker v. Robertson, 205 Ala. 434, 88 So. 418 (1921); Gray v. Weatherford, 227 Ala. 324, 149 So. 819 (1933).

Collateral references. — 33 C.J.S., Executors & Administrators, § 131.

§ 43-2-316. Supplemental inventories and appraisements.

The executor and administrator must make supplemental inventories of the decedent's estate coming to his knowledge or possession after making the first inventory; and an appraisement must be made of such estate by the appraisers, on oath, and in the same manner as the first appraisement was made. (Code 1852, §§ 1731, 1732; Code 1867, §§ 2054, 2055; Code 1876, §§ 2423, 2424; Code 1886, § 2073; Code 1896, § 120; Code 1907, § 2584; Code 1923, § 5808; Code 1940, T. 61, § 195.)

Collateral references. — 33 C.J.S., Executors & Administrators, § 134.

§ 43-2-317. Appointment of new appraisers.

New appraisers may be appointed by the court, from time to time, as may be necessary. (Code 1852, § 1733; Code 1867, § 2056; Code 1876, § 2425; Code 1886, § 2074; Code 1896, § 121; Code 1907, § 2585; Code 1923, § 5809; Code 1940, T. 61, § 196.)

§ 43-2-318. Exhibit showing condition of estate.

Six months after his appointment, and at any time thereafter when required by the court, either upon its own motion or upon the application of any person interested in the estate, the executor or administrator must render, for the information of the court, an exhibit under oath, showing the amount of all claims presented against the estate, and the names of the claimants, and all other matters necessary to show the condition of its affairs. (Code 1923, § 5810; Code 1940, T. 61, § 197.)

ARTICLE 14.

KEEPING ESTATES TOGETHER.

§ 43-2-330. Authorization by probate court to keep estate together; term.

The probate court may authorize the executor or administrator, on application made and good cause shown, to keep the real and personal estate, or any portion thereof, together for such length of time as the court may deem advisable, not exceeding 10 years, and employ laborers to cultivate, improve, keep in repair and carry on the plantation belonging to the estate. (Code 1852, § 1902; Code 1867, § 2263; Code 1876, § 2602; Code 1886, § 2210; Code 1896, § 278; Code 1907, § 2743; Code 1923, § 5982; Code 1940, T. 61, § 198.)

Cited in Pickens v. Pickens, 35 Ala. 442 (1860); Harrison v. Harrison, 39 Ala. 489 (1864); Cannon v. Copeland, 43 Ala. 259 (1869); Tabor v. Peters, 74 Ala. 90 (1883); Hinson v. Williamson, 74 Ala. 180 (1883).

Collateral references. — 33 C.J.S., Executors & Administrators, § 194.

§ 43-2-331. Extension of time upon showing of good cause.

Whenever any executor or administrator has kept an estate together, under the order of the probate court, for 10 years, the time may be extended annually, upon application and good cause shown, if the court is of the opinion that the interest of such estate demands such extension. (Code 1867, § 4431; Code 1876, § 2603; Code 1886, § 2211; Code 1896, § 279; Code 1907, § 2744; Code 1923, § 5983; Code 1940, T. 61, § 199.)

Cited in Houston v. Deloach, 43 Ala. 364 (1869).

§ 43-2-332. When distributed share kept and worked with undivided portion of estate.

When a share or shares of real or personal property of any decedent is or are set apart or distributed to any widow, heir at law or distributee of such decedent, and it appears to the satisfaction of the court that it is to the interest of the parties interested in the estate that such share or shares should be kept and worked together with such estate remaining undivided, the probate court, upon the application of the executor or administrator, and of the owner or owners of such share or shares, may order the executor or administrator to keep such share or shares, and work the same, together with the estate remaining undivided, for a term not exceeding 10 years; but such order must not be granted, if in conflict with the will of the testator. (Code 1867, § 2264; Code 1876, § 2604; Code 1886, § 2212; Code 1896, § 280; Code 1907, § 2745; Code 1923, § 5984; Code 1940, T. 61, § 200.)

§ 43-2-333. Payment of profits to share owners.

The executor or administrator must pay, at the end of each year, to the owner or owners of such share or shares a proportionate share of the profits arising from such estate, and is entitled to a credit for same; but if it shall appear, on a settlement of his accounts, that he has not paid the same, a decree therefor in favor of the owner or owners must be rendered by the probate court. (Code 1867, § 2265; Code 1876, § 2605; Code 1886, § 2213; Code 1896, § 281; Code 1907, § 2746; Code 1923, § 5985; Code 1940, T. 61, § 201.)

Collateral references. — 34 C.J.S., Executors & Administrators, § 492.

§ 43-2-334. Order authorizing hiring of laborers — Generally.

The probate court has power to grant orders authorizing administrators, in cases of intestacy, to hire a sufficient number of laborers to keep up and cultivate the plantation of their intestates, where it is deemed by the court advisable to order the same to be kept together for a term of years. (Code 1867, § 2266; Code 1876, § 2606; Code 1886, § 2214; Code 1896, § 282; Code 1907, § 2747; Code 1923, § 5986; Code 1940, T. 61, § 202.)

§ 43-2-335. Same — Petition; notice and hearing.

Before granting such order, the court must require the administrator to file a petition under oath, setting forth the facts upon which the application is based; and, upon the filing of such petition, the court must appoint a day for the hearing of the same, and must give 10 days' notice thereof by advertisement in some newspaper published in the county, or if there be no newspaper published in the county, then by posting the notice at the courthouse door. On the day appointed, the court must proceed to hear and determine the same upon the evidence adduced by the petitioner, or the other parties in interest, and any other evidence that the court may, in its discretion, cause to be adduced. Unless good cause be shown to the contrary, the court must grant such order, and must require the petitioner to return a written report of such hiring under oath, on or before a day specified in such order. (Code 1867, § 2266; Code 1876, § 2606; Code 1886, § 2215; Code 1896, § 283; Code 1907, § 2748; Code 1923, § 5987; Code 1940, T. 61, § 203.)

§ 43-2-336. Cultivation under direction of executor or administrator; reservation of dower.

When the estate of any decedent is kept together the real estate may be cultivated under the direction of the executor or administrator; but the dower of the widow must in all cases be reserved. (Code 1852, § 1903; Code 1867, § 2267; Code 1876, § 2607; Code 1886, § 2216; Code 1896, § 284; Code 1907, § 2749; Code 1923, § 5988; Code 1940, T. 61, § 204.)

Cross references. — As to abolition of dower generally, see § 43-8-57.

Cited in Tabor v. Peters, 74 Ala. 90 (1883).

§ 43-2-337. Preceding sections not to be construed so as to conflict with will.

The provisions of the preceding sections of this article must not be so construed as to conflict with the will of the testator. (Code 1852, § 1904; Code 1867, § 2268; Code 1876, § 2608; Code 1886, § 2217; Code 1896, § 285; Code 1907, § 2750; Code 1923, § 5989; Code 1940, T. 61, § 205.)

Collateral references. — 33 C.J.S., Executors & Administrators, § 195.

§ 43-2-338. Annual settlements.

(a) The executor or administrator must make annual settlements of such estates, as required in other cases, and in such settlements he must show how such estate has been managed, crops made, expenses incurred and the disposition of all moneys received; and he must also show the amounts appropriated and expended for each and every person entitled to any distribution from such estate.

(b) The accounts and vouchers, evidence and statement of the heirs and legatees must be filed, notice given and contest made, in the same manner as on annual settlements in other cases.

(c) Such settlement may be compelled by attachment, or the probate court may proceed in the same manner as in other cases, when an executor or administrator, being cited to make a settlement, fails to do so. (Code 1852, §§ 1905-1908; Code 1867, §§ 2269-2272; Code 1876, §§ 2609-2612; Code 1886, §§ 2218-2220; Code 1896, §§ 286-288; Code 1907, §§ 2751-2753; Code 1923, §§ 5990-5992; Code 1940, T. 61, §§ 206-208.)

Cross references. — As to settlements and distributions generally, see § 43-2-500 et seq.

Cited in Tyson v. Sanderson, 45 Ala. 364 (1871).

§ 43-2-339. Certain rights not affected by provisions of article.

The provisions of this article in relation to keeping estates together must not be so construed as to affect the rights of creditors, or to prevent any legatee or distributee from receiving his proportion of the estate on his arriving at full age. (Code 1852, § 1909; Code 1867, § 2273; Code 1876, § 2613; Code 1886, § 2221; Code 1896, § 289; Code 1907, § 2754; Code 1923, § 5993; Code 1940, T. 61, § 209.)

Cited in Neel v. Clay, 48 Ala. 252 (1872).

ARTICLE 15.

CLAIMS AND DEBTS.

Division 1.

Presentation.

Cross references. — As to actions against estate for trespass, waste, etc., see § 6-5-90. As to homestead and other exemptions from administration and payment of debts, see § 43-8-110 et seq.

§ 43-2-350. Time and manner of filing claims — Generally.

(a) All claims against the estate of a decedent, held by the personal representative of such decedent or by an assignee or transferee of such representative, or in which he has an interest, whether due or to become due, must be presented within six months after the grant of letters by filing the claims, or statement thereof, verified by affidavit, in the office of the judge of probate, in all respects as provided by section 43-2-352. All such claims not so presented and filed are forever barred, and the payment or allowance thereof is prohibited. But this subsection shall not apply to claims of executors or administrators to compensation for their services as such, nor to sums properly disbursed by them in the course of administration.

(b) All claims against the estate of a decedent, other than the claims referred to in subsection (a) of this section, whether due or to become due, must be presented within six months after the grant of letters testamentary or of administration; and if not presented within that time, they are forever barred and the payment or allowance thereof is prohibited. Such presentation must be made by filing a verified claim or verified statement thereof in the office of the judge of probate of the county in which the letters are granted. Claims which have not been filed and which are liens against the real or personal property of the decedent may be paid by the personal representative to protect the assets of the estate. The provisions of this subsection do not apply to heirs or legatees claiming as such. (Code 1852, §§ 1883, 1884; Code 1867, §§ 2239, 2240; Code 1876, §§ 2597, 2598; Code 1886, §§ 2081, 2082; Code 1896, §§ 129, 130, 132; Code 1907, §§ 2589, 2590, 2592; Code 1923, §§ 5814, 5815, 5817; Acts 1931, No. 722, p. 839; Acts 1931, No. 723, p. 840; Code 1940, T. 61, §§ 210, 211, 213.)

I. General Consideration.
II. Claims Held by Personal Representative.
III. Other Claims.
    A. Generally.
    B. Presentment.
    C. Claims Against the Estate.

I. GENERAL CONSIDERATION.

The six-months time limit contained with the nonclaim statute is jurisdictional in the sense that it is not subject to waiver by the court; the very language of the statute makes it applicable to "all claims against the estate of the decedent." Williams v. Phillips Petroleum Co., 453 F. Supp. 967 (S.D. Ala. 1978), aff'd, 614 F.2d 293 (5th Cir. 1980).

"All claims against the estate of the decedent" includes counterclaims. — The term "all claims against the estate of the decedent" as used in the nonclaim statute includes counterclaims as well as original claims brought against the estate. Motley v. Battle, 368 So. 2d 20 (Ala. 1979).

Where counterclaim against estate of deceased motorist was not filed within six months after the granting of the letters of administration, the failure to comply with the nonclaim statute could not be remedied by treating the counterclaim as relating back to the time that the claim of the deceased motorist arose. Motley v. Battle, 368 So. 2d 20 (Ala. 1979).

Motorist's counterclaim in wrongful death action seeking damages for personal injury is a tort claim and it is clearly a claim against the estate within the meaning of the nonclaim statute. Motley v. Battle, 368 So. 2d 20 (Ala. 1979).

Cited in Andrews v. Huckabee, 30 Ala. 143 (1857); Harrison v. Jones, 33 Ala. 258 (1858); McNeill v. McNeill, 36 Ala. 109 (1860); Bank of Montgomery v. Plannett, 37 Ala. 222 (1861); Harrison v. Harrison, 39 Ala. 489 (1864); Mahone v. Haddock, 44 Ala. 92 (1870); Clark v. Washington, 44 Ala. 291 (1870); Prince v. Prince, 47 Ala. 283 (1872); Cochran v. Martin, 47 Ala. 525 (1872); Beasley v. Waugh, 51 Ala. 156 (1874); Whitfield v. Woolf, 51 Ala. 202 (1874); Fretwell v. McLemore, 52 Ala. 124 (1875); Foster v. Holland, 56 Ala. 474 (1876); Hatchett v. Curbow, 59 Ala. 516 (1877); George v. George, 67 Ala. 192 (1880); Allen v. Elliott, 67 Ala. 432 (1880); Grimball v. Mastin, 77 Ala. 553 (1884); Farris v. Stoutz, 78 Ala. 130 (1884); Smith v. Gillam, 80 Ala. 296 (1885); Fearn v. Ward, 80 Ala. 555, 2 So. 114 (1887); Walker v. Johnson, 82 Ala. 347, 2 So. 744 (1887); Morrissett v. Carr, 127 Ala. 277, 27 So. 844 (1900); Stakely v. Executive Comm. of Foreign Missions of Presbyterian Church, 145 Ala. 379, 39 So. 653 (1905); Merrett v. Vincent Mercantile Co., 157 Ala. 576, 47 So. 731 (1908); Rives v. Cabel, 213 Ala. 206, 104 So. 420 (1925); Bartlett v. Jenkins, 213 Ala. 510, 105 So. 654 (1925); Metcalf v. Payne, 214 Ala. 81, 106 So. 496 (1925); Foster v. Foster, 219 Ala. 70, 121 So. 80 (1929); Arbo v. State Bank, 226 Ala. 52, 145 So. 318 (1932); Wright v. Menefee, 226 Ala. 55, 145 So. 315 (1932); Dirago v. Taylor, 227 Ala. 271, 150 So. 150 (1933); Whitaker v. Kennamer, 229 Ala. 80, 155 So. 855 (1934); Meador-Pasley Co. v. Hallmark, 26 Ala. App. 384, 160 So. 558 (1935); Walsh v. Walsh, 231 Ala. 305, 164 So. 822 (1935); Grist v. Carswell, 231 Ala. 442, 165 So. 102 (1935); Richards v. Williams, 231 Ala. 450, 165 So. 820 (1936); Soper v. Burns, 233 Ala. 492, 172 So. 598 (1937); White v. Blair, 234

Ala. 119, 173 So. 493 (1937); Esslinger v. Spragins, 236 Ala. 508, 183 So. 401 (1938); Crews v. United States Fid. & Guar. Co., 237 Ala. 14, 185 So. 370 (1938); Long v. Shumate, 237 Ala. 470, 187 So. 627 (1939); First Nat'l Bank v. Henderson, 243 Ala. 636, 11 So. 2d 366 (1942); Elliott v. First Nat'l Bank, 248 Ala. 360, 27 So. 2d 623 (1946); Ex parte Floyd, 250 Ala. 154, 33 So. 2d 340 (1947); Terry v. Gresham, 254 Ala. 349, 48 So. 2d 437· (1950); Ex parte Zepernick, 259 Ala. 493, 66 So. 2d 757 (1953); State v. Crocker, 38 Ala. App. 306, 83 So. 2d 261 (1955); Dorrough v. McKee, 264 Ala. 663, 89 So. 2d 77 (1956); Hamilton v. City of Anniston, 268 Ala. 559, 109 So. 2d 728 (1959); McElhaney v. Singleton, 270 Ala. 162, 117 So. 2d 375 (1960); Norton v. Liddell, 280 Ala. 353, 194 So. 2d 514 (1967); Dodd v. Lovett, 287 Ala. 131, 248 So. 2d 724 (1971).

Collateral references. — 34 C.J.S., Executors & Administrators, §§ 382-390, 394, 397, 707-710, 732-736.

Conduct of personal representative preventing filing of claims within time allowed by statute of nonclaim. 11 ALR 246, 66 ALR 1415.

Applicability of nonclaim statutes to claims arising under executory contract. 41 ALR 144, 47 ALR 896.

Applicability of nonclaim statute to claims for unpaid balance of stock subscription upon call made after the stockholder's death. 41 ALR 150, 156, 47 ALR 896.

Applicability of nonclaim statute in case of misappropriation of trust funds or fraudulent breach of trust by decedent. 41 ALR 169.

Applicability of statute of nonclaim to stockholder's superadded liability. 41 ALR 180, 51 ALR 772, 87 ALR 494.

Effect of recovery of judgment on unfiled or abandoned claim after expiration of time allowed for filing claims. 60 ALR 736.

Statutory provisions excusing under certain conditions compliance with requirement as to filing claim against decedent's estate, construction and application of. 71 ALR 940.

Succession tax as affected by attempted waiver of statute of nonclaim. 76 ALR 1456.

Nonclaim statute as applied to mortgage on real estate or mortgage debt. 78 ALR 1126.

Claim on decedent's contract of guaranty, suretyship, or endorsement, as contingent within statute of nonclaim. 94 ALR 1155.

Applicability of statute of nonclaim as between surviving partner and estate of deceased partner. 96 ALR 449, 157 ALR 1114.

Delay of claimant, after filing claim against decedent's estate, to press its establishment or enforcement. 100 ALR 241.

Statutes forbidding suit against representative of estate until expiration of prescribed period as affecting running of statute of nonclaim. 104 ALR 901.

Nonclaim statute as governing claim barred, subsequent to death of obligor, by general statute of limitations. 112 ALR 289.

Applicability of statute providing for a shortening period for filing claims against decedent's estate to existing claims and constitutionality of statute as so applied. 117 ALR 1208.

Personal claim of executor or administrator against estate, antedating decedent's death. 144 ALR 968.

Time for filing claim based on promise not to make a will. 32 ALR2d 380.

Claim of government or subdivision thereof as within provision of nonclaim statute. 34 ALR2d 1003.

Necessity of compliance with nonclaim statute before bringing suit in replevin against personal representative. 42 ALR2d 443.

Failure of personal representative to file proof of publication of notice of appointment or notice to creditors within specified time as tolling statute of nonclaim. 42 ALR2d 1218.

Amendment of claim against decedent's estate after expiration of time for filing claims. 56 ALR2d 627.

Exclusiveness of grounds enumerated in statute providing, under specified circumstances, extension of time for filing claims against decedent's estate. 57 ALR2d 1304.

Appealability of order, of court possessing probate jurisdiction, allowing or denying tardy presentation of claim to personal representative. 66 ALR2d 659.

Time limitation, under nonclaim statute, as to claim for unmatured payments under land contract. 99 ALR2d 275.

Running of statute of limitations as affected by doctrine of relation back of appointment of administrator. 3 ALR3d 1234.

Tort claim as within nonclaim statutes. 22 ALR3d 493.

Amount of claim filed against decedent's estate as limiting amount recoverable in action against estate. 25 ALR3d 1356.

Effect of delay in appointing administrator or other representative on cause of action accruing at or after death of person in whose favor it would have accrued. 28 ALR3d 1141.

Validity of claims against estate filed prior to publication of notice to creditors. 70 ALR3d 784.

II. CLAIMS HELD BY PERSONAL REPRESENTATIVE.

General basis of nonclaim statute. — The reason for the statutes of nonclaims was to prevent the payment of unjust, unconscionable or fraudulent claims that may be made against estates by personal representatives and other creditors, without giving notice to the parties in interest and affording them the opportunity to resist the demands. Burgess v. Burgess, 201 Ala. 631, 79 So. 193 (1918).

Purpose. — Creditors, or others interested in distribution of estate, have equal right with personal representative to insist on pleading of nonclaim, but primary purpose of section is to protect personal representative, and to provide for giving of notice to him. Roberts v. Grayson, 233 Ala. 658, 173 So. 38 (1937).

The purpose of the statute of nonclaims is to give notice to the personal representative of the nature, character and amount of the claim and to distinguish it from other claims so that it may be investigated and the question of liability determined. First Nat'l Bank v. Chichester, 352 So. 2d 1371 (Ala. Civ. App.), cert. denied, 352 So. 2d 1376 (Ala. 1977).

The purpose of the statute of nonclaim is to promote a speedy, safe and definitive settlement of estates, by giving the personal representative notice and knowledge of all claims against the estate. Motley v. Battle, 368 So. 2d 20 (Ala. 1979).

Subsection (a) of this section contemplates that relationship of creditor and debtor exist between the personal representative and the estate for there to be a claim against the estate. Myers v. Parker, 349 So. 2d 1136 (Ala. 1977).

Administration of estate is necessary before section may be a defense. — Though a failure to comply with this section is ordinarily a defense, it is not so when there is no administration of the estate. Merchants' Nat'l Bank v. McGee, 108 Ala. 304, 19 So. 356 (1896); Trotter v. Brown, 232 Ala. 147, 167 So. 310 (1936).

Prescribed mode of filing is exclusive. — The mode of presentation of claims under this section is limited to a public filing in "the office of the judge of probate," and not in the probate court, nor a presentment of them personally to the representative in lieu of such filing. Smith v. Nixon, 205 Ala. 223, 87 So. 326 (1921).

Failure to give notice of appointment does not suspend section. — As to failure of executor to give notice of appointment not serving to suspend running of this section, see Johnson v. Bain, 17 Ala. App. 71, 81 So. 849 (1919).

Proof of time of grant of letters. — Where issue is taken on pleading of this section, and plaintiff attempts to show a compliance with this section, it rests upon him to show when letters of administration were issued. Stewart v. L. Lasseter & Co., 4 Ala. App. 665, 59 So. 233 (1912).

Land cannot be sold to pay claims until section complied with. — A grant of administrator's application to sell lands of decedent to pay debts is error where administrator fails to establish compliance with this section. Little v.

Marx, 145 Ala. 620, 39 So. 517 (1905), and authorities therein cited. See also § 43-2-449, and notes thereto.

Not necessary to file claim to preserve a specific lien. — In order to preserve the debt as a charge upon the intestate's general estate, a filing as herein prescribed is necessary. Traweek v. Hagler, 199 Ala. 664, 75 So. 152 (1917). See also Burgess v. Burgess, 201 Ala. 631, 79 So. 193 (1918). But such filing is not necessary in order to preserve a specific lien upon intestate's property. Traweek v. Hagler, 199 Ala. 664, 75 So. 152 (1917). See also Rives v. Cabel, 213 Ala. 206, 104 So. 420 (1925). And a failure to present the claim for debt which supports the lien will not affect the specific lien in or title to the property. Rives v. Cabel, 213 Ala. 206, 104 So. 420 (1925). See also Chamblee v. Proctor, 203 Ala. 61, 82 So. 21 (1919).

Claim not filed is not available as setoff. — A claim against an estate, which has not been filed as required by law, is not available as a setoff against a debt owed to the estate by an executor. Webb v. Webb, 250 Ala. 194, 33 So. 2d 909 (1948).

Claim of funeral expenses is within subsection (a) of this section. — The claim for funeral expenses of a decedent is not a claim against his estate within subsection (b) of this section, but is one which comes within the provisions of subsection (a) of this section. It is a claim included in the words "sums properly disbursed by them in the course of administration." Roche Undertaking Co. v. De Bardeleben, 7 Ala. App. 232, 60 So. 1000 (1912).

Right to reimbursement arising from payment of mortgage indebtedness by widow to protect dower interest not within subsection (a) of this section. — The equitable right to reimbursement arising from the payment of the mortgage indebtedness by the widow to protect her interest (dower) in the real estate is not within the purview of subsection (a) of this section. That right is not the subject of a claim against the estate but rather a claim to an interest in, or part of, the estate. Myers v. Parker, 349 So. 2d 1136 (Ala. 1977).

Amount paid for improvement of testator's property during his lifetime. — Claim for amount paid by executor prior to testator's death for items used in improving property of testator during his lifetime should have been presented by the executor against the estate. Webb v. Webb, 250 Ala. 194, 33 So. 2d 909 (1948).

Administratrix's claim against decedent's estate for funeral expenses was held not required to be presented under § 43-2-352, limiting time for presentation of claims, but such claim falls within the claim indicated in this section. Canada v. Canada, 243 Ala. 109, 8 So. 2d 846 (1942).

Widow's claim for funeral and burial expenses which she paid is a preferred claim and does not require presentation. Gilbreath v. Levi, 270 Ala. 413, 119 So. 2d 210 (1959).

Noncompliance no bar to redemption from mortgage. — The failure to comply with this section — the statute of nonclaim — does not operate to bar the complainants' right to redeem from mortgage. Cunningham v. Andress, 267 Ala. 407, 103 So. 2d 722 (1958).

Burden on claimant to show compliance with section. — Where credit for money paid on a claim filed under this section is claimed by an administrator, the burden is on him to show a compliance with the provision herein contained. McKenzie v. Matthews, 153 Ala. 437, 44 So. 958 (1907).

III. OTHER CLAIMS.

A. Generally.

Limitation not affected by Constitution. — Section 100 of the Constitution does not affect the power of the legislature to provide for limitations in the interest of repose. This power may be applied against the state and its agencies notwithstanding § 100 of the Constitution. State v. Mudd, 273 Ala. 579, 143 So. 2d 171 (1962).

Purpose of subsection (b). — This subsection has been in force in this state a great many years. It was intended to facilitate a safe and speedy settlement of estates, by furnishing the personal representative the means of determining its financial status within 18 (now six) months after his appointment. Jones v. Lightfoot, 10 Ala. 17 (1846); Fretwell v. McLemore, 52 Ala. 124 (1875); Foster v. Holland, 56 Ala. 474 (1876); Owens v. Corbitt, 57 Ala. 92 (1876); McDowell v. Jones, 58 Ala. 25 (1877); Rhodes v. Hannah, 66 Ala. 215 (1880); Yniestra v. Tarleton, 67 Ala. 126 (1880); Taylor v. Robinson, 69 Ala. 269 (1881); Jones v. Drewry, 72 Ala. 311 (1882); McDowell v. Brantley, 80 Ala. 173 (1885).

One purpose of subsection (b) of this section is to enable the administrator to pay the claim if he ascertains it to be well founded. Barrett v. Fondren, 262 Ala. 537, 80 So. 2d 243 (1955).

The purpose of subsection (b) of this section is to promote a speedy, safe and definitive settlement of estates by giving the personal representative notice of all claims against the estate in his hands. Moore v. Stephens, 264 Ala. 86, 84 So. 2d 752 (1956).

Subsection (b) of this section does not specify the manner in which such claim shall be described, except that it shall be a "verified claim or a verified statement thereof," with direction as to the nature of the verification. Merchants Nat'l Bank v. Cotnam, 250 Ala. 316, 34 So. 2d 122 (1948).

Attempted avoidance of bar. — The facts and ruling in the case of Hamil v. Flowers, 184 Ala. 301, 63 So. 994 (1913), clearly show that a party will not be permitted to avoid the bar of subsection (b) of this section by attempting to recover in an action, the form and nature of which is not governed by these provisions.

A testator in his will may so change his estate as not to fall within this section. Bromberg v. First Nat'l Bank, 235 Ala. 226, 178 So. 48 (1937).

The claim of heirs of partner who advanced moneys to partnership, against estate of attorney and manager who acted as trustee of moneys received on behalf of partnership was not subject to this section where claim was to a specific trust and did not seek personal decree against the trustee's estate or personal representative. Bromberg v. First Nat'l Bank, 235 Ala. 226, 178 So. 48 (1937).

This can only be done by a clear declaration of trust. — A testator can only set aside requirements of this section by creating a trust upon some or all his property. A mere general declaration that his debts shall be paid out of his estate and a power of sale to pay them has been held many times in Alabama (contrary to the English rule) not to create a lien or trust sufficient to remove subsection (b) of this section or statute of limitations. But there must be the clear declaration of a trust for that purpose. Foster v. Featherston, 230 Ala. 268, 160 So. 689 (1935).

The requirement of this section as to presentation of claims against estate within six months from grant of letters testamentary or of administration does not apply to claims of a cestui que trust for whom decedent was trustee so long as trust fund or property can be traced and trust enforced by suitable proceedings, but where fund or property cannot be traced, and cestui que trust seeks redress as a general creditor of estate, he must present his claim. Esslinger v. Spragins, 236 Ala. 508, 183 So. 401 (1938).

An administrator with will annexed of payee of note who did not file claim on note in office of judge of probate within six months after grant of letters testamentary, as required by this section, could not maintain action on note against endorser's executors, on ground that this section did not apply because administrator sought to enforce rights to a trust fund, where administrator claimed as a creditor and sought to recover money in action on a note. Esslinger v. Spragins, 236 Ala. 508, 183 So. 401 (1938).

However, anyone can avoid this section by making a trust contract. Bromberg v. First Nat'l Bank, 235 Ala. 226, 178 So. 48 (1937).

A new promise by executor will not revive barred claim. — A new promise by the executor, after the expiration of the statutory period, will not remove the claim from the operation of this section. Branch Bank v. Hawkins, 12 Ala. 755 (1848).

Absence of the administrator from the state will not prevent the bar after it has commenced. Lowe v. Jones, 15 Ala. 545 (1849).

The state bank of Alabama is subject to the provisions of this section. Bank of State v. Gibson, 6 Ala. 814 (1844).

Where deceased mortgagor's son assumed payment of debts and expenses of administration which mortgagee paid, sum paid became part of mortgage debt, subject to defense of this section but to be paid primarily out of property assigned to son. Dirago v. Taylor, 227 Ala. 271, 150 So. 150 (1933).

Bank depositor a "trustee in invitum" and not within section. — A bank account which represented part of a loan secured to pay installments on mortgage and taxes on realty of depositor's mother, and which was secured by chattel mortgage on the mother's personalty was impressed with a "trust" to be used for purposes for which it was procured and the depositor was a "trustee in invitum" and upon death of the depositor the trust was not affected by this section. Winston v. Winston, 242 Ala. 45, 4 So. 2d 730 (1941).

Heirs and legatees are excepted only when claiming as such heirs, etc. — Subsection (b) of this section does not except from its operation the claim of an heir or legatee for a debt or claim against the estate, but for a claim to the estate or any part of the estate as such heir or legatee. Claims of heirs or legatees against an estate come under the operation of and must be presented as required by subsection (b). Rives v. Cabel, 213 Ala. 206, 104 So. 420 (1925).

The claim of heirs or legatees against the estate of a surety, growing out of the misfeasance or malfeasance of his principal, whether judicially ascertained or not, is barred if not presented to the administrator of the surety within the specified time. Fretwell v. McLemore, 52 Ala. 124 (1875).

B. Presentment.

"All claims" has been construed to mean every claim, or demand, existing against the testator or intestate at the time of his death, or subsequently accruing; every legal liability of either character, to which the personal representative can be made to answer, in courts of law or of equity, or which can charge the assets in his hands subject to administration. Fox v. Woods, 382 So. 2d 1118 (Ala. 1980).

Tort claims as well as contract claims are subject to bar established in subsection (b). Fox v. Woods, 382 So. 2d 1118 (Ala. 1980).

Bar against late claims set forth in subsection (b) cannot be waived by personal representative of decedent. Fox v. Woods, 382 So. 2d 1118 (Ala. 1980).

Time and manner of presenting a claim under state nonclaims statute is to be governed by the law of the state in which the claim is to be filed. Fox v. Woods, 382 So. 2d 1118 (Ala. 1980).

Where Michigan court properly obtained jurisdiction over defendant, executrix of estate, and Michigan judgment was valid in all regards, plaintiffs were still barred from asserting claim against defendant based on judgment by this section, due to their failure to timely present a claim against estate. Fox v. Woods, 382 So. 2d 1118 (Ala. 1980).

Claims represented by foreign judgments are not excepted from operation of this statute. Fox v. Woods, 382 So. 2d 1118 (Ala. 1980).

Although judgment against administrator obtained in sister state, claims nevertheless barred in Alabama where not presented within time limit set by this section. Fox v. Woods, 382 So. 2d 1118 (Ala. 1980).

Commencement of civil action is sufficient presentation. — A civil action filed within six months after the grant of letters is a sufficient presentation insofar as the purposes of that action are concerned. Barrett v. Fondren, 262 Ala. 537, 80 So. 2d 243 (1955).

The time is to be computed from the date of the letters testamentary and not from the date of publication of notice. McBroom v. Governor, 6 Port. 32 (1837); Cawthorne v. Weisinger, 6 Ala. 714 (1844).

The use of the word "within" as a limit of time enhances the last day, Rice v. J.H. Beavers & Co., 196 Ala. 355, 71 So. 659 (1916), and therefore where letters were granted on January 18, 1921, the claim was filed within 12 months when filed on January 18, 1922. Davenport v. Witt, 212 Ala. 114, 101 So. 887 (1924). See § 1-1-4 and the notes thereto.

Proof of time of grant of letters. — See Stewart v. L. Lasseter & Co., 4 Ala. App. 665, 59 So. 233 (1912).

When statute of limitations begins to run. — After presentation the statute of limitations does not run against the claim unless and until the claimants are by the administrator, or someone interested in the estate, notified to commence an action thereon. Nicholas v. Sands, 136 Ala. 267, 33 So. 815 (1903). See also § 6-2-9.

As to failure of representative to give notice of appointment not serving to suspend running of this section. See Johnson v. Bain, 17 Ala. App. 71, 81 So. 849 (1919).

A part payment is a fact tending to prove that the claim was presented in due time. Pharis v. Leachman, 20 Ala. 662 (1852).

Knowledge of personal representatives of deceased of a claim against the estate does not dispense with presentment. McDowell v. Jones, 58 Ala. 25 (1877); Borum v. Bell, 132 Ala. 85, 31 So. 454 (1902), overruled on other grounds, Lowery v. Pritchett, 204 Ala. 328, 85 So. 531 (1920). See also Jones v. Lightfoot, 10 Ala. 17 (1846); Boggs v. Branch Bank, 10 Ala. 970 (1847); Pipkin v. Hewlett, 17 Ala. 291 (1850).

Presentation is not necessary to preserve lien existing upon intestate's property, such as bank's lien based on depositor's guaranty of note. King v. Porter, 230 Ala. 112, 160 So. 101 (1935).

County not protected by maxim that no time runs against the state. — In county's action against personal representative of deceased surety on official bond of county treasurer to recover money lost to county by alleged devastavit of treasurer, wherein personal representative pleaded subsection (b) of this section, county was not entitled to protection of maxim "nullum tempus occurrit reipublicae," which means that no time runs against the commonwealth or state. Covington County v. O'Neal, 239 Ala. 322, 195 So. 234 (1939).

Claim against decedent for stockholder's liability in national bank, which was not assessed by comptroller until over one year after letters testamentary had been granted, held not barred by subsection (b) of this section requiring filing of claim within six months of grant of letters, since liability dated from order of comptroller finally determining claim, and since enforcement of such liability under federal statute could not be thwarted by state law. Soper v. Burns, 233 Ala. 492, 172 So. 598 (1937).

A claim against the estate of a stockholder of an insolvent corporation to recover an unpaid subscription for the benefit of creditors is barred under subsection (b) of this section where no action was taken for more than two years after the qualification of the executors and more than a year after authorizing its receiver to take steps for its enforcement. Barth v. Roberts, 297 F. 187 (5th Cir. 1924).

Burden of proof is on creditor to show proper presentment. — The burden of proof was upon the creditor, in each instance, to show due presentation to avert the bar of subsection (b) of this section and § 43-2-352. Barnes v. Bell, 231 Ala. 84, 163 So. 616 (1935).

Whether claim is presented within statutory period is for jury. — In action on note against administrators of deceased maker, whether claim was presented to administrators within statutory period held for jury. White v. Sowell, 231 Ala. 80, 163 So. 609 (1935).

C. Claims Against the Estate.

Claim may be within section though no action has accrued. — A claim may fall within the operation of subsection (b) of this section, though the action thereon has not accrued. It is enough that the claim, the right to demand in the future, certainly exists. McDowell v. Jones, 58 Ala. 25 (1877). See also § 43-2-375. It is only contingent claims — claims which may never accrue — that fall within the provisions postponing the presentation of claims accruing after the grant of letters. Farris v. Stoutz, 78 Ala. 130 (1884), cited in Chamblee v. Proctor, 203 Ala. 61, 82 So. 21 (1919). See also Floyd v. Clayton, 67 Ala. 265 (1880); Stakely v. Executive Comm. of Foreign Missions of Presbyterian Church, 145 Ala. 379, 39 So. 653 (1905). It thus appears that a clear distinction is taken by the supreme court of Alabama between claims which are certain and those which are contingent. Barth v. Roberts, 297 F. 187 (5th Cir. 1924); Moore v. Stephens, 264 Ala. 86, 84 So. 2d 752 (1956).

Claim on demand note signed by decedent and others, on which interest was paid by others after decedent's death, held not a "contingent," but "unconditional," claim barred because not presented within 12 months (now six months) after grant of letters of administration. North Birmingham Am. Bank v. White, 225 Ala. 72, 142 So. 47 (1932).

An heir's equitable claim for contribution or exoneration from personal estate for amount paid on decedent's mortgage to prevent foreclosure, was contingent until he paid off the indebtedness, and claim therefor filed 12 months (now six months) from time of such payment was timely, under subsection (b) of this section, since such statute of nonclaim does not begin to run until accrual of claim. Foster v. Foster, 219 Ala. 70, 121 So. 80 (1929).

A claim for breach of warranty of fee simple title by owner of an estate for life is not an accrued claim within the meaning of subsection (b) of this section requiring presentment. Being contingent it is not within the operation of subsection (b) of this section. Dallas Compress Co. v. Liepold, 205 Ala. 562, 88 So. 681 (1921).

An exception to the requirement of subsection (b) of this section is where the claim is a "contingent" one. Edgehill Corp. v. Hutchens, 282 Ala. 492, 213 So. 2d 225 (1968); Hartford Accident & Indem. Co. v. Kuykendall, 287 Ala. 36, 247 So. 2d 356 (1971).

The legislature, as a matter of public policy, did not intend to include "contingent claims" as being barred by a six-month period from the time of the appointment of an administrator or executor. Edgehill Corp. v. Hutchens, 282 Ala. 492, 213 So. 2d 225 (1968); Hartford Accident & Indem. Co. v. Kuykendall, 287 Ala. 36, 247 So. 2d 356 (1971).

Definitions of contingent claims. — See Edgehill Corp. v. Hutchens, 282 Ala. 492, 213 So. 2d 225 (1968).

Future rentals under a lease fell within the "contingent claims" exception to subsection (b) of this section. Edgehill Corp. v. Hutchens, 282 Ala. 492, 213 So. 2d 225 (1968).

Claim of cestui que trust for whom decedent was trustee. — The requirement of presentation of claims against an estate is inapplicable to the claim of a cestui que trust for whom the decedent was trustee so long as the trust fund or property can be traced and the trust enforced by appropriate proceedings. King v. Coosa Valley Mineral Prods. Co., 283 Ala. 197, 215 So. 2d 275 (1968).

Claim by widow for payment of mortgage due on decedent's property. — Widow who paid out of her own funds the balance due on a mortgage on decedent's property had no rights as a general creditor of the estate because she presented no claim as required by subsection (b) of this section, but she had the purely equitable right arising out of her payment of the mortgage indebtedness for the protection of her interest in the real estate. Gilbreath v. Levi, 270 Ala. 413, 119 So. 2d 210 (1959).

Claim for a homestead by the widow and minor children need not be filed as a claim against the estate. Gilbreath v. Levi, 270 Ala. 413, 119 So. 2d 210 (1959).

Claim based on devastavit of executor must be filed within nonclaim period. — Where a deceased executor or trustee has committed a devastavit with respect to properties held by him as executor or trustee, or where he has commingled the estate properties with his own in such manner that they cannot be specifically identified, a claim based on such acts must be presented within the nonclaim period. Marks v. Brightwell, 269 Ala. 506, 114 So. 2d 268 (1959).

Tort claims. — The use of the words "all claims" in subsection (b) of this section clearly denotes a legislative intention to include claims ex delicto as well as those ex contractu. Moore v. Stephens, 264 Ala. 86, 84 So. 2d 752 (1956).

Subsection (b) of this section is clear and unambiguous and must be construed to mean just what the words import, and the words "all claims against the estate of the decedent" should be construed to include all claims not specifically excepted, and thus to include tort claims. Moore v. Stephens, 264 Ala. 86, 84 So. 2d 752 (1956).

Where person injured in an automobile accident on February 2, 1952 died on September 8, 1952 without filing a claim for injuries sustained in the estate of the deceased driver whose estate was opened in probate court on February 14, 1952, a wrongful death action filed by the administrator of the estate of the injured person on December 8, 1952 was barred by the six months provision of subsection (b) of this section. The contingent claim exception did not apply. Moore v. Stephens, 264 Ala. 86, 84 So. 2d 752 (1956).

Section applies to state. — The legislature clearly intended that subsection (b) of this section should operate to bar the state of Alabama from presenting a claim after the time allowed by statute. State v. Crocker, 38 Ala. App. 306, 83 So. 2d 261 (1955).

Claims represented by foreign judgment are not excepted from subsection (b) of section. — Formerly "debts contracted out of the state" were excepted from the application of subsection (b) of this section. The omission is held to be a clear signification of the legislative will that such debts shall fall within the operation of the section. Jones v. Drewry, 72 Ala. 311 (1882).

Under this authority it was held that though a judgment was secured against the administrator in a sister state, the claims were nevertheless barred in Alabama where not presented within the time limit set by subsection (b) of this section. Reed v. Bloodworth, 200 Ala. 444, 76 So. 376 (1917).

Nor was a judgment against the administrator in the sister state (Illinois) of binding force against the executor under the appointment in the state of Alabama. Reed v. Bloodworth, 200 Ala. 444, 76 So. 376 (1917). See also Johnson v. McKinnon, 129 Ala. 223, 29 So. 696 (1901).

But claims arising after death of decedent are. — Subsection (b) of this section has no application to claims of third persons for services rendered after death of decedent (funeral expenses here). Claims such as these are by legal implication claims against the administrator or executor to the extent of assets of the estate in his hands, and are governed by subsection (a) of this section. Roche Undertaking Co. v. De Bardeleben, 7 Ala. App. 232, 60 So. 1000 (1912).

But a claim for a legacy which vested on the testator's death, though the time of payment was postponed, must be presented according to subsection (b) of this section. Fretwell v. McLemore, 52 Ala. 124 (1875); Foster v. Holland, 56 Ala. 474 (1876).

Contract claim not subject to subsection (b) of section. — A claim, under contract by which woman caring for testator to remain in testator's home or be paid $5,000.00 at election of testator's son out of residuary estate passing to son, was not subject to subsection (b) of this section. Murwin v. Birmingham Trust & Sav. Co., 237 Ala. 100, 185 So. 756 (1939).

Claim within subsection (b) of section. — In the case of Rhodes v. Hannah, 66 Ala. 215 (1880), the administrator of a deceased guardian was cited to make settlement of the guardianship. On the settlement it appeared that the deceased guardian had in his lifetime received an item of money of which he had made no account. This was an amount held to be due by the guardian as a debt, in the absence of a showing that he retained the specific fund, and that because he owed such debt to the ward, it should be presented as such against the estate of the deceased guardian.

In Taylor v. Robinson, 69 Ala. 269 (1881), it was held that a claim of heirs that an administrator has committed a devastavit, upon the death of such administrator, should be presented to his administrator under subsection (b) of this section. Cook v. Castleberry, 233 Ala. 650, 173 So. 1 (1911).

Claim by minority stockholders not barred. — A minority stockholders' complaint, alleging that assets of corporation were fraudulently diverted by directors prior to death of one director, did not on its face show that the claim as against estate of deceased director and his personal representative and trustee was barred by subsection (b) of this section, notwithstanding failure to allege that claim was filed in office of judge of probate of county in which estate was being administered. Holloway v. Osteograf Co., 240 Ala. 507, 200 So. 197 (1941).

§ 43-2-351. Same — Exception as to minors or persons of unsound mind.

The provisions of subsection (b) of section 43-2-350 do not apply to minors or persons of unsound mind who have no legal guardian at the time of the grant of letters testamentary or of administration; but such minors and persons of unsound mind are allowed six months after the appointment of a guardian, or, if none be appointed, six months after the removal of their respective disabilities, in which to present their claims. (Code 1852, § 1884; Code 1867, § 2240; Code 1876, § 2598; Code 1886, § 2082; Code 1896, § 131; Code 1907, § 2591; Code 1923, § 5816; Code 1940, T. 61, § 212.)

This section is a flaring notice, and indeed an express declaration, to the administrator that he is liable for all the claims herein mentioned though not presented within 12 months (now six months) from the grant of letters. Daniell v. Baldwin, 148 Ala. 292, 40 So. 421 (1906).

Claims under it remain debts throughout extended period. — The claim, the presentation of which is extended by this section, is placed on the same footing throughout the extended period as the claim of persons sui juris within the presentation period of 12 months (now six months). Throughout the extended period they constitute debts of the estate for which the assets are liable for payment. Daniell v. Baldwin, 148 Ala. 292, 40 So. 421 (1906).

Liability of administrator. — Presentation of a claim by a minor within 12 months (now six months) after removal of disability of nonage satisfies this section, and is entitled to be paid. And it is no defense to administrator's liability that, though he had sufficient assets to pay the claim, he had distributed the same in good faith without notice of the claim. Daniell v. Baldwin, 148 Ala. 292, 40 So. 421 (1906).

Nor will the voluntary settlement and distribution of assets discharge administrator from liability of a claim of a minor whose claim was not required to be presented before fixed settlement. Whetstone v. McQueen, 137 Ala. 301, 34 So. 229 (1903).

Sureties right of subrogation. — Where the administrator, without knowledge of a minor's claim, settled the estate prior to time allowed such minor for presenting his claim, and the surety of the administrator paid the claim upon which judgment had been secured against the administrator and the surety, such surety was entitled to be subrogated to the right of the administrator against the distributee. Baldwin v. Alexander, 145 Ala. 186, 40 So. 391 (1906).

Cited in Citizens' Mut. Ins. Co. v. Lott, 45 Ala. 185 (1871); Smith v. Fellows, 58 Ala. 467 (1877); Taylor v. Robinson, 69 Ala. 269 (1881); Massey v. Modawell, 73 Ala. 421 (1882); Burford v. Steele, 80 Ala. 147 (1885); McDowell v. Brantley, 80 Ala. 173 (1885); First Nat'l Bank v. Chichester, 352 So. 2d 1371 (Ala. Civ. App. 1977).

§ 43-2-352. Verification of claims.

The presentation must be made by filing a verified claim, or a verified statement thereof, in the office of the judge of probate in which letters are granted, and the same must be docketed with a note of the date of such presentation; and, if required, a statement must be given by such judge, showing the date of presentation. Every such claim or statement thereof so presented must be verified by the oath of the claimant or some person having knowledge of the correctness thereof, and that the amount claimed is justly due, or to become due, after allowing all proper credits. Any defect or insufficiency in the affidavit may be supplied by amendment at any time. All claims not presented within six months from the granting of letters testamentary or letters of administration shall be forever barred, and the payment or allowance thereof is prohibited. But this section shall not apply to claims of executors or administrators to compensation for their services as such, nor to sums properly disbursed by them in the course of administration. (Code 1852, § 1885; Code 1867, § 2241; Code 1876, § 2599; Code 1886, § 2083; Code 1896, § 133; Code 1907, § 2593; Code 1923, § 5818; Acts 1931, No. 717, p. 837; Code 1940, T. 61, § 214.)

I. General Consideration.
II. Presentment of Claim.
    A. In General.
    B. Filing.
    C. Verification.
III. Sufficiency of Statement of Claim.

I. GENERAL CONSIDERATION.

History of section. — Prior to the 1931 amendment this section provided that presentation of claims could be made to the executor or administrator. For cases construing this provision, see Hunley v. Shuford, 11 Ala. 203 (1847); Flinn v. Shackleford, 42 Ala. 202 (1868); Carrington v. Odom, 124 Ala. 529, 27 So. 510 (1900); Brannan v. Sherry, 195 Ala. 272, 71 So. 106 (1916).

Methods of presentation enumerated. — It will be seen from this section that claims may be presented in one of three ways: (1) by presenting the claim, duly verified, personally to the administrator or the executor (now omitted by the 1931 amendment). Peevey v. Farmers' & Merchants' Nat'l Bank, 132 Ala. 82, 31 So. 466 (1902). (2) By "filing" the claim, duly verified in the office of the judge of probate. Or (3) by filing a statement of the claim, duly verified, in the office of the judge of probate. Floyd v. Clayton, 67 Ala. 265 (1880). See also Brannan v. Sherry, 195 Ala. 272, 71 So. 106 (1916); Smith v. Nixon, 205 Ala. 223, 87 So. 326 (1921).

This section is a part of the "procedural law." First Nat'l Bank v. Henderson, 243 Ala. 636, 11 So. 2d 366 (1942).

Claims reported under section 43-2-702 not necessarily included. — Claims to be reported by administrator under § 43-2-702, are not necessarily claims which should be presented under this section. Gilbreath v. Levi, 270 Ala. 413, 119 So. 2d 210 (1959).

Claim of cestui que trust for whom decedent was trustee. — The requirement of presentation of claims against an estate is inapplicable to the claim of a cestui que trust for whom the decedent was trustee so long as the trust fund or property can be traced and the trust enforced by appropriate proceedings. King v. Coosa Valley Mineral Prods. Co., 283 Ala. 197, 215 So. 2d 275 (1968).

Noncompliance as affecting final settlement. — If at the end of 12 months (now six months) after the grant of letters, the estate of the intestate is ready for final settlement in all other respects, an outstanding claim not verified as required by this section furnishes sufficient reason for delay. Chamblee v. Proctor, 203 Ala. 61, 82 So. 21 (1919).

Though a mortgage is unaffected by a final settlement made prior to date when it is due, the debt to be preserved as a charge against the estate must be filed as herein required. Chamblee v. Proctor, 203 Ala. 61, 82 So. 21 (1919).

Claims upon which civil action brought are not excluded. — There is nothing in this section which excludes demands on which a civil action has been brought. Moss v. Mosley, 148 Ala. 168, 41 So. 1012 (1906).

Funeral expenses not included. — Claim of administratrix for funeral expenses of decedent is not required to be presented under this section, but such claims fall within the claim indicated in subsection (a) of § 43-2-350. This question was definitely declared in Foster v. Foster, 219 Ala. 70, 121 So. 80 (1929), and in Roche Undertaking Co. v. De Bardeleben, 7 Ala. App. 232, 60 So. 1000 (1912). Canada v. Canada, 243 Ala. 109, 8 So. 2d 846 (1942).

Where a mentally disturbed airman was negligently returned to duty and permitted to obtain a pistol with which he killed his former wife, it was held in an action against the United States that the district court erred in excluding the bill for the wife's funeral expenses on the ground that no claim had been filed against the estate and the time for filing claims had expired. Claims for funeral expenses of the decedent are not barred by the Alabama statute of nonclaims. Underwood v. United States, 356 F.2d 92 (5th Cir. 1966).

Allegation of noncompliance. — Where, on appeal, it is alleged in the brief that this section has not been complied with, the grounds for the assertion must be stated. Moore v. Robinson, 214 Ala. 412, 108 So. 233 (1926).

Burden of proof. — The person bringing a civil action on a claim against a decedent has the burden of proving presentation within the allowed time. W.L. Weller & Sons v. Rensford, 185 Ala. 333, 64 So. 366 (1914). And in one of the ways provided by this section. Brannan v. Sherry, 195 Ala. 272, 71 So. 106 (1916).

Question for jury. — Whether executors were liable for services rendered deceased by plaintiff held for jury. Hunt v. Murdock, 229 Ala. 277, 156 So. 841 (1934).

Cited in Dennis v. Coker, 34 Ala. 611 (1859); Clark v. Washington, 44 Ala. 291 (1870); Clement v. Nelson, 46 Ala. 634 (1871); Grace v. Martin, 47 Ala. 135 (1872); Brewer & Co. v. Moseley, 49 Ala. 79 (1873); Walker v. Wigginton, 50 Ala. 579 (1874); Hatchett v. Curbow, 59 Ala. 516 (1877); Agnew v. Walden, 95 Ala. 108, 10 So. 224 (1891); Rayburn v. Rayburn, 130 Ala. 217, 30 So. 365 (1901); Gillespie v. Campbell, 149 Ala. 193, 43 So. 28 (1907); Watson v. Hamilton, 210 Ala. 577, 98 So. 784 (1923); McClure v. Pettyjohn, 226 Ala. 156, 145 So. 478 (1932); Barnes v. Bell, 231 Ala. 84, 163 So. 616 (1935); Terry v. Gresham, 254 Ala. 349, 48 So. 2d 437 (1950); McElhaney v. Singleton, 270 Ala. 162, 117 So. 2d 375 (1960); First Nat'l Bank v. Chichester, 352 So. 2d 1371 (Ala. 1977).

II. PRESENTMENT OF CLAIM.

A. In General.

It is not necessary to repeat presentation on a change in the administration. Floyd v. Clayton, 67 Ala. 265 (1880).

Commencement of an action operates as presentment. — Commencement of an action within the statutory period, and its continued prosecution, operates as a presentment of the claim on which the action is founded. Barrett v. Fondren, 262 Ala. 537, 80 So. 2d 243 (1955).

Claim based on devastavit of executor must be filed within nonclaim period. — Where a deceased executor or trustee has committed a devastavit with respect to properties held by him as executor or trustee, or where he has commingled the estate properties with his own in such manner that they cannot be specifically identified, a claim based on such acts must be presented within the nonclaim period. Marks v. Brightwell, 269 Ala. 506, 114 So. 2d 268 (1959).

Heir or distributee may waive presentation of claims as provided by this section. Rikard v. O'Reilly, 232 Ala. 667, 169 So. 320 (1936).

Effect of statute changing mode of presenting claim. — Due presentation of claim against decedent's estate under statute then in force obviated necessity of doing anything further in matter of its presentation under subsequent statute changing mode of presenting such claims. White v. Long, 234 Ala. 610, 176 So. 297 (1937). See also White v. Sowell, 231 Ala. 80, 163 So. 609 (1935); White v. Blair, 234 Ala. 119, 173 So. 493 (1937).

Claim could not be amended after time for presentment so as to include attorney's fees. Burns v. Burns, 228 Ala. 61, 152 So. 48 (1933).

Admissibility of evidence to disprove presentation. — Conversations of deceased with administrator or statements by him to administrator in absence of plaintiff in action against administrator on note of deceased held not admissible to rebut evidence of presentation of claim, alleged to have been made at a different time and place. White v. Blair, 234 Ala. 119, 173 So. 493 (1937).

Evidence in action against administrators on intestate's note held sufficient to present jury question as to due presentation of claim against estate on such note. White v. Long, 234 Ala. 610, 176 So. 297 (1937).

B. Filing.

Best evidence as to "filing". — The docket entry, when made, is the best evidence of the filing of the claim or a statement thereof. And when sufficiently full it suffices to give the required information as to the character of the claim. The evidence so furnished is attended by at least a prima facie presumption of correctness. Kornegay v. Mayer, 135 Ala. 141, 33 So. 36 (1902); Roberts v. Grayson, 233 Ala. 658, 173 So. 38 (1937).

Sufficiency of filing. — Where a claim evidenced by note was presented at the probate office within the prescribed time, and an entry made on the record describing the claim and the note, though neither the note nor a copy was filed there, this was a sufficient compliance with this section. Agnew v. Walden, 84 Ala. 502, 4 So. 672 (1888); Agnew v. Walden, 95 Ala. 108, 10 So. 224 (1891). See also Halfman v. Ellison, 51 Ala. 543 (1874); Smith v. Fellows, 58 Ala. 467 (1877); Bibb v. Mitchell, 58 Ala. 657 (1877).

Filing of a claim against decedent's estate based on a note, which claim failed to state that deceased had made an express promise to pay the note after obtaining a discharge in bankruptcy, was held a substantial compliance with this section and sufficient to put administratrix on inquiry. First Nat'l Bank v. Henderson, 243 Ala. 636, 11 So. 2d 366 (1942).

Filing of claim against decedent's estate with filing notations showing claim was filed in "probate court" held not defective for failure of notation to recite that claim was filed in office of probate judge, where claim was filed by probate judge, who signed notation and claim remained on file in judge's office. Roberts v. Grayson, 233 Ala. 658, 173 So. 38 (1937).

In action on note against endorser's executors, pleadings alleging a failure to file verified claim within six months from date of issuance of letters testamentary were not defective because they alleged a failure to file verified claim or statement in probate court instead of in office of judge of probate as required by this section. Esslinger v. Spragins, 236 Ala. 508, 183 So. 401 (1938).

Filing of claim against decedent's estate as claim against estate of "Mrs. J. C. Jones," which name contained initials of decedent's husband rather than decedent's Christian name, held to comply with this section, as sufficient to give notice stimulating inquiry, especially where executrix was decedent's daughter. Roberts v. Grayson, 233 Ala. 658, 173 So. 38 (1937).

Filing claim in court without filing in office of probate judge not a valid presentation. — There is no authority, statutory or otherwise, for the effectuation of a valid presentation, to avert the bar of this section of a claim against a decedent's estate, by simply filing it, however complete the statement, in the court without having filed the claim in the office of the judge of probate as required by this section. W.L. Weller & Sons v. Rensford, 185 Ala. 333, 64 So. 366 (1914); Smith v. Nixon, 205 Ala. 223, 87 So. 326 (1921); Barnes v. Bell, 231 Ala. 84, 163 So. 616 (1935).

C. Verification.

The affidavit must state that the affiant "has knowledge of the correctness of the claims." Pickle v. Ezzell, 27 Ala. 623 (1855).

And an affidavit that an account against the estate is correct according to the creditor's best knowledge and belief is insufficient. Pickle v. Ezzell, 27 Ala. 623 (1855); Lay v. Clark, 31 Ala. 409 (1858); Dennis v. Coker, 34 Ala. 611 (1859).

Unless excepted to, the failure to verify will not defeat claim. — The omission to verify is not ground for rejecting the claim unless an exception to it is filed within the time required. Hollinger v. Holly, 8 Ala. 454 (1845).

Claim on note against estate presented to administrators within 12 months (now six months) of granting of letters of administration held not barred by failure to verify claim. White v. Sowell, 231 Ala. 80, 163 So. 609 (1935).

III. SUFFICIENCY OF STATEMENT OF CLAIM.

Necessary requisites for sufficient presentation. — To constitute a sufficient presentation, the nature and amount of the claims must be brought to the attention of the personal representative by someone authorized in law or fact to make the presentation, and the representative must be notified, expressly or impliedly, that the estate is looked to for payment. Smith v. Fellows, 58 Ala. 467 (1877). See also Posey v. Decatur Bank, 12 Ala. 802 (1848); Burns v. Burns, 228 Ala. 61, 152 So. 48 (1933); White v. Blair, 234 Ala. 119, 173 So. 493 (1937); White v. Long, 234 Ala. 610, 176 So. 297 (1937).

But the term "impliedly" used in Smith v. Fellows, 58 Ala. 467 (1877), does not mean that there may be an effective presentation as the result of implication. W.L. Weller & Sons v. Rensford, 185 Ala. 333, 64 So. 366 (1914), holding insufficient as a presentation the filing of a motion to be allowed to intervene in an action against an administrator where the motion is denied.

In a very early case (Bigger v. Hutchings, 2 Stew. 445 (1830)) it was said that the original bond, note or contract on which the debt accrued, or at least an abstract or copy, should be presented as evidence of the claim, and if the claim arose on an open account, unliquidated demand, verbal contract or legal liability, it should be reduced to writing, and be so presented.

Technical accuracy or certainty of description essential in pleadings need not be observed in statement of claim against estate, but statement must of itself inform personal representative of nature, character and amount of liability which statement imports, and must distinguish claim with reasonable certainty from all similar claims. Roberts v. Grayson, 233 Ala. 658, 173 So. 38 (1937); Merchants Nat'l Bank v. Cotnam, 250 Ala. 316, 34 So. 2d 122 (1948).

Thus, mere knowledge of personal representative as to claim against estate does not suffice to conform with this section, but there must be some formality of presentation. Roberts v. Grayson, 233 Ala. 658, 173 So. 38 (1937).

Claim for attorney's fees. — Fact that attorney's fees have accrued on note when claim is presented against estate should be brought to attention of administrator at that time so he can be advised as to amount claimed. White v. Blair, 234 Ala. 119, 173 So. 493 (1937).

Amendment after six months. — The fact that this section authorizes amendments to the affidavit is not conclusive that some other sort of amendment may not be made to a claim after six months when the amendment only makes certain or accurate some descriptive features of it. Merchants Nat'l Bank v. Cotnam, 250 Ala. 316, 34 So. 2d 122 (1948).

But where a claim as filed is fatally defective in substance so as not to be sufficient when tested by the rule which requires it to inform the administrator of its nature and amount and to distinguish itself from other such claims, it cannot be vitalized by an amendment after six months. Merchants Nat'l Bank v. Cotnam, 250 Ala. 316, 34 So. 2d 122 (1948).

Amendment of affidavit not too late. — Where complaint filed by judgment creditor in proceeding to remove administration of estate from probate court to circuit court and for discovery and an accounting showed that claim of judgment creditor against decedent's estate as originally filed in probate court and later made basis of judgment against personal representatives was not supported by sufficient affidavit as required by this section, and demurrers (now motions to dismiss) to the original complaint raising point were sustained, amendment of affidavit in probate court and of the complaint was held properly allowed as against contention that the amendment came too late. Moebes v. Kay, 241 Ala. 294, 2 So. 2d 754 (1941).

Claim for services rendered under agreement providing for share in decedent's estate. — Where a claim specifically stated the amount of it, and that it was due by an agreement with deceased that the promisee was to receive a sum equal to one fifth of the value of his estate, and that the promisee had performed her part of the agreement and that it was for services rendered, the claim was held to be sufficient although it did not give the date of the agreement, the substance of its terms, definitely when it was payable nor the nature of the services rendered. Merchants Nat'l Bank v. Cotnam, 250 Ala. 316, 34 So. 2d 122 (1948).

Although such claim did not state definitely when it was payable, the court held that the use of the word "estate" could reasonably be construed to mean what the valuation was at the time of the promisor's death. Merchants Nat'l Bank v. Cotnam, 250 Ala. 316, 34 So. 2d 122 (1948).

Collateral references. — 34 C.J.S., Executors & Administrators, §§ 394-435.

31 Am. Jur. 2d, Executors & Administrators, §§ 297-308.

Waiver of mortgage or other lien by filing claim as an unsecured one. 2 ALR 1132.

Necessity of presenting claim to executor or administrator before bringing suit. 34 ALR 362.

Presentation of claim as condition precedent to action on contingent claim. 34 ALR 372.

Presentation of claim for funeral expenses to executor or administrator. 34 ALR 375, 120 ALR 275.

Executor's or administrator's waiver of presentation of claim against estate before action brought thereon. 34 ALR 393.

Vendor under executory contract for sale of land as entitled to claim as creditor of the estate of vendee. 35 ALR 927.

Effect of recovery of judgment on unfiled or abandoned claim as to expiration of time allowed for filing claims. 60 ALR 736.

Necessity of presenting, probating, or prosecuting claims for allowance as affected by provision of will directing payment of debt. 65 ALR 861.

Sufficiency of notice of claim against decedent's estate. 74 ALR 368.

Amendment of statement of claim against decedent's estate, or verification thereof. 74 ALR 400, 402.

Nonclaim statute as applied to real estate mortgage or mortgage debt. 78 ALR 1126.

Effect of filing claim for mortgage on real estate against estate of deceased mortgagor. 78 ALR 1148.

Sufficiency of presentation of claim for mortgage on real estate. 78 ALR 1153.

Mortgage on real estate not yet due; contingency of claim. 78 ALR 1159.

Necessity of filing claim under Workmen's Compensation Act against estate of deceased employer. 94 ALR 889.

Guaranty, suretyship or endorsement, claim on decedent's contract of, as contingent. 94 ALR 1155.

Applicability of statute of nonclaim as between surviving partner and estate of deceased partner. 96 ALR 449, 157 ALR 1114.

Necessity of presenting claim against decedent's estate as affected by executor's or administrator's personal duty or obligation to claimant. 103 ALR 337.

Claims for taxes as within contemplation of statute requiring presentation of claims. 109 ALR 1370.

Condition precedent to suit for specific performance of contract to make will in favor of another or to will the latter a specified sum or property, presentation of same against decedent's estate as. 113 ALR 1070.

Effect of statement of claim against decedent's estate regarding debt apparently barred by statute of limitations. 119 ALR 426.

Claims for expenses of last sickness as within statute requiring presentation of claims against decedent's estate. 120 ALR 275.

Filing claim against estate of decedent as affecting or precluding other remedies against the estate. 120 ALR 1225.

Time for filing claim based on promise not to make a will. 32 ALR2d 380.

Necessity of compliance with nonclaim statute before bringing suit in replevin against personal representative. 42 ALR2d 443.

Amendment of claim against decedent's estate after expiration of time for filing claims. 56 ALR2d 627.

Necessity of presenting spouse's claim under separation agreement to personal representative of other spouse's estate. 58 ALR2d 1283.

Sufficiency of presentation of claim under statute dealing with existing intestate administration, upon discovery of will. 65 ALR2d 1207.

Tort claim as within nonclaim statutes. 22 ALR3d 493.

Presentation of claim to executor or administrator as prerequisite of its availability as counterclaim or setoff. 36 ALR3d 693.

§ 43-2-353. Revival of pending action considered as presentation.

The revival of any action pending against any person at the time of his death, which by law survives against his personal representative, by notice served on the executor or administrator within six months after the grant of letters, shall be considered as a presentation of the claim on which the action is founded. (Code 1852, § 1886; Code 1867, § 2242; Code 1876, § 2600; Code 1886, § 2084; Code 1896, § 134; Code 1907, § 2594; Code 1923, § 5819; Acts 1931, No. 719, p. 838; Code 1940, T. 61, § 215.)

Cited in Minor v. Thomasson, 236 Ala. 247, 182 So. 16 (1938); Penney v. Speake, 256 Ala. 359, 54 So. 2d 709 (1951); Barrett v. Fondren, 262 Ala. 537, 80 So. 2d 243 (1955).

§ 43-2-354. Notice and hearing; judgment; costs; appeals.

The personal representative of the estate of a decedent may give notice in writing to the claimant or anyone having a beneficial interest in a claim against the estate that such claim is disputed in whole or in part; if in part, specifying the part disputed. Thereupon the judge of the court having jurisdiction of the administration of the estate shall, on written application of either the personal representative or the claimant, hear and pass on the validity of such claim, or part thereof, first giving 10 days' notice of such hearing to the interested parties. If the claimant in such proceeding shall fail to recover upon the disputed part of such claim, he shall be taxed with the costs thereof. This section shall not apply to claims against estates declared insolvent. If the judgment on any such claim is rendered by a probate court, either party may, within 30 days after the rendition of such judgment, appeal to the circuit court of the county in which the administration of said estate is pending, and the trial of the validity of said claim in said circuit court shall be de novo, and upon demand of either party, filed in the circuit court within 30 days from the taking of said appeal, shall be tried by a jury. If the administration of an estate in which a claim is disputed is pending in the circuit court, the trial of the validity of said claim shall be by jury upon demand of either party filed within 30 days after written notice that the claim is disputed. In any event either party may appeal to the supreme court or court of civil appeals, as the case may be, from the judgment of the circuit court, such appeal to be taken within 42 days and as other appeals are taken. (Code 1896, § 2818; Code 1907, § 4857; Code 1923, § 8971; Acts 1939, No. 517, p. 806; Code 1940, T. 61, § 216; Acts 1943, No. 324, p. 308.)

Cross references. — See notes to § 6-2-9.

Constitutionality of former provisions. — See Tillery v. Commercial Nat'l Bank, 241 Ala. 653, 4 So. 2d 125 (1941); State v. Elliott, 246 Ala. 439, 21 So. 2d 310, appeal dismissed, 246 Ala. 442, 21 So. 2d 312 (1945).

Purpose and procedure. — A proceeding under this section does not lead to a moneyed judgment on which execution may issue. Its only purpose is to fix the rights of parties to a fund in trust, being administered in that court, so as to determine who is entitled to it on distribution. The procedure is similar to that relating to banks in liquidation. Tillery v. Commercial Nat'l Bank, 241 Ala. 653, 4 So. 2d 125 (1941); Ex parte Zepernick, 259 Ala. 493, 66 So. 2d 757 (1953); Coon v. Coon, 264 Ala. 127, 85 So. 2d 430 (1955).

The jurisdiction conferred by this section was never intended to be exclusive of the jurisdiction expressly conferred on the circuit court by the Constitution and by § 12-11-30. At most this section undertakes to confer partial concurrent jurisdiction to hear and determine the validity of a claim properly filed in the probate court if the required conditions are met. Ex parte Zepernick, 259 Ala. 493, 66 So. 2d 757 (1953).

While this section confers a partial concurrent jurisdiction on probate courts to determine the validity of a claim properly filed in the probate court, it does not abrogate the jurisdiction of circuit courts to determine the validity of such claims, the circuit court's jurisdiction being conferred by § 143 of the Constitution and by § 12-11-30. Norton v. Liddell, 280 Ala. 353, 194 So. 2d 514 (1967).

And is not available when an action is pending. — The remedy provided by this section is not available to the personal representative when an action is pending against him on the claim. Ex parte Zepernick, 259 Ala. 493, 66 So. 2d 757 (1953).

Even if the personal representative had taken the necessary steps to invoke the jurisdiction of the probate court prior to the filing of the action in the circuit court, the circuit court would nevertheless have jurisdiction of the subject matter. And the pendency of the prior action would have to be raised in a proper manner because of the pendency of the prior action. Ex parte Zepernick, 259 Ala. 493, 66 So. 2d 757 (1953).

Section applies where interested party objects to claim. — Where an interested party may perhaps object to a claim in a court in which an administration is pending, when its allowance would affect his financial standing in the estate, this section, though it names only the personal representative as the party who may object, was intended to apply to all such hearings though filed by some other interested person. In the instant case, the administrator objected and also an interested person objected. A different rule was not intended to apply to them separately. Willingham v. Starnes, 247 Ala. 30, 22 So. 2d 424 (1945).

Though this section names only the personal representative as the party who may object, it was intended to apply to all such hearings though filed by some other interested person. MacLaurin v. Kilgore, 272 Ala. 563, 133 So. 2d 252 (1961).

Parties can convert proceeding into common-law action. — Although a proceeding under this section is for the purpose of declaring a status, the parties with the consent of the court can convert it into a common-law action and have a personal judgment accordingly entered. Merchants Nat'l Bank v. Cotnam, 250 Ala. 316, 34 So. 2d 122 (1948).

But section does not authorize a money judgment. — The determination of a contest of claim authorized by this section does not lead to the rendition of a money judgment, and the procedure prescribed by this section was not intended as a substitute for the statutory method of a revivor of judgments by scire facias (now motion or other appropriate action) or the common-law civil action, which leads to the entry of such money judgment. Gant v. Gilmer, 245 Ala. 686, 18 So. 2d 542 (1944); Merchants Nat'l Bank v. Cotnam, 250 Ala. 316, 34 So. 2d 122 (1948).

This section was not intended as a substitute for a civil action which might lead to the entry of a moneyed judgment. Dodd v. Lovett, 282 Ala. 383, 211 So. 2d 799 (1968).

The determination of a contest of claim filed against an estate, as provided in this section, does not lead to a moneyed judgment. Dodd v. Lovett, 282 Ala. 383, 211 So. 2d 799 (1968).

A proceeding under this section, in a contest of a claim, is only to fix the rights to a fund in trust being administered so as to determine who is entitled to it on distribution. Such proceeding does not and cannot properly lead to a

moneyed judgment. White v. Hilbish, 282 Ala. 498, 213 So. 2d 230 (1968).

The determination of a contest or claim filed against an estate as authorized by this section does not ordinarily lead to a moneyed judgment. Humphrey v. Boschung, 287 Ala. 600, 253 So. 2d 769 (1971).

Nature of judgment. — A judgment rendered on a disputed claim against an estate in effect is a decree in the nature of a declaratory judgment to determine the validity of the claim. Coon v. Coon, 264 Ala. 127, 85 So. 2d 430 (1955).

A proceeding under this section is not intended to lead to a personal judgment, but is in the nature of a declaratory judgment to determine the validity of the claim which has been filed against the estate. Merchants Nat'l Bank v. Cotnam, 250 Ala. 316, 34 So. 2d 122 (1948); Cotnam v. Commissioner, 263 F.2d 119 (5th Cir. 1959).

This section prescribes the method of testing the validity of claims filed against the estates of decedents. Hicks v. Ward, 240 Ala. 236, 198 So. 705 (1940).

It has no application to insolvent estates. Elliott v. First Nat'l Bank, 248 Ala. 360, 27 So. 2d 623 (1946).

Nor does it apply to claim of heir to estate. — Where decedent's mother claimed decedent's entire estate because his wife had murdered him and he was survived only by his widow and his mother, such claim is not within the meaning of this section, and as the mother's rights are as an heir this section has no application. Ex parte Floyd, 250 Ala. 154, 33 So. 2d 340 (1947).

It is not material that the objection and notice as provided in this section was not literally observed. Willingham v. Starnes, 247 Ala. 30, 22 So. 2d 424 (1945).

Jurisdiction conferred on judge. — This section conferred jurisdiction on the judge of probate, or of a circuit court, to pass on the validity of the claim on the written application of the personal representative or claimant. This merely confers a right similar to that which applied to proceedings for the administration of trusts and receiverships and the liquidation of banks. Tillery v. Commercial Nat'l Bank, 241 Ala. 653, 4 So. 2d 125 (1941).

Matter of an accounting. — Where administrators alleged that claimants were indebted to estate on note secured by mortgage and on interest note, and that administrators could not ascertain, without an accounting, exact amount of balance due on notes over amount due on claims, and administrators sought reference to register and other relief, matter of accounting was not associated or connected with an independent equity so as to entitle administrators to equitable relief. Sumner v. Caldwell, 244 Ala. 149, 12 So. 2d 391 (1943).

Where claimants were indebted to estate on mortgage note. — In an action by administrators of estate which was in probate for adjudication of validity of separate claims filed by husband and wife against estate for services rendered decedent, wherein administrators alleged that claimants were indebted to estate on note secured by mortgage and on interest note, evidence was held to sustain trial court's conclusion as to amount due on mortgage and amount due on claims. Sumner v. Caldwell, 244 Ala. 149, 12 So. 2d 391 (1943).

Recovery precluded on "open account". — An account showing dates of labor done for and materials furnished to deceased in repairing buildings and the dates of credits was held an "open account," and limitation statute precluded recovery from deceased's executor for labor done or materials furnished more than three years before action on claim against the estate was brought. Ratliff v. Silvey, 30 Ala. App. 228, 3 So. 2d 328 (1941).

This section did not apply to an appeal from a judgment for the sale of land by an administrator to pay debts, though the judgment provided for payments of a claim out of the proceeds from the sale. Coon v. Coon, 264 Ala. 127, 85 So. 2d 430 (1955).

Validity of widow's claim as to exemptions. — The motion by administrator in circuit court, to which administration of an estate had been removed, for determination of validity of widow's claim as to exemptions was held not authorized by this section. Hicks v. Ward, 240 Ala. 236, 198 So. 705 (1940).

Section guarantees trial by jury. — From the language and history of the 1943 amendment to this section it is a fair conclusion that the legislature intended to guarantee an opportunity for trial by jury in proceedings under this section to determine validity of disputed claims against a solvent estate. Wilkerson v. Hagan, 265 Ala. 515, 92 So. 2d 901 (1957).

Final judgment. — The trial court's judgment disallowing a claim in its entirety was such a final judgment as would support an appeal. Harrison v. Harrison, 261 Ala. 648, 75 So. 2d 620 (1954).

No appeal directly to supreme court from judgment of probate court. — Sections 12-22-20 and 12-22-21, authorizing appeals either to supreme court or circuit court from final judgments, orders and decrees of probate court, do not apply to appeals from a judgment of probate court relating to validity of disputed claim in view of this section authorizing direct appeal only to circuit court in such cases. State v. Elliott, 246 Ala. 439, 21 So. 2d 310, appeal dismissed, 246 Ala. 442, 21 So. 2d 312 (1945).

But appeal lies to supreme court from judgment of circuit court to which administration has been removed. Schmale v. Bolte, 255 Ala. 115, 50 So. 2d 262 (1951).

Security for costs required upon appeal to circuit court. — The language and history of the 1943 amendment disclose a legislative intent to require any person appealing from the probate court to the circuit court to furnish security for costs as provided by § 12-22-25. Wilkerson v. Hagan, 265 Ala. 515, 92 So. 2d 901 (1957).

Appeal from probate court to circuit court was properly dismissed where security for costs was not furnished within 30 days from rendition of judgment in probate court. Wilkerson v. Hagan, 265 Ala. 515, 92 So. 2d 901 (1957).

The appealing party is required to give security for costs on appeal to the circuit court from the allowance of a claim against the estate. Culp v. Godwin, 295 Ala. 316, 329 So. 2d 88 (1976).

Amendment of defective security for costs. — This section gives the right of appeal "within 30 days after the rendition of such judgment" in the probate court, the appeal being "to the circuit court of the county in which the administration of said estate is pending." There is no statute which authorizes the amendment of a defective security for costs of appeal in such cases, after expiration of the 30-day period for taking an appeal. The Alabama cases approving the amendment of defective security for costs seem to be based on constitutional or statutory provisions authorizing such amendments. Clary v. Cassels, 258 Ala. 183, 61 So. 2d 692 (1952).

Cited in Meager v. Meager, 229 Ala. 680, 159 So. 216 (1934); Dudley v. Whatley, 244 Ala. 508, 14 So. 2d 141 (1943); Gilmer v. Gant, 246 Ala. 671, 22 So. 2d 176 (1945); Hyde v. Starnes, 247 Ala. 26, 22 So. 2d 421 (1945); Barnett v. Crumpton, 247 Ala. 572, 25 So. 2d 414 (1946); Webb v. Webb, 250 Ala. 194, 33 So. 2d 909 (1948); Bolte v. Schmale, 258 Ala. 373, 62 So. 2d 797 (1952); Brown v. First Nat'l Bank, 261 Ala. 565, 75 So. 2d 141 (1954); Barrett v. Fondren, 262 Ala. 537, 80 So. 2d 243 (1955); Ex parte Estes, 264 Ala. 20, 84 So. 2d 765 (1956); Evans v. Guy, 268 Ala. 107, 105 So. 2d 61 (1958); Arant v. Board of Adjustment, 271 Ala. 600, 126 So. 2d 100 (1960); Shirley v. McNeal, 272 Ala. 696, 133 So. 2d 873 (1961); Jacks v. Sullinger, 284 Ala. 223, 224 So. 2d 583 (1969); Austin v. Austin, 364 So. 2d 301 (Ala. 1978).

Collateral references. — 34 C.J.S., Executors & Administrators, §§ 436-455.

Division 2.

Payment and Preference.

Collateral references. — 34 C.J.S., Executors & Administrators, §§ 457-481.

31 Am. Jur. 2d, Executors & Administrators, §§ 351-357.

Liability to heirs, devisees, legatees, or distributees of executor or administrator or his bond in respect of invalid sale of property of the estate. 106 ALR 429.

Statutory provisions forbidding sale of homestead for purpose of paying decedent's debts or legacies. 116 ALR 85.

Mortgage or other encumbrance as affecting duty of executor or administrator of insolvent estate to sell real estate to pay debts, or duty of probate court to order such sale. 116 ALR 910.

Right or duty of executor or administrator to contest order directing sale of real estate for payment of debt. 126 ALR 903.

Rights and remedies of purchaser at sale by personal representative where sale is void or set aside because proceedings are imperfect or irregular, or where description of property is defective. 142 ALR 310.

§ 43-2-370. Property charged with payment of debts.

All the property of the decedent, except as otherwise provided, is charged with the payment of his debts, and, if necessary, may be sold for that purpose. (Code 1852, § 1737; Code 1867, § 2060; Code 1876, § 2429; Code 1886, § 2078; Code 1896, § 125; Code 1907, § 2596; Code 1923, § 5821; Code 1940, T. 61, § 217.)

Editor's note. — This section has been repeatedly cited in the cases which have been decided under § 43-2-410 (providing for sale of personalty) and § 43-2-441 (authorizing the sale of land where there is a will). For this reason, the practitioner is especially urged to refer to those sections.

Common-law rule as to realty. — At common law the real estate was never subject to payment of the debts of the decedent. But this rule has been changed by this section. Baldwin v. Alexander, 145 Ala. 186, 40 So. 391 (1906).

This section applies only to property in Alabama, and does not control property located elsewhere, or subject realty in another state to lien for existing debt of decedent in such other state. Murphree v. Starrett, 231 Ala. 123, 163 So. 647 (1935).

A legacy does not prevent the property willed from being a part of deceased's estate subject to administration. Jennings v. Jennings, 250 Ala. 130, 33 So. 2d 251 (1947).

Abatement of legacies where assets insufficient. — The general rule, in the absence of express interest of testator, where the assets prove insufficient to pay debts of estate and the legacies, is that the loss falls (1) upon the residuary, (2) then upon the general legacies and (3) then upon the specific devises or bequests. Powell v. Labry, 210 Ala. 248, 97 So. 707 (1923).

Bequests and devises to the widow are not to be used to pay debts until all other property has been exhausted. Rowe v. Newman, 290 Ala. 289, 276 So. 2d 412 (1972).

Life insurance is subject to decedent's debts. — Life insurance is, under this section, property subject to decedent's debts. Pope v. Carter, 210 Ala. 533, 98 So. 726 (1924); Perrydore v. Hester, 215 Ala. 268, 110 So. 403 (1926).

However, insurance payable to a named beneficiary is no part of the estate of the insured, is not subject to administration and, except for fraud, is not subject to payment of debts, whether or not there is reserved a right to change the beneficiary or whether or not such beneficiary has contract rights or equities in the insurance. Jennings v. Jennings, 250 Ala. 130, 33 So. 2d 251 (1947).

As are rents and income. — Rents or income from real property specifically devised are subject to the payment of debts under the same circumstances as lands. Powell v. Labry, 210 Ala. 248, 97 So. 707 (1923).

If the personal representative exercised a control over the real estate of his intestate, he held the rents in trust for those legally entitled thereto. Powell v. Labry, 210 Ala. 248, 97 So. 707 (1923).

Recovery from administrator in case of maladministration or conversion. — If there have been personal assets for the payment of debts and there has been a devastavit committed by the administrator through maladministration or conversion by him, the creditor must look first to the administrator and his sureties. If they are solvent, a legal remedy exists against them and this must be exhausted. But, with certain exceptions, all property of a decedent is charged with the payment of his debts. If the administrator has wasted or converted the personal assets, the lands of the decedent are not thereby ultimately relieved of the charge. Moebes v. Kay, 241 Ala. 294, 2 So. 2d 754 (1941).

Recovery from lands where administrator insolvent. — If the administrator and his sureties are wholly insolvent, so that no part of the debt can be realized from them, court will not require the creditor first to pursue his remedy against those whose duty it is to make good the loss occasioned by the devastavit. Resort to lands may be had by alleging and proving such insolvency. Moebes v. Kay, 241 Ala. 294, 2 So. 2d 754 (1941).

Presentation of claims. — As to necessity of proving compliance with requirement of presentation of claims, see Little v. Marx, 145 Ala. 620, 39 So. 517 (1905).

Cited in Boynton v. McEwen, 36 Ala. 348 (1860); Griffin v. Bland, 43 Ala. 542 (1869); Prince v. Prince, 47 Ala. 283 (1872); Dunlap v. Newman, 47 Ala. 429 (1872); Childress v. Harrison, 47 Ala. 556 (1872); Hudson v. Stewart, 48 Ala. 204 (1872); Harkins v. Bailey, 48 Ala. 376 (1872); Todd v. Neal, 49 Ala. 266 (1873); Williams v. Williams, 49 Ala. 439 (1873); Thornton v. Neal, 49 Ala. 590 (1873); Taylor v. Taylor, 53 Ala. 135 (1875); Scott v. Ware, 64 Ala. 174 (1879); Nelson v. Murfee, 69 Ala. 598 (1881); Murphy v. Vaughan, 226 Ala. 461, 147 So. 404 (1933); Bedsale v. Tiller, 236 Ala. 101, 181 So. 286 (1938); Vauss v. Thomas, 249 Ala. 449, 31 So. 2d 502 (1947); McClendon v. Straub, 193 F.2d 596 (5th Cir. 1952); Festorazzi v. First Nat'l Bank, 288 Ala. 645, 264 So. 2d 496 (1972); Tolar v. Tolar, 337 So. 2d 1284 (Ala. 1976); Dorough v. Johnson, 373 So. 2d 1082 (Ala. 1979).

Collateral references. — Liability of administration expenses of wife electing against the will. 89 ALR3d 315.

§ 43-2-371. Order of preference.

The debts against the estates of decedents are to be paid in the following order:

(1) The funeral expenses.

(2) The fees and charges of administration.

(3) Expenses of the last sickness.

(4) Taxes assessed on the estate of the decedent previous to his death.

(5) Debts due to employees, as such, for services rendered the year of the death of the decedent.

(6) The other debts of the decedent. (Code 1867, § 1741; Code 1876, § 2430; Code 1886, § 2079; Code 1896, § 126; Code 1907, § 2597; Code 1923, § 5822; Code 1940, T. 61, § 218.)

Cross references. — As to payment of state and federal estate taxes from estate property, see § 40-15-18.

The law implies a promise to reimburse one paying funeral expenses. — The amount of funeral expenses, when paid by a friend or relative, is regarded as money paid on request of the personal representative, and the law raises a promise to repay it, so far as he has assets. Gayle v. Johnston, 72 Ala. 254 (1882). And the burial of the dead being a public necessity, it may be furnished by a stranger. Hatchett v. Curbow, 59 Ala. 516 (1877). Both of the foregoing cases are cited with approval in Phillips v. First Nat'l Bank, 208 Ala. 589, 94 So. 801 (1922), wherein the bank in which decedent was a depositor, having paid the funeral

expenses was held entitled to reimbursement on showing necessity of payment.

Such expenses are the first to be paid. — Funeral expenses are not only lawful charge against all the estate of deceased subject to debt, but a first preferred charge under this section. Kennedy v. Parks, 217 Ala. 323, 116 So. 161 (1928).

They should be proportionate to the size of decedent's estate. — The expenses of burial must bear reasonable proportion to the condition and estate of the deceased; and if disproportionate, should be scaled to that standard. Hatchett v. Curbow, 59 Ala. 516 (1877), cited in Phillips v. First Nat'l Bank, 208 Ala. 589, 94 So. 801 (1922), in which the court said that the expenses which are chargeable upon the decedent's estate in favor of a stranger are those which are incident to the burial itself, and which cannot be postponed.

Where widow paid certain expenses from own personal money. — Taxes, funeral expenses and expenses of the last illness were debts of the decedent and a lawful charge against all of the estate of decedent, notwithstanding the fact that they had been paid by the widow from her personal moneys. Canada v. Canada, 243 Ala. 109, 8 So. 2d 846 (1942).

Testamentary provisions made for surviving widow are accorded priority over all other kinds of gifts in the will, and abate last. Dorough v. Johnson, 373 So. 2d 1082 (Ala. 1979).

All other bequests and devises should be exhausted before the bequest to the widow can be applied to payment of debts, claims, and expenses of administration. Rowe v. Newman, 290 Ala. 289, 276 So. 2d 412 (1972).

Administrative expenses of different settlement. — Costs incurred in the settlement of an estate where decedent, at the time of his death, was administrator, are not preferred claims against decedent's estate within the meaning of subdivision (2) of this section. Hullett v. Hood, 109 Ala. 345, 19 So. 419 (1896).

Reasonable costs, etc., in good faith incurred in litigation are allowed. — Under this section reasonable costs and expenses incurred in good faith in litigation are allowed. And the right of the personal representative to recover for these depends on the good faith in prosecuting or defending and not on the result of the litigation. First Nat'l Bank v. Watters, 201 Ala. 670, 79 So. 242 (1918).

Physician's fee allowed even though summoned after death. — In view of this section and § 43-2-372, if amount found in son's possession taken by father, part of which was paid for physicians summoned before it was known the son was dead, was reasonable and necessary, and other preferred claims would not be prejudiced thereby, the father was entitled to such deduction. Sewell v. Sewell, 199 Ala. 242, 74 So. 343 (1917).

Taxes against decedent's estate prior to his death are debts against the decedent for the payment of which the estate of such decedent is subject to sale. Canada v. Canada, 243 Ala. 109, 8 So. 2d 846 (1942).

But taxes assessed after death are not preferred. — Taxes assessed against an estate subsequent to the death of the decedent are not preferred claims. Pryor v. Davis, 109 Ala. 117, 19 So. 440 (1896).

Under this section the supreme court of Alabama has held that taxes assessed subsequent to the death of the decedent, e.g., estate taxes, are not preferred claims. Robertson v. United States, 281 F. Supp. 955 (N.D. Ala. 1968).

The federal estate tax liability, as the government admits, arises only upon the decedent's death. It therefore does not qualify under this section as a debt which is to be paid before the wife's one-third marital share is computed under former § 43-3-10. Cox v. United States, 421 F.2d 576 (5th Cir. 1970).

Claims for services rendered within the final year. — In order to establish a claim as preferred, for services (under subdivision (5) of the section) rendered the year of the decedent's death, the evidence as to the amount thereof must be sufficient to show clearly how much was earned and due in that year. Hullett v. Hood, 109 Ala. 345, 19 So. 419 (1896).

When estate probably insolvent unpreferred debts should not be paid in full. — Where an estate is in a probably insolvent condition the administrators are not justified in paying in full the unpreferred debts. They can do this only by themselves assuming the risks of a deficiency of assets. Byrd v. Jones, 84 Ala. 336, 4 So. 375 (1888).

Cited in Prince v. Prince, 47 Ala. 283 (1872); Sharp v. Sharp, 76 Ala. 312 (1884); Wommock v. Davis, 228 Ala. 362, 153 So. 611 (1934); Snodgrass v. United States, 308 F. Supp. 440 (N.D. Ala. 1968).

Collateral references. — 34 C.J.S., Executors & Administrators, §§ 458-461.

31 Am. Jur. 2d, Executors & Administrators, §§ 467-475.

Meaning of phrase "last sickness" and the like in statutes giving preference to expenses. 9 ALR 462.

Vendor under executory contract for sale of land as preferred creditor in case of vendee's death. 35 ALR 929.

State's prerogative right of preference at common law. 51 ALR 1355, 65 ALR 1331, 90 ALR 184, 167 ALR 640.

Foreclosure decree which ascertained amount of mortgage debt or other claim as judgment within statute relating to rank of claims against decedent's estate. 57 ALR 489.

Stockholder's superadded liability, rank or preference of claim against insolvent estate in respect of. 92 ALR 1040.

Expense of preserving assets before appointment of executor or administrator as entitled to priority. 108 ALR 393.

Priority in event of incompetent's death of claims incurred during guardianship over other claims against estate. 113 ALR 402.

Judgment against executor or administrator, or levy of attachment or execution against him, as affecting rank of creditor's claim against estate or his right in respect of property of estate. 121 ALR 656.

Statutory provisions as to classification or priority of claims against decedent's estate in respect of money or property received by decedent as trustee or fiduciary. 125 ALR 1487.

Foreign judgment, or judgment of sister state, rendered in lifetime of decedent, rank of, in settlement of debtor's estate after his death. 128 ALR 1400.

Personal claim of executor or administrator against estate, antedating death of decedent. 144 ALR 953.

Amount of funeral expenses allowable against decedent's estate. 4 ALR2d 995.

Rent accruing under lease after death of lessee as preferred claim or cost of administration. 22 ALR3d 814.

§ 43-2-372. No preference among debts of same class.

No executor or administrator must, before the expiration of six months from the grant of letters, give a preference in the payment of any debt over others of the same class; nor is a debt due and payable entitled to any preference over debts of the same class which are not due. (Code 1852, § 1742; Code 1867, § 2065; Code 1876, § 2431; Code 1886, § 2080; Code 1896, § 127; Code 1907, § 2598; Code 1923, § 5823; Code 1940, T. 61, § 219.)

Cross references. — See notes to § 43-2-371.

Effect of section. — This section prevents a creditor from acquiring a preference by any diligence on his part. Scott v. Ware, 64 Ala. 174 (1879).

Cited in McNeill v. McNeill, 36 Ala. 109 (1860).

§ 43-2-373. Payment of claims barred by statute of limitations.

No claim against the estate of a decedent whether in favor of the personal representative or any other person, which was barred by the statute of limitations at the time of the death of such decedent, shall be paid by or allowed to the personal representative, unless the payment of such claim be expressly directed by a testator in his will. (Code 1896, § 128; Code 1907, § 2599; Code 1923, § 5824; Code 1940, T. 61, § 220.)

Formerly the administrator could waive the statute. — Prior to the present status of this section an administrator could exercise a discretion to plead the statute as the decedent could in life, but not so as to charge real estate on account of the law applicable to the descent of such kind of property. Bond v. Smith, 2 Ala. 660 (1841); Pollard v. Scears, 28 Ala. 484 (1856); Steele v. Steele, 64 Ala. 438 (1879); Fleming v. Kirkland, 226 Ala. 222, 146 So. 384 (1933); May v. Mathers, 233 Ala. 654, 172 So. 907 (1937).

Administratrix cannot waive six-month statute within which materialmen's lien action must be brought and thus deprive general creditors of assets to which they are otherwise entitled. Fleming v. Kirkland, 226 Ala. 222, 146 So. 384 (1933).

This section applies to solvent and insolvent estates alike, and it is not incumbent upon the administrator of an insolvent estate to file objections under § 43-2-747 to the payment of claims barred at the time of death of decedent

within the required time, because such claims are barred and the administrator has no discretion as to their payment. Elliott v. First Nat'l Bank, 248 Ala. 360, 27 So. 2d 623 (1946).

But not to claims other than those barred at decedent's death. — The provisions of this section have no application to claims other than those which were barred at the time of the death of the decedent. Elliott v. First Nat'l Bank, 248 Ala. 360, 27 So. 2d 623 (1946).

An administrator has a discretion whether he will plead statute of limitations as to debt of decedent which was not barred at date of decedent's death, but administrator has no discretion with respect to debts which were barred before decedent's death and is prohibited from paying such debts. Jones v. Baswell, 246 Ala. 410, 20 So. 2d 715 (1945).

The personal representative of an estate has no discretion as to the payment of claims barred by statute of limitations at the time of decedent's death and not directed to be paid by will, and cannot by any act of commission or omission make such claims legal charges against the estate. Elliott v. First Nat'l Bank, 248 Ala. 360, 27 So. 2d 623 (1946).

Cited in Neil v. Cunningham, 2 Port. 171 (1835); Evans v. Steel, 2 Ala. 114 (1841); Camp

v. Hatter, 11 Ala. 151 (1847); McCaskle v. Amarine, 12 Ala. 17 (1847); Walsh v. Walsh, 231 Ala. 305, 164 So. 822 (1935); Brown v. First Nat'l Bank, 261 Ala. 565, 75 So. 2d 141 (1954).

Collateral references. — 34 C.J.S., Executors & Administrators, §§ 382, 735.

§ 43-2-374. When executor or administrator protected in payment of debts.

The payment of any debt against the estate of the executor or administrator, after six months from the grant of letters, protects him to the extent of the payment from liability on any other debt against such estate which had not been presented at the time of such payment. (Code 1852, § 1790; Code 1867, § 2117; Code 1876, § 2494; Code 1886, § 2086; Code 1896, § 136; Code 1907, § 2600; Code 1923, § 5825; Acts 1931, No. 722, p. 839; Code 1940, T. 61, § 221.)

§ 43-2-375. Payment of debts not due.

Any debt not due, which has been presented, may be paid by an executor or administrator after six months from the grant of letters, and the provisions of section 43-2-374 include such debts; but such payment must not be made unless the creditor accepts, in discharge of such debt, such an amount as, with interest from the day of payment to the day when such debt is due, would make the amount thereof. (Code 1852, § 1791; Code 1867, § 2118; Code 1876, § 2495; Code 1886, § 2087; Code 1896, § 137; Code 1907, § 2601; Code 1923, § 5826; Acts 1931, No. 717, p. 837; Code 1940, T. 61, § 222.)

Rule as to absolute maturity. — Under this section a claim against an estate for the price of land purchased by the decedent may be proved, although not then due, where it will become due absolutely at some definite or fixed time in the future. Jones v. Hert, 192 Ala. 111, 68 So. 259 (1915).

Cited in Mobile v. Dargan, 45 Ala. 310 (1871).

Collateral references. — 34 C.J.S., Executors & Administrators, §§ 466, 467.

Division 3.

Sale, Compromise and Settlement.

§ 43-2-390. Authorization to compromise or sell claims.

The probate court having jurisdiction of the estate may authorize any executor or administrator to compromise or sell any bad or doubtful claim due the estate, on the written application of the executor or administrator, verified by his affidavit, and stating the facts, supported by evidence satisfactory to the court, that such claim is bad or doubtful, and that a compromise or sale thereof will promote the interests of the estate. (Code 1876, § 2505; Code 1886, § 2088; Code 1896, § 138; Code 1907, § 2602; Code 1923, § 5827; Code 1940, T. 61, § 223.)

This section is for the greater security of the executor or administrator. Loveman v. Birmingham Ry., L. & P. Co., 149 Ala. 515, 43 So. 411 (1906); Arledge v. Ellison, 247 Ala. 190, 23 So. 2d 389 (1945).

They have full control over choses in action. — An executor or administrator has the full legal title to all choses in action due the estate of a decedent, and, in the absence of fraud, he may release, compound or discharge them, as fully as if he were the absolute owner, being answerable only for improvidence. Arledge v. Ellison, 247 Ala. 190, 23 So. 2d 389 (1945).

And a court's order under this section furnishes ample protection from personal liability. Waring v. Lewis, 53 Ala. 615 (1875); Van Hoose v. Bush, 54 Ala. 342 (1875); Butler v. Gazzam, 81 Ala. 491, 1 So. 16 (1886); Carr v. Illinois Cent. R.R., 180 Ala. 159, 60 So. 277 (1912).

They may make a settlement without court's authority. — This section does not prohibit the executor or administrator from settling a claim without the authority of the court. Logan v. Central Iron & Coal Co., 139 Ala. 548, 36 So. 729 (1904); Arledge v. Ellison, 247 Ala. 190, 23 So. 2d 389 (1945), involving notes and mortgage on land.

Therefore a pleading alleging that the administrator settled the claim sued on is not bad for failing to allege that he received a reasonable amount in satisfaction of the claim and that the settlement was authorized by the court. Loveman v. Birmingham Ry., L. & P. Co., 149 Ala. 515, 43 So. 411 (1906).

Cited in Thompson v. Acree, 69 Ala. 178 (1881).

Collateral references. — 34 C.J.S., Executors & Administrators, §§ 469, 536-542, 588.

31 Am. Jur. 2d, Executors & Administrators, §§ 257-259.

Relation back of letters testamentary or of administration to validate compromises and settlements made by administrators or executors before they received letters. 26 ALR 1366.

Authority of executor or administrator to make agreement to drop or compromise will contest or withdraw objections to probate. 42 ALR2d 1365.

Power of public administrator as to compromise of claims. 56 ALR2d 1196.

Power of executor or administrator in respect of waiver or compromise of claim due estate. 72 ALR2d 191.

Power and responsibility of executor or administrator to compromise claim against estate. 72 ALR2d 243.

§ 43-2-391. Notice and hearing.

Such application must not be heard until 10 days after the filing thereof, and notice thereof may be given to some person adversely interested whenever the court may deem just. When, or at such time as the court may continue the hearing, the court, satisfied that the claim is bad or doubtful, and that a sale or compromise thereof will promote the interests of the estate, must make and enter a decree directing the sale or compromise of the claim, as may be best for the interests of the estate. If a sale is decreed, it must be made by the executor or administrator at the courthouse of the county, or such other place as the court may direct, at public outcry to the highest bidder for cash, after having first given notice of the time and place thereof by publication, once a week for three successive weeks, in some newspaper published in the county, or if none is published therein, by posting notices for three weeks at the courthouse door, and three other public places in the county, or the notice may be given in any manner and for any time which may be directed by the court. (Code 1876, § 2505; Code 1886, § 2089; Code 1896, § 139; Code 1907, § 2603; Code 1923, § 5828; Code 1940, T. 61, § 224.)

Collateral references. — 34 C.J.S., Executors & Administrators, §§ 568-570, 574-578, 592-596.

§ 43-2-392. Report.

The executor or administrator shall make report, in writing and under oath, of such sale or compromise within 30 days thereafter; and when such report is made, the sale or compromise may be confirmed, unless good cause is shown for setting the same aside. (Code 1876, § 2506; Code 1886, § 2090; Code 1896, § 140; Code 1907, § 2604; Code 1923, § 5829; Code 1940, T. 61, § 225.)

Collateral references. — 34 C.J.S., Executors & Administrators, § 606.

Lack of final settlement of intestate's estate as affecting heir's right to partition of realty. 92 ALR3d 473.

§ 43-2-393. When executor or administrator may give note, etc., to extend or settle debt.

Any executor or administrator, by authority of the probate court given on his written application, may, in his representative capacity, give his note, bond or bill for the purpose of extending or settling a debt of the decedent, or settling a debt contracted by such representative for articles, or for work and labor for the estate; and for such note, bond or bill the estate is liable, and the executor or administrator is not personally liable. But the heirs, devisees, distributees or legatees must have 10 days' notice of such application. (Code 1867, § 2066; Code 1876, § 2432; Code 1886, § 2091; Code 1896, § 141; Code 1907, § 2605; Code 1923, § 5830; Code 1940, T. 61, § 226.)

Cited in Wilburn & Co. v. McCalley, 63 Ala. 436 (1879); McCalley v. Wilburn & Co., 77 Ala. 549 (1884); Soper v. Pointer, 67 F.2d 676 (5th Cir. 1933); Pointer v. Farmers' Fertilizer Co., 230 Ala. 87, 160 So. 252 (1935); Foster v. Featherston, 230 Ala. 268, 160 So. 689 (1935).

§ 43-2-394. Compounding with and discharge of debtor.

Whenever a debtor of the decedent is unable to pay all his debts, the executor or administrator, with the approbation of the court or judge thereof, may compound with him and give him a discharge, upon receiving a fair and just dividend of his effects. A compromise may also be authorized when it appears to be just, and for the best interest of the estate. (Code 1923, § 5831; Code 1940, T. 61, § 227.)

ARTICLE 16.

SALE OF PERSONAL PROPERTY.

Cross references. — As to renting and sale of real estate, see § 43-2-440 et seq.

Collateral references. — Validity of sales of property of deceased person before letters testamentary or of administration have been granted to the vendor. 26 ALR 1364.

Exchange of property as covered by power of sale. 63 ALR 1003.

Sale by executor or administrator to corporation of which he is an officer or stockholder, as voidable or as ground for surcharging his account. 105 ALR 449.

Confirmation by a court as affecting void or voidable character of sale made in violation of statute providing that no representative making sale shall be interested therein. 111 ALR 1362.

Authority of special or temporary administrator, or administrator pendente lite, to dispose of, distribute, lease, or encumber property of estate. 148 ALR 275.

Rights and duties of executor or administrator in respect of pledge of property to him by decedent. 154 ALR 203.

Conclusiveness of allowance of account of trustee or personal representative as respects self-dealing in assets of estates. 1 ALR2d 1060.

Right of an administrator with the will annexed, or trustee other than the person named in the will as such, to execute power of sale conferred by will. 9 ALR2d 1324.

Power of sale conferred on executor by testator as authorizing private sale. 11 ALR2d 955.

Power of executor to create easement, implied from power to sell. 44 ALR2d 573.

Power of public administrator to sell personalty of the estate. 56 ALR2d 1191.

Rights and remedies of one purchasing at executor's or administrator's sale where there was misrepresentation or mistake as to acreage or location of boundaries of tract sold. 69 ALR2d 254.

Fiduciary's power to sell property at price less than that specified in will creating power of sale. 100 ALR2d 1049.

§ 43-2-410. Power of sale conferred.

Any part of the personal property of a decedent, including land warrants and choses in action, may be sold only by order of the court, on the written application of the executor or administrator, verified by affidavit, in the following cases, unless, in such cases, power to sell is conferred by the will:

(1) For the payment of debts.

(2) To make distribution among the distributees or legatees.

(3) To prevent the waste or destruction of property liable to waste, or of a perishable nature, if it is proved that the sale would be beneficial to the estate. (Code 1852, § 1743; Code 1867, § 2067; Code 1876, § 2433; Code 1886, § 2092; Code 1896, § 142; Code 1907, § 2606; Code 1923, § 5832; Code 1940, T. 61, § 228.)

Jurisdiction to order a sale of personal property is derived solely from the section, and is special and limited. Hall v. Chapman, 35 Ala. 553 (1860).

A sale without order of the court is invalid. Wyatt v. Rambo, 29 Ala. 510 (1857). The record must show every fact essential to the jurisdiction. Pettit v. Pettit, 32 Ala. 288 (1858); Beene v. Collenberger, 38 Ala. 647 (1863).

The administrator of an insolvent estate cannot sell land or personalty of the estate without an order of the court. Batson v. Etheridge, 239 Ala. 535, 195 So. 873 (1940).

Direction in will for sale is no ground for such order by court. — In view of this section the fact that decedent's will directs the sale of his property is no ground for an order of sale by the probate court, and can give no validity thereto. Wilson v. Armstrong, 42 Ala. 168 (1868). See also Alabama Conference v. Price, 42 Ala. 39 (1868); Chandler v. Chandler, 87 Ala. 300, 6 So. 153 (1889).

Petition must show cause for sale. — The court has no jurisdiction to make an order for the sale of personal property, when the petition of the administrator does not allege or show the existence of a legal cause for the sale, and such

an order is a nullity. Hall v. Chapman, 35 Ala. 553 (1860). See also Wyatt v. Rambo, 29 Ala. 510 (1857); King v. Kent, 29 Ala. 542 (1857); Ikelheimer v. Chapman, 32 Ala. 676 (1858); Hatcher v. Clifton, 33 Ala. 301 (1858).

An application by an administrator for an order to sell certain described personal property left by his intestate, which alleges that in his opinion a sale of the property is necessary to pay the debts of the intestate, is sufficient to confer jurisdiction upon the probate court. Reynolds v. Kirkland, 44 Ala. 312 (1870).

Judgment creditor is not entitled to petition for sale. — A judgment creditor is not entitled to file a petition for the sale of decedent's personal property. But where the administrator joins in the petition the sale will not be void. Howell v. Randle, 171 Ala. 451, 54 So. 563 (1911).

Mere irregularities in primary proceedings will not void sale. — Mere irregularities in proceedings leading up to a decree for a sale of property by a probate court are not sufficient to avoid the decree upon the ground of want of jurisdiction. Carter v. Waugh, 42 Ala. 452 (1868); Gartman v. Lightner, 160 Ala. 202, 49 So. 412 (1908). See also Satcher v. Satcher, 41 Ala. 26 (1867).

Method of determining what is perishable property. — As to perishable property, all that is necessary to be shown is that the property in the hands of the court is likely to waste or be destroyed by keeping. If it is shown that, by keeping the article, it will necessarily become, or is likely to become, worthless to the creditor, and by consequence to the debtor, then it does not matter what the subject matter is. McCulloûgh v. McCulloûgh, 269 Ala. 417, 113 So. 2d 499 (1959).

Livestock held perishable. — It was held that it would be to the benefit of an estate to dispose of livestock because, under the existing circumstances, the livestock could not be taken care of without considerable time and expenditure. Accordingly, the court held that the livestock was perishable. McCulloûgh v. McCulloûgh, 269 Ala. 417, 113 So. 2d 499 (1959).

Sale of perishable property. — Where the record shows that application was made for the sale of property of an estate of perishable nature, and that the court was satisfied by proof that the property was of such nature, and that the sales would be beneficial to the estate, the sale was not void. Adkinson v. Wright, 46 Ala. 598 (1871).

And an averment, in a petition for sale, that the property is "of a character liable to waste or be consumed by fire," is sufficient to sustain the jurisdiction of the court. Harris v. Parker, 41 Ala. 604 (1868).

Such sale should be made immediately. — It is the duty of an administrator, on obtaining an order of sale, to sell the perishable property without delay, and if he fails to do so, and retains it until it deteriorates in value, he is chargeable with its value at the time it should have been sold. Steele v. Knox, 10 Ala. 608 (1846).

Nursery business a "joint adventure". — Upon death of one party to arrangement whereby such deceased party furnished capital for greenhouse and nursery business and surviving party was to plant shrubs and plants and to superintend their care and maintenance, court properly ordered sale of the property on petition of executors of the deceased party and over objection of surviving party, on ground that the arrangement was a "joint adventure" and not a "partnership," that the plants and shrubs were perishable and that sale was in the best interests of all parties. Pfingstl v. Solomon, 240 Ala. 58, 197 So. 12 (1940).

And properly ordered sold as perishable property. — Where executors of deceased party to joint adventure relating to greenhouse and nursery business sought to have court order sale of the property, court was not limited by this section, authorizing sale of perishable property of a decedent, but its jurisdiction was more extensive in scope and was based on its traditional powers to consider the joint adventure contract and the circumstances and to exercise its discretion in the best interests of all the parties. Pfingstl v. Solomon, 240 Ala. 58, 197 So. 12 (1940).

Title not in representative. — The probate court has no jurisdiction to order a sale of personal property at the instance of a personal representative, where the title in him, which devolved upon him at the death of his testator or intestate, has been divided by his assent to a legacy. Whorton v. Moragne, 62 Ala. 201 (1878).

Cited in Brown v. Hay, 1 Stew. & Port. 102 (1831); Sale v. Branch Bank, 1 Ala. 425 (1840); Erwin v. Branch Bank, 14 Ala. 307 (1848); Bryant v. Ingraham, 16 Ala. 116 (1849); Boyd v. Beck, 29 Ala. 703 (1857); Ikelheimer v. Chapman, 32 Ala. 676 (1858); McIntosh v. Reid, 45 Ala. 456 (1871); Arledge v. Ellison, 247 Ala. 190, 23 So. 2d 389 (1945); Tolar v. Tolar, 337 So. 2d 1284 (Ala. 1976); Dorough v. Johnson, 373 So. 2d 1082 (Ala. 1979).

Collateral references. — 34 C.J.S., Executors & Administrators, §§ 536-538, 543-545.

31 Am. Jur. 2d, Executors & Administrators, §§ 341-343.

§ 43-2-411. Notice of application.

Notice of such application must be given to some person adversely interested in such manner, and for such length of time, not less than three weeks, as the judge of probate may require; but when the property is perishable, and it is so specified in the application, no notice is required if the judge is satisfied of the truth of the allegations contained in the application. (Code 1867, § 2068; Code 1876, § 2434; Code 1886, § 2093; Code 1896, § 143; Code 1907, § 2607; Code 1923, § 5833; Code 1940, T. 61, § 229.)

Cited in Anderson v. McGowan, 45 Ala. 462 (1871); Lane v. Mickle, 46 Ala. 600 (1871).

Collateral references. — 34 C.J.S., Executors & Administrators, §§ 564, 565.

§ 43-2-412. Contesting application.

Any person interested may appear and contest such application, and show that no sale is required, or that it is more for the interest of the estate that other personal property should be sold. (Code 1852, § 1745; Code 1867, § 2069; Code 1876, § 2435; Code 1886, § 2094; Code 1896, § 144; Code 1907, § 2608; Code 1923, § 5834; Code 1940, T. 61, § 230.)

Collateral references. — 34 C.J.S., Executors & Administrators, §§ 553, 556.

§ 43-2-413. Notice of sale.

When the application is granted for the sale of any personal property, the executor or administrator must give notice of the day, place and terms of sale, and a description of the property to be sold, by advertisement for three successive weeks in some newspaper published in the county where the sale is to take place, or, by posting notice at the courthouse door and at three other public places in the county. But when the property is perishable, or the expense of keeping it is very great, the sale may be made after five days' notice, which may be given by one insertion in a newspaper published in the county where the sale is to take place, or, if there be no such paper, by posting at the courthouse door, and at three other public places in the county. In addition to the notice prescribed in this article, the court may direct the giving of notice by printed handbills, or posters, to be distributed and posted in the manner best calculated to give extended notice of the sale. (Code 1852, § 1746; Code 1867, § 2070; Code 1876, § 2436; Code 1886, § 2095; Code 1896, § 145; Code 1907, § 2609; Code 1923, § 5836; Code 1940, T. 61, § 231.)

Collateral references. — 34 C.J.S., Executors & Administrators, § 592.

§ 43-2-414. Hours of sale.

Such sale must not commence before 11:00 A.M., nor continue longer than 4:00 P.M.; and, if not completed within those hours, it may be continued from day to day. (Code 1852, § 1747; Code 1867, § 2071; Code 1876, § 2437; Code 1886, § 2096; Code 1896, § 146; Code 1907, § 2610; Code 1923, § 5837; Code 1940, T. 61, § 232.)

Collateral references. — 34 C.J.S., Executors & Administrators, § 594.

§ 43-2-415. Terms of sale.

Such sale may be for cash or on credit not exceeding 12 months, as the court may direct; and if on credit, notes or bonds, with at least two sufficient sureties, must be taken by the executor or administrator. (Code 1852, §§ 1748, 1752; Code 1867, §§ 2072, 2077; Code 1876, §§ 2438, 2444; Code 1886, § 2097; Code 1896, § 147; Code 1907, § 2611; Code 1923, § 5838; Code 1940, T. 61, § 233.)

Administrator must act with care of prudent businessman. — If an administrator in taking the bond or notes required by this section acts with such care as a prudent man would take in the management of his own business, it will be sufficient. Searcy v. Holmes, 45 Ala. 225 (1871).

Defense for omission to take security. —

Failure to take the security required by this section cannot be excused upon the ground that the distributee's husband was present and made no objection. Walls v. Grigsby, 42 Ala. 473 (1868).

Collateral references. — 34 C.J.S., Executors & Administrators, § 597.

§ 43-2-416. When bid rejected and sale postponed.

When the highest amount bid for the property, or any part thereof, is, in the opinion of the executor or administrator, greatly less than its fair value, he may withdraw the property and postpone the sale. (Code 1896, § 148; Code 1907, § 2612; Code 1923, § 5839; Code 1940, T. 61, § 234.)

Collateral references. — 34 C.J.S., Executors & Administrators, § 600.

§ 43-2-417. Resale upon failure of purchaser to comply with terms; liability for deficiency.

If the purchaser fails to comply with the terms of the sale, the executor or administrator may again proceed to advertise and sell the property. If, on another and a completed sale, the property sells for a less sum than the amount bid at the former sale, the purchaser so in default is liable to the executor, administrator or any person damaged for the deficiency, and also the expense of the sale. (Code 1896, § 149; Code 1907, § 2613; Code 1923, § 5840; Code 1940, T. 61, § 235.)

It is not necessary for the sale to be confirmed to support an action under this section. Culli v. House, 133 Ala. 304, 32 So. 254 (1902).

Collateral references. — 34 C.J.S., Executors & Administrators, §§ 602, 604.

§ 43-2-418. Completion, gathering and sale of crops commenced by decedent.

Any crop commenced by a decedent may be completed and gathered by the executor or administrator, and, the expenses of the plantation being deducted therefrom, is assets in his hands, and may be sold by him at private sale, either in or out of the state. (Code 1852, §§ 1750, 1901; Code 1867, §§ 2073, 2261, 2262; Code 1876, §§ 2439, 2440, 2441; Code 1886, § 2098; Code 1896, § 150; Code 1907, § 2614; Code 1923, § 5841; Code 1940, T. 61, § 236.)

No absolute duty to complete and gather crop. — Under this section it is optional with executor or administrator whether he shall complete and gather a growing crop. But whenever from the reasonable appearance of things, the interests of the estate are likely to be promoted thereby, then it is his duty to exercise the power given. Blair v. Murphree, 81 Ala. 454, 2 So. 18 (1886). See also Tayloe v. Bush, 75 Ala. 432 (1883).

The determination of this fact (the interest of the estate) will depend upon the state and character of the crop, the weather conditions, the resources of the estate and all other matters which enter into the control and cultivation and harvesting of crops. Hence the option thus conferred is not an arbitrary one. Wright v. Watson, 96 Ala. 536, 11 So. 634 (1892).

Any election or option, however, made by the personal representative pursuant to this section will furnish protection to him if it be such as would have been exercised by a man of ordinary care and prudence in the management of his own affairs. Wright v. Watson, 96 Ala. 536, 11 So. 634 (1892).

Where testator was not farming land himself. — The rule that the executor should exercise the power given when the interest of the estate is likely to be promoted thereby had no application where it appeared that the testator was not farming his land himself but was renting it and the rent was paid in cotton. Webb v. Webb, 250 Ala. 194, 33 So. 2d 909 (1948).

Crops pass to heir of intestate subject to administrator's right to sell. — Growing crops at the death of an intestate pass to the heir, subject to the administrator's authority under this section to convert it into assets by the exercise of his election pursuant to this section. Wright v. Watson, 96 Ala. 536, 11 So. 634 (1892). See also Blair v. Murphree, 81 Ala. 454, 2 So. 18 (1886).

Heir's interest becomes absolute when administrator asserts no authority. — Where nothing is done by the administrator towards cultivating or gathering the crop and he asserts no authority over it, but this is done by a son and heir at his expense, then the crop is the property of the heir and does not become assets of the estate. Wright v. Watson, 96 Ala. 536, 11 So. 634 (1892).

Cited in Goodgame v. Cole & Co., 12 Ala. 77 (1847); Wyatt v. Rambo, 29 Ala. 510 (1857); Mobile v. Dargan, 45 Ala. 310 (1871); Calhoun v. Fletcher, 63 Ala. 574 (1879); East Tenn., etc., R. Co. v. Bayliss, 74 Ala. 150 (1883); Loeb v. Richardson, 74 Ala. 311 (1883); Tayloe v. Bush, 75 Ala. 432 (1883); Eubank v. Clark, 78 Ala. 73 (1884).

§ 43-2-419. Sale of farm products.

All farm products coming into the hands of the executor or administrator as assets of the estate may be sold by him at public or private sale, at the reasonable market value, either in or out of the state. (Code 1923, § 5842; Code 1940, T. 61, § 237.)

§ 43-2-420. Assignment or transfer of mortgages, notes or accounts.

Executors and administrators may assign and transfer by endorsement, without recourse or warranty, any mortgages, notes or accounts belonging to a decedent, provided he receives the full amount due thereon, and provided said mortgages, notes or accounts shall have been entered on the inventory returned to the court. (Code 1923, § 5835; Code 1940, T. 61, § 238.)

Cited in Arledge v. Ellison, 247 Ala. 190, 23 So. 2d 389 (1945).

Collateral references. — 34 C.J.S., Executors & Administrators, § 654.

§ 43-2-421. Stock in trade.

(a) When any person engaged in mercantile business dies, leaving a stock of goods, wares and merchandise, and leaving no surviving partner in such business, the executor or administrator of his estate may sell such stock or goods, wares or merchandise, either at public or private sale, by wholesale or retail, upon first obtaining an order for such sale, as provided in subsection (b) of this section, from the probate court having jurisdiction of the estate.

(b) To obtain such order, the executor or administrator must file in such court an application in writing, verified by his oath, setting forth with reasonable certainty the kind, quantity and estimated value of such goods, wares or merchandise, and any facts or circumstances that may render it necessary or expedient to sell the same; and if it should appear to the court that it would benefit those interested in the estate that such order should be made, the court must make the same, and may, in its discretion, prescribe such terms and conditions of sale as may seem to the court most advantageous to those interested in the estate. Such sale must be made within one year from the making of such order. (Code 1867, §§ 2074, 2075; Code 1876, §§ 2442, 2443; Code 1886, §§ 2099, 2100; Code 1896, §§ 151, 152; Code 1907, §§ 2615, 2616; Code 1923, §§ 5843, 5844; Code 1940, T. 61, §§ 239, 240.)

Cited in Harris v. Parker, 41 Ala. 604 (1868); Goolsbee v. Fordham, 49 Ala. 202 (1873); Cousins v. Jackson, 52 Ala. 262 (1875).

§ 43-2-422. Returns of accounts of sales.

All accounts of sales of personalty made by the executor or administrator must be returned on oath, within 30 days after such sale, and must be recorded; and such returns may be compelled by attachment. (Code 1852, § 1753; Code 1867, § 2078; Code 1876, § 2445; Code 1886, § 2101; Code 1896, § 153; Code 1907, § 2617; Code 1923, § 5845; Code 1940, T. 61, § 241.)

Cited in Ex parte Russell, 29 Ala. 717 (1857); Hill v. Erwin, 44 Ala. 661 (1870); Searcy v. Holmes, 45 Ala. 225 (1871).

ARTICLE 17.

RENTING AND SALE OF REAL ESTATE.

Cross references. — As to conveyances by executors and administrators in cases of written agreements or contracts for the conveyance of lands where person executing the same dies before the execution of the conveyance, see § 35-4-320 et seq. As to sale of personal property, see § 43-2-410 et seq.

Collateral references. — Determination of price under testamentary option to buy real estate. 13 ALR4th 947.

Division 1.

For Payment of Debts and for Division.

Collateral references. — Implied power of executor to sell real estate. 23 ALR2d 1000.

Rights and remedies of one purchasing at executor's or administrator's sale where there was misrepresentation or mistake as to acreage or location of boundaries of tract sold. 69 ALR2d 254.

Fiduciary's power to sell property at price less than that specified in will creating power of sale. 100 ALR2d 1049.

§ 43-2-440. Renting of lands.

The executor or administrator may rent the decedent's lands at public outcry, or, when the interest of the estate requires it, privately; and such rent is assets; but when lands are rented privately, he must report such renting to the probate court of the proper county within 30 days thereafter. (Code 1852, § 1751; Code 1867, § 2076; Code 1876, § 2446; Code 1886, § 2102; Code 1896, § 154; Code 1907, § 2618; Code 1923, § 5846; Code 1940, T. 61, § 242.)

Claim of the executor to lands dominates that of the heir. — The power given by this section shows that the claim of the executor to the lands of the decedent dominates that of the heir. Griffith v. Rudisill, 141 Ala. 200, 37 So. 83 (1904).

Thus, this section authorizes the personal representative to intercept the possession of the heir or devisee to the real estate for the payment of debts. Powell v. Labry, 210 Ala. 248, 97 So. 707 (1923). See also Wright v. Watson, 96 Ala. 536, 11 So. 634 (1892).

But in order to recover lands from the heirs or devisees it must affirmatively appear that there is a necessity therefor under this article. Layton v. Hamilton, 214 Ala. 329, 107 So. 830 (1926).

Under the statutes the administrator may if advisable intervene, and by taking the necessary steps become the landlord, and collect the rents. Kelly v. Kelly, 250 Ala. 664, 35 So. 2d 686 (1948), judgment modified, 257 Ala. 105, 57 So. 2d 345 (1952).

Security need not be taken for rent. — Under this section an executor may rent lands without demanding security for the rent. Patapsco Guano Co. v. Ballard, 107 Ala. 710, 19 So. 777 (1895).

Reasonable diligence and fair judgment is required of representative. — Under this section the personal representative is bound only to reasonable diligence and the exercise of fair judgment in making rents. Patapsco Guano Co. v. Ballard, 107 Ala. 710, 19 So. 777 (1895).

Cited in Brown v. Hay, 1 Stew. & Port. 102 (1831); Erwin v. Branch Bank, 14 Ala. 307 (1848); Ex parte Swan, 23 Ala. 192 (1853); Henderson v. Renfro, 31 Ala. 101 (1857); Ikelheimer v. Chapman, 32 Ala. 676 (1858); Parkman v. Aicardi, 34 Ala. 393 (1859); Boynton v. McEwen, 36 Ala. 348 (1860); Neilson v. Cook, 40 Ala. 498 (1867); Griffin v. Bland, 43 Ala. 542 (1869); Searcy v. Holmes, 45 Ala. 225 (1871); Waller v. Ray, 48 Ala. 468 (1872); Melson v. Murfee, 69 Ala. 598 (1881); Morgan v. Casey, 73 Ala. 222 (1882); Vandegrift v. Abbott, 75 Ala. 487 (1883); Eubank v. Clark, 78 Ala. 73 (1884); Banks v. Speers, 97 Ala. 560, 11 So. 841 (1892); Murphy v. Vaughan, 226 Ala. 461, 147 So. 404 (1933); Hancock v. Watt, 233 Ala. 29, 169 So. 704 (1936); Smith v. Smith, 266 Ala. 118, 94 So. 2d 863 (1957); Tolar v. Tolar, 337 So. 2d 1284 (Ala. 1976).

Collateral references. — 33 C.J.S., Executors & Administrators, §§ 259, 265, 266.

31 Am. Jur. 2d, Executors & Administrators, §§ 249, 250.

§ 43-2-441. Authorization to sell — Where will exists.

Lands may be sold by the executor or by the administrator with the will annexed, for the payment of debts, when the will gives no power to sell the same for that purpose, and the personal estate is insufficient therefor. (Code 1852, § 1754; Code 1867, § 2079; Code 1876, § 2447; Code 1886, § 2103; Code 1896, § 155; Code 1907, § 2619; Code 1923, § 5847; Code 1940, T. 61, § 243.)

Editor's note. — As indicated in the notes to § 43-2-370, that section is so closely akin to this section, that the cases often cite the two together. Therefore, the notes to § 43-2-370 should be referred to in connection with the notes to this section.

When personalty is insufficient the duty to sell the realty is mandatory. — The duty to make sale of realty where there is insufficiency of personalty is mandatory, and it is the administrator's duty to intercept the rents and sell the land if need be to pay the creditors. Boyle v. Perkins, 211 Ala. 130, 99 So. 652 (1924); Ex parte Stephens, 233 Ala. 167, 170 So. 771 (1936).

And in these proceedings the administration represents the creditors as opposed to the heirs. Boyle v. Perkins, 211 Ala. 130, 99 So. 652 (1924).

Or the widow claiming to retain the lands until dower is assigned. Clark v. Knox, 70 Ala. 607 (1881).

Only the representative may apply to sell realty. — The right to prefer the application to have lands sold to pay debts devolves alone upon the personal representative. Henley v. Johnston, 134 Ala. 646, 32 So. 1009 (1902); Bolen v. Hoven, 143 Ala. 652, 39 So. 379 (1905). Therefore, it is essential that his appointment as administrator de bonis non be valid. Henley v. Johnston, 134 Ala. 646, 32 So. 1009 (1902). As to appointment of administrator de bonis non, see § 43-2-272 and notes thereto.

An heir cannot maintain a petition for the sale of the intestate's real estate to pay debts. Martin v. Williams, 18 Ala. 190 (1850); Chighizola v. Le Baron, 21 Ala. 406 (1852); Kirkbride v. Kelly, 167 Ala. 570, 52 So. 660 (1910).

His right to sell is wholly statutory. — An administrator's right to maintain a petition to sell lands of the intestate to pay debts is wholly statutory, and can be maintained by the administrator alone, in the manner and on the conditions prescribed. Kirkbride v. Kelly, 167 Ala. 570, 52 So. 660 (1910); Ex parte Stephens, 233 Ala. 167, 170 So. 771 (1936).

Right of representative to sell realty for payment of debts has priority over claims of heirs to realty. — When there is insufficient personal property for the payment of the debts of an estate, the executor has the sole and exclusive right to sell the real estate for the payment of the debts, and a complaint for sale of real estate and division of proceeds, filed in circuit court by a devisee who is not the executor under the will, does not take priority, because of an earlier filing, over a petition for sale of personal and real estate for payment of debts and division, alleging insufficiency of personal property for payment of debts. Hamilton v. Mayer, 345 So. 2d 1334 (Ala. 1977).

The proceedings under this section are in rem. — Since the decision of Wyman v. Campbell, 6 Port. 219 (1838), the supreme court has uniformly held to the doctrine that proceedings in the probate court for the sale of lands of an estate for the payment of debts are in the nature of proceedings in rem. DeBardelaben v. Stoudenmire, 48 Ala. 643 (1872); Lyons v. Hamner, 84 Ala. 197, 4 So. 26 (1887); Howell v. Hughes, 168 Ala. 460, 53 So. 105 (1910); Johnson v. Gartman, 173 Ala. 290, 55 So. 906 (1911).

An application to a court of probate for an order to sell land of a decedent for the payment of debts, when collaterally assailed, is regarded as a proceeding in rem, and jurisdiction of the thing, not of persons is the controlling element of its validity, but, when the regularity of the proceeding is presented on error or by appeal, it is regarded as in personam. Garrett v. Bruner, 59 Ala. 513 (1877).

It has been held that it is error to decree a sale of the land of a decedent without the previous appointment of a guardian ad litem for the infant heirs. Taylor v. Reese, 4 Ala. 121 (1842); Craig v. McGehee, 16 Ala. 41 (1849). But in Neville v. Kenney, 125 Ala. 149, 28 So. 452 (1900), the court held that where complainant, a minor heir, was not made a party to the proceedings, and no guardian ad litem was appointed for her, this did not invalidate the sale as to her, since the proceedings were in rem.

The jurisdiction of the court is special and limited. — The jurisdiction of the probate court to order a sale of lands for the payment of debts is statutory, special and limited. Hall v. Chapman, 35 Ala. 553 (1860); Robertson v. Bradford, 70 Ala. 385 (1881); Smith v. Smith, 266 Ala. 118, 94 So. 2d 863 (1957). It cannot be presumed on appeal but must appear from the record. Pettus v. McClannahan, 52 Ala. 55 (1875); Wilburn & Co. v. McCalley, 63 Ala. 436 (1879); Tyson v. Brown, 64 Ala. 244 (1879); Howell v. Hughes, 168 Ala. 460, 53 So. 105 (1910).

This jurisdiction attaches only when petition sets out grounds for sale. — Jurisdiction attaches when a petition stating a statutory ground for the order of sale is regularly filed and recognized by the order of the court. And this though parties in interest may not be personally notified of the pendency of the proceedings. Howell v. Hughes, 168 Ala. 460, 53 So. 105 (1910).

No title passes when the petition is insufficient. — A purchaser of lands at a sale under a probate decree, founded on a petition by an executor or administrator which does not contain averments necessary to give the court jurisdiction, acquires no legal title, and can convey none to a subpurchaser, but he may acquire an equity, enforceable against the heirs, if they receive their share of the purchase money paid. Wilson v. Holt, 83 Ala. 528, 3 So. 321 (1887).

Where a decedent's land was sold by an administrator under a void order, the circuit court, at the instance of the purchaser, or one claiming under him, to whom the administrator and sole heir conveyed a legal title, will by injunction prevent the cloud on the title caused by a second sale by an administrator de bonis non under a probate court order. Bell v. Craig, 52 Ala. 215 (1875).

Cannot order sale when it may be done under will. — A court of probate cannot order a sale of property to pay debts when it may be done under the power in a will. Riley v. Wilkinson, 247 Ala. 231, 23 So. 2d 582 (1945).

Existence of power under will must be negatived by petition. — A petition in the probate court, for a sale under this section, must negative the existence of a power of sale in the will, and a decree of sale on a petition failing to allege that fact is void. Howell v. Hughes, 168 Ala. 460, 53 So. 105 (1910). See also Moore v. Cottingham, 113 Ala. 148, 20 So. 994 (1896).

This has been repeatedly held both in the case of a direct attack upon the decree of the court, McCollum v. McCollum, 33 Ala. 711 (1859); Alabama Conference v. Price, 42 Ala. 39 (1868); Meadows v. Meadows, 73 Ala. 356 (1882); and in the case of a collateral attack. Hall v. Hall, 47 Ala. 290 (1872); Brock v. Frank, 51 Ala. 85 (1874); Arnett v. Bailey, 60 Ala. 435 (1877).

No sale of realty when there are no debts or personalty is sufficient. — The lands of a decedent will not be ordered sold for the payment of debts when there are no debts or when there are sufficient personal assets for their payment. Banks v. Speers, 97 Ala. 560, 11 So. 841 (1892).

Or, as stated in Baldwin v. Alexander, 145 Ala. 186, 40 So. 391 (1906), the existence of debts and the insufficiency of personal assets to pay them are essential conditions for resorting to the lands to pay the debts. Powell v. Labry, 210 Ala. 248, 97 So. 707 (1923).

A deficiency in the assets of an estate caused by maladministration or devastavit will not justify a sale of lands to pay debts. Speers v. Banks, 114 Ala. 323, 21 So. 834 (1897).

These debts must exist at time of death. — Probate courts possess no power to order sale of land belonging to a decedent's estate, except for the payment of debts in existence at the date of his death. Beadle v. Steele, 86 Ala. 413, 5 So. 169 (1888).

The jurisdiction does not extend to sales for the payment of debts contracted by the administrator. Beadle v. Steele, 86 Ala. 413, 5 So. 169 (1888); Bolen v. Hoven, 143 Ala. 652, 39 So. 379 (1905).

The lands of a decedent are chargeable under this section with debts owing by decedent at the time of his death, but not for costs and expenses of administration, when no debts are shown for the payment of which the lands are liable. Turley v. Hazelwood, 234 Ala. 186, 174 So. 616 (1937),

Until the period for presenting claims has elapsed necessity for sale is indeterminable. — Until the lapse of the period for the presentation of claims against the estate, it cannot be determined whether there is a real necessity to divert the possession of the real estate. And during the period for presenting claims (see §§ 43-2-350 through 43-2-352) it is within the sound discretion of a

personal representative to determine whether or not it is necessary. Powell v. Labry, 210 Ala. 248, 97 So. 707 (1923).

Proof of insufficiency of personalty. — See § 43-2-449, and notes thereto.

Intestate must have claim to estate before sale will be ordered. — The probate court has no jurisdiction to order the sale of land for the purpose of its distribution, under the petition of an administrator which alleges that it is of the estate of his intestate, when the latter had no claim to it whatever at the time of his death. Bishop v. Blair, 36 Ala. 80 (1860). See also Johnson v. Collins, 12 Ala. 322 (1847); McCain v. McCain, 12 Ala. 510 (1847); Pettit v. Pettit, 32 Ala. 288 (1858); Cothran v. McCoy, 33 Ala. 65 (1858).

A specific devise of realty does not affect its liability for debts. — Speaking with reference to debts, not legacies, this section makes the realty of a decedent subject to their payment when the personalty is not sufficient. And such liability is not affected by a specific devise of the property. Kelly v. Richardson, 100 Ala. 584, 13 So. 785 (1893); May v. Burns, 222 Ala. 68, 131 So. 232 (1930); Cater v. Howard, 230 Ala. 133, 159 So. 830 (1935); Hammond v. Bibb, 234 Ala. 192, 174 So. 634 (1937).

But before this liability attaches, both real and personal property, not specifically devised, shall be exhausted first. — See Lightfoot v. Lightfoot, 27 Ala. 351 (1855); Morgan v. Watkins, 214 Ala. 671, 108 So. 561 (1926); Hammond v. Bibb, 234 Ala. 192, 174 So. 634 (1937).

Title to the real property on the death of the decedent was held to be in the next of kin, subject to be divested by the administrator, as provided by this section and §§ 43-2-442 and 43-2-443. Little v. Gavin, 244 Ala. 156, 12 So. 2d 549 (1943).

To prevent sale heir may use the same defenses decedent could have used. — When an administrator asks an order to sell lands for the payment of debts under this section the heir at law, as the party in adverse interest, may plead the statute of limitations, or set up any other defense which would be available to the decedent himself, if the action were against him while living. Warren v. Hearne, 82 Ala. 554, 2 So. 491 (1887).

Abatement of legacies where assets insufficient. — See Powell v. Labry, 210 Ala. 248, 97 So. 707 (1923).

The devisees are the only necessary parties defendant to a petition for sale of the devised lands to pay debts. Williams v. Williams, 49 Ala. 439 (1873).

Administrator cum testamento annexo was a proper party to maintain suit for slander of title because, even though title to the property passed to the devisees upon the death of prior owner, such passing was subject to the payment of debts and charges against the estate and administrator had duty imposed by law to sell realty to pay debts in the event the personal estate is insufficient to pay the debts. Proctor v. Gissendaner, 579 F.2d 876 (5th Cir. 1978).

Where administration of estate was removed from probate court to circuit court, administratrix was removed along with proceedings to circuit court and was authorized to ask permission to proceed in circuit court with her petition filed in probate court for sale of lands for payment of debts of estate. And circuit court had no discretion as to whether to permit administratrix to proceed with petition to sell lands for payment of debts, or whether to allow Mokvant in original motion for sale to proceed, where such motion which was filed in circuit court prior to issue of letters of administration to administratrix was simply a motion for sale of lands for division among joint owners but motion did not trace title into joint owners. Ex parte Stephens, 233 Ala. 167, 170 So. 771 (1936).

Cited in Kitchell v. Jackson, 44 Ala. 302 (1870); Hill v. Erwin, 44 Ala. 661 (1870); Mobile v. Dargan, 45 Ala. 310 (1871); Shiver v. Shiver, 45 Ala. 349 (1871); Mosely v. Tuthill, 45 Ala. 621 (1871); Williams v. Williams, 49 Ala. 439 (1873); Wallace v. Nichols, 56 Ala. 321 (1876); Gibbs v. Hodge, 65 Ala. 366 (1880); Ford v. Ford, 68 Ala. 141 (1880); Quarles v. Campbell, 72 Ala. 64 (1882); Morgan v. Casey, 73 Ala. 222 (1882); Sharp v. Sharp, 76 Ala. 312 (1884); Griffith v. Rudisill, 141 Ala. 200, 37 So. 83 (1904); Nelson v. Atkins, 215 Ala. 88, 109 So. 882 (1926); Murphy v. Vaughan, 226 Ala. 461, 147 So. 404 (1933); Kelly v. Kelly, 250 Ala. 664, 35 So. 2d 686 (1948); Tolar v. Tolar, 337 So. 2d 1284 (Ala. 1976); Dorough v. Johnson, 373 So. 1082 (Ala. 1979).

Collateral references. — 33 C.J.S., Executors & Administrators, §§ 269, 274-277.

31 Am. Jur. 2d, Executors & Administrators, §§ 351-357.

Right to exercise power of sale of real estate after time limited by will. 31 ALR 1394.

Exchange of property as covered by power of sale. 63 ALR 1003.

Execution by executor empowered to sell or mortgage, of deed or mortgage without referring to power, as exercise thereof. 91 ALR 433, 127 ALR 248.

Power of sale of real estate given to executor as impliedly conferring right to possession. 94 ALR 1140.

Liability on bond of executor or administrator for proceeds of sale of real estate under power in will. 104 ALR 202.

Statutory provision permitting sale of homestead for purpose of paying decedent's debts or legacies. 116 ALR 85.

Mortgage or other encumbrance as affecting duty of executor or administrator of insolvent estate to sell real estate to pay debts, or duty of probate court to order such sale. 116 ALR 910.

Right or duty of executor or administrator as to contest of order directing sale of real estate for payment of debt. 126 ALR 903.

Remedies in event of delay in exercise of power to sell or rent estate conferred by will. 132 ALR 1473.

Implied power of executor to sell real property. 134 ALR 378, 23 ALR2d 1000.

Realty not specifically referred to in power nor devised by will as within power of sale conferred upon executor. 139 ALR 1143.

Rights and remedies of purchaser at judicial sale where sale is void or set aside because proceedings are imperfect or irregular, or where description of property is defective. 142 ALR 310.

Waiver or renunciation of right to administer decedent's estate as affecting power of sale. 153 ALR 239.

What constitutes public sale. 4 ALR2d 575.

Right of administrator with will annexed to execute power of sale conferred by will. 9 ALR2d 1324.

Power of sale conferred on executor by testator as authorizing private sale. 11 ALR2d 955.

Power of executor to create easement, implied from power to sell. 44 ALR2d 573.

Power of public administrator to sell realty of estate. 56 ALR2d 1191.

§ 43-2-442. Same — In case of intestacy.

In case of intestacy, lands may be sold by the administrator for the payment of debts, when the personal estate is insufficient therefor. (Code 1852, § 1755; Code 1867, § 2080; Code 1876, § 2448; Code 1886, § 2104; Code 1896, § 156; Code 1907, § 2620; Code 1923, § 5848; Code 1940, T. 61, § 244.)

Cross references. — See notes to § 43-2-441.

As to necessity for sale of entire interest of decedent, see notes to § 43-2-450.

Duty is mandatory. — The duty of an administrator to sell realty for payment of debts in case personalty is insufficient is "mandatory." Moebes v. Kay, 241 Ala. 294, 2 So. 2d 754 (1941); Dorrough v. McKee, 264 Ala. 663, 89 So. 2d 77 (1956).

When there are debts of an estate and the personalty is insufficient to satisfy said debts, it is mandatory that the administrator sell the lands of the estate to pay said debts. Smith v. Smith, 266 Ala. 118, 94 So. 2d 863 (1957); Gilmore v. Roberson, 273 Ala. 230, 139 So. 2d 604 (1962).

Administrator has only bare power. — In regard to the sale of lands for payment of debts, an administrator or executor has only a bare power over the lands. Gilmore v. Roberson, 273 Ala. 230, 139 So. 2d 604 (1962).

The existence of which depends upon necessity for its exercise. — While by no act of the heir or devisee can the power of the administrator to sell be frustrated, the existence of the power itself depends upon the existence of the necessity for its exercise — the payment of debts of the testator or intestate. Gilmore v. Roberson, 273 Ala. 230, 139 So. 2d 604 (1962).

When the necessity of sale does not exist, as where the heirs are willing to pay all of the debts or charges against the estate, it would be unconscionable to allow the personal representative to disturb the possession of the heir or of the devisee or of the alienee of the one or of the other. Gilmore v. Roberson, 273 Ala. 230, 139 So. 2d 604 (1962).

The administrator cannot be controlled by the heirs, nor take orders from them. The duty and responsibility is upon the administrator. Gilmore v. Roberson, 273 Ala. 230, 139 So. 2d 604 (1962).

The right of an administrator to sell land to pay debts of his intestate is wholly statutory, and he alone can do so on the conditions and in the manner prescribed by this section. Austin v. Eyster, 242 Ala. 402, 6 So. 2d 892 (1942); Smith v. Smith, 266 Ala. 118, 94 So. 2d 863 (1957).

If there was an original deficiency of personal assets for the payment of debts, then under the very terms of this section a sale of the realty is due as a matter of course, or, if these assets have become unavailing from depreciation or loss through no fault of the administrator or creditor, the realty may be sold, the result being the same as if there had been an original lack of personalty. Moebes v. Kay, 241 Ala. 294, 2 So. 2d 754 (1941).

And failure to sell realty may subject administrator to civil action. — Failure of administrator to sell realty in order to pay debts in case the personalty is insufficient may subject administrator to civil action by a creditor of the estate, in order that the creditor may secure judgment against the administrator as such, attended with the consequence of being personally liable therefor if the judgment is allowed to stand and execution issued and returned "no property." Moebes v. Kay, 241 Ala. 294, 2 So. 2d 754 (1941).

Or creditor may force a sale. — Where there is insufficient personalty for payment of intestate's debts; the initial duty to sell the land devolves upon administrator, and if he arbitrarily fails to act upon reasonable demand or after reasonable length of time, creditor may force a sale of realty upon allegation and proof of such facts. Moebes v. Kay, 241 Ala. 294, 2 So. 2d 754 (1941).

Presumption where creditor reduces claim to judgment. — The creditor may reduce his claim to a judgment and a presumption of a devastavit will arise against the administrator if the judgment is allowed to stand, but this will not estop the sureties on the bond from denying that such administrator had come into possession of assets with which to discharge the debts, and there being no devastavit in fact no action will lie against them. Moebes v. Kay, 241 Ala. 294, 2 So. 2d 754 (1941).

Realty of persons dying intestate in this state descends to the heirs at law subject to the payments of debts in event personalty is insufficient for that purpose. Moebes v. Kay, 241 Ala. 294, 2 So. 2d 754 (1941).

Personal representative may intercept possession of heirs. — This section permits the personal representative to intercept and take possession of land from the heirs or their vendee, if a necessity exists therefor. Johnson v. Sandlin, 206 Ala. 53, 89 So. 81 (1921).

Heir at law could not maintain petition to sell lands belonging to intestate decedent for division during pendency of action by administratrix for leave to sell land to pay debts of deceased on ground personal property was insufficient for that purpose. Austin v. Eyster, 242 Ala. 402, 6 So. 2d 892 (1942).

One heir may purchase entire estate. — Tenants in common are in a confidential relationship to each other by operation of law as to the joint property. And a cotenant cannot buy an outstanding adversary claim to the common estate and assert it for his exclusive benefit to the injury or prejudice of his co-owners. However, this rule does not prevent one heir from purchasing the entire estate at an administrator's sale for the purpose of subjecting the land to the payment of the debts of the decedent. Smith v. Smith, 266 Ala. 118, 94 So. 2d 863 (1957).

Court is vendor. — In an administrator's sale of deceased's lands to pay the debts of his intestate, the court is the vendor. Smith v. Smith, 266 Ala. 118, 94 So. 2d 863 (1957).

Sufficiency of petition. — A petition averring that the personal property of the estate is insufficient for the payment of debts, and that the sale of the land is necessary for that purpose is sufficient. Peavy v. Griffin, 152 Ala. 256, 44 So. 400 (1907). See also Cotton v. Holloway, 96 Ala. 544, 12 So. 172 (1892), wherein it is held that it is unnecessary to allege the amount of the debts or the value of the personalty, and overruling on this point, Abernathy v. O'Reilly, 90 Ala. 495, 7 So. 919 (1890), overruled on other grounds, Cotton v. Holloway, 96 Ala. 544, 12 So. 172 (1892). See also Garner v. Toney, 107 Ala. 352, 18 So. 161 (1895).

It is absolutely indispensable that the petition contain not only the above averment (insufficiency of personalty), but also the existence of debts. And unless it does this, the court is without jurisdiction and any decree rendered on the defective petition is a nullity even on collateral attack. Abernathy v. O'Reilly, 90 Ala. 495, 7 So. 919 (1890), overruled on other grounds, Cotton v. Holloway, 96 Ala. 544, 12 So. 172 (1892). See also Alford v. Alford, 96 Ala. 385, 11 So. 316 (1892), containing specific enumeration of the requisites of the petition. As to further contents of application, see § 43-2-444 and notes thereto.

Cited in Wiley v. White, 3 Stew. & Port. 355 (1833); Forward v. Armstead, 12 Ala. 124 (1847); Doe v. Riley, 28 Ala. 164 (1856); Griffin v. Bland, 43 Ala. 542 (1869); Kitchell v. Jackson, 44 Ala. 302 (1870); Spragins v. Taylor, 48 Ala. 520 (1872); Thornton v. Neal, 49 Ala. 590 (1873); Griffith v. Rudisill, 141 Ala. 200, 37 So. 83 (1904); Alvarez v. Warner, 201 Ala. 50, 77 So. 344 (1917); Turk v. Turk, 206 Ala. 312, 89 So. 457 (1921); Dirago v. Taylor, 227 Ala. 271, 150 So. 150 (1933); McGregor v. McGregor, 249 Ala. 75, 29 So. 2d 561 (1947); McClendon v. Straub, 193 F.2d 596 (5th Cir. 1952); Gibson v. Hall, 260 Ala. 539, 71 So. 2d 532 (1954); Bodiford v. Ganus, 276 Ala. 510, 164 So. 2d 701 (1964).

§ 43-2-443. Same — Sale for division.

Lands of an estate may be sold by order of the probate court having jurisdiction of the estate when the same cannot be equitably divided among the heirs or devisees, when an adult heir or devisee files his written consent that the land be sold. (Code 1852, § 1867; Code 1867, § 2221; Code 1876, § 2449; Code 1886, § 2105; Code 1896, § 157; Code 1907, § 2621; Code 1923, § 5849; Code 1940, T. 61, § 245.)

Initial procedure. — Under this section one or more of the adult heirs must become the actor by filing a written consent to the sale, whereas the duty to sell the lands where there is insufficient personalty to pay the debts is mandatory. Boyte v. Perkins, 211 Ala. 130, 99 So. 652 (1924).

Order of probate court for sale of land without written consent of adult heir or devisee was void. Forman v. McAnear, 219 Ala. 157, 121 So. 538 (1929); Dawkins v. Hutto, 222 Ala. 132, 131 So. 228 (1930).

Petition may be filed by administrator together with one or more heirs. — A petition contemplating a sale of real estate for division among the joint owners, including a distribution among the heirs of an intestate, may properly be filed by the administrator, together with one or more of the heirs of the intestate. McGowin v. Robinson, 251 Ala. 690, 39 So. 2d 237 (1949).

Priority of proceeding for division under section 35-6-20. — In a proceeding under § 35-6-20, wherein the heirs filed a complaint to sell lands of intestate for division, a plea in abatement (now motion to dismiss) by administrator which alleged that a petition had been filed in probate court by the administrator upon the request of an adult heir to sell the real estate for distribution among the heirs was insufficient where it appeared that lands of the intestate were not needed to pay the debts of the estate or costs of administration and the time for filing claims against the estate had expired, since to hold otherwise would give the administrator under this section, rights prior to those conferred upon the heirs at law under the provisions of § 35-6-20, contrary to legislative intent. Dorrough v. McKee, 264 Ala. 663, 89 So. 2d 77 (1956).

An action to sell land for distribution under § 35-6-20 does not have priority over an action under this section. Estate of Autry v. McDonald, 332 So. 2d 377 (Ala. 1976).

Lands in which decedent held equitable interest may be sold. — Under this section the probate court has jurisdiction to sell for division lands in which the decedent held only an equitable interest. Jones v. Woodstock Iron Co., 95 Ala. 551, 10 So. 635 (1892), where the authorities are collected.

In Vaughan v. Holmes, 22 Ala. 593 (1853), it was held that a purchaser of lands, who died before paying the entire purchase money, had such an inchoate interest or equity as was subject to sale under this section.

Intestate must have title at death. — Under this section the probate court has no jurisdiction to order the sale of land, the title to which intestate did not have at the time of his death, but which was taken after his death, in the name of the heirs, by the administrator who paid the balance of the purchase price out of the funds of the estate. Jones v. Woodstock Iron Co., 95 Ala. 551, 10 So. 635 (1892).

Administrator in preference to heir is entitled to intercept rents from real estate of decedent for payment of debts of estate when personal estate is insufficient therefor, under § 43-2-442, or for charges against the estate, and setting aside of dower under § 6-10-95, or for sale of land when same cannot be equitably divided, under this section. Johnson v. Moxley, 22 Ala. App. 1, 113 So. 651 (1926), rev'd on other grounds, 216 Ala. 466, 113 So. 656 (1927).

Averment as to seisin held sufficient. — The supreme court has held sufficient an averment that decedent died seised and possessed of the following described real estate, to wit "certain interests and rights not definitely known to your petitioner. . . ." Rucker v. Tennessee Coal, Iron & R.R., 176 Ala. 456, 58 So. 465 (1912).

Decree is not subject to collateral attack for irregularities. — The decree ordering sale under this section cannot be collaterally attacked because of irregularities, such as the omission of the name of any of the heirs, the court being one of general jurisdiction in regard to those matters. Conniff v. McFarlin, 178 Ala. 160, 59 So. 472 (1912).

Cited in England v. McLaughlin, 35 Ala. 590 (1860); Satcher v. Satcher, 41 Ala. 26 (1867); Brown v. Powell, 45 Ala. 149 (1871); McSwean v. Foulks, 46 Ala. 610 (1871); Smitha v. Flournoy, 47 Ala. 345 (1872); Avery v. Avery, 47 Ala. 505 (1872); Snedicor v. Mobley, 47 Ala. 517 (1872); Warnock v. Thomas, 48 Ala. 463 (1872); DeBardelaben v. Stoudenmire, 48 Ala. 643 (1872); Thornton v. Neal, 49 Ala. 590 (1873); Ford v. Garner, 49 Ala. 601 (1873); Calloway v. Kirkland, 50 Ala. 401 (1874); Bland v. Bowie, 53 Ala. 152 (1875); Gillespie v. Nabors, 59 Ala. 441 (1877); Moore v. Randolph, 70 Ala. 575 (1881); Bragg v. Beers, 71 Ala. 151 (1881); Clark v. Hughes, 71 Ala. 163 (1881); Farris v. Houston, 74 Ala. 162 (1883); Pollard v. Hanrick, 74 Ala. 334 (1883); Roulston v. Washington, 79 Ala. 529 (1885); Bolling v. Smith, 79 Ala. 535 (1885); Wilson v. Holt, 83 Ala. 528, 3 So. 321 (1887); McEvoy v. Leonard, 89 Ala. 455, 8 So. 40 (1890); Matthews v. Matthews, 104 Ala. 303, 16 So. 91 (1893); Griffith v. Rudisill, 141 Ala. 200, 37 So. 83 (1904); Roy v. Roy, 159 Ala. 555, 48 So. 793 (1909); Hardwick v. Hardwick, 164 Ala. 390, 51 So. 389 (1909); Spiers v. Zeigler, 175 Ala. 664, 57 So. 699 (1912); Snodgrass v. Snodgrass, 176 Ala. 160, 57 So. 474 (1912); Crowder v. Doe, 193 Ala. 470, 68 So. 1005 (1915); Dent v. Foy, 206 Ala. 454, 90 So. 317 (1921); Boyte v. Perkins, 211 Ala. 130, 99 So. 652 (1924); Nelson v. Atkins, 215 Ala. 88, 109 So. 882 (1926); Murphy v. Vaughan, 226 Ala. 461, 147 So. 404 (1933); Campbell v. Carter, 248 Ala. 294, 27 So. 2d 490 (1946); McGregor v. McGregor, 249 Ala. 75, 29 So. 2d 561 (1947); Hamilton v. Mayer, 345 So. 2d 1334 (Ala. 1977).

§ 43-2-444. Application for sale.

The application for the sale of lands, either for payment of debts or for division, must be made by the executor or administrator in writing, verified by affidavit, to the probate court having jurisdiction of the estate, must describe the lands accurately, must give the names of the heirs or devisees, and their places of residence and must also state whether any, and which of such heirs or devisees, are under the age of 19 years or of unsound mind; and such application may be contested by any party interested in the estate. (Code 1852, §§ 1759, 1868; Code 1867, §§ 2085, 2222; Code 1876, §§ 2450, 2453; Code 1886, § 2106; Code 1896, § 158; Code 1907, § 2622; Code 1923, § 5851; Code 1940, T. 61, § 246.)

Cross references. — See notes §§ 43-2-441 through 43-2-443.

Purpose of this section. — The purpose of this section is to require such a description of the land in the application that a decree can be rendered therein that will be so exact and accurate that a purchaser at a sale thereunder will know from the proceedings just what land he bought. Little v. Marx, 145 Ala. 620, 39 So. 517 (1905).

Filing of application by administrator is mandatory. — Unless the application is filed by the executor or administrator the probate court acquires no jurisdiction. Bolen v. Hoven, 143 Ala. 652, 39 So. 379 (1905).

And such application should be filed within 20 years. — Where one of several heirs has been in the possession of lands of a decedent for 20 years, holding adversely, notoriously and exclusively, by independent claim of right in himself, the application for a sale for distribution among the heirs authorized by this section should not be granted, although the statute does not, in terms, limit the time within which application must be made. Bozeman v. Bozeman, 82 Ala. 389, 2 So. 732 (1887).

Insufficiency of personalty is a jurisdictional fact. — This section, it will be noticed, does not, ex vi termini, require an allegation in the petition that the personal property belonging to the decedent's estate is insufficient for the payment of debts, and in construing it the supreme court has held that on direct attack by appeal the proceeding is in personam, but on collateral attack it is to be regarded as in rem. But in view of § 43-2-449, it is manifest that the insufficiency of personal property for the payment of the debts of the estate is the jurisdictional fact upon the existence of which the right and power of sale in such cases is made to depend. Cotton v. Holloway, 96 Ala. 544, 12 So. 172 (1892).

A purchaser of a homestead from the widow is a party interested in the estate, within the meaning of the last clause of this section, and this is true although at the time of the purchase said property had not been set apart to the widow as a homestead. Newell v. Johns, 128 Ala. 584, 29 So. 609 (1901).

Hence he cannot maintain an action to enjoin the sale, but must pursue his remedy by contesting the application hereunder. Spear v. Banks, 114 Ala. 323, 21 So. 834 (1897).

Sufficiency of description of lands. — Jurisdiction in a proceeding under this section is founded on the petition, and it does not attach where the land is not described with sufficient certainty. Kornegay v. Mayer, 135 Ala. 141, 33 So. 36 (1902).

In Alvarez v. Warner, 201 Ala. 50, 77 So. 344 (1917), it was said that the petition must conform to the requirement herein named.

An application describing certain lands by metes and bounds and seeking to sell all such lands, "except 150 acres thereof deeded by A. to B." on a certain date, but which does not describe or identify the land so deeded, is insufficient. Little v. Marx, 145 Ala. 620, 39 So. 517 (1905).

The description was insufficient in Rucker v. Tennessee Coal, Iron & R.R., 176 Ala. 456, 58 So. 465 (1912).

But was sufficient in Alvarez v. Warner, 201 Ala. 50, 77 So. 344 (1917).

Failure to indicate with any degree of accuracy the section, township and range in which the lands are located invalidates the petition. Henley v. Johnston, 134 Ala. 646, 32 So. 1009 (1902).

Petition must show residence and status of heirs. — It is reversible error where the petition fails to state the places of residence of heirs as herein required, and whether they are minors or married women. Bozeman v. Bozeman, 82 Ala. 389, 2 So. 732 (1887).

Answer of heir or devisee is appropriate to contest application. — Under this section formal pleadings are not required nor practiced and the answer of the heir or devisee is sufficient if it denies the existence of the debts for the payment of which the land is sought to be sold. Little v. Marx, 145 Ala. 620, 39 So. 517 (1905). See also Alvarez v. Warner, 201 Ala. 50, 77 So. 344 (1917).

Cited in Henderson v. Richardson, 5 Ala. 349 (1843); Beck v. Simmons, 7 Ala. 71 (1844); Hitchcock v. United States Bank, 7 Ala. 386 (1845); Perkins v. Winter, 7 Ala. 855 (1845); Holman v. Bank of Norfolk, 12 Ala. 369 (1847); Carrington & Co. v. Manning, 13 Ala. 611 (1848); Beall v. Williamson, 14 Ala. 55 (1848); Governor v. Wiley, 14 Ala. 172 (1848); Cloud v. Barton, 14 Ala. 347 (1848); McMorris v. Crawford, 15 Ala. 271 (1849); Lightfoot v. Lightfoot, 27 Ala. 351 (1855); Fields v. Goldsby, 28 Ala. 218 (1856); Stewart v. Stewart, 31 Ala. 207 (1857); Pearson v. Darrington, 32 Ala. 227 (1858); Pettit v. Pettit, 32 Ala. 288 (1858); Hoard v. Hoard, 41 Ala. 590 (1868); Page v. Matthew, 41 Ala. 719 (1868); Brown v. Powell, 45 Ala. 149 (1871); Shiver v. Shiver, 45 Ala. 349 (1871); Smitha v. Flournoy, 47 Ala. 345 (1872); Avery v. Avery, 47 Ala. 505 (1872); Snedicor v. Mobley, 47 Ala. 517 (1872); Spragins v. Taylor, 48 Ala. 520 (1872); DeBardelaben v. Stoudenmire, 48 Ala. 643 (1872); Bland v. Bowie, 53 Ala. 152 (1875); Hatchett v. Curbow, 59 Ala. 516 (1877); Whorton v. Moragne, 62 Ala. 201 (1878); Ford v. Ford, 68 Ala. 141 (1880); Clark v. Hughes, 71 Ala. 163 (1881); Gilchrist v. Shackleford, 72 Ala. 7 (1882); Griffith v. Rudisill, 141 Ala. 200, 37 So. 83 (1904); Crowder v. Doe, 193 Ala. 470, 68 So. 1005 (1915); Grayson v. Roberts, 229 Ala. 245, 156 So. 552 (1934); McGregor v. McGregor, 249 Ala. 75, 29 So. 2d 561 (1947); Estate of Autry v. McDonald, 332 So. 2d 377 (Ala. 1976).

Collateral references. — 33 C.J.S., Executors & Administrators, §§ 279, 280.

§ 43-2-445. Notice and hearing generally; time for hearing; appointment of guardian ad litem.

(a) The court must appoint a day, not less than 30 days from the time of making such application, for the hearing thereof, and must appoint a proper person, not a petitioner or of kin to a petitioner, as a guardian ad litem, to represent the minors or persons of unsound mind, if any there be, and must issue a citation to the heirs or devisees of full age, and residing in this state, notifying them of the application, and the day appointed for hearing the same, which must be served on them 10 days before the day appointed for the hearing.

(b) If such application be for the sale of land for the payment of debts, notice must also be given by publication, once a week for three successive weeks, in some newspaper published in the county, or by posting up notice at the courthouse door and three other public places in the county, at the discretion of the court. If no newspaper is published in the county, notices must be posted as above prescribed. (Code 1852, § 1869; Code 1867, §§ 2223, 2224; Code 1876, §§ 2451, 2454; Code 1886, §§ 2107, 2108; Code 1896, §§ 159, 160; Code 1907, §§ 2623, 2624; Code 1923, §§ 5852, 5853; Code 1940, T. 61, §§ 247, 248.)

Lack of notice. — The failure to give notice as herein prescribed will not render the proceedings void on collateral attack. Lyons v. Hamner, 84 Ala. 197, 4 So. 26 (1887). This because the proceedings are in rem. See on this point notes to § 43-2-441.

Cited in Doe v. Riley, 28 Ala. 164 (1856); Ex parte Russell, 29 Ala. 717 (1857); Summersett v. Summersett, 40 Ala. 596 (1867); Satcher v. Satcher, 41 Ala. 26 (1867); Snedicor v. Mobley, 47 Ala. 517 (1872); Williams v. Williams, 49 Ala. 439 (1873); Bland v. Bowie, 53 Ala. 152 (1875); Crowder v. Doe, 193 Ala. 470, 68 So. 1005 (1915).

Collateral references. — 34 C.J.S., Executors & Administrators, §§ 559, 564.

31 Am. Jur. 2d, Executors & Administrators, §§ 362-365.

§ 43-2-446. Notice to nonresidents.

If any of the heirs or devisees reside out of this state, such heirs or devisees may be brought into court by publication, once a week for three successive weeks, in a newspaper published in the county in which the application is made, or if none is published therein, then in the newspaper published nearest to the courthouse of such county. (Code 1852, § 1871; Code 1867, § 2227; Code 1876, § 2452; Code 1886, § 2109; Code 1896, § 161; Code 1907, § 2625; Code 1923, § 5854; Code 1940, T. 61, § 249.)

Cited in Thompson v. Acree, 69 Ala. 178 (1881); Goodwin v. Sims, 86 Ala. 102, 5 So. 587 (1889).

§ 43-2-447. Notice to unknown parties; appointment of special guardian; disposition of shares.

If it shall be averred in an application for the sale of lands for the payment of debts or for division, that the names of any of the heirs or devisees are unknown, that the petitioner has made diligent inquiry and cannot ascertain the same, the cause may proceed against them without naming them; but the court must make publication as in case of nonresidents, describing such unknown parties as near as may be by the character in which they are made parties and with reference to their interest in the lands sought to be sold, and must appoint a suitable and competent person not of kin or counsel to the petitioner, as special guardian to represent such unknown parties. The shares or interests of such unknown parties, in the proceeds of lands sold for division, shall be paid into court and there retained and paid out to the proper parties when ascertained. (Code 1896, § 162; Code 1907, § 2626; Code 1923, § 5855; Code 1940, T. 61, § 250.)

Cited in Swoope v. Darrow, 237 Ala. 692, 188 So. 879 (1939); Garrison v. Kelley, 257 Ala. 105, 57 So. 2d 345 (1952).

§ 43-2-448. Duties and compensation of guardian ad litem and special guardian.

The person appointed to represent minors, or persons of unsound mind, or unknown parties, must deny in writing the allegations contained in the application, and, if necessary, must employ counsel to defend the interests of those he represents. He is entitled to reasonable compensation, to be fixed by the court, and taxed and collected as costs. (Code 1867, § 2224; Code 1876, § 2454; Code 1886, § 2110; Code 1896, § 163; Code 1907, § 2627; Code 1923, § 5856; Code 1940, T. 61, § 251.)

Cited in Perkins v. Winter, 7 Ala. 855 (1845); Ex parte Russell, 29 Ala. 717 (1857); Stewart v. Stewart, 31 Ala. 207 (1857); Bland v. Bowie, 53 Ala. 152 (1875); Ford v. Ford, 68 Ala. 141 (1880); Garrison v. Kelley, 257 Ala. 105, 57 So. 2d 345 (1952).

§ 43-2-449. Proof of insufficiency of personalty.

On the day appointed for hearing an application for the sale of land for the payment of debts, or on any other day to which it is continued, the applicant must show to the court that the personal property of the estate is insufficient for the payment of debts; and such proof may be made by the deposition of disinterested witnesses, or by oral examination of disinterested witnesses in open court, which must be reduced to writing, and filed and carefully preserved, but not recorded and for all purposes shall be considered a part of the record. (Code 1852, § 1758; Code 1867, § 2084; Code 1876, § 2455; Code 1886, § 2111; Code 1896, § 164; Code 1907, § 2628; Code 1923, § 5857; Code 1940, T. 61, § 252.)

Purpose of this section. — The object of this section is to require very satisfactory proof of the salable value of the personal property, so as to show the necessity of resorting to the land of the decedent for the payment of his debts. Curtis v. Hunt, 158 Ala. 78, 48 So. 598 (1909).

Insufficiency of personalty is a jurisdictional fact. — The enactment of this section together with the omission from § 43-2-444, of the requirement of averring the insufficiency of personalty may be suggestive of a legislative intent that the jurisdiction should depend, not upon the averment of that fact, but upon its proof. Cotton v. Holloway, 96 Ala. 544, 12 So. 172 (1892). See also notes to § 43-2-444.

Which must be proved by disinterested witnesses. — The insufficiency of the personal property to pay debts must be proved as required by this section (that is, by deposition of disinterested witnesses) in order to authorize the sale. Little v. Marx, 145 Ala. 620, 39 So. 517 (1905).

Proof by one witness is sufficient. — The necessity for the sale hereunder may be proved by only one witness though this section uses the term "witnesses", this because by § 1-1-2 "the singular includes the plural, and the plural the singular." Thompson v. Boswell, 97 Ala. 570, 12 So. 809 (1893).

The uncontroverted deposition of one witness that the only personal property the deceased had was livestock, which died after her death, and that the deceased was indebted on a note given for the price of land, authorizes a decree of sale. Garner v. Toney, 107 Ala. 352, 18 So. 161 (1895).

Further proof is not necessary where estate is insolvent. — The declaration by the court that the estate is insolvent adjudicates the necessity to sell both the realty and personalty for the payment of debts, dispensing with other or further proof, and this is conclusive on the heirs. Dolan v. Dolan, 89 Ala. 256, 7 So. 425 (1890).

Depositions may be controverted by oral evidence. — The depositions read in the application for the sale of land for payment of decedent's debts may be controverted by oral evidence. Garner v. Toney, 107 Ala. 352, 18 So. 161 (1895).

Administrator as "disinterested witness". — The personal representative is a disinterested witness in respect of the character and identity of the personal property, but not such disinterested witness upon the question of value of that property. But a failure to object to the competency of administratrix to testify as to the value is a waiver thereof. Curtis v. Hunt, 158 Ala. 78, 48 So. 598 (1909).

Witness and administrator bearing same name. — The proceedings will not be held void on collateral attack on proof that one of the witnesses was of the same name as the administrator where it does not appear that the administrator was the same person who was examined as the witness. Kent v. Mansel, 101 Ala. 334, 14 So. 489 (1893).

Creditor is a competent witness. — Miller v. Mayer, 124 Ala. 434, 26 So. 892 (1899) holds that a creditor is a disinterested witness within the meaning of this section. See also Alford v. Alford, 96 Ala. 385, 11 So. 316 (1892). See also § 12-21-163.

Proof of existence of debts. — This section does not require the existence of decedent's debts to be proved by disinterested witnesses. Alford v. Alford, 96 Ala. 385, 11 So. 316 (1892); Miller v. Mayer, 124 Ala. 434, 26 So. 892 (1899).

It is asserted in Quarles v. Campbell, 72 Ala. 64 (1882), that the averment of the petition as to the existence of debts must be proved by depositions of disinterested witnesses. This statement was not necessary to the decision of the case, and is said not to "correctly state the law." Alford v. Alford, 96 Ala. 385, 11 So. 316 (1892).

Cited in Beck v. Simmons, 7 Ala. 71 (1844); Butler v. Merchants' Ins. Co., 14 Ala. 777 (1848); Upchurch v. Norsworthy, 15 Ala. 705 (1849); Fields v. Goldsby, 28 Ala. 218 (1856); Vauss v. Thomas, 249 Ala. 449, 31 So. 2d 502 (1947); Tolar v. Tolar, 337 So. 2d 1284 (Ala. 1976).

§ 43-2-450. Order of sale for payment of debts.

On the hearing of such application, if the court is satisfied that the personal property of the estate is insufficient to pay the debts, and when the application is by an executor or administrator with the will annexed, that no power is given by the will for that purpose, the court may direct the sale of all, or such portion of the real estate as may be necessary to pay the debts; and such sale may be had on such credit as the court may direct, not exceeding two years. (Code 1852, § 1760; Code 1867, § 2086; Code 1876, § 2456; Code 1886, § 2112; Code 1896, § 165; Code 1907, § 2629; Code 1923, § 5858; Code 1940, T. 61, § 253.)

Cross references. — As to sufficiency of petition, see notes to §§ 43-2-441, 43-2-442 and 43-2-444.

Land may be sold only when personal property insufficient. — The lands of a decedent can be ordered sold only when the personal property in the estate is insufficient to pay the debts or for division. Cox v. United States, 421 F.2d 576 (5th Cir. 1970).

Sale must be of decedent's entire interest in parcel sold. — The legislature intended by this section and § 43-2-464 to empower the judge of probate to sell a part or parcel of the realty of a decedent's estate when the debts owed by the estate were not enough to require the sale of all the realty owned by the deceased at the time of his death, but the judge of probate can only authorize the sale of the entire interest which the decedent had in that part or parcel to be sold. Smith v. Smith, 266 Ala. 118, 94 So. 2d 863 (1957).

Court may not sell lands reserving mineral interest. — The probate court was without statutory authority to sell the lands reserving the mineral interest to the heirs. Smith v. Smith, 266 Ala. 118, 94 So. 2d 863 (1957).

Cited in Hill v. Erwin, 44 Ala. 661 (1870); Quarles v. Campbell, 72 Ala. 64 (1882); Moore v. Cottingham, 113 Ala. 148, 20 So. 994 (1896); Miller v. Mayer, 124 Ala. 434, 26 So. 892 (1899); Cottingham v. Moore, 128 Ala. 209, 30 So. 784 (1900); Myers v. Parker, 349 So. 2d 1136 (Ala. 1977).

Collateral references. — 34 C.J.S., Executors & Administrators, § 574.

§ 43-2-451. Proof of facts on application to sell for division; order of sale.

The facts stated in an application to sell land for distribution may be proved or disproved by the deposition of disinterested witnesses, or by oral examination of disinterested witnesses in open court, which must be reduced to writing, filed and recorded; and if the facts stated in such application are proven to the satisfaction of the court by the evidence, the court may order a sale of the land, which must be sold on such terms as the court may direct, not exceeding a credit of three years. (Code 1852, § 1872; Code 1867, § 2228; Code 1876, § 2457; Code 1886, § 2113; Code 1896, § 166; Code 1907, § 2630; Code 1923, § 5859; Code 1940, T. 61, § 254.)

Affidavit is not essential. — Under this section no affidavit is required setting forth the cause for making the depositions herein provided for. Bozeman v. Bozeman, 83 Ala. 416, 3 So. 784 (1888).

The deposition of one disinterested witness is sufficient on collateral attack though there be minors interested. Thompson v. Boswell, 97 Ala. 570, 12 So. 809 (1893).

Sale must precede ascertainment of attorney's fee. — A sale under this section (or under § 35-6-62, for purpose of partition) should be had before ascertaining the amount of solicitor's fees authorized by § 34-3-60. This because the sale price of the land is an essential factor in determining the amount of these fees. Graham v. Graham, 207 Ala. 648, 93 So. 660 (1922).

Cited in Brown v. Brown, 41 Ala. 215 (1867); Kitchell v. Jackson, 44 Ala. 302 (1870); Brown v. Powell, 45 Ala. 149 (1871); Garrett v. Lynch, 45 Ala. 204 (1871); Dugger v. Tayloe, 46 Ala. 320 (1871); Avery v. Avery, 47 Ala. 505 (1872); Ketchum v. Creagh, 53 Ala. 224 (1875); Van Hoose v. Bush, 54 Ala. 342 (1875); Calloway v. Kirkland, 57 Ala. 476 (1876); Smith v. Wert, 64 Ala. 34 (1879); Moore v. Randolph, 70 Ala. 575 (1881); Cox v. United States, 421 F.2d 576 (5th Cir. 1970).

§ 43-2-452. When depositions required.

No order for the sale of land belonging to any estate, whether for the payment of debts, or for division, must be made when there are minors or persons of unsound mind or unknown parties interested in such estate, unless the probate court has taken evidence by deposition, showing the necessity of such sale; and such evidence must be taken, whether the allegations in the petition are denied or not by the guardian appointed by the court to represent the minors or persons of unsound mind or unknown parties; and any order of sale and sale, made without a compliance with the requisitions of this section, shall be wholly void. (Code 1867, § 2225; Code 1876, § 2458; Code 1886, § 2114; Code 1896, § 167; Code 1907, § 2631; Code 1923, § 5861; Code 1940, T. 61, § 255.)

Notice of guardian's appointment may be served on mother. — In ejectment, where defendant claimed through an administrator's sale and plaintiff claimed by inheritance, alleging that a guardian ad litem had not been properly appointed for him in the proceedings for such sale because of failure to serve notice before the appointment, and that it was therefore void, it was held that the trial court erred in declining to allow defendant to prove notice of the appointment of a guardian ad litem, served on the mother of the minor. Crowder v. Doe, 193 Ala. 470, 68 So. 1005 (1915).

Sale for benefit of minor. — Under this section, it was error to refuse to allow defendant to prove that depositions were taken to show that the sale would be of interest to the minors. Crowder v. Doe, 193 Ala. 470, 68 So. 1005 (1915).

Proof of order and confirmation of sale. — It is error to refuse to allow proof of the order of sale, the confirmation thereof and the deeds to the purchasers. Crowder v. Doe, 193 Ala. 470, 68 So. 1005 (1915).

One witness is sufficient to prove necessity of sale of decedent's land to pay debts. Thompson v. Boswell, 97 Ala. 570, 12 So. 809 (1893).

Cited in Gee v. Pharr, 5 Ala. 586 (1843); Brown v. Powell, 45 Ala. 149 (1871); Garrett v. Lynch, 45 Ala. 204 (1871); Bruce v. Strickland, 47 Ala. 192 (1872); Smitha v. Flournoy, 47 Ala. 345 (1872); Avery v. Avery, 47 Ala. 505 (1872); Spragins v. Taylor, 48 Ala. 520 (1872); Bland v. Bowie, 53 Ala. 152 (1875); Bibb v. Bishop Cobbs Orphan Home, 61 Ala. 326 (1878); Robertson v. Bradford, 70 Ala. 385 (1881); Quarles v. Campbell, 72 Ala. 64 (1882); Curtis v. Hunt, 158 Ala. 78, 48 So. 598 (1909).

§ 43-2-453. Evidence of title.

In applications to the probate court for the sale of lands, the patent or deed shall be sufficient evidence to authorize the court to proceed and hear the application. (Code 1867, § 2129; Code 1876, § 2473; Code 1886, § 2131; Code 1896, § 186; Code 1907, § 2651; Code 1923, § 5881; Code 1940, T. 61, § 275.)

Deed showing intestate's title to undivided interest admissible. — Under this section it is error to exclude as evidence a deed showing title in the intestate to an undivided half interest in the land at the time of his death. Hunt v. Curtis, 151 Ala. 507, 44 So. 54 (1907).

§ 43-2-454. Dismissal of application upon failure of proof.

If, on the hearing of the application, the facts are not proved, the same must be dismissed at the cost of the applicant, for which execution may issue against him and his sureties. (Code 1852, § 1761; Code 1867, § 2087; Code 1876, § 2459; Code 1886, § 2115; Code 1896, § 168; Code 1907, § 2632; Code 1923, § 5862; Code 1940, T. 61, § 256.)

Cited in Gillespie v. Nabors, 59 Ala. 441 (1877).

Collateral references. — 34 C.J.S., Executors & Administrators, § 573.

§ 43-2-455. Advertisement of sale.

When the application for the sale of land for the payment of debts or division is granted and the land directed to be sold, the executor or administrator must give notice of the day, place and terms of sale, and a description of the property to be sold, by advertisement for three successive weeks in some newspaper published in the county where the sale is to take place; and in case of a sale of lands lying in one body, but in more than one county, such notice must be given in each of the counties. If there is no such paper published in the county or in any county in which notice is required to be given, then, as to the county having no such paper, the notice must be given by posting at the courthouse door, and at three other public places in the county. In addition to the notice prescribed in this section, the court may direct the giving of notice by printed handbills or posters, to be distributed and posted in the manner best calculated to give extended notice of the sale. (Code 1852, § 1762; Code 1867, § 2088; Code 1876, § 2460; Code 1886, § 2116; Code 1896, § 169; Code 1907, § 2633; Code 1923, § 5863; Code 1940, T. 61, § 257.)

Cited in Fields v. Goldsby, 28 Ala. 218 (1856); McIntosh v. Reid, 45 Ala. 456 (1871); United States v. Hiles, 318 F.2d 56 (5th Cir. 1963).

Collateral references. — 34 C.J.S., Executors & Administrators, § 592.

§ 43-2-456. Applicability of sections 43-2-414, 43-2-416 and 43-2-417.

Sections 43-2-414, 43-2-416 and 43-2-417 are applicable to sales of real estate. (Code 1897, § 170; Code 1907, § 2634; Code 1923, § 5864; Code 1940, T. 61, § 258.)

§ 43-2-457. How purchase money secured.

The executor or administrator must secure the purchase money by taking notes or bonds of the purchaser, with sufficient sureties, or taking a purchase money mortgage. (Code 1852, § 1763; Code 1867, § 2089; Code 1876, § 2461; Code 1886, § 2117; Code 1896, § 171; Code 1907, § 2635; Code 1923, § 5865; Code 1940, T. 61, § 259.)

The named security is exclusive. — Under this section the court has no power to authorize, nor the executor to demand security of a different character, and a purchaser is entitled to tender his notes or bonds with two sureties, and demand a confirmation of the sale. Howison v. Oakley, 118 Ala. 215, 23 So. 810 (1898).

Notice of resale to defaulting purchaser. — Purchaser, making no attempt to comply with laws of sale, is not entitled to notice of action setting aside sale and ordering resale. But if his failure only amounts to giving of insufficient notes, then he is entitled to notice before resale. Griel v. Randolph, 108 Ala. 601, 18 So. 609 (1895); Howison v. Oakley, 118 Ala. 215, 23 So. 810 (1898); Oakley v. Howison, 131 Ala. 505, 32 So. 644 (1902).

Cited in Hill v. Erwin, 44 Ala. 661 (1870); Searcy v. Holmes, 45 Ala. 225 (1871); McIntosh v. Reid, 45 Ala. 456 (1871); Cruikshank v. Luttrell, 67 Ala. 318 (1880); May v. Green, 75 Ala. 162 (1883); Morgan v. Virginia-Carolina Chem. Co., 213 Ala. 551, 106 So. 136 (1925).

Collateral references. — 33 C.J.S., Executors & Administrators, § 290.

§ 43-2-458. Place of sale.

Lands may be sold at such place in the county where they lie, as the court may direct; and if they lie in one body, but in more than one county, they may be sold in either of the counties, as the court may direct. (Code 1852, § 1764; Code 1867, § 2090; Code 1876, § 2462; Code 1886, § 2118; Code 1896, § 172; Code 1907, § 2636; Code 1923, § 5866; Code 1940, T. 61, § 260.)

Court may specify place of sale. — The omission of the order of sale to specify the place of sale, as required by this section, is fatal to the validity of the sale. And no power is vested by law in the administrator to select the place. Bozeman v. Bozeman, 82 Ala. 389, 2 So. 732 (1887).

Cited in Ex parte Russell, 29 Ala. 717 (1857);

Brown v. Brown, 41 Ala. 215 (1867); Kitchell v. Jackson, 44 Ala. 302 (1870); Boynton v. Nelson, 46 Ala. 501 (1871); Smitha v. Flournoy, 47 Ala. 345 (1872); Calloway v. Kirkland, 50 Ala. 401 (1874); Sanders v. Robertson, 57 Ala. 465 (1876); Cruikshank v. Luttrell, 67 Ala. 318 (1880).

Collateral references. — 31 Am. Jur. 2d, Executors & Administrators, § 379.

§ 43-2-459. Report and examination of sale — Generally.

The executor or administrator must, within 30 days after such sale, report on oath his proceedings to the court, which report must show whether or not the executor or administrator has any personal pecuniary interest in the sale, whether he is, directly or indirectly, a purchaser at such sale; and the court must examine the same, and may also examine witnesses in relation thereto. (Code 1852, § 1765; Code 1867, § 2091; Code 1876, § 2463; Code 1886, § 2119; Code 1896, § 173; Code 1907, § 2637; Code 1923, § 5867; Code 1940, T. 61, § 261.)

Facts considered in confirming sales. — This section and § 43-2-462 limit the power of the court in passing on the question of confirming sales to three issues: (1) fairness of the sale; (2) adequacy of price; (3) sufficiency or solvency of the sureties, and if the court is satisfied on these three points, it must confirm the sale, and failure in details of the order of sale as to advertising and selling in subdivisions are not of themselves sufficient reason for refusing to confirm a sale of the fairness of which the court is satisfied. Meadows v. Meadows, 81 Ala. 451, 1 So. 29 (1887). See also § 43-2-462 and the notes thereto.

Cited in Mosley v. Tuthill, 45 Ala. 621 (1871); McSwean v. Faulks, 46 Ala. 610 (1871); Field v. Gamble, 47 Ala. 443 (1872); Spragins v. Taylor, 48 Ala. 520 (1872); Fretwell v. McLemore, 52 Ala. 124 (1875); Cruikshank v. Luttrell, 67 Ala. 318 (1880); Thomas v. Caldwell, 136 Ala. 518, 34 So. 949 (1903).

§ 43-2-460. Same — Notice and hearing.

If it appears from the report of the personal representative provided for in section 43-2-459 that he has a personal interest in such sale, or that he was, directly or indirectly, the purchaser at such sale, or if the court is satisfied from the examination of witnesses in relation to the report as provided for in section 43-2-459 that he has such personal interest in the sale adverse to the interest of the heirs or devisees, or that he was, directly or indirectly, the purchaser at such sale, the court shall set a day for the hearing of such report for confirmation, of which hearing the court shall give the adverse parties at least 10 days' notice in any mode or manner to be directed by the court. (Code 1907, § 2638; Code 1923, § 5868; Code 1940, T. 61, § 262.)

Executor may purchase at his own sale. — Under proper safeguards, an executor with a personal interest in the property sold can become the purchaser at his own sale. Batson v. Etheridge, 239 Ala. 535, 195 So. 873 (1940).

Proceedings for review where land purchased by administrator. — Even if the land is bought by the administrator himself, or his attorney for him, this section and § 43-2-461 provide a way by which that matter can be inquired into in the proceedings for confirmation of the sale and for vacating the sale if the sale was not fairly conducted or the price was grossly inadequate. Conniff McFarlin, 178 Ala. 160, 59 So. 472 (1912).

Collateral references. — 33 C.J.S., Executors & Administrators, § 286.

§ 43-2-461. Setting aside sale; resale.

(a) If, on such examination, the court is satisfied that the sale was not fairly conducted, or that the amount for which the land, or any portion of the same, sold was greatly less than its real value, the court may vacate such sale, either in whole or in part.

(b) If it is made to appear to the court previous to the confirmation of such sale, that the sureties taken on the notes or bonds of the purchasers or the security given are insufficient, such sale, as to every such purchaser, must not be confirmed until he gives security for the purchase money to the satisfaction of the court; and if such security is not given within 10 days the sale must be vacated as to the purchaser thus failing.

(c) When any sale of land is vacated, in whole or in part, according to the provisions of subsections (a) and (b) of this section, the court must direct another sale to be had, which must be advertised and conducted in all respects as is provided for the sale of lands under the provisions of this division. (Code 1852, §§ 1766-1768; Code 1867, §§ 2092-2094; Code 1876, §§ 2464-2466; Code 1886, §§ 2120-2122; Code 1896, §§ 174-176; Code 1907, §§ 2639-2641; Code 1923, §§ 5869-5871; Code 1940, T. 61, §§ 263-265.)

Sale may be set aside for inadequacy of price. — When the court is satisfied that a sale has been fairly conducted, it is not authorized to set it aside unless the amount for which the property was sold was greatly less than the real value of the same, and an offer to raise the bid $3,000.00 (one sixth of the price paid) does not show this fact. Schloss-Sheffield Steel & Iron Co. v. Borden, 201 Ala. 628, 79 So. 190 (1918).

Notice of resale to defaulting purchaser. — See same catchline under notes to § 43-2-457.

Purchaser must be notified of insufficiency of security. — Where the two sureties on notes given by the purchaser are found to be insufficient such purchaser is entitled to notice of this fact and a reasonable opportunity to furnish satisfactory sureties before the court is justified in vacating the sale and ordering a resale at his risk. Howison v. Oakley, 118 Ala. 215, 23 So. 810 (1898).

Sufficiency of complaint. — A complaint for the recovery of loss sustained by a second sale, which failed to aver that the purchaser had such notice and opportunity, or facts from which such notice and opportunity followed by necessary inference, was insufficient. Howison v. Oakley, 118 Ala. 215, 23 So. 810 (1898).

Want of confirmation will not avoid liability of purchaser for failure to keep his bid good. — See Culli v. House, 133 Ala. 304, 32 So. 254 (1902).

Second sale is at purchaser's risk. — The second sale of the land is made at the risk of the purchaser at the first sale, who fails to comply with the terms of the purchase, though this section does not so specify. This is a condition implied by law in every judicial sale. Thomas v. Caldwell, 136 Ala. 518, 34 So. 949 (1903).

Destruction of property before confirmation of first sale. — The destruction of the buildings on the land before confirmation of the first sale will not be a defense to the purchaser's liability, though these structures served to induce his bid. Thomas v. Caldwell, 136 Ala. 518, 34 So. 949 (1903). See also Haralson v. George, 56 Ala. 295 (1876).

When a master or commissioner accepts a bid at a judicial sale there is created an anomalous relation between the court and the bidder. All the commissioner can do is to accept the bid subject to the court's approval. And though there is a lack of mutuality the bidder is nevertheless bound from the moment of the conditional acceptance of his bid, and the court, as vendor, may in the exercise of a proper discretion either accept, through confirmation, or reject the bid. When the sale is confirmed the confirmation relates back to the day of the sale, Haralson v. George, 56 Ala. 295 (1876), and the transaction for the first time assumes the nature of a completed contract binding the court as well as the purchaser. The purchaser is therefore regarded as the owner from the day of his purchase (which is the time of the conditional acceptance by the master of his bid), and as said in Haralson v. George, supra, he bears "the loss if the thing sold perishes, or deteriorates in value, and is entitled to any appreciation in value or accretions to the thing during the time necessarily intervening between the sale and the confirmation."

Cited in Hutton v. Williams, 35 Ala. 503 (1860); McSwean v. Faulks, 46 Ala. 610 (1871); Field v. Gamble, 47 Ala. 443 (1872); Cruikshank v. Luttrell, 67 Ala. 318 (1880); Lowe v. Guice, 69 Ala. 80 (1881).

Collateral references. — 33 C.J.S., Executors & Administrators, §§ 286, 294. 34 C.J.S., Executors & Administrators, § 604.

§ 43-2-462. Confirmation of sale.

Whenever the court is satisfied that such sale was fairly conducted, and the land sold for an amount not greatly less than its real value, and the purchase money is paid, or sufficiently secured, by mortgage or other personal security, it must make an order confirming such sale; but such order of confirmation shall not be made until after the expiration of 10 days after the report of sale is filed. (Code 1852, § 1769; Code 1867, § 2095; Code 1876, § 2467; Code 1886, § 2123; Code 1896, § 177; Code 1907, § 2642; Code 1923, § 5872; Code 1940, T. 61, § 266.)

Editor's note. — The sale is inchoate, as shown in the notes to § 43-2-461, until it is confirmed under this section. The cases cited in the notes to §§ 43-2-459 through 43-2-461 dealing with the steps leading up to the order of confirmation, necessarily bear upon the provisions herein contained. Reference should be made to those notes.

Facts considered in confirming sale. — See notes to § 43-2-459.

This section takes no account of irregularities which are not shown to affect the result of the sale, as to its fairness and the adequacy of the price. Parker v. Clayton, 248 Ala. 632, 29 So. 2d 139 (1947).

Discretion of court. — The matter of confirmation rests peculiarly upon the wise discretion of the court. Its decision is of weighty consideration on review. Campbell v. Carter, 248 Ala. 294, 27 So. 2d 490 (1946).

Cited in Hill v. Erwin, 44 Ala. 661 (1870); Field v. Gamble, 47 Ala. 443 (1872); Evans v. English, 61 Ala. 416 (1878); Matthews v. McDade, 72 Ala. 377 (1882); Roulston v. Washington, 79 Ala. 529 (1885); Reed v. Hughes, 192 Ala. 162, 68 So. 334 (1915).

Collateral references. — 34 C.J.S., Executors & Administrators, §§ 607-611.

31 Am. Jur. 2d, Executors & Administrators, §§ 392-395.

Conclusiveness on purchaser of provisions of order or decree of confirmation regarding terms and conditions. 95 ALR 1492.

Rights and remedies of purchaser at sale by personal representative where sale is void or set aside because proceedings are imperfect or irregular, or where description of property is defective. 142 ALR 310.

Rights and remedies of one purchasing at executor's or administrator's sale where there was misrepresentation or mistake as to acreage or location of boundaries of tract sold. 69 ALR2d 254.

§ 43-2-463. Report of payment of purchase money.

When lands have been sold on credit, and when the whole of the purchase money has been paid, the executor or administrator must, within 30 days after such complete payment has been made, report the fact of such payment to the court of probate. If he fails to do so within the time specified in this section, such report may be compelled of him in the manner provided by section 43-2-465. (Code 1896, § 178; Code 1907, § 2643; Code 1923, § 5873; Code 1940, T. 61, § 267.)

Collateral references. — 34 C.J.S., Executors & Administrators, § 606.

§ 43-2-464. Conveyance.

After such confirmation, and when the whole of the purchase money has been paid by the purchaser, or his heirs, or any other person holding under him, directly or derivatively, on the application of such purchaser, or his heirs, or such other person holding under him, or of the executor or administrator, the court must order a conveyance to be made to such purchaser, or to his heirs, or to such other person holding under him, as the case may be, by the executor or administrator, or such other person as the court may appoint, conveying all the right, title and interest which the decedent had, at the time of his death, in such lands; and such order shall operate to vest the right, title and interest of the decedent in such purchaser, or his heirs, or such other person holding under him. (Code 1852, § 1770; Code 1867, § 2096; Code 1876, § 2468; Code 1886, § 2124; Code 1896, § 179; Code 1907, § 2644; Code 1923, § 5874; Code 1940, T. 61, § 268.)

All the land is charged with purchase price. — Title under this section cannot be made until the whole of the purchase money for the land has been paid, and all of the land must remain as security for the entire price. And the unpaid heirs may subject the whole of the lands to the satisfaction of their demand. Washington v. Bogart, 119 Ala. 377, 24 So. 245 (1898). And the title of the heirs is not divested until the purchase money has been paid in full. Gardner v. Kelsoe, 80 Ala. 497, 2 So. 680 (1887).

On the principle just set forth it is held that a judgment creditor of one who purchased land at an administrator's sale without paying all the purchase price has no lien on the interest of those heirs who have been fully paid and satisfied for their share in the land. Washington v. Bogart, 119 Ala. 377, 24 So. 245 (1898).

Administrator as purchaser. — The application for an order of conveyance of title under this section by an administrator who becomes a purchaser at a sale of his intestate's lands must be regarded as made in his capacity of purchaser. And notice to the heirs is essential to the validity of the order. Bogart v. Bell, 112 Ala. 412, 20 So. 511 (1896). And such administrator must show that he has paid the price to the heirs. Ligon v. Ligon, 84 Ala. 555, 4 So. 405 (1888). See also Snow v. Bray, 198 Ala. 398, 73 So. 542 (1916).

Third party as purchaser. — But when the application is made by the administrator for an order of conveyance of title to a purchaser other than himself, notice to heirs is not essential to its validity. Ligon v. Ligon, 84 Ala. 555, 4 So. 405 (1888).

Entry of decree and execution of deed are prerequisites to valid sale. — The purchase of realty by an administrator from the estate of his decedent is void where the report of sale was endorsed by the clerk of the probate court as approved, but there was no decree affirming such sale nor any deed executed by a commissioner to a purchaser. Snow v. Bray, 198 Ala. 398, 73 So. 542 (1916).

Insufficiency of report of sale. — The insufficiency of the report of an administrator's sale to authorize the making of title is no ground for excluding it as evidence of the facts recited. Webb v. Ballard, 97 Ala. 584, 12 So. 106 (1892).

Copy of probate court's decree is admissible. — Copy of probate court's decree, confirming report of administrator's sale of land offered in evidence, held admissible, in view of this section, as color of title in defense to action for breach of covenant of seisin in a timber deed. Belsher v. Russell, 218 Ala. 597, 119 So. 659 (1928).

Cited in Mobile v. Dargan, 45 Ala. 310 (1871); McIntosh v. Reid, 45 Ala. 456 (1871); Solomon v. Ross, 49 Ala. 198 (1873); Corbitt v. Clenny, 52 Ala. 480 (1875); Ketchum v. Creagh, 53 Ala. 224 (1875); Van Hoose v. Bush, 54 Ala. 342 (1875); Dugger v. Tayloe, 60 Ala. 504 (1877); Stabler v. Spencer, 64 Ala. 496 (1879); Anderson v. Bradley, 66 Ala. 263 (1880); Cruikshank v. Luttrell, 67 Ala. 318 (1880); Landford v. Dunklin, 71 Ala. 594 (1882); Matthews v. McDade, 72 Ala. 377 (1882); Mobile Life Ins. Co. v. Randall, 74 Ala. 170 (1883); Pollard v. Hanrick, 74 Ala. 334 (1883).

Collateral references. — 33 C.J.S., Executors & Administrators, § 289.

§ 43-2-465. Right of purchaser to cite executor or administrator to report sale.

(a) If the executor or administrator fails, within the time required by law, to report any sale of lands made by him under the provisions of this article, the purchaser, or his heirs, or any other person claiming under him directly or derivatively, may, on motion in the probate court, have citation to issue to such executor or administrator, citing him to appear within 20 days from the date of the service of the citation, and report the sale; and if such executor or administrator is then a nonresident of the state, or his place of residence is unknown to the party asking for the citation, the court, on affidavit being made of either of these facts, must cause service of such citation to be made by publication, once a week for three successive weeks, in some newspaper published in the county, or if none is published therein, in the newspaper published nearest to the courthouse of such county.

(b) If the executor or administrator fails to appear and report the sale, as required by such citation, the probate court must, on the day such executor or administrator is cited to appear, or on such other day as may be set by the court, proceed to hear evidence touching the regularity of the sale, the compliance with the terms of sale, and the adequacy of the price bid for the lands; and if from the evidence the court is satisfied that the sale was regular and fair, that the purchase money has been paid or secured, according to the terms of sale, and that the amount bid at the sale is an adequate price for the lands, an order confirming the sale, and, if the sale was for cash, and the purchase money has been paid, designating and authorizing some person to convey the title to the lands to the party entitled thereto, must be made. (Code 1886, §§ 2125, 2126; Code 1896, §§ 180, 181; Code 1907, §§ 2645, 2646; Code 1923, §§ 5875, 5876; Code 1940, T. 61, §§ 269, 270.)

Cited in Robertson v. Bradford, 70 Ala. 385 (1881).

§ 43-2-466. Disposition of dower interest.

(a) In all cases where, under the provisions of this article, the lands of a decedent can be ordered to be sold by the probate court, the widow may file in the office of the judge of probate her written consent, that her dower interest in the land may be sold, so as to vest in the purchaser the complete title; and thereupon, the court must order such dower interest to be sold with the residue of the lands.

(b) When the sale is confirmed, the court, on application of the widow, must make an order that a fair equivalent for the dower interest be paid to her by the personal representative, when the purchase money is collected, the value of such interest to be ascertained by proof, having regard to the age and health of the widow, but in no case to exceed one third of the purchase money. (Code 1852, §§ 1873-1875; Code 1867, §§ 2229-2231; Code 1876, §§ 2469-2471; Code 1886, §§ 2127, 2128; Code 1896, §§ 182, 183; Code 1907, §§ 2647, 2648; Code 1923, §§ 5877, 5878; Code 1940, T. 61, §§ 271, 272; Acts 1945, No. 447, p. 686.)

Cross references. — As to abolition of dower generally, see § 43-8-57.

Sale of dower presupposes consent. — This section prohibits the probate court from selling dower interest without the written consent of the widow. Boyles v. Wallace, 208 Ala. 213, 93 So. 908 (1922); Hopkins v. Crews, 220 Ala. 149, 124 So. 202 (1929). See also Hamby v. Hamby, 165 Ala. 171, 51 So. 732 (1910).

Without such previous written consent, both the order of sale and the sale made are subject, whether expressed or not, to the right of dower. And the same rule is applicable to quarantine. Clancy v. Stephens, 92 Ala. 577, 9 So. 522 (1891).

Consent vests title in purchaser. — The consent of the widow as herein prescribed will serve to vest a complete title in the purchaser at the sale of the lands. Hamby v. Hamby, 165 Ala. 171, 51 So. 732 (1910).

"Consent" illustrated. — The written reply of a widow to a counterclaim, denying counterclaimants ownership in lands, and averring widow's ownership and asking for division, satisfies the requirement of consent in this section. Boyles v. Wallace, 208 Ala. 213, 93 So. 908 (1922).

A position taken in the pleadings can operate as a written consent of a widow to the sale of her dower interest in a sale for division as required by this section. Compton v. Cook, 259 Ala. 256, 66 So. 2d 176 (1953).

Petition by widow and administratrix that she be authorized to sell lands for cash for the purpose of making a division of the estate among the heirs and that the court ascertain the portion of the purchase price to be awarded her in lieu of her dower interest in the property was tantamount to the filing of her written consent that her dower interest in the property be sold, as provided by this section. McGregor v. McGregor, 249 Ala. 75, 29 So. 2d 561 (1942), appeal dismissed, 250 Ala. 662, 35 So. 2d 685 (1948).

Where administratrix is also deceased's widow, whose dower and homestead rights are involved, she is in the position of representing conflicting interests, if the sole party plaintiff in action to sell deceased's realty for payment of debts, and in such case, she should also be made a party individually. Davidson v. Quigley, 243 Ala. 555, 11 So. 2d 138 (1942).

Purchaser of dower interest is protected. — The purchaser of the widow's dower interest for a valuable consideration succeeds to her rights and will be protected. And he is entitled to have the value of the dower paid to him. Long v. Long, 195 Ala. 560, 70 So. 733 (1916).

When compensation in lieu of dower allowed. — The widow may elect to take a lump sum award in lieu of dower in only three situations. Compensation in gross is allowed if both parties agree when the land out of which dower is demanded has been sold to another by the husband prior to his death. This section provides that in all cases where the lands of the decedent can be ordered sold, the widow may consent that her dower interest be sold. In such a case subsection (b) of this section requires that the court, upon request of the widow, order the personal representative to pay the widow a fair equivalent of her dower interest. Cox v. United States, 421 F.2d 576 (5th Cir. 1970).

Section as it read at time of death governs. — This section as it read at the time of the death of the husband, and not as amended subsequent to his death but prior to the date on which the sale of the land was confirmed, governs the computation of the amount allowable to a widow out of the proceeds of the sale of land which belonged to her husband as a fair equivalent for her dower interest. McGregor v. McGregor, 249 Ala. 75, 29 So. 2d 561 (1947), appeal dismissed, 250 Ala. 662, 35 So. 2d 685 (1948).

Purchase of widow's dower interest. — A plaintiff in a partition action, who purchases the widow's dower interest for a valuable consideration, is entitled to have the value of the dower paid to him where he had succeeded to her right. Long v. Long, 195 Ala. 560, 70 So. 733 (1916).

Cited in Sherard v. Sherard, 33 Ala. 488 (1859); Whitworth v. Oliver, 39 Ala. 286 (1864); Snedicor v. Mobley, 47 Ala. 517 (1872); Clark v. Bernstein, 49 Ala. 596 (1873); Bradford v. Bradford, 66 Ala. 252 (1880); Cruikshank v. Luttrell, 67 Ala. 318 (1880); Gordon, etc., Co. v. Tweedy, 71 Ala. 202 (1881); Brake v. Graham, 214 Ala. 10, 106 So. 188 (1925); Schwab v. Schwab, 255 Ala. 218, 50 So. 2d 435 (1951); Dorough v. Johnson, 373 So. 2d 1082 (Ala. 1979).

Collateral references. — 28 C.J.S., Dower, §§ 1, 2, 61-65. 34 C.J.S., Executors & Administrators, § 637.

§ 43-2-467. Correction of mistake in description of lands sold.

(a) When a mistake has been made in the description of lands of a decedent sold in good faith under an order of the probate court, either in the petition, order or other proceedings, the court ordering the sale has authority, on the written application of the purchaser, or his heirs or personal representatives, or any person holding under him, verified by affidavit, to correct such mistake. The application must contain a correct description of the lands sold, and must state the facts, and the names, ages and places of residence of the personal representatives and heirs or devisees of such decedent, if known, and if there be no personal representative, that fact must be stated; and, upon the filing of such application, the court must appoint a day for the hearing, of which, and of the nature of the application, notice must be given, by personal service, to the personal representative of such decedent, and such of his heirs as are of age, and are of sound mind, if residents of the state at least 20 days before the day appointed for the hearing, and also by publication, once a week for three successive weeks, in some newspaper published in the county, or if none is published therein, in a newspaper published nearest to the courthouse thereof. If there is no personal representative of the estate of such decedent, the court must appoint an administrator ad litem to represent the estate in such proceeding; and the court must also appoint a guardian ad litem for such of the heirs or devisees as are under the age of 19 years, or are of unsound mind.

(b) If, upon the hearing, the court is satisfied from the evidence adduced, that the sale of such lands was made in good faith, and that a mistake was made in the description of the lands sold, as stated in the application, a decree must be made and entered, correcting the mistake. If the purchase money has been fully paid, and a deed executed, the court must order the personal representative, or, if there be none, the administrator ad litem, to execute to the party making the application a new deed, conveying to him the lands according to the description as corrected. (Code 1867, § 2128; Code 1876, § 2472; Code 1886, §§ 2129, 2130; Code 1896, §§ 184, 185; Code 1907, §§ 2649, 2650; Code 1923, §§ 5879, 5880; Code 1940, T. 61, §§ 273, 274.)

General effect. — This section creates no new contract between the parties, and imposes no additional burdens or obligations. It merely reforms the record evidence so as to make it speak the truth as to the real contract. Brown v. Williams, 87 Ala. 353, 6 So. 111 (1889), overruled on other grounds, 122 Ala. 188, 25 So. 50 (1899).

The purpose of this section. — The whole purpose of such proceeding is to correct, by reformation, a mistake in the description of the lands sold, and to authorize such rectification of error by the execution of a new deed conveying to the purchaser or applicant "the lands according to the description as corrected." Brown v. Williams, 87 Ala. 353, 6 So. 111 (1889), overruled on other grounds, 122 Ala. 188, 25 So. 50 (1899).

Misdescription is the only thing corrected. — The legal effect of a proceeding under this section is only to accomplish a single purpose. It only corrects the misdescription in the lands sold and conveyed, and places the purchaser or applicant holding under him in pre-

cisely the position he would have occupied had there been no misdescription in the lands sold. In other respects the validity of the proceedings is unaffected. Brown v. Williams, 87 Ala. 353, 6 So. 111 (1889), overruled on other grounds, 122 Ala. 188, 25 So. 50 (1899).

Application is made by purchaser or one claiming under him. — An amendment of the petition and decree, by correcting a mistake in the description of the lands, must be made at the instance of the purchaser, or someone claiming under him, and cannot be made at the instance of the administrator of the decedent. Lee v. Williams, 85 Ala. 189, 3 So. 718 (1888).

Mistake as to amount of land to be sold may be corrected. — Where a mistake as to amount of land to be sold is made in advertising the sale, and the auctioneer announces that the whole lot would be sold, and the purchaser in good faith buys what he thinks is the whole of the lot, and subsequently discovers a mistake in the description, it is held that the mistake may be corrected under this section. Gomez v. Gomez, 155 Ala. 158, 45 So. 637 (1908).

Lapse of 17 years is no bar to right. — The lapse of 17 years since the alleged mistake was committed constitutes no bar to its correction where no adverse possession in hostility to applicant's title is shown. Brown v. Williams, 87 Ala. 353, 6 So. 111 (1889), overruled on other grounds, 122 Ala. 188, 25 So. 50 (1899).

Cited in Doe v. Hardy, 52 Ala. 291 (1875); Jarrell v. Farmers Nat'l Bank, 253 Ala. 119, 43 So. 2d 116 (1949).

Collateral references. — Rights and remedies of purchaser at sale by personal representative where sale is void or set aside because of proceedings are imperfect or irregular, or where description of property is defective. 142 ALR 310.

Rights and remedies of one purchasing at executor's or administrator's sale where there was misrepresentation or mistake as to acreage or location of boundaries of tract sold. 69 ALR2d 254.

§ 43-2-468. Sale or division of land received on compromise.

Real estate received by an executor or administrator in payment of any bad or doubtful claim, on a compromise of such claim made under an order of the probate court, may be distributed by the court having jurisdiction of the estate, by sale or division, upon the same proceedings as are had for the sale or division of real estate of decedents; but such real estate, or the proceeds thereof, if sold, must otherwise be treated and distributed as personal property. (Code 1867, § 2132; Code 1876, § 2507; Code 1886, § 2132; Code 1896, § 187; Code 1907, § 2652; Code 1923, § 5882; Code 1940, T. 61, § 276.)

Cited in Mobile v. Dargan, 45 Ala. 310 (1871); Cochran v. Martin, 47 Ala. 525 (1872); Clark v. Moses, 50 Ala. 326 (1874); Cruikshank v. Luttrell, 67 Ala. 318 (1880).

Division 2.

Sale of Land for Payment of Legacies.

Collateral references. — 34 C.J.S., Executors & Administrators, §§ 492, 543.

§ 43-2-480. Authorization to sell.

Lands of an estate may be ordered sold by the probate court having jurisdiction of the estate for the payment of pecuniary legacies, when such legacies are expressly or by necessary implication made a charge on such lands and the will does not confer upon the personal representative the power or authority to make sale of lands for such purpose. (Acts 1923, No. 481, p. 632; Code 1923, § 5883; Code 1940, T. 61, § 277.)

Cited in Murphy v. Vaughan, 226 Ala. 461, 147 So. 404 (1933).

Collateral references. — 31 Am. Jur. 2d, Executors & Administrators, § 356.

§ 43-2-481. Application for sale.

The application for the sale of lands for the payment of legacies must be made by the executor by petition, verified by affidavit, to the probate court having jurisdiction of the estate. It must describe the lands accurately and give the names of the devisees and their places of residence and must state whether any and which such devisees are under the age of 19 years or of unsound mind, and must also show that the lands prayed to be sold are charged or chargeable, expressly or by necessary implication, with the payment of pecuniary legacies, and that no power is given the personal representative to sell the lands for such purpose. (Acts 1923, No. 481, p. 632; Code 1923, § 5884; Code 1940, T. 61, § 278.)

§ 43-2-482. Notice; proceedings; order of sale.

Notice of the filing of such petition must be given as provided by law on petition by the personal representative to sell lands for division or for the payment of debts, and testimony shall be taken and all other proceedings had and the sale, if ordered, shall be made as now provided by law for the sale of lands by personal representatives for the payment of debts. (Acts 1923, No. 481, p. 632; Code 1923, § 5885; Code 1940, T. 61, § 279.)

ARTICLE 18.

SETTLEMENTS AND DISTRIBUTIONS.

Cross references. — As to correction by circuit court of errors by probate court regarding settlements of estates, see § 12-11-60.

Division 1.

General Provisions.

Collateral references. — 31 Am. Jur. 2d, Executors & Administrators, §§ 506-549.
Expiration of statutory period for settling estate as affecting removal of executor or administrator. 8 ALR 178.

§ 43-2-500. When annual or partial settlement required.

Every executor or administrator must make annual settlements of his administration; and he may, when necessary for the interests of the estate, be required to make a settlement at any time. (Code 1852, § 1801; Code 1867, § 2136; Code 1876, § 2508; Code 1886, § 2133; Code 1896, § 201; Code 1907, § 2666; Code 1923, § 5899; Code 1940, T. 61, § 293.)

Cross reference. — As to annual settlements when estate kept together, see § 43-2-338.

Section does not limit power of testator. — This section does not impose any limitations upon the power of a testator in disposing of his estate, or provide for the manner of its distribution, so far as concerns those who take under his will. Burch v. Gaston, 182 Ala. 467, 62 So. 508 (1913), giving effect to discretionary power in administering the trust, vested in executor by will.

The probate judge may issue citations on his own motion under this section, or on the application of distributees or legatees, requiring a settlement. Burch v. Gaston, 182 Ala. 467, 62 So. 508 (1913).

Restraint of power. — Under this section the probate court had jurisdiction to require a settlement as to purely executorial duties at the instance of creditors, or of a grandchild who had become entitled to so much of the estate as survived the trust. And hence, the probate judge will not be restrained by prohibition or otherwise, from citing such executors to a settlement, where the petition for the writ of prohibition did not show upon whose application the citation for a settlement was issued. Burch v. Gaston, 182 Ala. 467, 62 So. 508 (1913).

Annual or partial settlements are considered as prima facie correct, but they may be surcharged and falsified by distributees on final settlement. Brazeale v. Brazeale, 9 Ala. 491 (1846); Willis v. Willis, 9 Ala. 330 (1846); Tayloe v. Bush, 75 Ala. 432 (1883).

Credits allowed on annual settlements must be allowed on final settlement in the absence of satisfactory evidence of their incorrectness. Dickie v. Dickie, 80 Ala. 57 (1885).

When the administration is removed into circuit court, that court may require such settlement, whether partial or final, as the condition of the estate would have rendered proper if the administration had remained in the probate court. Stein v. Gordon, 10 So. 631 (Ala. 1892).

Cited in Carrington & Co. v. Manning, 13 Ala. 611 (1848); Benford v. Daniels, 13 Ala. 667 (1848); Gerald v. Bunkley, 17 Ala. 170 (1849); Marion County v. Brown, 43 Ala. 112 (1869); Cook v. Cook, 69 Ala. 294 (1881); Walsh v. Walsh, 231 Ala. 305, 164 So. 822 (1935); Pinckard v. Ledyard, 251 Ala. 648, 38 So. 2d 580 (1948); Robertson v. United States, 310 F.2d 199 (5th Cir. 1962).

Collateral references. — 34 C.J.S., Executors & Administrators, § 910.

§ 43-2-501. When final settlement may be made.

Final settlement may be made at any time after six months from the grant of letters, if the debts are all paid and the condition of the estate in other respects will admit of it. (Code 1852, § 1821; Code 1867, § 2157; Code 1876, § 2528; Code 1886, § 2134; Code 1896, § 202; Code 1907, § 2667; Code 1923, § 5900; Acts 1931, No. 719, p. 838; Code 1940, T. 61, § 294.)

When action for "final settlement" may be brought. — A complaint alleging misconduct on the part of an administrator and requesting an accounting from him as an individual as to matters therein specified is not an action to compel a final settlement of the estate, which, under this section, cannot be brought until the expiration of the time specified. Baker v. Mitchell, 109 Ala. 490, 20 So. 40 (1896). See also Eastburn v. Canizas, 193 Ala. 574, 69 So. 459 (1915).

Allegation as to condition of estate. — When a bill seeks to compel a final settlement of a decedent's estate, it must show that the estate is ready for such a settlement. Baker v. Mitchell, 109 Ala. 490, 20 So. 40 (1896).

Enforced settlement before expiration of time specified. — A settlement cannot be enforced until after the expiration of the time

specified unless the executor or administrator becomes satisfied before that time that the estate is solvent, and so reports; in which event he may "obtain an order of distribution as to the whole or any part of the property," as provided in § 43-2-640. Jackson v. Rowell, 87 Ala. 685, 6 So. 95 (1889), decided prior to the 1949 amendment of § 43-2-640. See also Carroll v. Richardson, 87 Ala. 605, 6 So. 342 (1889).

Cited in Lary v. Craig, 30 Ala. 631 (1857); Rogers v. Boyd, 33 Ala. 175 (1858); Harrison v. Harrison, 39 Ala. 489 (1864); Avery v. Avery, 47 Ala. 505 (1872); Hooper v. Smith, 57 Ala. 557 (1877); Cook v. Cook, 69 Ala. 294 (1881); Minor v. Thomasson, 236 Ala. 247, 182 So. 16 (1938); Barrett v. Fondren, 262 Ala. 537, 80 So. 2d 243 (1955).

Collateral references. — 34 C.J.S., Executors & Administrators, § 904.

§ 43-2-502. Filing of account, etc. — Generally.

In making settlements of an administration, the executor or administrator must proceed as follows:

He must make out an account between himself and the estate he represents, charging himself with all the assets of the deceased which have come into his possession, except the lands, and crediting himself with all the credits he is by law entitled to; which account, verified by his oath, must be filed with the judge of probate of the court having jurisdiction.

With such account he must also file the vouchers and written evidence in his possession, on which he relies to sustain the credit side of such account.

He must, at the same time, file a statement, on oath, of the names of the heirs and legatees of such estate, specifying particularly which are under the age of 19 years; and, if any of them are persons of unsound mind, it must be stated; but if the names, ages or condition of such heirs or legatees are unknown and they reside out of the state, they may be made parties as unknown heirs or legatees.

He must state the sum of funds of the estate which he has used for his own benefit, the time and the profit resulting from such use, if over legal interest, or, if he has not so used any of the funds of the estate for his own benefit, he must expressly deny on oath that he has so used such funds, and any party interested in the estate may contest the same.

He shall be allowed all reasonable premiums paid on his bond as administrator or executor. (Code 1852, § 1802; Code 1867, § 2137; Code 1876, § 2509; Code 1886, § 2135; Code 1896, § 203; Code 1907, § 2668; Code 1923, § 5901; Code 1940, T. 61, § 295.)

When jurisdiction attaches. — Jurisdiction for final settlement in probate court begins upon filing accounts and vouchers with statement of the heirs invoking the court's jurisdiction for such settlement and an order entered setting day, directing notice, etc. Ex parte McLendon, 212 Ala. 403, 102 So. 696 (1924).

If the personal representatives collected money belonging to decedent, during his lifetime, this constituted a debt for which they were liable to him, and when they procured their appointment as personal representatives of his estate and accepted that office, said indebtedness due from them to the decedent was transmuted from a chose in action to a chose in possession in their hands in their representative capacity, as assets of said estate, for which they were required to account in the final settlement of said estate in the administration proceedings. Faust v. Faust, 248 Ala. 660, 29 So. 2d 133 (1947).

Refusal to approve alleged payments to legatee in excess of amount shown by vouchers filed with executor's account held not error, where it did not appear that books, which were only other evidence offered, were regular, kept in due course and that items were entered at time of transaction recorded. Grist v. Carswell, 231 Ala. 442, 165 So. 102 (1935).

Avoidance of decree for omitting name of heir. — The allegations in a complaint to the effect that administrator made a false affidavit in filing names of legatees under this section, omitting therefrom the plaintiff's name, and fraudulently concealing from the probate court her relationship to decedent, and as a result of

which, the plaintiff received nothing from the estate, and that she had no knowledge of the proceedings until day when the action was commenced, were held sufficient to avoid decree on final settlement. Fidelity & Deposit Co. v. Hendrix, 215 Ala. 555, 112 So. 117 (1927), discussing liability of sureties on administrator's bond after distribution of assets pursuant to final decree.

Intervention by court for fraud in accounting. — The failure of the administrator to honestly account for all funds coming into his hands belonging to the estate is a fraud which authorizes the intervention of a court, if such fraud is not due to fault or negligence of plaintiff, and was an element entering into the decree which deprived the heirs of their distributive share. Fidelity & Deposit Co. v. Hendrix, 215 Ala. 555, 112 So. 117 (1927).

Oath not conclusive. — The exculpatory oath does not conclude the question whether the administrator used or received any benefit from the funds in his hands. Elmore v. Cunninghame, 208 Ala. 15, 93 So. 814 (1922).

Cited in Sankey v. Sankey, 8 Ala. 601 (1845); Otis v. Dargan, 53 Ala. 178 (1875); Waring v. Lewis, 53 Ala. 615 (1875); Pinney v. Werborn, 72 Ala. 58 (1882).

Collateral references. — 34 C.J.S., Executors & Administrators, §§ 850, 851.

Employment of attorney at expense of estate, by executor or administrator who is himself an attorney. 18 ALR 635.

Allowance of retaining fee paid by executor to attorneys. 21 ALR 1445.

Rent, on death of landlord, as part of his estate. 31 ALR 4.

Allowances for expenses and disbursements by executor or administrator after revocation of letters of administration. 31 ALR 846.

Reimbursement of executor or administrator held personally liable for torts. 44 ALR 676, 127 ALR 687.

Effect of judgment recovered on unfiled or abandoned claim after expiration of time allowed for filing claim. 60 ALR 736.

Allowance out of estate for services of attorney not employed by executor or administrator in connection with settlement of estate or accounting of personal representative. 79 ALR 530, 533, 142 ALR 1459, 1465, 1467.

Right to allowance for broker's commission or other expenses incurred in sale of real property or collection of rent. 91 ALR 829, 155 ALR 1314.

Exercise of power which one possesses as trustee but not as executor before settlement of his account as executor, as affecting his rights and liabilities as executor. 94 ALR 1464.

Right of executor or administrator to allowance of attorneys' fees and expenses incident to controversy over surcharging account. 101 ALR 806.

Purchase or sale to corporation of which he is an officer or stockholder by executor or administrator as ground for sucharging his account. 105 ALR 449.

Amount of assets of incompetent decedent's estate as diminished by claims incurred during guardianship. 113 ALR 402.

Surchargeability of executor or administrator in respect of mortgage investment, as affected by matters relating to value of property. 117 ALR 871.

Credit for amount paid for tombstone or monument. 121 ALR 1115.

Right of executor or administrator to credit on account of advances to distributees before obtaining order of distribution. 126 ALR 780.

Right to credit personal claim of executor or administrator against estate antedating death of decedent. 144 ALR 962.

United States savings bonds as assets of holder's estate. 168 ALR 245, 173 ALR 550, 37 ALR2d 1221, 39 ALR2d 698, 40 ALR2d 788, 51 ALR2d 163.

Depreciation in value of securities, liability for, as affected by appreciation of other securities. 171 ALR 1422.

Costs and other expenses incurred by administrator or executor whose appointment was improper as chargeable against estate. 4 ALR2d 164.

Rights and liabilities of personal representative with respect to completion of improvements. 5 ALR2d 1250.

Accountability of personal representative for his use of decedent's real estate. 31 ALR2d 243.

Right to allowance out of estate of attorneys' fees incurred in attempt to establish or defeat will. 40 ALR2d 1407.

Compensation of attorney for executor or administrator as affected by representation of heir or other beneficiary in controversy with other heirs or beneficiaries. 47 ALR2d 1104.

Tort claimant against decedent's estate as person or party interested, or as creditor, entitled to object to account or report of personal representative. 87 ALR2d 1231.

Liability of executor or administrator, or his bond, for loss caused to estate by act or default of his agent or attorney. 28 ALR3d 1191.

§ 43-2-503. Same — Liability for failure to file statement.

If such statement is not filed, the executor or administrator and his sureties are liable for all damages arising therefrom. (Code 1852, § 1804; Code 1867, § 2139; Code 1876, § 2511; Code 1886, § 2136; Code 1896, § 204; Code 1907, § 2669; Code 1923, § 5902; Code 1940, T. 61, § 296.)

Collateral references. — 34 C.J.S., Executors & Administrators, §§ 835, 847-849.

§ 43-2-504. Appointment of guardian ad litem.

The court must appoint a competent attorney-at-law as guardian ad litem to represent the interests of minors and persons of unsound mind interested in such settlement. (Code 1852, § 1803; Code 1867, § 2138; Code 1876, § 2510; Code 1886, § 2137; Code 1896, § 205; Code 1907, § 2670; Code 1923, § 5903; Code 1940, T. 61, § 297.)

Appointment is necessary. — Infants, of themselves, are incapable of electing whether they will account for advancements, or be excluded from the distribution, on final settlement of the estate, and their exclusion, without previous appointment of a guardian ad litem, is erroneous. Wilson v. Wilson, 18 Ala. 176 (1850).

A decree without the appointment required by this section is void. Willis v. Willis, 16 Ala. 652 (1849); Clack v. Clack, 20 Ala. 461 (1852); Searcy v. Holmes, 43 Ala. 608 (1869); Bruce v. Strickland, 47 Ala. 192 (1872); Petty v. Britt, 46 Ala. 491 (1873).

Unless regular guardian is present. — There is no necessity for appointing a guardian ad litem when the minor's regular guardian is present and representing him. Jones v. Fellows, 58 Ala. 343 (1877); Hatcher v. Dillard, 70 Ala. 343 (1881).

Assent of appointee is necessary. — The appointment required by this section is not complete until the assent to act of the person appointed is signified. Laird v. Reese, 43 Ala. 148 (1869).

Appointment renders settlement binding. — When the infant is represented by guardians the decree of settlement is as binding against him as against an adult. Otis v. Dargan, 53 Ala. 178 (1875); Waring v. Lewis, 53 Ala. 615 (1875); Hutton v. Williams, 60 Ala. 133 (1877); Hatchett v. Blanton, 72 Ala. 423 (1882); Modawell v. Hudson, 80 Ala. 265 (1885).

Cited in Webb v. Webb, 250 Ala. 194, 33 So. 2d 909 (1948).

Collateral references. — 34 C.J.S., Executors & Administrators, § 848.

§ 43-2-505. Time for settlement; notice generally.

(a) Upon the filing of such account, vouchers, evidence, and statement, the judge of probate must appoint a day for such settlement, and must give notice of the same, by publication in some newspaper published in the county, for three successive weeks; or, if none is published in the county, by posting such notice at the courthouse and three other public places in such county, for the same length of time; but if the settlement be only an annual one, publication shall only be given by posting up notices as above provided. If the settlement is a final one, the probate judge must also give 10 days' notice of the day set for making the settlement to every adult distributee resident in the state whose place of residence is known or can be ascertained with reasonable diligence, and to all sureties on the bond of the administrator or executor.

(b) Such notice must state the name of the executor or administrator, the name of the deceased, the day appointed for settlement and the nature of the settlement, whether annual or final.

(c) If the heirs or legatees are of age and waive publication in a newspaper, notice must, in such case, be given by posting the same at the courthouse door. (Code 1852, §§ 1805-1807; Code 1867, §§ 2140-2142; Code 1876, §§ 2512-2514; Code 1886, §§ 2138-2140; Code 1896, §§ 206-208; Code 1907, §§ 2671-2673; Code 1923, §§ 5904-5906; Acts 1931, No. 705, p. 829; Code 1940, T. 61, §§ 298-300; Acts 1953, No. 757, p. 1020.)

The purpose of the notice is apparent — that all persons interested may examine the account and prepare, if necessary, to contest it. Robinson v. Steele, 5 Ala. 473 (1843); Jenkins v. Jenkins, 16 Ala. 693 (1849).

This section provides for alternative modes of giving notice. — This section provides for two modes of giving notice of settlement, but they are in the alternative and resort cannot be had to the second mode without

showing impossibility of compliance with the first. Hence, if the record shows that notice was given by posting, it must also affirmatively show that no newspaper was published in the county. Bruce v. Strickland, 47 Ala. 192 (1872).

Publication must be for three consecutive weeks, and "three consecutive times" will not suffice. Jenkins v. Jenkins, 16 Ala. 693 (1849).

Notice to infant distributees. — There

need not be personal service on infants represented by guardian ad litem. Trawick v. Trawick, 67 Ala. 271 (1880). See also Stabler v. Cook, 57 Ala. 22 (1876); Hutton v. Williams, 60 Ala. 107 (1877).

Notice to a succeeding administrator must be given personally. Hatchett v. Billingslea, 65 Ala. 16 (1880).

Notice of annual settlement will not support a decree of final settlement. King v. Collins, 21 Ala. 363 (1852); Sims v. Waters, 65 Ala. 442 (1880); Daughdrill v. Daughdrill, 108 Ala. 321, 19 So. 185 (1896).

Notice to sureties. — See Stone v. Vaughn, 232 Ala. 120, 167 So. 297 (1936), holding this section inapplicable to surety on resigned executor's bond.

Record must show notice. — The record must show affirmatively that the parties had notice. Bruce v. Strickland, 47 Ala. 192 (1872).

Cited in Watson v. May, 8 Ala. 177 (1845); Sankey v. Sankey, 8 Ala. 601 (1845); Hamilton v. Adams, 15 Ala. 596 (1849); Wright v. Clough, 17 Ala. 490 (1850); Crothers v. Ross, 17 Ala. 816 (1851); Hollis v. Caughman, 22 Ala. 478 (1853); McRee v. McRee, 34 Ala. 165 (1859); Frierson v. Travis, 39 Ala. 150 (1863); Bogia v. Darden, 41 Ala. 322 (1867); Searcy v. Holmes, 43 Ala. 608 (1869).

Collateral references. — 34 C.J.S., Executors & Administrators, § 846.

Right to notice of proceedings to settle account of surety on bond of executor or administrator. 93 ALR 1366.

§ 43-2-506. Settlement by consent without notice.

In any case in which an administration is conducted pursuant to letters testamentary or letters of administration with the will annexed granted in this state and all legatees and distributees named in the will are of age and proof is made that all legal charges against the estate have been paid in full, the probate court, upon verified petition of the personal representative consented to by written instrument properly executed and acknowledged by all legatees and distributees, may approve a consent settlement without notice or publication or posting. In any case in which an administration is conducted pursuant to letters testamentary or letters of administration granted in this state and such administration in this state is ancillary to a primary administration in another state, and proof is made that all legal charges against the estate in this state have been paid in full and the balance of the assets of the estate in this state have been delivered to the executor or personal representative in the state of primary administration, the probate court, upon verified petition of the executor or personal representative appointed in this state consented to by the executor or personal representative in the state of primary administration, may approve a consent settlement without notice or publication or posting. In all other cases, when all heirs and next of kin are of age and proof is made that all legal charges against the estate have been paid in full, the probate court, upon verified petition of the personal representative consented to by written instrument properly executed and acknowledged by all heirs and next of kin, may approve a consent settlement without notice or publication or posting. In any of the above enumerated cases in which a minor or person of unsound mind may be a distributee or legatee and such minor or person of unsound mind has a guardian, duly appointed by any court of this state, and such guardian is not adversely interested to his ward in said settlement, such guardian may approve a consent settlement as evidenced by his consent in writing, if properly executed and acknowledged. (Acts 1943, No. 414, p. 380; Acts 1951, No. 808, p. 1410; Acts 1965, 2nd Ex. Sess., No. 136, p. 188.)

Collateral references. — 34 C.J.S., Executors & Administrators, § 836.

§ 43-2-507. Auditing of account; proof of credits.

On the day appointed or any other day to which the settlement is continued, the court must proceed to examine and audit the account; and, on such auditing, the executor or administrator must produce satisfactory proof of the correctness of each item on the credit side of the account which may be made by the affidavit or oral examination of witnesses or by any other legal evidence. (Code 1852, §§ 1808-1810; Code 1867, §§ 2143-2145; Code 1876, §§ 2515-2517; Code 1886, § 2141; Code 1896, § 209; Code 1907, § 2674; Code 1923, § 5907; Code 1940, T. 61, § 302.)

Vouchers as satisfactory proof. — On final settlement of administrator's account, court was held to have authority to accept vouchers as the satisfactory proof required by this section of each item on the credit side of account. Stanley v. Beck, 242 Ala. 574, 7 So. 2d 276 (1942).

Allowance of costs of litigation. — On a settlement of his account, an administrator is properly allowed items of cost, attorney's fees and fees for guardian ad litem. Howard v. Rutherford, 149 Ala. 661, 43 So. 30 (1907).

Burden of proof of credits. — This section places the burden of proving the correctness of items of credit of the account on the administrator where objections are filed to an item therein. Hines v. Baldwin, 211 Ala. 322, 100 So. 466 (1924).

Cited in Hamilton v. Adams, 15 Ala. 596 (1849); West, etc., Co. v. Snodgrass, 17 Ala. 549 (1850); Crothers v. Ross, 17 Ala. 816 (1850); Shadden v. Sterling, 23 Ala. 518 (1853); Bendall v. Bendall, 24 Ala. 295 (1854); Moore v. Baker, 39 Ala. 704 (1866); Marion County v. Brown, 43 Ala. 112 (1869); Waller v. Ray, 48 Ala. 468 (1872); Marsh v. Richardson, 49 Ala. 430 (1873); Hutton v. Williams, 60 Ala. 133 (1877).

§ 43-2-508. Satisfaction of claims.

Any judge of probate, clerk or register of any circuit court or officer of any other court in Alabama having jurisdiction of partial or final settlement of estates of deceased persons shall be authorized to satisfy any claim legally filed against such estates and recorded in the solvent docket book in the office of the probate court, when satisfied from the evidence presented on a partial or final settlement that such claims have been paid.

Such satisfaction shall have the effect of notifying all interested parties that evidence of payment of such debt has been filed in the court.

For each such satisfaction, the officer shall be paid a fee of $.25.

A cancelled check for the amount claimed, properly endorsed by the claimant, may be considered as proof of the payment of such claim, and further proof of payment shall not be required. (Acts 1939, No. 68, p. 109; Code 1940, T. 61, § 303; Acts 1975, No. 1222, § 1.)

Collateral references. — 34 C.J.S., Executors & Administrators, § 805.

§ 43-2-509. Liability of executor or administrator for interest or profits.

If any executor or administrator uses any of the funds of the estate for his own benefit, he is accountable for any profit made thereon or legal interest. (Code 1852, § 1813; Code 1867, § 2148; Code 1876, § 2520; Code 1886, § 2142; Code 1896, § 210; Code 1907, § 2675; Code 1923, § 5908; Code 1940, T. 61, § 304.)

An administrator prima facie is chargeable with interest under this section upon all receipts until disbursement, and must discharge himself by oath. King v. Cabiness, 12 Ala. 598 (1847), cited in Hollis v. Caughman, 22 Ala. 478 (1853); Farmer v. Farmer, 26 Ala. 671 (1855); Harrison v. Harrison, 39 Ala. 489 (1864), overruled on other grounds, Fretwell v. McLemore, 52 Ala. 124 (1875); Clark v. Knox, 70 Ala. 607 (1881).

And delay in settlement renders him liable therefor. — The rulings of the Alabama court have settled the doctrine that an administrator who delays, without sufficient cause, settlement and distribution for an unreasonable time, is liable for interest, though he may have kept the money unemployed and in safe deposit. Mims v. Mims, 39 Ala. 716 (1866); Clark v. Knox, 70 Ala. 607 (1881); Clark v. Hughes, 71 Ala. 163 (1881); Englehardt v. Yung, 76 Ala. 534 (1884).

And executor who mingles funds of estate with his own is chargeable with interest. Farmer v. Farmer, 26 Ala. 671 (1855); Pearson v. Darrington, 32 Ala. 227 (1858); Harrison v. Harrison, 39 Ala. 489 (1864), overruled on other grounds, Fretwell v. McLemore, 52 Ala. 124 (1875); Ivey v. Coleman, 42 Ala. 409 (1868).

This applies where executor deposits estate funds in his private account. Collins v. Clements, 199 Ala. 618, 75 So. 165 (1917).

Deposit in bank where executor owns stock. — In Elmore v. Cunninghame, 208 Ala. 15, 93 So. 814 (1922), it is held that under this section an executor is not chargeable with interest on estate funds deposited in a bank in which he was a stockholder. The court based its decision on the ruling in Johnson v. Holifield, 82 Ala. 123, 2 So. 753 (1887), to the effect that an executor was not chargeable with interest on funds that he "deposited" with a partnership of which he was a member. However, the court observed that if the question presented in the Johnson case was up for original decision it was exceedingly doubtful whether the view there taken would be acceptable. See also Noble v. Jackson, 124 Ala. 311, 26 So. 955 (1899).

Administrator is not chargeable with interest on commissions which he had paid himself in anticipation of their allowance from date of allowance thereof on annual settlement. Walsh v. Walsh, 231 Ala. 305, 164 So. 822 (1935).

Nor where collections are small compared with costs. — The administrator is not liable for interest on rents, where the rent collected is small compared with the costs of settlement and distribution. Eubank v. Clark, 78 Ala. 73 (1884).

Compound interest will not be charged unless it is shown that the executor used the funds or was guilty of willful neglect. Powell v. Powell, 10 Ala. 900 (1846); Smith v. Kennard, 38 Ala. 695 (1863).

Cited in Benford v. Gibson, 15 Ala. 521 (1849); Hamilton v. Adams, 15 Ala. 596 (1849); Rhodes v. Turner, 21 Ala. 210 (1852); Molett v. Keenan, 22 Ala. 484 (1853); Bendall v. Bendall, 24 Ala. 295 (1854); Roundtree v. Snodgrass, 36 Ala. 185 (1860); Raines v. Raines, 51 Ala. 237 (1874); Wright v. Evans, 53 Ala. 103 (1875); Ditmar v. Bogle, 53 Ala. 169 (1875); First Nat'l Bank v. Weaver, 225 Ala. 160, 142 So. 420 (1932); Stone v. Vaughn, 232 Ala. 120, 167 So. 297 (1936); Webb v. Webb, 250 Ala. 194, 33 So. 2d 909 (1948); Wilkerson v. Wilkerson, 257 Ala. 633, 60 So. 2d 343 (1952); Papan v. Papan, 362 So. 2d 902 (Ala. 1978).

Collateral references. — 33 C.J.S., Executors & Administrators, § 239.

§ 43-2-510. Credit for expenses of minor distributees.

(a) When the estate of a decedent is solvent, the executor or administrator, out of the assets in his hands, may defray the necessary and reasonable expenses of maintaining and educating minors who are entitled to distribution therein, and who have no legal guardian; and, upon any partial or final settlement by him, the probate court must allow him credit for such expenses, to be charged against the shares of such minors and deducted therefrom on any distribution of the estate.

(b) An executor or administrator defraying such expenses must file with his account for a settlement a separate account of the amounts paid therefor on account of each of such minors accompanied by proper vouchers, showing the amounts and for what expended. (Code 1876, §§ 2644, 2645; Code 1886, §§ 2159, 2160; Code 1896, §§ 227, 288; Code 1907, §§ 2676, 2677; Code 1923, §§ 5909, 5910; Code 1940, T. 61, §§ 305, 306.)

Law prior to adoption of section. — The right to the credit herein allowed was recognized in equity before the adoption of this section. Cary v. Simmons, 87 Ala. 524, 6 So. 416 (1889).

Items of board against the distributees are properly allowed against their distributive shares on final settlement and distribution by the administrator. Howard v. Rutherford, 149 Ala. 661, 43 So. 30 (1907). See also Glover v. Hill, 85 Ala. 41, 4 So. 613 (1888), holding administrator entitled to "reasonable value" of the board of the minors.

Money paid to disencumber property to minor. — An administrator is not entitled to allowance for money paid to disencumber the property of minor heirs, the money not being paid in the course of administration since the property did not come to them from the estate. Cary v. Simmons, 87 Ala. 524, 6 So. 416 (1889).

Collateral references. — 34 C.J.S., Executors & Administrators, § 851.

§ 43-2-511. Contest of account — Generally.

Any person interested may appear and contest any item of the account and may examine the executor or administrator or any other witness and may introduce any legal evidence in support of his contest. (Code 1852, § 1812; Code 1867, § 2147; Code 1876, § 2519; Code 1886, § 2143; Code 1896, § 211; Code 1907, § 2678; Code 1923, § 5911; Code 1940, T. 61, § 307.)

Heir of estate is interested person. — Under this section a mother of deceased, and heir of her estate, is interested therein, and may appear and contest items in the account. Hines v. Baldwin, 211 Ala. 322, 100 So. 466 (1924).

Also a grantee of heirs. — A grantee of real estate of a deceased person, conveyed to him by the heirs, is entitled to be admitted as a party to the accounting under this section, where the lands conveyed to him are subsequently recovered by administrator on pretense of paying debts owing, and the grantee is entitled to the rents collected by the administrator. Spear v. Banks, 125 Ala. 227, 27 So. 979 (1900), holding that an assignee of an integral share of the estate is within this section.

But creditors of the heirs have no such interest, under this section, as entitles them to oppose the application for settlement. Owens v. Thurmond, 40 Ala. 289 (1866).

Showing insolvency of estate. — A creditor contesting the final account of outgoing administrators may show the insolvency of the estate, although it has not been formally declared insolvent, to determine whether such administrators are entitled to credits for the payment of unpreferred debts. And he may show that the allowance of the unauthorized item would render the estate insolvent. The fact that a complaint is pending in the circuit court, alleging that such creditor's claim had been paid, does not bar him from contesting in the probate court. Byrd v. Jones, 84 Ala. 336, 4 So. 375 (1888).

As to when and by whom estate reported insolvent, see § 43-2-701 and notes thereto.

As to burden of proof of credits. — See Hines v. Baldwin, 211 Ala. 322, 100 So. 466 (1924).

Failure to contest precludes review. — Administrator de bonis non, failing to contest any item of executor's account or reserve exceptions to allowance thereof, could not review decree settling executor's account. Grist v. Carswell, 231 Ala. 442, 165 So. 102 (1935).

Cited in Waller v. Ray, 48 Ala. 468 (1872); Chancellor v. Chancellor, 177 Ala. 44, 58 So. 423 (1912).

§ 43-2-512. Same — Showing of failure to discharge trust, etc.

Upon final settlement, any person contesting may also show that the executor or administrator has failed to charge himself with or to account for all the assets of the decedent received by him, or that he has failed to collect the same, or any portion thereof, or that by any abuse of, or failure to discharge his trust, such assets or any portion thereof have been depreciated, injured or destroyed. (Code 1852, § 1824; Code 1867, § 2160; Code 1876, § 2532; Code 1886, § 2150; Code 1896, § 218; Code 1907, § 2679; Code 1923, § 5912; Code 1940, T. 61, § 308.)

Cited in Henderson v. Renfro, 31 Ala. 101 (1857); Grace v. McKissack, 49 Ala. 163 (1873); Tayloe v. Bush, 75 Ala. 432 (1883); Crews v. United States Fid. & Guar. Co., 237 Ala. 14, 185 So. 370 (1938); Webb v. Webb, 250 Ala. 194, 33 So. 2d 909 (1948).

§ 43-2-513. Same — Examination of witnesses.

The depositions of witnesses may be taken on interrogatories and read in evidence, or witnesses examined orally, by any party to the settlement, in the same cases, for the same causes and under the same rules as depositions are taken and read, or as witnesses are examined in civil actions. (Code 1852, § 1812; Code 1867, § 2147; Code 1876, § 2519; Code 1886, § 2144; Code 1896, § 212; Code 1907, § 2680; Code 1923, § 5913; Code 1940, T. 61, § 309.)

§ 43-2-514. Same — Reduction or disallowance of item.

If any item as charged by the executor or administrator is reduced or not allowed, the costs of the contest in relation to such item must be paid by the executor or administrator, otherwise, by the party contesting. (Code 1852, § 1814; Code 1867, § 2149; Code 1876, § 2521; Code 1886, § 2145; Code 1896, § 213; Code 1907, § 2681; Code 1923, § 5914; Code 1940, T. 61, § 310.)

In general. — Where there is a contest between administrator and distributee, as to ownership of fund and the administrator loses, he is liable for the costs. Jones v. Deyer, 16 Ala. 221 (1849). See also Pinckard v. Pinckard, 24 Ala. 250 (1854); Smyley v. Reese, 53 Ala. 89 (1875).

Costs on appeal. — This section does not make an administrator liable for costs on appeal, when an order allowing him credit is reversed. Moody v. Hemphill, 71 Ala. 169 (1881).

Cited in Henderson v. Renfro, 31 Ala. 101 (1857).

Collateral references. — 34 C.J.S., Executors & Administrators, § 943.

§ 43-2-515. Same — Withdrawal of item.

The executor or administrator may, before the decision of the court on any item, withdraw the same; but in such case he must pay the costs of the contest as to such item. (Code 1852, § 1815; Code 1867, § 2150; Code 1876, § 2522; Code 1886, § 2146; Code 1896, § 214; Code 1907, § 2682; Code 1923, § 5915; Code 1940, T. 61, § 311.)

§ 43-2-516. Decree passing account as stated.

On auditing the account, the court must state the same and render a decree passing it as stated; and the same must be recorded. (Code 1852, § 1816; Code 1867, § 2152; Code 1876, § 2523; Code 1886, § 2147; Code 1896, § 215; Code 1907, § 2683; Code 1923, § 5916; Code 1940, T. 61, § 312.)

Cited in Marion County v. Brown, 43 Ala. 112 (1869).

§ 43-2-517. Appointment and compensation of special guardian.

The jurisdiction of the probate court to make partial or final settlements or distributions of the estates of decedents is not affected by the fact that the executor or administrator making the settlement is also guardian of any heir or distributee, devisee or legatee of the decedent; but in such case the court must appoint a special guardian, without bond, to represent such heir or distributee, devisee or legatee on the settlement and distribution; and, upon final settlement, any decree to which such ward may be entitled must be rendered against the executor or administrator in the name of the special guardian for the use of the ward; and thereafter the executor or administrator, in the capacity of guardian, shall be accountable for such decree. The special guardian shall be entitled to reasonable compensation for his services and for the services of counsel properly employed to be allowed by the court and to be paid by such general guardian out of the estate of the ward. (Code 1876, § 2529; Code 1886, § 2148; Code 1896, § 216; Code 1907, § 2684; Code 1923, § 5917; Code 1940, T. 61, § 313.)

The express purpose of this section is to authorize the probate court to proceed to final settlement in cases where the administrator is also the guardian of some of the heirs or distributees. Swope v. Swope, 178 Ala. 172, 59 So. 661 (1912) (dissenting opinion).

The chief purpose of the enactment of this section was to change a rule that the probate court had no jurisdiction to make decree of final settlement of the administration of an estate when the administrator was also guardian of a minor heir and distributee of said estate, and give such jurisdiction to the probate court. Lane v. Lane, 240 Ala. 447, 199 So. 870 (1940).

Liability of executor or administrator unchanged. — By the provision in this section, "and thereafter the executor or administrator, in the capacity of guardian, shall be accountable for such decree," it was not intended to change the law fixing the liability of his two bonds as such. When the administrator was declared thereafter to be accountable for the decree as guardian, it means that he should be accountable on principles of law which fix his liability as guardian to account. Lane v. Lane, 240 Ala. 447, 199 So. 870 (1940).

Subsequent decree of settlement of guardianship was unwarranted. — Where decedent's estate consisted of an amount of damages for decedent's unlawful death in Florida railroad accident, and decedent's husband, who acted as administrator and as guardian for minor children, as administrator, collected damages from railroad and used proceeds to purchase land, title to which was taken in husband's name, and Florida statutes concerning death actions were not pleaded and proved in proceeding on final settlement of husband's guardianship accounts, and at time of settlement of administration in probate court, fund arising from damages was not in being and administrator was insolvent, a subsequent decree of settlement of guardianship was held unwarranted in so far as it charged husband, as guardian, and surety on guardian's bond, with amounts charged against husband, individually and as administrator, in favor of special guardian for children under decree in settlement of administration. Lane v. Lane, 240 Ala. 447, 199 So. 870 (1940).

And reversal of one decree did not affect the other. — Where decree was rendered against decedent's husband, who had acted as administrator and as guardian for minor children, individually and as administrator, in favor of special guardian for children on final settlement of administration in probate court reversal of decree against husband, as guardian, and against surety on guardian's bond in proceeding on final settlement of guardianship accounts, insofar as decree erroneously charged certain items against husband, as guardian, and surety was held not to affect decree against husband, as administrator. Lane v. Lane, 240 Ala. 447, 199 So. 870 (1940).

Cited in Carswell v. Spencer, 44 Ala. 204 (1870); Tankersly v. Pettis, 61 Ala. 354 (1878); Alexander v. Alexander, 70 Ala. 212 (1881).

§ 43-2-518. Reexamination of items included in previous settlements.

Upon the final settlement, any item of account included in any previous settlement may be reexamined; but its allowance in the previous settlement is presumptive evidence of its correctness. (Code 1852, § 1823; Code 1867, § 2159; Code 1876, § 2531; Code 1886, § 2149; Code 1896, § 217; Code 1907, § 2685; Code 1923, § 5918; Code 1940, T. 61, § 314.)

Settlement held not final. — A settlement in which an executrix procured the withdrawal of objections to an item, and the allowance of the item, on the faith of an agreement between the objectors and herself which was not carried out by her, is not a final settlement within the meaning of this section. McKeitchen v. Rich, 204 Ala. 588, 86 So. 377 (1920). See also Lehman v. Robertson, 84 Ala. 489, 4 So. 728 (1888).

The burden of proof is on the attacking party to overcome the presumption of this section. Newberry v. Newberry, 28 Ala. 691 (1856); Ivey v. Coleman, 42 Ala. 409 (1868); Sheppard v. Gill, 49 Ala. 162 (1873); Eubank v. Clark, 78 Ala. 73 (1884); Dickie v. Dickie, 80 Ala. 57 (1885).

Previous settlements of administrator and decrees thereon are presumed to be correct under this section, and burden of showing error is on a person with an interest in previous settlements to overcome the presumption of veracity. Stumpf v. Wiles, 235 Ala. 317, 179 So. 201 (1938).

Items of account and allowances approved on annual settlement prior to final settlement are prima facie conclusive, and impose on person objecting thereto burden to establish impropriety of items on final settlement. Walsh v. Walsh, 231 Ala. 305, 164 So. 822 (1935).

Cited in Ditmar v. Bogle, 53 Ala. 169 (1875); Radford v. Morris, 66 Ala. 283 (1880).

§ 43-2-519. Notice of annual or partial settlement; conclusiveness of order or decree; reopening account.

Whenever any administrator or executor shall file any annual, partial or final settlement in any court having jurisdiction thereof, the court shall, at the request of such administrator or executor, require that notice thereof be given in the same manner as required by law in cases of final settlements, and any order or decree of the court on such settlement after such notice shall be final and conclusive as to all items of receipts and disbursements and other transactions and matters shown therein, and as to all fees and compensation fixed or allowed to any such administrator, executor or attorney, and appeals therefrom shall and must be taken in the manner provided for from any other final decrees of such court. Thereafter, at any time prior to final settlement, the account may be reopened by the court on motion or petition of the administrator, executor, beneficiary or other party having an interest in the estate for amendment or revision, if it later appears that the account is incorrect, either because of fraud or mistake. (Acts 1936, Ex. Sess., No. 128, p. 90; Code 1940, T. 61, § 315.)

Cited in Wilkerson v. Wilkerson, 257 Ala. 633, 60 So. 2d 343 (1952).

Collateral references. — 34 C.J.S., Executors & Administrators, § 903.

Division 2.

Compelling Settlement by Existing Executor or Administrator.

Collateral references. — 31 Am. Jur. 2d, Executors & Administrators, §§ 509-549.

§ 43-2-530. Authorization to compel settlement.

Any executor or administrator may be required by citation to file his accounts and vouchers and to make a settlement, notwithstanding any provision in any will or other instrument to the contrary; and, if after service of the citation, he fails to file his accounts and vouchers for a settlement on the day named in the citation, the probate court or other court having jurisdiction of the said estate may compel him to do so by attachment or may proceed to state the account against him from the materials on file or such other information as may be accessible, charging him with such assets as may have come to his hands. (Code 1852, § 1817; Code 1867, § 2153; Code 1876, § 2524; Code 1886, § 2155; Code 1896, § 223; Code 1907, § 2686; Acts 1919, No. 440, p. 566; Code 1923, § 5919; Code 1940, T. 61, § 316.)

Cross references. — See § 43-2-311 and notes thereto.

Settlement is mandatory. — Under this section the duty to make settlement is mandatory. Naugher v. Hinson, 211 Ala. 278, 100 So. 221 (1924).

And if the accounts and vouchers are not filed by the day named in the citation the court should proceed as herein prescribed. Adams v. Walsh, 190 Ala. 516, 67 So. 432 (1914).

Cited in Duffee v. Buchanan, 8 Ala. 27 (1845); Moore v. Baker, 39 Ala. 704 (1866); Childress v. Childress, 49 Ala. 237 (1873); v. , 51 Ala. 79 (1874); Vincent v. Daniel, 59 Ala. 602 (1877); May v. Carlisle, 68 Ala. 135 (1880); Little v. Ennis, 207 Ala. 111, 92 So. 167 (1922); Wright v. Menefee, 226 Ala. 55, 145 So. 315 (1932); Pinckard v. Ledyard, 251 Ala. 648, 38 So. 2d 580 (1949).

§ 43-2-531. Issuance of citation; notice; when court required to examine, audit or restate account.

After stating such account, the court must issue a citation to such executor or administrator to appear on a day therein named and file his accounts and vouchers for settlement or that the account so stated will be passed, which must be served on him at least 10 days before the day named therein; and must also give notice of such settlement by publication, as in case of settlements voluntarily made by executors and administrators; and, if on the day named such executor or administrator fails to appear and file his accounts and vouchers for settlement, as required by law, the court must proceed to examine the account so stated and audit and, if necessary, restate the same. (Code 1852, §§ 1818, 1819; Code 1867, §§ 2154, 2155; Code 1876, §§ 2525, 2526; Code 1886, § 2156; Code 1896, § 224; Code 1907, § 2687; Code 1923, § 5920; Code 1940, T. 61, § 317.)

Cross references. — See notes to § 43-2-532.

Allegation and presumption as to notice. — A complaint by an administratrix to set aside a decree on an account stated by the probate court must allege that plaintiff did not receive the statutory notice, and was not present at the hearing. Adams v. Walsh, 190 Ala. 516, 67 So. 432 (1914).

The presumption on appeal is that in the absence of such allegation such notice was fully given and that administratrix was present at the hearing. Adams v. Walsh, 190 Ala. 516, 67 So. 432 (1914).

Cited in Cook v. Cook, 69 Ala. 294 (1881); Booker v. State, 76 Ala. 22 (1884).

§ 43-2-532. Proceedings on settlement of account.

On the day appointed for auditing such account, any person may attend on the part of such executor or administrator and show that he is entitled to additional credits; and any person interested may attend and contest any item of such account or in any previous account, or may show assets not accounted for, or that such executor or administrator has failed to collect any assets from want of due diligence, or that, by any abuse of, or failure to discharge his trust, such assets or any portion thereof have been injured, destroyed or depreciated; and, in case of such proof, the executor or administrator must be charged therewith; and, upon such settlements, decrees must be rendered as upon settlements voluntarily made. (Code 1886, § 2157; Code 1896, § 225; Code 1907, § 2688; Code 1923, § 5921; Code 1940, T. 61, § 318.)

Administrator afforded protection. — This section and § 43-2-531 indicate that this article is intended not only for the protection of the distributees of the estate but of the administrator as well. Adams v. Walsh, 190 Ala. 516, 67 So. 432 (1914).

Cited in Crews v. United States Fid. & Guar. Co., 237 Ala. 14, 185 So. 370 (1938).

Collateral references. — 34 C.J.S., Executors & Administrators, §§ 917-920.

§ 43-2-533. Setting aside decree.

If, however, such executor or administrator appears and files his accounts and vouchers for settlement and pays such costs as have accrued upon the proceedings had under sections 43-2-530 through 43-2-532, the court may set aside such decree and proceed as if none had been rendered. (Code 1852, § 1820; Code 1867, § 2156; Code 1876, § 2527; Code 1886, § 2158; Code 1896, § 226; Code 1907, § 2689; Code 1923, § 5922; Code 1940, T. 61, § 319.)

Cited in Vincent v. Daniel, 59 Ala. 602 (1877).

Collateral references. — 34 C.J.S., Executors & Administrators, §§ 912, 921.

Division 3.

Compelling Settlement of Executor or Administrator Whose Authority Has Ceased.

Collateral references. — 31 Am. Jur. 2d, Executors & Administrators, §§ 603-623.

§ 43-2-550. Final settlement required following death, removal or resignation of executor or administrator.

When an executor or administrator dies, resigns or is removed, or his letters are revoked, or his authority ceases from any cause, he must within one month after his authority ceases or, in case of his death, his personal representative must or, in case of his removal from the state, his sureties must, within six months after the grant of letters, file his accounts, vouchers and statement of heirs and legatees for and must make final settlement of the administration of, such executor or administrator, of which settlement notice must be given in the same manner; and such settlement must be conducted and governed, except as otherwise provided in this article, by the same rules and provisions of law as other final settlements by executors or administrators. (Code 1852, § 1876; Code 1867, §§ 2165, 2232; Code 1876, §§ 2537, 2590; Code 1886, § 2173; Code 1896, § 241; Code 1907, § 2692; Acts 1923, No. 492, p. 655; Code 1923, § 5925; Code 1940, T. 61, § 320.)

Cross references. — See notes to § 43-2-252.

Reason for enactment of section. — At common law, if an administrator committed a devastavit, his administrator, upon his death, was not liable at law. It was regarded at law as a personal tort which did not survive. It resulted that his administrator could not be required to settle the former administration. The remedy was in equity. This led to the enactment of this section, under which the administrator of the estate of a deceased administrator must make settlement of the former administration. Cowan v. Perkins, 214 Ala. 155, 107 So. 63 (1926).

Purpose of settlement. — The settlement under this section is to ascertain what the estate of the deceased administrator owes, growing out of the trust left unsettled. Boyte v. Perkins, 211 Ala. 130, 99 So. 652 (1924).

Delay in filing accounts renders executor liable for interest. — Under this section the resigning executor should be charged interest on any balance in his hands, for delay in filing his accounts within a reasonable time after the one month expires. Elmore v. Cunninghame, 208 Ala. 15, 93 So. 814 (1922).

Such delay is not justified by removal of administration to circuit court. — Under this section the removal of administration from the probate court after the resignation of the executor is not ground for delay in filing accounts. Elmore v. Cunninghame, 208 Ala. 15, 93 So. 814 (1922).

Nor by state of war or prevalence of epidemic. — That World War I was in progress, it not being shown that the executor was absent on that account, and the prevalence of the flu epidemic, with which the executor was not shown to have been afflicted, was held to be no excuse for delay in filing his accounts. Elmore v. Cunninghame, 208 Ala. 15, 93 So. 814 (1922).

Necessary parties to action for settlement. — Ordinarily, administrator de bonis non or ad litem would be necessary party to action for settlement and distribution of intestate's estate where administrator was deceased. Cook v. Castleberry, 233 Ala. 650, 173 So. 1 (1937).

But where settlement of decedent's estate was sought, all debts were paid, and all heirs of decedent and distributees of his estate were represented, administrator de bonis non or ad litem was not necessary party, notwithstanding administrator was deceased. Cook v. Castleberry, 233 Ala. 650, 173 So. 1 (1937).

Venue of action for settlement. — Complaint against administratrix for settlement and distribution of estate of which her decedent was administrator held properly filed in court of county to which administration was removed, regardless of residence of parties. Cook v. Castleberry, 233 Ala. 650, 173 So. 1 (1937).

Cited in Lyon v. Odom, 31 Ala. 234 (1857); Whitworth v. Oliver, 39 Ala. 286 (1864); Harrison v. Harrison, 39 Ala. 489 (1864); Searcy v. Holmes, 43 Ala. 608 (1869); Chisholm v. Arrington, 43 Ala. 610 (1869); Cunningham v. Beard, 44 Ala. 317 (1870); Cogburn v. McQueen, 46 Ala. 551 (1871); Waller v. Ray, 48 Ala. 468 (1872); Seawell v. Buckley, 54 Ala. 592 (1875); Stallworth v. Farnham, 64 Ala. 259 (1879); Glenn v. Billingslea, 64 Ala. 345 (1879); Hatchett v. Billingslea, 65 Ala. 16 (1880); Buchanan v. Thomason, 70 Ala. 401 (1881); Eubank v. Clark, 78 Ala. 73 (1884); Sampey v. Sowell, 93 Ala. 447, 9 So. 600 (1891); Wright v.

Menefee, 226 Ala. 55, 145 So. 315 (1932); Lindsey v. Lindsey, 226 Ala. 489, 147 So. 425 (1933); Blue v. United States Fid. & Guar. Co., 228 Ala. 239, 153 So. 150 (1934); Stone v. Vaughn, 232 Ala. 120, 167 So. 297 (1936); Willett v. First Nat'l Bank, 234 Ala. 577, 176 So. 344 (1937); Crews v. United States Fid. & Guar. Co., 237 Ala. 14, 185 So. 370 (1938);

Clark v. Glenn, 249 Ala. 342, 31 So. 2d 507 (1947); Ex parte Lange, 268 Ala. 422, 108 So. 2d 335 (1959); Marks v. Brightwell, 269 Ala. 506, 114 So. 2d 268 (1959); First Nat'l Bank v. United States, 176 F. Supp. 768 (M.D. Ala. 1959).

Collateral references. — 34 C.J.S., Executors & Administrators, § 911.

§ 43-2-551. Making succeeding executor or administrator party to settlement.

The remaining or succeeding executor or administrator of the estate of the decedent, if there be one, must be made a party to such settlement and, if a resident of this state, must have personal notice of the time of making the same served on him at least 10 days before the day appointed therefor. (Code 1867, § 2166; Code 1876, § 2538; Code 1886, § 2174; Code 1896, § 242; Code 1907, § 2693; Code 1923, § 5926; Code 1940, T. 61, § 321.)

Cross references. — See notes to § 43-2-550.

Cited in Sampey v. Sowell, 93 Ala. 447, 9 So. 600 (1891); Lindsey v. Lindsey, 226 Ala. 489, 147 So. 425 (1933); Merrill v. Zera, 265 Ala. 390, 91 So. 2d 472 (1956).

§ 43-2-552. Decree for balance — Generally.

If there remains any act of administration to be done, other than making settlement and distribution or payment of legacies, and there is a remaining or succeeding executor or administrator, a decree must be rendered in his favor for the amount found due on such settlement, and for the delivery of any personal property in the hands of the executor or administrator whose authority has ceased or, if dead, of his personal representative; but if more than six months have elapsed from the original grant of letters and there remains no other act of administration to be done than making distribution or payment of legacies, and the estate is solvent, the court must at once proceed to decree distribution or payment of legacies directly to those entitled; or, if in the case last mentioned, there are money assets in the hands of the outgoing executor or administrator, or, if dead, of his personal representative, in excess of a sum sufficient for the payment of debts and expenses of further administration, such excess must be distributed, or legacies paid therefrom, directly to those entitled, without passing through the hands of the remaining or succeeding administrator. (Code 1852, § 1877; Code 1867, § 2233; Code 1876, § 2591; Code 1886, § 2175; Code 1896, § 243; Code 1907, § 2694; Code 1923, § 5927; Code 1940, T. 61, § 322.)

Cross references. — See notes to § 43-2-550.

Intent of section. — This section is intended to prescribe what decrees shall be rendered on settlements made under § 43-2-550. Boyte v. Perkins, 211 Ala. 130, 99 So. 652 (1924).

This section deals with two distinct classes of cases: First, where an administrator has resigned or been removed, and is accounting for his own doings in the administration of his trust. Secondly, comes the provision for delivery of any personal property which may be in the hands of the outgoing administrator, or if dead, in the hands of his personal representative. Boyte v. Perkins, 211 Ala. 130, 99 So. 652 (1924).

In the first case the administrator and the

sureties on his bond are responsible for the amount found due on the settlement. A decree goes against him as though he were making a final settlement of his trust. But the decree in the second case (for the delivery of personal property in his hands) applies to "his personal representative." Boyte v. Perkins, 211 Ala. 130, 99 So. 652 (1924).

Decree has no preference over other claims. — The decree is a claim against the estate of the decedent and is given no preference over other debts of the decedent. Boyte v. Perkins, 211 Ala. 130, 99 So. 652 (1924).

Surety of deceased administrator is not bound. — The decree rendered against personal representative of deceased administratrix for settlement of former administration, under this section and § 43-2-550 does not bind the surety of deceased administratrix, there being no privity between such surety and administrator of his principal. The remedy is by accounting against the surety, whose liability accrues upon the death of the administrator. Cowan v. Perkins, 214 Ala. 155, 107 So. 63 (1926).

Revival of decree. — A decree against the personal representative of a deceased administratrix obtained under this section may, under § 43-2-134, be revived against the administratrix de bonis non of the deceased administratrix. Cowan v. Perkins, 214 Ala. 158, 107 So. 66 (1926).

Enforcement by execution. — A decree under this section, directing execution against the representative as in § 43-2-150 (providing for enforcements of judgments and decrees against representatives) to be followed by an execution against his sureties under § 43-2-151, is not contemplated, since the settlement hereunder relates to no maladministration on his part. Boyte v. Perkins, 211 Ala. 130, 99 So. 652 (1924). See also Cowan v. Perkins, 214 Ala. 155, 107 So. 63 (1926).

Ordering distribution of assets of two estates. — Where the widow of a decedent was appointed his administratrix and died before making final settlement and the same person was appointed administrator for the estate of the original decedent and that of the widow, after the expiration of six months from the issue of letters as to each estate separately, there being no debts unpaid or owing by either estate, the court in which both administrations were pending could, at the instance of the distributees or one of them, cause a distribution of all assets of both estates. Merrill v. Zera, 265 Ala. 390, 91 So. 2d 472 (1956).

Cited in Lyon v. Odom, 31 Ala. 234 (1857); Searcy v. Holmes, 45 Ala. 225 (1871); Hendricks v. Thornton, 45 Ala. 299 (1871); Waring v. Lewis, 53 Ala. 615 (1875); Stallworth v. Farnham, 64 Ala. 259 (1879); Glenn v. Billingslea, 64 Ala. 345 (1879); Hatchett v. Billingslea, 65 Ala. 16 (1880); Lindsey v. Lindsey, 226 Ala. 489, 147 So. 425 (1933); Patterson v. First Nat'l Bank, 261 Ala. 601, 75 So. 2d 471 (1954).

§ 43-2-553. Same — Decree in favor of outgoing executor or administrator; insolvent estates.

If, on such settlement, a balance is ascertained to be due from the estate of such decedent to the deceased or outgoing executor or administrator, the probate court may, if six months have elapsed from the grant of original letters, render a decree in favor of the outgoing executor or administrator or, if dead, of his personal representative, against the remaining or succeeding executor or administrator for such balance; and if the estate is solvent, payment thereof may be enforced by execution against him, to be levied on any effects of such estate in his hands unadministered; but if the estate is insolvent, such decree is to be paid as other claims against insolvent estates; and if such balance or any part thereof is for expenses of administration necessarily incurred, such balance, or such part thereof as may be for such expenses, shall be a preferred claim against such estate and shall be paid as other preferred claims are paid. (Code 1867, § 2167; Code 1876, § 2539; Code 1886, § 2176; Code 1896, § 244; Code 1907, § 2695; Code 1923, § 5928; Code 1940, T. 61, § 323.)

Cross references. — See § 43-2-552 and notes thereto.

Cited in Cunningham v. Beard, 44 Ala. 317 (1870); Stallworth v. Farnham, 64 Ala. 259 (1879); Glenn v. Billingslea, 64 Ala. 345 (1879);

Hatchett v. Billingslea, 65 Ala. 16 (1880); Buchanan v. Thomason, 70 Ala. 401 (1881); Davis v. Sowell & Co., 77 Ala. 262 (1884); Eubank v. Clark, 78 Ala. 73 (1884).

§ 43-2-554. When execution may be stayed.

The probate court may stay execution on any decree rendered under the provisions of section 43-2-553, for any time not exceeding six months, if, in the judgment of the court, the interest of the estate requires extension. (Code 1867, § 2168; Code 1876, § 2540; Code 1886, § 2177; Code 1896, § 245; Code 1907, § 2696; Code 1923, § 5929; Code 1940, T. 61, § 324.)

Cross references. — See notes to §§ 43-2-552 and 43-2-553.

Cited in Cunningham v. Beard, 44 Ala. 317 (1870).

§ 43-2-555. Stating account or compelling settlement by attachment.

If such outgoing executor or administrator or, if dead, his personal representative or, in case of his removal from the state, his sureties fail to make settlement within the time required by this division, the court may, of its own motion or on the application of any party in interest, compel him or his sureties to do so by attachment, or may state the account against him or his sureties from the materials on file or such other information as may be accessible to the court, charging him or his personal representative or his sureties with such assets as may have come into the hands of such executor or administrator. (Code 1852, § 1881; Code 1867, § 2234; Code 1876, § 2592; Code 1886, § 2178; Code 1896, § 246; Code 1907, § 2697; Acts 1923, No. 492, p. 655; Code 1923, § 5930; Code 1940, T. 61, § 325.)

Cited in Whitworth v. Oliver, 39 Ala. 286 (1864); Glenn v. Billingslea, 64 Ala. 345 (1879); Hatchett v. Billingslea, 65 Ala. 16 (1880);

Crews v. United States Fid. & Guar. Co., 237 Ala. 14, 185 So. 370 (1938).

§ 43-2-556. Issuance of citation; notice; when court required to examine, audit or restate account.

After stating such account, the court must issue citation to such executor or administrator or, if dead, to his personal representative or, in case of his removal from the state, to his sureties to appear on a day therein named and to file his account and vouchers for settlement, or that the account so stated will be passed, which must be served on him, or, if dead, on his personal representative or, in case of his removal from the state, his sureties at least 10 days before the day named therein; and must also give notice of such settlement by publication, as in case of final settlements voluntarily made by executors or administrators; and if, on the day named, such executor or administrator or, if dead, his personal representative or, in case of his removal from the state, his sureties fail to appear and file his accounts and vouchers for settlement, as required by law, the court must proceed to examine the account, audit and, if necessary, restate the same. (Code 1852, § 1879; Code 1867, § 2235; Code 1876, § 2593; Code 1886, § 2179; Code 1896, § 247; Code 1907, § 2698; Acts 1923, No. 492, p. 655; Code 1923, § 5931; Code 1940, T. 61, § 326.)

Notice to surety. — Surety, on resigning executor's bond, need not be notified of proceeding for final accounting under this section, in absence of executor's removal from state.

Stone v. Vaughn, 232 Ala. 120, 167 So. 297 (1936).

Cited in Lyon v. Odom, 31 Ala. 234 (1857).

§ 43-2-557. Proceedings on final settlement of account.

On the day appointed for auditing such account, any person may attend on the part of such executor or administrator or, if dead, of his personal representative or, in case of his removal from the state, his sureties and show that he is entitled to additional credits; and any person interested may attend and contest any item of such account or in any previous account, or may show assets not accounted for, or that such executor or administrator has failed to collect any assets from want of due diligence, or that, by any abuse of or failure to discharge his trust, such assets, or any portion thereof, have been injured, destroyed or depreciated; and, in case of such proof, the executor or administrator or, if dead, his personal representative or, in case of his removal from the state, his sureties must be charged therewith. On such settlements, decrees must be rendered as upon like settlements voluntarily made. (Code 1852, § 1880; Code 1867, § 2236; Code 1876, § 2594; Code 1886, § 2180; Code 1896, § 248; Code 1907, § 2699; Acts 1923, No. 492, p. 655; Code 1923, § 5932; Code 1940, T. 61, § 327.)

Cited in Chisholm v. Arrington, 43 Ala. 610 (1869).

§ 43-2-558. Setting aside decree.

If, however, such executor or administrator or, if dead, his personal representative or, in event of his removal from the state, his sureties appear and file his accounts and vouchers for settlement and pay such costs as have accrued upon the proceedings had under sections 43-2-555 through 43-2-557, the court may set aside such decree and proceed as if none had been rendered. (Code 1886, § 2181; Code 1896, § 249; Code 1907, § 2700; Acts 1923, No. 492, p. 655; Code 1923, § 5933; Code 1940, T. 61, § 328.)

§ 43-2-559. Other actions not barred.

The proceedings for the settlement of the accounts of deceased or outgoing executors or administrators provided for in this division do not prevent any action by the remaining or succeeding executor or administrator, or by any other person entitled thereto, against such executor or administrator or his personal representative for any property remaining in his hands or for any other cause of action. (Code 1852, § 1882; Code 1867, § 2238; Code 1876, § 2596;

Code 1886, § 2182; Code 1896, § 250; Code 1907, § 2701; Code 1923, § 5934; Code 1940, T. 61, § 329.)

Enforcing vendor's lien. — Under this section a remaining administrator may maintain an action to enforce a vendor's lien against a co-administrator. Langley v. Langley, 121 Ala. 70, 25 So. 707 (1899).

Cited in Hendricks v. Thornton, 45 Ala. 299 (1871); Hatchett v. Billingslea, 65 Ala. 16 (1880).

§ 43-2-560. Settlement by sureties of deceased executor or administrator — Filing account and vouchers.

In case of the death of an executor or administrator who had not made a final settlement of his executorship or administration, and where letters of administration or testamentary have not been granted on his estate, the sureties on his official bond may proceed to make settlement of his administration of said estate as executor or administrator in the probate court having jurisdiction thereof by filing an account and vouchers for final settlement with the heirs and distributees, or with the administrator de bonis non, or cestui que trust, or minors and guardian ad litem, where minors are interested. (Acts 1915, No. 98, p. 138; Code 1923, § 5935; Code 1940, T. 61, § 330.)

The evident purpose of this section and section 43-2-552 was to provide a remedy at law where no personal representative of the deceased administrator has been appointed. Blue v. United States Fid. & Guar. Co., 228 Ala. 239, 240, 153 So. 150 (1934).

This section and sections 43-2-561 through 43-2-564 are limited to cases wherein there is no personal representative of the estate of the deceased administrator. Cowan v. Perkins, 214 Ala. 155, 107 So. 63 (1926).

No effect on section 43-2-550. — This section and §§ 43-2-561 through 43-2-564 do not modify or repeal § 43-2-550, requiring settlement to be made by the personal representative of the deceased administrator, if there is one. Cowan v. Perkins, 214 Ala. 155, 107 So. 63 (1926).

Procedure. — This section and §§ 43-2-561 through 43-2-564 do not contemplate separate proceedings in the probate court against the administrator and against his surety. Cowan v. Perkins, 214 Ala. 155, 107 So. 63 (1926).

Cited in Crews v. United States Fid. & Guar. Co., 237 Ala. 14, 185 So. 370 (1938).

Collateral references. — 34 C.J.S., Executors & Administrators, § 957.

§ 43-2-561. Same — Making representative of deceased executor or administrator party to settlement.

Should an administrator or executor of such deceased executor or administrator be appointed at any time before final decree, any party to the proceeding may, on motion, have such executor or administrator of such deceased executor or administrator made a party to such settlement on 10 days' notice. (Acts 1915, No. 98, p. 138; Code 1923, § 5936; Code 1940, T. 61, § 331.)

Cross references. — See notes to § 43-2-560.

Cited in Crews v. United States Fid. & Guar. Co., 237 Ala. 14, 185 So. 370 (1938).

§ 43-2-562. Same — Petition for order requiring sureties to make settlement.

In any case where an executor or administrator shall die without having made a final settlement of his administration and a successor is appointed, such succeeding executor or administrator or the heirs and distributees, legatees or cestui que trust may, by petition to the court in which such estate is pending, have an order requiring the sureties on such bond to make settlement of such estate in said court after 10 days' notice of the day fixed by the court or judge thereof. (Acts 1915, No. 98, p. 138; Code 1923, § 5937; Code 1940, T. 61, § 332.)

Cross references. — See notes to § 43-2-560.

Cited in Crews v. United States Fid. & Guar. Co., 237 Ala. 14, 185 So. 370 (1938).

§ 43-2-563. Same — Conclusiveness of settlement.

In all such cases provided for in section 43-2-562, the settlement therein provided for shall be final and conclusive against such sureties save the right of review by appeal or otherwise as now provided by law. (Acts 1915, No. 98, p. 138; Code 1923, § 5938; Code 1940, T. 61, § 333.)

Cross references. — See notes to § 43-2-560.

Cited in Crews v. United States Fid. & Guar. Co., 237 Ala. 14, 185 So. 370 (1938).

§ 43-2-564. Same — Execution against sureties.

Execution and all other final process may issue against the said sureties on said bond to enforce said judgments. (Acts 1915, No. 98, p. 138; Code 1923, § 5939; Code 1940, T. 61, § 334.)

Cross references. — See notes to § 43-2-560.

Cited in Crews v. United States Fid. & Guar. Co., 237 Ala. 14, 185 So. 370 (1938).

Division 4.

Compelling Payment of Legacies.

§ 43-2-580. When legatee or widow entitled to compel payment.

After the expiration of six months from the grant of letters testamentary, or of administration, with the will annexed, if there are more than sufficient assets in the hands of such executor or administrator to pay the debts of the deceased, any legatee may apply to the probate court of the county in which letters were granted to compel the payment of his legacy; and a widow who has dissented from her husband's will or her personal representative, if she is dead, shall have like remedy to compel the payment of the distributive share to which she may be entitled. (Code 1852, § 1772; Code 1867, § 2098; Code 1876, § 2475; Code 1886, § 2192; Code 1896, § 260; Code 1907, § 2736; Code 1923, § 5975; Acts 1931, No. 726, p. 841; Code 1940, T. 61, § 335.)

Time limitation and interest. — Until the lapse of the time specified, payment of a legacy when will does not specify time of payment cannot be compelled since it is not considered due until this time. And the sum does not bear interest, unless in exceptional cases, until this time. Walker v. Johnson, 82 Ala. 347, 2 So. 744 (1887). See also Carroll v. Richardson, 87 Ala. 605, 6 So. 342 (1889).

Since a legatee's application to compel payment cannot be brought within six months from the granting of letters testamentary, it follows, absent a testamentary directive to the contrary, that interest is not due where the payment of the legacy is made within this six-month period. Hancock v. Hancock, 334 So. 2d 873 (Ala. 1976).

Cited in Johnston v. Fort, 30 Ala. 78 (1857); McReynolds v. Jones, 30 Ala. 101 (1857); McAllister v. Thompson, 32 Ala. 497 (1858); Mason v. Pate, 34 Ala. 379 (1859); Cawlfield v. Brown, 45 Ala. 552 (1871); Charles v. Stickney, 50 Ala. 86 (1873); Whitfield v. Woolf, 51 Ala. 202 (1874); Millsap v. Stanley, 50 Ala. 319 (1874); Stelzenmuller v. Carroll, 272 Ala. 13, 127 So. 2d 842 (1961).

Collateral references. — 34 C.J.S., Executors & Administrators, § 487.

§ 43-2-581. Application.

The application for such purpose must be in writing, verified by affidavit; must set forth the applicant's claim and must allege a sufficiency of assets in the hands of such executor or administrator to pay the same after discharging the debts of the testator, charges on his estate and other legacies entitled to priority of payment. (Code 1852, § 1773; Code 1867, § 2099; Code 1876, § 2476; Code 1886, § 2193; Code 1896, § 261; Code 1907, § 2737; Code 1923, § 5976; Code 1940, T. 61, § 336.)

§ 43-2-582. Time for hearing; notice to executor or administrator.

The court must appoint a day for hearing such application, and a citation must be issued and served on the executor or administrator notifying him of the grounds of such application and of the day appointed for hearing the same, 10 days before such day. (Code 1852, § 1774; Code 1867, § 2100; Code 1876, § 2477; Code 1886, § 2194; Code 1896, § 262; Code 1907, § 2738; Code 1923, § 5977; Code 1940, T. 61, § 337.)

§ 43-2-583. Conduct of hearing; when payment or delivery directed.

On the day appointed or on any other day to which the hearing of the application may be continued, the court must hear the same; and, if it appears that the applicant is a legatee and that after the payment of his legacy there will be a sufficiency of assets to pay all the debts which have been presented, charges and other legacies which are entitled to priority, the court may direct the payment or delivery of such legacy, or any part thereof, according to the proof of assets and of the other legacies in the same degree with that of the applicant, on the legatee's executing a refunding bond according to the provisions of section 43-2-584. (Code 1852, § 1775; Code 1867, § 2101; Code 1876, § 2478; Code 1886, § 2195; Code 1896, § 263; Code 1907, § 2739; Code 1923, § 5978; Code 1940, T. 61, § 338.)

Cited in Coleman v. Holmes, 44 Ala. 124 (1870).

Collateral references. — 34 C.J.S., Executors & Administrators, § 482.

§ 43-2-584. Refunding bond.

Such refunding bond must be payable to the executor or administrator with the will annexed and must be in double the amount directed to be paid or in double the value of the property to be delivered, to be ascertained by the appraisement or other evidence satisfactory to the court, with at least two sufficient sureties, conditioned to refund the amount paid or to return the property or pay the value thereof, with interest on such amount or value from the time the same was received, should the assets prove insufficient to discharge the other debts presented and charges and other legacies entitled to priority of payment. (Code 1852, § 1776; Code 1867, § 2102; Code 1876, § 2479; Code 1886, § 2196; Code 1896, § 264; Code 1907, § 2740; Code 1923, § 5979; Code 1940, T. 61, § 339.)

§ 43-2-585. Enforcement of payment or delivery.

If the legacy is not payable in money, the value thereof as ascertained under section 43-2-584 must be entered of record; and, if the amount directed to be paid or the property directed to be delivered is not paid or delivered within 60 days after such order, an execution may issue for such amount or the value of such property against such executor or administrator and his sureties. (Code 1852, § 1777; Code 1867, § 2104; Code 1876, § 2481; Code 1886, § 2197; Code 1896, § 265; Code 1907, § 2741; Code 1923, § 5980; Code 1940, T. 61, § 340.)

§ 43-2-586. Applicability of sections 43-2-581 through 43-2-585 to widow.

Sections 43-2-581 through 43-2-585 apply to the widow who has dissented from her husband's will and seeks to compel the payment of her distributive share or, if she is dead, to her administrator or executor. (Code 1867, § 2103; Code 1876, § 2480; Code 1886, § 2198; Code 1896, § 266; Code 1907, § 2742; Code 1923, § 5981; Code 1940, T. 61, § 341.)

Division 5.

Arbitration on Settlement of Estates.

§ 43-2-600. When matters of controversy may be referred to arbitration.

On the settlement of the estate of a decedent, when such estate is free from debt, the probate court in which such settlement may be pending has authority to refer all matters of controversy arising in such settlement to arbitration, if, in the opinion of the court, the interests of the parties can be best subserved thereby and the parties, or their attorneys, consent thereto. (Code 1867, § 2169; Code 1876, § 2541; Code 1886, § 2183; Code 1896, § 251; Code 1907, § 2702; Code 1923, § 5940; Code 1940, T. 61, § 342.)

Controversy not arising in settlement. — This section does not apply to a controversy between the administrator and persons claiming under intestate's widow, as to whether exemptions, which had been set apart to the widow, on her death reverted to her husband's estate, or belonged to such persons as heirs of the widow. And any order or judgment of such court in the matter, though by consent, is without jurisdiction and void. Holdsombeck v. Fancher, 112 Ala. 469, 20 So. 519 (1896).

Petition must show pendency of settlement in probate court. — The petition to the probate court praying for submission to arbitration under this section must show that the settlement of the estate was pending in the probate court. Holdsombeck v. Fancher, 112 Ala. 469, 20 So. 519 (1896).

Collateral references. — 34 C.J.S., Executors & Administrators, § 442.

§ 43-2-601. Consent by guardian.

If any person interested in such estate is an infant or of unsound mind, his guardian shall have authority to consent to the reference to arbitration, which consent must be in writing, and, when so given, shall be binding on such person as fully and effectually as if he were of full age or of sound mind. (Code 1867, § 2170; Code 1876, § 2542; Code 1886, § 2184; Code 1896, § 252; Code 1907, § 2703; Code 1923, § 5941; Code 1940, T. 61, § 343.)

§ 43-2-602. Appointment of arbitrators.

The arbitrators must not exceed three in number and must be entirely disinterested and must be appointed by order of the probate court. (Code 1867, § 2171; Code 1876, § 2543; Code 1886, § 2185; Code 1896, § 253; Code 1907, § 2704; Code 1923, § 5942; Code 1940, T. 61, § 344.)

§ 43-2-603. Award — Generally.

The arbitrators must make their award in writing, and, within 10 days after making the same, they must return it to such court; and, if approved by the court, it must be entered of record and shall be final and conclusive upon all the parties. But such award must not be approved until after the expiration of 10 days from the time it is returned to the court. (Code 1867, § 2172; Code 1876, § 2544; Code 1886, § 2186; Code 1896, § 254; Code 1907, § 2705; Code 1923, § 5943; Code 1940, T. 61, § 345.)

§ 43-2-604. Same — Force and effect; execution.

If such award, or any part thereof, is for the payment of money, it shall, when approved and entered of record, have the force and effect of a judgment at law in favor of the person to whom the money may be awarded; and execution may issue thereon as in other cases. (Code 1867, § 2173; Code 1876, § 2545; Code 1886, § 2187; Code 1896, § 255; Code 1907, § 2706; Code 1923, § 5944; Code 1940, T. 61, § 346.)

§ 43-2-605. Same — Setting aside; second reference.

If such award is not approved by the court, it must be set aside; and the court may refer the matters again to the same or other arbitrators. (Code 1867, § 2174; Code 1876, § 2546; Code 1886, § 2188; Code 1896, § 256; Code 1907, § 2707; Code 1923, § 5945; Code 1940, T. 61, § 347.)

§ 43-2-606. Same — Objections.

Any of the parties may, within 10 days after such award has been returned to the court, file objections to the same; and, if objections are filed, the court must appoint a day, not less than 30 days from the filing of such objections, to hear and determine the same, notice of which must be given as now required by law in cases of applications for final settlements of the estates of decedents by executors or administrators. (Code 1867, § 2175; Code 1876, § 2547; Code 1886, § 2189; Code 1896, § 257; Code 1907, § 2708; Code 1923, § 5946; Code 1940, T. 61, § 348.)

§ 43-2-607. Applicability of certain sections in Title 6.

Sections 6-6-4 through 6-6-10 and 6-6-13 are made applicable to the settlement of estates by arbitration. (Code 1867, § 2176; Code 1876, § 2548; Code 1886, § 2190; Code 1896, § 258; Code 1907, § 2709; Code 1923, § 5947; Code 1940, T. 61, § 349.)

Division 6.

Distribution or Division on Final Settlement.

Collateral references. — 34 C.J.S., Executors & Administrators, §§ 482-535.

Right of retainer in respect of indebtedness of heir, legatee, or distributee. 1 ALR 993, 30 ALR 775, 75 ALR 878, 110 ALR 1384, 164 ALR 717.

Declaration of rights or declaratory judgments affecting the distribution of estate. 12 ALR 77, 19 ALR 1124, 50 ALR 42, 68 ALR 110, 87 ALR 1205, 114 ALR 1361, 142 ALR 8.

Postponing distribution until payment of debts or settlement of estate as violating rule against perpetuities. 13 ALR 1033.

Liability of estate for administrator's failure to distribute estate. 44 ALR 676, 127 ALR 687.

Specific performance of oral family settlement involving real property as affected by doctrine of part performance. 101 ALR 994.

Payment or delivery of legacy or distributive share before decree of distribution as defense to action by legatee or distributee against personal representative or surety on his bond. 121 ALR 1069.

Fees of executor or administrator as applicable to discharge of his indebtedness to decedent. 123 ALR 1285.

Share of executor or administrator as beneficiary of estate, as subject to charge in respect of his liability in his fiduciary capacity. 123 ALR 1320.

Duty of executor or administrator c.t.a. as to delivery of specifically bequeathed personal property not need for payment of debts. 127 ALR 1071.

Decree of distribution as res judicata on questions of construction of will. 136 ALR 1185.

Right of consul to receive distributive share or legacy payable to his national. 157 ALR 118.

Time for payment of legacy or distributive shares and reasonableness of delay by personal representative sought to be personally charged with interest. 18 ALR2d 1395, 1417.

Personal representative's right to retainer or setoff, against debtor's distributive share of estate, of debt barred by statute of limitations. 39 ALR2d 675.

Validity of agreement among beneficiaries for distribution and manner of proportion other than that provided by will. 29 ALR3d 8.

Family settlement of intestate's estate. 29 ALR3d 174.

§ 43-2-620. Orders of distribution — Generally.

On the final settlement of an estate, the court may make such orders of distribution as may be necessary, and, on the confirmation of the same, may render a decree thereon, and the property must be delivered according to such decree; or, if there is money only to be divided, it may render a decree in favor of each distributee entitled to the same, for his distributive share, against the executor or administrator. (Code 1852, § 1822; Code 1867, § 2158; Code 1876, § 2530; Code 1886, § 2161; Code 1896, § 229; Code 1907, § 2710; Code 1923, § 5948; Code 1940, T. 61, § 350.)

Distribution is properly made by a single decree, assigning to each heir separately his distributive share. King v. Brown, 108 Ala. 68, 18 So. 935 (1896).

Which should specify amount due each distributee. — In decreeing distribution, the court should specify the amount to be paid each distributee. Davis v. Davis, 6 Ala. 611 (1844); Sankey v. Sankey, 8 Ala. 601 (1845).

A decree in favor of infants should be in their names by guardians, if any, but if in infant's name alone, it is not reversible error. Sankey v. Sankey, 6 Ala. 607 (1844); Green v. Fagan, 15 Ala. 335 (1849).

Wrongful application of funds. — Under this section and § 43-2-640 an executor who prematurely assents to a legacy and permits assets to pass to the legatee which should go to creditors of the estate is responsible therefor without regard to directions in the will. Handley v. Heflin, 84 Ala. 600, 4 So. 725 (1888).

Cited in Mason v. Pate, 34 Ala. 379 (1859); Rives v. Flinn, 47 Ala. 481 (1872); Avery v. Avery, 47 Ala. 505 (1872); Franklin v. Pollard Mill Co., 88 Ala. 318, 6 So. 685 (1889).

§ 43-2-621. Same — To whom directed; contents.

All orders of distribution must be directed to three disinterested persons appointed by the court, must specify the property to be divided, the persons and their respective shares and must require them to return their proceedings on a day specified in such order. (Code 1852, § 1792; Code 1867, § 2119; Code 1876, § 2496; Code 1886, § 2162; Code 1896, § 230; Code 1907, § 2713; Code 1923, § 5951; Code 1940, T. 61, § 351.)

§ 43-2-622. Same — Oath; return; exceptions to report.

(a) The persons therein named, or a majority of them, must proceed to make distribution according to such order, having first taken an oath to make such distribution fairly and impartially, if the same can be made, which oath may be administered by the executor or administrator, and must return their proceedings in writing, signed by them, to the court by the day specified in such order.

(b) If the property cannot be divided equitably without a sale of all or some portion thereof, the commissioners must so report.

(c) Any person may file exceptions to the report of the commissioners within 30 days after the day appointed for the return or, if returned at any time thereafter, within 30 days after the return. (Code 1852, §§ 1793-1795; Code 1867, §§ 2120-2122; Code 1876, §§ 2497-2499; Code 1886, §§ 2163-2165; Code 1896, §§ 231-233; Code 1907, §§ 2714-2716; Code 1923, §§ 5952-5954; Code 1940, T. 61, §§ 352-354.)

Collateral references. — 34 C.J.S., Executors & Administrators, § 528.

§ 43-2-623. Confirming or setting aside distribution; when sale may be directed.

The court, for causes shown on such exceptions, or otherwise, may set aside such distribution and direct another distribution or, if the same is just, may confirm it; or, if it appears from such report that the property cannot be equitably divided without a sale of all or some portion thereof, it may direct a sale of all or any portion of the personal property. (Code 1852, § 1796; Code 1867, § 2123; Code 1876, § 2500; Code 1886, § 2166; Code 1896, § 234; Code 1907, § 2717; Code 1923, § 5955; Code 1940, T. 61, § 355.)

§ 43-2-624. How sale advertised and made.

Such a sale must be advertised and made as sales of personal property under the order of the court for the payment of debts. (Code 1852, § 1797; Code 1867, § 2124; Code 1876, § 2501; Code 1886, § 2167; Code 1896, § 235; Code 1907, § 2718; Code 1923, § 5956; Code 1940, T. 61, § 356.)

Cross references. — As to sale of personal property, see § 43-2-410 et seq.

§ 43-2-625. Delivery of property upon confirmation.

Upon the confirmation of any order of distribution, the executor or administrator must deliver the property to the persons entitled thereto. (Code 1852, § 1798; Code 1867, § 2125; Code 1876, § 2502; Code 1886, § 2168; Code 1896, § 236; Code 1907, § 2719; Code 1923, § 5957; Code 1940, T. 61, § 357.)

§ 43-2-626. Division, sale or assignment of judgments or claims.

(a) Any judgments or claims in favor of the estate, which are not collected at the time of final distribution, may be divided among the persons entitled, on final distribution; or, if such division cannot be equitably made, may be sold as other personal property.

(b) The executor or administrator must assign any such judgment or claim to the distributee, legatee or purchaser, as the case may be; and such person is entitled to collect the same by civil action or otherwise. (Code 1852, §§ 1799, 1800; Code 1867, §§ 2126, 2127; Code 1876, §§ 2503, 2504; Code 1886, §§ 2169, 2170; Code 1896, §§ 237, 238; Code 1907, §§ 2720, 2721; Code 1923, §§ 5958, 5959; Code 1940, T. 61, §§ 358, 359.)

Cited in Offutt v. Vance, 42 Ala. 243 (1868); Moorer v. Moorer, 87 Ala. 545, 6 So. 289 (1889).

§ 43-2-627. Setting off indebtedness of distributee or legatee.

(a) If, on final settlement, any distributee or legatee owes the estate any debt, contracted with the decedent in his lifetime or with the executor or administrator in his representative capacity, the court shall allow the same in favor of the executor or administrator, as a setoff against the distributive share of such distributee or legatee and shall decree satisfaction of his distributive share to the extent of such debt or demand; but the distributee or legatee may make any defense to the setoff that would be available to him in a direct proceeding for the recovery of the debt.

(b) In no case shall a decree be rendered in favor of the executor or administrator against such distributee or legatee for the excess, when the debt is greater in amount than the distributive share; nor shall the executor or administrator be prevented from prosecuting a civil action in the proper court for any excess that may be due him from such distributee or legatee. (Code 1886, §§ 2171, 2172; Code 1896, §§ 239, 240; Code 1907, §§ 2722, 2723; Code 1923, §§ 5960, 5961; Code 1940, T. 61, §§ 360, 361.)

Jurisdiction of probate court. — The only jurisdiction conferred upon the probate court is to ascertain that the distributee's indebtedness is equal to or exceeds his distributive share. It is not within its jurisdiction to ascertain the amount of the excess and render a decree therefor. Caldwell v. Caldwell, 121 Ala. 598, 25 So. 825 (1899).

Liability to testator's estate of his surviving partner for assets thereof, which he collected and for which he never accounted, is not a "debt contracted with the decedent in his lifetime or with the executor," and hence does not come within this section. But such liability may be deducted from the legacy or distributive share of the debtor. Noble v. Tait, 140 Ala. 469, 37 So. 278 (1904).

No time limitation. — The right to deduct from the share of a legatee a sum due from him to the estate as surviving partner of a testator is not affected by the mere efflux of time. Noble v. Tait, 140 Ala. 469, 37 So. 278 (1904).

Defense of discharge in bankruptcy by distributee relieves him from liability of a debt contracted with decedent in his lifetime, and prevents setoff under this section by administrator. Dent v. Foy, 210 Ala. 475, 98 So. 390 (1923).

Cited in Caldwell v. Caldwell, 183 Ala. 590, 62 So. 951 (1913); McAleer v. Cawthon, 215 Ala. 674, 112 So. 251 (1927); Martin v. Martin, 267 Ala. 600, 104 So. 2d 302 (1958).

Collateral references. — 34 C.J.S., Executors & Administrators, § 494.

Right of retainer in respect of indebtedness of heir, legatee, or distributee. 1 ALR 991, 30 ALR 775, 75 ALR 878, 110 ALR 1384, 164 ALR 717.

Personal claim of executor or administrator antedating death of decedent. 144 ALR 943.

§ 43-2-628. Discharge of executor or administrator from liability.

When the estate has been fully administered and it is shown by the executor or administrator, by the production of satisfactory vouchers, that he has paid all sums of money due from him and delivered up, under the order of the court, all the property of the estate to the parties entitled and performed all the acts lawfully required of him, the court must make a judgment or decree discharging him from all liability as such executor or administrator. (Code 1923, § 5962; Code 1940, T. 61, § 362.)

Final settlement and distribution must precede order of discharge. — After discharge of an administratrix no further authority to act on behalf of the estate exists. Under this section, final settlement and distribution must precede an order of discharge. Humphrey v. Boschung, 47 Ala. App. 310, 253 So. 2d 760 (1970), aff'd, 287 Ala. 600, 253 So. 2d 769 (1971).

§ 43-2-629. Disposition of personal estate of foreign decedent.

(a) When administration is taken out in this state on the estate of any person who, at the time of his death, was an inhabitant of any other state or country, his personal estate, after the payment of debts and charges on his estate, must be disposed of according to his last will, if probated in this state and, if no such will is probated in this state, according to the law of the state or country of which he was an inhabitant.

(b) Upon the settlement of such estate and after the payment of all debts for which the same is liable in this state, the residue of the personal estate may be distributed and disposed of according to the provisions of subsection (a); or it may be transmitted or paid over to the executor or administrator of the state or country where the deceased had his domicile. (Code 1852, §§ 1826, 1827; Code 1867, §§ 2163, 2164; Code 1876, §§ 2535, 2536; Code 1886, §§ 2153, 2154; Code 1896, §§ 221, 222; Code 1907, §§ 2711, 2712; Code 1923, §§ 5949, 5950; Code 1940, T. 61, §§ 363, 364.)

Division 7.

Distribution Before Settlement.

Cited in Beck v. Simmons, 7 Ala. 71 (1844); Moore v. Clay, 7 Ala. 742 (1845); Powell v. Williams, 14 Ala. 476 (1848); Kemp v. Coxe, 14 Ala. 614 (1848); Crothers v. Ross, 17 Ala. 816 (1850); Williamson v. Mason, 18 Ala. 87 (1850); Wyatt v. Rambo, 29 Ala. 510 (1857); McReynolds v. Jones, 30 Ala. 101 (1857); Harrison v. Harrison, 39 Ala. 489 (1864); Mosely v. Tuthill, 45 Ala. 621 (1871); Whitfield v. Woolf, 51 Ala. 202 (1874); Zeigler v. Zeigler, 226 Ala. 61, 145 So. 571 (1933); Ingalls Iron Works Co. v. Ingalls, 177 F. Supp. 151 (N.D. Ala. 1959).

Collateral references. — 31 Am. Jur. 2d, Executors & Administrators, §§ 550-602.

§ 43-2-640. Authorization to make distribution — Distribution by executor or administrator.

When the executor or administrator is satisfied that the estate is solvent, he may, after six months from the date of the grant of letters testamentary or of administration, make distribution of the whole or any part of the property without obtaining an order of court, or he may so report it and obtain an order of distribution as to the whole, or any part of the property; but, in such case, if the distribution or the order is made before a final settlement of such estate, neither the distribution, the order, nor the proceedings thereon are a defense in any action brought against such executor or administrator as such. (Code 1852, § 1771; Code 1867, § 2097; Code 1876, § 2474; Code 1886, § 2191; Code 1896, § 259; Code 1907, § 2724; Code 1923, § 5963; Code 1940, T. 61, § 365; Acts 1949, No. 614, p. 945.)

§ 43-2-641. Same — Distribution by court after six months from grant of letters.

(a) The court may also, in case of intestacy, make an order of distribution out of the assets of the decedent, on the application of any person entitled to distribution, after six months from the grant of letters.

(b) The order of the court, made after six months from the grant of letters on the application of any legatee or person entitled to distribution, is a protection to the executor or administrator, to the extent of the amount or value of the legacy or share ordered to be paid or distributed. (Code 1852, §§ 1778, 1789; Code 1867, §§ 2105, 2116; Code 1876, §§ 2482, 2493; Code 1886, §§ 2199, 2209; Code 1896, §§ 267, 277; Code 1907, §§ 2725, 2735; Code 1923, §§ 5964, 5974; Acts 1931, No. 727, p. 841; Code 1940, T. 61, §§ 366, 376.)

As to compelling payment of legacy where time not specified in will. — See Walker v. Johnson, 82 Ala. 347, 2 So. 744 (1887).
Cited in Johnston v. Fort, 30 Ala. 78 (1857); Lary v. Craig, 30 Ala. 631 (1857); Harrison v. Meadors, 41 Ala. 274 (1868); Ward v. Oates, 42 Ala. 225 (1868); Martin v. State, 47 Ala. 564 (1872); Zeigler v. Zeigler, 226 Ala. 61, 145 So. 571 (1933).

§ 43-2-642. Contents of application.

Such application must be in writing, verified by affidavit, must specify the share to which the applicant is entitled and must allege that the assets of the decedent are more than sufficient to pay the debts of the decedent and the charges on his estate. (Code 1852, § 1779; Code 1867, § 2106; Code 1876, § 2483; Code 1886, § 2200; Code 1896, § 268; Code 1907, § 2726; Code 1923, § 5965; Code 1940, T. 61, § 367.)

Cited in Avery v. Avery, 47 Ala. 505 (1872); Brewer & Co. v. Moseley, 49 Ala. 79 (1873).

§ 43-2-643. Time for hearing; notice.

A day must be appointed for the hearing of such application, and a citation must be issued and served on the administrator 10 days before the day appointed, notifying him of the grounds of the application and the day of hearing the same. (Code 1852, § 1780; Code 1867, § 2107; Code 1876, § 2484; Code 1886, § 2201; Code 1896, § 269; Code 1907, § 2727; Code 1923, § 5966; Code 1940, T. 61, § 368.)

§ 43-2-644. When distribution made; limit on amount.

On the day appointed, or on any other day to which the application may be continued, if the court is satisfied from the evidence that the assets are more than sufficient to pay the debts and charges, it may make an order of distribution for such portion of the distributive share of the applicant as may be authorized by the evidence; but, in making such order, the court must not exceed the share to which the applicant would be entitled on a final settlement and distribution. (Code 1852, §§ 1781, 1782; Code 1867, §§ 2108, 2109; Code 1876, §§ 2485, 2486; Code 1886, § 2202; Code 1896, § 270; Code 1907, § 2728; Code 1923, § 5967; Code 1940, T. 61, § 369.)

Cited in Cunningham v. Beard, 44 Ala. 317 (1870).
Collateral references. — 34 C.J.S., Executors & Administrators, §§ 524, 525.

§ 43-2-645. Refunding bonds — Required; terms and conditions.

Such order must not in any case be made, unless the applicant gives a refunding bond, with two sufficient sureties, to be approved by the judge of probate, payable to the administrator, in double the amount distributed to the applicant or in double the value of his share of the property directed to be distributed, to be ascertained by the appraisement or other evidence and entered of record, and conditioned to refund the amount directed to be paid, or to return the property received on such distribution, or to pay the value thereof and interest on such amount or value from the time the same was received, if the assets are insufficient to discharge the debts and charges against the estate. (Code 1852, § 1782; Code 1867, § 2109; Code 1876, § 2486; Code 1886, § 2203; Code 1896, § 271; Code 1907, § 2729; Code 1923, § 5968; Code 1940, T. 61, § 370.)

Cited in Johnston v. Fort, 30 Ala. 78 (1857).

§ 43-2-646. Same — Recordation; transcript as evidence.

All refunding bonds provided for in this division must be recorded by the judge of probate and then delivered to the executor or administrator; and a transcript of any such bond as recorded, duly certified, is evidence to the same extent as the original would have been if produced. (Code 1852, § 1784; Code 1867, § 2111; Code 1876, § 2488; Code 1886, § 2205; Code 1896, § 273; Code 1907, § 2731; Code 1923, § 5970; Code 1940, T. 61, § 372.)

§ 43-2-647. Same — Bond stands as security; action on bond.

(a) Such refunding bond stands as security for the executor or administrator, should the assets in his hands, after any payment of money or delivery of property under the order of the court, prove insufficient to pay the debts, claims and charges against the estate, and the executor or administrator pays the same; and also as security for the creditors of the estate; and any creditor may bring a civil action thereon.

(b) The extent of the recoveries on such bond is the amount or value of the property received by the legatee or distributee and interest on such amount or value from the date of its receipt; and the value of property received may be proved by the entry of record, made according to the provisions of this division or other evidence; and civil actions may be brought on such bond from time to time in the name of any person aggrieved until the whole amount of the liability, as determined by this section, is recovered. (Code 1852, §§ 1785-1787; Code 1867, §§ 2112-2114; Code 1876, §§ 2489-2491; Code 1886, §§ 2206, 2207; Code 1896, §§ 274, 275; Code 1907, §§ 2732, 2733; Code 1923, §§ 5971, 5972; Code 1940, T. 61, §§ 373, 374.)

Cited in Whitfield v. Woolf, 51 Ala. 202 (1874).

§ 43-2-648. Same — Rights of parties among themselves.

Any party making a payment on any refunding bond taken under this division, may recover against the parties to any other refunding bond such an amount as shall be in the same proportion to the amount collected from the plaintiff, as the amount of money and value of the property delivered on both bonds bears to the amount of money or property delivered on the bond of the defendant. (Code 1852, § 1788; Code 1867, § 2115; Code 1876, § 2492; Code 1886, § 2208; Code 1896, § 276; Code 1907, § 2734; Code 1923, § 5973; Code 1940, T. 61, § 375.)

§ 43-2-649. Costs.

If any application made under the provisions of this division is determined against the applicant, he must pay the costs. (Code 1852, § 1783; Code 1867, § 2110; Code 1876, § 2487; Code 1886, § 2204; Code 1896, § 272; Code 1907, § 2730; Code 1923, § 5969; Code 1940, T. 61, § 371.)

Division 8.

Presumption of Settlement After 20 Years.

§ 43-2-660. When presumption arises.

When the administration of the estate of a deceased person shall be pending in any court, and the records of such court shall show that letters testamentary or letters of administration on such estate were issued and that 20 years or more have elapsed since six months after such letters were issued, without further action in said cause, or if any further action was taken in said cause, and 20 or more years have elapsed since any such action, and if all bequests and legacies provided for in a will being administered in such cause have been payable or demandable for more than 20 years, and if the executor or administrator in such cause shall not for 20 or more years have made any payment or partial payment or promise of payment of any claim against such estate or of any bequest, devise or distributive share due from such estate, then it shall be conclusively presumed that final settlement of said estate has been made by the executor or administrator thereof and that all debts of said estate, all legacies and bequests due by said estate, and all distributive shares in said estate have been paid to the persons entitled thereto. (Acts 1953, No. 687, p. 939, § 1.)

State policy expressed. — As a matter of public policy, and for the repose of society, it has long been the settled policy of this state, as of others, that antiquated demands will not be considered by the courts, and that, without regard to any statute of limitations, there must be a time beyond which human transactions will not be inquired into. Melton v. Melton, 288 Ala. 452, 261 So. 2d 887 (1972).

Conclusive presumption. — It is settled that, after a period of 20 years without any payment, settlement or other recognition of liability, mortgages and liens will be conclusively presumed to have been paid and settlements

will be conclusively presumed to have been
made by administrators, trustees, agents and
other persons occupying fiduciary positions.
Melton v. Melton, 288 Ala. 452, 261 So. 2d 887
(1972).

Collateral references. — 34 C.J.S., Executors & Administrators, § 842.

§ 43-2-661. Petition to establish presumption.

An executor, administrator or surety on the bond of the executor or administrator of said estate, or the heirs or next of kin of such executor, administrator or surety may file a petition or complaint, verified by affidavits, in the court in which such a cause is pending, alleging the existence of the facts that raise the presumptions stated in section 43-2-660, and, upon the filing of such petition or complaint and giving security for costs of the proceeding, the court must appoint a day for the hearing of such petition or complaint and must give notice of the same by publication in some newspaper published in the county for three successive weeks or, if none is published in the county, by posting such notice at the courthouse and three other public places in such county for the same length of time; and the court must also give 10 days' notice to every adult distributee resident in the state and to all sureties on the bond of the administrator or executor in said cause, of the day set for hearing the petition or complaint. (Acts 1953, No. 687, p. 939, § 2.)

§ 43-2-662. Notice of hearing on petition.

Such notice must state the name of the executor or administrator, the name of the deceased and the day appointed for the hearing of the petition or complaint. If all heirs and legatees are of age and waive publication in a newspaper, notice must, in such case be given by posting the same at the courthouse door. (Acts 1953, No. 687, p. 939, §§ 3, 4.)

§ 43-2-663. Contest.

Any person interested may appear and contest any statement in the petition or complaint and may examine the parties or any other witness and may introduce any legal evidence in support of his contest. (Acts 1953, No. 687, p. 939, § 5.)

§ 43-2-664. Order after hearing.

Should the court find the allegations of the petition or complaint to be true, it shall enter an order, decree or judgment in said cause discharging the executor or the administrator and the sureties on their official bonds from all liability growing out of the administration of said estate. Should it find otherwise, the court shall dismiss the petition or complaint. (Acts 1953, No. 687, p. 939, § 6.)

Division 9.

Compensation, Commissions, Fees, etc.

Collateral references. — 34 C.J.S., Executors & Administrators, §§ 852-881.

31 Am. Jur. 2d, Executors & Administrators, §§ 486-505.

Death of executor or administrator as affecting right to compensation. 7 ALR 1595.

Preference of legacy to executor as compensation for services as regards abatement of legacy. 34 ALR 1272.

Lien on, or outstanding interest in, property, as affecting computation of commissions of executors or administrators. 46 ALR 239.

Right of executor or administrator to commission on stock dividends. 55 ALR 710.

Right to extra compensation for services other than attorney's services. 66 ALR 512.

Faults in administration as affecting rights to commissions. 83 ALR 726.

Rights of person, natural or corporate, named as trustee and executor to double commission. 84 ALR 667, 85 ALR2d 537.

Right to commission in respect of debt of personal representative himself to estate. 88 ALR 189.

Broker's commission incurred in sale of real property, allowance of, as affecting commissions of personal representatives. 91 ALR 836, 155 ALR 1214.

Change in statute after decedent's death and before final settlement as affecting compensation. 91 ALR 1421.

Loss or depreciation of assets for which executor or administrator is not responsible as affecting the amount of his compenation. 110 ALR 994.

Validity, construction, and effect of provisions of will to effect that legacy or devise to executor is made in consideration of, or contemplation of, services to be rendered after testator's death, in carrying on testator's business or in administering or caring for estate. 116 ALR 361.

Interlocutory order of one judge concerning compensation as binding on another judge in same case. 132 ALR 76.

Executor's fee prior to establishment of trust as chargeable to corpus or income. 135 ALR 1322.

Appraised value of estate as shown by inventory, or value at time of settlement as basis for determining commissions of executor or administrator. 173 ALR 1346.

Costs and other expenses incurred by administrator or executor whose appointment was improper as chargeable against estate. 4 ALR2d 160.

Fiduciary's compensation on estate assets distributed in kind. 32 ALR2d 778.

Will limiting amount of fees of executor. 19 ALR3d 520.

Resignation or removal of executor or administrator as affecting his compensation. 96 ALR3d 1102.

§ 43-2-680. Executors and administrators may be allowed fair compensation, etc.

Executors and administrators may be allowed such commissions on all receipts and disbursements by them, as such, as may appear to the probate court to be a fair compensation for their trouble, risk and responsibility, not to exceed two and one-half percent on the receipts and the same percentage on the disbursements; and the court may also allow actual expenses, and, for special or extraordinary services, such compensation as is just, and such premiums as an executor or administrator may have paid a guaranty company for making his bond. (Code 1852, § 1825; Code 1867, § 2161; Code 1876, § 2533; Code 1886, § 2151; Code 1896, § 219; Code 1907, § 2690; Code 1923, § 5923; Code 1940, T. 61, § 377.)

I. General Consideration.
II. When Commissions Allowed on Receipts and Disbursements.
III. Amount of Commission.
IV. Actual Expenses.
V. Special or Extraordinary Services.

I. GENERAL CONSIDERATION.

The language of this section is permissive, rather than mandatory. While it allows the court to set a reasonable compensation for efforts of the administrator or executor, it does not require that such compensation be granted. The allowance is a matter of judicial determination. Smith v. McNaughton, 378 So. 2d 703 (Ala. 1979); Armstrong v. Alabama Nat'l Bank, 404 So. 2d 675 (Ala. 1981).

Code sections which provide for awarding administrator's commissions, attorney's fees, and expenses are permissive, not mandatory. Aird v. Thomas, 408 So. 2d 500 (Ala. 1981).

Common-law rule. — At common law administrators and executors were not entitled to any compensation for their personal trouble and loss of time in the performance of their duties. Kenan v. Graham, 135 Ala. 585, 33 So. 699 (1903).

But the established practice in Alabama, from an early date, was to allow executors and administrators a reasonable compensation for their trouble. Phillips v. Thompson, 9 Port. 664 (1839); Carroll v. Moore, 7 Ala. 615 (1845).

Special administrators are included within the term "administrators" as employed in this section. But such an administrator is not entitled to commissions on the valuation of the assets of the estate. Wright v. Wilkerson, 41 Ala. 267 (1867).

The statute which provides for a special administrator does not make any enactment as to his compensation. But certainly the maximum features of the present section have application. This section makes the allowance a matter of judicial determination. Hale v. Cox, 240 Ala. 622, 200 So. 772 (1941); Crossley v. Davies, 253 Ala. 275, 44 So. 2d 439 (1950).

Executor's commission is not due before final settlement. — Under this section an executor is not entitled to his commissions before final settlement, and if he retains, prior to that time, an amount to which he presumes he will become entitled, he should be charged with interest on the sum from the time of its appropriation to the date of final settlement. Kenan v. Graham, 135 Ala. 585, 33 So. 699 (1903).

Stepmother's acts as executrix not chargeable against child's share. — Where deceased's widow served as executrix under will which was later vacated on contest and it appeared that widow's conduct had been consistently opposed to interest of decedent's child by a former marriage, and that child had received no substantial benefit from estate on account of widow's acts, trial court properly ruled that widow's acts, in administering estate and trust established in will, should not be chargeable

against child's share in estate. Hale v. Cox, 240 Ala. 622, 200 So. 772 (1941).

Cited in King v. Keith, 257 Ala. 463, 60 So. 2d 47 (1952); Taylor v. First Nat'l Bank, 279 Ala. 624, 189 So. 2d 141 (1966); Hancock v. Hancock, 334 So. 2d 873 (Ala. 1976); Papan v. Papan, 362 So. 2d 902 (Ala. 1978).

Collateral references. — Liability of administration expenses of wife electing against the will. 89 ALR3d 315.

II. WHEN COMMISSIONS ALLOWED ON RECEIPTS AND DISBURSEMENTS.

This section has been held to refer to cash transactions only. Wright v. Wilkerson, 41 Ala. 267 (1867). That does not mean that cash money must be handled, but the transaction must be one which is so regarded and properly so interpreted. Walsh v. Walsh, 231 Ala. 305, 164 So. 822 (1935).

The term "receipts" as used in the section means pecuniary assets, and does not embrace assets which are not money or currency. Wright v. Wilkerson, 41 Ala. 267 (1867).

The term "receipts" as used in this section is not limited, but the commissions allowable are on all receipts. There is no logical distinction to be drawn between receipts of money from a banking institution paid over to the administrator and money paid over to him by private individuals. Anderson v. McClure, 252 Ala. 660, 42 So. 2d 353 (1949).

The word "receipts" as used in § 26-5-16 should carry the same meaning as the same word has been given in this section dealing with commissions to which executors and administrators are entitled. It has traditionally been defined to mean the value of the estate coming into the hands of the fiduciary. Gordon v. Brunson, 287 Ala. 535, 253 So. 2d 183 (1971).

Disbursements must be allowed by court. — In computing the compensation of an administrator, all disbursements except those properly allowed by the court should be excluded. Pryor v. Davis, 109 Ala. 117, 19 So. 440 (1896).

"Commission" should not be paid on proceeds arising from sale of land for division. — The commission provided in this section should not include the proceeds of the sale of land for division, but that § 43-2-681 applies to such fund, and since two and one-half percent of it exceeds $100.00, the latter figure should be treated as the maximum. Walsh v. Walsh, 231 Ala. 305, 164 So. 822 (1935).

Assets not in possession or unadministered should not be counted in ascertaining the commission. So commission should not be allowed on lands sold by a preceding administrator. Moore v. Randolph, 70 Ala. 575 (1881).

No commission upon appraised value of property not sold. — An executor is not entitled to a commission upon the appraised value of property, where the condition of the estate does not require a sale and it is divided among the legatees or distributees. Wilson v. Wilson, 30 Ala. 670 (1857); Jenkins v. Jenkins, 33 Ala. 731 (1859).

Sale of intestate's lands under agreement of heirs. — Where the intestate's lands are sold under written agreement of the heirs, part of the price being paid in cash and the remainder in notes made payable to, and received by, the heirs in payment of their respective shares, the proceeds of such sales or notes are not proper matters of the administrator's accounts, and he is not entitled to commissions thereon. Key v. Jones, 52 Ala. 238 (1875).

Forfeiture or deprivation of commissions. — An administrator who is guilty of willful default or gross negligence in the management of the estate cannot be heard to complain that commissions have not been allowed him. Hall v. Wilson, 14 Ala. 295 (1848).

And it is frequently stated that compensation to executors and administrators should be refused only in cases of fraud, willful default or gross negligence, causing loss to the estate. Powell v. Powell, 10 Ala. 900 (1846); Gould v. Hayes, 19 Ala. 438 (1851); Bendall v. Bendall, 24 Ala. 295 (1854); Stewart v. Stewart, 31 Ala. 207 (1857); Smith v. Kennard, 38 Ala. 695 (1863).

So failure to file accounts, failure to fulfill orders of court and false representations in procuring appointment have been the basis of disallowing compensation in May v. Carlisle, 68 Ala. 135 (1880); Pearson v. Darrington, 32 Ala. 227 (1858); and Hall v. Santangelo, 178 Ala. 447, 60 So. 168 (1912), respectively.

Executor held not guilty of willful default or gross negligence in the discharge of his duties so as to justify the court in denying to him compensation, although he failed to keep proper records and perhaps misconceived his duties and powers in some respects. Wilkerson v. Wilkerson, 257 Ala. 633, 60 So. 2d 343 (1952).

III. AMOUNT OF COMMISSION.

Section provides the maximum commission. — So long as the executor's commission does not exceed the maximum authorized by this section, its amount is largely discretionary with the trial court. Collins v. Clements, 199 Ala. 618, 75 So. 165 (1917). This section is a legislative declaration, that no case can arise in which the maximum provided by it would not furnish sufficient consideration. Noble v. Jackson, 124 Ala. 311, 26 So. 955 (1899).

Section 43-2-681 is a limitation on this section, so that in computing the maximum allowance under this section there must be deducted the amount of the proceeds of the sale of land for division, and the commission is computed on the balance with the addition of a maximum of $100.00 as compensation for services in connection with that transaction. Walsh v. Walsh, 231 Ala. 305, 164 So. 822 (1935).

Rule as to court's discretion. — Under this section the commissions allowed an administrator are within the sound discretion of the court not exceeding the maximum herein fixed. Collins v. Clements, 199 Ala. 618, 75 So. 165 (1917); Boyte v. Perkins, 211 Ala. 130, 99 So. 652 (1924); Walsh v. Walsh, 231 Ala. 305, 164 So. 822 (1935); Anderson v. McClure, 252 Ala. 660, 42 So. 2d 353 (1949).

This discretion of the court has but two limitations: (1) The allowance must be a fair compensation, (2) and must not exceed the percentage herein named. Noble v. Jackson, 124 Ala. 311, 26 So. 955 (1899).

Whether deceased's widow, who was named as executrix in contested will, and who served as special administrator during contest, which was successful, should be allowed compensation for her services as special administrator, as well as its amount, was a matter of judicial discretion, not controlled by this section or other rule. Hale v. Cox, 240 Ala. 622, 200 So. 772 (1941).

The award of executor fees is largely within the discretion of the trial judge. Armstrong v. Alabama Nat'l Bank, 404 So. 2d 675 (Ala. 1981).

Court's discretion applied to compensation of administrator ad colligendum. — Since this section provides that "the court may also allow . . . for special or extraordinary services, such compensation as is just," etc., the matter of allowances for special or extraordinary services of an administrator ad colligendum is governed by the same principle and is likewise within judicial discretion. Crossley v. Davies, 253 Ala. 275, 44 So. 2d 439 (1950).

Computation of compensation. — The condition and value of the estate should be a controlling consideration in all cases. Pinckard v. Pinckard, 24 Ala. 250 (1854); Kenan v. Graham, 135 Ala. 585, 33 So. 699 (1903).

The court in making the allowance is to look to the loss of time, risk and responsibility, which are demanded by the nature of the trust and to allow such a reasonable remuneration as a prudent and just man would, in view of the circumstances, consider a fair compensation, without, however, being governed by business charges usually made for like services. When thus allowed the compensation is not, and should not be but little, if anything, more than liberal indemnity. Gould v. Hays, 25 Ala. 426

(1854); Newberry v. Newberry, 28 Ala. 691 (1856); Kenan v. Graham, 135 Ala. 585, 33 So. 699 (1903); Armstrong v. Alabama Nat'l Bank, 404 So. 2d 675 (Ala. 1981).

Although the commissions, within the maximum herein prescribed, are largely discretionary with the trial court, this rule has exceptions, one of which is that where the estate is very large and does not require extraordinary service and trouble and the compensation as fixed by the trial court is more than fair, it is the duty of the court on appeal to correct and reduce it. Rice v. First Nat'l Bank, 212 Ala. 352, 102 So. 700 (1925), and the authorities there cited. In this case the percentage prescribed was held excessive and was reduced.

And in Noble v. Jackson, 124 Ala. 311, 26 So. 955 (1899), the estate was a large one and the maximum there given was excessive, but the case was reversed on another point and the supreme court said that it would not "forestall the probate judge's discretion in fixing the amount upon another hearing."

The allowance of additional compensation for special or extraordinary services is within the discretion of the hearing court, having due regard to the time expended, the particular circumstances of the administration, the ends accomplished and the character of special services rendered. Anderson v. McClure, 252 Ala. 660, 42 So. 2d 353 (1949).

Where the estate has but few undisputed debts, its property consisting most largely of stocks, bonds or solvent securities, involving only ordinary care and attention in their handling and distribution, and of real estate which may be readily rented, and at the proper time divided or sold for division among those entitled, and the value of the estate is large, and liberal compensation may and often should be, less than the maximum statutory allowance, but never greater, even if the administration involves much care, attention and trouble. If extraordinary services are rendered, these may be compensated for beyond the statutory allowance, owing to the particular services rendered, and the attending conditions and circumstances. Armstrong v. Alabama Nat'l Bank, 404 So. 2d 675 (Ala. 1981).

Facts of each case govern. — What shall be allowed below or up to the maximum limit prescribed by this section is to be determined according to the circumstances of each particular case. Kenan v. Graham, 135 Ala. 585, 33 So. 699 (1903); Smith v. McNaughton, 378 So. 2d 703 (Ala. 1979).

Effect of stipulation in will on allowance. — A provision in a will that the executor shall be "liberally" paid does not authorize or permit an allowance greater than that here prescribed, although it may in some cases call for a smaller allowance. Kenan v. Graham, 135 Ala. 585, 33 So. 699 (1903), the court saying that the word "liberally" as there employed means a compensation just and fair.

Where testator bequeathed to his executor a specified amount for the purpose of carrying out certain provisions of his will expressly requiring that out of that amount there should be paid "all expenses which might be incurred in executing these provisions," it was held, in Ivey v. Coleman, 42 Ala. 409 (1868), that an extra allowance to the executor for this service would be creating a charge upon the residuum of the estate, in direct conflict with the will.

In Waddy v. Hawkins, 31 Va. (4 Leigh) 458 (1833), a testator directed that his executors should be handsomely paid out of his estate, for their trouble in discharging the trust, there being no extraordinary trouble in the administration. The court held that nothing should be allowed beyond the usual commissions. Kenan v. Graham, 135 Ala. 585, 33 So. 699 (1903).

IV. ACTUAL EXPENSES.

Editor's note. — As will be noticed the section expressly declares that the executor or administrator may be allowed his actual expenses. This subject is closely connected with the allowance of compensation for special or extraordinary services, and the cases under the next succeeding analysis line of this annotation should be examined. As the case law of Alabama pertaining to this point alone is comparatively meager, it is thought that a resume of decisions of other states pertaining to this subject may be serviceable.

It is generally held that the expenses may include proper traveling expenses, proper clerk hire, room rent, accounting services, auctioneer fees, expenses for keeping records where necessary, court costs and, as will be seen under the next analysis line, counsel fees. It does not follow that because in some cases some expenses are reasonable that they will be reasonable in others. It would not be proper to add as expense what should be in the commissions. And generally, the representative is not entitled to office rent, although there are cases where in the administration of a large estate such an expense may be justified. Each case must more or less be a rule unto itself.

Expenses of repairs of household furniture. — In Pinckard v. Pinckard, 24 Ala. 250 (1854) it was held that expenses of repairs in household furniture belonging to the estate may be properly allowed.

Attorney's fees are an item of expense. — This section provides that executors may be allowed actual expenses, including premiums paid a guaranty company for making his bond.

Attorney's fees are a proper item of such expense. Turley v. Hazelwood, 234 Ala. 186, 174 So. 616 (1937).

The charge for a reasonable attorney's fee was properly allowed to executor. Wilkerson v. Wilkerson, 257 Ala. 633, 60 So. 2d 343 (1952).

Expenses incurred in attempting to establish will are charge against realty. — The expenses incurred by executor for bond and attorney's fee in unsuccessfully attempting, in good faith, to establish will under which executor claimed were chargeable against land of estate, where personalty was insufficient to pay debt owing at testator's death, notwithstanding that executor did not pay such expenses. Turley v. Hazelwood, 234 Ala. 186, 174 So. 616 (1937).

When finding of register will not be disturbed. — The finding of register on oral evidence and confirmation thereof by trial court, as to amount allowed administrator for services of attorney would not be disturbed where there was a dispute in the evidence as to what was a reasonable attorney's fee and sum allowed was within amount fixed by this section. Stumpf v. Wiles, 235 Ala. 317, 179 So. 201 (1938).

Repairs on testator's car. — Executor properly allowed expenditures for repairs on car of testator used in connection with his duties as executor. Wilkerson v. Wilkerson, 257 Ala. 633, 60 So. 2d 343 (1952).

V. SPECIAL OR EXTRAORDINARY SERVICES.

Examples of extraordinary services. — Where, on final settlement, it appears that an administrator had invested in property, charging himself with the sums so invested, he should be allowed a reasonable compensation for the investment, if it was for the benefit of the estate. Gerald v. Bunkley, 17 Ala. 170 (1850).

It was held in Craig v. McGehee, 16 Ala. 41 (1849), that an executor was entitled to fair compensation for her services in superintending a plantation. See also Reese v. Gresham, 29 Ala. 91 (1856).

Where an administrator gave his full time for 18 months, kept an excellent set of books and performed numerous other duties, the court found that such were extraordinary services warranting a reasonable compensation above the statutory commission. Anderson v. McClure, 252 Ala. 660, 42 So. 2d 353 (1949).

Examples of services not extraordinary. — Making inventories or sales, or keeping accounts, O'Neill v. Donnell, 9 Ala. 734 (1846); ordinary attendance on an action brought by the executor, Holman v. Sims, 39 Ala. 709 (1866); and making inquiries as to evidence in an action against the estate when the representative was in an adjoining county on his own business, Dockery v. McDowell, 40 Ala. 476 (1867), have all been held not to constitute special or extraordinary services entitling to compensation under the last clause of this section.

Nor does the fact that one of the executors transacted most of the business, in itself, characterize his services as extraordinary, meriting compensation as such. Noble v. Jackson, 132 Ala. 230, 31 So. 450 (1902).

Acting as or procuring services as attorney. — In a proper case an attorney at law who is an administrator may be allowed reasonable counsel fees. Pinckard v. Pinckard, 24 Ala. 250 (1854); Gould v. Hays, 25 Ala. 426 (1854); Bates v. Vary, 40 Ala. 421 (1867); Morgan v. Nelson, 43 Ala. 586 (1869); Alexander v. Bates, 127 Ala. 328, 28 So. 415 (1900).

In such case the rule is not to allow the executor or administrator acting as an attorney the usual professional charges for such services, but to allow him a compensation fixed and determined by the inquiry, what is fair and reasonable in view of all the circumstances of the estate. Harris v. Martin, 9 Ala. 895 (1846); Bendall v. Bendall, 24 Ala. 295 (1854); Teague v. Corbitt, 57 Ala. 529 (1877); Clark v. Knox, 70 Ala. 607 (1881).

So an administrator ad litem, who is also an attorney, is entitled, not to the usual professional charges, but to a fair and reasonable allowance therefor. Clark v. Knox, 70 Ala. 607 (1881).

As to procuring the services of an attorney, it is the established rule that when an executor or administrator, in good faith, procures the aid and advice of counsel to direct him in the performance of his duties, paying only such compensation as is fair and reasonable, when considered in connection with the value of the estate and the services rendered, to allow him a credit for such compensation. Pickens v. Pickens, 35 Ala. 442 (1860); Smyley v. Reese, 53 Ala. 89 (1875).

Neither the register nor the judge can take judicial notice of the value of professional service as attorney, rendered by an administrator, and if no objection is made before the register, and no exception reserved to his action, in the matter of an allowance to the administrator for such services, the judge has no authority to reduce the allowance. Clark v. Knox, 70 Ala. 607 (1881).

§ 43-2-681. Commissions on money or property sold or distributed.

Upon the appraised value of all personal property and the amount of money and solvent notes distributed by executors or administrators, they shall be allowed the same commissions as upon disbursements. For selling lands solely for division, they shall be allowed two and one-half percent commission on the amount received, but in no case more than $100.00; except, that when sold under the terms of a will, this section shall not apply. (Code 1867, § 2162; Code 1876, § 2534; Code 1886, § 2152; Code 1896, § 220; Code 1907, § 2691; Code 1923, § 5924; Code 1940, T. 61, § 378.)

Cross references. — See notes to § 43-2-680.

Commissions on disbursements in payment of debts and other outlay in course of administration do not cover all commissions due upon final settlement and distribution of the estate. Henry v. Griffith, 242 Ala. 598, 7 So. 2d 560 (1942).

Allowance not excessive. — Allowance of $1,500.00 commissions to executor was held not excessive, where allowance did not exceed maximum allowed by this section and the winding up of estate involved much time, labor and responsibility, and was well and faithfully performed. Henry v. Griffith, 242 Ala. 598, 7 So. 2d 560 (1942).

Cited in Armstrong v. Alabama Nat'l Bank, 404 So. 2d 675 (Ala. 1981).

Collateral references. — 34 C.J.S., Executors & Administrators, §§ 862, 863, 865, 866.

Lien on, or outstanding interest in, property, as affecting computation of commissions of executors or administrators. 46 ALR 239.

Right of executor or administrator to commission on stock dividends. 55 ALR 710.

Faults in administration as affecting right to commission. 83 ALR 726.

Broker's commission incurred in sale of real property, allowance of, as affecting commissions of personal representative. 91 ALR 836, 155 ALR 1314.

Change in statute after decedent's death and before final account as affecting commissions. 91 ALR 1421.

Loss or depreciation of assets for which executor or administrator is not responsible as affecting the amount of his commission. 110 ALR 994.

Appraised value of estate as shown by inventory, or value at time of settlement as basis for determining commissions of executor or administrator. 173 ALR 1346.

Fiduciary's compensation on estate assets distributed in kind. 32 ALR2d 778.

Right to double compensation where same person (natural or corporate) acts as executor and trustee. 85 ALR2d 537.

§ 43-2-682. Court may allow compensation or attorney's fees up to time of settlement.

Upon any annual, partial or final settlement made by any administrator or executor, the court having jurisdiction thereof may fix, determine and allow the fees or other compensation to which any such administrator or executor is entitled from an estate up to the time of such settlement, and may also fix, determine and allow an attorney's fee or compensation, to be paid from such estate to attorneys representing such administrator or executor, for services rendered to the time of such settlement. (Acts 1936, Ex. Sess., No. 128, p. 90; Code 1940, T. 61, § 379.)

Fee allowance not mandatory. — Code sections which provide for awarding administrator's commissions, attorney's fees, and expenses are permissive, not mandatory. Aird v. Thomas, 408 So. 2d 500 (Ala. 1981).

Cited in King v. Keith, 257 Ala. 463, 60 So. 2d 47 (1952); Hancock v. Hancock, 334 So. 2d 873 (Ala. 1976).

Collateral references. — 34 C.J.S., Executors & Administrators, §§ 860, 940.

Right to allowance out of estate for attorney's fees incurred in attempt to establish or defeat will. 10 ALR 783, 40 ALR2d 1407.

Employment of attorney at expense of estate, by executor or administrator who is himself an attorney. 18 ALR 635.

Allowance of retaining fee paid by executor to attorneys. 21 ALR 1445.

Power of probate court to require return by attorney to estate of overpayment on account of fees or services. 70 ALR 478.

Allowance out of estate for services of attorney not employed by executor or administrator in connection with settlement of estate or accounting of personal representative. 79 ALR 530, 533, 142 ALR 1459.

Right of executor or administrator to allowance of attorneys' fees and expenses incident to controversy of surcharging account. 101 ALR 806.

Validity and effect of provisions in will regarding attorney's fees. 148 ALR 362.

Attorney's fees, costs and expenses incurred by administrator or executor whose appointment was improper as chargeable against estate. 4 ALR2d 164.

Compensation of attorney for executor or administrator as affected by representation of heir or other beneficiary in controversy with other heirs or beneficiaries. 47 ALR2d 1104.

Personal liability of executor or administrator for fees of attorney employed by him for benefit of the estate. 13 ALR3d 518.

Amount of compensation of attorney for services in administration of decedent's estate in absence of contract or statute fixing amount. 59 ALR3d 152.

Liability of estate for legal services of attorney employed by estate attorney without consent of executor or administrator. 83 ALR3d 1160.

§ 43-2-683. Previous fees considered upon final settlement.

In the allowance of fees to executors or administrators and their attorneys on final settlement, the court shall take into consideration such fees as may have been allowed and paid to them prior to such final settlement, but such administrators or executors shall be entitled to full credit for any fees allowed and paid on any annual or partial settlement after notice given as provided for in case of final settlements. (Acts 1936, Ex. Sess., No. 128, p. 90; Code 1940, T. 61, § 380.)

Division 10.

Summary Distribution of Small Estates.

Cross references. — As to disposition of small bank deposits of deceased persons, see §§ 5-5A-38, 5-5A-39. As to disposition of small accounts of deceased persons in savings and loan associations, see § 5-16-46. As to disposition of small credit union accounts upon death of depositor, see § 5-17-16.

§ 43-2-690. Short title.

This division shall be known as the "Alabama Small Estates Act." (Acts 1975, 3rd Ex. Sess., No. 145, § 1.)

§ 43-2-691. Definitions.

For the purposes of this division, the following words and phrases shall have the meanings respectively ascribed to them by this section:

(1) DISTRIBUTEES. The persons who are entitled to the personal property of a decedent under the terms of a testamentary disposition or under the Alabama descent and distribution statutes.

605

(2) DEVISEES. The persons who are entitled to the personal property of a decedent under the terms of a testamentary disposition.

(3) HEIRS. The persons who are entitled to the personal property of a decedent under the Alabama descent and distribution statutes.

(4) ESTATE. All the personal property of a decedent who owns no real property at the time of his death.

(5) PERSONAL REPRESENTATIVE. Such term includes an executor, administrator, administrator with the will annexed and special administrator.

(6) PERSON. Such term includes natural persons and corporations. (Acts 1975, 3rd Ex. Sess., No. 145, § 2.)

§ 43-2-692. Petition for summary distribution; probate judge to take possession of assets of estate; when surviving spouse or distributees entitled to personal property without administration.

(a) The surviving spouse, if there is one, otherwise the distributees of an estate of personal property only, may initiate a proceeding for summary distribution of the estate by filing a petition as hereinafter provided in the probate judge's office of the county in which the decedent was domiciled at death. The petition shall include a description of the estate of the decedent. The judge of probate or his duly authorized clerk shall take actual possession of any liquid or negotiable assets and constructive possession of all other personal property of the decedent.

(b) The surviving spouse or distributee shall have a defeasible right to the personal property of the decedent without awaiting the appointment of a personal representative or the probate of a will if all of the following conditions exist:

(1) The value of the entire estate does not exceed $3,000.00;

(2) The decedent died a resident of this state;

(3) No petition for the appointment of a personal representative is pending or has been granted;

(4) At least 45 days have elapsed since the filing of a petition for summary distribution under this division and at least 21 days have elapsed since the first notice thereof was published as hereinafter provided;

(5) All funeral expenses of the decedent have been paid, or alternatively, that arrangements for the payment out of the estate of the decedent of all unpaid funeral expenses have been made by the surviving spouse or other distributee;

(6) If the decedent died intestate, the awards due under Alabama descent and distribution statutes to the surviving spouse and to the child or children have been determined by the probate judge, and a certified copy of such determination has been transmitted to the surviving spouse and the child or children;

(7) If the decedent died testate, a document purporting to be his will, which on its face, is properly executed, witnessed and attested in compliance with Alabama law, has been duly filed in the probate judge's office;

(8) Notice of the filing of a petition for a summary distribution under this division must be published once a week for three successive weeks in a newspaper of general circulation in the county in which the decedent was domiciled, or if there is no newspaper of general circulation in such county, then notice thereof must be posted at the county courthouse for three weeks;

(9) All claims against the decedent's estate have been paid or arrangements for the payment out of the estate of the decedent have been made by the surviving spouse or other distributee according to the following priority:

a. First, to each person entitled to payment for any funeral expenses owed by the decedent or his estate; then

b. To the judge of probate for fees and charges incurred in the proceedings for summary distribution; then

c. To any person entitled to payment for expenses incurred in the decedent's last illness; then

d. To the state of Alabama, the county and any municipality therein for taxes assessed on the estate of the decedent previous to his death; then

e. To each secured creditor under article 9 of Title 7 of this Code; then

f. To each unsecured lienholder; then

g. To each remaining general unsecured creditor of the decedent; then

h. To each surviving spouse, child or other distributee who is entitled to take under Alabama's descent and distribution laws, or, alternatively, to each devisee entitled to take under any testamentary disposition of the decedent. (Acts 1975, 3rd Ex. Sess., No. 145, § 3.)

§ 43-2-693. Entry of order directing summary distribution; delivery and release of assets by probate judge.

When all of the applicable conditions enumerated in subsection (b) of section 43-2-692 concur, the judge of probate shall enter an order directing a summary distribution of the estate; and he shall thereupon deliver such liquid or negotiable assets of the estate as have come into his possession and shall release his constructive possession of the other personal property of the decedent to the surviving spouse or distributee entitled to the defeasible interest in the property. (Acts 1975, 3rd Ex. Sess., No. 145, § 4.)

§ 43-2-694. Transfer of property or evidence of rights therein to surviving spouse or distributees.

Upon delivering a copy of the judge's order for summary distribution or an affidavit executed by any person having knowledge of the fact and alleging the concurrence of the conditions listed in subsection (b) of section 43-2-692 showing the defeasible right therein, together with a copy of the decedent's will if the claim is under such will, such spouse or distributee shall be entitled to have the decedent's property or the evidence of the decedent's ownership in such property transferred to him by any person owing any money to the decedent's estate, having custody of any personal property of the decedent or acting as a registrar or transfer agent of any evidence of interest, indebtedness, property or right of the deceased therein. (Acts 1975, 3rd Ex. Sess., No. 145, § 5.)

§ 43-2-695. Limitation on defeasible rights of surviving spouse or distributees.

The defeasible right of the surviving spouse or distributees provided for by this division shall be subject only to any preexisting rights to administer the estate or probate the will, or to the superior rights of any other person to such personal property. (Acts 1975, 3rd Ex. Sess., No. 145, § 6.)

§ 43-2-696. Effect of transfer pursuant to affidavit.

The person making payment, delivery, transfer or issuance of personal property or evidence thereof pursuant to the affidavit prescribed in section 43-2-694 shall be discharged and released to the same extent as if made to a personal representative of the decedent, and he shall not be required to see the application thereof or to inquire into the truth of any statement in the affidavit if made by any other person. If any person to whom such affidavit is delivered refuses to pay, deliver, transfer or issue any personal property or evidence thereof, it may be recovered or its payment, delivery, transfer or issuance compelled in an action brought for such purpose by or on behalf of the person entitled thereto under sections 43-2-692 and 43-2-695 upon proof of the defeasible right declared by such sections. Any person to whom payment, delivery, transfer or issuance is made shall be answerable and accountable therefor to any personal representative of the estate or to the surviving spouse or minor children of the decedent who shall proceed against such person, or to any other person having a superior right to the decedent's estate. (Acts 1975, 3rd Ex. Sess., No. 145, § 7.)

ARTICLE 19.

INSOLVENT ESTATES.

Division 1.

General Provisions.

When estate declared insolvent. — Under this article the estate of a decedent can be declared insolvent only when the real and personal property is insufficient for the payment of the debts. Banks v. Speers, 97 Ala. 560, 11 So. 841 (1892); Gilbreath v. Levi, 270 Ala. 413, 119 So. 2d 210 (1959).

Cited in Hitchcock v. United States Bank, 7 Ala. 386 (1845); Glover v. Chandler, 11 Ala. 161 (1847); Forward v. Armstead, 12 Ala. 124 (1847); Aikin v. Bloodgood, 12 Ala. 221 (1847); Scott v. Dansby, 12 Ala. 714 (1848); Burk v. Jones, 13 Ala. 167 (1848); Beall v. Williamson, 14 Ala. 55 (1848); Pipkin v. Hewlett, 17 Ala. 291 (1850); Ewing v. Peck, 17 Ala. 339 (1850); Snedicor v. Davis, 17 Ala. 472 (1850); Gould v. Hayes, 19 Ala. 438 (1851); Lee v. Leachman, 22 Ala. 452 (1853); Long v. McDougald, 23 Ala. 413 (1853); Shadden v. Sterling, 23 Ala. 518 (1853); Shackelford v. King, 24 Ala. 158 (1854); Amason v. Nash, 24 Ala. 279 (1854); Smith & Co. v. Mallory, 24 Ala. 628 (1854); Raines v. Raines, 30 Ala. 425 (1857); Prince v. Prince, 47 Ala. 283 (1872); Christian v. Morris, 50 Ala. 585 (1874); Newell v. Bradford, 187 Ala. 251, 65 So. 800 (1914); Cassady v. Davis, 245 Ala. 93, 15 So. 2d 909 (1943); Barrett v. Fondren, 262 Ala. 537, 80 So. 2d 243 (1955).

Collateral references. — 34 C.J.S., Executors & Administrators, §§ 667-687.

31 Am. Jur. 2d, Executors & Administrators, §§ 312-315.

See also Am. Jur. and ALR references under § 43-2-371.

§ 43-2-700. Order and preference of payment of debts.

When the real and personal property of any decedent is insufficient for the payment of the debts, the proceeds arising from the sale thereof must be distributed as directed by section 43-2-371 in proportion to the amounts due to each class of creditors, in the order in such section specified. (Code 1852, § 1828; Code 1867, § 2177; Code 1876, § 2549; Code 1886, § 2222; Code 1896, § 290; Code 1907, § 2755; Code 1923, § 5994; Code 1940, T. 61, § 381.)

Cited in Hames v. Irwin, 214 Ala. 422, 108 So. 253 (1926).

Collateral references. — 34 C.J.S., Executors & Administrators, § 685.

§ 43-2-701. Report of insolvency—Generally.

Whenever the executor or administrator of any estate is satisfied that the property of the estate is insufficient to pay its debts, he must file with the judge of probate of the court having jurisdiction of the estate a report in writing that such estate is, to the best of his knowledge and belief, insolvent. (Code 1852, § 1829; Code 1867, § 2178; Code 1876, § 2550; Code 1886, § 2223; Code 1896, § 291; Code 1907, § 2756; Code 1923, § 5995; Code 1940, T. 61, § 382.)

When decree follows as matter of course. — Where report of insolvency of decedent's estate, properly verified by the administrator, discloses insolvency and there is no contest, a decree of insolvency follows as a matter of course. Martin v. Cothran, 240 Ala. 619, 200 So. 609 (1941).

Time of reporting insolvency. — The administrator may report the insolvency of the estate immediately after his appointment, if he is satisfied that this is its condition. Hullett v. Hood, 109 Ala. 345, 19 So. 419 (1896).

Administrator is the only one who may report insolvency. — No one has the right to invoke the jurisdiction of the probate court so as to establish the insolvency of the estate judicially except the administrator and it is attributable to his neglect if he fails to do so. And his breach of duty in this respect will not prejudice the rights of the creditors. Byrd v. Jones, 84 Ala. 336, 4 So. 375 (1888). As to right of creditor to show insolvency of estate, see notes to § 43-2-511.

The failure of an administrator to ascertain the insolvency of an estate is not a bar to the right of the widow of the intestate to proceed independently and have such insolvency ascertained judicially in her own name. Medley v. Shipes, 177 Ala. 94, 58 So. 304 (1912).

Insolvency may be determined by parties not concerned with homestead. — A proceeding for judicial ascertainment as to insolvency of decedent's estate may be instituted, contested and issue determined among parties having no concern with the succession to the fee in decedent's homestead. Martin v. Cothran, 240 Ala. 619, 200 So. 609 (1941).

Cited in Feagan v. Kendall, 43 Ala. 628 (1869); Prince v. Prince, 47 Ala. 283 (1872); McDowell v. Jones, 58 Ala. 25 (1877); Hatchett v. Curbow, 59 Ala. 516 (1877); Julian v. Woolbert, 202 Ala. 530, 81 So. 32 (1919); Crossland v. First Nat'l Bank, 226 Ala. 679, 148 So. 418 (1933); Elliott v. First Nat'l Bank, 248 Ala. 360, 27 So. 2d 623 (1946).

Collateral references. — 34 C.J.S., Executors & Administrators, §§ 669-672.

§ 43-2-702. Same—Statement to be filed with report.

He must file with such report:

(1) A statement of all the goods and chattels, evidences of debt and other personal property, with the estimated value of each, and the amount of money belonging to such estate;

(2) A full statement of the real property of the deceased, or any interest therein, and estimated value thereof;

(3) A full statement of the claims against the estate which have come to his knowledge, the character and amount of each claim and the name and residence of each creditor, if known; and

(4) A full statement of the names and ages of all heirs or distributees and their places of residence. (Code 1852, § 1830; Code 1867, § 2179; Code 1876, § 2551; Code 1886, § 2224; Code 1896, § 292; Code 1907, § 2757; Code 1923, § 5996; Code 1940, T. 61, § 383.)

Report not limited to claims that must be presented. — Claims referred to by the administrator are not necessarily claims which should be presented under § 43-2-352. Gilbreath v. Levi, 270 Ala. 413, 119 So. 2d 210 (1959).

Cited in Sims v. Canfield, 2 Ala. 555 (1841); Reed v. Minell & Co., 30 Ala. 61 (1857); Raines v. Raines, 30 Ala. 425 (1857); Thornton v. Moore, 61 Ala. 347 (1878); Banks v. Speers, 97 Ala. 560, 11 So. 841 (1892); Elliott v. First Nat'l Bank, 248 Ala. 360, 27 So. 2d 623 (1946).

§ 43-2-703. Same — Affidavit accompanying report and statement.

Such report and statement must be accompanied by an affidavit of the executor or administrator to the effect that they are correct to the best of his knowledge, information and belief. (Code 1852, § 1831; Code 1867, § 2180; Code 1876, § 2552; Code 1886, § 2225; Code 1896, § 293; Code 1907, § 2758; Code 1923, § 5997; Code 1940, T. 61, § 384.)

Cited in Raines v. Raines, 30 Ala. 425 (1857); Elliott v. First Nat'l Bank, 248 Ala. 360, 27 So. 2d 623 (1946); Gilbreath v. Levi, 270 Ala. 413, 119 So. 2d 210 (1959).

§ 43-2-704. Time for hearing; notice of hearing.

The probate court, on the filing of such report and statements, must appoint a day, not less than 30 nor more than 60 days therefrom, to hear and determine the same and must give notice to the creditors of and to all persons interested in the estate of the filing of the report and the day appointed to hear and determine the same by publication, once a week for three successive weeks, in some newspaper published in the county or, if none is published therein, in a newspaper published nearest to the courthouse of such county, and by posting such notice at the courthouse door for the same length of time and by forwarding such notice by mail to all creditors and to all adult heirs or distributees whose places of residence are known, and shall appoint guardians ad litem for all heirs or distributees who are minors or of unsound mind. Upon the day appointed or on any other day to which the hearing is continued, the court must proceed to hear and determine such report. (Code 1852, §§ 1832, 1833;

Code 1867, §§ 2181, 2182; Code 1876, §§ 2553, 2554; Code 1886, §§ 2226, 2227; Code 1896, §§ 294, 295; Code 1907, §§ 2759, 2760; Code 1923, §§ 5998, 5999; Code 1940, T. 61, §§ 385, 386.)

Cited in Thompson v. Acree, 69 Ala. 178 (1881); Cassady v. Davis, 245 Ala. 93, 15 So. 2d 909 (1943); Elliott v. First Nat'l Bank, 248 Ala. 360, 27 So. 2d 623 (1946).

§ 43-2-705. Trial of issue of insolvency to be by jury.

Any creditor or other person interested in the estate may make an issue as to the correctness of such report by denying in writing that the estate is insolvent, which issue must be tried by a jury on the application of any party; but only one issue must be made, in which any number of the creditors or persons interested in the estate may join at any time before the determination thereof. (Code 1852, §§ 1834, 1837; Code 1867, §§ 2183, 2186; Code 1876, §§ 2555, 2558; Code 1886, § 2228; Code 1896, § 296; Code 1907, § 2761; Code 1923, § 6000; Code 1940, T. 61, § 387.)

Decree is inadmissible except against persons interested in estate. — Under this section a decree of insolvency is inadmissible in evidence except as against a party interested in the estate, and who could hereunder make issue as to the correctness of the report of insolvency. Bush v. Coleman, 121 Ala. 548, 25 So. 569 (1899).

Cited in Hine v. Hussey, 45 Ala. 496 (1871).

§ 43-2-706. Payment of costs.

If such issue is decided against the executor or administrator, the report must be dismissed, and execution for the costs may issue against him and his sureties; but if it is decided in his favor, the costs must be paid by the contesting creditor, or parties interested in the estate, or out of the estate, as the court may direct. (Code 1852, §§ 1835, 1836; Code 1867, §§ 2184, 2185; Code 1876, §§ 2556, 2557; Code 1886, § 2229; Code 1896, § 297; Code 1907, § 2762; Code 1923, § 6001; Code 1940, T. 61, § 388.)

§ 43-2-707. Declaration of insolvency.

If no person contests the correctness of the report or if the issue is decided against contestant, the court must declare the estate insolvent and must make an order for the executor or administrator on a day therein named, not less than 30 nor more than 60 days therefrom, to appear and make a settlement of his administration; and of such order, and of the day appointed for such settlement, notice must be given by the judge of probate as is required by section 43-2-704. (Code 1852, §§ 1838, 1839; Code 1867, §§ 2187, 2188; Code 1876, §§ 2559, 2560; Code 1886, § 2230; Code 1896, § 298; Code 1907, § 2763; Code 1923, § 6002; Code 1940, T. 61, § 389.)

The primary objective of a decree of insolvency as to decedent's estate is procedural, and the further course of administration for the protection of all interest concerned is controlled thereby. Martin v. Cothran, 240 Ala. 619, 200 So. 609 (1941).

Cited in Feagan v. Kendall, 43 Ala. 628 (1869); Prince v. Prince, 47 Ala. 283 (1872);

Wilson v. Barnes, 49 Ala. 134 (1873); Clay v. Gurley, 62 Ala. 14 (1878); Wright v. Dunklin, 83 Ala. 317, 3 So. 597 (1888); Elliott v. First Nat'l Bank, 248 Ala. 360, 27 So. 2d 623 (1946); King v. Keith, 257 Ala. 463, 60 So. 2d 47 (1952);

Gilbreath v. Levi, 270 Ala. 413, 119 So. 2d 210 (1959).

Collateral references. — 34 C.J.S., Executors & Administrators, § 674.

§ 43-2-708. Second declaration by succeeding administrator not necessary.

An estate of a decedent having once been declared insolvent, it shall not be necessary for any succeeding administrator to apply for or obtain a declaration or decree of insolvency; but a declaration of insolvency once had, and remaining unreversed, shall continue and apply to and be effectual under all subsequent administrations, as if obtained under each of them. (Code 1867, § 4424; Code 1876, § 2589; Code 1886, § 2261; Code 1896, § 329; Code 1907, § 2766; Code 1923, § 6005; Code 1940, T. 61, § 392.)

Cross references. — As to decree of insolvency substituting for proof of existence of debts in sale of lands after insolvency, see notes to § 43-2-790.

§ 43-2-709. Appeals.

(a) Any party to the proceedings to declare an estate insolvent may appeal to the supreme court or court of civil appeals from the decree or order declaring the estate insolvent or dismissing the report within 42 days from the rendition of such order or decree in the manner provided by law for appeals from the probate court in other similar or like proceedings.

(b) If an appeal has been taken on a contest as to the report of insolvency, the case must, on motion, be continued during the pendency of such appeal. (Code 1852, § 1861; Code 1867, § 2210; Code 1876, § 2582; Code 1886, § 2252; Code 1896, § 320; Code 1907, §§ 2764, 2765; Code 1923, §§ 6003, 6004; Code 1940, T. 61, §§ 390, 391.)

Cited in Crossland v. First Nat'l Bank, 226 Ala. 679, 148 So. 418 (1933).

Division 2.

Nomination and Election of Administrators of Insolvent Estates.

§ 43-2-720. When creditors may make nomination; who may be nominated.

On the day appointed for the settlement of the administration of an estate declared insolvent or on any day to which the same is continued, the creditors present or represented may nominate to the court any fit person, an inhabitant of this state, as administrator of the property, rights and credits of such estate unadministered. (Code 1852, § 1840; Code 1867, § 2189; Code 1876, § 2561; Code 1886, § 2231; Code 1896, § 299; Code 1907, § 2767; Code 1923, § 6006; Code 1940, T. 61, § 393.)

Cited in Snedicor v. Mobley, 47 Ala. 517 (1872); Clay v. Gurley, 62 Ala. 14 (1878); Cassady v. Davis, 245 Ala. 93, 15 So. 2d 909 (1943).

§ 43-2-721. Voting procedure generally; proof of claims required.

(a) In making the nomination, each creditor, in person or represented, votes as follows:

(1) On claims held by any one creditor, not exceeding in the aggregate $1,000.00, one vote for each $100.00; and

(2) On claims held by any one creditor, exceeding in the aggregate $1,000.00, 10 votes for the first $1,000.00, and one for every additional $500.00.

(b) Every creditor is entitled to one vote, and no creditor to more than 20.

(c) The nomination must be made in the presence and under the direction of the court. The amount of claims held by any creditor must be proved by affidavit, as required by section 43-2-352. The court may require other evidence of the correctness and amount of the claim. (Code 1852, §§ 1841, 1842; Code 1867, §§ 2190, 2191; Code 1876, §§ 2562, 2563; Code 1886, §§ 2232, 2233; Code 1896, §§ 300, 301; Code 1907, §§ 2768, 2769; Code 1923, §§ 6007, 6008; Code 1940, T. 61, §§ 394, 395.)

Cited in Calhoun v. Fletcher, 63 Ala. 574 (1879).

§ 43-2-722. Person receiving plurality appointed administrator.

The person receiving a plurality of votes must be appointed by the court administrator of the property, rights and credits of the estate unadministered. (Code 1852, § 1843; Code 1867, § 2192; Code 1876, § 2564; Code 1886, § 2234; Code 1896, § 302; Code 1907, § 2770; Code 1923, § 6009; Code 1940, T. 61, § 396.)

§ 43-2-723. Discretion of court upon failure of creditors to attend.

If none of the creditors attend at the time appointed or if, from any other cause, no appointment of such administrator is made, the court may, in its discretion, continue the former executor or administrator or may appoint any fit person, or the general administrator of the county or, should there be none, the sheriff of the county, to administer the estate according to the provisions of this division. (Code 1852, § 1845; Code 1867, § 2194; Code 1876, § 2566; Code 1886, § 2235; Code 1896, § 303; Code 1907, § 2771; Code 1923, § 6010; Code 1940, T. 61, § 397.)

Cited in McDonald v. McDonald, 50 Ala. 26 (1873); Elliott v. First Nat'l Bank, 248 Ala. 360, 27 So. 2d 623 (1946).

§ 43-2-724. Former letters revoked upon appointment; property vested in administrator.

Whenever an administrator is appointed under the provisions of this division, any former grant of letters on the estate is thereby revoked; and the property of such estate is thereby vested in such administrator. (Code 1852, § 1846; Code 1867, § 2195; Code 1876, § 2567; Code 1886, § 2237; Code 1896, § 305; Code 1907, § 2773; Code 1923, § 6012; Code 1940, T. 61, § 399.)

General effect of this section. — The provisions of this section are effective though the insolvency proceedings did not ipso facto terminate the authority of the personal representative for certain purposes. Julian v. Woolbert, 202 Ala. 530, 81 So. 32 (1919). And though the acts of the personal representative, if he continues to administer the estate after such declaration of insolvency (no other administrator having been appointed in his stead), are valid, and the sureties on his bond remain bound as if no declaration of insolvency has been made. Clay v. Gurley, 62 Ala. 14 (1878).

Cited in Cogburn v. McQueen, 46 Ala. 551 (1871); Snedicor v. Mobley, 47 Ala. 517 (1872); Lambert v. Mallett, 50 Ala. 73 (1873); Thames v. Herbert, 61 Ala. 340 (1878); Elliott v. First Nat'l Bank, 248 Ala. 360, 27 So. 2d 623 (1946).

§ 43-2-725. Vacancy.

Whenever a vacancy occurs in the office of such administrator, the court, on motion of any creditor of the estate, may order another meeting of creditors, and hold another election, and make the appointment of the person elected, in all respects, as upon the first meeting of the creditors. (Code 1852, § 1844; Code 1867, § 2193; Code 1876, § 2565; Code 1886, § 2236; Code 1896, § 304; Code 1907, § 2772; Code 1923, § 6011; Code 1940, T. 61, § 398.)

Division 3.

Filing and Allowing Claims Against Insolvent Estates.

Cited in Sims v. Canfield, 2 Ala. 555 (1841); Jordan v. Hazard, 10 Ala. 221 (1846); Carrington & Co. v. Manning, 13 Ala. 611 (1848); Erwin v. Branch Bank, 14 Ala. 307 (1848); Ridgell v. Dale, 16 Ala. 36 (1849); Guild v. Guild, 16 Ala. 121 (1849); Delage v. Hazzard, 16 Ala. 196 (1849); Lewis v. Stein, 16 Ala. 214 (1849); Kennedy v. Townsley, 16 Ala. 239 (1849); Seaborn v. State, 20 Ala. 15 (1852); Sterne v. State, 20 Ala. 43 (1852); Lawson v. State, 20 Ala. 65 (1852); Weaver v. Weaver, 23 Ala. 789 (1853); Locke v. Palmer, 26 Ala. 312 (1855); Reed v. Minell & Co., 30 Ala. 63 (1857); McDougald v. Rutherford, 30 Ala. 253 (1857); Bell v. Andrews, 34 Ala. 538 (1859); Puryear v. Puryear, 34 Ala. 555 (1859); Phillips v. Beene, 38 Ala. 248 (1862); Flinn v. Shackleford, 42 Ala. 202 (1868); Clement v. Nelson, 46 Ala. 634 (1871); Prince v. Prince, 47 Ala. 283 (1872); Brewer & Co. v. Moseley, 49 Ala. 79 (1873); McGehee v. Lomax, 49 Ala. 131 (1873); Walker v. Wigginton, 50 Ala. 579 (1874); Shelton v. Carpenter, 60 Ala. 201 (1877); Mitchell v. Pitts, 61 Ala. 219 (1878); Guard v. Hale, 64 Ala. 479 (1879); Moore v. Winston, 66 Ala. 296 (1880); Clark v. Guard, 73 Ala. 456 (1882); Barnes v. Bell, 231 Ala. 84, 163 So. 616 (1935).

Collateral references. — 34 C.J.S., Executors & Administrators, §§ 679-682.

Right of executor or administrator of insolvent estate to take advantage of failure to record, or file, or refile a conveyance or mortgage executed by his decedent. 91 ALR 299.

Rank or preference of claim against insolvent estate in respect to stockholder's superadded liability. 92 ALR 1040.

Mortgage or other encumbrance as affecting duty of executor or administrator of insolvent estate to sell real estate to pay debts, or duty of probate court to order such sale. 116 ALR 910.

§ 43-2-740. Time and manner of filing claims — Generally.

Every person having any claim against the estate declared insolvent must file the same in the office of the judge of probate as provided by subsection (b) of section 43-2-350. Any defect or insufficiency in the affidavit may be supplied by amendment at any time. And when, prior to the declaration of insolvency, a claim has been filed in the office of the judge of probate, as required by said section, such claim shall be considered as duly filed under this section. (Code 1852, § 1847; Code 1867, § 2196; Code 1876, § 2568; Code 1886, § 2238; Code 1896, § 306; Code 1907, § 2774; Code 1923, § 6013; Acts 1931, No. 721, p. 839; Code 1940, T. 61, § 400.)

In general. — This section in effect makes the statute of nonclaim applicable to insolvent estates. Murdock v. Rousseau, 32 Ala. 611 (1858); Ray v. Thompson, 43 Ala. 434 (1869); Watson v. Rose, 51 Ala. 292 (1874). And claims not filed according to the section are barred. Hollinger v. Holly, 8 Ala. 454 (1845); Plowman v. Thornton, 52 Ala. 559 (1875). But the allowance of a claim duly filed under the section is a matter of right secured by the section (when no objections are taken under § 43-2-747). Clark v. Knox, 70 Ala. 607 (1881).

Who may present claims. — Under this section it has been held that a party having an equitable title to a demand (Hogan v. Calvert, 21 Ala. 194 (1852)), a surety who pays a debt for his principal (Powe v. Tyson, 15 Ala. 221 (1849)), an indorser who pays a note (Henry v. Black, 24 Ala. 417 (1854)), and an administrator of a deceased guardian, may file their claims against the estate.

Creditors must file claims within time limit. — Under this section a creditor who fails to file his claim within the time limit herein set cannot recover against the insolvent's estate, though the estate may have been transferred by the deceased debtor to a fraudulent donee. Herstein v. Walker, 85 Ala. 37, 4 So. 262 (1888), aff'd, 90 Ala. 477, 7 So. 821 (1890).

Judgments. — The requirements of this section apply to judgments entered before the decree of insolvency against the intestate, and not to judgments entered against an administrator. Woodall v. Wright, 142 Ala. 205, 37 So. 846 (1904). But see Gamble v. Dunklin, 48 Ala. 425 (1872). See also Reid v. Nash, 23 Ala. 733 (1853).

Civil actions commenced before insolvency. — This section does not apply to a claim on which a civil action had been commenced against the estate before insolvency. Erwin v. McGuire, 44 Ala. 499 (1870); Waller v. Nelson, 48 Ala. 531 (1872).

Statement, verification and filing. — The purpose of this section is complied with when the statement and affidavit fairly disclose an existing liability preferred against the estate. Thornton v. Moore, 61 Ala. 347 (1878). No particular form is required. Hogan v. Calvert, 21 Ala. 194 (1852). And a copy or substantial statement of the claim is sufficient. Rutherford v. Branch Bank, 14 Ala. 92 (1848). See also Hunley v. Shuford, 11 Ala. 303 (1847); Rowdon v. Young, 12 Ala. 234 (1847).

The amount of a note placed in attorney's hand need not be specified. Stubbs v. Beene, 37 Ala. 627 (1861).

Time of verification. — It is no objection to a claim against an insolvent estate, filed under this section, that the affidavit, though made after intestate's death, was in fact made before the estate was declared insolvent. Norvill v. Williams, 35 Ala. 551 (1860). See also Shortridge v. Easley, 10 Ala. 520 (1846); Brown & Co. v. Easly, 10 Ala. 564 (1846); Gilbert v. Brashear, 12 Ala. 191 (1847); Rutherford v. Branch Bank, 14 Ala. 92 (1848); Planters', etc., Bank v. Smith, 14 Ala. 416 (1848); Gaffney v. Williamson, 21 Ala. 112 (1852).

Verification before an officer of another state is presumed to be correct. — See Carhart v. Clark, 31 Ala. 396 (1858).

But the affidavit must show that the claim is just and subsisting. Lay v. Clark, 31 Ala. 409 (1858). See also Fox v. Lawson, 44 Ala. 319 (1870).

Failure to docket the verified claim does not invalidate the filing. But when the creditor relies on a filing made before the decree of insolvency, he must show verification and docketing, so as to afford opportunity for objections. Henderson v. Henderson, 67 Ala. 519 (1880).

Time of filing. — The section does not require the rejection of a claim filed before declaration of insolvency. Levert v. Read, 54 Ala. 529 (1875).

Sufficient affidavits. — Affidavit of claimant's bookmaker in Trowbridge v. Pinckard, 31 Ala. 424 (1858), of an agent in Planters', etc., Bank v. Smith, 14 Ala. 416 (1848), and of claimant's attorney in Erwin v. McGuire, 44 Ala. 499 (1870), have all been held sufficient.

An account for a tombstone is within the section. Hatchett v. Curbow, 59 Ala. 516 (1877).

Revivor of decree. — See Sharp v. Herrin, 32 Ala. 502 (1858). See also Hollinger v. Holly,

8 Ala. 454 (1845); Campbell v. Campbell, 11 Ala. 730 (1847); Brasher v. Lyle, 13 Ala. 524 (1848); Bartol v. Calvert, 21 Ala. 42 (1852); Hogan v. Calvert, 21 Ala. 194 (1852).

§ 43-2-741. Same — Time allowed certain minors and persons of unsound mind.

The provisions of section 43-2-740, as to the time within which claims are to be filed, do not apply to infants and persons of unsound mind who have no legal guardian at the time of the declaration of insolvency; but such minors and persons of unsound mind are allowed six months after the appointment of a guardian or, if none be appointed, six months after the removal of their respective disabilities in which to file their claims. (Code 1852, § 1848; Code 1867, § 2197; Code 1876, § 2569; Code 1886, § 2239; Code 1896, § 307; Code 1907, § 2775; Code 1923, § 6014; Code 1940, T. 61, § 401.)

Cross references. — See notes to § 43-2-740.

Cited in Sharp v. Herrin, 32 Ala. 502 (1858); Beene v. Phillips, 37 Ala. 312 (1861); Warfield v. Ravesies, 38 Ala. 518 (1863); Robinson v. Richards, 45 Ala. 354 (1871).

§ 43-2-742. Same — Claims verified in another state.

When a claim against such estate is verified by the oath of a person out of this state, but within the United States, such oath may be made before a notary public, justice of the peace or any judge or clerk of a court of record or a commissioner of such state. When made before a justice of the peace, it must be certified that such officer was a justice of the peace and that his attestation is genuine, by some judge of a court of record or a commissioner of said state; but, when made before either of the other officers specified, no other proof of the taking of such oath is necessary than the certificate of such officer. (Code 1852, § 1849; Code 1867, § 2198; Code 1876, § 2570; Code 1886, § 2240; Code 1896, § 308; Code 1907, § 2776; Code 1923, § 6015; Code 1940, T. 61, § 402.)

Cited in Garrett v. Lynch, 44 Ala. 324 (1870).

§ 43-2-743. Same — Claims verified in foreign country.

When such oath is taken out of the United States, it may be taken before any judge or clerk of a court of record, mayor or chief magistrate of any county, city, borough or town, notary public or diplomatic, consular or commercial agent of the United States. No proof of the taking of such oath is necessary, other than the certificate of such officer. (Code 1852, § 1850; Code 1867, § 2199; Code 1876, § 2571; Code 1886, § 2241; Code 1896, § 309; Code 1907, § 2777; Code 1923, § 6016; Code 1940, T. 61, § 403.)

§ 43-2-744. Receipt for claim; endorsement by judge.

The judge of probate must, when required, give a receipt for such claim to the claimant, his agent or attorney and must endorse on the claim the day when the same was filed and sign his name thereto. (Code 1852, § 1851; Code 1867, § 2200; Code 1876, § 2572; Code 1886, § 2242; Code 1896, § 310; Code 1907, § 2778; Code 1923, § 6017; Code 1940, T. 61, § 404.)

Cited in Clement v. Nelson, 46 Ala. 634 (1871).

§ 43-2-745. Claims docket.

Such judge must keep a docket of all the claims thus filed, which must be at all times, during office hours, subject to the inspection of the administrator and creditors of, or any person interested in, the estate. (Code 1852, § 1852; Code 1867, § 2201; Code 1876, § 2573; Code 1886, § 2243; Code 1896, § 311; Code 1907, § 2779; Code 1923, § 6018; Code 1940, T. 61, § 405.)

§ 43-2-746. When claim allowed without further proof.

If no opposition is made, in the manner provided in section 43-2-747, within six months after the time when the estate was declared insolvent, such claim must be allowed against the estate without further proof. (Code 1852, § 1853; Code 1867, § 2202; Code 1876, § 2574; Code 1886, § 2244; Code 1896, § 312; Code 1907, § 2780; Code 1923, § 6019; Code 1940, T. 61, § 406.)

Claims within section. — Claims to be "allowed against the estate without further proof," merely because they were filed verified in nine months (now six), and not objected to in 12 months (now six), must be of a character which, if objected to, the probate court can determine their correctness on "an issue to be made up between the claimant and the objector," under § 43-2-747. Chandler v. Wynne, 85 Ala. 301, 4 So. 653 (1888).

Unopposed claims are debts against personal representative and assets. — Claims filed against an insolvent estate, and not objected to in time, become ascertained and fixed debts against the personal representative and against the personal assets in his hands. And they are open only to defenses which accrue after the time for filing objections has expired. Chandler v. Wynne, 85 Ala. 301, 4 So. 653 (1888).

Claims which were barred by limitations at the time of decedent's death and not directed to be paid by will, could not be allowed against insolvent estate notwithstanding fact that the administrator did not file objections to such claims within six months as required by § 43-2-747. Such claims were barred by § 43-2-373 and the administrator had no discretion as to the payment of such claims. Elliott v. First Nat'l Bank, 248 Ala. 360, 27 So. 2d 623 (1946).

Cited in Pickle v. Ezzell, 27 Ala. 623 (1855); Hardy v. Meachem, 33 Ala. 457 (1859); Flinn v. Shackleford, 42 Ala. 202 (1868); Prince v. Prince, 47 Ala. 283 (1872); Thames v. Herbert, 61 Ala. 340 (1878); Thornton v. Moore, 61 Ala. 347 (1878); Guard v. Hale, 64 Ala. 479 (1879).

§ 43-2-747. Objections.

At any time within six months after the declaration of insolvency, the administrator or any creditor, heir, legatee, devisee or distributee may object to the allowance of any claim filed against the estate by filing objections thereto in writing; and, thereupon, the court must cause an issue to be made up between the claimant and objector, in which issue the correctness of such claim must be tried as in a civil action, if required; and, if it is found for the claimant to the whole amount thereof, the same must be allowed and such claimant recover the costs of the trial of such issue; but, if against the claimant, the claim must be rejected, and the party contesting recovers the cost of the trial of such issue. (Code 1852, § 1854; Code 1867, § 2203; Code 1876, § 2575; Code 1886, § 2245; Code 1896, § 313; Code 1907, § 2781; Code 1923, § 6020; Acts 1931, No. 732, p. 843; Code 1940, T. 61, § 407.)

Character of objections. — Objections which under this section must be filed within the prescribed time, and which may be litigated thereunder to a final determination, are those questioning the merits or validity of the particular claim for matters apart from its status in respect of its filing. Christopher v. Stewart, 133 Ala. 348, 32 So. 11 (1901), and authorities cited. See also Chandler v. Wynne, 85 Ala. 301, 4 So. 653 (1888).

Unsettled partnership claim. — The validity of a claim for a balance on an unsettled partnership account filed by a surviving partner against his deceased partner's insolvent estate cannot be determined by the probate court on an issue "between the claimant and the objector." Chandler v. Wynne, 85 Ala. 301, 4 So. 653 (1888).

Claims barred by statute of limitations. — It is not incumbent upon the administrator of an insolvent estate to file objections under this section to the payment of claims barred by statute of limitations at the time of death of the decedent because such claims are barred by § 43-2-373, which section applies to solvent and insolvent estates alike. The administrator is not required to plead the statute of limitations, and has no discretion as to the payment of such claims. Elliott v. First Nat'l Bank, 248 Ala. 360, 27 So. 2d 623 (1946).

The time prescribed by this section cannot be enlarged by agreement between the probate judge and the administrator. Hardy v. Meachem, 33 Ala. 457 (1859).

Failure to file objections cuts off the right

to contest. Thames v. Herbert, 61 Ala. 340 (1878); Christopher v. Stewart, 133 Ala. 348, 32 So. 11 (1901).

Time of objections. — Objections for failure to verify may be had, under this section, at any time before or on the settlement. Pickle v. Ezzell, 27 Ala. 623 (1855); Carhart v. Clark, 31 Ala. 396 (1858).

Jury trial may be had when demanded. — With respect to insolvent estates this section provides that objections to claims must be tried in the probate court, and the supreme court has held that such provisions confer a right to a jury trial in that court when demanded. Tillery v. Commercial Nat'l Bank, 241 Ala. 653, 4 So. 2d 125 (1941).

Judge decides issues when no jury is demanded. — Where an issue is made up under this section, and a jury is not demanded, it is the duty of the judge to decide the issues under the rules prevailing in courts of law. Nooe v. Garner, 70 Ala. 443 (1881).

Cited in Brasher v. Lyle, 13 Ala. 524 (1848); Rutherford v. Branch Bank, 14 Ala. 92 (1848); Goodwin v. McGehee, 15 Ala. 232 (1849); Lees v. Brownings, 15 Ala. 495 (1849); Amason v. Nash, 19 Ala. 104 (1851); Lee v. Leachman, 22 Ala. 452 (1853); Weaver v. Weaver, 23 Ala. 789 (1853); McDougald v. Rutherford, 30 Ala. 253 (1857); Prince v. Prince, 47 Ala. 283 (1872); Miller v. Parker, 47 Ala. 312 (1872); David v. Malone, 48 Ala. 428 (1872); Blankenship v. Nimmo, 50 Ala. 506 (1874); Hatchett v. Curbow, 59 Ala. 516 (1877); Moore v. Winston, 66 Ala. 296 (1880).

§ 43-2-748. Allowance of due part of claim.

If a part only of such claim is found to be due, it must be allowed for that amount and the costs paid by either party, or in such proportion by either party as the court may direct. (Code 1852, § 1855; Code 1867, § 2204; Code 1876, § 2576; Code 1886, § 2246; Code 1896, § 314; Code 1907, § 2782; Code 1923, § 6021; Code 1940, T. 61, § 408.)

Cross references. — See notes to § 43-2-747.

§ 43-2-749. Debt not due.

Any creditor whose debt is not due must file the same as if due and thereupon must be considered as a creditor under this division; and he is entitled to his dividend or such an amount as, with the interest added from the time of payment to the maturity of the debt, would be equal to the amount thereof. (Code 1852, § 1862; Code 1867, § 2211; Code 1876, § 2583; Code 1886, § 2253; Code 1896, § 321; Code 1907, § 2783; Code 1923, § 6022; Code 1940, T. 61, § 409.)

Cited in Marston v. Rowe, 43 Ala. 271 (1869).

§ 43-2-750. Claim allowed after partial distribution.

Any creditor of an insolvent estate, whose claim is allowed after a partial distribution, must be allowed out of the remaining assets of such estate, if sufficient, such an amount as will give him his just dividend. (Code 1852, § 1863; Code 1867, § 2212; Code 1876, § 2584; Code 1886, § 2254; Code 1896, § 322; Code 1907, § 2784; Code 1923, § 6023; Code 1940, T. 61, § 410.)

§ 43-2-751. Action by creditor to recover dividend.

(a) Any creditor of an insolvent estate, whose claim is not barred, may bring a civil action against any person who has received any dividend of such estate and may recover from him such an amount of the dividend he has received as shall be in the same proportion thereto as the claim of the plaintiff bears to the debts of the estate distributed, including the claim of the plaintiff.

(b) But, in such action, the defendant may reduce the recovery, by showing that such dividend has been reduced by the recovery or payment of the claims of other creditors of such estate in the like proportion.

(c) In such action, the plaintiff must pay the costs, unless he proves that he has exhibited his claim and demanded of the defendant his proportion of the dividend received by him before the commencement of the action. (Code 1852, §§ 1864-1866; Code 1867, §§ 2213-2215; Code 1876, §§ 2585-2587; Code 1886, §§ 2255-2257; Code 1896, §§ 323-325; Code 1907, §§ 2785-2787; Code 1923, §§ 6024-6026; Code 1940, T. 61, §§ 411-413.)

Cited in Clark v. Guard, 73 Ala. 456 (1882).

Division 4.

Settlement of Insolvent Estates.

Cited in Burk v. Jones, 13 Ala. 167 (1848); Carrington & Co. v. Manning, 13 Ala. 611 (1848); Lapsley v. Goldsby, 14 Ala. 73 (1848); Rutherford v. Branch Bank, 14 Ala. 92 (1848); Goodwin v. McGehee, 15 Ala. 232 (1849); Weaver v. Weaver, 23 Ala. 789 (1853);

McDougald v. Rutherford, 30 Ala. 253 (1857); Christian v. Morris, 50 Ala. 585 (1874); Eubank v. Clark, 78 Ala. 73 (1884).

Collateral references. — 34 C.J.S., Executors & Administrators, § 687.

§ 43-2-770. When settlement must be made.

Every executor or administrator of an insolvent estate must make a settlement of his accounts, as such, at such time as the court may appoint, not less than six months nor more than 12 months from the time the estate is declared insolvent. (Code 1852, § 1856; Code 1867, § 2205; Code 1876, § 2577; Code 1886, § 2247; Code 1896, § 315; Code 1907, § 2788; Code 1923, § 6027; Acts 1931, No. 729, p. 842; Code 1940, T. 61, § 414.)

§ 43-2-771. Decree.

At such settlement, the court must decree to each creditor whose claim has been allowed, as provided in this article, his proportion of all moneys then found due from such executor or administrator, reserving in his hands a ratable proportion of such moneys for such claims as may be then contested and undecided; and a similar settlement and distribution must be made at least every six months thereafter, at such times as the court may appoint, until the estate is finally settled and distributed. (Code 1852, § 1857; Code 1867, § 2206; Code 1876, § 2578; Code 1886, § 2248; Code 1896, § 316; Code 1907, § 2789; Code 1923, § 6028; Code 1940, T. 61, § 415.)

Execution may issue upon decree. — The decrees in favor of the creditors for their pro rata share under this section are in the nature of final decrees upon which execution may issue. Lehman v. Robertson, 84 Ala. 489, 4 So. 728 (1888).

Cited in Corr v. Shackelford, 68 Ala. 241 (1880); Otis v. McMillan & Sons, 70 Ala. 46 (1881); Clark v. Guard, 73 Ala. 456 (1882).

Division 5.

Sale of and Actions for Lands of Insolvent Estates.

§ 43-2-790. Application for order for sale — Generally.

On the application of an executor or administrator of an estate which has been declared insolvent for an order for the sale of lands belonging to the estate for the payment of debts, he shall be allowed to obtain such order without taking any evidence to show the necessity of such sale. (Code 1886, § 2258; Code 1896, § 326; Code 1907, § 2790; Code 1923, § 6029; Code 1940, T. 61, § 416.)

Decree of insolvency as proof of debts. — In Meadows v. Meadows, 78 Ala. 240 (1884), the supreme court treating this section said: "We think the legislative intent was to substitute the decree of insolvency for proof that there were debts of the estate to be paid, and that the personal assets were insufficient therefor." This holding was approved in King v. Gilreath, 154 Ala. 129, 45 So. 89 (1907). But it makes only a prima facie case, for to hold it conclusive would be, perhaps, to make it unconstitutional. Chandler v. Wynne, 85 Ala. 301, 4 So. 653 (1888). See also Henley v. Johnston, 134 Ala. 646, 32 So. 1009 (1902).

The administrator of an insolvent estate is unable to bind the estate by his contract, and therefore the estate cannot be "estopped" by his conduct. Batson v. Etheridge, 239 Ala. 535, 195 So. 873 (1940).

Sufficiency of petition. — A petition for sale of real estate which averred that some years before the estate had been regularly declared insolvent is sufficient to call into existence the jurisdiction of the probate court to sell the land. King v. Gilreath, 154 Ala. 129, 45 So. 89 (1907).

Record need not show that sale was necessary. — Under this section the failure of the record to show that evidence of the necessity for the sale was taken is not an irregularity. Friedman v. Shamblin, 117 Ala. 454, 23 So. 821 (1898).

Cited in Rucker v. Tennessee Coal, Iron & R.R., 176 Ala. 456, 58 So. 465 (1912); Loeb v. Callaway, 250 Ala. 524, 35 So. 2d 198 (1948).

§ 43-2-791. Same — Form and contents; verification; notice to heirs and devisees.

Such application shall be in writing, verified by affidavit, shall contain an accurate description of the lands sought to be sold and shall set forth the names and places of residence of the heirs or devisees and whether they are under or over the age of 19 years; and the court shall give notice to such heirs or devisees of the filing of such application and of the day appointed to hear the same by publication once a week for three successive weeks in some newspaper published in the county or, if none is published therein, in the newspaper published nearest to the courthouse of such county, by posting notice at the courthouse door for the same length of time and by forwarding notices to those whose places of residence are known. If any of the heirs or devisees are unknown, they may be made parties in the manner provided by section 43-2-447. (Code 1886, § 2259; Code 1896, § 327; Code 1907, § 2791; Code 1923, § 6030; Code 1940, T. 61, § 417.)

Nature of proceedings. — The proceeding hereunder is in rem and if the application contains the necessary averments to give the court jurisdiction, errors thereafter committed by the court, such as failure to notify the parties in adverse interest, or to appoint a guardian ad litem, will not render the order of sale void on collateral attack. Friedman v. Shamblin, 117 Ala. 454, 23 So. 821 (1898).

Evidence need not be taken. — This section, adopted while the preceding one was in force, must be construed as dispensing with the necessity of taking evidence when the application is made after the decree of insolvency, even though some of the heirs be minors. Friedman v. Shamblin, 117 Ala. 454, 23 So. 821 (1898).

§ 43-2-792. Action by administrator for recovery of lands.

The administrator of an insolvent estate may maintain an action for the recovery of lands of the estate in every case in which such action might be maintained by him if the estate was solvent. (Code 1867, § 2216; Code 1876, § 2588; Code 1886, § 2260; Code 1896, § 328; Code 1907, § 2792; Code 1923, § 6031; Code 1940, T. 61, § 418.)

Cited in Wilkins v. Sorrells, 45 Ala. 272 (1871); Landford v. Dunklin, 71 Ala. 594 (1882); Morgan v. Casey, 73 Ala. 222 (1882).

Division 6.

Report or Decree of Insolvency as Affecting Pending Civil Actions.

§ 43-2-810. Continuance upon showing of insolvency.

During the progress of any civil action against an executor or administrator, he may show that such estate has been reported insolvent; and, upon such showing, the case must be continued until the final disposition of such report. (Code 1852, § 1858; Code 1867, § 2207; Code 1876, § 2579; Code 1886, § 2249; Code 1896, § 317; Code 1907, § 2793; Code 1923, § 6032; Code 1940, T. 61, § 419.)

Administrator must be defendant. — This section and § 43-2-811 afford protection only where the administrator is defendant. McDonald v. Cox, 104 Ala. 379, 16 So. 113 (1893).

Failure to interpose defense. — In Lambert v. Mallett, 50 Ala. 73 (1873), it was said that, while the judgment is certainly conclusive of any defense the administrator might have interposed (under this section or § 43-2-811), if circumstances beyond his control have since made the estate insolvent, the administrator ought not, in good conscience, to be held personally accountable. Smith v. Alabama Great S.R.R., 212 Ala. 166, 102 So. 118 (1924).

Duty of sheriff to levy. — But so long as the judgment stands against the administrator it is conclusive, and it is the duty of the sheriff to make levy when he holds execution against him. In other words, the refuge of this section and § 43-2-811 afforded the administrator does not affect the sheriff's liability for failure to make levy. Smith v. Alabama Great S.R.R., 212 Ala. 166, 102 So. 118 (1924).

Cited in Murdock v. Rousseau, 32 Ala. 611 (1858); Gamble v. Dunklin & Co., 48 Ala. 425 (1872); Cunningham v. Lindsay, 77 Ala. 510 (1884).

§ 43-2-811. Special plea of insolvency.

The executor or administrator may, at any time before judgment, plead specially that the estate has been declared insolvent; and, in such case, the other issues must be tried and judgment entered thereon. (Code 1852, § 1859; Code 1867, § 2208; Code 1876, § 2580; Code 1886, § 2250; Code 1896, § 318; Code 1907, § 2794; Code 1923, § 6033; Code 1940, T. 61, § 420.)

Cross references. — See notes to § 43-2-810. As to appeals from final judgments or decrees against insolvent estates, see § 12-22-2 and notes thereto.

Nature of plea. — Even though a plea of insolvency does not answer the whole complaint or any certain part of it, and though it does not constitute a plea in bar, it is something more than a mere suggestion, and should be allowed to remain on file. Therefore, judgment on demurrer (now motion to dismiss) which took the plea from the files was error. Lavergne v. Evans Bros. Constr. Co., 166 Ala. 289, 52 So. 318 (1910).

Cited in Godbold v. Roberts, 7 Ala. 662 (1845); Desha v. Holland, 12 Ala. 513 (1847); Crothers v. Ross, 17 Ala. 816 (1850); Bartol v. Calvert, 21 Ala. 42 (1852); Lee v. Leachman, 22 Ala. 452 (1853); McEachin v. Reid, 40 Ala. 410 (1867); Erwin v. McGuire, 44 Ala. 499 (1870); Nunn v. Givham, 45 Ala. 370 (1871); Gamble v. Dunklin & Co., 48 Ala. 425 (1872); Nicholson v. Mobile, etc., R. Co., 49 Ala. 205 (1873); Christian v. Morris, 50 Ala. 585 (1874).

§ 43-2-812. Judgment certified to probate court; execution for costs.

If such judgment is for the plaintiff, and it is shown to the court that such estate has been declared insolvent, an order must be made to the effect that no execution issue on such judgment, but that the same be certified to the proper probate court. Upon a certified copy of such judgment being filed as a claim against the estate, it must be allowed with the costs against such estate, unless shown to have been obtained by collusion; and when such judgment is certified, the clerk may demand of the plaintiff payment of all costs incurred in obtaining the same. If the plaintiff fails for 20 days after the judgment is so certified to pay such costs, execution may issue against him for the same as in other cases. (Code 1852, § 1860; Code 1867, § 2209; Code 1876, § 2581; Code 1886, § 2251; Code 1896, § 319; Code 1907, § 2795; Code 1923, § 6034; Code 1940, T. 61, § 421.)

Cross references. — See notes to §§ 43-2-810 and 43-2-811.

This section applies to judgments obtained after the estate is declared insolvent, and the next section applies to judgments before decree of insolvency. Ouchita Nat'l Bank v. Fulton, 195 Ala. 34, 70 So. 722 (1916).

Satisfaction of judgment. — Judgments under this section are certified to the court of probate for equal allowance with the other debts of the insolvent estate, and shares only pari passu with them in the disbursement. Chandler v. Wynne, 85 Ala. 301, 4 So. 653 (1888).

Judgment under this section will support an appeal. — A judgment under this section is a settlement of the rights litigated between the parties and possesses the characteristics of a final judgment so as to support an appeal. Coffey v. Norwood, 81 Ala. 512, 3 So. 8, 8 So. 199 (1887).

Cited in Leigh v. Smith, 5 Ala. 583 (1843); Cogburn v. McQueen, 46 Ala. 551 (1871); McKinney v. Benagh, 48 Ala. 358 (1872); Gamble v. Dunklin & Co., 48 Ala. 425 (1872); Dudley v. Witter, 51 Ala. 456 (1874); Seals v. Holloway, 77 Ala. 344 (1884).

§ 43-2-813. Effect of order or decree of insolvency certified to other courts after judgment or decree therein rendered.

After judgment or decree has been rendered in any court against an executor or administrator for any debt, damages or costs, if the estate is subsequently declared insolvent, such personal representative may file a certified copy of the decree or order of the probate court declaring such estate insolvent with the clerk or register of the court in which such judgment or decree was rendered against the personal representative; whereupon, it shall be the duty of such clerk or register to certify back to the probate court a copy of such judgment or decree for payment in the probate court as other claims against insolvent estates, after which no execution shall issue or be further enforced against such executor or administrator or sureties personally by the court rendering such judgment or decree. (Code 1907, § 2796; Code 1923, § 6035; Code 1940, T. 61, § 422.)

Section is valid. — The validity of this section is not subject to question. Fulton v. Eggler, 200 Ala. 269, 76 So. 35 (1917).

Purpose of this section. — This section was evidently intended, not only to relieve administrators from personal liability upon such judgments after complying with same, reconciling on this point, Woodall v. Wright, 142 Ala. 205, 37 So. 846 (1904), but also to make the judgment a fixed charge against the estate, and requiring the "payment" of same as other claims are paid, that is, in the same proportion.

Ouchita Nat'l Bank v. Fulton, 195 Ala. 34, 70 So. 722 (1916).

Judgment is incontestable in probate court. — The judgment under this section need not be established or proved, but must be certified for payment, which in effect makes it incontestable in the probate court as authorized by § 43-2-812 as the judgments obtained under § 43-2-811. Ouchita Nat'l Bank v. Fulton, 195 Ala. 34, 70 So. 722 (1916). Whether such judgments could be contested in some other tribunal for fraud or collusion is not decided by the court. This stated construction of the section is expressly approved in Fulton v. Eggler, 200 Ala. 269, 76 So. 35 (1917).

Applicable in circuit court. — The application and effect of this section is not confined to the administration of an estate in a probate court but follows the estate upon its removal into the circuit court. Fulton v. Eggler, 200 Ala. 269, 76 So. 35 (1917).

CHAPTER 3.

TRANSFERRED AND REPEALED.

Article 1.

Descents.

Article 2.

Advancements.

ARTICLE 1.

DESCENTS.

§§ 43-3-1 through 43-3-12. Repealed by Acts 1982, No. 82-399, § 8-102, effective January 1, 1983.

ARTICLE 2.

ADVANCEMENTS.

§§ 43-3-30 through 43-3-34. Repealed by Acts 1982, No. 82-399, § 8-102, effective January 1, 1983.

§ 43-3-35. Transferred.

Code commissioner's note. — Section 43-3-35, as set out in the original 1975 Code, has been renumbered as § 43-8-50.

§ 43-3-36. Transferred.

Code commissioner's note. Section 43-3-36, as set out in the original 1975 Code, has been renumbered as § 43-8-51.

§ 43-3-37. Transferred.

Code commissioner's note. — Section 43-3-37, as set out in the original 1975 Code, has been renumbered as § 43-8-52.

§ 43-3-38. Transferred.

Code commissioner's note. — Section 43-3-38, as set out in the original 1975 Code, has been renumbered as § 43-8-53.

§ 43-3-39. Transferred.

Code commissioner's note. — Section
43-3-39, as set out in the original 1975 Code,
has been renumbered as § 43-8-54.

CHAPTER 4.

ADOPTION OF ADULTS FOR PURPOSES OF INHERITANCE.

Cross references. — As to adoption of children, see § 26-10-1 et seq.

Collateral references. — Modern status of law as to equitable adoption or adoption by estoppel. 97 ALR3d 347.

§ 43-4-1. Petition for order of adoption; recordation of order.

Any resident of Alabama over the age of 19 years desiring to adopt another adult person so as to make such person capable of inheriting his real and personal estate may file a petition for an order of adoption in the office of the probate judge of the county where he resides. Such petition shall be attested by two witnesses and acknowledged by the petitioner before the judge of probate and shall contain the name, sex and age of the person to be adopted, and the name the petitioner wishes such person to be known by. The petition for adoption shall be accompanied by the notarized written consent to the adoption by the person to be adopted. After the filing of the petition for adoption and the filing of the consent of the person to be adopted the probate judge shall make an order of adoption in accordance with the petition. The order, the petition, and the consent shall be recorded in the office of the judge of probate and be made a permanent record therein. (Acts 1973, No. 1083, p. 1843, § 1.)

Cross references. — As to transfer of adoption proceedings from probate court to district court, see § 12-12-35.

Cited in Gissendanner v. Slade, 382 So. 2d 1127 (Ala. 1980).

Collateral references. — 2 C.J.S., Adoption of Persons, §§ 57, 133, 153.

2 Am. Jur. 2d, Adoption, § 11.

Adoption of adult. 21 ALR3d 1012.

§ 43-4-2. Notice of order to registrar of vital statistics.

Upon the entry of a final order of adoption under this chapter, the judge or the clerk of the court shall notify the registrar of vital statistics of the state board of health and send such registrar a copy of such order, petition and consent. (Acts 1973, No. 1083, p. 1843, § 2.)

§ 43-4-3. Relationship of adopted person to adopter and children of adopter; rights of inheritance of adopted person and descendants; right of inheritance from natural parents not barred.

For the purposes of inheritance of property under the laws of descent and distribution, an adopted person shall bear the same relation to his adopter and the natural and adopted children of the adopter as if he were the natural child of such adopting person. It is intended hereby to give an adopted person all right of inheritance from the person who adopts him and through him from his natural and adopted children, and to give to the adopting person and his natural and adopted kindred all rights of inheritance from the adopted person and his descendants, including adopted children, the same as if such adopted person were born to the adopting person as a legitimate child. An adopted person's surviving spouse and descendants, including adopted children, shall inherit through such adopted person from the adopting person and his children the same as if he were born to the adopting person in lawful wedlock. Where an adopter is the spouse of a natural parent of an adopted child, such natural and adopted parent and kindred shall inherit from the adopted child the same as natural parents and kindred unless otherwise specifically provided in the final decree of adoption. Nothing in this chapter shall be construed as debarring a legally adopted person from inheriting property from his natural parents or other kin. (Acts 1973, No. 1083, p. 1843, § 3.)

Cross references. — As to disclaimer of any property, property right, or interest in property, see § 43-8-290 et seq.

Collateral references. — 2 C.J.S., Adoption of Persons, §§ 145-151.

What law in point of time governs as to inheritance from or through adoptive parent. 18 ALR2d 960.

Right of adopted child to inherit from kindred of adoptive parent. 43 ALR2d 1183.

What law in point of time governs inheritance from or through adopted person. 52 ALR2d 1228.

Conflict of laws as to adoption as affecting descent and distribution of decedent's estate. 87 ALR2d 1240.

Right of children of adopted child to inherit from adopting parent. 94 ALR2d 1200.

Right of adopted child to inherit from intestate natural grandparent. 60 ALR3d 631.

§ 43-4-4. Prior vested rights not affected.

The provisions of this chapter shall not be construed to affect adversely any rights which have vested prior to the effective date of its enactment, and nothing herein shall be considered to change, modify or repeal in any respect the provisions of chapter 10 of Title 26 of this Code relating to the adoption of minor children. (Acts 1973, No. 1083, p. 1843, § 4.)

Collateral references. — Adoption as affecting right of inheritance through or from natural parent or other natural kin. 37 ALR2d 333.

CHAPTER 5.

TRANSFERRED AND REPEALED.

Cross references. — As to abolition of dower and curtesy, see § 43-8-57.

ARTICLE 1.

GENERAL PROVISIONS.

§§ 43-5-1 through 43-5-5. Repealed by Acts 1982, No. 82-399, § 8-102, effective January 1, 1983.

ARTICLE 2.

RELINQUISHMENT.

§§ 43-5-20 through 43-5-23. Repealed by Acts 1982, No. 82-399, § 8-102, effective January 1, 1983.

ARTICLE 3.

ASSIGNMENT.

§ 43-5-40. Transferred.

Code commissioner's note. — Section 43-5-40, as set out in the original 1975 Code, has been renumbered as § 43-8-114.

§§ 43-5-41 through 43-5-53. Repealed by Acts 1982, No. 82-399, § 8-102, effective January 1, 1983.

CHAPTER 6.

ESCHEATS.

Constitution. — For constitutional provision as to disposition of estates of deceased persons who die without leaving a will or heir, see Const., § 258, as amended by Amendment No. 111.

Duty of administrator. — Under this chapter it is the duty and right of an administrator to see that estate property goes to the person entitled thereto, and although an order of the probate court dismissing his escheat proceedings, and finding that the property descended to certain claimants would protect him, yet he may appeal therefrom. McKenzie v. Jensen, 195 Ala. 36, 70 So. 678 (1916).

Cited in Hammett v. Smith, 5 Ala. 156 (1843); Hitchcock v. United States Bank, 7 Ala. 386 (1845); Harrison v. Harrison, 9 Ala. 470 (1846); Kelly v. Kelly, 9 Ala. 908 (1846); Fowler v. Trewhit, 10 Ala. 622 (1846); McMekin v. Bobo, 12 Ala. 268 (1847); Roberts v. Trawick, 13 Ala. 68 (1848); Carrington & Co. v. Manning, 13 Ala. 611 (1848); Jones v. Deyer, 16 Ala. 221 (1849); Crothers v. Ross, 17 Ala. 816 (1850); Coster v. Brack, 19 Ala. 210 (1851); Denson v. Autrey, 21 Ala. 205 (1852); Lightfoot v. Lightfoot, 27 Ala. 351 (1855); Van Wagner v. Chapman, 29 Ala. 172 (1856); Matheson v. Hearin, 29 Ala. 210 (1856); Horton v. Sledge, 29 Ala. 478 (1856); King v. Kent, 29 Ala. 542 (1857); Jay v. Martin, 49 Ala. 192 (1873); Kelly v. Garrett, 67 Ala. 304 (1880); McKenzie v. Jensen, 212 Ala. 92, 101 So. 755 (1924); Morgan County Nat'l Bank v. Nelson, 244 Ala. 374, 13 So. 2d 765 (1943).

Collateral references. — 30A C.J.S., Escheat, §§ 1-4.

27 Am. Jur. 2d, Escheats, § 1 et seq.

Unclaimed deposits required by public utility. 43 ALR2d 1276.

Escheat of estate of illegitimate. 48 ALR2d 778.

Escheat of personal property of intestate domiciled or resident in other state. 50 ALR2d 1375.

§ 43-6-1. Repealed by Acts 1982, No. 82-399, § 8-102, effective January 1, 1983.

Cross references. — For provision relating to subject matter of repealed section, see § 43-8-44.

§ 43-6-2. Notice by representative.

The personal representative of any person leaving property not devised or bequeathed, or where the devisees or legatees are incapable of taking and such representative is unable to ascertain any lawful heirs or distributees or persons capable of taking within six months after the grant of letters testamentary or of administration, must give notice thereof in some newspaper published in the state once a week for three successive weeks; but it shall not be necessary for any personal representative to institute escheat proceedings under this chapter until the debts of the decedent have been paid. (Code 1852, § 2065; Code 1867, § 2457; Code 1876, § 2852; Code 1886, § 1937; Code 1896, § 1753; Code 1907, § 3919; Code 1923, § 7615; Code 1940, T. 16, § 26.)

§ 43-6-3. Contents of notice.

Such notice must contain the name of the deceased, as near as may be, a description of his person, the place where he was or is supposed to have been born, the place where he died, or was known to reside, and a description of the property of which he died seised and possessed. (Code 1852, § 2066; Code 1867, § 2458; Code 1876, § 2853; Code 1886, § 1938; Code 1896, § 1754; Code 1907, § 3920; Code 1923, § 7616; Code 1940, T. 16, § 27.)

Cited in Bibb v. Bishop Cobbs Orphan Home, 61 Ala. 326 (1878).

Collateral references. — Necessity and sufficiency of notice to support title by escheat to defendant's estate. 48 ALR 1342.

§ 43-6-4. Disposition of personalty when no heir appears.

If no heir or person entitled to receive such estate appears or is ascertained within 12 months after such publication, the money and proceeds of the personal assets must be paid to the judge of probate, after deducting the expenses of administration. (Code 1852, § 2067; Code 1867, § 2459; Code 1876, § 2854; Code 1886, § 1939; Code 1896, § 1755; Code 1907, § 3921; Code 1923, § 7617; Code 1940, T. 16, § 28.)

Collateral references. — 30A C.J.S., Escheat, § 20.
27 Am. Jur. 2d, Escheats, § 40 et seq.

§ 43-6-5. Disposition of real estate when no heir appears.

If, after two years from the publication of such notice, no heir or person entitled to receive such estate appears, the real estate must be sold by such personal representative, under the direction of the judge of probate of the county in which letters testamentary or of administration were granted and upon such notice as real estate is sold by executors and administrators; and the proceeds thereof must, after deducting all expenses and allowances, be paid to such judge. (Code 1852, § 2068; Code 1867, § 2460; Code 1876, § 2855; Code 1886, § 1940; Code 1896, § 1756; Code 1907, § 3922; Code 1923, § 7618; Code 1940, T. 16, § 29.)

Collateral references. — 30A C.J.S., Escheat, § 20.
27 Am. Jur. 2d, Escheats, § 40 et seq.

§ 43-6-6. Decree against personal representative for failure to pay over proceeds.

The judge of probate may render decrees against such personal representative, in the name of the state, for the money or proceeds of the property, under the provisions of this chapter, and enforce the same as other decrees by the judge of probate against executors or administrators are enforced. (Code 1852, § 2069; Code 1867, § 2461; Code 1876, § 2856; Code 1886, § 1941; Code 1896, § 1757; Code 1907, § 3923; Code 1923, § 7619; Code 1940, T. 16, § 30.)

Collateral references. — 30A C.J.S., Escheat, § 20.

§ 43-6-7. Payment of receipts to state treasurer.

The judge of probate must, within three months after the receipt thereof, pay to the treasurer all moneys he may receive under the provisions of this chapter, and, failing so to do, he is liable as a defaulter and also forfeits $300.00, one half to the state, and the other half to any one suing for the same; and, on the trial, the certificate of the treasurer is presumptive evidence of his failure to make such payment. (Code 1852, § 2070; Code 1867, § 2462; Code 1876, § 2857; Code 1886, § 1942; Code 1896, § 1758; Code 1907, § 3924; Code 1923, § 7620; Code 1940, T. 16, § 31.)

Collateral references. — 30A C.J.S., Escheat, § 20.

§ 43-6-8. Action by state to recover personal property distributed without authority.

The state may enforce its right to any personal property to which it is entitled under the provisions of this chapter by action against any person into whose possession the same may come; and, if any personal representative pays any money or delivers any property to which the state is, under the provisions of this chapter, entitled, to any person not authorized to receive the same, such personal representative and his sureties are liable to the state for the amount of such money or value of such property and interest thereon from the time of such payment or delivery. (Code 1852, § 2072; Code 1867, § 2464; Code 1876, § 2858; Code 1886, § 1943; Code 1896, § 1759; Code 1907, § 3925; Code 1923, § 7621; Code 1940, T. 16, § 32.)

Collateral references. — 30A C.J.S., Escheat, § 20.
Necessity of judicial proceeding to vest title to real property in state by escheat. 23 ALR 1237, 79 ALR 1364.

§ 43-6-9. Duty of probate judge to attend to interest of state.

It is the official duty of the judge of probate of each county to attend to the interest of the state intended to be secured by the provisions of this chapter. (Code 1852, § 2073; Code 1867, § 2465; Code 1876, § 2859; Code 1886, § 1944; Code 1896, § 1760; Code 1907, § 3926; Code 1923, § 7622; Code 1940, T. 16, § 33.)

CHAPTER 7.

UNIFORM SIMULTANEOUS DEATH ACT.

Collateral references. — 22 Am. Jur. 2d, Death, §§ 297, 298, 314. 23 Am. Jur. 2d, Descent & Distribution, § 103.

Construction, application, and effect of Uniform Simultaneous Death Act. 39 ALR3d 1332.

§ 43-7-1. Short title.

This chapter may be cited as the Uniform Simultaneous Death Act. (Acts 1949, No. 542, p. 852, § 8.)

§ 43-7-2. No sufficient evidence of survivorship; disposition of property of decedents.

Where the title to property or the devolution thereof depends upon priority of death and there is no sufficient evidence that the persons have died otherwise than simultaneously, the property of each person shall be disposed of as if he had survived, except as provided otherwise in this chapter. (Acts 1949, No. 542, p. 852, § 1.)

Collateral references. — 26A C.J.S., Descent & Distribution, § 10.

§ 43-7-3. Beneficiaries of another person's disposition of property.

Where two or more beneficiaries are designated to take successively by reason of survivorship under another person's disposition of property and there is no sufficient evidence that these beneficiaries have died otherwise than simultaneously, the property thus disposed of shall be divided into as many equal portions as there are successive beneficiaries and these portions shall be distributed respectively to those who would have taken in the event that each designated beneficiary had survived. (Acts 1949, No. 542, p. 852, § 2.)

§ 43-7-4. Joint tenants or tenants by the entirety.

Where there is no sufficient evidence that two joint tenants or tenants by the entirety have died otherwise than simultaneously, the property so held shall be distributed one half as if one had survived and one half as if the other had survived. If there are more than two joint tenants and all of them have so died, the property thus distributed shall be in the proportion that one bears to the whole number of joint tenants. (Acts 1949, No. 542, p. 852, § 3.)

§ 43-7-5. Insurance policies.

Where the insured and the beneficiary in a policy of life or accident insurance have died and there is no sufficient evidence that they have died otherwise than simultaneously, the proceeds of the policy shall be distributed as if the insured had survived the beneficiary. (Acts 1949, No. 542, p. 852, § 4.)

Court must be reasonably satisfied that beneficiary survived the insured. — The court, before it can decide in favor of the personal representative of the deceased beneficiary, must be reasonably satisfied from the evidence that she survived the insured. Liberty Nat'l Life Ins. Co. v. Brown, 119 F. Supp. 920 (M.D. Ala. 1954).

§ 43-7-6. Chapter not retroactive.

This chapter shall not apply to the distribution of the property of a person who died before September 7, 1949. (Acts 1949, No. 542, p. 852, § 5.)

§ 43-7-7. Chapter not applicable if decedent provides otherwise.

This chapter shall not apply in the case of wills, living trusts, deeds or contracts of insurance wherein provision has been made for distribution of property different from the provisions of this chapter or wherein provision is made for a presumption as to the order of survivorship if there is no sufficient evidence that the persons died otherwise than simultaneously, in which event full effect shall be given to the presumption so provided as to the order of survivorship. (Acts 1949, No. 542, p. 852, § 6; Acts 1951, No. 949, p. 1619.)

Collateral references. — Construction of provision as to which of two or more parties shall be deemed the survivor in case of death simultaneously, in a common disaster, or within a specified period of time. 40 ALR3d 359.

§ 43-7-8. Uniformity of interpretation.

This chapter shall be so construed and interpreted as to effectuate its general purpose to make uniform the law in those states which enact it. (Acts 1949, No. 542, p. 852, § 7.)

CHAPTER 8.

PROBATE CODE.

Effective date. — The act which added this chapter became effective January 1, 1983. For special transition provisions, see § 43-8-8.

ARTICLE 1.

GENERAL PROVISIONS.

§ 43-8-1. General definitions.

Subject to additional definitions contained in the subsequent articles which are applicable to specific articles or divisions, and unless the context otherwise requires, in this chapter, the following words shall have the following meanings:

(1) BENEFICIARY. As it relates to trust beneficiaries, includes a person who has any present or future interest, vested or contingent, and also includes the owner of an interest by assignment or other transfer and as it relates to a charitable trust, includes any person entitled to enforce the trust.

(2) CHILD. Includes any individual entitled to take as a child under this chapter by intestate succession from the parent whose relationship is involved and excludes any person who is only a stepchild, a foster child, a grandchild or any more remote descendant.

(3) COURT. The court having jurisdiction in matters relating to the affairs of decedents. This court in Alabama is known as the probate court.

(4) DAYS. That period of time as computed in accordance with section 1-1-4 and Rule 6(a), Alabama Rules of Civil Procedure.

(5) DEVISE. When used as a noun, means a testamentary disposition of real or personal property and when used as a verb, means to dispose of real or personal property by will.

(6) DEVISEE. Any person designated in a will to receive a devise. In the case of a devise to an existing trust or trustee, or to a trustee or trust described by will, the trust or trustee is the devisee and the beneficiaries are not devisees.

(7) DISTRIBUTEE. Any person who has received property of a decedent from his personal representative other than as creditor or purchaser. A testamentary trustee is a distributee only to the extent of distributed assets or increment thereto remaining in his hands. A beneficiary of a testamentary trust to whom the trustee has distributed property received from a personal representative is a distributee of the personal representative. For purposes of this provision, "testamentary trustee" includes a trustee to whom assets are transferred by will, to the extent of the devised assets.

(8) ESTATE. Includes the property of the decedent whose affairs are subject to this chapter as originally constituted and as it exists from time to time during administration.

(9) EXEMPT PROPERTY. That property of a decedent's estate which is described in section 43-8-111.

(10) FIDUCIARY. Includes personal representative, guardian and trustee.

(11) FOREIGN PERSONAL REPRESENTATIVE. A personal representative of another jurisdiction.

(12) GUARDIAN. A person who has qualified as a guardian of a minor or incompetent person pursuant to testamentary or court appointment, but excludes one who is merely a guardian ad litem.

(13) HEIRS. Those persons, including the surviving spouse, who are entitled under the statutes of intestate succession to the property of a decedent.

(14) INTERESTED PERSON. Any person having an enforceable right or claim, which may be affected by the proceeding, and may include heirs, devisees, children, spouses, creditors, beneficiaries and any others having a property right in or claim against a trust estate or the estate of a decedent which may be affected by the proceeding. "Interested person" also includes persons having priority for appointment as personal representative, and other fiduciaries representing interested persons. The meaning of "interested person" as it relates to particular persons may vary from time to time and must be determined according to the particular purposes of, and matter involved in, any proceeding.

(15) ISSUE OF A PERSON. All his lineal descendants of all generations, with the relationship of parent and child at each generation being determined by the definitions of child and parent contained in this chapter.

(16) LEASE. Includes an oil, gas, or other mineral lease.

(17) LETTERS. Includes letters testamentary and letters of administration.

(18) MINOR. A person who is under 19 years of age.

(19) MORTGAGE. Any conveyance, agreement or arrangement in which property is used as security.

(20) NONRESIDENT DECEDENT. A decedent who was domiciled in another jurisdiction at the time of his death.

(21) ORGANIZATION. Includes a corporation, government or governmental subdivision or agency, business trust, estate, trust, partnership or association, two or more persons having a joint or common interest, or any other legal entity.

639

(22) PARENT. Includes any person entitled to take, or who would be entitled to take if the child died without a will, as a parent under this chapter by intestate succession from the child whose relationship is in question and excludes any person who is only a stepparent, foster parent, or grandparent.

(23) PERSON. An individual, a corporation, an organization, or other legal entity.

(24) PERSONAL REPRESENTATIVE. Includes executor, administrator, successor personal representative, special administrator, and persons who perform substantially the same function under the law governing their status.

(25) PROPERTY. Includes both real and personal property or any interest therein and means anything that may be the subject of ownership.

(26) SECURITY. Includes any note, stock, treasury stock, bond, debenture, evidence of indebtedness, certificate of interest or participation in an oil, gas or mining title or lease or in payments out of production under such a title or lease, collateral trust certificate, transferable share, voting trust certificate, or, in general, any interest or instrument commonly known as a security, or any certificate of interest or participation, any temporary or interim certificate, receipt or certificate of deposit for, or any warrant or right to subscribe to or purchase, any of the foregoing.

(27) SETTLEMENT. In reference to a decedent's estate, includes the full process of administration, distribution, accounting and closing.

(28) STATE. Includes any state of the United States, the District of Columbia, the Commonwealth of Puerto Rico, and any territory or possession subject to the legislative authority of the United States.

(29) SUCCESSOR PERSONAL REPRESENTATIVE. A personal representative who is appointed to succeed a previously appointed personal representative.

(30) SUCCESSORS. Those persons, other than creditors, who are entitled to property of a decedent under his will or this chapter.

(31) TESTACY PROCEEDING. A proceeding to establish a will or determine intestacy.

(32) TRUST. Includes any express trust, private or charitable, with additions thereto, wherever and however created. It also includes a trust created or determined by judgment or decree under which the trust is to be administered in the manner of an express trust. "Trust" excludes other constructive trusts, and it excludes resulting trusts, guardianships, curatorships, personal representatives, custodial arrangements pursuant to chapter 5 of Title 35, business trusts providing for certificates to be issued to beneficiaries, common trust funds, voting trusts, security arrangements, liquidation trusts, and trusts for the primary purpose of paying debts, dividends, interest, salaries, wages, profits, pensions, or employee benefits of any kind, and any arrangement under which a person is nominee or escrowee for another.

(33) TRUSTEE. Includes an original, additional, or successor trustee, whether or not appointed or confirmed by court.

(34) WILL. Includes codicil and any testamentary instrument which merely appoints an executor or revokes or revises another will. (Acts 1982, No. 82-399, § 1-201.)

Commentary

The definitions contained in this section are adopted substantially from the Uniform Probate Code (UPC) § 1-201. Where Alabama terminology is clearly different, the definitions have been adapted to use Alabama terminology, but those instances are few. Prior to enactment of this act, Title 43 of the Alabama Code 1975 did not have a comparable definitions section, but the definitions that are codified in this section generally are consistent with the use of the terms in Title 43.

Collateral references. — 96 C.J.S., Wills, §§ 20, 117, 134, 148, 315, 317, 322, 323, 359, 371, 423, 425, 434, 516, 550, 578, 613, 643 to 718, 748, 788, 1004 to 1061, 1082, 1088, 1129. 39 Am. Jur. 2d, Guardians and Wards, § 11;

79 Am. Jur. 2d, Wills, §§ 23, 27, 28, 38, 39, 125, 178 to 182, 191, 841, 842; 80 Am. Jur. 2d, Wills, §§ 882, 900, 1098 to 1121, 1164, 1192, 1195, 1216 to 1221, 1515, 1536, 1667, 1755.

§ 43-8-2. Construction of chapter; purposes and policies.

(a) This chapter shall be liberally construed and applied to promote its underlying purposes and policies.

(b) The underlying purposes and policies of this chapter are:

(1) To simplify and clarify the law concerning the affairs of decedents;

(2) To discover and make effective the intent of a decedent in the distribution of his property. (Acts 1982, No. 82-399, § 1-102.)

Collateral references. — 82 C.J.S., Statutes, §§ 371-373.

73 Am. Jur. 2d, Statutes, §§ 32, 161-167.

§ 43-8-3. Supplementary effect of principles of law and equity.

Unless displaced by the particular provisions of this chapter, the principles of law and equity supplement its provisions. (Acts 1982, No. 82-399, § 1-103.)

§ 43-8-4. Construction against implied repeal.

This chapter is a general act intended as a unified coverage of its subject matter and no part of it shall be deemed impliedly repealed by subsequent legislation if it can reasonably be avoided. (Acts 1982, No. 82-399, § 1-105.)

Collateral references. — § 2 C.J.S., Statutes, §§ 292, 300.

73 Am. Jur. 2d, Statutes, §§ 392-407.

§ 43-8-5. Relief against fraud; limitations.

Whenever fraud has been perpetrated in connection with any proceeding or in any statement filed under this chapter or if fraud is used to avoid or circumvent the provisions or purposes of this chapter, any person injured thereby may obtain appropriate relief against the perpetrator of the fraud or restitution from any person (other than a bona fide purchaser) benefitting from the fraud, whether innocent or not. Any proceeding must be commenced within one year after the discovery of the fraud or from the time when the fraud should have been discovered, but no proceeding may be brought against one not a perpetrator of the fraud later than five years after the time of the commission of the fraud. This section has no bearing on remedies relating to fraud practiced on a decedent during his lifetime which affects the succession of his estate. (Acts 1982, No. 82-399, § 1-106.)

Commentary

This is an overriding provision that provides an exception to the procedures and limitations provided in this act or otherwise in the Code of Alabama. The remedy of a party wronged by fraud is intended to be supplementary to other protections provided in this act and can be maintained outside the process of settlement of the estate. Thus, if a will which is known to be a forgery is probated, and the forgery is not discovered until after the period for contest has run, the defrauded heirs still could bring a fraud action under this section. If a will is fraudulently concealed after the testator's death and its existence not discovered until after the basic five year period under Alabama law has elapsed, there still may be an action under this section. However, if there is fraudulent misrepresentation or concealment in the preparation of the claim, a later suit may be brought under this section against the personal representative for damages; or restitution may be obtained from those distributees who benefit by the fraud. In any case innocent purchasers for value are protected.

Any action under this section is subject to usual rules of res judicata; thus, if an heir discovers the forgery, and then there is a formal probate proceeding of which the heir is given notice, followed by an order of complete settlement of the estate, the heir could not bring a subsequent action under this section but would be bound by the litigation in which the issue could have been raised.

The usual rules for securing relief for fraud on a court would govern, however.

The final limitation in this section is designed to protect innocent distributees after a reasonable period of time. There is no limit (other than the one year from discovery of the fraud) against the wrongdoer. But there ought to be some limit after which innocent persons who have built up expectations in good faith cannot be deprived of the property by a restitution action.

The time of "discovery" of a fraud is a fact question to be determined in the individual case. In some situations persons may not actually know that a fraud has been perpetrated but have such strong suspicion and evidence that a court may conclude there has been a discovery of the fraud at that stage. On the other hand there is no duty to exercise reasonable care to discover fraud; the burden should not be on the heirs and devisees to check on the honesty of the other interested persons or the fiduciary.

The Uniform Probate Code (UPC) provides for commencing a proceeding within two years after the discovery of the fraud. This time limitation has been changed in the Alabama Probate Code to one year after discovery to be consistent with § 6-2-3 (1975).

Collateral references. — 37 C.J.S., Fraud, §§ 1-45, 70-73.

37 Am. Jur. 2d, Fraud and Deceit, §§ 1-19.

Person taking under probate of forged or fraudulent will as trustee ex maleficio. 52 ALR 779.

Concealment of or failure to disclose existence of person interested in estate as extrinsic fraud which will support attack on judgment in probate proceedings. 113 ALR 1235.

Statute limiting time for probate of will as applicable to will probated in another jurisdiction. 87 ALR2d 721.

What circumstances excuse failure to submit will for probate within time limit set by statute. 17 ALR3d 1361.

§ 43-8-6. Rules of evidence; evidence as to death or status; presumption of death.

In proceedings under this chapter the rules of evidence in courts of general jurisdiction including any relating to simultaneous deaths, are applicable unless specifically displaced by the chapter. In addition, the following rules relating to determination of death and status are applicable:

(1) A certified or authenticated copy of a death certificate purporting to be issued by an official or agency of the place where the death purportedly occurred is prima facie proof of the fact, place, date and time of death and the identity of the decedent;

(2) A certified or authenticated copy of any record or report of a governmental agency, domestic or foreign, that a person is missing, detained, dead, or alive is prima facie evidence of the status and of the dates, circumstances and places disclosed by the record or report;

(3) A person who is absent for a continuous period of five years, during which he has not been heard from, and whose absence is not satisfactorily explained after diligent search or inquiry is presumed to be dead. His death is presumed to have occurred at the end of the period unless there is sufficient evidence for determining that death occurred earlier. (Acts 1982, No. 82-399, § 1-107.)

Commentary

Subdivisions (1) and (2) are consistent with Ala. R. Civ. P. 44. Subdivision (2) is consistent with §§ 12-21-90 and 12-21-91 (1975).

Subdivision (3) is inconsistent with section 1 of the Uniform Absence as Evidence of Death and Absentees' Property Act (1938). It is also inconsistent with § 43-2-231 (1975) which provides for a presumption of death after seven years absence from the place of last domicile in this state. Recent revisions of statutes have tended to shorten the period after which there is a presumption. Preexisting Alabama law was also ambiguous if taken literally. Therefore, this section adopts the five-year period of the UPC.

The preliminary paragraph is designed to accommodate the Uniform Simultaneous Death Act, which is codified as §§ 43-7-1 through 43-7-8 (1975).

Collateral references. — 25A C.J.S., Death, §§ 6-10.

22 Am. Jur. 2d, Death and Death Actions, §§ 299-303.

Death certificate as evidence. 17 ALR 359; 42 ALR 1454; 96 ALR 324.

§ 43-8-7. Effect of acts by holder of general power of appointment, etc., on beneficiaries.

For the purpose of granting consent or approval with regard to the acts or accounts of a personal representative or trustee, including relief from liability or penalty for failure to post bond, or to perform other duties, and for purposes of consenting to modification or termination of a trust or to deviation from its terms, the sole holder or all co-holders of a presently exercisable general power of appointment, including one in the form of a power of amendment or revocation, are deemed to act for beneficiaries to the extent their interests (as objects, takers in default, or otherwise) are subject to the power. (Acts 1982, No. 82-399, § 1-108.)

Commentary

"General power" as used in this section, is intended to refer to the common law concept, rather than to tax or other statutory meanings. A general power, as used herein, is one which enables the power holder to draw absolute ownership to himself.

There was no comparable provision formerly in the Alabama Code, but this provision is an attempt to codify common law. This section is designed to supplement rather than to change preexisting Alabama law.

Collateral references. — 72 C.J.S., Powers, §§ 30, 50.

62 Am. Jur. 2d, Powers, §§ 39-46.

Share of beneficiary of trust or of decedent's estate, who is also trustee or executor or administrator, as subject to charge in respect of his liability in his fiduciary capacity. 123 ALR 1320.

Accountability of personal representative for his use of decedent's real estate. 31 ALR2d 243.

Power and standing of personal representative of deceased promisee to enforce a contract made for benefit of a third party. 76 ALR2d 231.

§ 43-8-8. Effective date; transition provisions.

(a) This chapter takes effect on January 1, 1983.

(b) Except as provided elsewhere in this chapter, on January 1, 1983:

(1) The chapter applies to any wills of decedents dying thereafter;

(2) An act of any personal representative or guardian done before January 1, 1983 in any proceeding and any accrued right is not impaired by this chapter. If a right is acquired, extinguished or barred upon the expiration of a prescribed period of time which has commenced to run by the provisions of any statute before January 1, 1983, the provisions shall remain in force with respect to that right; and

(3) Any rule of construction or presumption provided in this chapter applies to instruments executed before January 1, 1983 unless there is a clear indication of a contrary intent. (Acts 1982, No. 82-399, § 8-101.)

§ 43-8-9. Savings provision for counties of Jefferson and Mobile.

No provision of this chapter shall be construed to void, alter, or modify, when invoked, the equity jurisdiction or powers of Jefferson and Mobile counties. (Acts 1982, No. 82-399, § 8-103.)

ARTICLE 2.

APPLICABILITY, JURISDICTION AND VENUE, AND IMPLIED OATH.

§ 43-8-20. Applicability of chapter.

Except as otherwise provided in this chapter, this chapter applies to:
  (1) The affairs and estates of decedents domiciled in this state; and
  (2) The property of nonresidents located in this state or property coming into the control of a fiduciary who is subject to the laws of this state. (Acts 1982, No. 82-399, § 1-301.)

Collateral references. 33 C.J.S., Executors and Administrators, §§ 1, 3, 12.

31 Am. Jur. 2d, Executors and Administrators, §§ 1, 8-11.

§ 43-8-21. Venue; multiple proceedings; transfer.

(a) Where a proceeding under this chapter could be maintained in more than one place in this state, the court in which the proceeding is first commenced has the exclusive right to proceed.

(b) If proceedings concerning the same estate are commenced in more than one court of this state, the court in which the proceeding was first commenced shall continue to hear the matter, and the other courts shall hold the matter in abeyance until the question of venue is decided, and if the ruling court determines that venue is properly in another court, it shall transfer the proceeding to the other court.

(c) If the court finds that in the interest of justice a proceeding or a file should be located in another court of this state, the court making the finding may transfer the proceeding or file to the other court. (Acts 1982, No. 82-399, § 1-303.)

Commentary

Subsection (a) — McDonnell v. Farrow, 132 Ala. 227, 31 So. 475 (1902); Beasley v. Howell, 117 Ala. 499, 22 So. 989 (1898) are in accord.

Subsection (c) — sections 43-1-38 and 43-1-77 (1975) are in accord.

Collateral references. — 92 C.J.S., Venue, §§ 126-128.

77 Am. Jur. 2d, Venue, §§ 25, 48-52.

§ 43-8-22. Filed documents deemed to include oath or affirmation.

Except as otherwise specifically provided in this chapter or by rule, every document filed with the court under this chapter including applications, petitions, and demands for notice, shall be deemed to include an oath, affirmation, or statement to the effect that its representations are true as far as the person executing or filing it knows and penalties for perjury may follow deliberate falsification therein. (Acts 1982, No. 82-399, § 1-310.)

Commentary

There was no comparable section in the Alabama Code previous to this act. However, there are numerous places in the Alabama Code where oaths are required for the documents involved. The effect of this section is to provide that it will be "deemed" (or assumed, if you will) that any person submitting a document for filing in the estate of a decedent makes an oath that the document is true to the best of his knowledge without the oath having to be expressly attached to each document.

Collateral references. 70 C.J.S., Perjury, § 24.

60 Am. Jur. 2d, Perjury, § 13.
61 Am. Jur. 2d, Pleadings, §§ 2, 26.

ARTICLE 3.

INTESTATE SUCCESSION.

§ 43-8-40. Intestate estate generally.

Any part of the estate of a decedent not effectively disposed of by his will passes to his heirs as prescribed in the following sections of this chapter. (Acts 1982, No. 82-399, § 2-101.)

Commentary

Preexisting Alabama law was in accord with this section. Former § 43-1-7 (1975).

I. General Consideration.
II. Decisions Under Prior Law.

I. GENERAL CONSIDERATION.

Collateral references. — 26A C.J.S., Descent & Distribution, §§ 1-18.

23 Am. Jur. 2d, Descent & Distribution, §§ 41-53.

Constitutionality of statute repealing, modifying or changing course of descent and distribution of property. 103 ALR 223.

Family settlement of intestate estate. 29 ALR3d 174.

Right to probate subsequently discovered will as affected by completed prior proceedings in intestate administration. 2 ALR4th 1315.

II. DECISIONS UNDER PRIOR LAW.

Editor's note. — In light of the similarity of the subject matter, decisions under former § 43-1-7 are included in the annotations for this section.

In general. — The real estate of a decedent, not devised to his executors, nor to any other person, descends to his heirs at law, who instantly are invested with the title, and may exert it, with all its incidents until the administrator, by actual civil action, or in some other legal mode, indicates his intention to assert the power reposed to him by statute. The title of the heirs is subject to the exercise of the statutory power. Patton v. Crow, 26 Ala. 426 (1855).

Testator must make valid disposition to defeat heirs. — A testator can only defeat his heirs at law or distributees by making a distribution of his property, and if any portion of it remain undisposed of by will, the heirs at law or next of kin are entitled to it, notwithstanding it may appear that the testator did not intend that they should succeed to it. Denson v. Autrey, 21 Ala. 205 (1852); Banks v. Sherrod, 52 Ala. 267 (1875).

Defeat of heirs is disfavored. — Estates by implication to defeat the heirs at law of the testator are disfavored, and must be based upon clear evidence found in the will itself and the circumstances attending its execution, showing an intention on the part of the testator not only to deprive the heirs of their inheritance, but indicating who should take. Caldwell v. Caldwell, 204 Ala. 161, 85 So. 493 (1920); Greil Mem. Hosp. v. First Ala. Bank, 387 So. 2d 778 (Ala. 1980).

Effect of lapse of bequest to child predeceasing testator. — Where testator directed that his executor sell his plantation and divide the proceeds, giving one sixth to each of testator's five children and one eighteenth to each of three grandchildren, and the will did not contain a residuary clause, lapse of bequest to child predeceasing testator without descendants did not work a failure of conversion of the land into money so that a surviving child and the sole heir of a deceased child was entitled to have the land sold for division because the land descended to the parties as joint owners under the laws of descent and distribution. Warrick v. Woodham, 243 Ala. 585, 11 So. 2d 150 (1942).

Estate not disposed of administered as in case of intestacy. — Estate not disposed of by will, confiding responsibility of making fair division of testatrix' property among her heirs and distributees to her nephew on qualifying as executor, should be administered as in case of intestacy where he failed to qualify. Parrish v. Gamble, 234 Ala. 220, 174 So. 303 (1937).

Property which lapses under a bequest or devise or which is not subject to any residuary clause of a will, must necessarily go by inheritance under the law of descent and distribution. The title to real estate may not remain in limbo. Hill v. Quinlan, 12 B.R. 824 (M.D. Ala. 1981).

One of the prime purposes of a residuary clause is to avoid the state of intestacy directed toward all property not disposed of by will. Greil Mem. Hosp. v. First Ala. Bank, 387 So. 2d 778 (Ala. 1980).

Where sole legatee predeceases the testatrix, bequest fails. — Where testatrix bequeathed all her personal property to a named brother who died before her, and there was no residuary clause, the bequest lapses. Caldwell v. Caldwell, 204 Ala. 161, 85 So. 493 (1920).

Advancements not considered in partial intestacy. — In cases of partial intestacy, advancements are not required to be brought into hotchpot to entitle the parties to share in the property undisposed of by the will. Greene v. Speer, 37 Ala. 532 (1861).

Charge of legacies on lands must be a devise, a disposition of the lands, or they must pass as in case of intestacy. Banks v. Sherrod, 52 Ala. 267 (1875).

Provision relating to wife's remarriage. — As to construction of a will, which provided that property should be divided according to law upon wife's remarriage, see Bell v. Mason, 10 Ala. 334 (1846).

Lost will exception. — Recognition of the importance of the ultimate effect of the testamentary administration of a decedent's estate, as opposed to its passing under Alabama's descent and distribution statutes, has led the court to consistently uphold and apply the exception to proving wills for probate and permit less stringent standards to govern in cases seeking to establish lost wills. Anderson v. Griggs, 402 So. 2d 904 (Ala. 1981).

§ 43-8-41. Share of the spouse.

The intestate share of the surviving spouse is as follows:

(1) If there is no surviving issue or parent of the decedent, the entire intestate estate;

(2) If there is no surviving issue but the decedent is survived by a parent or parents, the first $100,000.00 in value, plus one-half of the balance of the intestate estate;

(3) If there are surviving issue all of whom are issue of the surviving spouse also, the first $50,000.00 in value, plus one-half of the balance of the intestate estate;

(4) If there are surviving issue one or more of whom are not issue of the surviving spouse, one-half of the intestate estate;

(5) If the estate is located in two or more states, the share shall not exceed in the aggregate the allowable amounts under this chapter. (Acts 1982, No. 82-399, § 2-102.)

Commentary

This section gives the surviving spouse a larger share than most preexisting statutes on descent and distribution. In doing so, it reflects the desires of most married persons, who almost always leave all of a moderate estate or at least one-half of a larger estate to the surviving spouse when a will is executed. A husband or wife who desires to leave the surviving spouse less than the share provided by this section may do so by executing a will, subject of course to possible election by the surviving spouse to take an elective share of one-third under article 4 of this chapter. Moreover, in the small estate (less than $50,000 after homestead allowance, exempt property, and allowances) the surviving spouse is given the entire estate if there are only children who are issue of both the decedent and the surviving spouse; the result is to avoid protective proceedings as to property otherwise passing to their minor children.

See § 43-8-252 for the definition of spouse which controls for purposes of intestate succession.

The comparable provisions in Alabama statutes were contained in former §§ 43-3-1 (1975) and 43-3-10 (1981). In addition, the surviving spouse in Alabama can get homestead. These additional rights are included in comments to subsequent sections of this act. This section will give the surviving spouse a larger share of the intestate estate than that spouse would get under prior Alabama statutes. However, this provision seems to reflect more closely what most testators do in their wills.

Editor's note. — In light of the similarity of the subject matter, decisions under former § 43-3-10 are included in the annotations for this section.

Where widow was entitled to all of deceased husband's personal estate at his death, her vested interest in proceeds of war risk insurance passed to her husband and son in equal parts as distributees of her estate on her death. McGilvary v. Reynolds, 224 Ala. 435, 140 So. 417 (1932).

Personalty is nonterminable interest and qualifies for marital deduction. — The personalty provided for the wife is given absolutely and is a nonterminable interest which qualifies for the marital deduction. Cox v. United States, 421 F.2d 576 (5th Cir. 1970).

The wife's marital share of personalty descends subject only to debts and charges against the estate. Cox v. United States, 421 F.2d 576 (5th Cir. 1970).

Widow's remarriage not a forfeiture. — The remarriage of the widow of a person presumed dead did not work a forfeiture of her rights under former § 43-3-10. Quicksey v. Hall, 260 Ala. 162, 69 So. 2d 698 (1954).

Widow named as beneficiary of war risk policy by veteran leaving no children or their descendants takes the whole of the policy, and on her death any unpaid installments can be collected by administrator of veteran's estate and distributed to widow's children as distributees of her estate. Jones v. Gaillard, 241 Ala. 571, 4 So. 2d 131 (1941).

The widow may dissent from the will. — When a widow dissented from a will under former § 43-1-15, she was entitled to all personal property where there were no children, and on her death her heirs at law became owners of such personal property. Cogburn v. Callier, 213 Ala. 38, 104 So. 328 (1925).

Even after qualifying as executrix. — Where a husband died without children, leaving only an estate of personalty, but by his will bequeathing certain amounts to his sisters, and his widow filed the will for probate and qualified as executrix, but later dissented from the will in view of former § 43-3-10, she was entitled to all the personalty although she had accepted the will by qualifying as executrix and action was brought by the legatees against the widow as executrix to recover the amount of the legacy. Eastburn v. Canizas, 193 Ala. 574, 69 So. 459 (1915).

And she may repudiate a contract to make will. — A contract to make a will could not be enforced against the widow of a party who married him without knowing of the existence of the contract, at least as to so much of the estate as given her by former § 43-3-10. Mayfield v. Cook, 201 Ala. 187, 77 So. 713 (1918).

Withdrawal of widow's dissent unadvisedly made permissible. — The Alabama courts recognize the power of the court to permit a seasonable withdrawal of a widow's dissent to a will unadvisedly made. First Nat'l Bank v. United States, 328 F. Supp. 1339 (N.D. Ala. 1971).

Where widow dissents, her rights achieve priority and would not be subject to abatement for estate taxes. — Where widow within the time limits set by Alabama law filed a dissent from the will, asking instead for her distributive share and dower in her husband's estate, her rights would have come ahead of the claims of the other devisees and legatees under the will, and would not have been subject to pro

rata abatement for estate taxes. First Nat'l Bank v. United States, 328 F. Supp. 1339 (N.D. Ala. 1971).

Widow's right is consideration for payment of debts of husband. — Where a widow, entitled under the statutes to the whole of her deceased husband's estate, gives notes for debts owed by the husband, and the estate is solvent, she cannot plead lack of consideration for the notes. The burden of proof is on the widow to show facts which will relieve her of obligation. Vaughan v. Bass, 10 Ala. App. 388, 64 So. 543 (1914).

Collateral references. — 26A C.J.S., Descent & Distribution, §§ 48-60.

23 Am. Jur. 2d, Descent & Distribution, § 110.

Effect of joint estate, community estate or estate by entireties, of death of both tenants in same disaster. 18 ALR 105.

Treatment of widow's allowance and exemptions in computing share to which she is entitled under Statute of Distribution in case of death of husband intestate or of her election to take against will. 98 ALR 1325.

What passes under provision of will that spouse shall take share of estate allowed or provided by law, or a provision of similar import. 36 ALR2d 147.

§ 43-8-42. Share of heirs other than surviving spouse.

The part of the intestate estate not passing to the surviving spouse under section 43-8-41, or the entire intestate estate if there is no surviving spouse, passes as follows:

(1) To the issue of the decedent; if they are all of the same degree of kinship to the decedent they take equally, but if of unequal degree, then those of more remote degree take by representation;

(2) If there is no surviving issue, to his parent or parents equally;

(3) If there is no surviving issue or parent, to the issue of the parents or either of them by representation;

(4) If there is no surviving issue, parent or issue of a parent, but the decedent is survived by one or more grandparents or issue of grandparents, half of the estate passes to the paternal grandparents if both survive, or to the surviving paternal grandparent, or to the issue of the paternal grandparents if both are deceased, the issue taking equally if they are all of the same degree of kinship to the decedent, but if of unequal degree those of more remote degree take by representation; and the other half passes to the maternal relatives in the same manner; but if there be no surviving grandparent or issue of grandparent on either the paternal or the maternal side, the entire estate passes to the relatives on the other side in the same manner as the other half. (Acts 1982, No. 82-399, § 2-103.)

Commentary

This section provides for inheritance by lineal descendants of the decedent, parents and their descendants, and grandparents and collateral relatives descended from grandparents; in line with modern policy, it eliminates more remote relatives tracing through great-grandparents.

In general, the principle of representation (which is defined in § 43-8-45) is adopted as the pattern which most decedents would prefer.

If the pattern of this section is not desired, it may be avoided by a properly executed will or, after the decedent's death, by renunciation by particular heirs under article 11 of this chapter.

The comparable provisions to this section were in former § 43-3-1 (1975). Former § 43-3-10 (1981) incorporates by reference the distribution scheme of former § 43-3-1 (1975) and both sections are affected by this section. Except for perhaps a larger share of the intestate estate, which will be received by the surviving spouse under the provisions of § 43-8-41, the distribution scheme for intestate property will not be different under this section than under prior Alabama statutes in 99% of the cases. The major difference between prior Alabama statutes and this act occurs when this act would cut off relatives more remote than descendants of grandparents. Most modern revisions of probate statutes have followed this pattern. It will have the effect of cutting off persons only in a rare case and the demands of notice strongly support this policy.

Another difference in this act and prior Alabama provisions is with regard to representation. Previously Alabama statutes only permitted representation to lineal descendants of the intestate and lineal descendants of parents of the intestate. Former §§ 43-3-2 and 43-3-3 (1975). This act extends representation to lineal descendants of grandparents also. Therefore, this act is more limited than prior Alabama provisions in one respect and it extends Alabama provisions in another respect.

The point at which the stocks will be determined for purposes of representation will be changed by subdivision (1) as compared with prior Alabama law. See former §§ 43-3-2 and 43-3-3 (1975). Under subdivision (1), the stocks will be determined at the nearest degree in which there is a living descendant. Previously in Alabama, the stocks were determined in the first degree of kinship. The provision of this subdivision, however, probably follows the wishes of most testators when they focus on what their desires would be if everyone in the first degree of their descending line (children) should predecease the testator.

I. General Consideration.
II. Decisions Under Prior Law.
    A. In General.
    B. Establishment and Determination of Heirship.
    C. Title of Heirs or Distributees.
    D. Rents and Profits, Income and Accumulations.
    E. Claims of Estate Against Heirs or Distributees.
    F. Conveyances and Other Transactions Between Heirs or Distributees.
    G. Actions Between Heirs or Distributees.
    H. Conveyance of Property by Heirs or Distributees.
    I. Assignments of Distributive Shares.
    J. Rights and Liabilities of Purchasers from or Assignees of Distributees.
    K. Actions by Heirs or Distributees.
    L. Actions Against Heirs or Distributees.
    M. Conveyances and Incumbrances by Heirs.
    N. Rights and Remedies of Creditors of Heirs or Distributees.

I. GENERAL CONSIDERATION.

Cross references. — As to disclaimer of any property, property right, or interest in property, see article 11 of this chapter.

Collateral references. — 26A C.J.S., Descent & Distribution, § 25.

23 Am. Jur. 2d, Descent & Distribution, §§ 54-63.

Succession to property as affected by death in common disaster in absence of presumption or proof of survivorship. 43 ALR 1348.

Right of one other than grandchild of intestate to take under statute providing that if any child of intestate be dead the heirs of such child shall inherit his share. 93 ALR 1511.

Particular articles within statute giving to surviving spouse or children certain specific items of personal property of deceased. 158 ALR 313.

Descent and distribution to nieces and nephews as per stirpes or per capita. 19 ALR2d 191.

Family settlement of intestate's estate. 29 ALR3d 174.

II. DECISIONS UNDER PRIOR LAW.

A. In General.

Editor's note. — In light of the similarity of the subject matter, decisions under former §§ 43-3-1 and 43-3-10 are included in the annotations for this section.

Inapplicability to real property devised by will. — Section providing for descent of real estate applies only to the real estate of persons dying intestate, and real property devised by will is not subject thereto. Riggan v. Johnson, 268 Ala. 201, 105 So. 2d 101 (1958).

Heirs are those appointed by law in absence of will. — The heirs at law of a deceased person are those who, in the absence of a will, are appointed by law to inherit his real estate. Hatter v. Quina, 216 Ala. 225, 113 So. 47 (1927); White v. Fowler, 245 Ala. 209, 16 So. 2d 399 (1944).

A man's heirs are ascertainable when he dies, and if one of them thereafter dies, his heirs are not heirs of first decedent, but inherit from their immediate ancestor, subject to administration of his estate. White v. Fowler, 245 Ala. 209, 16 So. 2d 399 (1944).

Rule of "the blood of the first purchaser" not adopted in Alabama. — The controlling principle of our statute providing for the descent of property is that it shall descend to the intestate's next of kin, whether of the blood of his ancestor or not, and not that an intestate's ancestral estate shall descend only to those who are of the blood of the ancestor from whom it came. Caffee v. Thompson, 262 Ala. 684, 81 So. 2d 358 (1955).

It was not the intention of the framers of our statute of descents, that, on failure of lineal descendants, the estate should only descend to those collateral relations who are of the blood of the first purchaser, which is the fifth canon of descents as laid down by Blackstone in his Commentaries. Caffee v. Thompson, 262 Ala. 684, 81 So. 2d 358 (1955).

The homestead statutes and the descent and distribution statutes should be treated in pari materia and as formulating a consistent whole in the matter of descents. Shull v. Shull, 252 Ala. 320, 40 So. 2d 708 (1949).

The provisions of the Workmen's Compensation Act are not to be construed in such a manner as to disinherit the heirs at law of a decedent simply because he was subject to a compensation act at the time of his death and proceeds from a recovery should be distributed under the Alabama descent and distribution statute as the wrongful death statute directs. Sanders v. Hertz Equip. Rental Corp., 339 F. Supp. 777 (S.D. Ala.), modified sub nom. Sanders v. Shockley, 468 F.2d 88 (5th Cir. 1972).

Burden of debts and charges against estate controlled by section 40-15-18. — Section 40-15-18 deals specifically with the burden of estate taxes and would under the doctrine of expressio unius control general provisions in relation to the burden of debts and charges against the estate. Snodgrass v. United States, 308 F. Supp. 440 (N.D. Ala. 1968), aff'd, 427 F.2d 150 (5th Cir. 1970).

Modification by statutes regulating effect of adoption. — The general statutes of inheritance are modified and set aside by statutes regulating the effect of adoption only so far as there is some specific provision in the statutes for adoption inconsistent with the application, in such cases, of the general inheritance statutes. Franklin v. White, 263 Ala. 223, 82 So. 2d 247 (1955).

Legal title to personal assets, not exempt from administration and payment of debts or charges against estate, at death of intestate passes to personal representative. Sovereign Camp, W.O.W. v. Snider, 227 Ala. 126, 148 So. 831 (1933).

The interests of distributees of personalty at death of intestate are secondary and are not converted into unqualified ownership except through administration. Sovereign Camp, W.O.W. v. Snider, 227 Ala. 126, 148 So. 831 (1933).

Sole heir of beneficiary of fraternal policy was entitled to recover proceeds of policy where beneficiary died intestate day after death of insured leaving personalty worth less than $1,000.00, and where proof of death was furnished to insurer within time provided by policy. Sovereign Camp, W.O.W. v. Snider, 227 Ala. 126, 148 So. 831 (1933).

Proper parties to complaint to settle estate. — A complaint to settle an estate, brought by relations, must aver that the plaintiffs are all the parties taking under the statute, all the collateral relations being necessary parties. Word v. Word, 90 Ala. 81, 7 So. 412 (1890). This rule applies vice versa. Gardner v. Kelsoe, 80 Ala. 497, 2 So. 680 (1887).

Descent of lands is subject to the payment of debts. Banks v. Speers, 97 Ala. 560, 11 So. 841 (1892).

Right of distributee to settle claim after administrator appointed. — Where a person dies intestate with a cause of action for his death surviving to his administrator, and there is only one distributee, if the distributee settles the claim with the party against whom the right exists after an administrator is appointed the settlement is void and the administrator can proceed to recover for the death of his intestate. See Newell v. Bushard, 204 Ala. 73, 85 So. 274 (1920).

On death of beneficiary and sole heir of insured in war risk policy, remaining installments must be distributed to those who would take as of date of insured's death. Hunter v. James, 225 Ala. 610, 144 So. 576 (1932).

Sale for debts defeats title of heir. — The title of an heir to realty owned by deceased is defeasible and is completely defeated by sale for the payment of the debts of decedent. Ex parte Stephens, 233 Ala. 167, 170 So. 771 (1936); Bedsole v. Tiller, 236 Ala. 101, 181 So. 286 (1938).

Right of administrator to sell lands to pay debts is wholly statutory, and administrator alone can do so on conditions and manner prescribed in statute. Ex parte Stephens, 233 Ala. 167, 170 So. 771 (1936).

Priority of mother and father over brothers and sisters. — The law of descent gives the mother and father of an intestate priority over the intestate's brothers and sisters. Hudson v. Reed, 259 Ala. 340, 66 So. 2d 909 (1953).

Brothers and sisters of the half blood. — "Brothers and sisters" include those of the half blood. Children, or their descendants, of an intestate, or an intestate dying without children, leaving brothers and sisters or their descendants, take by representation without regard to degrees, that is, the children or grandchildren take the same share that their deceased parents would have inherited if living. Cox v. Clark, 93 Ala. 400, 9 So. 457 (1891).

Intestate's whole brother took property, devised and bequeathed to intestate by his aunt, to exclusion of half-brothers and half-sisters and children of deceased half-brothers and half-sisters who were not of aunt's blood. Purcell v. Sewell, 223 Ala. 73, 134 So. 476 (1931).

Intestate's whole brother, half-brothers, half-sisters and children of deceased half-brothers and half-sisters held in "same degree" within statute governing descent of ancestral estates. Purcell v. Sewell, 223 Ala. 73, 134 So. 476 (1931).

Grandparents take before uncles and aunts. Rucker v. Jackson, 180 Ala. 109, 60 So. 139 (1912).

Death of infant with vested remainder. — Where right to take as remaindermen was limited to children of named life tenant, the interest of life tenant's child vested on its death in infancy, to mother and father in equal parts. McWhorter v. Cox, 239 Ala. 441, 195 So. 435 (1940).

Recovery for death of deceased. — Where an infant died, and left surviving him a father and minor sisters, the father, if fit to serve, was entitled to administer the estate, which consisted of a right of action for the wrongful death of a minor. Nichols v. Smith, 186 Ala. 587, 65 So. 30 (1914).

Devise to sister and to nieces and nephews. — A will providing that residuary estate should be divided into four equal shares, and that one of shares was devised to children of each of testatrix' three deceased brothers and sisters, and the fourth to a living sister, devised residuary estate to named persons who would have taken if there had been no will and no person entitled to take in preference to or along with the brothers and sisters and their descendants. Henry v. Griffith, 242 Ala. 598, 7 So. 2d 560 (1942).

Husband and wife take prior to remote kindred. — Prior to the Code of 1896, any kindred, however remote, were preferred as heirs over husband and wife, in accordance with the doctrines of the common law. Former § 43-3-1 evinced an unmistakable legislative purpose to prefer husband or wife as heir over such remoter kindred. Indeed, language could not be plainer nor purpose clearer, for the express condition upon which alone these unpreferred next of kin could take as heirs was that there be "no husband or wife." Lake v. Russell, 180 Ala. 199, 60 So. 850 (1913).

Widow and children as heirs. — Where decedent left both widow and children (adults and minors) at the time of his death, and said children were the "next of kin" or other heirs, there could be no question but that the widow and children were heirs under the statute. Bishop v. Johnson, 242 Ala. 551, 7 So. 2d 281 (1942).

B. Establishment and Determination of Heirship.

May be barred by limitation and laches. — The claim of "heirs or legatees claiming as such," exempted from subsection (b) of § 43-2-350, is the claim of title, whether derived from statutes of descents and distribution, or by will, to property of the estate — the right to the specific property in the hands of the administrator, unadministered and unconverted, as contradistinguished from a claim or a devisavit, or a default creating merely the relation of debtor and creditor. Fretwell v. McLemore, 52 Ala. 124 (1875).

The claim of heirs or legatees against the estate of a surety, growing out of the misfeasance or malfeasance of his principal, whether judicially ascertained or not, is barred if not presented to the administrator of the surety within 18 (now six) months. Fretwell v. McLemore, 52 Ala. 124 (1875).

No decree except on proof of title. — Where the only son of a deceased daughter left neither child, father, mother, nor maternal grandmother living at the time of his death, being one of the heirs at law of the decedent, it could not be assumed that his four maternal aunts were his only heirs and next of kin, when the fact was not averred, and it was not shown that he left no grandfather, nor paternal grandmother, nor paternal uncles or aunts. Gardner v. Kelsoe, 80 Ala. 497, 2 So. 680 (1887).

Sufficiency of evidence to prove fact. — Recital of the names of the minor children and heirs of W., in an act authorizing them to sell their interests in land, if evidence of who they were, did not, in the absence of other evidence, overcome a recital in the deed that the persons therein named were, at date of its execution, his only children and heirs. Scotch Lumber Co. v. Sage, 132 Ala. 598, 32 So. 607 (1902).

An admission that F., if present, would testify that he was a brother-in-law of W., deceased, and that W. died soon after the Civil War, was never married and left a mother who had been dead about 15 years, and five named sisters was an admission that the mother and five sisters were all of the heirs left by W. at his death. Hooper v. Bankhead, 171 Ala. 626, 54 So. 549 (1911).

C. Title of Heirs or Distributees.

No title can be asserted directly from intestate. — The next of kin and distributees of an intestate can receive their rights only through an administration of his estate, and can assert no title directly from the intestate. Lockhart v. Cameron, 29 Ala. 355 (1856).

Title attaches by operation of law. — The right of a distributee attaches upon the death of the intestate, and accrues by operation of law under the statute of distributions. The subsequent division only serves to define, convert into a legal right and reduce to possession an equity which before existed in the form of a chose in action. Perryman v. Greer, 39 Ala. 133 (1863).

And no estoppel occurs by covenants of ancestor. — An heir, claiming an independent title in himself, is not estopped to assert it by the mere force of covenants of his ancestor. C.W. Zimmerman Mfg. Co. v. Wilson, 147 Ala. 275, 40 So. 515 (1906).

Title and rights of heir, as affected by statutory powers of personal representative. — On the death of a person intestate, seized of a heritable estate of lands, the title descends eo instanti, and vests in the heir, and with it all the common-law rights and incidents of ownership, subject to the exercise by the administrator of the statutory power with which he is clothed for the purposes of administration, and until these statutory powers are effectually asserted by the administrator the title and rights of the heir remain unimpaired and unaffected. Cockrell v. Coleman, 55 Ala. 583 (1876); Calhoun v. Fletcher, 63 Ala. 574 (1879); Steele v. Steele, 64 Ala. 438 (1879); Turner v. Kelly, 67 Ala. 173 (1880); Cruikshank v. Luttrell, 67 Ala. 318 (1880); Nelson v. Murfee, 69 Ala. 598 (1881); Baldwin v. Alexander, 145 Ala. 186, 40 So. 391 (1906); McMillan v. State, 160 Ala. 115, 49 So. 668 (1909); Rucker v. Tennessee Coal, Iron & R.R., 176 Ala. 456, 58 So. 465 (1912); Randolph v. Vails, 180 Ala. 82, 60 So. 159 (1912).

Under the Alabama statutes, as at common law, the title to lands on the death of the ancestor descends immediately to the heir at law, but unlike the rule of the common law, it does not vest in the heir absolutely, but the descent may be intercepted, and the possession claimed and held by the personal representative, for the purpose of administration. Nelson v. Murfee, 69 Ala. 598 (1881).

Title of heir upon death of vendor before conveyance. — On the death of a vendor before conveyance, his heir takes the title in trust for the vendee, and must convey on payment of the purchase money, which, however, when paid, goes to the vendor's personal representatives. Flomerfelt v. Siglin, 155 Ala. 633, 47 So. 106 (1908).

A distributee of an intestate's estate has only an equitable interest in the personalty, which will not support detinue, the legal title thereto vesting in the personal representative when appointed. Huddleston v. Huey, 73 Ala. 215 (1882).

Distributees have no title to the personal assets of decedent's estate, and are not appointed by law to demand or receive them. All their interest is secondary, and is capable of conversion into unqualified ownership only through the process of administration. Costephens v. Dean, 69 Ala. 385 (1881).

And cannot compel distribution until letters of administration have been granted. — The distributees or next of kin can maintain no action for the mere purpose of distribution, until letters of administration have been granted on the estate of the decedent, since the law casts the title to all the personal estate upon the personal representative. Gardner v. Gantt, 19 Ala. 666 (1851).

Actions on contracts must be in name of real beneficiaries. Norwich Union fire Ins. Co. v. Prude, 145 Ala. 297, 40 So. 322 (1906).

D. Rents and Profits, Income and Accumulations.

Heirs are entitled to receive. — On the death of an intestate, the legal title to his lands at once descends to and vests in his heirs, subject to the statutory powers conferred on the administrator, and until their estate is divested by the exercise of such powers, they are entitled to receive and hold the rents, issues and profits. Chighizola v. Le Baron, 21 Ala. 406 (1852); Branch Bank v. Fry, 23 Ala. 770 (1853); Patton v. Crow, 26 Ala. 426 (1855); Cockrell v. Coleman, 55 Ala. 583 (1876); Calhoun v. Fletcher, 63 Ala. 574 (1879); Cruikshank v. Luttrell, 67 Ala. 318 (1880).

As between the administrator and the heirs, the latter are not responsible for rents received, or damages, until the statute power is asserted in some lawful mode, on the principle that, in law, they are the owners, and may lawfully expend the usufruct, until advised of the necessity to apply it otherwise. Chighizola v. Le Baron, 21 Ala. 406 (1852); Branch Bank v. Fry, 23 Ala. 770 (1853); Patton v. Crow, 26 Ala. 426 (1855); Cockrell v. Coleman, 55 Ala. 583 (1876); Calhoun v. Fletcher, 63 Ala. 574 (1879); Gayle v. Johnson, 80 Ala. 388 (1885).

Rents received by an administrator after the widow has taken possession of the land allotted her as dower belonged exclusively to the heirs and distributees. Munden v. Bailey, 70 Ala. 63 (1881).

And may commence civil action and recover. — Though an administrator by statute is invested with power to rent the real estate of his decedent, and, under its provisions, may recover rents accruing on the demise of his decedent, until the administrator asserts this power by notice to the tenant or by actual civil action, the heir may commence an action for and recover rent falling due after the death of his ancestor. Masterson v. Girard, 10 Ala. 60 (1846).

An heir may commence a civil action for the recovery of rents accruing after the death of his ancestor whose estate has been declared insolvent, if neither the administrators nor creditors object. Branch Bank v. Fry, 23 Ala. 770 (1853).

But rents accruing previous to the lessor's death go to the personal representative, and not to the heir. Brewster v. Buckholts, 3 Ala. 20 (1841).

E. Claims of Estate Against Heirs or Distributees.

The court has no power to allow the set-off of a debt, due to the estate by one of the distributees, against the share of such distributee. Bondurant v. Thompson, 15 Ala. 202 (1849).

F. Conveyances and Other Transactions Between Heirs or Distributees.

Voluntary divisions upheld. — Although the legal title to a distributive share of the estate of an intestate can only be acquired through administration, yet where the distributees are all adults, and the distributees, by agreement, divide the estate, and there is no unfairness, a court will uphold the division. Perryman v. Greer, 39 Ala. 133 (1863); McCaa v. Woolf, 42 Ala. 389 (1868).

Though commissioners appointed to make distribution of an estate cannot require one distributee to pay a sum of money to another, yet, if the parties adopt the division, with its terms, and act on it, they are bound thereby. Allen v. Raney, 19 Ala. 68 (1851).

A. conveyed by deed to his son B. certain slaves, with the understanding that, at the death of the father, the son should divide them equally with his sister, who was then the wife of D. When A. died, the son claimed the slaves absolutely until his own death, after which D., on valuable consideration, sold and released to the distributees of B.'s estate "all the right, title, claim, interest, and demand" which he "then had or might thereafter recover in and to the goods and chattels, rights and credits, lands and tenements of B. or A. deceased." Held, that the deed of D. embraced the claim of his wife to the slaves, it not appearing that he had any other claim or demand against the estate of B. at the time of its execution. Hamilton v. Clement, 17 Ala. 201 (1850).

An agreement by one of several heirs and her husband, to accept from the other heirs a certain sum in full settlement of the question of advances, is a sufficient consideration for an agreement by the other heirs to pay such sum. Campbell v. Larmore, 84 Ala. 499, 4 So. 593 (1888).

Where the husband obtains possession of his wife's share in an intestate's personal estate, under a division voluntarily made by the distributees, he thereby acquires an equitable title, which a court will uphold and enforce. McCaa v. Woolf, 42 Ala. 389 (1868).

G. Actions Between Heirs or Distributees.

All of excluded heirs need not be joined. — Where, on the death of the owner of land, one of his heirs, being in possession, denied possession to the other heirs, each of them was entitled to be let in, and, in an action for that purpose, it was not material whether all of the excluded heirs joined. Butler v. Butler, 133 Ala. 377, 32 So. 579 (1902).

An action may be maintained against those in possession. — Where an intestate leaves no debts, and there has been no administration of his estate, an action may be maintained by one of the distributees, against those in possession, for distribution of the estate, an accounting of the portion wasted or converted, and a recovery of plaintiff's portion, although possession of defendants be adverse to the title of plaintiff. Teal v. Chancellor, 117 Ala. 612, 23 So. 651 (1898).

And complaint may be amended to make wife of defendant a party. — A complaint by one of the distributees of an estate, against her codistributees, for the recovery of her distributive share, may be amended so as to make the wife of a defendant a party defendant, to allege that she claimed and was using some of the property, but had no interest therein, and to ask that her claim be canceled, and that she and her husband be charged with the property converted, to the extent of plaintiff's interest. Teal v. Chancellor, 117 Ala. 612, 23 So. 651 (1898).

H. Conveyance of Property by Heirs or Distributees.

Heir or devisee may alienate lands subject to exercise of the statutory powers of the personal representative. Rucker v. Tennessee Coal, Iron & R.R., 176 Ala. 456, 58 So. 465 (1912).

Proof of the death of the owner of land, leaving a widow, who had one child, and who had lived on the land since the owner's death, and who had rented it for a specified quantity of cotton a year, did not show the invalidity of a mortgage on the land executed by the widow, as dower might have been assigned her of the land embraced in the mortgage, vesting in the mortgagee her life estate, or as she might have acquired the land in fee, in the absence of any surviving children, or father or mother, or brother or sister of the deceased owner. Penny v. Weems, 139 Ala. 270, 35 So. 883 (1904).

I. Assignments of Distributive Shares.

The interest of a distributee in an unsettled estate is the subject of assignment. Graham v. Abercrombie, 8 Ala. 552 (1845).

A widow may assign her interest in her deceased husband's estate, and such assignment is sufficient to pass such interest to the assignees. Powell v. Powell, 10 Ala. 900 (1846).

Heirs of a decedent, who have assigned to another all their interest in the decedent's real estate, are not, on an accounting by the administrator for the rents and profits, entitled to any share thereof. Spear v. Banks, 125 Ala. 227, 27 So. 979 (1900).

J. Rights and Liabilities of Purchasers from or Assignees of Distributees.

Assignee invested with rights of distributee. — The interest of a distributee in an unsettled estate is the subject of assignment. If one is made, it divests the interest of the distributee, so that no proceeding can be had by his representatives against the administrator. His assignee is thereby invested with all his rights, and they may be asserted by him in his own name. Graham v. Abercrombie, 8 Ala. 552 (1845).

The assignment of a debt secured by a mortgage by the heirs and devisees of the mortgagee will pass an equity which will prevail against all but creditors whose rights are affected. Cook v. Parham, 63 Ala. 456 (1879).

Unless it is shown that the estate of a decedent owes no debts, and has no administrator, an action on a note which belonged to the estate cannot be maintained by one who claims title thereto by transfer from the heirs and distributees. Knight v. Knight, 103 Ala. 484, 15 So. 834 (1894).

When one claims as assignee of a distributee the sum due in this character cannot be joined with a sum due to him in right of his wife. Petty v. Wafford, 11 Ala. 143 (1847).

K. Actions by Heirs or Distributees.

When distributee may commence civil action without administration. — When all the debts against a decedent's estate have been paid, and no other act of administration is necessary than the making of final settlement and distribution, distributees may, without the appointment and intervention of an administrator de bonis non, maintain an action to compel a settlement and distribution of an estate in which their ancestor was a distributee. Alexander v. Alexander, 70 Ala. 212 (1881).

Nature of remedy and conditions precedent. — An heir may maintain ejectment, to recover land of decedent. Wilson v. Kirkland, 172 Ala. 72, 55 So. 174 (1911).

Upon a sale of land by commissioners, on the petition of the heirs for distribution among them, the vendor's lien remains unimpaired in the heirs who own the land, and this lien may be enforced by them. McIntosh v. Reid, 45 Ala. 456 (1871).

When the bond for title showed that the title was in a third person, and the obligor never procured a conveyance of the title to the obligee, nor obtained it himself, the heir of the obligee could not commence an action in his own name for a breach of the condition, whether that breach happened before or after the death of his ancestor. Allen v. Greene, 19 Ala. 34 (1851).

Where one of several brothers and sisters, having title to personal property, dies in infancy, the remaining brothers can not commence a civil action to recover the property until administration is taken out of the estate of the infant. Miller v. Eatman, 11 Ala. 609 (1847).

An heir has no capacity to commence a civil action to enforce any claim owned by the estate or to bring its debtors to a settlement, without showing either that the administrator refuses to do so, or is in collusion with the debtor, or occupies a position antagonistic to his duties as administrator. Tillery v. Tillery, 155 Ala. 495, 46 So. 582 (1908).

In an action to recovery a distributive share in an estate, it was error in the judge to direct the master to take an account, and, after ascertaining the amount due plaintiff, to apportion it among the several defendants, and, if they did not pay on request to issue execution, as such acts involved the exercise of judicial power, and therefore the defendants could not be deprived of their right of exception and appeal to the judge. McCartney v. Calhoun, 11 Ala. 110 (1847).

Interest of parties and widow's right to file petitions. — When petition was filed by decedent's widow in 1874, and alleged that she and her two infant children were the joint owners and tenants of described lands, containing 160 acres, were each entitled to one-third interest therein, and acquired their joint ownership therein by reason of being the widow and minor children of said decedent, who died in said county, and whose estate was insolvent, these averments were sufficient, on collateral attack, to show the interest of the respective parties, and the widow's right to file the petition. Morgan v. Farned, 83 Ala. 367, 3 So. 798 (1888).

Construction of contract between heirs. — Where an agreement specified that the administrator should account for the rent of the property only for certain years, it was error for the court, in determining the portion each heir should contribute for the redemption of a mortgage against the land, to charge one of the heirs with rent of the land for other years than those specified. Caldwell v. Caldwell, 183 Ala. 590, 62 So. 951 (1913).

Laches. — A delay of 14 years by heirs before attempting to enforce a lien upon the land of the ancestor created by an agreement among the heirs was held not to constitute laches, where there were no adverse rights asserted, and no prejudice resulted from the delay. Caldwell v. Caldwell, 183 Ala. 590, 62 So. 951 (1913).

Parties. — A posthumous child may claim by descent as an heir of its father, and may join with its elder borthers and sisters in an action for the recovery of the possession of the lands descended. Bishop v. Hampton, 11 Ala. 254 (1847).

An action for damages for failure of a purchaser of a decedent's land, sold under a decree of the probate court for partition among heirs, to complete the sale, may be properly brought in the name of the heirs. Howison v. Oakley, 118 Ala. 215, 23 So. 810 (1898).

A guardian who had loaned his ward's money and had taken a note and mortgage therefor to himself as such guardian afterwards settled his accounts and paid the ward in full. Held that, though such guardian died intestate and no administration of his estate was had, yet where his wife and children were living, and none of the children were under the disability of minority and his debts were paid, such wife and children could commence an action in their own names to foreclose such mortgage. Wright v. Robinson, 94 Ala. 479, 10 So. 319 (1891).

To a complaint for partition and an accounting, which alleged that plaintiff's ancestor was seized jointly with defendant of certain land, that deceased left no debts, and that there had been no administration on his estate in this state, the administrator of deceased was not a necessary party. Stevenson v. Anderson, 87 Ala. 228, 6 So. 285 (1889).

Where there were no debts against the estate of a deceased person, and administration had been finally closed, his heirs and distributees could maintain an action on a written obligation payable to deceased, or for money had and received to his use. Wooten v. Steele, 98 Ala. 252, 13 So. 563 (1893).

To a complaint filed by distributee, for a settlement of the administration on a decedent's estate, the personal representative of a deceased distributee is not a necessary party, where there are no debts outstanding against his estate, nor when his estate has been settled, and his rights and interests have become vested in his surviving child, as sole distributee and heir at law, who is made a party to the complaint. Baines v. Barnes, 64 Ala. 375 (1879).

After the death of the wife, there being no administrator of her estate, and no debts against it, her sole legatee and devisee may maintain an action against the surviving husband for an account of waste committed during his life. De Bardeleben v. Stoudenmire, 82 Ala. 574, 2 So. 488 (1887).

An action cannot be maintained by the heirs or next of kin of a deceased legatee to recover his share in an estate, but the administrator of such deceased legatee is the proper party plaintiff. Sullivan v. Lawler, 72 Ala. 68 (1882).

On the death of the wife, without issue and intestate, being a distributee of the estate of her deceased father, her surviving husband was properly joined with the other distributees as plaintiff in a complaint which sought to compel a settlement of the administration of the estate. Baines v. Barnes, 64 Ala. 375 (1879).

Pleadings and evidence. — Where two of three heirs die, a complaint by the survivor to recover their interests in the estate must aver that the other two died leaving no debts, though they died at the ages of 12 and 14, respectively. Morris v. Morris, 58 Ala. 443 (1877).

Though the court will dispense with an administration where an intestate leaves no debts, and will entertain a complaint by his distributees based on their equitable title to his personalty, in a complaint to enforce a lien on land for unpaid purchase money, evidenced by a note given by defendant to the intestate, where plaintiffs merely aver that they are the "only heirs at law" of such intestate, it is not sufficiently shown that they were entitled to succeed to his personal estate, and the complaint is demurrable (now subject to motion to dismiss) on that ground. Hopkins v. Miller, 92 Ala. 513, 8 So. 750 (1891).

In an action for damages for failure of a purchaser of land sold by an administrator for partition among heirs to complete the sale, a complaint alleging "that plaintiffs are the heirs at law of [said] deceased" was sufficient to show that they were all the heirs. Howison v. Oakley, 118 Ala. 215, 23 So. 810 (1898).

Distributees cannot maintain an action to enforce a vendor's lien on land sold by their decedent upon the sole averment that he died about 13 years before the filing of the complaint and no administration had ever been had. Costephens v. Dean, 69 Ala. 385 (1881).

In an action by heirs for wrongfully cutting timber after intestate's death, evidence that after such cutting the estate was reported insolvent, and the property from which the timber was cut was assigned to the widow and the minor heirs as a homestead, was inadmissible to show that the right of action was in the widow, where it did not appear that the entire estate did not exceed the exemption allowed by law, or that the homestead assigned was less than the amount of such exemption, so that the same would vest absolutely in the widow and minors, irrespective of the solvency of the estate as otherwise the fee would not vest in them until judicial ascertainment of the insolvency of the estate. Louisville & N.R.R. v. Hill, 155 Ala. 334, 22 So. 163 (1897).

L. Actions Against Heirs or Distributees.

When a complaint to redeem lands seeks to divest title out of the heirs of decedent, and vest the same in plaintiffs, it is indispensible — to obtain the relief sought — that such heirs should be made parties defendant. Smith v. Murphy, 58 Ala. 630 (1877).

M. Conveyances and Incumbrances by Heirs.

Rights and liabilities of purchasers in general. — Where lands acquired from intestate were fraudulently conveyed by the heirs to purchasers taking with notice of the fraud, such conveyances were no obstacle to an action to subject them to reimbursement of the administrator's surety for the payment of a judgment recovered against him on a debt of the intestate. Baldwin v. Alexander, 145 Ala. 186, 40 So. 391 (1906).

Actions against heirs, distributees or purchasers. — When the property of a deceased debtor, real and personal, exceeds the statutory exemptions in value and extent, and the widow and children take possession of it, without administration on his estate, the creditor may maintain an action against them to enforce payment of his debt. Cameron v. Cameron, 82 Ala. 392, 3 So. 148 (1887), overruled on other grounds, Jackson v. Sheffield, 107 Ala. 358, 18 So. 106 (1894).

In a proceeding against heirs by a creditor, on behalf of himself and other creditors, to subject to the payment of their claims the lands of the deceased debtor, plaintiff could not, by an amended complaint, ask the foreclosure of a mortgage given to secure his individual debt, since the original complaint was not filed to enforce a separate, individual right, but a right had in common with others. Scott v. Ware, 64 Ala. 174 (1879).

Where judgment was recovered against an administrator, in an action on the debt of the intestate, lands could not, by scire facias (now motion or appropriate action) against the heirs, be made liable to execution. Bells v. Robinson, 1 Stew. 193 (1827).

Conditions precedent. — Before a creditor of the ancestor can proceed against the heirs to collect his claim, he must exhaust his remedy against the personal representatives. Ledyard v. Johnston, 16 Ala. 548 (1849).

Such parts of the estate of a deceased person as have regularly passed into the hands of the distributees will not, where the administrator has committed a devastavit, be subjected to the satisfaction of a debt due by the estate until after the creditor has exhausted his remedy against the administrator and his sureties. Pyke v. Searcy, 4 Port. 52 (1836).

Where both the lands and personal property are liable for a decedent's debts, a claim for damages for breach of decedent's contract will not lie against the heirs in the first instance. The claim for damages should be presented in due course of administration and be asserted against the personal representative of the decedent. C.W. Zimmerman Mfg. Co. v. Wilson, 147 Ala. 275, 40 So. 515 (1906).

Defenses. — In proceedings to subject the lands of a decedent to the payment of debts, the heirs or devisees may avail themselves of any defense against such debts which the decedent, if living, could have set up, or which would be available to the personal representative in an action against him, and they may also rely on defenses which the personal representative has, by his own acts or laches, precluded himself from making. Scott v. Ware, 64 Ala. 174 (1879).

Parties. — To a complaint which seeks to subject to the satisfaction of the plaintiff's claim the undivided interest of a distributee in an estate, while yet in the hands of the administrator, all the distributees are necessary parties. Chapman v. Hamilton, 19 Ala. 121 (1851).

On a complaint by a creditor to subject property of his deceased debtor in the hands of heirs to the payment of his debt, notice must be given to the personal representative by service of process, if within the reach of process, otherwise, by publication, before a judgment can be entered. Darrington v. Borland, 3 Port. 9 (1836), overruled on other grounds, Starke v. Wilson, 65 Ala. 576 (1878).

Pleading. — It is not necessary that a complaint to enforce a subsequent promise by the heirs, founded on a valid claim against their ancestor, and a lien created by them for its payment, should aver due presentment of the claim against the estate. Grimball v. Mastin, 77 Ala. 553 (1884).

A complaint against the heirs and distributees to enforce a claim which had not been presented for allowance within the time limited by statute is demurrable (now subject to motion to dismiss) if it fails to allege facts excepting the claim from the statute. Farris v. Stoutz, 78 Ala. 130 (1884).

Evidence. — There being no privity between the personal representative and the heir or devisee, a judgment against the former is not binding on the latter, nor even evidence, as against him, of any other fact than its rendition, of which it is evidence against all the world. Scott v. Ware, 64 Ala. 174 (1879).

N. Rights and Remedies of Creditors of Heirs or Distributees.

Interests or rights which may be subjected. — A distributee's undivided interest in an unsettled estate may be set apart, by his judgment creditor, and subjected to the satisfaction of his demand, proper proceedings being had. Lang v. Brown, 21 Ala. 179 (1852).

Until distribution of an estate is made, the legal title to the assets remains in the personal representative, no matter where the possession is. But if, after the debts are paid, the distributees, with the assent of the administrator, make an amicable division of the property, or agree to keep it together in common, it will be subject to the payment of their debts, in the proportion of their several interests. Brashear v. Williams, 10 Ala. 630 (1846).

Effect of indebtedness of heirs or distributees to estate. — Under former law a minor over 18 years of age could make a valid bequest of personalty, or subject it to the payment of legacies, but, on failure or insufficiency of personalty, the legacy could not become a charge on the realty which descended to the heir. Banks v. Sherrod, 52 Ala. 267 (1875).

Where surplus money arising from the sale of decedent's land for the payment of his debts remains in the hands of the personal representative for distribution, he is entitled to retain the share of an heir or distributee in payment of a debt which the latter owes the estate, in preference to the claim of a judgment creditor of such heir or distributee. Nelson v. Murfee, 69 Ala. 598 (1881).

An administratrix and codistributee of an estate, having wasted and misapplied a considerable portion of the assets, conveyed by deed all her right, title and interest in the estate to her children and codistributees. A judgment creditor of the administratrix filed his complaint for an account and settlement of the estate, and requested that the deed be set aside, and the share of the administratrix in the estate be subjected to the payment of his judgment. Held that, in the absence of fraud, the codistributees had, under the deed, a lien on the share of the administratrix as distributed prior to the lien of the creditor. Brown v. Lang, 14 Ala. 719 (1848).

Actions and other proceedings by creditors. — A creditors' complaint will lie to reach interest of the debtor in an undistributed estate. Brown v. Lang, 14 Ala. 719 (1848); Lang v. Brown, 21 Ala. 179 (1852).

When creditors of a deceased debtor, not having reduced their claim to judgment as against the estate, seek by complaint to reach the property alleged to have been fraudulently conveyed by the executor, who is also the sole devisee, and who has been removed from the office of executor, a personal representative of the estate must be brought before the court as a party, and the failure to make him a party, though not objected to in the court below, is a fatal defect which the supreme court is bound to notice on appeal by the plaintiffs. Gibbs v. Hodge, 65 Ala. 366 (1880).

An execution purchaser of a distributee's share of the realty, but not of the personalty, cannot have a decree in his own name for that share upon a final sale and distribution, since the probate court has no power to render a decree in favor of an assignee, unless he is a purchaser of the entire interest of the distributee's share of the estate. Simmons v. Knight, 35 Ala. 105 (1859).

§ 43-8-43. Requirement that heir survive decedent for five days.

Any person who fails to survive the decedent by five days is deemed to have predeceased the decedent for purposes of homestead allowance, the exempt property and intestate succession, and the decedent's heirs are determined accordingly. If the time of death of the decedent or of the person who would otherwise be an heir, or the times of death of both, cannot be determined, and it cannot be established that the person who would otherwise be an heir has survived the decedent by five days, it is deemed that the person failed to survive for the required period. This section is not to be applied where its application would result in a taking of intestate estate by the state under section 43-8-44. (Acts 1982, No. 82-399, § 2-104.)

Commentary

This section is a limited version of the type of clause frequently found in wills to take care of the common accident situation, in which several members of the same family are injured and die within a few days of each other. The Uniform Simultaneous Death Act (§§ 43-7-1 through 43-7-8) provides only a partial solution, since it applies only if there is no proof that the parties died otherwise than simultaneously. This section requires an heir to survive by five days in order to succeed to decedent's intestate property; for a comparable provision as to wills, see § 43-8-220. This section avoids multiple administrations and in some instances prevents the property from passing to persons not desired by the decedent. The five-day period will not hold up administration of a decedent's estate because § 43-2-45 (1975) precludes the issuance of letters of administration until the expiration of five days after the death of the intestate. The last sentence prevents the survivorship requirement from affecting inheritances by the last eligible relative of the intestate who survives him for any period.

I.R.C. § 2056(b)(3) makes it clear that an interest passing to a surviving spouse is not made a "terminable interest" and thereby disqualified for inclusion in the marital deduction by its being conditioned on failure of the spouse to survive a period not exceeding six months after the decedent's death, if the spouse in fact lives for the required period. Thus, the intestate share of a spouse who survives the decedent by five days is available for the marital deduction. To assure a marital deduction in cases where one spouse fails to survive the other by the required period, the decedent must leave a will. The marital deduction is not a problem in the typical intestate estate. The statute should accommodate the typical estate to which it applies, rather than the unusual case of an unplanned estate involving large sums of money.

Collateral references. — 26A C.J.S., Descent & Distribution, §§ 1-18.

23 Am. Jur. 2d, Descent & Distribution, § 103.

Decree directing distribution of estate to person who is dead. 25 ALR 1563.

Time interval contemplated by provision of will or of statute of descent and distribution

with reference to death of two persons simultaneously or approximately at same time. 173
ALR 1254.

§ 43-8-44. When estate passes to state.

If there is no taker under the provisions of this article, the intestate estate
passes to the state of Alabama. (Acts 1982, No. 82-399, § 2-105.)

Commentary

Prior Alabama law was in accord. Former § 43-3-1 (1975).

I. General Consideration.
II. Decisions Under Prior Law.

I. GENERAL CONSIDERATION.

Collateral references. — 30A C.J.S.,
Escheat, § 2.

27 Am. Jur. 2d, Escheat, §§ 1-4, 11.

Necessity of judicial proceeding to vest title
to real property in state by escheat. 23 ALR
1237; 79 ALR 1364.

Necessity and sufficiency of notice to support
title by escheat to decedent's estate. 48 ALR
1342.

Constitutionality, construction and application of statutes relating to disposition of old
bank deposits. 151 ALR 836.

Inheritance from illegitimate. 48 ALR 759.

Escheat of personal property of intestate
domiciled or resident in another state. 50
ALR2d 1375.

Uniform Disposition of Unclaimed Property
Act. 98 ALR2d 304.

II. DECISIONS UNDER PRIOR LAW.

Editor's note. — In light of the similarity of
the subject matter, decisions under former
§ 43-6-1 are included in the annotations for this
section.

Constitution. — For constitutional provision as to disposition of estates of deceased
persons who die without leaving a will or heir,
see Const., § 258, as amended by Amendment
No. 111.

**Devise over after trust created by will
lapsed.** — Where testatrix left no persons capable of inheriting from her will, created a trust
for the support of a specified person and made
a devise over at her death of any part of the
undisposed   property   to   specified
brothers-in-law of testatrix who pre-deceased
her with no provision for that contingency in
the will, the undisposed of portion of the trust
estate after the sister-in-law's death would
escheat to the state. Morgan County Nat'l Bank
v. Nelson, 244 Ala. 374, 13 So. 2d 765 (1943).

**When devisees died prior to the death of
testatrix,** their devises lapsed and would have
gone to the next of kin of testatrix, if she had
had such, and they did not survive to the other
devisees as on the death of a joint tenant, but
since testatrix died without further devising or
bequeathing devisees' shares, and left no kin or
husband capable of inheriting, they escheated
to the state. Morgan County Nat'l Bank v.
Nelson, 244 Ala. 374, 13 So. 2d 765 (1943).

Duty of administrator. — It is the duty and
right of an administrator to see that estate
property goes to the person entitled thereto, and
although an order of the probate court
dismissing his escheat proceedings, and finding
that the property descended to certain claimants would protect him, yet he may appeal
therefrom. McKenzie v. Jensen, 195 Ala. 36, 70
So. 678 (1916).

§ 43-8-45. Division of estate where representation is involved.

If representation is called for by this chapter, the estate is divided into as
many shares as there are surviving heirs in the nearest degree of kinship and
deceased persons in the same degree who left issue who survive the decedent,
each surviving heir in the nearest degree receiving one share and the share of
each deceased person in the same degree being divided among the issue of such
deceased heir in the same manner. (Acts 1982, No. 82-399, § 2-106.)

Commentary

Under the system of intestate succession in effect in some states, property is directed to be divided "per stirpes" among issue or descendants of identified ancestors. Applying a meaning commonly associated with the quoted words, the estate is first divided into the number indicated by the number of children of the ancestor who survive, or who leave issue who survive. If, for example, the property is directed to issue "per stirpes" of the intestate's parents, the first division would be by the number of children of parents (other than the intestate) who left issue surviving even though no person of this generation survives. Thus, if the survivors are a child and a grandchild of a deceased brother of the intestate and five children of his deceased sister, the brother's descendants would divide one-half and the five children of the sister would divide the other half. Yet, if the parent of the brother's grandchild also had survived, most statutes would give the seven nephews and nieces equal shares because it is commonly provided that if all surviving kin are in equal degree, they take per capita.

The section rejects this pattern and keys to a system which assures that the first and principal division of the estate will be with reference to a generation which includes one or more living members.

Alabama previously provided for representation in former §§ 43-3-2 and 43-3-3 (1975). See Comment to § 43-8-42 for the comparison of the prior Alabama provisions and the provisions in this act. The effect of this section, however, is to provide where the stirpes are to be determined when representation is needed. Alabama is silent on this question, which in effect means that the stirpes will be determined at the nearest degree of kinship to the intestate. This section follows the pattern that has become quite popular in drafting wills and one which most testators seem to want when they focus on the question.

I. General Consideration.
II. Decisions Under Prior Law.

I. GENERAL CONSIDERATION.

Collateral references. — 26A C.J.S., Descent & Distribution, § 23.

23 Am. Jur. 2d, Descent & Distribution, § 63.

II. DECISIONS UNDER PRIOR LAW.

Editor's note. — In light of the similarity of the subject matter, decisions under former §§ 43-3-2 and 43-3-3 are included in the annotations for this section.

Devise to sister and to nieces and nephews. — Where testatrix expressly directed a division into four shares, and bequeathed one share to the class, who, at the time of the testatrix's death, should represent her deceased sister and one share to the class who should represent each of two deceased brothers, and the fourth to a living sister "or should she be dead to her children or their descendants share and share alike per stirpes," it was held that the will devised and bequeathed the residuary estate to the same persons and in the same shares they would have taken under the law of descent and distributions had there been no will, where no other person is in being entitled to take in preference to or along with brothers and sisters and their descendants. Henry v. Griffith, 242 Ala. 598, 7 So. 2d 560 (1942).

Under former § 43-3-3 cousins could not take by representation. Hall v. Proctor, 239 Ala. 211, 194 So. 675 (1940); Hall v. Proctor, 242 Ala. 636, 7 So. 2d 764 (1942).

§ 43-8-46. Inheritance by relatives of half blood.

Relatives of the half blood inherit the same share they would inherit if they were of the whole blood. (Acts 1982, No. 82-399, § 2-107.)

Commentary

Prior Alabama law (former § 43-3-5 (1975)) made no distinction between relatives of the whole blood and relatives of the half blood in the same degree, unless the inheritance came to the intestate by descent, devise, or gift from one of his ancestors; in which case all those who were not of the blood of such ancestor were excluded from the inheritance as against those of the same degree. The provision with regard to half-bloods was the only vestige of ancestral property remaining in Alabama law. The statute was difficult to construe and the policy supporting the concept seems to be gone. This section eliminates this exception to the rule that no distinction is made against heirs of the half blood. The section is a small step in terms of policy and a giant step in terms of clarity of the statutes.

Collateral references. — 26A C.J.S., Descent & Distribution, § 36.
23 Am. Jur. 2d, Descent & Distribution, §§ 46, 47.

Rights of inheritance in ancestral property as between kindred of whole and half blood. 141 ALR 976.

§ 43-8-47. Inheritance by afterborn heirs.

Relative of the decedent conceived before his death but born thereafter inherit as if they had been born in the lifetime of the decedent. (Acts 1982, No. 82-399, § 2-108.)

Commentary

Alabama law previously included only posthumous children of the intestate. Former § 43-3-6 (1975). A posthumous child under this section includes not only a posthumous child of the testator but also a child of any relative conceived before the death of the decedent but born subsequent to his death. This may extend application of the pretermitted heir statute and require notice to persons previously not contemplated by the Alabama statutes. This section includes any relative fitting the test. Only a few cases will likely come within this extension of applicable persons.

I. General Consideration.
II. Decisions Under Prior Law.

I. GENERAL CONSIDERATION.

Cross reference. — As to inclusion of posthumous children in terms "heirs," "issue" or "children," see § 35-4-8.

Collateral references. — 26A C.J.S., Descent & Distribution, § 29.
23 Am. Jur. 2d, Descent & Distribution, §§ 87-89.

II. DECISIONS UNDER PRIOR LAW.

Editor's note. — In light of the similarity of the subject matter, decisions under former § 43-3-6 are included in the annotations for this section.

A posthumous child may claim by descent as an heir of its father. Bishop v. Hampton, 11 Ala. 254 (1847).

An infant is in esse, for the purpose of taking an estate for its benefit, from the time of conception, provided it be born alive, and after such a period of fetal existence that its continuance in life may be reasonably expected. Nelson v. Iverson, 24 Ala. 9 (1853).

If born alive. — An unborn child is considered as having an existence for certain purposes beneficial to it, but the existence is conditional and imperfect, and confers no right of property until it is born alive. Gillespie v. Nabors, 59 Ala. 441 (1877).

Rents and profits during time child is en ventre sa mere. — In the case of descent the presumptive heir may enter and receive the profits from the estate for his own use until the birth of the child en ventre sa mere. Bishop v. Hampton, 11 Ala. 254 (1847).

§ 43-8-48. Parent and child relationship.

If, for purposes of intestate succession, a relationship of parent and child must be established to determine succession by, through, or from a person:

(1) An adopted person is the child of an adopting parent and not of the natural parents except that adoption of a child by the spouse of a natural parent has no effect on the right of the child to inherit from or through either natural parent;

(2) In cases not covered by subdivision (1) of this section, a person born out of wedlock is a child of the mother. That person is also a child of the father, if:

a. The natural parents participated in a marriage ceremony before or after the birth of the child, even though the attempted marriage is void; or

b. The paternity is established by an adjudication before the death of the father or is established thereafter by clear and convincing proof, but the paternity established under this paragraph is ineffective to qualify the father or his kindred to inherit from or through the child unless the father has openly treated the child as his, and has not refused to support the child. (Acts 1982, No. 82-399, § 2-109.)

Commentary

The definition of "child" and "parent" in § 43-8-1 incorporates the meanings established by this section, thus extending them for all purposes of the Code. See § 43-8-252 for the definition of "spouse" for purposes of intestate succession.

The provisions in this section are essentially the provisions of UPC § 2-109, except that subdivision (1) has been changed relative to the rights of the adopted child to continue to inherit from natural parents. The change is a retention of Alabama law (§ 26-10-5(c) (1975)) on this point.

Inheritance rights of adopted children and illegitimate children were contained in scattered provisions of the Alabama Code. See, former § 43-3-7 and §§ 43-7-8, 26-10-5 through 26-10-7, 26-11-1 and 26-11-2 (1975). Inheritance by a child adopted under the laws of a foreign state is also covered. Section 26-10-6 (1975).

With regard to inheritance rights of adopted children, this section apparently reaches the same intended effect as the preexisting Alabama statutes and this section is much simpler in wording. The preexisting Alabama law is complex and under some possible constructions has very questionable support from a policy standpoint.

Note that § 26-10-5 (1975) provides that where an adopter is the spouse of a natural parent of an adopted child, such natural and adopted parent and kindred shall inherit from the adopted child the same as natural parents and kindred unless otherwise specifically provided in the final order of adoption. Except for the suggestion in § 26-10-5 (1975) that a court in the order of adoption may provide otherwise, the same result will follow under this act.

With regard to inheritance rights of illegitimate children, Alabama law was not changed as the rights relate to the mother. If the father attempts to legitimate the child through a marriage to the mother, Alabama law was not changed, but may be clarified slightly by this section. The rights of a child born out of wedlock to inherit from a father go farther than prior Alabama statutes, but the law codified here is consistent with recent Alabama case law. See, Everage v. Gibson, 372 So. 2d 829 (Ala. 1979); Shelly v. Woodyard, 382 So. 2d 516 (Ala. 1980). The difference in the codification in this section and prior Alabama case law is that there is no time limitation in this section on when a child may attempt to establish paternity against the father except that the adjudication must be before the father's death. The case law in Alabama at the time of the enactment of this chapter was that paternity must be established during the father's lifetime and within two years of birth. Everage v. Gibson, 372 So. 2d 829 (Ala. 1979); Shelly v. Woodyard, 382 So. 2d 516 (Ala. 1980). Because there are serious reservations about the constitutionality of the two-year limitation, it has not been made a part of this section.

I. General Consideration.
II. Decisions Under Prior Law.

I. GENERAL CONSIDERATION.

Cross references. — As to legitimation of children, see § 26-11-1 et seq.

Collateral references. — 2 C.J.S., Adoption of Children, §§ 63-65. 10 C.J.S., Bastards, §§ 24-30. 26A C.J.S., Descent & Distribution, § 28.

2 Am. Jur. 2d, Adoption, §§ 92-99. 10 Am. Jur. 2d, Bastards, §§ 133-165. 23 Am. Jur. 2d, Descent & Distribution, §§ 41-44.

Illegitimate child as a "child" within statute limiting the right of amount of disposition by will by one survived by a child. 23 ALR 400.

Inheritance by, from or through illegitimate. 24 ALR 570; 83 ALR 1330; 48 ALR2d 759; 60 ALR2d 1182.

Denial of, or expression of doubt as to, paternity or other relationship as estoppel to assert right of inheritance by virtue of such relationship. 33 ALR 579.

Right of child legitimated by marriage of parents to take by inheritance from kindred of parents. 64 ALR 1124.

What constitutes a "marriage" within meaning of a statute legitimating issue of all marriages null in law. 84 ALR 499.

Statute regarding status or rights of children born out of wedlock as applicable to children born before it became effective. 140 ALR 1323.

What amounts to recognition within statutes affecting the status or rights of illegitimates. 33 ALR2d 705.

Inheritance from illegitimate. 48 ALR2d 759.

Conflict of laws as to legitimacy or legitimation or as to rights of illegitimates, as affecting descent and distribution of decedent's estate. 87 ALR2d 1274.

Inheritance by illegitimate from or through mother's ancestors or collateral kindred. 97 ALR2d 1101.

Inheritance by illegitimate from mother's other illegitimate children. 7 ALR3d 677.

Right of adopted child to inherit from intestate natural grandparent. 60 ALR3d 631.

Legitimation by marriage to natural father of child born during mother's marriage to another. 80 ALR3d 219.

II. DECISIONS UNDER PRIOR LAW.

Editor's note. — In light of the similarity of the subject matter, decisions under former §§ 43-3-7 and 43-3-8 are included in the annotations for this section.

Former § 43-3-7 did not violate equal protection of law by discriminating on basis of illegitimacy. Everage v. Gibson, 372 So. 2d 829 (Ala. 1979), cert. denied, 445 U.S. 931, 100 S. Ct. 1322, 63 L. Ed. 2d 765 (1980).

In order to claim the right to inherit from intestate father's estate, a child born out of wedlock may prove legitimation by the marriage of his parents plus a clear and unambiguous recognition of the child by the father. Or, such child may introduce a written, attested and filed declaration of legitimation. Finally, the child may show a judicial determination of paternity made within two years of birth and during the father's lifetime. Everage v. Gibson, 372 So. 2d 829 (Ala. 1979), cert. denied, 445 U.S. 931, 100 S. Ct. 1322, 63 L. Ed. 2d 765 (1980).

Section liberally construed. — Although former § 43-3-7 was in derogation of the common law, it was basically remedial and beneficent, and was to be liberally construed in order to carry out its obvious purpose of assuaging the harsh and unjust rule of the common law. Hudson v. Reed, 259 Ala. 340, 66 So. 2d 909 (1953).

Repudiation of common-law rule. — Former § 43-3-7 repudiated the common-law rule that prevented a bastard from inheriting from any but his own offspring, and made him quasi-legitimate. See Butler v. Elyton Land Co., 84 Ala. 384, 4 So. 675 (1888).

The heritable blood of the common law could flow only out of the civil contract of marriage between man and wife. The heritable blood of an illegitimate flows from the veins of the mother alone. The statute in favor of illegitimates, like the general statute of descents and distribution, follows the lead of the natural affections, and seeks to make such provision as the mother would probably make. Williams v. Witherspoon, 171 Ala. 559, 55 So. 132 (1911).

The policy of the state toward children born outside of the marriage relation was modified by former § 43-3-7 from that of the common law. Hunt v. United States Steel Corp., 274 Ala. 328, 148 So. 2d 618 (1963).

Bastard made the heir of its mother as fully as if born in wedlock. — Former §§ 43-3-7 and 43-3-8 were placed in the Code as a part of the general system of laws governing descents and distributions. And, if it be inquired why in express terms they failed to make the bastard and his descendants the heirs of his mother, an obvious answer is that by their very terms they made the bastard as much the child and heir of his mother as if he were born in lawful wedlock, that is, fully legitimated him for the purpose of heirship and succession, and as though he never were a bastard. This being accomplished by these sections, it must have been intended, by their association with the other general statutes of descent and distribution, that further legitimate descent in the bastard line was sufficiently cared for by those general statutes, if such specification were needed. Indeed, it would seem that considerations of verbal economy and statutory condensation would forbid a needless repetition of any of those provisions. Foster v. Lee, 172 Ala. 32, 55 So. 125 (1911); Everage v. Gibson, 372 So. 2d 829 (Ala. 1979), cert. denied, 445 U.S. 931, 100 S. Ct. 1322, 63 L. Ed. 2d 765 (1980).

Former §§ 43-3-7 and 43-3-8 were complete within themselves, but were a part of an entire system of statutes on the subject of descents and distributions, and were to be construed in pari materia with them. Butler v. Elyton Land Co., 84 Ala. 384, 4 So. 675 (1888); Moore v. Terry, 220 Ala. 47, 124 So. 80 (1929);

Hudson v. Reed, 259 Ala. 340, 66 So. 2d 909 (1953).

Proof of paternity is immaterial. — A bastard who is not legitimated may only inherit from his mother or her descendants, even though his paternity is satisfactorily shown. Moore v. Terry, 220 Ala. 47, 124 So. 80 (1929).

Bastards are heirs only of their mothers, and of her other bastard children, if any, and not of any kindred on the part of their mothers, although all their kindred on the part of their mothers are still made the heirs of bastards. Foster v. Lee, 172 Ala. 32, 55 So. 125 (1911).

But the legitimate child of a bastard may inherit from the bastard's mother. — The legitimate child of a deceased bastard may inherit from the bastard's mother, and such a child succeeds to the parent's right of inheritance from a bastard brother or sister. The legitimate child of a bastard has all the rights of any child as to the parent, and the bastard parent can transmit to his or her legitimate child all the rights he or she has equally with any other parent. Foster v. Lee, 172 Ala. 32, 55 So. 125 (1911).

There can be no question about a legitimate child having the right to inherit from his illegitimate half brother. — And it has been held that a bastard's uncles of the half blood on the side of the bastard's mother are the bastard's "next of kin" and entitled to his estate, if the bastard dies intestate and leaves no surviving wife, mother, brothers or sisters, or their descendants. Mostilla v. Ash, 234 Ala. 626, 176 So. 356 (1937).

An illegitimate child can inherit from his kindred on the part of his mother in like manner as if he had been lawfully begotten of his mother. Hudson v. Reed, 259 Ala. 340, 66 So. 2d 909 (1953).

The illegitimate children of an illegitimate mother can inherit from their mother's legitimate half brother, when their mother and her half brother have the same mother. Hudson v. Reed, 259 Ala. 340, 66 So. 2d 909 (1953).

Rights under Workmen's Compensation Law. — The illegitimate children of a deceased female employee are entitled to death benefits under the Workmen's Compensation Law of this state, but not so the illegitimate children of a male employee. Hunt v. United States Steel Corp., 274 Ala. 328, 148 So. 2d 618 (1963).

Elimination of bastard's natural father. — In determining who was entitled to an intestate bastard's estate as his next of kin, bastard's natural father and descendants on his side were required to be eliminated. Mostilla v. Ash, 234 Ala. 626, 176 So. 356 (1937).

§ 43-8-49. Advancements.

If a person dies intestate as to all his estate, property which he gave in his lifetime to an heir is treated as an advancement against the latter's share of the estate only is declared in a contemporaneous writing by the decedent or acknowledged in writing by the heir to be an advancement. For this purpose the property advanced is valued as of the time the heir come into possession or enjoyment of the property or as of the time of death of the decedent, whichever first occurs. If the recipient of the property fails to survive the decedent, the property is not taken into account in computing the intestate share to be received by the recipient's issue, unless the declaration or acknowledgment provides otherwise. (Acts 1982, No. 82-399, § 2-110.)

Commentary

This section alters the common law relating to advancements by requiring written evidence of the intent that an inter vivos gift be an advancement. The statute is phrased in terms of the donee being an "heir" because the transaction is regarded as of decedent's death; of course, the donee is only a prospective heir at the time of the transfer during lifetime. Most inter vivos transfers today are intended to be absolute gifts or are carefully integrated into a total estate plan. If the donor intends that any transfer during lifetime be deducted from the donee's share of his estate, the donor may either execute a will so providing or, if he intends to die intestate, charge the gift as an advance by a writing within this section. This section applies only when the decedent died intestate and not when he leaves a will. This application is in accord with prior Alabama law as stated in Little v. Ennis, 207 Ala. 111, 92 So. 167 (1922).

This section applies to advances to collaterals (such as nephews and nieces) as well as to lineal descendants. The statute does not spell out the method of taking account of the advance, since this process is well settled by the common law and is not a source of litigation. Provisions for advancements in the Alabama statutes were previously included in ten sections. Former §§ 43-3-30 through 43-3-34 and §§ 43-3-35 through 43-3-39 (1975). The concept in Alabama extended only to children and other lineal descendants of the intestate, but a written acknowledgment of the advancement was not necessary. Former § 43-3-30 (1975). If the person, who received an advancement, predeceased the intestate, in Alabama lineal descendants and heirs of the recipient were charged with the advancement in determining their share. Former § 43-3-33 (1975). This result will be changed under this section.

I. General Consideration.
II. Decisions Under Prior Law.

I. GENERAL CONSIDERATION.

Collateral references. — 26A C.J.S., Descent & Distribution, §§ 91-115.

3 Am. Jur. 2d, Advancements, §§ 1-19.

Widow's statutory distributive share as affected by advancements to others, or by provisions of will that legatees shall take certain indebtedness owing to testator as part of their share. 76 ALR 1420.

II. DECISIONS UNDER PRIOR LAW.

Editor's note. — In light of the similarity of the subject matter, decisions under former §§ 43-3-30, 43-3-32 and 43-3-34 are included in the annotations for this section.

An advancement is a provision made by a parent to his child of money or property, the entire interest in which passes out of the former in his lifetime, though it is not necessary in all cases that it should take effect in possession before his death. Grey v. Grey, 22 Ala. 233 (1853).

Not all gifts to children constitute advancements. — In the distributees of Mitchell v. Mitchell, 8 Ala. 414 (1845), it is said in the opinion: "It must be a marriage portion, or 'something to set up in the world with.'"

Property sent home by a father to his daughter and son-in-law, on their marriage, must be regarded as an advancement, unless at the time a less estate is declared or limited. Barnett v. Branch Bank, 22 Ala. 642 (1853); Rumbly v. Stainton, 24 Ala. 712 (1854).

A mere subscription to stock in the name of the heir is not sufficient to constitute an advancement. Butler v. Merchants' Ins. Co., 14 Ala. 777 (1848).

Death intestate contemplated. — Former § 43-3-30 contemplated death intestate, and children of decedent were not liable thereunder for advances made to them when the father had made a will, although he died intestate as to part of his property devised to his wife, who predeceased him. The law contemplated that the devisor by his will provided against advances. Little v. Ennis, 207 Ala. 111, 92 So. 167 (1922).

And a perfected gift is essential to an advancement. — When a conveyance of land was void because not properly attested, it could not be treated as an advancement. The gift must be perfected before there can be a deduction of it as an advancement. Glover v. Woodward, 204 Ala. 63, 85 So. 270 (1920).

Presumption that gifts by parent to child are advancements. — When money or property was given by a parent to his child, it would be presumed to be an advancement under former § 43-3-30, unless the nature of the gift repelled such presumption, as in the case of trifling presents, money expended for education, etc. Dent v. Foy, 210 Ala. 475, 98 So. 390 (1923).

Gift must be made in anticipation of the future share of the child in the estate of the parent. Malone v. Malone, 106 Ala. 567, 17 So. 676 (1895); Dent v. Foy, 210 Ala. 475, 98 So. 390 (1923).

Advancements will not be liable for debts or costs of administering. — Advancements cannot be made liable for the debts of the estate of the decedent; they will not be liable for costs and expenses of the estate; they cannot be set apart as exempt to the widow and minors of the decedent from administration; they do not become a part of the assets of the estate to be administered; but they must be considered in the division and distribution only of the estate, as part of the estate, among the children or their descendants. Dent v. Foy, 210 Ala. 475, 98 So. 390 (1923).

Unless made fraudulently. — Where advances are fraudulently made and the estate of the deceased is insufficient to pay creditors, the creditors may by a creditors' complaint brought against the children subject the advances to the payment of their claims. Handley v. Heflin, 84 Ala. 600, 4 So. 725 (1888).

Widow's rights. — Widow held not entitled, upon the distribution of her husband's estate, to have the advancements made by him to his children in his lifetime collated for her benefit, but only entitled to a share of what remained, exclusive of such advancements. Logan v. Logan, 13 Ala. 653 (1848); Andrews v. Hall, 15 Ala. 85 (1848).

Valuation of shares in partition, etc. — Shares in partition or distribution are, as to the corpus of the property, to be valued at the time when they became the actual property of the heir or distributee. Turner v. Kelly, 67 Ala. 173 (1880).

When a parent makes an advancement to children, reserving a life estate, the value of the property when it is actually delivered to the children is the amount to be brought into the estate when the distributive share is sought. Wilks v. Greer, 14 Ala. 437 (1848).

§ 43-8-50. Controversy as to advancements — How issue made up and tried.

Controversies as to advancements are cognizable before the probate court, on the application, either of a party who has received an advancement, or of a party in interest, who alleges that an advancement has been made; and upon demand of either party, an issue in writing shall be made up under the direction of the court and tried by a jury as in other cases of contested fact. (Code 1867, § 1904; Code 1876, § 2268; Code 1886, § 1931; Code 1896, § 1469; Code 1907, § 3773; Code 1923, § 7384; Code 1940, T. 16, § 20; Code 1975, § 43-3-35.)

Code commissioner's note. — This section was originally codified as § 43-3-35 of the 1975 Code.

The section eliminates the necessity for technical pleading. — It is unnecessary that pleadings in a controversy relating to advancements be technically formed, in view of this section, the issues being made in writing as directed by the probate court. Dent v. Foy, 210 Ala. 475, 98 So. 390 (1923).

When a prima facie case is made out by the complainants, the burden of proof shifts to the defendants, who claim no advancements were made. Dent v. Foy, 210 Ala. 475, 98 So. 390 (1923).

It is not applicable in partition action. — This section has reference to controversies as to advancements, whether they have been made or not and their amounts, and it does not authorize the probate court in partition actions to adjust and equalize advancements among tenants in common where the lands descend from a common ancestor. Bozone v. Daniel, 39 So. 774 (Ala. 1905).

Testimony as to transaction with deceased. — Section 12-21-163, providing that no interested person shall testify as to any transaction with deceased person whose estate is interested, did not disqualify the distributees from testifying in an action, under this section, as to whether gifts made by decedent to them were intended as advancements or absolute gifts, title having passed at the time of the delivery, as the estate had no interest. Dent v. Foy, 210 Ala. 475, 98 So. 390 (1923).

Cited in Benagh v. Turrentine, 60 Ala. 557 (1877).

Collateral references. — 26A C.J.S., Descent & Distribution, § 108.

3 Am. Jur. 2d, Advancements, § 67 et seq.

§ 43-8-51. Same — Discovery of advancements.

Pending administration of an estate, on the application of the executor or administrator, or someone interested in the estate, to the probate court where the administration is, alleging on oath that an advancement has been made by the decedent, and that the value of such advancement is not expressed in any conveyance or receipt, within the applicant's knowledge, or in any charge made by the decedent, the judge of probate must issue citation to the distributee or heir alleged to have received such advancement, requiring him, within a specified time, not less than 30 nor more than 60 days, to report on oath a list of the property received, the time when and the value of the same when received, or to deny on oath having received any advancement from the decedent. If the party alleged to have received the advancement is a nonresident of the state, notice must be given by publication once a week for three successive weeks in some newspaper published in the county, or if no paper is published in the county, then in one published in the adjoining county, requiring him to answer within a specified time, not less than 40 days, nor more than 90 days. (Code 1867, § 1905; Code 1876, § 2269; Code 1886, § 1932; Code 1896, § 1470; Code 1907, § 3774; Code 1923, § 7385; Code 1940, T. 16, § 21; Code 1975, § 43-3-36.)

Code commissioner's note. — This section was originally codified as § 43-3-36 of the 1975 Code.

Cited in Comer v. Shehee, 129 Ala. 588, 30 So. 95 (1900).

§ 43-8-52. Same — Proceedings and answer upon death of distributee.

In case of the death of any distributee or heir alleged to have received advancements, his legal representatives or heirs at law shall be required to report or answer in the same manner as set forth in section 43-8-51; and if they are residents of this state, notice must be given by citation, and if nonresidents, by publication, as provided for in cases embraced in section 43-8-51. If any of the heirs at law of such deceased distributee or heir are minors or persons of unsound mind, the probate court must appoint a suitable guardian ad litem for them, who shall deny the allegation contained in such application, and demand proof thereof. (Code 1867, § 1906; Code 1876, § 2270; Code 1886, § 1933; Code 1896, § 1471; Code 1907, § 3775; Code 1923, § 7386; Code 1940, T. 16, § 22; Code 1975, § 43-3-37.)

Code commissioner's note. — This section was originally codified as § 43-3-37 of the 1975 Code.

§ 43-8-53. Same — Contest of answer.

Upon the rendition of the report or answer of the distributee or heir alleged to have received an advancement, or of his legal representatives or heirs, if deceased, if the executor or administrator, or any of the parties interested in such estate are not satisfied with the report or answer, on the ground that the same does not set forth all the property received or advanced, or does not set forth the true value of the property at the time it was received or advanced, or is not satisfied that the report or answer is true, then, in either case, such party may file objections thereto, stating the grounds of the objections, and the judge of probate must set a day, at such time as he may think proper, for hearing and determining, according to the evidence, as to the amount of property advanced, the time when advanced, and its value when received. He must give all the parties interested notice of such objections, and of the time set for hearing the same, by citation, if residents of this state, or if nonresidents, by publication in some newspaper published in the county, or if no paper is published in the county, then in one published in an adjoining county, once a week for three successive weeks. (Code 1867, § 1907; Code 1876, § 2271; Code 1886, § 1934; Code 1896, § 1472; Code 1907, § 3776; Code 1923, § 7387; Code 1940, T. 16, § 23; Code 1975, § 43-3-38.)

Code commissioner's note. — This section was originally codified as § 43-3-38 of the 1975 Code.

Cited in Clements v. Hood, 57 Ala. 459

(1876); Thompson v. Acree, 69 Ala. 178 (1881).

Collateral references. — 26A C.J.S., Descent & Distribution, §§ 108-115.

§ 43-8-54. Same — Consequence of failure to answer.

In case any distributee or heir, or the legal representatives of heirs at law of any distributee or heir alleged to have received an advancement, and on whom a citation has been personally served as above provided, fail or neglect to return a report, as required, or fail to answer such application, denying that he has received any advancement, such failure or neglect to report or answer shall be considered by the probate court as prima facie evidence that such person has received his full proportionate part of such estate. In case any nonresident against whom publication has been made fails or neglects to return a report as required, or to answer such application, denying that he has received any advancement, the court may proceed to take evidence ex parte as to the matters alleged in such application. (Code 1867, § 1908; Code 1876, § 2272; Code 1886, § 1935; Code 1896, § 1473; Code 1907, § 3777; Code 1923, § 7388; Code 1940, T. 16, § 24; Code 1975, § 43-3-39.)

Code commissioner's note. — This section was originally codified as § 43-3-39 of the 1975 Code.

Cited in Brown v. Powell, 45 Ala. 149 (1871).

§ 43-8-55. Against whom debts owed to decedent charged.

A debt owed to the decedent is not charged against the intestate share of any person except the debtor. If the debtor fails to survive the decedent, the debt is not taken into account in computing the intestate share of the debtor's issue. (Acts 1982, No. 82-399, § 2-111.)

Commentary

Alabama law was previously uncertain as to the particular point made in this section. Insofar as a testate situation is concerned and a lapse occurs because the legatee predeceases the testator, prior law in Alabama was contrary to the provisions of this section in that the debt owed the decedent was charged against the share taken by persons claiming through the debtor. Kling v. Goodman, 236 Ala. 297, 181 So. 745 (1938). However, the change follows most modern revisions of probate laws and it is consistent with the treatment of advancements in this act.

Collateral references. — 26A C.J.S., Descent & Distribution, § 129.

23 Am. Jur. 2d, Descent & Distribution, §§ 157-159.

§ 43-8-56. Alien status not a disqualification to inheriting.

No person is disqualified to take as an heir because he or a person through whom he claims is or has been an alien. (Acts 1982, No. 82-399, § 2-112.)

Commentary

The purpose of this section is to eliminate the ancient rule that an alien cannot acquire or transmit land by descent, a rule based on the feudal notions of the obligations of the tenant to the king. Although there never was a corresponding rule as to personalty, this section is phrased in light of the basic premise of the act that distinctions between real and personal property should be abolished.

This section has broader vitality in light of the decision of the United States Supreme Court in Zschernig v. Miller, 88 S.Ct. 664, 389 U.S. 429, 19 L.Ed.2d 683 (1968) holding unconstitutional a state statute providing for escheat if a nonresident alien cannot meet three requirements: the existence of a reciprocal right of a United States citizen to take property on the same terms as a citizen or inhabitant of the foreign country, the right of United States citizens to receive payment here of funds from estates in the foreign country, and the right of the foreign heirs to receive the proceeds of the local estate without confiscation by the foreign government. The rationale was that such a statute involved the local probate court in matters which essentially involve United States foreign policy, whether or not there is a governing treaty with the foreign country. Hence, the statute is "an intrusion by the state into the field of foreign affairs which the Constitution entrusts to the President and the Congress."

This section is in accord with prior Alabama law. See, Ala. Const. art. I, § 34 (1901) and § 35-1-1 (1975).

Collateral references. — 3 Am. Jur. 2d, Aliens and Citizens, § 17.

Relation of treaty to state and federal law. 4 ALR 1377; 134 ALR 882.

Declaratory judgment as to aliens. 19 ALR 1137; 50 ALR 42; 68 ALR 110; 87 ALR 1205; 114 ALR 1361; 142 ALR 8.

Necessity of judicial proceedings to vest title to real property in state by escheat. 23 ALR 1237; 79 ALR 1364.

Escheat of property of alien corporation. 23 ALR 1247; 79 ALR 1364.

Escheat as affecting contract for sale or lease to alien. 79 ALR 1366.

§ 43-8-57. Dower and curtesy abolished.

The estates of dower and curtesy are abolished. (Acts 1982, No. 82-399, § 2-113.)

Commentary

The provisions of this Code replace the common law concepts of dower and curtesy and their statutory counterparts. Those estates provided both a share in intestacy and a protection against disinheritance.

This section is contrary to prior Alabama law. See, former §§ 43-3-1 through 43-3-11, 43-5-1, 43-5-20 through 43-5-23, 43-5-40 through 43-5-53 (1975). Protection for the surviving spouse is otherwise provided under this Code.

Collateral references. — 25 C.J.S., Curtesy, § 1. 28 C.J.S., Dower, §§ 1, 6. 25 Am. Jur. 2d, Dower and Curtesy, §§ 1, 2.

Constitutionality of statutes in relation to dower. 10 ALR3d 212.

§ 43-8-58. Share of persons related to decedent through two lines.

A person who is related to the decedent through two lines of relationship is entitled to only a single share, based on the relationship which would entitle him to the larger share. (Acts 1982, No. 82-399, § 2-114.)

Commentary

Applying § 43-8-48 (1) the prospects of double inheritance are present to the point where this section seems desirable. The section has potential application in the not uncommon case where a deceased person's brother or sister marries the spouse of the decedent and adopts a child of the former marriage; it would block inheritance through two lines if the adopting parent died thereafter leaving the child as a natural and adopted grandchild of its grandparents.

671

Collateral references. — 26A C.J.S., 23 Am. Jur. 2d, Descent & Distribution, § 61. Descent & Distribution, § 20.

ARTICLE 4.

ELECTIVE SHARE OF SURVIVING SPOUSE; ABATEMENT.

§ 43-8-70. Right of surviving spouse to elective share.

(a) If a married person domiciled in this state dies, the surviving spouse has a right of election to take an elective share of the estate. The elective share shall be the lesser of:

(1) All of the estate of the deceased reduced by the value of the surviving spouse's separate estate; or

(2) One-third of the estate of the deceased.

(b) The "separate estate" of the surviving spouse shall include:

(1) All property which immediately after the death of the decedent is owned by the spouse outright or in fee simple absolute;

(2) All legal and equitable interests in property the possession or enjoyment of which are acquired only by surviving the decedent; and

(3) All income and other beneficial interests:

a. Under a trust;

b. In proceeds of insurance on the life of the decedent; and

c. Under any broad-based nondiscriminatory pension, profit-sharing, stock bonus, deferred compensation, disability, death benefit or other such plan established by an employer.

(c) If a married person not domiciled in this state dies, the right, if any, of the surviving spouse to take an elective share in property in this state is governed by the law of the decedent's domicile at death. (Acts 1982, No. 82-399, § 2-201.)

Commentary

Under the common law, a widow was entitled to dower, which was a life estate in a fraction of lands of which her husband was seized of an estate of inheritance at any time during the marriage. Dower encumbers titles and provides inadequate protection for widows in a society which classifies most wealth as personal property. Hence states have tended to substitute a forced share in the whole estate for dower and the widower's comparable common-law right of curtesy.

Few existing forced share statutes make adequate provisions for transfer by means other than succession to the surviving spouse and others. This section is one that takes into consideration other means of support the surviving spouse may have through his or her separate property. The separate property, as defined in this section, will include lifetime inter-spousal transfers and other inter-vivos financial arrangements the deceased spouse may have made for the survivor, but it also will include property the surviving spouse may have received from other sources. Including all separate property of the surviving spouse emphasizes the protective nature of the right and it avoids difficult tracing problems which could occur if the computation of the share included only separate property of the surviving spouse derived from the deceased spouse. Simplifying the computation was a consideration in choosing the approach adopted in this section for taking into account inter-vivos arrangements the deceased spouse may have made for the surviving spouse.

Another premise on which this section is based is that both spouses (whether or not both spouses are actually employed outside the home) do contribute to any estate accumulated by spouses. Any attempt to place an exact measurement of the relative contributions of each spouse could lead to very complex valuation problems. Simplification of the computation again was a basis for adopting an approach that does not require exact measurement of the value of each spouse's contribution to the estate. However, it was concluded, based on the premise that both spouses contribute to their combined estate, that the surviving spouse should be entitled to some share of the deceased spouse's estate, unless the surviving spouse has substantial separate property.

The provisions of this section are not entirely that of the UPC nor are they exactly the provisions of any statute in any other state, but ideas have been drawn from several statutes in other states in an attempt to provide a simplified approach to achieve policies on which there is rather broad agreement and support. Of course, a person can avoid the forced share by either ante-nuptial or post-nuptial agreements.

Prior Alabama provisions were in former § 43-1-15 (1975).

I. General Consideration.
II. Decisions Under Prior Law.

I. GENERAL CONSIDERATION.

Collateral references. — 97 C.J.S., Wills, §§ 1237-1267.

80 Am. Jur. 2d, Wills, §§ 1607-1610, 1652.

When is widow put to her election between provision made for her by her husband's will and her dower, homestead, or community right. 22 ALR 437, 68 ALR 507; 171 ALR 649.

Codicil as affecting application of statute as to election to take under or against will. 87 ALR 836.

Direction in will that provision for wife shall be in lieu of other rights or claims as requiring election as between rights in respect of intestate property or property not validly disposed of by will and provisions of will. 93 ALR 1384.

Parol or extrinsic evidence to show intention of testator as to election by beneficiary. 94 ALR 199.

When one to whom policy of life insurance is payable is put to election as between his rights under the policy and right to take under provision in will. 110 ALR 1317.

Doctrine of election or estoppel as applicable against beneficiary of will where provision for other beneficiary is invalid, not for reasons personal to former, but because of statute. 112 ALR 377.

Law in effect at time of execution of will or at time of death of testator as controlling. 129 ALR 859.

Doctrine of election as applicable where testator after the execution of the will transferred to one beneficiary the subject of a specific devise or bequest to another. 147 ALR 735.

Necessity of election between will and rights under a contract by testator to leave property at death. 152 ALR 898.

Joint, mutual, and reciprocal wills. 169 ALR 9.

Legacy accepted by surviving spouse in lieu of dower or other marital rights as charge upon real estate, where personalty is insufficient to pay legacy. 2 ALR2d 607.

Validity and effect of will clause disinheriting children if surviving spouse elects to take against will. 32 ALR2d 895.

Rights of surviving spouse taking under or against will as affected by provision in will directing conversion. 33 ALR2d 1280.

Right to elect against will as barred by separation agreement. 34 ALR2d 1040.

Compensation of legatees disappointed by another's election against will, out of renounced provision. 36 ALR2d 306.

Determination as to whether testator intended to dispose of property belonging to devisee or legatee so as to put latter to election. 60 ALR2d 736.

Doctrine of election where will purports to give devisee or legatee property he already owns. 60 ALR2d 789.

Election by spouse to take under or against will as exercisable by agent or personal representative. 83 ALR2d 1077.

Abandonment, desertion, or refusal to support on part of surviving spouse as affecting marital rights in deceased spouse's estate. 13 ALR3d 446.

II. DECISIONS UNDER PRIOR LAW.

Editor's note. — In light of the similarity of the subject matter, decisions under former § 43-1-15 are included in the annotations for this section.

Common law changed. — The common-law principle was that gifts or devises to a wife by a husband did not exclude the wife from dower, unless the intent to exclude her was expressed or the incompatibility of dower and the gift or devise was clear and manifest. Dower was regarded as a right conferred and favored by law, paramount to the will of the husband, beyond his power of disposition; and a gift or devise proceeding from the volition and bounty of the husband was deemed rather as a cumulative provision for the wife than as a satisfaction of her clear legal rights. The statutes of this state have reversed this rule of the common law, and the presumption under their operation is that a gift or bequest or devise to the wife is intended to exclude her, not only from dower, but from the share of the personal estate to which she is entitled under the statute of distributions, unless it is expressed, or clearly appears from the will, that the gift or bequest or devise was intended as cumulative to dower, and the right of distribution. Green v. Green, 7 Port. 19 (1838); McLeod v. McDonnel, 6 Ala. 236 (1844); Hillard v. Binford, 10 Ala. 977 (1847); Vaughan v. Vaughan, 30 Ala. 329 (1857); Adams v. Adams, 39 Ala. 274 (1864); Dean v. Hart, 62 Ala. 308 (1878).

Purpose of former § 43-1-15 was to place widow's claims beyond husband's control. — Neither the letter nor the spirit of former § 43-1-15 could be carried out, without according to the widow the same interest, and in the same form, as the statute confers in case of intestacy. Its purpose was to place her claims entirely beyond her husband's control. To hold otherwise would clothe the husband with power to bequeath specifically the most desirable half of his estate, and thus cast his widow upon the refuse for her distributive share. McReynolds v. Jones, 30 Ala. 101 (1857).

Husband may not, against wife's dissent, make provision for her different from dower rights and distributive share. Merchants' Nat'l Bank v. Hubbard, 222 Ala. 518, 133 So. 723 (1931).

General effect. — Former § 43-1-15, by enlarging the privilege of dissenting and extending it to "all cases," conferred on the widow the power to obstruct arbitrary disposition of the personalty which might be deemed unjust. Though no provision whatever was made for her in the will, she could dissent therefrom, and take such portion of the personal estate as she would be entitled to in case of intestacy. While the first section of the Act of 1912 only entitled the widow, in case of dissent, to take her dower, former § 43-1-15 entitled her to take both her dower in the land and the portion of the personal estate to which she would be entitled if her husband had died intestate. McGhee v. Stephens, 83 Ala. 466, 3 So. 808 (1888).

Former § 43-1-15 had to be construed with sections providing for descent and distribution of an intestate's estate, since the effect of a widow's dissent from her deceased husband's will is that she takes of his estate such property as she would have taken if he had died intestate (subject, of course, to the exception clause of the section). Stelzenmuller v. Carroll, 272 Ala. 13, 127 So. 2d 842 (1961).

Our statutes deny to the husband the power to make a will giving the wife a less estate than she would take without a will. She need merely dissent therefrom, with statutory limitations. Cook v. Morton, 241 Ala. 188, 1 So. 2d 890 (1941).

No presumption of undue influence on part of wife. — The fact that a wife has received more under her husband's will than under the dower and homestead laws, and the laws of distribution in case of intestacy would not raise a presumption of undue influence, since such laws merely deal with estates not disposed of by will and proceed on the hypothesis that the decedent will make a will if the laws do not dispose of his estate as he desires. Cook v. Morton, 241 Ala. 188, 1 So. 2d 890 (1941).

All lands of which husband was seised included. — There was nothing in the phraseology of former § 43-1-15 which limited its application to lands held at the decease of the testator, but when fairly construed, it embraced all lands of which the husband was seised at any time during the coverture. Sanders v. Wallace, 118 Ala. 418, 24 So. 354 (1898).

Widow's dissent from will bequeathing her a life estate accelerates remainder. — Dissent by the widow from the will of her husband with consequent renunciation by the widow of a life estate bequeathed to her by her husband is equivalent to its termination by the widow's death and accelerates a remainder provided by the will to take effect at her death. Decker v. Decker, 251 Ala. 278, 37 So. 2d 204 (1948).

Even where there is an alternative substitutional gift. — Where there is an alternative substitutional gift, this will not prevent acceleration, unless an intent to the contrary is manifest, and when acceleration occurs, the interests of alternative substitutional remaindermen are eliminated. Decker v. Decker, 251 Ala. 278, 37 So. 2d 204 (1948).

And she is not limited to homestead and dower. — A widow, dissenting from her husband's will by which she received a life estate in all of his property, was not limited to homestead and dower. She was also entitled to such portion of the personal estate as she would have been entitled to in case of intestacy. Decker v. Decker, 251 Ala. 278, 37 So. 2d 204 (1948).

Widow to either take by the will or claim her dower. — Former § 43-1-15 in terms, placed the dower and distributive share of a dissenting widow in the place of the provision made for her by the will, and precluded the conclusion that there could be a right to both. She could not take that which the will gave and also that which the law substituted for it. Adams v. Adams, 39 Ala. 274 (1864).

Widow's right to dissent from will is favored. Dorsey v. Dorsey, 224 Ala. 496, 140 So. 540 (1932).

Failure to dissent barred right of dower. — Under former § 43-1-15, as under former statutes, the failure of the widow to timely dissent from the will of her deceased husband was a bar to her right of dower, if the will made any provision for her which did not appear to have been intended as an addition to her dower. Adams v. Adams, 39 Ala. 264 (1864).

Wife's failure to dissent from husband's will amounted to forfeiture of dower rights and distributive share. Merchants' Nat'l Bank v. Hubbard, 222 Ala. 518, 133 So. 723 (1931).

By creating trust for wife, removable on contingency which had not occurred at his death, testator provided for her, making dissent prerequisite to distributive share. Fitzgerald v. Rogers, 223 Ala. 576, 137 So. 661 (1931).

Effect of widow's dissent from will. — The effect of this dissent is simply to annul the provisions of the will in her favor, to blot them out, and leave them as if from death or any other cause she had become incapable of taking. Former § 43-1-15 did not contemplate that it should in any other respect disappoint and nullify the arrangements of the will, destroy the rights it conferred, or create new and distinct rights in those who were strangers to the will. The whole purpose of the section was accomplished when she obtained that which the law would have given her if her husband had died intestate. Whatever she renounced, of necessity resulted to the indemnity of those who were injured by her renunciation. Dean v. Hart, 62 Ala. 308 (1878).

The effect of a widow's dissent from the will of her husband is that she takes of his estate such property as she would have taken had he died intestate. Mitchell v. Mitchell, 278 Ala. 670, 180 So. 2d 266 (1965).

Probate court decides as to proper dissent. — The question as to whether the widow has properly dissented from the will is to be settled by the probate court regardless of the fact that civil actions, to compel the widow as executrix to pay over certain legacies, are pending in the circuit court. Eastburn v. Canizas, 193 Ala. 574, 69 So. 459 (1915).

Proceedings under will not bar to privilege of dissent. — The fact that a widow filed the will for probate, was appointed under its terms executrix and proceeded with the administration thereof, clearly had no effect to bar her dissent. Eastburn v. Canizas, 193 Ala. 574, 69 So. 459 (1915). This same question received consideration in Reaves v. Garrett, 34 Ala. 558 (1859); Harrison v. Harrison, 39 Ala. 489 (1864); Key v. Jones, 52 Ala. 238 (1875).

Widow's right to dissent from will is not cut off by joining in petition to probate will, by acting as executrix or by declaration of satisfaction with will. Dorsey v. Dorsey, 224 Ala. 496, 140 So. 540 (1932).

The rights of a widow under the homestead statutes are fixed by the death of her husband and by the law in force at the time of his death. Hicks v. Huggins, 405 So. 2d 1324 (Ala. Civ. App.), cert. denied, 405 So. 2d 1328 (Ala. 1981).

No dissent is necessary to justify the widow to claim the homestead and personalty exemptions provided by law. Johnson v. Johnson, 252 Ala. 366, 41 So. 2d 287 (1949).

Widow entitled to exemption of personalty without dissent. — Where a decedent leaves a last will and testament, by which he disposes of all his property, the widow is not required to dissent from the will in order to become entitled to the exemption of personal property provided by statute. Hubbard v. Russell, 73 Ala. 578 (1883).

Widow who makes an election unadvisedly. — Although a widow is not concluded by an election unadvisedly made, she cannot avoid it while retaining the property which she has received by virtue of it; her only remedy against such election is to obtain relief on the restoration of what she has received. Adams v. Adams, 39 Ala. 274 (1864).

It is manifest justice that she should avoid the election only upon a restoration of what she has received. Steele v. Steele, 64 Ala. 438 (1879).

Equitable relief. — Transaction entered into by widow unadvisedly, whereby she parted with dower right and distributive share, with persons standing in fiduciary relation, could be relieved against in court. Dorsey v. Dorsey, 224 Ala. 496, 140 So. 540 (1932).

Where others have not acted thereon. — Widow's unadvised election will not bind her in court, if she restores what she received and others have not acted thereon so as to be prejudiced by her dissent thereafter. Merchants' Nat'l Bank v. Hubbard, 222 Ala. 518, 133 So. 723 (1931).

Wife's agreement during coverture not to dissent. — Wife's agreement, during coverture, not to dissent from husband's will was virtually agreement to forego dower and distributive share in consideration of provisions of will. Merchants' Nat'l Bank v. Hubbard, 222 Ala. 518, 133 So. 723 (1931).

Binding on husband. — Contract or acquiescence in will during husband's lifetime, to prevent wife from dissenting, must be intended to be binding or acted upon by husband. Merchants' Nat'l Bank v. Hubbard, 222 Ala. 518, 133 So. 723 (1931).

And is enforceable. — Widow's contract, during or before coverture, to release dower and distributive share, was enforceable when founded on adequate consideration, fair, reasonable, equal in all terms and mutual in operation and effect. Merchants' Nat'l Bank v. Hubbard, 222 Ala. 518, 133 So. 723 (1931).

But widow is not estopped when agreement falls short of adequacy. — Court should not declare estoppel against widow to dissent from will, though widow, in husband's lifetime, acquiesced therein, when provision falls short of adequacy of consideration and circumstances would not justify specific performance of a contract. Merchants' Nat'l Bank v. Hubbard, 222 Ala. 518, 133 So. 723 (1931).

Burden is upon husband to show adequacy. — Burden is upon husband or representatives to show fairness and adequacy of provision for wife to estop her from dissenting from will by reason of agreement during lifetime. Merchants' Nat'l Bank v. Hubbard, 222 Ala. 518, 133 So. 723 (1931).

What constitutes election. — Widow's mere intention not to dissent from will, as expressed in conversations or declarations, does not constitute "election." Merchants' Nat'l Bank v. Hubbard, 222 Ala. 518, 133 So. 723 (1931).

Bare acquiescence, without full, deliberate and intelligent choice, does not constitute widow's "election" not to dissent from will. Merchants' Nat'l Bank v. Hubbard, 222 Ala. 518, 133 So. 723 (1931).

Widow's "election" not to dissent does not result from circumstance that she stated that certain legatees would receive something under will. Merchants' Nat'l Bank v. Hubbard, 222 Ala. 518, 133 So. 723 (1931).

"Election" not to dissent does not result from widow's filing will for probate, though she receives letters testamentary and proceeds with administration. Merchants' Nat'l Bank v. Hubbard, 222 Ala. 518, 133 So. 723 (1931).

Receipt of money as trustee and occupancy of homestead not inconsistent with dissent. — Widow's receipt of money as trustee under will and her occupancy of homestead held not inconsistent with disaffirmance. Merchants' Nat'l Bank v. Hubbard, 222 Ala. 518, 133 So. 723 (1931).

Widow's priority as to creditors. — Although the widow's right of dower was superior to the claims of creditors, devisees or legatees, when she elected to accept the testamentary provision made for her in lieu of dower and it became necessary to sell lands for the payment of debts, her rights had to yield to the claim of the creditors, though superior to that of legatees or devisees. Steele v. Steele, 64 Ala. 438 (1879).

An insane widow is incapable of entering a dissent. Copeland v. Turner, 273 Ala. 609, 143 So. 2d 625 (1962).

Effect of forbearance to dissent by personal representative of widow. — In forbearing to dissent, the personal representative of the widow is no less a purchaser for value than was the widow in her forbearance during lifetime. Rowe v. Newman, 290 Ala. 289, 276 So. 2d 412 (1972).

A widow could not enlarge a dower interest into a fee simple title by dissenting from her husband's will, although she might have taken a fee in the event he had died without one. Mitchell v. Mitchell, 278 Ala. 670, 180 So. 2d 266 (1965).

Widow's marital share upon dissent treated with greater protection than specific bequests. — The widow's marital share upon dissent from her husband's will is treated with greater protection than specific bequests which lapse if necessary when she elects to take against the will. Cox v. United States, 421 F.2d 576 (5th Cir. 1970).

§ 43-8-71. Right of election personal to surviving spouse.

The right of election of the surviving spouse may be exercised only by the surviving spouse during his lifetime. If a guardian, custodian, curator, or conservator has been appointed for the surviving spouse, the right of election may be exercised only by order of the court upon petition of the fiduciary or upon the court's own initiative, after finding that exercise is necessary to provide adequate support for the surviving spouse during his probable life expectancy. (Acts 1982, No. 82-399, § 2-203.)

Commentary

This section is UPC § 2-203 modified to reflect the present status of representation of persons by fiduciaries in Alabama.

This section allows exercise of the right of election by the surviving spouse only. The surviving widower currently has no right of election.

However, this section allows the court to order upon petition of the guardian or its own initiative the exercise of election for a protected person in such a manner as to provide the surviving spouse with the elective share in order to provide adequate maintenance and support for such spouse during said spouse's probable life.

The court shall determine whether such election is necessary under the circumstances.

The section alters the standard utilized by the court in its determination of whether to allow election for a protected person. It also removes the requirement of hearing the testimony of at least two disinterested witnesses to determine that such dissent is to the surviving widow's best interest.

I. General Consideration.
II. Decisions Under Prior Law.

I. GENERAL CONSIDERATION.

Collateral references. — 97 C.J.S., Wills, §§ 1245, 1246, 1266.

80 Am. Jur. 2d, Wills, §§ 1611-1616.

Election by spouse to take under or against will as exercisable by agent or personal representative. 83 ALR2d 1077.

Factors considered in making election for incompetent to take under or against will. 3 ALR3d 6.

Time within which election must be made for incompetent to take under or against will. 3 ALR3d 119.

Who may make election for incompetent to take under or against will. 21 ALR3d 320.

II. DECISIONS UNDER PRIOR LAW.

Editor's note. — In light of the similarity of the subject matter, decisions under former § 43-1-17 are included in the annotations for this section.

Right conferred is personal. — The right given a sane widow to dissent from her husband's will is personal to the widow. Copeland v. Turner, 273 Ala. 609, 143 So. 2d 625 (1962). See also, Crenshaw v. Carpenter, 69 Ala. 572 (1881).

Hence, guardian or next friend cannot make an election. — Guardian or next friend does not have the right to make an election on behalf of the insane widow. Copeland v. Turner, 273 Ala. 609, 143 So. 2d 625 (1962); First Ala.

Bank v. Coker, 408 So. 2d 510 (Ala. 1982).

But can only petition court for order allowing dissent. — The guardian or next friend is simply given the right to petition the probate court for an order allowing the dissent. Copeland v. Turner, 273 Ala. 609, 143 So. 2d 625 (1962); First Ala. Bank v. Coker, 408 So. 2d 510 (Ala. 1982).

Whether or not an insane widow's interest will be best subserved by a dissent must be determined from all the facts and circumstances in a particular case. Copeland v. Turner, 273 Ala. 609, 143 So. 2d 625 (1962).

No hard and fast rule should be laid down. — In determining whether or not it is to the interest of an insane widow to dissent from a will, no hard and fast rule should be laid down. Copeland v. Turner, 273 Ala. 609, 143 So. 2d 625 (1962).

Evidence was not sufficient as a matter of law to sustain the trial court's finding that it was in the best interest of the widow for the court to authorize a dissent where the two disinterested witnesses who testified that it was in the incompetent widow's best interest to dissent were both the widow's sisters-in-law who knew little of the facts and consequences of the will. First Ala. Bank v. Coker, 408 So. 2d 510 (Ala. 1982).

Legal status of insane widow. — An insane widow or one acting for her does not come into court for the purpose of dissenting from her husband's will on like terms and in the

same legal status as if she were sane. Copeland
v. Turner, 273 Ala. 609, 143 So. 2d 625 (1962).

§ 43-8-72. Waiver of right to elect and of other rights.

The right of election of a surviving spouse and the rights of the surviving
spouse to homestead allowance, exempt property and family allowance, or any
of them, may be waived, wholly or partially, before or after marriage, by a
written contract, agreement, or a waiver signed by the party waiving after fair
disclosure. Unless it provides to the contrary, a waiver of "all rights" (or
equivalent language) in the property or estate of a present or prospective
spouse or a complete property settlement entered into after or in anticipation
of separation or divorce is a waiver of all rights to elective share, homestead
allowance, exempt property and family allowance by each spouse in the property of the other at death and a renunciation by each of all benefits which
would otherwise pass to him from the other by intestate succession or by virtue
of the provisions of any will executed before the waiver or property settlement.
(Acts 1982, No. 82-399, § 2-204.)

Commentary

The right to homestead allowance is conferred by § 43-8-110, that to exempt
property by § 43-8-111, and that to family allowance by § 43-8-112. The right to
renounce interests passing by testate or intestate succession is recognized by article
11 of this chapter. The provisions of this section, permitting a spouse or prospective
spouse to waive all statutory rights in the other spouse's property seem desirable
in view of the common and commendable desire of parties to second and later
marriages to insure that property derived from prior spouses passes at death to the
issue of the prior spouses instead of to the newly acquired spouse. The operation of
a property settlement as a waiver and renunciation takes care of the situation
which arises when a spouse dies while a divorce suit is pending.

Prior Alabama law was essentially identical to this section. See former § 43-5-20
(1975). Allison v. Stevens, 269 Ala. 288, 112 So. 2d 451 (1959); Rash v. Bogart, 226
Ala. 284, 146 So. 814 (1933); Merchants' National Bank of Mobile v. Hubbard, 222
Ala. 518, 133 So. 723 (1931); Crownover v. Crownover, 216 Ala. 286, 113 So. 42
(1927); and Richter v. Richter, 180 Ala. 218, 60 So. 880 (1913). Waiver of homestead
and exempt property is permitted by § 6-10-120 (1975). The procedure is changed
somewhat by this section but the effect is in accord with prior Alabama law.

The UPC, like prior Alabama law (see Allison v. Stevens, 269 Ala. 288, 112 So.
2d 457 (1959)) requires adequate consideration or that the agreement was entered
into knowingly after full disclosure and knowledge of the value of the estate in
order to be valid.

Editor's note. — In light of the similarity of
the subject matter, decisions under former
§ 43-5-20 are included in the annotations for
this section.

**Effect on right of occupancy and pro-
ceeds.** — Wife's release of homestead and
dower rights by joining in husband's mortgage
did not affect her rights to free occupancy and

proceeds of all land before homestead was set
apart and dower assigned after husband's
death, such income and her part of crops being
her individual property, not property of husband's estate. Whitehead v. Boutwell, 218 Ala.
109, 117 So. 623 (1928).

**Consideration moving to wife or to hus-
band only.** — Wife who joined with her hus-

band in a conveyance of land she could require a consideration inuring to herself as a condition on which she renounced her right to dower, or she could validly and effectually release her right thereto without such consideration and upon a consideration moving to her husband only. Allison v. Stevens, 269 Ala. 288, 122 So. 2d 451 (1959).

Collateral references. — 97 C.J.S., Wills, §§ 1245, 1246, 1266.

80 Am. Jur. 2d, Wills, § 1656.

What amounts to election by widow to take under or against will. 82 ALR 1509.

Waiver or abandonment of, or estoppel to assert, prior renunciation of, or election to take against, spouse's will. 29 ALR2d 227.

Time within which election must be made for incompetent to take under or against will. 3 ALR3d 119.

§ 43-8-73. Procedure for making election; petition; time limit; notice and hearing; withdrawal of demand; order of court; enforcement of order.

(a) The surviving spouse may elect to take his elective share by filing with the court and mailing or delivering to the personal representative, if any, a petition for the elective share within six months after the date of death, or within six months after the probate of the decedent's will, whichever limitation last expires.

The court may extend the time for election for cause shown by the surviving spouse before the time for election has expired.

(b) The surviving spouse shall give notice of the time and place set for hearing to persons interested in the estate whose interests will be adversely affected by the taking of the elective share.

(c) The surviving spouse may withdraw his demand for an elective share at any time before entry of a final determination by the court.

(d) After notice and hearing, the court shall determine the amount of the elective share and shall order its satisfaction from the assets of the estate. If it appears that a fund or property included in the estate has not come into the possession of the personal representative, or has been distributed by the personal representative, the court nevertheless shall fix the liability of any person who has any interest in the fund or property or who has possession thereof, whether as trustee or otherwise. The proceeding may be maintained against fewer than all persons against whom relief could be sought, but no person is subject to contribution in any greater amount than he would have been if relief had been secured against all persons subject to contribution.

(e) The order or judgment of the court may be enforced as necessary in suit for contribution or payment in other courts of this state or other jurisdictions. (Acts 1982, No. 82-399, § 2-205.)

Commentary

The language of this section has the effect of clearing included, nonprobate transfers to persons other than the surviving spouse of the lien of any possible elective share proceeding unless the spouse's action is commenced within six months after death. This bar on efforts to recapture nonprobate assets for an elective share does not apply to probate assets. Probate assets may be controlled by a will that may not be offered for probate until as late as five years from death. As to these, the limitation on the surviving spouse's proceeding is six months after the probate.

A dissent in Alabama previously had to be made in writing and deposited with the judge of probate within six months from the probate of the will. Former § 43-1-16 (1975). Prior Alabama law regarding the revocation of an election can be found in Merchants' National Bank of Mobile v. Hubbard, 222 Ala. 518, 133 So. 723 (1931), which permits recognition of a widow's revocation of election provided other distributees have not acted upon her election to their detriment. The primary difference between this section and prior Alabama law is in the provisions to whom notice must be given under this section. Under prior Alabama law the widow was not required to give notice to the interested persons.

I. General Consideration.
II. Decisions Under Prior Law.

I. GENERAL CONSIDERATION.

Collateral references. — 97 C.J.S., Wills, §§ 1249, 1250.

80 Am. Jur. 2d, Wills, §§ 1622-1624.

Time for election on behalf of incompetent to take under or against will, 74 ALR 452, 147 ALR 336.

Validity of election to take under or against will as affected by fact that it was filed before probate of will or grant of letters. 120 ALR 1270.

Extension of time within which spouse may elect to accept or renounce will. 59 ALR3d 767.

II. DECISIONS UNDER PRIOR LAW.

Editor's note. — In light of the similarity of the subject matter, decisions under former § 43-1-16 are included in the annotations for this section.

The dissent must be made in writing, and within one year (now six months) from the probate of the will, and although she may not be concluded by an election made unadvisedly, or in ignorance of facts calculated to influence her choice, the widow cannot treat such election as a nullity, nor avoid it, except upon the restoration of what she has received under it. Steele v. Steele, 64 Ala. 438 (1879).

And administrator cannot dissent for widow. — The widow's right to dissent from the will of the deceased husband is personal to her and cannot be exercised by the administrator in the event of her death, without having expressed her dissent. Donald v. Portis, 42 Ala. 29 (1868).

Dissent filed after death of widow held sufficient compliance. — Where a widow executed in writing her dissent from her husband's will, and handed it to a friend with instructions to file it in the office of the probate judge, and then died, if the dissent was filed by the person to whom it was entrusted, after her death, but within the period prescribed by law this was a sufficient compliance. McGrath v. McGrath, 38 Ala. 246 (1862).

§ 43-8-74. Entitlement of surviving spouse to certain benefits regardless of election.

A surviving spouse is entitled to homestead allowance, exempt property, and family allowance, whether or not he elects to take an elective share. (Acts 1982, No. 82-399, § 2-206.)

Commentary

The election does not result in a loss of benefits under the will (in the absence of renunciation) because those benefits are charged against the elective share under §§ 43-8-70 and 43-8-75 (a).

Former § 43-1-15 (1975) did not apply expressly to a widower. This section and former § 43-1-15 (1975) are consistent if the widow is not mentioned in the will; however, if the widow is mentioned the two sections are inconsistent.

Previously in Alabama, if the widow dissented from the will, she could not also take property devised or bequeathed to her under the will. See, Merchants' Nat'l Bank of Mobile v. Hubbard, 222 Ala. 518, 133 So. 723 (1931); Dean v. Hart, 62 Ala. 308 (1878); and Pearson v. Darrington, 32 Ala. 227 (1858).

This section does not alter the ability of a testator, by express provision in the will, from putting a surviving spouse to an election between accepting the devises provided or accepting the family exemptions provided by law. This matter is dealt with in §§ 43-8-110 through 43-8-113.

Collateral references. — 97 C.J.S., Wills, §§ 1244, 1285, 1286.

80 Am. Jur. 2d, Wills, §§ 1651-1656.

When is widow put to her election between provision made for her by her husband's will and her dower, homestead, or community right. 22 ALR 437; 68 ALR 507; 171 ALR 649.

Direction in will that provision for wife shall be in lieu of other rights or claims as requiring election as between rights in respect of intestate property or property not validly disposed of by will and provisions of will. 93 ALR 1384.

When one to whom policy of life insurance is payable is put to election as between his rights

under the policy and right to take under provision in will. 110 ALR 1317.

Necessity of election between will and rights under a contract by testator to leave property at death. 152 ALR 898.

Right to elect against will as barred by separation agreement. 34 ALR2d 1040.

Effect of testamentary gift on widow's right to fixed statutory allowance or allowance for support. 97 ALR2d 1319.

Abandonment, desertion, or refusal to support on part of surviving spouse as affecting marital rights in deceased spouse's estate. 13 ALR3d 446.

§ 43-8-75. How elective share satisfied; what property applied first; apportionment of others' liability for balance of elective share.

(a) In the proceeding for an elective share, values included in the estate which pass or have passed to the surviving spouse, or which would have passed to the surviving spouse but were renounced, are applied first to satisfy the elective share and to reduce any contributions due from other recipients of transfers included in the estate. For purposes of this subsection, the electing spouse's beneficial interest in any life estate or in any trust shall be computed as if worth one-half of the total value of the property subject to the life estate, or of the trust estate, unless higher or lower values for these interests are established by proof; provided, however, that, to the extent that the electing spouse's beneficial interest is a life estate or is an interest in a trust and is coupled with a general power of appointment (whether exercisable by deed or by will or by either), the beneficial interest shall be computed as being equal to two-thirds of the total value of the property subject to the life estate, or of the trust estate, with respect to which the general power of appointment exists.

(b) Remaining property of the estate is so applied that liability for the balance of the elective share of the surviving spouse is equitably apportioned among the recipients of the estate in proportion to the value of their interests therein. (Acts 1982, No. 82-399, § 2-207.)

Commentary

The provisions of this section generally follow UPC § 2-207, except that the provision in subsection (a) relative to valuation of an interest coupled with a general power of appointment has been added. Sections 43-8-110 through 43-8-112 have the effect of giving a spouse certain exempt property and allowances in addition to the amount of the elective share.

Prior Alabama law was contrary in that if a widow dissented from the will, she thereby renounced devises and bequests to her under the will. See, former § 43-1-15 (1975); Merchants' Nat'l Bank of Mobile v. Hubbard, 222 Ala. 518, 133 So. 723 (1931). See also, Comment to § 43-8-74.

Section 43-8-74 and subsection (a) of this section have the effect of protecting a decedent's plan as far as it provides values for the surviving spouse. The spouse is not compelled to accept the benefits devised by the decedent, but if these benefits are rejected, the values involved are charged to the electing spouse as if the devises were accepted. The second sentence of subsection (a) provides a rebuttable presumption of the value of a life estate or an interest in a trust, when this form of benefit is provided for an electing spouse by the decedent's plan.

Collateral references. — 97 C.J.S., Wills, §§ 1285, 1288.

80 Am. Jur. 2d, Wills, §§ 1641-1644.

Legacy accepted by surviving spouse in lieu of dower or other marital rights as charge upon real estate, where personalty is insufficient to pay legacy. 2 ALR2d 607.

Validity and effect of will clause disinheriting children if surviving spouse elects to take against will. 32 ALR2d 895.

Who must bear loss occasioned by election against will. 36 ALR2d 291.

§ 43-8-76. Order of abatement.

(a) Except as provided in subsection (b) of this section and except as provided in connection with the share of the surviving spouse who elects to take an elective share, shares of distributees abate, without any preference or priority as between real and personal property, in the following order:

(1) Property not disposed of by the will;

(2) Residuary devises;

(3) General devises;

(4) Specific devises.

For purposes of abatement, a general devise charged on any specific property or fund is a specific devise to the extent of the value of the property on which it is charged, and upon the failure or insufficiency of the property on which it is charged, a general devise to the extent of the failure or insufficiency. Abatement within each classification is in proportion to the value of property each of the beneficiaries would have received if full distribution of the property had been made in accordance with the terms of the will.

(b) If the will expresses an order of abatement, or if the testamentary plan or the express or implied purpose of the devise would be defeated by the order of abatement stated in subsection (a) of this section, the shares of the distributees abate as may be found necessary to give effect to the intention of the testator.

(c) If the subject of a preferred devise is sold or used incident to administration, abatement shall be achieved by appropriate adjustments in, or contribution from, other interests in the remaining assets. (Acts 1982, No. 82-399, § 2-208.)

Commentary

A testator may determine the order in which the assets of his estate are applied to the payment of his debts. If he does not, then the provisions of this section express rules which may be regarded as approximating what testators generally want. The statutory order of abatement is designed to aid in resolving doubts concerning the intention of a particular testator, rather than to defeat his purpose. Hence, subsection (b) directs that consideration be given to the purpose of a testator. This may be revealed in many ways. Thus, it is commonly held that, even in the absence of statute, general legacies to a wife, or to persons with respect to which the testator is in loco parentis, are to be preferred to other legacies in the same class because this accords with the probable purpose of the legacies.

Prior Alabama law seems to be consistent with this section. See, Ullmann v. First National Bank of Mobile, 273 Ala. 154, 137 So. 2d 496 (1961); and Festorazzi v. First National Bank of Mobile, 288 Ala. 645, 264 So. 2d 496 (1972). It may be (but it is unclear) that there is a preference for real property in abatement in Alabama because of the statute which provides for a preference for land when a sale is necessary for the payment of debts. See, § 43-2-441 (1975). There is a preference for the surviving spouse when property is being taken for the payment of debts, claims and expenses of administration. Rowe v. Newman, 290 Ala. 289, 276 So. 2d 412 (1972).

Collateral references. — 97 C.J.S., Wills, §§ 1289, 1290.

80 Am. Jur. 2d, Wills, §§ 1641-1644.

Compensation of legatees disappointed by another's election against will, out of renounced provision. 36 ALR2d 306.

ARTICLE 5.

SPOUSE AND CHILDREN NOT PROVIDED FOR IN WILL.

§ 43-8-90. Omitted spouse.

(a) If a testator fails to provide by will for his surviving spouse who married the testator after the execution of the will, the omitted spouse shall receive the same share of the estate he would have received if the decedent left no will unless it appears from the will that the omission was intentional or the testator provided for the spouse by transfer outside the will and the intent that the transfer be in lieu of a testamentary provision be reasonably proven.

(b) In satisfying a share provided by this section, the devises made by the will abate as provided in section 43-8-76. (Acts 1982, No. 82-399, § 2-301.)

Commentary

Section 43-8-137 provides that a will is not revoked by a change of circumstances occurring subsequent to its execution other than as described by that section. This section reflects the view that the intestate share of the spouse is what the decedent would want the spouse to have if he had thought about the relationship of his old will to the new situation. One effect of this section should be to reduce the number of instances where a spouse will claim an elective share.

This section is like § 2-301 of the UPC except in subsection (a) "be reasonably proven" is substituted for "shown by statements of the testator or from the amount of the transfer or other evidence." Although the wording is somewhat different and the order of stating the principles is not the same, the effect of this section is in accord with former § 43-1-15 (1975) and it is clear that this section applies to a spouse of either sex. Parker v. Hall, 362 So. 2d 875 (Ala. 1978) declared former § 43-1-8 (1975) unconstitutional in that it only applied to wills of females. Even if former § 43-1-8 (1975) were made applicable to both males and females, it would be changed by this section.

Collateral references. — 26A C.J.S., Descent & Distribution, § 48.

79 Am. Jur. 2d, Wills, § 68.

Construction, application and effect of statutes which deny or qualify right of widow or surviving husband to elect against will of other spouse. 87 ALR 228.

What constitutes transfer outside the will precluding surviving spouse from electing statutory share under Uniform Probate Code, § 2-301. 11 ALR4th 1213.

§ 43-8-91. Pretermitted children.

(a) If a testator fails to provide in his will for any of his children born or adopted after the execution of his will, the omitted child receives a share in the estate equal in value to that which he would have received if the testator had died intestate unless:

(1) It appears from the will that the omission was intentional;

(2) When the will was executed the testator had one or more children and devised substantially all his estate to the other parent of the omitted child; or

(3) The testator provided for the child by transfer outside the will and the intent that the transfer be in lieu of a testamentary provision be reasonably proven.

(b) If at the time of execution of the will the testator fails to provide in his will for a living child solely because he believes the child to be dead, the child receives a share in the estate equal in value to that which he would have received if the testator had died intestate.

(c) In satisfying a share provided by this section, the devisees made by the will abate as provided in section 43-8-76. (Acts 1982, No. 82-399, § 2-302.)

Commentary

This section provides for both the case where a child was born or adopted after the execution of the will and not foreseen at the time and thus not provided for in the will, and the rare case where a testator omits one of his existing children because of the mistaken belief that the child is dead. This section is similar to UPC § 2-302 except that in subdivision (a)(3) "be reasonably proven" is substituted for "shown by statements of the testator or from the amount of the transfer or other evidence." This section is not intended to alter the rules of evidence applicable to statements of a decedent.

Although the sections dealing with advancement and ademption by satisfaction (§§ 43-8-49 and 43-8-231) provide that a gift during lifetime is not an advancement or satisfaction unless the testator's intent is evidenced in writing, this section may permit oral evidence to establish a testator's intent that lifetime gifts or nonprobate transfers such as life insurance or joint accounts are in lieu of a testamentary provision for a child born or adopted after the will. Here there is no real contradiction of testamentary intent, since there is no provision in the will itself for the omitted child.

To preclude operation of this section it is not necessary to make any provision, even nominal in amount, for a testator's present or future children; a simple recital in the will that the testator intends to make no provision for then living children or any the testator thereafter may have, would meet the requirement of subdivision (a)(1).

Subdivision (a)(1) of this section corresponds to the Alabama law contained in former § 43-1-9 (1975). The remainder of the section differs from prior Alabama law relating to pretermitted children. Former § 43-1-9 (1975) stated that "whenever a testator has a child born after the making of his will, either in his lifetime or after his death, or adopted after the making of his will, and no provision is made in the will in any way for such contingency, such birth or adoption operates as a revocation of the will, so far as to allow such child to take the same share of the estate of the testator as if he had died intestate." Under this section, this same rule would apply unless (a) when the will was executed the testator had one or more children and devised substantially all his estate to the other parent of the omitted child or (b) the testator provided for the omitted child by transfer outside the will and the intent that the transfer be in lieu of a testamentary provision be reasonably proven.

The general principle upon which this section is based is the same as the principle supporting former § 43-1-9 (1975). That principle is to preclude unintentional pretermission of a child. See, Shackelford v. Washburn, 180 Ala. 168, 60 So. 318 (1912). The purpose of subsection (a) of this section is to prescribe the character of evidence necessary to avoid application of this statute to any will and prior Alabama law is in accord. See, Shackelford v. Washburn, 180 Ala. 168, 60 So. 318 (1912). Subdivision (a)(1) of this section is clearly in accord with the prior Alabama statute. Id. Subdivision (a)(2) probably is within the most recent construction of the Alabama statute. See, Thomas v. Reynolds, 234 Ala. 212, 174 So. 753 (1937); but cf., Boackle v. Bloom, 272 Ala. 490, 132 So. 2d 586 (1961). Subdivision (a)(3) probably is an extension of prior Alabama law. Through the definition of "children" in this Code, this section will be extended to children legitimated subsequent to the execution of a will. This result will be contrary to the previous construction of the Alabama statute. See, Foster v. Anderson, 287 Ala. 111, 248 So. 2d 707 (1971).

685

Subsection (b) is an adaptation of the concept referred to as dependent relative revocation. Subsection (b) would permit what might be a desirable result without necessitating a revocation of the whole will. The approach would seem to more nearly carry out the intent of the testator. The concept of dependent relative revocation probably is part of the common law of Alabama, although the courts have not had an opportunity to apply it in a case. See, Franklin v. Rogue, 245 Ala. 379, 17 So. 2d 405 (1944).

There was previously no Alabama statute corresponding to subsection (b).

Under subsection (c) and § 43-8-76, any intestate estate will first be applied to satisfy the share of a pretermitted child. Prior Alabama law is in accord with this subsection. Former § 43-1-9 (1975).

I. General Consideration.
II. Decisions Under Prior Law.

I. GENERAL CONSIDERATION.

Collateral references. — 26A C.J.S., Descent & Distribution, §§ 43-46.

79 Am. Jur. 2d, Wills, §§ 632-641.

Intention of testator as regards child not provided for by will as affecting applicability of statutes to prevent disinheritance of children. 65 ALR 472.

Nature of, and remedies for enforcement of, the interest which a pretermitted child takes by virtue of statute where parent leaves will. 123 ALR 1073.

Illegitimate child as within contemplation of statute regarding rights of child pretermitted by will, or statute preventing disinheritance of child. 142 ALR 1447.

Disinheritance provision or mere nominal bequest as affecting application of statute for benefit of pretermitted children. 152 ALR 723.

What, other than express disinheritance or bequest, avoids application of statute for benefit of pretermitted or afterborn children. 170 ALR 1317.

Adoption of child as revoking will. 24 ALR2d 1085.

Statutory revocation of will by subsequent birth or adoption of child. 97 ALR2d 1044.

Conflict of laws as to pretermission of heirs. 99 ALR3d 724.

II. DECISIONS UNDER PRIOR LAW.

Editor's note. — In light of the similarity of the subject matter, decisions under former § 43-1-9 are included in the annotations for this section.

Former status of adopted child. — Prior to 1956 an adopted child did not become a pretermitted heir upon the death of his adoptive parent if his adoption was made final after the execution of the will. Hamilton v. Smith, 264 Ala. 199, 86 So. 2d 283 (1956).

Common-law doctrine. — At common law the subsequent marriage and the birth of issue of a testator operated as an unqualified revocation of his will in toto. The birth of issue alone had no effect upon the will, and such issue was cut out of participating in any property devised by such will. At common law, however, it was well settled that if provision was made in the will for a future wife and child or children, in the event of a subsequent marriage and birth of issue, then such will was not impliedly revoked by a subsequent marriage and birth of issue. Woodliff v. Dunlap, 187 Ala. 255, 65 So. 936 (1914).

Reason for rule. — The true reason at common law for the implied revocation of a will where there was a subsequent marriage and birth of issue of the testator not provided for by the testator was that the testator executed the will with "a tacit condition annexed to the will when made that it should not take effect if there should be a total change in the situation of the testator's family." Woodliff v. Dunlap, 187 Ala. 255, 65 So. 936 (1914); Foster v. Martin, 286 Ala. 709, 246 So. 2d 435 (1971).

Inconsistency of common-law rule remedied. — The inconsistency of the common-law rule that subsequent marriage and birth of issue of testator revoked will, in absence of provision for such contingency, but that birth of issue alone did not do so, was remedied by statute giving child born after execution of will statutory share of testator's estate, in absence of provision for such contingency. Thomas v. Reynolds, 234 Ala. 212, 174 So. 753 (1937).

General principle. — It is clear that the principle upon which all statutes providing for pretermitted children are based is whether pretermission was unintentional, although it may not be expressly so stated in the statute. To say that a testator may dispose of his estate by a will duly executed, and yet that he may not disinherit any of his heirs, even though he indicates a clear intention to do so, is absurd. Shackelford v. Washburn, 180 Ala. 168, 60 So. 318 (1912).

Purpose. — The legislative intent manifested by incorporating into former § 43-1-9 the words "and no provision is made in the will in any way for such contingency" was to particularly prescribe the character of evidence necessary to preclude the application of this section to the will, and to guard against the uncertainty of looking into the mind of the testator or testatrix through extrinsic facts depending on parol testimony. This was the holding in Shackelford v. Washburn, 180 Ala. 168, 60 So. 318 (1912), when read in the light of Gay v. Gay, 84 Ala. 38, 4 So. 42 (1888), and reaffirmed in Woodliff v. Dunlap, 187 Ala. 255, 65 So. 936 (1914), and Ensley v. Hodgson, 212 Ala. 526, 103 So. 465 (1925). Toomer v. Van Antwerp Realty Corp., 238 Ala. 87, 189 So. 549 (1939).

This interpretation does not preclude evidence going to show the circumstances and condition of the testator, the property to be disposed of and the objects of the testator's bounty, to aid the court in the interpretation of language of doubtful meaning, used in the will and designed to provide for the contingency, or where other legal and competent evidence admitted in the case raises a latent ambiguity as to the meaning of such language. Chambers v. Ringstaff, 69 Ala. 140 (1881); Fowlkes v. Clay, 205 Ala. 523, 88 So. 651 (1921); Thomas v. Reynolds, 234 Ala. 212, 174 So. 753 (1937); Money v. Money, 235 Ala. 15, 176 So. 817 (1937); Toomer v. Van Antwerp Realty Corp., 238 Ala. 87, 189 So. 549 (1939).

Proper application of the law requires consideration of all the statutes which come into play when one dies intestate. Risher v. United States, 465 F.2d 1 (5th Cir. 1972).

Right to property. — The pretermission section creates and confers upon natural born and adopted children a right to property which would not be theirs without the section. Foster v. Martin, 286 Ala. 709, 246 So. 2d 435 (1971).

Children legitimated subsequent to execution of will. — Children, legitimated by a testator subsequent to the execution of his will and for whom no provision is made in the will, do not share in the estate as pretermitted heirs. Foster v. Anderson, 287 Ala. 111, 248 So. 2d 707 (1971).

Each after-born child must be provided for. — In Ensley v. Hodgson, 212 Ala. 526, 103 So. 465 (1925), a will was considered and held not to provide for the contingency of after-born children except as to a child with which the testator's wife was pregnant when the will was made and another child born subsequently was entitled to share in the estate.

Where testator's will made no provision for any of his eight children living when the will was made and there was nothing in the will indicating that testator contemplated having after-born children, a child born after the making of the will was entitled to take a child's part the same as if the father had died intestate. Boackle v. Bloom, 272 Ala. 490, 132 So. 2d 586 (1961).

Effect on powers of widow as executrix. — Where the testator bequeathed all his property to his wife and gave her unqualified power to sell any and all of the property she might deem best, the subsequent birth of issue unprovided for in the will did not revoke the widow's power to sell as executrix, but merely imposed on her the duty to account to the after-born children for their interest in the proceeds of the property sold. Woodliff v. Dunlap, 187 Ala. 255, 65 So. 936 (1914).

Statutes of descent and distribution as standard and yardstick. — Pretermission section, by reference, sets up the statutes of descent and distribution as the standard and yardstick by which the share of the pretermitted child shall be measured, and declares the method of apportionment in satisfaction of the share and the right to compel contribution from the devisee or devisees under the will. Toomer v. Van Antwerp Realty Corp., 238 Ala. 87, 189 So. 549 (1939).

In short, pretermission section, when read into the will, makes the will provide for the pretermitted child or children as though such provision had been written into the will by the testatrix. Toomer v. Van Antwerp Realty Corp., 238 Ala. 87, 189 So. 549 (1939).

Where widow's separate estate was in excess of her dower and distributive share, so that she would not have been entitled to any property on decedent's intestate death, pretermitted child would have been entitled to one half of the deceased father's personal property under the intestacy statute and was thus entitled to one half of the property under the will through the operation of the pretermitted heir statute, which allows the pretermitted child to take the same share of the testator's estate as if he had died intestate. Risher v. United States, 465 F.2d 1 (5th Cir. 1972).

Birth of issue does not revoke will in toto. — The birth of children to testatrix after making of will devising all of property to testatrix' husband and making no provision for children did not revoke the will in its entirety, but only insofar as to allow children to take same share of estate of testatrix as if she had died intestate. Toomer v. Van Antwerp Realty Corp., 238 Ala. 87, 189 So. 549 (1939).

Failure to make provision for children in will creates trust. — Where testatrix in will executed prior to birth of her children devised all property to husband without provision for children, title to her property passed to husband under will, impressed with a trust and the duty to account to the children who were also beneficiaries of the estate. Toomer v. Van Antwerp Realty Corp., 238 Ala. 87, 189 So. 549 (1939).

Son made beneficiary after execution of will became co-owner of proceeds of insurance policy. — Insured's son, made beneficiary of life insurance policy jointly with insured's daughter, originally named as sole beneficiary therein, after execution of insured's will bequeathing policy to her, became co-owner of death benefits thereunder on insured's death, notwithstanding such bequest. Carter v. First Nat'l Bank, 237 Ala. 47, 185 So. 361 (1938).

Expression of feeling that wife would provide suitably for children. — Section giving child born after execution of will a statutory share of testator's estate, in absence of provision for such contingency, did not apply to a will which was executed several months before birth of testator's third child, and which left testator's estate to wife without making any bequest to children for expressed reason that testator felt that wife would deal justly with and provide suitably for children. Thomas v. Reynolds, 234 Ala. 212, 174 So. 753 (1937).

Evidence may be introduced to interpret doubtful language. — Although applicability of section providing for revocation of prior will upon birth of a child is dependent upon absence of any provision in will for that contingency, evidence relating to circumstances of testator, property to be disposed of and object of testator's bounty, may be introduced to aid court in interpreting doubtful language in will, or where other evidence raises a latent ambiguity as to meaning thereof. Toomer v. Van Antwerp Realty Corp., 238 Ala. 87, 189 So. 549 (1939).

Sufficient provision in will. — A will by a young married woman without children whereby she gives to her husband all her property "notwithstanding I may have a child or children living at may death" satisfies the requirements of pretermission section. Shackelford v. Washburn, 180 Ala. 168, 60 So. 318 (1912).

Children are entitled to share in administration of estate. — Where administration of estate of testatrix who has made no provision for children born subsequent to execution of will is had without any accounting or contribution in favor of the pretermitted children, they may, on timely application to court, have administration of estate opened and be let in to participate therein. Toomer v. Van Antwerp Realty Corp., 238 Ala. 87, 189 So. 549 (1939).

Presumption of full settlement where more than 20 years had elapsed. — Where more than 20 years had elapsed after death of testatrix without any question as to failure of will to provide for children subsequently born, the presumption would be indulged, in the interest of repose, that full settlement had been made with children. Toomer v. Van Antwerp Realty Corp., 238 Ala. 87, 189 So. 549 (1939).

Delay of more than 40 years foreclosed judicial investigation. — Although sale of land devised to husband by testatrix, who had made him executor under will making no provision for children subsequently born, was a breach of the trust imposed upon husband as executor and armed children with right to proceed to obtain their share in estate, their delay of more than 40 years until after death of husband foreclosed judicial investigation, and all things would be presumed in the interest of repose. Toomer v. Van Antwerp Realty Corp., 238 Ala. 87, 189 So. 549 (1939).

When shares pass under will. — Where testatrix made no provision in will for her children born subsequent to execution thereof, the share in her estate of children surviving her but dying before receipt thereof passed under will to devisee, and not under statutes of descent and distribution. Toomer v. Van Antwerp Realty Corp., 238 Ala. 87, 189 So. 549 (1939).

Administrator cum testamento annexo was proper party to maintain suit for slander of title because, even though title to the property passed to the devisees upon the death of prior owner, such passing was subject to the payment of debts and charges against the estate and administrator had duty imposed by law to sell realty to pay debts in the event the personal estate was insufficient to pay the debts. Proctor v. Gissendaner, 579 F.2d 876 (5th Cir. 1978).

ARTICLE 6.

EXEMPT PROPERTY AND ALLOWANCES.

§ 43-8-110. Homestead allowance.

(a) A surviving spouse of a decedent who was domiciled in this state is entitled to a homestead allowance of $6,000.00. If there is no surviving spouse, each minor child and each dependent child of the decedent is entitled to a homestead allowance amounting to $6,000.00 divided by the number of minor and dependent children of the decedent. The homestead allowance is exempt from and has priority over all claims against the estate. Homestead allowance is in addition to any share passing to the surviving spouse or minor or dependent child by the will of the decedent unless otherwise provided in the will, by intestate succession or by way of elective share.

(b) The value of any constitutional right of homestead in the family home received by a surviving spouse or child shall be charged against that spouse or child's homestead allowance to the extent that the family home is part of the decedent's estate or would have been but for the homestead provision of the Constitution. (Acts 1982, No. 82-399, § 2-401.)

Commentary

See § 43-8-252 for the definition of "spouse" which controls in this article. Also, see § 43-8-43. Waiver of homestead is covered by § 43-8-72. "Election" between a provision of a will and homestead is not required unless the will so provides.

A set dollar amount for homestead allowance was dictated by the desirability of having a certain level below which administration may be dispensed with or be handled summarily, without regard to the size of allowances under § 43-8-111. The "small estate" line is controlled largely, though not entirely, by the size of the homestead allowance.

Another reason for a set amount is related to the fact that homestead allowance may prefer a decedent's minor or dependent children over his other children. It was felt desirable to minimize the consequence of application of an arbitrary age line among children of the testator.

In Alabama, homestead from the estate of the husband has been in value $6,000.00 and in area 160 acres for the widow and minor children during the life of the widow or the minority of the children. Former § 6-10-60 (1975). When the homestead set apart for the widow and minor children, or either, constituted all the real estate owned in Alabama by the decedent at the time of his death, title to such homestead vested absolutely in the widow, the children (minors and adults) and the descendants of deceased children. Former § 6-10-62 (1975).

If all debts had been paid and the homestead was not devised by will, the homestead in Alabama vested in the widow and minor children without limitation as to value. Former § 6-10-60 (1975). If the decedent had no homestead, the widow and minor children were entitled to have the homestead exemption from any other real estate which conformed to the limitations on homestead in lieu of homestead. Section 6-10-61 (1975). However, in order to be entitled to the homestead exemption, the decedent must have died with a homestead or other real property from which a homestead could be carved or which could be sold so that $6,000.00 in lieu of homestead could be taken. See, Geohegan v. Geohegan, 272 Ala. 514, 133 So. 2d 50 (1961).

Collateral references. — 40 C.J.S., Homesteads, §§ 239-291.
40 Am. Jur. 2d, Homestead, §§ 1-3, 156.

§ 43-8-111. Exempt property.

If the decedent was domiciled in this state at the time of death the surviving spouse is entitled to receive, in addition to the homestead allowance, property of a value not exceeding $3,500.00 in excess of any security interests therein in household furniture, automobiles, furnishings, appliances and personal effects. If there is no surviving spouse, children of the decedent are entitled jointly to the same value. If encumbered chattels are selected and if the value in excess of security interests, plus that of other exempt property, is less than $3,500.00, or if there is not $3,500.00 worth of exempt property in the estate, the spouse or children are entitled to other assets of the estate, if any, to the extent necessary to make up the $3,500.00 value. Rights to exempt property and assets needed to make up a deficiency of exempt property have priority over all claims against the estate, except that the right to any assets to make up a deficiency of exempt property shall abate as necessary to permit prior payment of homestead allowance and family allowance. These rights are in addition to any benefit or share passing to the surviving spouse or children by the will of the decedent unless otherwise provided, by intestate succession, or by way of elective share. (Acts 1982, No. 82-399, § 2-402.)

Commentary

Unlike the exempt values described in §§ 43-8-110 and 43-8-112, the exempt values described in this section are available in a case where the decedent left no spouse but left only adult children. The possible difference between beneficiaries of the exemptions described by §§ 43-8-110 and 43-8-112, and this section, explain the provision in this section which establishes priorities.

Section 43-8-72 covers waiver of exempt property rights. This section indicates that a decedent's will may put a spouse to an election with reference to exemptions, but that no election is presumed to be required.

In Alabama previously, certain specific personal property was exempt in favor of the widow and minor children (former § 6-10-63 (1975)), but the property exempted had only a remote relation, if any, to the needs of or property held by persons in a modern society. An additional exemption was allowable to an amount of $2,000.00 in value. Former § 6-10-64 (1975). Wages and salary of the decedent/employee in a sum not exceeding $2,000.00 could be paid to the surviving spouse, or if there was no surviving spouse, to the person having actual custody and control of the decedent's minor children. Payment of these wages discharged the debtor from further liability, but the money received had to be counted as part of the personalty exempted to the recipient. Former § 6-10-65 (1975).

Collateral references. — 35 C.J.S., Exemptions, § 23.

80 Am. Jur. 2d, Wills, § 1653.

§ 43-8-112. Family allowance.

In addition to the right to homestead allowance and exempt property, if the decedent was domiciled in this state, the surviving spouse and minor children whom the decedent was obligated to support and children who were in fact being supported by him are entitled to a reasonable allowance in money out of the estate for their maintenance during the period of administration, which allowance may not continue for longer than one year if the estate is inadequate to discharge allowed claims. The allowance may be paid as a lump sum or in periodic installments. It is payable to the surviving spouse, if living, for the use of the surviving spouse and minor and dependent children; otherwise to the children, or persons having their care and custody; but in case any minor child or dependent child is not living with the surviving spouse, the allowance may be made partially to the child or his guardian or other person having his care and custody, and partially to the spouse, as their needs may appear. The family allowance is exempt from and has priority over all claims but does not have priority over the homestead allowance.

The family allowance is not chargeable against any benefit or share passing to the surviving spouse or children by the will of the decedent unless otherwise provided in the will, by intestate succession, or by way of elective share. The death of any person entitled to family allowance terminates his right to allowances not yet paid. (Acts 1982, No. 82-399, § 2-403.)

Commentary

The allowance provided by this section does not qualify for the marital deduction under the Federal Estate Tax Act because the interest is a nonqualified terminable interest. A broad code must provide the best possible protection for the family in all cases, even though this may not provide desired tax advantages for certain larger estates. In estates falling in the federal estate tax bracket where careful planning may be expected, it is important to the operation of formula clauses that the family allowance be clearly terminable or clearly nonterminable. With this section clearly creating a terminable interest, estate planners can create a plan which will operate with certainty. Finally, in order to facilitate administration of this allowance without court supervision it is necessary to provide a fairly simple and definite framework.

In determining the amount of the family allowance, account should be taken of both the previous standard of living and the nature of other resources available to the family to meet current living expenses until the estate can be administered and assets distributed. While the death of the principal income producer may necessitate some change in the standard of living, there must also be a period of adjustment. If the surviving spouse has a substantial income, this may be taken into account. Whether life insurance proceeds payable in a lump sum or periodic installments were intended by the decedent to be used for the period of adjustment or to be conserved as capital may be considered. A living trust may provide the needed income without resorting to the probate estate. If a husband has been the principal source of family support, a wife should not be expected to use her capital to support the family.

Obviously, need is relative to the circumstances, and what is reasonable must be decided on the basis of the facts of each individual case. Note, however, that under § 43-8-113 the personal representative may not determine an allowance of more than $500.00 per month for one year; a court order would be necessary if a greater allowance is reasonably necessary.

Alabama previously had no comparable section. Section 6-10-67 (1975) included the concept of permitting use of the exempt property before it was actually set apart.

Collateral references. — 34 C.J.S., Executors and Administrators, §§ 323, 324.

31 Am. Jur. 2d, Executors and Administrators, §§ 324-339, 470.

§ 43-8-113. Source, determination and documentation of exempt property and allowances; petition for relief by personal representative or interested person.

If the estate is otherwise sufficient, property specifically devised is not used to satisfy rights to homestead and exempt property. Subject to this restriction, the surviving spouse, the guardians of the minor children, or children who are adults may select property of the estate as homestead allowance and exempt property. The personal representative may make these selections if the surviving spouse, the children or the guardians of the minor children are unable or fail to do so within a reasonable time or if there are no guardians of the minor children. The personal representative may execute an instrument or deed of distribution to establish the ownership of property taken as homestead allowance or exempt property. He may determine the family allowance in a lump sum not exceeding $6,000.00 or in periodic installments not exceeding $500.00 per month for one year, and may disburse funds of the estate in payment of the family allowance and any part of the homestead allowance payable in cash. The personal representative or any interested person aggrieved by any selection, determination, payment, proposed payment, or failure to act under this section may petition the court for appropriate relief, which relief may provide a family allowance larger or smaller than that which the personal representative determined or could have determined. (Acts 1982, No. 82-399, § 2-404.)

Commentary

Procedures for setting apart exemptions to the widow and minor children in Alabama are stated in §§ 6-10-80 through 6-10-107 (1975).

Collateral references. — 35 C.J.S., Exemptions, § 138. 40 C.J.S., Homesteads, §§ 209, 210.

40 Am. Jur. 2d, Homesteads, §§ 158-177.

§ 43-8-114. Widow may retain dwelling, etc., until assignment of dower.

The widow may retain possession of the dwelling house where her husband most usually resided next before his death, with the offices and buildings appurtenant thereto and the plantation connected therewith until her dower is assigned her, free from the payment of rent. (Code 1852, § 1359; Code 1867, § 1630; Code 1876, § 2238; Code 1886, § 1900; Code 1896, § 1515; Code 1907, § 3824; Code 1923, § 7437; Code 1940, T. 34, § 50; Code 1975, § 43-5-40.)

Code commissioner's note. — This section was originally codified as § 43-5-40 of the 1975 Code.

Editor's note. — The following cases were decided prior to abolition of dower by § 43-8-57.

The widow is entitled to quarantine as incidental right to dower. — The residence of the husband, not of the wife, at the time of his death is the controlling fact which entitles the widow to quarantine as an incidental right to dower. Clancy v. Stephens, 92 Ala. 577, 9 So. 522 (1891).

This right to remain in possession is the widow's so-called "quarantine" right incidental to dower, and it is the residence of the husband next before his death, and not of the wife at the time of his death, which is the controlling fact. Clark v. McWaters, 286 Ala. 559, 243 So. 2d 670 (1971).

Quarantine is an incident of dower. Both rights perish with the death of the widow. Hale v. Cox, 240 Ala. 622, 200 So. 772 (1941); Taylor v. United States, 388 F.2d 849 (5th Cir. 1967).

Which she may enforce until dower is assigned. — A widow retaining use of a deceased husband's land may so hold until dower is assigned without having to account for rents, income and profits, and the burden of having dower assigned is upon the owner of the fee, but failure to have dower assigned and permitting widow to retain possession without more does not deprive the owner of the fee. Lynch v. Jackson, 235 Ala. 90, 177 So. 347 (1937).

Before dower is assigned, and during widow's lifetime, right of quarantine continues, and, if widow or heirs wish to change status, they may do so by causing an assignment of dower. Hale v. Cox, 240 Ala. 622, 200 So. 772 (1941).

The right is limited to certain property. — In view of this section and former § 6-10-60, widow's right of immediate possession and use of property at time of husband's death was limited to house and lot last occupied by him, since neither her homestead nor quarantine rights would entitle her to possession of his other houses and lots at that time. Lester v. Stroud, 212 Ala. 635, 103 So. 692 (1925).

It is not a property right. — This section giving a widow right to possession of a dwelling house, with appurtenances free of rent, till dower assigned, gives her no property right that would by such occupancy defeat the ultimate title and right of possession descending to heirs. Chavers v. Mayo, 202 Ala. 128, 79 So. 594 (1918).

Nor an estate of inheritance. — The widow's right of quarantine is but an incident to dower and neither is a heritable estate, both perish with the widow, hence the heirs of the widow cannot revive an action for quarantine. Clancy v. Stephens, 92 Ala. 577, 9 So. 522 (1891).

Possession is not adverse to husband's heirs. — The right given under this section is a mere continuance of the possession of the deceased husband, and, however long the possession may have been continued, it was without the elements or constituents of a possession hostile and adverse to the heirs of the husband. Foy v. Wellborn, 112 Ala. 160, 20 So. 604 (1896); White v. Williams, 260 Ala. 182, 69 So. 2d 847 (1954).

Possession by widow who was entitled to life estate until her dower was assigned, by virtue of this section, was not adverse to remaindermen, in absence of facts showing that she openly asserted a hostile title. Bank of Columbia v. McElroy, 231 Ala. 454, 165 So. 105 (1935); White v. Williams, 260 Ala. 182, 69 So. 2d 847 (1954).

And statute of limitations does not run against owner while widow's possession is under right of quarantine. — A divestiture of the widow's dower right, as by a release to the heir or tenant, or other act amounting to a relinquishment of a dower, brought to the notice of the legal owner, would enable her thereafter to set up a possession which would be adverse, and to perfect and prove ownership thereunder according to the usual rules. But, so long as the right of quarantine accompanies her possession, it excludes the owner's right to the possession, and is sufficient to defeat any action he might bring therefor. While such is the status of the parties, no mere claim or assertion of ownership, however often and openly made, would start the statute of limitations to run against the owner, to whom the right of entry and the cause of action have not accrued. White

v. Williams, 260 Ala. 182, 69 So. 2d 847 (1954).

The widow is entitled by law to the full amount of rents and profits from the land during quarantine. Jay v. Jay, 289 Ala. 513, 268 So. 2d 788 (1972).

Under the provisions of this section the widow is entitled to the rents and profits of the homestead and the plantation connected therewith, regardless of area. Jay v. Jay, 289 Ala. 513, 268 So. 2d 788 (1972).

Widow is entitled to rents and profits from quarantine but not from dowable lands until assignment. — Unless dower is set apart to widow in her lifetime neither she nor her personal representative is ever entitled to rents and profits of land in which she may have been dowable, except that which accrued from her quarantine rights, but as soon as dower is assigned in her lifetime, her rights in the part included in the assignment vest in her as of date of husband's death. Hale v. Cox, 240 Ala. 622, 200 So. 772 (1941).

She may rent the property. — The object of this section is to provide for her a support until dower is allotted, on which she may enter. For this purpose she may rent the premises, and if the administrator, or heir, or any other person, receives the rents, she is entitled to recover them. Reeves v. Brooks, 80 Ala. 26 (1885).

She may cut reasonable amount of timber. — The doweress being in possession by virtue of this section is entitled to a reasonable amount of wood off the land for fuel, fences, agricultural erections and other necessary improvements, but to no more. Lowery v. Rowland, 104 Ala. 420, 16 So. 88 (1893).

And convert crops into assets. — In Blair v. Murphree, 81 Ala. 454, 2 So. 18 (1886), it was held, that a widow having the right to retain possession, under this section, is entitled to all the benefits that right confers, except those the statute itself denies her, and if the personal representative does not take the necessary steps to convert the crops into assets of the estate, the crop belongs to the widow.

Her right is not affected by sale under execution. — In Callahan v. Nelson, 128 Ala. 871, 29 So. 555 (1900), it was held, that the widow was entitled to remain in possession by virtue of this section, where the property in question was sold under execution to satisfy the husband's debts.

Where neither dower nor the homestead could be allotted to the widow in kind, the only alternative was to sell the property and award the widow her money in lieu of homestead and dower as provided by law. Beck v. Beck, 288 Ala. 479, 262 So. 2d 596 (1972).

Insanity is not a bar to right. — Insanity of the wife at the time of her husband's death and subsequent removal to an insane hospital does not bar the widow of her right given under this section and she can maintain or defend that possession by action against any and all persons not showing a better title, and may recover the rents and profits against anyone coming into possession without right. Clancy v. Stephens, 92 Ala. 577, 9 So. 522 (1891).

Removal or rental is not forfeiture. — Neither the removal from and renting the premises, instead of remaining in actual occupancy, nor her subsequent marriage, works a forfeiture of her quarantine. Foy v. Wellborn, 112 Ala. 160, 20 So. 604 (1896).

Consent is necessary to divest widow of right. — A sale by the personal representative of the husband for the payment of his debts does not divest the widow of her rights under this section and the purchaser acquires no right thereunder in the absence of written consent given by the widow prior to the sale as provided under § 43-2-466. Clancy v. Stephens, 92 Ala. 577, 9 So. 522 (1891).

Effect of divorce a vinculo for abandonment. — In Hinson v. Bush, 84 Ala. 368, 4 So. 410 (1888), overruling Williams v. Hale, 71 Ala. 83 (1881), it was held that a wife who had been divorced a vinculo for abandonment cannot under any circumstances claim dower at the death of the husband.

Effect of exclusion of homestead. — Although certain land could not be a part of what the law denominates the "homestead" it may be subject to the widow's right of quarantine occupancy as provided by this section. Jackson v. Rowell, 87 Ala. 685, 6 So. 95 (1889).

Rights of grantee of widow's dower interest. — The right given under this section is not an estate in the land, which can be sold under execution at law, or alienated. It terminates whenever the widow deprives herself of the right to dower by release to the heir, or in any other manner. Boynton v. Sawyer, 35 Ala. 497 (1860).

Conveyance of the widow's entire dower interest and her removal from the homestead entitled the grantee only to the rents or mesne profits to which the widow would have been entitled had she abandoned the homestead without conveying her dower interest. Norton v. Norton, 94 Ala. 481, 10 So. 436 (1892).

Payment of mortgage by widow. — Where a widow paid the interest on a mortgage given by husband on the homestead property, and had reduced the principal, held that, on settlement of her account as administratrix, she was improperly charged with interest on the mortgage, in view of this section, where she had already been charged with interest on rents which she should have held as administratrix. Boyte v. Perkins, 211 Ala. 130, 99 So. 652 (1924).

Sufficiency of pleadings. — In Grimmer v. Grimmer, 17 Ala. App. 616, 88 So. 44 (1920), it was held that pleadings of a widow in an action for rent under a contract, providing that the widow should pay stipulated rental for occupancy of the lessor's share of an undivided 215 acres of land, setting up that the property was occupied as the homestead plantation of the widow's husband, and that no dower, etc., had been assigned to her, were insufficient to bring her completely within this section, it not appearing that the lessor was not a co-owner with the husband instead of his heir.

Decree assigning dower to widow terminates her possessory right to all lands of deceased husband not allotted to her. Bowdoin v. Bowdoin, 225 Ala. 618, 144 So. 819 (1932).

She is not entitled, pending appeal without supersedeas from probate court decree assigning dower, to injunction restraining heirs from interfering with possession of lands not allotted to her. Bowdoin v. Bowdoin, 225 Ala. 618, 144 So. 819 (1932).

Cited in Springle v. Shields, 17 Ala. 295 (1850); Doe v. Webb, 18 Ala. 810 (1851); Pharis v. Leachman, 20 Ala. 662 (1852); McLaughlin v. Godwin, 23 Ala. 846 (1853); Boynton v. Sawyer, 35 Ala. 497 (1860); Slatter v. Meek, 35 Ala. 528 (1860); Harrison v. Boyd, 36 Ala. 203 (1860); Boyd v. Harrison, 36 Ala. 533 (1860);

McAllister v. McAllister, 37 Ala. 484 (1861); Waters v. Williams, 38 Ala. 680 (1863); Harrison v. Harrison, 39 Ala. 489 (1864); Griffin v. Bland, 43 Ala. 542 (1869); Pizzala v. Campbell, 46 Ala. 35 (1871); Benagh v. Turrentine, 60 Ala. 557 (1877); Calhoun v. Fletcher, 63 Ala. 574 (1879); Humes v. Scruggs, 64 Ala. 40 (1879); Tillman v. Spann, 68 Ala. 102 (1880); Steele v. Tutwiler, 68 Ala. 107 (1880); Jenks v. Terrell, 73 Ala. 238 (1882); Farris v. Houston, 74 Ala. 162 (1883); Barber v. Williams, 74 Ala. 331 (1883); Melton v. Andrews, 76 Ala. 586 (1884); James v. Clark, 89 Ala. 606, 7 So. 161 (1889); Bank of Hartselle v. Brindley, 213 Ala. 405, 104 So. 803 (1925); Whitehead v. Boutwell, 218 Ala. 109, 117 So. 623 (1928); Williams v. Anthony, 219 Ala. 98, 121 So. 89 (1929); Hopkins v. Crews, 220 Ala. 149, 124 So. 202 (1929); Gravely v. Phillips, 23 Ala. App. 471, 127 So. 248 (1930); Haney v. Ray, 253 Ala. 224, 43 So. 2d 889 (1950); Dauphin v. Gatlin, 256 Ala. 34, 53 So. 2d 580 (1951); McClendon v. Straub, 193 F.2d 596 (5th Cir. 1952); Ray v. Fowler, 265 Ala. 65, 89 So. 2d 573 (1956); Smith v. Persons, 285 Ala. 48, 228 So. 2d 806 (1969).

Collateral references. — 28 C.J.S., Dower, § 99.

ARTICLE 7.

WILLS GENERALLY.

I. General Consideration.
II. Decisions Under Prior Law.

I. GENERAL CONSIDERATION.

Collateral references. — 94 C.J.S., Wills, §§ 1, 91-107.

79 Am. Jur. 2d, Wills, §§ 56, 70, 167, 169, 179.

Rights and duties of life tenant with power to anticipate or enjoy principal. 2 ALR 1243; 27 ALR 1381; 69 ALR 825; 114 ALR 946.

Want of trustee as invalidating charitable trust. 5 ALR 315.

Admissibility and probative force, on issue as to mental condition, of evidence that one had been adjudged incompetent or insane, or had been confined in insane asylum. 7 ALR 568; 68 ALR 1309.

Experimental evidence as to possibility of testator seeing and hearing attesting witnesses. 8 ALR 18; 85 ALR 479.

Character as witness of one who signed will for another purpose. 8 ALR 1075.

Blind persons testamentary capacity. 9 ALR 1416; 37 ALR 603.

Capacity of inmate of house of prostitution to take by will. 16 ALR 457; 31 ALR2d 321.

Epilepsy as affecting testamentary capacity. 16 ALR 1418.

Husband or wife of beneficiary as attesting witness to will. 25 ALR 308.

Testator's name in body of instrument as sufficient signature where statute does not require will to be signed at end. 29 ALR 891.

Manner of signing as affecting sufficiency of signature of testator. 31 ALR 682; 42 ALR 954; 114 ALR 1110.

Duty of attesting witness with respect to mental capacity of testator. 35 ALR 79.

Membership in, or other connection with, club, society, association or corporation as disqualifying one as witness to will in which it is beneficiary. 53 ALR 211.

Evidence as to signature of testator other than that of subscribing witnesses. 63 ALR 1202.

Evidence as to time of affixing testator's signature, other than testimony of subscribing witnesses. 63 ALR 1204.

Effect of illegibility of signature. 64 ALR 208.

Competency of attesting witness who is not benefited by will except as it revokes an earlier will. 64 ALR 1306.

Heirs' or next of kins' right to attack devise to corporation on ground of its incapacity to take. 69 ALR 1359.

Codicil as validating will or codicil which was invalid or inoperative at time of its purported execution. 87 ALR 836; 21 ALR2d 821.

Discontinuance of active functions of religious or other society as affecting its right to legacy or devise. 91 ALR 840.

Merger or association with other organization as affecting legacy or devise to religious or other society. 91 ALR 840.

Necessity that subscription of attesting witnesses to will be made in presence of each other. 99 ALR 554.

Power of tenant in fee simple conditional to dispose of property by devise. 114 ALR 614.

Acknowledgment of signature by testator or witness to will as satisfying statutory requirement that testator or witness sign in the presence of each other. 115 ALR 689.

Necessity of, and what amounts to, request on part of testator to witnesses to attest or subscribe will. 125 ALR 414.

Necessity that attesting witness to will not signed by testator in his presence shall have seen latter's signature on paper. 127 ALR 384.

Law in effect at time of execution of will or time of death of testator as controlling. 129 ALR 862.

Proof, or possibility of proof of will without testimony of attesting witnesses as affecting application of statute relating to invalidation of will, or of devise or legacy, where attesting witness is beneficiary under will. 133 ALR 1286.

Capacity of minor to make soldiers' and sailors' will. 137 ALR 1310; 147 ALR 1297; 148 ALR 1384; 149 ALR 1452; 150 ALR 1417; 151 ALR 1453; 152 ALR 1450.

Right of alien enemy to take by inheritance or will. 137 ALR 1328; 147 ALR 1297; 150 ALR 1418; 152 ALR 1450.

Capacity of one sentenced to life imprisonment to take under will. 139 ALR 1315.

Insane delusion as invalidating will. 175 ALR 882.

Power and capacity of bank to take devise or bequest. 8 ALR2d 454.

Reversion left by grant to one for life and afterwards, either absolutely or contingently, to grantor's heirs or next of kin as subject to disposition by will. 16 ALR2d 714.

Devisability of possibility of reverter, or right of reentry for breach of condition subsequent. 16 ALR2d 1246.

Enlarged interest acquired by testator after execution of will as passing by devise or bequest. 18 ALR2d 519.

Validity of will drawn by layman, who, in so doing, violated criminal statute forbidding such activities by one other than licensed attorney. 18 ALR2d 918.

Place of signature on holographic will. 19 ALR2d 926.

Codicil as validating will or codicil which was invalid or inoperative at time of its purported execution. 21 ALR2d 821.

Right of witness to nuncupative will to take as beneficiary thereunder. 28 ALR2d 796.

Legality of testamentary gift to illegitimate. 34 ALR2d 10.

Felonious killing of testator as affecting slayer's rights as beneficiary under will. 36 ALR2d 960.

Signature on informal testamentary letter. 40 ALR2d 740.

Option to purchase real estate as subject to creation by will. 44 ALR2d 1215.

"Attestation" or "witnessing" of will, required by statute, as including witnesses' subscription. 45 ALR2d 1365.

Failure of attesting witness to write or state place of residence as affecting will. 55 ALR2d 1053.

Sufficiency of publication of will. 60 ALR2d 124.

Effect of failure of attesting witness to observe testator's capacity. 69 ALR2d 662.

Fingerprints as signature on will. 72 ALR2d 1267.

Amount or value of testamentary gift as affecting application of statute invalidating will attested by beneficially interested witness. 73 ALR2d 1230.

Competency of named executor as subscribing witness to will. 74 ALR2d 283.

What constitutes presence of testator in witnessing of his will. 75 ALR2d 318.

Sufficiency, as to form, of signature to holographic will. 75 ALR2d 895.

Adopted child as within class in testamentary gift. 86 ALR2d 12.

Admissibility, on issue of testamentary capacity, of previously executed wills. 89 ALR2d 177.

Guardianship of adult as affecting testamentary capacity. 89 ALR2d 1120.

Requirement that holographic will be entirely in handwriting of testator as affected by appearance of printed matter or handwriting of another. 89 ALR2d 1198.

Validity of will as affected by fact that witnesses signed before testator. 91 ALR2d 737.

Exception or proviso in statute invalidating testamentary gift to subscribing witness, saving the share witness would take in absence of will. 95 ALR2d 1256.

Validity of will signed by testator with the assistance of another. 98 ALR2d 824.

Validity of will signed by testator's mark or symbol, or partial or abbreviated signature. 98 ALR2d 841.

Determination of absolute or conditional nature of will. 1 ALR3d 1048.

What amounts to "last sickness" or the like within requirement that nuncupative will be made during last sickness. 8 ALR3d 952.

Testamentary capacity as affected by use of intoxicating liquor or drugs. 9 ALR3d 15.

"Pour-over" provisions from will to inter vivos trust. 12 ALR3d 56.

Competency of interested witness to testify to signature or handwriting of deceased. 13 ALR3d 404.

Necessity of laying foundation for opinion of attesting witness as to mental condition of testator or testatrix. 17 ALR3d 503.

Place of signature of attesting witness. 17 ALR3d 705.

What circumstances excuse failure to submit will for probate within time limit set by statute. 17 ALR3d 1361.

Testator's illiteracy or lack of knowledge of language in which will is written as affecting its validity. 37 ALR3d 889.

Validity and construction of testamentary gift to political party. 41 ALR3d 833.

Bequest of shares in Massachusetts or business trusts. 88 ALR3d 704.

Effect of testamentary gift to child conditioned upon specified arrangements for parental control. 11 ALR4th 940.

Wills: gift to persons individually named but also described in terms of relationship to testator or another as class gift. 13 ALR4th 978.

II. DECISIONS UNDER PRIOR LAW.

Editor's note. — In light of the similarity of the subject matter, decisions under former chapter 1 of title 43 are included in the annotations for this section.

"Will" defined. — A will is a disposition of real and personal property, to take effect after the death of the testator. 4 Kent Com. 501. A will is the legal declaration of man's intentions which he wills to be performed after his death. 2 Black. Com. t. p. 417. A will is the declaration of the mind, either by word or writing, in disposing of an estate, and to take place after the death of the testator. Carthew 38; 7 Bac. ab. 299.

A will is defined to be an instrument by which a person makes a disposition of his property to take effect after his decease, and which is, in its own nature, ambulatory and revocable during his life. It is this ambulatory and revocable quality which forms the characteristics of a will. Daniel v. Hill, 52 Ala. 430 (1875).

Intent of testator governs. — A cardinal principle in the construction of wills is to ascertain the intent of the testator, and give it effect if it is not prohibited by law. Smith v. Smith, 157 Ala. 79, 47 So. 220 (1908); Castleberry v.

Stringer, 176 Ala. 250, 57 So. 849 (1912).

Wills speak only from the death of the testator, and must be construed as they would have been construed at the moment of death, and without regard to the consequences resulting from subsequent events, which were probably not foreseen or anticipated at the making of the will. Taylor v. Harwell, 65 Ala. 1 (1880); Blakeney v. Du Bose, 167 Ala. 627, 52 So. 746 (1910).

Skill of scrivener will be considered. — Facts showing that the person drawing the paper was unskilled will be considered in construing the will. May v. Ritchie, 65 Ala. 602 (1880); Findley v. Hill, 133 Ala. 229, 32 So. 497 (1901); Castleberry v. Stringer, 176 Ala. 250, 57 So. 849 (1912).

Contract to make a will is valid. — All the authorities agree that one may, for a valuable consideration, renounce the absolute power to dispose of his estate at pleasure, and bind himself by contract to dispose of his property by will to a particular person, and that such contract may be enforced in the courts after his decease, either by an action for its breach against the personal representative, or, in a proper case, by action in the nature of specific performance against his heirs, devisees or personal representative. The validity of such agreements is supported by an unbroken current of authorities, both English and American. Bolman v. Overall, 80 Ala. 451, 2 So. 624 (1887).

Bequests held valid. — An executory bequest of money to "Pilgrims' Rest Association," "to be loaned out by commissioners to be appointed by said association, and the interest to be equally divided annually between the ministers having charge of churches in said association," and a similar bequest to "Vienna and Cochran's Mill Beat," to be received and loaned out by three commissioners elected by the people of the beats, the interest to be collected annually, "and applied by said commissioners to the education and tuition of all the pauper and poor children of said beats whose parents are not able to support them," are both valid. Williams v. Pearson, 38 Ala. 299 (1862).

A bequest to "the Baptist Societies for Foreign and Domestic Missions, and the American and Foreign Bible Society," is valid and sufficiently specific, and if societies can be found, which were organized and known by those names at the time of the testator's death, they will be considered the societies referred to in the will, and capable of taking the bequest, whether incorporated or not. Carter v. Balfour, 19 Ala. 814 (1851).

A bequest for the erection of monuments to the memory of certain designated persons is valid. Gilmer v. Gilmer, 42 Ala. 9 (1868).

697

Bequest held invalid. — A bequest to a church, "to be used in solemn masses for the repose of my soul," held not valid. Festorazzi v. St. Joseph's Catholic Church, 104 Ala. 327, 18 So. 394 (1894).

Definite action is required to exclude heirs. — Heirs are appointed by the law to succeed to the estate of which a valid disposition is not made by will. "Plain words are required to disinherit them." Though it may appear that the testator did not intend that his heir or next of kin should take his estate, real or personal, and intended to exclude them from succession to it, yet, if he fails to make a valid devise or gift to another, they will take under the statute of descents and distributions. Denson v. Autrey, 21 Ala. 205 (1852); Banks v. Sherrod, 52 Ala. 267 (1875).

Void nuncupative will could not be established on ground of ignorance or mistake as to change of law. — A nuncupative will bequeathing personal property of more than $500.00 in value, which was void under former § 43-1-31, could not be established on the ground of the decedent's ignorance or mistake as to the change in the law in this respect made by the Code. Erwin v. Hamner, 27 Ala. 296 (1855).

Division 1.

Execution of Will.

§ 43-8-130. Who may make a will.

Any person 18 or more years of age who is of sound mind may make a will. (Acts 1982, No. 82-399, § 2-501.)

Commentary

This section states a uniform minimum age of 18 for capacity to execute a will. "Minor" is defined in § 43-8-1, and involves a different age than that prescribed here.

Under prior law, all persons over the age of 18 years, and of sound mind, could dispose of their personal property by will in Alabama. Former § 43-1-2 (1975). Persons over the age of 19 years, and of sound mind, could dispose of their interests in real property in Alabama. Former § 43-1-1 (1975). Married persons over the age of 18 years were relieved of the disabilities of minority. Sections 30-4-15 and 30-4-16 (1975). Apparently prior Alabama law is in accord with this section.

I. General Consideration.
II. Decisions Under Prior Law.

I. GENERAL CONSIDERATION.

Cross references. — As to authority of married women to dispose of separate estates by last will and testament, see § 30-4-14. As to right of aliens to devise property, see § 35-1-1. As to persons who may convey lands by deed or will, see § 35-4-1.

Collateral references. — 94 C.J.S., Wills, §§ 5, 15.

79 Am. Jur. 2d, Wills, §§ 54-62.

Epilepsy as affecting testamentary capacity. 16 ALR 1418.

Admissibility of evidence other than testimony of subscribing witnesses to prove due execution of will or testamentary capacity. 63 ALR 1195.

Admissibility of evidence of reputation on issue of mental condition, or testamentary or contractual capacity or incapacity. 105 ALR 1443.

Illustrations of instructions or requested instructions as to effect of unnaturalness or unreasonableness of provisions of will on question of testamentary capacity or undue influence. 137 ALR 989.

Admissibility and probative force, on issue of competency to execute an instrument, of evidence of incompetency at other times. 168 ALR 969.

Insane delusion as invalidating a will. 175 ALR 882.

Admissibility, on issue of testamentary capacity, of previously executed wills. 89 ALR2d 177.

Effect of guardianship of adult on testamentary capacity. 89 ALR2d 1120.

Testamentary capacity as affected by use of intoxicating liquor or drugs. 9 ALR3d 15.

Partial invalidity of will: may parts of will be upheld notwithstanding failure of other parts for lack of testamentary mental capacity or undue influences. 64 ALR3d 261.

Sufficiency of evidence that will was not accessible to testator for destruction, in proceeding to establish lost will. 86 ALR3d 980.

Base for determining amount of bequest of a specific percent or proportion of estate or property. 87 ALR3d 605.

Condition that devisee or legatee shall renounce, embrace, or adhere to specified religious faith. 89 ALR3d 984.

II. DECISIONS UNDER PRIOR LAW.

Editor's note. — In light of the similarity of the subject matter, decisions under former §§ 43-1-1 and 43-1-2 are included in the annotations for this section.

Law of domicile governs. — The testamentary disposition of personal property is governed by the law of the testator's domicile. Varner v. Bevil, 17 Ala. 286 (1850).

Testamentary capacity as to personalty is governed by the law of the last domicile. Daniel v. Hill, 52 Ala. 430 (1875).

Common-law rule. — By the common law infants were incapable of devising real estate. Females of the age of 12 years, and males of 14, could make a valid disposition of personal estate by will. 1 Jar. on Wills, 29; Banks v. Sherrod, 52 Ala. 267 (1875).

Creation of charges on realty included. — The capacity to devise lands includes the creation of all charges on real estate by last will. Banks v. Sherrod, 52 Ala. 267 (1875).

What mental capacity is required. — A total deprivation of reason is not requisite to destroy testamentary capacity. Dementia and idiocy are not the only forms of incapacity. A competent testator must not only have mind and memory, but mind and memory enough to understand the business in which he is engaged. Stubbs v. Houston, 33 Ala. 55 (1858).

That the testator should make a valid will, it is not necessary that his memory should be perfect and his mind wholly unimpaired. If he had memory and mind enough to recollect the property he was about to bequeath, and the persons to whom he wished to will it, and the manner in which he wished it disposed of and to know and understand what he was engaged in, he had, in contemplation of the law, a sound mind, and his great age, bodily infirmity and impaired mind would not vitiate a will made by one possessing such capacity. Coleman v. Robertson, 17 Ala. 84 (1849); Taylor v. Kelly, 31 Ala. 59 (1857); Leeper v. Taylor, 47 Ala. 221 (1872).

Capacity for ordinary business is not necessary. — There may be a competency to make a will, without such capacity as would enable a man to transact the ordinary business of life. Feebleness of intellect, or the childishness and fretfulness of old age, not amounting to mental unsoundness, might make one unfit for the business transactions of life, which would require prompt action upon newly presented subjects with combinations to which the mind was unaccustomed, and yet there might be a full capacity to make a will. Stubbs v. Houston, 33 Ala. 55 (1858).

"Heirs" may mean children. — Where the word "heirs" was used in an instrument, and from the evidence showing the circumstances which attended the making of the will and the fact that the will showed it was drawn by an unskilled person, the necessary construction required it, the word "heirs" would be held to mean children. Fellows, etc., Co. v. Tann, 9 Ala. 999 (1846); Powell v. Glenn, 21 Ala. 458 (1852); Flanagan v. State Bank, 32 Ala. 508 (1858); Twelves v. Nevill, 39 Ala. 175 (1863); May v. Ritchie, 65 Ala. 602 (1880); Campbell v. Noble, 110 Ala. 382, 19 So. 28 (1895); Findley v. Hill, 133 Ala. 229, 32 So. 497 (1902); Castleberry v. Stringer, 176 Ala. 250, 57 So. 849 (1912).

Decedent cannot pass to legatee title to property which could not pass by descent. — Legatee's rights as to specific property bequeathed by will do not vest on testator's death when property would become part of latter's estate without will, as decedent cannot by will pass to legatee title to property which would not pass by descent without will. Carter v. First Nat'l Bank, 237 Ala. 47, 185 So. 361 (1938).

§ 43-8-131. Execution and signature of will; witnesses.

Except as provided within section 43-8-135, every will shall be in writing signed by the testator or in the testator's name by some other person in the testator's presence and by his direction, and shall be signed by at least two persons each of whom witnessed either the signing or the testator's acknowledgment of the signature or of the will. (Acts 1982, No. 82-399, § 2-502.)

Commentary

The formalities for execution of a witnessed will have been reduced to a minimum. Execution under this section normally would be accomplished by signature of the testator and of two witnesses; each of the persons signing as witnesses must "witness" any of the following: the signing of the will by the testator, an acknowledgment by the testator that the signature is his, or an acknowledgment by the testator that the document is his will. Signing by the testator may be by mark under general rules relating to what constitutes a signature; or the will may be signed on behalf of the testator by another person signing the testator's name at his direction and in his presence. There is no requirement that the testator publish the document as his will, or that he request the witnesses to sign, or that the witnesses sign in the presence of the testator or of each other. The testator may sign the will outside the presence of the witnesses, if he later acknowledges to the witnesses that the signature is his or that the document is his will, and they sign as witnesses. There is no requirement that the testator's signature be at the end of the will; thus, if he writes his name in the body of the will and intends it to be his signature, this would satisfy the statute. The intent is to validate wills which meet the minimal formalities of the statute.

This section is substantially like UPC § 2-502, except that it is at this point that this Alabama act rejects the idea of permitting holographic wills in the historic sense *i.e.,* a will entirely in the handwriting of the testator and valid without witnesses) to be validly executed in Alabama. This decision leaves the Alabama law as it was. The section does not reject the proposition that a holographic will of a nonresident of Alabama could be admitted to transfer property in Alabama if the holographic will is valid in the domicile of the decedent. See § 43-8-135, *infra.*

In Alabama all wills shall be in writing, signed by the testator or in the testator's name in his presence by his direction. Goldsmith v. Gates, 205 Ala. 632, 88 So. 861 (1921) (testator blind). Prior law required that there shall be at least two witnesses to every will who subscribe their names in the presence of the testator. Former § 43-1-30 (1975). However, it is not necessary that the attestation be at the personal request of the testator if it is done in the testator's presence with his knowledge and consent. Ritchey v. Jones, 210 Ala. 204, 97 So. 736 (1923). If it should develop that the instrument was signed by the testator after the witnesses subscribed and not in their presence, the will is void. Reynolds v. Massey, 219 Ala. 265, 122 So. 2d 29 (1929). Yet it is not necessary for a witness to actually see the testator sign the instrument; just an acknowledgment to the witness by the testator that he executed the will is sufficient. *Id.* In summary, prior Alabama law is in accord with this section.

I. General Consideration.
II. Decisions Under Prior Law.
    A. In General.
    B. Will Must Be in Writing.
    C. Signing by the Testator.
    D. Attestation.
    E. Signing by the Witnesses.
    F. In the Presence of the Testator.

I. GENERAL CONSIDERATION.

Collateral references. — 94 C.J.S., Wills, § 167-199.

79 Am. Jur. 2d, Wills, §§ 183-198.
Manner of signing as affecting sufficiency of signature of testator. 31 ALR 682; 42 ALR 954; 114 ALR 1110.

Effect of illegibility of signature of testator or witness to will. 64 ALR 208.

Acknowledgment of signature by testator or witness to will as satisfying statutory requirement that testator or witness sign in the presence of each other. 115 ALR 689.

Admissibility of testator's declarations upon the issue of the genuineness or due execution of purported will. 62 ALR2d 855.

Will or instrument in form of will as sufficient memorandum of contract to devise or bequeath. 94 ALR2d 921.

Necessity that attesting witness realize instrument was intended as will. 71 ALR3d 877.

II. DECISIONS UNDER PRIOR LAW.

A. In General.

Editor's note. — In light of the similarity of the subject matter, decisions under former § 43-1-30 are included in the annotations for this section.

Common-law rule. — By the common law, wills of personal property were valid and operative, though not written or signed by the testator, or attested by witnesses, if written in accordance with his instructions, and the rule of the common law prevailed here until the adoption of the Code of 1852. Barnewall v. Murrell, 108 Ala. 366, 18 So. 831 (1895).

Purpose. — Statutes of this character are enacted for the purpose of removing uncertainty as to the execution of wills and to safeguard testators against frauds and impositions. Riley v. Riley, 36 Ala. 496 (1860); Dawkins v. Dawkins, 179 Ala. 666, 60 So. 289 (1877); Elston v. Price, 210 Ala. 579, 98 So. 573 (1923); Weaver v. Grant, 394 So. 2d 15 (Ala. 1981).

A will is an instrument by which a person makes disposition of his property to become effective after his death, and is in its own nature ambulatory and revocable, during the life of the testator. Blacksher Co. v. Northrup, 176 Ala. 190, 57 So. 743 (1911).

An instrument purporting to devise real or personal property, but signed only by one witness, is ineffectual for any purpose. There is no such thing under Alabama statutes as a will which does not dispose of property. Blacksher Co. v. Northrup, 176 Ala. 190, 57 So. 743 (1911).

Lost instrument. — Before a lost instrument can be admitted to probate as a will it must be established that the will was signed by the testator and attested as required. Allen v. Scruggs, 190 Ala. 654, 67 So. 301 (1914); Jordan v. Ringstaff, 212 Ala. 414, 102 So. 895 (1925).

A lost will may be established by the testimony of a single witness who read it, or heard it read and remembered its contents, and proof of the substance of a lost instrument as a will is sufficient, and the exact words need not be shown. Lovell v. Lovell, 270 Ala. 720, 121 So. 2d 901 (1960).

In a proceeding to probate an alleged lost or destroyed will, the burden is on the proponent to establish, to the reasonable satisfaction of the judge or jury trying the facts: (1) the existence of a will — an instrument in writing, signed by the testator or some person in his presence, and by his direction, and attested to by at least two witnesses, who must subscribe their names thereto in the presence of the testator; (2) the loss or destruction of the instrument; (3) the nonrevocation of the instrument by the testator; (4) the contents of the will in substance and effect. Barksdale v. Pendergrass, 294 Ala. 526, 319 So. 2d 267 (1975).

The provisions of former §§ 43-1-30 and 43-1-33 and § 43-8-167 contemplate "will-in-hand" situations which obviously supply a court with the necessary contents of the will at issue. Proof has not been allowed of the requisites of former §§ 43-1-30 and 43-1-33 as to a lost will unless that proof is also sufficient to invoke the exception method of proving a will for probate and the only and ultimate end of proving the valid execution of any will. Anderson v. Griggs, 402 So. 2d 904 (Ala. 1981).

The republication of a will, whether express or constructive, must contain the essential ingredients, that, being in writing, and signed by the testator, he makes it known as such to a competent number of witnesses, whose attestation is made in writing, in the presence of the testator. Barker v. Bell, 49 Ala. 284 (1873).

Testamentary executors and guardians are such only as are named by a will executed in accordance with law, as under the provisions of § 43-2-20, letters may not be granted to them until after the will has been admitted to probate. Blacksher v. Northrup, 176 Ala. 190, 57 So. 743 (1911).

Documents must meet requirements of statutes to be admitted to probate. — The Alabama statutes require certain formalities for wills, and are in the nature of statutes of frauds, and only such documents as meet the requirements of the statutes will be admitted to probate. First Nat'l Bank v. Klein, 285 Ala. 505, 234 So. 2d 42 (1970).

Changes in will must comply with statute. — If alterations or additions to a will are not made as the statute requires, they are mere nullities, and the will as it existed at the time of execution is unaffected in validity. Calhoun v. Thomas, 274 Ala. 111, 145 So. 2d 789 (1962).

Regardless of the thoughts or contemplation of the testator, until there is a change, or alteration or revocation in the mode required by statute, the legal presumption is that the result of all thought and contemplation was a determination to adhere to the will as executed. Calhoun v. Thomas, 274 Ala. 111, 145 So. 2d 789 (1962).

B. Will Must Be In Writing.

What "writing" includes. — Under section requiring will to be in writing, "writing" includes printing on paper, or part writing and printing or part typewritten and part written. Stuck v. Howard, 213 Ala. 184, 104 So. 500 (1925).

Separate sheets of paper permissible. — It is of no consequence that the will was written upon separate sheets of paper. And, had these sheets remained disconnected, this would not have been an objection to its validity, or have afforded an inference of its revocation by the testatrix. Barnewall v. Murrell, 108 Ala. 366, 18 So. 831 (1895); Woodruff v. Hundley, 127 Ala. 640, 29 So. 98 (1900).

C. Signing by the Testator.

Constructions of British statute apply. — Former § 43-1-30, so far as it related to the signing, was a substantial transcript of that part of the 5th section 29th Car. II, ch. 3, which related to the signing of the will, and therefore the construction which had been put upon that part of the British statute, and settled as its construction, by the British decisions before the adoption of our statute, was to be regarded as the construction which our legislature intended to be put upon that part of the statute. Armstrong v. Armstrong, 29 Ala. 538 (1857); Plemons v. Tarpey, 262 Ala. 209, 78 So. 2d 385 (1955).

Testator need not write his own name. — It is not essential that the testator should write his own name. The British statute, as well as our own, allows a will to be signed for him by another, and his name, when written by another for him, in his presence and by his direction, will have the same effect as if it had been written by himself. Although his name is not written by himself, nor subscribed to the will, yet, if it be written in the beginning of the will by another, in his presence and under his direction, and if it be acknowledged by him to the attesting witnesses at the time he calls on them to attest and subscribe it, it will be as effectual as if with his own pen he had written it. Armstrong v. Armstrong, 29 Ala. 538 (1857); Goldsmith v. Gates, 205 Ala. 632, 88 So. 861 (1921).

The fact that the testator was assisted, because of physical defect or weakness, in writing his signature to the will, makes it nonetheless his individual, conscious and voluntary act, if the testator was so conscious of the act and its effect or the attending circumstances and surroundings were such as to show that it was his conscious, voluntary individual act. Thus the fact that testator was about 85 years of age and almost blind, and that the son actually wrote testator's name to the will, while testator (the father) rested his hand on the back of the son's hand, did not fail of statutory requirement. Goldsmith v. Gates, 205 Ala. 632, 88 So. 861 (1921).

Witnesses may sign for testator. — It seems to be settled that such signing for the testator may be made by a person who is one of the subscribing witnesses to the will. Riley v. Riley, 36 Ala. 496 (1860).

Witnesses need not be present when testator signs. — It is well settled that the witnesses need not be present when the testator signs the will, nor need they sign their attestation in the presence of each other. Hoffman v. Hoffman, 26 Ala. 535 (1855); Woodcock v. McDonald, 30 Ala. 411 (1857); Woodruff v. Hundley, 127 Ala. 640, 29 So. 98 (1900); Ritchey v. Jones, 210 Ala. 204, 97 So. 736 (1923); Massey v. Reynolds, 213 Ala. 178, 104 So. 494 (1925).

It is not necessary for the witnesses to actually see the testator sign his name. Barksdale v. Pendergrass, 294 Ala. 526, 319 So. 2d 267 (1975).

An acknowledgment by the testator to the witnesses of his signature to the instrument is sufficient. Woodruff v. Hundley, 127 Ala. 640, 29 So. 98 (1900).

Signing after witnesses subscribe. — If instrument propounded as will was not signed by testator until after witnesses subscribed, and not in their presence, it was not duly attested, under the statute, and was void. Reynolds v. Massey, 219 Ala. 265, 122 So. 29 (1929); Whitt v. Forbes, 258 Ala. 580, 64 So. 2d 77 (1953).

Signature of testator need not be at end of will. — If the testator with his own pen writes his own name in the beginning of the will, thus "I, James Armstrong," with the design of giving it authority, and acknowledges it to be his writing when he calls the subscribing witnesses to attest it, and, if, at the time of acknowledgment, he does not intend to subscribe it, the signing is sufficient, without any subscription of his name at the bottom. Armstrong v. Armstrong, 29 Ala. 538 (1857).

Location of signature is not controlling. — The location of the signature of the testator is not controlling; the intent with which the signatures are affixed is the essential of the statute. Plemons v. Tarpey, 262 Ala. 209, 78 So. 2d 385 (1955).

It may be anywhere on face of instrument. — The statute not fixing the location of the signature of a testator to a will, but merely providing that it shall be in writing and signed, it may be placed at the top, in the margin or anywhere on the face of the instrument provided it is affixed thereto with the intention of authenticating it as the testator's completed testamentary act. Plemons v. Tarpey, 262 Ala. 209, 78 So. 2d 385 (1955).

Charge properly stated law. — In will contest, given charges that witnesses to will must have seen testator sign his name or testator must have acknowledged to witnesses that signature affixed to will was his signature were held proper statements of the law. Little v. Sugg, 243 Ala. 196, 8 So. 2d 866 (1942).

But instruction imposed a greater burden on proponent than required. — Where the evidence was undisputed that testator signed will in the presence of all subscribing witnesses, but was in conflict as to whether testator said anything after he signed the will, instruction that, if testator did not sign will in presence of subscribing witnesses and did not acknowledge his signature to them, they must find for contestants, imposed a greater burden on proponent than the law required. Towles v. Pettus, 244 Ala. 192, 12 So. 2d 357 (1943).

When no acknowledgment necessary. — When the testator or someone in his presence and by his direction affixes the testator's signature on the will as the act of its completion, in the presence of the subscribing witnesses, and the witnesses subscribe in his presence, no acknowledgment is necessary to its valid execution. Towles v. Pettus, 244 Ala. 192, 12 So. 2d 357 (1943); Staples v. Harris, 264 Ala. 629, 89 So. 2d 167 (1956).

Proof of signing. — Signing by the testator was proved where brother of testator testified that he was present in the room; that he saw the testator sign the will; that the testator asked the two attesting witnesses to "witness my will," which they did; that he was familiar with testator's handwriting, and that the signature on the will was the testator's signature. Staples v. Harris, 264 Ala. 629, 89 So. 2d 167 (1956).

Two subscribing witnesses can establish a prima facie case of execution of will even if there are additional witnesses; the statutes do not require the testimony of all subscribing witnesses. Culver v. King, 362 So. 2d 221 (Ala. 1978).

But, the better practice, in regard to proving a prima facie case of execution of a will, is to call all the witnesses to the execution. Culver v. King, 362 So. 2d 221 (Ala. 1978).

D. Attestation.

Purpose of statute requiring that will must be attested to by at least two witnesses is to remove uncertainty as to the execution of wills and safeguard testators against frauds and impositions. Culver v. King, 362 So. 2d 221 (Ala. 1978).

What is sufficient attestation. — To constitute an efficacious "attestation" of a will, act intended by testator to operate as a signing by him must either be done in presence of subscribing witnesses or, if previously affixed, be acknowledged to them as his act by express words or necessary implication from his conduct at the time of attestation. Reynolds v. Massey, 219 Ala. 265, 122 So. 29 (1929); Whitt v. Forbes, 258 Ala. 580, 64 So. 2d 77 (1953).

The testator may acknowledge to the subscribing witnesses that it is his signature on the instrument by his express words or by implication from his conduct and from the surrounding circumstances. Barksdale v. Pendergrass, 294 Ala. 526, 319 So. 2d 267 (1975).

Attestation distinguished from subscription. — Attestation consists in the witnesses seeing that those things exist and are done which the statute requires. Attestation is the act of the senses; subscription is the act of the hand; the one is mental; the other mechanical. To attest the signature means to take note mentally that the signature exists as a fact. If this is done, and the attestor also subscribes his name, the statute is complied with. The essential thing is that by the signature he meant to affirm that the deceased executed the will in his presence. Elston v. Price, 210 Ala. 579, 98 So. 573 (1923); Whitt v. Forbes, 258 Ala. 580, 64 So. 2d 77 (1953).

A witness is a "subscribing attesting witness" when he sees testator sign his name on the will, or sees testator's name on it, and has his acknowledgment that he (testator) signed the will before or at the time the witness subscribed his name to it. Stuck v. Howard, 213 Ala. 184, 104 So. 500 (1925); Staples v. Harris, 264 Ala. 629, 89 So. 2d 167 (1956).

Attestation is required. — While a subscribing witness need not be present when testator signs the will, he must attest it — that is, must see him sign it, or see his name on it, and have his acknowledgment that it is his signature — before or at the time the subscribing witness subscribes his name to it as such. Ritchey v. Jones, 210 Ala. 204, 97 So. 736 (1923); Massey v. Reynolds, 213 Ala. 178, 104 So. 494 (1925).

An instrument, not attested by two witnesses, is inoperative as a will. Arrington v. Brown, 235 Ala. 196, 178 So. 218 (1938).

No attestation clause is required. — The statute does not require an attestation clause. Hence its complete omission would have no effect upon the validity of the will. A fulfillment of the statutory requirements is all that is necessary, and this may be proven without any recital of the fact in the will or in an attestation clause attached to it. No particular form of words is essential to constitute an attestation. Woodruff v. Hundley, 127 Ala. 640, 29 So. 98 (1900); Massey v. Reynolds, 213 Ala. 178, 104 So. 494 (1925); Fulks v. Green, 246 Ala. 392, 20 So. 2d 787 (1945).

Attestation need not be at testator's personal request. — It is not necessary that the attestation be at the personal request of the testator (Lockridge v. Brown, 184 Ala. 106, 63 So. 524 (1913)), but it is sufficient if done in his presence with his knowledge and with his consent, expressed or implied. Ritchey v. Jones, 210 Ala. 204, 97 So. 736 (1923); Fulks v. Green, 246 Ala. 392, 20 So. 2d 787 (1945); Barksdale v. Pendergrass, 294 Ala. 526, 319 So. 2d 267 (1975).

How testator's acknowledgment to witnesses is proved. — In view of the statute, the testator's acknowledgment to the subscribing witnesses that the signature on the instrument is his may be proved by his words, or by his acts, or by circumstances surrounding him and them when subscribing or by a combination of all three — his words, his acts and circumstances surrounding them. Massey v. Reynolds, 213 Ala. 178, 104 So. 494 (1925). But no formal words or acts are necessary to constitute such "acknowledgment." Stuck v. Howard, 213 Ala. 184, 104 So. 500 (1925); Fulks v. Green, 246 Ala. 392, 20 So. 2d 787 (1945); Staples v. Harris, 264 Ala. 629, 89 So. 2d 167 (1956).

Testator does not have to inform witnesses that it is his will. — Under the law the testator does not have to inform the subscribing witnesses that the instrument is his will, or give them information as to its contents. Leverett v. Carlisle, 19 Ala. 80 (1851); Barnewall v. Murrell, 108 Ala. 366, 18 So. 831 (1895); Goldsmith v. Gates, 205 Ala. 632, 88 So. 861 (1921); Massey v. Reynolds, 213 Ala. 178, 104 So. 494 (1925); Fulks v. Green, 246 Ala. 392, 20 So. 2d 787 (1945); Barksdale v. Pendergrass, 294 Ala. 526, 319 So. 2d 267 (1975).

An attesting witness need not know the document he attests is a will. Weaver v. Grant, 394 So. 2d 15 (Ala. 1981).

An attesting witness must possess, at the minimum, an intent to witness some document. Weaver v. Grant, 394 So. 2d 15 (Ala. 1981).

Witnesses must intend to act as witnesses. — Regardless of what it is that is attested, the witnesses must intend to act as witnesses, or the will is not valid. The mere presence of persons during the performance of the acts required by statute, coupled with the fact that they sign the will, is not sufficient unless the witnesses have the requisite animus attestandi. Weaver v. Grant, 394 So. 2d 15 (Ala. 1981).

A subscribing witness to a will is not called upon to testify to attestation of other witness, but only to presence of testator, testator's signature and attestation and subscription by witness in testator's presence. Fulks v. Green, 246 Ala. 392, 20 So. 2d 787 (1945).

Proof of execution otherwise than by testimony of attesting witnesses. — If from forgetfulness, the subscribing witnesses should fail to prove the formal execution of the will, other evidence is admissible to supply the deficiency. And even if the subscribing witnesses all swear that the will was not duly executed they may be contradicted, and the will supported by other witnesses or by circumstances. Staples v. Harris, 264 Ala. 629, 89 So. 2d 167 (1956).

Attestation in separate instrument. — The attestation of a will executed in Germany was evidenced by an instrument termed a protocol, referring to and attached to the will. The attestation clause was thus part and parcel of the will itself sufficient to satisfy the requirements of the law. Johnston v. King, 250 Ala. 571, 35 So. 2d 202 (1948).

Question for jury. — In will contest, on ground that will was not executed in conformity with law, charge given for proponents, which assumed that testator's name was on paper when it was subscribed by attesting witnesses, held invasive of the province of jury. Reynolds v. Massey, 219 Ala. 265, 122 So. 29 (1929).

In will contest, on ground that will was not executed in conformity with law, charges given at proponents' request, which gave effect to alleged will as carrying ex facie evidence of its due execution, and assuming that attesting witnesses subscribed their names under word "witness," held, under evidence, erroneous and invasive of province of jury. Reynolds v. Massey, 219 Ala. 265, 122 So. 29 (1929).

In will contest, whether will was duly and legally executed was for jury. Street v. Street, 246 Ala. 683, 22 So. 2d 35 (1945).

E. Signing by the Witnesses.

Section relating to execution of wills operated upon jurisdiction of the court, and a decree was void which admitted to probate a will having only one witness. Blacksher Co. v. Northrup, 176 Ala. 190, 57 So. 743 (1911).

The legislature unquestionably has the power to prescribe rules for the execution of wills, before a right has been vested in the devisee, legatee or heir, by the death of the testator, and it was, therefore, entirely competent for it to fix the number of witnesses which were essential to the validity of any will, whether made before or after the passage of the statute. Hoffman v. Hoffman, 26 Ala. 535 (1855).

When provision as to number of witnesses applies. — The provision decreasing the number of witnesses from three to two applied to every will of real estate, where the testator died after the statute went into operation. Hoffman v. Hoffman, 26 Ala. 535 (1855).

What signature of witness implies. — One who writes his name as witness at request of testator and in his presence, under word "witness" or other equivalent phrase, impliedly certifies thereby that he saw testator sign his name to the instrument, saw testator's name thereon and that testator acknowledged that his name on instrument was his signature. Massey v. Reynolds, 213 Ala. 178, 104 So. 494 (1925); Staples v. Harris, 264 Ala. 629, 89 So. 2d 167 (1956).

Extra witnesses do not invalidate will. — The validity of a will attested as required by law is not impaired by the fact that two other witnesses signed their names as witnesses when not in the presence of the testator. Jones v. Brooks, 184 Ala. 115, 63 So. 978 (1913).

Witness who is able to write must sign own name. — In Riley v. Riley, 36 Ala. 496 (1860), it was held that one subscribing witness could not write the name of another subscribing witness, when the latter was able to write and did not physically participate in the signing. Elston v. Price, 210 Ala. 579, 98 So. 573 (1923).

When witness may use mark for signature. — Where the testator signs his own name to a will, the attestation may be by witnesses who subscribe their names by merely making their marks. Garrett v. Heflin, 98 Ala. 615, 13 So. 326 (1893); Wade v. Cole, 200 Ala. 691, 77 So. 234 (1917).

Where the testator signs by mark only, the attestation must be by two witnesses who write their own names. Dawkins v. Dawkins, 179 Ala. 666, 60 So. 289 (1912).

In such case a mark, whether it be the usual cross, or some peculiar mark, or combination of marks or symbols, habitually used by the witness in lieu of his written name, does not answer the statutory requirement. The requirement is that an attesting witness must write his name, and not merely meaningless marks which any illiterate witness might adopt as his own substitute therefor. Wade v. Cole, 200 Ala. 691, 77 So. 234 (1917).

Where a testatrix could not write and her name was signed to a will in her presence, by her direction, by one of the witnesses, it was essential that both witnesses should subscribe their own names; hence if one of them was only able to write one of the capital letters of his name and could not complete the name without the involuntary guidance of his hand by the other witness, the will was not legally executed. Dawkins v. Dawkins, 179 Ala. 666, 60 So. 289 (1912).

Meaning of "subscribe". — To "subscribe" was not intended to be used in its literal, primary sense, but in its broader meaning to attest by signing the witness' name as an act done with the intention of his witnessing the execution of the will. Hughes v. Merchants' Nat'l Bank, 256 Ala. 88, 53 So. 2d 386 (1951); Weaver v. Grant, 394 So. 2d 15 (Ala. 1981).

Constructions of English statute apply. — The provisions of former § 43-1-30 relating to the subscription of testamentary documents by attesting witnesses were a substantial counterpart or transcript of the English statute; thus the supreme court would look to the decisions of the English courts for guiding precedence. Hughes v. Merchants' Nat'l Bank, 256 Ala. 88, 53 So. 2d 386 (1951).

Location of signatures is not controlling. — The location of the signatures of the subscribing witnesses is not controlling, but the intent with which the signatures are affixed is the essential. Plemons v. Tarpey, 262 Ala. 209, 78 So. 2d 385 (1955).

Essential for valid signing is intent. — The essential for a valid signing, wherever the local position on the instrument, is that the signature must have been placed there with the intent of authenticating the document as the testator's completed testamentary act. Plemons v. Tarpey, 262 Ala. 209, 78 So. 2d 385 (1955).

Witnesses may affix signatures on any part of will. — A compliance with the law does not require that the attesting witnesses sign their names at the foot or end of the will, but the proviso is met by the attesting witnesses affixing their respective signatures on any part of the will with the intention of attesting it, the essential thing being that by their signatures they intended to affirm that the testator executed the will in their presence. Hughes v. Merchants' Nat'l Bank, 256 Ala. 88, 53 So. 2d 386 (1951); Plemons v. Tarpey, 262 Ala. 209, 78 So. 2d 385 (1955).

Knowledge of nature of instrument witnessed. — Testimony of subscribing witnesses to will that will was executed by testatrix in their presence and that they each signed the will as attesting witnesses as required by law made out a prima facie case for proponents, notwithstanding that one witness did not understand at the time that it was the will of testatrix she was witnessing. Fulks v. Green, 246 Ala. 392, 20 So. 2d 787 (1945).

F. In the Presence of the Testator.

Requirement substantially same as English statute of frauds. — The requirement that the witnesses shall subscribe their names in the presence of the testator is substantially the same, so far as here material, as was the language of the English statute of frauds from which it was borrowed, and with the statutes of other states. Johnston v. King, 250 Ala. 571, 35 So. 2d 202 (1948).

Within view of testator is sufficient. — A will, to be attested in the presence of the testator, must be witnessed within his view. It is not necessary to prove that he actually saw the witnesses attest the will; it is sufficient if, from their relative positions, he could see them. Hill v. Barge, 12 Ala. 687 (1848); Allen v. Jones, 259 Ala. 98, 65 So. 2d 217 (1953); Stanley v. Kelley, 267 Ala. 379, 102 So. 2d 16 (1958).

Witnesses need not sign in presence of each other. — It is not necessary that the witnesses should sign the will in the presence of each other. Hoffman v. Hoffman, 26 Ala. 535 (1855).

Burden of proof is on proponent. — Proponent has burden of proving witnesses' subscription in testator's presence. Green v. Davis, 228 Ala. 162, 153 So. 240 (1934); Allen v. Jones, 259 Ala. 98, 65 So. 2d 217 (1953).

Witnesses did not subscribe will "in testator's presence," where testator was in parked automobile and witnesses were inside bank through window of which testator might possibly have seen witnesses, but could not have seen will. Green v. Davis, 228 Ala. 162, 153 So. 240 (1934).

Testimony held sufficient to show due execution of will. — Subscribing witnesses' testimony, corroborated by signatures, that testator signed will in their presence with witness' pen which witnesses used in signing will as such at same time and place held sufficient to show due execution. Graves v. Graves, 228 Ala. 642, 154 So. 788 (1934).

Evidence sustained finding that will was attested in the presence of the testator. — See Stanley v. Kelley, 267 Ala. 379, 102 So. 2d 16 (1958).

§ 43-8-132. Self-proved will — Form and execution; how attested will made self-proved; effect.

(a) Any will may be simultaneously executed, attested, and made self-proved, by acknowledgment thereof by the testator and affidavits of the witnesses, each made before an officer authorized to administer oaths under the laws of the state where execution occurs and evidenced by the officer's certificate, under official seal, in substantially the following form:

"I, _____, the testator, sign my name to this instrument this ____ day of _____, 19__, and being first duly sworn, do hereby declare to the undersigned authority that I sign and execute this instrument as my last will and that I sign it willingly (or willingly direct another to sign for me), that I execute it as my free and voluntary act for the purposes therein expressed, and that I am 19 years of age or older, of sound mind, and under no constraint or undue influence."

_____

Testator

"We, _____, _____, the witnesses, sign our names to this instrument, being first duly sworn, and do hereby declare to the undersigned authority that the testator signs and executes this instrument as his last will and that he signs it willingly (or willingly directs another to sign for him), and that each of us, in the presence and hearing of the testator, hereby signs this will as witness to the testator's signing, and that to the best of our knowledge the testator is 19 years of age or older, of sound mind, and under no constraint or undue influence."

_____
Witness
_____
Witness

State of _____
County of _____

"Subscribed, sworn to and acknowledged before me by _____
_____, the testator and subscribed and sworn to before me by
_____, and _____, witnesses, this _____ day of
_____ , 19__.

SEAL

(Signed) _____

_____
(Official Capacity of Officer)

(b) An attested will may at any time subsequent to its execution be made self-proved by the acknowledgment thereof by the testator and the affidavits of the witnesses, each made before an officer authorized to administer oaths under the laws of the state where the acknowledgment occurs and evidenced by the officer's certificate, under the official seal, attached or annexed to the will in substantially the following form:

"STATE OF _____
COUNTY OF _____

We, _____, _____, and _____, the testator and the witnesses, respectively, whose names are signed to the attached or foregoing instrument, being first duly sworn, do hereby declare to the undersigned authority that the testator signed and executed the instrument as his last will and that he had signed willingly (or willingly directed another to sign for him), and that he executed it as his free and voluntary act for the purposes therein expressed, and that each of the witnesses, in the presence and hearing of the testator, signed the will as witness and that to the best of his knowledge the testator was at that time 19 years of age or older, of sound mind and under no constraint or undue influence."

_____
Testator
_____
Witness
_____
Witness

"Subscribed, sworn to and acknowledged before me by _____,

the testator, and subscribed and sworn to before me by _____, and _____, witnesses, this _____ day of _____, 19__.

SEAL   (SIGNED)_____

                                        (Official capacity of officer)

(c) If the will is self-proved, as provided in this section, compliance with signature requirements for execution is conclusively presumed, other requirements of execution are presumed subject to rebuttal without the testimony of any witness, and the will shall be probated without further proof, unless there is proof of fraud or forgery affecting the acknowledgment or affidavit. (Acts 1981, 3rd Ex. Sess., No. 81-1209; Code 1975, § 43-1-30.1.)

Commentary

This section was enacted as a free-standing act in Acts 1982, No. 82-1209. A self-proved will may be admitted to probate as provided in this section without the testimony of any subscribing witness, but otherwise it is treated no differently than a will not self-proved. Thus, a self-proved will may be contested (except in regard to signature requirements), revoked, or amended by a codicil in exactly the same fashion as a will not self-proved.

The "conclusive presumption" described here would foreclose questions such as whether the witnesses signed in the presence of the testator. It would not preclude proof of undue influence, lack of testamentary capacity, revocation or any relevant proof that the testator was unaware of the contents of the document.

Although the Alabama court has talked in terms of a "self-proving document" in referring to a will (see, Reynolds v. Massey, 219 Ala. 265, 122 So. 29 (1929)), it is fair to conclude that Alabama did not have prior to this act the self-proving mechanism which is provided by this section.

Effective date. — The act which added this section became effective December 4, 1981.

Code commissioner's note. — This section was formerly codified as § 43-1-30.1 of the 1975 Code, as amended.

Collateral references. — 95 C.J.S., Wills, § 312.

80 Am. Jur. 2d, Wills, § 1008.

Testator's name in body of instrument as sufficient signature where statute does not require will to be signed at end. 29 ALR 891.

Fingerprints as signature. 72 ALR2d 1267.

Validity of wills signed by mark, stamp or symbol or partial or abbreviated signature. 98 ALR2d 841.

Sufficiency of testator's acknowledgment of signature from his conduct and the surrounding circumstances. 7 ALR3d 317.

Place of signature of attesting witness. 17 ALR3d 705.

Testator's illiteracy or lack of knowledge of language in which will is written as affecting its validity. 37 ALR3d 889.

When is will signed at "end" or "foot" as required by statute. 44 ALR3d 701.

§ 43-8-133. Same — Making attested will self-proved.

An attested will may be made self-proved through compliance with section 43-8-132 or as otherwise provided by law. (Acts 1982, No. 82-399, § 2-504.)

§ 43-8-134. Who may witness will.

(a) Any person generally competent to be a witness may act as a witness to a will.

(b) A will or any provision thereof is not invalid because the will is signed by an interested witness. (Acts 1982, No. 82-399, § 2-505.)

Commentary

This section simplifies the law relating to interested witnesses. Interest no longer disqualifies a person as a witness, nor does it invalidate or forfeit a gift under the will. Of course, the purpose of this change is not to foster use of interested witnesses, and attorneys will continue to use disinterested witnesses to execution of wills. But the rare and innocent use of a member of the testator's family on a home-drawn will would no longer be penalized. This change does not increase appreciably the opportunity for fraud or undue influence. A substantial gift by will to a person who is one of the witnesses to the execution of the will would itself be a suspicious circumstance, and the gift could be challenged on grounds of undue influence. The requirement of disinterested witnesses has not succeeded in preventing fraud and undue influence; and in most cases of undue influence, the influencer is careful not to sign as witness but to use disinterested witnesses.

In Alabama a suitable attestor is one who at the time of execution was competent to testify in court as to the facts of the execution. Kumpe v. Coons, 62 Ala. 448 (1869) (beneficiary was a competent witness). Section 43-1-39 (1975). Subsequent incompetency of a witness will not invalidate a will, if the witness was competent at the time of attestation. Section 43-1-39 (1975). This section did not change Alabama law.

Collateral references. — 94 C.J.S., Wills, § 185.

79 Am. Jur. 2d, Wills, §§ 283-288.

Competency, as witness attesting will, of attorney named therein as executor's attorney. 30 ALR3d 1361.

§ 43-8-135. Choice of law as to validity of execution.

A written will is valid if executed in compliance with section 43-8-131 or if its execution complies with the law at the time of execution of the place where the will is executed, or with the law of the place where at the time of execution or at the time of death the testator is domiciled, has a place of abode or is a national. (Acts 1982, No. 82-399, § 2-506.)

Commentary

This section permits probate of wills in this state under certain conditions even if they are not executed in accordance with the formalities of § 43-8-131. Such wills must be in writing but otherwise are valid if they meet the requirements for execution of the law of the place where the will is executed (when it is executed in another state or country) or the law of testator's domicile, abode or nationality at either the time of execution or the time of death. Thus, if testator is domiciled in State 1 and executes a typed will merely by signing it without witnesses in State 2 while on vacation there, the court of this state would recognize the will as valid if the law of either State 1 or State 2 permits execution by signature alone. Or if a national of Mexico executes a written will in this state which does not meet the requirements of § 43-8-131 but meets the requirements of Mexican law, the will would be recognized as validly executed under this section. The purpose of this section is to provide a wide opportunity for validation of expectations of testators.

Alabama had no statute exactly comparable to this section. Generally, Alabama followed the rule that testamentary dispositions of real property were governed by the law of the state of situs. Varner v. Bevil, 17 Ala. 286 (1850). The law of the domicile of the decedent at death controlled the disposition of personal property. Goodman v. Winter, 64 Ala. 410 (1879). However, if the will has been admitted to probate in another state, it will be admitted to probate in Alabama. Section 43-1-52 (1975); Carter v. Davis, 275 Ala. 250, 154 So. 2d 9 (1963).

A similar provision relating to choice of law as to revocation is not included. Revocation by subsequent instruments are covered. Revocations by act, other than partial revocations, do not cause much difficulty in regard to choice of laws.

Collateral references. — 94 C.J.S., Wills, § 150.

79 Am. Jur. 2d, Wills, § 62.

Retrospective application of statute concerning execution of wills. 111 ALR 910.

Construction of reference in will to statute where pertinent provisions of statute are subsequently changed by amendment or repeal. 63 ALR3d 603.

§ 43-8-136. Revocation by writing or by act; when witnesses required.

(a) A will or any part thereof is revoked by a subsequent will which revokes the prior will or part expressly or by inconsistency.

(b) A will is revoked by being burned, torn, canceled, obliterated, or destroyed, with the intent and for the purpose of revoking it by the testator or by another person in his presence by his consent and direction. If the physical act is by someone other than the testator, consent and direction of the testator must be proved by at least two witnesses. (Acts 1982, No. 82-399, § 2-507.)

Commentary

This section is UPC § 2-507 modified to retain the Alabama rule that precludes partial (or pro tanto) revocation of a will by physical act. Law v. Law, 83 Ala. 432, 3 So. 752 (1887). The section also retains the Alabama rule that if the physical act is performed by someone other than the testator, the testator's consent and direction must be proved by at least two witnesses. See former § 43-1-33 (1975).

Revocation of a will may be by either a subsequent will or an act done to the document. If revocation is by a subsequent will, it must be properly executed. This section employs the traditional language which has been interpreted by the courts in many cases. It leaves to the court the determination of whether a subsequent will which has no express revocation clause is inconsistent with the prior will so as to revoke it wholly or partially, and in the case of an act done to the document the determination of whether the act is a sufficient burning, tearing, canceling, obliteration or destruction and was done with the intent and for the purpose of revoking. The latter necessarily involves exploration of extrinsic evidence, including statements of testator as to intent.

The section specifically permits partial revocation by a subsequent instrument executed as a will, but not by physical act. The court is free to apply its own doctrine of dependent relative revocation.

The section does not affect prior law in regard to the case of accidental destruction which is later confirmed by revocatory intention.

The section should remove the uncertainty caused in Alabama by the line of cases stemming from Bruce v. Sierra, 175 Ala. 517, 57 So. 709 (1912). The section is consistent with what seems to be the present position of the Alabama court as stated in Anderson v. Griggs, 402 So. 2d 904 (Ala. 1981).

I. General Consideration.
II. Decisions Under Prior Law.

I. GENERAL CONSIDERATION.

Collateral references. — 95 C.J.S., Wills, § 262. 96 C.J.S., Wills, § 1106.

79 Am. Jur. 2d, Wills, §§ 498-509, 540-546.

Necessity that later will refer to earlier will in order to effect revocation under statutes providing that a will may be revoked by a subsequent will declaring the revocation. 28 ALR 691.

Implied revocation of will by later will. 51 ALR 652; 59 ALR2d 11.

Validity, construction and effect of provisions of will relating to its modification or revocation. 72 ALR 871.

Revocation of earlier will by revoking clause in a lost will or other lost instrument. 94 ALR 1024.

Revocation by ratification or adoption of physical destruction or mutilation of will without testator's knowledge or consent in first instance. 99 ALR 524.

Necessity that physical destruction or mutilation of will be done in testator's presence in order to effect revocation. 100 ALR 1520.

Possibility of avoiding or limiting effect of clause in later will purporting to revoke all former wills. 125 ALR 936.

Destruction or cancellation, actual or presumed, of one copy of will executed in duplicate, as revocation of other copy. 17 ALR2d 805.

Effect of testator's attempted physical alteration of will after execution. 24 ALR2d 514.

Revocation as affected by invalidity of some or all of the dispositive provisions of later will. 28 ALR2d 526.

Revocation of will by nontestamentary writing. 22 ALR3d 1346.

Admissibility of testator's declarations on issue of revocation of will, in his possession at time of his death, by mutilation, alteration or cancellation. 28 ALR3d 994.

Revocation of witnessed will be holographic will or codicil, where statute requires revocation by instrument of equal formality as will. 49 ALR3d 1223.

Testator's failure to make new will, following loss of original will by fire, theft or similar casualty, as constituting revocation of original will. 61 ALR3d 958.

II. DECISIONS UNDER PRIOR LAW.

Editor's note. — In light of the similarity of the subject matter, decisions under former § 43-1-33 are included in the annotations for this section.

Former § 43-1-33 set out the exclusive means, with the exceptions therein noted, by which the revocation of a will could be effectuated. Parker v. Foreman, 252 Ala. 77, 39 So. 2d 574 (1949); Kelley v. Sutliff, 257 Ala. 371, 59 So. 2d 65 (1952).

Strict adherence to requirements of former § 43-1-33 was necessary to accomplish an effective revocation because said section provided the only method by which a will could be revoked. Anderson v. Griggs, 402 So. 2d 904 (Ala. 1981).

And there is no scope for the application of the common-law doctrine of implied revocation of a will by reason of changes in the family status or domestic relations of the testatrix where the statutory method of revocation is exclusive by specific terms of the statute. Parker v. Foreman, 252 Ala. 77, 39 So. 2d 574 (1949).

How will revoked. — Will may be revoked by making a subsequent will or by its destruction with intention of revoking it by testator himself, or by some other person in his presence and by his direction, provided proof of destruction by one other than testator must be by two witnesses. Vaughn v. Vaughn, 217 Ala. 364, 116 So. 427 (1928).

Mere influence inducing testator to destroy will is not sufficient to prevent the effect of revocation by its destruction if intentionally done in the manner provided by statute. Vaughn v. Vaughn, 217 Ala. 364, 116 So. 427 (1928).

Revocation must be in mode required by statute. — Regardless of the thoughts or contemplation of the testator, until there is a change or alteration or revocation in the mode required by the statute, the legal presumption is that the result of all thought and contemplation was a determination to adhere to the will as executed. Calhoun v. Thomas, 274 Ala. 111, 145 So. 2d 789 (1962).

Revocation is an act of the mind which must be demonstrated by some visible sign or action as set out by law. Woodruff v. Hundley, 127 Ala. 640, 29 So. 98 (1900); Allen v. Scruggs, 190 Ala. 654, 67 So. 301 (1914).

Mere intention to revoke is insufficient. — It is not infrequent that testators entertain thoughts, or have in contemplation changes or alterations or revocations of gifts or directions they may have expressed in their executed wills. The fact that such thoughts have been entertained, or such changes or alterations or revocations contemplated, cannot affect the validity of a duly-executed will in its integrity, or in any of its parts. Until there is change or alteration or revocation in the mode appointed by law, the legal presumption is that the result of all thought and contemplation was a determination to adhere to the will as executed. Slaughter v. Stephens, 81 Ala. 418, 2 So. 145 (1887); Barnewall v. Murrell, 108 Ala. 366, 18 So. 831 (1895).

Words alone do not revoke. — In Law v. Law, 83 Ala. 432, 3 So. 752 (1888), it was said "that no revocation can be effected by mere words of mouth, or nuncupative declaration, any more than could be done under the English statute of frauds. It requires one or more of the specific acts mentioned in this section — a burning, tearing, cancelling or obliterating with the intention to revoke — or a new will or codicil, properly executed and attested." Woodruff v. Hundley, 127 Ala. 640, 29 So. 98 (1900); Allan v. Allan, 353 So. 2d 1157 (Ala. 1977).

Two things must concur in order to revoke. — All the destroying in the world without intention will not revoke a will, nor all the intention in the world without destroying. There must be two. There must be the act as well as the animus. Both must concur in order to constitute a legal revocation. Allen v. Scruggs, 190 Ala. 654, 67 So. 301 (1914).

What constitutes tearing, cancelling, etc. — To what extent an obliteration of the instrument must extend to be effectually revocatory cannot be stated with any great degree of particularity. The paper must certainly be materially mutilated, so that, if unexplained by accompanying declarations, an intent to revoke may be inferred from its appearance, taken in connection with the act itself. Woodruff v. Hundley, 127 Ala. 640, 29 So. 98 (1900).

Removal of fastenings is not a tearing of will. — The removing of the fastenings holding the sheets of paper together by the testatrix was not a tearing of the will. Woodruff v. Hundley, 127 Ala. 640, 29 So. 98 (1900).

The words "annulled" and "void," written on the face of the will in the handwriting of the testator, with intention at the time of writing the same to revoke the will, is a sufficient revocation. Franklin v. Bogue, 245 Ala. 379, 17 So. 2d 405 (1944).

Presumption as to revocation. — Although it be shown that a will was once executed, yet if it remained in the possession of the testator, and cannot be found after his death, the presumption of law is that it was destroyed animo revocandi. The declarations of the testator are admissible strengthen or repel this presumption when the will is not produced. Weeks v. McBeth, 14 Ala. 474 (1848); Allen v. Scruggs, 190 Ala. 654, 67 So. 301 (1914).

When the will is shown to have been in the possession of the testator, and is not found at his death, the presumption arises that he destroyed it for the purpose of revocation.

Barksdale v. Pendergrass, 294 Ala. 526, 319 So. 2d 267 (1975).

May be rebutted. — The presumption may be rebutted, and the burden of rebutting it is on the proponent. Jaques v. Horton, 76 Ala. 238 (1884); Barksdale v. Pendergrass, 294 Ala. 526, 319 So. 2d 267 (1975).

A subsequent legally executed will revokes a prior one. Kelley v. Sutliff, 262 Ala. 622, 80 So. 2d 636 (1955).

A subsequent will legally executed revokes a prior will without any proof of the contents of the will. Wilson v. Bostick, 151 Ala. 536, 44 So. 389 (1907); Bruce v. Sierra, 175 Ala. 517, 57 So. 709 (1912).

Except where subsequent writing is intended as a codicil. — If the instrument and the proof connected therewith showed that it was intended as a mere codicil, the execution of same does not revoke the former will in its entirety. In other words, if it definitely appears from the subsequent instrument and the evidence that it was not the intention of the testator to revoke the former will, but to merely make certain changes therein, the latter will be treated as a codicil, and should be proved in connection with the former, and the two should be considered and construed together. Kohlenberg v. Shaw, 198 Ala. 571, 73 So. 932 (1917); Kelley v. Sutliff, 257 Ala. 371, 59 So. 2d 65 (1952).

Subsequent codicil does not revoke prior one. — The rule that the writing of a second will revokes the first will, unless the former is referred to and preserved by the subsequent, or unless it is clear that the second will was intended as a codicil to be read together with the will, does not extend to codicils. First Nat'l Bank v. First Nat'l Bank, 348 So. 2d 1041 (Ala. 1977).

An attempted codicil not properly attested is not effective, and the will must be read as originally written and executed. Calhoun v. Thomas, 274 Ala. 111, 145 So. 2d 789 (1962).

Elements of a revoking will. — It is plain that a revoking will must be executed with all due formality, and the compliance with every legal requirement must appear affirmatively as follows: (1) The will must be in writing; (2) It must be signed by the testator, or someone for him; (3) It must be attested by at least two witnesses; (4) The witnesses must subscribe their names in the presence of the testator. Bruce v. Sierra, 175 Ala. 517, 57 So. 709 (1912).

To show revocation of a will by the execution of a subsequent will, the following is required: (1) The will must be in writing; (2) it must be signed by the testator, or someone for him; (3) it must be attested by at least two witnesses; and (4) the witnesses must subscribe their names in the presence of the testator. Allan v.

Allan, 353 So. 2d 1157 (Ala. 1977); Forrester v. Putman, 409 So. 2d 773 (Ala. 1981).

It is not every duly executed will that revokes all those previously executed. Whether so or not depends upon the purpose of the testator in making them, to be inferred from legal evidence to that end. This evidence is usually furnished by the instruments themselves, in the light of facts known to the testator in making them. Kelley v. Sutliff, 257 Ala. 371, 59 So. 2d 65 (1952).

In Bruce v. Sierra, 175 Ala. 517, 57 So. 709 (1912), it was held that under § 6174, Code 1907, a subsequent will legally executed revokes a prior will without proof of the contents of the will. This has been modified so as not to apply where the will expressly negatives an intention to revoke the prior will. Wheat v. Wheat, 236 Ala. 52, 181 So. 243 (1938); Pugh v. Perryman, 257 Ala. 187, 58 So. 2d 117 (1952); Brooks v. Everett, 271 Ala. 354, 124 So. 2d 105 (1960).

Declarations by testator held inadmissible to prove revocation. — Declarations by a testator, made subsequent to the execution of a will, that he had revoked it, held not admissible to prove revocation. Allen v. Scruggs, 190 Ala. 654, 67 So. 301 (1914).

Statements by testator under oath revoke will. — Where testator, by positive statement under oath, before attesting witness, stated that former will had "been lost, destroyed or stolen," and "that said will is void, as a new will has been made since that time," the lost will was revoked, though the subsequent will cannot be found or was not made or executed as required by law. The doctrine of dependent, relative revocation has no application. Luther v. Luther, 211 Ala. 352, 100 So. 497 (1924).

The burden of showing revocation as provided by law is on contestants. Luther v. Luther, 211 Ala. 352, 100 So. 497 (1924); Allan v. Allan, 353 So. 2d 1157 (Ala. 1977).

Where a testator delivered a will to one of the beneficiaries for safekeeping, and the will was lost, the contestant has the burden to prove that it was destroyed animo revocandi. Allen v. Scruggs, 190 Ala. 654, 67 So. 301 (1914); Hodge v. Joy, 207 Ala. 198, 92 So. 171 (1921).

Allegations or revocation. — An allegation that a second will "was itself destroyed by said B with the intention of revoking it" is the legal equivalent of an allegation that testator burned, tore, canceled or obliterated the will with such intent as specified by law. Barksdale v. Davis, 114 Ala. 623, 22 So. 17 (1897), overruled on other grounds, Alexander v. Gibson, 176 Ala. 258, 57 So. 760 (1912).

An allegation that the alleged testator "made and executed, in the presence of witnesses, as required by law, another will, covering the same property, thereby revoking said alleged will," sufficiently charges the execution of such other will. Barksdale v. Davis, 114 Ala. 623, 22 So. 17 (1897), overruled on other grounds, Alexander v. Gibson, 176 Ala. 258, 57 So. 760 (1912).

Joint will is revocable. — A writing purporting to be a will, executed by two persons, making a posthumous disposition of the property of the one who may first die, in favor of the other, and requiring the survivor to pay the expenses of the last sickness and burial of the decedent, and such debts as may be proved against his estate, is the separate will of the first decedent, and is revocable as are other wills. Schumaker v. Schmidt, 44 Ala. 454 (1870).

The evidence of one witness is insufficient to show a revocation of a second will by the burning of the same by any other than the testator himself. Wilson v. Bostick, 151 Ala. 536. 44 So. 389 (1907).

Fact that a writing declared the will revoked, instead of containing terms revoking in praesenti, is immaterial. Luther v. Luther, 211 Ala. 352, 100 So. 497 (1924).

The provisions of former §§ 43-1-30 and 43-1-33 and § 43-1-44 contemplate "will-in-hand" situations which obviously supply a court with the necessary contents of the will at issue. Proof has not been allowed of the requisites of former §§ 43-1-30 and 43-1-33 as to a lost will unless that proof is also sufficient to invoke the exception method of proving a will for probate and the only and ultimate end of proving the valid execution of any will. Anderson v. Griggs, 402 So. 2d 904 (Ala. 1981).

Exception allowed for probating lost will cannot be read into and made an exception to revocation statute. One who offers to prove a lost will for the purpose of revoking a former one must be prepared to live by the terms of the lost document; and what the law recognizes as an exception for the purpose of rendering an estate testate, the law cannot recognize as an exception for the limited purposes of revoking a will, thus rendering the estate intestate in derogation of the revocation statute. Anderson v. Griggs, 402 So. 2d 904 (Ala. 1981).

To permit revocation by use of the lost will exception, in derogation of the statutory requisites for revocation, produces the one result least likely to carry out a testator's intent: to die testate. Anderson v. Griggs, 402 So. 2d 904 (Ala. 1981).

Contents of lost will may be proved by one witness. — Where the evidence showed the due execution of a will which had since been lost, the contents of the lost instrument could be proved by one witness, though the statute requires two subscribing witnesses to make it a valid will. Hodge v. Joy, 207 Ala. 198, 92 So. 171 (1921).

A lost will may be established by the testimony of a single witness who read it, or heard it read, and remembered its contents, and proof of the substance of a lost instrument as a will is sufficient, and the exact words need not be shown. Brooks v. Everett, 271 Ala. 354, 124 So. 2d 105 (1960).

Revoked will is absolutely void. — From the date of the revocation, the revoked will ceases to be a testamentary disposition of the maker's estate. Such revoked will is nothing. It can have no effect as a will. And if the party who made it desires to make a testamentary disposition of his estate, he must make a new will, in the manner required by the statute. Barker v. Bell, 46 Ala. 216 (1871).

Revival of revoked will. — It is clearly the law in this state that after a "good" revocation, a will can be revived only by the expressed intention of the testator himself. Clark v. Clark, 280 Ala. 644, 197 So. 2d 447 (1967).

A codicil which, through mistake of the typist, referred by date to a previous will which had been revoked did not have the effect of reviving the previous will. Clark v. Clark, 280 Ala. 644, 197 So. 2d 447 (1967).

New will may be in same words as old. — In making a new will a testator may use the same form of words, without variations, as often as he pleases, and the same written or printed document that'was used at first, but the process of making the will must be the same each time, that is, it must be done as prescribed by the statute. Barker v. Bell, 46 Ala. 216 (1871).

§ 43-8-137. Revocation by divorce or annulment; revival by remarriage; no revocation by other changes or circumstances.

If after executing a will the testator is divorced or his marriage annulled, the divorce or annulment revokes any disposition or appointment of property made by the will to the former spouse, any provision conferring a general or special power of appointment on the former spouse, and any nomination of the former spouse as executor, trustee, or guardian, unless the will expressly provides otherwise. Property prevented from passing to a former spouse because of revocation by divorce or annulment passes as if the former spouse failed to survive the decedent, and other provisions conferring some power or office on the former spouse are interpreted as if the spouse failed to survive the decedent. If provisions are revoked solely by this section, they are revived by testator's remarriage to the former spouse. For purposes of this section, divorce or annulment means any divorce or annulment which would exclude the spouse as a surviving spouse within the meaning of section 43-8-252(b). A decree of separation which does not terminate the status of husband and wife is not a divorce for purposes of this section. No change of circumstances other than as described in this section revokes a will. (Acts 1982, No. 82-399, § 2-508.)

Commentary

The section deals with what is sometimes called revocation by operation of law. It provides for revocation by a divorce or annulment only. No other change in circumstances operates to revoke the will. Of course, a specific devise may be adeemed by transfer of the property during the testator's lifetime except as otherwise provided in this act; although this is occasionally called revocation, it is not within the present section. The provisions with regard to invalid divorce decrees parallel those in § 43-8-252. Neither this section nor § 43-8-252 includes "divorce from bed and board" as an event which affects devises or marital rights on death.

But see § 43-8-72 providing that a complete property settlement entered into after or in anticipation of separation or divorce constitutes a renunciation of all benefits under a prior will, unless the settlement provides otherwise.

Alabama law is not changed by this section in that a divorce revokes any provision for a spouse in a will. Former § 43-1-8 (1975). Alabama's statute did not provide expressly that property affected by the revocation caused by a divorce passes as if the spouse failed to survive the testator, as this section provides, but this is a possible construction which a court might reach in Alabama. See, First Church of Christ, Scientist v. Watson, 286 Ala. 270, 239 So. 2d 194 (1970). This section, therefore, goes into more detail and is more explicit with regard to the effect of a divorce on a will, but it cannot be stated that Alabama law was inconsistent with this section.

Although this section does not provide for revocation of a will by subsequent marriage of the testator, the spouse may be protected by § 43-8-90 or an elective share under § 43-8-70.

I. General Consideration.
II. Decisions Under Prior Law.

I. GENERAL CONSIDERATION.

Collateral references. — 95 C.J.S., Wills, § 287.

79 Am. Jur. 2d, Wills, §§ 586-589.

Illegitimacy of child as affecting revocation of will by subsequent birth of child. 18 ALR 91; 38 ALR 1344.

Divorce or separation as affecting person entitled to devise or bequest to "husband," "wife" or "widow." 75 ALR2d 1413.

Statutory revocation of will by subsequent birth or adoption of child. 97 ALR2d 1044.

Validity and construction of testamentary gift conditioned upon beneficiary's remaining married. 28 ALR3d 1325.

Divorce as affecting will previously executed by husband or wife. 71 ALR3d 1297.

Devolution of gift over upon spouse predeceasing testator where gift to spouse fails because of divorce. 74 ALR3d 1108.

Validity of statutes or rule providing that marriage or remarriage of woman operates as revocation of will previously executed by her. 99 ALR3d 1020.

II. DECISIONS UNDER PRIOR LAW.

Editor's note. — In light of the similarity of the subject matter, decisions under former § 43-1-8 are included in the annotations for this section.

Former statutory provision that woman's will was revoked by her subsequent marriage was unconstitutional denial of equal protection because it clearly and impermissibly treated females differently from males. Parker v. Hall, 362 So. 2d 875 (Ala. 1978).

Strict construction. — Statutes such as former § 43-1-8 are in derogation of the general power to make a will, are in the nature of exceptions thereto, and must be accorded a strict construction, and no obtrusion to include a class not clearly comprehended therein will be recognized or permitted. Parker v. Foreman, 252 Ala. 77, 39 So. 2d 574 (1949).

Divorced wife of testator not entitled to letters testamentary. Jeffries v. Boyd, 269 Ala. 177, 112 So. 2d 210 (1959).

Divorce revokes only that portion of will which makes provision for former spouse. — The former spouse can take nothing under the provisions of the will, but the entire will is not revoked, only that portion which makes provision for the former spouse. First Church of Christ v. Watson, 286 Ala. 270, 239 So. 2d 194 (1970).

Property to pass as if former spouse failed to survive. — Property which is prevented from passing to the former spouse because of revocation by divorce should pass as if the former spouse failed to survive the decedent, unless a contrary intention is apparent from the provisions of the will. First Church of Christ v. Watson, 286 Ala. 270, 239 So. 2d 194 (1970).

Former spouse not entitled to be named executrix. — The former spouse is not entitled to be named executrix of her former husband's estate even though the husband had appointed "my wife" as the executrix. First Church of Christ v. Watson, 286 Ala. 270, 239 So. 2d 194 (1970).

Divorce of wife of testator is not equivalent to her death. — It is not necessary to go so far as to declare that the divorce of the wife of the testator is equivalent to her death. After her divorce, she is no longer the wife of the testator and does not survive as his widow. First Church of Christ v. Watson, 286 Ala. 270, 239 So. 2d 194 (1970).

§ 43-8-138. When will revived on revocation of subsequent will.

(a) If a second will which, had it remained effective at death, would have revoked the first will in whole or in part, is thereafter revoked by acts under section 43-8-136, the first will is revoked in whole or in part unless it is evident from the circumstances of the revocation of the second will or from testator's contemporary or subsequent declarations in writing, signed by the testator and attested as prescribed in section 43-8-131, that he intended the first will to take effect as executed.

(b) If a second will which, had it remained effective at death, would have revoked the first will in whole or in part, is thereafter revoked by a third will, the first will is revoked in whole or in part, except to the extent it appears from the terms of the third will that the testator intended the first will to take effect. (Acts 1982, No. 82-399, § 2-509.)

Commentary

This section adopts a limited revival doctrine. If testator executes will number 1 and later executes will number 2 revoking will number 1 and still later revokes will number 2 by act such as destruction, there is a question as to whether testator intended to die intestate or have will number 1 revived as his last will. Under this section will number 1 can be probated as testator's last will if his intent to that effect can be established by testator's declarations in writing. This section differs from the UPC § 2-509 in that under the UPC provisions testator's declaration of intent to revive could be oral declarations as well as written declarations. This section limits effective declarations of intent to revive to written declarations of such intent. If will number 2 is revoked by a third will, will number 1 would remain revoked except to the extent that will number 3 showed an intent to have will number 1 effective.

Prior Alabama law probably was in accord with the UPC provision, but this section alters the UPC provision by permitting declarations of intent to revive to declarations "in writing". Former § 43-1-34 (1975), provided that the making of any subsequent will or writing, and the cancellation, destruction, or revocation thereof did not revive any will previously executed, unless it appeared, by the terms of such revocation, that it was the intention of the testator to revive and give effect to the first will; or unless, after such cancellation or destruction, the testator duly republished the previous will. Apparently oral declarations of an intent to revive an earlier revoked will can be effective to revive the earlier will when the oral declarations accompany the revocation of a subsequent will by physical act. Fuller v. Nazal, 259 Ala. 598, 67 So. 2d 806 (1953). It is not clear that oral declarations of intent to revive an earlier will would be effective if the oral declarations were made subsequent to the physical act which revoked a later will, although this intent would be effective under the UPC provisions. Barker v. Bell, 49 Ala. 284 (1873) indicates that "republish" as used in former § 43-1-34 really means re-execution. There can be no revival of a first will if the will has been destroyed or mutilated, and you cannot have an oral republication. *Id.* A memorandum, executed with the formality of executing a will, will suffice to revive a previously revoked will in Alabama. Price v. Marshall, 255 Ala. 447, 52 So. 2d 149 (1951).

I. General Consideration.
II. Decisions Under Prior Law.

I. GENERAL CONSIDERATION.

Collateral references. — 95 C.J.S., Wills, §§ 298, 301.

79 Am. Jur. 2d, Wills, §§ 684-693.

Revocation of later will as reviving earlier will. 28 ALR 911; 162 ALR 1072.

II. DECISIONS UNDER PRIOR LAW.

Editor's note. — In light of the similarity of the subject matter, decisions under former § 43-1-34 are included in the annotations for this section.

After a good revocation a will can be revived only by the expressed intention of the testator himself. Allen v. Bromberg, 147 Ala. 317, 41 So. 771 (1906).

Two methods are provided for reviving a prior will revoked by a subsequent will: (1) By the cancellation, destruction or revocation of the second will in terms which declare the intent to revive the first will, and (2) After a cancellation or destruction of a last will by the republication of the previous will. The first alternative in effect provides that the same act should both cancel, destroy or revoke the second will and revive the first one. Fuller v. Nazal, 259 Ala. 598, 67 So. 2d 806 (1953).

By codicil. — A codicil may not revoke a last will and revive a prior one by mere implication. For a codicil to have the effect of reviving a will previously revoked by reference to the date of such prior will, the intention of the testator to revoke the intervening will and to revive such revoked will must be clearly expressed in the face of the codicil either by express words referring to the prior will as having been revoked and declaring an intention to revive the same or by a disposition of the testator's property inconsistent with any other intention. A reference to the revoked will merely by the date of its execution and its subscribing witnesses is not alone sufficient in and of itself to impart such an intent. Fuller v. Nazal, 259 Ala. 598, 67 So. 2d 806 (1953); Clark v. Clark, 280 Ala. 644, 197 So. 2d 447 (1967).

If the codicil does not in and of itself show an intent on the part of the testator to revoke the last will and to revive a prior one, and is manifestly ambiguous in referring to the prior will as the last will when in fact the subsequent will, still unrevoked, was his last will, it becomes necessary and proper to resort to evidence aliunde to determine the intent of the testator with respect to the issue. See Fuller v. Nazal, 259 Ala. 598, 67 So. 2d 806 (1953), holding that the trial court properly allowed in evidence the testimony of the testator's banker and his attorney, who drafted the codicil, tending to show that a mistake with respect to which will the codicil was intended refer had been made, as well as the testator's relevant declarations and statements made with reference to the will, including several letters to the appellee, all tending to show that he had no intention of revoking his last will and of reviving the former one, but all the while thought the last will was in full force and effect.

Memorandum testamentary in nature may revive. — A 1946 instrument was a legal will and its effect was to revoke a 1945 will. After the destruction by testatrix of the 1946 will, a memorandum was efficacious to revive the 1945 will since it possessed all the elements of a testamentary document. Price v. Marshall, 255 Ala. 447, 52 So. 2d 149 (1951).

Republication when signatures torn off. — There can be no republication of a will that has been revoked by tearing off the names of the maker and the attesting witnesses, unless the will is re-signed and re-attested, as required by law. The signing of the will and the attestation of this signature are essential formalities that cannot be dispensed with. Barker v. Bell, 46 Ala. 216 (1871).

§ 43-8-139. Incorporation by reference.

Any writing in existence when a will is executed may be incorporated by reference if the language of the will manifests this intent and describes the writing sufficiently to permit its identification. (Acts 1982, No. 82-399, § 2-510.)

Commentary

Prior Alabama law is not changed by this section. See, First National Bank of Birmingham v. Klein, 285 Ala. 505, 234 So. 2d 42 (1970); Mastin v. First National Bank of Mobile, 278 Ala. 251, 177 So. 2d 808 (1965); Arrington v. Brown, 235 Ala. 196, 178 So. 218 (1938).

Collateral references. — 95 C.J.S., Wills, § 624.

79 Am. Jur. 2d, Wills, §§ 199-209.

Letter as a will or codicil. 54 ALR 917; 40 ALR2d 698.

Notation on note or securities as a will or codicil. 62 ALR 292.

§ 43-8-140. Testamentary additions to trusts.

A devise or bequest, the validity of which is determinable by the law of this state, may be made by a will to the trustee of a trust established or to be established by the testator and some other person or by some other person (including a funded or unfunded life insurance trust, although the trustor has reserved any or all rights of ownership of the insurance contracts) if the trust is identified in the testator's will and its terms are set forth in a written instrument (other than a will) executed before or concurrently with the execution of the testator's will or in the valid last will of a person who has predeceased the testator (regardless of the existence, size, or character of the corpus of the trust). The devise is not invalid because the trust is amendable or revocable, or because the trust was amended after the execution of the will or after the death of the testator. Unless the testator's will provides otherwise, the property so devised (1) is not deemed to be held under a testamentary trust of the testator but becomes a part of the trust to which it is given and (2) shall be administered and disposed of in accordance with the provisions of the instrument or will setting forth the terms of the trust, including any amendments thereto made before the death of the testator (regardless of whether made before or after the execution of the testator's will), and, if the testator's will so provides, including any amendments to the trust made after the death of a testator. A revocation or termination of the trust before the death of the testator causes the devise to lapse. (Acts 1982, No. 82-399, § 2-511.)

Commentary

This is section 1 of the Uniform Testamentary Additions to Trusts Act.

Former § 43-1-4 (1975) and this section are in accord except that this section allows the trust to be amended after the death of the testator if the testator specifically so stated, while Alabama did not allow such amendment prior to this act.

Collateral references. — 96 C.J.S., Wills, §§ 1004-1022.

79 Am. Jur. 2d, Wills, § 209.

§ 43-8-141. Reference to events of independent significance.

A will may dispose of property by reference to acts and events which have significance apart from their effect upon the dispositions made by the will, whether they occur before or after the execution of the will or before or after the testator's death. The execution or revocation of a will of another person is such an event. (Acts 1982, No. 82-399, § 2-512.)

Commentary

Prior Alabama case law and this section apparently are in accord. See, First National Bank of Birmingham v. Klein, 285 Ala. 505, 234 So. 2d 42 (1970).

Collateral references. — 96 C.J.S., Wills, §§ 974-976.

80 Am. Jur. 2d, Wills, §§ 1548-1556.

Excuse for delay in complying with condition of bequest or devise, beyond time allowed by will. 26 ALR 929.

Provision in devise requiring devisee to pay money as creating a charge or a condition. 62 ALR 589.

Effect of prevention, by colegatee or codevisee or a third person, of a legatee or devisee from performing the condition upon which the gift rests. 76 ALR 1342.

Right of legatee or devisee and duty of executor in respect of legacy or devise, payment of which is by the terms of will conditional upon performance of some act or course of conduct by legatee or upon some future event. 110 ALR 1354.

Validity of provision of will that makes devise or legacy dependent upon some future act by testator. 152 ALR 1238.

Absence of limitation over in event of nonperformance of condition as to conduct or obligation of devisee, legatee or grantee, as affecting operation of condition. 163 ALR 1152.

Testamentary gift to one named as executor or trustee as conditioned upon his qualifying or serving as such. 61 ALR2d 1380.

Construction of will provision for gift over if first taker dies without issue and if some other contingency occurs, where there is death without issue but the other contingency does not occur. 73 ALR2d 466.

Determination of absolute or conditional nature of will. 1 ALR3d 1048.

Validity of condition of gift depending on divorce or separation. 14 ALR3d 1219.

Validity of testamentary provision making gift to person or persons meeting specified qualification and authorizing another to determine who qualifies. 74 ALR3d 1073.

Wills: condition that devisee or legatee shall renounce, embrace, or adhere to specified religious faith. 89 ALR3d 984.

Division 2.

Probate of Will.

§ 43-8-160. Who may have will probated.

Upon the death of a testator, any executor, devisee, or legatee named in the will, or any person interested in the estate, or who has custody of such will may have the will proved before the proper probate court. (Code 1852, § 1620; Code 1867, § 1939; Code 1876, § 2303; Code 1886, § 1975; Code 1896, § 4272; Code 1907, § 6181; Code 1923, § 10607; Code 1940, T. 61, § 33; Code 1975, § 43-1-36.)

Code commissioner's note. — This section was originally codified as § 43-1-36 of the 1975 Code.

Option to buy stock from testator is sufficient interest. — A resident of Alabama holding option from nonresident testator who died out of the state to purchase stock in Alabama corporation owned by testator at time of death had an equitable interest in such stock as assets of testator's estate in Alabama which constituted such an interest in testator's estate as to entitle optionee to seek probate of testator's will. Nashville Trust Co. v. Cleage, 246 Ala. 513, 21 So. 2d 441 (1945).

Decree admitting will to probate would not be dismissed merely on the asserted ground that the will was admitted to probate on the petition of one without authority to have the will probated. Smith v. Chism, 262 Ala. 417, 79 So. 2d 45 (1955).

Alignment of parties. — The latter part of § 43-8-190 which directs the probate court to align the parties between the person making the application for probate, as plaintiff, and the person contesting the validity of the will, as defendant, is directory rather than mandatory in light of this section and §§ 43-8-190 and

43-8-198. Hooper v. Huey, 293 Ala. 63, 300 So. 2d 100 (1974), overruled on other grounds, Bardin v. Jones, 371 So. 2d 23 (1979).

Cited in Woodruff v. Hundley, 127 Ala. 640, 29 So. 98 (1900); McDonnell v. Jordan, 178 U.S. 229, 20 S. Ct. 886, 44 L. Ed. 1048 (1900); Tankersley v. Tankersley, 270 Ala. 571, 120 So. 2d 744 (1960).

Collateral references. — 80 Am. Jur. 2d, Wills, § 887.

Relative rights to real property as between purchasers from or through decedent's heirs and devisees under will subsequently sought to be established. 22 ALR2d 1107.

Right to probate subsequently discovered will as affected by completed prior proceedings in intestate administration. 2 ALR4th 1315.

§ 43-8-161. Time limit for probate.

Wills shall not be effective unless filed for probate within five years from the date of the death of the testator. If the testator was not an inhabitant of this state at the time of his or her death, the will may be admitted to probate in this state pursuant to section 43-8-175, provided the will was admitted to probate, within five years from the date of death, in the state, territory or country where the testator resided at the time of death; provided further, that the probate in the state of the will of an inhabitant of another state, territory or country shall not be effective against persons purchasing from the heirs of such testator if such purchase was made more than five years after the death of the testator and prior to February 24, 1959. (Acts 1945, No. 196, p. 322; Acts 1949, No. 336, p. 501; Acts 1959, No. 587, p. 1475, § 1; Code 1975, § 43-1-37.)

Code commissioner's note. — This section was originally codified as § 43-1-37 of the 1975 Code.

"File for probate" indicates that the filing is for the specific purpose of probate, which is "the act or process of proving a will." Russell v. Maxwell, 387 So. 2d 156 (Ala. 1980).

The "file for probate" language of this section connotes action beyond turning the will over to a clerk for recordation and involves some further action such as making application to probate the will to evidence an intent to probate the will. Russell v. Maxwell, 387 So. 2d 156 (Ala. 1980).

Verbal application for probate. — While the better practice is to require an application or petition for probate to be in writing, verbal applications have been recognized if the probate court deemed such an application adequate to call into exercise its jurisdiction to take proof. Russell v. Maxwell, 387 So. 2d 156 (Ala. 1980).

When statute of limitations began to run. — Eo instanti upon enactment limitation section began to run against probate of will and against will itself as operative disposition of property. Gilbert v. Partain, 222 Ala. 459, 133 So. 2 (1931).

It was not the legislative intent in the adoption of this section to place it within the power of a legatee under a will, who obtained possession thereof, to deprive other legatees of rights by fraudulently concealing the existence of the will. Fuller v. Qualls, 241 Ala. 673, 4 So. 2d 418 (1941).

Wills not probated are inefficacious to pass title or confer rights. Fuller v. Qualls, 241 Ala. 673, 4 So. 2d 418 (1941).

Court must revoke letters of administration where will proved within five years. — Under statute dictating that if after letters of administration have been granted, will is proved and executor appears and complies with requisite requirements, probate court must revoke letters of administration and grant letters testamentary to executor, a will located within five years of death of the testator should not be denied probate solely because the estate has been fully administered and settled in accordance with the laws of intestacy of Alabama. Gross v. Slye, 360 So. 2d 333 (Ala. 1978).

Section is a statute of limitations. — While this section is so worded as to operate against wills as well as proceedings to probate the same, it is nevertheless a statute of limitations, intended to cut off the remedy. Fuller v. Qualls, 241 Ala. 673, 4 So. 2d 418 (1941); Sharpe v. Booker, 263 Ala. 592, 83 So. 2d 313 (1955).

And is tolled where fraud is proven. — Section 6-2-3 is in pari materia with this section and must be construed as tolling the running of this section, where the party invoking the remedy alleges and proves fraud as the basis of the right to proceed. Fuller v. Qualls, 241 Ala. 673, 4 So. 2d 418 (1941).

The predecessor of § 6-2-3 is in pari materia with the predecessor of this section and must be construed as tolling the five-year provision, where the party attempting to invoke the remedy alleges and proves fraud as the basis of the right to proceed. Russell v. Maxwell, 387 So. 2d 156 (Ala. 1980).

And will may be probated after five years. — The devisee of estate in remainder was entitled to probate of will, notwithstanding that more than five years had elapsed between testator's death and filing of petition for probate of will, where life tenant concealed existence of will from devisee, and devisee had no knowledge of existence of will until death of life tenant, and petition was filed within a year after discovery of will. Fuller v. Qualls, 241 Ala. 673, 4 So. 2d 418 (1941).

Termination of spouse's interests by her death prior to probate of decedent's will. — Where, according to the terms of the will, death of the decedent's spouse prior to the probate of the will would have terminated the interest bequeathed to her, since the will could have been filed for probate within a period of five years from the date of the testator's death, there existed at the time of his death a possible contingency that the spouse might survive the decedent by more than six months and die thereafter before the will was probated. This possible contingency defeated the exception in the marital deduction provisions of the Internal Revenue Code of 1954. Silvey v. United States, 265 F. Supp. 235 (N.D. Ala. 1966).

Cited in Rice v. Park, 223 Ala. 317, 135 So. 472 (1931); Johnston v. Rothenberg, 270 Ala. 304, 118 So. 2d 744 (1960).

Collateral references. — 95 C.J.S., Wills, §§ 356-360.

79 Am. Jur. 2d, Wills, §§ 874, 875, 877, 878.

Statute requiring production of will for probate or declaring consequences of failure or delay in that regard. 119 ALR 1259.

Relative rights to real property as between purchaser from or through decedent's heirs and devisees under a will subsequently sought to be established as affected by statutes of limitation relating to time for probate of will. 22 ALR2d 1119.

What circumstances excuse failure to submit will for probate within time limit set by statute. 17 ALR3d 1361.

Statute limiting time for probate of will as applicable to will probated in another jurisdiction. 87 ALR2d 721.

Right to probate subsequently discovered will as affected by completed prior proceedings in intestate administration. 2 ALR4th 1315.

§ 43-8-162. Where will probated.

Wills must be proved in the several probate courts as follows:

(1) When the testator, at the time of his death, was an inhabitant of the county, in the probate court of such county.

(2) When the testator, not being an inhabitant of the state, dies in the county, leaving assets therein, in the probate court of such county.

(3) When the testator, not being an inhabitant of the state, dies out of the county, leaving assets therein, in the probate of the county in which such assets, or any part thereof, are.

(4) When the testator, not being an inhabitant of the state, dies, not leaving assets therein, and assets thereafter come into any county, in the probate court of any county into which such assets are brought.

(5) In the probate court of the county designated by testator in the will if the testator owns property in such county at the time of his death. (Code 1852, § 1621; Code 1867, § 1940; Code 1876, § 2304; Code 1886, § 1976;

Code 1896, § 4273; Code 1907, § 6182; Code 1923, § 10609; Code 1940, T. 61, § 35; Code 1975, § 43-1-38.)

Code commissioner's note. — This section was originally codified as § 43-1-38 of the 1975 Code.

"Inhabitant" means domiciliary resident. — The word "inhabitant," as used in this section regulating the probate of wills, is the synonym of domiciliary resident, and means one who has his domicile in the particular county. A person's domicile is that place in which his habitation is fixed, without any present intention of removing; and it embraces both the fact of residence, and the intention to remain. Merrill v. Morrissett, 76 Ala. 433 (1884).

The word "inhabitant" in the sense of this section is synonymous with "domiciliary." Ambrose v. Vandeford, 277 Ala. 66, 167 So. 2d 149 (1964).

Death at certain place is no evidence of domicile. — The casual death of a person at a given place very clearly can have no tendency to show that his domicile was there, unless the fact stands alone and unexplained by any rebutting evidence. It is the fact of such person being there at all, and not his death, which may sometimes constitute a prima facie case of domicile. Somerville v. Somerville, 5 Ves. Jr. 750; Merrill v. Morrissett, 76 Ala. 433 (1884).

One who casually dies anywhere may hastily prepare his will, even when almost in articulo mortis; but persons, especially when exercising great deliberation, are not accustomed to appoint executors to administer upon their estates in foreign jurisdictions and places distant from their domiciles. Ambrose v. Vandeford, 277 Ala. 66, 167 So. 2d 149 (1964).

"Domicile". — Domicile is a residence at a particular place accompanied by an intent to remain there permanently, or for an indefinite length of time. Ambrose v. Vandeford, 277 Ala. 66, 167 So. 2d 149 (1964).

Allegation of domicile. — Under subdivision (1) of this section, a petition to probate a will in the probate court of M. county, properly averred that at the time of her death testatrix was an inhabitant thereof. McDonnell v. Farrow, 132 Ala. 227, 31 So. 475 (1902).

Domicile once acquired continues until a new one is acquired. Ambrose v. Vandeford, 277 Ala. 66, 167 So. 2d 149 (1964).

Change of domicile consists of physical presence in the new domicile with the concurrent intent of remaining there for an indefinite time. Ambrose v. Vandeford, 277 Ala. 66, 167 So. 2d 149 (1964).

Declarations of domicile by deceased are admissible to show intent. Ambrose v.

Vandeford, 277 Ala. 66, 167 So. 2d 149 (1964).

The declaration by decedent that he did not intend to live in Bessemer again, made to his son while he was hospitalized, clearly tended to establish the decedent's intent to abandon his Bessemer domicile. Ambrose v. Vandeford, 277 Ala. 66, 167 So. 2d 149 (1964).

Exercise of franchise. — When a man's domicile is the subject of inquiry, the scale has often been made to turn by a single fact, as, that he exercised the right of political franchise in a particular state or county. Ambrose v. Vandeford, 277 Ala. 66, 167 So. 2d 149 (1964).

Recitals of domicile or place of residence in wills and deeds are generally regarded as not conclusive, but only prima facie, and capable of being rebutted by proof to the contrary. Ambrose v. Vandeford, 277 Ala. 66, 167 So. 2d 149 (1964).

Prior probate in state of testator's domicile is not necessary for probate of a foreign will in this state under this section. Kelley v. Sutliff, 262 Ala. 622, 80 So. 2d 636 (1955).

In view of subdivision (3) of this section, where a testator dies out of the state, having a domicile outside the state, leaving real estate within the state and county, it was not a condition precedent to the attaching of the jurisdiction of the probate court of the county, upon the petition to probate the will, that such will should be first probated in the state of the testator's domicile. Jaques v. Horton, 76 Ala. 238 (1884); Frederick v. Wilbourne, 198 Ala. 137, 73 So. 442 (1916).

Nonresident testator who owned stock in Alabama corporation when he dies outside the state, though certificate representing such stock was held in the state of his residence, left assets in Alabama in county of principal place of business of corporation within this section. Nashville Trust Co. v. Cleage, 246 Ala. 513, 21 So. 2d 441 (1945).

Exclusive jurisdiction of probate court. — The probate of wills in Alabama is a matter within the exclusive jurisdiction of the probate court. It cannot be accomplished unilaterally by a designated representative. Silvey v. United States, 265 F. Supp. 235 (N.D. Ala. 1966).

Assuming, arguendo, that the decedent's spouse, designated to be executrix in the will, had the exclusive right to offer the will for probate and thereafter to letters testamentary, this right may not be equated with the power to appoint the entire interest to herself or her estate exercisable by herself alone or in all events without the intervention of the probate court. Silvey v. United States, 265 F. Supp. 235 (N.D. Ala. 1966).

The probate of a will is a matter resting exclusively in the jurisdiction of the probate court. Wachter v. Davis, 215 Ala. 659, 111 So. 917 (1927); Ex parte Russell, 239 Ala. 641, 196 So. 718 (1940).

Collateral attack on jurisdiction. — Where the statutory jurisdictional averment was made in the petition for probate filed in Jefferson county, and issue was joined on the question and a hearing held, which resulted in a finding by the probate court of Jefferson county that the decedent was an inhabitant of Jefferson county at the time of her death, the decision of the court as to the jurisdictional fact cannot collaterally be called in question. Orton v. Cheatham, 293 Ala. 639, 309 So. 2d 94 (1975).

Sufficiency of evidence. — Where evidence offered consisted largely of certain documents such as deceased's driver's license, car registration receipt, an identification card, etc., and these documents listed his address as of the time of the issuance of the document, such evidence possessed no probative force in tending to show the decedent's domicile during the critical period after he was overwhelmed by a physical illness which proved fatal in a few months. Ambrose v. Vandeford, 277 Ala. 66, 167 So. 2d 149 (1964).

Cited in Broughton v. Bradley, 34 Ala. 694 (1859); McDonnell v. Jordan, 178 U.S. 229, 20 S. Ct. 886, 44 L. Ed. 1048 (1900); Kelley v. Sutliff, 257 Ala. 371, 59 So. 2d 65 (1952); Mallette v. Merchants Nat'l Bank, 286 Ala. 37, 236 So. 2d 694 (1970); Davis v. State, 348 So. 2d 844 (Ala. Crim. App. 1977).

Collateral references. — 95 C.J.S., Wills, §§ 351-355.

79 Am. Jur. 2d, Wills, § 852.

Establishment of will lost before testator's death. 34 ALR 1304.

Relation back of probate of will in support of title or rights of persons claiming under or through devisees. 48 ALR 1035.

Probate fees or taxes as a property tax or an excise tax. 103 ALR 91.

Necessity of revocation of probate of prior will before probate of later will, or effect of probate after prior probate. 107 ALR 249; 157 ALR 1351.

Power and duty of probate court to set aside admission of forged instrument to probate as a will. 115 ALR 473.

Jurisdiction in proceedings for probate of will to adjudicate as to other wills not offered for probate. 119 ALR 1099.

Relative rights to real property as between purchasers from or through decedent's heirs and devisees under a foreign will subsequently sought to be established. 22 ALR2d 1107.

Probate, in state where assets are found, of will of nonresident which has not been admitted to probate in state of domicile. 20 ALR3d 1033.

§ 43-8-163. Probate not prevented by subsequent incompetency of witnesses.

If the witnesses attesting the execution of any will are competent at the time of their attestation, their subsequent incompetency, from whatever cause it may arise, must not prevent the probate of such will, if otherwise satisfactorily proved. (Code 1852, § 1612; Code 1867, § 1931; Code 1876, § 2295; Code 1886, § 1967; Code 1896, § 4264; Code 1907, § 6173; Code 1923, § 10599; Code 1940, T. 61, § 25; Code 1975, § 43-1-39.)

Code commissioner's note. — This section was originally codified as § 43-1-39 of the 1975 Code.

Cited in Barker v. Bell, 46 Ala. 216 (1871).

Collateral references. — 94 C.J.S., Wills, § 185.

79 Am. Jur. 2d, Wills, § 288.

Competency, as witness attesting will, of attorney named therein as executor's attorney. 30 ALR3d 1361.

§ 43-8-164. Notice to surviving spouse and next of kin — Generally.

Whenever an application is made to prove a will in this state, at least 10 days' notice must be given to the surviving spouse and next of kin, or either of them, residing and being within the state, before such application is heard. (Code 1852, § 1632; Code 1867, § 1951; Code 1876, § 2315; Code 1886, § 1987;

Code 1896, § 4284; Code 1907, § 6193; Code 1923, § 10622; Code 1940, T. 61, § 48; Code 1975, § 43-1-41.)

Code commissioner's note. — This section was originally codified as § 43-1-41 of the 1975 Code.

This section differs from common-law rule. — The attempt to trace resemblances between the methods of proving and contesting wills under this section and under the system which it supersedes suggests certain analogies, which are apt to mislead, as the proceedings under the two systems are widely dissimilar in important particulars. This section does not contemplate any such ex parte proceeding as the old proof in common form. Notice to the widow (now surviving spouse) and next of kin of the decedent, and an opportunity for them to contest, are required whenever a will is offered for probate. Knox v. Paull, 95 Ala. 505, 11 So. 156 (1892).

At common law no notice was required. — Wills of personal property could at common law be probated either in common form or in solemn form. A probate in common form was permitted without notice to parties in interest and without affording them an opportunity to contest. They were not required to abide by the result of such a summary proceeding if they chose to demand that the will be proved in solemn form, which involved a citation to all persons interested in the estate so as to bind them by the decree rendered. Knox v. Paull, 95 Ala. 505, 11 So. 156 (1892).

This section contemplates notice to surviving spouse and next of kin. — It is perfectly plain that the statutory system of probating and contesting wills contemplates that the widow (now surviving spouse) and next of kin shall have notice of any application for the probate of a will of the decedent, and that before any instrument is admitted to probate as a last will and testament, all persons interested therein, or in the estate of the decedent if he died intestate, should have an opportunity to contest its validity in the probate court. Knox v. Paull, 95 Ala. 505, 11 So. 156 (1892).

The probate of a will is a proceeding in rem, because it operates upon the thing itself,

defining its status. Deslonde v. Darrington, 29 Ala. 92 (1856).

Yet the widow (now surviving spouse) and next of kin are entitled to personal notice. Hine v. Hussey, 45 Ala. 496 (1871).

Failure to give notice is a mere irregularity. — The failure to give the widow (now surviving spouse) and next of kin the notice required by this section is a mere irregularity, which can only be taken advantage of in a direct proceeding to set aside the probate. Sowell v. Sowell, 40 Ala. 243 (1866); Hall v. Hall, 47 Ala. 290 (1872); Knox v. Paull, 95 Ala. 505, 11 So. 156 (1892).

The provision in this section for notice to next of kin is directory only, the failure to give it is a mere irregularity, in no way affecting the validity of the probate on collateral attack. Caverno v. Webb, 239 Ala. 671, 196 So. 723 (1940); Hawkins v. Sanders, 260 Ala. 585, 72 So. 2d 81 (1954).

A court may set aside a decree against a party on allegation and proof that he was not served, provided he shows he has a meritorious claim, but it will not set aside the judgment of a court of general jurisdiction merely because the record does not show the service of notice. As against such attack, it is conclusive. Hawkins v. Sanders, 260 Ala. 585, 72 So. 2d 81 (1954).

And does not render probate void. — The probate of a will in the probate court is not void, although notice to the widow (now surviving spouse) or next of kin or to both is not given. Hawkins v. Sanders, 260 Ala. 585, 72 So. 2d 81 (1954).

Waiver of notice by an illegitimate son not properly legitimated is of no effect under this section. Johnson v. Barnett, 240 Ala. 413, 199 So. 804 (1941).

Cited in Kirby v. Anders, 26 Ala. 466 (1855); McDonnell v. Jordan, 178 U.S. 229, 20 S. Ct. 886, 44 L. Ed. 1048 (1900); Griffin v. Milligan, 177 Ala. 57, 58 So. 257 (1912).

Collateral references. — 95 C.J.S., Wills, §§ 309, 370.

§ 43-8-165. Same — Minors.

If any of the next of kin are minors, such notice may be served as provided by the Alabama Rules of Civil Procedure; and in addition to the service above provided for minors, the court must appoint a guardian ad litem who is disinterested and who shall be an attorney-at-law and who does not represent any party having an interest adverse to such minors; and notice shall issue to such guardian ad litem. Such guardian shall accept service and agree to represent the minors in the proof and probate of the will, and if he fail to accept service and agree to appear for the minors within 10 days after service, the court appoint another guardian ad litem, upon whom notice must be served, and he must agree to accept service and represent the minors as is provided in the first instance, and the will must not be probated until a guardian ad litem has agreed to accept the appointment and to represent the minors in the proof and probate of the will, which acceptance and agreement must be in writing and filed with the papers in the cause, and notice must be given to such guardian ad litem in all proceedings to contest the probate of the will. (Code 1896, § 4285; Code 1907, § 6194; Code 1923, § 10623; Code 1940, T. 61, § 49; Code 1975, § 43-1-42.)

Code commissioner's note. — This section was originally codified as § 43-1-42 of the 1975 Code.

Cross references. — As to rules of supreme court relative to service of process, see A.R.C.P., Rule 4 et seq. As to authority of guardian ad litem to contest will, see notes to § 43-8-190.

The duties of a guardian ad litem are substantial and extend to any matter which comes to his attention which would defeat the will, if necessary, to protect the ward's interest. Ex parte Petty, 249 Ala. 393, 31 So. 2d 575 (1947).

§ 43-8-166. Same — Persons outside state.

If either the surviving spouse or next of kin reside and are without the state, notice of such application must be given by publication once a week for three successive weeks in a newspaper published in the county in which such application is made, and if no paper is published therein, by posting of the same at the courthouse three weeks before such application is heard. In lieu of the notice herein provided, notice may be had on such persons as provided by the Alabama Rules of Civil Procedure. (Code 1852, § 1633; Code 1867, § 1952; Code 1876, § 2316; Code 1886, § 1988; Code 1896, § 4286; Code 1907, § 6195; Code 1923, § 10624; Code 1940, T. 61, § 50; Code 1975, § 43-1-43.)

Code commissioner's note. — This section was originally codified as § 43-1-43 of the 1975 Code.

Cited in Kirby v. Anders, 26 Ala. 466 (1855).

§ 43-8-167. Mode of proving will generally.

(a) Wills offered for probate, except nuncupative wills, must be proved by one or more of the subscribing witnesses, or if they be dead, insane or out of the state or have become incompetent since the attestation, then by the proof of the handwriting of the testator, and that of at least one of the witnesses to the will. Where no contest is filed, the testimony of only one attesting witness is sufficient.

(b) If none of the subscribing witnesses to such will are produced, their insanity, death, subsequent incompetency or absence from the state must be satisfactorily shown before proof of the handwriting of the testator, or any of the subscribing witnesses, can be received; in addition to the methods already provided, the will of a person serving in the armed forces of the United States, executed while such person is in the actual service of the United States, or the will of a seaman, executed while such seaman was at sea, shall be admitted to

725

probate when either or all of the subscribing witnesses is out of the state at the time said will is offered for probate, or when the places of address of such witness or witnesses are unknown upon the oath of at least three credible witnesses, that the signature to said will is in the handwriting of the person whose will it purports to be. Such will so proven shall be effective to devise real property as well as to bequeath personal property of all kinds. (Code 1852, §§ 1624, 1625; Code 1867, §§ 1943, 1944; Code 1876, §§ 2307, 2308; Code 1886, §§ 1979, 1980; Code 1896, §§ 4276, 4277; Code 1907, §§ 6185, 6186; Code 1923, §§ 10613, 10614; Code 1940, T. 61, §§ 39, 40; Acts 1945, No. 78, p. 75; Code 1975, § 43-1-44.)

Code commissioner's note. — This section was originally codified as § 43-1-44 of the 1975 Code.

Editor's note. — The "lost will exception" referred to in Anderson v. Griggs, 402 So. 2d 904 (Ala. 1981), below, dates back to Skeggs v. Horton, 82 Ala. 352, 2 So. 110 (1886). In Skeggs, the Alabama Supreme Court held, for the first time, that a "lost will may be established by testimony of a single witness, who read and remembers the contents of the will." This holding had the effect of "relaxing the demands of this section in cases attempting to probate lost wills."

Common-law rule. — The rule of the common law prevailing in this state, as declared in Bowling v. Bowling, 8 Ala. 538 (1945), was that, on a contest in the court of probate of the validity of a will purporting to pass lands, the proponent was bound to call all the subscribing witnesses. But if any of these witnesses had become incompetent, or were dead or without the state, and, of consequence, without the jurisdiction of the court, the proponent was relieved from the duty of calling them, and could satisfy the burden resting upon him in this respect by making proof of their handwriting. Barnewall v. Murrell, 108 Ala. 366, 18 So. 831 (1895).

Section adopts common-law. — This section does not dispense with the necessary proof that the will was attested by at least two witnesses and in fact this section is nothing more than a legislative declaration of the common law. Woodruff v. Hundley, 127 Ala. 640, 29 So. 98 (1900).

This section recognizes a rule of ancient origin which is seemingly grounded in the law of evidence, which makes the testimony of the subscribing witnesses the best evidence of its due execution and attestation, and where their evidence is available requires that they be called to prove the execution of wills offered for probate. Whitt v. Forbes, 258 Ala. 580, 64 So. 2d 77 (1953).

Secondary evidence is admissible in absence of primary proof. — Under this section a will, upon formal contest, must be proved by both subscribing witnesses, or if one is not available, his absence must be accounted for to get secondary evidence of his attestation, as only in the absence of primary proof should secondary evidence be resorted to. Barnett v. Freeman, 197 Ala. 142, 72 So. 395 (1916); Ferrell v. Minnifield, 275 Ala. 388, 155 So. 2d 345 (1963).

This section was intended to prescribe and prescribes a definite rule regulating the admission of that which may be appropriately termed secondary evidence when the primary evidence of the execution of wills is not attainable. The proper construction of its words, and their real sense and meaning, is that, if any one or more of the subscribing witnesses, because of the events or the disabilities mentioned, cannot be produced, there may be a resort to the secondary evidence for which it provides, the equivalent in degree of the unattainable primary evidence. Woodruff v. Hundley, 127 Ala. 640, 29 So. 98 (1900).

The trial judge was justified in his action permitting several witnesses to give secondary evidence as to the handwriting or signatures of the testator and that of a deceased subscribing witness, when taken in connection with the efforts to locate the absent or unavailing witness, and if the court so found, then the proof of the testator's signature and that of the deceased witness was sufficient to show due execution under this section. Ray v. McClelland, 274 Ala. 363, 148 So. 2d 221 (1963).

Two subscribing witnesses can establish prima facie case of execution of will even if there are additional witnesses; the statutes do not require the testimony of all subscribing witnesses. Culver v. King, 362 So. 2d 221 (Ala. 1978).

But, the better practice, in regard to proving a prima facie case of execution of a will, is to call all the witnesses to the execution. Culver v. King, 362 So. 2d 221 (Ala. 1978).

The provisions of former §§ 43-1-30, 43-1-33 and this section contemplate "will-in-hand" situations which obviously supply a court with the necessary contents of the will at issue. Proof has not been allowed of the requisites of former §§ 43-1-30 and 43-1-33 as to a lost will unless that proof is also sufficient to invoke the exception method of proving a will for probate and the only and ultimate end of proving the valid execution of any will. Anderson v. Griggs, 402 So. 2d 904 (Ala. 1981).

The lost will exception was developed in keeping with the public policy favoring the testamentary disposition of the decedent's estate. The beneficent purpose of the lost will exception is self-evident. To require strict compliance with the statutory requisites of proof, where the document itself is lost, would defeat rather than enhance the public policy explicit in the law to effect the last intent of the deceased with respect to the disposition of his property. To effect that intent, then, the exception's field of operation must necessarily be limited to proof of the lost will for probate. Otherwise, the application of the exception to allow less than the statutory requisites of proof for the limited purpose of revoking a prior will would defeat the very purpose for which the exception exists. Anderson v. Griggs, 402 So. 2d 904 (Ala. 1981).

The exception, which relaxes the requisite proof for probating a lost will, is in keeping with the public policy of this state in carrying out the last intent of the testator. Anderson v. Griggs, 402 So. 2d 904 (Ala. 1981).

One of the requirements to be met is that the single testifying witness "remember the contents" of the lost will which he read or which was read to him. Anderson v. Griggs, 402 So. 2d 904 (Ala. 1981).

Exception allowed for probating lost will cannot be read into and made an exception to revocation statute. One who offers to prove a lost will for the purpose of revoking a former one must be prepared to live by the terms of the lost document; and what the law recognizes as an exception for the purpose of rendering an estate testate, the law cannot recognize as an exception for the limited purpose of revoking a will, thus rendering the estate intestate in derogation of the revocation statute. Anderson v. Griggs, 402 So. 2d 904 (Ala. 1981).

To permit revocation by use of the lost will exception, in derogation of the statutory requisites for revocation, produces the one result least likely to carry out a testator's intent: to die testate. Anderson v. Griggs, 402 So. 2d 904 (Ala. 1981).

Condition of subscribing witnesses. — It is undoubted law that any deficiency in the evidence of subscribing witnesses, as to the due execution or identity of the instrument may be supplied by the evidence of other witnesses. If, from forgetfulness, the subscribing witnesses should fail to prove the formal execution of the

will, other evidence is admissible to supply the deficiency, or if the subscribing witnesses all swear that the will was not duly executed, they may be contradicted, and the will supported by other witnesses or by circumstances. Hall v. Hall, 38 Ala. 131 (1861); Barnewall v. Murrell, 108 Ala. 366, 18 So. 831 (1895); Reynolds v. Massey, 219 Ala. 265, 122 So. 29 (1929).

Where the fact that the subscribing witnesses were living precluded proof of a will by the handwriting of the testator and one witness pursuant to this section, and such witnesses testified that they did not see testator's name on instrument which they, by him, were requested to sign, and that they did not receive testator's acknowledgment that he signed the instrument, the court did not err in allowing an attesting but nonsubscribing witness to testify as to things evidencing the intention of the testator to have the will properly signed, witnessed and attested, the will otherwise appearing on its face to have been properly executed. Stuck v. Howard, 213 Ala. 184, 104 So. 500 (1925).

Where subscribing witnesses testified that they saw no writing on document propounded as will not even word "witness," under which names appear, instrument had none of elements of self-proving document, and attestation clause was without force to raise a presumption of due execution, under this section. Reynolds v. Massey, 219 Ala. 265, 122 So. 2d (1929).

Under this section, where testimony of subscribing witnesses to will is available, and their testimony identifies document as one which they subscribed, document should be received in evidence for inspection of triers of fact, showing its form and purport as of testamentary nature. Reynolds v. Massey, 219 Ala. 265, 122 So. 29 (1929).

Contradictory evidence to be viewed with caution. — In view of the mode prescribed by this section and § 43-8-168 of proving of wills, contradictory oral evidence of a subscribing witness is to be viewed with great caution and scanned with grave suspicion, because it contradicts his written testimony, and is contrary to the confidence placed in him by the testator. Massey v. Reynolds, 213 Ala. 178, 104 So. 494 (1925).

When a will is contested, there should be proof of execution as provided by this section in either the probate court or the circuit court. Ferrell v. Minnifield, 275 Ala. 388, 155 So. 2d 345 (1963).

Cited in Whitaker v. Kennamer, 229 Ala. 80, 155 So. 855 (1934).

Collateral references. — 94 C.J.S., Wills, § 209, 95 C.J.S., Wills, §§ 392-395, 409-413. 80 Am. Jur. 2d, Wills, § 970.

Admissibility of other than testimony of subscribing witness to prove execution of will or testamentary capacity. 63 ALR 1195.

Admissibility and credibility of testimony of subscribing witness tending to impeach execution of will or testamentary capacity of testator. 79 ALR 394.

Necessity of affirmative evidence of testamentary capacity to make prima facie case in will contest. 110 ALR 675.

Proof, or possibility of proof, of will without testimony of attesting witness as affecting application of statute relating to invalidation of will, or of devise or legacy where attesting witness is beneficiary under will. 133 ALR 1286.

Testimony of attesting witnesses as to the time of interlineations and changes appearing on face of will. 34 ALR2d 662.

Proof of due execution of lost will. 41 ALR2d 393.

§ 43-8-168. Depositions of witnesses.

When the subscribing witnesses, or any of them, reside out of the state, or are physically unable or in any case in which depositions are authorized to be taken in circuit court, the judge of probate may issue a commission to take the testimony of such witnesses in proof of such will. (Code 1852, § 1626; Code 1867, § 1945; Code 1876, § 2309; Code 1886, § 1981; Code 1896, § 4278; Code 1907, § 6187; Code 1923, § 10615; Code 1940, T. 61, § 41; Code 1975, § 43-1-45.)

Code commissioner's note. — This section was originally codified as § 43-1-45 of the 1975 Code.

Cross reference. — See notes to § 43-8-167.

Collateral references. — 95 C.J.S., Wills, §§ 311, 444.

§ 43-8-169. Recordation of witnesses' testimony.

If it appears, on the proof taken before the judge of probate, that the will was duly executed, the testimony of the witnesses must be reduced to writing by him, signed by the witnesses and, with the will, immediately recorded in a book provided and kept for that purpose. (Code 1852, § 1627; Code 1867, § 1946; Code 1876, § 2310; Code 1886, § 1982; Code 1896, § 4279; Code 1907, § 6188; Code 1923, § 10616; Code 1940, T. 61, § 42; Code 1975, § 43-1-46.)

Code commissioner's note. — This section was originally codified as § 43-1-46 of the 1975 Code.

Three sections govern recordation of wills. — Sections 35-4-91, 35-4-94 and this section are the only statutes relating to the recording of wills. Sheridan v. Schimpf, 120 Ala. 475, 24 So. 940 (1898).

Distinction between will and conveyance. — While, technically speaking, a will may be a conveyance, or statutes relating to the registration and record of wills and conveyances seem to preserve an evident distinction between the two. Sheridan v. Schimpf, 120 Ala. 475, 24 So. 940 (1898).

This section is directory only. — The provisions of this section requiring, if it appears on the proof taken before the judge of probate that the will was duly executed, that the testimony of the witnesses be reduced to writing by the judge, signed by the witnesses, and, with the

will, recorded in a book provided for the purpose, are also directory, and a failure to comply therewith will not avoid the probate. Reese v. Nolen, 99 Ala. 203, 13 So. 677 (1893).

Evidence recorded under this section is admissible in circuit court. — Evidence heard in the probate court and preserved in accordance with this section is admissible in a proceeding in circuit court to attack the validity of the will, under the direct provisions of § 43-8-202. Stephens v. Richardson, 189 Ala. 360, 66 So. 497 (1914). See notes under § 43-8-202.

And will be accorded a prima facie effect. — The evidence of the attesting witness, taken in writing in the probate court under this section, is admissible in the circuit court and is sufficient to establish prima facie the execution of the will. Cummings v. McDonnell, 189 Ala. 96, 66 So. 717 (1914).

Record of nonprobated will is not notice. — This section does not authorize the recording of a will until after probate, and hence such record of a nonprobated will was not constructive notice of the rights of remaindermen as against the mortgages of the life tenant in possession for more than five years. Sheridan v. Schimpf, 120 Ala. 475, 24 So. 940 (1898).

Cited in Lyons v. Campbell, 88 Ala. 462, 7 So. 250 (1890); Whitaker v. Kennamer, 229 Ala. 80, 155 So. 855 (1934); Hancock v. Frazier, 264 Ala. 202, 86 So. 2d 389 (1956).

§ 43-8-170. Certificate endorsed on will.

Every will so proved must have a certificate endorsed thereon, setting forth in substance that such will had been duly proved and recorded, with the proof, specifying also the date of the probate, the book in and page or pages on which it is recorded. Such endorsement must be signed by such judge of probate. (Code 1852, § 1628; Code 1867, § 1947; Code 1876, § 2311; Code 1886, § 1983; Code 1896, § 4280; Code 1907, § 6189; Code 1923, § 10617; Code 1940, T. 61, § 43; Code 1975, § 43-1-47.)

Code commissioner's note. — This section was originally codified as § 43-1-47 of the 1975 Code.

Transcript need not show that original endorsement was made. — Every will, properly admitted to probate, must have endorsed on it the certificate required by this section, but it is not necessary that a transcript, properly certified, should show that such endorsement was made on the original will. Hall v. Hall, 47 Ala. 290 (1872).

Proof of title by will. — In order to prove title to real estate under a will, the record of its probate, or the will endorsed with the certificate of the probate judge as provided by this section and § 43-8-171, must be introduced.

Collum v. Price, 185 Ala. 556, 64 So. 88 (1913).

Where original certificate is lost there may be a substitution. — Where the certificate of probate of a will endorsed on the original will under this section and the original files were lost, the probate court had inherent jurisdiction under § 12-20-26, to cause substitution of the lost documents. Baxley v. Jackson, 216 Ala. 411, 113 So. 500 (1927).

Cited in Whitaker v. Kennamer, 229 Ala. 80, 155 So. 855 (1934); McGregor v. Shipp, 238 Ala. 221, 189 So. 740 (1939); Kelley v. Sutliff, 257 Ala. 371, 59 So. 2d 65 (1952).

Collateral references. — 95 C.J.S., Wills, § 499.

§ 43-8-171. Admission of will in evidence.

Every will, so proved or endorsed, may be read in evidence in any court of the state, without further proof thereof; and the record of such will and proof or a transcript thereof, certified by the judge of probate, must be received as evidence to the same extent as if the original will was produced, and the same proof made. (Code 1852, § 1629; Code 1867, § 1948; Code 1876, § 2312; Code 1886, § 1984; Code 1896, § 4281; Code 1907, § 6190; Code 1923, § 10618; Code 1940, T. 61, § 44; Code 1975, § 43-1-48.)

Code commissioner's note. — This section was originally codified as § 43-1-48 of the 1975 Code.

Will was admissible without further proof. — A will which had been admitted to probate and on which was endorsed a certificate by the probate judge in form prescribed by statute was admissible in evidence without further proof. McGregor v. Shipp, 238 Ala. 221, 189 So. 740 (1939); Ray v. McClelland, 274 Ala. 363, 148 So. 2d 221 (1962).

And was sufficient to establish ownership of mortgage. — On complaint to redeem from mortgage wherein defendant filed counterclaim to foreclose, will of mortgagee which had been admitted to probate and on which was endorsed certificate by probate judge in statutory form which showed that mortgage passed under residuary clause to defendant was sufficient to establish defendant's ownership of mortgage. McGregor v. Shipp, 238 Ala. 221, 189 So. 740 (1939).

Cited in Whitaker v. Kennamer, 229 Ala. 80, 155 So. 855 (1934); Smith v. Bryant, 263 Ala. 331, 82 So. 2d 411 (1955).

Collateral references. — 95 C.J.S., Wills, §§ 389, 390.

Wills: challenge in collateral proceeding to decree admitting will to probate, on ground of fraud inducing complainant not to resist probate. 84 ALR3d 1119.

§ 43-8-172. Protection of bona fide purchasers, etc.

Any will which is not propounded for probate in this state within 12 months from the date of the death of the testator shall be inoperative and void as to bona fide purchasers, mortgagees or pledgees (and those claiming under them) of property or any interest therein from the executors, administrators, heirs at law, devisees, distributees of the estate of such deceased or anyone claiming under them, provided such purchasers acquire their interest in such property prior to the time such will is propounded for probate in this state and without actual notice of such will.

The provisions of this section shall not affect the right of any beneficiary entitled thereto under any such will to follow the proceeds from the sale of any such property in lieu of such property in the hands of the executors, administrators, heirs at law or distributees of such estate. (Acts 1939, No. 42, p. 45; Code 1940, T. 61, § 51; Code 1975, § 43-1-49.)

Code commissioner's note. — This section was originally codified as § 43-1-49 of the 1975 Code.

Collateral references. — 95 C.J.S., Wills, §§ 356-360.

Relation back of probate of will in support of title or rights of persons claiming under or through devisee. 48 ALR 1035.

Relative rights to real property as between purchasers from or through decedent's heirs and devisees under will subsequently sought to be established. 22 ALR2d 1107.

§ 43-8-173. Withdrawal of will before probate.

When any will is filed with the probate judge or in the probate court for the purpose of probating the same, and it becomes necessary to withdraw said will before it is probated, the probate judge shall have the same recorded in the book in which are recorded probated wills, but shall mark or have written on the page or pages of the record where recorded the following: "Recorded Before Being Probated." The probate judge shall not allow any will filed with him or his office for the purpose of probating to be removed from such office by anyone until it is so recorded, and in the event such will is lost, destroyed or mutilated, the record of such will and certified transcripts therefrom shall be given the same force and effect as could be given the original. (Code 1923, § 10619; Code 1940, T. 61, § 45; Code 1975, § 43-1-50.)

Code commissioner's note. — This section was originally codified as § 43-1-50 of the 1975 Code.

§ 43-8-174. Withdrawal of will for proof out of state.

Whenever any will has been proved and recorded for six months in any county of this state, as required by this article, and such will is required to be proved out of this state, the judge of probate may, on the application of the executor, duly sworn to, allow him to withdraw the will. (Code 1852, § 1631; Code 1867, § 1950; Code 1876, § 2314; Code 1886, § 1986; Code 1896, § 4283; Code 1907, § 6192; Code 1923, § 10621; Code 1940, T. 61, § 47; Code 1975, § 43-1-51.)

Code commissioner's note. — This section was originally codified as § 43-1-51 of the 1975 Code. § 43-8-175. Probate of foreign will.

§ 43-8-175. Probate of foreign will.

When the testator was not, at the time of his or her death, an inhabitant of this state, but was an inhabitant of some other state or territory of the United States of America, or of some other territory, district or country subject to the jurisdiction of the United States of America, and his or her will has been duly proved in any other state of the United States of America, or in any territory, district or country subject to the jurisdiction of the United States of America, it may be admitted to probate in the proper court of this state in the manner following: If the will has been admitted to probate out of the state of Alabama, but within another state of the United States of America, or within any territory, district or country subject to the jurisdiction of the United States of America, such will, or copy of the same, and the probate thereof must be certified and authenticated as provided in 28 U.S.C.A., § 1738. Upon the presentation to the probate judge of any such will, already admitted to probate out of the state of Alabama, but in another state of the United States of America, or in any territory, district or country subject to the jurisdiction of the United States of America, authenticated as herein provided for, he shall, without notice or further proceedings, enter a decree admitting said will to probate, and shall record the same, together with a certificate of probate, in a record kept for that purpose. If the will has been admitted to probate elsewhere than in some other state of the United States of America, or some territory, district or country subject to the jurisdiction of the United States of America, if such will purports or undertakes to dispose of, or if it has the effect of disposing of, any land or real estate situated within the state of Alabama, such will, in order to be valid to that end, shall be probated in all respects, including notice to the next of kin of the testator or testatrix, as wills are required to be probated in the courts of the state of Alabama, upon original proceedings to probate wills in this state, and shall be subject to be contested and controverted in the same manner as wills are subject to be contested and controverted when offered or propounded for original probate and record in the courts of this state. If the will has been admitted to probate elsewhere than in some other state of the United States of America, or some territory, district or country subject to the jurisdiction of the United States of America, if such will purports or undertakes to dispose of, or if it has the effect of disposing of, any personal

731

property situated within the state of Alabama, such will, in order to be valid to that end, shall be probated in all respects, including notice to the next of kin of the testator or testatrix, as wills are required to be probated in the courts of the state of Alabama, upon original proceedings to probate wills in this state, and shall be subject to be contested and controverted when offered or propounded for original probate and record in the courts of this state. (Code 1852, § 1630; Code 1867, § 1949; Code 1876, § 2313; Code 1886, § 1985; Code 1896, § 4282; Code 1907, § 6191; Code 1923, § 10620; Acts 1931, No. 82, p. 162; Code 1940, T. 61, § 46; Acts 1945, No. 153, p. 193; Acts 1951, No. 988, p. 1663, § 1; Acts 1959, 1st Ex. Sess., No. 92, p. 151; Code 1975, § 43-1-52.)

Code commissioner's note. — This section was originally codified as § 43-1-52 of the 1975 Code.

This section is independent from section 43-2-192. — There is no interdependence between this section and § 43-2-192. The one provides how a will proved in another state may be probated in this state. The other provides for issue of letters testamentary to an executor named in a will probated in another state. That there is a distinction between the filing of a copy of such a will in this state and the probating of such will in this state appears from the terms of the two statutes. Certainly it could not be contended that a foreign will could be probated in this state by proceeding under § 43-2-192, else there would have been no purpose in the enactment of this section. That the two statutes were intended to accomplish different purposes is apparent. Having resorted to one, seeking only such benefits as may be derived therefrom, as in §§ 43-2-190 through 43-2-200, appellants cannot be said to be bound to observe the requirements of the other from which greater benefits may be derived. Fields v. Baker, 259 Ala. 336, 67 So. 2d 10 (1953).

This section and section 43-8-199 are in pari materia. Carter v. Davis, 275 Ala. 250, 154 So. 2d 9 (1963).

Effect of section. — This section withdraws from courts of probate all jurisdiction over the contestation of wills which have already been probated in the state or territory of the United States wherein the testator was living at the time of his death. Carter v. Davis, 275 Ala. 250, 154 So. 2d 9 (1963).

In other cases state is final judge of validity. — Except as provided by this section, the state of Alabama has not surrendered its exclusive authority to determine itself the existence of will or no will, to govern the devise of real estate situated within its borders. Frederick v. Wilbourne, 198 Ala. 137, 73 So. 442 (1916).

Failure to give notice where foreign will probated. — Where a foreign will is admitted to probate under this section, a failure to give the requisite statutory notice to the widow (now surviving spouse) and next of kin of the application for such probate does not render void the judgment of the court establishing the probate. In such case the judgment, being designed to establish the status of a thing, binds the res, even in the absence of any personal notice to interested parties. Dickey v. Vann, 81 Ala. 425, 8 So. 195 (1886). As to notice, see § 43-8-164 and notes.

Effect of a foreign will attested by only one witness. — See Sullivan v. Rabb, 86 Ala. 433, 5 So. 746 (1889).

Function of state court. — When a will, which has already been probated in the state or territory of the United States wherein the testator was living at the time of his death, is presented for probate in Alabama, the only inquiries the court of this state can make are whether the foreign probate was granted by a court having jurisdiction, and whether the will and probate is properly authenticated. Ascertaining these facts, the duty of the court then becomes ministerial, not judicial, and that duty is the record of the will and probate. The law intervenes and attaches to the probate not only the faith and credit it commanded within the jurisdiction pronouncing the sentence, but the value and dignity of a domestic decree of probate. Carter v. Davis, 275 Ala. 250, 154 So. 2d 9 (1963).

Nonresident's domicile may be decided by county probate court to dispose of local assets. — Neither the provisions of this section nor the full faith and credit clause of the U.S. Const., article IV, § 1, operates to prevent the probate court of Jefferson county, in disposing of local assets, to determine anew the question of domicile of a District of Columbia decedent at the instance of any interested party who is not bound by participation in the district probate proceeding. National Sav. & Trust Co. v. Herrick, 269 Ala. 133, 112 So. 2d 191 (1958).

Cited in Wood v. Mathews, 53 Ala. 1 (1875); Marx v. Leob, 228 Ala. 196, 153 So. 266 (1933); Keeley v. Sutliff, 262 Ala. 622, 80 So. 2d 636 (1955); Johnston v. Rothenberg, 270 Ala. 304, 118 So. 2d 744 (1960).

Collateral references. — 95 C.J.S., Trusts, §§ 350, 389.

Division 3.

Contesting Validity of Will.

§ 43-8-190. Who may contest will; filing objections; making up issue; trial by jury.

A will, before the probate thereof, may be contested by any person interested therein, or by any person, who, if the testator had died intestate, would have been an heir or distributee of his estate, by filing in the court where it is offered for probate allegations in writing that the will was not duly executed, or of the unsoundness of mind of the testator, or of any other valid objections thereto; and thereupon an issue must be made up, under the direction of the court, between the person making the application, as plaintiff, and the person contesting the validity of the will, as defendant; and such issue must, on application of either party, be tried by a jury. (Code 1852, § 1634; Code 1867, § 1953; Code 1876, § 2317; Code 1886, § 1989; Code 1896, § 4287; Code 1907, § 6196; Code 1923, § 10625; Code 1940, T. 61, § 52; Code 1975, § 43-1-70.)

Code commissioner's note. — This section was originally codified as § 43-1-70 of the 1975 Code.

    I. General Consideration.
    II. Contest Prior to Probate.
    III. Who May Contest.
    IV. Grounds of Contest.
    V. Trial by Jury.
    VI. Proceedings and Judgment.
    VII. Appeal.

I. GENERAL CONSIDERATION.

Cross reference. — As to the contest in circuit court after probate, see notes to § 43-8-199.

Editor's note. — In Alabama a will may be contested in two ways: (1) Before probate a contest may be instituted in the probate court under this section; or (2) After probate and within six months thereof a contest may be instituted under § 43-8-199. Infants and lunatics are allowed a longer time to contest by the provisions of § 43-8-201.

Since the parties who may contest, the grounds of contest and the method of procedure are very similar in both cases, the notes under both this section and § 43-8-199 should be considered when dealing with a case under either.

Burden of proving lack of requisite capacity is cast upon the party who contests validity of a will. In order to survive a motion for directed verdict in a will contest, a contestant must produce at least a scintilla of evidence in support of his or her claim. Koonce v. Mims, 402 So. 2d 942 (Ala. 1981).

Cited in Dunlap v. Robinson, 28 Ala. 100 (1856); Coghill v. Kennedy, 119 Ala. 641, 24 So. 459 (1898); McDonnell v. Jordan, 178 U.S. 229, 20 S. Ct. 886, 44 L. Ed. 1048 (1900); Ex parte Winn, 226 Ala. 447, 147 So. 625 (1933); Whitaker v. Kennamer, 229 Ala. 80, 155 So. 855 (1934); Bradford v. Fletcher, 248 Ala. 483, 28 So. 2d 313 (1946); Johnston v. King, 250 Ala. 571, 35 So. 2d 202 (1948); Kelley v. Sutliff, 257 Ala. 371, 59 So. 2d 65 (1952); Allen v. Jones, 259 Ala. 98, 65 So. 2d 217 (1953); Fields v. Baker, 259 Ala. 336, 67 So. 2d 10 (1953); Fuller v. Nazal, 259 Ala. 598, 67 So. 2d 806 (1953); Smith v. Bryant, 263 Ala. 331, 82 So. 2d 411 (1955); Baker v. Baker, 266 Ala. 210, 95 So. 2d 101 (1957); Carruba v. Meeks, 274 Ala. 714, 150 So. 2d 195 (1963); Fletcher v. DeLoach, 360 So. 2d 316 (Ala. 1978); Bardin v. Jones, 371 So. 2d 23 (Ala. 1979).

Collateral references. — 95 C.J.S., Wills, §§ 365-368, 372-382.

79 Am. Jur. 2d, Wills, § 844.

Preference to successful contestant of will in selection of administrator from among members of class equally entitled. 1 ALR 1250.

Admissibility and probative force of adjudication of insanity on issue of testamentary capacity. 7 ALR 568; 68 ALR 1309.

Fact that testatrix and beneficiaries are inmates of houses of prostitution as undue influence. 16 ALR 457; 31 ALR2d 321.

Epilepsy as affecting testamentary capacity. 16 ALR 1418.

Mistake as to relationship or status of legatee or devisee. 17 ALR 247.

Public administrator's or state's right to file caveat to, or contest will. 18 ALR 79; 56 ALR2d 1183.

Fraud as distinguished from undue influence as ground for contesting will. 28 ALR 787; 92 ALR 790.

Right of creditor of heir to contest will. 46 ALR 1490; 128 ALR 963.

Contract to refrain from contesting will. 55 ALR 811.

Estoppel by conduct during testator's life to dissent from or attack validity of will. 74 ALR 659.

Right to interest on legacy as affected by contest of will. 75 ALR 179.

Admissibility of evidence of good character of party for truth and honesty on issue of fraud in procuring will. 78 ALR 648.

Election by contestant to claim as beneficiary under an earlier will or as heir or next of kin, necessity of, as condition of contesting will. 82 ALR 885.

Codicil as affecting application of statutory provision to will, or previous codicil not otherwise subject, or as obviating objections to lack of testamentary capacity, undue influence, or defective execution otherwise fatal to will. 87 ALR 836.

Third person's undue influence in which immediate beneficiary did not participate. 96 ALR 613.

Application to probate later will as subject to restrictions on contest of earlier will. 107 ALR 249; 157 ALR 1351.

Right of assignee of expectancy to contest will. 112 ALR 84.

Right of heir or next of kin to contest will as affected by gift or conveyance or prior will by which he is disinherited in whole or part. 112 ALR 1405.

Adoption intended but not affected as giving standing to contest will. 112 ALR 1422.

Right of heirs, next of kin, or others who would have benefited by denial of probate of will, to share in the consideration for an agreement, to which they were not parties, to withdraw objection to probate. 120 ALR 1495.

Amount of attorney's compensation in absence of contract or statute fixing amount. 143 ALR 672; 56 ALR2d 13.

Status as husband or wife, prospective heir, or next of kin of living person who is entitled but does not exercise or consent to exercise right to contest will, as enabling one to do so where not otherwise qualified. 149 ALR 1270.

Right of consul to contest will on behalf of nonresident national. 157 ALR 114.

Contingent interest as sufficient to entitle one to oppose or contest will or codicil. 162 ALR 843.

Insane delusion as invalidating will. 175 ALR 882.

Right of debtor or of person claimed to be liable to estate to contest will or challenge its admission to probate. 15 ALR2d 864.

Codicil as validating will or prior codicil invalid because of want of testamentary capacity or undue influence or fraud. 21 ALR2d 830.

Right to contest will or attack its validity. 28 ALR2d 116.

Right of executor or administrator to contest will or codicil of his decedent. 31 ALR2d 756.

Validity and enforceability of agreement to drop or compromise will contest or withdraw objections to probate, or of agreement to induce others to do so. 42 ALR2d 1319.

Gift or other voluntary transfer by husband as fraud on wife. 49 ALR2d 521.

Decedent's spouse as a proper party to contest will. 78 ALR2d 1060.

Effect of guardianship of adult or testamentary capacity. 89 ALR2d 1120.

Right of trustee named in earlier will to contest, or seek to revoke probate of, later will. 94 ALR2d 1409.

Testamentary capacity as affected by use of intoxicating liquor or drugs. 9 ALR3d 15.

Partial invalidity of will: may parts of will be upheld notwithstanding failure of other parts for lack of testamentary mental capacity or undue influence. 64 ALR3d 261.

Existence of illicit or unlawful relation between testator and beneficiary as evidence of undue influence. 76 ALR3d 743.

Validity of condition that a will beneficiary must renounce, embrace or adhere to a particular religious faith. 89 ALR3d 984.

Modern status: inheritability or descendability of right to contest will. 11 ALR4th 907.

II. CONTEST PRIOR TO PROBATE.

The probate of a will is defined to be the proof before an officer authorized by law that the instrument offered to be proved or recorded is the last will and testament of the deceased person whose testamentary act it is alleged to be. Allen v. Pugh, 206 Ala. 10, 89 So. 470 (1921).

No contest under this section after probate. — A will, whether of real or personal property, must now be proved in the probate court, before any legal rights can be asserted under it, and it may be contested in that court before it has been admitted to probate. When it has once been probated in that court in the mode prescribed by the statute, it cannot be contested except by filing of a complaint in a circuit court by a person interested therein who has not already contested it. Knox v. Paull, 95 Ala. 505, 11 So. 156 (1892).

Contest in circuit court is extension of right. — In the construction of this section it has been several times declared that the right to contest thereunder in circuit court is but an extension of the right to contest in the probate court. Kaplan v. Coleman, 180 Ala. 267, 60 So. 885 (1912); Ex parte Walter, 202 Ala. 281, 80 So. 119 (1918); Allen v. Pugh, 206 Ala. 10, 89 So. 470 (1921).

Examination of witnesses to establish will is part of probate. — In providing for the contest of a will before the probate thereof, it is clear that this section requires the filing of the contest before the examination of the witnesses whose testimony would establish the will, the word "probated" being referable to the proving of the will on the day set therefor, rather than to the mere endorsement of the certificate of probate on the will as evidence of the fact of probate. Allen v. Pugh, 206 Ala. 10, 89 So. 470 (1921).

This section applies only in will contest cases. Meriwether v. Reynolds, 289 Ala. 361, 267 So. 2d 434 (1972).

III. WHO MAY CONTEST.

Cross reference. — See notes under the same analysis line under § 43-8-199 in considering the following annotations.

Persons having material interest must be made parties. — The general rule is that all persons having a material interest, legal or equitable, in the subject matter of an action, must be made parties, either as plaintiffs or defendants. Rowe v. Newman, 290 Ala. 289, 276 So. 2d 412 (1972).

The divorced former wife of testator has a material interest in the question whether she has a right to payment of a claim for alimony, and her right to such payment cannot be determined while she is not a party to the proceeding. Rowe v. Newman, 290 Ala. 289, 276 So. 2d 412 (1972).

Meaning of "any person interested therein". — The settled construction of the phrase "any person interested therein" is that it embraces any person who has an interest in the estate disposed of, which would be conserved by

defeating the probate of the will, or jeopardized or impaired by its establishment. Montgomery v. Foster, 91 Ala. 613, 8 So. 349 (1890); Elmore v. Stevens, 174 Ala. 228, 57 So. 457 (1912); Stephens v. Richardson, 189 Ala. 360, 66 So. 497 (1914); Braasch v. Worthington, 191 Ala. 210, 67 So. 1003 (1915).

Any person, whether he is interested for or against the will, may offer a will for probate in Alabama, and such person will not be estopped to contest the validity of the instrument in the same proceedings. Hooper v. Huey, 293 Ala. 63, 300 So. 2d 100 (1974), overruled on other grounds, Bardin v. Jones, 371 So. 2d 23 (Ala. 1979).

The phrase "any person interested therein" is not limited to persons named as beneficiaries in the will, but includes any person with a direct interest in the estate disposed of by the will, i.e., the interest referred to is not in the will itself but in its operation. Tomaras v. Papadeas, 358 So. 2d 428 (Ala. 1978).

A contestant of a will must have some direct legal or equitable interest in the decedent's estate, in privity with him, whether as heir, purchaser or beneficiary under another will, which would be destroyed or injuriously affected by the establishment of the contested will. Allen v. Pugh, 206 Ala. 10, 89 So. 470 (1921).

One named as beneficiary in will filed for probate has right as "person interested therein" to contest will or attached codicil pursuant to section. Baker v. Bain, 237 Ala. 618, 188 So. 681 (1939).

Testator's nephews and nieces, who were beneficiaries under will, were "parties in interest" entitled to contest codicil injuriously affecting them. Baker v. Bain, 237 Ala. 618, 188 So. 681 (1939).

The creditor of an heir is not a party interested within this section. Montgomery v. Foster, 91 Ala. 613, 8 So. 349 (1890); Lockard v. Stephenson, 120 Ala. 641, 24 So. 996 (1899), overruled on other grounds, Braasch v. Worthington, 191 Ala. 210, 67 So. 1003 (1915).

A contestant of a will must have some direct legal or equitable interest, etc.

Under this section, if a person has a direct legal or equitable interest in the decedent's estate, in privity with the decedent, whether as heir, purchaser or beneficiary under another will, which would be destroyed or injuriously affected by the establishment of the contested will, he has standing to contest the will. Pruitt v. Pruitt, 343 So. 2d 495 (Ala. 1976).

One having the right to contest a will may do so only once; however, any party aggrieved by the ruling in the probate court may appeal under § 12-22-21. Elsworth v. Rini, 388 So. 2d 953 (Ala. 1980).

Such interest may be acquired by purchase or descent. — Any person who has acquired an interest in the estate by purchase or descent from an heir or distributee — and, it would seem, from a devisee or legatee — which would be injuriously affected by the establishment of the will may contest it in the probate court, if such interest was acquired prior to the probate of the will. Allen v. Pugh, 206 Ala. 10, 89 So. 470 (1921).

Certain persons not interested in the will may contest it. — This section expressly names one class of persons, who, though not named in the will, may contest it. These persons are those who, if the testator had died intestate, would have been an heir or distributee of his estate, clearly demonstrating that the legislature construed the words "interested therein" as referring to and including only such persons as took an interest in the estate of testatrix under and by virtue of the provisions of the will. Lockard v. Stephenson, 120 Ala. 641, 24 So. 996 (1899), overruled on other grounds, Braasch v. Worthington, 191 Ala. 210, 67 So. 1003 (1915).

Persons not in interest assisting contestant have no legal right. — It is a person in interest who files the allegations in writing who alone has the right to determine the issue under the direction of the court, to summon, examine and cross-examine witnesses, and who is alone liable for costs in the event the contest fails. All other persons, whether interested in the estate or not, who obtain a voice in the conduct of the contest in the probate court by rendering financial or other assistance to the contestant of record, do so merely by and through him. They do not exercise a statutory right, but merely an imperfect right granted by the contestant. Breeding v. Grantland, 135 Ala. 497, 33 So. 544 (1903).

Other contestants must come in when one person has filed contest. — Where one person has filed a contest, others so entitled must become contestants, if at all, by making themselves parties to the contest pending, since the issue is in rem, and must be single and complete as to all the parties. Rainey v. Ridgway, 148 Ala. 524, 41 So. 632 (1906); Allen v. Pugh, 206 Ala. 10, 89 So. 470 (1921).

Forfeiture of interest under will by contesting it. — Where the clause of forfeiture declares that any child who "resists the probate" of the will, "or petitions to break or set it aside," shall forfeit all interest under it, and the property devised or bequeathed to him shall then go to those who have not "opposed" it, a child who, without making himself a party to a contest instituted by another devisee, actively interfered in behalf of the contestant, advising and aiding him, is equally within the prohibition, and his interest under the will is forfeited,

although the contest was never brought to a trial, but was abandoned. Donegan v. Wade, 70 Ala. 501 (1881).

Guardian ad litem. — The duties of the guardian, under an appointment in accordance with § 43-8-165, are in fact defensive in character and his objections to the probate of the will are not properly to be designed as a civil action but grow out of his duties to represent the minor in the proof and probate of the will. Ex parte Petty, 249 Ala. 393, 31 So. 2d 575 (1947).

Actions of guardian as affecting minor. — The fact that a guardian ad litem made general denial of the allegations of a petition propounding a will for probate and demanded strict proof of the same did not make the minor by his guardian ad litem a party defendant to the contest, and in such sense as to prevent his exercise of the right of contest. Bowe v. Pierson, 206 Ala. 250, 89 So. 711 (1921).

An heir at law, who would have inherited from decedent if he had died intestate, had the right to contest decedent's will under the provisions of this section. Hornaday v. First Nat'l Bank, 259 Ala. 26, 65 So. 2d 678 (1952).

Legatee may contest later will or codicil. — A legatee in a will may either under this section before probate, or under § 43-8-199 after probate, contest either a later will or a later codicil which injuriously affects his status under the prior instrument. Curry v. Holmes, 249 Ala. 545, 32 So. 2d 39 (1947); Binford v. Penney, 255 Ala. 20, 49 So. 2d 665 (1950).

Waiver of misjoinder of contestants. — When the probate of a will is contested by one of the testator's children, who is a married woman, if it is improper to join her husband with her as a contestant, the misjoinder is waived by joining issue and going to trial on the merits, and is not available on motion in arrest of judgment. Blake v. Harlan, 80 Ala. 37 (1885).

IV. GROUNDS OF CONTEST.

In general. — It is manifest that the provisions of this section and § 43-8-191 were introduced to change the policy of the law obtaining prior to their adoption, by requiring the contestant, by written procedure, to set forth the grounds upon which he expects to contest the validity of the proposed will, and to confine the trial, after proof of the due execution of the will, to the issues which his allegations tender. The purpose of the change was that which underlies the law of pleading generally, that the parties may be certainly advised of the issues to be tried, and the court enabled to proceed intelligently in adjudicating their rights. In subservience of this general rule, it is a familiar principle of pleading that the plaintiff must distinctly allege the facts upon which he relies for relief. Mere general statements or conclusions will not suffice. Barksdale v. Davis, 114 Ala. 623, 22 So. 17 (1897), overruled on other grounds, Alexander v. Gibson, 176 Ala. 258, 57 So. 760 (1912).

A will must have been "offered for probate" before it can be contested in either the probate or the circuit court. Hooper v. Huey, 293 Ala. 63, 300 So. 2d 100 (1974), overruled on other grounds, Bardin v. Jones, 371 So. 2d 23 (Ala. 1912).

Facts should be stated in alleging right to contest. — Instead of the conclusions of law, an application to contest should allege the facts constituting the relationship between the plaintiff and the deceased, and the facts out of which his interest in the will arose, and thus have enabled the court to determine for itself whether he would have been an heir or distributee of the estate, or had such an interest in the will as qualified him to contest its probate. Montgomery v. Foster, 91 Ala. 613, 8 So. 349 (1890); Ellis v. Crawson, 147 Ala. 294, 41 So. 942 (1906).

A general statement is not sufficient. — Upon a contest of a will, when fraud or undue influence is relied upon, the burden is upon the contestant to prove it. The opposite party is only required to prove the due execution of the will according to the statute. It is as essential, therefore, that such party be informed, by distinct averments, of the facts constituting the fraud or undue influence, so as to be prepared to meet them, as that such information be so given to any party in any judicial proceeding; hence there can be no well-founded reason for holding that the legislature intended, when it required that the contest be in writing and set forth the grounds relied on, that only a general statement of such grounds, conveying to the opposite party practically no information of value to him in the preparation of his cause, should be sufficient. Barksdale v. Davis, 114 Ala. 623, 22 So. 17 (1897), overruled on other grounds, Alexander v. Gibson, 176 Ala. 258, 57 So. 760 (1912).

Where a bill, as the ground of contest, averred that the execution of the alleged will was procured by fraud and misrepresentation, without averring any facts constituting the alleged fraud and misrepresentation, this is an insufficient averment, and in this respect the bill was open to demurrer. The rule is, where fraud is charged, facts constituting the fraud should be stated. Ellis v. Crawson, 147 Ala. 294, 41 So. 942 (1906).

Any objection which goes to the validity of the alleged will is a ground of contest. — And all of the grounds of objection to the validity of the will may be averred in the contest. And the same thing may be done where the proceeding to contest is in the circuit court

under § 43-8-199. Ellis v. Crawson, 147 Ala. 294, 41 So. 942 (1906).

The proof of any one of them is sufficient. — This section contemplates the allegation of any number of objections to the validity of the will, proof of any one of which is sufficient to justify the rejection of the will. The fact that these various objections are subdivided and numbered, and that one subdivision contains two or more objections, does not render it necessary to prove all of those contained in such subdivision. Moore v. Heineke, 119 Ala. 627, 24 So. 374 (1898), overruled on other grounds, Alexander v. Gibson, 176 Ala. 258, 57 So. 760 (1912).

Party having the right to contest is not bound to treat original will and codicils thereto as a unit for the purpose of contest either before or after probate. Binford v. Penney, 255 Ala. 20, 49 So. 2d 665 (1950).

What constitutes undue influence. — The undue influence necessary to overturn a testamentary disposition of one's estate must be of such a character as to overpower the will of the testator, and substitute another will in its stead. It is said by the text-writers on this branch of legal learning, "that the influence to vitiate the act must amount to force and coercion, destroying the free-agency." It must not be the influence of affection or attachment, or the desire to gratify the wishes of another. And there must be evidence of such importunity, or coercion, as could not be resisted, so that motive impelling the testator was tantamount to force or fear. 1 Williams on Wills, 42; 1 Jar. on Wills, 39; Leverett v. Carlisle, 19 Ala. 80 (1851); Gilbert v. Gilbert, 22 Ala. 529 (1853); Dunlap v. Robinson, 28 Ala. 100 (1856); Taylor v. Kelly, 31 Ala. 59 (1857); Pool v. Pool, 35 Ala. 12 (1859); Hall v. Hall, 38 Ala. 131 (1861); 1 Redf. Law of Wills, 514 et seq.; Leeper v. Taylor, 47 Ala. 221 (1872). See also Daniel v. Hill, 52 Ala. 430 (1875).

A presumption of undue influence arises when a person stands in a confidential relation to the testator, dominates the relationship and procures the execution of the will by participation in undue activity. This presumption does not arise, however, where the testator is the parent and the person active in the procurement of the will is the testator's child. Nottage v. Jones, 388 So. 2d 923 (Ala. 1980).

When it appears that the child has obtained a general dominance over the parent, and has been active in procuring a will giving a favoring position over the other children, the presumption of undue influence arises. Nottage v. Jones, 388 So. 2d 923 (Ala. 1980).

Averment of fraud must set out the particular facts. — If fraud be relied upon, the general charge that a fraud was committed is, of course, not sufficient, but the particular facts constituting the fraud must be stated, otherwise the opposite party would be practically without information of what he was called upon to defend. Barksdale v. Davis, 114 Ala. 623, 22 So. 17 (1897), overruled on other grounds, Alexander v. Gibson, 176 Ala. 258, 57 So. 760 (1912).

But not so when undue influence is averred. — In defining the necessary averments in the contest of a will for undue influence, as distinguished from fraud, it has been held that it was not necessary to allege with particularity the quo modo the result complained of was accomplished, but only that it was accomplished by undue influence exerted by named persons. Alexander v. Gibson, 176 Ala. 258, 57 So. 760 (1912); Barnett v. Freeman, 197 Ala. 142, 72 So. 395 (1916).

Examples of sufficient averment. — One averment in a contest stated it "was not duly executed according to law," and another averment therein stated it "was not duly and legally executed." These averments are each sufficient. They each state a valid ground of contest; and the court did not err in overruling demurrers of petitioners to each of them. Massey v. Reynolds, 213 Ala. 178, 104 So. 494 (1925).

A bill averred that the said M.L. was "mentally unable to make a will," at the time of making of the alleged will. It may be that this may be taken as averment of that "unsoundness of mind" which incapacitated her to make a will, but the bill in this respect might be improved. Ellis v. Crawson, 147 Ala. 294, 41 So. 942 (1906).

V. TRIAL BY JURY.

Jury not essential unless demanded. — It is not made the imperative duty of the judge to cause a jury to be summoned, in every case of a contested will, only to be discharged, if neither party should require a jury. The duty does not arise until one of the parties makes application for the trial of the issues by a jury. Jaques v. Horton, 76 Ala. 238 (1884).

History of right to jury. — The right of trial by jury in a will contest case existed in Alabama at the time of adoption of the 1901 Constitution. Gilbreath v. Wallace, 292 Ala. 267, 292 So. 2d 651 (1974).

Failure to demand jury at beginning not a waiver. — It would seem the better practice that a party who desires that a jury shall pass on the issue should make his application at the time the contest is interposed, but his failure to do so is not a waiver of the right. Stedham v. Stedham, 32 Ala. 525 (1958).

Right to waive after demanding jury. — Where contestants, after demanding a jury to try the issue, filed a written waiver of that demand, this did not prevent the plaintiffs under this section from afterwards demanding a jury to try the issue in the probate court, if they desired. And hence the demand for a jury trial can be withdrawn without the consent of the other party. Massey v. Reynolds, 213 Ala. 178, 104 So. 494 (1925).

Effect of dispensing with jury. — Dispensing with a trial by jury restored the case to the position in which it would have been, if neither party had made application, in the first instance, for a jury. Jaques v. Horton, 76 Ala. 238 (1884).

VI. PROCEEDINGS AND JUDGMENT.

How issues made up. — The section is silent as to how the issue shall be made up. If the contest was by a complaint in a circuit court, the proponent would file an answer admitting or denying the material allegations of the contest. By analogy it would appear that the proponent may, by permission of the court, specifically set out the issues of fact to be tried by way of replication to a contest filed in the probate court. If such proceedings are prolix, redundant, unnecessary or improper, the parts thereof transcending the rules of pleading should be stricken on motion. Barnett v. Freeman, 197 Ala. 142, 72 So. 395 (1916); Miller v. Whittington, 202 Ala. 406, 80 So. 499 (1918).

The issue to be made up under the direction of the court as provided in this section does not contemplate formal replications and subsequent pleadings as on a common-law trial, except by permission of the court, as found appropriate. Mindler v. Crocker, 245 Ala. 578, 18 So. 2d 278 (1944); Thigpen v. Walker, 251 Ala. 426, 37 So. 2d 923 (1948).

Contestants of a will are the defendants. — In a contest before the probate court respecting the validity of a will, the proponent is the party plaintiff, and the contestants are the defendants, and the other heirs-at-law, or distributees, though notified of the proceeding, are not parties to it, unless they come forward and make themselves parties. Blakey v. Blakey, 33 Ala. 611 (1859).

But latter part of section directory. — The latter part of this section which directs the probate court to align the parties between the person making the application for probate, as plaintiff, and the person contesting the validity of the will, as defendant, is directory rather than mandatory in light of this section and §§ 43-8-160 and 43-8-198. Hooper v. Huey, 293 Ala. 63, 300 So. 2d 100 (1974), overruled on other grounds, Bardin v. Jones, 371 So. 2d 23 (Ala. 1979).

Grounds of contesting become part of record. — When the probate of a will is contested, the grounds of contest are required to be filed in writing, and become part of the record, and secondary evidence of them cannot be received, without proper proof of their loss or destruction, as in case of other writings. Donegan v. Wade, 70 Ala. 501 (1881).

Judgment follows verdict. — When the probate of a will is contested, and an issue of devisavit vel non is submitted to a jury, who find in favor of the will, the judgment necessarily follows the verdict, and the verdict being rendered on Saturday morning, while the court is in session, the judgment is properly entered and dated as of that day, although entry was not actually made until ten o'clock at night, after the expiration of office hours. Lanier v. Richardson, 72 Ala. 134 (1884).

Proceedings may not be collaterally attacked. — A proceeding for the probate of a will is in the nature of a proceeding in rem, and, until set aside or reversed, is conclusive on all persons, and cannot be collaterally impeached for irregularities which may have intervened in the proceedings after the jurisdiction of the court attached. Hall v. Hall, 47 Ala. 290 (1872).

Valid contest prior to transfer. — There must be pending in the probate court a valid contest when the judge of the probate court enters the order transferring the contest to the circuit court. Hooper v. Huey, 293 Ala. 63, 300 So. 2d 100 (1974), overruled on other grounds, Bardin v. Jones, 371 So. 2d 23 (Ala. 1979).

Pending contest in circuit court not sufficient basis for refusal of probate court to act on contest and demand for transfer relating to earlier will. — Fact that later will and codicil had been previously admitted and were being contested in the circuit court was not a sufficient basis for probate court to take no action on a petition for probate, contest and demand for transfer filed later pertaining to an earlier will. Cagle v. Reeves, 353 So. 2d 787 (Ala. 1977).

After probate court has no jurisdiction to entertain contest. — The jurisdiction of the probate court to entertain a proceeding contesting a will is a statutory and limited jurisdiction, and after the proceeding to probate the will has eventuated in a final decree admitting the will to probate, the court is without jurisdiction to entertain a contest. Ex parte Pearson, 241 Ala. 467, 3 So. 2d 5 (1941).

Burden of proving due execution. — In will contests the burden of proving due execution of the will is on proponent. Whitt v. Forbes, 258 Ala. 580, 64 So. 2d 77 (1953).

When there is a contest in the probate court under this section, the burden of proof is on the proponent and remains with him throughout to prove to the reasonable satisfaction of the court or jury trying the issue that the instrument was duly executed and is valid. Hancock v. Frazier, 264 Ala. 202, 86 So. 2d 389 (1956).

Where burden of showing mental incapacity is on contestants. — Where the contestees introduce the original will and the depositions of the attesting witnesses, the burden of establishing mental incapacity is on the contestant, and the court properly denied the contestant's motion to require contestees to introduce all of their affirmative testimony with reference to the sanity of testator. West v. Arrington, 200 Ala. 420, 76 So. 352 (1917).

Where burden of showing fraud and undue influence is also on them. — One attacking a will for fraud and undue influence does not shift the burden of proof to the proponent of the will by merely showing confidential relations between the beneficiary and testatrix, but where, in addition, circumstances of suspicion are shown, such as that the beneficiary aided in the preparation or procurement of the will, the burden shifts to proponent to show that the instrument was not superinduced by undue influence. McElhaney v. Jones, 197 Ala. 303, 72 So. 531 (1916).

In order for the contestant to raise a presumption of undue influence the evidence must establish: (1) A confidential relationship between a favored beneficiary and testator; (2) that the influence of or for the beneficiary was dominant and controlling in that relationship; and (3) undue activity on the part of the dominant party in procuring the execution of the will. Pruitt v. Pruitt, 343 So. 2d 495 (Ala. 1976).

VII. APPEAL.

Party not contesting cannot appeal. — On appeal, persons who were not parties to the proceeding in probate are not concerned (Blakey v. Blakey, 33 Ala. 611 (1859)), and an appeal cannot be prosecuted by any person in interest who was not a party to the record. Clemens v. Patterson, 38 Ala. 721 (1863); Allen v. Pugh, 206 Ala. 10, 89 So. 470 (1921).

Nature of appellate proceeding. — In a will contest the appellate proceeding is a continuation of the original, leading to a judgment on the merits, which is conclusive of the issue, and a case cannot be remanded to let in additional evidence, and under the mandate of the appellate court directing probate nothing remains for the probate court to do except to enter a formal certificate of probate. Allen v. Pugh, 206 Ala. 10, 89 So. 470 (1921).

§ 43-8-191. Time for trial; continuance; summoning witnesses.

Upon the institution of such contest, a day must be appointed for the trial thereof, and the trial may, on good cause shown by either party, be continued to any other day; and the judge of probate must, on application of either party, issue subpoenas for witnesses to appear on the day fixed for such trial, and may resummon them to any day to which the same may be continued. (Code 1852, §§ 1635, 1636, 1640; Code 1867, §§ 1934, 1955, 1959; Code 1876, §§ 2318, 2323; Code 1886, § 1990; Code 1896, § 4288; Code 1907, § 6197; Code 1923, § 10626; Code 1940, T. 61, § 52; Code 1975, § 43-1-71.)

Code commissioner's note. — This section was originally codified as § 43-1-71 of the 1975 Code.

Cited in Baker v. Bain, 237 Ala. 618, 188 So. 681 (1939).

§ 43-8-192. Drawing and summoning of jurors; penalty for default.

(a) The jury for the trial of such contest must be drawn and summoned as provided by law.

(b) Any person summoned as a juror who shall, without legal cause or good excuse, fail to attend at the time and place required, shall be guilty of a contempt of court and may be punished by the court by a fine of not exceeding $100.00. (Code 1852, §§ 1637-1639; Code 1867, §§ 1956-1958; Code 1876, §§ 2320-2322; Code 1886, §§ 1991, 1992; Code 1896, §§ 4289, 4290; Code 1907, §§ 6198, 6199; Acts 1909, No. 227, p. 305; Code 1923, §§ 10627, 10628; Code 1940, T. 61, §§ 54, 55; Code 1975, § 43-1-72.)

Code commissioner's note. — This section was originally codified as § 43-1-72 of the 1975 Code.

Cross reference. — As to drawing and summoning jurors generally, see § 12-16-70 et seq.

Order of challenges in discretion of court. — The order in which the challenges are required to be presented in a will contest is not prescribed, and this is a matter resting in the sound discretion of the trial court, and will not be revised unless there has been an abuse of that discretion to the injury of the party complaining. Whitsett v. Belue, 172 Ala. 256, 54 So. 677 (1911).

Proceedings presumed regular upon collateral attack. — When the probate of a will, or of parts only of the paper purporting to be a will, is collaterally attacked, it is not necessary that the record shall affirmatively show notice of the application, the appointment of a guardian ad litem for the infants or the summoning or waiver of a jury; in the absence of averment and proof to the contrary, the proceedings in the several matters will be presumed to have been regular. Acklen v. Goodman, 77 Ala. 521 (1884).

This section applies only in will contest cases. Meriwether v. Reynolds, 289 Ala. 361, 267 So. 2d 434 (1972).

Cited in Baker v. Bain, 237 Ala. 618, 188 So. 681 (1939); Rowell v. McCollough, 270 Ala. 576, 120 So. 2d 729 (1960).

Collateral references. — 95 C.J.S., Wills, §§ 430, 431, 437, 449.

§ 43-8-193. Proceedings against defaulting witness.

If any witness, being duly summoned, fails to attend, the judge of probate shall enter up a conditional fine against him, not exceeding $50.00, and shall thereupon issue a notice to such witness to appear at a term of said court, not more than 30 days from the date of such notice and show cause why such fine should not be made absolute. The proceedings thereafter shall be governed by the same rules, and such witness shall be subject to the same liabilities, except as to the amount of the fine, as are provided by law in cases of defaulting witnesses in the circuit court. (Code 1852, § 1642; Code 1867, § 1961; Code 1876, § 2325; Code 1886, § 1993; Code 1896, § 4291; Code 1907, § 6200; Code 1923, § 10629; Code 1940, T. 61, § 56; Code 1975, § 43-1-73.)

Code commissioner's note. — This section was originally codified as § 43-1-73 of the 1975 Code.

Cited in Baker v. Bain, 237 Ala. 618, 188 So. 681 (1939).

§ 43-8-194. Depositions of witnesses; rules governing procedure.

For the trial of such contest, depositions of witnesses may be taken in like cases, for the same causes and in the same manner, as depositions are taken in civil actions in the circuit court. In all matters relating to the organization and impaneling of the jury, to the evidence, mode of proceeding and investigation and determination of such contest, not specially provided for by this article, the court shall proceed and be governed by the same rules and regulations, so far as applicable, as prevail in courts of law in civil cases. (Code 1852, §§ 1641, 1643; Code 1867, §§ 1960, 1962; Code 1876, §§ 2324, 2326; Code 1886, § 1994; Code 1896, § 4292; Code 1907, § 6201; Code 1923, § 10630; Code 1940, T. 61, § 57; Code 1975, § 43-1-74.)

Code commissioner's note. — This section was originally codified as § 43-1-74 of the 1975 Code.

§ 43-8-195. Admission or rejection of will.

When the judgment of the probate court is against the validity of the will, the probate thereof must be rejected; otherwise, the will must be admitted to probate. (Code 1852, § 1647; Code 1867, § 1965; Code 1876, § 2329; Code 1886, § 1995; Code 1896, § 4293; Code 1907, § 6202; Code 1923, § 10631; Code 1940, T. 61, § 58; Code 1975, § 43-1-75.)

Code commissioner's note. — This section was originally codified as § 43-1-75 of the 1975 Code.

Judgment follows verdict. — When the jury return their verdict in favor of the will, the judgment of the court establishing it is a matter of course, unless the verdict is set aside and a new trial granted. Lanier v. Richardson, 72 Ala. 134 (1882).

When appellate court directs the judgment of primary court. — On appeal from a judgment and decree of the probate court, in the matter of the contested probate of a will, the evidence having been submitted to the court without the intervention of a jury and being all set out in the record, the appellate court, on reversing the judgment of the primary court, will direct that court what judgment to enter in the case. Leeper v. Taylor, 47 Ala. 221 (1872).

Cited in Baker v. Bain, 237 Ala. 618, 188 So. 681 (1939).

Collateral references. — 95 C.J.S., Trusts, §§ 501, 577.

80 Am. Jur. 2d, Wills, § 1035.

Who is "adverse party" entitled to notice of appeal. 88 ALR 444.

Who entitled to appeal from decree admitting will to probate or denying probate. 88 ALR 1158.

§ 43-8-196. Costs.

The costs of any contest under the provisions of this article must be paid by the party contesting if he fails; otherwise, it must be paid by the plaintiff or out of the estate, or in such proportion by the plaintiff or out of the estate as the court may direct; and for the costs directed to be paid by the plaintiff or defendant, execution may be issued as in other cases; and the costs directed to be paid out of the estate may be collected as other claims against an estate are collected. (Code 1852, §§ 1649, 1650, 1653; Code 1867, §§ 1967, 1968, 1971; Code 1876, §§ 2331, 2332, 2335; Code 1886, § 1996; Code 1896, § 4294; Code 1907, § 6203; Code 1923, § 10632; Code 1940, T. 61, § 59; Code 1975, § 43-1-76.)

Code commissioner's note. — This section was originally codified as § 43-1-76 of the 1975 Code.

Nonresident will-contestant may be required to give security for costs. Ex parte Winn, 226 Ala. 447, 147 So. 625 (1933).

When administrator contests in good faith he is entitled to reimbursement out of estate. — When the probate of a will is contested by an administrator previously appointed, the costs are properly adjudged against him individually, if he fails, but, if he acted in good faith, he is entitled to reimbursement out of the estate on settlement of his accounts. Bradley v. Andress, 30 Ala. 80 (1857).

Sole heir and distributee, at whose request administrator successfully contested probate of alleged will, was held to be in no position to object to the allowance out of estate of reasonable expenses incurred by administrator in connection with the prosecution of such will contest. Stanley v. Beck, 242 Ala. 574, 7 So. 2d 276 (1942).

Even though contest is lost. — If an administrator in good faith contests probate of a will, even though he loses contest, court may allow his costs out of the estate. Stanley v. Beck, 242 Ala. 574, 7 So. 2d 276 (1942).

Administrator ad colligendum held entitled to costs expended in propounding will for probate, which terminated unsuccessfully, though costs were taxed against him personally. Mitchell v. Parker, 227 Ala. 676, 151 So. 842 (1933).

When contest compromised court may tax costs against estate. — Where a will contest failed because of compromise by the parties, it was within the court's discretion to tax costs against decedent's estate under this section. Harris v. Harris, 211 Ala. 144, 99 So. 913 (1924).

Section held applicable to will contest transferred to circuit court. — The provisions of this section were applicable to a will contest which the original transcript disclosed was filed in the probate court of DeKalb County but was later transferred to the circuit court under the provisions of § 43-8-198. Clark v. Clark, 287 Ala. 42, 247 So. 2d 361 (1971).

This section is applicable to will contest cases filed originally in circuit court. — The supreme court has said it can conceive of no logical reason why the provisions of this section should be applicable to will contest cases tried in the circuit court after transfer from the probate court, but not applicable to will contest cases filed originally in the circuit court under the provisions of § 43-8-199. Clark v. Clark, 287 Ala. 42, 247 So. 2d 361 (1971).

Cited in Taylor v. Kelly, 31 Ala. 59 (1857); Baker v. Bain, 237 Ala. 618, 188 So. 681 (1939).

Collateral references. — 95 C.J.S., Wills, §§ 328, 558-572.

80 Am. Jur. 2d, Wills, §§ 1092-1097.

§ 43-8-197. Change of venue.

(a) At any time before the trial of such contest, either party may remove the same to another county by proceeding as is required in civil actions in the circuit court; and when an order for the removal of the trial of such contest is made, the judge of probate must transmit the will, subpoenas and all other papers belonging, and a transcript of all the entries of record relating thereto, to the judge of the probate court of the county to which the trial is ordered to be removed. Such judge of probate must proceed to try the case in the same manner as prescribed for the judge of probate of the county from which it has been removed.

(b) If the judgment is rendered in the probate court to which it has been removed, and no appeal is taken within 30 days thereafter, such judgment must be certified by the judge of such probate court, and the will and other papers be returned to the probate court from which the trial was removed; and the will must be probated or rejected in such probate court as such judgment may be for or against the validity of the will.

(c) If, on the removal of the trial, the costs are directed to be paid out of the estate, a bill of costs must be made out by the judge of probate trying the same and certified to the judge of probate of the county from which the trial was removed; and such bill of costs may be taxed by motion in the court in which the trial was had, and the same may be recertified to such judge of probate. (Code 1852, §§ 1644, 1651, 1652; Code 1867, §§ 1963, 1964, 1966, 1969, 1970; Code 1876, §§ 2327, 2328, 2330, 2333, 2334; Code 1886, §§ 1997-1999; Code 1896, §§ 4295-4297; Code 1907, §§ 6204-6206; Code 1923, §§ 10633-10635; Code 1940, T. 61, §§ 60-62; Code 1975, § 43-1-77.)

Code commissioner's note. — This section was originally codified as § 43-1-77 of the 1975 Code.

Cited in McDonnell v. Jordan, 178 U.S. 229, 20 S. Ct. 886, 44 L. Ed. 1048 (1900); Baker v. Bain, 237 Ala. 618, 188 So. 681 (1939).

Collateral references. — 95 C.J.S., Wills, § 355. 96 C.J.S., Wills, § 1081.

§ 43-8-198. Transfer of contest to circuit court; appeal from judgment of circuit court; certification of judgment, etc., to probate court.

Upon the demand of any party to the contest, made in writing at the time of filing the initial pleading, the probate court, or the judge thereof, must enter an order transferring the contest to the circuit court of the county in which the contest is made, and must certify all papers and documents pertaining to the contest to the clerk of the circuit court, and the case shall be docketed by the clerk of the circuit court and a special session of said court may be called for the trial of said contest or, said contest may be tried by said circuit court at any special or regular session of said court. The issues must be made up in the circuit court as if the trial were to be had in the probate court, and the trial had in all other respects as trials in other civil cases in the circuit court. An appeal to the supreme court may be taken from the judgment of the circuit court on such contest within 42 days after the entry of such judgment. After a final determination of the contest, the clerk of the circuit court shall certify the transcript of all judgments of the circuit court in such proceedings, together with all of the papers and documents theretofore certified to the circuit court by the probate court, back to the probate court from which they were first certified to the circuit court, and thereafter shall be recorded in the probate court as all other contested wills are recorded in the probate court. (Code 1923, § 10636; Code 1940, T. 61, § 63; Acts 1947, No. 712, p. 552; Code 1975, § 43-1-78.)

Code commissioner's note. — This section was originally codified as § 43-1-78 of the 1975 Code.

Editor's note. — The Alabama supreme court held in Bardin v. Jones, 371 So. 2d 23 (Ala. 1979) that the circuit court, following transfer of a will contest to it under this section, can consider any issues presented in an appropriate pleading under the Rules of Civil Procedure, provided those issues could properly have been raised in a will contest. The court then went on to state that any language to the contrary in Hooper v. Huey, 293 Ala. 63, 300 So. 2d 100 (1974), below, is disapproved.

Circuit court can consider issues presented under Rules of Civil Procedure pleading. — The circuit court following transfer of a will contest to it under this section can consider any issues presented in an appropriate pleading under the Rules of Civil Procedure, provided those issues can properly be raised in a will contest. Bardin v. Jones, 371 So. 2d 23 (Ala. 1979).

This section must be read in conjunction with § 43-8-190. Bardin v. Jones, 371 So. 2d 23 (Ala. 1979).

A will must have been "offered for probate" before it can be contested in either the probate or the circuit court. Hooper v. Huey, 293 Ala. 63, 300 So. 2d 100 (1974), overruled on other grounds, Bardin v. Jones, 371 So. 2d 23 (Ala. 1979).

Who may contest will. — An adopted daughter of a deceased brother of testatrix has no such interest in the estate, nor is she so related to testatrix, as to have a right under this section to contest the probate of the will. Gamble v. Cloud, 263 Ala. 336, 82 So. 2d 526 (1955).

The words "must transfer the contest" have been regarded as mandatory. Ex parte Stephens, 259 Ala. 361, 66 So. 2d 901 (1953).

Example of "initial pleading". — A written request by one filing contest of codicil to will before dismissal of another's contest thereof to transfer case from probate court to circuit court for jury trial was second contestant's "initial pleading" within this section requiring such transfer on written demand of any party to contest at time of filing initial pleading. Baker v. Bain, 237 Ala. 618, 188 So. 2d 681 (1939).

Jurisdiction statutory and limited. — The jurisdiction conferred on the circuit court as a court of law by this section is a statutory and limited jurisdiction, and to warrant the exercise of that jurisdiction there must be pending in the probate court a valid contest when the probate court or the judge thereof enters the order transferring the contest to the circuit court. Ex parte Pearson, 241 Ala. 467, 3 So. 2d 5 (1941); Thigpen v. Walker, 251 Ala. 426, 37 So. 2d 923

(1948); Ex parte Stephens, 259 Ala. 361, 66 So. 2d 901 (1953); Bardin v. Jones, 371 So. 2d 23 (Ala. 1979).

The jurisdiction conferred on the circuit court to try contests of wills is a statutory and limited jurisdiction. Hooper v. Huey, 293 Ala. 63, 300 So. 2d 100 (1974), overruled on other grounds, Bardin v. Jones, 371 So. 2d 23 (Ala. 1979).

Probate of the will is essential to the circuit court's jurisdiction, and the declaratory judgment law was not intended to confer upon the circuit court jurisdiction in admitting or refusing to admit a purported will to probate. Hooper v. Huey, 293 Ala. 63, 300 So. 2d 100 (1974), overruled on other grounds, Bardin v. Jones, 371 So. 2d 23 (Ala. 1979).

Jurisdiction statutory and limited. — Where there was neither a transfer of a contest to the circuit court according to this section, nor a circuit court contest of a will admitted to probate according to § 43-1-79, a circuit court's jurisdiction over a will contest is statutory and limited. The circuit court had jurisdiction over the later will only to the extent of determining whether it revoked the earlier will. Forrester v. Putman, 409 So. 2d 773 (Ala. 1981).

Although this section empowers the circuit court to hear contests, its grant of jurisdiction is limited. Nottage v. Jones, 388 So. 2d 923 (Ala. 1980).

Jurisdictional defect cured where action remanded. — Although initially the circuit court did not have proper jurisdiction because the contestants failed to file a contest in the probate court, this jurisdictional defect was cured when the circuit court remanded the action to the probate court where a contest was filed. Nottage v. Jones, 388 So. 2d 923 (Ala. 1980).

Pending contest in circuit court not sufficient basis for refusal of probate court to act on contest and demand for transfer relating to earlier will. — Fact that later will and codicil had been previously admitted and were being contested in the circuit court was not a sufficient basis for probate court to take no action on a petition for probate, contest and demand for transfer filed later pertaining to an earlier will. Cagle v. Reeves, 353 So. 2d 787 (Ala. 1977).

Valid contest must be pending before transfer. — Under the language and judicial interpretation of this section, there must be a valid will contest pending in the probate court before the probate judge can transfer the contest to the circuit court. Nottage v. Jones, 388 So. 2d 923 (Ala. 1980).

Contest is an extension of probate proceeding. — This section and §§ 43-8-199 and 43-8-200 demonstrate that the contest of a will subsequent to its probate, is but an extension of the probate proceeding — a proceeding not inter partes but in rem. Mitchell v. Nixon, 200 F.2d 50 (5th Cir. 1952).

The circuit court may consider only those issues transferred to it from the probate court and the resolution of these issues must be certified back to the probate court. Hooper v. Huey, 293 Ala. 63, 300 So. 2d 100 (1974), overruled on other grounds, Bardin v. Jones, 371 So. 2d 23 (Ala. 1979). But see editor's note, above.

Alignment of parties. — The latter part of § 43-8-190 which directs the probate court to align the parties between the person making the application for probate, as plaintiff, and the person contesting the validity of the will, as defendant, is directory rather than mandatory in light of this section and §§ 43-8-160 and 43-8-190. Hooper v. Huey, 293 Ala. 63, 300 So. 2d 100 (1974), overruled on other grounds, Bardin v. Jones, 371 So. 2d 23 (Ala. 1979).

Appeal to supreme court. — Where demurrer (now motion to dismiss) to the contest of one contestant was sustained, and contestant having failed to amend the contest within the time allowed, the court dismissed it, the judgment of dismissal was in all respects final insofar as concerned the contest of that contestant and was appealable to the supreme court as authorized by this section. Gamble v. Cloud, 263 Ala. 336, 82 So. 2d 526 (1955).

Appeal taken over 30 (now 42) days after entry of judgment must be dismissed. Wildman v. Wildman, 222 Ala. 409, 132 So. 891 (1931).

A docket sheet notation is a sufficient order pursuant to this section. Cook v. Cook, 396 So. 2d 1037 (Ala. 1981).

Cited in Ex parte Petty, 249 Ala. 393, 31 So. 2d 575 (1947); Curry v. Holmes, 249 Ala. 545, 32 So. 2d 39 (1947); State v. Le Croy, 254 Ala. 637, 49 So. 2d 553 (1950); Hornaday v. First Nat'l Bank, 259 Ala. 26, 65 So. 2d 678 (1952); Hiller v. Goodwin, 258 Ala. 700, 65 So. 2d 152 (1953); Allen v. Jones, 259 Ala. 98, 65 So. 2d 217 (1953); Fields v. Baker, 259 Ala. 336, 67 So. 2d 10 (1953); Hubbard v. Moseley, 261 Ala. 683, 75 So. 2d 658 (1954); Smith v. Bryant, 263 Ala. 331, 82 So. 2d 411 (1955); Baker v. Baker, 266 Ala. 210, 95 So. 2d 101 (1957); Foster v. Shepherd, 269 Ala. 94, 110 So. 2d 894 (1959); Harris v. Martin, 271 Ala. 52, 122 So. 2d 116 (1960); Grady v. Wallace, 272 Ala. 119, 130 So. 2d 21 (1961); Romano v. Romano, 277 Ala. 207, 168 So. 2d 236 (1964); Ivey v. Byrd, 286 Ala. 183, 238 So. 2d 349 (1970); Clark v. Clark, 287 Ala. 42, 247 So. 2d 361 (1971); Owens v. Burton, 340 So. 2d 24 (Ala. 1976); Fletcher v. DeLoach, 360 So. 2d 316 (Ala. 1978); Rabon v. Rabon, 360 So. 2d 971 (Ala. 1978).

Collateral references. — 95 C.J.S., Wills, §§ 316, 353, 354, 1076.

§ 43-8-199. Contest in circuit court after admission to probate — Generally.

Any person interested in any will who has not contested the same under the provisions of this article, may, at any time within the six months after the admission of such will to probate in this state, contest the validity of the same by filing a complaint in the circuit court in the county in which such will was probated. (Code 1852, § 1654; Code 1867, § 1972; Code 1876, § 2336; Code 1886, § 2000; Code 1896, § 4298; Code 1907, § 6207; Code 1923, § 10637; Acts 1931, No. 733, p. 844; Code 1940, T. 61, § 64; Code 1975, § 43-1-79.)

Code commissioner's note. — This section was originally codified as § 43-1-79 of the 1975 Code.

I. GENERAL CONSIDERATION.

Cross reference. — See editor's note under § 43-8-190.

History of section. — This section has existed in this state since the year 1806, having undergone a change in phraseology, but not in meaning, in passing through our various codes enacted since that time. Knox v. Paull, 95 Ala. 505, 11 So. 156 (1892). Its effect was to confer on courts of equity a jurisdiction which they never before possessed, the power to set aside a probated will for fraud, forgery or other ground affecting the validity of the paper. Another purpose was to shorten the time within which a judgment establishing a will could be disturbed, or the validity of the will, as such, assailed; or, as said in Johnson v. Glasscock, 2 Ala. 218 (1841), where the statute of 1806 was construed, "to provide a period of limitation much shorter than before was known after which the will admitted to probate ceases to be the subject of controversy, and becomes entirely conclusive on parties interested." Watson v. Turner, 89 Ala. 220, 8 So. 20 (1889). The origin, history and purpose of this section are fully discussed in the case of Knox v. Paull, 95 Ala. 505, 11 So. 156 (1892).

Before 1836, our statutes had established a peculiar jurisdiction and system for their proof and contestation, and for the final determination of their validity or invalidity. The probate embraced all wills, whether of real or personal estate. The jurisdiction was given to the orphans' court to determine, in the first instance, the question of will or no will, and, according to its decision of that question, to allow or disallow probate. If it disallowed probate, its decree was conclusive upon all persons, until reversed or set aside in some recognized legal mode. If it allowed probate, any person interested in the will might contest its validity by bill in chancery filed within five years from the time of such probate. Hunt v. Acre, 28 Ala. 580 (1856).

Prior to the enactment of this section or its progenitors there was no jurisdiction in equity for contesting a will. This section creates such jurisdiction. Carter v. Davis, 275 Ala. 250, 154 So. 2d 9 (1963).

Early construction. — This section was construed in Hardy v. Hardy, 26 Ala. 524 (1855). The decision reached in that case, and the reasoning of the court, establish the following propositions: (1) That the jurisdiction conferred by the act of 1806 (Clay, Dig. p. 598, § 15) on courts of chancery to entertain bills of this nature contesting the validity of wills already proved in courts of probate was exclusive; (2) That a court of probate therefore no longer possessed its ancient jurisdiction to set aside the probate of a former will and permit the probate of a later one; (3) That the lapse of five years was a bar to any contest in either forum. Watson v. Turner, 89 Ala. 220, 8 So. 20 (1890).

Purpose of section. — This section and its predecessors were enacted so as to allow a rea-

sonable time after a formal and regular probate for a contest of the validity of the will by all who did not make a contest in the probate court. Smith v. Bryant, 263 Ala. 331, 82 So. 2d 411 (1955).

The purpose of this section and its progenitors is to give an additional opportunity to contest the validity of a will which has been admitted to probate in the probate court. Carter v. Davis, 275 Ala. 250, 154 So. 2d 9 (1963).

Effect of section. — This section merely confers upon the circuit court the jurisdiction of the probate court as to the contest of a will, and that court therefore in such a proceeding — in the exercise of this special statutory power — exercises a limited jurisdiction. Cox v. Johnson, 80 Ala. 22 (1855); McEvoy v. Leonard, 89 Ala. 455, 8 So. 40 (1890); Ex parte Walter, 202 Ala. 281, 80 So. 119 (1918).

It creates a new right. — This section is not merely one of limitation, but creates a new, substantive and independent right, which may be exercised within the time prescribed. Wachter v. Davis, 215 Ala. 659, 111 So. 917 (1927); Smith v. Bryant, 263 Ala. 331, 82 So. 2d 411 (1955); Odom v. Odom, 272 Ala. 164, 130 So. 2d 10 (1961).

Doubtless the former period of five years was found to work inconvenience and hardship to those interested in the validity of the will, and was for this reason shortened to 12 months (now six months). The section is not primarily a limitation, but rather an extension, and its purpose is to allow to contestants coming within its terms the full period of 12 months (now six months) after probate for the initiation of a contest. Kaplan v. Coleman, 180 Ala. 267, 60 So. 885 (1912); Ex parte Walter, 202 Ala. 281, 80 So. 119 (1918).

This section confers a right to contest upon any party adversely interested who has not contested the will in the probate court and upon any ground disclosing that the will as probated was not the last will and testament of the decedent in whole or in part. In such case the probate of the original will is vacated that the last will and testament, the original and the codicil, be then admitted to probate and become effective as of the date of the death of the testator. Caverno v. Webb, 239 Ala. 671, 196 So. 723 (1940).

The right of contest of a will in the circuit court is purely of statutory creation and this section creates a new substantive and independent right. Ferrell v. Minnifield, 275 Ala. 388, 155 So. 2d 345 (1963).

Which is but an extension of right to contest in probate court. — While this section creates a new and independent right, it is but an extension of the right to contest in the probate court. Carter v. Davis, 275 Ala. 250, 154 So. 2d 9 (1963).

And which is unhampered by any question of neglect to contest in first instance. Cain v. Burger, 219 Ala. 10, 121 So. 17 (1929).

It supplies the sole remedy. — Where a person interested in an estate failed to join a will contest in the probate court, after appeal from that court his only remedy was to contest in the circuit court under this section. Allen v. Pugh, 206 Ala. 10, 89 So. 470 (1921).

For the probate of a will is a judgment in rem and binding on the whole world so long as it stands; it is not subject to collateral attack and its validity can be contested and vacated only by seasonable appeal or by complaint filed to contest as authorized by this section. Hardy v. Hardy, 26 Ala. 524 (1855); Kaplan v. Coleman, 180 Ala. 267, 60 So. 885 (1912).

This section and section 43-8-175 are in pari materia. Carter v. Davis, 275 Ala. 250, 154 So. 2d 9 (1963).

No contest where will already probated in another state. — The legislature did not intend to permit the contest of a will probated in this state, when such will has already been probated in the state or territory of the United States wherein the testator was living at the time of his death. Carter v. Davis, 275 Ala. 250, 154 So. 2d 9 (1963).

"Month" within the meaning of this section means a calendar month, the time from any day of any of the months as adjusted in the calendar to the corresponding day of the next month, if any; if not, to the last day of the next month. Odom v. Odom, 272 Ala. 164, 130 So. 2d 10 (1961).

Matter for legislature. — The fact that this section practically permits parties to repeat a contest of the validity of a will by one of them refraining from participating of record in the contest in the probate court is a matter for the legislature, and not for the courts. Breeding v. Grantland, 135 Ala. 497, 33 So. 544 (1903).

This section does not limit the grounds of contest, but authorizes a contest upon the ground of revocation by a later will, or revocation pro tanto by a codicil. Caverno v. Webb, 239 Ala. 671, 196 So. 723 (1940).

Jurisdiction statutory and limited. — Where there was neither a transfer of a contest to the circuit court according to § 43-8-198, nor a circuit court contest of a will admitted to probate according to this section, a circuit court's jurisdiction over a will contest is statutory and limited. The circuit court had jurisdiction over the later will only to the extent of determining whether it revoked the earlier will. Forrester v. Putman, 409 So. 2d 773 (Ala. 1981).

Cited in Hill v. Barge, 12 Ala. 687 (1848); Lewis v. Elrod, 38 Ala. 17 (1861); Hall v. Hall, 47 Ala. 290 (1872); Waddell v. Lanier, 54 Ala.

440 (1875); Harwell v. Lehman, etc., Co., 72 Ala. 344 (1882); Matthews v. McDade, 72 Ala. 377 (1882); Brierfield Coal & Iron Co. v. Gay, 106 Ala. 615, 17 So. 618 (1895); McDonnell v. Jordan, 178 U.S. 229, 20 S. Ct. 886, 44 L. Ed. 1048 (1900); Frederick v. Wilbourne, 198 Ala. 137, 73 So. 442 (1916); Crawford v. Walter, 202 Ala. 235, 80 So. 73 (1918); Miller v. Whittington, 202 Ala. 406, 80 So. 499 (1918); Cronheim v. Loveman, 225 Ala. 199, 142 So. 550 (1932); Alexander v. Alexander, 227 Ala. 322, 150 So. 142 (1933); Upshaw v. Eubank, 227 Ala. 653, 151 So. 837 (1933); Thompson v. Earnest, 228 Ala. 641, 154 So. 797 (1934); Whitaker v. Kennamer, 229 Ala. 80, 156 So. 855 (1934); Cook v. Morton, 236 Ala. 237, 181 So. 904 (1938); Ex parte Pettus, 245 Ala. 349, 17 So. 2d 409 (1944); Hartley v. Alabama Nat'l Bank, 247 Ala. 651, 25 So. 2d 680 (1946); Ex parte Curry, 248 Ala. 384, 27 So. 2d 630 (1946); Bradford v. Fletcher, 248 Ala. 483, 28 So. 2d 313 (1946); State v. Le Croy, 254 Ala. 637, 49 So. 2d 553 (1950); Kelley v. Sutliff, 257 Ala. 371, 59 So. 2d 65 (1952); Staples v. Harris, 264 Ala. 629, 89 So. 2d 167 (1956); Carruba v. Meeks, 274 Ala. 714, 150 So. 2d 195 (1963); Romano v. Romano, 277 Ala. 207, 168 So. 2d 236 (1964); Hicks v. Allred, 281 Ala. 464, 204 So. 2d 813 (1967); Hooper v. Huey, 293 Ala. 63, 300 So. 2d 100 (1974); Hinton v. Nelson, 294 Ala. 24, 310 So. 2d 879 (1975); Owens v. Burton, 340 So. 2d 24 (Ala. 1976); Jackson v. Davis, 398 So. 2d 242 (Ala. 1981).

Collateral references. — See collateral references under § 43-8-190.

II. WHO MAY CONTEST.

Any person entitled to share in the distribution of estate may contest. — It is the settled law of this state that any person entitled to share in the distribution of an estate, whether as devisee, legatee or as an heir at law, without showing any special equity, has the right to have the administration of such estate settled in the circuit court. Bromberg v. Bates, 98 Ala. 621, 13 So. 557 (1893).

Thus, there can be no doubt but that a contest under this section may be instituted by any person who could have contested the will under § 43-8-190, but has neglected to do so. Stephens v. Richardson, 189 Ala. 360, 66 So. 497 (1914); Braasch v. Worthington, 191 Ala. 210, 67 So. 1003 (1915); Allen v. Pugh, 206 Ala. 10, 89 So. 470 (1921); Carter v. Davis, 275 Ala. 250, 154 So. 2d 9 (1963).

A beneficiary has the right to contest a will under this section. Binford v. Penney, 255 Ala. 20, 49 So. 2d 665 (1950).

It is clear that the phrases "any person interested therein," in § 43-8-190, and "any person interested in any will," in this section, do not mean simply any person who is named as a beneficiary in the will, but rather any person who has a direct interest in the estate disposed of by will, in other words, the "interest" intended is not literally an interest in the will itself, but in its operation. Braasch v. Worthington, 191 Ala. 210, 67 So. 1003 (1915).

Testator's nephews and nieces, who were beneficiaries under will, were "parties in interest" entitled to contest codicil injuriously affecting them. Baker v. Bain, 237 Ala. 618, 188 So. 681 (1939).

Where the heir at law of a decedent, who willed real property to others, conveyed all of the real property disposed of by the will to another, but the conveyance of part of it provided for a reversion on breach of conditions, the heir was interested in the establishment of the will, and might contest its validity by a complaint under this section. Stephens v. Richardson, 189 Ala. 360, 66 So. 497 (1914).

Legatees who are the children of the living heirs of the testator are not entitled to contest. Braasch v. Worthington, 191 Ala. 210, 67 So. 1003 (1915).

Provided the interest was acquired before probate. — The authorities generally hold that the right of contest is a personal and not a property right, and therefore cannot pass by transfer or descent, and that every would-be contestant under statutes authorizing any person "interested in the will" to contest it after probate must show that he acquired his interest before the probate of the will. Allen v. Pugh, 206 Ala. 10, 89 So. 470 (1921); Cain v. Burger, 219 Ala. 10, 121 So. 17 (1929).

And provided he has not contested before. — A judgment in the probate court, establishing a will on contestation, is final and conclusive, as against all persons who joined therein. Those only who do not contest in that court can resort to the circuit court. To contest in the probate court it is necessary to state some valid objection to the will; the same rule applies when the will is contested in the circuit court. Lyons v. Campbell, 88 Ala. 462, 7 So. 250 (1890).

One having the right to contest a will may do so only once; however, any party aggrieved by the ruling in the probate court may appeal under § 12-22-21. Elsworth v. Rini, 388 So. 2d 953 (Ala. 1980).

Notice of prior contest in immaterial. — Though a person entitled to contest a will was duly served with notice of a proceeding to contest in the probate court, he may nevertheless afterwards contest it by a complaint in the circuit court. Knox v. Paull, 95 Ala. 505, 11 So. 156 (1892).

As is giving aid in prior contest. — A person interested in a will may contest it in the circuit court even though he previously aided in a contest under § 43-8-190, and paid a portion of the attorneys' fees, if he was not in fact a contestant in the prior contest. Breeding v. Grantland, 135 Ala. 497, 33 So. 544 (1903).

This section is available to any person, who would take by descent in case of intestacy. Hall v. Proctor, 242 Ala. 636, 7 So. 2d 764 (1942).

Having an interest as heir or distributee, in an estate which would pass under the will, if valid, constitutes the "interest in the will," which entitles such person to contest its validity when it is propounded for probate. Hall v. Proctor, 242 Ala. 636, 7 So. 2d 764 (1942).

Legatee. — See analysis line III in notes to § 43-8-190.

A legatee under a will, having no interest in the estate of the decedent, does not have sufficient interest to entitle him to contest the will. Whatley v. Hamilton, 271 Ala. 438, 124 So. 2d 436 (1960).

A contestant of a will must have some direct legal or equitable interest in the decedent's estate, in privity with him, whether as heir, purchaser or beneficiary under another will, which would be destroyed or injuriously affected by the establishment of the contested will. Baker v. Baker, 266 Ala. 210, 95 So. 2d 101 (1957).

The executor named in a will in his representative capacity had no such interest insofar as the averments of his complaint disclosed, as would entitle him to contest the will. Baker v. Baker, 266 Ala. 210, 95 So. 2d 101 (1957).

Executor cannot force independent party to contest. — The executor of a will has no right, under the guise of an action for its construction, to bring into court anyone having an independent right to contest it, and thus anticipate and precipitate such contest against the latter's will, and in advance of the time to which he is authorized by the statute to postpone such action. Kaplan v. Coleman, 180 Ala. 267, 60 So. 885 (1912).

Contract for contest by cousins and aunt. — A contract, after will was propounded for probate, for contest of will by cousins and aunt, who alone was heir or distributee entitled to contest will, and for passing of specific share of estate to cousins and aunt in event of successful contest, did not give cousins such an "interest in will" as to entitle them after aunt's death to contest will after probate. Hall v. Proctor, 242 Ala. 636, 7 So. 2d 764 (1942).

Contest rights died with aunt. — If will of deceased was invalid, Alabama lands of deceased who left only aunt and cousins as survivors descended only to aunt, who as next of kin alone could contest will, and contest right died with aunt without passing to aunt's descendants or deceased's next of kin becoming such after aunt's death. Hall v. Proctor, 242 Ala. 636, 7 So. 2d 764 (1942).

III. THE CONTEST AFTER ADMISSION TO PROBATE.

A. Nature.

Cross reference. — As to the trial by a jury, see notes to § 43-8-202.

Contest is between living parties. — In either proceeding — the contests in the courts of probate, or by complaint in the circuit court — the parties claiming under the will are in fact the actors, bound to support it affirmatively, while the heir, or next kin, is in the relation of a defendant. In either court, the controversy is between living parties. The estate of the testator is not interested. The interests of those claiming to succeed to it, either by operation of law, or by operation of the instrument propounded as a will, are alone involved. The estate remains intact, undiminished, whatever may be the result of the controversy, and the subject-matter of investigation is not a transaction with or statement by the decedent, but an act of his in its nature ambulatory and revocable, taking effect only by his death. Kumpe v. Coons, 63 Ala. 448 (1879).

It is a proceeding in rem. — Proceedings to probate or to set aside the probate of wills are proceedings in rem and not in personam; such proceedings are exclusively to determine the status of the res, and not the rights of the parties. Hunt v. Acre, 28 Ala. 580 (1856); McCann v. Ellis, 172 Ala. 60, 55 So. 303 (1911); Ex parte Walter, 202 Ala. 281, 80 So. 119 (1918); Newman v. Martin, 210 Ala. 485, 98 So. 465 (1923).

The contest of a will by complaint in the circuit court is a proceeding in rem, entirely of statutory creation, and is limited to determining the validity of the will. Nesmith v. Vines, 248 Ala. 72, 26 So. 2d 265 (1946).

Sections 43-8-198, 43-8-200 and this section demonstrate that the contest of a will subsequent to its probate is but an extension of the probate proceeding — a proceeding not inter partes but in rem. Mitchell v. Nixon, 200 F.2d 50 (5th Cir. 1952).

And is entirely statutory. — Not only is the contest of the will, by complaint in circuit court, under this section, a proceeding in rem, but it is one entirely of statutory creation. Ex parte Walter, 202 Ala. 281, 80 So. 119 (1918); Nesmith v. Vines, 248 Ala. 72, 26 So. 2d 265 (1946).

The right of contest of a will in circuit court if purely of statutory creation. Ex parte Russell, 239 Ala. 641, 196 So. 718 (1940); Kelley v. Sutliff, 262 Ala. 622, 80 So. 2d 636 (1955); Baker v. Baker, 266 Ala. 210, 95 So. 2d 101 (1957).

The jurisdiction of the circuit court is statutory and limited, and that jurisdiction can only be quickened into exercise by a complaint filed in the circuit court, by a person who has not contested and is interested in the estate of the decedent if the will is set aside, within "six months after the admission of such will to probate." Ex parte Pearson, 241 Ala. 467, 3 So. 2d 5 (1941).

Is limited. — The jurisdiction and authority of the circuit court is limited to the trial of the issues presented by the contest after which the case must be certified back to the probate court. Thigpen v. Walker, 251 Ala. 426, 37 So. 2d 923 (1948).

The sole and only appropriate purpose of the proceeding brought under this section is the contest, the revocation, of a will already admitted to probate. Kelley v. Sutliff, 262 Ala. 622, 80 So. 2d 636 (1955).

It is not such an action as would give federal court jurisdiction. — A proceeding to contest a will after its admission to probate under this section, being merely a matter of procedure ancillary to the original probate, is not such an action inter partes as would give a federal court jurisdiction. Mitchell v. Nixon, 200 F.2d 50 (5th Cir. 1952).

What constitutes a contest under section. — The attempt to set aside a probated will, by proving a later one, or by attaching to it a codicil with inconsistent provisions, is a contest of the validity of the former will. Watson v. Turner, 89 Ala. 220, 8 So. 20 (1890).

A will is contested, under the provisions of this section, by a party in interest, by filing in the court where it is offered for probate allegations in writing that the will was not duly executed, or of the unsoundness of mind of the testator or of any other valid objections thereto, and thereupon an issue must be made up under the direction of the court between the person making the application as plaintiff and the person contesting the validity of the will as defendant. Breeding v. Grantland, 135 Ala. 497, 33 So. 544 (1903).

Rules in inter partes proceedings apply. — Though a will contest where the testatrix's testamentary capacity was attacked is a proceeding in rem, yet, as it also partakes of the nature of a proceeding inter partes, the rules of evidence and procedure obtaining in the case of any customary proceeding inter partes apply. Kay v. Elston, 205 Ala. 307, 87 So. 525 (1920).

A complaint to contest will after probate must aver facts which against apt demurrer (now motion to dismiss) sufficiently disclose that plaintiff has an interest in will within this section. Hall v. Proctor, 242 Ala. 636, 7 So. 2d 764 (1942).

Failure of complaint to state time of probate. — See Baker v. Baker, 266 Ala. 210, 95 So. 2d 101 (1957).

Averment in complaint was subject to motion to dismiss as mere "conclusion". — An averment in complaint by aunt and cousins to contest, after probate, will of Tennessee woman leaving personalty and realty in Tennessee and Alabama, that aunt and cousins were next of kin and heirs at law entitled to share in distribution of estate under Alabama and Tennessee laws, was subject to demurrer (now motion to dismiss) as being mere "conclusion" as to property rights passing under such laws. Hall v. Proctor, 242 Ala. 636, 7 So. 2d 764 (1942).

The dismissal of complaint to contest will after probate, as incapable of amendment, was not error, where trial court gave full and repeated opportunities to plaintiffs to amend by setting up facts entitling plaintiffs to contest, and plaintiffs were unable to do so. Hall v. Proctor, 242 Ala. 636, 7 So. 2d 764 (1942).

Proof of execution. — Upon a contest, the execution of the will must be proved by both subscribing witnesses, or if one is not available, his absence must be accounted for before resorting to secondary evidence. Ferrell v. Minnifield, 275 Ala. 388, 155 So. 2d 345 (1963).

The failure to offer proof of execution by two subscribing witnesses, or to account for the absence of one, in the event of a contest, will not sustain a judgment in favor of the proponents of the will. Ferrell v. Minnifield, 275 Ala. 388, 155 So. 2d 345 (1963).

Evidence of the probated will and the probate proceedings are admissible when a will is contested for the first time in an action in circuit court under this section, even though the proceedings show the testimony of only one subscribing witness to the will. Ferrell v. Minnifield, 275 Ala. 388, 155 So. 2d 345 (1963).

Where the proceedings in the probate court show by proof of two witnesses, or one and a proper accounting for the other that the will was properly executed, it is not necessary to produce the same witnesses again in a contest in the circuit court or to take the same steps to prove the execution of the will, in view of § 43-8-202, which makes the evidence taken in probate court admissible in the circuit court. Ferrell v. Minnifield, 275 Ala. 388, 155 So. 2d 345 (1963).

And validity of will is prima facie sustained. — Where the execution of a will is proved in the probate court by both subscribing witnesses or if one is not available, by accounting for his absence before resorting to secondary evidence, and the probate proceedings are introduced into evidence in a contest in circuit court the validity of the will is prima facie sustained and the proponents may then rest their case. Ferrell v. Minnifield, 275 Ala. 388, 155 So. 2d 345 (1963).

Contest filed too late. — Since under § 1-1-4, the time within which a will contest

must be filed is computed by excluding the first day and including the last, a contest filed on the 26th of February to a will probated on August 25th was invalid. Odom v. Odom, 272 Ala. 164, 130 So. 2d 10 (1961).

A complaint, after probate, to contest will of Tennessee woman dying in Tennessee, purporting to dispose of woman's personalty, and her realty in Tennessee, must plead Tennessee laws of descent and distribution, under which such realty and personalty pass. Hall v. Proctor, 242 Ala. 636, 7 So. 2d 764 (1942).

A "favored beneficiary," within rule that confidential rélations and activity by a "favored beneficiary" in the execution of a will raises a prima facie presumption of undue influence, is one who in the circumstances of the particular case has been favored over others having equal claim to testator's bounty, by an unnatural discrimination which leads to a natural inference that advantage has been taken by one in position to do so. Cook v. Morton, 241 Ala. 188, 1 So. 2d 890 (1941).

Confidential relations and activity by favored beneficiary in execution of will raise a prima facie presumption of undue influence, casting on proponent the burden of proof on such issue. Cook v. Morton, 241 Ala. 188, 1 So. 2d 890 (1941).

Nuncupative will. — For a contest under this section of a nuncupative will, see Johnston v. Glasscock, 2 Ala. 218 (1841).

B. Similarity to Contest Before Probate.

Editor's note. — Section 43-8-190 provides for the contest before probate and the full annotations under that section should be consulted in connection with the following notes.

Will must have been admitted to probate. — Under this section the admission of the will to probate in the probate court is a condition precedent to the circuit court's jurisdiction of the will contest. Wachter v. Davis, 215 Ala. 659, 111 So. 917 (1927); Ex parte Russell, 239 Ala. 641, 196 So. 718 (1940); Ferrell v. Minnifield, 275 Ala. 388, 155 So. 2d 345 (1963).

It is necessary to show the probate of the will in the probate court because the probate of the will in the probate court is essential to the jurisdiction of the circuit court. Smith v. Bryant, 263 Ala. 331, 82 So. 2d 411 (1955).

An original contest in the circuit court may only be filed after admission of a will to probate. Cagle v. Reeves, 353 So. 2d 787 (Ala. 1977).

Character of proceeding same as in probate court. — If the application for probate is not contested in the probate court, but the heirs or distributees afterwards seek to set aside the probate by complaint in circuit court, which is a statutory substitute for probate in solemn form, the character of the proceeding is not changed so far as the estate is concerned, though it is an adversary action between the parties claiming under and against the will. Kumpe v. Coons, 63 Ala. 448 (1879).

Thus, where certain matter alleged is not ground for a contest in the probate court it could not be made so by a complaint filed under this section. Newman v. Martin, 210 Ala. 485, 98 So. 465 (1923).

The same general rules apply. — When the investigation is in circuit court, the same general rules prevail as when the contest is in the probate court, and the same general laws are applicable in both courts as when a will is probated in the ecclesiastical courts in solemn form, only changed so as to be adapted to the particular remedies. Lyons v. Campbell, 88 Ala. 462, 7 So. 250 (1890).

But the parties are not designated as plaintiff and defendant. — Where there is the contest of a will in the circuit court under the provisions of this section, there is no requirement in the section as to who shall be designated as plaintiff and who shall be designated as defendant. Crawford v. Walter, 202 Ala. 235, 80 So. 73 (1918); Smith v. Bryant, 263 Ala. 331, 82 So. 2d 411 (1955).

One or more items may be contested. — In the circuit court, equally as well as in the probate court, there may be valid reasons for contesting one or more items, leaving the remainder of the will unaffected. If not allowed this privilege or right, the heir or distributee would oftentimes be debarred from contesting such items, though procured by fraud or undue influence, because unable to show the entire will to be tainted thereby. Such denial would violate the principles of natural justice, and, under the clauses of the will which are the result of the free will of the testator, furnish protection to fraud or undue importunity on the part of one legatee. Lyons v. Campbell, 88 Ala. 462, 7 So. 250 (1890).

If fraud or undue influence, on the part of one or more devisees or legatees under the will affected the whole will, then no portion thereof can be upheld. Florey v. Florey, 24 Ala. 241 (1854). However, if the evidence shows that the will was in part the effect of undue influence, and in part the "act of the testator's own free will," in such case the will is not wholly void, and the latter part must stand, although the will be annulled as to the former. Lewis v. Martin, 210 Ala. 401, 98 So. 635 (1923).

Manner of trial. — The respondent, who is in effect the proponent, should first introduce the proceedings in the probate court, that is the petition to probate the will, the order fixing the time for hearing and giving notice, testimony of the attesting witnesses and proof of will, the decree admitting the will to probate and the will itself. The complainant, who is in effect the

contestant, should then introduce testimony on which the alleged invalidity of the will is based. The respondent should then introduce the rebuttal testimony, if any. The respondent should then make the opening argument to the jury, the complainant should then make the argument for complainant and the respondent should have the closing argument. Smith v. Bryant, 263 Ala. 331, 82 So. 2d 411 (1955); Hancock v. Frazier, 264 Ala. 202, 86 So. 2d 389 (1956).

The burden of proof in a contest in the circuit court is the same whether the case is tried with a jury or without a jury. As to the taking of depositions of witnesses prior to trial, there is no rule of procedure prescribing when that shall be done. When the trial is based on depositions, without a jury, counsel must prepare notes of the evidence which has been taken and which they intend to use. The court in considering the case should then apply the rule fixing the burden of proof. Hancock v. Frazier, 264 Ala. 202, 86 So. 2d 389 (1956).

Those claiming under will must show affirmatively its validity. — When the probate of a will is contested in the circuit court under this section, those who claim under the probated will must show affirmatively its validity and become the actors. Smith v. Bryant, 263 Ala. 331, 82 So. 2d 411 (1955).

The claimants under a disputed will have the burden on a contest to prove to the reasonable satisfaction of the court that testator did sign the will propounded for probate and did cause it to be attested by two witnesses who subscribed their names thereto in the presence of the testator. Hancock v. Frazier, 264 Ala. 202, 86 So. 2d 389 (1956).

On a will contest in circuit court, the burden of proof is on the proponents of the will of proving to the court's reasonable satisfaction that the testator signed the will and caused it to be attested by two witnesses who subscribed their names thereto in the presence of the testator. Ferrell v. Minnifield, 275 Ala. 388, 155 So. 2d 345 (1963).

Plaintiff not bound by statement in probate court. — The fact that the file in the probate court showed a signed statement by the plaintiff in a contest in circuit court that she consented that the instrument be immediately admitted to probate and recorded as the last will and testament of her father did not preclude proof by such plaintiff in the circuit court of the facts in the case. Smith v. Bryant, 263 Ala. 331, 82 So. 2d 411 (1955).

C. Issues and Judgment.

The issues are confined to the question of "will or no will," and therefore to the determination of the status of the res and matters pertaining thereto, and is not to be extended to questions concerning the rights of the parties. Ex parte Walter, 202 Ala. 281, 80 So. 119 (1918).

In a contest of a will by complaint in circuit court, the issues are confined to the question of "will or no will." Nesmith v. Vines, 248 Ala. 72, 26 So. 2d 265 (1946).

And if the contest is successful, the judgment is conclusive that there is no will, either in whole or in part, as the contest may be framed and the proof shown. Kaplan v. Coleman, 180 Ala. 267, 60 So. 885 (1912).

Thus, a judgment under this section which declares the whole will invalid as to certain heirs and valid as to others, is erroneous. McCann v. Ellis, 172 Ala. 60, 55 So. 303 (1911).

And contest cannot be joined in action to set aside deeds. — The contest of a will cannot be joined in an action to set aside and cancel deeds executed by testator, and alleged to have been procured through fraud, undue influence and mental incapacity of the grantor. Nesmith v. Vines, 248 Ala. 72, 26 So. 2d 265 (1946).

Judgment becomes conclusive evidence. — The judgment establishing the codicil as a part of the last will, revoking pro tanto the original will, becomes conclusive evidence that the two instruments should be admitted to probate in the probate court upon application. Caverno v. Webb, 239 Ala. 671, 196 So. 723 (1940).

A judgment of "will" or "no will" was not required where the trial court had erroneously overruled contestant's objection to the lack of proper proof of the execution of the will, and had ruled that the execution of the will had been sufficiently proved and admitted it in evidence, upon the proof of one subscribing witness since, had the trial court sustained contestant's objection to the will, then in all probability the proponents would have produced the other subscribing witness, or accounted for a failure to do so, and resorted to secondary evidence. Ferrell v. Minnifield, 275 Ala. 388, 155 So. 2d 345 (1963).

§ 43-8-200. Same — Parties; conclusiveness of judgment.

In the event a contest of the probate of a will is instituted in the circuit court, as is or may be authorized by law, all parties interested in the probate of the will, as devisees, legatees or otherwise, as well as those interested in the testator if he had died intestate, as heirs, distributees or next of kin, shall be made parties to the contest; and if there be minors or persons of unsound mind interested in the estate or in the probate of the will, they shall be represented by their legal guardian, if such they have; if they have no such guardian, the court shall appoint an attorney-at-law as guardian ad litem to represent their interest in the contest, and the final judgment in such contest proceedings shall be conclusive as to all matters which were litigated or could have been litigated in such contest; and no further proceedings shall ever be entertained in any courts of this state to probate or contest the probate of such will. (Code 1923, § 10638; Code 1940, T. 61, § 65; Code 1975, § 43-1-80.)

Code commissioner's note. — This section was originally codified as § 43-1-80 of the 1975 Code.

Guardian ad litem required for contestee only. — Where contestant of will alleged to be of unsound mind commenced the action by next friend, failure of trial court to appoint guardian ad litem for contestant held not to render judgment in will contest erroneous on its face, since this section requiring apppointment of guardian ad litem for party to will contest of unsound mind applied only to contestee of will. Thompson v. Earnest, 228 Ala. 641, 154 So. 797 (1934).

The last part of this section is not to be construed to prevent proceedings to effectuate the judgment entered in the contest proceedings. It merely declares the finality of the contest in circuit court. Caverno v. Webb, 239 Ala. 671, 196 So. 723 (1940).

Cited in Mitchell v. Nixon, 200 F.2d 50 (5th Cir. 1952); Goldthwaite v. Disciplinary Bd., 408 So. 2d 504 (Ala. 1982).

Collateral references. — 95 C.J.S., Wills, §§ 550, 581.

80 Am. Jur. 2d, Wills, § 1035.

§ 43-8-201. Same — Additional time for contest by infants and persons of unsound mind.

After the expiration of such six months, the validity of the will can only be contested by infants and persons of unsound mind who had no legal guardian at the time the will was admitted to probate, or who were not represented by a guardian ad litem, who are allowed 12 months after the appointment of a guardian, or, if none be appointed, 12 months from the termination of their respective disabilities in which to contest such will, but in no case to exceed 20 years from the time the will was admitted to probate; and also provided there has not been one contest instituted and prosecuted to final judgment in the circuit court as is provided for in sections 43-8-199 and 43-8-200; in which case the final judgment of the circuit court, court of civil appeals or supreme court shall be final and conclusive against all parties. (Code 1852, § 1656; Code 1867, § 1974; Code 1876, § 2338; Code 1886, § 2002; Code 1896, § 4299; Code 1907, § 6208; Code 1923, § 10639; Acts 1931, No. 731, p. 843; Code 1940, T. 61, § 66; Code 1975, § 43-1-81.)

Code commissioner's note. — This section was originally codified as § 43-1-81 of the 1975 Code.

Infants must have been potential contestants. — The additional extension given by this section was limited to infants who were potential contestants at the time of probate. Allen v. Pugh, 206 Ala. 10, 89 So. 470 (1921).

Minor's rights not affected. — The fact that some of the heirs at law of the deceased are barred under the statute by lapse of time from proceeding in circuit court to contest the will does not affect the right of a minor who is not barred, from maintaining her complaint for that purpose. Ellis v. Crawson, 147 Ala. 294, 41 So. 942 (1906).

Affidavits as to mental condition held insufficient. — Where issue decided in will contest judgment was whether contestant was of unsound mind so as to permit bringing contest 10 years after probate of will, affidavits of mental condition of contestant were insufficient to support review, since merely cumulative. Thompson v. Earnest, 228 Ala. 641, 154 So. 797 (1934).

Collateral references. — 94 C.J.S., Wills, §§ 8, 16-21.

§ 43-8-202. Same — Trial of issues by jury; consideration of witnesses' testimony.

The circuit court may, in such case, direct an issue to be tried by a jury, and on the trial before the jury, or hearing before the circuit judge, the testimony of the witnesses reduced to writing by the judge of probate, according to section 43-8-169, is evidence to be considered by the judge or jury. (Code 1852, § 1655; Code 1867, § 1973; Code 1876, § 2337; Code 1886, § 2001; Code 1896, § 4300; Code 1907, § 6209; Code 1923, § 10640; Code 1940, T. 61, § 67; Code 1975, § 43-1-82.)

Code commissioner's note. — This section was originally codified as § 43-1-82 of the 1975 Code.

In general. — The method of establishing the fact that the statutory requirements have been fulfilled need not be by the same kind or character of evidence in the circuit court as is required and as was pursued in the probate court. To hold that the attesting witnesses would again have to be produced or the same steps taken to prove same as the statute requires in the probating of the will in the probate court would, in effect, emasculate so much of this section as makes the written testimony taken under § 43-8-169 in the probate court admissible evidence in a contest of this character. Cummings v. McDonnell, 189 Ala. 96, 66 So. 717 (1914).

Written testimony is admissible. — Generally speaking, under this section, depositions of witnesses to the will, taken in the probate court upon the uncontested probate of the instrument, are admissible in a subsequent contest. Kay v. Elston, 205 Ala. 307, 87 So. 525 (1920).

In a trial under this section it was held error to refuse to allow the introduction in evidence of the testimony of a witness, taken by the judge of probate in substantial compliance with § 43-8-169, and it cannot be said that the mere fact of said witness's examination on this trial averted any effective prejudice to appellant attending the refusal to admit the matter stated. Stephens v. Richardson, 189 Ala. 360, 66 So. 497 (1914).

Unsigned depositions were admissible when not objected to. — In a will contest, unsigned depositions of witnesses to the will taken in the probate court on the uncontested probate were properly admitted, for, as objection was made on other specific grounds, the objection that the depositions were not signed was waived. Kay v. Elston, 205 Ala. 307, 87 So. 525 (1920).

Nature of the issue. — Where the complaint contesting the validity of the will alleged that the instrument had never been executed by the testatrix, and the answer specifically denied such allegations and specifically averred that the testatrix did sign the paper purporting to be a will, the only issue which could be framed for a jury under this section was the genuineness of the will; evidence of undue influence or fraud should not therefore have been received. Stephens v. Richardson, 189 Ala. 360, 66 So. 497 (1914).

Jury trial a matter of right. — This section is one of the cases where disputed facts are submitted to a jury as a matter of right. Alabama, T. & N. Ry. v. Aliceville Lumber Co., 199 Ala. 391, 74 So. 441 (1916); Lewis v. Martin, 210 Ala. 401, 98 So. 635 (1923); Nesmith v. Vines, 248 Ala. 72, 26 So. 2d 265 (1946).

Under this section when a jury is demanded, the duty upon the court to submit the issues to a jury is mandatory. Curry v. Holmes, 249 Ala. 545, 32 So. 2d 39 (1947).

Provided it is demanded. — It is not the duty of the judge, ex mero motu, to award an issue to be tried by a jury in all cases of a contested will before him. It is only when a jury is demanded by one of the parties that he is without discretion, and must award the issue. Mathews v. Forniss, 91 Ala. 157, 8 So. 661 (1890).

Where the right of trial by jury of controverted issues of fact was duly demanded and had as a matter of right under this section,

and not by the grace of the court, the verdict of that jury was not merely advisory to the court, but was required by law to be made the basis of the final judgment entered in said case. Lewis v. Martin, 210 Ala. 401, 98 So. 635 (1923).

And such demand is made before case is submitted. — To be availing, a demand for a jury trial must be made before the case is submitted, or else it is waived. Mathews v. Forniss, 91 Ala. 157, 8 So. 661 (1890).

Nature of such trial. — The jury may be empanelled by the judge, or he may direct the issues to a court of law for trial by jury. Ex parte Colvert, 188 Ala. 650, 65 So. 964 (1914); Hicks v. Allred, 281 Ala. 464, 204 So. 2d 813 (1967).

Any exceptions properly reserved will be considered on appeal. — When the issue devisavit vel non is tried by a jury and the verdict of the jury is made the basis of a final judgment of the circuit court, then the supreme court, upon appeal from such judgment, will consider any exceptions which were properly reserved during the trial of the issue by the jury. Ex parte Colvert, 188 Ala. 650, 65 So. 964 (1914).

Directed verdict on issue of undue influence not error. — In will contest after probate, giving affirmative charge (now directed verdict) for proponent on issue of undue influence was held not reversible error, notwithstanding that wife who was principal beneficiary had caused lawyer to come for notes prepared by testator to aid lawyer in preparing will, that evidence may have tended to show conference between testator and wife in preparing the notes, that preparation of will was not in keeping with prior declarations of testator, and that wife in accordance with testator's direction retained will in her possession, and did not reveal its existence until testator's death. Cook v. Morton, 241 Ala. 188, 1 So. 2d 890 (1941).

Judgment of probate court has no probative value. — On a contest in circuit court the judgment in the probate court has no probative value, and only serves to give direction to the order of procedure. Hancock v. Frazier, 264 Ala. 202, 86 So. 2d 389 (1956).

Note of testimony. — In the hearing of a contest in circuit court the testimony of the witnesses in probate court which has been reduced to writing should be shown in a note of testimony when a note is necessary. Hancock v. Frazier, 264 Ala. 202, 86 So. 2d 389 (1956).

Production of same witnesses unnecessary. — In view of this section which makes the evidence taken in probate court admissible in the circuit court, where the proceedings in the probate court show, by proof of two witnesses, or one and a proper accounting for the other, that the will was properly executed it is not necessary to produce the same witnesses again in a contest in the circuit court or to take steps to prove the execution of the will. Ferrell v. Minnifield, 275 Ala. 388, 155 So. 2d 345 (1963).

Cited in Miller v. Whittington, 202 Ala. 406,

80 So. 499 (1918); Ex parte Curry, 248 Ala. 384, 27 So. 2d 630 (1946).

Collateral references. — 95 C.J.S., Wills, §§ 445, 579.

ARTICLE 8.

CONSTRUCTION OF WILLS.

§ 43-8-220. Requirement that devisee survive testator by five days.

A devisee who does not survive the testator by five days is treated as if he predeceased the testator, unless the will of decedent contains some language dealing explicitly with simultaneous deaths or deaths in a common disaster, or requiring that the devisee survive the testator or survive the testator for a stated period in order to take under the will. (Acts 1982, No. 82-399, § 2-601.)

Commentary

This section parallels § 43-8-43 requiring an heir to survive by five days in order to inherit.

There was no comparable section previously in the Alabama law. Therefore, Alabama did not have a requirement that a devisee survive for any particular length of time in order to take. However, anti-simultaneous death clauses are routinely put in wills in order to reduce litigation, among other reasons. Such clauses may still be drafted into wills, but this section will tend to reduce litigation by eliminating some of the cases where order of death is an issue.

Collateral references. — 96 C.J.S., Wills, § 719.

80 Am. Jur. 2d, Wills, §§ 1698-1700.

Decree directing distribution of estate to person who is dead. 25 ALR 1563.

Time interval contemplated by provision of will or of statute of descent and distribution with reference to death of two persons simulta-neously or approximately at same time. 173 ALR 1254.

Relinquishment of interest by life beneficiary in possession as accelerating remainder of which there is substitutional gift in case primary remainderman does not survive life beneficiary. 7 ALR4th 1084.

§ 43-8-221. Choice of law as to meaning and effect of wills.

The meaning and legal effect of a disposition in a will shall be determined by the local law of a particular state selected by the testator in his instrument unless the application of that law is contrary to the provisions relating to the elective share described in sections 43-8-70 through 43-8-75, the provisions relating to exempt property and allowances described in sections 43-8-110 through 43-8-113, or any other public policy of this state otherwise applicable to the disposition. (Acts 1982, No. 82-399, § 2-602.)

Commentary

New York Estates, Powers & Trusts Law, Sec. 3-5.1(h) and Illinois Probate Act, Sec. 896(b) direct respect for a testator's choice of local law with reference to personal and intangible property situated in the enacting state. This provision goes further and enables a testator to select the law of a particular state for purposes of interpreting his will without regard to the location of property covered thereby. This section should be accepted as necessary and desirable to add to the utility of wills. Choice of law regarding formal validity of a will is in § 43-8-135.

The explicit reference to the elective share described in article 4 of this chapter, and the exemptions and allowances described in article 6 of this chapter, embody policies of this state which may not be circumvented by a testator's choice of applicable law.

Collateral references. — 95 C.J.S., Wills, §§ 587, 692.

80 Am. Jur. 2d, Wills, § 1122.

Conflict of laws respecting revocation of will. 9 ALR2d 1412.

Conflict of laws as regards survival of cause of action and revival of pending action upon death of party. 42 ALR2d 1170.

Escheat of personal property of intestate domiciled or resident in another state. 50 ALR2d 1375.

Right of nonresident surviving spouse or minor children to allowance of property exempt from administration or to family allowance from local estate of nonresident decedent. 51 ALR2d 1026.

What law governs in determining who are "heirs," "heirs at law," "issue," "next of kin," or the like, who will take legacy or bequest under terms of will. 52 ALR2d 490.

Conflict of laws as to legitimacy or legitimation or as to rights of illegitimates, as affecting descent and distribution of decedent's estate. 87 ALR2d 1274.

Conflict of laws regarding election for or against will, and effect in one jurisdiction of election in another. 69 ALR3d 1081.

§ 43-8-222. Controlling effect of intention of testator.

The intention of a testator as expressed in his will controls the legal effect of his dispositions. The rules of construction expressed in the succeeding sections of this article apply unless a contrary intention is indicated by the will. (Acts 1982, No. 82-399, § 2-603.)

Commentary

Alabama law is unchanged by this section. Werneth v. Hanly, 262 Ala. 219, 78 So. 2d 299 (1955); Baker v. Wright, 257 Ala. 697, 60 So. 2d 825 (1952).

Collateral references. — 95 C.J.S., Wills, §§ 586-588.

80 Am. Jur. 2d, Wills, §§ 1127-1139.

Admissibility of extrinsic evidence upon issue of testamentary intent. 21 ALR2d 319.

Validity, construction, and application of statutory requirement that will beneficiary survive testator for specified time. 88 ALR3d 1339.

§ 43-8-223. Construction of will to pass all property, including after-acquired property.

A will is construed to pass all property which the testator owns at his death including property acquired after the execution of the will. (Acts 1982, No. 82-399, § 2-604.)

Commentary

In the absence of a contrary intention appearing in the will, or in the instrument conveying the estate, or in the instrument by which the property is acquired, a general bequest or devise will dispose of all property held by the decedent at death including after-acquired property. Former §§ 43-1-6 and 43-1-12 (1975); Wagar v. Marshburn, 241 Ala. 73, 1 So. 2d 303 (1941); Balkeney v. DuBose, 167 Ala. 627, 52 So. 746 (1910).

Editor's note. — In light of the similarity of the subject matter, decisions under former § 43-1-6 are included in the annotations for this section.

Legal estate in land not necessary. — It is not essential that the testator should be seized of a legal estate at the time when the will is made. If he has an equitable estate merely, it is governed by precisely the same rules as if it was purely legal. Meader v. Sorsby, 2 Ala. 712 (1841).

Wills should be construed to uphold **rather than defeat devises.** Rowe v. Newman, 290 Ala. 289, 276 So. 2d 412 (1972).

Will conveying whole estate. — See Elyton Land Co. v. McElrath, 53 F. 763 (5th Cir. 1893).

Collateral references. — 95 C.J.S., Wills, § 615. 96 C.J.S., Wills, §§ 756, 821.

80 Am. Jur. 2d, Wills, §§ 1175, 1356-1362.

Extent of rights of surviving spouse who elects to take against will in profits of or increase in value of estate accruing after testator's death. 7 ALR4th 989.

§ 43-8-224. Anti-lapse provision; applicability to deceased devisees and to class gifts.

If a devisee who is a grandparent or a lineal descendant of a grandparent of the testator is dead at the time of execution of the will, fails to survive the testator, or is treated as if he predeceased the testator, the issue of the deceased devisee who survive the testator by five days take in place of the deceased devisee and if they are all of the same degree of kinship to the devisee they take equally, but if of unequal degree then those of more remote degree take by representation. One who would have been a devisee under a class gift if he had survived the testator is treated as a devisee for purposes of this section whether his death occurred before or after the execution of the will. (Acts 1982, No. 82-399, § 2-605.)

Commentary

This section prevents lapse by death of a devisee before the testator if the devisee is a relative and leaves issue who survives the testator. A relative is one related to the testator by kinship and is limited to those who can inherit under § 43-8-42 (through grandparents); it does not include persons related by marriage. Issue include adopted persons and illegitimates to the extent they would inherit from the devisee; see §§ 43-8-1 and 43-8-48. While not by any express holding, the Alabama court seems to agree by implication that Alabama's lapse statute includes adopted children. Kirkley v. Bailey, 282 Ala. 115, 209 So. 2d 398 (1968). This section is expressly applicable to class gifts, thereby eliminating a frequent source of litigation. It also applies to the so-called "void" gift, where the devisee is dead at the time of execution of the will. This effect, though contrary to some decisions, seems justified. It still seems likely that the testator would want the issue of a person included in a class term but dead when the will is made to be treated like the issue of another member of the class who was alive at the time the will was executed but who died before the testator.

Alabama's lapse statute was former § 43-1-13, which prevented lapse if the devise or bequest was to a "child or other descendant of the testator. ..." This section is broader, therefore, than the previous Alabama statute. In addition, this section attempts to answer some questions, e.g., questions arising from "void gifts" and class gifts, which were not answered by the previous Alabama statute and which have not been answered specifically by case law in Alabama. This section seems to answer these questions according to the probable intent of the testator.

The five day survival requirement stated in § 43-8-220 does not require issue who would be substituted for their parent by this section to survive their parent by any set period.

Section 43-8-45 describes the method of division when a taking by representation is directed by this act.

Editor's note. — In light of the similarity of the subject matter, decisions under former § 43-1-13 are included in the annotations for this section.

General effect of section. — Former § 43-1-13 forbade the lapse of a devise or legacy because the legatee or devisee, being a descendant of the testator, died before the testator, if such legatee or devisee left a descendant. And it substituted the descendants of the legatee or devisee, for such legatee or devisee, to the right of receiving the legacy or devise; and provided for an apportionment among such descendants, of the property bequeathed, in a manner conformable to the law which would have governed, if the devisee or legatee had survived the testator and died intestate. Jones v. Jones, 37 Ala. 646 (1861); Kling v. Goodman, 236 Ala. 297, 181 So. 745 (1938).

No distinction could be made between devises and legacies in the operation of former § 43-1-13. Jones v. Jones, 37 Ala. 646 (1861).

Deceased legatee's child gets what legatee would have received. — Where testatrix devised estate to children share and share alike, and one of legatees who was indebted to testatrix predeceased her, leaving descendants, deceased legatee's children upon death of testatrix were entitled to legatee's share less the amount of indebtedness owed to testatrix, in same manner as legatee would have shared had he survived testatrix. Kling v. Goodman, 236 Ala. 297, 181 So. 745 (1938).

Legacy which descends to the descendants of the named legatee as substituted legatees is the same legacy and subject to the same rules in making distribution between them and other legatees named in will. Kling v. Goodman, 236 Ala. 297, 181 So. 745 (1938).

Where testator directed his executor to sell a plantation and divide the proceeds giving one-sixth to each of testator's five children and one-eighteenth to each of three grandchildren

and the will did not contain a residuary clause, death of one child leaving a daughter as sole heir prior to testator's death did not work a "lapse" as to his interest but it passed to the daughter, and death of another child without descendants worked a lapse as to his interest which was required to be administered and distributed as in case of intestacy. Warrick v. Woodham, 243 Ala. 585, 11 So. 2d 150 (1942).

Legatee's debt is an asset of the estate. — Where testatrix devised estate to children share and share alike and legatee indebted to testatrix predeceased her, leaving children, legatee's indebtedness would be charged as an asset of the estate of the testatrix to be divided amont the legatees, of which deceased legatee's share, less the amount of indebtedness, would be distributed among his descendants. Kling v. Goodman, 236 Ala. 297, 181 So. 745 (1938).

Death of remainderman. — Where a remainderman dies during the continuance of the life estate his rights are vested in his descendants. Pierce v. Fulmer, 165 Ala. 344, 51 So. 728 (1910).

Devise to predeceased brothers-in-law lapsed. — Under will bequeathing one-third of testatrix' residuary estate in trust to be used for the support of testatrix' sister-in-law, any part of gift remaining undisposed of after the sister-in-law's death to be given equally to testator's two brothers-in-law, brothers-in-law were held devisees in remainder and their gifts lapsed where they predeceased testatrix with no provision for that contingency in the will. Morgan County Nat'l Bank v. Nelson, 244 Ala. 374, 13 So. 2d 765 (1943).

And complaint showed on its face that claimants had no interest. — Bill (now complaint) alleging that devisees who were testatrix' brothers-in-law predeceased her with no provision for that contingency in the will, and failing to allege that devisees left heirs or distributees, established that the devises lapsed, and therefore showed on its face that if such heirs or distributees existed they had no interest in the subject matter of the will. Morgan County Nat'l Bank v. Nelson, 244 Ala. 374, 13 So. 2d 765 (1943).

Collateral references. — 96 C.J.S., Wills, §§ 719-746, 921-973, 1197-1222.

80 Am. Jur. 2d, Wills, §§ 1403-1411, 1671, 1672.

Time of ascertainment of membership with respect to devise or bequest to class which takes effect at testator's death. 6 ALR2d 1342.

Validity and construction of limitation over to another in event that original beneficiary should die before payment or receipt of devise or legacy. 59 ALR3d 1043.

§ 43-8-225. Effect of failure of testamentary provisions.

(a) Except as provided in section 43-8-224 if a devise other than a residuary devise fails for any reason, it becomes a part of the residue.

(b) Except as provided in section 43-8-224 if the residue is devised to two or more persons and the share of one of the residuary devisees fails for any reason, his share passes to the other residuary devisee, or to other residuary devisees in proportion to their interests in the residue. (Acts 1982, No. 82-399, § 2-606.)

Commentary

If a devise fails by reason of lapse and the conditions of § 43-8-224 are met, the latter section governs rather than this section. There is also a special rule for renunciation contained in article 11 of this chapter; a renounced devise may be governed by either § 43-8-224 or this section, depending on the circumstances.

With regard to subsection (a) of this section, Alabama prior to this Act made a distinction between real and personal property. Alabama has been in accord with the provision for personal property. First National Bank of Mobile v. Hartwell, 232 Ala. 413, 168 So. 446 (1936); Caldwell v. Caldwell, 204 Ala. 161, 85 So. 493 (1920); Woodroof v. Hundley, 147 Ala. 287, 39 So. 907 (1905). For real property, all lapsed devises became intestate property and passed to the testator's heirs at law (Powell v. Pearson, 222 Ala. 199, 1313 So. 571 (1930); Little v. Ennis, 207 Ala. 111, 92 So. 167 (1922); Johnson v. Holifield, 82 Ala. 123, 2 So. 753 (1886), but if the testator had no heirs competent to take the real property, it went to the residuary devisee. Former § 43-1-5 (1975).

Since there is no distinction between real and personal property under this act, the provision seems consistent with Alabama policy.

With regard to subsection (b) of this section, Alabama law may have been to the contrary where one of several residuary legatees died before the testator. In such a case and if the residuary estate was to be held by them in common, the portion of the deceased legatee did not survive to his co-legatees, but went to the testator's next of kin according to the statute of distribution. Hamlet v. Johnson, 26 Ala. 557 (1855). The Alabama case is a very old case, however, and this section is consistent with other provisions of this act.

Collateral references. — 96 C.J.S., Wills, §§ 1223-1226.

79 Am. Jur. 2d, Wills, §§ 1147-1153, 1671, 1673.

Validity, construction and effect of express provisions in will for severance of good from bad in event of partial invalidity. 80 ALR 1210.

Effect of residuary clause to pass property acquired by testator's estate after his death. 39 ALR3d 1390.

May parts of will be upheld notwithstanding failure of other parts for lack of testamentary mental capacity or undue influence. 64 ALR3d 261.

§ 43-8-226. Specific devise of securities; change in securities; accessions; nonademption.

(a) If the testator intended a specific devise of certain securities rather than the equivalent value thereof, the specific devisee is entitled only to:

(1) As much of the devised securities as is a part of the estate at time of the testator's death;

(2) Any additional or other securities of the same entity derived from the securities specifically devised and owned by the testator by reason of action initiated by the entity excluding any acquired by exercise of purchase options;

(3) Securities of another entity derived from the securities specifically devised and owned by the testator as a result of a merger, consolidation, reorganization or other similar action initiated by the entity; and

(4) Any additional securities of the entity owned by the testator as a result of a plan of reinvestment if it is a regulated investment company, which is defined in section 851 of the Federal Internal Revenue Code of 1954 as amended.

(b) Distributions prior to death with respect to a specifically devised security not provided for in subsection (a) of this section are not part of the specific devise. (Acts 1982, No. 82-399, § 2-607.)

Commentary

Alabama did not previously seem to have any statement of law comparable to subsection (a) of this section. The Alabama case of Ullmann v. First National Bank of Mobile, 273 Ala. 154, 137 So. 2d 765 (1961) discusses ademption when there is a specific bequest of securities, but the case is not directly in point and seems consistent as to policy.

Subsection (b) of this section is intended to codify existing law to the effect that cash dividends declared and payable as of a record date occurring before the testator's death do not pass as a part of the specific devise even though paid after death. See § 4, Revised Uniform Principal and Income Act. Alabama has not enacted the Revised Uniform Principal and Income Act. Subsection (b) is consistent with § 19-3-273, which is part of an earlier Uniform Principal and Income Act that has been enacted in Alabama.

Collateral references. — 96 C.J.S., Wills, §§ 756, 1172-1181.
80 Am. Jur. 2d, Wills, §§ 1701, 1716.

§ 43-8-227. Nonademption of specific devises in certain cases; proceeds of sale, condemnation, insurance or foreclosure; sale by guardian or curator.

(a) A specific devisee has the right to the remaining specifically devised property and:

(1) Any balance of the purchase price (together with any security interest) owing from a purchaser to the testator at death by reason of sale of the property;

(2) Any amount of a condemnation award for the taking of the property unpaid at death;

(3) Any proceeds unpaid at death on fire or casualty insurance on the property; and

(4) Property owned by testator at his death as a result of foreclosure, or obtained in lieu of foreclosure, of the security for a specifically devised obligation.

(b) If specifically devised property is sold by a guardian or curator, or if a condemnation award or insurance proceeds are paid to a guardian or curator as a result of condemnation, fire, or casualty, the specific devisee has the right to a general pecuniary devise equal to the net sale price, the condemnation award, or the insurance proceeds. This subsection does not apply if after the sale, condemnation or casualty, it is adjudicated that the disability of the testator has ceased and the testator survives the adjudication by one year. The right of the specific devisee under this subsection is reduced by any right he had under subsection (a) of this section. (Acts 1982, No. 82-399, § 2-608.)

Commentary

The intent of this section is to prevent ademption in all cases involving sale, condemnation or destruction of specifically devised assets where testator's death occurred before the proceeds of the sale, condemnation or any insurance, had been paid to the testator.

Prior Alabama law can be said to be in accord with the general policy stated in this section. Former § 43-1-10 provided that "when any testator, after making his will, makes any contract for the conveyance of any property devised in such will, and the whole or any part of the purchase money remains unpaid to such testator at his death, the disposition of the property by such contract is not a revocation of the devise, . . . unless it clearly appears by the contract, or some other instrument in writing to be intended as a revocation . . . ." However this section specifically mentions additional situations. Alabama did not previously have any statement of law specifically covering the situation mentioned in subsection (b) of this section.

Cross references. — As to disclaimer of any property, property right, or interest in property, see article 11 of this chapter.

Editor's note. — In light of the similarity of the subject matter, decisions under former § 43-1-10 are included in the annotations for this section.

In general. — It seems to be the intention of the legislature to declare that an alteration of the estate devised or bequeathed does not, per se, revoke the will, but that whatever interest remains in the testator passes by the will to his devisee or legatee, unless the intention to revoke expressly appears. Powell v. Powell, 30 Ala. 697 (1857); Sims v. Moore, 288 Ala. 630, 264 So. 2d 484 (1972).

Effect of former section. — One effect of former § 43-1-10 was to avoid the revocation of a will by the simple act of a contract to sell or a sale of the property devised thereby, and another was to substitute, for the property so contracted away by the will-maker, the unpaid purchase money therefor, whether it be all or only a part. When recovered by the executor of the testator, the prescription of said section was that it be paid to the devisee of such property, that is, the devised property that the testator, in life, had sold or contracted to sell. Scarbrough v. Scarbrough, 176 Ala. 141, 57 So. 820 (1912); Boise v. Merry, 266 Ala. 286, 96 So. 2d 448 (1957); Benedict v. Little, 288 Ala. 638, 264 So. 2d 491 (1972).

Former section as part of every devise. — It may be said that former § 43-1-10 was written into every devise of lands situate in Alabama, as if to say, on the face of the will, "I devise this land or any unpaid purchase money due me thereon at my death, to the persons named in the will." Phillips v. Phillips, 213 Ala. 27, 104 So. 234 (1925).

The application of former § 43-1-10 was not restricted to contracts to sell property. Sims v. Moore, 288 Ala. 630, 264 So. 2d 484 (1972).

But extended to any contract to convey property. — Under former § 43-1-10, the disposition of property by any contract for its conveyance prevented a revocation of a devise of the property by the testator in his will, and passed the unpaid purchase money to the devisee. Sims v. Moore, 288 Ala. 630, 264 So. 2d 484 (1972).

Where no intention to revoke a devise is made to appear by the contract for conveyance, the principal balance payable under such a sale contract goes to the devisee of lands, subject to the use of the lands by the executor for payment of estate taxes. Rowe v. Newman, 290 Ala. 289, 276 So. 2d 412 (1972).

Intent to exclude unpaid purchase money must be expressed in writing. — Former § 43-1-10 declared the unpaid purchase money should not be taken out of the operation of the devise unless such intent was clearly expressed by an instrument in writing. Slaughter v. Stephens, 81 Ala. 418, 2 So. 145 (1887); Boise v. Merry, 266 Ala. 286, 96 So. 2d 448 (1957). And hence parol evidence that testator was keeping the proceeds from the sale of devised land separate, and evidence as to his intentions and declarations of intent relating thereto, was incompetent in an action for construction of the will. Phillips v. Phillips, 213 Ala. 27, 104 So. 234 (1925).

Money held in this state is subject to administration by courts of state. — In view of former § 43-1-10, unpaid purchase money of devised lands sold by testator prior to death, and held in the state, was subject to administration and distribution by the courts of the state, although the testator at the time of his death was domiciled in another state. Phillips v. Phillips, 213 Ala. 27, 104 So. 234 (1925).

Collateral references. — 96 C.J.S., Wills, §§ 1172-1181.

80 Am. Jur. 2d, Wills, § 1701.

Property purchased with proceeds of sale of subject of devise or bequest as passing thereunder. 3 ALR 1497.

§ 43-8-228. Nonexoneration.

A specific devise passes subject to any mortgage interest existing at the date of death, without right of exoneration, regardless of a general directive in the will to pay debts. (Acts 1982, No. 82-399, § 2-609.)

Commentary

This section governs the substantive rights of the devisee. The common-law rule of exoneration of the specific devise is abolished by this section, and the contrary rule is adopted.

Apparently Alabama has previously followed the common-law rule, but the courts have tended to go to some length to find some hint of the testator's intention. See Fulenwider v. Birmingham Trust & Savings Company, 222 Ala. 95, 130 So. 801 (1930); Pitts v. Campbell, 173 Ala. 604, 55 So. 500 (1911). If the testator desires that the property pass to the distributee subject to a mortgage, lien or other charge, that desire will be given effect. Austin v. Pepperman, 278 Ala. 551, 179 So. 2d 299 (1965). This section will help to clarify the ambiguity in Alabama.

For the rule as to exempt property, see § 43-8-111.

Collateral references. — 80 Am. Jur. 2d, Wills, §§ 1761, 1762, 1765.

Validity of provisions of instrument creating legal estate attempting to exempt it from claims of creditors. 80 ALR 1007.

Direction in will for payment of debts and expenses as subjecting exempt homestead to their payment. 103 ALR 257.

Direction in will for payment of debts of testator, or for payment of specified debt, as affecting debts or debt barred by limitation. 109 ALR 1441.

Conclusiveness of testator's statement as to amount of debt or advancement to be charged against legacy or devise. 98 ALR2d 273.

Right of heir or devisee to have realty exonerated from lien thereon at expense of personal estate. 4 ALR3d 1023.

§ 43-8-229. Exercise of power of appointment.

A general residuary clause in a will, or a will making general disposition of all of the testator's property, does not exercise a power of appointment held by the testator unless specific reference is made to the power or there is some other indication of intention to include the property subject to the power. (Acts 1982, No. 82-399, § 2-610.)

Commentary

Although this act generally has avoided any provisions relating to powers of appointment, there is a great need for a clear statement of the rule on the subject of exercise of a power of appointment by a will purporting to dispose of all of the donee's property, whether by a standard residuary clause or a general recital of property passing under the will. The rule stated in this section is based on two reasons: (1) This is still the majority rule in the United States; and (2) Most powers of appointment are created in marital deduction trusts and the donor would prefer to have the property pass under his trust instrument unless the donee affirmatively manifests an intent to exercise the power. Prior Alabama law is in accord with the rule stated in this section. United States v. Merchants National Bank of Mobile, 261 F.2d 570 (5th Cir. 1958); Mastin v. Merchants National Bank of Mobile, 278 Ala. 261, 177 So. 2d 817 (1965); Cramton v. Rutledge, 157 Ala. 141, 47 So. 214 (1908). See also, Jones, "Consequences of an Ineffective Appointment — Capture," 18 Ala. L. Rev. 229 (1966).

Under this section and § 43-8-222 the intent to exercise the power is effective if it is "indicated by the will." This wording permits a court to find the manifest intent if the language of the will interpreted in light of all the surrounding circumstances shows that the donee intended an exercise, except, of course, if the donor has conditioned exercise on an express reference to the original creating instrument. In other words, the rule on interpretation of the donee's will would be available.

Collateral references. — 72 C.J.S., Powers, § 40.

Am. Jur. 2d, Powers of Appointment and Alienation, §§ 39-46.

Disposition of all or residue of testator's property, without referring to power of appointment, as constituting sufficient manifestation of intention to exercise power, in absence of statute. 15 ALR3d 346.

Marriage of testator or birth of testator's child as revoking child's will previously made in exercise of power of appointment. 92 ALR3d 1244.

§ 43-8-230. Construction of generic terms to accord with relationships as defined for intestate succession; when person born out of wedlock treated as child of father.

Half bloods, adopted persons, and persons born out of wedlock are included in class gift terminology and terms of relationship in accordance with rules for determining relationships for purposes of intestate succession. However, a person born out of wedlock is not treated as the child of the father unless the person is openly and notoriously so treated by the father. (Acts 1982, No. 82-399, § 2-611.)

Commentary

The purpose of this section is to facilitate a modern construction of gifts, usually class gifts, in wills.

Unless the language of the creating instrument expressly excludes an adopted child of a child of the creator of the interest, an adopted child is within the term "descendant" and is permitted to take as a descendant through an adopting parent. Zimmerman v. First National Bank of Birmingham, 348 So. 2d 1359 (Ala. 1977); McCaleb v. Brown, 344 So. 2d 485 (Ala. 1977); but *cf.*, Whitfield v. Matthews, 334 So. 2d 876 (Ala. 1976). Unless there is a clear statement expressing a contrary intent, there is a presumption in Alabama today that adopted children are within class designations applying to natural children of the adopting parents. Seller's v. Blackwell, 378 So. 2d 1106 (Ala. 1979); Gotlieb v. Klotzman, 369 So. 2d 798 (Ala. 1979); Southside Baptist Church v. Drennen, 362 So. 2d 854 (Ala. 1978). An adopted child can be excluded from an estate by the testator. Palmore v. Inghram, 373 So. 2d 312 (Ala. 1979).

Unless a child born out of wedlock is legitimated under one of the methods provided for legitimation in Alabama, a child "born out of wedlock" will not be included with class designations usually applying to natural children of the father. Shelly v. Woodyard, 382 So. 2d 810 (Ala. 1980); Cowart v. Wheeler, 378 So. 2d 732 (Ala. 1979); Everage v. Gibson, 372 So. 2d 829 (Ala. 1979).

Section 26-10-5 provides that an adopted child "shall be invested with every legal right, privilege, obligation, and relation in respect to education, maintenance and the rights of inheritance to real estate, and to the distribution of personal estate on the death of such adopting parent or parents as if born to them in lawful wedlock." The rights of inheritance by half bloods were previously stated in former § 43-3-5 and the rights of inheritance for bastards were previously stated in former § 43-3-7. Legitimation of bastards is prescribed in §§ 26-11-1 through 26-11-3. However, the statutes referred to here are not directly in point on rules of construction for wills in Alabama.

This section states rules of construction which are consistent with the treatment of these persons in intestacy under this act and which are consistent with current constitutional analyses of these terms. The section also seems to be consistent with the present trend of judicial construction of these terms by the Alabama court.

Collateral references. — 95 C.J.S., Wills, §§ 643-718.

80 Am. Jur. 2d, Wills, §§ 1459-1475.

Illegitimate child as a "child" within statute limiting the right or amount of disposition by will by one survived by a child. 23 ALR 400.

Right of illegitimate to take under testamentary gift to "heirs." 27 ALR2d 1232.

Testamentary gift to class or group of specified relationship as including those of half-blood. 49 ALR2d 1362.

Adopted child as within class in testamentary gift, 86 ALR2d 12.

Wills: Gift to persons individually named but also described in terms of relationship to testator or another as class gift. 13 ALR4th 978.

§ 43-8-231. Ademption by satisfaction.

Property which a testator gave in his lifetime to a person is treated as a satisfaction of a devise to that person in whole or in part, only if the will provides for deduction of the lifetime gift, or the testator declares in a contemporaneous writing that the gift is to be deducted from the devise or is in satisfaction of the devise, or the devisee acknowledges in writing that the gift is in satisfaction. For purposes of partial satisfaction, property given during lifetime is valued as of the time the devisee came into possession or enjoyment of the property or as of the time of death of the testator, whichever occurs first. (Acts 1982, No. 82-399, § 2-612.)

Commentary

This section parallels § 43-8-49 on advancements and follows the same policy of requiring written evidence that lifetime gifts are to be taken into account in distribution of an estate, whether testate or intestate. Although courts traditionally call this "ademption by satisfaction" when a will is involved, and "advancement" when the estate is intestate, the difference in terminology is not significant. Some wills expressly provide for lifetime advances by a hotchpot clause. Where the will is silent the above section would require either the testator to declare in writing that the gift is an advance or satisfaction or the devisee to acknowledge the same in writing. The second sentence on value accords with § 43-8-49 and would apply if property such as stock is given. If the devise is specific, a gift of the specific property during lifetime would adeem the devise by extinction rather than by satisfaction, and this section would be inapplicable. If a devisee to whom an advancement is made predeceases the testator and his issue take under § 43-8-224, they take the same devise as their ancestor; if the devise is reduced by reason of this section as to the ancestor, it is automatically reduced as to his issue. In this respect the rule in testacy differs from that in intestacy; see § 43-8-49.

In Alabama prior to this act, the intention of the testator was the controlling factor in determining whether a particular legacy or devise was adeemed by satisfaction (Roberts v. Weatherford, 10 Ala. 72 (1846) or by the transfer of property. Ullman v. First National Bank of Mobile, 273 Ala. 154, 137 So. 2d 765 (1961); Willis v. Barrow, 218 Ala. 549, 119 So. 678 (1929). A charge or incumbrance on any real or personal property as security did not affect an ademption, unless it appeared from the will, or the instrument creating the charge or incumbrance, that such was the intention of the testator. Former § 43-1-11 (1975). Therefore, prior Alabama law seems to be consistent with this section. However, this section was enacted because the probable effect will be to reduce litigation by specifically providing how the testator's intention that a property transfer is an ademption by satisfaction must be stated in a contemporaneous writing.

I. General Consideration.
II. Decisions Under Prior Law.

I. GENERAL CONSIDERATION.

Collateral references. — 96 C.J.S., Wills, § 1178.
80 Am. Jur. 2d, Wills, §§ 1719-1734.

II. DECISIONS UNDER PRIOR LAW.

Editor's note. — In light of the similarity of the subject matter, decisions under former § 43-1-11 are included in the annotations for this section.

Subsequent mortgage on entire property does not per se revoke prior bequests. — Where the entire subject matter of the bequests was covered by a mortgage, former § 43-1-11 presented an insuperable barrier to the conclusion that the bequests were revoked by the subsequent mortgage. Stubbs v. Houston, 33 Ala. 55 (1859).

The mortgage could not, of itself, effect a revocation of such a bequest, nor could any subsequent conveyance of a part of the property, or change in its character, effect such revocation. Any interest, or right of redemption or other right remaining in the testator at his death, would fall within the operation of the bequest. Stubbs v. Houston, 33 Ala. 55 (1859).

Ademption of legacy. — A legacy of a thing which is not in existence or has been disposed of, so that it does not form part of testator's estate at time of his death, is extinguished or adeemed. Carter v. First Nat'l Bank, 237 Ala. 47, 185 So. 361 (1938).

ARTICLE 9.

MISCELLANEOUS PROVISIONS.

§ 43-8-250. Contracts concerning succession, etc.; no presumption of nonrevocation from joint or mutual wills.

A contract to make a will or devise, or not to revoke a will or devise, or to die intestate, if executed after January 1, 1983, can be established only by:

(1) Provisions of a will stating material provisions of the contract;

(2) An express reference in a will to a contract and extrinsic evidence proving the terms of the contract; or

(3) A writing signed by the decedent evidencing the contract.

The execution of a joint will or mutual wills does not create a presumption of a contract not to revoke the will or wills. (Acts 1982, No. 82-399, § 2-701.)

Commentary

It is the purpose of this section to tighten the methods by which contracts concerning succession may be proved. Oral contracts not to revoke wills have given rise to much litigation in a number of states; and in many states if two persons execute a single document as their joint will, this gives rise to a presumption that the parties had contracted not to revoke the will except by consent of both.

This section requires that either the will must set forth the material provisions of the contract, or the will must make express reference to the contract and extrinsic evidence prove the terms of contract, or there must be a separate writing signed by the decedent evidencing the contract. Oral testimony regarding the contract is permitted if the will makes reference to the contract, but this provision of the statute is not intended to affect normal rules regarding admissibility of evidence.

This section is consistent with prior Alabama law. Section 8-9-2 (1975) requires that every agreement, contract or promise to make a will or to devise or bequeath any real or personal property or right, title or interest therein must be in writing and subscribed by the party to be charged. However, this section states explicitly and clearly a rule which otherwise requires some deduction from the Alabama cases. See, Wagar v. Marshburn, 241 Ala. 73, 1 So. 2d 303 (1941); Allen v. Bromberg, 163 Ala. 620, 50 So. 884 (1909); and Allen v. Bromberg, 147 Ala. 317, 41 So. 771 (1906). But *cf.,* Walker v. Yarbrough, 200 Ala. 458, 76 So. 390 (1917).

Collateral references. — 94 C.J.S., Wills, § 111.

79 Am. Jur. 2d, Wills, §§ 63, 64, 327, 384, 385, 387, 501, 768-770.

Right of beneficiary to enforce contract between third persons to provide for him by will. 2 ALR 1193; 33 ALR 739; 73 ALR 1395.

Remedies for breach of decedent's agreement to devise, bequeath, or leave property as compensation for services. 69 ALR 14; 106 ALR 742.

Construction of contract not to make a will. 32 ALR2d 370.

Remedies during promisor's lifetime for breach of agreement to give property at death. 8 ALR3d 930.

Measure of damages for breach of contract to will property. 65 ALR3d 632.

§ 43-8-251. Renunciation of succession.

Renunciation of succession shall be through compliance with Article 11 of this chapter or as otherwise provided by law. (Acts 1982, No. 82-399, § 2-801.)

Commentary

Alabama has a comprehensive disclaimer of property interests act, the provisions of which are also adopted for application in this act. The Alabama Uniform Disclaimer of Property Interests Act (Article 11 of this chapter) is drafted so that a person following the requirements of that act will not only affect disposition of property interests, but certain tax benefits will result under Internal Revenue Code of 1954 (as amended) § 2518. At common law, a disclaimer or renunciation "seasonably made" was effective to determine disposition of property interests. That common-law rule is not inconsistent with the Alabama Disclaimer of Property Interests Act and therefore probably still provides another means of affecting the disposition of property interests even though the tax benefits might not be achieved. The phrase here, "as otherwise provided by law," recognizes that the common-law rule may still be applicable to affect dispositions of property interests, plus it will prevent conflicts if the Alabama legislature subsequently provides other means for disclaiming property interests.

Collateral references. — 96 C.J.S., Wills, §§ 1148, 1150, 1151.
80 Am. Jur. 2d, Wills, §§ 1597-1606.

§ 43-8-252. Effect of divorce, annulment, or decree of separation.

(a) A person who is divorced from the decedent or whose marriage to the decedent has been annulled is not a surviving spouse unless, by virtue of a subsequent marriage, he is married to the decedent at the time of death. A decree of separation which does not terminate the status of husband and wife is not a divorce for purposes of this section.

(b) For purposes of sections 43-8-40 through 43-8-49, 43-8-55 through 43-8-58, 43-8-70 through 43-8-76, 43-8-90, 43-8-91, and 43-8-110 through 43-8-113, a surviving spouse does not include:

(1) A person who obtains or consents to a final decree or judgment of divorce from the decedent or an annulment of their marriage, which decree or judgment is not recognized as valid in this state, unless they subsequently participate in a marriage ceremony purporting to marry each to the other, or subsequently live together as man and wife;

(2) A person who, following a decree or judgment of divorce or annulment obtained by the decedent, participates in a marriage ceremony with a third person; or

(3) A person who is a party to a valid proceeding concluded by an order purporting to terminate all marital property rights. (Acts 1982, No. 82-399, § 2-802.)

Commentary

See § 43-8-137 for similar provisions relating to the effect of divorce to revoke devises to a spouse.

The effect of divorce on testamentary provisions for a spouse of Alabama decedents is covered in former § 43-1-8 (1975). The effect is a pro tanto revocation of that portion of the will. Because the section applied only to the will of a woman, former § 43-1-8 (1975) was declared unconstitutional. Parker v. Hall, 362 So. 2d 875 (Ala. 1978).

Although some preexisting statutes barred the surviving spouse for desertion or adultery, this section requires some definitive legal act to bar the surviving spouse. Normally, this is divorce. Subsection (a) of this section states an obvious proposition, but subsection (b) of this section deals with the difficult problem of invalid divorce or annulment, which is particularly frequent as to foreign divorce decrees but may arise as to a local decree where there is some defect in jurisdiction; the basic principle underlying these provisions is estoppel against the surviving spouse. Where there is only a legal separation, rather than a divorce, succession patterns are not affected; but if the separation is accompanied by a complete property settlement, this may operate under § 43-8-72 as a renunciation of benefits under a prior will and by intestate succession.

This section is consistent with prior Alabama law. A divorce from the bonds of matrimony barred the wife of her dower and of any distributive share in the personal estate of her husband. Former § 43-5-4 (1975); Hinson v. Bush, 84 Ala. 368, 4 So. 410 (1887). There was previously no similar provisions applying to a husband with regard to the estate of a deceased wife, but this situation has occurred because a surviving husband had no curtesy-type interest in the estate of a deceased wife unless the wife died intestate. Former § 43-3-12 (1975; Repealed 1981). Whenever it has had the opportunity, the Alabama supreme court in recent years has tended to treat both females and males alike relative to property rights. Therefore, it is assumed that the Alabama court, if given the opportunity, would treat surviving husbands the same as surviving wives in the circumstances covered by this section and thus consistent with this section.

Prior Alabama law also was in accord with the provision that a divorce a mensa et thoro (bed and board) does not terminate the wife's marital rights in her husband's estate, which are terminated only by a divorce a vinculo. Section 30-2-30 (1975); Drake v. Drake, 262 Ala. 609, 80 So. 2d 268 (1955); Adair v. Adair, 258 Ala. 293, 62 So. 2d 437 (1952).

With regard to subdivision (b)(1) of this section, prior Alabama law is in accord. Prudential Insurance Company of America v. Lewis, 306 F. Supp. 1177 (N.D. Ala. 1969). Subdivision (b)(3) of this section follows prior Alabama law. Mussey v. Mussey, 251 Ala. 439, 37 So. 2d 921 (1948).

I.　General Consideration.
II.　Decisions Under Prior Law.

I. GENERAL CONSIDERATION.

Collateral references. — 95 C.J.S., Wills, §§ 293, 564.

79 Am. Jur. 2d, Wills, §§ 586-588.

Divorce or separation as affecting person entitled to devise or bequest to husband, wife or widow. 75 ALR2d 1413.

Devolution of gift over upon spouse predeceasing testator where gift to spouse fails because of divorce. 74 ALR3d 1108.

Husband's death as affecting periodic payment provision of separation agreement. 5 ALR4th 1153.

II. DECISIONS UNDER PRIOR LAW.

Editor's note. — In light of the similarity of the subject matter, decisions under former § 43-5-4 are included in the annotations for this section.

Former section no bar to children's rights. —- Former § 43-5-4 did not conclude the homestead rights of the children of the marriage, although it barred the divorced wife's right to dower in the realty by her husband, and any distributive right in his personalty. Chamboredon v. Fayet, 176 Ala. 211, 57 So. 845 (1912).

But was an absolute bar to dower. — A wife divorced a vinculo could not under any circumstances claim dower after death of her husband, such right being expressly excluded by statute. McLaughlin v. McLaughlin, 202 Ala. 16, 79 So. 354 (1918).

A final judgment of divorce terminated a wife's dower interest. Consequently, she had no interest in the land following the divorce. Reed v. Ray, 409 So. 2d 814 (Ala. 1982).

Foreign divorce. — A divorce from the bonds of matrimony barred the wife's dower, unless preserved by the lex rei sitae. McLaughlin v. McLaughlin, 202 Ala. 16, 79 So. 354 (1918).

Divorce a vinculo for abandonment. — A wife who was divorced, a vinculo matrimonii, for her voluntary abandonment of her husband's bed and board, could not under any circumstances claim dower at the death of her husband. Hinson v. Bush, 84 Ala. 368, 4 So. 410 (1888).

Complaint by divorced wife to remove cloud on title, based on fee ownership under divorce decree, held not to show independent equity for protection of plaintiff's inchoate rights, under former § 43-5-4, such as would permit maintenance of action without proof of possession, since divorce was bar to dower. Frazier v. Espalla, 218 Ala. 487, 119 So. 209 (1928).

§ 43-8-253. Effect of homicide on intestate succession, wills, joint assets, life insurance and beneficiary designations; effect of bona fide purchase by third party or good faith payment by obligor, etc.

(a) A surviving spouse, heir or devisee who feloniously and intentionally kills the decedent is not entitled to any benefits under the will or under articles 3 through 10 of this chapter, and the estate of decedent passes as if the killer had predeceased the decedent. Property appointed by the will of the decedent to or for the benefit of the killer passes as if the killer had predeceased the decedent.

(b) Any joint tenant who feloniously and intentionally kills another joint tenant thereby effects a severance of the interest of the decedent so that the share of the decedent passes as his property and the killer has no rights by survivorship. This provision applies to joint tenancies with the right of survivorship and tenancies in common during the respective lives of the grantees with cross-contingent remainders in fee to the survivor in real and personal property, joint and multiple-party accounts in banks, savings and loan associations, credit unions and other institutions, and any other form of co-ownership with survivorship incidents.

(c) A named beneficiary of a bond, life insurance policy, or other contractual arrangement who feloniously and intentionally kills the principal obligee or the person upon whose life the policy is issued is not entitled to any benefit under the bond, policy or other contractual arrangement, and it becomes payable as though the killer had predeceased the decedent.

(d) Any other acquisition of property or interest by the killer shall be treated in accordance with the principles of this section.

(e) A final judgment of conviction of felonious and intentional killing is conclusive for purposes of this section. In the absence of a conviction of felonious and intentional killing the court may determine by a preponderance of evidence whether the killing was felonious and intentional for purposes of this section.

(f) This section does not affect the rights of any person who, before rights under this section have been adjudicated, purchases from the killer for value and without notice property which the killer would have acquired except for this section, but the killer is liable for the amount of the proceeds or the value of the property. Any insurance company, bank, or other obligor making payment according to the terms of its policy or obligation is not liable by reason of this section unless prior to payment it has received at its home office or principal address written notice of a claim under this section. (Acts 1982, No. 82-399, § 2-803.)

Commentary

A growing group of states have enacted statutes dealing with the problems covered by this section, and uniformity appears desirable. The section is confined to intentional and felonious homicide and excludes the accidental manslaughter killing.

At first it may appear that the matter dealt with is criminal in nature and not a proper matter for probate courts. However, the concept that a wrongdoer may not profit by his own wrong is a civil concept, and the probate court is the proper forum to determine the effect of killing on succession to property of the decedent. There are numerous situations where the same conduct gives rise to both criminal and civil consequences. A killing may result in criminal prosecution for murder and civil litigation by the murdered person's family under wrongful death statutes. While a conviction in the criminal prosecution under this section is treated as conclusive on the matter of succession to the murdered person's property, acquittal does not have the same consequences. This is because different considerations as well as a different burden of proof enter into the finding of guilty in the criminal prosecution. Hence, it is possible that the defendant on a murder charge may be found not guilty and acquitted, but if the same person claims as an heir or devisee of the decedent, he may in the probate court be found to have feloniously and intentionally killed the decedent and thus be barred under this section from sharing in the estate. An analogy exists in the tax field, where a taxpayer may be acquitted of tax fraud in a criminal prosecution but found to have committed the fraud in a civil proceeding. In many of the cases arising under this section there may be no criminal prosecution because the murderer has committed suicide.

This section codifies "public policy" under prior Alabama law, which applied the principle that a person cannot benefit from his own wrongdoing. Weaver v. Hollis, 247 Ala. 47, 22 So. 2d 525 (1945). A similar result has been reached with regard to proceeds of a life insurance policy. American Life Insurance Company v. Anderson, 246 Ala. 588, 21 So. 2d 791 (1945); Protective Life Insurance Company v. Linson, 245 Ala. 493, 17 So. 2d 761 (1944).

As to the conclusive effect of a prior criminal conviction under subsection (e) of this section, Alabama courts have not previously afforded the conviction the same probative effect. The record of conviction of the beneficiary could be introduced as evidence of guilt to preclude recovery, but this conviction was merely prima facie evidence. The beneficiary could attempt to rebut the presumption. Sovereign Camp

W.O.W. v. Gunn, 227 Ala. 400, 150 So. 491 (1933). The treatment of a conviction as in this section seems more logical, however.

Collateral references. — 26A C.J.S., Descent & Distribution, § 47. 46 C.J.S., Insurance, § 1190. 48A C.J.S., Joint Tenancy, §§ 1, 2. 94 C.J.S., Wills, § 104.

20 Am. Jur. 2d, Cotenancy and Joint Ownership, § 8. 23 Am. Jur. 2d, Descent & Distribution, §§ 94-102. 44 Am. Jur. 2d, Insurance, §§ 1741-1745. 79 Am. Jur. 2d, Wills, §§ 170, 171.

Right of murderer to take as beneficiary under will of victim. 36 ALR2d 960.

§ 43-8-254. Appointment of debtor as executor.

The appointment of a debtor as an executor is not a discharge of the debt, unless it is so directed in the will. (Code 1852, § 1606; Code 1867, § 1927; Code 1876, § 2291; Code 1886, § 1952; Code 1896, § 4258; Code 1907, § 6167; Code 1923, § 10592; Code 1940, T. 61, § 17; Code 1975, § 43-1-14.)

Code commissioner's note. — This section was originally codified as § 43-1-14 of the 1975 Code.

Collateral references. — 96 C.J.S., Wills, § 1146.

§ 43-8-255. Administrators with will annexed have same powers as executors.

Administrators with the will annexed have the same powers and authority over the estates which executors named in the will would have, and their acts are as effectual for all purposes. (Code 1923, § 10595; Code 1940, T. 61, § 22; Code 1975, § 43-1-18.)

Code commissioner's note. — This section was originally codified as § 43-1-18 of the 1975 Code.

Cross references. — As to disclaimer of any property, property right, or interest in property, see article 11 of this chapter.

§ 43-8-256. Testator may preclude corporation from becoming surety on bond of executor or administrator.

Whenever any testator, by the terms of his will, so provides, no corporation shall be accepted upon the bond of any executor or administrator of such testator. (Code 1896, § 3097; Code 1907, § 1512; Code 1923, § 2645; Code 1940, T. 61, § 23; Code 1975, § 43-1-19.)

Code commissioner's note. — This section was originally codified as § 43-1-19 of the 1975 Code.

ARTICLE 10.

CUSTODY OF WILLS.

§ 43-8-270. Duty of custodian of will after death of testator; liability.

After the death of a testator and on request of an interested person, any person having custody of a will of the testator shall deliver it with reasonable promptness to a person able to secure its probate and if none is known, to an appropriate court. Any person who wilfully fails to deliver a will is liable to any person aggrieved for the damages which may be sustained by the failure. Any person who wilfully refuses or fails to deliver a will after being ordered by the court in a proceeding brought for the purpose of compelling delivery is subject to the penalty for contempt of court. (Acts 1982, No. 82-399, § 2-901.)

Commentary

This section is UPC § 2-902 slightly modified. A person authorized by a court to accept delivery of a will from a custodian may, in addition to a registrar or clerk, be a universal successor or other person authorized under the law of another nation to carry out the terms of a will.

The adoption of this section causes no significant change in Alabama law. Former § 43-1-40 provided that a person who had the custody of a will should forthwith after notice or information of the death of the testator, deliver such will into the probate court which had jurisdiction thereof, or to the executor named in the will; and if a person, without reasonable cause, neglected so to deliver a will after being duly cited for the purpose by such court, he would be deemed guilty of contempt of court. The prior Alabama statute further provided that upon application to the probate court by any person interested, the judge had to issue a citation to any person alleged to have the custody or possession of any last will, requiring such person to produce the will; and any person, who failed to produce such will or make an affidavit, could be committed to jail; and he was also liable to all persons interested for all damages caused by withholding the will. Former § 43-1-40 (1975).

Collateral references. — 95 C.J.S., Wills, § 305.
79 Am. Jur. 2d, Wills, §§ 832-838.

ARTICLE 11.

UNIFORM DISCLAIMER OF PROPERTY INTERESTS.

Effective date. — The act which added this article became effective on March 31, 1981, and the provisions were retroactively effective as of January 1, 1981.

§ 43-8-290. Short title.

This article may be cited as the Alabama Uniform Disclaimer of Property Interests Act. (Acts 1981, No. 81-156, § 1; Code 1975, § 35-17-1.)

Code commissioner's note. — This section was originally codified as § 35-17-1 of the 1975 Code.

§ 43-8-291. Right to disclaim interest in property.

(a) A person, or the representative of a deceased, incapacitated person, protected person, incompetent or ward, who is an heir, next of kin, devisee, legatee, grantee, donee, surviving joint tenant, person succeeding to a disclaimed interest, beneficiary under a testamentary or nontestamentary instrument or contract, or appointee under a power of appointment exercised by a testamentary or nontestamentary instrument, or to whom any property or interest therein devolves, by whatever means, may disclaim in whole or in part the right of succession to any property or interest therein by delivering or filing a written disclaimer under this article.

(b) A surviving joint tenant may disclaim as a separate interest any property or interest therein devolving to him by right of survivorship. A surviving joint tenant may disclaim the entire interest in any property or interest therein that is the subject of a joint tenancy devolving to him, if the joint tenancy was created by act of a deceased joint tenant, if the survivor did not join in creating the joint tenancy.

(c) The right to disclaim exists notwithstanding any limitation on the interest of the disclaimant in the nature of a spendthrift provision or similar restriction. (Acts 1981, No. 81-156, § 2; Code 1975, § 35-17-2.)

Code commissioner's note. — This section was originally codified as § 35-17-2 of the 1975 Code.

Collateral references. — 26A C.J.S., Descent & Distribution, § 76. 48 C.J.S., Joint Tenancy, § 1. 78 C.J.S., Property, § 15.

23 Am. Jur. 2d, Descent & Distribution, §§ 165, 171, 174. 63 Am. Jur. 2d, Property, § 45.

§ 43-8-292. Filing and delivery of disclaimer.

(a) Except as provided in subsection (c) of this section, if the property or interest has devolved to the disclaimant under a testamentary instrument or by the laws of intestacy, the disclaimer shall be filed, as to a present interest, not later than nine months after the death of the deceased owner or deceased donee of a power of appointment and, if of a future interest, not later than nine months after the event determining that the taker of the property or interest has become finally ascertained and his interest is indefeasibly vested. The disclaimer shall be filed in the probate court of the county in which proceedings for the administration of the estate of the deceased owner or deceased donee of the power have been commenced or, if they have not been commenced, in which they could be commenced. A copy of the disclaimer shall be delivered in person or mailed by registered or certified mail to any personal representative or other fiduciary of the decedent or donee of the power.

(b) Except as provided in subsection (c) of this section, if the property or interest has devolved to the disclaimant under a nontestamentary instrument or contract, the disclaimer shall be delivered or filed, as to a present interest, not later than nine months after the effective date of the nontestamentary instrument or contract and, as to a future interest, not later than nine months after the event determining that the taker of the property or interest has become finally ascertained and his interest is indefeasibly vested. If the person entitled to disclaim does not have actual knowledge of the existence of the interest, the disclaimer shall be delivered or filed not later than nine months after he has actual knowledge of the existence of the interest. The effective date of a revocable instrument or contract is the date on which the maker no longer has power to revoke it or to transfer to himself or another the entire legal and equitable ownership of the interest. The disclaimer or a copy thereof shall be delivered in person or mailed by registered or certified mail to the trustee or other person who has legal title to, or possession of, the interest disclaimed.

(c) In any case, as to a transfer creating an interest in the disclaimant made after December 31, 1976, and subject to tax under chapter 11, 12, or 13 of the Internal Revenue Code of 1954, as amended, a disclaimer intended as a qualified disclaimer thereunder must specifically so state and must be delivered not later than nine months after the later of the date the transfer is made or the day on which the person disclaiming attains age 21.

(d) If real property or an interest therein is disclaimed, a copy of the disclaimer instrument may be filed for record in the office of the probate judge of the county in which the property or interest disclaimed is located. (Acts 1981, No. 81-156, § 3; Code 1975, § 35-17-3.)

Code commissioner's note. — This section was originally codified as § 35-17-3 of the 1975 Code.

Collateral references. — 26A C.J.S., Descent & Distribution, § 76. 48 C.J.S., Joint Tenancy, § 1. 73 C.J.S., Property, § 15.

23 Am. Jur. 2d, Descent & Distribution, § 174.

§ 43-8-293. Form of disclaimer.

The disclaimer shall:

(1) Be in writing;

(2) Describe the property or interest disclaimed;

(3) Declare the disclaimer and extent thereof; and

(4) Be signed by the disclaimant. (Acts 1981, No. 81-156, § 4; Code 1975, § 35-17-4.)

Code commissioner's note. — This section was originally codified as § 35-17-4 of the 1975 Code.

Collateral references. — 26A C.J.S., Descent & Distribution, § 76. 48 C.J.S., Joint Tenancy, § 1. 73 C.J.S., Property, § 15.

23 Am. Jur. 2d, Descent & Distribution, § 174.

§ 43-8-294. Effect of disclaimer.

(a) If the property or interest devolved to a disclaimant under a testamentary instrument or under the laws of intestacy and the deceased owner or donee of a power of appointment has not provided for another disposition, it devolves as if the disclaimant had predeceased the decedent or, if the disclaimant was designated to take under a power of appointment exercised by a testamentary instrument, as if the disclaimant had predeceased the donee of the power. Any future interest that takes effect in possession or enjoyment after the termination of the estate or interest disclaimed takes effect as if the disclaimant had died before the event determining that the taker of the property or interest had become finally ascertained and his interest is indefeasibly vested. A disclaimer relates back for all purposes to the date of death of the decedent, or of the donee of the power, or the determinative event, as the case may be.

(b) If the property or interest devolved to a disclaimant under a nontestamentary instrument or contract and the instrument or contract does not provide for another disposition:

(1) It devolves as if the disclaimant had died before the effective date of the instrument or contract; and

(2) A future interest that takes effect in possession or enjoyment at or after the termination of the disclaimed interest takes effect as if the disclaimant had died before the event determining that the taker of the property or interest had become finally ascertained and his interest indefeasibly vested.

A disclaimer relates back for all purposes to the effective date of the instrument or contract or the date of the determinative event, as the case may be.

(c) The disclaimer or the written waiver of the right to disclaim is binding upon the disclaimant or person waiving and all persons claiming through or under him. (Acts 1981, No. 81-156, § 5; Code 1975, § 35-17-5.)

Code commissioner's notes. — This section was originally codified as § 35-17-5 of the 1975 Code.

Collateral references. — 26A C.J.S., Descent & Distribution, § 76. 48 C.J.S., Joint Tenancy, § 1. 73 C.J.S., Property, § 15.

23 Am. Jur. 2d, Descent & Distribution, §§ 165, 171, 174. 63 Am. Jur. 2d, Property, § 45.

§ 43-8-295. Waiver and bar.

The right to disclaim property or an interest therein is barred by:

(1) An assignment, conveyance, encumbrance, pledge, or transfer of the property or interest, or a contract therefor;

(2) A written waiver of the right to disclaim;

(3) An acceptance of the property or interest or a benefit thereunder; or

(4) A sale of the property or interest under judicial sale made before the disclaimer is effected. (Acts 1981, No. 81-156, § 6; Code 1975, § 35-17-6.)

Code commissioner's note. — This section was originally codified as § 35-17-6 of the 1975 Code.

Collateral references. — 26A C.J.S., Descent & Distribution, § 76. 48 C.J.S., Joint Tenancy, § 1. 73 C.J.S., Property, § 15.

23 Am. Jur. 2d, Descent & Distribution, §§ 165, 171, 174. 63 Am. Jur. 2d, Property, § 45.

§ 43-8-296. Remedy not exclusive.

This article does not abridge the right of a person to waive, release, disclaim, or renounce property or an interest therein under any other statute. (Acts 1981, No. 81-156, § 7; Code 1975, § 35-17-7.)

Code commissioner's note. — This section was originally codified as § 35-17-7 of the 1975 Code.

Collateral references. — 26A C.J.S., Descent & Distribution, § 76. 48 C.J.S., Joint Tenancy, § 1. 73 C.J.S., Property, § 15.

23 Am. Jur. 2d, Descent & Distribution, §§ 165, 171, 174. 63 Am. Jur. 2d, Property, § 45.

§ 43-8-297. Uniformity of application and construction.

This article shall be applied and construed to effectuate its general purpose to make uniform the law with respect to the subject of this article among states enacting it. It is the intent of the legislature of the state of Alabama by this article to clarify the laws of this state with respect to the subject matter hereof in order to ensure the ability of persons to disclaim interests in property without the imposition of federal and state estate, inheritance, gift and transfer taxes. This article is to be interpreted and construed in accordance with, and in furtherance of, that intent. (Acts 1981, No. 81-156, § 8; Code 1975, § 35-17-8.)

Code commissioner's note. — This section was originally codified as § 35-17-8 of the 1975 Code.

§ 43-8-298. Applicability of article.

An interest in property that exists on the effective date of this article as to which, if a present interest, the time for delivering or filing a disclaimer under this article has not expired or, if a future interest, the interest has not become indefeasibly vested or the taker finally ascertained, may be disclaimed within nine months after the effective date of this article. (Acts 1981, No. 81-156, § 10; Code 1975, § 35-17-9.)

Code commissioner's note. — This section was originally codified as § 35-17-9 of the 1975 Code.

Acts 1981, No. 81-156, § 10, was approved by the governor on March 31, 1981, and became retroactively effective January 1, 1981.

TABLE.

This table indicates the derivation of new chapter 8 of Title 43.

New Chapter 8	Acts1982, No. 82-399	Prior Code transferred	Repealed Code relating to similar subject
43-8-1	1-201		
43-8-2	1-102		
43-8-3	1-103		
43-8-4	1-105		
43-8-5	1-106		
43-8-6	1-107		
43-8-7	1-108		
43-8-8	8-101		
43-8-9	8-103		
43-8-20	1-301		
43-8-21	1-303		
43-8-22	1-310		
43-8-40	2-101		43-1-7
43-8-41	2-102		43-3-1, 43-3-10
43-8-42	2-103		43-3-1, 43-3-2, 43-3-3, 43-3-10
43-8-43	2-104		
43-8-44	2-105		43-3-1
43-8-45	2-106		43-3-2, 43-3-3
43-8-46	2-107		43-3-5
43-8-47	2-108		43-3-6
43-8-48	2-109		43-3-7, 43-3-8
43-8-49	2-110		43-3-30 through 43-3-34
43-8-50		43-3-35	
43-8-51		43-3-36	
43-8-52		43-3-37	
43-8-53		43-3-38	
43-8-54		43-3-39	
43-8-55	2-111		
43-8-56	2-112		
43-8-57	2-113		
43-8-58	2-114		
43-8-70	2-201		
48-8-71	2-203		43-1-15
43-8-72	2-204		43-1-17
43-8-73	2-205		43-5-20
43-8-74	2-206		43-1-16
43-8-75	2-207		43-1-15
43-8-76	2-208		43-1-15
43-8-90	2-301		
43-8-91	2-302		43-1-15
43-8-110	2-401		43-1-9
43-8-111	2-402		
43-8-112	2-403		
43-8-113	2-404		
43-8-114		43-5-40	
43-8-130	2-501		43-1-1, 43-1-2
43-8-131	2-502		43-1-30

New Chapter 8	Acts 1982, No. 82-399	Prior Code transferred	Repealed Code relating to similar subject
43-8-132	*		
43-8-133	2-504		
43-8-134	2-505		
43-8-135	2-506		
43-8-136	2-507		43-1-33
43-8-137	2-508		43-1-8
43-8-138	2-509		43-1-34
43-8-139	2-510		
43-8-140	2-511		43-1-4
43-8-141	2-512		
43-8-160		43-1-36	
43-8-161		43-1-37	
43-8-162		43-1-38	
43-8-163		43-1-39	
43-8-164		43-1-41	
43-8-165		43-1-42	
43-8-166		43-1-43	
43-8-167		43-1-44	
43-8-168		43-1-45	
43-8-169		43-1-46	
43-8-170		43-1-47	
43-8-171		43-1-48	
48-8-172		43-1-49	
43-8-173		43-1-50	
43-8-174		43-1-51	
43-8-175		43-1-52	
43-8-190		43-1-70	
43-8-191		43-1-71	
43-8-192		43-1-72	
43-8-193		43-1-73	
43-8-194		43-1-74	
43-8-195		43-1-75	
43-8-196		43-1-76	
43-8-197		43-1-77	
43-8-198		43-1-78	
43-8-199		43-1-79	
43-8-200		43-1-80	
43-8-201		43-1-81	
43-8-202		43-1-82	
43-8-220	2-601		
43-8-221	2-602		
43-8-222	2-603		
43-8-223	2-604		43-1-6, 43-1-12
43-8-224	2-605		43-1-13
43-8-225	2-606		43-1-5
43-8-226	2-607		
43-8-227	2-608		43-1-10
43-8-228	2-609		
43-8-229	2-610		
43-8-230	2-611		

* Derived from Acts 1981, No. 81-1209.

New Chapter 8	Acts 1982, No. 82-399	Prior Code transferred	Repealed Code relating to similar subject
43-8-231	2-612		43-1-11
43-8-250	2-701		
43-8-251	2-801		
43-8-252	2-802		43-5-4
43-8-253	2-803		
43-8-254		43-1-14	
43-8-255		43-1-18	
43-8-256		43-1-19	
43-8-270	2-901		43-1-40
43-8-290		35-17-1	
43-8-291		35-17-2	
43-8-292		35-17-3	
43-8-293		35-17-4	
43-8-294		35-17-5	
43-8-295		35-17-6	
43-8-296		35-17-7	
43-8-297		35-17-8	
43-8-298		35-17-9	

TITLE 44.

YOUTH SERVICES.

CHAPTER 1.

DEPARTMENT OF YOUTH SERVICES AND YOUTH SERVICES BOARD.

Cited in Carter v. Coosa Valley Youth Servs., 378 So. 2d 1145 (Ala. Civ. App. 1979).

ARTICLE 1.

GENERAL PROVISIONS.

Cross references. — As to child care generally, see § 38-7-1 et seq.
Collateral references. — 47 Am. Jur. 2d, Juvenile Courts & Delinquent & Dependent Children, §§ 1-70.

§ 44-1-1. Purpose of chapter.

The purpose of this chapter is to promote and safeguard the social well-being and general welfare of the youth of the state through a comprehensive and coordinated program of public services for the prevention of juvenile delinquency and the rehabilitation of delinquent youth. This state program shall provide the following:

(1) Social and educational services and facilities for any youth whom a juvenile judge deems in need of such state services;

(2) The establishment of standards for social and educational services and facilities for such youth;

(3) Cooperation with public and voluntary agencies, organizations and citizen groups in the development and coordination of programs and activities directed toward the prevention, control and treatment of delinquency;

(4) The promotion and improvement of community conditions, programs and resources to aid parents in discharging their responsibilities for the care, development and well-being of their children; and

(5) The promotion of improved communications between the public and voluntary agencies and bodies of this state responsible for said youth and the juvenile courts of this state. (Acts 1973, No. 816, p. 1261, § 1.)

§ 44-1-2. Definitions.

The following terms, wherever used in this chapter, shall have the following respective meanings unless the content thereof indicates otherwise:

(1) AFTERCARE. A youth is released by the department from a state training school operated by the department, wherein the department releases legal custody, supervision, and the right to return until further order of the juvenile court. "Aftercare" means a legal status created by order of the committing court at the time of release from a state training school whereby a youth is permitted to return to the community subject to supervision by the court or any agency designated by the court and subject to return to the court at any time during the aftercare period.

(2) BOARD. The Alabama youth services board.

(3) BOARD MEMBER. Any member of the Alabama youth services board.

(4) COMMITTED YOUTH. Any youth committed to the legal custody of the department upon a finding of delinquency and a finding by a juvenile judge that said youth is in need of care and/or treatment in a state training school; provided, that such term shall not include any youth so committed upon a finding of in need of supervision or dependency.

(5) DEPARTMENT. The department of youth services established in this chapter.

(6) DETENTION or DETENTION CARE. Temporary care in a detention facility.

(7) DETENTION FACILITY. A facility licensed by the department, other than a jail, affording secure custody for children and youths.

(8) DIRECTOR. The Alabama youth services director.

(9) DISCHARGE. A complete release of a committed youth by the department without further supervision.

(10) FOSTER CARE FACILITY or GROUP HOME. Any place providing care for one or more youths alleged or adjudicated delinquent, exclusive of the state training schools.

(11) GUARDIAN. Any parent who has legal custody of the person or property of a youth or a person or agency who has custody of the person or property of the said youth pursuant to a court order.

(12) JUVENILE COURT. Any court having jurisdiction over juveniles pursuant to Amendment No. 328 of the Constitution of the state and Title 12 of this Code.

(13) JUVENILE CODE. Chapter 15 of Title 12 of this Code.

(14) LEGAL CUSTODY. A legal status created by a court order embodying the following rights and responsibilities: the right to have physical possession of the youth; the right and the duty to protect, train and discipline him; the responsibility to provide him with food, clothing, shelter, education and medical, dental and hospital care and the right to determine where and with whom he shall reside.

(15) MAINTENANCE. All general expenses for care such as food, clothing, shelter, education and medical, dental and hospital care, transportation and other necessary or incidental expenses or money payments therefor.

(16) PROBATION. A legal status created by a court order following adjudication in a delinquency or in need of supervision case whereby a youth is permitted to remain in the community, subject to supervision by the court or any agency designated by the court and subject to return to the court at any time during the probation period.

(17) PROBATION SERVICES. a. The making of investigations, reports and recommendations to the court as directed by this Code;

b. The receiving and examining of complaints and charges of delinquency for the purpose of considering the commencement of proceedings under this Code;

c. The supervision of a child placed on probation by order of the court;

d. The supervision of a child placed on aftercare by order of the court;

e. The making of appropriate referrals to other private or public agencies of the community, if their assistance appears to be needed or desirable;

f. The taking into custody and detaining of a youth who is under the supervision and care of the department as a delinquent where there is reasonable cause to believe that the youth's health or safety or that of another is in imminent danger, or that he may abscond or be moved from the jurisdiction of the court, or when ordered by the court pursuant to the Juvenile Code; and

g. The performing of all other functions designated by the Juvenile Code or by order of the court pursuant thereto.

(18) STATE. The state of Alabama.

(19) TRAINING SCHOOL. An institution operated by the department for the rehabilitation of delinquent youth.

(20) YOUTH. Prior to January 1, 1978, such term means an individual under the age of 17 or under 19 years of age who committed the act of delinquency with which he is charged before reaching the age of 17 years. After December 31, 1977, such term means an individual under the age of 18 or under 19 years of age who committed the act of delinquency with which he is charged before reaching the age of 18 years, and for the purpose of continuing to provide services only, jurisdiction obtained by the court in the case of a youth shall be retained by it until the youth becomes 21 years of age unless terminated prior thereto by order of the judge of the juvenile court.

(21) YOUTH SERVICES. The duties and functions which are authorized or required by this chapter to be provided by the department with respect to the establishment and enforcement of standards of treatment for youths. (Acts 1973, No. 816, p. 1261, § 2.)

§ 44-1-3. Alabama Boys Industrial School, Alabama Training School for Girls and Alabama Industrial School — Control; priority as to use of funds of department; legal custody of inhabitants.

The Alabama Boys Industrial School, the Alabama Training School for Girls and the Alabama Industrial School shall be under the control of the youth services board. All duties, responsibilities, authority, power, assets, appropriations, liabilities, contractual rights and obligations and property rights, whether accruing or vesting in the aforementioned institutions before or after September 5, 1973, shall be vested in the youth services board. It is the intention of the legislature that out of moneys available to the board the first priority shall be given to insuring that the services provided by the financial resources available to the Alabama Boys Industrial School, the Alabama Training School for Girls and the Alabama Industrial School shall be maintained at least at the level existing on January 22, 1975. All youths in the custody of or committed to the Alabama Boys Industrial School, the Alabama Training School for Girls and the Alabama Industrial School shall be in the legal custody of the department of youth services. (Acts 1973, No. 816, p. 1261, § 7.)

§ 44-1-4. Same — Separate advisory boards; regulations.

The department of youth services shall establish separate advisory boards for the Alabama Boys Industrial School, the Alabama Training School for Girls and the Alabama Industrial School. Any regulation of the aforementioned institutions in existence on January 22, 1975, shall be made a regulation of the department on January 22, 1975, and shall continue in force until repealed or amended by the board. (Acts 1973, No. 816, p. 1261, § 7.)

§ 44-1-5. Same — Continuation of rights, etc., of employees; personal leave for teachers.

(a) Employees of the Alabama Boys Industrial School, the Alabama Training School for Girls and the Alabama Industrial School holding positions on January 22, 1975, shall become employees of the department of youth services on the date of such transfer. Such employees of the abovementioned institutions shall continue to enjoy employment conditions, including salary, housing and office arrangements, at a level no less than those enjoyed prior to transfer to the department.

(b) The youth services board shall grant personal leave to any teacher employed by the board at Alabama Boys Industrial School, Alabama Training School for Girls and the Alabama Industrial School at Mt. Meigs up to five days annually, noncumulative, during the time such schools are in session. Two days of personal leave shall be granted upon the request of the teacher with full pay and three days may, at the discretion of the board, be granted with part pay or with full pay. The teacher shall, whenever possible, notify the board five days in advance of the time such leave is to be taken; however, when such notice is not practical, leave may be taken in the same manner and under the procedures governing sick leave. (Acts 1973, No. 816, p. 1261, § 7; Acts 1975, No. 1057, § 1.)

§ 44-1-6. Same — Restrictions on appropriations.

All moneys appropriated to the Alabama Industrial School, Alabama Boys Industrial School and the Alabama Training School for Girls from the special education trust funds shall be used solely for the operations of these institutions. (Acts 1973, No. 816, p. 1261, § 34.)

§ 44-1-7. Same — Donations and endowment funds.

In order to make provision for the proper preservation and application of donations from private sources by gift, devise or otherwise, heretofore made to the board of trustees of the Alabama Boys Industrial School, the board of trustees of the Alabama Training School for Girls or the board of trustees of the Alabama Industrial School for the uses and purposes intended by the private donors and in order to encourage future donations from private sources by way of gift, devise or otherwise to said schools and assure prospective private donors of the use thereof at the particular school or schools designated as the object of donations and to prohibit the diversion of past and future donations to said schools from the uses and purposes for which the same were made, the advisory board of each school is authorized and empowered to serve as trustee or trustees for an endowment trust fund for its respective school set up under an agreement with a bank or banks organized either under the national banking laws or the banking laws of this state and having trust powers, to accept donations from private sources for the benefit of the particular school involved, manage the trust property in a prudent manner in accordance with sound financial principles and pay out so much of the income therefrom and/or of the principal as may be required by appropriate resolutions adopted and approved by the youth services board and, in the event of disestablishment of the particular school, to provide for the termination of its endowment trust fund and transfer of trust property then on hand to the department of youth services for use for the particular uses and purposes of each separate endowment fund then included in the trust, or, if such use has ceased to be practicable, then for such use as in the department's judgment constitutes an equitable approximation of such uses and purposes. The trustee or trustees of any endowment trust fund established pursuant to this section shall periodically, not less than once every three years, make a full accounting of its handling of the trust estate to the youth services board, and written approval of the trustee's or trustees' accounts by said board shall be final and binding and have the same full force and effect as a partial final settlement or final settlement, as the case may be, had the accounting been accomplished through judicial proceedings. The advisory board of said school is prohibited from authorizing or directing any payment out of the endowment trust fund of said school for any purposes contrary to the expressed uses and purposes of the private donors of a donation constituting a part of the school's endowment trust fund. (Acts 1973, No. 816, p. 1261, § 37.)

§ 44-1-8. Confinement of youth in adult penal institutions.

The department of youth services shall not have the power, by virtue of the vesting in it of the legal custody of a youth or of anything contained in this chapter, to confine any youth in any adult jail or adult penal institution now or hereafter established, except under conditions set forth in section 12-15-61. (Acts 1973, No. 816, p. 1261, § 25.)

§ 44-1-9. Detention without order or warrant of escaped youths.

A committed youth who has been placed by the department of youth services in any state training school and who has escaped or run away therefrom may be taken into custody without warrant or order of the state youth services director by a peace officer or employee designated by the department. Any youth taken into custody pursuant to this section shall be detained in a suitable place designated by the department until determination concerning his further care and treatment is made. (Acts 1973, No. 816, p. 1261, § 27.)

§ 44-1-10. Penalties; enforcement of chapter.

(a) Violations of the provisions of this chapter shall be penalized or punished as follows:

(1) Any person, partnership, corporation or association that violates the provisions of this chapter or any regulations promulgated under the authority delegated to the youth services board or to the state youth services director, after notice of such violation served upon such person, partnership, corporation or association by United States registered or certified mail to the last known address thereof, shall be liable to pay to the department of youth services a penalty of $50.00 per day for each day such violation continues after receipt of such notice.

(2) Any person, group of persons, association or corporation who

a. Conducts, operates or acts as a foster care facility or detention facility without a license or an approval to do so in violation of the provisions of this chapter;

b. Makes materially false statements in order to obtain a license or permit;

c. Fails to keep the records and make the reports provided under this chapter;

d. Advertises any service not authorized by license or permit held;

e. Publishes any advertisement in violation of this chapter; or

f. Violates any other provision of this chapter or any reasonable rule or regulation adopted and published by the department for the enforcement of the provisions of this chapter

shall be guilty of a misdemeanor and shall be fined not less than $100.00 nor more than $1,000.00 or be imprisoned in the county jail not longer than one year, or both; and, in case of an association or corporation, imprisonment may be imposed upon its officers who knowingly participated in the violation.

(3) Any person who shall allow, assist, aid or abet in the escape of any juvenile confined by court action or pursuant to the authority of the board or department shall be guilty of a misdemeanor and, upon conviction, shall be punished by a fine of not more than $100.00 or by imprisonment in the county jail in the county in which such act shall occur at hard labor for the said county for not more than 90 days, or by both such fine and imprisonment as the court may decide.

(4) Any member of the legislature, any member of the board, any employee of the department or any holder of any office of the state who takes any contract for work or services for the board, the department or any of their agencies, or is employed in any way under such contract or sells any goods or supplies to the board, the department or any of their agencies, or is in any way pecuniarily interested in any such contract or sale as principal or agent must, on conviction, be fined not less than $50.00 nor more than $1,000.00 and also shall forfeit his office or employment.

(b) It shall be the duty of every district attorney or assistant district attorney to institute action for the enforcement of the provisions of this chapter or prosecute action for the violation of the provisions of this chapter, or both. (Acts 1973, No. 816, p. 1261, § 35.)

ARTICLE 2.

DEPARTMENT OF YOUTH SERVICES.

§ 44-1-20. Created; composition and principal offices.

There is hereby created and established a department of the state to be known as the department of youth services. The department shall be composed of the youth services board, the director and such divisions and administrative sections as the board may establish. The principal offices of the department shall be located at the state capital. The department shall have the powers and duties and shall perform the functions prescribed in this chapter. (Acts 1973, No. 816, p. 1261, § 3.)

Cited in Alabama Youth Servs. Bd. v. Ellis, 350 So. 2d 405 (Ala. 1977).

§ 44-1-21. State youth services director.

(a) The state youth services director shall have at a minimum a master's degree in behavioral or social science or a related field from an accredited school and shall have at least six years' experience in the field of services to children and youth, with at least three years of that experience being in the field of juvenile delinquency services. The last three years of such experience must have been in an administrative and/or management position with demonstrated competence as indicated by promotion or other indications of responsibility.

(b) The director may be removed from office by a vote of nine members of the board for reasons fully set forth in the minutes of the meeting at which such removal takes place.

(c) The director shall have the following powers and duties:

(1) Subject to the provisions of the state merit system, to appoint all officers and employees of the department, or to authorize any superintendent, division or bureau head or other administrator to select with his approval all staff members and employees.

(2) To exercise supervision over all the officers and employees of the department, and should any such officer or employee fail to perform faithfully any of the duties which are lawfully prescribed for him or if he fails or refuses to observe or conform to any rule, regulation or policy of the board, to remove him from office, in conformity with the state merit system law.

(3) To make agreements with the heads of other executive departments of the state providing for the coordination of the functions of the various departments of the state.

(4) Serve as the administrator of the Interstate Compact on Juveniles. (Acts 1973, No. 816, p. 1261, § 11.)

Cross references. — As to merit system, see § 36-26-1 et seq. As to administration of interstate compact on juveniles, see § 44-2-2.

§ 44-1-22. Employees of department.

The employees of the department of youth services shall be governed by the personnel merit system rules and regulations of the state personnel department. Employees of institutions and agencies which are transferred to the department under the provisions of this chapter, who have been so employed for six months immediately preceding such date, shall remain in their respective employments and shall be considered to meet the requirements of the department in terms of training and experience; but nothing herein shall be construed to prevent or preclude the removal of an employee for cause in the manner provided by law. (Acts 1973, No. 816, p. 1261, § 14.)

Cross references. — As to merit system, see § 36-26-1 et seq.

§ 44-1-23. Legal counsel.

The state youth services director shall be authorized, subject to the provisions of the state merit system law, to appoint legal counsel for the department. Such counsel shall be commissioned as assistant attorney generals; except, that they shall devote their entire time to the business of the department. Salaries for such counsel will be paid by the department. (Acts 1973, No. 816, p. 1261, § 16.)

§ 44-1-24. Powers and duties of department generally.

The department of youth services shall have the following powers, duties and functions:

(1) To provide services for youths who have run away from their own communities in this state or from their home communities in other states to this state, and to provide such services, care or cost for such youths as may be required pursuant to the provisions of the Interstate Compact on Juveniles;

(2) To provide for the expansion of local detention care for youths alleged to be delinquent pending court hearing;

(3) To encourage the expansion of juvenile probation services to youths alleged or adjudged to be delinquent or in need of supervision;

(4) To establish and promulgate reasonable minimum standards for juvenile probation services;

(5) To establish and promulgate reasonable minimum standards for juvenile probation officers and certify any applicant meeting such standards for the position of juvenile probation officer;

(6) To secure the provision of medical, hospital, psychiatric, surgical or dental service, or payment of the cost of such services, as may be needed for committed youths;

(7) To license and subsidize foster care facilities or group homes for youths alleged to be delinquent pending hearing before a juvenile court or adjudged delinquent following such hearing, including detention, examination, study, care, treatment and training;

(8) To establish, maintain and subsidize programs to train employees of the department, juvenile courts and law enforcement personnel in such subject matters and techniques as may be necessary to assure efficient and effective administration of such services in accordance with the purpose of this chapter;

(9) To make and enforce all rules and regulations which are necessary and appropriate to the proper accomplishment of the duties and functions vested in the department by law with respect to youth services and which do not conflict with or exceed the provisions of law vesting such duties and functions in the department;

(10) To enter into contracts with any other state or federal agency or with any private person, organization or group capable of contracting, if it finds such action to be in the public interest;

(11) Upon approval of the attorney general of the state, to file and prosecute civil actions in any court in the name of the department to enforce the provisions of this chapter and to enforce such rules and regulations as may be duly promulgated under the provisions of this chapter. Such civil actions may include actions for an injunction to restrain any person, agency or organization from violating any provision of this chapter or any rule or regulation duly promulgated under the provision of this chapter;

(12) To accept gifts, trusts, bequests, grants, endowments or transfers of property of any kind and prudently to manage such property in accordance with sound financial principles;

(13) To prescribe for and furnish forms to clerks of probate and juvenile courts for use in connection with any action to be taken under the provisions of this chapter;

(14) To enter into reciprocal agreements with appropriate agencies of other states relative to youth services programs; and

(15) To engage in research in the field of youth services, to enter into contracts with public or voluntary organizations, including educational institutions, and with individuals for the purpose of securing such research and to make provisions for any pay grants to such organizations or individuals in accordance with the rules of the department, as may be necessary to secure the performance of such research. (Acts 1973, No. 816, p. 1261, §§ 13, 14.)

§ 44-1-25. Development of department program.

The department of youth services shall develop a workable program of youth services as follows:

(1) Collect statistics, information and data concerning the need for and condition of rehabilitative services to delinquent youth or youth in need of supervision throughout the state;

(2) Disseminate information to the public and to appropriate public and private agencies and organizations within the state on the conditions and needs thus ascertained;

(3) Serve in a consultative and licensing capacity and develop materials and standards concerning delinquent youth within the state;

(4) Enlist the participation of citizens and representatives of other agencies and organizations in the planning and development throughout the state of an adequate youth services program as provided for in this chapter;

(5) Cooperate with and assist other public and voluntary agencies and organizations in the development and coordination of programs and activities for youths, particularly those programs and activities which contribute to the prevention or treatment of delinquency;

(6) Collaborate with others in the establishment of statewide and local planning bodies, or assist and cooperate with any such existing bodies which are concerned with promoting the physical, mental, emotional and social well-being of youths;

(7) Assist local communities in making surveys of conditions contributing to delinquency and of the facilities and services provided to rehabilitate committed youths; and

(8) Prescribe and furnish uniform procedures and forms for all law enforcement agencies and court clerks to use in reporting contacts with youths. (Acts 1973, No. 816, p. 1261, § 12.)

§ 44-1-26. Salary subsidies for probation services; juvenile probation officers; responsibilities of department of pensions and security.

(a) The department of youth services shall provide salary subsidies for probation services to all Alabama counties. The department shall expend funds to match at least half of the probation officers' salaries according to the following formula. At a minimum, each county will receive funding for one juvenile probation officer per 20,000 population or fraction thereof. The department shall use the last federal decennial census for these determinations. The various counties shall provide the necessary matching funds for these subsidies. If there are counties of under 30,000 population which do not provide matching funds, the department is authorized at its discretion to fully subsidize one probation officer per such county.

(b) The department of youth services shall establish and promulgate reasonable minimum standards for certification of juvenile probation officers. Any person serving as a juvenile probation officer as of September 5, 1973, shall be considered to meet the requirements of the department. The existing level of state support for county juvenile probation officers employed by counties as of September 5, 1973, shall not be reduced. All funds expended by the department will be contingent upon the recipients of said funds meeting the standards established by the department.

(c) The responsibilities of the department of pensions and security exercised pursuant to law relating to probation, parole and foster care services to a minor who is an adjudicated delinquent shall cease effective January 1, 1976, it being the intention of the legislature that these functions shall be performed by the department of youth services. Any responsibilities of the department of pensions and security relating to probation services to a court when a petition alleging delinquency has been filed shall cease effective January 1, 1976; provided, that the authority of the department of pensions and security to continue to give services and provide foster care for a child who is dependent, neglected or under insufficient guardianship shall continue; provided further, that the department of pensions and security, if appointed by a court of competent jurisdiction, shall perform the functions of a probation officer of the court in cases involving children who are dependent, neglected, under insufficient guardianship and otherwise handicapped children. (Acts 1973, No. 816, p. 1261, § 8.)

§ 44-1-27. Standards for programs and youth detention facilities; licensing and inspection of youth detention and foster care facilities.

(a) The department of youth services is authorized and directed to establish and promulgate reasonable minimum standards for the construction and operation of detention facilities, programs for the prevention and correction of youth delinquency, in-service training for probation officers, consultation from local officials and subsidies to local delinquency projects. The said standards shall include, but not be limited to, reasonable minimum standards for detention facilities, foster care facilities, group homes, correctional institutions and aftercare services.

(b) No county or city in the state nor any public or private agency, group, corporation, partnership or individual shall establish, maintain or operate any detention facility or any foster care facility for youths found delinquent or in need of supervision by a juvenile court without a license from the department. A license shall be required on an annual basis or as determined by the department. The department shall revoke the license of any city, county or public or private agency, group, corporation or individual conducting, operating or acting as a detention facility or foster care facility caring for children and youths alleged or adjudged to be delinquent or in need of supervision that fails to meet the standards prescribed by the department. The department is authorized to visit and inspect any public or voluntary detention facility, foster care facility or group home as it deems necessary.

(c) The department is authorized to develop standards for probation and aftercare services. The department shall provide consultation upon request by the juvenile court judges and staffs of the county administered programs as to the standards for probation and aftercare services and shall conduct in-service training to aid in the development of services which are in accord with the standards. (Acts 1973, No. 816, p. 1261, § 9.)

§ 44-1-28. Subsidies for youth detention facilities.

The functions and facilities related to youth detention facilities, licensed by the department of youth services of each county or counties, acting together may, upon the express written agreement of each such county or such counties acting together and the department, receive funds from the department according to formulae for disbursement established by the department and in accordance with the terms of written agreements between each such county or such counties acting together and the department, relative to detention care. Any county or counties acting together shall retain control of such detention functions and detention facilities and shall continue to have financial responsibility for their operation, unless otherwise provided for by the department. All detention programs and facilities shall maintain standards prescribed by the department. All funds expended by the department will be contingent upon the recipients of said funds meeting the standards established by the department. (Acts 1973, No. 816, p. 1261, § 10.)

§ 44-1-29. Competitive bids; conflicts of interest.

Any purchase and any construction or supply contract of the department of youth services in an amount in excess of $500.00 shall be made or let by competitive bids through the state purchasing agent or otherwise, as the board may direct. No purchases, except for rights-of-way, shall be made from, nor shall any sales be made to, any member of the legislature, any member of the youth services board, any employee of the department or any other person holding an office of the state. (Acts 1973, No. 816, p. 1261, § 20.)

§ 44-1-30. Study and evaluation of youth in custody of department.

When the legal custody of a youth has been vested in the department of youth services by order of the juvenile judge, the department shall, under rules established by it, study and evaluate such youth and investigate all pertinent circumstances of his behavior and life in order to prepare a service plan while he or she is detained in the state training schools. Data concerning such youth secured in any previous study and evaluation undertaken under this chapter may be utilized by the department in lieu of or in supplementation of a new study and evaluation. The police authorities, the school authorities and other public officials and agencies of the state or any county or municipality in the state shall, upon the request of the department, promptly make available to the department all pertinent information in their possession with respect to a youth whose custody is vested in the department; provided, that this section shall not require any disclosure which would be inconsistent with the requirements of any federal statute or regulation under which grants are made to the state or any state law. The department shall make available its findings pursuant to this section to any juvenile court in the state. (Acts 1973, No. 816, p. 1261, § 21.)

§ 44-1-31. Guardianship of youth in custody of department.

If, at any time while legal custody of a youth is vested in the department of youth services, the department learns that he or she, for any reason does not have a natural or adoptive parent in a position to exercise effective guardianship or a legally appointed guardian of his or her person, the department may thereupon file a petition in the appropriate court for the appointment of a guardian of the person or property of such youth. No officer or employee of the department shall accept appointment as the guardian of a youth whose legal custody is vested in the department. (Acts 1973, No. 816, p. 1261, § 22.)

§ 44-1-32. Determination of social service plan.

(a) When legal custody of a youth has been vested in the department of youth services and so long as such legal custody is so vested in the department, the department may, after an objective consideration of all available information, take one of the following social service actions:

(1) The department may place the youth in a state training school within the state or in another state in accordance with the provisions of the Interstate Compact on Juveniles, under such conditions as it believes best designed for his welfare or the protection of the public;

(2) The department may release the youth to the jurisdiction of the committing court;

(3) The department may arrange temporary return or a trial visit of the youth to his own home, as often as conditions appear desirable; and

(4) The department may revoke or modify any social service plan as often as conditions appear desirable.

(b) The committing court shall be kept informed by the department of the physical location of the youth at all times. (Acts 1973, No. 816, p. 1261, § 23.)

§ 44-1-33. Authorization of medical, psychiatric, surgical and dental treatment.

(a) The state youth services director or his delegate may authorize major surgery or medical treatment to be performed upon any committed youth or general anesthetic to be administered to a committed youth when it is deemed necessary by a licensed medical physician and approval by the parent or guardian is acquired. If such approval is not given or the parent or guardian is unavailable for two weeks, the director or his delegate may apply to the juvenile court in the county where the child is confined for an order to undertake such surgery or treatment. A ruling must be made within 24 hours by the said juvenile judge.

(b) The state youth services director or his delegate may authorize major surgery or medical treatment to be performed upon any committed youth or general anesthetic to be administered to a committed youth when it is deemed an emergency situation where a child has suffered serious injury or is experiencing severe pain or his or her life is endangered and such judgment is made by a licensed medical physician. The director shall within 48 hours notify in writing the juvenile court in the county where the child is confined and the parent or guardian of such action. A copy of the report shall be sent to the committing court. (Acts 1973, No. 816, p. 1261, § 24.)

§ 44-1-34. Review of committed youth.

The department of youth services shall make a periodic review in the case of each youth whose legal custody is vested in the department who has not been finally discharged. Such review shall be in the form of a written report to the committing court and shall include study of all pertinent circumstances of his personal and family situation and shall be for the purpose of determining whether existing decisions, orders and dispositions in his case should be modified or continued in force. Such review may be made as frequently as the department deems necessary and shall be made with respect to every youth at least every nine months. (Acts 1973, No. 816, p. 1261, § 26.)

§ 44-1-35. Petition for examination or review by director or court.

In the event any committed youth has not been examined as provided in section 44-1-30 or has not been reviewed within nine months of a previous review as provided in section 44-1-34, such youth or his parent or guardian shall be entitled to petition the state youth services director for such examination or review and to have his petition given prompt consideration in accordance with appropriate rules established therefor. In the event such petition to the director has not been granted or where it has not been acted upon within 30 days, such youth or his parent or guardian shall be entitled to petition the committing court for such examination and review, and the same shall be granted. Pending the determination of such a petition by the court, the authority of the department of youth services to take such action as it may deem necessary with respect to such youth shall in no way be affected. (Acts 1973, No. 816, p. 1261, § 28.)

§ 44-1-36. Commitment of mentally ill or retarded youth to state hospital; discharge of rehabilitated youth; release of youth into aftercare; termination or extension of orders of commitment.

(a) In the event a committed youth shall be diagnosed in writing as mentally ill to the degree that said youth is unable to profit from the programs operated by the department of youth services for the benefit of delinquent youth, the department may petition the proper juvenile court for the commitment of the said youth to the state hospital for the mentally ill. The diagnosis must be made by a person who is legally and professionally qualified under the laws of Alabama to make such a diagnosis.

(b) In the event a committed youth shall be diagnosed in writing as mentally retarded to the degree that said youth is unable to profit from the programs operated by the department for the benefit of delinquent youth, the department may petition the proper juvenile court for the commitment of the said youth to the state hospital for the mentally retarded. The diagnosis must be made by a person who is legally and professionally qualified under the laws of Alabama to make such a diagnosis.

(c) A committed youth shall be discharged who, in the judgment of the director, has gained optimal rehabilitation from the programs of the department and will not be received again by the department under the original commitment order.

(d) A committed youth shall be released into aftercare when the department determines that said youth is no longer in need of the services of the state training schools and can function within open society under the supervision of a probation officer in accordance with terms and conditions as established by the committing court. The department shall notify the committing court in writing at least 10 days in advance of the release. The committing court, at the time of release into aftercare, shall then invest custody in a party which the court deems suitable.

(e) The committing court shall have jurisdiction to extend an order of commitment during the time of aftercare and to issue further orders in relation to the investment of legal custody in some other party until the youth reaches his twenty-first birthday only upon proper petitions being filed with the said court by a probation officer alleging all reasons for any aftercare extension or change of legal custody. A hearing shall be held in said juvenile court within 10 days after the filing of the petition to determine whether the youth's aftercare should be extended, for no more than six months.

(f) When a committed youth has fulfilled his period of commitment, he or she shall be discharged from the department's custody, and any recommitment to the department must be based on a new offense and a new hearing.

(g) In the event that a youth has not been discharged prior to the expiration of two years from the date of the entry of the original commitment order, the department must request either:

(1) The termination of the commitment order and the issuance of such other orders respecting the legal custody and continued supervision of the youth as may be warranted under the circumstances, or

(2) The extension of the original order for a further specifically limited period of time, on the grounds that such extension is necessary for the welfare of the youth or for the public interest, such extension not to exceed the date upon which the youth will reach the age of 21 years.

There must be a hearing at which the youth and his or her parent, guardian or counsel are present. The committing court shall have jurisdiction until the youth reaches his twenty-first birthday to issue an extension of its original commitment order. If the department does not act as prescribed in this subsection, custody awarded by the commitment order is terminated, and such order as regards such youth has no further force and effect after the expiration of two years.

(h) Upon the youth's reaching his twenty-first birthday, custody awarded by the commitment order is terminated, and such order as regards such person has no further force and effect. (Acts 1973, No. 816, p. 1261, § 29.)

§ 44-1-37. Clothing, money and transportation to be furnished upon release.

The department of youth services shall insure that each youth it releases from the state training schools has clothing, transportation to his home or to the place at which a suitable home or employment has been found for him and such an amount of money as the rules of the department shall authorize. (Acts 1973, No. 816, p. 1261, § 30.)

§ 44-1-38. Records of examinations, etc.

The department of youth services shall keep adequate written records of all social studies and examinations and of the conclusions based thereon and of all major decisions and orders concerning the disposition or treatment of every youth for whom the department provided social services and care pursuant to this chapter. (Acts 1973, No. 816, p. 1261, § 31.)

§ 44-1-39. Restrictions on release or use of records.

(a) It shall be unlawful, except for purposes directly connected with the administration of this chapter, or as herein provided, and in accordance with regulations of the department of youth services, for any person or persons to solicit, disclose, receive or make use of, or authorize, knowingly permit, participate in or acquiesce in the use of any information concerning any youth for whom the department provides social services or care in accordance with the provisions of this chapter and derived from the records, papers, files or communications of the department, or of any agency or facility utilized by the department in providing services to any youth or acquired in the course of the performance of official duties.

(b) Nothing contained in this section shall preclude the disclosure of information secured in the performance of functions under this chapter upon order of the court which vested legal custody of the youth in the department, in any one of the following circumstances:

(1) In subsequent proceedings for delinquency involving the same youth;

(2) To other youth care agencies which subsequently provide services to the said youth;

(3) In any issue of custody before a court in which the court finds that such disclosure is necessary to protect the general welfare of the youth; or

(4) For research purposes where anonymity is preserved. (Acts 1973, No. 816, p. 1261, § 32.)

§ 44-1-40. Agreements with federal government.

The department of youth services is authorized to serve as an agent of the state in entering into agreements with any appropriate agency of the federal government to provide care and treatment for a youth found by a federal court to be delinquent and committed to the custody of the attorney general of the United States. Such agreement shall be upon such terms and conditions and shall provide for such compensation as may be mutually agreed upon between the department and the appropriate agency of the federal government. Funds received as compensation under such agreement shall be placed in the state treasury and are hereby appropriated for the use of the department for carrying out the provisions of this chapter. (Acts 1973, No. 816, p. 1261, § 33.)

ARTICLE 3.

YOUTH SERVICES BOARD.

§ 44-1-50. Created; principal offices.

There is hereby created and established the Alabama youth services board. The principal offices of the board shall be located at the state capital. The board shall have the powers and duties and shall perform the functions described in this Code. (Acts 1973, No. 816, p. 1261, § 4.)

Cited in Alabama Youth Servs. Bd. v. Ellis, 350 So. 2d 405 (Ala. 1977).

§ 44-1-51. Membership; officers; appointment, term of office and compensation of members; filling of vacancies; records of proceedings.

(a) The governor shall be the ex officio chairman of the youth services board.

(b) The board shall be composed of 18 voting members, five of whom shall be the commissioner of the state department of pensions and security, the state superintendent of education, the commissioner of the state department of mental health, the state health officer and the director of the Alabama law enforcement planning agency, each of whom may delegate his or her vote to any agent or employee of the said agencies by written notification 10 days prior to a meeting of the board.

(c) The chairman, vice-chairman and secretary of the board shall be elected by the members thereof. The chairman shall vote only in the case of a tie.

(d) The speaker of the Alabama house of representatives shall appoint two members to be selected from the membership of said house and the presiding officer of the Alabama senate shall appoint two members to be selected from the membership of said senate. The president of the Alabama council of juvenile court judges shall appoint one member to be selected from the membership of said council. The chairman of the Alabama chief probation officers association shall appoint one member to be selected from the membership of said association. The governor shall appoint the remaining seven members of the board, as representatives of the public, one such member to be selected from each of the congressional districts of the state as they existed on January 19, 1972.

(e) The term of each member representative of the public appointed by the governor shall be determined by lot at the first meeting of the board following September 3, 1973. Two of such members shall serve five-year terms, two shall serve two-year terms and one each shall serve three, four and six-year terms, respectively. Thereafter, the term of any such member representative of the public shall be six years. The terms of office of the appointed legislative members shall be for the duration of their respective elected terms of office to the senate or house of representatives. The term of office of the member representative of the Alabama council of juvenile court judges and the member representative of the chief probation officers association shall be six years.

(f) If any appointed legislative member should die, cease to be a member of the legislature or resign from the board, such vacancy shall be filled by the speaker of the house or presiding officer of the senate, such member to be selected from the respective legislative body. Vacancies in other positions appointed by the speaker of the house of representatives or the presiding officer of the senate shall be filled by said appointing authorities. If the appointed juvenile court judge should die, cease to be a juvenile court judge or resign from the board, the president of the Alabama council of juvenile court judges shall appoint a successor for the unexpired term of such a member. If the appointed chief probation officer should die, cease to be a probation officer or resign from the board, the chairman of the Alabama chief probation officers association shall appoint a successor for the unexpired term of such a member. If a vacancy occurs in the appointed membership, upon certification thereof by the board, the governor shall appoint a person to fill the vacancy for the unexpired term of said member. If any person holding any state office named in this section should cease to hold such office by reason of death, resignation, expiration of term of office or for any other reason, then his successor in office shall take his place as a member of the board.

(g) No member of the board shall draw any salary in addition to that now authorized by law for any service he may render or for any deed he may perform in connection with the board. The member representative of the Alabama council of juvenile court judges, the member representative of the Alabama chief probation officers association and each member representative of the public shall receive $25.00 per day and mileage expense at the state rate of mileage reimbursement while attending meetings of the board or while engaged in other official duties at the request of the board. The legislative members shall receive their regular legislative compensation and mileage when actively engaged in board business.

(h) All proceedings of the board shall be reduced to writing by the secretary of the board, shall be signed by at least six members of the board and shall be recorded in a substantially bound book and filed in the office of the secretary, who shall be the custodian of the records of the board. Copies of such proceedings, when certified by the secretary of the board, shall be received in all courts as prima facie evidence of the matters and things therein set forth. (Acts 1973, No. 816, p. 1261, § 5; Acts 1980, No. 80-741, p. 1506.)

§ 44-1-52. Powers.

The youth services board shall have the following powers:

(1) To appoint the state youth services director and to fix his salary.

(2) To institute and defend legal proceedings in any court of competent jurisdiction and proper venue.

(3) To contract with any private person, organization or entity or any combination thereof capable of contracting, if it finds such act to be in the public interest.

(4) To establish and promulgate reasonable rules, policies, orders and regulations for the carrying out of its duties and responsibilities.

(5) To purchase or lease land or to acquire property by eminent domain and to purchase, lease, let, sell, exchange or otherwise transfer property, land or buildings in order to carry out its duties and responsibilities under the provisions of this chapter. (Acts 1973, No. 816, p. 1261, §§ 6, 15.)

§ 44-1-53. Meetings; quorum.

The youth services board may hold such meetings as are convenient and necessary, which shall be at least annually, to carry out its duties and responsibilities at such place or places within the state as it may direct. A quorum consisting of any nine members of the board shall be competent to act at all regular or special meetings. Special meetings may be called by the chairman of the board or by any three members of the board upon one week's written notice to every member of the board, which notice shall state the purpose of the meeting. (Acts 1973, No. 816, p. 1261, § 15.)

§ 44-1-54. Court review of board orders or decisions.

Any person aggrieved by any final order or decision of the youth services board may have a review of such order or decision in the circuit court of Montgomery county, provided a complaint is filed within 15 days of the date of such order or decision, charging that such order or decision was arbitrary, illegal or capricious. The review granted by this section shall be cumulative with that provided elsewhere in the laws of Alabama. (Acts 1973, No. 816, p. 1261, § 17.)

§ 44-1-55. Annual report to governor.

As soon after the end of a fiscal year as practicable, the youth services board shall print and send to the governor of Alabama a report to include the activities of the board, the need for facilities under its jurisdiction, juvenile service conditions in the state, plans for the future, financial reports for the preceding year and the names and addresses of the members of the board. A sufficient number of copies of such report shall be printed and distributed to the members of the legislature of Alabama. (Acts 1973, No. 816, p. 1261, § 18.)

§ 44-1-56. Budget requests.

Each biennium the youth services board shall present to the governor a request for funds based on projected needs for juvenile services in the state, together with a budget showing proposed expenditures. The governor shall include in his appropriation bill a request for funds to meet the reasonable financial needs of the department. (Acts 1973, No. 816, p. 1261, § 19.)

ARTICLE 4.

YOUTH SERVICES DEPARTMENT DISTRICT.

Effective date. — The act which added this article becomes effective October 1, 1983.

§ 44-1-70. Department of youth services designated "youth services department district."

The department of youth services as presently constituted by law is hereby designated as a special school district of the state to be known as the "youth services department district," hereinafter referred to as the district. The relationship existing between the district and the state board of education shall be the same as that of local boards of education to the state board. (Acts 1982, No. 82-485, § 1.)

§ 44-1-71. Superintendent of education for youth services department district — Appointment and qualifications.

There is hereby established the position of superintendent of education for the district which shall be filled by the appointment of the governing board of the department of youth services upon the recommendation of the director of said department, and the superintendent shall serve at the pleasure of, and be directly responsible to, the director. The superintendent shall possess such qualifications as may be specified by the youth services board and as provided by section 16-9-2. (Acts 1982, No. 82-485, § 2.)

§ 44-1-72. Same — Responsibility; annual budget.

The superintendent of the district shall have the general responsibility for administering and supervising the educational programs of the youth services department as approved by the department director. The superintendent shall have the specific duty of submitting the department's annual educational budget recommendations to the director, which shall be based on any funds made available to the department for such educational purposes. The final annual budget shall be approved by the board upon submission by the director. (Acts 1982, No. 82-485, § 3.)

§ 44-1-73. Funding.

The youth services board and the state board of education shall cooperatively establish a funding formula which reflects the educational needs of the students assigned to its custody. The funds for the educational programs shall be appropriated by the legislature from the special educational trust fund and shall be used only for educational purposes, except when the board determines an emergency situation exists; and upon such a determination the board, as recommended by the director, may transfer funds between items of educational and noneducational sources of funding. (Acts 1982, No. 82-485, § 4.)

§ 44-1-74. Retention of certain personnel; employment and status of new teaching personnel; merit system coverage of nonteaching personnel.

As of October 1, 1983, all personnel who have been employed by the department of youth services for at least six months shall remain in their respective jobs and shall be considered to meet all requirements of the department in terms of training and experience; but nothing herein shall be construed to prevent or preclude the removal of an employee for cause in the manner provided by law. The employment of any new teaching personnel after October 1, 1983, shall be on a probationary or nontenured status with the expectation of attaining tenure under the state's tenure law after three consecutive years of service and reemployment for the fourth year. The employment of nonteaching personnel after October 1, 1983, shall continue to be under the provisions and protection of the state merit system. (Acts 1982, No. 82-485, § 5.)

Cross references. — As to tenure of employment of teachers, see § 16-24-1 et seq.

§ 44-1-75. Salary schedule for teachers; leaves, benefits and insurance.

The youth services director shall work with the superintendent and the teaching staffs on each of the three campuses to develop a salary schedule for teachers. In placing teachers, granted tenure in section 44-1-74, on the resulting salary schedule, no teacher shall be placed at a salary level lower than that held on October 1, 1983. In addition to developing this salary schedule, the director and superintendent shall work together with teachers to arrange replacement of all leaves and benefits previously enjoyed by the teachers of the department under the state merit system. For purposes of obtaining hospital/medical benefits and life insurance, teaching personnel shall remain under the state employees' hospital/medical and life insurance plans until such time as statewide hospital/medical and life insurance plans are developed for all state teachers. (Acts 1982, No. 82-485, § 6.)

§ 44-1-76. Relationship of board of youth services and superintendent to state board of education; powers and duties of board and superintendent; functioning of district.

The board of youth services and the superintendent of education of the special school district shall stand in the same relationship to the state board of education as do local boards of education and local superintendents of education. The powers, duties and responsibilities of the board of youth services, the superintendent, and the functioning of the district shall be the same as provided for in sections 16-8-10 and 16-11-18. (Acts 1982, No. 82-485, § 7.)

§ 44-1-77. Construction of article.

The provisions of this article shall be construed in pari materia with the provisions of law contained in Title 44, chapters 1 and 2, and shall supersede and repeal such provisions of law only to the extent there exists a conflict herewith. (Acts 1982, No. 82-485, § 9.)

CHAPTER 2.

INTERSTATE COMPACT ON JUVENILES.

ARTICLE 1.

GENERAL PROVISIONS.

Collateral references. — 16 C.J.S., Constitutional Law, § 138.

§ 44-2-1. Legislative findings and declaration of policy.

(a) It is hereby found and declared:

(1) That juveniles who are not under proper supervision and control or who have absconded, escaped or run away are likely to endanger their own health, morals and welfare and the health, morals and welfare of others;

(2) That the cooperation of this state with other states is necessary to provide for the welfare and protection of juveniles and of the people of this state.

(b) It shall therefore be the policy of this state, in adopting the Interstate Compact on Juveniles, to cooperate fully with other states:

(1) In returning juveniles to such other states whenever their return is sought; and

(2) In accepting the return of juveniles whenever a juvenile residing in this state is found or apprehended in another state and in taking all measures to initiate proceedings for the return of such juveniles. (Acts 1965, No. 675, p. 1214, § 1.)

Collateral references. — Extradition of juveniles. 73 ALR3d 700.

Validity, construction and applications of Uniform Child Custody Jurisdiction Act. 96 ALR3d 968.

§ 44-2-2. Compact administrator.

The state youth services director shall be the compact administrator and, acting jointly with like officers of other party states, shall promulgate rules and regulations to carry out more effectively the terms of the compact. The compact administrator is hereby authorized, empowered and directed to cooperate with all departments, agencies and officers of and in the government of this state and its subdivisions in facilitating the proper administration of the compact or of any supplementary agreement or agreements entered into by this state hereunder. (Acts 1965, No. 675, p. 1214, § 3.)

§ 44-2-3. Supplementary agreements.

The compact administrator is hereby authorized and empowered to enter into supplementary agreements with appropriate officials of other states pursuant to the compact. In the event that such supplementary agreement shall require or contemplate the use of any institution or facility of this state or require or contemplate the provision of any service by this state, said supplementary agreement shall have no force or effect until approved by the head of the department or agency under whose jurisdiction said institution or facility is operated or whose department or agency will be charged with the rendering of such service. (Acts 1965, No. 675, p. 1214, § 4.)

§ 44-2-4. Financial arrangements.

The compact administrator may make or arrange for any payments necessary to discharge any financial obligations imposed upon this state by the compact or by any supplementary agreement entered into thereunder. (Acts 1965, No. 675, p. 1214, § 5.)

§ 44-2-5. Responsibilities of state courts, departments, agencies and officers.

The courts, departments, agencies and officers of this state and its subdivisions shall enforce this compact and shall do all things appropriate to the effectuation of its purposes and intent which may be within their respective jurisdictions. (Acts 1965, No. 675, p. 1214, § 6.)

§ 44-2-6. Additional procedures not precluded.

In addition to any procedure provided in Articles IV and VI of the compact for the return of any runaway juvenile, the particular states, the juvenile or his parents, the courts or other legal custodian involved may agree upon and adopt any other plan or procedure legally authorized under the laws of this state and the other respective party states for the return of any such runaway juvenile. (Acts 1965, No. 675, p. 1214, § 7.)

§ 44-2-7. Execution and text of compact.

The governor is hereby authorized and directed to execute a compact on behalf of this state with any other state or states legally joining therein in the form substantially as follows:

The contracting states solemnly agree:

Article I. Findings and Purposes.

That juveniles who are not under proper supervision and control, or who have absconded, escaped or run away, are likely to endanger their own health, morals and welfare, and the health, morals and welfare of others. The cooperation of the states party to this compact is therefore necessary to provide for the welfare and protection of juveniles and of the public with respect to (1) cooperative supervision of delinquent juveniles on probation or parole; (2) the return, from one state to another, of delinquent juveniles who have escaped or absconded; (3) the return, from one state to another, of nondelinquent juveniles who have run away from home; and (4) additional measures for the protection of juveniles and of the public, which any two or more of the party states may find desirable to undertake cooperatively. In carrying out the provisions of this compact the party states shall be guided by the noncriminal, reformative and protective policies which guide their laws concerning delinquent, neglected or dependent juveniles generally. It shall be the policy of the states party to this compact to cooperate and observe their respective responsibilities for the prompt return and acceptance of juveniles and delinquent juveniles who become subject to the provisions of this compact. The provisions of this compact shall be reasonably and liberally construed to accomplish the foregoing purposes.

Article II. Existing Rights and Remedies.

That all remedies and procedures provided by this compact shall be in addition to and not in substitution for other rights, remedies and procedures, and shall not be in derogation of parental rights and responsibilities.

Article III. Definitions.

That, for the purposes of this compact, "delinquent juvenile" means any juvenile who has been adjudged delinquent and who, at the time the provisions of this compact are invoked, is still subject to the jurisdiction of the court that has made such adjudication or to the jurisdiction or supervision of an agency or institution pursuant to an order of such court; "probation or parole" means any kind of conditional release of juveniles authorized under the laws of the states party hereto; "court" means any court having jurisdiction over delinquent, neglected or dependent children; "state" means any state, territory or possession of the United States, the District of Columbia, and the Commonwealth of Puerto Rico; and "residence" or any variant thereof means a place at which a home or regular place of abode is maintained.

Article IV. Return of Runaways.

(a) That the parent, guardian, person or agency entitled to legal custody of a juvenile who has not been adjudged delinquent but who has run away without the consent of such parent, guardian, person or agency may petition the appropriate court in the demanding state for the issuance of a requisition for his return. The petition shall state the name and age of the juvenile, the name of the petitioner and the basis of entitlement to the juvenile's custody, the circumstances of his running away, his location if known at the time application is made, and such other facts as may tend to show that the juvenile who has run away is endangering his own welfare or the welfare of others and is not an emancipated minor. The petition shall be verified by affidavit, shall be executed in duplicate, and shall be accompanied by two certified copies of the document or documents on which the petitioner's entitlement to the juvenile's custody is based, such as birth certificates, letters of guardianship, or custody decrees. Such further affidavits and other documents as may be deemed proper may be submitted with such petition. The judge of the court to which this application is made may hold hearing thereon to determine whether for the purposes of this compact the petitioner is entitled to the legal custody of the juvenile, whether or not it appears that the juvenile has in fact run away without consent, whether or not he is an emancipated minor, and whether or not it is in the best interest of the juvenile to compel his return to the state. If the judge determines, either with or without a hearing, that the juvenile should be returned, he shall present to the appropriate court or to the executive authority of the state where the juvenile is alleged to be located a written requisition for the return of such juvenile. Such requisition shall set forth the name and age of the juvenile, the determination of the court that the juvenile has run away without the consent of a parent, guardian, person or agency entitled to his legal custody, and that it is in the best interest and for the protection of such juvenile that he be returned. In the event that a proceeding for the adjudication of the juvenile as a delinquent, neglected or dependent juvenile is pending in the court at the time when such juvenile runs away, the court may issue a requisition for the return of such juvenile upon its own motion, regardless of the consent of the parent, guardian, person or agency entitled to legal custody, reciting therein the nature and circumstances of the pending proceeding. The requisition shall in every case be executed in duplicate and shall be signed by the judge. One copy of the requisition shall be filed with the compact administrator of the demanding state, there to remain on file subject to the provisions of law governing records of such court. Upon the receipt of a requisition demanding the return of a juvenile who has run away, the court or the executive authority to whom the requisition is addressed shall issue an order to any peace officer or other appropriate person directing him to take into custody and detain such juvenile. Such detention order must substantially recite the facts necessary to the validity of its issuance hereunder. No juvenile detained upon such order shall be delivered over to the officer whom the court demanding him shall have appointed to receive him, unless he shall first be taken forthwith before a judge of a court in the state, who shall inform him of the demand made for his return, and who may appoint counsel or guardian ad litem for him. If the judge of such court shall find that the requisition is in order, he shall deliver such juvenile over to the officer whom the court demanding him shall have appointed to receive him. The judge, however, may fix a reasonable time to be allowed for the purpose of testing the legality of the proceeding.

Upon reasonable information that a person is a juvenile who has run away from another state party to this compact without the consent of a parent, guardian, person or agency entitled to his legal custody, such juvenile may be taken into custody without a requisition and brought forthwith before a judge of the appropriate court who may appoint counsel or guardian ad litem for such juvenile and who shall determine after a hearing whether sufficient cause exists to hold the person, subject to the order of the court, for his own protection and welfare, for such a time not exceeding 90 days as will enable his return to another state party to this compact pursuant to a requisition for his return from a court of that state. If, at the time when a state seeks the return of a juvenile who has run away, there is pending in the state wherein he is found any criminal charge, or any proceeding to have him adjudicated a delinquent juvenile for an act committed in such state, or if he is suspected of having committed within such state a criminal offense or an act of juvenile delinquency, he shall not be returned without the consent of such state until discharged from prosecution or other form of proceeding, imprisonment, detention or supervision for such offense or juvenile delinquency. The duly accredited officers of any state party to this compact, upon the establishment of their authority and the identity of the juvenile being returned, shall be permitted to transport such juvenile through any and all states party to this compact, without interference. Upon his return to the state from which he ran away, the juvenile shall be subject to such further proceedings as may be appropriate under the laws of that state.

(b) That the state to which a juvenile is returned under this article shall be responsible for payment of the transportation costs of such return.

(c) That "juvenile" as used in this article means any person who is a minor under the law of the state of residence of the parent, guardian, person or agency entitled to the legal custody of such minor.

Article V. Return of Escapees and Absconders.

(a) That the appropriate person or authority from whose probation or parole supervision a delinquent juvenile has absconded or from whose institutional custody he has escaped shall present to the appropriate court or to the executive authority of the state where the delinquent juvenile is alleged to be located a written requisition for the return of such delinquent juvenile. Such requisition shall state the name and age of the delinquent juvenile, the particulars of his adjudication as a delinquent juvenile, the circumstances of the breach of the terms of his probation or parole or of his escape from an institution or agency vested with his legal custody or supervision, and the location of such delinquent juvenile, if known, at the time the requisition is made. The requisition shall be verified by affidavit, shall be executed in duplicate, and shall be accompanied by two certified copies of the judgment, formal adjudication, or order of commitment which subjects such delinquent juvenile to probation or parole or to the legal custody of the institution or agency concerned. Such further affidavits and other documents as may be deemed proper may be submitted with such requisition. One copy of the requisition shall be filed with the compact administrator of the demanding state, there to remain on file subject to the provisions of law governing records of the appropriate court. Upon the receipt of a requisition demanding the return of a delinquent juvenile who has absconded or escaped, the court or the executive authority to whom the requisition is addressed shall issue an order to any peace officer or other appropriate person directing him to take into custody and detain such delinquent juvenile. Such detention order must substantially recite the facts necessary to the validity of its issuance hereunder. No delinquent juvenile detained upon such order shall be delivered over to the officer whom the appropriate person or authority demanding him shall have appointed to receive him, unless he shall first be taken forthwith before a judge of an appropriate court in the state, who shall inform him of the demand made for his return and who may appoint counsel or guardian ad litem for him. If the judge of such court shall find that the requisition is in order, he shall deliver such delinquent juvenile over to the officer whom the appropriate person or authority demanding him shall have appointed to receive him. The judge, however, may fix a reasonable time to be allowed for the purpose of testing the legality of the proceeding.

Upon reasonable information that a person is a delinquent juvenile who has absconded while on probation or parole, or escaped from an institution or agency vested with his legal custody or supervision in any state party to this compact, such person may be taken into custody in any other state party to this compact without a requisition. But in such event, he must be taken forthwith before a judge of the appropriate court, who may appoint counsel or guardian ad litem for such person and who shall determine, after a hearing, whether sufficient cause exists to hold the person subject to the order of the court for such a time, not exceeding 90 days, as will enable his detention under a detention order issued on a requisition pursuant to this article. If, at the time when a state seeks the return of a delinquent juvenile who has either absconded while on probation or parole or escaped from an institution or agency vested with his legal custody or supervision, there is pending in the state wherein he is detained any criminal charge or any proceeding to have him adjudicated a delinquent juvenile for an act committed in such state, or if he is suspected of having committed within such state a criminal offense or an act of juvenile delinquency, he shall not be returned without the consent of such state until discharged from prosecution or other form of proceeding, imprisonment, detention or supervision for such offense or juvenile delinquency. The duly accredited officers of any state party to this compact, upon the establishment of their authority and the identity of the delinquent juvenile being returned, shall be permitted to transport such delinquent juvenile through any and all states party to this compact, without interference. Upon his return to the state from which he escaped or absconded, the delinquent juvenile shall be subject to such further proceedings as may be appropriate under the laws of that state.

(b) That the state to which a delinquent juvenile is returned under this article shall be responsible for the payment of the transportation costs of such return.

Article VI. Voluntary Return Procedure.

That any delinquent juvenile who has absconded while on probation or parole, or escaped from an institution or agency vested with his legal custody or supervision in any state party to this compact, and any juvenile who has run away from any state party to this compact, who is taken into custody without a requisition in another state party to this compact under the provisions of Article IV (a) or of Article V (a), may consent to his immediate return to the state from which he absconded, escaped or ran away. Such consent shall be given by the juvenile or delinquent juvenile and his counsel or guardian ad litem if any, by executing or subscribing a writing, in the presence of a judge of the appropriate court, which states that the juvenile or delinquent juvenile and his counsel or guardian ad litem, if any, consent to his return to the demanding state. Before such consent shall be executed or subscribed, however, the judge, in the presence of counsel or guardian ad litem, if any, shall inform the juvenile or delinquent juvenile of his rights under this compact. When the consent has been duly executed, it shall be forwarded to and filed with the compact administrator of the state in which the court is located and the judge shall direct the officer having the juvenile or delinquent juvenile in custody to deliver him to the duly accredited officer or officers of the state demanding his return, and shall cause to be delivered to such officer or officers a copy of the consent. The court may, however, upon the request of the state to which the juvenile or delinquent juvenile is being returned, order him to return unaccompanied to such state and shall provide him with a copy of such court order; in such event a copy of the consent shall be forwarded to the compact administrator of the state to which said juvenile or delinquent juvenile is ordered to return.

Article VII. Cooperative Supervision of Probationers and Parolees.

(a) That the duly constituted judicial and administrative authorities of a state party to this compact (herein called "sending state") may permit any delinquent juvenile within such state, placed on probation or parole, to reside in any other state party to this compact (herein called "receiving state") while on probation or parole, and the receiving state shall accept such delinquent juvenile, if the parent, guardian or person entitled to the legal custody of such delinquent juvenile is residing or undertakes to reside within the receiving state. Before granting such permission, opportunity shall be given to the receiving state to make such investigations as it deems necessary. The authorities of the sending state shall send to the authorities of the receiving state copies of pertinent court orders, social case studies and all other available information which may be of value to and assist the receiving state in supervising a probationer or parolee under this compact. A receiving state, in its discretion, may agree to accept supervision of a probationer or parolee in cases where the parent, guardian or person entitled to the legal custody of the delinquent juvenile is not a resident of the receiving state, and if so accepted the sending state may transfer supervision accordingly.

(b) That each receiving state will assume the duties of visitation and of supervision over any such delinquent juvenile and in the exercise of those duties will be governed by the same standards of visitation and supervision that prevail for its own delinquent juveniles released on probation or parole.

(c) That, after consultation between the appropriate authorities of the sending state and of the receiving state as to the desirability and necessity of returning such a delinquent juvenile, the duly accredited officers of a sending state may enter a receiving state and there apprehend and retake any such delinquent juvenile on probation or parole. For that purpose, no formalities will be required, other than establishing the authority of the officer and the identity of the delinquent juvenile to be retaken and returned. The decision of the sending state to retake a delinquent juvenile on probation or parole shall be conclusive upon and not reviewable within the receiving state, but if, at the time the sending state seeks to retake a delinquent juvenile on probation or parole, there is pending against him within the receiving state any criminal charge or any proceeding to have him adjudicated a delinquent juvenile for any act committed in such state or if he is suspected of having committed within such state a criminal offense or an act of juvenile delinquency, he shall not be returned without the consent of the receiving state until discharged from prosecution or other form of proceeding, imprisonment, detention or supervision for such offense or act of juvenile delinquency. The duly accredited officers of the sending state shall be permitted to transport delinquent juveniles being so returned through any and all states party to this compact, without interference.

(d) That the sending state shall be responsible under this article for paying the costs of transporting any delinquent juvenile to the receiving state or of returning any delinquent juvenile to the sending state.

Article VIII. Responsibility for Costs.

(a) That the provisions of Articles IV (b), V (b) and VII (d) of this compact shall not be construed to alter or affect any internal relationship among the departments, agencies and officers of and in the government of a party state, or between a party state and its subdivisions, as to the payment of costs, or responsibilities therefor.

(b) That nothing in this compact shall be construed to prevent any party state or subdivision thereof from asserting any right against any person, agency or other entity in regard to costs for which such party state or subdivision thereof may be responsible pursuant to Articles IV (b), V (b) or VII (d) of this compact.

Article IX. Detention Practices.

That, to every extent possible, it shall be the policy of states party to this compact that no juvenile or delinquent juvenile shall be placed or detained in any prison, jail or lockup nor be detained or transported in association with criminal, vicious or dissolute persons.

Article X. Supplementary Agreements.

That the duly constituted administrative authorities of a state party to this compact may enter into supplementary agreements with any other state or states party hereto for the cooperative care, treatment and rehabilitation of delinquent juveniles whenever they shall find that such agreements will improve the facilities or programs available for such care, treatment and rehabilitation. Such care, treatment and rehabilitation may be provided in an institution located within any state entering into such supplementary agreement. Such supplementary agreements shall (1) provide the rates to be paid for the care, treatment and custody of such delinquent juveniles, taking into consideration the character of facilities, services and subsistence furnished; (2) provide that the delinquent juvenile shall be given a court hearing prior to his being sent to another state for care, treatment and custody; (3) provide that the state receiving such a delinquent juvenile in one of its institutions shall act solely as agent for the state sending such delinquent juvenile; (4) provide that the sending state shall at all times retain jurisdiction over delinquent juveniles sent to an institution in another state; (5) provide for reasonable inspection of such institutions by the sending state; (6) provide that the consent of the parent, guardian, person or agency entitled to the legal custody of said delinquent juvenile shall be secured prior to his being sent to another state; and (7) make provision for such other matters and details as shall be necessary to protect the rights and equities of such delinquent juveniles and of the cooperating states.

Article XI. Acceptance of Federal and Other Aid.

That any state party to this compact may accept any and all donations, gifts and grants of money, equipment and services from the federal or any local government, or any agency thereof and from any person, firm or corporation, for any of the purposes and functions of this compact, and may receive and utilize the same subject to the terms, conditions and regulations governing such donations, gifts and grants.

Article XII. Compact Administrators.

That the governor of each state party to this compact shall designate an officer who, acting jointly with like officers of other party states, shall promulgate rules and regulations to carry out more effectively the terms and provisions of this compact.

Article XIII. Execution of Compact.

That this compact shall become operative immediately upon its execution by any state as between it and any other state or states so executing. When executed it shall have the full force and effect of law within such state, the form or execution to be in accordance with the laws of the executing state.

Article XIV. Renunciation.

That this compact shall continue in force and remain binding upon each executing state until renounced by it. Renunciation of this compact shall be by the same authority which executed it, by sending six months' notice in writing of its intention to withdraw from the compact to the other states party hereto. The duties and obligations of a renouncing state under Article VII hereof shall continue as to parolees and probationers residing therein at the time of withdrawal until retaken or finally discharged. Supplementary agreements entered into under Article X hereof shall be subject to renunciation as provided by such supplementary agreements, and shall not be subject to the six months' renunciation notice of the present article.

Article XV. Severability.

That the provisions of this compact shall be severable and if any phrase, clause, sentence or provision of this compact is declared to be contrary to the Constitution of any participating state or of the United States or the applicability thereof to any government, agency, person or circumstances is held invalid, the validity of the remainder of this compact and the applicability thereof to any government, agency, person or circumstances shall not be affected thereby. If this compact shall be held contrary to the Constitution of any state participating therein, the compact shall remain in full force and effect as to the remaining states and in full force and effect as to the state affected as to all severable matters. (Acts 1965, No. 675, p. 1214, § 2.)

ARTICLE 2.

INTERSTATE COMPACT ON THE PLACEMENT OF CHILDREN.

§ 44-2-20. Text of compact.

The Interstate Compact on the Placement of Children is hereby enacted into law and entered into with all other jurisdictions legally joining therein in form substantially as follows:

Article I.

Purpose and Policy.

It is the purpose and policy of the party states to cooperate with each other in the interstate placement of children to the end that:

(a) Each child requiring placement shall receive the maximum opportunity to be placed in a suitable environment and with persons or institutions having appropriate qualifications and facilities to provide a necessary and desirable degree and type of care.

(b) The appropriate authorities in a state where a child is to be placed may have full opportunity to ascertain the circumstances of the proposed placement, thereby promoting full compliance with applicable requirements for the protection of the child.

(c) The proper authorities of the state from which the placement is made may obtain the most complete information on the basis of which to evaluate a projected placement before it is made.

(d) Appropriate jurisdictional arrangements for the care of children will be promoted.

Article II.

Definitions.

As used in this compact:

(a) "Child" means a person who, by reason of minority, is legally subject to parental, guardianship or similar control.

(b) "Sending agency" means a party state, or officer or employee thereof; a subdivision of a party state, or officer or employee thereof; a court of a party state; a person, corporation, association, charitable agency or other entity which sends, brings or causes to be sent or brought any child to another party state.

(c) "Receiving state" means the state to which a child is sent, brought or caused to be sent or brought, whether by public authorities or private persons or agencies, and whether for placement with state or local public authorities or for placement with private agencies or persons.

(d) "Placement" means the arrangement for the care of a child in a family free or boarding home or in a child-caring agency or institution but does not include any institution caring for the mentally ill, mentally defective or epileptic or any institution primarily educational in character, and any hospital or other medical facility.

Article III.

Conditions for Placement.

(a) No sending agency shall send, bring or cause to be sent or brought into any other party state any child for placement in foster care or as a preliminary to a possible adoption unless the sending agency shall comply with each and every requirement set forth in this article and with the applicable laws of the receiving state governing the placement of children therein.

(b) Prior to sending, bringing or causing any child to be sent or brought into a receiving state for placement in foster care or as a preliminary to a possible adoption, the sending agency shall furnish the appropriate public authorities in the receiving state written notice of the intention to send, bring or place the child in the receiving state. The notice shall contain:

(1) The name, date and place of birth of the child.

(2) The identity and address or addresses of the parents or legal guardian.

(3) The name and address of the person, agency or institution to or with which the sending agency proposed to send, bring or place the child.

(4) A full statement of the reasons for such proposed action and evidence of the authority pursuant to which the placement is proposed to be made.

(c) Any public officer or agency in a receiving state which is in receipt of a notice pursuant to paragraph (b) of this article may request of the sending agency, or any other appropriate officer or agency of or in the sending agency's state, and shall be entitled to receive therefrom, such supporting or additional information as it may deem necessary under the circumstances to carry out the purpose and policy of this compact.

(d) The child shall not be sent, brought or caused to be sent or brought into the receiving state until the appropriate public authorities in the receiving state shall notify the sending agency, in writing, to the effect that the proposed placement does not appear to be contrary to the interests of the child.

Article IV.

Penalty for Illegal Placement.

The sending, bringing or causing to be sent or brought into any receiving state of a child in violation of the terms of this compact shall constitute a violation of the laws respecting the placement of children of both the state in which the sending agency is located or from which it sends or brings the child and of the receiving state. Such violation may be punished or subjected to penalty in either jurisdiction in accordance with its laws. In addition to liability for any such punishment or penalty, any such violation shall constitute full and sufficient grounds for the suspension or revocation of any license, permit or other legal authorization held by the sending agency which empowers or allows it to place, or care for children.

Article V.

Retention of Jurisdiction.

(a) The sending agency shall retain jurisdiction over the child sufficient to determine all matters in relation to the custody, supervision, care, treatment and disposition of the child which it would have had if the child had remained in the sending agency's state, until the child is adopted, reaches majority, becomes self-supporting or is discharged with the concurrence of the appropriate authority in the receiving state. Such jurisdiction shall also include the power to effect or cause the return of the child or its transfer to another location and custody pursuant to law. The sending agency shall continue to have financial responsibility for support and maintenance of the child during the period of the placement. Nothing contained herein shall defeat a claim of jurisdiction by a receiving state sufficient to deal with an act of delinquency or crime committed therein.

(b) When the sending agency is a public agency, it may enter into an agreement with an authorized public or private agency in the receiving state providing for the performance of one or more services in respect of such case by the latter as agent for the sending agency.

(c) Nothing in this compact shall be construed to prevent a private charitable agency authorized to place children in the receiving state from performing services or acting as agent in that state for a private charitable agency of the sending state; nor to prevent the agency in the receiving state from discharging financial responsibility for the support and maintenance of a child who has been placed on behalf of the sending agency without relieving the responsibility set forth in paragraph (a) hereof.

Article VI.

Institutional Care of Delinquent Children.

A child adjudicated delinquent may be placed in an institution in another party jurisdiction pursuant to this compact but no such placement shall be made unless the child is given a court hearing on notice to the parent or guardian with opportunity to be heard, prior to his being sent to such other party jurisdiction for institutional care and the court finds that:

1. Equivalent facilities for the child are not available in the sending agency's jurisdiction; and

2. Institutional care in the other jurisdiction is in the best interest of the child and will not produce undue hardship.

Article VII.

Compact Administrator.

The executive head of each jurisdiction party to this compact shall designate an officer who shall be general coordinator of activities under this compact in his jurisdiction and who, acting jointly with like officers of other party jurisdictions, shall have power to promulgate rules and regulations to carry out more effectively the terms and provisions of this compact.

Article VIII.

Limitations.

This compact shall not apply to:

(a) The sending or bringing of a child into a receiving state by his parent, step-parent, grandparent, adult brother or sister, adult uncle or aunt or his guardian and leaving the child with any such relative or nonagency guardian in the receiving state.

(b) Any placement, sending or bringing of a child into a receiving state pursuant to any other interstate compact to which both the state from which the child is sent or brought and the receiving state are party, or to any other agreement between said states which has the force of law.

Article IX.

Enactment and Withdrawal.

This compact shall be open to joinder by any state, territory or possession of the United States, the District of Columbia, the Commonwealth of Puerto Rico and, with the consent of congress, the government of Canada or any province thereof. It shall become effective with respect to any such jurisdiction when such jurisdiction has enacted the same into law. Withdrawal from this compact shall be by the enactment of a statute repealing the same, but shall not take effect until two years after the effective date of such statute and until written notice of the withdrawal has been given by the withdrawing state to the governor of each other party jurisdiction. Withdrawal of a party state shall not affect the rights, duties and obligations under this compact of any sending agency therein with respect to a placement made prior to the effective date of withdrawal.

Article X.

Construction and Severability.

The provisions of this compact shall be liberally construed to effectuate the purposes thereof. The provisions of this compact shall be severable and if any phrase, clause, sentence or provision of this compact is declared to be contrary to the constitution of any party state or the United States or the applicability thereof to any government, agency, person or circumstance is held invalid, the validity of the remainder of this compact and the applicability thereof to any government, agency, person or circumstance shall not be affected thereby. If this compact shall be held contrary to the constitution of any state party thereto, the compact shall remain in full force and effect as to the remaining states and in full force and effect as to the state affected as to all severable matters. (Acts 1979, No. 79-675, p. 1192.)

Section applied prospectively. — Whether a statute operates prospectively or retrospectively is a matter of legislative intent. Statutes generally will be held to operate prospectively unless the purpose and intention of the legislature to give them a retrospective effect clearly appears. After a careful review of this section, the court is unable to discern any intent that its provisions be applied retrospectively. Hanlon v. Mooney, 407 So. 2d 554 (Ala. Civ. App.), rev'd on other grounds, 407 So. 2d 559 (Ala. 1981).

§ 44-2-21. Financial responsibility.

Financial responsibility for any child placed pursuant to the provisions of the Interstate Compact on the Placement of Children shall be determined in accordance with the provisions of Article V thereof in the first instance. However, in the event of partial or complete default of performance thereunder, the provisions of sections 30-4-50 through 30-4-82, also may be invoked. (Acts 1979, No. 79-675, p. 1192.)

§ 44-2-22. Department of pensions and security to act as appropriate public authority.

The [term] "appropriate public authorities" as used in Article III of the Interstate Compact on the Placement of Children shall, with reference to this state, mean the department of pensions and security of the state of Alabama and said department shall receive and act with reference to notices required by said Article III. (Acts 1979, No. 79-675, p. 1192.)

§ 44-2-23. Commissioner of department of pensions and security to be appropriate authority in the receiving state.

As used in paragraph (a) of Article V of the Interstate Compact on the Placement of Children the phrase "appropriate authority in the receiving state" with reference to this state shall mean the commissioner of the department of pensions and security. (Acts 1979, No. 79-675, p. 1192.)

§ 44-2-24. Authority to enter into agreements; commissioner of department of pensions and security to approve financial commitments or obligations.

The officers and agencies of this state and its subdivisions having authority to place children are hereby empowered to enter into agreements with appropriate officers or agencies of or in other party states pursuant to paragraph (b) of Article V of the Interstate Compact on the Placement of Children. Any such agreement which contains a financial commitment or imposes a financial obligation of this state or subdivision or agency thereof shall not be binding unless it has the approval in writing of the commissioner of the department of pensions and security or his designated agent. (Acts 1979, No. 79-675, p. 1192.)

§ 44-2-25. Governor to act as executive head.

As used in Article VI [Article VII] of the Interstate Compact on the Placement of Children, the term "executive head" means the governor. The governor of each state party to this compact shall designate an officer who, acting jointly with like officers of other party states, shall promulgate rules and regulations to carry out more effectively the terms and provisions of this compact. (Acts 1979, No. 79-675, p. 1192.)

§ 44-2-26. Commissioner of department of pensions and security to be compact administrator.

The commissioner of the state department of pensions and security shall be the compact administrator and, acting jointly with like officers of other party states, shall promulgate rules and regulations to carry out more effectively the terms of the compact. The compact administrator is hereby authorized, empowered and directed to cooperate with all departments, agencies and officers of and in the government of this state and its subdivisions in facilitating the proper administration of the compact or any supplementary agreement or agreements entered into by this state hereunder. (Acts 1979, No. 79-675, p. 1192.)

CHAPTER 3.

REGIONAL CUSTODY AND CARE OF YOUTHS UNDER
JURISDICTION OF JUVENILE COURT.

Cited in Carter v. Coosa Valley Youth
Servs., 378 So. 2d 1145 (Ala. Civ. App. 1979).

§ 44-3-1. Definitions.

The following words and phrases used in this chapter, and others evidently intended as the equivalent thereof, shall, in the absence of clear implication herein otherwise, be given the following respective interpretations herein:

(1) ALABAMA DEPARTMENT OF YOUTH SERVICES. The state department of that name or any other department created by the legislature in lieu of said department.

(2) BOARD OF DIRECTORS. That body of persons selected in accordance with the articles of incorporation and bylaws of a corporation formed pursuant to this chapter.

(3) COUNTY. Any county in this state.

(4) FACILITIES. Structures, equipment and furnishings, or any other part or combination thereof, which are used, useful or capable of use, and the use thereof in connection with the implementation and operation of programs as defined herein.

(5) GOVERNING BODY. A county commission, board of revenue or other like governing body of a county, or the council, commission or other like governing body of an incorporated municipality.

(6) PROGRAMS. The use of various behavioral programs in the care and supervision of children. All programs are to be in compliance with the minimum standards as established by the Alabama department of youth services as defined herein. (Acts 1978, No. 620, p. 880, § 1.)

§ 44-3-2. Authorization for creation by counties and municipalities of regional, nonprofit public corporations for provision of temporary care and custody of youths under juvenile court jurisdiction.

All counties and incorporated municipalities in this state are hereby authorized and empowered to form regional, nonprofit, public corporations which shall provide for the temporary care and custody of youths who have been placed under the jurisdiction of a juvenile court. (Acts 1978, No. 620, p. 880, § 2.)

Collateral references. — 43 C.J.S., Infants, §§ 6, 7, 9, 10, 12.

47 Am. Jur. 2d, Juvenile Courts and Delinquent and Dependent Children, § 29.

§ 44-3-3. Effect of formation of corporations upon presently existing juvenile facilities and programs and corporations.

Any corporation so created shall be a public, nonprofit corporation and may be organized as a successor to presently existing juvenile facilities and programs. Members in presently existing corporations shall automatically retain membership in any successor corporation formed after the passage of this chapter. (Acts 1978, No. 620, p. 880, § 3.)

§ 44-3-4. Service areas of corporations.

The service area of such corporation shall be those present and future Alabama counties who are members of a corporation formed for the purpose of providing temporary care and custody to those children who are placed with the corporation by order of a judge exercising juvenile court jurisdiction or otherwise placed under the authority of existing law. (Acts 1978, No. 620, p. 880, § 4.)

§ 44-3-5. Corporations to be governed by boards of directors; selection and meetings of boards of directors.

Such corporation shall be governed by a board of directors selected from member counties or municipalities, as the case may be, as may be specified in the bylaws of the corporation. The board of directors shall hold regular quarterly meetings and such meetings as may be called from time to time by the chairman of the board who shall be selected in accordance with procedure as outlined in the bylaws. The annual meeting of the corporation shall be held in conjunction with the last board of directors meeting in the calendar year. (Acts 1978, No. 620, p. 880, § 5.)

§ 44-3-6. Powers of corporations generally.

Pursuant to the provisions of this chapter, such corporation, in acting through the board of directors, shall have all the powers of a corporation as granted by the laws of Alabama. (Acts 1978, No. 620, p. 880, § 6.)

Collateral references. — 14 C.J.S., Charities, §§ 68, 69, 72.

§ 44-3-7. Amendment of articles of incorporation of corporations.

The articles of incorporation of such corporation may be amended as specified in the articles of incorporation. (Acts 1978, No. 620, p. 880, § 7.)

§ 44-3-8. Admission of governing bodies into membership of corporations.

Any governing body in the state as defined in this chapter may submit a letter of application to the corporation's chairman of the board of directors. Said letter shall be in compliance with admission procedures as established by the board. Upon approval of a majority of board members present at a regularly scheduled board meeting, new members shall be admitted into the corporation and the number of directors representing that body will be determined by the existing board. (Acts 1978, No. 620, p. 880, § 8.)

§ 44-3-9. Appropriations to corporations by governing bodies.

All governing bodies, as defined in this chapter, are hereby authorized to appropriate and pay over to the corporation a respective share of the costs of operation of the facilities and programs of said corporation and the construction, renovation or operation of any future facility or programs as determined by the board of directors. (Acts 1978, No. 620, p. 880, § 9.)

§ 44-3-10. Responsibility of boards of directors for control and direction of facilities and programs.

Nothing in this chapter shall be construed to mean that the facilities and programs, provided for herein, are to be under the control or direction of any person other than the board of directors, who shall require the facilities and programs of the corporation to be in compliance with the minimum standards of construction, maintenance and operation adopted by state regulatory agencies and laws of the state of Alabama. (Acts 1978, No. 620, p. 880, § 10.)

§ 44-3-11. Exemption from taxation of corporations, property, income, etc.

Such corporation authorized herein, and its property, including bonds, conveyances, mortgages, leases and all income from such property, and operation of programs shall be exempt from all taxation that shall be imposed on said corporation for the privilege of engaging in any of the activities authorized by this chapter. (Acts 1978, No. 620, p. 880, § 11.)

§ 44-3-12. Commencement of existence of corporations.

Such corporation authorized herein shall come into being upon the filing of the articles of incorporation with the office of probate judge in the county in which its principal facility is located. (Acts 1978, No. 620, p. 880, § 12.)

Collateral references. — 18 C.J.S., Corporations, §§ 23-26.

18 Am. Jur. 2d, Corporations, § 24.

CODE OF ALABAMA
1975

1990 Cumulative Supplement

ANNOTATED

Prepared by

The Editorial Staff of the Publishers

Under the Direction of

A. D. Kowalsky, S. C. Willard, W. L. Jackson, K. S. Mawyer,
S. C. Gorman, M. A. Sancilio and T. R. Troxell

VOLUME 22

1982 REPLACEMENT VOLUME

*Including Acts through the 1990 Regular Session and
annotations taken through Southern Reporter,
Second Series, Volume 557, Page 805*

**Place in Pocket of Corresponding Volume of Main Set.
This Supersedes Previous Supplement, Which
May Be Retained for Reference Purposes.**

The Michie Company
Law Publishers
Charlottesville, Virginia
1990

THIS SUPPLEMENT CONTAINS

Constitutions:

All amendments to the Alabama Constitution of 1901 ratified through June 5, 1990.

All amendments proposed to the Alabama Constitution of 1901 which are subject to referendum and which had not been voted upon as of June 5, 1990.

Statutes:

All laws of a general and permanent nature enacted by the Alabama Legislature through the 1989 Extraordinary Session and 1990 Regular Session of the Legislature. Local laws and general laws of local application are not included in this supplement.

Rules of Alabama Supreme Court:

Rules promulgated by the Supreme Court of Alabama through June 1, 1990.

Annotations:

Annotations or constructions of Alabama statutes and the 1901 Constitution of Alabama and amendments thereto by the Alabama Supreme Court, the Alabama Courts of Appeal, the Supreme Court of the United States and other federal courts, taken from the following:

Southern Reporter, Second Series, through volume 557, p. 805.
Federal Reporter, Second Series, through volume 897, p. 1158.
Federal Supplement, through volume 731, p. 529.
Federal Rules Decisions, through volume 129, p. 355.
Bankruptcy Reporter, through volume 110, p. 1011.
Supreme Court Reporter, through volume 110, p. 1515.
Opinions of the Clerk of the Supreme Court of Alabama.

References to:

Corpus Juris Secundum.
American Jurisprudence, Second Edition.
American Law Reports, First Series.
American Law Reports, Second Series.
American Law Reports, Third Series.
American Law Reports, Fourth Series.

Cross references to related provisions of the Code and the Alabama Constitution of 1901.

References to applicable or related federal statutes.

Tables:

Acts of Legislature to 1975 Code.

3

Index:

A cumulative replacement index to the statutes, constitutional amendments and rules contained in this supplement and the bound volumes of the Code of Alabama.

User's Guide

In order to assist both the legal profession and the layman in obtaining the maximum benefit from the Code of Alabama, a User's Guide has been included herein. This guide contains comments and information on the many features found within the Code of Alabama intended to increase the usefulness of this set of laws to the user. See Volume 1 of this set for the complete User's Guide.

CODE OF ALABAMA

1990 Cumulative Supplement

TITLE 41.

STATE GOVERNMENT.

CHAPTER 1.

GENERAL PROVISIONS.

§ 41-1-5. Nepotism in state service prohibited.

Constitutionality. — See State v. Taylor, 437 So. 2d 482 (Ala. 1983).

It does not apply to gubernatorial, etc.

A judge is not subordinate, and cannot under the Constitution be subordinate, either to the executive or to the legislative branch. Neither can exercise any control or supervision over a judge, once appointed. Thus, the perceived evil which the Anti-Nepotism Act seeks to address does not arise in judicial appointments. State v. Taylor, 437 So. 2d 482 (Ala. 1983).

The constitutional requirement of strict separation of powers between an executive department, a legislative department, and a judicial department supplies in a more fundamental and forceful way protection against any interference by the appointing authority with an appointed judge. State v. Taylor, 437 So. 2d 482 (Ala. 1983).

§ 41-1-7. Issuance of securities in fully registered form without coupons.

(a) The state, and each county, municipality, board of education, political subdivision, public instrumentality, public corporation or other public entity howsoever identified, which is authorized by law to issue bonds, warrants, notes, certificates of indebtedness or other securities howsoever identified is hereby further authorized to issue any such securities in fully registered form without coupons.

(b) This law shall not repeal any existing law which authorizes the issuance of securities in any other form but no such existing law shall be construed to prohibit the issuance of securities in the form permitted by subsection (a) hereof or to require that securities be issued in any form other than that permitted hereby. (Acts 1983, 1st Ex. Sess., No. 83-74, p. 77.)

Cross references. — As to authority of counties to make loans in anticipation of taxes, see ch. 10, T. 11. As to warrant issued in anticipation of ad valorem taxes, see ch. 11A, T. 11. As to warrants issued in anticipation of gasoline taxes, see ch. 11, T. 11. As to securities issued in anticipation of grants, see ch. 11B, T. 11. As to authority of municipalities and public corporations to issue securities in anticipation of grants, see ch. 64, T. 11. As to authority of municipalities, counties and public corporations to issue securities in anticipation of receipt of grants, see ch. 81A, T. 11.

§ 41-1-8. Issuance of securities with facsimile signatures of officers and facsimile of corporate seal.

(a) In any instance where any bond, warrant, note, certificate of indebtedness or other security howsoever designated is authorized to be issued by the state, or by any county, municipality, board of education, political subdivision, public instrumentality, public corporation or other public entity howsoever identified and is required or permitted to be executed, attested, registered other than as to ownership or authenticated by one or more of its officers or other persons, a facsimile of the signature of any one or more of the officers or persons executing, attesting, registering or authenticating the same may be imprinted or reproduced on such security if such security is required to be authenticated by the manual signature of the duly designated registrar of such securities, or an authorized officer of such registrar. Any seal required or permitted to be affixed or impressed on such security may be imprinted or otherwise reproduced thereon in facsimile.

(b) This law shall not repeal or supersede any other law which authorizes execution, attestation, registration or authentication of securities by facsimile signature or imprinting or other reproduction thereon of any seal, but shall be construed as cumulative authorization thereof. (Acts 1983, 1st Ex. Sess., No. 83-76, p. 81.)

Cross references. — As to authority of counties to make loans in anticipation of taxes, see ch. 10, T. 11. As to warrant issued in anticipation of ad valorem taxes, see ch. 11A, T. 11. As to warrants issued in anticipation of gasoline taxes, see ch. 11, T. 11. As to securities issued in anticipation of grants, see ch. 11B, T. 11. As to authority of municipalities and public corporations to issue securities in anticipation of grants, see ch. 64, T. 11. As to

authority of municipalities, counties and public corporations to issue securities in anticipation of receipt of grants, see ch. 81A, T. 11.

§ 41-1-9. Issuance of interest bearing securities, etc.

In any instance where any bond, warrant, note, certificate of indebtedness or other securities howsoever designated is authorized to be issued by the state, or by any county, municipality, board of education, political subdivision, public instrumentality, public corporation or other public entity howsoever identified; any such security may bear one or more rates of interest, or no interest, or interest may be payable through one or more payments which reflect compound interest computed at specified intervals on accrued but unpaid interest, or through a discount in the sales price for such security equivalent to compound interest on such security for all or part of the term thereof, or through any combination of the foregoing methods of providing for the payment of interest, and any such amounts shall be payable at such time or times as may be provided in the proceedings authorizing any such security, regardless of the requirements of any other provision of law authorizing the issuance of any such security. (Acts 1983, 4th Ex. Sess., No. 83-923, p. 205, § 1.)

§ 41-1-10. Section 41-1-9 deemed declarative of existing law.

The provisions of § 41-1-9 shall be deemed declarative of existing law and shall not be construed in a manner adverse to the validity of, or the lawfulness of the interest payable with respect to, (i) any bonds, warrants, notes, certificates of indebtedness or other securities at any time issued by any issuer described in section 41-1-9 hereof, or (ii) any debt at any time incurred by any private person, corporation or other legal entity. (Acts 1983, 4th Ex. Sess., No. 83-923, p. 205, § 2.)

CHAPTER 4.

DEPARTMENT OF FINANCE.

ARTICLE 1.

GENERAL PROVISIONS.

§ 41-4-5. Appointment of employees; officers and employees subject to merit system.

The director of finance shall, subject to the provisions of the merit system, have the right to appoint any employee in the department. All employees and officers of the department of finance, including the chiefs of divisions, except as otherwise provided for in this chapter, shall be subject to the merit system.

(Acts 1939, No. 112, p. 144; Code 1940, T. 55, § 72; Acts 1983, No. 83-438, p. 619, § 1.)

§ 41-4-8. Powers and duties of department as to educational and eleemosynary institutions.

Collateral references. — Validity and application of governmental limitation on permissible amount or proportion of fundraising expenses or administrative costs of charitable organizations. 15 ALR4th 1163.

ARTICLE 2.

DIRECTOR OF FINANCE.

§ 41-4-33.2. Applicability of section; use of public funds, etc., by ambulance services, etc., authorized; penalty for unauthorized use; final disposition of property.

(a) This section shall apply to voluntary nonprofit ambulance services and voluntary nonprofit rescue squads which are operated as a public service for the benefit of the citizens of this state. It is declared that said ambulance services and rescue squads are quasi-public entities that are entitled to receive and use public funds or property appropriated, donated or loaned to them by the state or any county or municipal governing body.

(b) All surplus property owned by the state to be disposed of by sale at auction by the finance department shall first be screened by the state board of health ambulance advisory board created in section 22-18-5, and the Alabama Association of Rescue Squads, Inc., to determine if such property may be of use by volunteer ambulance services or volunteer rescue squads respectively. If said entities find such property to be useful to voluntary ambulance services or rescue squads, then the state finance director shall loan said property to the voluntary services. The state finance director is authorized to promulgate necessary rules to implement this section.

(c) Any property transferred to a volunteer ambulance service or rescue squad under the provisions of this section shall be used exclusively for ambulance and rescue purposes. The use of any such property other than on the business of the volunteer ambulance service or rescue squad is expressly prohibited. Any violation of the provision of this section shall be a Class A misdemeanor punishable as provided under Title 13A.

Final disposition of all properties loaned as a result of this section shall rest with the finance department of the state. (Acts 1984, No. 84-619, p. 1257.)

ARTICLE 3.

DIVISION OF CONTROL AND ACCOUNTS.

§ 41-4-50. Established; functions and duties.

There shall be in the department of finance the division of control and accounts. The functions and duties of the division of control and accounts shall be as follows:

(1) To keep all books, records and accounts relating to the finances of the state government (including the budget accounts) which are authorized or required to be kept by the department of finance, in accordance with recognized standards of public accounting and in such a manner as at all times to reveal the true financial status of the state government and of each special fund and account in the state treasury.

(2) To control and make records of all payments into and out of the state treasury and each special fund and account therein.

(3) To audit currently all receipts and receivables.

(4) To preaudit and determine the correctness and legality of every claim and account submitted for the issuance of a warrant and to determine that funds have been appropriated and allotted and are then available in the state treasury for the payment of such claim or account before any warrant on the state treasury shall be issued; except, that the preaudit of claims for unemployment compensation or public assistance or child welfare or income tax refunds shall be performed by the department or departments having charge of the other functions and duties relating to unemployment compensation, or public assistance, or child welfare, or income tax refunds subject to the general supervision of the division of control and accounts.

(5)a. To draw every warrant authorized to be drawn upon the state treasury and any fund therein, whether a special or earmarked fund or not.

b. Any law to the contrary notwithstanding, any or all warrants issued by the division of control and accounts may be transferred or deposited electronically or by other acceptable methods to any financial institution capable of handling direct deposits by electronic transfer or other acceptable methods if written approval is given by the original payee of said warrant. The state comptroller shall maintain files on all written approvals given by original payees and separate records on all transfers of funds authorized in this subsection and shall furnish sufficient documentation for the purpose of auditing and reconciling such electronic financial transactions.

(6) To secure such information and data, to prepare or make such studies and reports and to perform such other functions and duties of the department of finance as may from time to time be assigned by the director of finance. (Acts 1939, No. 112, p. 144; Code 1940, T. 55, § 81; Acts 1984, 1st Ex. Sess., No. 84-789, p. 180.)

ARTICLE 4.

DIVISION OF THE BUDGET.

§ 41-4-81. Budget officer.

(a) The division of the budget shall be headed by and under the direction, supervision and control of an officer who shall be designated the budget officer. The budget officer may be employed from within or without the classified service; such budget officer shall be appointed by and serve at the pleasure of the director of finance, with the approval of the governor. The budget officer shall be entitled to the same benefits as any person in the classified service.

(b) Any person who may be serving as such budget officer on the effective date of this section, who is not reemployed as such budget officer under the provisions of this section, and who prior to such employment as budget officer was a member of the state merit system, may elect to return to the merit system job classification previously held. (Acts 1939, No. 112, p. 144; Acts 1939, No. 144, p. 190; Code 1940, T. 55, § 92; Acts 1983, No. 83-438, p. 619, §§ 1, 2.)

§ 41-4-93. Lapsing of appropriations.

The term "unencumbered balances," as used in this section, must be given its natural, plain, ordinary and commonly understood meaning. Mitchell v. State Child Abuse & Neglect Prevention Bd., 512 So. 2d 778 (Ala. Civ. App. 1987).

Sections 26-16-30 through 26-16-33 do not evidence a legislative intent to exempt children's trust fund from the general reversion requirements of this section. Mitchell v. State Child Abuse & Neglect Prevention Bd., 512 So. 2d 778 (Ala. Civ. App. 1987).

ARTICLE 5.

DIVISION OF PURCHASING.

Code commissioner's note. — The heading of this article was changed in view of the change of the name of the Division of Purchases and Stores to the Division of Purchasing by Acts 1989, No. 89-947.

Division 1

General Provisions.

§ 41-4-110. Established; functions and duties; contracts for stationery, printing, paper and fuel.

(a) There shall be in the department of finance the division of purchasing. The functions and duties of the division of purchasing shall be as follows:

(1) To purchase all personal property, except alcoholic beverages, which shall be purchased by the alcoholic beverage control board and except as

otherwise provided by law, for the state and each department, board, bureau, commission, agency, office and institution thereof.

(2) To make and supervise the execution of all contracts and leases for the use or acquisition of any personal property unless otherwise provided by law.

(3) To fix standards of quality and quantity and to develop standard specifications for all personal property acquired by the state or any department, board, bureau, commission, agency, office or institution thereof.

(4) To maintain records as to prices and sources of supply of such personal property, such records to be open to the inspection of any state, county, municipal or other public officer or employee charged with the duty of acquiring any such property or article for his department, board, bureau, commission, agency, office, institution, county, municipal corporation or local public body.

(5) To manage, supervise and control all printing and binding for the state and for each department, board, bureau, commission, agency, office and institution thereof and the distribution of all printed matter and to make and supervise the execution of all contracts with respect thereto, unless otherwise provided by law.

(6) To require the periodic reporting of all purchases of furniture, fixtures, supplies, material, equipment and other personal property, except printing, and all contracts and leases for the use or acquisition thereof by or for counties, the purchase, contract or lease price of which is $100.00 or more, and to require information in connection therewith, to prescribe forms and fix the time for submitting such reports, and, when requested by any county, municipal corporation and other local public body (including any board of education) to make such purchases, contracts or leases for it. It shall be the duty of every county to make such report on forms furnished by the department of finance, whenever requested so to do, but not more than once every 30 days.

(7) To perform such other functions and duties of the department of finance as may from time to time be assigned by the director of finance.

(b) As long as the Constitution so requires, all stationery, printing, paper and fuel used in the legislative and other departments of the government shall be furnished, and the printing, binding and distribution of the laws, journals, departmental reports and all other printing, binding and repairing and furnishing the halls and rooms used for the meetings of the legislature and its committees shall be performed under contract, to be given to the lowest responsible bidder below a maximum price, under such regulations as have been or may be prescribed by law and as may be promulgated by the director of finance. No member or officer of any department of the government shall be in any way interested in such contracts, and all such contracts shall be subject to the approval of the governor, the auditor and the treasurer. All contracts not required to be approved by a named officer or officers by the Constitution shall be subject to the approval of the director of finance, who may, however, provide for the automatic approval thereof by compliance with the general rules or regulations promulgated by him. (Acts 1939, No. 112, p. 144; Code 1940, T. 55, § 108; Acts 1989, No. 89-947, p. 1866, § 1.)

The 1989 amendment, effective May 19, 1989, deleted former subdivisions (a)(3) and (a)(4), pertaining to the distribution of furniture, fixtures, etc., and the perpetual inventory of such, and redesignated former subdivisions (a)(5) through (a)(9) as present subdivisions (a)(3) through (a)(7).

§ 41-4-111. Purchasing agent.

The division of purchasing shall be headed by and be under the direction, supervision and control of an officer who shall be designated the purchasing agent. The purchasing agent shall be appointed by the director of finance with the approval of the governor. (Acts 1939, No. 112, p. 144; Code 1940, T. 55, § 108; Acts 1989, No. 89-947, p. 1866, § 2.)

The 1989 amendment, effective May 19, 1989, substituted "division of purchasing " for "division of purchases and stores" in the first sentence.

§ 41-4-113. Procedure for obtaining supplies or materials for departments or institutions.

Unless otherwise provided by law, when the head of any department of the state shall desire any office supplies or materials or other articles of use or necessity, written application shall be made therefor to the division of purchasing, sworn to and stating by items the articles desired and needed, showing out of what fund they are to be paid, that the articles are necessary, that the amount of the requisition is not excessive, and that no part of the same will be used except in conducting the public business. Such application shall be kept on file in the office of the division of purchasing. (Acts 1923, No. 85, p. 67; Code 1923, § 43; Acts 1939, No. 112, p. 144; Code 1940, T. 55, § 109; Acts 1989, No. 89-947, p. 1866, § 3.)

The 1989 amendment, effective May 19, 1989, substituted "division of purchasing" for "division of purchases and stores" throughout the section.

Division 2.

Public Printing and Binding.

§ 41-4-130. Public printing and binding to be done under contract.

(a) The acts and journals of the legislature, the revenue laws of each session of the legislature, in separate pamphlets, the reports of the decisions of the supreme court, the reports of the decisions of the court of civil appeals and the court of criminal appeals, the annual or biennial reports of all officials, boards, commissions, bureaus, departments and institutions, which are required by law to make such reports, and all handbooks, pamphlets, blanks, bulletins, circulars, notices, reports, messages and forms used, published or required by all such officials, boards, commissions, bureaus, departments and institutions, and also by the clerk of the supreme court, the clerk of the court of civil appeals, the clerk of the court of criminal appeals, and all bills, papers, documents and reports ordered by and for the use of the legislature or either house thereof, shall be printed, or printed and bound, as the case may be, and the records of the supreme court, the court of civil appeals and the court of criminal appeals shall be bound as ordered by the clerks of said courts, under contract as provided in this division. No printing or binding for the state shall be done under contracts made in pursuance of the provisions of this division other than such as are covered and provided for in this division. This division shall not apply, however, to printing and binding required by any college, vocational-technical school or trade school subject to the jurisdiction and control of the state board of education; such printing and binding shall be performed or furnished under contracts let on a competitive bidding basis by the purchasing agent or chief executive officer of the institution affected.

(b) With regard to the preparation and printing of the journals of the house and senate, the clerk of the house and the secretary of the senate are hereby authorized to prepare the journal from their respective chambers in such form or state of completion, including camera ready drafts or other forms, as the clerk or secretary deem necessary or appropriate, including the final form for printing. The clerk of the house and the secretary of the senate are each hereby further authorized to prepare a final bound and printed journal in their sole discretion, provided that all other time requirements for their final printing are met. (Code 1896, § 3385; Code 1907, § 1647; Code 1923, § 2895; Acts 1939, No. 112, p. 144; Code 1940, T. 55, § 110; Acts 1967, No. 223, p. 592; Acts 1990, No. 90-224, § 1.)

The 1990 amendment, effective April 3, 1990, added subsection (b).

§ 41-4-131. Classification of public printing and binding.

The printing and binding authorized in section 41-4-130, for the purposes of the contracts provided in this division, shall be divided into classes, each class to be let in a separate contract:

Class 1. The reports of the decisions of the supreme court, the court of civil appeals and the court of criminal appeals.

Class 2(a). The acts passed by the legislature.

Class 2(b). The journals of the house and senate, unless the clerk of the house or the secretary of the senate elect to bind and print their own respective journals as provided in subsection (b) of section 41-4-130 above.

Class 3. Annual or biennial reports of all officials, boards, commissions, bureaus, departments and institutions which are required by law, and all handbooks, pamphlets or bulletins which the commissioner of agriculture and industries is or may be authorized by law to publish, and all other pamphlets or documents of a public nature, the publication of which is ordered by the governor in pursuance of law.

Class 4. All messages of the governor to the legislature, all bills, documents and reports ordered by and for the use of the legislature or either house thereof while in session; all blanks, circulars, notices and forms used in the office of or ordered by the governor, or by any other state official, board, commission, bureau or department, or by the clerks of the supreme court, the court of civil appeals and the court of criminal appeals; and all blanks and forms ordered by and for the use of the secretary of the senate and clerk of the house of representatives, and binding the original records and opinions of the supreme court, the court of civil appeals and the court of criminal appeals. (Code 1896, § 3386; Code 1907, § 1648; Code 1923, § 2896; Acts 1939, No. 112, p. 144; Code 1940, T. 55, § 111; Acts 1949, No. 28, p. 42; Acts 1990, No. 90-224, § 1.)

The 1990 amendment, effective April 3, 1990, rewrote the description of Class 2(b).

§ 41-4-134. Opening of bids; acceptance of bids; rejection and readvertisement of bids.

The director of finance must, after the twentieth and before the thirtieth day of the month in which bids are received, open the same in the presence of the governor, auditor and treasurer, or any two of them, and the director of finance, by and with the approval of the governor, auditor and treasurer, any two concurring, or in the case of Class 2(a) printing as defined in section 41-4-131 with the approval of the clerk of the house and the secretary of the senate or in the case of Class 2(b) printing if the clerk of the house or secretary of the senate elect not to print and bind their own respective journals, then with the approval of said clerk and secretary, shall select the lowest responsible bidder, either for the classes separately or for the classes combined, as may be to the best interest of the state, but no bid unaccompanied by a bond as required in this division shall be considered. If, in the judgment of a majority of the said officers present, the public interest can be served best thereby, all the proposals, or all for either class, may be rejected, whereupon the director of finance shall advertise again in all respects as in the first instance for proposals to do the public printing or binding, or that class of it, the bids for which were rejected, and, upon the coming in of the new bids, they shall be considered, passed on and accepted or rejected, and in the last event, advertisement made again as provided in this division with respect to the proposals first made. (Code 1896, § 3390; Code 1907, § 1652; Code 1923, § 2899; Acts 1939, No. 112, p. 144; Code 1940, T. 55, § 114; Acts 1983, No. 83-431, p. 612, § 1; Acts 1990, No. 90-224, § 1.)

The 1990 amendment, effective April 3, 1990, near the middle of the first sentence, deleted "or 2(b)" following "Class 2 (a)" and inserted "or in the case of Class 2(b) printing if the clerk of the house or secretary of the senate elect not to print and bind their own respective journals, then with the approval of said clerk and secretary" preceding "shall select the lowest responsible bidder."

§ 41-4-136. Contract and bond to be approved by governor, auditor and treasurer; filing of bonds.

All contracts for public printing and binding and all bonds to secure the faithful performance of the same shall be approved by the governor, auditor and treasurer, or in the case of Class 2(a) or 2(b) printing as defined in section 41-4-131 with the approval of the clerk of the house and the secretary of the senate, and a new or additional bond may be required whenever they deem it necessary; but the giving of such new or additional bond shall in no way affect the liability of the sureties on the original or any existing bond. All such bonds must be filed and recorded in the office of the secretary of state. (Code 1896, § 3392; Code 1907, § 1654; Code 1923, § 2901; Code 1940, T. 55, § 116; Acts 1983, No. 83-431, p. 612, § 2.)

§ 41-4-139. Where printing to be done.

The printing and binding in Classes 2(a), 2(b) and 4 must be done in the state of Alabama. All other printing and binding enumerated in classes 1 and 3 may be done wherever the best work at the lowest bid can be had. (Code 1896, § 3395; Code 1907, § 1657; Code 1923, § 2906; Code 1940, T. 55, § 119; Acts 1983, No. 83-431, p. 612, § 3; Acts 1990, No. 90-224, § 1.)

The **1990 amendment,** effective April 3, 1990, substituted "state of Alabama" for "city of Montgomery" in the first sentence.

§ 41-4-145. Preparation of journals.

The journals must be prepared with a title page and index and must be bound and lettered as specified or prepared by the clerk of the house or secretary of the senate. (Code 1852, § 76; Code 1867, § 112; Code 1876, § 124; Code 1886, § 216; Code 1896, § 3405; Code 1907, § 1666; Code 1923, § 2915; Code 1940, T. 55, § 128; Acts 1990, No. 90-224, § 1.)

The **1990 amendment,** effective April 3, 1990, substituted "bound and lettered as specified or prepared by the clerk of the house or secretary of the senate" for "substantially half-bound and lettered."

§ 41-4-147. Penalty for not delivering copies of acts to printer.

For each day's delay of the secretary of the senate, if he elects not to bind and print the journal within his office, clerk of the house, if he elects not to bind and print the journal within his office, secretary of state, director of the legislative reference service or other officer in furnishing the printer the copy required in printing the acts and journals at the time prescribed for delivery, such officer shall forfeit the sum of $20.00, to be deducted by the comptroller from salary first accruing thereafter. The comptroller must not pay to such officer any salary accruing next after the period when such copy should have been by law delivered to the printer without first having received and filed in his office, as a voucher, the certificate of such officer that copy for the acts or journals, as the case may be, has been delivered by him to the printer within the time prescribed by law. (Acts 1949, No. 27, p. 39, § 13; Acts 1990, No. 90-224, § 1.)

The 1990 amendment, effective April 3, 1990, in the first sentence, inserted "if he elects not to bind and print the journal within his office" following both "secretary of the senate" and "clerk of the house."

§ 41-4-148. Style of printing and quality of paper of acts and journals; index.

(a) The acts of the legislature shall be printed on paper of the same weight and quality as that required for the supreme court's reports, in 10-point type solid, 26 pica ems wide and not less than 44 lines on the page. The pages must be sewed to two strong tapes and be bound in the best quality American buckram.

(b) The journals shall be printed and bound to such specifications as provided by the secretary of the senate and clerk of the house, respectively. It is further provided that the said clerk and secretary are authorized to bind and print entirely the journal for their respective houses; or, alternatively, the said clerk and secretary may prepare the draft for the state printer in such final form as deemed appropriate.

(c) Each journal shall be provided with an index, which shall be prepared by the secretary of the senate or the clerk of the house, as the case may be, within 30 days from receipt of said journal's galley sheets for the entire legislative session from the printer, unless the said secretary or clerk shall elect to bind and print the journal within his own office.

(d) The acts shall be provided with an index, which shall be prepared by the legislative reference service within 10 days after receipt of a paged copy of the acts from the printer. (Acts 1949, No. 27, p. 39, § 5; Acts 1990, No. 90-224, § 1.)

The 1990 amendment, effective April 3, 1990, in subsection (a), deleted "affidavit required to be printed in the journals," following "The titles of acts" in the third sentence; rewrote subsection (b), and in subsection (c) substituted "said journal's galley sheets for the entire legislative session from the printer, unless the said secretary or clerk shall elect to bind and print the journal within his own office" for "a paged copy from the printer" at the end of the subsection.

§ 41-4-150. When acts and journals must be printed and delivered by printer.

(a) The printer must, within 90 days after being furnished a copy of the last act, print, as herein provided, package or box in complete sets and distribute pursuant to an address list furnished by the secretary of state, 1,300 copies of the bound acts, which copies shall be indexed, stitched, half-bound and lettered.

(b) If the house and senate elect to contract with the state printer, then within 180 days after receipt of the copy from the secretary of the senate and clerk of the house of representatives, which period shall include the 30 days mentioned in subsection (c) of section 41-4-148, the printer must distribute in packaged or boxed sets pursuant to an address list furnished by the secretary of state, 450 copies of the journal of each house, which copies shall also be indexed, bound and lettered. (Acts 1949, No. 27, p. 39, § 6; Acts 1959, No. 403, p. 1035; Acts 1975, No. 1161, p. 2285, § 1; Acts 1986, Ex. Sess., No. 86-711, p. 125; Acts 1990, No. 90-224, § 1.)

The 1990 amendment, effective April 3, 1990, at the beginning of subsection (b), substituted "If the house and senate elect to contract with the state printer, then within 180 days" for "Within 180 days."

§ 41-4-156. Printing of acts and resolutions in pamphlet form — Distribution to certain officers, departments, etc.; certain officers to keep pamphlets in books until acts published in permanent form.

(a) Within three working days after an enrolled bill or joint resolution has been delivered to and filed in the office of the secretary of state, it shall be numbered, in the order in which it is received, and a copy of each local or general act shall be placed in the hands of the printer by the secretary of the senate or clerk of the house, as the case may be. The printer must immediately print 1,700 copies in slip or pamphlet form in accordance with section 41-4-158, which the printer must distribute as follows: two copies for every member and officer of the legislature, which copies shall be delivered to the secretary of the senate and the clerk of the house of representatives, 25 copies to the supreme court library, 15 copies to the legislative reference service, 20 copies to the law library at the University of Alabama, 50 copies to the department of archives and history, one copy to every judge of a court of record, circuit court clerk, register of the circuit court, district court clerk, district attorney, deputy district attorney, county commission chairman, municipal clerk, and sheriff, and the remainder shall be delivered to the secretary of state.

(b) Each probate judge, circuit court clerk, register of the circuit court, district court clerk, county commission chairman, municipal clerk, and sheriff shall preserve in his office, in a book kept for that purpose, each pamphlet furnished him until the acts are published in permanent form. Pamphlet acts shall be open to public inspection during regular business hours. (Acts 1949, No. 27, p. 39, § 7; Acts 1975, No. 1161, p. 2285, § 1; Acts 1981, No. 81-347, p. 503; Acts 1982, 2nd Ex. Sess., No. 82-763, p. 238, § 2.)

§ 41-4-160. Bond of printer of acts and journals; deductions from contract price for failure to perform within time.

(a) In making the contracts for publication of the acts and journals, if applicable, the state purchasing agent shall require the printer to give bond, in such sum as he may direct, conditioned that the acts and journals shall be printed as herein provided and be delivered as herein required.

(b) In the event the printer fails to perform his contract within the time prescribed for performance, the comptroller must cause to be deducted from the contract price, as liquidated damages, $100.00 for each day's delay; except that the printer shall be allowed one day for each day his performance is delayed by reason of the neglect of duty by a state official or by strike or vis major. (Acts 1949, No. 27, p. 39, § 11; Acts 1990, No. 90-224, § 1.)

The 1990 amendment, effective April 3, 1990, inserted "if applicable" following "acts and journals" near the beginning of subsection (a).

ARTICLE 11.

TELECOMMUNICATIONS DIVISION.

Effective date. — The act which added this article became effective April 19, 1990.

§ 41-4-280. Definitions.

For the purposes of this article, the following words and phrases shall have the meanings ascribed:

(1) DEPARTMENT. The department of finance.

(2) AGENCY. Any agency, department, board, commission, office, agency or institution of the state, except those agencies and institutions excluded by section 41-4-291.

(3) ELECTROMAGNETIC TRANSMISSION EQUIPMENT. Any transmission medium, switch, instrument, inside wiring system or other facility which is used, in whole or in part, to provide any transmission.

(4) EQUIPMENT SUPPORT CONTRACT. A contract which covers a specific class or classes of telecommunications equipment and all features associated with that class, through which state agencies may purchase or lease the item specified by issuing a purchase order under the terms of the contract without the necessity of further competitive bidding.

(5) PROCUREMENT. The buying, purchasing, renting, leasing, lease/purchasing or otherwise obtaining telecommunications equipment, systems or related services, as well as all activities engaged in, resulting in or expected to result in buying, purchasing, renting, leasing or otherwise obtaining telecommunications equipment.

(6) TELECOMMUNICATIONS EQUIPMENT, SYSTEMS, RELATED SERVICES.

a. All devices, such as telephone instruments, modulators, coders, etc., used to convert voices or digital data into a form suitable for transmission, by electric current or electromagnetic wave, from one point to another point;

b. All devices, such as telephone receivers, demodulators, decoders, etc., used to receive an electric current or electromagnetic wave containing voice information or digital data, and/or to convert this information into usable form;

c. All wiring, waveguides, optical fibers, or other physical means used to convey electric currents or electromagnetic waves containing voice information or digital data;

d. All switches, networks, branch exchanges, software, and other devices used to selectively interconnect devices which use electric current or electromagnetic waves for the purpose of communicating voice signals or digital data from one point to another;

e. All maintenance of the types of devices and means listed above in (i) through (iv), and all consulting, designs, or management services related to these devices, their interconnection, and their use.

(7) TELECOMMUNICATIONS SYSTEM LEASE CONTRACT. A contract between a supplier of telecommunications systems, including equipment and related services, and any agency as authorized by the department through which telecommunications systems, including equipment and related services, may be leased. (Acts 1990, No. 90-553, § 1.)

§ 41-4-281. Legislative declaration; purpose.

The legislature hereby declares it essential for the creation and maintenance of an efficient, modern, economically feasible, telecommunications system for Alabama state government that a telecommunications division be established under the jurisdiction of the department of finance. The purposes of this act shall be to coordinate and promote efficiency in the acquisition, operation and maintenance of all telecommunications equipment, systems and networks being used by agencies of the state and further to coordinate the compatibility of such equipment, systems and networks so as to promote a uniform, compatible communications system for agencies of state government. (Acts 1990, No. 90-553, § 2.)

§ 41-4-282. Rules and regulations.

The department may promulgate rules and regulations governing the manner in which the authority and duties of the telecommunications division as prescribed in this article shall be carried out. The department shall employ competent personnel necessary to carry out its purposes under rules promulgated by the state personnel department and in accord with the Merit System Act. (Acts 1990, No. 90-553, § 3.)

§ 41-4-283. Powers and duties of department.

The department is hereby authorized and empowered to exercise such duties and powers necessary to effectuate the purposes of this article, including the following:

(1) Provide effective management of state telecommunications resources and implement annual plans and procurement;

(2) Manage, plan and coordinate all telecommunications systems under the jurisdiction of the state. This centralized management function shall be provided through the following activities:

a. Administration of existing systems including coordination of activities, vendors, service orders and billing/record-keeping functions;

b. Planning of new systems or services;

c. Design of replacement systems;

d. Project management during specification writing, bid letting, proposal evaluation and contract negotiations;

e. Implementation supervision of new systems and ongoing support;

f. Implementation of long-term state plans;

g. Management of telecommunications networks. (Acts 1990, No. 90-553, § 4.)

§ 41-4-284. Additional duties of department.

The department shall have the following additional duties:

(1) To establish and coordinate through either state ownership or commercial leasing, all telecommunications systems and services affecting the management and operations of the state.

(2) To act as the centralized approving authority for the acquisition of all telecommunications systems or services provided to state agencies whether obtained through lease or purchase, including pay telephones located on premises owned by the state or any of its agencies.

(3) To charge respective user agencies for their proportionate cost of the installation, maintenance and operation of the telecommunications systems and services, including the operation of the telecommunications division.

(4) To develop coordinated telecommunications systems or services within and among all state agencies and require, where appropriate, cooperative utilization of telecommunications equipment, facilities and services by aggregating users.

(5) To review, coordinate, approve or disapprove all requests by state agencies for the procurement, through purchase or lease, of telecommunications systems or services including telecommunications proposals, studies and consultation contracts.

(6) To establish and define telecommunications system and service specifications and designs so as to assure compatibility of telecommunications systems and services within state government.

(7) To provide a continuous, comprehensive analysis and inventory of telecommunications costs, facilities and systems within state government.

(8) To advise and provide consultation to agencies with respect to telecommunications management planning and related matters including training within state government in telecommunications technology and system use. (Acts 1990, No. 90-553, § 5.)

§ 41-4-285. Written approval of department required for lease purchase, etc., of telecommunications system by agency.

No agency shall rent, lease, lease/purchase, or in any way own or pay for the operation of any telecommunications system out of any funds available for that purpose without the written approval of the department. (Acts 1990, No. 90-553, § 6.)

§ 41-4-286. Department authorized to contract on behalf of agency; appropriation dependency clause.

The department may, on behalf of any state agency, enter into an equipment support contract with a vendor of telecommunications equipment for the purchase, lease or lease/purchase of such equipment subject to the competitive bid law. Such contracts shall be valid for not more than five fiscal years and must include the following annual appropriation dependency clause: "The continuation of the contract is contingent upon the appropriation by the legislature of funds to fulfill the requirements of the contract. If the legislature fails to appropriate sufficient monies to provide for the continuance of the contract, or if funds from other sources are not available, the contract shall terminate on the date of the beginning of the fiscal year for which funds are not appropriated or available." (Acts 1990, No. 90-553, § 7.)

§ 41-4-287. Trade-in of equipment.

The department shall have the authority to allow the trade-in of telecommunications equipment the value of which may be credited against the cost of replacement equipment purchased in accordance with Alabama competitive bidding laws. This authority may be exercised with the approval of the state purchasing agent. (Acts 1990, No. 90-553, § 8.)

§ 41-4-288. Additional contract requirements.

The department may enter into contracts for the lease of telecommunications equipment, systems or related services in accordance with the following provisions:

(1) The department may directly contract for or approve contracts for regulated or tariffed telecommunications services upon determination that the application of such service is in the best interests of the State of Alabama.

(2) Such contracts shall be valid for not more than five fiscal years. (Acts 1990, No. 90-553, § 9.)

§ 41-4-289. Telecommunications revolving fund.

All user fees collected, direct appropriations, and other funds received under the provisions of this article shall be deposited into a revolving fund in the state treasury designated as the telecommunications revolving fund, and the director of finance is authorized to make deposits and expenditures from time to time from such fund to carry out the purposes of this article. All balances of revenue, income and receipts remaining in the telecommunications revolving fund at the end of the fiscal year shall carry over to the next fiscal year and shall not revert to the state general fund or any other fund under the provisions of section 41-4-93. (Acts 1990, No. 90-553, § 10.)

§ 41-4-290. Exemptions — Public safety, criminal justice, highway maintenance and construction.

The provisions of this article shall not apply to two-way radio communications equipment, systems or networks operated by state agencies for purposes related to public safety, the administration of criminal justice or highway maintenance and construction operations. (Acts 1990, No. 90-553, § 11.)

§ 41-4-291. Same — Education television commission, post-secondary education system, public colleges and universities; technical consultation and procurement; long distance service.

The provisions of this article shall not apply to the education television commission, the post-secondary education system or any public college or university. Upon request, the department of finance shall provide technical consultation and procurement services for telecommunications to the education television commission, the post-secondary education system and public colleges and universities. The education television commission, the post-secondary education system and public colleges and universities shall continue to be provided in-state and out-of-state long distance service by the telecommunications division of the department of finance, so long as funding is provided to the telephone revolving fund from the Alabama special educational trust fund, and shall not be required to pay any additional charge for such service. (Acts 1990, No. 90-553, § 12.)

§ 41-4-292. Sunset provision.

The telecommunications division of the finance department shall be subject to the provisions of the Alabama Sunset Law of 1981, and shall be classified an enumerated agency under section 41-20-3, and shall terminate in 1992 unless continued as therein provided and, if continued, shall be reviewed every two years thereafter and terminated unless then continued as provided by said law. (Acts 1990, No. 90-553, § 13.)

§ 41-4-293. Exemption of legislative and judicial branches.

The legislative and judicial branches of government are exempt from the requirements of this article. (Acts 1990, No. 90-553, § 14.)

ARTICLE 12.

DIVISION OF RISK MANAGEMENT.

Effective date. — The act which added this article became effective April 25, 1990.

§ 41-4-300. Division created.

There shall be created within the department of finance the division of risk management. (Acts 1990, No. 90-672, § 1.)

§ 41-4-301. Function, powers and duties.

The function, powers and duties of the division of risk management shall be as follows:

(1) To carry out the provisions of section 41-15-1 et seq., relating to the state insurance fund and section 36-1-6.1 relating to the state liability insurance fund.

(2) To assist and advise the finance director on insurance and bonding matters;

(3) To provide information and recommendations to the legislature when requested;

(4) To provide programs and/or guidelines leading to premium and financial risk reductions, to include collection and investment of premiums, rate making, and claims administration.

(5) To make, with the approval of the finance director, rules and regulations necessary to implement the provisions of this article. (Acts 1990, No. 90-672, § 2.)

§ 41-4-302. Administration of insurance programs.

The division of risk management shall have the authority to institute, manage and administer programs of insurance, not specifically enumerated herein and which do not conflict with existing laws, upon a determination by the director of finance and the governor that such insurance program or programs serve the best interests of the state. (Acts 1990, No. 90-672, § 3.)

§ 41-4-303. Applicability of article; coverage of risk management program.

The provisions of this article shall not apply to: universities and colleges; the state docks; or county and city boards of education, except as is already required by section 41-15-1 et seq., relating to the state insurance fund. Provided however that universities and colleges may elect to participate in, and be covered by, such risk management program. A university or college may elect to participate in and be covered by such program by giving notice thereof to the division of risk management not less than six months prior to the beginning of the fiscal year in which such university or college desires to begin participation in and coverage by such program. Any university or college which elects to be covered by such risk management program may terminate such participation and coverage by giving notice thereof to the division of risk management not less than six months prior to the beginning of the fiscal year such university or college desires to terminate such participation and coverage. (Acts 1990, No. 90-672, § 3.)

§ 41-4-304. Commingling of funds proscribed.

There shall be no commingling of funds between various self-insured programs. (Acts 1990, No. 90-672, § 4.)

§ 41-4-305. Risk manager; appointment; compensation.

The division of risk management shall be headed by and under the supervision, direction and control of an officer who shall be designated "risk manager." The risk manager shall be appointed and compensated, subject to the provisions of the state merit system, by the director of finance, with the approval of the governor. Salary of said risk manager shall be paid from self-insured programs on a basis determined by the finance director. (Acts 1990, No. 90-672, § 5.)

§ 41-4-306. Additional employees.

The director of finance may employ and compensate such additional employees as may be needed, in accordance with the merit system. (Acts 1990, No. 90-672, § 6.)

CHAPTER 5.

DEPARTMENT OF EXAMINERS OF PUBLIC ACCOUNTS.

§ 41-5-21. Examiners to make sworn reports of audits.

Cited in Peevy v. State, 460 So. 2d 248 (Ala. Crim. App. 1984).

CHAPTER 6A.

DEPARTMENT OF ENERGY.

Code commissioner's note. — As to the transfer of the department of energy and the functions, duties, etc., provided by this chapter, see § 41-23-1.

CHAPTER 7.

BUREAU OF TOURISM AND TRAVEL.

§ 41-7-1. Created; composition; powers and duties.

(a) There is created hereby a state bureau of tourism and travel, hereinafter referred to as the bureau, composed of a division of records and reports and such other divisions as the director determines to be necessary.

(b) The bureau shall, with the advice and assistance of the advisory board provided for in section 41-7-3, have exclusive power and authority to plan and conduct all state programs of information and publicity designed to attract tourists to the state of Alabama. It shall be the duty of the principal administrator of each department, board, commission, institution, agency and office, upon request, to assist the director of publicity in preparing news items of general interest relating to tourism. (Acts 1943, No. 253, p. 223, §§ 2, 4; Acts 1951, No. 712, p. 1250, § 1; Acts 1984, No. 84-273, p. 459, § 1.)

§ 41-7-5. Director may contract with and spend funds in support of southern travel directors council.

The director of the bureau of tourism and travel may, with the approval of the governor, enter into contracts and agreements with the organization known as the southern travel directors council, a regional travel advertising and promotion agency, for the purpose of expanding and extending the state's tourist advertising program. The director may, with the governor's approval, spend a sum not exceeding $15,000.00 per annum for the support of the council, such expenditures to be made from legislative appropriations for tourist advertising. (Acts 1967, No. 269, p. 775; Acts 1984, No. 84-273, p. 459, § 1.)

CHAPTER 8.

ALABAMA PUBLIC LIBRARY SERVICE.

ARTICLE 1.

GENERAL PROVISIONS.

§ 41-8-2. Executive board generally.

The executive board of the Alabama public library service shall consist of seven members appointed by the governor, of which one member shall be from each congressional district. Such members shall be qualified electors of the state and shall have resided in the state for five years next preceding their appointment and shall live in the congressional district which he or she represents. Appointments shall be for five years, and all vacancies, including expired and unexpired terms, shall be filled by the governor by appointment. Provided, however, present members of the executive board shall continue in office until the first expiration of the term of any member, at which time and thereafter each board member shall represent the congressional district in which he or she resides with no two members residing in the same district, and any vacancies, for whatever reason, shall be filled accordingly. Members of the executive board shall be allowed $10.00 per day, not to exceed 20 days per year, plus travel expenses pursuant to article 2 of chapter 7 of Title 36. It shall be the duty and power of the executive board to conduct the affairs of the public library service, to administer the funds received from the treasury that are allocated to the public library service and to be responsible for the program and for such other activities as would naturally be administered by such an executive board. (Acts 1939, No. 171, p. 297; Code 1940, T. 55, § 279; Acts 1959, No. 600, p. 1488; Acts 1988, No. 88-338, p. 514.)

§ 41-8-9. "Registration records" defined.

As used in section 41-8-10, the term "registration records" includes any information which a library requires a patron to provide in order to become eligible to borrow books and other materials, and the term "circulation records" includes all information which identifies the patrons utilizing particular books and any other library materials in any medium or format. (Acts 1983, No. 83-565, p. 866, § 1.)

Cross references. — As to free public libraries, see ch. 90, T. 11. As to the establishment of libraries, see § 16-11-23. As to general provisions relating to libraries, see ch. 21, T. 16.

§ 41-8-10. Registration, etc., records of public libraries to be confidential; right of parents to inspect records.

It is recognized that public library use by an individual should be of confidential nature. Any other provision of general, special or local law, rule or regulation to the contrary notwithstanding, the registration and circulation records and information concerning the use of the public, public school, college and university libraries of this state shall be confidential. Registration and circulation records shall not be open for inspection by, or otherwise available to, any agency or individual except for the following entities: (a) the library which manages the records; (b) the state education department for a library under its jurisdiction when it is necessary to assure the proper operation of such library; or (c) the state public library service for a library under its jurisdiction when it is necessary to assure the proper operations of such library. Aggregate statistics shown from registration and circulation records, with all personal identification removed, may be released or used by a library for research and planning purposes. Provided however, any parent of a minor child shall have the right to inspect the registration and circulation records of any school or public library that pertain to his or her child. (Acts 1983, No. 83-565, p. 866, § 2.)

Cross references. — As to free public libraries, see ch. 90, T. 11. As to the establishment of libraries, see § 16-11-23. As to general provisions relating to libraries, see ch. 21, T. 16.

CHAPTER 8A.

ALABAMA LAW ENFORCEMENT PLANNING AGENCY.

Code commissioner's note. — As to the transfer of the law enforcement planning agency and the functions, duties, etc., provided by this chapter, see § 41-23-1.

CHAPTER 9.

BOARDS AND COMMISSIONS.

31

ARTICLE 3.

COUNCIL ON THE ARTS AND HUMANITIES.

§ 41-9-41. Establishment; composition; qualifications and appointment of members.

There is hereby established a state commission to be known as the Alabama state council on the arts, to consist of 15 members, broadly representative of all fields of the performing and fine arts, to be appointed by the governor from among citizens of Alabama who are widely known for their competence and experience in connection with the performing and fine arts. In making such appointments, due consideration shall be given to the recommendations made by representative civic, educational and professional associations and groups concerned with or engaged in the production or presentation of the performing and fine arts generally. (Acts 1967, No. 551, p. 1300, § 2; Acts 1969, No. 1065, p. 1986, § 1; Acts 1987, No. 87-659, p. 1167.)

§ 41-9-43. Executive director, consultants, advisors, etc.

Code commissioner's note. — Acts 1983, 2nd Ex. Sess., No. 83-131, § 1 made a technical correction in this section which was included in the section as set out in the bound volume.

ARTICLE 4.

BOARD OF ADJUSTMENT.

Division 1.

General Provisions.

Cited in State v. McCurley, 412 So. 2d 1233
(Ala. Crim. App. 1981).

§ 41-9-60. Purpose of division.

Agencies of the state legislature not subject to Administrative Procedure Act. — The board of adjustment is not subject to the Alabama Administrative Procedure Act (AAPA) because it is an agency of the state legislature and is thus specifically excepted from the definition of an agency to which the AAPA applies. Medical Laundry Serv. v. Board of Adjustment, 486 So. 2d 1305 (Ala. Civ. App. 1986).

§ 41-9-62. Claims within jurisdiction of board generally; employees of municipalities, counties, etc., not within jurisdiction of board, etc.

Exclusive jurisdiction over contract dispute involving Alabama State University. — The state board of adjustment had exclusive jurisdiction over a contract dispute involving Alabama State University, and the circuit court did not err in dismissing the university's appeal of an adverse decision of the board of adjustment. Alabama State Univ. v. State Bd. of Adjustment, 541 So. 2d 567 (Ala. Civ. App. 1989).

§ 41-9-64. Claims for death to be made by personal representative; distribution of proceeds of claim.

Collateral references.
Effect of settlement with and acceptance of release from one wrongful death beneficiary upon liability of tort-feasor to other beneficiaries or decedent's personal representative. 21 ALR4th 275.

§ 41-9-65. Limitation periods for presentation of claims.

Cross references. — For requirement that attorney general be served with a copy of any lawsuit seeking damages from negligent or wrongful acts committed by state employees while in the performance of their duties, see § 36-1-6.1.

Collateral references.
Governmental tort liability for failure to provide police protection to specifically threatened crime victim. 46 ALR4th 948.

§ 41-9-68. Determination of amount of injury or damage and entry of award for payment of damages generally.

Measure of injured person's rights, etc.
Provisions whereby the board of adjustment adjusts claims is just such a set of rules securing plaintiff's interest in the instant contract. The fact that the Supreme Court of Alabama has referred to the board of adjustment procedures as a mere matter of grace does not alter this conclusion. The language of the Alabama statute directs the board of adjustment to determine the amount of dam-

age and directs the treasurer of the state to pay pursuant to the awards of the board. Medical Laundry Serv. v. Board of Trustees, 840 F.2d 840, modified, 856 F.2d 128 (11th Cir.), cert. denied, — U.S. —, 109 S. Ct. 77, 102 L. Ed. 2d 53 (1988).

Collateral references. — Modern status of rule excusing governmental unit from tort liability on theory that only general, not particular, duty was owed under circumstances. 38 ALR4th 1194.

§ 41-9-69. Determination of agency, commission, etc., of state inflicting injury or damage and entry of award for payment of damages out of funds appropriated thereto.

Measure of injured person's rights under this section. — The provisions whereby the board of adjustment "adjusts" claims is just such a set of rules securing plaintiff's interest in the instant contract. The fact that the Supreme Court of Alabama has referred to the board of adjustment procedures as a mere matter of grace, does not alter this conclusion. The language of the Alabama statute directs the board of adjustment to determine the amount of damage and directs the treasurer of the state to pay pursuant to the awards of the board. Medical Laundry Serv. v. Board of Trustees, 840 F.2d 840, modified, 856 F.2d 128 (11th Cir.), cert. denied, — U.S. —, 109 S. Ct. 77, 102 L. Ed. 2d 53 (1988).

Collateral references. Governmental tort liability for failure to provide police protection to specifically threatened crime victim. 46 ALR4th 948.

§ 41-9-70. Limitation on amount of award for personal injury or death.

Collateral references. — Validity and construction of statute or ordinance limiting the kinds or amount of actual damages recoverable in tort action against governmental unit. 43 ALR4th 19.

Recovery of damages for grief or mental anguish resulting from death of child — modern cases. 45 ALR4th 234.

Governmental tort liability for failure to provide police protection to specifically threatened crime victim. 46 ALR4th 948.

Excessiveness and adequacy of damages for personal injuries resulting in death of minor. 49 ALR4th 1076.

Excessiveness or adequacy of damages awarded for personal injuries resulting in death of persons engaged in professional, white collar, and nonmanual occupations. 50 ALR4th 787.

Recovery in death action for failure to diagnose incurable disease which caused death. 64 ALR4th 1232.

§ 41-9-71. Secretary of board to prepare, etc., history of cases, etc., and deliver to certain agencies, etc., certified copy of findings and awards of board; comptroller to draw warrant in favor of persons, etc., found entitled to damages, etc.

The secretary of the board of adjustment shall make a record of and file in the office of the secretary of state a history of the case, together with the findings and awards of the board of adjustment, and shall deliver to the agencies, commissions, boards, institutions or departments against whom the award is made and by whom payment must be made a certified copy of its findings and awards.

Upon receipt of such a copy of the findings and awards of the board of adjustment, the agencies, commissions, boards, institutions or departments will voucher and certify same to the comptroller of the state of Alabama who is authorized and directed to draw his warrant in favor of the person or persons, association or corporation found by the board of adjustment to be entitled to the damages in the amount of the damages so certified, and he shall charge the same to the appropriation as directed in said findings or awards. (Acts 1935, No. 546, p. 1164; Code 1940, T. 55, § 341; Acts 1984, 1st Ex. Sess., No. 84-758, p. 130.)

§ 41-9-72. Payment by treasurer of warrants drawn pursuant to findings and awards of board.

Measure of injured person's rights under this section. — The provisions whereby the board of adjustment "adjusts" claims is just such a set of rules securing plaintiff's interest in the instant contract. The fact that the Supreme Court of Alabama has referred to the board of adjustment procedures as a mere matter of grace does not alter this conclusion.

The language of the Alabama statute directs the board of adjustment to determine the amount of damage and directs the treasurer of the state to pay pursuant to the awards of the board. Medical Laundry Serv. v. Board of Trustees, 840 F.2d 840, modified, 856 F.2d 128 (11th Cir.), cert. denied, — U.S. —, 109 S. Ct. 77, 102 L. Ed. 2d 53 (1988).

§ 41-9-73. Appropriations for payment of awards, etc.

There is hereby appropriated annually out of the general fund of the state of Alabama, the state insurance fund, the fund of the department of corrections, the special educational trust fund, the special mental health fund or any other fund of the state, to be determined by the board of adjustment, an amount, not exceeding $1,000,000.00 for each fiscal year, as may be necessary to pay the claims ordered paid by the board of adjustment and its expenses. There is also hereby appropriated, for each fiscal year, an additional amount, not exceeding $175,000.00, from funds of the state highway department to pay the claims chargeable against the highway department which are ordered paid by the board of adjustment and its expenses. There is also appropriated, in addition to the foregoing appropriations, from the state general fund to the state board of adjustment, the sum of $400,000.00 for each fiscal year for the purpose of paying death benefits covered under the provisions of article 1 of chapter 30 of Title 36 of this Code. (Acts 1935, No. 546, p. 1164; Code 1940, T. 55, § 343; Acts 1951, No. 943, p. 1609; Acts 1963, No. 307, p. 786, § 1; Acts 1965, 1st Ex. Sess., No. 218, p. 286; Acts 1977, No. 675, p. 1166; Acts 1982, No. 82-576, § 1; Acts 1989, No. 89-870, p. 1745.)

The 1989 amendment, effective May 17, 1989, substituted "$1,000,000.00" for "$750,000.00" in the first sentence, and substituted "$400,000.00" for "$200,000.00" in the last sentence.

Collateral references. — Validity and construction of statute or ordinance limiting the kinds or amount of actual damages recoverable in tort action against governmental unit. 43 ALR4th 19.

§ 41-9-74. Board to pay judgments against board of corrections officials; limitations, exceptions, etc.

This provision does not express the intent of the legislature to waive sovereign immunity; rather, the legislature appears to reaffirm Alabama's sovereign immunity and simply to limit payments made pursuant to the statute to $100,000. This construction of this section is consistent with Alabama's traditional reluctance to waive its sovereign immunity. Williams v. Bennett, 689 F.2d 1370 (11th Cir. 1982), cert. denied, 464 U.S. 932, 104 S. Ct. 335, 78 L. Ed. 2d 305 (1983).

This section makes no mention of suits against the state or against the board itself as an independent political body. Instead, the statute indicates that its indemnity provision runs to individuals by specifically listing those employees who may claim the benefit of its coverage. In addition, the provision that awards will be paid only to the extent that coverage is not provided by an insurance carrier suggests further that payments pursuant to the statute were intended to be nothing more than an insurance supplement for individuals, and perhaps to afford some measure of relief to plaintiffs required to sue those who might otherwise be judgment proof individuals. Williams v. Bennett, 689 F.2d 1370 (11th Cir. 1982), cert. denied, 464 U.S. 932, 104 S. Ct. 335, 78 L. Ed. 2d 305 (1983).

Because of Alabama's unequivocal affirmation of sovereign immunity, and because this section fails to represent a clear expression of intent to waive that immunity in federal court, the Alabama board of corrections may not be subject to suit; however, while its officials and/or employees may not be sued in their official capacities, they are individually subject to suits for acts or omissions in connection with their official duties. Williams v. Bennett, 689 F.2d 1370 (11th Cir. 1982), cert. denied, 464 U.S. 932, 104 S. Ct. 335, 78 L. Ed. 2d 305 (1983).

This section was designed to be an employment benefit, analogous to liability insurance, for any Alabama correctional employee who may be sued individually for acts arising in the course of employment. Williams v. Bennett, 689 F.2d 1370 (11th Cir. 1982), cert. denied, 464 U.S. 932, 104 S. Ct. 335, 78 L. Ed. 2d 305 (1983).

A state municipality does not waive its eleventh amendment immunity by purchasing liability insurance. Williams v. Bennett, 689 F.2d 1370 (11th Cir. 1982), cert. denied, 464 U.S. 932, 104 S. Ct. 335, 78 L. Ed. 2d 305 (1983).

Waiver of a state's eleventh amendment immunity can be found only when evidenced by the most express language or by such overwhelming implications from the text as will leave no room for any other reasonable construction. Williams v. Bennett, 689 F.2d 1370 (11th Cir. 1982), cert. denied, 464 U.S. 932, 104 S. Ct. 335, 78 L. Ed. 2d 305 (1983).

Division 2.

Escrow Accounts for Benefit
of Crime Victims.

§ 41-9-80. Entity contracting with convicted felon to pay money to board; felony upon failure to pay; escrow account for crime victim who recovers judgment against felon.

Collateral references. — Validity, construction, and application of "Son of Sam" laws regulating or prohibiting distribution of crime-related book, film, or comparable revenues to criminals. 60 ALR4th 1210.

§ 41-9-84. Action to defeat division purpose null and void.

Collateral references. — Validity, construction, and application of "Son of Sam" laws regulating or prohibiting distribution of crime-related book, film, or comparable revenues to criminals. 60 ALR4th 1210.

ARTICLE 6.

BUILDING COMMISSION AND BUILDING CODE.

Division 1.

Building Commission.

§ 41-9-141. Powers and duties generally; appointment, etc., of officers, employees and agents; adoption of rules, regulations and plans; approval and allocation of funds; notice of meetings required.

Cited in Wyatt v. State Bldg. Comm'n, 418 So. 2d 145 (Ala. Civ. App. 1982).

Division 2.

Minimum Building Standards Code.

§ 41-9-161. Promulgation, distribution and enforcement of code of minimum building standards by commission generally.

Collateral references. — Recovery of punitive damages for breach of building or construction contract. 40 ALR4th 110.

§ 41-9-163. Requirements of building code; erection or acquisition of state building or construction or public schoolhouse not conforming to code; operation of private school, hotel, etc., not conforming to code.

Collateral references.
Recovery, under strict liability in tort, for injury or damage caused by defects in building or land. 25 ALR4th 351.

§ 41-9-166. Adoption, etc., of building code by municipalities and counties.

Cited in Robertson v. Baldwill County, 538 So. 2d 33 (Ala. Civ. App. 1988).

Division 3.

Energy Conservation Building Code.

§ 41-9-171. Promulgation, distribution and enforcement of code of minimum building standards for buildings constructed or remodeled with state funds by building commission generally.

Collateral references.

Recovery of punitive damages for breach of

building or construction contract. 40 ALR4th 110.

ARTICLE 8.

STATE DEVELOPMENT OFFICE.

§ 41-9-201. Creation; composition; encouragement by governor of comprehensive and coordinated planning and programming of state governmental affairs; furnishing of personnel, equipment, etc., to office by departments or agencies.

(a) There is hereby created the Alabama development office within the office of the governor and directly under his supervision and control. The Alabama development office shall consist of the governor as the state planning and development officer and a chief administrative officer to be designated as director of development, who shall be a person possessed with extensive responsible experience in development of economic, human and physical resources and promotion of industrial and commercial development and who shall be appointed by the governor and serve at his pleasure at a salary of any reasonable amount not to exceed by $25,742.00 the highest authorized salary for employees of the Alabama development office who are subject to the provisions of the merit system law. In fixing such salary, the governor shall give due consideration of the salaries of comparable positions in other states and in private industry. All other employees necessary to carry out the duties and functions of the Alabama development office shall be employed subject to the provisions of the merit system law.

(b) The governor, through the Alabama development office, shall encourage comprehensive and coordinated planning and programming of the affairs of state government.

(c) The governor may direct any state department or other agency of state government directly under his control and supervision to furnish the Alabama development office with such personnel, equipment and services as are necessary to enable it to carry out its responsibilities and duties and prescribe the terms thereof, including reimbursement of costs thereof. (Acts 1969, No. 657, p. 1187, § 2; Acts 1987, No. 87-591, p. 1029.)

ARTICLE 8A.

OFFICE OF STATE PLANNING AND FEDERAL PROGRAMS.

Code commissioner's note. — As to the transfer of the office of state planning and federal programs and the functions, duties, etc., provided by this article, see § 41-23-1.

ARTICLE 10.

HISTORICAL COMMISSIONS.

Cross reference. — As to historic preservation commissions and architectural review boards, see § 11-68-1 et seq.

Division 1.

Alabama Historical Commission.

§ 41-9-249.1. Contracts for recovery or salvage of archaeological treasure, etc.

(a) Notwithstanding any provision of law to the contrary, the Alabama historical commission may enter into contracts with any group or person for the recovery or salvage of archaeological treasure, sunken or abandoned ships and wrecks of the sea, or parts thereof or their contents, which are determined to be located on state owned lands, or on private land if the written consent of the owner thereof is first obtained. Such contracts shall be on forms approved by the commission and may provide for fair compensation to the salvager, and owner of the private land where applicable, in terms of a percentage of the reasonable cash value of the objects recovered or at the discretion of the commission, of a fair share of the objects recovered. The amount constituting a fair share shall be determined by the commission, taking into consideration the circumstances of each operation, and the reasonable cash value may be determined by contractual agreement for appraisal by qualified experts or by representatives of the contracting parties. Each contract shall provide for the termination of any right in the salvager thereunder upon the violation of any of the terms thereof. Each contract shall be approved by both the state finance director and the governor. The distribution of the state's share of the recovery or salvage shall be as follows:

(1) All archaeological treasure and artifacts shall be placed in the custody and control of the Alabama historical commission.

(2) All monetary proceeds from the sale of any recovered or salvaged archaeological treasure or artifacts including but not limited to gold, silver or other precious metal shall be deposited with the state treasurer to the credit of the state general fund.

(b) The provisions of this section are supplemental. It shall be construed in pari materia with other laws regulating salvage and excavation of antiquities; however, those laws or parts of laws which are in direct conflict or

40

inconsistent herewith are hereby repealed. (Acts 1984, 2nd Ex. Sess., No. 85-53, p. 75.)

Division 5.

Tannehill Furnace and Foundry Commission.

The Tannehill commission was created as an arm of the state of Alabama, existing to carry forth the important function of holding, maintaining, and preserving state lands of historical significance for the benefit of the citizens. This governmental function is recognized by the legislative language which repeatedly emphasizes the commission's purpose to preserve the Tannehill lands as an exhibit of the state's iron and steelmaking heritage. Deal v. Tannehill Furnace & Foundry Comm'n, 443 So. 2d 1213 (Ala. 1983).

The Tannehill commission's character, its function, and its funding identify the commission as the state of Alabama for purposes of Ala. Const., § 14. Deal v. Tannehill Furnace & Foundry Comm'n, 443 So. 2d 1213 (Ala. 1983).

Tannehill commission members and park superintendent were immune from claims of plaintiff injured from dive into a creek located within the park where evidence shows park personnel discouraged swimming by placing warning signs around the creek. Such act clearly fell within exercise of discretion central to the function of such commission as contained in § 41-9-320. Deal v. Tannehill Furnace & Foundry Comm'n, 443 So. 2d 1213 (Ala. 1983).

§ 41-9-320. Creation; purpose.

Cited in Deal v. Tannehill Furnace & Foundry Comm'n, 443 So. 2d 1213 (Ala. 1983).

§ 41-9-321. Composition; appointment and terms of office of members; vacancies.

The commission shall be composed of 18 members, one of whom shall be appointed by the board of trustees of the University of Alabama, one of whom shall be appointed by the board of trustees of the University of Montevallo, and one of whom shall be a member of the Alabama historical commission, chosen by such commission in the manner prescribed by it. Fourteen members shall be appointed by the governor and the remaining member who shall by virtue of historical background be knowledgeable about the early Alabama iron industry, be chosen by the commission membership and designated "historian." Four of the first members appointed by the governor shall be appointed for eight-year terms, four shall be appointed for six-year terms, four shall be appointed for four-year terms, and two shall be appointed for two-year terms. Beginning in 1990, future appointments by the governor shall include no less than three seats each to persons legally residing in Jefferson, Tuscaloosa and Bibb counties. The first members appointed by the board of trustees of the University of Alabama and the University of Montevallo and the first member representative of the Alabama historical commission shall be appointed for two-year terms. Successors to these first members shall all be appointed for eight-year terms. The term of the historian shall be set by the commission.

Vacancies on the board during a term shall be filled for the unexpired portion of the term in the same manner and by the same appointing authority as the member whose place is being filled. (Acts 1969, No. 994, p. 1760, § 4; Acts 1989, No. 89-1004, § 1.)

The 1989, Ex. Sess. amendment, effective December 22, 1989, in the first paragraph, in the first sentence substituted "18 members" for "16 members" and inserted "one of whom shall be appointed by the board of trustees of the University of Montevallo" following "University of Alabama," substituted the present second sentence for the former second sentence which read "The remaining 14 members shall be appointed by the governor," inserted the present fourth sentence, inserted "of Alabama and the University of Montevallo" in the fifth sentence and added the last sentence.

Cited in Deal v. Tannehill Furnace & Foundry Comm'n, 443 So. 2d 1213 (Ala. 1983).

§ 41-9-322. Members not to receive pay, etc.; payment of expenses of members; conflicts of interest of members or employees of commission.

Cited in Deal v. Tannehill Furnace & Foundry Comm'n, 443 So. 2d 1213 (Ala. 1983).

§ 41-9-323. Meetings generally; quorum; organization and procedure; seal; officers; requirement of bond from treasurer.

Ten members of the commission shall constitute a quorum for the transaction of business. Additional meetings may be held at such times and places within the state as may be necessary, desirable or convenient upon call of the chairman or, in the case of his absence or incapacity, of the vice-chairman or on the call of any three members of the commission. The commission shall determine and establish its own organization and procedure in accordance with the provisions of this division, and shall have an official seal. The commission shall elect its chairman, its vice-chairman, its secretary and its treasurer, and such officers shall hold office for a period of one year or until a successor is elected. Neither the secretary nor the treasurer need be members of the commission. The commission may require that the treasurer thereof be bonded in an amount to be determined by the commission. (Acts 1969, No. 994, p. 1760, § 7; Acts 1989, No. 89-1004, § 1.)

The 1989, Ex. Sess. amendment, effective December 22, 1989, deleted the former first sentence which read "The commission shall hold an annual meeting in the city of Tuscaloosa" and substituted "Ten members of the commission shall constitute a quorum for the transaction of business" for "Eight members shall constitute a quorum for the transaction of business" in the present first sentence of this section.

Cited in Deal v. Tannehill Furnace & Foundry Comm'n, 443 So. 2d 1213 (Ala. 1983).

§ 41-9-324. Commission a body corporate.

The Tannehill commission was created as an arm of the state of Alabama, existing to carry forth the important function of holding, maintaining, and preserving state lands of historical significance for the benefit of the citizens. This governmental function is recognized by the legislative language which repeatedly emphasizes the commission's purpose to preserve the Tannehill lands as an exhibit of the state's iron and steelmaking heritage. Deal v. Tannehill Furnace & Foundry Comm'n, 443 So. 2d 1213 (Ala. 1983).

The Tannehill commission's character, its function, and its funding identify the commission as the state of Alabama for purposes of Ala. Const., § 14. Deal v. Tannehill Furnace & Foundry Comm'n, 443 So. 2d 1213 (Ala. 1983).

§ 41-9-325. Commission a state agency; commission to have exclusive control over Tannehill furnace and foundry; rule making and police power.

The Tannehill commission was created as an arm of the state of Alabama, existing to carry forth the important function of holding, maintaining, and preserving state lands of historical significance for the benefit of the citizens. This governmental function is recognized by the legislative language which repeatedly emphasizes the commission's purpose to preserve the Tannehill lands as an exhibit of the state's iron and steelmaking heritage. Deal v. Tannehill Furnace & Foundry Comm'n, 443 So. 2d 1213 (Ala. 1983).

The Tannehill commission's character, its function, and its funding identify the commission as the state of Alabama for purposes of Ala. Const., § 14. Deal v. Tannehill Furnace & Foundry Comm'n, 443 So. 2d 1213 (Ala. 1983).

§ 41-9-326. Acquisition of property; borrowing of money and issuance of revenue bonds.

Cited in Deal v. Tannehill Furnace & Foundry Comm'n, 443 So. 2d 1213 (Ala. 1983).

§ 41-9-327. Operation, etc., of park or historic site; entry into agreements with civic organizations, etc.; acceptance of gratuitous services and employment of hostesses, guards, etc.

Cited in Deal v. Tannehill Furnace & Foundry Comm'n, 443 So. 2d 1213 (Ala. 1983).

§ 41-9-328. Appropriations by counties and municipalities.

Cited in Deal v. Tannehill Furnace & Foundry Comm'n, 443 So. 2d 1213 (Ala. 1983).

§ 41-9-329. Exemption from taxation of commission and income, properties, etc., thereof.

The Tannehill commission was created as an arm of the state of Alabama, existing to carry forth the important function of holding, maintaining, and preserving state lands of historical significance for the benefit of the citizens. This governmental function is recognized by the legislative language which repeatedly emphasizes the commission's purpose to preserve the Tannehill lands as an exhibit of the state's iron and steelmaking heritage. Deal v. Tannehill Furnace & Foundry Comm'n, 443 So. 2d 1213 (Ala. 1983).

The Tannehill commission's character, its function, and its funding identify the commission as the state of Alabama for purposes of Ala. Const., § 14. Deal v. Tannehill Furnace & Foundry Comm'n, 443 So. 2d 1213 (Ala. 1983).

§ 41-9-330. Insurance programs for employees.

Cited in Deal v. Tannehill Furnace &
Foundry Comm'n, 443 So. 2d 1213 (Ala. 1983).

Division 6.

St. Stephens Historical Commission.

§ 41-9-335. Creation, purpose and composition of St. Stephens histori-
cal commission; terms; compensation; acquisition of
property; expenses of appropriation, reconstruction, etc.,
of property; annual meetings, procedures; elections; appropriation and expenditure of funds.

(a) A board of trustees to be known as the St. Stephens historical
commission is hereby authorized to be appointed and established for the
purpose of acquiring, maintaining, protecting and promoting certain properties of historical interest at St. Stephens, in Washington county, in the
general vicinity of the site of the first territorial capital of Alabama. Said
board shall be comprised of seven members, and the first six enumerated
appointees designated herein shall serve for terms of one, two, three, four,
five, and six years, respectively, with subsequent appointees serving for terms
of six years. The ex officio board member shall serve a term on the board
concurrent with the serving of the term of the elected public office.

(b) The board of trustees of the St. Stephens historical commission shall
consist of:

(1) Two members appointed by the governor;

(2) One member appointed by the Alabama historical commission;

(3) Two members appointed by the Washington county historical society;

(4) One member appointed by the Washington county commission; and

(5) One ex officio, full member who shall be the member of the Alabama
house of representatives representing the geographical community of St.
Stephens in Washington county.

(c) Such trustees shall serve without compensation other than payment of a
per diem allowance and travel expenses in attending meetings of the board or
in performing any actual service under the direction of the board, such
expenses to be paid in accordance with article 2 of chapter 7 of Title 36. Such
expenses shall be payable out of any appropriation, donation or grant, upon
warrant of the comptroller, after the account for such expenses has been
approved by the board of trustees or the treasurer thereof.

(d) Said board of trustees, within its discretion, may acquire title, possession or control of such properties and also of objects of historic interest at St.
Stephens as it may deem necessary or proper to be constructed, reconstructed,
maintained, preserved and protected on behalf of the state of Alabama, mark
in suitable manner the places or locations of historic interest at such point
and prepare and publish for distribution pamphlets or other printed matter

with respect thereto. The expenses incurred for such purposes by the board of trustees shall be paid out of the appropriation upon warrant drawn by the comptroller, supported by an itemized account thereof approved by the board of trustees or the treasurer thereof.

(e) The board of trustees of the St. Stephens historical commission shall hold an annual meeting at St. Stephens in Washington county each September on a day designated by the chairman. Four members shall constitute a quorum for the transaction of business. Additional meetings may be held at such times and places within the state as may be necessary, desirable or convenient, upon call of the chairman or, in the case of his absence or incapacity, of the vice-chairman or on the call of any five members of the said board.

(f) The board shall determine and establish its own procedure in accordance with the provisions of this division, and shall have an official seal.

(g) The board shall elect its chairman, its vice-chairman, its secretary and its treasurer, and such officers shall hold office for a period of two years or until a successor is elected. The board may require that the treasurer thereof be bonded in an amount to be determined by the board.

(h) The board is authorized to appropriate and expend funds and to cooperate financially and otherwise with the Washington county historical society, the county of Washington and any other historical organization, county or municipality in this state to acquire, establish, maintain, and promote historical sites in and around the present community of St. Stephens, in the vicinity of the first territorial capital of Alabama. (Acts 1988, No. 88-335, p. 510, § 1.)

§ 41-9-336. Authorization for county or municipality to appropriate public funds for commission; acquisition, etc. of roads, bridges, etc., on commission land.

The county commission of any county or governing body of any municipality in this state or any other public or private agency or any historical organization shall be authorized, by resolution duly adopted and recorded, to appropriate any available public funds not otherwise pledged to the use of the St. Stephens historical commission and shall be authorized to acquire, construct and maintain roads and bridges and other public facilities and improvements on commission owned or controlled land. (Acts 1988, No. 88-335, p. 510, § 2.)

§ 41-9-337. Employees treated same as state employees for insurance or benefits purposes; employer's contributions to such programs; part-time employees.

(a) All full-time employees of the St. Stephens historical commission shall be treated as state employees for the purpose of participating in any insurance programs and other fringe benefits provided for state employees.

(b) The commission is hereby authorized and empowered to pay the employer's contributions to any such programs out of any funds appropriated them or available to them for any purpose whatsoever, and it may deduct the employees' contributions for such programs by means of payroll deductions or otherwise from any salary or compensation paid said employees.

(c) Part-time employees may be employed from time to time as needed. (Acts 1988, No. 88-335, p. 510, § 3.)

ARTICLE 11.

USS ALABAMA BATTLESHIP COMMISSION.

§ 41-9-341. Members not to receive pay, etc.; payment of expenses of members; conflicts of interest of members or employees of commission; penalty.

No member of the commission shall receive any pay or emolument for the discharge of his duties. Commission members and employees of the commission shall be reimbursed for actual expenses incurred on behalf of the commission in the development, operation, promotion, and expansion of its programs and activities. All such expenses are to be paid from the funds of the commission.

It shall be unlawful for any member of the commission or any employee thereof to charge, receive or obtain, either directly or indirectly, any fee, commission, retainer or brokerage out of the funds of the commission, and no member of the commission or officer or employee thereof shall have any interest in any land, materials or contracts sold to or made or negotiated with the commission or with any member or employee thereof acting in his capacity as a member or employee of such commission. Violation of any provision of this section shall be a misdemeanor and, upon conviction, shall be punishable by removal from membership or employment and by a fine of not less than $100.00 or by imprisonment not to exceed six months or both. (Acts 1963, No. 481, p. 1028, § 3; Acts 1988, 1st Ex. Sess., No. 88-900, p. 467, § 1.)

§ 41-9-343. Executive committee.

The commission may, at its discretion, create and provide for an executive committee of not fewer than five members and delegate to such committee such powers and authority as are deemed advisable by the commission; except, that the executive committee may not be empowered to issue revenue or any other bonds or execute any lease or contract for a period in excess of one year or execute any contract for an amount in excess of $100,000.00. The commission shall notify the governor when any member misses three consecutive meetings and the commission shall recommend that said member shall be removed by the governor for cause. (Acts 1963, No. 481, p. 1028, § 6; Acts 1985, No. 85-703, p. 1156, § 1.)

§ 41-9-345. Employees.

The commission may hire such laborers, artisans, caretakers, technicians, stenographers and administrative employees and supervisory and professional personnel as may be necessary or advisable for the carrying out in the most efficient and beneficial manner of the purposes and provisions of this article; and may at its discretion offer to its employees any benefits offered to employees of the state of Alabama. (Acts 1963, No. 481, p. 1028, § 10; Acts 1985, No. 85-703, p. 1156, § 2.)

§ 41-9-347. Commission to establish, operate, etc., memorial park and acquire, exhibit, etc., battleship USS Alabama.

The commission created under this article shall itself establish, operate and maintain a state memorial park to honor the Alabamians who participated so valiantly in all armed conflicts of the United States, which shall be under the exclusive management and control of the commission as a separate agency of the state government as provided for in this article, the principal purpose and function of which shall be to acquire, transport, berth, renovate, equip, maintain and exhibit the battleship USS Alabama as a permanent public memorial. (Acts 1963, No. 481, p. 1028, § 1; Acts 1985, No. 85-703, p. 1156, § 3.)

§ 41-9-349. Powers and duties of commission generally.

The commission shall have the duty and authority to acquire the battleship USS Alabama (BB60) and to select and improve appropriate sites for the permanent or temporary berthing of said vessel, taking into consideration factors, including, but not limited to, the accessibility of same, the location of nearby roads and highways, scenic attractions, esthetic value, cost, cooperation with federal, state, county, municipal and other governmental authorities, protection from the hazards of weather, fire and sea and any other factors which may affect the suitability of such site for the establishment of the ship as a temporary or permanent memorial and exhibit.

The commission may accept public or private gifts, grants and donations for the purposes of this article, may make and enter into contracts with other governmental departments, agencies and boards, either federal, state or municipal, and with private persons and corporations, may transport the ship to and berth the same at temporary and permanent park sites, ready the ship for visitation by the public, establish and provide for a proper charge for admission to the ship and otherwise renovate, maintain and operate the ship as a permanent memorial and exhibit.

The commission shall have full, complete and exclusive jurisdiction over the vessel, the sites and the related exhibits and shall have the power and authority to allocate funds from its treasury for the fulfillment and accomplishment of its duties and responsibilities in such manner as may be necessary and appropriate for the perfection of the purposes of this article, including the power to lease lands of the commission whenever the commission shall find any such action to be in furtherance of the purposes for which the commission was organized, and the authority to pledge revenues from its income from long term leases, future revenues from admissions and any other sources as may from time to time be necessary or desirable.

No lease may be entered into for longer than 25 years with option to renew every five year-period thereafter. (Acts 1963, No. 481, p. 1028, § 7; Acts 1965, 1st Ex. Sess., No. 169, p. 220, § 1; Acts 1988, 1st Ex. Sess., No. 88-900, p. 467, § 2.)

§ 41-9-355. Loan from state docks department; commission may borrow from banks pending such loan and pledge loan as security; $50,000.00 outstanding indebtedness forgiven.

(a) At such time as existing revenue bond covenants of the Alabama state docks department are satisfied as a result of any refunding of revenue bond issues of the Alabama state docks department that are outstanding as of August 1, 1963, the Alabama state docks department shall loan $50,000.00 to the USS Alabama battleship commission from the trust fund that will be released to the Alabama state docks department as a result of said refunding. This loan shall be repaid to the Alabama state docks department from the proceeds of the first revenue issue authorized under this article.

Pending said loan from the Alabama state docks department from the released trust fund, the USS Alabama battleship commission is hereby authorized to borrow from any bank or banks in the state of Alabama such sums up to $50,000.00 as are needed to carry out the purposes of this article. The USS Alabama battleship commission may pledge as collateral for this loan or loans the above described loan that will be received from the Alabama state docks department.

(b) Having issued no bonds as of May 29, 1985, and having no intentions to do so, the $50,000.00 outstanding indebtedness to the Alabama state docks department is hereby forgiven. (Acts 1963, No. 481, p. 1028, § 17; Acts 1985, No. 85-703, p. 1156, § 4.)

ARTICLE 15.

SPACE SCIENCE EXHIBIT COMMISSION.

§ 41-9-430. Creation; commission a public body corporate; commission to provide, etc., facilities for exhibits of national aeronautics and space administration, department of army, etc.; commission empowered to provide lodging for visitors, etc.

There is hereby created and established a state agency to be known as the Alabama space science exhibit commission, which shall be a public body corporate with all the powers and privileges of a corporation, for the purpose of providing for and participating in the management and control of facilities to house and display such visual exhibits of space exploration and hardware used therefor as may be made available by the national aeronautics and space administration. Such facility shall constitute a permanent housing for the national aeronautics and space administration exhibit, which shall be open to the general public and shall be located at a place to be designated and made available in Madison county for a nominal cost through the cooperation of the department of the army or at such other locations as the commission may deem appropriate.

The commission is further empowered to provide such facilities as will be mutually agreed upon between the commission and department of the army for the housing and display of army weaponry and mementos of national defense.

The commission is further empowered to establish an energy information and exhibit center in order to provide information to the public on research and development in the field or energy as developed by the national aeronautics and space administration, the department of the army, the energy research and development administration, other federal and state agencies, including universities and colleges, and other public and private sectors engaged in energy related activities.

The commission is further empowered to construct or otherwise acquire, whether by purchase, construction, exchange, gift, lease or otherwise, lodging and other similar facilities, including parking facilities and facilities for meetings, (provided said items are constructed within one mile of the Alabama Space and Rocket Center), for use by visitors to the permanent exhibit of the commission and users of the commission's visitors' center. In connection therewith, the commission may acquire any land or construct or acquire buildings or other improvements and all real and personal properties deemed necessary by the commission for such purpose, whether or not now in existence. The commission may lease to others any such facilities and may also lease lands of the commission on which such facilities may be constructed and charge and collect rent therefor, and terminate any such lease upon the failure of the lessee to comply with any of the obligations thereof. The commission may also sell, exchange, or convey and grant options to any lessee to acquire any such facilities and may lease lands of the commission on which such facilities may be constructed whenever the commission shall find any such action to be in furtherance of the purpose for which the commission was organized. (Acts 1965, No. 863, p. 1605, § 1; Acts 1966, Ex. Sess., No. 408, p. 553; Acts 1976, No. 587, p. 799; Acts 1983, No. 83-576, p. 895, § 1.)

§ 41-9-431. Composition; qualifications, appointment, terms of office and removal of members; vacancies; chairman; compensation and expenses of members; meetings generally; quorum; executive committee.

The commission created by section 41-9-430 shall consist of 18 members, to be appointed by the governor, who shall be bona fide residents and qualified voters of this state, at least three of whom shall be residents of Madison county. The remaining members of the commission shall be appointed from throughout the state in such manner as to provide general statewide representation on the commission, but all members shall be qualified persons of unquestioned loyalty to this country who are knowledgeable and interested in national defense and space exploration and in the promotion of interest in such fields. Nine of the original members shall be appointed for terms of four years, and nine members shall be appointed for terms of eight years. Thereafter, all members shall serve for terms of eight years. All members shall serve until their successors are appointed and qualified, but any member may be removed by the governor for just cause. Vacancies shall be filled in the same manner as original appointments are made.

The first chairman of the commission shall be appointed by the governor from among the original appointees. Thereafter, each succeeding chairman shall be selected by the other members of the commission.

Members of the commission shall serve without compensation.

Members and employees of the commission shall be reimbursed for actual expenses incurred on behalf of the commission in the development, operation, promotion and expansion of its programs and activities.

The commission shall hold at least one annual meeting at the site of the exhibit, and one half of the members shall constitute a quorum for the transaction of any business which may properly come before the commission at any such meeting.

The commission shall be authorized to provide for an executive committee of not fewer than five of its members to whom it may delegate such powers and authority as the commission may deem to be advisable. (Acts 1965, No. 863, p. 1605, § 2; Acts 1985, 2nd Ex. Sess., No. 85-987, p. 333, § 1.)

§ 41-9-432. Powers generally.

The commission shall be authorized:

(1) To investigate and select an available site for housing the exhibits, including the surrounding grounds, in cooperation with the department of the army and the community, taking into consideration all pertinent factors affecting the suitability of such site;

(2) To acquire by rent or lease agreement or otherwise the necessary housing facilities and to establish, improve and enlarge the available facility, including providing it with necessary equipment, furnishings, landscaping and related facilities, including parking areas and ramps, roadways, sewers, curbs and gutters;

(3) To enter into such contracts and cooperative agreements with the local, state and federal governments, with agencies of such governments, including the department of the army and the national aeronautics and space administration, with private individuals, corporations, associations and other organizations as the commission may deem necessary or convenient to carry out the purpose of this article, such contracts and agreements to include leases to private industry;

(4) To borrow money from private sources or such other sources as may be acceptable to the commission under such terms and conditions as may be provided by law and, in order to provide security for the repayment of any such private loans, to pledge such future revenues from admissions and any other sources as may from time to time be necessary or desirable;

(5) To issue and sell, subject to the approval of the governor, interest-bearing general obligation bonds not in excess of $1,900,000.00 in principal amount as authorized by constitutional amendment. Such bonds shall be general obligations of the state of Alabama with full faith and credit and taxing power of the state to be pledged to the prompt and faithful payment of the principal of the bonds and the interest thereon. The proceeds from the sale of such bonds shall be used exclusively for the purpose of paying the expenses incurred in the sale and issuance thereof and for the construction, establishment, improvement or enlargement and equipment of building facilities and related grounds, including the renewal or replacement of structural parts of such facility, but not including the purchase of the site for such facility;

(6) To issue and sell at any time and from time to time its revenue bonds for the purpose of providing funds to acquire, enlarge, improve, equip and maintain a facility and for the payment of obligations incurred for such purposes. The principal and interest on any such revenue bonds shall be payable solely out of the revenues derived from the project;

(7) To borrow money and in evidence of such borrowing to issue and sell at any time and from time to time its revenue bonds (in addition to those authorized under subdivisions (5) and (6) hereof) for the purpose of carrying out the commission's power to construct or acquire lodging facilities, as set out in section 41-9-430, the principal of and interest on which shall be payable solely out of the revenues and receipts derived by the commission from the operation, leasing or sale of the lodging facilities. The resolution under which such revenue bonds are authorized to be issued and any mortgage and deed of trust or trust indenture securing same may contain any agreements and provisions respecting the operation, maintenance and insurance of the property covered by said mortgage and deed of trust or trust indenture, the use of the revenues and receipts subject to such mortgage and deed of trust or trust indenture, the creation and mainte-nance of special funds from such revenues and receipts, the rights, duties and remedies of the parties to any such instrument and the parties for the benefit of whom such instrument is made and the rights and remedies available in the event of default as the commission shall deem advisable

and which are not in conflict herewith. Each pledge, agreement, mortgage and deed of trust or trust indenture made for the benefit or security of any of such revenue bonds of the commission shall continue effective until the principal of and interest on the bonds for the benefit of which the same were made shall have been fully paid. In the event of default in such payment or in any agreements of the commission made as a part of the contract under which such revenue bonds were issued, whether contained in the proceedings authorizing those bonds or in any mortgage and deed of trust or trust indenture executed as security therefor, said payment may be enforced by mandamus, the appointment of a receiver, or either of said remedies, and foreclosure of such mortgage and deed of trust or trust indenture may, if provided for in said instrument, be had;

(8) To make such contracts in the issuance of its bonds as may seem necessary or desirable to assure their marketability and to provide for their retirement by a pledge of all or any revenue which may come to the commission from the investment of the proceeds of the sale of such bonds or from any other source whatsoever;

(9) To accept public or private gifts, grants and donations;

(10) To acquire property by purchase, lease, gift or license, such power not to include the purchase of a site for the facility;

(11) To allocate and expend funds from all donations, income and revenue from any source whatsoever coming into its treasury for the fulfillment and accomplishment of its duties and responsibilities in such manner as may be necessary and appropriate for the perfection of the purposes of this article;

(12) To sell, convey, transfer, mortgage, lease or donate any property, franchise, grant, easement, license or lease or interest therein which it may own and to transfer, assign, sell, mortgage, convey or donate any right, title or interest which it may have in any lease, contract, agreement, license or property;

(13) To employ an executive director and such additional personnel as may be necessary to accomplish the purposes of this article. The executive director and such additional personnel as may be employed by the commission will serve at the pleasure of the commission. The commission shall fix the compensation of the executive director, and such additional personnel and such compensation shall be paid from the funds of the commission. The commission shall designate the duties and authority of the executive director and such additional personnel. The executive director and such additional personnel shall not be subject to the provisions of the state Merit System Act; provided, however, that they shall be eligible for participation in the state health insurance plan and benefits as provided in sections 36-29-1 through 36-29-12, and they shall be eligible for participation in the state employees' retirement system under the provisions of section 36-27-6 governing counties, cities, towns and other quasi-public organizations of the state;

(14) To make such rules and regulations as the commission may deem necessary and desirable to provide for the operation, management and

control of the facility in cooperation with the department of the army and with the national aeronautics and space administration; and

(15) To expend funds of the commission in the development, operation, promotion and expansion of the programs and activities of the commission including the franchising, nationally and internationally, of the United States Space Camp, a youth science program developed and owned by the commission; and

(16) To perform such other acts necessary or incidental to the accomplishment of the purposes of this article, whether or not specifically authorized in this section, and not otherwise prohibited by law. (Acts 1965, No. 863, p. 1605, § 3; Acts 1969, No. 280, p. 611, § 1; Acts 1971, No. 2339, p. 3772; Acts 1983, No. 83-567, p. 868, § 2; Acts 1985, 2nd Ex. Sess., No. 85-987, p. 333, § 1.)

§ 41-9-435. Liability upon revenue bonds issued by commission.

All revenue bonds issued by the commission shall be solely and exclusively the obligations of the commission and shall not create an obligation or debt of the state or of any county or of any municipality within the state. All revenue bonds issued by the commission for the purpose of providing lodging facilities shall be payable solely out of the revenues and receipts derived from the operation, leasing or sale by the commission of such lodging facilities as may be designated in the proceedings of the commission under which the bonds shall be authorized to be issued.

The principal of and interest on any such revenue bonds shall be secured by a pledge of the revenues and receipts out of which the same may be payable and may be secured by a mortgage and deed of trust or trust indenture conveying as security for such revenue bonds all or any part of the property of the commission from which the revenues or receipts so pledged may be derived. (Acts 1965, No. 863, p. 1605, § 6; Acts 1983, No. 83-567, p. 868, § 3.)

ARTICLE 23.

CRIMINAL JUSTICE INFORMATION
CENTER COMMISSION.

Division 2.

*Collection, Dissemination, etc., of
Criminal Data.*

§ 41-9-621. Powers and duties of commission as to collection, dissemination, etc., of crime and offender data, etc., generally.

The commission, acting through the director of the Alabama criminal justice information center, shall:

(1) Develop, operate and maintain an information system which will support the collection, storage, retrieval, analysis and dissemination of all

crime and offender data described in this article consistent with those principles of scope, security and responsiveness prescribed by this article;

(2) Cooperate with all criminal justice agencies within the state in providing those forms, procedures, standards and related training assistance necessary for the uniform operation of the statewide ACJIC crime reporting and criminal justice information system;

(3) Offer assistance and, when practicable, instruction to all criminal justice agencies in establishing efficient systems for information management;

(4) Compile statistics on the nature and extent of crime in Alabama and compile data for planning and operating criminal justice agencies; provided, that such statistics shall not identify persons. The commission shall make available all such statistical information obtained to the governor, the legislature, the judiciary and any such other governmental agencies whose primary responsibilities include the planning, development or execution of crime reduction programs. Access to such information by such governmental agencies shall be on an individual written request basis or in accordance with the approved operational procedure, wherein must be demonstrated a need to know, the intent of any analyses and dissemination of such analyses, and shall be subject to any security provisions deemed necessary by the commission;

(5) Periodically publish statistics, no less frequently than annually, that do not identify persons and report such information to the chief executive officers of the agencies and branches of government concerned; such information shall accurately reflect the level and nature of crime in this state and the general operation of the agencies within the criminal justice system;

(6) Make available, upon request, to all criminal justice agencies in this state, to all federal criminal justice and criminal identification agencies and to state criminal justice and criminal identification agencies in other states any information in the files of the ACJIC which will aid these agencies in crime fighting; for this purpose the ACJIC shall operate 24 hours per day, seven days per week;

(7) Cooperate with other agencies of this state, the crime information agencies of other states and the uniform crime reports and national crime information center systems of the federal bureau of investigation or any entity designated by the federal government as the central clearinghouse for criminal justice information systems in developing and conducting an interstate, national and international system of criminal identification, records and statistics;

(8) Provide the administrative mechanisms and procedures necessary to respond to those individuals who file requests to view their own records as provided for elsewhere in this article and to cooperate in the correction of the central ACJIC records and those of contributing agencies when their accuracy has been successfully challenged either through the related contributing agencies or by court order issued on behalf of the individual;

(9) Institute the necessary measures in the design, implementation and continued operation of the criminal justice information system to ensure the privacy and security of the system. Such security measures must meet standards to be set by the commission as well as those set by the nationally operated systems for interstate sharing of such information; and

(10) Designate in writing agents or employees of the ACJIC who shall be and are hereby constituted peace officers of the state of Alabama with full and unlimited police power and jurisdiction to enforce the laws of this state pertaining to the operation and administration of the Alabama criminal justice information system and the storage, use and dissemination of information processed therein. (Acts 1975, No. 872, p. 1716, § 10; Acts 1986, Ex. Sess., No. 86-714, p. 129.)

§ 41-9-630. Furnishing of other identifying data to center by criminal justice agencies generally; furnishing of information in criminal identification files.

Collateral references. — Criminal law: dog scent discrimination lineups. 63 ALR4th 143.

ARTICLE 25.

MUSIC HALL OF FAME BOARD.

§ 41-9-682. Function and powers generally.

(a) It shall be the function and main purpose of the board to honor those, living or dead, who, by achievement or service, have made outstanding and lasting contributions to music in Alabama or elsewhere. The board may adopt such rules, regulations and bylaws as may be needed to carry out its functions. Also, it may conduct surveys and polls and may appoint such committees and representatives as it may determine necessary or desirable. The board may acquire, construct, install, equip, lease, manage and operate buildings and other facilities consisting of any one or more of the following to be located in Colbert county, Alabama: (i) a music hall of fame and exhibition facility for the display of busts, statues, plaques, books, papers, computerized figures, memorabilia, records, films, audio tapes, video tapes, compact disks, recordings, pictures and other exhibits relating to music and musicians, (ii) a library, research and educational center for the collection and documentation of music and for music education and enrichment programs, (iii) an audio-visual auditorium/theatre, (iv) a recording studio, or (v) other facilities necessary or useful in connection with the use of any of the aforesaid facilities, including sites and equipment for any of the aforesaid facilities.

(b) Pursuant to the constitutional amendment authorizing the creation of the Alabama music hall of fame authority, the members of the Alabama music hall of fame board shall serve ex officio as members of such authority which shall be a public body corporate with all the powers and privileges of a corporation for the purposes of providing for and participating in the management and control of any of its facilities. The authority may acquire, construct, install, equip, lease, manage and operate buildings and other facilities consisting of any one or more of the following to be located in Colbert county, Alabama: (i) a music hall of fame and exhibition facility for the display of busts, statues, plaques, books, papers, computerized figures, memorabilia, records, films, audio tapes, video tapes, compact disks, recordings, pictures and other exhibits relating to music and musicians, (ii) a library, research and educational center for the collection and documentation of music and for music education and enrichment programs, (iii) an audio-visual auditorium/theatre, (iv) a recording studio, or (v) other facilities necessary or useful in connection with the use of any of the aforesaid facilities, including sites and equipment for any of the aforesaid facilities.

(c) The authority shall have the following powers, together with all powers incidental thereto or necessary to the discharge thereof:

(1) To adopt, alter and repeal bylaws, not inconsistent with the provisions of this section, for the regulation and conduct of its affairs and business;

(2) To acquire, whether by purchase, construction, exchange, gift, lease or otherwise and to improve, maintain, equip and furnish one or more projects, including all real and personal properties which the members of the authority may deem necessary in connection therewith, regardless of whether or not any such projects shall then be in existence;

(3) To lease to others any or all of its projects and properties and to charge and collect rent therefor and to terminate any such lease upon the failure of the lessee to comply with any of the obligations thereof;

(4) To receive and accept, from any source, aid or contributions of money, property, labor or other items of value for furtherance of any of its purposes, subject to any conditions not inconsistent herewith, including, but without limitation to, gifts or grants from any department, agency or instrumentality of the United States of America;

(5) To procure such insurance and guarantees as the members of the authority may deem advisable, including, but without limitation to, insurance or guarantees against any loss in connection with any of its projects, property or assets and for payment of any bonds or other obligations issued by the board, in such amounts and from such public or private entities, as it may deem advisable, and to pay premiums or other charges for any such insurance or guarantees;

(6) To borrow money and to sell and issue its bonds for any authority function, use or purpose;

(7) To mortgage, pledge, assign or grant security interests in any or all of its projects and properties or any part or parts thereof, as security for the payment of the principal of and interest on any bonds issued by the board, or as security for any agreements made in connection therewith, whether then owned or thereafter acquired, and to pledge the revenues from which said bonds are payable as security for the payment of the principal of and interest on said bonds and any agreements made in connection therewith;

(8) To appoint, employ, contract with, and provide for the compensation of, such officers, employees and agents, including, but without limitation to, engineers, architects, construction contractors, attorneys, management consultants, and fiscal advisers, as the business of the authority may require;

(9) To invest any funds of the authority that the members of the authority may determine are not presently needed for any of its corporate purposes in obligations of the United States of America and interest-bearing bank and savings and loan association deposits and in any investments eligible under then applicable law for the investment of trust funds by fiduciaries, or any thereof;

(10) To enter into a management agreement or agreements with any person or firm for the management by said person or firm for the authority of any of its projects and properties upon such terms and conditions as may be mutually agreeable;

(11) To sell, exchange, donate and convey any or all of its projects, properties and assets whenever its members shall find any such action to be in furtherance of the purposes for which the authority was created; and

(12) To make, enter into, and execute such contracts, agreements, leases and other instruments and to take such other actions as may be necessary or convenient to accomplish any purpose for which the authority was created or to exercise any power expressly granted hereunder.

(d) All revenue bonds issued by the board shall be payable solely out of the revenues and other receipts of the board as may be designated in the proceedings of the authority under which the bonds shall be authorized to be issued.

(e) The principal of and interest on the bonds issued by the board shall be secured by a pledge of the revenues and other receipts out of which the same may be payable and may be secured by a trust indenture evidencing such pledge or by a foreclosable mortgage and deed of trust conveying as security for such bonds all or any part of the property of the board from which the revenues so pledged may be derived. The resolution under which the bonds are authorized to be issued or any such trust indenture or mortgage may contain any agreements and provisions respecting the maintenance and insurance of the property covered by such trust indenture or mortgage, the use of the revenues subject to such trust indenture or mortgage, the creation and maintenance of special funds from such revenues, the rights, duties and remedies of the parties to any such instrument and the parties for the benefit of whom such instrument is made and the rights and remedies available in the event of default as the authority shall deem advisable and which are not in conflict with the provisions of this section.

(f) All bonds issued by the authority shall be signed by its chairman and attested by its secretary; provided, that a facsimile of the signature of any one or more of said officers executing or attesting any such bonds may be printed or otherwise reproduced on any such bonds in lieu of said officer or officers manually signing the same if such bonds are required to be authenticated by the manual signature of the duly authorized registrar of such bonds, or an authorized officer of such registrar.

(g) Any such bonds may be executed and delivered by the authority at any time and from time to time, shall be in such form and denominations and of such tenor and maturities, shall contain such provisions permitting or restricting redemption of such bonds prior to their maturities, shall contain such provisions not inconsistent with the provisions of this section, and shall bear such rate or rates of interest, payable and evidenced in such manner, as may be provided by resolution of the authority. Bonds of the authority may be sold at either public or private sale in such manner and at such price or prices and at such times as determined by the authority to be advantageous. The authority may pay all expenses, premiums and commissions which the authority may deem necessary or advantageous in connection with any financing done by it.

(h) All revenue bonds issued by the authority shall be solely and exclusively an obligation of the authority and shall not create an obligation or debt of the state or any county or municipality within the state, or a charge on the credit or taxing powers of the state or any county or municipality within the state. Any revenue bonds issued by the authority shall be limited or special obligations of the authority payable solely out of the revenues and other receipts of the authority specified in the proceedings authorizing those bonds.

(i) All moneys derived from the sale of any bonds issued by the authority shall be used solely for the purpose or purposes for which the same are authorized, including, without limitation to, the establishment of reserve funds as security for the payment of the principal of (and premium, if any) and interest on the bonds, and any costs and expenses incidental thereto. Such costs and expenses may include but shall not be limited to (i) the fiscal, consulting, legal and other expenses incurred in connection with the issuance of the bonds, (ii) in the case of bonds issued to pay costs of construction, interest on such bonds prior to and during such construction and for not exceeding one year after completion of such construction, and (iii) except in the case of refunding bonds, interest to accrue on such bonds for a period ending not later than two years from their date.

(j) Any bonds issued by the authority may from time to time be refunded by the issuance, by sale or exchange, of refunding bonds payable from the same or different sources for the purpose of paying all or any part of the principal of the bonds to be refunded, any redemption premium required to be paid as a condition to the redemption prior to maturity of any such bonds that are to be so redeemed in connection with such refunding, any accrued and unpaid interest on the bonds to be refunded, any interest to accrue on each bond to be refunded to the date on which it is to be paid, whether at maturity or by redemption prior to maturity, and the expenses incurred in connection with such refunding; provided, that unless duly called for redemption pursuant to provisions contained therein, the holders of any such bonds then outstanding and proposed to be refunded shall not be compelled without their consent to surrender their outstanding bonds for such refunding. Any refunding bonds may be sold by the authority at public or private sale at such price or prices as may be determined by it to be most advantageous, or may be exchanged for the bonds or other obligations to be refunded. Any refunding bonds issued by the board shall be issued and may be secured in accordance with the foregoing provisions of this section.

(k) The authority, its property and income and all bonds issued by the authority, the income from such bonds or from the investment of such income and all conveyances, leases, mortgages and deeds of trust by or to the authority shall be exempt from all taxation of any nature.

(*l*) The authority is hereby vested with full authority, except as limited herein, and in the constitution as amended, to provide for the terms of its bonds and to provide for the sale and issuance thereof.

(m) The full faith and credit of the state of Alabama shall be pledged to pay the principal, interest and premium (if any) of such bonds of the authority only as provided in such amendment or amendments to the constitution of Alabama of 1901, which amendment or amendments may be adopted and ratified before or after July 23, 1987.

(n) The provisions of this section shall be construed liberally, it being the purpose to provide in this state appropriate housing facilities for displaying to the general public exhibits of the Alabama music hall of fame board and for the management and control of displays by such means as may be feasible and agreed upon. (Acts 1977, No. 645, p. 1093, § 3; Acts 1987, No. 87-613, p. 1063, § 1; Acts 1988, 1st Ex. Sess., No. 88-918, p. 512, § 118).

Code commissioner's note. — Sections 1 and 2 of Acts 1987, No. 87-613 provide for the amendment of this section, as set out above, upon the ratification of a constitutional amendment by the qualified electors of this state, creating the Alabama music hall of fame authority. Amendment No. 489, relating to the Alabama Music Hall of Fame, was approved at the election held on November 8, 1988.

§ 41-9-683. Solicitation and acceptance of gifts, etc.; exemption from taxation.

Collateral references. — Exemption of nonprofit theater or concert hall from local property taxation. 42 ALR4th 614.

ARTICLE 26.

ALABAMA INDIAN AFFAIRS COMMISSION.

§§ 41-9-700 through 41-9-707. Repealed by Acts 1984, No. 84-257, p. 423, § 12, effective May 8, 1984.

Cross references. — As to voluntary check-off designation of state tax returns for Alabama Indian affairs commission, see § 40-18-59.

§ 41-9-708. Creation; administration; composition; qualifications; chairman; terms of office; recognition and representation of additional Indian tribes, bands, and groups.

(a) There is hereby created and established the Alabama Indian affairs commission, hereinafter called the commission, which shall be administered under the direction and supervision of the joint committee on administrative regulations, as provided by section 41-22-22.

(b) The commission shall be composed of at least 11 members. All members of the commission must reside in Alabama. Members shall include a member of the state senate, appointed by the lieutenant governor, and a member of the house of representatives, appointed by the speaker of the house of representatives, seven Indian representatives from the seven tribes, bands, or groups in the state of Alabama, and one member at large. The governor shall appoint seven Indian members from recommendations submitted by each of the seven Indian tribes, bands or groups, principally geographically located as follows: The Poarch Band of Creeks of Escambia county, one member; the Mowa Band of Choctaws of southwest Alabama, one member; the Star Clan of Muscogee Creeks of Pike county, one member; the Echota Cherokees of Alabama, one member; the Cherokees of northeast Alabama, one member; the Cherokees of southeast Alabama, one member; and the Ma-Chis Lower Creek Indian Tribe, one member. Each of the seven identified groups shall have one member. The commission shall appoint one Alabama resident, who is a member of a federally recognized Indian tribe, band or group, that is not a member of any tribe represented on this commission. The governor shall appoint one member at large, who may be Indian or non-Indian; provided, however, that the majority of the members of the commission shall always be Indian. All above stated tribes, bands, and groups shall be state recognized upon passage of this article. The commission shall have the power to recognize additional Indian tribes, bands or groups. The commission shall adopt appropriate procedure for such recognition process. Any recognized Indian tribe, band, or group shall be entitled to have one representative on the commission who shall be appointed for an initial term of three years by the governor and subject thereafter to the same requirements and privileges as specified in subsections (b) and (c) and any other applicable sections. Said member shall be granted the same voting powers accorded other members.

(c) The commission shall elect a chairman of the commission from among its members. Members serving by virtue of their office within state government shall serve so long as they hold that office. The terms of office for all other members shall be for four years each, except for the initial appointments which shall be as follows: Four members for two years; two members for three years; and two members for four years. The initial term of office for persons who are granted membership upon the recognition of their tribe, band or group by the commission shall be as provided in subsection (b). The initial term and all subsequent terms of office of the member representing the Ma-Chis Lower Creek Indian Tribe shall be four years. Each member shall serve until his successor is appointed. Members shall be eligible for reappointment. Upon the death, disability, resignation, removal or refusal to serve of any member, the governor shall appoint a qualified member of that tribe, band or group to fill the unexpired term of office. (Acts 1984, No. 84-257, p. 423, § 1; Acts 1985, No. 85-738, p. 1188, § 1.)

Code commissioner's note. — Acts 1984, No. 84-677, provides that Acts 1984, No. 84-257 shall be known as the "Davis-Strong Act."

§ 41-9-709. Purpose.

The purpose of this commission shall be to deal fairly and effectively with Indian affairs; to bring local, state, federal resources into focus for the implementation or continuation of meaningful programs for Indian citizens of the state of Alabama; to provide aid for Indians as needs demonstrate; to assist Indian communities in social and economic development; to promote recognition of the right of Indians to pursue cultural and religious traditions considered by them to be sacred and meaningful to the American Indian; and to establish appropriate procedures to provide for legal recognition of any future Indian organization who desires state recognition. (Acts 1984, No. 84-257, p. 423, § 2.)

§ 41-9-710. Powers and duties.

It shall be the duty of the commission to study, consider, accumulate, compile, assemble and disseminate information on any aspect of Indian affairs; to investigate relief needs of Indians of Alabama and to provide technical assistance in the preparation of plans for the alleviation of such needs; to confer with appropriate officials of local, state and federal governments and agencies of those concerned with Indian affairs to encourage and implement coordination of applicable resources to meet the needs of Indians in Alabama; to cooperate with and secure the assistance of the local, state and federal governments or any agencies thereof in formulating any such programs, and to coordinate such programs with any program regarding Indian affairs adopted or planned by the federal government to the end that the Alabama Indian affairs commission secure the full benefit of such programs; provided, however, that such commission is hereby authorized to directly seek and receive from the federal government any grants, funds or other benefits which may be available for Indians; to review all proposed or pending legislation and amendments to existing state legislation affecting Indians in Alabama; and to conduct public hearings on matters relating to Indian affairs. (Acts 1984, No. 84-257, p. 423, § 3.)

§ 41-9-711. Compensation.

The members of the Alabama Indian affairs commission shall receive no compensation for their services, other than reimbursement for travel and other expenses actually incurred in the performance of their official duties. (Acts 1984, No. 84-257, p. 423, § 4.)

§ 41-9-712. Time of meeting; notice; quorum; proxy vote prohibited.

(a) The commission shall meet monthly, and at such times that it shall deem necessary. Special meetings may be called by the chairman or by a petition signed by a majority of the members of the commission. Ten-days notice shall be given in writing prior to the meeting date. Such notice shall describe the matters to be discussed at the meeting.

(b) A simple majority of the members of the commission shall constitute a quorum for the transaction of business at every monthly meeting of the commission or any special called meetings for the purpose of transacting business.

(c) Proxy vote shall not be permitted. (Acts 1984, No. 84-257, p. 423, § 5.)

§ 41-9-713. Executive director.

The commission shall hire an executive director for the commission. Such director shall serve as secretary of the commission and as chief administrator and executive officer of the commission, having general charge of the work of the commission under its direction, and shall hire such other personnel as may be necessary in carrying out the provisions of this article with the approval of the commission. The executive director shall always serve at the discretion of the commission. (Acts 1984, No. 84-257, p. 423, § 6.)

§ 41-9-714. Authority to receive gifts, etc.

The commission is authorized to receive, and hold, gifts, devises, bequests of money, real estate and other things of value to be used in the support and development of its work for the commission. (Acts 1984, No. 84-257, p. 423, § 7.)

§ 41-9-715. Perpetual appropriation.

There is hereby appropriated out of funds in the state treasury, not otherwise appropriated, the sum of $125,000.00 perpetually funded for the commission, which shall begin May 8, 1984, for the operation of the commission, which funds shall be disbursed in accordance with a financial management system approved by the legislative council. (Acts 1984, No. 84-257, p. 423, § 8.)

§ 41-9-716. Annual report.

The commission shall prepare a written annual report giving an account of its proceedings, transactions, findings and recommendations. This report shall be submitted to the governor and the legislature. The report will become a matter of public record and will be maintained in the state department of archives and history. (Acts 1984, No. 84-257, p. 423, § 9.)

§ 41-9-717. Fiscal records; annual audit; bond of certain members, etc., required.

(a) Fiscal records shall be kept by the executive director or his/her designee, and will be subject to annual audit by the state examiner of public accounts. The audit report will become a part of the annual report.

(b) Commission members or employees of the commission who are responsible for receiving and disbursing commission funds shall be bonded in an amount satisfactory to the commission, but not less than $50,000.00. (Acts 1984, No. 84-257, p. 423, § 10.)

ARTICLE 28.

ALABAMA SENIOR CITIZENS HALL OF FAME.

§ 41-9-740. Establishment; purpose.

There is hereby created and established an organization which shall be known as the "Alabama Senior Citizens Hall of Fame." The purpose of such organization shall be to bestow honor and recognition upon a deserving citizen or citizens for their outstanding accomplishments, service and contributions to the lives of older American citizens. (Acts 1983, No. 83-674, p. 1063, § 1.)

§ 41-9-741. Composition.

The Alabama Senior Citizens Hall of Fame shall be composed of not more than 100 living members, and no more than 10 of such members shall be elected to membership in any calendar year. Each person elected for membership shall be a citizen of Alabama who shall be chosen for accomplishment or service greatly benefiting the lives of older American citizens. No more than 25 percent of the elected members at any time shall be from the political field. (Acts 1983, No. 83-674, p. 1063, § 2.)

§ 41-9-742. Election of members.

(a) The initial 10 members of the said Hall of Fame shall be elected by a committee appointed for such purpose by the governor. Such committee shall be composed of one person from each congressional district of the state and three members appointed at-large from the state. Upon the election of the first 10 members to the Alabama Senior Citizens Hall of Fame the committee shall stand discharged from any further duties and obligations and shall be dissolved.

(b) Thereafter, new members, not to exceed 10 in any calendar year, shall be elected by the existing members of the Senior Citizens Hall of Fame. A majority vote of the existing members shall be necessary for the election of each new member, and new members shall be chosen in order of the highest number of votes received.

(c) Nominations for new members shall be made by the existing members and in writing by citizens of the state. (Acts 1983, No. 83-674, p. 1063, § 3.)

§ 41-9-743. Election of chairman; term of office; appointment of secretary.

The members of the said Hall of Fame shall elect among themselves a chairman and shall fix his term of office. The chairman shall preside over meetings, direct the business of the academy and perform such other duties as may be prescribed or delegated to him by the said organization. The members shall appoint one of their number as secretary, who shall keep minutes of each meeting. The commission on aging shall provide such clerical assistance as may be needed by the Senior Citizens Hall of Fame. (Acts 1983, No. 83-674, p. 1063, § 4.)

§ 41-9-744. Annual meetings required; time and place of meetings; quorum; promulgation of rules and regulations.

The said organization shall meet at least once annually to award new memberships and shall hold such other meetings as necessary to carry out its purpose. The time and place of meetings shall be designated by the members. A majority of the members shall constitute a quorum for conducting business. The said Hall of Fame may make rules and regulations necessary to carry out its purposes and functions as prescribed in this article. (Acts 1983, No. 83-674, p. 1063, § 5.)

§ 41-9-745. Reimbursement for actual and necessary expenses.

The members of the Alabama Senior Citizens Hall of Fame shall be reimbursed for actual and necessary expenses upon approval of the chairman out of any funds appropriated to said Alabama Senior Citizens Hall of Fame and processed in the manner provided by law. (Acts 1983, No. 83-674, p. 1063, § 6.)

ARTICLE 29.

ALABAMA SMALL BUSINESS OFFICE OF ADVOCACY.

§ 41-9-760. Created; purpose.

There is hereby created, within the Alabama development office, the Alabama small business office of advocacy for the purpose of aiding, counselling, assisting and protecting, insofar as possible, the interests of small business concerns in order to preserve free competitive enterprise and maintain a healthy state economy; and to provide information and assistance to citizens interested in entering into commercial activity. (Acts 1984, No. 84-262, p. 445, § 1.)

§ 41-9-761. Definitions.

For purposes of this article, the following words and phrases shall have the following meanings:

(1) SMALL BUSINESS. A small business, as defined in section 25-10-3.

(2) OFFICE. The Alabama small business office of advocacy.

(3) DIRECTOR. The director of the Alabama small business office of advocacy.

(4) A.D.O. The Alabama development office. (Acts 1984, No. 84-262, p. 445, § 2.)

§ 41-9-762. Director and other employees.

(a) The management of the office created by this article shall be vested in a director, who shall be designated by the director of the A.D.O.

(b) The A.D.O. director may assign other A.D.O. employees or other employees in the state merit system and exempt positions in the various executive branch departments to assist the director for such periods of time as are necessary to enable the director to carry out his responsibilities. (Acts 1984, No. 84-262, p. 445, § 3.)

§ 41-9-763. Duties and functions.

The duties and functions of the office shall include all of the following:

(1) Serve as the principal advocate in the state on behalf of small businesses, including, but not limited to, advisory participation in the consideration of all legislation and administrative regulations which affect small businesses.

(2) Establish a central reference program and general counseling service to assist small businesses.

(3) Represent the views and interests of small businesses before other state agencies whose policies and activities may affect small businesses.

(4) Enlist the cooperation and assistance of public and private agencies, businesses, and other organizations in disseminating information about the

programs and services provided by state government which are of benefit to small businesses, and information on how small businesses can participate in, or make use of, those programs and services.

(5) Evaluate the efforts of state agencies, businesses, and industry to assist minority small business enterprises, and make such recommendations as may be appropriate to assist the development and strengthening of minority and other small business enterprises.

(6) Consult with experts and authorities in the fields of small business investment, venture capital investment, and commercial banking and other comparable financial institutions involved in the financing of business, and with individuals with regulatory, legal, economic, or financial expertise, including members of the academic community, and individuals who generally represent the public interest.

(7) Determine the desirability of developing a set of rational, objective criteria to be used to define small business, and to develop such criteria, if appropriate.

(8) To provide a center of information where a person interested in establishing a commercial facility or engaging in a commercial activity may be informed of any registration, license, or other approval of a state regulatory agency that is required for that facility or activity or of the existence of standards, criteria, or requirements which the laws of this state require that facility or activity to meet. (Acts 1984, No. 84-262, p. 445, § 4.)

§ 41-9-764. Information required of state agencies requiring regulatory approval, etc.

Each state agency which requires a permit, license, or other regulatory approval or maintains standards or criteria with which an activity or facility must comply shall inform the office of the following:

(1) The activity or facility that is subject to regulation.

(2) The existence of any threshold levels which would exempt the activity or facility from regulation.

(3) The nature of the regulatory program.

(4) The amount of any fees.

(5) How to apply for any permits or regulatory approvals.

(6) A brief statement of the purpose of requiring the permit or regulatory approval or requiring compliance with the standards or criteria. (Acts 1984, No. 84-262, p. 445, § 5.)

§ 41-9-765. State agencies required to disclose establishment of new regulatory programs, etc.

Each state agency shall promptly inform the office of any changes in the information provided under this article or the establishment of a new regulatory program. The information provided to or disseminated by the office shall not be binding upon the regulatory program of a state agency. (Acts 1984, No. 84-262, p. 445, § 6.)

§ 41-9-766. Toll-free telephone number authorized.

For the purpose of implementing the provisions of this article, the office shall establish a toll-free telephone number. (Acts 1984, No. 84-262, p. 445, § 7.)

§ 41-9-767. State agencies required to furnish to director documents, etc., necessary to carry out functions; annual report.

Each agency of the state shall furnish to the director such reports, documents, and information as the director deems necessary to carry out his functions under this article. The office shall prepare and submit a written annual report to the governor and to the legislature, that describes the activities and recommendations of the office. (Acts 1984, No. 84-262, p. 445, § 8.)

ARTICLE 30.

TENNESSEE VALLEY EXHIBIT COMMISSION.

§ 41-9-780. Creation; powers and privileges generally; purpose.

There is hereby created and established a state agency to be known as the Tennessee valley exhibit commission of Alabama, which shall be a public body corporate with all the powers and privileges of a corporation, for the purpose of providing for and participating in the management and control of facilities to house and display such visual exhibits of energy related hardware and examples of technology used therefor as may be made available by the Tennessee valley authority, the energy research and development administration, other federal and state agencies, including universities and colleges, and other public and private sectors engaged in energy related activities. Such facility shall constitute a permanent housing for the Tennessee valley exhibit, which shall be open to the general public and shall be located at a place to be designated in the vicinity of the Muscle Shoals area for a nominal cost through the cooperation of the Tennessee valley authority or at such other locations as the commission may deem appropriate. The commission is further empowered to provide facilities for the housing and display of energy related hardware and technology, navigational river and tributary development practices, agriculture technology and innovations, and wildlife and environmental practices and protections, and mankind and his historical achievements and mementos of the Tennessee valley authority. All such facilities shall be principally constructed out of oolitic shadow vein Alabama limestone. The commission is further empowered to establish an information and exhibit center in order to provide information to the public on research and development in the field of energy related hardware and technology, navigational river and tributary development practices, agriculture technology and innovations, wildlife and environmental practices and protections and mankind and his historical achievements as developed by the Tennessee

67

valley authority, the energy research and development administration, other federal and state agencies, including universities and colleges, and other public and private sectors engaged in energy related activities. (Acts 1984, No. 84-292, p. 551, § 1; Acts 1985, No. 85-655, p. 1024, § 1.)

Bonds. — Bonds proposed to be issued by the Tennessee Valley Exhibit Commission, when analyzed according to the "standard" set out in Edmonson v. State Indus. Dev. Auth., 279 Ala. 206, 184 So. 2d 115 (1966), did not create a new debt of the state and were not prohibited by the state constitution because: (1) By this section the proposed bonds are payable from revenues of the Project, the TVA "in lieu of taxes" payments being used only if the revenues are insufficient to pay the bond obligations; (2) the legislation creating the Commission and authorizing the issuance of the bonds states specifically that the bonds will not be obligations of the state; (3) the authorizing legislation limits the appropriation and pledge of non-Commission moneys to the TVA "in lieu of taxes" payments; and (4) the authorizing legislation specifically states that the Commission's bonds shall not create a pledge of the faith and credit of the state and prohibits the appropriating of any state funds except the TVA payments. McBurney v. Ruth, 527 So. 2d 1265 (Ala. 1988).

§ 41-9-781. Composition; terms; vacancies; chairman; compensation; meetings; quorum; executive committee.

The commission created herein shall consist of 16 members, to be appointed by the governor, and shall be bona fide residents and qualified voters of this state. The 16 members of the commission shall be appointed one each from the following counties of: Blount, Cherokee, Colbert, Cullman, DeKalb, Etowah, Franklin, Jackson, Lauderdale, Lawrence, Limestone, Madison, Marion, Marshall, Morgan and Winston in such a manner as to provide general representation on the commission, but all members shall be qualified persons of unquestioned loyalty to their country who are knowledgeable and interested in energy, river development, agriculture, wildlife and mankind and in the promotion of interest in such fields. Eight of the original members shall be appointed for terms of four years, and eight members shall be appointed for terms of eight years. Thereafter, all members shall serve for terms of eight years. All members shall serve until their successors are appointed and qualified, but any member may be removed by the governor for just cause. Vacancies for any reason whatsoever shall be filled in the same manner as original appointments are made. The first chairman of the commission shall be appointed by the governor from among the original appointees. Thereafter, each succeeding chairman shall be selected by the other members of the commission. Members of the commission shall serve without compensation. The commission shall hold at least one annual meeting at the site of the exhibit, and one half of the members shall constitute a quorum for the transaction of any business which may properly come before the commission at any such meeting. The commission shall be authorized to provide for an executive committee of not fewer than five of its members to whom it may delegate such powers and authority as the commission may deem to be advisable. (Acts 1984, No. 84-292, p. 551, § 2; Acts 1985, No. 85-655, p. 1024, § 1.)

§ 41-9-782. Authority of commission generally.

The commission shall be authorized:

(1) To investigate and select an available site for housing the exhibits, including the surrounding grounds, in cooperation with the Tennessee valley authority and the community, taking into consideration all pertinent factors affecting the suitability of such site;

(2) To acquire by rent or lease agreement or otherwise the necessary housing facilities and to establish, improve and enlarge the available facility, including providing it with necessary equipment, furnishings, landscaping and related facilities, including parking areas and ramps, roadways, sewers, curbs and gutters;

(3) To enter into such contracts and cooperative agreements with the local, state and federal governments, with agencies of such governments, including the Tennessee valley authority, with private individuals, corporations, associations and other organizations as the commission may deem necessary or convenient to carry out the purpose of this article, such contracts and agreements to include leases to private industry;

(4) To borrow money from private sources or such other sources as may be acceptable to the commission under such terms and conditions as may be provided by law and, in order to provide security for the repayment of any such private loans, to pledge such future revenues from admissions and any other sources as may from time to time be necessary or desirable;

(5) To issue and sell at any time, and from time to time, its revenue obligations for the purpose of providing funds to acquire, construct, enlarge, improve, equip and maintain a facility and for the payment of obligations incurred for such purposes. The principal and interest on any such obligations shall be payable from revenues derived from the project and from such other sources (including, to the extent applicable, the TVA payments referred to in section 41-9-783) as the commission may deem necessary to provide sufficient security for the marketing of said obligations. In addition to any obligations of the commission that shall be payable from any other source or sources, the commission is further authorized to issue and sell revenue obligations in an aggregate principal amount of not to exceed $5,000,000.00 to construct and equip the information and exhibit center as provided for in section 41-9-780, for the benefit of which the said TVA payments shall be pledged and appropriated as hereinafter provided. Any revenue obligations issued by the commission may thereafter at any time (whether before, at or after the maturity thereof) and from time to time be refunded by the issuance of refunding obligations, which revenue obligations or refunding obligations may be sold by the commission at public or private sale at such price or prices as may be determined by its executive committee to be most advantageous. The commission may pay all expenses, premiums and commissions which its executive committee may deem necessary and advantageous in connection with any financing done by it. Neither the full faith and credit nor taxing powers of the state of

Alabama or any political subdivision thereof shall be pledged to the payment of the principal of, premium, if any, on or interest on said obligations;

(6) To make such contracts in the issuance of its obligations as may seem necessary or desirable to assure their marketability and to provide for their retirement by a pledge of all or any revenue which may come to the commission from the investment of the proceeds of the sale of such obligations or from any other source whatsoever;

(7) To accept public or private gifts, grants and donations;

(8) To acquire property by purchase, lease, gift or license, such power not to include the purchase of a site for the facility;

(9) To receive and deposit into the state treasury funds from all donations, income and revenue from any source whatsoever coming into the commission and expend such funds for the fulfillment and accomplishment of its duties and responsibilities in such manner as may be necessary and appropriate for the perfection of the purposes of this article. However, such funds shall be paid out only by warrant of the comptroller upon the treasurer, upon itemized vouchers, approved by the executive director; provided, that no funds shall be withdrawn or expended except as budgeted and allotted according to the provisions of sections 41-4-80 through 41-4-96 and sections 41-19-1 through 41-19-12, and only in amounts as stipulated in the general appropriation or other appropriation bills;

(10) To sell, convey, transfer, lease or donate any property, franchise, grant, easement, license or lease or interest therein which it may own and to transfer, assign, sell, convey or donate any right, title or interest which it may have in any lease, contract, agreement, license or property;

(11) To employ an executive director and such additional personnel as may be necessary to accomplish the purposes of this article. The executive director and such additional personnel as may be employed by the commission will serve at the pleasure of the commission. The commission shall fix the compensation of the executive director, and such additional personnel and such compensation shall be paid from any funds of the commission. The commission shall designate the duties and authority of the executive director and such additional personnel. The executive director and such additional personnel shall not be subject to the provisions of the state Merit System Act; provided, however, that they shall be eligible for participation in the state health insurance plan and benefits as provided, and they shall be eligible for participation in the state employees' retirement system under the provisions governing counties, cities, towns and other quasi-public organizations of the state;

(12) To make such rules and regulations as the commission may deem necessary and desirable to provide for the operation, management and control of the facility; and

(13) To perform such other acts necessary or incidental to the accomplishment of the purposes of this article, whether or not specifically authorized in this section, and not otherwise prohibited by law. (Acts 1984, No. 84-292, p.

551, § 3; Acts 1985, No. 85-655, p. 1024, § 1; Acts 1986, No. 86-501, p. 980, § 1; Acts 1987, No. 87-586, p. 957, § 1; Acts 1990, No. 90-531, § 1.)

The 1990 amendment, effective April 19, 1990, in subdivision (5), in the third sentence added "In addition to any obligations of the commission that shall be payable from any other source or sources, the" at the beginning, substituted "aggregate principal amount of not to exceed five (5)" for "amount not to exceed 3.5," and added "for the benefit of which the said TVA payments shall be pledged and appropriated as hereinafter provided" at the end of the sentence, in the fourth sentence inserted "revenue obligations or refunding obligations" and deleted "or which may be exchanged for the revenue obligations to be refunded" at the end of the sentence.

§ 41-9-783. Revenue bonds deemed exclusive obligation of commission — Appropriation and pledge of TVA payments.

All revenue obligations issued by the commission shall be solely and exclusively the obligations of the commission and shall not create an obligation or debt of the state or of any county or of any municipality within the state. For the purpose of providing additional funds to enable the commission to pay at their respective maturities the principal of and the interest on an issue of revenue bonds in an amount not to exceed $3,500,000.00 to pay the costs of constructing and equipping the said information and exhibit center or to pay the principal of and the interest on any revenue refunding bonds issued to refund any revenue bonds that shall be issued for that purpose, there is hereby irrevocably pledged to such purpose and hereby appropriated such amounts as may be necessary for such purpose from the revenues retained by the state of Alabama from the in-lieu-of-taxes payments made by Tennessee valley authority following the distribution of a portion of such payments to certain counties in the state of Alabama as provided in section 40-28-2, or any successor law or statute. In order to carry out the said pledge and appropriation, the entire revenues so retained by the state of Alabama from the aforesaid in-lieu-of-taxes payments made by Tennessee valley authority (which are herein called the "TVA payments") in each fiscal year of the state of Alabama shall be deposited in the state treasury to the credit of a special fund to be called the "Tennessee valley exhibit commission trust fund" (herein called the "trust fund"), until an amount equal to the principal of and the interest on any such revenue bonds or revenue refunding bonds that shall come due in the then next succeeding fiscal year shall be on deposit in the trust fund. Further, for the purpose of providing additional funds to enable the commission to pay at their respective maturities the principal of and the interest on a second issue of revenue bonds of the commission in a principal amount not to exceed $1,500,000.00, the net proceeds of which shall be used to pay the costs of constructing and equipping the said information and exhibit center or to pay the principal of and the interest on any revenue refunding bonds issued to refund any revenue bonds that shall be issued for that purpose, there is hereby irrevocably pledged to such purpose and hereby appropriated, in addition to all amounts that shall have heretofore been so pledged and appropriated for the benefit of the aforesaid issue of revenue bonds of the commission in an amount not to exceed $3,500,000.00, such amounts from the TVA payments as may be necessary to pay all such principal and interest at their respective maturities. In order to carry out any such pledge and appropriation for the benefit of each of the foregoing issues of revenue bonds of the commission the entire TVA payments in each fiscal year shall be deposited to the credit of the trust fund until an amount equal to the principal of and the interest on each of the aforesaid issues of revenue bonds of the commission, or any revenue refunding bonds that shall be issued by the commission to refund any such revenue bonds, maturing in the then next succeeding fiscal year shall be on deposit in the trust fund. The amounts deposited into the trust fund in each fiscal year shall be disbursed and are hereby appropriated to the extent necessary to pay at their respective maturities, or to redeem under the terms thereof, the principal of and the interest on each of the foregoing issues of revenue bonds of the commission, or any revenue refunding bonds that may be issued to refund either of the said issues of revenue bonds that shall be so issued for such purpose.

In each fiscal year of the state of Alabama, beginning in the fiscal year in which any such revenue bonds are issued by the commission, all moneys retained by the state of Alabama from the TVA payments shall be so deposited into the trust fund until the amount on deposit in the trust fund shall equal the total principal and interest becoming payable with respect to the said revenue bonds or revenue refunding bonds in the next succeeding fiscal year of the state. After the said amount shall have been deposited into the trust fund in each fiscal year, all other moneys retained by the state of Alabama from TVA payments shall be credited to the state general fund. Not less than 30 days before the end of each fiscal year, beginning with the fiscal year in which the said revenue bonds shall be issued, the executive director of the commission shall determine whether or not the net revenues of the commission derived from all sources whatsoever during the then current fiscal year, after payment of all the costs of operating the said information and exhibit center and all other expenses of the commission, shall be sufficient or insufficient to pay the principal and interest that will come due during the next succeeding fiscal year on those bonds of the commission for payment of which TVA payments have been pledged. Not less than 15 days before the end of each fiscal year the executive director of the commission shall file a notification with the director of finance stating whether such net revenues shall be sufficient or insufficient to pay the said principal and interest coming due in the next succeeding fiscal year. If the said executive director shall determine that the said net revenues of the commission shall not be sufficient to pay the said principal and interest during the then next succeeding fiscal year of the state, he shall so state in the said notification and shall specify the amount of any expected deficiency, supported by such documentation as shall be deemed appropriate by the director of finance. Upon receipt of said notification and such other documentation as he may specify, the director of finance shall cause to be transferred, and to the extent herein provided there is hereby in such event appropriated to the commission, solely for the purpose of paying such principal and interest, an amount equal to the lesser of (i) the amount of any expected deficiency as determined by the director of finance or (ii) the entire amount then on deposit in the trust fund. Following any such transfer, all moneys retained by the state of Alabama from TVA payments shall again be deposited into the trust fund until an amount equal to the entire principal and interest coming due on the said bonds in the then next succeeding fiscal year shall again be on deposit in the trust fund, after which all moneys retained by the state of Alabama from TVA payments shall again be credited to the state general fund.

If at the end of any fiscal year of the commission there shall be on deposit in the state treasury any surplus funds for the account of the commission, after payment of the principal of and the interest on any outstanding revenue bonds of the commission and all costs of operating, maintaining and improving all facilities of the commission in each such fiscal year, such surplus moneys shall first be applied to the reimbursement to the trust fund of all moneys previously withdrawn from the trust fund for the account of the commission, with interest at the legal rate on all such moneys from the date of their withdrawal from the trust fund. If, after all moneys so withdrawn from the trust fund shall have been repaid with interest thereon, any such surplus moneys shall be on deposit in the state treasury for the account of the commission, such surplus moneys shall be transferred into the general fund of the state promptly after the close of each such fiscal year.

At such time as the entire principal of and the interest on any revenue bonds or revenue refunding bonds issued by the commission for the payment of which TVA payments have been pledged have been paid, no further TVA payments shall be deposited into the trust fund, and all moneys then on deposit in the trust fund shall be paid into the general fund. (Acts 1984, No. 84-292, p. 551, § 4; Acts 1985, No. 85-655, p. 1024, § 1; Acts 1987, No. 87-586, p. 957, § 2; Acts 1990, No. 90-531, § 2.)

The 1990 amendment, effective April 19, 1990, in the first paragraph, added the fourth and fifth sentences, and in the last sentence substituted "each of the foregoing issues of revenue bonds of the commission," for "any revenue bonds that may at any time be issued by the commission for the purpose of paying the costs of constructing and equipping the said information and exhibit center" and "refund either of the said issues of" for "refund any," and added the next to the last paragraph.

§ 41-9-784. Additional authority and power.

In view of the unique character and complexity of the duties and responsibilities imposed on the commission by this article, it is hereby specifically provided that the commission shall have, in addition to the power and authority enumerated in section 41-9-782, the right, power and authority to:

(1) Develop and institute a program of promotion and advertising of the exhibits and facilities provided for by this article, said program of promotion and advertising to be conducted by the commission both within

and without the state in such manner and to such extent as may be deemed economically advisable and appropriate by the commission;

(2) Purchase and acquire items of tangible personal property on a competitive bid basis in the manner prescribed by law for the purchase of such items by state trade schools, state junior colleges and state colleges and universities under the supervision and control of the state board of education, the city and county boards of education, the district boards of education of independent school districts, the county commissions and the governing bodies of the municipalities of the state and the governing boards of instrumentalities of counties and municipalities;

(3) Operate itself or, in its discretion enter into lease agreement with a person or agency of its choosing to operate, all concessions located in or on the grounds and facilities operated by the commission, any such lease agreement to be so designated as to provide maximum services and convenience to the patrons of the exhibit center and to provide reasonable revenue return to the commission. (Acts 1984, No. 84-292, p. 551, § 5.)

§ 41-9-785. Maintenance of accurate records and books required; audit.

It shall be the duty of the commission to maintain at all times accurate records and books of account covering revenues and expenditures which shall be subject to the audit of the department of examiners of public accounts.(Acts 1984, No. 84-292, p. 551, § 6.)

§ 41-9-786. Obligations, etc., exempt from taxation.

The commission, its property and income and all obligations issued by the commission, the income from such obligations or from the investment of such income and all conveyances, leases, mortgages and deeds of trust by or to the commission shall be exempt from all taxation in the state of Alabama. (Acts 1984, No. 84-292, p. 551, § 7; Acts 1985, No. 85-655, p. 1024, § 1.)

§ 41-9-787. Article liberally construed.

The provisions of this article shall be construed liberally, it being the purpose to provide in this state appropriate housing facilities for displaying to the general public exhibits of such hardware, technology, innovations, achievements, mementos, practices and protections as enumerated in section 41-9-780, and for providing for the management and control of that portion of the display furnished and supplied by the Tennessee valley authority by such means as may be feasible and agreed upon. (Acts 1984, No. 84-292, p. 551, § 8; Acts 1985, No. 85-655, p. 1024, § 1.)

ARTICLE 31.

CAHABA TRACE COMMISSION.

§ 41-9-800. Cahaba Trace commission created; members.

There is hereby created a commission to be known as the Cahaba Trace commission to consist of 23 members who shall be appointed by the governor of Alabama and shall be bona fide residents and qualified voters of the county represented. Said members shall be confirmed by the senate. Two shall be residents of St. Clair county, two shall be residents of Jefferson county, two shall be residents of Shelby county, two shall be residents of Autauga county, two shall be residents of Tuscaloosa county, three shall be residents of Bibb county, two shall be residents of Perry county, two shall be residents of Hale county, two shall be residents of Dallas county, two shall be residents of Lowndes county and two shall be residents of Montgomery county. Said members appointed by the governor shall constitute the board of directors of the commission and shall be the voting members of the commission. The board, at its discretion, may appoint as many advisory members as it deems necessary. (Acts 1985, 2nd Ex. Sess., No. 85-945, p. 285, § 1; Acts 1988, No. 88-298, p. 458, § 1.)

§ 41-9-801. Terms of office; appointment of new members; chairman.

Members of the commission shall serve for terms of office as follows: One member from each county shall serve for two years and the remaining member of each county shall serve for four years. Two of Bibb county's members shall be appointed for an initial term of four years and one for an initial term of two years. The initial members from Autauga county shall serve one year and two years, respectively. Upon the expiration of the original term of office of commission members, all successor voting members shall be appointed for four-year terms, providing for approximately one-half membership vacancies every two years.

All board members shall serve until their successors are appointed and qualified. New members shall be appointed by the governor from nominations submitted by the Cahaba Trace commission. The first chairman of the commission shall be elected by the board of directors from among its voting membership. Annually thereafter, each succeeding chairman shall be selected by all the members of the commission. (Acts 1985, 2nd Ex. Sess., No. 85-945, p. 285, § 2; Acts 1988, No. 88-298, p. 458, § 1.)

§ 41-9-802. Headquarters; meetings; quorum; chairman, vice-chairman, secretary, and treasurer; bonding of treasurer.

The headquarters of the commission shall be located in Bibb county. The commission shall hold an annual meeting and one-half of the voting members shall constitute a quorum for the transaction of business. Additional meetings may be held at such times as may be considered necessary, desirable or convenient, upon call of the chairman, or in the case of his absence or incapacity, of the vice-chairman. The commission shall elect a chairman, vice-chairman, secretary and treasurer, and such officers shall hold office for a period of one year or until a successor is elected. Neither secretary nor treasurer need be members of the commission. The commission may require that the treasurer be bonded in an amount to be determined by the commission. (Acts 1985, 2nd Ex. Sess., No. 85-945, p. 285, § 3.)

§ 41-9-803. Rules and regulations; executive committee.

The commission shall have the right to adopt such rules and regulations as may be necessary to carry out the intent and purpose of the commission, and shall be authorized to provide for an executive committee of not fewer than three members to whom such powers and authority as the commission may deem to be advisable shall be delegated. (Acts 1985, 2nd Ex. Sess., No. 85-945, p. 285, § 4.)

§ 41-9-804. Members not to receive pay or emoluments; expenses; fees, etc., from commission funds prohibited; interest in contracts, etc., with commission prohibited; penalty for violation of section.

No member of the commission shall receive any pay or emolument other than actual expenses incurred in the discharge of his duties as a member of the commission. All such expenses are to be paid from the funds of the commission. Further, it shall be unlawful for any member of the commission or any employee thereof to charge, receive or obtain, either directly or indirectly, any fee, commission, retainer or brokerage out of the funds of the commission, and no members of the commission or officer or employee thereof shall have any interest in any land, materials or contracts sold to or made or negotiated with the commission, or with any member or employee thereof acting in his capacity as a member of such commission. Any person violating the provisions of this section, upon conviction, shall be guilty of a Class C misdemeanor and shall be removed from the commission. (Acts 1985, 2nd Ex. Sess., No. 85-945, p. 285, § 5.)

§ 41-9-805. Cahaba Trace fund.

The commission shall establish, and maintain at such lawful depository or depositories as it shall select, a "Cahaba Trace fund" composed of the money or moneys which may come into its hands from admission, inspection fees, gifts, donations, grants, bequests, loans, bond issues, governmental appropriations or other sources, either public or private. Such funds shall be used by the commission to pay for the purposes herein set forth, and the servicing, retirement or amortization of any bonds or other evidences of indebtness issued by the commission. (Acts 1985, 2nd Ex. Sess., No. 85-945, p. 285, § 6.)

§ 41-9-806. Powers of commission.

The commission shall be authorized:

(1) To investigate and select available sites for housing historic exhibits, including the surrounding grounds, with such state, federal or local agencies and governments and private individuals, corporations, associations or other organizations as may be involved, taking into consideration all pertinent factors affecting the suitability of such sites; to acquire, transport, renovate, maintain and exhibit appropriate and suitable military, or historic units, articles, exhibits and attractions; to have full, complete and exclusive jurisdiction over the sites and any related exhibits;

(2) To promote tourism throughout the Cahaba valley by attending travel shows; issuing news releases, calendars of events and newsletters; publishing brochures and pamphlets; constructing mobile travel exhibits; producing films and other visual presentations as may be necessary; and advertising in magazines and/or newspapers;

(3) To acquire by rent or lease agreement or otherwise the necessary housing facilities; and to establish, improve and enlarge available facilities, including providing them with necessary equipment, furnishings, landscaping and related facilities, including parking areas and ramps, roadways, sewers, curbs and gutters;

(4) To enter into such contracts and cooperative agreements with the local, state and federal governments, with agencies of such governments, with private individuals, corporations, associations and other organizations as the commission may deem necessary or convenient to carry out the purposes of the commission with such contracts and agreements to include leases to private industry;

(5) To borrow money from private sources, the state emergency fund or such other source as may be acceptable to the commission under such terms and conditions as may be provided by law, and, in order to provide security for the repayment of any such private loans, the commission shall have the authority to pledge such future revenues from admissions and any other sources as may from time to time be necessary or desirable;

(6) To issue and sell at any time and from time to time its revenue bonds for the purpose of providing funds to acquire, enlarge, improve, equip and maintain its property, and for the payment of obligations incurred for such purposes. The principal and interest on any such revenue bonds shall be payable solely out of the revenues derived from the project;

(7) To make such contracts in the issuance of its bonds as may seem necessary or desirable to assure their marketability and to provide for their retirement by a pledge of all or any revenue which may come to the commission from the investment of the proceeds of the sale of such bonds or from any other source whatsoever;

(8) To accept public or private gifts, grants, and donations;

(9) To acquire property by purchase, lease, gift or license; and to dispose of any property of the commission when, in the opinion of the commission, such disposition is deemed expedient;

(10) To allocate and expend funds from all donations, income and revenue from any source whatsoever coming into its treasury for the fulfillment and accomplishment of its duties and responsibilities in such manner as may be necessary and appropriate for the perfection of the purposes of this article;

(11) To sell, convey, transfer, lease or donate any property, franchise, grant, easement, license, or lease or interest therein which it may own, and to transfer, assign, sell, convey or donate any right, title or interest which it may have in any lease, contract, agreement, license or property;

(12) To hire such laborers, artisans, caretakers, technicians, stenographers and administrative employees and supervisory and professional personnel as may be necessary or advisable for the carrying out in the most efficient and beneficial manner of the purposes and provisions of the commission;

(13) To employ an executive director who shall serve at the pleasure of the commission, who shall be responsible directly to the commission, whose compensation shall be fixed by the commission, whose duties and authority shall be designated by the commission and who shall be paid from funds of the commission;

(14) To make such rules and regulations as the commission may deem necessary and desirable to provide for the operation, management and control of its facilities; and

(15) To perform such other acts necessary or incidental to the accomplishment of the purposes of the commission, whether or not specifically authorized in this section, and not otherwise prohibited by law.

The commission shall constitute a public body corporate and shall have, in addition to those powers set forth specifically in this section, all powers necessary or convenient to effect the purposes for which it has been established, together with all powers incidental thereto or necessary to the discharge of its said powers and duties. (Acts 1985, 2nd Ex. Sess., No. 85-945, p. 285, § 7.)

§ 41-9-807. Exemption from taxation.

The commission, its property and income and all bonds issued by the commission, the income from such bonds or from the investment of such income and all conveyances, leases, mortgages and deeds of trust by or to the commission shall be exempt from all taxation in the state of Alabama. (Acts 1985, 2nd Ex. Sess., No. 85-945, p. 285, § 8.)

§ 41-9-808. Obligation of state not created by commission obligations.

All obligations incurred by the commission shall be solely and exclusively an obligation of the commission and shall not create an obligation or debt of the state of Alabama or any county or municipality of either. (Acts 1985, 2nd Ex. Sess., No. 85-945, p. 285, § 9.)

§ 41-9-809. Records of revenues and expenditures; audits.

The commission shall maintain at all times accurate records and books of account covering revenues and expenditures. Such records and books shall be available for audit at any time by the department of examiners of public accounts, and shall be audited at least every two years in the same manner as audits are made of other state agencies and departments. (Acts 1985, 2nd Ex. Sess., No. 85-945, p. 285, § 10.)

§ 41-9-810. State park or museum not authorized by article.

Nothing in this article shall be construed to grant authority to establish a state park or museum. (Acts 1985, 2nd Ex. Sess., No. 85-945, p. 285, § 11.)

ARTICLE 32.

ALABAMA TURKEY HUNTERS HALL OF FAME.

§ 41-9-830. Alabama turkey hunters hall of fame created; board membership; meetings; quorum; compensation; terms of office; vacancies.

There shall be created and established as herein provided a board and a facility to be designated and known as the Alabama turkey hunters hall of fame and the Alabama turkey hunters hall of fame museum. The board shall be composed of nine members and the initial members of the board shall be appointed by the city of Linden, Alabama. The board shall meet semi-annually and at such other times as its rules and by-laws may prescribe. A quorum of seven members of the board must be present for business to be conducted. The members of the board shall not be compensated for their services. Members of the board shall serve for terms of three years. The board will fill vacancies as they occur and shall have full and final right of choosing succeeding members. (Acts 1986, No. 86-202, p. 266, § 1.)

§ 41-9-831. Location of board, museum, and other quarters.

The board shall be domiciled in the city of Linden in Marengo county, where it shall maintain a museum and such other quarters as may be considered suitable and appropriate for conducting its affairs. (Acts 1986, No. 86-202, p. 266, § 2.)

§ 41-9-832. Function and purpose of board; election to Alabama turkey hunters hall of fame.

It shall be the function and main purpose of the board to honor noteworthy and exceptionally skilled turkey hunters. It shall elect to the Alabama turkey hunters hall of fame such individuals who are nominated for election and who receive a unanimous vote of the board of directors with at least a quorum of the board present. (Acts 1986, No. 86-202, p. 266, § 3.)

§ 41-9-833. Donations; board responsible for museum; exemption from taxation.

The board may solicit and accept donations, contributions and gifts of money and property, and all gifts made to the board shall be exempt from taxation in Alabama. The board shall specifically be responsible for the establishment and operation of a museum. All property, money, income, resources and activities of the board shall likewise be exempt from taxation. (Acts 1986, No. 86-202, p. 266, § 4.)

ARTICLE 33.

ALABAMA MEN'S HALL OF FAME.

§ 41-9-850. Creation of board known as Alabama men's hall of fame; members; meetings; quorum; terms of office; chairman; secretary.

There shall be created and established as herein provided a board to be designated and known as the Alabama men's hall of fame. The board shall be composed of 19 members: five of whom shall be members of the women's committee of 100 for Birmingham; two members shall be appointed by the governor from each of the United States Congressional Districts, except District Number 6, as such districts are presently established, for a total of 12 members appointed from said districts; and the governor and the director of the department of archives and history who shall serve as voting members of the board. The initial members of the board of directors of the hall shall be appointed by the governor of the state of Alabama. The board shall meet semiannually and at such other times as its rules and bylaws may prescribe. A quorum for all meetings shall be a majority of those present and voting.

The newly created board of directors' membership shall serve for three years. After this initial period of organization, a rotation policy for members of the board shall go into effect and each member shall serve one, two, or three years in addition to the three-year minimum period. Five members shall rotate off the board in 1989, five more in 1990, and four more in 1991 unless a member should be reappointed to the board for an additional three-year term. Members appointed to fill vacancies shall serve for a term of three years on the board of directors.

The perpetuation of the board shall result from choices made by the board to fill all vacancies as they occur because of rotation, resignation, or incapacitation. The board shall have full and final right of choosing succeeding members.

The chairman of the board of directors shall be elected annually by the board of directors, and may not serve more than two consecutive years.

The chairman of the board shall appoint a secretary. (Acts 1987, No. 87-717, p. 1407, § 1.)

§ 41-9-851. Location of Alabama men's hall of fame.

The location of the hall shall be in the Library Building, Samford University, Birmingham, Alabama. All items pertaining to the hall shall be housed at the same location. (Acts 1987, No. 87-717, p. 1407, § 2.)

§ 41-9-852. Purpose; selection of persons to be installed in hall of fame.

The purpose of the Alabama men's hall of fame shall be to recognize those men native to or identified most closely with the state of Alabama who have made significant contributions on a state, national, or international scale within their professional or personal fields of activity and concern. The number of persons chosen to be installed at each noted period shall not exceed the following:

(1) The first selection meeting of the board of directors shall choose not more than five persons, who must be deceased for a minimum of two years.

(2) Once every year after the first selection meeting, the board may choose not more than three new members of the hall. These new members must be deceased, for a minimum of two years, at the time of their selection. (Acts 1987, No. 87-717, p. 1407, § 3.)

§ 41-9-853. Donations, contributions and gifts; exemptions from taxation.

The board may solicit and accept donations, contributions and gifts of money and property, and all gifts made to the board shall be exempt from taxation in Alabama. All property, money, income, resources and activities of the board shall likewise be exempt from taxation. (Acts 1987, No. 87-717, p. 1407, § 4.)

ARTICLE 34.

ALABAMA PEACE OFFICERS' HALL OF FAME.

§ 41-9-870. Creation of Alabama peace officers' hall of fame board; members; meetings; quorum.

The Alabama peace officers' hall of fame board is hereby created and established. The board shall be composed of seven law enforcement officers, no two of whom shall be from the same congressional district, elected for a term of four years by the board itself. Board members shall be prohibited from serving consecutive terms. The board shall annually elect one of the members to serve as chairman. The initial board members shall be appointed as follows, viz: The member from Congressional District No. 1 shall be appointed by the Alabama Peace Officers' Association; the member from Congressional District No. 2 shall be appointed by the Alabama Sheriffs' Association; the member from Congressional District No. 3 shall be appointed by the Fraternal Order of Police; the member from Congressional District No. 4 shall be appointed by the Alabama League of Municipalities; the member from Congressional District No. 5 shall be appointed by the Alabama Association of County Commissioners; the member from Congressional District No. 6 shall be appointed by the Alabama Association of Chiefs of Police, and the member from Congressional District No. 7 shall be appointed by the Alabama State Troopers Association. Members of the board shall not be compensated for their services. The board shall meet annually at the office of the Alabama peace officers' association, and at such other times and places as its rules and bylaws may prescribe. A majority of the members shall constitute a quorum for the transaction of business. (Acts 1987, No. 87-718, p. 1408, § 1.)

§ 41-9-871. Function and purpose of board; rules, regulations, and bylaws.

It shall be the function and main purpose of the board to honor those living or dead, who by achievement or service, have made outstanding and lasting contributions to law enforcement in Alabama. The board may adopt such rules, regulations, and bylaws as it deems necessary to carry out its functions and duties. (Acts 1987, No. 87-718, p. 1408, § 2.)

§ 41-9-872. Donations, contributions and gifts; exemption from taxation.

The board may solicit and accept donations, contributions and gifts of money and property or services, and all gifts made to the board shall be exempt from all taxation in Alabama. All property, money, and income, of the board shall likewise be exempt from taxation. (Acts 1987, No. 87-718, p. 1408, § 3.)

§ 41-9-873. Expenditure of appropriations and donated funds.

The board may spend all appropriations of public money made for the use of the board and may expend funds donated or contributed for its use. (Acts 1987, No. 87-718, p. 1408, § 4.)

ARTICLE 35.

ALABAMA CHIROPRACTORS' HALL OF FAME.

§ 41-9-880. Creation; composition; meetings; quorum.

The Alabama chiropractors' hall of fame board is hereby created and established. The board shall be composed of the executive committee of the Alabama state chiropractic association. The board shall meet annually at the office of the Alabama state chiropractic association and at such other times and places as its rules and bylaws may prescribe. A majority of the members shall constitute a quorum for the transaction of business. Members who cannot attend a meeting may appoint another member of the state chiropractic association to serve in their place for that meeting. (Acts 1988, 1st Ex. Sess., No. 88-874, p. 409, § 1.)

§ 41-9-881. Purpose of board; adoption of rules, regulations, and bylaws.

It shall be the function and main purpose of the board to honor those living or dead, who by achievement or service, have made outstanding and lasting contributions to the profession and exhibited outstanding civic service in Alabama. The board may adopt such rules, regulations, and bylaws as it deems necessary to carry out its functions and duties. (Acts 1988, 1st Ex. Sess., No. 88-874, p. 409, § 2.)

§ 41-9-882. Solicitation and acceptance of donations, contributions, etc.; exemption from taxation.

The board may solicit and accept donations, contributions and gifts of money and property or services, and all gifts made to the board shall be exempt from all taxation in Alabama. All property, money and income of the board shall likewise be exempt from taxation. (Acts 1988, 1st Ex. Sess., No. 88-874, p. 409, § 3.)

§ 41-9-883. Expenditure of appropriations and other funds.

The board may receive and spend all appropriations of public money made for the use of the board and may expend funds donated or contributed for its use. (Acts 1988, 1st Ex. Sess., No. 88-874, p. 409, § 4.)

CHAPTER 10.

AUTHORITIES.

Article 11.

Alabama Mental Health Finance Authority.

86

ARTICLE 1.

GENERAL PROVISIONS.

§ 41-10-1. Alabama building authority.

Code commissioner's note. — The reference to "Acts of 1951" in the first sentence is incorrect. The correct reference is "Acts of 1955."

Acts 1990, No. 90-600 amends section 18 of Act No. 205 of 1955 Legislature, p. 501, Acts of 1955, relating to the Alabama Building Authority.

§ 41-10-2. Alabama building finance authority.

Code commissioner's note. — Acts 1990, No. 90-601 amends section 25 of Act No. 658 of

1961 Legislature, p. 807, Acts of 1961, relating to the Alabama Building Finance Authority.

ARTICLE 2.
INDUSTRIAL DEVELOPMENT AUTHORITY.

Division 1.
General Provisions.

Code commissioner's note. — Sections 41-10-20 to 41-10-32 have been designated as Division 1 of Article 2 of Chapter 10 of Title 41.

§ 41-10-26.1. Exercise of powers granted to airport authorities.

Any industrial development authority organized and incorporated under the provisions of chapter 10 of Title 41, which owns and utilizes property that has airport facilities is hereby authorized and empowered to exercise those powers granted to airport authorities under section 4-3-11. (Acts 1988, No. 88-337, p. 514.)

§ 41-10-27. Issuance and sale of bonds for purpose of making grants for certain purpose authorized; terms and conditions of grants.

Code commissioner's note. — Acts 1983, No. 83-925, effective December 21, 1983, authorizes the state industrial development authority to sell and issue bonds not exceeding $6,000,000.00 in principal amount in addition to those heretofore authorized to be issued by it; prescribes certain additional powers and duties of the authority, including: (a) the power to make grants from the proceeds of the said additional bonds to counties, municipalities, and local industrial development boards for the purposes of making certain local surveys incidental to industrial development and to grade and drain industrial sites and the means of access thereto; and (b) the power to establish a revolving loan fund of up to $3,000,000.00 from the proceeds of the said additional bonds, and to make loans from such fund to local industrial development boards, subject to certain limitations, for the purpose of encouraging construction of buildings for industrial development purposes, with such loans to be made on a participating basis and to be repaid by any recipient board upon entry into a lease or sale of any such building; provides that the authority may issue and sell such bonds for the purpose of making the said grants and loans; provides for the execution, form and terms of such bonds and for the terms of sale thereof; provides that such bonds and the income therefrom shall be exempt from taxation, that such bonds may be used to secure deposits of funds of the state and its political subdivisions, instrumentalities and agencies, shall be legal for investment of fiduciary funds and funds of the teachers' retirement system of Alabama, the employees' retirement system of Alabama, and the state insurance fund, and shall not create an obligation or debt of the state; provides for the deposit, investment and disposition of the proceeds of the sale of the bonds of the authority; makes an appropriation and pledge of funds from the special tax levied by sections 40-25-2 and 40-25-23, to the extent necessary to pay the principal of and interest on bonds of the authority; authorizes the authority to pledge the funds so appropriated for the payment of the principal of and interest on its bonds; provides that such principal and interest shall be payable solely from the funds so appropriated; and provides that the state treasurer shall be the custodian of the funds of the authority.

Acts 1984, No. 84-309, § 4, declares that the provisions of this act shall satisfy in full the contingency set out in § 4 of Act No. 83-925, with respect to issuance of certain additional bonds by the state industrial development authority.

Acts 1984, No. 84-801, effective June 14, 1984, amends § 3 of Acts 1983, No. 83-925, which authorizes a bond issuance by the state industrial development authority, so as to provide additional powers and duties of the authority and to authorize the authority to make certain grants of money to economic development councils.

Acts 1987, No. 87-550, effective July 22, 1987, authorizes the state industrial development authority to sell and issue from time to time its bonds not exceeding $6,000,000 in principal amount in addition to those heretofore authorized to be issued by it; prescribes certain additional powers and duties of the authority, including the power to make grants from the proceeds of the said additional bonds to counties, municipalities and local industrial development boards, economic development councils and airport authorities, subject to certain limitations, for the purposes of making certain local surveys incidental to industrial development and to grade and drain industrial sites and the means of access thereto; to provide that the authority may issue and sell such bonds for the purpose of making the said grants; provides for the execution, form and terms of such bonds and for the terms of sale thereof; provides that such bonds and the income therefrom shall be exempt from taxation, that such bonds may be used to secure deposits of funds of the state and its political subdivisions, instrumentalities and agencies, shall be legal for investment of fiduciary funds and funds of the teachers' retirement system of Alabama, the employees' retirement system of Alabama, and the state insurance fund, and shall not create an obligation or debt of the state; provides for the deposit, investment and disposition of the proceeds of the sale of the bonds of the authority; makes an appropriation and pledge of funds from the special tax levied by sections 40-25-2 and 40-25-23, to the extent necessary to pay the principal of and interest on bonds of the authority; authorizes the authority to pledge the funds so appropriated for the payment of the principal of and interest on its bonds; provides that such principal and interest shall be payable solely from the funds so appropriated; and provides that the state treasurer shall be the custodian of the funds of the authority.

Collateral references. — Adverse impact upon existing business as factor affecting validity and substantive requisites of issuance, by state or local governmental agencies, of economic development bonds in support of private business enterprise. 39 ALR4th 1096.

Division 2.

State Ceiling.

§ 41-10-35. Legislative findings and intent.

The Internal Revenue Code of 1986, as amended, imposes a "state ceiling" upon the aggregate principal amount of "private activity bonds" which may be issued in any calendar year by or on behalf of a state and its political subdivisions and instrumentalities, and establishes a method of allocating the available state ceiling within each state. Authority is granted by the Internal Revenue Code, however, to the states to provide for a different formula for allocation of the state ceiling. The legislature has found and determined that the allocation method contained in the Internal Revenue Code is ill-suited for the needs of the state of Alabama and that the provisions of this division will result in a more equitable and efficient distribution of the state ceiling available to the state and will therefore promote the economic and industrial development of the state. It is the intent of the legislature by the passage of this division to establish a method of allocation of the available state ceiling in the state and to delegate to the state industrial development authority substantial responsibility for the administration of the bond allocation plan established by this division. (Acts 1988, 1st Ex. Sess., No. 88-870, p. 382, § 1.)

§ 41-10-36. Definitions.

Unless the context requires otherwise, the terms defined in this section shall have the following meanings for purposes of this division:

(1) AFFECTED BOND. Any obligation or portion thereof which is required under the terms of the code to receive an allocation of the state ceiling as a condition for the exclusion of interest on such obligation from the gross income of the recipient thereof for federal income tax purposes.

(2) ALLOCATION. An allocation of a portion of the state ceiling issued by the authority pursuant to the provisions of this division.

(3) APPLICATION. An application for an allocation, submitted by an issuer under the provisions of this division.

(4) APPLICATION FOR CARRYFORWARD ALLOCATION. Any application filed with the authority seeking an elective carryforward of unused limitation for a "carryforward purpose" as defined in section 146(f)(5) of the code.

(5) AUTHORITY. The state industrial development authority, a public corporation of the state, organized and existing under Act No. 662, enacted at the 1965 Regular Session of the legislature of Alabama.

(6) CARRYFORWARD ALLOCATION. An elective carryforward of state ceiling for a "carryforward purpose" which may be granted by the authority under the provisions of section 41-10-39 and section 146(f) of the code.

(7) CODE. The Internal Revenue Code of 1986, as amended, including any successor provision to any code section or subsection referred to herein.

(8) EXEMPT FACILITY BOND. Any obligation described as such in section 142(a) of the Code, other than bonds, the proceeds of which are to be used to provide airports or docks and wharves within the meaning of sections 142(a)(1) and 142(a)(2), respectively, and includes any obligation issued to finance air and water pollution control facilities under the provisions of section 103(b)(4)(F) of the Internal Revenue Code of 1954, as amended, to the extent permitted under any transitional or effective date provision of the code.

(9) ISSUER. The state, any agency or instrumentality of the state and any county, municipality or public corporation authorized by or pursuant to the Constitution or laws of the state to issue affected bonds.

(10) LOCAL ISSUER. Any issuer which is a county, municipality, or public corporation organized by or pursuant to approval by a county or municipality (or pursuant to approval by two or more counties or municipalities or both) and which is authorized by or pursuant to the constitution or laws of the state to issue affected bonds.

(11) MANUFACTURING FACILITY. Any facility which is used in the manufacturing or production of tangible personal property (including processing resulting in a change in the condition of such property), and includes any facility devoted to an activity described in Standard Industrial Classification (SIC) Code Major Groups 20 through 39, or to agricultural activities, and further includes office facilities related to the foregoing so long as such

office facilities are located on the premises of the manufacturing facility to which they are related.

(12) PRIVATE ACTIVITY BOND has the same meaning as that specified for such term in section 141(a) of the code.

(13) QUALIFIED MORTGAGE BOND has the same meaning as that specified for such term in section 143(a)(1)(A) of the code.

(14) QUALIFIED REDEVELOPMENT BOND has the same meaning as that specified for such term in section 144(c) of the code.

(15) QUALIFIED RESIDENTIAL RENTAL PROJECT has the same meaning as that specified for such term in section 142(d) of the code.

(16) QUALIFIED SMALL ISSUE BOND has the same meaning as that specified for such term in section 144(a) of the code.

(17) QUALIFIED STUDENT LOAN BOND has the same meaning as that specified for such term in section 144(b) of the code.

(18) REMAINING STATE CEILING. The total state ceiling for calendar year 1988, less the amount thereof which, as of September 27, 1988, has been allocated by the governor of the state pursuant to the provisions of Executive Order No. 22 of the governor, and less the amount thereof which, as of September 27, 1988, has been allocated to, or otherwise used by, local issuers for the issuance of affected bonds issued prior to September 27, 1988. The amount of the remaining state ceiling shall be determined by the authority pursuant to section 41-10-38(b)(2).

(19) STATE. The state of Alabama.

(20) STATE CEILING. The maximum principal amount of affected bonds permitted to be issued in the state during a calendar year under the provisions of section 146 of the code. Under the provisions of the code in effect on September 27, 1988, based upon the most recent estimate of the population of the state made by the bureau of census, the state ceiling for calendar year 1988 is $201,050,000. In the event that the provisions of section 146 of the code are amended subsequent to September 27, 1988, or upon the publication by the bureau of census of revised estimates of the population of the state from time to time, the amount of the state ceiling available for allocation hereunder shall be revised in accordance with the provisions of section 146 of the code. (Acts 1988, 1st Ex. Sess., No. 88-870, p. 382, § 2.)

U.S. Code. — The Internal Revenue Code of 1986, referred to in this section, is codified primarily in Titles 23, 26 and 42 of the United States Code.

§ 41-10-37. Allocation procedure.

Allocations of the state ceiling shall be granted by the authority in response to applications filed with the authority by any issuer in the following manner:

(1) Each application shall be made by an instrument in writing signed by an officer or agent of the issuer and shall contain (i) the names and addresses of the issuer, the proposed lessee, purchaser or user of the project to be financed (if applicable), and bond counsel, (ii) the maximum principal

amount of affected bonds proposed to be issued, (iii) a brief description of the project to be financed, and (iv) a brief description of the affected bonds proposed to be issued, identifying such bonds as "Exempt Facility Bonds," "Qualified Mortgage Bonds", "Qualified Small Issue Bonds" (and if "Qualified Small Issue Bonds," further indicating whether the project to be financed constitutes a "Manufacturing Facility"), "Qualified Student Loan Bonds," or "Qualified Redevelopment Bonds." In addition, a copy of any notification required by law to be filed with the Alabama securities commission in connection with the issuance of the bonds which are the subject of the application shall also be filed with the authority together with the application. All applications shall be mailed or otherwise delivered to the authority at such address and in such manner as may be specified by the authority.

(2) Each application and each request for an extension of an allocation shall be accompanied by an administrative fee in such amount as may be determined by the authority.

(3) All applications shall be processed and all allocations shall be made by the authority in accordance with the provisions of section 41-10-38.

(4) Each allocation of state ceiling granted by the authority prior to December 1 of any calendar year shall expire upon the earlier of (i) 60 calendar days following the date of allocation, or (ii) midnight on November 30 of the calendar year in which the allocation is made, unless a notification confirming issuance of the bonds has been received by the authority as described in subdivision (5) below, subject to extension for such period as may be permitted at the discretion of the authority for good cause shown. Any application which has expired may be renewed by resubmission of a new application. Any allocation granted by the authority on or after December 1 of any year shall expire at such time as may be designated by the authority in such allocation. The foregoing provisions of this subdivision (4) shall not apply to carryforward allocation, which shall be effective for the period provided in section 146(f)(3) of the code.

(5) Every allocation shall be subject to the condition subsequent that a notification confirming the issuance of bonds pursuant to such allocation must be received in the office of the president of the authority within such period of time following the date of issuance of the bonds as may be provided by the authority. The confirmation required hereby may be executed by any officer, representative or agent of the issuer, by hand delivery, or by regular, certified or registered mail, and shall be effective upon receipt at the office of the president of the authority. Failure to provide a confirmation within the specified period shall authorize the authority to revoke the allocation for which the confirmation is required; provided, however, that the authority shall waive any such revocation upon a reasonable and timely showing of good cause for such failure or undue hardship that would be caused by the said revocation, and any such revocation shall be subject to review by a court of competent jurisdiction.

(6) On December 1 of each calendar year, any portion of the state ceiling previously allocated by the authority, for which a confirmation of issuance has not been received by the authority as required by subdivision (5) above shall revert to the authority, to be allocated along with any other portion of the state ceiling then available, to issuers of affected bonds at the discretion of the authority, subject to the duty of fairness and impartiality in the granting of allocations set forth in section 41-10-40. Applications for allocations to be made during the month of December shall be submitted to the authority in the manner required in subdivisions (1) and (2) above. (Acts 1988, 1st Ex. Sess., No. 88-870, p. 382, § 3.)

§ 41-10-38. Allocation formulae.

(a) The state ceiling for calendar year 1989 and thereafter is hereby allocated in its entirety to the state, and no other governmental unit, issuer, or other entity of any type shall have or utilize any portion of the state ceiling for such year except in accordance with this division. The state ceiling for calendar year 1989 and thereafter shall be redistributed by the authority to issuers of affected bonds in the chronological order of receipt of completed applications, subject to the limitations, reservations and further provisions of this subsection.

(1) There is hereby reserved for Alabama housing finance authority 25 percent of the state ceiling for each calendar year, to be used for the issuance of exempt facility bonds for qualified residential rental projects and for the issuance of qualified mortgage bonds, in such relative principal amounts as shall be determined by the board of directors of Alabama housing finance authority. The reservation of state ceiling hereby granted to Alabama housing finance authority shall extend until December 24 of each calendar year. Any portion thereof which shall be voluntarily released by Alabama housing finance authority in favor of the authority or which shall remain unused as of 5:00 P.M., central standard time, on December 24, shall revert to the authority and shall be available for reallocation under subdivision (a)(5) below. If, during any calendar year, the provisions of the code as then in effect shall not provide an exclusion from gross income for interest on bonds or other obligations issued by Alabama housing finance authority, the reservation contained in this subdivision (a)(1) shall revert to the authority and shall be subject to allocation by the authority under subdivision (5) below.

(2) There is hereby reserved for Alabama higher education loan corporation 10 percent of the state ceiling for each calendar year, to be used for the issuance of qualified student loan bonds. The reservation of state ceiling hereby granted to Alabama higher education loan corporation shall extend until December 24 of each calendar year. Any portion thereof which shall be voluntarily released by Alabama higher education loan corporation in favor of the authority or which shall remain unused as of 5:00 P.M., central standard time, on December 24 shall revert to the authority and shall be

available for reallocation under subdivision (a)(5) below. If, during any calendar year, the provisions of the code as then in effect shall not provide an exclusion from gross income for interest on bonds or other obligations issued by Alabama higher education loan corporation, the reservation contained in this subdivision (a)(2) shall revert to the authority and shall be subject to allocation by the authority under subdivision (5) below.

(3) Subject to the provisions of subdivision (a)(6) below, 35 percent of the state ceiling for each calendar year is hereby reserved for issuers of qualified small issue bonds which are issued to finance manufacturing facilities.

(4) Subject to the provisions of subdivision (a)(6) below, 15 percent of the state ceiling for each calendar year is hereby reserved for issuers of exempt facility bonds.

(5) Subject to the duty of fairness and impartiality set forth in section 41-10-40, the remaining 15 percent of the state ceiling for each calendar year not provided for in subdivisions (1), (2), (3) and (4) above, together with any amounts which shall revert to the authority under section 41-10-37(f) or subdivisions (1) and (2) above, is hereby reserved for the authority, to be allocated to issuers of affected bonds in the discretion of the authority.

(6) Subject to the duty of fairness and impartiality set forth in section 41-10-40, should the authority determine that inefficient use has been or is being made of the reservations contained in subdivisions (2), (3) and (4) above, or should the authority determine for any other reason that such reservations are inappropriate, the authority may, from time to time, reallocate all or any part of such reservations in accordance with subdivision (5) above.

(b) The legislature has found and determined that the method for allocating the state ceiling contained in section 146 of the code, as applicable to the state immediately prior to September 27, 1988, including particularly the provisions therein requiring that one-half of the state ceiling be distributed among local issuers on the basis of population, does not permit the full utilization of the state ceiling. In many instances, the amount of state ceiling available to local issuers under the provisions of the code are inadequate to permit the issuance of affected bonds in the principal amounts needed. In order to promote the complete and efficient utilization of the state ceiling available for use in calendar year 1988 as of September 27, 1988, the following provisions shall be applicable to affected bonds issued on or after September 27, 1988:

(1) The remaining state ceiling for calendar year 1988 is hereby allocated in its entirety to the state, and from and after September 27, 1988, no other governmental unit, issuer or other entity of any type shall have or utilize any portion of the remaining state ceiling for such year except in accordance with this division. The remaining state ceiling shall be allocated during calendar year 1988, in the discretion of the authority, to issuers of affected bonds upon receipt of completed applications subject to the further provisions of this subsection (b).

(2) The authority shall take all necessary and appropriate steps to determine the amount of the remaining state ceiling as soon as practicable after the passage of this division. In order to assist the authority in such determination, each county, municipality and other local issuer in the state shall be required to report to the authority such information as the authority may request with respect to the principal amount of affected bonds issued by such entities during calendar year 1988 and prior to September 27, 1988. The authority shall also review the records of the Alabama securities commission maintained under article 5 of chapter 6 of Title 8 as a further means of determining the amount of state ceiling heretofore used by local issuers in calendar year 1988 otherwise than pursuant to the provisions of Executive Order No. 22. (Acts 1988, 1st Ex. Sess., No. 88-870, p. 382, § 4.)

§ 41-10-39. Carryforward allocation procedure.

Applications for carryforward allocations may be submitted to the authority on or after December 1 of each calendar year. The authority shall grant such carryforward allocations in its sole discretion, giving due regard to the likelihood of the use of the remaining state ceiling prior to December 31 of such year, and shall use its best efforts to assure that any remaining and unallocated state ceiling is used to satisfy applications for carryforward allocations. (Acts 1988, 1st Ex. Sess., No. 88-870, p. 382, § 5.)

§ 41-10-40. Duty of fairness and impartiality in granting allocations.

Anything contained in this division to the contrary notwithstanding, the authority shall have a duty to administer the state ceiling allocation program created in this division fairly and impartially. In making any decision entrusted to its discretion, including particularly the granting of allocations or the reallocation of portions of the state ceiling among categories of affected bonds, or the revocation or waiver of revocation of an allocation, the authority shall give paramount importance to the fair, impartial and efficient discharge of its powers. Actions of the authority shall be subject to review by a court of competent jurisdiction to assure adherence to such standards of fairness and impartiality, which court may grant such legal and equitable remedies as it may deem necessary in order to assure such adherence; provided, however, that no member or director of the authority shall have any personal liability for the actions of the authority in connection with the allocation program. (Acts 1988, 1st Ex. Sess., No. 88-870, p. 382, § 6.)

§ 41-10-41. Forms, regulations, and interpretations; employment of attorneys, agents, etc.

The authority may do all other things necessary or desirable to carry out the purpose of this division, including the establishment of fees to be paid with each application. The authority is hereby empowered to adopt and promulgate such rules, policies, regulations and forms as it may deem necessary or desirable to carry out the purposes of this division. The authority is hereby specifically authorized to adopt such rules and regulations, including rules and regulations limiting the principal amount of allocations to be granted to local issuers, as it may determine to be necessary or desirable to promote the fair and efficient distribution of the state ceiling among local issuers. The authority shall have the power to employ attorneys, agents or independent contractors to assist the authority in the administration of its duties hereunder. (Acts 1988, 1st Ex. Sess., No. 88-870, p. 382, § 8.)

§ 41-10-42. Designation of official for certifications.

The president of the authority is hereby designated as the state official authorized to make certifications required by section 149(e)(2)(F) of the code. (Acts 1988, 1st Ex. Sess., No. 88-870, p. 382, § 9.)

§ 41-10-43. Confirmation of prior allocations.

All allocations of state ceiling applicable to the state made prior to September 27, 1988, pursuant to executive orders of the governor of the state are hereby ratified and confirmed. (Acts 1988, 1st Ex. Sess., No. 88-870, p. 382, § 10.)

ARTICLE 3.

SOUTHERN PRODUCTS MART AUTHORITY.

§ 41-10-54. Powers of authority generally; acquisition by eminent domain of real property or rights owned by railroads or utilities not authorized.

Collateral references. — Eminent domain: industrial park or similar development as public use justifying condemnation of private property. 62 ALR4th 1183.

ARTICLE 4.

STATE PRODUCTS MART AND COLISEUM AUTHORITIES.

§ 41-10-92. Powers of corporation — Eminent domain.

Collateral references. — Eminent domain: industrial park or similar development as public use justifying condemnation of private property. 62 ALR4th 1183.

ARTICLE 5.

HISTORICAL PRESERVATION AUTHORITIES.

Cross reference. — As to historic preservation commissions and architectural review boards, see § 11-68-1 et seq.

ARTICLE 7.

ALABAMA SHAKESPEARE FESTIVAL THEATRE FINANCE AUTHORITY.

§ 41-10-200. Declaration of purpose and legislative findings.

The legislature has found and determined and does hereby declare that it is necessary, desirable and in the best interest of the citizens of this state that provision be made for the establishment of a public corporation to acquire, enlarge, improve, expand, replace, own, operate, lease and dispose of properties to the end that such corporation may be able to promote public interest in, and aid in the development of, The Alabama Shakespeare Festival, Inc., a not-for-profit corporation created under the laws of Alabama, and to provide certain facilities for use by said not-for-profit corporation and to vest such public corporation with all powers, rights and privileges that may be necessary to enable it to accomplish such purposes. (Acts 1983, No. 83-408, p. 580, § 1.)

§ 41-10-201. Definitions.

The following words and phrases used in this article, and others evidently intended as the equivalent thereof, shall, in the absence of clear implication herein otherwise, be given the following respective interpretations herein:

(1) AUTHORITY. The public corporation organized pursuant to the provisions of this chapter.

(2) BOARD. The board of directors of the authority.

(3) BONDS. Bonds, notes, certificates, bond anticipation notes, grant anticipation notes or revenue anticipation notes or any other evidence of indebtedness representing an obligation to pay money.

(4) DIRECTOR. A member of the board of the authority.

(5) PERSON. Unless limited to a natural person by the context in which it is used, a person, corporation, association, partnership or cooperative.

(6) PROJECT. Land, any building or other improvement thereon or thereto, and any personal properties, whether or not now in existence, deemed necessary or suitable for use incident to or in connection with any theatrical or educational undertakings of the not-for-profit corporation known as The Alabama Shakespeare Festival, Inc.

(7) STATE. The state of Alabama. (Acts 1983, No. 83-408, p. 580, § 2.)

§ 41-10-202. Incorporation of authority; procedure.

(a) The governor, the state treasurer and the director of finance may incorporate and organize a public corporation, with the power and authority hereinafter provided, by proceeding according to the provisions of this chapter. To organize such a corporation, the governor, the state treasurer and the director of finance shall present to the secretary of state of Alabama an application signed by them which shall set forth:

(1) The name and official designation of each of the applicants, together with a certified copy of the commission evidencing each applicant's right to office;

(2) The date on which each applicant was inducted into office and the term of office of each of the applicants;

(3) The name of the proposed corporation, which shall be "Alabama Shakespeare Festival Theatre finance authority";

(4) The location of the principal office of the proposed corporation, which shall be in the state;

(5) The period of duration of the proposed corporation (if the duration is to be perpetual, subject to the provisions of section 41-10-213 hereof that fact shall be stated); and

(6) Any other matter relating to the incorporation of the proposed corporation that the applicants may choose to insert and that is not inconsistent with this chapter or the laws of the state.

(b) The application shall be subscribed and sworn to by each of the applicants before an officer authorized by the laws of the state to take acknowledgments to deeds.

(c) The secretary of state shall examine the application; and, if he finds that it substantially complies with the requirements of this section, he shall receive and file it and record it in an appropriate book of records in his office.

(d) When the application has been made, filed and recorded as herein provided, the secretary of state shall make and issue to the applicants a certificate of incorporation pursuant to this article under the great seal of the state, and shall record the certificate with the application. There shall be no fees paid to the secretary of state for any work done in connection with the incorporation or dissolution of the authority. (Acts 1983, No. 83-408, p. 580, § 3.)

§ 41-10-203. Board of directors; members; terms; vacancies; qualifications; expenses; quorum; impeachment; copies of proceedings as evidence.

(a) The authority shall be governed by a board of directors, and all powers of the authority shall be exercised by the board or pursuant to its authorization.

(b) The board shall consist of five directors. The chancellor of the University of Alabama and the president of Auburn University shall be ex officio members of the board. The remaining three directors shall be appointed by the governor in the manner hereinafter prescribed, as soon as may be practicable after the incorporation of the authority, for staggered terms as follows: The governor shall appoint two directors each of whose initial terms shall begin immediately upon his respective appointment and shall end on September 30 in the fifth calendar year next following the calendar year in which the certificate of incorporation of the authority was issued; and the governor shall appoint the remaining director whose initial term shall begin immediately upon his appointment and shall end on September 30 in the tenth calendar year next following the calendar year in which the certificate of incorporation of the authority was issued. Thereafter, the term of office of each appointed director shall be 10 years, commencing on the October 1 next following the September 30 on which the term of the immediate predecessor director ended. If at any time there should be a vacancy on the board not heretofore provided for, a successor director shall be appointed by the governor to serve for the unexpired term applicable to such vacancy. If the term of office of any appointed director shall expire prior to the reappointment of such director or prior to the appointment of his successor, such director shall continue to serve until his successor is appointed and qualified, and if such director is reappointed for a new term after the expiration of the immediately preceding term which he has been serving, his new term of office shall be deemed to have commenced on the October 1 next following the expiration of such immediately preceding term. Directors shall be eligible for reappointment.

(c) Each appointed director shall, at the time of his appointment and at all times during his term of office, be a qualified elector of the state; and a failure by any appointed director to remain so qualified during such term shall cause a vacancy of the office of such director. No officer or employee of the state or of any county, city or town therein shall be eligible for appointment as a director. The acceptance by an appointed director of any office or employment which, had such director held such office or been so employed at the time of his appointment as a director, would have rendered him ineligible for appointment as a director, shall cause a vacancy of the office of such director. Each director shall serve without compensation, except that he may be reimbursed for expenses actually incurred by him in and about the performance of his duties.

(d) A majority of the directors in office shall constitute a quorum for the transaction of business. No vacancy in the membership of the board or the voluntary disqualification or abstention of any member thereof shall impair the right of a quorum of the board to exercise all the powers and duties of the authority. All proceedings of the board shall be reduced to writing by the secretary of the authority and maintained in the permanent records of the authority. Copies of such proceedings, when certified by the secretary of the authority under the seal of the authority, shall be received in all courts as evidence of the matters therein certified. (Acts 1983, No. 83-408, p. 580, § 4.)

§ 41-10-204. Officers.

The officers of the authority shall consist of a chairman, vice-chairman, secretary, treasurer and such other officers as the board shall deem necessary or appropriate. The chairman and the vice-chairman shall be elected by the board from the membership thereof, and the secretary, the treasurer and any other officers of the authority may, but need not, be members of the board and shall also be elected by the board. The offices of secretary and treasurer may, but need not, be held by the same person. (Acts 1983, No. 83-408, p. 580, § 5.)

§ 41-10-205. Powers of authority; open meetings required.

(a) The authority shall have the following powers, together with all powers incidental thereto or necessary to the discharge thereof in corporate form:

(1) To have succession by its corporate name for the duration of time (which may be perpetuity, subject to the provisions of section 41-10-213) specified in its certificate of incorporation;

(2) To sue and be sued in its own name in civil suits and actions, and to defend suits against it;

(3) To adopt and make use of a corporate seal and to alter the same at pleasure;

(4) To adopt, alter and repeal bylaws, not inconsistent with the provisions of this article, for the regulation and conduct of its affairs and business;

(5) To acquire, whether by purchase, construction, exchange, gift, lease or otherwise and to improve, maintain, equip and furnish one or more projects, including all real and personal properties which the board may deem necessary in connection therewith, regardless of whether or not any such projects shall then be in existence;

(6) To lease to others any or all of its projects and to charge and collect rent therefor and to terminate any such lease upon the failure of the lessee to comply with any of the obligations thereof;

(7) To receive and accept, from any source, aid or contributions of money, property, labor or other items of value for furtherance of any of its purposes, subject to any conditions not inconsistent herewith or with the laws of this state pertaining to such contributions, including, but without limitation to, gifts or grants from any department, agency or instrumentality of the United States of America;

(8) To procure such insurance and guarantees as the board may deem advisable, including, but without limitation to, insurance or guarantees against any loss in connection with any of its property or assets and for payment of any bonds or other obligations issued by the authority, in such amounts and from such public or private entities, as it may deem advisable, and to pay premiums or other charges for any such insurance or guarantees;

(9) To borrow money and to sell and issue its bonds for any corporate function, use or purpose authorized herein;

(10) To mortgage, pledge, assign or grant security interests in any or all of its projects or any part or parts thereof, as security for the payment of the principal of and interest on any bonds issued by the authority, or as security for any agreements made in connection therewith, whether then owned or thereafter acquired, and to pledge the revenues from which said bonds are payable as security for the payment of the principal of and interest on said bonds and any agreements made in connection therewith;

(11) To appoint, employ, contract with, and provide for the compensation of, such officers, employees and agents, including, but without limitation to, engineers, architects, construction contractors, attorneys, management consultants, and fiscal advisers, as the business of the authority may require; provided, however, that no director or member of his or her firm, business, partnership or corporation shall be employed or compensated by the authority;

(12) To invest any funds of the authority that the board may determine are not presently needed for any of its corporate purposes in obligations of the United States of America and interest-bearing bank and savings and loan association deposits and in any investments eligible under then applicable law for the investment of trust funds by fiduciaries, or any thereof;

(13) To enter into a management agreement or agreements with any person for the management by said person for the authority of any of its properties upon such terms and conditions as may be mutually agreeable;

(14) To sell, exchange, donate and convey any or all of its properties whenever its board shall find any such action to be in furtherance of the purposes for which the authority was organized; and

(15) To make, enter into, and execute such contracts, agreements, leases and other instruments and to take such other actions as may be necessary or convenient to accomplish any purpose for which the authority was organized or to exercise any power expressly granted hereunder.

(b) All meetings of the board of the authority for any purpose shall be open to the public. (Acts 1983, No. 83-408, p. 580, § 6.)

§ 41-10-206. Bonds.

(a) *Source of payment.* — All bonds issued by the authority shall be payable solely out of the revenues and other receipts of the authority as may be designated in the proceedings of the board under which the bonds shall be authorized to be issued.

(b) *Pledge of revenues and other security.* — The principal of an interest on any bonds issued by the authority shall be secured by a pledge of the revenues and other receipts out of which the same may be payable and may be secured by a trust indenture evidencing such pledge or by a foreclosable mortgage and deed of trust conveying as security for such bonds all or any part of the property of the authority from which the revenues so pledged may be derived. The resolution under which the bonds are authorized to be issued or any such trust indenture or mortgage may contain any agreements and provisions respecting the maintenance and insurance of the property covered by such trust indenture or mortgage, the use of the revenues subject to such trust indenture or mortgage, the creation and maintenance of special funds from such revenues, the rights, duties and remedies of the parties to any such instrument and the parties for the benefit of whom such instrument is made and the rights and remedies available in the event of default as the board shall deem advisable and which are not in conflict with the provisions of this article.

(c) *Execution.* — All bonds issued by the authority shall be signed by its chairman or vice-chairman and attested by its secretary, and the seal of the authority shall be affixed thereto, and any interest coupons applicable to the bonds of the authority shall be signed by its chairman or vice-chairman; provided, that a facsimile of the signature of one, but not both, of said officers may be printed or otherwise reproduced on any such bonds in lieu of his manually signing the same, a facsimile of the seal of the authority may be printed or otherwise reproduced on any such bonds in lieu of being manually affixed thereto, and a facsimile of the signature of its chairman or vice-chairman may be printed or otherwise reproduced on any such interest coupons in lieu of his manually signing the same.

(d) *General provisions respecting form, interest rate, maturities, sale and negotiability of bonds.* — Any such bonds may be executed and delivered by the authority at any time and from time to time, shall be in such form and denominations and of such tenor and maturities, shall contain such provisions permitting or restricting redemption of such bonds prior to their maturities, shall contain such provisions not inconsistent with the provisions of this article, and shall bear such rate or rates of interest, payable and evidenced in such manner, as may be provided by resolution of its board. Bonds of the authority may be sold at either public or private sale in such manner and at such price or prices and at such times as determined by the board of directors to be advantageous. The authority may pay all expenses, premiums and commissions which the board may deem necessary or advantageous in connection with any financing done by it. Whether or not any bonds of the authority, and any interest coupons appertaining thereto, are of such form and character as to be negotiable instruments under the terms of Title 7, all bonds, except bonds registered as to principal or as to both principal and interest, and any interest coupons applicable thereto issued by the authority shall be construed to be negotiable instruments although payable solely from a specified source.

(e) *Nature of obligation and source of payment.* — All obligations created and all bonds issued by the authority shall be solely and exclusively an obligation of the authority and shall not create an obligation or debt of the state or a charge on its credit or taxing powers. Any bonds issued by the authority shall be limited or special obligations of the authority payable solely out of the revenues and other receipts of the authority specified in the proceedings authorizing those bonds. (Acts 1983, No. 83-408, p. 580, § 7.)

§ 41-10-207. Proceeds from sale of bonds.

All moneys derived from the sale of any bonds issued by the authority shall be used solely for the purpose or purposes for which the same are authorized, including, but without limitation to, the establishment of reserve funds as security for the payment of the principal of (and premium, if any) and interest on the bonds, and any costs and expenses incidental thereto. Such costs and expenses may include but shall not be limited to (1) the fiscal, consulting, legal and other expenses incurred in connection with the issuance of the bonds, (2) in the case of bonds issued to pay costs of construction, interest on such bonds prior to and during such construction and for not exceeding one year after completion of such construction, and (3) except in the case of refunding bonds, interest to accrue on such bonds for a period ending not later than two years from their date. (Acts 1983, No. 83-408, p. 580, § 8.)

§ 41-10-208. Refunding bonds.

Any bonds issued by the authority may from time to time be refunded by the issuance, by sale or exchange, of refunding bonds payable from the same or different sources for the purpose of paying all or any part of the principal of the bonds to be refunded, any redemption premium required to be paid as a condition to the redemption prior to maturity of any such bonds that are to be so redeemed in connection with such refunding, any accrued and unpaid interest on the bonds to be refunded, any interest to accrue on each bond to be refunded to the date on which it is to be paid, whether at maturity or by redemption prior to maturity, and the expenses incurred in connection with such refunding; provided, that unless duly called for redemption pursuant to provisions contained therein, the holders of any such bonds then outstanding and proposed to be refunded shall not be compelled without their consent to surrender their outstanding bonds for such refunding. Any refunding bonds may be sold by the authority at public or private sale at such price or prices as may be determined by its board to be most advantageous, or may be exchanged for the bonds or other obligations to be refunded. Any refunding bonds issued by the authority shall be issued and may be secured in accordance with the provisions of section 41-10-206. (Acts 1983, No. 83-408, p. 580, § 9.)

§ 41-10-209. Exemption from taxation.

The property and income of the authority, all bonds issued by the authority, the income from such bonds, conveyances by or to the authority, and leases, mortgages and deeds of trust or trust indentures by or to the authority shall be exempt from all taxation in the state of Alabama. The authority shall be exempt from all taxes levied by any county, incorporated city or town, or other political subdivision of the state, including, but without limitation to, license and excise taxes imposed in respect of the privilege of engaging in any of the activities in which the authority may engage. The authority shall not be obligated to pay or allow any fees, taxes or costs to the judge of probate of any county of this state in respect of its incorporation or the recording of any document. (Acts 1983, No. 83-408, p. 580, § 10.)

Collateral references. — Exemption of nonprofit theater or concert hall from local property taxation. 42 ALR4th 614.

§ 41-10-210. Exemption from usury and interest laws.

The authority shall be exempt from the laws of the state of Alabama governing usury or prescribing or limiting interest rates, including, but without limitation to, the provisions of chapter 8 of Title 8. (Acts 1983, No. 83-408, p. 580, § 11.)

§ 41-10-211. Freedom of authority from state supervision and control; inapplicability of code of ethics.

(a) This article is intended to aid the state through the furtherance of the purposes of the chapter by providing an appropriate and independent instrumentality of the state with full and adequate powers to fulfill its functions. Except as expressly provided in this article, no proceeding, notice or approval shall be required for the incorporation of the authority, the issuance of any bonds, the execution of any mortgage and deed of trust or trust indenture, or the exercise of any other of its powers by the authority. Neither a public hearing nor the consent of the state department of finance shall be prerequisite to the issuance of bonds by the authority.

(b) The directors, the officers and employees of the authority shall not be subject to the provisions of chapter 25 of Title 36 or to the rules and promulgations by the Alabama ethics commission. (Acts 1983, No. 83-408, p. 580, § 12.)

§ 41-10-212. Exemption from competitive bid laws.

All contracts made by the authority shall be exempt from the laws of the state now or hereafter in effect that require competitive bids, including, but without limitation to, the provisions of article 3 of chapter 16 of this title. (Acts 1983, No. 83-408, p. 580, § 13.)

§ 41-10-213. Dissolution of authority and vesting of title to its property.

At any time when the authority has no bonds or other obligations outstanding, its board may adopt a resolution, which shall be duly entered upon its minutes, declaring that the authority shall be dissolved. Upon filing for record of a certified copy of the said resolution in the office of the secretary of state, the authority shall thereupon stand dissolved and in the event it owned any property at the time of its dissolution, the title to all its properties shall thereupon pass to and vest in the board of trustees of the University of Alabama. (Acts 1983, No. 83-408, p. 580, § 14.)

§ 41-10-214. Article cumulative.

The provisions of this article are cumulative and shall not be deemed to repeal existing laws, except to the extent such laws are clearly inconsistent with provisions of this article. (Acts 1983, No. 83-408, p. 580, § 15.)

§ 41-10-215. Liberal construction of article.

This article is remedial in nature and shall be liberally construed to effect its purposes. (Acts 1983, No. 83-408, p. 580, § 16.)

ARTICLE 8.

AFRICATOWN, U.S.A. STATE PARK AND
HISTORIC PRESERVATION AUTHORITY.

§ 41-10-230. Short title.

This article shall be known and cited as "The Africatown, U.S.A. Act of 1985." (Acts 1985, 2nd Ex. Sess., No. 85-950, p. 292, § 1.)

§ 41-10-231. "Authority" defined.

The word "authority" as used throughout this article shall mean "The Africatown, U.S.A. Historic Preservation Authority" unless the context clearly intends a different meaning. (Acts 1985, 2nd Ex. Sess., No. 85-950, p. 292, § 2.)

§ 41-10-232. Africatown, U.S.A. state park to be included in listings of state parks; use of park.

In order to preserve and interpret to the public the historic and cultural properties at and near Africatown, U.S.A. in Mobile county, the commissioner of the state department of conservation and natural resources shall include the descriptions of lands and boundaries contained in section 41-10-233 on any registry or listings of state parks. The Africatown, U.S.A. state park shall be comprised of those facilities authorized in section 41-10-234 and shall be utilized as a park for recreational use by the general public and for no other and different purpose, as stated in the deed conveying said property to the city of Prichard. (Acts 1985, 2nd Ex. Sess., No. 85-950, p. 292, § 3.)

§ 41-10-233. Africatown, U.S.A. state park established; description of boundaries.

There is hereby established in the city of Prichard, Alabama, the Africatown, U.S.A. state park to recognize the significance of Africatown, U.S.A. in American history and culture and to commemorate African heritage in the United States of America, with boundaries described as follows: All that portion of the southeast quarter and the southwest quarter of the northeast quarter of section 18, township 3 south, range 2 west, located south of Chickasawbogue creek, excepting that part of the southeast quarter located east of the west line of the Basil Chastang claim.

Beginning at the southeast corner of section 18, township 3 south, range 2 west, thence run westerly a distance of 350 feet along the south line of said section 18 to a point; thence run north 12° 09' east, a distance of 1,663 feet to the point of beginning of the parcel of land herein conveyed; thence run south 45° 00' east along the south line of lot 1 in the Basil Chastang claim a distance of approximately 1,050 feet to the point of intersection with the east line of the right of way of the Alabama power company; thence run northeasterly along the east line of this right of way to its intersection with the south edge of Chickasawbogue creek; thence run westerly along the south edge of Chickasawbogue creek to a point where the south edge of Chickasawbogue creek intersects the east line of section 18, township 3 south, range 2 west; thence run south along the said east line of section 18 a distance of approximately 700 feet to a point; thence run north 12° 09' east a distance of approximately 50 feet to the point of beginning. All of the aforesaid being a portion of lot 1 in the Basil Chastang claim as recorded in the office of the judge of probate of Mobile county, Alabama, in Deed Book 128 N.S., Page 3, and all of fractional southwest quarter of section 18, township 3 south, range 1 west. The aforesaid parcels of land contain 150 acres, more or less. (Acts 1985, 2nd Ex. Sess., No. 85-950, p. 292, § 4.)

§ 41-10-234. Agreements with city of Prichard as to development, administration, etc., of park.

The governor is authorized to enter into agreements with the city of Prichard for supervision and maintenance of the park and for construction on a portion of the land as authorized, certain administrative facilities including the institute of ethnic science and technology, a visitor's center, museum, theatre, library and other facilities including a zoo for the interpretation of the historical-cultural features of the park and area and the cultural technology employed.

Such park shall be developed, administered and maintained by the city of Prichard through agreement with the state of Alabama and by standards of interpretation and scientific management for state parks. Nothing in this section precludes the city of Prichard from entering into contracts with private sector and public sector agencies to carry out the provisions of this section. The mayor of the city of Prichard is hereby authorized to implement the terms and conditions of this section. (Acts 1985, 2nd Ex. Sess., No. 85-950, p. 292, § 5.)

§ 41-10-235. Commemorative markers and plaques.

The state of Alabama, in recognition of the Africatown, U.S.A. settlement, to American history and culture, hereby authorizes and empowers the city of Prichard to enter into negotiations for the acquisition of, and to acquire, by conveyance, gift or bequest, rights to place commemorative markers and plaques to commemorate historical and cultural sites and landscapes, including natural wetlands, which bear significance to the cultural history of Africatown, U.S.A. as associated with the historical events relating to the Clotilde as recognized by the Alabama historical commission in Montgomery. (Acts 1985, 2nd Ex. Sess., No. 85-950, p. 292, § 6.)

§ 41-10-236. State advisory committee to Africatown, U.S.A. state park.

There is hereby established a state advisory committee to the Africatown, U.S.A. state park which shall include the director of the state historical commission, the director of the department of conservation and natural resources, the director of the state department of tourism and travel, the mayor of the city of Prichard, Alabama, a member selected by the black heritage council, the state representative and state senator representing the legislative districts in which the Africatown, U.S.A. state park is located, and the senators and representatives representing the legislative districts in which the commemorative sites are located, a member of the Africatown, U.S.A. historic preservation authority, and five other persons to be appointed by the governor, at least one of whom shall be a descendent of the Africans brought over on the Clotilde and at least one of whom shall be a representative of the corporate community of Mobile county to be selected by the Mobile area chamber of commerce and three persons appointed from the state of

Alabama at large who shall have a demonstrated concern for protecting the historical and cultural resources of this state.

The duties of the advisory committee shall include coordination with the state historical commission, the state department of conservation and natural resources and the city of Prichard to assure the most advantageous development and interpretation of Alabama's cultural resources and the most efficient management of the park. (Acts 1985, 2nd Ex. Sess., No. 85-950, p. 292, § 7.)

§ 41-10-237. Functions of institute of ethnic science and technology as to black heritage resources and programs.

The institute of ethnic science and technology shall serve as a state resource for reviews, research and informational update on planning, design and management of the park as an African-American state heritage resource and for support to the state department of tourism and information in the development of a black heritage program. Such institute shall also work with state universities for teaching, research and public service programs on Alabama black settlements and heritage resources. (Acts 1985, 2nd Ex. Sess., No. 85-950, p. 292, § 8.)

§ 41-10-238. Establishment of Africatown, U.S.A. historic preservation authority; duties.

In accordance with "The Historical Preservation Authorities Act of 1979," excluding any sections relating to the national register of historic places as a qualifying element to establish a public corporation and exempting any corporation formed under the authority of said act from any listing on the national register of historic places, a public corporation may be formed under the provisions of this section and said act for purposes of establishing the Africatown, U.S.A. historic preservation authority. It shall be the duty of the authority to study, consider, accumulate, compile, assemble and disseminate information on any aspect of Africatown, U.S.A. state park; to confer with appropriate officials of local, state and federal governments and agencies on matters related to any national and international recognition for Africatown, U.S.A. state park; to cooperate with and secure assistance of local, state, federal and international governments or any agencies thereof in formulating related programs; and, to coordinate such programs with any program relating to Africatown, U.S.A. state park that is adopted or planned by the federal government to the end that the authority may secure the full benefit of such program; provided, however, that such authority is hereby authorized to directly seek and receive from the federal government any grants, funds or other benefits which may be available for the Africatown, U.S.A. state park. (Acts 1985, 2nd Ex. Sess., No. 85-950, p. 292, § 9.)

Cross references. — As to the Historical Preservation Authorities Act of 1979, see § 41-10-135, et seq.

§ 41-10-239. Property rights not to be affected by article; sections imposing licensing requirements, taxes, etc., are void if such requirements not otherwise imposed.

It is the intent of this article that it shall not restrict or impair the real, personal or mixed property in which any individual person, industry, business, utility, industrial development board or similar board or authority, public or private corporation or the Alabama state docks department has any legal, equitable, absolute or conditional right, title or interest, whether by fee simple, leasehold, easement, possession, contract, license, permit or any other form of ownership or other rights thereto whatsoever or any existing or future rights of way required by the state of Alabama highway department for the construction of Interstate Route I-210 and the construction of the new Cochrane bridge and its roadway approaches and any future connections to or between these two highway facilities. In the event that any individual person, industry, business, utility, industrial development board or similar board or authority, public or private corporation or the Alabama state docks department or the state of Alabama highway department shall at any time be required to obtain any license, permit or other certificate, or be made subject to any tax, assessment, fine, penalty, law, rule, regulation, ruling, ordinance or order of any city, county, state, federal or other governmental, quasi-governmental or public entity or any agency of any of them, to which such individual person, industry, business, utility, industrial development board or similar board or authority, public or private corporation or the Alabama state docks department or the state of Alabama highway department would not have been subject in the absence of this article, then, notwithstanding any severability provision herein to the contrary, any section or sections of this article causing that effect shall immediately become null and void without any further legislative or judicial action. (Acts 1985, 2nd Ex. Sess., No. 85-950, p. 292, § 10.)

§ 41-10-240. Injunction to protect property interests under § 41-10-239.

Any person who has any interest in real, personal, or mixed property as described in section 41-10-239 herein may enjoin the violation of, or enforce compliance with, this article or any program adopted hereunder. (Acts 1985, 2nd Ex. Sess., No. 85-950, p. 292, § 11.)

ARTICLE 9.

ALABAMA JUDICIAL BUILDING AUTHORITY.

§ 41-10-260. Definitions.

The following terms, wherever used in this article, shall have the following respective meanings unless the context clearly indicates otherwise:

(1) AUTHORITY. The public corporation organized pursuant to the provisions of this article.

(2) BOARD OF DIRECTORS. The board of directors of the authority.

(3) BONDS. When used with reference to debt instruments issued by the authority, means bonds, notes and other forms of indebtedness.

(4) BUILDING COMMISSION. The building commission created by Act No. 128 adopted at the 1945 Regular Session of the legislature of the state, and any successor agency thereto.

(5) CHIEF JUSTICE. The chief justice of the supreme court of the state of Alabama.

(6) GOVERNMENT SECURITIES. Any bonds or other obligations which as to principal and interest constitute direct obligations of, or are unconditionally guaranteed by, the United States of America, including obligations of any federal agency to the extent such obligations are unconditionally guaranteed by the United States of America and any certificates or any other evidences of an ownership interest in such obligations of, or unconditionally guaranteed by, the United States of America or in specified portions thereof (which may consist of the principal thereof or the interest thereon).

(7) JUDICIAL FACILITIES. One or more buildings, and the site or sites therefor, to be constructed and acquired in the city of Montgomery, Alabama and designed primarily for the use by tne unified judicial system, including the supreme court of the state of Alabama, the court of criminal appeals, the court of civil appeals, the state law library and the administrative office of courts, and any equipment and other facilities necessary or useful in connection with such building(s), including courtrooms, conference rooms, library facilities, educational facilities, furnishings, offices, file rooms, parking facilities and the like.

(8) PERMITTED INVESTMENTS.

a. Government securities;

b. Bonds, debentures, notes or other evidences of indebtedness issued by any of the following agencies, to the extent that such obligations are secured by the full faith and credit of the United States of America: bank for cooperatives; federal intermediate credit banks; federal financing bank; federal home loan banks; federal farm credit bank; export-import bank of the United States; federal land banks; or farmers home administration, or any other agency or corporation which has been or may hereafter be created by or pursuant to an act of the congress of the United States as an agency or instrumentality thereof, the bonds, debentures, participation certificates or notes of which are unconditionally guaranteed by the United States of America;

c. Bonds, notes, pass through securities or other evidences of indebtedness of the Government National Mortgage Association and participation certificates of the Federal Home Loan Mortgage Corporation;

d. Full faith and credit obligations of any state, provided that at the time of purchase such obligations are rated at least "AA" by Standard & Poor's Corporation and at least "Aa" by Moody's Investors Service;

e. Public housing bonds issued by public agencies or municipalities and fully secured as to the payment of both principal and interest by contracts with the United States of America, or temporary notes, preliminary notes or project notes issued by public agencies or municipalities, in each case fully secured as to the payment of both principal and interest by a requisition or payment agreement with the United States of America;

f. Time deposits evidenced by certificates of deposit issued by banks or savings and loan associations which are members of the federal deposit insurance corporation or the federal savings and loan insurance corporation, provided that, to the extent such time deposits exceed available federal deposit insurance, such time deposits are fully secured by obligations described in paragraphs a., b., c. and e. above, which at all times have a market value (exclusive of accrued interest) at least equal to such bank time deposits so secured, including interest, and which meet the greater of 100 percent collateralization or the "AA" collateral levels established by Standard & Poor's Corporation for structured financings;

g. Repurchase agreements for obligations of the type specified in paragraphs a, b, c and e above, provided such repurchase agreements are fully collateralized and secured by such obligations which have a market value (exclusive of accrued interest) at least equal to the purchase price of such repurchase agreements and which are held by a depository satisfactory to the state treasurer in such manner as may be required to provide a perfected security interest in such obligations, and which meet the greater of 100 percent collateralization or the "AA" collateral levels established by Standard & Poor's Corporation for structured financings; and

h. Uncollateralized investment agreements with, or certificates of deposit issued by, banks or bank holding companies, the senior long-term securities of which are rated at least "AA" by Standard & Poor's Corporation and at least "Aa" by Moody's Investors Service.

(9) STATE. The state of Alabama.

(10) UNIFIED JUDICIAL SYSTEM. The unified judicial system of the state as constituted at the time of the adoption of this article or at any time subsequent thereto.

(11) Pronouns when used in this article shall include all applicable genders. (Acts 1986, No. 86-420, p. 627, § 1.)

§ 41-10-261. Legislative intent; liberal construction.

It is the intent of the legislature by the passage of this article to authorize the incorporation by the governor, the director of finance and the chief justice of a public corporation for the purpose of acquiring, constructing, installing, equipping, operating and maintaining judicial facilities, and to vest such corporation with all powers, authority, rights, privileges, and titles that may be necessary to enable it to accomplish such purpose. This article shall be liberally construed in conformity with the purpose expressed. (Acts 1986, No. 86-420, p. 627, § 2.)

§ 41-10-262. Authority to incorporate.

The governor, the director of finance, the lieutenant governor, the speaker of the house, and the chief justice may become a public corporation with the powers and authorities hereinafter provided, by proceeding according to the provisions of this article. (Acts 1986, No. 86-420, p. 627, § 3.)

§ 41-10-263. Procedure for incorporation.

To become a corporation, the governor, the director of finance, the lieutenant governor, the speaker of the house, and the chief justice shall present to the secretary of state an application signed by each of them which shall set forth:

(1) The name, official designation, and official residence of each of the applicants, together with a certified copy of the document evidencing each applicant's right to office;

(2) The date on which each applicant was inducted into office and the term of office of each of the applicants;

(3) The name of the proposed corporation, which shall be "Alabama judicial building authority";

(4) The location of the principal office of the proposed corporation, which shall be Montgomery, Alabama; and

(5) Any other matter relating to the incorporation which the applicants may choose to insert and which is not inconsistent with this article or the laws of the state. The application shall be subscribed and sworn to by each of the applicants before an officer authorized by the laws of the state to take acknowledgments to deeds.

The secretary of state shall examine the application and, if he finds that it substantially complies with the requirements of this section and that the name proposed in the application is not identical with that of a person or other corporation in the state or so nearly similar thereto as to lead to confusion and uncertainty, he shall receive and file it and record it in an appropriate book of records in his office. (Acts 1986, No. 86-420, p. 627, § 4.)

§ 41-10-264. Certificate of incorporation; no fees for incorporation or dissolution.

When the application has been made, filed, and recorded as provided in section 41-10-263, the secretary of state shall make and issue to the applicants a certificate of incorporation pursuant to this article, under the great seal of the state, and shall record the certificate with the application, whereupon the applicants shall constitute a public corporation of the state under the name proposed in the application. There shall be no fees paid to the secretary of state for any work done in connection with the incorporation or dissolution of the authority. (Acts 1986, No. 86-420, p. 627, § 5.)

§ 41-10-265. Members, directors and officers of authority; quorum; vacancies; no additional salary for service to authority; effect of resolutions; record of proceedings; establishment of legislative oversight committee.

The applicants named in the application and their respective successors in office shall constitute the members of the authority. The governor shall be the chairman of the authority, the chief justice shall be the vice chairman of the authority and the director of finance shall be the secretary of the authority. The state treasurer shall be the treasurer of the authority but shall not be a member of the authority. The authority, at its option, may appoint an assistant secretary who shall not be a member of the authority. The members of the authority shall constitute all the members of the board of directors of the authority, which shall be the governing body of the authority. The presence of any three members of the said board of directors shall constitute a quorum for the transaction of business. No vacancy in the membership of the board of directors or the voluntary disqualification or abstention of any member thereof shall impair the right of a quorum of the board of directors to act. Should any person holding any state office named in this section cease to hold such office by reason of death, resignation, expiration of his term of office, or for any other reason, then his successor in office shall take his place as a member, officer, or director, as the case may be, of the authority. No member, officer, or director of the authority shall draw any salary in addition to that now authorized by law for any service he may render or for any duty he may perform in connection with the authority. All resolutions adopted by the board of directors shall constitute actions of the authority, and all proceedings of the board of directors shall be reduced to writing by the secretary or assistant secretary of the authority and shall be recorded in a substantially bound book and filed in the office of the director of finance. Copies of such proceedings, when certified by the secretary of the authority under the seal of the authority, shall be received in all courts as prima facie evidence of the matters and things therein certified.

There shall be established a legislative oversight committee to provide consultation and advice to the board of directors concerning the efficient operation of the authority. The oversight committee shall consist of three members of the house of representatives appointed by the speaker of the house, at least one of which shall be a member of the ways and means committee and one of which shall be a member of the house judiciary committee, and three members of the senate appointed by the lieutenant governor, at least one of which shall be a member of the committee on finance and taxation and one of which shall be a member of the senate judiciary committee. After their initial appointment, the members of the oversight committee shall be named at each organizational session of the legislature, and all members shall serve until their successors are properly qualified. All members of the oversight committee shall be entitled to their actual expenses incurred in the performance of their duties as members of the committee. (Acts 1986, No. 86-420, p. 627, § 6.)

§ 41-10-266. Meetings of board of directors.

The board of directors of the authority shall meet at such times upon such notice as it shall determine. (Acts 1986, No. 86-420, p. 627, § 7.)

§ 41-10-267. Powers of authority.

The authority shall have the following powers among others specified in this article:

(1) To have succession by its corporate name until dissolved as provided in this article;

(2) To sue and be sued and to prosecute and defend, at law or in equity, in any court having jurisdiction of the subject matter and of the parties thereto;

(3) To have and to use a corporate seal and to alter the same at pleasure;

(4) To make and alter all needful bylaws, rules and regulations for the transaction of the authority's business and the control of its property and affairs;

(5) To provide for the acquisition, construction, installation, equipping, operation and maintenance of judicial facilities;

(6) To receive, take and hold by sale, gift, lease, devise or otherwise, real and personal property of every description, and to manage the same;

(7) To acquire by purchase, gift, or the exercise of the power of eminent domain, or any other lawful means, and to transfer, convey or cause to be conveyed to the state, any real, personal or mixed property;

(8) To exercise the right of eminent domain as freely and completely as, and in the same manner as, the state is empowered to exercise such right;

(9) To borrow money and issue its bonds in evidence thereof subject to the provisions of this article;

(10) As security for payment of the principal of and the interest on its bonds, to pledge any funds or revenues from which its bonds may be made payable and to arrange for and provide such additional security for its bonds, including letters of credit, bond insurance policies, surety bonds and

the like, as the board of directors shall determine to be necessary or desirable;

(11) To make and enter into such contracts, leases, agreements and other actions as may be necessary or desirable to accomplish any corporate purpose and to exercise any power necessary for the accomplishment of the purposes of the authority or incidental to the powers expressly set out herein; and

(12) To appoint and employ such attorneys, accountants, financial advisors, underwriters, trustees, depositories, registrars, fiscal agents and other advisors, agents and independent contractors as may, in the judgment of the board of directors, be necessary or desirable. (Acts 1986, No. 86-420, p. 627, § 8.)

§ 41-10-268. Authorization, issuance and sale of bonds.

The authority is hereby authorized from time to time to sell and issue its interest-bearing or noninterest-bearing bonds, in one or more series, not to exceed an aggregate principal amount of $40,000,000.00, excluding refunding bonds described in section 41-10-277, for the purpose of providing funds for the acquisition, construction, installation and equipping of judicial facilities, and for payment of obligations incurred for any of said purposes.

Bonds of the authority may be in such form and denominations, may be of such tenor, may be payable in such installments and at such time or times not exceeding 30 years from their date, may be payable at such place or places, may be redeemable at such times and under such conditions, may bear interest at such rate or rates payable and evidenced in such manner or may be structured to bear no interest or to reflect compound interest and may be secured in such manner, all as shall not be inconsistent with the provisions of this article and as may be provided in the proceedings of the board of directors whereunder said bonds shall be authorized to be issued. Bonds of the authority may be sold at such price or prices and at such time or times as the board of directors may consider advantageous, either at public or private sale and by negotiation or by competitve bid. Bonds of the authority sold by competitive bid must be sold, whether on sealed bids or at public auction to the bidder whose bid reflects the lowest net interest cost to the authority for the bonds being sold, computed from their date to their respective maturities; provided, that if no bid acceptable to the authority is received, it may reject all bids. The authority may fix the terms and conditions under which each sale of bonds may be held; provided, that such terms and conditions shall not conflict with any of the requirements of this article. The authority may allow or pay, from the proceeds of sale of its bonds, all expenses, fees, premiums, discounts, insurance premiums and commissions as the board of directors may deem necessary or advantageous in connection with the authorization, sale and issuance of its bonds. Neither a public hearing nor consent of the state department of finance of any other department or agency of the state shall be a prerequisite to the issuance of bonds by the authority. All bonds issued by the authority shall contain a recital that they are issued pursuant to the provisions of this article, which recital shall be conclusive evidence that the said bonds have been duly authorized pursuant to the provisions of this article. (Acts 1986, No. 86-420, p. 627, § 9.)

§ 41-10-269. Execution of bonds.

All bonds of the authority shall be signed by its chairman or vice chairman, and the seal of the authority shall be affixed thereto and attested by its secretary or assistant secretary. The signatures of the chairman, vice chairman, secretary and assistant secretary may be facsimile signatures and a facsimile of the seal of the authority may be imprinted on the bonds if the board of directors, in its proceedings with respect to issuance of such bonds, provides for manual authentication of such bonds by a trustee or paying agent or by named individuals who are employees of the state and who are assigned to the department of finance or office of the state treasurer. Delivery of bonds so executed shall be valid notwithstanding any changes in officers or in the seal of the authority after the signing and sealing of such bonds. (Acts 1986, No. 86-420, p. 627, § 10.)

§ 41-10-270. Use of proceeds from sale of bonds.

All proceeds derived from the sale of any bonds (except refunding bonds) by the authority remaining after payment of the expenses of issuance thereof shall be turned over to the state treasurer, shall be carried in a special account of the state treasury to the credit of the authority, and shall be subject to be drawn on by the authority solely for the purposes of funding any required reserve fund, acquiring, constructing, installing and equipping judicial facilities and paying all reasonable and necessary expenses incidental thereto, including interest which shall accrue on said bonds during the construction of said judicial facilities. Any balance of said proceeds thereafter remaining shall, upon completion of said judicial facilities and the payment of all costs in connection therewith, be used for the redemption of bonds of the authority at the earliest permissible date. (Acts 1986, No. 86-420, p. 627, § 11.)

§ 41-10-271. Acquisition, construction, etc., of judicial facilities; award of contract; payments under contract; building commission expenses; revision of plans.

The authority shall proceed with the acquisition, construction, installation and equipping of the judicial facilities as soon as may be practicable following the sale of the authority's bonds. Such acquisition, construction, installation and equipping shall be done by the authority under the supervision of the building commission upon the award of a contract or contracts for each part of the work to the lowest responsible bidder after advertisement for and public opening of sealed bids; provided, that for the purpose of determining the lowest responsible bidder, the invitation for bids and the bidding documents shall be so arranged that alternates from the base bid shall constitute cumulative deductions from the base bid in the event such alternates should be selected. All such contracts shall be lump sum contracts and shall be awarded and executed by the authority to the respective lowest responsible bidders following determination by the building commission of the lowest responsible bidder. Payments made under any such contracts shall be only upon the contractor's written, verified statements when approved by the building commission or its agent, in such amounts as the building commission may approve as having been then earned under such contracts. The building commission shall be reimbursed for all reasonable direct costs incurred by it in connection with such acquisition, construction, installation and equipping, including expenses and fees for the preparation of plans, specifications and contract documents and supervision and inspection of the work. Such plans and specifications may be revised and extras may be added to the contracts only when approved by the building commission and only to the extent that funds are available therefor. (Acts 1986, No. 86-420, p. 627, § 12.)

§ 41-10-272. Creation of fund for payment of bonds.

For the purpose of providing funds for the payment of the principal of, premium, if any, and interest on the bonds issued by the authority under the provisions of this article, there is hereby created and irrevocably pledged to the payment of such obligations a special and continuing fund which shall consist of all receipts and income from rents contracted for and received by the authority under leases of the judicial facilities constructed with the proceeds from the sale of bonds. Moneys on deposit in said fund shall not be diverted or used for any other purpose if needed for the payment of the principal of, premium, if any, or interest on the bonds of the authority. (Acts 1986, No. 86-420, p. 627, § 13.)

§ 41-10-273. Security for bonds; collection and application of revenues pledged to payment of bonds; terms of leases of judicial facilities; maintenance and insurance of judicial facilities; reserve and other funds; rights of holders of bonds upon default.

Any resolution of the board of directors authorizing the issuance of bonds may contain any provision or agreement customarily contained in instruments securing evidences of indebtedness, including, without limiting the generality of the foregoing, a pledge, transfer or assignment of any leases of any judicial facilities out of the revenues from which such bonds are payable and a pledge of such revenues. Any such resolution may also contain provisions respecting the collection and application of any revenues pledged to the payment of the authority's bonds, the terms to be incorporated in lease agreements respecting judicial facilities out of the revenues from which such bonds are payable, the maintenance of and insurance on such judicial facilities, the creation and maintenance of reserve and other special funds from such revenues or from the proceeds of the authority's bonds, and the rights and remedies available in the event of default to the holders of the bonds, all as the authority may deem advisable and as shall not be in conflict with the provisions of this article. If there be any default by the authority in the payment of the principal of or interest on the bonds or in any of the agreements on the part of the authority which may properly be included in any resolution in which any of the bonds are authorized to be issued, any holder of any of the bonds may either at law or in equity, by suit, action, mandamus or other proceeding, enforce payment and compel performance of all duties of the board of directors and officers of the authority, and shall be entitled, as a matter of right and regardless of the sufficiency of any such security or the availability of any other remedy, to the appointment of a receiver in equity with all the power of such receiver for the maintenance, insurance, and leasing of the judicial facilities covered by such resolution and the collection and application of such revenues; provided, however, that no such resolution shall grant any lien subject to foreclosure, nor shall such resolution be construed so as to compel the sale of any of the judicial facilities of the authority in satisfaction of the bonds secured thereby. Any such resolution may contain provisions regarding the rights and remedies of the holders of the bonds and may contain provisions restricting the individual rights of action of the holders of the bonds. (Acts 1986, No. 86-420, p. 627, § 14.)

§ 41-10-274. State treasurer to disburse funds for payment of bonds.

From the fund to be pledged pursuant to section 41-10-272 hereof, the state treasurer is authorized and directed to pay the principal of, premium, if any, and interest on the bonds as such principal and interest shall respectively mature, and is further authorized and directed to set up and maintain appropriate records pertaining thereto. (Acts 1986, No. 86-420, p. 627, § 15.)

§ 41-10-275. Terms and conditions of leasing by authority.

The authority, as lessor, and the unified judicial system, as lessee (acting by and through the chief justice or his designee) are hereby authorized to enter into a lease or leases for the use and occupancy of the judicial facilities constructed by the authority under the provisions of this article by the unified judicial system, including the supreme court, the court of criminal appeals, the court of civil appeals, the state law library and the administrative office of courts. Such lease or leases may commence, at the discretion of the authority and the lessee, at such time as the judicial facilities are completed and available for occupancy or at such time as the site for such judicial facilities is made available for construction of the judicial facilities. The responsibilities for control, management and maintenance of the judicial facilities shall be, and any lease entered by the authority, as lessor, shall provide that the control, management and maintenance of such facilities are, vested in the lessee.

Should any space become vacant in the judicial facilities constructed by the authority, the authority may enter into a lease or leases with any public entity. If any space remains vacant after an attempt to lease to public entities, the authority may enter into a lease with private entities but only in order to prevent default in the bonds of the authority. Any such lease with a private entity shall not be for the purpose of competing with private enterprise or for lending public credit but shall be solely for the use and benefit of the holders of the authority's bonds to avoid default thereon and to insure the prompt payment of the principal thereof and interest thereon when due. No free space shall be available in the said judicial facilities so long as the principal of or interest on any bonds, including refunding bonds, issued by the authority remains unpaid. The authority may also enter into leases with respect to concession space such as space for a cafeteria, lunch room, or vending machines, if it shall determine that such concession will not interfere with, but will better serve, the occupants of the said judicial facilities and that the use of a portion of the judicial facilities by concessionaires will not adversely affect the holders of the authority's bonds.

Leases by the authority of the judicial facilities financed from the proceeds of the authority's bonds shall provide for rental payments sufficient to pay debt service on the bonds of the authority due and payable during the term of such leases. Rental payments shall be due in advance on the first day of the fiscal year and shall, upon being so paid, entitle the lessee to quiet possession and maintenance, repairs, utilities and other customary office building services, as agreed upon in the lease for the remainder of said fiscal year. The rental payment for the first year or part of a year shall be due and payable when the authority notifies the lessee that the space is tenantable, and the rent for the remainder of the then current fiscal year shall be prorated in the same proportion as the number of days then remaining in the then current fiscal year bears to the total number of days in such fiscal year. Notwithstanding the foregoing, leases of the judicial facilities may provide for monthly rental payments so long as the obligation of the lessee to make such rental payments during the term of the lease is absolute and unconditional.

Leases by the authority may contain and grant to the lessee successive options of renewing the said lease on the terms specified therein for any subsequent fiscal year, provided that no lease to the state or any agency or department thereof, nor liability for the payment of rent, shall ever be for a term longer than one fiscal year. So long as the state or any department or agency thereof is the lessee of the judicial facilities, the obligation to pay rent and each covenant on the part of the state or such department or agency, shall be paid and performed solely out of the current revenues of the state for the fiscal year for which the lease is effective. Any such lease may contain appropriate provisions as to the method by which the lessee may, at its election, exercise any of the said options of renewal.

In the event that the judicial facilities of the authority or any portion thereof should become vacant or not be used by the unified judicial system, including the supreme court, the court of criminal appeals, the court of civil appeals, the state law library and the administrative office of courts, then such entities shall not rent, purchase, acquire, construct or lease any office, courtroom, library or similar facility so long as the judicial facilities of the authority or any portion thereof shall remain vacant or unused and so long as any of the bonds of the authority shall remain outstanding and unpaid. (Acts 1986, No. 86-420, p. 627, § 16.)

§ 41-10-276. Investment of proceeds from sale of bonds; disposition of investment income.

Any portion of the principal proceeds derived from the sale of the bonds which the board of directors may determine is not then needed for any of the purposes for which the bonds are authorized to be issued shall, on order of the authority, be invested by the state treasurer in permitted investments which mature at such time or times as the authority shall direct. Any such investments may, at any time and from time to time on order of the authority, be sold or otherwise converted by the state treasurer into cash. The income derived from any such investments shall be disbursed on order of the authority for any purpose for which it may lawfully expend funds. (Acts 1986, No. 86-420, p. 627, § 17.)

§ 41-10-277. Refunding bonds.

Any bonds issued by the authority may from time to time thereafter be refunded by the issuance of refunding bonds of the authority. Any such refunding bonds may be issued regardless of whether the bonds to be refunded shall have then matured or shall thereafter mature, and such refunding may be effected either by sale of the refunding bonds and the application of the proceeds thereof to the payment or redemption of the bonds so refunded or by exchange of the refunding bonds for those to be refunded thereby; provided, that the holders of any bonds so to be refunded shall not be compelled without their consent to surrender their bonds for payment or exchange prior to the date on which they are payable or, if they are called for redemption, prior to the date on which they may be redeemed by the authority according to their terms. Any refunding bonds of the authority shall be payable solely from and secured by the revenues out of which the bonds to be refunded thereby were payable. The proceeds derived from any sale of refunding bonds remaining after paying the expenses of their issuance shall be applied to the purchase, redemption or payment of the principal of, premium, if any, and accrued but unpaid interest on the bonds refunded thereby. Pending the application of said proceeds to the purchase, redemption or payment of such outstanding bonds, the said proceeds may be invested in permitted investments pursuant to an escrow or trust agreement providing for the future application of such proceeds to the purchase, redemption or payment of such outstanding bonds.

Bonds refunded prior to their maturity with the proceeds of refunding bonds shall be defeased if the authority, in its proceedings regarding issuance of the refunding bonds, provides for and establishes a trust or escrow fund comprised of moneys or government securities, or both, sufficient to pay, when due, the entire principal of, premium, if any, and interest on the refunded bonds; provided, that such government securities shall not be subject to redemption prior to their maturities other than at the option of the holder thereof. Upon the establishment of such a trust or escrow fund, the refunded bonds shall no longer be deemed to be outstanding, shall no longer be secured by the funds pledged therefor in section 41-10-272, shall no longer be obligations of the authority and shall be secured solely by and payable from the moneys and government securities deposited in such trust or escrow fund. (Acts 1986, No. 86-420, p. 627, § 18.)

§ 41-10-278. Presumption of validity of bonds and publication of notice thereof; civil action challenging validity.

Any resolution authorizing any bonds hereunder shall contain a recital that they are issued pursuant to the provisions of this article, which recital shall be conclusive evidence that said bonds have been duly authorized pursuant to the provisions of this article, notwithstanding the provisions of any other law now in force or hereafter enacted or amended. Upon the passage of any resolution providing for the issuance of bonds under the provisions of this article, the authority may, in its discretion, cause to be published once in each of two consecutive weeks in a newspaper published and having general circulation in the city of Montgomery a notice in substantially the following form (the blanks being first properly filled in):

Alabama judicial building authority, a public corporation in the state of Alabama, on the _____ day of _____, 19_____, adopted a resolution providing for the issuance of _____ dollars principal amount of bonds of said authority. Any action or proceeding questioning the validity of said resolution or said bonds or the pledge and agreements made in said resolution for the benefit thereof, or the proceedings under which said bonds, pledge and agreements were authorized, must be commenced within twenty days after the first publication of this notice.

Alabama judicial building authority

By _____

Its chairman

Any civil action or proceeding in any court seeking to set aside or invalidate a resolution providing for the issuance of bonds under the provisions of this article or to contest the validity of any such bonds, or the validity of any pledge or agreement made therefor, must be commenced within 20 days after the first publication of said notice. After the expiration of 20 days following such first publication, no right of action or defense founded upon the validity of the resolution or other proceedings, if any, or of the bonds, or of the pledge or agreements, shall be asserted. In the event of such publication the validity of such resolution, proceedings, bonds, pledge or agreements shall not be open to question in any court upon any ground whatever, except in a civil action or proceeding commenced within such period. Any such action and any action to protect or enforce any rights under the provisions of this article shall be brought in the circuit court of Montgomery county. (Acts 1986, No. 86-420, p. 627, § 19.)

§ 41-10-279. Exemption from taxation.

The properties of the authority and the income therefrom, all lease agreements made by the authority, all bonds issued by the authority and the income therefrom and all lien notices, mortgages, assignments and financing statements filed with respect thereto shall be forever exempt from any and all taxation in the state. (Acts 1986, No. 86-420, p. 627, § 20.)

§ 41-10-280. Bonds constitute negotiable instruments; registration of transfers.

All bonds (and income therefrom) issued by the authority shall be construed to be negotiable instruments subject to the registration provisions pertaining to transfers, even though they are payable from a limited source. (Acts 1986, No. 86-420, p. 627, § 21.)

§ 41-10-281. Obligations not debt of state.

All contracts made, obligations incurred and bonds issued by the authority shall be solely and exclusively obligations of the authority and shall not create obligations or debts of the state. (Acts 1986, No. 86-420, p. 627, § 22.)

§ 41-10-282. Bonds are lawful security for state deposits; investment of state, retirement, and other fiduciary funds in bonds of authority.

Any bonds issued by the authority may be used by the holders thereof as security for deposits of any funds belonging to the state or to any instrumentality, agency or political subdivision of the state in any instance where security for such deposits may be required or permitted by law. Any surplus in any state fund and any retirement or trust fund, where the investment thereof is permitted or required by law, may be invested in bonds issued by the authority. Unless otherwise directed by the court having jurisdiction thereof, or the document that is the source of authority, a trustee, executor, administrator, guardian, or one acting in any other fiduciary capacity may, in addition to any other investment powers conferred by law and with the exercise of reasonable business prudence, invest trust funds in the bonds of the authority. (Acts 1986, No. 86-420, p. 627, § 23.)

§ 41-10-283. Earnings of authority.

The authority shall be a nonprofit corporation, and no part of its net earnings remaining after payment of its expenses shall inure to the benefit of any private entity. (Acts 1986, No. 86-420, p. 627, § 24.)

§ 41-10-284. Dissolution of authority.

At any time when the bonds and other obligations of the authority have been paid in full, the authority may be dissolved upon the filing with the secretary of state of a written statement for dissolution, reciting payment in full of all bonds and other obligations of the authority, which statement shall be subscribed by each of the members of the authority and which shall be sworn to by each such member before an officer authorized to take acknowledgments to deeds. Upon the filing of said written statement for dissolution, the authority shall cease and any property owned by it at the time of its dissolution shall pass to the state. The secretary of state shall file and record the written statement for dissolution in an appropriate book of record in his office, and shall make and issue, under the great seal of the state, a certificate that the authority is dissolved, and shall record the said certificate with the written statement for dissolution. (Acts 1986, No. 86-420, p. 627, § 25.)

ARTICLE 10.

ALABAMA SPACE SCIENCE EXHIBIT
FINANCE AUTHORITY.

§ 41-10-300. Definitions.

For the purposes of this article, the following terms shall have the meanings respectively ascribed to them by this section:

(1) AUTHORITY. The public corporation organized pursuant to the provisions of this article.

(2) COMMISSIONER. The Alabama space science exhibit commission established pursuant to and under the provisions of article 15 of chapter 9 this title, and its successors as the state agency established for the purposes set out in said article 15.

(3) CODE. The Code of Alabama, 1975, as amended.

(4) REFUNDING BONDS. Those refunding bonds issued under the provisions of section 41-10-312.

(5) STATE. The state of Alabama.

(6) BONDS. Those bonds, including without limitation refunding bonds, issued under the provisions of this article.

(7) FACILITIES. Includes exhibit facilities, educational facilities and any other facilities or lands necessary or useful in connection with exhibit facilities or educational facilities, including, without limiting the generality of the foregoing, offices, camp counselors' quarters, warehouses, garages,

storage facilities, food services facilities and hotel and motel facilities used in connection with the commission's exhibit facilities or educational facilities.

(8) EXHIBIT FACILITIES. Facilities of the types provided for in the aforesaid article 15, together with the land on which such facilities are located.

(9) EDUCATIONAL FACILITIES. Without limiting the generality of the foregoing, a building or buildings containing classrooms, offices, support facilities and teaching and exhibit facilities related to the exhibits of the commission, dormitories and dining facilities for the accommodation of students located adjacent to or on the site of the commission's exhibits, and the land on which such facilities are located. (Acts 1986, No. 86-546, p. 1093, § 1.)

§ 41-10-301. Purpose of article and construction thereof.

It is the intent of the legislature, by the passage of this article, to authorize the incorporation of a public corporation for the purposes of acquiring land, constructing and equipping facilities, leasing such facilities to the commission (or others, to the extent provided for herein), and providing financing therefor, and to vest such corporation with all powers, authority, rights, privileges and titles that may be necessary to enable it to accomplish such purposes. This article shall be liberally construed in conformity with the purpose herein stated. (Acts 1986, No. 86-546, p. 1093, § 2.)

§ 41-10-302. Incorporation of authority.

Any three individual citizens of the state selected for such purpose by the commission and approved by the governor of the state may become a public corporation with the power and authority provided in this article by proceeding according to the provisions hereof. (Acts 1986, No. 86-546, p. 1093, § 3.)

§ 41-10-303. Certificate of incorporation — Application.

To become a corporation, the three individuals selected pursuant to section 41-10-302 hereof shall present to the secretary of state of Alabama an application signed by them which shall set forth:

(1) The name and residence of each of the applicants, together with a certified copy of all documents evidencing each applicant's selection by the commission and approval by the governor;

(2) The name of the proposed corporation, which shall be the "Alabama space science exhibit finance authority";

(3) The location of the principal office of the proposed corporation; and

(4) Any other matter relating to the incorporation of the proposed corporation which the applicants may choose to insert and which is not inconsistent with this article.

The application shall be subscribed and sworn to by each of the applicants before an officer authorized by the laws of this state to take acknowledgements to deeds. The secretary of state shall examine the application, and if he finds that it substantially complies with the requirements of this section, he shall receive and file it and record it in an appropriate book of records in his office. (Acts 1986, No. 86-546, p. 1093, § 4.)

§ 41-10-304. Same — Issuance.

When the application has been made, filed and recorded as provided in section 41-10-303 hereof, the secretary of state shall make and issue to the applicants a certificate of incorporation pursuant to this article, under the great seal of the state, and shall record the certificate with the application, whereupon the applicants shall constitute a public corporation of the state under the name proposed in the application. (Acts 1986, No. 86-546, p. 1093, § 5.)

§ 41-10-305. Members; officers; directors; quorum; vacancies; salaries and expenses; liability.

The applicants named in the application and their respective successors in office shall constitute the members of the authority. At the time of initial selection by the commission of the individual citizens to incorporate the authority pursuant to section 41-10-302, the commission shall designate one of such persons to serve an initial term of two years, one to serve an initial term of four years, and one to serve an initial term of six years. Each succeeding appointment of a member of the authority thereafter shall be for a term of six years. The members shall be eligible to succeed themselves. The members shall select from among themselves a president of the authority, a secretary of the authority and a treasurer of the authority. The members of the authority shall constitute all the members of the board of directors of the authority, which shall be the governing body of the authority. A majority of the members of the said board of directors shall constitute a quorum for the transaction of business. Upon the expiration of the term of office of any member of the authority or in the event any member of the authority ceases to be a member of the authority, by reason of death, resignation, removal of his residence from the state of Alabama or for any other reason, then the commission shall, with the concurrence of the governor, select a successor in office to take his place as a member of the authority. No member, officer or director of the authority shall draw any salary for any service he may render or for any duty he may perform in connection with the authority, but may be reimbursed by the authority for reasonable expenses incurred in carrying out the business of the authority. No member, officer, director or employee of the authority shall be personally liable for any debt, obligation or liability of the authority. (Acts 1986, No. 86-546, p. 1093, § 6.)

§ 41-10-306. Resolutions and proceedings of board of directors.

All resolutions adopted by the board of directors shall constitute actions of the authority, and all proceedings of the board of directors shall be reduced to writing by the secretary of the authority, shall be signed by the members of the authority and shall be recorded in a substantially bound book and filed in the office of the secretary of state. Copies of such proceedings, when certified by the secretary of the authority under the seal of the authority, shall be received in all courts as prima facie evidence of the matters and things therein certified. (Acts 1986, No. 86-546, p. 1093, § 7.)

§ 41-10-307. Powers of authority.

The authority shall have the following powers among others specified in this article:

(1) To have succession in its corporate name until the principal of and interest on all bonds issued by it shall have been fully paid and until it shall have been dissolved as provided herein;

(2) To maintain actions and have actions maintained against it and to prosecute and defend in any court having jurisdiction of the subject matter and of the parties thereof;

(3) To have and to use a corporate seal and to alter such seal at pleasure;

(4) To establish a fiscal year;

(5) To acquire and hold title to real and personal property and to sell, convey, mortgage or lease the same as provided in this article;

(6) To provide for the construction, reconstruction, alteration and improvement of facilities and for the procurement of sites and equipment for such facilities and for the lease thereof;

(7) To lease facilities to the state, the commission or any other agency or instrumentality of the state designated to perform the activities of the commission;

(8) To anticipate by the issuance of its bonds, subject to the provisions of this article, the receipt of the rent and revenues from such facilities;

(9) As security for the payment of the principal of and interest on its bonds, to enter into any lawful covenant, to grant mortgages upon or security interests in its facilities and to pledge the rents and revenues from such facilities;

(10) To appoint a bank or savings and loan association as a depositary for funds of the authority;

(11) To invest as provided in this article the proceeds from the sale of its bonds pending need therefor; and

(12) To appoint and employ such attorneys, agents and employees as the business of the authority may require, subject to the merit system where applicable. (Acts 1986, No. 86-546, p. 1093, § 8.)

§ 41-10-308. Temporary loans in anticipation of issuance of bonds.

In anticipation of issuance of bonds under this article, the authority may, from time to time, borrow such sums as may be needed for any of the purposes for which bonds are authorized to be issued under this article, and in evidence of the moneys so borrowed may issue its promissory notes. The principal of and the interest on notes so issued may, from time to time, be refunded by refunding notes or by bonds in anticipation of the issuance of which such notes were issued. All such notes, whether initial issues or refunding issues, may bear interest from their dates until their maturities at such rate or rates as may be deemed acceptable by the board of directors, not to exceed 15 percent per annum, shall mature within three years from their date, and the principal thereof, premium, if any, and interest thereon shall be payable solely from the proceeds of the refunding notes issued to refund any such notes outstanding, the proceeds from the sale of bonds in anticipation of the issuance of which any such notes were issued and the sources from which bonds may be made payable pursuant to section 41-10-319, all as may be provided in the resolution of the board of directors under which such notes may be issued. (Acts 1986, No. 86-546, p. 1093, § 9.)

§ 41-10-309. Execution of bonds and notes.

The bonds and notes of the authority shall be executed by the manual or facsimile signature of either its president or its treasurer, as shall be provided in the resolution under which such securities shall be issued, and the seal of the authority or a facsimile thereof shall be affixed to any bonds so issued and attested by the manual or facsimile signature of its secretary; provided, that if bonds are executed entirely by facsimile, such bonds shall be authenticated by the manual signature of the bond trustee, registrar or paying agent. If, after any of the bonds shall be so signed, whether manually or by facsimile, any such officer shall for any reason vacate his said office, the bonds so signed may nevertheless be delivered at any time thereafter as the act and deed of the authority. (Acts 1986, No. 86-546, p. 1093, § 10.)

§ 41-10-310. Authority to issue bonds.

For the purpose of providing funds for the acquisition of sites, for the construction, reconstruction, alteration and improvement of facilities, for the procurement and installation of equipment therefor and for payment of obligations incurred and the principal of and interest on any temporary loans made for any of the said purposes, the authority is hereby authorized, from time to time, to sell and issue its bonds (other than refunding bonds) in such aggregate principal amounts as may be determined by the board of directors of the authority to be necessary for the said purposes. (Acts 1986, No. 86-546, p. 1093, § 11.)

§ 41-10-311. Authority to issue refunding bonds.

The authority may, from time to time, sell and issue its refunding bonds for the purpose of refunding any matured or unmatured bonds of the authority at the time outstanding and paying any premiums necessary to be paid to redeem any such bonds so to be refunded and all expenses incurred in connection therewith. Such refunding bonds shall be subrogated and entitled to all priorities, rights and pledges to which the bonds refunded thereby were entitled. (Acts 1986, No. 86-546, p. 1093, § 12.)

§ 41-10-312. Specifications and priority of bonds.

Any bonds of the authority may be executed and delivered by it at any time and from time to time, shall be in such form and denominations and of such tenor and maturities, shall bear such rate or rates of interest, fixed or floating, payable and evidenced in such manner, may contain provisions for redemption prior to maturity and may contain other provisions not inconsistent with this section, all as may be provided by the resolution of the board of directors whereunder such bonds are authorized to be issued; provided that no bond of the authority shall have a specified maturity date later than 30 years after its date. In the event that the authority shall make more than one pledge of the same revenues, such pledges shall, unless otherwise provided in the resolution or resolutions authorizing the earlier issued bonds, take precedence in the order of the adoption of the resolutions in which the pledges are made; provided, that each pledge for the benefit of refunding bonds shall have the same priority as the pledge for the benefit of the bonds refunded thereby. (Acts 1986, No. 86-546, p. 1093, § 13.)

§ 41-10-313. Price of bonds; competitive bidding; notice of sale; expenses of sale.

Bonds of the authority may be sold at such price or prices and at such time or times as the board of directors of the authority may consider advantageous, at public or private sale. If bonds are to be sold by competitive bid on sealed bids or at public auction, the bonds may be sold only to the bidder whose bid reflects the lowest effective borrowing cost to the authority for the bonds being sold; provided, that if no bid acceptable to the authority is received, it may reject all bids. Notice of each such sale by competitive bids shall be given by publication in either a financial journal or a financial newspaper published in the city of New York, New York, and also by publication in a newspaper published in the state of Alabama, each of which notices must be published at least one time not less than 10 days before the date fixed for such sale. The board of directors may fix the terms and conditions under which such sale by competitive bids may be held; provided that such terms and conditions shall not conflict with any of the requirements of this article. The authority may pay out of the proceeds of the sale of its bonds all expenses, including publication and printing charges, fiscal agents' fees, attorneys' fees and other expenses which said board of directors may deem necessary and advantageous in connection with the authorization, advertisement, sale, execution and issuance of such bonds. Neither a public hearing nor consent of the state shall be a prerequisite to the issuance or sale of bonds by the authority. (Acts 1986, No. 86-546, p. 1093, § 14.)

§ 41-10-314. Investment of trust funds in bonds of authority.

Any trust fund, where the investment thereof is permitted or required by law, may be invested in bonds issued by the authority. Unless otherwise directed by the court having jurisdiction thereof or the document which is the source of authority, a trustee, executor, administrator, guardian or one acting in any other fiduciary capacity may, in addition to any other investment powers conferred by law and with the exercise of reasonable business prudence, invest trust funds in the bonds of the authority. (Acts 1986, No. 86-546, p. 1093, § 15.)

§ 41-10-315. Security for deposit of governmental funds.

Any bonds issued by the authority may be used by the holders thereof as security for deposits of any funds belonging to the state or to any instrumentality, agency or political subdivision of the state in any instance where security for such deposits may be required or permitted by law. (Acts 1986, No. 86-546, p. 1093, § 16.)

§ 41-10-316. Disposition of proceeds of bonds.

(a) All proceeds derived from the sale of any bonds, except refunding bonds, sold by the authority, remaining after payment of the expenses of issuance thereof, shall be held by the authority and used solely for the purposes of:

(1) Acquiring land for and constructing, reconstructing and equipping thereon one or more facilities;

(2) Paying all reasonable and necessary expenses incidental thereto, including filing, recording, surveying, legal and engineering fees and expenses;

(3) Paying the interest which will accrue on the said bonds during the period required for the construction and equipment of the said facilities and for a period not exceeding six months after the completion thereof; and

(4) Paying the principal of and interest on all then outstanding notes theretofore issued by the authority pursuant to the provisions hereof.

The balance of the said proceeds thereafter remaining shall be set aside as additional security for the bonds or shall be used to pay, purchase or redeem bonds as may be provided in the proceedings authorizing their issuance.

(b) All proceeds from the sale of refunding bonds issued by the authority that remain after paying the expenses of their issuance may be used only for the purpose of refunding the principal of and any unpaid and accrued interest on the outstanding bonds of the authority for the refunding of which the refunding bonds are authorized to be issued, together with any premium that may be necessary to be paid in order to redeem or retire such outstanding bonds. (Acts 1986, No. 86-546, p. 1093, § 17.)

§ 41-10-317. Investment of proceeds.

Any portion of the principal proceeds derived from the sale of the bonds which the board of directors of the authority may determine is not then needed for any of the purposes for which the bonds are authorized to be issued shall, on order of the authority, be invested in such manner as the board of directors of the authority shall direct in any securities which are direct and general obligations of the United States of America or the principal of and interest on which are unconditionally and irrevocably guaranteed by the United States of America, or in certificates of deposit insured by an agency of the United States. Any such securities may, at any time and from time to time on order of the authority, be sold or otherwise converted into cash. The income derived from any such investments shall be disbursed on order of the authority for any purpose for which it may lawfully expend funds. (Acts 1986, No. 86-546, p. 1093, § 18.)

§ 41-10-318. Security for bonds.

The principal of, premium, if any, and interest on the bonds of the authority shall be secured by any or all of the following, as the authority may determine:

    (1) The rent and revenues from the lease or use of one or more facilities of the authority;

    (2) The proceeds from any sale of any facilities of the authority;

    (3) Any bond proceeds remaining unexpended upon completion of all facilities to be constructed with such bond proceeds and the payment of the cost thereof;

    (4) Any insurance proceeds which the authority may receive by reason of its ownership of any of the facilities; and

    (5) Any mortgage upon or security interest in one or more facilities of the authority, granted in connection with the issuance of such bonds.

The authority shall have authority to transfer and assign any lease or mortgage of any of its facilities as security for the payment of such principal, premium, if any, and interest. The bonds may be issued under, and secured by, a resolution which may, but need not, provide for an indenture of trust covering one or more facilities of the authority. Such resolution or such indenture of trust may contain any provision or agreement customarily contained in instruments securing evidences of indebtedness, including, without limiting the generality of the foregoing, provisions respecting the collection and application of any receipts pledged to the payment of bonds, the terms to be incorporated in lease agreements respecting the facilities, the maintenance and insurance thereof, the creation and maintenance of reserve and other special funds from such receipts and the rights and remedies available in the event of default to the holders of the bonds or to the trustee for the holders of the bonds or under any indenture of trust, all as the authority may deem advisable and as shall not be in conflict with the provisions of this article; provided, however, that in making such agreements or provisions the authority shall not have the power to obligate itself except with respect to its facilities, and the application of the rents, revenues and other moneys and assets which it is authorized in this article to pledge. (Acts 1986, No. 86-546, p. 1093, § 19.)

§ 41-10-319. Rights of holders of bonds upon default.

If there by any default by the authority in the payment of the principal of or interest on the bonds or in any of the agreements on the part of the authority which may properly be included in any resolution or indenture of trust securing such bonds, any holder of any of the bonds or the trustee for the bondholders under any resolution or indenture of trust, if so authorized therein, may, by an action, mandamus or other proceedings, enforce payment of such items and foreclosure upon any mortgage or security interest granted as security for such bonds and compel performance of all duties of the directors and officers of the authority and shall be entitled, as a matter of right and regardless of the sufficiency of any such security or the availability of any other remedy, to the appointment of a receiver with all the power of such receiver for the maintenance, insurance and leasing of the facilities and property covered by such resolution or such indenture of trust and the collection and application of the receipts therefrom. Any such resolution or indenture of trust may contain provisions regarding the rights and remedies of any trustee thereunder and the holders of the bonds and may contain provisions restricting the individual rights of action of the holders of the bonds. (Acts 1986, No. 86-546, p. 1093, § 20.)

§ 41-10-320. Bonds and coupons deemed negotiable instruments.

All bonds issued by the authority, while not registered, shall be construed to be negotiable instruments even though they are payable from a limited source. All coupons applicable to any bonds issued by the authority, while the applicable bonds are not registered as to both principal and interest, shall likewise be construed to be negotiable instruments although payable from a limited source. (Acts 1986, No. 86-546, p. 1093, § 21.)

§ 41-10-321. Obligations, bonds and notes not debts of state.

All obligations incurred by the authority and all bonds and notes issued by it shall be solely and exclusively an obligation of the authority, payable solely from the sources which may under the provisions of this article be pledged to the payment thereof. No obligation incurred by the authority and no bond or note issued by it shall create an obligation or debt of the state or of the commission. (Acts 1986, No. 86-546, p. 1093, § 22.)

§ 41-10-322. Conveyance of property by commission; right to possession.

The chairman of the commission is authorized upon direction and authorization of the commission to execute and deliver, at any time and from time to time, an appropriate deed or deeds conveying to the authority:

(1) Any facilities belonging to the commission,

(2) Any unimproved real property belonging to the commission which the commission determines to be needed by the authority for the construction of facilities, and

(3) Any improved real property and any personal property associated therewith belonging to the commission which the commission determines to be needed by the authority for the construction, reconstruction or improvement of facilities, for such consideration as the commission shall determine to be appropriate. No concurrence in the conveyance evidenced by any such deed by any state official or any other person or persons shall be necessary or prerequisite to the validity of any such conveyance.

Upon delivery of any such deed to the authority, it thereby shall be invested with all right and title that the commission had in the property conveyed thereby, subject to the right of reverter to the commission of all such property upon the dissolution of the authority provided for in section 41-10-330 hereof. The authority shall be entitled to immediate possession of all such property upon execution of the deed thereto. (Acts 1986, No. 86-546, p. 1093, § 23.)

§ 41-10-323. Plans for construction of facilities.

All facilities constructed by the authority shall be constructed according to plans and specifications of architects or engineers, or both, selected by the commission. Such plans and specifications shall be approved by the authority. (Acts 1986, No. 86-546, p. 1093, § 24.)

§ 41-10-324. Leasing to commission and other agencies.

(a) The authority is hereby authorized to enter into a lease or leases of any one or more facilities constructed, acquired, reconstructed, renovated or improved by the authority under the provisions of this article, to and with the commission or any other agency of the state which may be charged with the responsibility for the operation of the commission's facilities. The commission and any such other agency of the state and each of them are hereby authorized to lease any such facilities from the authority. No such lease shall, however, be for a term longer than the then current fiscal year of the state, but any such lease may contain a grant to the commission or any state agency of successive options of renewing said lease on the terms specified therein for any subsequent fiscal year or years of the state; provided, that liability for the payment of rent shall never be for a term longer than one fiscal year.

(b) Rent payments by the commission, the state, or any of its agencies shall be due and payable not less often than once each fiscal year at such time or times as shall be specified in the lease respecting the facilities leased and shall, upon being so paid, entitle the commission, the state or such agency to quiet possession of the facilities leased for such fiscal year. Said rent for such fiscal year shall be payable, and any such covenent with respect thereto on the part of the commission, the state or any of its agencies (as the case may be) shall be performed, solely out of the current revenues of the commission, the state or such agency for such fiscal year. The rent payable and the covenants to be performed by the commission, the state or any of its agencies under the provisions of said lease shall never be deemed to create a debt of the state within the meaning of the constitution.

(c) In the event that there shall be any default in the payment of any rent required to be paid or in the performance of any covenant required to be performed by the commission, the state or any of its agencies under the provisions of any such lease, while such lease is in effect, the authority and any pledgee of such lease may, by any appropriate proceedings instituted within the time permitted by law, enforce and compel the payment of such rent and the performance of such covenants. No free use shall be made of any facilities of the authority so long as the principal of or interest on any bonds, including refunding bonds, issued by the authority remains unpaid.

(d) In the event that any facility of the authority should become vacant or not be used by the commission or one of the state agencies, then neither the commission, the state nor any agency, board, bureau, commission, public corporation or department of the state shall rent, purchase, acquire, construct or lease any facilities or renew any lease of any facilities, nor shall it use any such facilities other than those of the authority, so long as any facility of the authority shall remain vacant or unused. (Acts 1986, No. 86-546, p. 1093, § 25.)

§ 41-10-325. Lease of vacant facilities to prevent default on bonds.

If at any time any facility constructed or acquired by the authority is, or is about to be, vacant or unused as a result of there being no lease for such facility in effect for the current fiscal year, then, but only in such event, in order to prevent default on its bonds, the authority is hereby authorized to lease such facility to any other agency, department, bureau or commission of the state, any municipal corporation, public corporation, county, or other public body in the state, or any agency of the federal government. Any such lease shall not be for the purpose of lending public credit but shall be solely to avoid default on the authority's bonds and to insure the prompt payment of the principal thereof and interest thereon when due. (Acts 1986, No. 86-546, p. 1093, § 26.)

§ 41-10-326. Special funds for payment of bonds, insurance, and other expenses.

In the resolution or proceedings authorizing the issuance of any bonds or any temporary loan or in any indenture of trust, the authority may provide for the establishment of one or more special funds for the payment of the principal of, or interest on, the bonds or notes, one or more reserve funds therefor and a fund, or funds, for the payment of insurance premiums or other expenses with respect to the ownership and leasing of the facilities. Any such special funds shall be held as trust funds pursuant to agreement with such trustee bank or banks as may be designated by the commission. The authority shall establish and maintain appropriate records pertaining to such funds. Such records shall be available at all reasonable times to public inspection. (Acts 1986, No. 86-546, p. 1093, § 27.)

§ 41-10-327. Exemption from taxation.

The properties of the authority and the income therefrom, all lease agreements made by the authority and all bonds and promissory notes issued by the authority, the interest thereon, the coupons, if any, applicable thereto, the income therefrom and all lien notices with respect thereto, and all purchases and uses of property by the authority shall be forever exempt from any and all taxation in the state or in any county, municipality or political subdivision thereof. (Acts 1986, No. 86-546, p. 1093, § 28.)

§ 41-10-328. Venue for actions.

Any action to protect or enforce any rights under the provisions of this article shall be brought in the circuit court of Madison county, Alabama. (Acts 1986, No. 86-546, p. 1093, § 29.)

§ 41-10-329. No fees for incorporation or dissolution.

There shall be no fees paid to the secretary of state for any work done in connection with the incorporation or dissolution of the authority. (Acts 1986, No. 86-546, p. 1093, § 30.)

§ 41-10-330. Dissolution.

When all bonds and securities issued by the authority and all obligations assumed by it under the provisions of this article shall have been paid in full, the then president of the authority may thereupon execute and deliver in the name of, and in behalf of, the authority an appropriate deed or deeds, to which the seal of the authority shall be affixed and attested by the secretary of the authority, conveying all facilities, properties and other assets then owned by the authority to the commission, or such agency of the state as shall at the time have succeeded to the rights and duties of the commission. The then directors of the authority may at such time file with the secretary of state a written statement, subscribed and sworn to by each of them, reciting the payment in full of all bonds theretofore issued by the authority and the execution and delivery of such deed or deeds, which statement shall be filed by the secretary of state and recorded with the certificate of incorporation of the authority, and thereupon the authority shall stand dissolved. (Acts 1986, No. 86-546, p. 1093, § 31.)

§ 41-10-331. Exemption of leases of facilities from competitive bid laws.

All leases of facilities made by the authority shall be exempt from the provisions and requirements of chapter 16 of this title of the code. (Acts 1986, No. 86-546, p. 1093, § 32.)

§ 41-10-332. Exemption from sunset law.

The authority shall not be governed by the provisions of chapter 20 of this title of the code (originally enacted as Act No. 512 of the 1976 Regular Session of the legislature of Alabama). (Acts 1986, No. 86-546, p. 1093, § 33.)

ARTICLE 11.

ALABAMA MENTAL HEALTH FINANCE
AUTHORITY.

Code commissioner's note. — Section 23 of Acts 1988, No. 88-475 provides that Act No. 277, adopted at the 1967 Regular Session of the Legislature of Alabama, which provided for the Alabama Mental Health Building Authority, is hereby repealed.

Cross references. — As to pledge of certain revenues for payment on bonds issued by the Alabama mental health finance authority under this article, see § 28-3-203.

§ 41-10-350. Legislative findings and purpose.

The legislature hereby finds and declares that it is necessary, desirable and in the public interest that additional facilities be made available in this state for mental health purposes. It is the intention of the legislature by the passage of this article to authorize the formation of a public corporation for the purpose of providing for the acquisition, construction, improvement and equipment of the mental health facilities (including improvements to existing facilities), and to authorize the said corporation, in order to provide for payment of the costs of the said facilities, to anticipate the proceeds of that portion of a special state tax (originally levied by Act No. 275, adopted at the 1967 regular session of the legislature of Alabama), that was levied for mental health purposes by the issuance of the bonds of the said corporation payable solely from the proceeds of the said tax. (Acts 1988, No. 88-475, p. 739, § 1.)

§ 41-10-351. Definitions.

The following terms hereafter used in this article shall have the following respective meanings:

(1) AUTHORITY. The public corporation organized pursuant to the provisions of this article.

(2) BONDS. The bonds issued under the provisions of this article.

(3) COMMISSIONER. The commissioner of mental health and mental retardation.

(4) DEPARTMENT. The department of mental health and mental retardation provided for in chapter 50 of subtitle 2 of Title 22.

(5) DIRECTORS. The board of directors of the authority.

(6) MENTAL HEALTH FACILITIES. Any one or more of the following: hospitals and other facilities of any kind for treatment and care of the mentally ill and mentally retarded; regional or community-based mental health centers; regional or community-based facilities for treatment and care of the mentally ill or the mentally retarded; regional or community-based centers for the treatment of alcoholism or drug addiction; and improvements to existing state hospitals or other facilities for the treatment and care of the mentally ill and the mentally retarded.

(7) COMMUNITY FACILITIES. Facilities operated by regional community mental health boards established pursuant to section 22-51-2, community mental health centers, associations for retarded citizens and community substance abuse programs certified by the Alabama department of mental health and mental retardation that provide services for the treatment and care of individuals with mental or emotional illnesses, mental retardation, alcoholism or drug addiction.

(8) OVERSIGHT COMMITTEE. The mental health capital outlay oversight committee created in section 22-50-25.

(9) PERMITTED INVESTMENTS. United States securities, certificates of deposit fully secured by United States securities and shall include investments in such obligations of the United States of America or its agencies under a repurchase agreement.

(10) UNITED STATES SECURITIES. Direct general obligations of the United States of America (including obligations of the state and local government series) and the obligations of any other agency or corporation which has been or may hereafter be created by or pursuant to an act of the congress of the United States as an agency or instrumentality thereof, the bonds, debentures, participation certificates or notes of which are unconditionally guaranteed by the United States of America.

(11) RETIREMENT SYSTEMS OF ALABAMA. The state employees' retirement system created pursuant to chapter 27 of Title 36, and the teachers' retirement system created pursuant to chapter 25 of Title 16.

The definitions hereinabove set forth shall be deemed applicable whether the words defined are used in the singular or the plural. Any pronoun or pronouns used herein shall be deemed to include both the singular and the plural and to cover all genders. (Acts 1988, No. 88-475, p. 739, § 2; Acts 1988, 1st Ex. Sess., No. 88-862, p. 359, § 1.)

§ 41-10-352. Authority for incorporation of Alabama mental health finance authority; members.

The governor, the commissioner, the director of finance, the chairman of the oversight committee and the vice-chairman of the oversight committee may become a public corporation with the powers hereinafter provided, by proceeding according to the provisions of section 41-10-353 of this article. (Acts 1988, No. 88-475, p. 739, § 3.)

§ 41-10-353. Application for authority to incorporate.

To become a corporation, the governor, the commissioner, the director of finance, the chairman of the oversight committee and the vice-chairman of the oversight committee shall present to the secretary of state of Alabama an application signed by them which shall set forth: (1) the name, official designation, and official residence of each of the applicants; (2) the date on which each applicant was inducted or elected into office and the term of office of each applicant; (3) the name of the proposed corporation, which shall be the Alabama mental health finance authority; (4) the location of the principal office of the proposed corporation; and (5) any other matter relating to the incorporation which the applicants may choose to insert and which is not inconsistent with this article or the laws of the state of Alabama. The application shall be subscribed and sworn to by each of the applicants before an officer authorized by the laws of this state to take acknowledgments to deeds. The secretary of state shall examine the application and, if he finds that it substantially complies with the requirements of this section, he shall receive and file it and record it in an appropriate book of records in his office. (Acts 1988, 88-475, p. 739, § 4.)

§ 41-10-354. Certificate of incorporation; no fee or compensation to secretary of state.

When the application has been made, filed, and recorded as herein provided, the applicants shall constitute a public corporation under the name proposed in the application, and the secretary of state shall make and issue to the applicants a certificate of incorporation under the great seal of the state and shall record the certificate with the application. No fees or compensation shall be paid to the secretary of state for any service rendered or work performed in connection with the authority, its incorporation, dissolution or records. (Acts 1988, No. 88-475, p. 739, § 5.)

§ 41-10-355. Members of authority; officers; payment of bonds of authority; quorum; vacancies; compensation; record of proceedings and use thereof as evidence; meetings.

The applicants named in the application and their respective successors in office shall constitute the members of the authority. The governor shall be the president of the authority, the commissioner shall be the vice-president thereof, and the director of finance shall be the secretary thereof. The state treasurer shall be treasurer of the authority, shall act as custodian of the funds of the authority, and shall pay the principal of and interest on the bonds of the authority out of the funds hereinafter provided for; provided, that the state treasurer may designate one or more banks either within or without the state as the paying agent with respect to any series of bonds issued under this article. The members of the authority shall constitute all the members of the board of directors of the authority, and the presence of any three members of the directors shall constitute a quorum for the transaction of business. Should any person holding any office named in this section cease to hold office by reason of death, resignation, expiration of his term of office, or for any other reason, then his successor in office shall take his place as a member and officer of the authority. No member, officer, or director of the authority shall draw any salary in addition to that now authorized by law for any service he may render or for any duty he may perform in connection with the authority. All proceedings had and done by the directors shall be reduced to writing by the secretary of the authority, shall be signed by each of the directors, and shall then be recorded in a substantially bound book, which shall be kept in the office of the director of finance. Copies of such proceedings, when certified by the secretary of the authority, under the seal of the authority, shall be received in all courts as prima facie evidence of the matters and things therein certified. The board of directors of the authority shall meet at such times and upon such notice as it shall determine. (Acts 1988, No. 88-475, p. 739, § 6.)

§ 41-10-356. Powers of authority.

The authority shall have the following powers among others specified in this article:

(1) To have succession by its corporate name until dissolved as provided in this article;

(2) To sue and be sued and to prosecute and defend, at law or in equity, in any court having jurisdiction of the subject matter and of the parties thereto;

(3) To have and to use a corporate seal and to alter the same at pleasure;

(4) To make and alter all needful bylaws, rules and regulations for the transaction of the authority's business and the control of its property and affairs;

(5) To provide for the acquisition, construction, installation, equipping, operation and maintenance of mental health facilities, including the equipping and improvement of existing mental health facilities;

(6) To receive, take and hold by sale, gift, lease, devise or otherwise, real and personal property of every description, and to manage the same;

(7) To acquire by purchase, gift, or any other lawful means, and to transfer, convey or cause to be conveyed to the state, any real, personal or mixed property;

(8) To borrow money and issue its bonds in evidence thereof subject to the provisions of this article;

(9) To anticipate by the issuance of its bonds the receipt of the revenues herein appropriated and pledged, all in the manner hereinafter provided;

(10) As security for payment of the principal of and the interest on its bonds, to pledge the proceeds of the appropriation and pledge herein provided for and any funds or revenues from which its bonds may be made payable and to arrange for and provide such additional security for its bonds, including letters of credit, bond insurance policies, surety bonds, all as the board of directors shall determine to be necessary or desirable;

(11) To make and enter into such contracts, leases, agreements and other actions as may be necessary or desirable to accomplish any corporate purpose and to exercise any power necessary for the accomplishment of the purposes of the authority or incidental to the powers expressly set out herein;

(12) To appoint and employ such attorneys, accountants, financial advisors, underwriters, trustees, depositories, registrars, fiscal agents and other advisors, agents and independent contractors as may, in the judgment of the directors, be necessary or desirable; provided that in selecting and engaging the services of such attorneys (including, without limitation, bond counsel and counsel to the authority), accountants, financial advisors, underwriters and other advisors, agents or contractors, whether in connection with an issue or series of bonds or any ongoing matters of the authority, the authority shall in every case request proposals from qualified parties offering such services by publishing a request for proposals once a week for two consecutive weeks in newspapers published or having a general circulation in the cities of Birmingham, Montgomery, Huntsville and Mobile, shall fully and fairly review all of such proposals, and shall award such engagement to the proposing party in each case whose proposal is most advantageous to the state; and

(13) To enter into any necessary financial instruments, or obligations, or both, of the retirement systems of Alabama in order to provide financing for projects of the authority; provided further that principal and interest payments on any such instrument or obligation shall be payable solely from such funds as may from time to time be appropriated for the use and support of the department of mental health and mental retardation, including the taxes appropriated and pledged in section 41-10-365; provided further that any short-term securities developed between said authority and the

retirement systems of Alabama for construction purposes shall bear an interest rate equal to other commercial paper purchases of the retirement system and further any intermediate or long-term securities shall bear an interest rate equal to or greater than the actuarial interest rate assumption and not less than 50 basis points above comparable U.S. treasury bonds. Fifty percent of all funds expended for facilities provided for by the Alabama mental health finance authority, under the provisions of this article, inclusive of any and all amendments to such article, shall be designated for community facilities as defined within the article. (Acts 1988, No. 88-475, p. 739, § 7; Acts 1988, 1st Ex. Sess., No. 88-862, p. 359, § 1.)

§ 41-10-357. Authorization to issue bonds; limitation on use of proceeds.

For the purpose of acquiring, constructing, installing and equipping mental health facilities, the authority is hereby authorized to issue and sell from time to time its bonds, which bonds may be in the form of interest-bearing bonds or noninterest-bearing bonds. The aggregate principal amount of bonds issued under this article shall (other than refunding bonds) not exceed $100,000,000.00. Provided, however, that the proceeds from the bonds issued under the provisions of this article shall not be utilized for the construction, installing or equipping of community crisis stabilization units unless there is no available existing hospital beds that can be leased for said purposes within the community where such facility is to be operated. (Acts 1988, No. 88-475, p. 739, § 8.)

§ 41-10-358. Form, terms, denominations, etc., of bonds; limitation on maturity date, redemption.

The bonds, which may be issued in one or more series, shall be in such forms and denominations and of such tenor and maturities, shall, if issued as interest-bearing bonds, bear such rate or rates of interest payable and evidenced in such manner, shall be payable in such installments, at such time or times and at such place or places, and may contain other provisions not inconsistent with this article, all as may be provided in the resolution or resolutions of the directors wherein the bonds are authorized to be issued; provided, that none of the bonds shall have a specified maturity date later than 30 years after its date. The authority may at its election retain in the resolution or resolutions under which any of the bonds are issued an option to redeem all or any thereof and at such redemption price or prices and after such notice or notices and on such dates and on such terms and conditions as may be set forth in said resolution or resolutions and as may be briefly recited in the bonds with respect to which such option of redemption is retained. (Acts 1988, No. 88-475, p. 739, § 9.)

§ 41-10-359. Execution and delivery of bonds; designation of bonds for community facilities.

The bonds shall be signed by the president of the authority and attested by its secretary; provided, that a facsimile of the signatures of both of said officers may be printed or otherwise reproduced on any of the bonds in lieu of their being manually signed if the proceedings under which the bonds are issued provide for the manual authentication of such bonds by officers or employees of the state designated by the authority. The seal of the authority shall be impressed on the bonds; provided, that a facsimile of said seal may be printed or otherwise reproduced on any of the bonds in lieu of being manually impressed thereon. Delivery of bonds so executed shall be valid notwithstanding any changes in officers subsequent to the signing of such bonds.

Fifty percent of the bonds issued under the provisions of this article shall be designated for community mental illness, mental retardation, and substance abuse facilities operated by regional community mental health boards established under section 22-51-2, community mental health centers, associations for retarded citizens, and/or community substance abuse programs, all of which must be certified by the Alabama department of mental health and mental retardation. Such community facilities may include, but shall not be limited to, those community facilities identified in the department of mental health and mental retardation's capital construction plan. (Acts 1988, No. 88-475, p. 739, § 10.)

§ 41-10-360. Sale of bonds at public auction; rejection of bids; notice of sale; terms and conditions of sale; expenses, fees, etc.; recital that bonds issued pursuant to article.

Each series of the bonds shall be sold at such time or times as the directors may determine at public sale pursuant to competitive bidding, either on sealed bids or at public auction, to the bidder whose bid reflects the lowest total net interest cost to the authority for the bonds being sold, computed from the date of those at the time being sold to their respective maturities; provided, that if no bid acceptable to the authority is received it may reject all bids. Notice of the sale of any bonds at public sale shall be given either (1) by publication in either a financial journal or a financial newspaper published in the city of New York, New York, or (2) by publication in a newspaper published in the state which is customarily published not less often than six days during each calendar week, which notice must be published at least one time not less than 10 days prior to the date fixed for the sale. The authority may fix the terms and conditions under which each sale of bonds may be held. The authority may pay out of the proceeds from the sale of the bonds all expenses, fees, premiums, discounts, insurance premiums and commissions and letters of credit or other credit enhancement fees as the directors may deem necessary or advantageous. Neither a public hearing nor consent by the state department of finance or any other department or agency shall be a prerequisite to the issuance of any of the bonds. All bonds issued by the authority shall contain a recital that they are issued pursuant to the provisions of this article, which recital shall be conclusive evidence that the said bonds have been duly authorized pursuant to the provisions of this article. (Acts 1988, No. 88-475, p. 739, § 11.)

§ 41-10-361. Liability upon bonds of authority; authorization of authority to pledge for payment of principal and interest of bonds; bonds deemed negotiable instruments.

The bonds shall not be general obligations of the authority but shall be payable solely out of the funds appropriated and pledged therefor in section 41-10-365 of this article. As security for the payment of the principal of and interest on the bonds issued by it under this article, the authority is hereby authorized and empowered to pledge for payment of the said principal and interest the funds that are appropriated and pledged in section 41-10-365 of this article for payment of the said principal and interest. All such pledges made by the authority shall take precedence in the order of the adoption of the resolutions containing such pledges. All bonds issued by the authority pursuant to the provisions of this article shall be solely and exclusively obligations of the authority and shall not be an obligation or debt of the state. The bonds shall be construed to be negotiable instruments although payable solely from a specified source as herein provided. (Acts 1988, No. 88-475, p. 739, § 12.)

§ 41-10-362. Exemption from taxation of bonds and income of authority; use of bonds as security for deposits of state funds; investment of trust funds in bonds.

The bonds and the income therefrom shall be exempt from all taxation in the state. Any of the bonds may be used by the holder thereof as security for the deposit of any funds belonging to the state or to any instrumentality or agency of the state in any instance where security for such deposits may be required by law. Unless otherwise directed by the court having jurisdiction thereof, or by the document that is the source of authority, a trustee, executor, administrator, guardian, or one acting in any other fiduciary capacity may, in addition to any other investment powers conferred by law and with the exercise of reasonable business prudence, invest trust funds in any of the bonds. (Acts 1988, No. 88-475, p. 739, § 13.)

§ 41-10-363. Refunding bonds; proceeds of sale of refunding bonds.

Any bonds issued by the authority under this article may from time to time thereafter be refunded by the issuance of refunding bonds of the authority. Any such refunding bonds may be issued whether the bonds to be refunded shall have then matured or shall thereafter mature, and such refunding may be effected either by sale of the refunding bonds and the applications of the proceeds thereof to the payment or redemption of the bonds so refunded or by exchange of the refunding bonds for those to be refunded thereby; provided, that the holders of any bonds so to be refunded shall not be compelled without their consent to surrender their bonds for payment or exchange prior to the date on which they are payable or, if they are called for redemption, prior to the date on which they may be redeemed by the authority according to their terms. Any refunding bonds may be issued in such aggregate principal amount as the authority shall deem necessary to effect such refunding. The proceeds derived from any sale of refunding bonds remaining after payment of the expenses of their issuance shall be applied in accordance with the proceedings of the authority under which such refunding bonds are issued. Pending the application of said proceeds to the purchase, redemption or payment of such outstanding bonds, the said proceeds may be invested in permitted investments pursuant to a trust agreement providing for the future application of such proceeds to the purchase, redemption or payment of such outstanding bonds. Bonds refunded prior to their maturity with the proceeds of refunding bonds shall be deemed not outstanding if the authority, in the proceedings under which such refunding bonds are issued, establishes a trust fund comprised of cash or permitted investments, or both, sufficient to pay in accordance with the provisions of such trust fund, when due, the entire principal of, premium, if any, and interest on the refunded bonds; provided, that such government securities shall not be subject to redemption prior to their maturities other than at the option of the holder thereof. Upon the establishment of such a trust fund, the refunded bonds shall no longer be deemed to be outstanding, shall no longer be secured by the funds pledged therefor in section 41-10-365 hereof, shall no longer be obligations of the authority and shall be secured solely by and payable from the moneys and investments deposited in such trust fund. (Acts 1988, No. 88-475, p. 739, § 14.)

§ **41-10-364. Proceeds of bonds, other than refunding bonds; special fund to pay costs of acquisition, construction, etc., of mental health facilities; such work supervised by building commission; such work subject to competitive bidding; disposition of moneys remaining.**

The proceeds of the bonds, other than refunding bonds, remaining after paying the expenses of their sale and issuance shall be turned into the state treasury, shall be carried in a special fund to be designated the mental health facilities building fund, and shall be subject to be drawn on by the authority for the purpose of paying costs of acquisition, construction, improvement and equipping of mental health facilities in the state.

For the purposes of this article, the improvement of a facility shall be deemed to include the renovation, modernization, remodeling, and equipment thereof and the construction of additions thereof, and the construction of a facility shall be deemed to include the acquisition of real estate sites and equipment therefor. For purposes of this article, equipment shall mean any item of personal property having an estimated useful life of at least 10 years.

The preparation of all plans and specifications for any building, or capital improvements to a building, constructed wholly or in part with any of the proceeds from the sale of the bonds and all work done hereunder in constructing buildings and capital improvements thereto shall be supervised by Alabama building commission, or any agency that may be designated by the legislature as its successor. All work done in the construction of buildings and all purchases of equipment shall be made on the basis of competitive bidding in the manner provided by law. Any moneys remaining on deposit in the mental health facilities building fund shall, upon completion of the acquisition and construction of mental health facilities and the payment of all costs in connection therewith, be applied either to redemption of bonds on the earliest date on which they are by their terms subject to redemption or otherwise utilized by the authority in connection with the refunding of bonds. (Acts 1988, No. 88-475, p. 739, § 15.)

§ 41-10-365. Sinking fund for payment of principal and interest on bonds of authority.

For the purpose of providing funds to enable the authority to pay at their respective maturities the principal of and interest on any bonds issued by it under the provisions of this article and to accomplish the objects of this article, there are hereby irrevocably pledged to such purpose and there are hereby appropriated so much as may be necessary for such purpose of (a) the receipts from the tax levied by sections 40-25-2 and 40-25-41 and required to be distributed to the authority in accordance with the provisions of section 40-25-23 and, (b) to the extent that the receipts from said tax shall be insufficient for such purpose, the receipts from the tax levied by Acts 1988, 1st Ex. Sess., No. 88-869, that are required to be distributed to the authority pursuant to the provisions of Acts 1988, 1st Ex. Sess., No. 88-869. All moneys hereby appropriated and pledged shall constitute a sinking fund for the purpose of paying the principal of (premium, if any) and the interest on the bonds herein authorized. (Acts 1988, No. 88-475, p. 739, § 16; Acts 1988, 1st Ex. Sess., No. 88-862, p. 359, § 1.)

§ 41-10-366. Contracts, etc., do not create obligations of state.

All contracts made, obligations incurred and bonds issued by the authority shall be solely and exclusively obligations of the authority and shall not create obligations or debts of the state. (Acts 1988, No. 88-475, p. 739, § 17.)

§ 41-10-367. Investment of surplus proceeds from sale of bonds; disbursement of income derived from such investments.

Any portion of the principal proceeds derived from the sale of the bonds which the board of directors may determine is not then needed for any of the purposes for which the bonds are authorized to be issued shall, on order of the authority, be invested by the state treasurer in permitted investments which mature at such time or times as the authority shall direct. Any such investments may, at any time and from time to time on order of the authority, be sold or otherwise converted by the state treasurer into cash. The income derived from any such investments shall be disbursed on order of the authority for any purpose for which it may lawfully expend funds. (Acts 88, No. 88-475, p. 739, § 18.)

§ 41-10-368. Authority is nonprofit corporation.

The authority shall be a nonprofit corporation, and no part of its net earnings remaining after payment of its expenses shall inure to the benefit of any private entity. (Acts 1988, No. 88-475, p. 739, § 19.)

§ 41-10-369. Dissolution of authority; disposition of property upon dissolution of authority.

At any time when the bonds and other obligations of the authority have been paid in full, the authority may be dissolved upon the filing with the secretary of state of a written statement for dissolution, reciting payment in full of all bonds and other obligations of the authority and which shall be sworn to by each such member before an officer authorized to take acknowledgments to deeds. Upon the filing of said written statement for dissolution, the authority shall cease and any property owned by it at the time of its dissolution shall pass to the state. The secretary of state shall file and record the written statement for dissolution in an appropriate book of record in his office, and shall make and issue, under the great seal of the state, a certificate that the authority is dissolved, and shall record the said certificate with the written statement for dissolution. (Acts 1988, No. 88-475, p. 739, § 20.)

§ 41-10-370. Payment of principal and interest on bonds and maintenance of records pertaining thereto by state treasurer.

Out of the revenues appropriated and pledged in section 41-10-365 of this article, the state treasurer is authorized and directed to pay the principal of and interest on the bonds at the respective maturities of the said principal and interest, and he is further authorized and directed to set up and maintain appropriate records pertaining thereto. In the event that the state treasurer designates any bank as the paying agent with respect to any bonds, the state treasurer shall make available to such bank, not later than one business day prior to the date on which any principal of or interest on such bonds is due and payable, funds sufficient to pay such principal and interest due on such date. (Acts 1988, No. 88-475, p. 739, § 21.)

§ 41-10-371. Power of authority to pay and make agreements with the United States to exempt interest of bonds from federal income tax.

The authority shall have the power to make such payments to the United States as the directors deem necessary to cause the interest on any bonds of the authority to be and remain exempt from federal income taxation. The authority shall have the power to make agreements respecting the investment of funds of the authority necessary in order that the interest income on bonds of the authority be and remain exempt from federal income taxation. (Acts 1988, No. 88-475, p. 739, § 22.)

ARTICLE 12.

ALABAMA SUPERCOMPUTER AUTHORITY.

Effective date. — The act which added this article became effective May 11, 1989.

§ 41-10-390. Short title.

This article shall be known as the Alabama Supercomputer Authority Act. (Acts 1989, No. 89-704, p. 1402, § 1.)

§ 41-10-391. Legislative findings of fact and declaration of intent; construction of article.

The legislature hereby makes the following findings of fact and declares its intent to be: Supercomputer technology is expected to have a significant impact on the research capabilities of research institutions, governmental agencies and private industries. The police power of the state authorizes the state to promote the prosperity and general welfare of its citizens. The development of supercomputer technology will greatly enhance research capabilities of the state's major research institutions and governmental agencies, and will attract industry to the state. For these reasons, it is the intent of the legislature by the passage of this article to exercise its police power to authorize the incorporation by the governor, the director of finance, the director of the Alabama development office, the lieutenant governor and the speaker of the house, of a public corporation for the purpose of planning, acquiring, developing, administering and operating a statewide supercomputer and related telecommunications system, and to vest such corporation with all powers, authorities, rights, privileges and titles that may be necessary to enable it to accomplish such purpose. This article shall be liberally construed in conformity with the purpose expressed.

It shall be the duty of the authority to establish, administer and operate such supercomputer system for the primary purpose of providing state-of-the-art technology in supercomputer processing for scientific research and development to governmental agencies, educational institutions, private-sector businesses and industries. (Acts 1989, No. 89-704, p. 1402, § 2.)

§ 41-10-392. Authorization and procedure for incorporation generally.

The governor, the director of finance, the director of the Alabama development office, the lieutenant governor and the speaker of the house may become a public corporation with the powers and authorities hereinafter provided, by proceeding according to the provisions of this article. (Acts 1989, No. 89-704, p. 1402, § 3.)

§ 41-10-393. Filing of application for incorporation with secretary of state; contents and execution thereof; filing and recordation of application by secretary of state.

To become a public corporation, the governor, the director of finance, the director of the Alabama development office, the lieutenant governor and the speaker of the house, shall present to the secretary of state an application signed by each of them which shall set forth (1) the name, official designation, and official residence of each of the applicants together with a certified copy of the document evidencing each applicant's right to office; (2) the date on which each applicant was inducted into office and the term of office of each of the applicants; (3) the name of the proposed public corporation, which shall be "Alabama supercomputer authority"; (4) the location of the principal office of the proposed public corporation, which shall be Montgomery, Alabama; and (5) any other matters relating to the incorporation which the applicants may choose to insert and which is not inconsistent with this article or the laws of the state, including any provisions necessary or appropriate to secure qualification as a nonprofit corporation exempt from federal income tax under section 501(c)(3) of the Internal Revenue Code. The application shall be sworn and subscribed to by each of the applicants before an officer authorized by the laws of the state to take acknowledgements to deeds. The secretary of state shall examine the application and, if he or she finds that it substantially complies with the requirements of this section and that the name proposed in the application is not identical with that of a person or other corporation in the state or so nearly similar thereto as to lead to confusion and uncertainty, he or she shall receive and file it and record it in an appropriate book of records in his or her office. (Acts 1989, No. 89-704, p. 1402, § 4.)

U.S. Code. — The federal Internal Revenue Code, referred to in this section, is codified primarily in Titles 23, 26 and 42, U.S.C.

§ 41-10-394. Issuance and recordation of certificate of incorporation
          by secretary of state; secretary of state to receive no fees
          in connection with incorporation, dissolution, etc., of
          authority.

When the application has been made, filed and recorded as provided in the
preceding section, the secretary of state shall make and issue to the applicants
a certificate of incorporation pursuant to this article, under the great seal of
the state, and shall record the certificate with the application, whereupon the
applicants shall constitute a public corporation of the state under the name
proposed in the application. No fee shall be paid to the secretary of state for
any work done in connection with the incorporation or dissolution of the
authority. (Acts 1989, No. 89-704, p. 1402, § 5.)

§ 41-10-395. Officers and directors of authority; reduction to writing,
          recordation and filing of proceedings of board of direc-
          tors; admissibility in evidence of proceedings of board.

(a) The authority shall be governed by a board of directors, constituted as
provided for in this section. All powers of the authority shall be exercised by
said board or pursuant to its authorization. The directors shall elect officers of
the board. The presence of a majority of the members of the board of directors,
or their designees, shall constitute a quorum for the transaction of business.
No vacancy on the board of directors or the voluntary disqualification or
abstention of any director thereof shall impair the right of a quorum of the
board of directors to act. Any action which may be taken at a meeting of the
directors or committee of directors may be taken without a meeting if a
consent in writing, setting forth the action so taken, is signed by all the
directors or all the members of the committee of directors, as the case may be.
Such consent shall have the same force and effect as a unanimous vote and
may be stated as such in any articles or documents filed with either the
probate judge or the secretary of state.

(b) The number of directors of the authority shall be selected as follows: The
director of finance and the director of the Alabama development office each
shall be a director, ex-officio. The speaker of the house shall appoint a member
of the house and the lieutenant governor shall appoint a member of the
senate. The governor shall appoint as directors one representative of each of
the doctoral-degree-granting public institutions of higher education in the
state of Alabama as nominated by the president of each such institution. The
governor shall appoint four representatives from the business sector and two
additional members of the board of directors as shall, in his or her judgment,
be necessary for the proper and efficient functioning of the authority, so that
the representation on the board of directors shall encompass the university,
state government, and business sectors of the state.

(c) Directors other than those appointed at the time the authority is
initially established, and except for ex-officio directors, shall be selected for
four-year terms expiring on August 31 of the respective year. The governor

shall, at his or her discretion, indicate a length of initial term for initial appointees of from one to four years, so that each year the term of one-quarter of the members of the board of directors other than ex-officio directors shall expire. Any vacancy on the board of any director, other than an ex-officio director, shall be filled by appointment by the governor, speaker of the house or lieutenant governor, as appropriate, for the remainder of that term. Directors may be reappointed for successive terms. Should any ex-officio director cease to hold such office by reason of death, resignation, expiration of his or her term of office, or for any other reason, then his or her successor in office shall take his or her place as an officer or director of the authority. No officer or director shall draw any salary in addition to that now authorized by law for any service he or she may render or for any duty he or she may perform in connection with the authority.

(d) All resolutions adopted by the board of directors shall constitute actions of the authority, and all proceedings of the board of directors shall be reduced to writing by the secretary and shall be recorded in a substantially bound book and filed in the office of the director of finance. Copies of such proceedings, when certified by the secretary under the seal of the authority, shall be received in all courts as prima facie evidence of the matters and things therein certified. The board of directors of the authority shall meet at such times upon such notice as it shall determine or upon call of the chairperson. (Acts 1989, No. 89-704, p. 1402, § 6.)

§ 41-10-396. Powers of authority generally.

The authority shall have the following powers among others specified in this article:

(1) To have succession by its corporate names until dissolved as provided in this article;

(2) To institute legal proceedings in any court of competent jurisdiction to enforce its contractual, statutory and other rights; provided that the authority shall be considered an instrumentality of the state of Alabama and entitled to the sovereign immunity of the state; provided further, that any claim, demand or action against the authority, or any of its directors, officers, employees or agents arising out of their official capacities, shall be presented to the board of adjustment, which shall have exclusive jurisdiction of any such claim, demand or action;

(3) To have and to use a corporate seal and to alter the same at pleasure;

(4) To make and alter all needful bylaws, rules and regulations for the transaction of the authority's business and the control of its property and affairs;

(5) To acquire, improve, maintain, equip, repair, furnish and administer supercomputer and related communications equipment and facilities which the authority may determine to be necessary and not inconsistent with the provisions of this article;

(6) To make the time and resources of the supercomputer system and the other facilities and equipment of the authority available to federal, state

and local governmental agencies, divisions, boards, and public corporations, including universities and other educational and research institutions and organizations; and to the businesses, industries, and others for such fees or charges as the authority shall determine to best support, promote and encourage research; and to the businesses and industries under such preferences, priorities, procedures, and policies as the board shall deem appropriate;

(7) To receive and accept from any source aid or contributions of money, property, labor or other items of value for furtherance of any of its purposes, subject to any limitations not inconsistent herewith or with the laws of this state pertaining to such contributions, including, but without limitation to, gifts or grants from any department, agency or entity of the federal, state or local government or business and industry;

(8) To procure such insurance and guarantees as the authority may deem advisable, including, but without limitation to, insurance and guarantees against any loss in connection with any of its property or assets, tangible or intangible, in such amounts and from such public or private entities as it may deem appropriate, and to pay premiums or other charges for such insurance or guarantees;

(9) To acquire by purchase, gift or any other lawful means, and to transfer, convey or cause to be conveyed to the state of Alabama, any real, personal or mixed property;

(10) To make and enter into such contracts, leases, agreements and other actions as may be necessary or desirable to accomplish any corporate purpose and to exercise any power necessary for the accomplishment of the purposes of the authority or incidental to the powers expressly set out herein;

(11) To appoint and employ such attorneys, accountants, technical consultants and other advisors, agents and independent contractors as may, in the judgment of the authority, be necessary or desirable; and

(12) To make and enter into such contracts and agreements as may be necessary to provide technical personnel and services required for the development, maintenance and operation of the supercomputer telecommunications system, and associated functions. (Acts 1989, No. 89-704, p. 1402, § 7.)

§ 41-10-397. Employment of a chief executive officer and staff.

The authority may employ a chief executive officer who shall serve at the pleasure of the board of directors of the authority. The chief executive officer shall perform such duties as may be assigned to him or her by the authority and such duties as are required of him or her by law. He or she shall receive such compensation as may properly be fixed by the authority. In addition, he or she shall be entitled to remuneration for his or her necessary traveling expenses consistent with the general law.

The qualifications of the chief executive officer shall be determined by the authority.

The chief executive officer may employ, with the approval of the authority, such professional, technical and clerical persons as may be authorized by the authority; and the authority, upon the recommendation of the chief executive officer, shall define the duties and fix the compensation of such employees. Said employees shall serve at the pleasure of the authority. The authority shall comply with the required procedures so that said employees shall be eligible to participate in the state employees' retirement system. (Acts 1989, No. 89-704, p. 1402, § 8.)

§ 41-10-398. Authority to have no proprietary interest in intellectual property.

The authority and its employees shall have no proprietary interest or property right in any product, process, idea, concept or procedure subject to protection under a copyright, patent or trade secret law, which was developed, invented or discovered through the utilization of its supercomputer and associated resources. (Acts 1989, No. 89-704, p. 1402, § 9.)

§ 41-10-399. Confidentiality of data; inapplicability of public record laws; use of data by authority; requirements for contractual agreements for supercomputer services.

(a) The privacy, security and confidentiality of data collected, stored, processed or disseminated by the supercomputer system under the provisions of this article are the responsibility of the person, organization or entity collecting, storing, processing or disseminating such data.

(b) Data collected, stored, processed or disseminated through utilization of the supercomputer system under the provisions of this article are not subject to the requirements of the public record laws of the state of Alabama, and are therefore not subject to public disclosure by the authority.

(c) The authority shall not access, use or disseminate any data collected, stored, processed or disseminated by the supercomputer system under the provisions of this article without the prior written approval of the owner of such data. For the purposes of this article, the person, governmental entity, educational institution, business or industry contracting for supercomputer services with the authority shall be the owner of all data collected, stored, processed or disseminated under the terms of said contract.

(d) The authority shall require that each person, governmental entity, educational institution, business or industry receiving supercomputer services from the authority enter into a contractual agreement setting forth the following:

(1) All fees and charges for use of the supercomputer system;

(2) Each party's responsibility for the privacy, security and confidentiality of data, as well as any privacy, security and confidentiality requirements the user shall require in its use of the supercomputer system;

(3) That the authority, its directors, officers, employees and agents shall not be liable for damages caused by system malfunctions, hardware or software malfunctions, or other errors or omissions associated with the development, maintenance, use and operations of the supercomputer system, or the collection, storage, processing or dissemination of data through the supercomputer system;

(4) That the user will remove any program or data which the authority determines, in its sole discretion, may cause harm or damage to the authority's equipment, or to the data or programs of other users of the supercomputer;

(5) That the supercomputer system user shall comply in all respects with rules and regulations promulgated by the authority under the provisions of this article;

(6) That all statutory and/or governmental regulatory restrictions for the maintenance, storage, use or dissemination of data entered into the supercomputer system by the user shall be brought to the attention of the authority;

(7) Any other requirements or procedures deemed necessary by the authority for the administration and operation of the supercomputer system. (Acts 1989, No. 89-704, p. 1402, § 10.)

§ 41-10-400. Establishment of the "supercomputer system fund."

There is hereby established in the state treasury a special fund to be known as the "supercomputer system fund", which shall be used exclusively for the operation of the authority. All fees, charges, grants, gifts, appropriations or other moneys received by the authority from any source whatsoever shall be deposited in said fund. All funds contained in this special fund at the end of any fiscal year of the state of Alabama are hereby reappropriated to the authority for the purposes specified in this article. (Acts 1989, No. 89-704, p. 1402, § 11.)

§ 41-10-401. Exemption from taxation of properties, income, etc., of authority.

The properties of the authority and the income therefrom, all lease agreements made by the authority and all lien notices, mortgages, assignments and financing statements filed with respect thereto shall be forever exempt from any and all taxation of the state of Alabama. (Acts 1989, No. 89-704, p. 1402, § 12.)

§ 41-10-402. Liability upon contracts, obligations, etc., of authority.

All contracts made and obligations incurred by the authority shall be solely and exclusively obligations of the authority and shall not create debts of the state of Alabama. (Acts 1989, No. 89-704, p. 1402, § 13.)

§ 41-10-403. Operation of authority as nonprofit corporation.

The authority shall be a nonprofit corporation, and no part of its net earnings remaining after payment of its expenses shall inure to the benefit of any private person or entity. (Acts 1989, No. 89-704, p. 1402, § 14.)

§ 41-10-404. Transfer of certain assets to authority.

Upon issuance of the certificate of incorporation, any unencumbered funds appropriated to the department of finance, division of data systems management, for capital outlay and operation and maintenance of the supercomputer system, are hereby transferred to the supercomputer system fund to be expended in accordance with the provisions of this article.

Upon issuance of the certificate of incorporation and pursuant to a written transfer, assignment or conveyance by the state of Alabama to the authority, all contracts, leases, management agreements, real or personal property acquired by the state of Alabama and utilized in the operation of a supercomputer center and system by the Alabama department of finance, shall be transferred, assigned or conveyed to the authority without payment or other consideration. Upon such assignment, transfer or conveyance, the state of Alabama shall have no further obligations or rights to or under the items or subject matters so assigned, transferred or conveyed. (Acts 1989, No. 89-704, p. 1402, § 15.)

§ 41-10-405. Duplication of services to be avoided.

The authority shall not duplicate the services provided to agencies, departments, boards, bureaus, commissions and institutions of the state of Alabama by the Alabama department of finance. All telecommunications services used by the authority must have prior approval of the data systems management division, department of finance, state of Alabama. (Acts 1989, No. 89-704, p. 1402, § 16.)

§ 41-10-406. Dissolution of authority; title to property of authority to rest in state upon dissolution of authority.

At any time when the incorporators named in section 41-10-393 determine that the services provided by the authority are no longer of benefit to the entities served by the authority and that all obligations of the authority have been paid in full, the authority may be dissolved upon the filing with the secretary of state of a written statement for dissolution, which shall be subscribed by each of the incorporators of the authority and which shall be sworn to by each such incorporator before an officer authorized to take acknowledgements to deeds. Upon the filing of said written statement for dissolution, the authority shall cease and any property or other asset owned by it at the time of dissolution shall pass to the state of Alabama exclusively for purposes of section 501(c)(3) of the Internal Revenue Code. The secretary of state shall file and record the written statement for dissolution in an appropriate book of record in his or her office and shall make and issue, under the great seal of the state, a certificate that the authority is dissolved, and shall record the said certificate with the written statement for dissolution. (Acts 1989, No. 89-704, p. 1402, § 17.)

U.S. Code. — The federal Internal Revenue Code, referred to in this section, is codified primarily in Titles 23, 26 and 42, U.S.C.

ARTICLE 13.

REAL ESTATE COMMISSION BUILDING AUTHORITY.

———

Effective date. — The act which added this article became effective April 12, 1990.

§ 41-10-420. Legislative intent.

The legislature finds that the real estate commission has acquired certain real property in Montgomery, Alabama, title to which is in the name of the state of Alabama, for the purpose of erecting a building to house the offices of the real estate commission. The real estate commission has also received authority from the legislature to expend certain of its funds in the construction of such a facility. The legislature further finds that the real estate commission is unable to complete this building project without additional funding provided through temporary financing arrangements. Therefore, it is in the best interest of the state of Alabama and real estate commission to establish a public corporation with the powers and authority necessary to construct and lease to the commission a facility adequate to serve the needs of the commission. (Acts 1990, No. 90-293, § 1.)

§ 41-10-421. Real estate commission building authority established; composition; powers.

There is hereby established the real estate commission building authority composed of the governor, the chairman of the real estate commission, the director of the state building commission, the lieutenant governor and the speaker of the house who together with the board of directors of the real estate commission shall be a public corporation for the purposes herein stated. Such corporation shall have all the powers, authorities, rights, privileges and title that may be necessary to enable it to implement the purposes of this article.

The provisions of this article shall be liberally construed. (Acts 1990, No. 90-293, § 2.)

§ 41-10-422. Commission to become public corporation.

To become a public corporation, the governor, the chairman of the real estate commission, the director of the state building commission, the lieutenant governor and the speaker of the house, shall present to the secretary of state an application signed by each of them which shall set forth (1) the name, official designation, and official residence of each of the applicants together with a certified copy of the document evidencing each applicant's right to office; (2) the date on which each applicant was inducted into office and the term of office of each of the applicants; (3) the name of the proposed public corporation, which shall be "real estate commission building authority"; (4) the location of the principal office of the proposed public corporation, which shall be Montgomery, Alabama; and (5) any other matters relating to the incorporation which the applicants may choose to insert and which is not inconsistent with this article or the laws of the state, including any provisions necessary or appropriate to secure qualification as a nonprofit corporation exempt from federal income tax under section 501(c)(3) of the Internal Revenue Code. The application shall be sworn and subscribed to by each of the applicants before an officer authorized by the laws of the state to take acknowledgements to deeds. The secretary of state shall examine the application and, if he or she finds that it substantially complies with the requirements of this section and that the name proposed in the application is not identical with that of a person or other corporation in the state or so nearly similar thereto as to lead to confusion and uncertainty he or she shall receive and file it and record it in an appropriate book of records in the office of the secretary of state. (Acts 1990, No. 90-293, § 3.)

§ 41-10-423. Certificate of incorporation.

When the application has been made, filed and recorded as provided in section 41-10-422, the secretary of state shall make and issue to the applicants a certificate of incorporation pursuant to this article, under the great seal of the state, and shall record the certificate with the application, whereupon the applicants shall constitute a public corporation of the state under the name proposed in the application. No fee shall be paid to the secretary of state for any work done in connection with the incorporation or dissolution of the authority. (Acts 1990, No. 90-293, § 4.)

§ 41-10-424. Board of directors.

(a) The authority shall be governed by a board of directors, constituted as provided for in this section. All powers of the authority shall be exercised by said board or pursuant to its authorization. The directors shall elect officers of the board. The presence of a majority of the members of the board of directors, or their designees, shall constitute a quorum for the transaction of business. No vacancy on the board of directors or the voluntary disqualification or abstention of any director thereof shall impair the right of a quorum of the board of directors to act. Any action which may be taken at a meeting of the directors or committee of directors may be taken without a meeting if a consent in writing, setting forth the action so taken, is signed by all the directors or all the members of the committee of directors, as the case may be. Such consent shall have the same force and effect as a unanimous vote and may be stated as such in any articles or documents filed with either the probate judge or the secretary of state.

(b) The number of directors of the authority shall be selected as follows: The director of the state building commission, the chairman of the real estate commission each shall be a director, ex-officio. The speaker of the house shall appoint a member of the house and the lieutenant governor shall appoint a member of the senate. The governor shall appoint as director one designee for himself. The members of the real estate commission as constituted by section 34-27-7, shall also serve ex-officio and all shall be entitled the same privileges.

(c) Directors other than those appointed at the time the authority is initially established, and except for ex-officio directors, shall be selected for four-year terms expiring on August 31 of the respective year. Any vacancy on the board of any director, other than an ex-officio director, shall be filled by appointment by the governor, speaker of the house or lieutenant governor, as appropriate, for the remainder of that term. Directors may be reappointed for successive terms. Should any ex-officio director cease to hold such office by reason of death, resignation, expiration of his or her term of office, or for any other reason, then his or her successor in office shall take his or her place as an officer or director of the authority. No officer or director shall draw any salary in addition to that now authorized by law for any service he or she may render or for any duty he or she may perform in connection with the authority.

(d) All resolutions adopted by the board of directors shall constitute actions of the authority, and all proceedings of the board of directors shall be reduced to writing by the secretary and shall be recorded in a substantially bound book and filed in the office of the real estate commission. Copies of such proceedings, when certified by the secretary under the seal of the authority, shall be received in all courts as prima facie evidence of the matters and things therein certified. The board of directors of the authority shall meet at such times upon such notice as it shall determine or upon call of the chairperson. (Acts 1990, No. 90-293, § 5.)

§ 41-10-425. Powers of the authority.

The authority shall have the following powers among others specified in this article:

(1) To have succession by its corporate names until dissolved as provided in this article;

(2) To institute or maintain legal proceedings in any court of competent jurisdiction to enforce its contractual, statutory and other rights;

(3) To have and to use a corporate seal and to alter the same at pleasure;

(4) To make and alter all needful bylaws, rules and regulations for transaction of the authority's business and the control of its property affairs;

(5) The authority may, from time to time, borrow an amount not to exceed $400,000.00, as may be needed, to acquire, hold title to real property, to prepare and construct facilities and to sell, convey, lease, leaseback or rent and maintain that certain property located in the city of Montgomery, Montgomery county, Alabama, which is owned by and in the name and interest of the state of Alabama and the real estate commission, and in evidence of the moneys so borrowed may issue its promissory notes or other acceptable security as required;

The principal and interest on its debt shall be paid by the authority solely from its revenues from any source whatsoever, when due as deemed by the authority to be in its best interests and upon terms of written agreement and as recorded in its minutes. It is specifically provided that the authority shall not issue its revenue bonds;

(6) To receive and accept from any source aid or contributions of money, property, labor or other items of value for furtherance of any of its purposes subject to any limitations not inconsistent herewith or with the laws of this state pertaining to such contributions, including, but without limitation to, gifts or grants from any department, agency or entity of the federal, state or local government or business and industry;

(7) To procure such insurance and guarantees as the authority may deem advisable, including, but without limitation to, insurance and guarantees against any loss in connection with any of its property or assets, tangible or intangible, in such amounts and from such public or private entities as it may deem appropriate, and to pay premiums or other charges for such insurance or guarantees;

(8) To acquire by purchase, gift or any other lawful means, and transfer, convey or cause to be conveyed to the state of Alabama, any real, personal or mixed property;

(9) To make and enter into such contracts, leases, agreements and other actions as may be necessary or desirable to accomplish any corporate purpose and to exercise any power necessary for the accomplishment of the purposes of the authority or incidental to the powers expressly set out herein;

(10) To appoint and employ such attorneys, accountants, technical consultants and other advisors, agents and independent contractors as may in the judgment of the authority, be necessary or desirable; however, administrative support may be provided to the authority by the real estate commission;

(11) To make and enter into such contracts and agreements as may be necessary to provide technical personnel and services required for the implementation of this article; and

(12) To lease facilities to the state, the commission or any other agency or instrumentality of the state designated to perform the activities of the commission. (Acts 1990, No. 90-293, § 6.)

§ 41-10-426. Notes of the authority.

The notes of the authority shall be executed by the manual or facsimile signature of either its president or its treasurer, as shall be provided in the resolution under which such securities shall be issued, and the seal of the authority or a facsimile thereof shall be affixed to any instruments so issued and attested by the manual or facsimile signature of its secretary; provided, that if such are executed entirely by facsimile, the notes shall be authenticated by the manual signature of the trustee, registrar or paying agent if any. If, after any of the notes shall be so signed, whether manually or by facsimile, any such officer shall for any reason vacate his said office, the notes so signed may nevertheless be redeemed at any time thereafter as the act and deed of the authority. (Acts 1990, No. 90-293, § 7.)

§ 41-10-427. Authority authorized to sell, rent, etc., set charges or rents or make rent adjustments necessary to meet obligations.

For the purpose of providing funds for the acquisition and preparation of sites, for the construction, reconstruction, alteration and improvement of facilities, for the procurement and installation of equipment therefor and for payment of obligations incurred and the principal of and interest on any temporary loans made for any of the said purposes, the authority is hereby authorized, from time to time, to sell, rent, lease, leaseback, set charges or rents and to make rent adjustments necessary to meet such obligations and to use other revenues from any sources or income from said property. At no time shall any indebtedness or obligations or liabilities be that of the state of Alabama. (Acts 1990, No. 90-293, § 8.)

§ 41-10-428. Resolutions adopted and all proceedings of board of directors to be recorded and filed; copies received in all courts as prima facie evidence.

All resolutions adopted by the board of directors shall constitute actions of the authority, and all proceedings of the board of directors shall be reduced to writing by the secretary of the authority, which shall be signed by the members of the authority and shall be recorded in a substantially bound book and filed in the office of the secretary of state. Copies of such proceedings, when certified by the secretary of the authority under the seal of the authority, shall be received in all courts as prima facie evidence of the matters and things therein certified. (Acts 1990, No. 90-293, § 9.)

§ 41-10-429. Properties, etc., forever exempt from any and all taxation.

The properties of the authority and the income therefrom, all lease agreements made by the authority and all lien notices, mortgages, assignments and financing statements filed with respect thereto shall be forever exempt from any and all taxation of the state of Alabama and its political subdivisions. (Acts 1990, No. 90-293, § 10.)

§ 41-10-430. Contracts and obligations not debts of state.

All contracts made and obligations incurred by the authority shall be solely and exclusively obligations of the authority and shall not create debts of the state of Alabama. (Acts 1990, No. 90-293, § 11.)

§ 41-10-431. Authority as nonprofit corporation.

The authority shall be a nonprofit corporation, and no part of its net earnings remaining after payment of its expenses shall inure to the benefit of any private person or entity. (Acts 1990, No. 90-293, § 12.)

§ 41-10-432. Funds appropriated for Alabama real estate commission building authority fund; state to have no further obligations or rights after property, contracts, etc., assigned, transferred or conveyed.

Upon issuance of the certificate of incorporation, all funds appropriated from the real estate commission fund for purposes of capital outlay by Acts of Alabama 88-777 and 88-953, which remain unspent or unencumbered, are hereby transferred to a fund in the state treasury to be known as the Alabama real estate commission building authority fund. All funds received by the authority from any source whatsoever shall be deposited into such fund. Moneys contained therein are hereby appropriated for the purposes set forth in this article; said funds shall not revert to any other fund at the end of a fiscal year but are hereby reappropriated to the authority to be expended for any lawful purpose.

Upon issuance of the certificate of incorporation and pursuant to a written transfer, assignment or conveyance by the state of Alabama to the authority, all contracts, leases, management agreements, real or personal property acquired by the state of Alabama for the purpose of erecting a facility for the real estate commission, shall be transferred, assigned or conveyed to the authority without payment or other consideration. Upon such assignment, transfer or conveyance, the state of Alabama shall have no further obligations or rights to or under the items or subject matters so assigned, transferred or conveyed. (Acts 1990, No. 90-293, § 13.)

§ 41-10-433. Dissolution of authority.

At any time when the incorporators named in this article determine that the services provided by the authority are no longer of benefit to the entities served by the authority and that all obligations of the authority have been paid in full, the authority may be dissolved upon the filing with the secretary of state of a written statement for dissolution, which shall be subscribed by each of the incorporators of the authority and which shall be sworn to by each such incorporator before an officer authorized to take acknowledgements to deeds. Upon the filing of said written statement for dissolution, the authority shall cease and any property or other asset owned by it at the time of dissolution shall pass to the state of Alabama exclusively for purposes of section 501(c)(3) of the Internal Revenue Code. The secretary of state shall file and record the written statement for dissolution in an appropriate book of record in his or her office and shall make and issue, under the great seal of the state, a certificate that the authority is dissolved, and shall record the said certificate with the written statement for dissolution. (Acts 1990, No. 90-293, § 14.)

ARTICLE 14.

ALABAMA BUILDING RENOVATION FINANCE AUTHORITY.

Effective date. — The act which added this article became effective April 23, 1990.

§ 41-10-450. Legislative intent.

It is the intent of the legislature by the passage of this article to authorize the incorporation of the governor, the director of finance, and the state treasurer as a public corporation for the sole purpose of renovating, reconstructing, improving, altering, equipping, operating and maintaining or contracting for the renovation, reconstruction, improvement, alteration, equipment, operation and maintenance of public office buildings, including the state capitol, and to vest such corporation with all powers, authority, rights, privileges, and titles that may be necessary to enable it to accomplish such purpose. This article shall be liberally construed in conformity with the purpose expressed. (Acts 1990, No. 90-602, § 1.)

§ 41-10-451. Definitions.

The following terms, wherever used in this article, shall have the following respective meanings unless the context clearly indicates otherwise:

(1) AUTHORITY. The public corporation organized pursuant to the provisions of this article.

(2) BONDS. The bonds issued under the provisions of this article.

(3) GOVERNMENT SECURITIES. Any bonds or other obligations which as to principal and interest constitute direct obligations of, or are unconditionally guaranteed by, the United States of America, including obligations of any federal agency to the extent such obligations are unconditionally guaranteed by the United States of America and any certificates or any other evidences of an ownership interest in such obligations of, or unconditionally guaranteed by, the United States of America or in specified portions thereof (which may consist of the principal thereof or the interest thereon).

(4) PERMITTED INVESTMENTS. (i) Government securities; (ii) bonds, debentures, notes or other evidences of indebtedness issued by any of the following agencies: bank for cooperatives; federal intermediate credit banks; federal financing bank; federal home loan banks; federal farm credit bank; export-import bank of the United States; federal land banks, or farmers home administration or any other agency or corporation which has been or may hereafter be created by or pursuant to an act of the congress of the United States as an agency or instrumentality thereof; (iii) bonds, notes, pass through securities or other evidences of indebtedness of government national mortgage association and participation certificates of federal home loan mortgage corporation; (iv) full faith and credit obligations of any state, provided that at the time of purchase such obligations are rated at least "AA" by Standard & Poor's Corporation and at least "Aa" by Moody's Investors Service; (v) public housing bonds issued by public agencies or municipalities and fully secured as to the payment of both principal and interest by contracts with the United States of America, or temporary notes, preliminary notes or project notes issued by public agencies or municipalities, in each case fully secured as to the payment of both principal and interest by a requisition or payment agreement with the United States of America; (vi) time deposits evidenced by certificates of deposit issued by banks or savings and loan associations which are members of the federal deposit insurance corporation, provided that, to the extent such time deposits exceed available federal deposit insurance, such time deposits are fully secured by obligations described in clauses (i), (ii), (iii), and (v) above, which at all times have a market value (exclusive of accrued interest) at least equal to such bank time deposits so secured, including interest and which meet the greater of 100 percent collateralization or the "AA" collateral levels established by Standard & Poor's Corporation for structured financings, (vii) repurchase agreements for obligations of the type specified in clauses (i), (ii), (iii), and (v) above, provided such repurchase agreements are fully collateralized and secured by such obligations which

have a market value (exclusive of accrued interest) at least equal to the purchase price of such repurchase agreements and which are held by a depository satisfactory to the state treasurer in such manner as may be required to provide a perfected security interest in such obligations, and which meet the greater of 100 percent collateralization or the "AA" collateral levels established by Standard & Poor's Corporation for structured financings; and (viii) uncollateralized investment agreements with, or certificates of deposit issued by, banks or bank holding companies, the senior long-term securities of which are rated at least "AA" by Standard & Poor's Corporation and at least "Aa" by Moody's Investors Service.

(5) REFUNDING BONDS. Those refunding bonds authorized in this article to be sold and issued by the authority.

(6) STATE. The state of Alabama.

(7) Pronouns when used in this article shall include all applicable genders. (Acts 1990, No. 90-602, § 2.)

§ 41-10-452. Power to incorporate.

The governor, the director of finance, and the state treasurer may become a public corporation with the power and authority hereinafter provided, by proceeding according to the provisions of this article. (Acts 1990, No. 90-602, § 3.)

§ 41-10-453. Provisions for incorporation.

To become a corporation, the governor, the director of finance, and the state treasurer shall present to the secretary of state of Alabama an application signed by them which shall set forth: (1) the name, official designation, and official residence of each of the applicants, together with a certified copy of the document evidencing each applicant's right to office; (2) the date on which each applicant was inducted into office and the term of office of each of the applicants; (3) the name of the proposed corporation, which shall be the Alabama building renovation finance authority; (4) the location of the principal office of the proposed corporation; and (5) any other matter relating to the incorporation which the applicants may choose to insert and which is not inconsistent with this article or the laws of the state. The application shall be subscribed and sworn to by each of the applicants before an officer authorized by the laws of this state to take acknowledgements to deeds. The secretary of state shall examine the application and, if he finds that it substantially complies with the requirements of this section, he shall receive and file it and record it in an appropriate book of records in his office. (Acts 1990, No. 90-602, § 4.)

§ 41-10-454. Consummation of incorporation.

When the application has been made, filed, and recorded as provided in section 41-10-453, the secretary of state shall make and issue to the applicants a certificate of incorporation pursuant to this article, under the great seal of the state, and shall record the certificate with the application, whereupon the applicants shall constitute a public corporation and agency of the state under the name proposed in the application. There shall be no fees paid to the secretary of state for any work done in connection with the incorporation or dissolution of the authority. (Acts 1990, No. 90-602, § 5.)

§ 41-10-455. Members, directors and officers of the authority.

The applicants named in the application and their respective successors in office shall constitute the members of the authority. The governor shall be the president of the authority, the director of finance shall be the secretary of the authority and the state treasurer shall be treasurer of the authority. The members of the authority shall constitute all the members of the board of directors of the authority, which shall be the governing body of the authority. A majority of the members of the said board of directors shall constitute a quorum for the transaction of business. Should any person holding any state office named in this section cease to hold such office by reason of death, resignation, expiration of his term of office, or for any other reason, then his successor in office shall take his place as a member, officer, or director, as the case may be, of the authority. No member, officer, or director of the authority shall draw any salary in addition to that now authorized by law for any service he may render or for any duty he may perform in connection with the authority. All resolutions adopted by the board of directors shall constitute actions of the authority, and all proceedings of the board of directors shall be reduced to writing by the secretary of the authority, shall be signed by the members of the authority, and shall be recorded in a substantially bound book and maintained in the office of the director of finance. Copies of such proceedings, when certified by the secretary of the authority, under the seal of the authority, shall be received in all courts as prima facie evidence of the matters and things therein certified. (Acts 1990, No. 90-602, § 6.)

§ 41-10-456. Powers of the authority.

The authority shall have the following powers among others specified in this article: (1) to have succession by its corporate name until dissolved as provided in this article; (2) to sue and be sued and to prosecute and defend, at law or in equity, in any court having jurisdiction of the subject matter and of the parties thereto; (3) to have and to use a corporate seal and to alter the same at pleasure; (4) to make and alter all needful bylaws, rules and regulations for the transaction of the authority's business and the control of its property and affairs; (5) to establish a fiscal year; (6) to provide for the renovation, reconstruction, improvement, alteration, equipment, operation and maintenance of public office building facilities, including the state capitol, and for the procurement of sites and equipment for such facilities; (7) to receive, take and hold by sale, gift, lease, devise or otherwise, real and personal property of every description, and to manage the same; (8) to acquire by purchase, gift, or any other lawful means, and to transfer, convey or cause to be conveyed to the state, any real, personal or mixed property; (9) to borrow money and issue its bonds in evidence thereof subject to the provisions of this article; (10) to anticipate by the issuance of its bonds as hereinafter limited the receipt of the revenues from such public office buildings; (11) as security for the payment of the principal of and interest on its bonds, to enter into any lawful covenant and to pledge the revenues from such public office buildings; (12) to invest as hereinafter provided the proceeds from the sale of its bonds pending need therefor; (13) to make and enter into such contracts, leases, agreements and other actions as may be necessary or desirable to accomplish any corporate purpose and to exercise any power necessary for the accomplishment of the purposes of the authority or incidental to the powers expressly set out herein; (14) to appoint and employ such attorneys, agents, advisors, independent contractors, and employees as may, in the judgment of the board of directors, be necessary or desirable; and (15) to contract, lease and make lease arrangements as hereinafter provided for the use and occupation of all or any part of the public office buildings renovated, reconstructed, altered, maintained or improved by it, other than the state capitol. (Acts 1990, No. 90-602, § 7.)

§ 41-10-457. Power of condemnation.

The authority shall have the same powers of eminent domain which shall be exercised in the same manner and under the same conditions as are provided by law for the exercise of the powers of eminent domain by the state of Alabama. (Acts 1990, No. 90-602, § 8.)

§ 41-10-458. Authorization of bonds.

The authority is hereby authorized from time to time to sell and issue its bonds, not exceeding $29,500,000.00, exclusive of refunding bonds, in aggregate principal amount, for the purpose of providing funds for the renovation, reconstruction, improvement and alteration of public office building facilities, including the state capitol, for the procurement of equipment therefor, and for payment of obligations incurred for any of said purposes. (Acts 1990, No. 90-602, § 9.)

§ 41-10-459. Refunding bonds.

The authority may from time to time sell and issue its refunding bonds for the purpose of refunding any matured or unmatured bonds of the authority at the time outstanding and paying any premiums necessary to be paid to redeem any bonds so to be refunded; provided, however, that no refunding bonds shall be issued unless the present value of all debt service on the refunding bonds (computed with a discount rate equal to the true interest rate of the refunding bonds and taking into account all underwriting discount and other issuance expenses) shall not be greater than 95 percent of the present value of all debt service on the bonds to be refunded (computed using the same discount rate and taking into account the underwriting discount and other issuance expenses originally applicable to such bonds) determined as if such bonds to be refunded were paid and retired in accordance with the schedule of maturities (considering mandatory redemption as a scheduled maturity) provided at the time of their issuance. Provided further that the average maturity of the refunding bonds, as measured from the date of issuance of such refunding bonds, shall not exceed by more than three years the average maturity of the bonds to be refunded, as also measured from such date of issuance, with the average maturity of any principal amount of bonds to be determined by multiplying the principal of each maturity by the number of years (including any fractional part of a year) intervening between such date of issuance and each such maturity, taking the sum of all such products, and then dividing such sum by the aggregate principal amount of bonds for which the average maturity is to be determined. Such refunding bonds shall be subrogated and entitled to all priorities, rights and pledges to which the bonds refunded thereby were entitled. (Acts 1990, No. 90-602, § 10.)

§ 41-10-460. Execution of bonds.

All bonds of the authority shall be signed by its president, and the seal of the authority shall be affixed thereto and attested by its secretary. The signatures of the president and secretary may be facsimile signatures and a facsimile of the seal of the authority may be imprinted on the bonds if the board of directors, in its proceedings with respect to issuance of such bonds, provides for manual authentication of such bonds by a trustee or paying agent or by named individuals who are employees of the state and who are assigned to the department of finance or office of the state treasurer. Delivery of bonds so executed shall be valid notwithstanding any changes in officers or in the seal of the authority after the signing and sealing of such bonds. (Acts 1990, No. 90-602, § 11.)

§ 41-10-461. Sale of bonds.

Bonds may be sold by the authority from time to time in series, and if sold in more than one series may all be authorized in one initial resolution of the board of directors with the pledges therefor made in such initial resolution although some of the details applicable to each series may be specified in the respective resolutions under which the different series are issued. Each series of the bonds may be sold at public or private sale, as determined by the authority, at such price or prices as the authority shall determine, and, if sold at public sale either on sealed bids or at public auction, to the bidder whose bid reflects the lowest total net interest cost to the authority for the series of the bonds being sold, computed from the date of those at the time being sold to their respective maturities and taking into account any premium or discount named in the bid therefor; provided, that if in the event of public sale of the bonds no bid acceptable to the authority is received it may reject all bids. Notice of each public sale shall be given by publication in either a financial journal or a financial newspaper published in the city of New York, New York, and also by publication in a newspaper published in the state which is customarily published not less than five days during each calendar week, each of which notices must be published at least one time not less than 10 days prior to the date fixed for the sale. The board of directors may fix the terms and conditions under which each such sale may be held; provided, that such terms and conditions shall not conflict with any of the requirements of this article. Approval by the governor of the terms and conditions under which any of the bonds may be issued shall be requisite to their validity, which approval signed by the governor shall be entered on the minutes of the respective meetings of the board of directors at which the series of the bonds proposed to be issued are authorized or sold. (Acts 1990, No. 90-602, § 12.)

§ 41-10-462. Bonds of the authority.

Any bonds of the authority may be executed and delivered by it at any time and from time to time, shall be in such form and denominations and of such tenor and maturities, shall bear such rate or rates of interest, payable and evidenced in such manner, may contain provisions for redemption prior to maturity, and may contain other provisions not inconsistent herewith, all as may be provided by the resolution of the board of directors whereunder such bonds are authorized to be issued; provided, that no bond of the authority shall have a specified maturity date later than 30 years after its date. Each bond of the authority having a specified maturity date more than 10 years after its date shall be made subject to redemption at the option of the authority at the end of the 10th year after its date, and on any interest payment date thereafter, under such terms and conditions and at such premiums, if any, as may be provided in the resolution under which such bond is authorized to be issued. The authority may pay out the proceeds of the sale of its bonds all expenses, including fees and disbursements of attorneys, accountants, fiscal agents, financial advisors and other consultants, fees and disbursements of trustees, escrow agents, registrars, paying agents, transfer agents, depositories for safekeeping, authenticating agents, agents for the delivery and payment of bonds, fees and commissions of bond insurers and credit enhancers, printing costs and other customary bond issuance expenses. Bonds issued by the authority shall not be general obligations of the authority but shall be payable solely out of the funds referred to in section 41-10-471. In the event the authority shall make more than one pledge of the same revenues, such pledges shall take precedence in the order of the adoption of the resolutions in which the pledges are made; provided, that each pledge for the benefit of refunding bonds shall have the same priority as the pledge for the benefit of the bonds refunded thereby. Neither a public hearing nor consent of the state department of finance or any other department or agency of the state shall be a prerequisite to the issuance of bonds by the authority. (Acts 1990, No. 90-602, § 13.)

§ 41-10-463. Investment of proceeds from sale of bonds.

Any portion of the principal proceeds derived from the sale of the bonds which the board of directors of the authority may determine is not then needed for any of the purposes for which the bonds are authorized to be issued shall, on order of the authority, be invested by the state treasurer in permitted investments. Any such securities may, at any time and from time to time on order of the authority, be sold or otherwise converted by the state treasurer into cash. The income derived from any such investments shall be disbursed on order of the authority for any purpose for which the authority may lawfully expend funds. (Acts 1990, No. 90-602, § 14.)

§ 41-10-464. Exemption from taxation.

The properties of the authority and the income therefrom, all lease agreements made by the authority, and all bonds issued by the authority and the income therefrom and all lien notices filed with respect thereto shall be forever exempt from any and all taxation in the state of Alabama. (Acts 1990, No. 90-602, § 15.)

§ 41-10-465. Bonds constitute negotiable instruments.

All bonds issued by the authority shall be construed to have all the qualities and incidents of negotiable instruments subject to the registration provisions pertaining to transfers. (Acts 1990, No. 90-602, § 16.)

§ 41-10-466. Obligations not a debt of the state.

All obligations incurred by the authority and all bonds issued by it shall be solely and exclusively an obligation of the authority and shall not create an obligation or debt of the state of Alabama. (Acts 1990, No. 90-602, § 17.)

§ 41-10-467. Bonds may be used to secure deposit and for investment of fiduciary funds.

The state and all public officers, municipal corporations, political subdivisions, and public bodies, all banks, bankers, trust companies, savings banks and institutions, building and loan associations, savings and loan associations, investment companies, and other persons carrying on a banking business, all insurance companies, insurance associations and other persons carrying on an insurance business and all executors, administrators, guardians, trustees and other fiduciaries may legally invest any sinking funds, moneys or other funds belonging to them or within their control in any bonds of the authority, and such bonds shall be authorized security for all public deposits, it being the purpose of this article to authorize any persons, firms, corporations, associations, political subdivisions, bodies, and officers, public or private, to use any funds owned or controlled by them, including, but not limited to, sinking, insurance, investment, retirement, compensation, pension and trust funds, and funds held on deposit, for the purchase of any such bonds, and that any such bonds shall be authorized security for all public deposits. However, nothing contained in this article with regard to legal investments shall be construed as relieving any person, firm or corporation from any duty of exercising reasonable care in selecting securities. (Acts 1990, No. 90-602, § 18.)

§ 41-10-468. Use of the proceeds from sale of bonds.

All proceeds derived from the sale of any bonds (except refunding bonds) sold by the authority remaining after payment of the expenses of issuance thereof shall be turned over to the state treasurer, shall be carried by the state treasurer in a special account to the credit of the authority, and shall be subject to be drawn on by the authority solely for the purposes of renovating, reconstructing, improving, altering and equipping one or more public office buildings, including the state capitol, and all reasonable and necessary expenses incidental thereto, including interest which shall accrue on said bonds during the renovation, reconstruction, improvement, alteration and equipping of said buildings and for a period not exceeding one year thereafter. The authority is specifically authorized and empowered to expend bond proceeds to pay a portion of the cost of renovation and equipping of the state capitol even though the said state capitol shall not be owned by the authority. Any balance of said proceeds thereafter remaining shall, upon completion of renovation of the building or buildings for which the bonds were issued and the payment of all costs in connection therewith, be transferred to the reserve fund account of the authority or used to redeem bonds issued by the authority as may be determined by the board of directors of the authority. (Acts 1990, No. 90-602, § 19.)

§ 41-10-469. Use of proceeds of refunding bonds.

The proceeds of refunding bonds shall be applied, together with any other moneys legally available therefor, to the payment of the expenses authorized by this article and to the payment of the principal of, premium, if any, and interest due and to become due on any outstanding bonds to be refunded thereby and, if so required by resolution of the authority, shall be deposited in the state treasury in an interest account to pay interest on refunding bonds, and in the state treasury in a reserve account to further secure the payment of the principal of, premium, if any, and interest on any refunding bonds. The expenses authorized by this article shall include, in addition to expenses authorized by other sections hereof, all expenses that the board of directors may deem necessary or advantageous in connection with the sale and issuance of such refunding bonds, including without limitation, the expenses of selling and issuing such refunding bonds (including any discount reflected in the purchase price thereof paid to the authority), fees and disbursements of attorneys, accountants, fiscal agents, financial advisors and other consultants, fees and disbursements of trustees, escrow agents, registrars, paying agents, transfer agents, depositories for safekeeping, authenticating agents, agents for the delivery and payment of bonds, fees and commissions of bond insurers and credit enhancers, printing costs and other customary bond issuance expenses. To the extent not required for the immediate payment of outstanding bonds or for deposit into an interest account or a reserve account, proceeds of refunding bonds together with any other moneys legally available therefor, shall be deposited with the state treasurer, in trust, to be held separate and apart from all other funds of the state, or, with the approval of the state treasurer, shall be deposited in trust, on such terms as the state treasurer shall approve, with one or more trustees or escrow agents, which trustees or escrow agents shall be trust companies or national or state banks, located either within or without the state, having powers of a trust company. Any such proceeds or moneys deposited in trust with the state treasurer or with one or more trustees or escrow agents shall be applied solely to the payment when due of the principal of, premium, if any, and interest due and to become due on the outstanding bonds on or prior to the redemption date or maturity date thereof, as the case may be. Any such proceeds or moneys so held by the state treasurer or deposited with one or more trustees or escrow agents, may be invested in government securities; provided, such government securities shall not be subject to redemption prior to their maturity other than at the option of the holder thereof. Except as provided in the immediately succeeding sentence, neither the government securities nor moneys so deposited with the state treasurer, or with one or more trustees or escrow agents, shall be withdrawn or used for any purpose other than, and shall be held in trust for, the payment of the principal of, redemption premium, if any, and interest on such outstanding bonds to be refunded thereby; provided that any cash received from such principal or interest payments on such government securities deposited with the state treasurer, or with one or more trustees or escrow agents, (a) to the extent such cash will not be required at any time for such purpose, shall be retained by, or paid over to the state treasurer, as the case may be, for deposit to the account of the authority, and (b) to the extent such cash will be required for such purpose at a later date, shall, to the extent practicable and legally permissible, be reinvested in government securities maturing at times and in amounts sufficient to pay when due the principal of, premium, if any, and interest on such outstanding bonds on and prior to such redemption date or maturity date thereof, as the case may be, and interest earned from such reinvestments to the extent not required for the payment of such outstanding bonds shall be retained by, or paid over to the state treasurer, as the case may be, for deposit to the account of the authority. Notwithstanding anything to the contrary contained herein: (a) moneys on deposit pursuant to the provisions of this section may be applied and government securities so deposited may be redeemed and sold and the proceeds thereof applied to (i) the purchase of the outstanding bonds which were refunded by the deposit with the state treasurer or with one or more trustees or escrow agents of such moneys and government securities and immediately thereafter all outstanding bonds so purchased shall be cancelled, or (ii) the purchase of different government securities; provided, however, that the moneys and government securities on deposit with the state treasurer or with one or more trustees or escrow agents after such purchase and cancellation of such outstanding bonds or such purchase of different government securities shall be sufficient to pay when due the principal of, premium, if any, and interest on all other outstanding bonds in respect of which such moneys and government securities were deposited on or prior to the redemption date or maturity date thereof, as the case may be; and (b) in the event that on any date, as a result of any purchases and cancellations of outstanding bonds or any purchases of different government securities as provided in this sentence, the total amount of moneys and government securities remaining on deposit with the state treasurer or with one or more trustees or escrow agents, is in excess of the total amount which would have been required to be deposited with the state treasurer or trustee or escrow agent on such date in respect of the remaining outstanding bonds for which such deposit was made in order to pay when due the principal of, premium, if any, and interest on such remaining outstanding bonds, the state treasurer shall deposit the amount of such excess in the account of the authority, or the trustee or escrow agent shall, upon the direction of the state treasurer, pay the amount of such excess to the state treasurer for deposit to the account of the authority.

The state treasurer, acting in the capacity of trustee, may name one or more trust companies, national banks, or state banks, located either within or without the state, to act as the state treasurer's depository for any funds escrowed pursuant to the provisions of this section.

All applications of proceeds of refunding bonds or other moneys deposited in trust for the payment of outstanding bonds as provided in this section, including without limitation the investment thereof and the sale of any related government securities, shall be at the direction of the authority, but subject to the prior approval of the state treasurer. Any such approval of the state treasurer may be given at any time, including without limitation at the time of the adoption by the board of directors of any resolution relating to any bonds and, once given, such approval shall be irrevocable.

Moneys on deposit in any reserve account created pursuant to the provisions of this section shall be invested by the state treasurer at the direction of the authority in permitted investments which mature at such time or times as the authority shall direct. Interest income earned from such investments shall be deposited as received by the state treasurer in the account of the authority. (Acts 1990, No. 90-602, § 20.)

§ 41-10-470. Conveyance to authority by state.

The governor of Alabama is authorized to execute and deliver immediately before or simultaneously with the issuance of the first bonds of the authority an appropriate deed or deeds conveying to the authority any land belonging to the state situated in the city and county of Montgomery upon which the following buildings are located, such buildings being referred to herein by their commonly known names:
(1) Alabama State House
(2) Folsom Administrative Building
(3) Public Health Building
(4) Judicial Building
(5) Public Safety Building
(6) Archives and History Building
(7) State Office Building.
Upon delivery of such deed or deeds to the authority it thereby shall be invested with all rights and title that the state of Alabama had in the property conveyed thereby, subject to the right of reverter to the state upon the dissolution of the authority. The consideration for said conveyance shall be the authority's agreement to reconvey said land to the state, with all improvements thereon free of charge, immediately before the dissolution of the authority. Said consideration is hereby conclusively determined to be valuable, adequate and fair. Immediately prior to its dissolution the authority shall also convey to the state all other assets acquired by the authority, whether by purchase, gift, grant or otherwise, provided the terms of the grant are not violated thereby. (Acts 1990, No. 90-602, § 21.)

§ 41-10-471. Creation of fund for the benefit of the bonds.

For the purpose of providing funds for the payment of the principal of and interest on the bonds issued by the authority under the provisions of this article, there is hereby created and irrevocably pledged to the payment of such obligations a special and continuing trust fund which shall consist of all receipts and income from rents contracted for and received by the authority under leases of the building or buildings constructed or renovated with the proceeds from sale of the bonds and any other income of the authority. (Acts 1990, No. 90-602, § 22.)

§ 41-10-472. Pledge and lien for benefit of bonds.

In the proceedings authorizing the issuance of any of its bonds, the authority is authorized and empowered to pledge for the payment of the principal of and interest on such bonds at the respective maturities of said principal and interest, and to agree to use solely for such purpose, all the revenues which under the provisions of section 41-10-471 are provided for the payment of the said principal and interest. In said proceedings the authority may further provide and create, as security for the payment of said principal and interest, a statutory lien upon the buildings and properties, other than the state capitol, for the acquisition and construction or renovation of which the bonds are issued. Such statutory lien shall not be subject to foreclosure and, in the event of default in the payment of any such principal or interest, the remedies thereunder shall be limited to a remedy by way of mandamus and to the appointment, as a matter of right, by any court having equity powers and having jurisdiction over the authority, of a receiver in equity with all the powers of such a receiver, except the power to sell the said buildings and properties. Upon the issuance of any bonds pursuant to this article the authority shall file in the office of the judge of probate of Montgomery county, Alabama, an instrument reciting the issuance of such bonds and the pledge of said revenues and the creation of said statutory lien as security therefor, and the filing of such instrument shall constitute constructive notice of said pledge and lien. Such instrument shall be received and recorded by said judge of probate upon the payment of the fee for the recording of mortgages but no tax shall be payable with respect thereto. (Acts 1990, No. 90-602, § 23.)

§ 41-10-473. State treasurer to disburse funds.

Out of the revenues referred to in section 41-10-471, the state treasurer is authorized and directed to pay the principal of and interest on the bonds as such principal and interest shall respectively mature, and he is further authorized and directed to set up and maintain appropriate records pertaining thereto. (Acts 1990, No. 90-602, § 24.)

§ 41-10-474. Terms and conditions of leasing by authority.

The authority and the executive head of any agency, board, commission, public corporation, bureau or department of the state of Alabama, or the successor in office and duties of such executive head, are hereby authorized to enter into a lease or leases for the use and occupancy of offices and storage space in the public office buildings renovated, reconstructed, improved, altered or equipped and owned by the authority under the provisions of this article. Such executive heads are hereby separately authorized to enter into lease agreements for the use and occupancy of any space in the said buildings.

The authority and the director of finance on behalf of the finance department are hereby authorized to enter into a lease or leases for the use and occupancy of any or all of said buildings. In such event, the finance department may sublease space in said buildings upon such terms and conditions as may be determined by the director of finance. (Acts 1990, No. 90-602, § 25.)

§ 41-10-475. Presumption of validity of bonds and publication of notice thereof.

Any resolution authorizing any bonds hereunder shall contain a recital that they are issued pursuant to the provisions of this article, which recital shall be conclusive evidence that said bonds have been duly authorized pursuant to the provisions of this article, notwithstanding the provisions of any other law now in force or hereafter enacted or amended. Upon the passage of any resolution providing for the issuance of bonds under the provisions of this article, the authority may, in its discretion, cause to be published once in each of two consecutive weeks in a newspaper published and having general circulation in the city of Montgomery a notice in substantially the following form (the blanks being first properly filled in):

Alabama Building Renovation Finance Authority, a public corporation and agency of the State of Alabama, on the _____ day of _____, _____, adopted a resolution providing for the issuance of _____ dollars principal amount of bonds of said authority. Any action or proceeding questioning the validity of said resolution or said bonds or the pledge and agreements made in said resolution for the benefit thereof, or the proceedings under which said bonds, pledge and agreements were authorized, must be commenced within 20 days after the first publication of this notice.

Alabama building renovation finance authority

By _____

Its President

Any action or proceeding in any court seeking to set aside or invalidate a resolution providing for the issuance of bonds under the provisions of this article or to contest the validity of any such bonds, or the validity of any pledge or agreement made therefor, must be commenced within 20 days after the first publication of said notice. After the expiration of 20 days following such first publication, no right of action founded upon questioning or challenging in any way the validity of the resolution or other proceedings, if any, or of the bonds, or of the pledge and agreements, shall be asserted. In the event of such publication the validity of such resolution, proceedings, bonds, pledge and agreements shall not be open to question in any court upon any ground whatever, except in an action or proceeding commenced within such period. Any such action and any action to protect or enforce any rights under the provisions of this article shall be brought in the circuit court of Montgomery county. (Acts 1990, No. 90-602, § 26.)

§ 41-10-476. Power to make payments and to make agreements respecting investment of funds.

The authority shall have the power to make such payments to the United States of America as the directors deem necessary to cause the interest on any bonds of the authority to be and remain exempt from federal income taxation. The authority shall have the power to make agreements respecting the investment of funds of the authority necessary in order that the interest income on bonds of the authority be and remain exempt from federal income taxation. (Acts 1990, No. 90-602, § 27.)

§ 41-10-477. Dissolution of the authority.

When all securities issued by the authority and all obligations assumed by it under the provisions of this article shall have been paid in full, the then president of the authority shall thereupon execute and deliver in the name of and in behalf of the authority an appropriate deed, or deeds, to which the seal of the authority shall be affixed and attested by the secretary of the authority, whereby there shall be conveyed to the state all the buildings, properties and other assets then owned by the authority. The then officers and directors of the authority shall at such time file with the secretary of state a written statement, subscribed and sworn to by each of them, reciting the payment in full of all bonds therefore issued by the authority and the execution and delivery of such deed or deeds to the state, which statement shall be filed by the secretary of state and recorded with the certificate of incorporation of the authority, whereupon the authority shall stand dissolved. (Acts 1990, No. 90-602, § 28.)

ARTICLE 15.

ALABAMA STATE PARKING DECK AUTHORITY.

Effective date. — The act which added this article became effective April 23, 1990.

§ 41-10-490. Definitions.

For the purposes of this article, the following terms shall have the meanings respectively ascribed to them by this section:

(1) AUTHORITY. The public corporation organized pursuant to the provisions of this article.

(2) CODE. The Code of Alabama 1975, as amended.

(3) REFUNDING BONDS. Those refunding bonds issued under the provisions of section 41-10-502.

(4) STATE. The state of Alabama.

(5) BONDS. Those bonds, including without limitation refunding bonds, issued under the provisions of this article.

(6) FACILITIES. A multi-storied vehicle parking and storage facility and appurtenanaces necessary or incidental to the operation of such facility, to be constructed and erected on, or attached to, that block of land bounded by the following streets: Pelham, Jackson, Washington, and South Ripley in the Capitol Complex in the city of Montgomery, Alabama.

(7) PERMITTED INVESTMENTS. United States securities, certificates of deposit fully secured by United States securities and shall include investments in such obligations of the United States of America or its agencies under a repurchase agreement.

(8) UNITED STATES SECURITIES. Direct general obligations of the United States of America (including obligations of the state and local government series) and the obligations of any other agency corporation which has been or may hereafter be created by or pursuant to an act of the congress of the United States as an agency or instrumentality thereof, the bonds, debentures, participation certificates or notes of which are unconditionally guaranteed by the United States of America. (Acts 1990, No. 90-603, § 1.)

§ 41-10-491. Purpose of article and construction.

It is the intent of the legislature, by the passage of this article, to authorize the incorporation of a public corporation for the purposes of acquiring land, constructing and equipping facilities, leasing such facilities to state agencies (or others, to the extent provided for herein), and providing financing therefor, and to vest such corporation with all powers, authority, rights, privileges and titles that may be necessary to enable it to accomplish such purposes. This article shall be liberally construed in conformity with the purpose herein stated. (Acts 1990, No. 90-603, § 2.)

§ 41-10-492. Authority as public corporation.

The state finance director, the state budget officer and one person appointed by the governor, one person appointed by the speaker of the house and one person appointed by the lieutenant governor, may become a public corporation with the power and authority provided in this article by proceeding according to the provisions hereof. Those persons appointed by the governor, lieutenant governor and speaker of the house shall serve at the pleasure of the official appointing them and until their replacements have been appointed. The state treasurer shall be treasurer of the authority, shall act as custodian of the funds of the authority, and shall pay the principal of and interest on the bonds of the authority out of the funds hereinafter provided for; provided, that the state treasurer may designate one or more banks either within or without the state as the paying agent with respect to any series of bonds issued under this article. (Acts 1990, No. 90-603, § 3.)

§ 41-10-493. Application for certificate of incorporation.

To become a corporation, the individuals selected pursuant to section 41-10-492 shall present to the secretary of state of Alabama an application signed by them which shall set forth:

(1) The name and residence of each of the applicants, together with a certified copy of all documents evidencing each applicant's selection or the office he holds;

(2) The name of the proposed corporation, which shall be the "Alabama state parking deck authority";

(3) The location of the principal office of the proposed corporation, which shall be in the office of the director of finance in Montgomery, Alabama; and

(4) Any other matter relating to the incorporation of the proposed corporation which the applicants may choose to insert and which is not inconsistent with this article.

The application shall be subscribed and sworn to by each of the applicants before an officer authorized by the laws of this state to take acknowledgements to deeds. The secretary of state shall examine the application, and if he finds that it substantially complies with the requirements of this section, he shall receive and file it and record it in an appropriate book of records in his office. (Acts 1990, No. 90-603, § 4.)

§ 41-10-494. Certificate of incorporation.

When the application has been made, filed and recorded as provided in section 41-10-493, the secretary of state shall make and issue to the applicants a certificate of incorporation pursuant to this article, under the great seal of the state, and shall record the certificate with the application, whereupon the applicants shall constitute a public corporation of the state under the name proposed in the application. (Acts 1990, No. 90-603, § 5.)

§ 41-10-495. Members; directors; quorum; vacancies; salaries; officers.

The applicants named in the application and their respective successors in office shall constitute the members of the authority. The members shall be eligible to succeed themselves. The members of the authority shall constitute all the members of the board of directors of the authority, which shall be the governing body of the authority. A majority of the members of the said board of directors shall constitute a quorum for the transaction of business. No member, officer or director of the authority shall draw any salary for any service he may render or for any duty he may perform in connection with the authority, but may be reimbursed by the authority for reasonable expenses incurred in carrying out the business of the authority. No member, officer, director or employee of the authority shall be personally liable for any debt, obligation or liability of the authority. The finance director shall serve as president of the authority, the state budget officer shall serve as secretary of the authority. The treasurer of the atate of Alabama shall be the treasurer of the authority. (Acts 1990, No. 90-603, § 6.)

§ 41-10-496. Resolutions and proceedings of board of directors.

All resolutions adopted by the board of directors shall constitute actions of the authority, and all proceedings of the board of directors shall be reduced to writing by the secretary of the authority, shall be signed by the members of the authority and shall be recorded in a substantially bound book and filed in the office of the state finance director. Copies of such proceedings, when certified by the secretary of the authority under the seal of the authority, shall be received in all courts as prima facie evidence of the matters and things therein certified. (Acts 1990, No. 90-603, § 7.)

§ 41-10-497. Powers generally.

The authority shall have the following powers among others specified in this article:

(1) To have succession in its corporate name until the principal of and interest on all bonds issued by it shall have been fully paid and until it shall have been dissolved as provided herein;

(2) To maintain actions and have actions maintained against it and to prosecute and defend in any court having jurisdiction of the subject matter and of the parties thereof;

(3) To have and to use a corporate seal and to alter such seal at pleasure;

(4) To establish a fiscal year;

(5) To acquire and hold title to real and personal property and to sell, convey, mortgage or lease the same as provided in this article;

(6) To provide for the construction, reconstruction, alteration and improvement of facilities and for the procurement of sites and equipment for such facilities and for the lease thereof;

(7) To lease facilities to the state, or any agency or instrumentality of the state;

(8) To anticipate by the issuance of its bonds, subject to the provisions of this article, the receipt of the rent and revenues from such facilities;

(9) As security for the payment of the principal of and interest on its bonds, to enter into any lawful covenant, to grant mortgages upon or security interests in its facilities and to pledge the rents and revenues from such facilities;

(10) To invest as provided in this act the proceeds from the sale of its bonds pending need therefor;

(11) To appoint and employ such attorneys, agents and employees as the business of the authority may require, subject to the merit system where applicable; and

(12) To perform such other acts and duties as are necessary to carry out the provisions of this article. (Acts 1990, No. 90-603, § 8.)

§ 41-10-498. Temporary loans in anticipation of issuance of bonds.

In anticipation of issuance of bonds under this article, the authority may, from time to time, borrow such sums as may be needed for any of the purposes for which bonds are authorized to be issued under this article, and in evidence of the moneys so borrowed by issue its promissory notes. The principal of and the interest on notes so issued may, from time to time, be refunded by refunding notes or by bonds in anticipation of the issuance of which such notes were issued. All such notes, whether initial issues or refunding issues, may bear interest from their dates until their maturities at such rate or rates as may be deemed acceptable by the board of directors, not to exceed 15 percent per annum, shall mature within three years from their date, and the principal thereof, premium, if any, and interest thereon shall be payable solely from the proceeds of the refunding notes issued to refund any such notes outstanding, the proceeds from the sale of bonds in anticipation of the issuance of which any such notes were issued and the sources from which bonds may be made payable pursuant to section 41-10-509 of this article, all as may be provided in the resolution of the board of directors under which such notes may be issued. (Acts 1990, No. 90-603, § 9.)

§ 41-10-499. Execution of bonds and notes.

The bonds and notes of the authority shall be executed by the manual or facsimile signature of either its president or its secretary, as shall be provided in the resolution under which such securities shall be issued, and the seal of the authority or a facsimile thereof shall be affixed to any bonds so issued and attested by the manuals or facsimile signature of its secretary; provided, that if bonds are executed entirely by facsimile, such bonds shall be authenticated by the manual signature of the bond trustee, registrar or paying agent or by named individuals who are employees of the state and who are assigned to the department of finance or office of the state treasurer. The seal of the authority shall be impressed on the bonds, and a facsimile of said seal may be printed or otherwise reproduced on any of the bonds in lieu of being manually impressed thereon. If, after any of the bonds shall be so signed, whether manually or by facsimile, any such officer shall for any reason vacate his said office, the bonds so signed may nevertheless be delivered at any time thereafter as the act and deed of the authority. (Acts 1990, No. 90-603, § 10.)

§ 41-10-500. Bonds authorization.

For the purpose of providing funds for the acquisition of sites, for the construction, reconstruction, alteration and improvement of facilities, for the procurement and installation of equipment therefor and for payment of obligations incurred and the principal of and interest on any temporary loans made for any of the said purposes, the authority is hereby authorized, from time to time, to sell and issue its bonds (other than refunding bonds) in an aggregate principal amount not to exceed $13,000,000.00. (Acts 1990, No. 90-603, § 11.)

§ 41-10-501. Sale and issuance of refunding bonds.

The authority may, from time to time, sell and issue its refunding bonds, without limitation as to principal amount, for the purpose of refunding any matured or unmatured bonds of the authority at the time outstanding and paying any premiums necessary to be paid to redeem any such bonds so to be refunded and all expenses incurred in connection therewith. Such refunding bonds shall be subrogated and entitled to all priorities, rights and pledges to which the bonds refunded thereby were entitled. (Acts 1990, No. 90-603, § 12.)

§ 41-10-502. Specifications and priority of bonds.

Any bonds of the authority may be executed and delivered by it at any time and from time to time, shall be in such form and denominations and of such tenor and maturities, shall bear such rate or rates of interest, fixed or floating, payable and evidenced in such manner, may contain provisions for redemption prior to maturity and may contain other provisions not inconsistent with this section, all as may be provided by the resolution of the board of directors whereunder such bonds are authorized to be issued; provided that no bond of the authority shall have a specified maturity date later than 20 years after its date. At its election, the authority may retain in the resolution(s) under which any of the bonds are issued an option to redeem all or any thereof and at such redemption price(s) and after such notice(s) and on such dates and on such terms and conditions as may be set forth in said resolution(s) and as may be briefly recited in the bonds with respect to which such option of redemption is retained. In the event that the authority shall make more than one pledge of the same revenues, such pledges shall, unless otherwise provided in the resolution or resolutions authorizing the earlier issued bonds, take precedence in the order of the adoption of the resolutions in which the pledges are made; provided, that each pledge for the benefit of refunding bonds shall have the same priority as the pledge for the benefit of the bonds refunded thereby. (Acts 1990, No. 90-603, § 13.)

§ 41-10-503. Sale of bonds.

Bonds of the authority may be sold at such price or prices and at such time or times as the board of directors of the authority may consider advantageous, at public or private sale. If bonds are to be sold by competitive bid on sealed bids or at public auction, the bonds may be sold only to the bidder whose bid reflects the lowest effective borrowing cost to the authority for the bonds being sold; provided, that if no bid acceptable to the authority is received, it may reject all bids. Notice of each such sale by competitive bids shall be given by publication in either a financial journal or a financial newspaper published in the city of New York, New York, and also by publication in a newspaper published in the state of Alabama, each of which notices must be published at least one time not less than 10 days before the date fixed for such sale. The board of directors may fix the terms and conditions under which such sale by competitive bids may be held; provided that such terms and conditions shall not conflict with any of the requirements of this article. The authority may pay out of the proceeds of the sale of its bonds all expenses, including publication and printing charges, fiscal agents' fees, attorneys' fees and other expenses which said board of directors may deem necessary and advantageous in connection with the authorization, advertisement, sale, execution and issuance of such bonds. Neither a public hearing nor consent of the state shall be a prerequisite to the issuance or sale of bonds by the authority. (Acts 1990, No. 90-603, § 14.)

§ 41-10-504. Bonds of authority eligible for investment of trust funds.

Any trust fund, where the investment thereof is permitted or required by law, may be invested in bonds issued by the authority. Unless otherwise directed by the court having jurisdiction thereof or the document which is the source of authority, a trustee, executor, administrator, guardian or one acting in any other fiduciary capacity may, in addition to any other investment powers conferred by law and with the exercise of reasonable business prudence, invest trust funds in the bonds of the authority. (Acts 1990, No. 90-603, § 15.)

§ 41-10-505. Security for deposit of governmental funds.

Any bonds issued by the authority may be used by the holders thereof as security for deposits of any funds belonging to the state or to any instrumentality, agency or political subdivision of the state in any instance where security for such deposits may be required or permitted by law. (Acts 1990, No. 90-603, § 16.)

§ 41-10-506. Disposition of proceeds of bonds.

(a) All proceeds derived from the sale of any bonds, except refunding bonds, sold by the authority, remaining after payment of the expenses of issuance thereof, shall be turned over to the state treasurer, shall be carried by him in a special account to the credit of the authority, and shall be subject to be drawn on by the authority solely for the purposes of:

(1) Acquiring land for and constructing, reconstructing and equipping thereon one or more facilities;

(2) Paying all reasonable and necessary expenses incidental thereto, including filing, recording, surveying, legal and engineering fees and expenses;

(3) Paying the interest which will accrue on the said bonds during the period required for the construction and equipment of the said facilities and for a period not exceeding six months after the completion thereof; and

(4) Paying the principal of and interest on all then outstanding notes theretofore issued by the authority pursuant to the provisions hereof.

The balance of the said proceeds thereafter remaining shall be set aside as additional security for the bonds or shall be used to pay, purchase or redeem bonds as may be provided in the proceedings authorizing their issuance.

(b) All proceeds from the sale of refunding bonds issued by the authority that remain after paying the expenses of their issuance may be used only for the purpose of refunding the principal of and any unpaid and accrued interest on the outstanding bonds of the authority for the refunding of which the refunding bonds are authorized to be issued, together with any premium that may be necessary to be paid in order to redeem or retire such outstanding bonds. (Acts 1990, No. 90-603, § 17.)

§ 41-10-507. Investment of proceeds.

Any portion of the principal proceeds derived from the sale of the bonds which the board of directors of the authority may determine is not then needed for any of the purposes for which the bonds are authorized to be issued shall, on order of the authority, be invested by the state treasurer in permitted investments which mature at such time or times as the authority shall direct. Any such investments may, at any time and from time to time on order of the authority, be sold or otherwise converted by the state treasurer into cash. The income derived from any such investments shall be disbursed on order of the authority for any purpose for which it may lawfully expend funds. (Acts 1990, No. 90-603, § 18.)

§ 41-10-508. Security.

The principal of, premium, if any, and interest on the bonds of the authority shall be secured by any or all of the following, as the authority may determine:

(1) The rent and revenues from the lease or use of one or more facilities of the authority;

(2) The proceeds from any sale of any facilities of the authority;

(3) Any bond proceeds remaining unexpended upon completion of all facilities to be constructed with such bond proceeds and the payment of the cost thereof;

(4) Any insurance proceeds which the authority may receive by reason of its ownership of any of the facilities; and

(5) Any mortgage upon or security interest in one or more facilities of the authority, granted in connection with the issuance of such bonds.

The authority shall have authority to transfer and assign any lease or mortgage of any of its facilities as security for the payment of such principal, premium, if any, and interest. The bonds may be issued under, and secured by, a resolution which may, but need not, provide for an indenture of trust covering one or more facilities of the authority. Such resolution or such indenture of trust may contain any provision or agreement customarily contained in instruments securing evidences of indebtedness, including, without limiting the generality of the foregoing, provisions respecting the collection and application of any receipts pledged to the payment of bonds, the terms to be incorporated in lease agreements respecting the facilities, the maintenance and insurance thereof, the creation and maintenance of reserve and other special funds from such receipts and the rights and remedies available in the event of default to the holders of the bonds or to the trustee for the holders of the bonds or under any indenture of trust, all as the authority may deem advisable and as shall not be in conflict with the provisions of this article; provided, however, that in making such agreements or provisions the authority shall not have the power to obligate itself except with respect to its facilities, and the application of the rents, revenues and other moneys and assets which it is authorized in this article to pledge. (Acts 1990, No. 90-603, § 19.)

§ 41-10-509. Enforcement upon default.

If there be any default by the authority in the payment of the principal of or interest on the bonds or in any of the agreements on the part of the authority which may properly be included in any resolution or indenture of trust securing such bonds, any holder of any of the bonds or the trustee for the bondholders under any resolution or indenture of trust, if so authorized therein, may, by an action, mandamus or other proceedings, enforce payment of such items and foreclosure upon any mortgage or security interest granted as security for such bonds and compel performance of all duties of the directors and officers of the authority and shall be entitled, as a matter of right and regardless of the sufficiency of any such security or the availability of any other remedy, to the appointment of a receiver with all the power of such receiver for the maintenance, insurance and leasing of the facilities and property covered by such resolution or such indenture of trust and the collection and application of the receipts therefrom. Any such resolution or indenture of trust may contain provisions regarding the rights and remedies of any trustee thereunder and the holders of the bonds and may contain provisions restricting the individual rights of action of the holders of the bonds. (Acts 1990, No. 90-603, § 20.)

§ 41-10-510. Bonds and coupons deemed negotiable instruments.

All bonds issued by the authority shall be construed to be negotiable instruments even though they are payable from a limited source. All coupons applicable to any bonds issued by the authority shall likewise be construed to be negotiable instruments although payable from a limited source. (Acts 1990, No. 90-603, § 21.)

§ 41-10-511. Obligations, bonds and notes not debt of state.

All obligations incurred by the authority and all bonds and notes issued by it shall be solely and exclusively an obligation of the authority, payable solely from the sources which may under the provisions of this article be pledged to the payment thereof. No obligation incurred by the authority and no bond or note issued by it shall create an obligation or debt of the state. (Acts 1990, No. 90-603, § 22.)

§ 41-10-512. Conveyance of land to corporation; conveyance of improvements back to state.

The governor of Alabama or the officers of any public corporation, as appropriate, are authorized and directed to execute and deliver immediately before or simultaneously with the issuance of the first series of the bonds of the corporation contemplated by this article appropriate deeds conveying to the corporation the title to that block of land bounded by the following streets: Pelham, Jackson, Washington, and South Ripley in the Capitol Complex in the city of Montgomery, Alabama. The consideration for said conveyances shall be the corporation's undertaking to reconvey said land with improvements free of charge to the state immediately before the dissolution of the corporation. Since the land would otherwise remain unimproved, said consideration is hereby conclusively determined to be valuable, adequate and fair. Immediately prior to its dissolution the corporation shall also convey to the state the title to that block of land bounded by the following streets: Pelham, Jackson, Washington, and South Ripley in the Capitol Complex in the city of Montgomery, Alabama acquired for construction of buildings thereon whether by purchase, gift, grant, or otherwise provided the terms of the grant are not violated thereby. (Acts 1990, No. 90-603, § 23.)

§ 41-10-513. Facilities construction.

All facilities constructed by the authority shall be constructed according to plans and specifications of architects or engineers, or both, selected by the authority. The parking deck shall be planned and constructed in such a manner as to accommodate the construction of a mirror image of the persons office building. All such plans and specifications shall be approved by the authority and by the state building commission. (Acts 1990, No. 90-603, § 24.)

§ 41-10-514. Leasing to state agencies.

(a) The authority is hereby authorized to enter into one or more leases of all or any part or portion of the facilities constructed, acquired, reconstructed, renovated or improved by the authority under the provisions of this article, to any agency of the state. Any agency of the state and each of them is hereby authorized to lease any such facilities from the authority. No such lease shall, however, be for a term longer than the then current fiscal year of the state, but any such lease may contain a grant to any state agency of successive options of renewing said lease on the terms specified therein for any subsequent fiscal year or years of the state; provided, that liability for the payment of rent shall never be for a term longer than one fiscal year.

(b) Rent payments by the state, or any of its agencies shall be due and payable at such time or times as shall be specified in the lease respecting the facilities leased and shall, upon being so paid, entitle the state or such agency to quiet possession of the facilities leased for such fiscal year. Said rent shall be payable, and any such covenant with respect thereto on the part of the state of any of its agencies (as the case may be) shall be performed, solely out of the current revenues of the state or such agency for such fiscal year. The rent payable and the covenants to be performed by the state or any of its agencies under the provisions of said lease shall never be deemed to create a debt of the state within the meaning of the Constitution.

(c) In the event that there shall be any default in the payment of any rent required to be paid or in the performance of any covenant required to be performed by the state or any of its agencies under the provisions of any such lease, while such lease is in effect, the authority and any pledgee of such lease may, by any appropriate proceedings instituted within the time permitted by law, enforce and compel the payment of such rent and the performance of such covenants. No free use shall be made of any facilities of the authority so long as the principal of or interest on any bonds, including refunding bonds, issued by the authority remains unpaid.

(d) In the event that any facility owned by the authority should become vacant or not be used by one of the state agencies, then neither the state nor any agency, board, bureau, commission, public corporation or department of the state shall rent, purchase, acquire, construct or lease any facilities or renew any lease of any facilities, nor shall it use any such facilities other than those owned by the authority, so long as any facility owned by the authority shall remain vacant or unused. (Acts 1990, No. 90-603, § 25.)

§ 41-10-515. Leasing to county, municipal corporation, agency of federal government, etc.

If at any time any facility constructed or acquired by the authority is, or is about to be, vacant or unused as a result of there being no lease for such facility in effect for the current fiscal year, then, but only in such event, in order to prevent default on its bonds, the authority is hereby authorized to lease such facility to any other agency, department, bureau or commission of the state, any municipal corporation, public corporation, county, or other public body in the state, or any agency of the federal government, and lastly, and in no other order of priority, to a private person, firm or corporation. Any such lease shall not be for the purpose of lending public credit but shall be solely to avoid default on the authority's bonds and to insure the prompt payment of the principal thereof and interest thereon when due. (Acts 1990, No. 90-603, § 26.)

§ 41-10-516. Special funds.

For the purpose of providing funds for the payment of the principal of and interest on the bonds issued by the authority under the provisions of this article, there is hereby created and irrevocably pledged to the payment of such obligations a special and continuing trust fund which shall consist of all receipts and income from rents contracted for and received by the authority under leases of the facility or facilities constructed with the proceeds from the sale of the bonds. There shall be created within said special and continuing trust fund a reserve fund account of said authority in the state treasury in which shall be placed as trust fund and held separate and apart from all other moneys of the state or of the authority, (1) any moneys left after the completion of the facility and the payment of all costs in connection therewith and in connection with the issuance of the bonds, and, (2) all excess rentals and other surplus income from the facility or facilities constructed with the proceeds from the sale of the bonds remaining each fiscal year after payment of all charges and expenses of operating and maintaining such facility or facilities during such fiscal year, including all payments required to be made during such fiscal year with respect to the bonds issued for such facility or facilities. Said reserve fund shall be held by the state treasurer in trust for the authority and the holders of its bonds and may be invested at the direction of the authority. Said reserve fund shall be used to pay, when due and payable, any installment of principal or interest or both on the bonds for which said fund was created which cannot be paid out of current revenues or other moneys of the authority. Said funds shall not be diverted or used for any other purpose. There shall also be created in said special and continuing trust fund an account thereof in which shall be deposited, segregated and held only the amounts reasonably estimated to be necessary for the maintenance, operation and upkeep of said facilities with all excess moneys at the end of each fiscal year being transferred to the reserve fund. (Acts 1990, No. 90-603, § 27.)

§ 41-10-517. Exemption from taxation.

The properties of the authority and the income therefrom, all lease agreements made by the authority and all bonds and promissory notes issued by the authority, the interest thereon, the coupons, if any, applicable thereto, the income therefrom and all lien notices with respect thereto, and all purchases and use of property by the authority shall be forever exempt from any and all taxation in the state or in any county, municipality or political subdivision thereof. (Acts 1990, No. 90-603, § 28.)

§ 41-10-518. Venue for actions.

Any action to protect or enforce any rights under the provisions of this article shall be brought in the circuit court of Montgomery county, Alabama. (Acts 1990, No. 90-603, § 29.)

§ 41-10-519. Fees of secretary of state.

There shall be no fees paid to the secretary of state for any work done in connection with the incorporation or dissolution of the authority. (Acts 1990, No. 90-603, § 30.)

§ 41-10-520. Interest on bonds exempt from federal income tax.

The authority shall have the power to make such payments to the United States of America as the directors deem necessary to cause the interest on any bonds of the authority to be and remain exempt from federal income taxation. The authority shall have the power to make agreements respecting the investment of funds of the authority necessary in order that the interest income on bonds of the authority be and remain exempt from federal income taxation. (Acts 1990, No. 90-603, § 31.)

§ 41-10-521. Dissolution.

When all bonds and securities issued by the authority and all obligations assumed by it under the provisions of this article shall have been paid in full, the then president of the authority may thereupon execute and deliver in the name of, and in behalf of, the authority an appropriate deed or deeds, to which the seal of the authority shall be affixed and attested by the secretary of the authority, conveying all facilities, properties and other assets then owned by the authority to such agency of the state as shall be designated by the governor. The then directors of the authority may at such time file with the secretary of state a written statement, subscribed and sworn to by each of them, reciting the payment in full of all bonds theretofore issued by the authority and the execution and delivery of such deed or deeds, which statement shall be filed by the secretary of state and recorded with the certificate of incorporation of the authority, and thereupon the authority shall stand dissolved. (Acts 1990, No. 90-603, § 32.)

§ 41-10-522. Exemption of leases of facilities from competitive bid laws.

All leases of facilities made by the authority shall be exempt from the provisions and requirements of chapter 16 of this title of the code. (Acts 1990, No. 90-603, § 32.)

§ 41-10-523. Exemption from sunset law.

The authority shall not be governed by the provisions of chapter 20 of this title of the code (originally enacted as Act No. 512 of the 1976 Regular Session of the legislature of Alabama). (Acts 1990, No. 90-603, § 33.)

CHAPTER 11.

ALABAMA ACADEMY OF HONOR.

Sec.
41-11-6. Maximum amount and use of annual
appropriation.

———

Code commissioner's note. — Section two of Acts 1990, No. 90-106 provides: "The existence of the academy of honor created and functioned pursuant to sections 41-11-1 through 41-11-6, Code of Alabama 1975, is hereby continued, and said code sections are hereby expressly preserved."

§ 41-11-6. Maximum amount and use of annual appropriation.

The academy shall receive an annual appropriation not to exceed $6,000.00, which shall be fixed by the legislature during each regular session thereof. The appropriation provided shall be used by the academy to pay for stationery, membership certificates, membership pins or plaques or the like, an annual banquet for members and such other necessary or appropriate expenses incurred in carrying out the purposes of the academy. (Acts 1965, 3rd Ex. Sess., No. 15, p. 219, § 6; Acts 1990, No. 90-106, § 3.)

The 1990 amendment, effective March 7, 1990, substituted an annual appropriation of $6,000.00 for an annual appropriation of $2,000.00.

CHAPTER 13.

PUBLIC RECORDS.

ARTICLE 1.

GENERAL PROVISIONS.

§ 41-13-5. Destruction, etc., of public records having no significance, importance or value.

Any public records, books, papers, newspapers, files, printed books, manuscripts, tapes or other public records which have no significance, importance or value may, upon the advice and recommendation of the custodian thereof and upon the further advice, recommendation and consent of the state or local government records commission be destroyed or otherwise disposed of. The state and local government records commissions are hereby authorized and empowered to make such orders, rules, and regulations as may be necessary or proper to carry the provisions of this section into effect. (Acts 1945, No. 293, p. 486, § 3; Acts 1987, No. 87-658, p. 1165, § 1.)

ARTICLE 2.

STATE AND LOCAL GOVERNMENT RECORDS COMMISSIONS.

§ 41-13-22. Local government records commission created; composition; certain members subject to removal; compensation of members generally; meetings.

There is hereby created a local government records commission consisting of 12 members as follows: the director of the department of archives and history, who shall be the chairman of the commission; the chief examiner of the department of examiners of public accounts; the attorney general; the secretary of state; one member from the University of Alabama, to be designated by the head of the department of history; one member from Auburn University, to be designated by the head of the department of history; one probate judge who is not a chairman of a county commission; two chairmen of county commissions who are not also probate judges; one county tax assessor and two city clerks, to be appointed by the governor. The representatives of the University of Alabama and Auburn University, the probate judges, the two chairmen of county commissions, the tax assessors, and the two city clerks may be removed by the governor at any time. No salary or compensation shall be allowed any member of the commission except expenses incurred in the performance of their duties, which expenses shall be paid pursuant to article 2 of chapter 7 of Title 36. The commission shall hold regular quarterly meetings in January, April, July and October of each year and at other times upon the call of the chairman. (Acts 1955, No. 565, p. 1226, § 7; Acts 1987, No. 87-658, p. 1165, § 1.)

§ 41-13-23. Local government commission to make determination as to county, municipal, etc., records to be preserved or destroyed, etc., after microfilming; classification of records; officials not to cause destruction, etc., of records without prior approval of commission.

The local government records commission shall be charged with the responsibility of determining which county, municipal, and other local government records shall be permanently preserved because of historical value and which county, municipal, and other local government records may be destroyed or otherwise disposed of after they have been microfilmed. The commission may classify the different types of records accordingly.

No county, municipal, or other local government official shall cause any county, municipal, or other local government record to be destroyed or otherwise disposed of without first obtaining the approval of the local government records commission. (Acts 1955, No. 565, p. 1226, § 8; Acts 1987, No. 87-658, p. 1165, § 1.)

Collateral references. — Defamation: privilege accorded state or local governmental administrative records relating to private individual member of public. 40 ALR4th 318.

What constitutes legitimate research justifying inspection of state or local public records not open to inspection by general public. 40 ALR4th 333.

§ 41-13-24. Conduct of surveys by state and local government records commissions authorized; issuance, etc., by commissions of regulations classifying public records, etc.

(a) Both the state records commission and the local government records commission are hereby empowered to conduct surveys of public records in carrying out the provisions of this chapter.

(b) Both commissions shall from time to time issue regulations classifying all public records and shall prescribe the period for which records of each class shall be retained. Such records may be permanent or for a lesser number of years. Such regulations may from time to time be amended or repealed. Prior to issuing such regulations, both the state records commission and the local government records commission shall consider the following factors:

(1) Actions at law and administrative proceedings in which the production of public records might be necessary or desirable;

(2) State and federal statutes of limitation applicable to such actions or proceedings;

(3) The availability of information contained in public records from other sources;

(4) The actual or potential historical value of certain public records; and

(5) Such other matters as the commissions shall deem pertinent in order that public records be retained for as short a period as is commensurate with the interests of the public. (Acts 1955, No. 565, p. 1226, § 10; Acts 1987, No. 87-658, p. 1165, § 1.)

Collateral references. — Defamation: privilege accorded state or local governmental administrative records relating to private individual member of public. 40 ALR4th 318.

What constitutes legitimate research justifying inspection of state or local public records not open to inspection by general public. 40 ALR4th 333.

§ 41-13-25. Payment of expenses of certain members of state and local government records commissions.

The expenses allowed by law for the county, municipal, and other local government officials who are members of the local government records commission shall be paid pursuant to article 2 of chapter 7 of Title 36. The expenses allowed by law for the representatives of the University of Alabama and Auburn University who are members of either the state records commission or the local government records commission shall be paid by their respective institutions. (Acts 1955, No. 565, p. 1226, § 11; Acts 1987, No. 87-658, p. 1165, § 1.)

ARTICLE 3.

PHOTOGRAPHING OR MICROPHOTOGRAPHING OF RECORDS.

§ 41-13-41. Photographing or microphotographing of state records centralized in department of archives and history; charges for photographing or microphotographing.

Collateral references. — What constitutes legitimate research justifying inspection of state or local public records not open to inspection by general public. 40 ALR4th 333.

CHAPTER 14.

STATE FUNDS GENERALLY.

ARTICLE 1.

STATE DEPOSITARIES.

§ 41-14-2. Application for designation as state depositary to be filed with state treasurer, etc.; verified statement as to assets and liabilities, capital stock, etc., and deposit of bonds or securities to accompany application.

Before any bank or trust company shall be designated as a state depositary, it shall file with the state treasurer an application in writing to be designated as a state depositary under the terms of this article.

Such bank or trust company shall accompany such application with a statement, verified by the affidavit of its president or other executive head, setting forth the amount of its paid-in capital stock, the amount of its surplus and undivided profits, its principal place of business, the length of time it has been engaged in business and its assets and liabilities at the time of making application.

Such bank or trust company shall also accompany the application with a deposit of bonds or securities in an amount not less than $10,000.00 par or face value or with receipts of an authorized holder of such bonds or securities evidencing the fact that bonds or securities in an amount not less than $10,000.00 par or face value are being held by such authorized holder as security for the deposit of state funds, such bonds or securities to be released only to the lawful holder of such receipts upon presentation of the receipts. A copy of such application and statement shall be filed with the director of finance.

The only bonds or securities which can be accepted as security or for which receipts can be accepted as security for the purposes set forth in this section are the direct obligations of the state of Alabama or the direct obligations of the United States government, the bonds and other securities issued by the Alabama highway finance corporation, the bonds and other securities issued by the Alabama public schools corporation and the bonds to secure the payment of which any rentals or revenues of the state docks department have been pledged prior to January 1, 1948, and other securities of the type which may be used to secure deposits of the state under section 41-14-35. All securities or receipts so deposited must be accepted at market or par value determined at the discretion of the state treasurer. Such securities or receipts therefor shall be registered in the name of the bank or trust company depositing the same, and the securities or receipts therefor shall be kept and held by the treasurer, and it shall be so stated in said application, as a security to the state for the faithful performance of the duties of such bank or trust company as a state depositary and that the bank or trust company will well and truly account for and pay over any moneys or funds of the state upon the check or order of the treasurer.

The securities money shall be deposited exclusively for the purposes set forth in this section with and held by a trust department of a bank organized under the laws of this state or under the laws of the United States having their principal place of business in this state which may be the same bank as holds the deposit, or a federal reserve bank or branch thereof or a federal home loan bank serving savings institutions located in this state or deposited for safekeeping with any third party bank or trust company organized either under the laws of the state of Alabama or of the United States having their principal place of business in this state, each of which shall be an authorized holder. The authorized holder shall issue a receipt for such securities in accordance with this section. (Code 1907, § 642; Code 1923, § 892; Acts 1939, No. 195, p. 349; Code 1940, T. 55, § 380; Acts 1943, No. 14, p. 17, § 1; Acts 1947, No. 411, p. 301, § 1; Acts 1990, No. 90-638, § 1.)

The 1990 amendment, effective April 25, 1990, in the third paragraph, in the first sentence substituted "receipts of an authorized holder of such bonds or securities" for "federal reserve bank receipts," and "such authorized holder" for "a federal reserve bank"; rewrote the fourth paragraph, and added the last paragraph.

§ 41-14-6. Depositaries to remit to treasurer state funds received, etc., in excess of authorized amount; withdrawal of state funds from and revocation of authority to act as state depositary of bank or trust company failing to remit surplus state funds to treasurer. Repealed by Acts 1990, No. 90-638, § 3, effective April 25, 1990.

ARTICLE 2.

DEPOSIT OF STATE FUNDS.

§ 41-14-32. Determination of income from time deposits, open accounts; determination of funds needed for projected monthly expenditures and payments; depositaries of funds needed for projected daily expenditures; excess funds to be deposited in time deposits, open accounts, in state depositaries; investment of funds which will be in treasury 30 days or less. Repealed by Acts 1990, No. 90-638, § 4, effective April 25, 1990.

§ 41-14-33. Execution by state treasurer of contracts with state depositories covering time deposits, open account; early withdrawal; payment and rate of interest.

(a) The state treasurer is authorized to enter into contracts with the state depositories for the deposit of state funds in time deposits, open account, having maturities of 91 days, six months or one year; provided that any such contract for a time deposit, open account, having a maturity of 91 days shall provide for early withdrawal of funds upon written notice delivered at least 14 days (or the minimum period of time as is prescribed by applicable banking regulation then in effect) prior to the date of withdrawal.

(b) The rate of interest to be paid on each time deposit, open account, of 91 days, six months and one year maturity shall correspond to the rate borne by United States treasury obligations of comparable maturity and shall be calculated as the average auction rate for United States treasury bills with maturities of 91 days and 26 weeks, respectively, as established at the four most recent auctions held immediately prior to the execution of the contract for such time deposit, open account, or where the maturity of the time deposit, open account, is one year, as established at the most recent auction for United States treasury bills with maturities of one year held immediately prior to the execution of the contract.

(c) The interest shall be payable in accordance with section 41-14-34. (Acts 1967, No. 3, p. 336, § 4; Acts 1971, 1st Ex. Sess., No. 62, p. 99; Acts 1975, 1st Ex. Sess., No. 1, § 2; Acts 1989, No. 89-868, p. 1743.)

The 1989 amendment, effective May 17, 1989, rewrote this section.

§ 41-14-34. How interest on time deposits, open account, calculated and paid; emergency withdrawal of funds on time deposit, open account.

(a) Interest shall be calculated on the basis of the contracts existing with respect to time deposits, open account, and shall be payable monthly to the state treasurer and by that officer paid into the state treasury to the credit of the general fund of the state.

(b) In the event of an emergency, the treasurer is authorized to comply with applicable banking regulations in order to receive all or any portion of the funds placed on time deposits, open account, on shorter notice than the agreement provides and to forfeit such amount of accrued and unpaid interest as may be required by such regulations. (Acts 1967, No. 3, p. 336, § 5; Acts 1983, 1st Ex. Sess., No. 83-80, p. 86.)

§ 41-14-35. Security for state money deposited in state depositaries in demand deposits and time deposits, open account.

(a) All state money deposited in state depositaries in demand accounts and time deposits, open account, shall be secured as required by section 5-5A-28 and article 1 of this chapter; provided, however, that for amounts deposited in time deposits, open account, and in demand accounts there may also be accepted as security for said deposits bonds and other securities issued by any agency or instrumentality of the United States of America, any general obligation bonds or securities of any of the various states of the continental United States or any of their instrumentalities which have a rating of "A" or better by Moody's Investors Rating Services, Inc., New York City, or any successor firm to that corporation, any general obligation bonds or warrants of any county or any municipality of the state of Alabama, warrants or securities of any county secured by a pledge of the special road, bridge and public building tax authorized by article XI, section 215 of the Constitution, bonds or warrants of any county or city board of education secured by a pledge of taxes levied under the authority of constitutional amendment 3 or any other constitutional amendment authorizing the levying of special ad valorem taxes for schools or secured by a pledge of county or city sales taxes, any gasoline tax anticipation warrants secured by a pledge of gasoline tax revenues derived from the gasoline excise tax levied by the state and distributed to counties under section 40-17-74 or any successor statute, electric, natural gas, sewer and water revenue bonds issued by any municipality of the state of Alabama or any board created by or with the consent of any such municipality, and mortgage-backed securities acceptable to the state treasurer in accordance with subsection (d) of this section, which securities may be issued and held in either definitive or book entry form. All securities and other collateral may be held by any federal reserve bank or branch thereof or a federal home loan bank serving savings institutions located in this state, by any bank which operates a trust department, or by such other depository as may be examined, supervised or regulated by the board of governors of the federal reserve system or the state banking department. Banks which exercise trust powers may hold collateral as security for deposits situated in that bank, or in any other bank or other depository.

(b) To be eligible to secure state deposits, revenue or limited obligation bonds or warrants must have a current average annual debt service coverage of at least two times.

(c) No security shall be required for the amount of any deposit or account to the extent said deposit or account is insured by the federal deposit insurance corporation or any successor federal insurance corporation or agency.

(d) The state treasurer is authorized to disapprove any security offered or pledged as collateral. (Acts 1967, No. 3, p. 336, § 6; Acts 1990, No. 90-638, § 2.)

The 1990 amendment, effective April 25, 1990, in subsection (a), in the first sentence substituted "section 5-5A-28" for "section 5-1-14" near the beginning, deleted "and" preceding "electric, natural gas, sewer and water revenue bonds" near the end, added the language beginning "and mortgage-backed securities acceptable" at the end of the sentence, added the second and third sentences, and added "or any successor federal insurance corporation or agency" at the end of subsection (c).

CHAPTER 15.

STATE INSURANCE FUND.

The 1990 amendment, effective April 19, 1990, substituted "direct physical loss" for "loss by fire, lightning, windstorm and hail or fire and all the perils included under extended coverage," inserted "and contents for the perils as may be determined by the finance director," and inserted "machinery," preceding "furni- ture, fixtures or."

§ 41-15-1. Creation; purpose.

There shall be a fund, to be known as the state insurance fund, carried by the state treasurer for the purpose of insuring direct physical loss on buildings and contents for the perils as may be determined by the finance director in which title in whole or in part is vested in the state of Alabama or any of its agencies or institutions or in which funds provided by the state have been used for the purchase of the land, construction of the building, purchase or maintenance of any equipment, machinery, furniture, fixtures or supplies in such buildings and public school buildings together with the contents of all such buildings; provided, that this section shall neither repeal nor in any manner affect the provisions of any local act of the legislature or any general act of local application authorizing city or county boards of education or district boards of education of independent school districts to insure school buildings and property either in the state insurance fund or in an insurance company, whichever in the opinion of such board provides the best coverage for such school buildings and property. (Acts 1923, No. 593, p. 769; Code 1923, § 8539; Code 1940, T. 28, § 317; Acts 1949, No. 675, p. 1045, § 1; Acts 1957, No. 596, p. 833, § 1; Acts 1990, No. 90-569, § 1.)

Cross references. — As to the division of risk management, see art. 12, ch. 4, T. 41.

§ 41-15-2. Department of finance to administer chapter; administrator of state insurance fund.

The department of finance is hereby constituted and designated as the agency through which this chapter shall be administered, and the director of said department is empowered with such authority as may be necessary to carry out its purposes.

The director of said department, with the approval of the governor, may appoint a risk manager, as administrator of the state insurance fund, who is familiar with insurance customs and practices and is otherwise qualified by actual experience in the underwriting of risks and adjustment of losses, to assist the director of said department in carrying out the purpose of this chapter. The said risk manager, shall install and keep an accurate system of accounting and statistical records and shall adjust losses, make appraisals of insured properties for insurance purposes, when necessary, and shall handle or supervise the handling of all other details incident to carrying out the provisions of this chapter. The risk manager, shall furnish to the department of finance each month a statement showing in detail the accumulated income and disbursements during the fiscal year, together with a financial statement showing assets and liabilities of the state insurance fund. At the close of each fiscal year the risk manager, shall furnish to the said department an annual statement of the affairs of the state insurance fund. The unearned net premium computed on a pro rata basis shall be considered as a liability and carried as a reserve. Said risk manager, shall file with the said department a bond in the penal sum of $10,000.00, executed by a surety company authorized to do business in this state, conditioned upon faithful performance of his duties, payable to the state of Alabama. (Acts 1923, No. 593, p. 769; Code 1923, § 8540; Acts 1936-37, Ex. Sess., No. 219, p. 260; Acts 1939, No. 112, p. 144; Code 1940, T. 28, § 318; Acts 1949, No. 675, p. 1045, § 2; Acts 1990, No. 90-569, § 2.)

The 1990 amendment, effective April 19, 1990, substituted "risk manager" for "actuary" throughout the section, in the second paragraph, in the first sentence substituted "a risk manager" for "an actuary" and "insurance customs" for "insurance custom," and "insured properties" for "state-owned properties" in the second sentence.

§ 41-15-3. Inspection and appraisal of property.

The director of finance may make or cause to be made a survey and appraisal of all property, to assist in the determination of the amount of insurance to be carried on the several properties and to classify all exposures or property. (Acts 1923, No. 593, p. 769; Code 1923, § 8541; Acts 1939, No. 112, p. 144; Code 1940, T. 28, § 319; Acts 1990, No. 90-569, § 3.)

The 1990 amendment, effective April 19, 1990, rewrote this section.

§ 41-15-4. Value for which state property to be insured; annual certification to department of finance of description and value of buildings and equipment; insuring of county school buildings; inspection of public property and distribution of copies of reports thereof.

(a) All covered property shall be insured for no more than its replacement cost and shall be insured for no less than 80 percent of its actual cash value. Replacement cost coverage may be provided with an amount of insurance as agreed upon by the proper insuring authority and the risk manager based upon a written statement of values. Replacement cost shall be the cost to repair or replace property with comparable materials of like kind and quality by generally accepted construction methods or technology to serve the same function as the lost or damaged property. Actual cash value shall be replacement cost less depreciation. No payment for a loss shall exceed the limit of the policy.

(b) The officer or person having charge by law of insuring any public building, contents, machinery, and equipment shall annually certify to the department of finance the description and the value of all buildings, contents, machinery and equipment under his supervision or control on forms prescribed by the department for the purpose of showing the character of the risk and determining the rate of premium. No coverage shall be issued unless such certificate is on file in the office of the department of finance or the director has waived, in writing, the filing of the same.

(c) Buildings, contents, machinery and equipment owned by any county, city, or school district and used for school purposes or under control of a board of education may be insured under the provisions of this chapter.

(d) The department of finance may cause to be surveyed, annually, if practicable, all public property coming within the provisions of this chapter, and the officer or person in charge of the public property shall receive a copy of such report. A survey shall be an examination of property for physical discrepancies, construction characteristics, usage or occupancy. (Acts 1923, No. 593, p. 769; Code 1923, § 8542; Acts 1936-37, Ex. Sess., No. 219, p. 260; Acts 1939, No. 112, p. 144; Code 1940, T. 28, § 320; Acts 1949, No. 675, p. 1045, § 3; Acts 1990, No. 90-569, § 4.)

The 1990 amendment, effective April 19, 1990, rewrote this section.

§ 41-15-5. Basis upon which premiums charged generally; reinsurance.

The net premium charged shall be based on the current commercial rate with not less than a 40 percent discount. The risk manager with the approval of the director of finance may purchase such reinsurance as may in the opinion of the risk manager, be necessary for the proper distribution of the risk. The risk manager shall collect such reinsurance upon any loss sustained and pay the same into the state insurance fund. (Acts 1923, No. 593, p. 769; Code 1923, § 8543; Acts 1936-37, Ex. Sess., No. 219, p. 260; Acts 1939, No. 112, p. 144; Code 1940, T. 28, § 321; Acts 1949, No. 675, p. 1045, § 4; Acts 1967, No. 435, p. 1104; Acts 1990, No. 90-569, § 5.)

The 1990 amendment, effective April 19, 1990, rewrote this section.

§ 41-15-6. Payment of premiums generally.

All premiums shall be paid to the department of finance, not later than 60 days from the effective date of such insurance or renewal thereof, by the treasurer or executive officer of the agency affected. Such funds shall be promptly transmitted to the state treasurer, who shall place the same to the credit of the state insurance fund. Upon failure or refusal of any officer to comply with the provisions of this section with regard to the payment of premiums, the state comptroller shall, when requested by the director of the department of finance, deduct from any funds due or which may become due the delinquent amount of unpaid premiums and pay the same to the state insurance fund. (Acts 1923, No. 593, p. 769; Code 1923, § 8544; Acts 1936-37, Ex. Sess., No. 219, p. 260; Acts 1939, No. 112, p. 144; Code 1940, T. 28, § 322; Acts 1949, No. 675, p. 1045, § 5; Acts 1990, No. 90-569, § 6.)

The 1990 amendment, effective April 19, 1990, deleted "of such" following "All" at the beginning of the first sentence.

§ 41-15-7. Pro rata premiums. Repealed by Acts 1990, No. 90-569, §§ 7, 12, effective April 19, 1990.

§ 41-15-8. Resolution of disagreements between department of finance and person in charge of state property as to value of property, premium rates, etc.

In the event a disagreement arises between the department of finance and any person or persons in charge of any insured property as to its replacement cost or actual cash value or the amount payable under the claim for loss or the proper premium rate or rates, the matter in disagreement shall be determined by a third person to be agreed upon by the director of finance on the one hand and the person or persons disagreeing with him on the other. In case of inability to agree on such third person, the governor shall appoint a third person to determine the question, and his decision thereon shall be binding on all parties concerned. (Acts 1923, No. 593, p. 769; Code 1923, § 8552; Acts 1936-37, Ex. Sess., No. 219, p. 260; Acts 1939, No. 112, p. 144; Code 1940, T. 28, § 326; Acts 1990, No. 90-569, § 8.)

The 1990 amendment, effective April 19, 1990, substituted "insured property as to its replacement cost or actual cash value" for "state property as to its true value" in the first sentence.

§ 41-15-9. Director of finance may prescribe forms of policies, etc., and make rules and regulations for administration of chapter.

The director of finance is authorized to prescribe insurance coverages, forms of policies, proofs of losses and other forms; to define terms; make rules and regulations; to provide additional experience and schedule rating factors and appropriate deductibles from losses as may be necessary or expedient for the proper administration of the provisions of this chapter. (Acts 1923, No. 593, p. 769; Code 1923, § 8553; Acts 1936-37, Ex. Sess., No. 219, p. 260; Code 1940, T. 28, § 327; Acts 1949, No. 675, p. 1045, § 8; Acts 1990, No. 90-569, § 9.)

The 1990 amendment, effective April 19, 1990, inserted "insurance coverages," deleted "and" following "other forms," inserted "define terms," deleted "such" preceding "rules," and added the language beginning "to provide additional experience" and ending "deductibles from losses."

§ 41-15-10.1. Repealed by Acts 1984, No. 84-313, p. 694, § 1, effective May 16, 1984.

Code commissioner's note. — Acts 1984, No. 84-313, § 2, provides: "Such amounts as have heretofore been transferred to the state general fund from the state insurance fund pursuant to Act No. 80-90, or any part thereof, may be transferred back from the state general fund to the state insurance fund, with interest at eight percent per annum, whenever the state finance director, with the approval of the governor, determines that there are sufficient funds in the state general fund."

§ 41-15-11. Limitations upon expenditure of funds; employees subject to merit system.

No part of the funds provided for in section 41-15-10 shall be used to increase the salary of any state employee. Only the salary of the designated risk manager, stenographic secretary, inspector, clerical force and such other employees and expenses as may be necessary for the efficient administration of the provisions of this chapter shall be paid from these funds. Such expenditures shall be limited to that amount appropriated by the legislature.

All employees as provided in this section shall be subject to the Merit System Act. (Acts 1923, No. 593, p. 769; Code 1923, § 8550; Acts 1936-37, Ex. Sess., No. 219, p. 260; Code 1940, T. 28, § 325; Acts 1949, No. 675, p. 1045, § 7; Acts 1957, No. 596, p. 833, § 2; Acts 1990, No. 90-569, § 10.)

The 1990 amendment, effective April 19, 1990, in the first paragraph substituted "risk manager and such other employees and expenses" for "administrator, stenographic secretary, inspector, clerical force and such other expense" in the second sentence and deleted "and all such expenditures shall be limited to six percent of the amount of premiums written in each year or so much thereof as may be required" at the end of the last sentence.

CHAPTER 15A.

PENNY TRUST FUND.

Code commissioner's note. — This chapter was contingent on the passage of a constitutional amendment providing for a "penny trust fund." The amendment, proposed by Acts 1989, No. 89-462, was voted on June 5, 1990 and passed. The amendment was proclaimed ratified on July 13, 1990 and became Amendment No. 512.

Cross references. — For constitutional amendment establishing the "penny trust fund," see Amendment No. 512 in Volume 2 of this Code.

§ 41-15A-1. Authorization, procedures, and forms.

The state treasurer is authorized to accept gifts, donations, and bequests from any person, association, company, or corporation wishing to contribute voluntarily to the penny trust fund. Any person, association, company, or corporation may deposit funds in the penny trust fund through the auspices of the state treasurer or in the appropriately designated depository. The state treasurer may seek the voluntary participation of banks, financial institutions, or other businesses in receiving and transferring donations to the penny trust fund. The state treasurer shall promulgate rules and regulations governing the procedures and administration for the voluntary donations, contributions, and transfers to the penny trust fund. Donation and transmittal forms and promotional materials may be developed and distributed as authorized by the state treasurer. (Acts 1989, No. 89-667, p. 1325, § 1.)

§ 41-15A-2. Division of proceeds.

Proceeds from the penny trust fund which are dedicated for the promotion of the public health shall be deposited in the general fund and divided as follows:

(1) Fifty percent to the department of public health for its programs to reduce infant mortality and/or improve child health;

(2) Fifty percent to the department of public health for its indigent health care programs.

Proceeds from the penny trust fund which are dedicated for the promotion of the public schools shall be deposited in the Alabama special educational trust fund and divided as follows:

(1) Twenty-five percent for programs to prevent substance abuse, including the employment of school counselors;

(2) Twenty-five percent for the immunization of children;

(3) Twenty-five percent for programs to promote health and disease prevention including the employment of school nurses;

(4) Twenty-five percent for student nutrition and nutritional education. (Acts 1989, No. 89-667, p. 1325, § 2.)

§ 41-15A-3. Tax deduction.

Donations and bequests to the penny trust fund by individuals, associations, corporations, and companies shall be exempt from all county and municipal taxes and deductible from state taxes in accordance with section 40-18-15. (Acts 1989, No. 89-667, p. 1325, § 3.)

§ 41-15A-4. Income tax return.

Taxpayers who file income tax returns and who are entitled to an income tax refund from the state department of revenue sufficient to make a donation to the penny trust fund may designate a sum as a voluntary donation from their refunds and such amounts shall be credited to the penny trust fund. The state department of revenue shall print on the face of the appropriate state income tax forms a space for the taxpayers to designate that a donation is to be made to the penny trust fund from the income tax refund due. The space for designating the donation shall provide for a checkoff box with the dollar amount to be voluntarily entered by the taxpayer, commencing for the tax year 1990 and thereafter. (Acts 1989, No. 89-667, p. 1325, § 4.)

§ 41-15A-5. State and local public funds.

No state, county, or municipal funds are to be deposited into the penny trust fund. (Acts 1989, No. 89-667, p. 1325, § 5.)

CHAPTER 16.

PUBLIC CONTRACTS.

ARTICLE 1.

GENERAL PROVISIONS.

§ 41-16-1. Withdrawal by contractor of amounts retained from payments under contract.

Cited in Urban San. Corp. v. City of Pell City, 662 F. Supp. 1041 (N.D. Ala. 1986).

§ 41-16-3. Timely execution of state contracts required.

Whenever the state of Alabama is a party to any contract, said contract must be executed by all parties in a timely fashion. When a party to a contract, other than the state, has fully executed his responsibility under the contract and there remains only the payment of funds by the state, said payment must be made in a timely manner. If the amount due by the state is not in dispute, payment must be made within 30 days after the other party has completed his portion of the contract and presented a proper invoice. If the amount payable is not paid within 30 days, interest on said amount shall be charged. Said interest rate shall be the legal amount currently charged by the state. Said interest shall be paid from the same fund or source from which the contract principal is paid. If the amount due by the state is in dispute, the state is hereby required to notify the other party of the fact that it was questioning the amount of the invoice within 15 days after receipt of the invoice. (Acts 1984, No. 84-407, p. 954.)

Collateral references. — Amount of appropriation as limitation on damages for breach of contract recoverable by one contracting with government agency. 40 ALR4th 998.

ARTICLE 2.

COMPETITIVE BIDDING ON PUBLIC CONTRACTS GENERALLY.

Cross references. — As to nonapplicability of competitive bid laws to a county industrial development authority, and its directors, officers, etc., see § 11-92A-19.

§ 41-16-20. Contracts for which competitive bidding required generally.

All contracts of whatever nature for labor, services or work or for the purchase or lease of materials, equipment, supplies or other personal property, involving $5,000.00 or more made or on behalf of any state department, board, bureau, commission, committee, institution, corporation, authority or office shall, except as otherwise provided in this article, be let by free and open competitive bidding, on sealed bids, to the lowest responsible bidder. (Acts 1957, No. 343, p. 452, § 1; Acts 1961, No. 870, p. 1365; Acts 1976, No. 751, p. 1032, § 1; Acts 1989, No. 89-687, p. 1351, § 1.)

The 1989 amendment, effective May 11, 1989, substituted "$5,000.00" for "$2,000.00."

Cited in Urban San. Corp. v. City of Pell City, 662 F. Supp. 1041 (N.D. 1986).

Collateral references.
Waiver of competitive bidding requirements for state and local public building and construction contracts. 40 ALR4th 968.

§ 41-16-21. Contracts for which competitive bidding not required generally; certain institutions, state agencies, etc., exempt from provisions of article relating to powers, duties, etc., of department of finance; said institutions, etc., to establish and maintain facilities necessary for competitive bidding in operation and management thereof; contracts entered into in violation of article declared void.

(a) Competitive bids shall not be required for utility services where no competition exists or where rates are fixed by law or ordinance, and the competitive bidding requirements of this article shall not apply to: the purchase of insurance by the state; contracts for the securing of services of attorneys, physicians, architects, teachers, superintendents of construction, artists, appraisers, engineers or other individuals possessing a high degree of professional skill where the personality of the individual plays a decisive part; contracts of employment in the regular civil service of the state; tourist advertising by the state bureau of tourism and travel authorized under section 41-7-4 or advertising of the state parks by the department of conservation and natural resources; purchases of alcoholic beverages only by the alcoholic beverage control board; purchases for any hospital or campus medical facility which has a total licensed bed capacity of no less than 800 beds at the time of passage of this act, operated by any state department, except the department of mental health and mental retardation, board, bureau, commission, committee, institution, upon approval of the governing board of said institution, corporation, authority or office; purchases by the state highway department of local materials from any property owners in the vicinity of a project on which such local materials shall be used or purchases and contracts for repair of equipment used in the construction and maintenance of highways by the state highway department; purchases of products made or manufactured by the blind or visually handicapped under the direction or supervision of the Alabama Institute for Deaf and Blind in accordance with sections 21-2-1 through 21-2-4; purchases of maps or photographs purchased from any federal agency; purchases of manuscripts, maps, books, pamphlets or periodicals purchased for the use of any state library or any other library in the state supported in whole or in part by state funds; contractual services and purchases of commodities for which there is only one vendor or supplier; contractual services and purchases of personal property, which by their very nature are impossible of award by competitive bidding; barter transactions by the department of corrections; and purchases, contracts or repairs by the state docks department when it is deemed by the director of state docks and the secretary-treasurer of the state docks department that such purchases, contracts or repairs are impractical of award by competitive bidding due to the exigencies of time or interference with the flow of commerce; provided, that the director of state docks and the secretary-treasurer of the state docks department shall place a sworn statement in writing in the permanent file or records setting out the emergency relied upon and the necessity for negotiation instead of proceeding by competitive bidding in said instance, and such sworn statement shall be open to public inspection. A copy of such sworn statement shall be furnished forthwith to the chief examiner of public accounts.

(b) All educational and eleemosynary institutions governed by a board of trustees or other similar governing body and the state docks department shall be exempt from the provisions of this article which relate to the powers, duties, authority, restrictions and limitations conferred or imposed upon the department of finance, division of purchases and stores; provided, however, that the said educational and eleemosynary institutions, the state docks department and the other state agencies exempted from the provisions of this article or any part hereof shall let by free and open competitive bidding on sealed bids to the lowest responsible bidder all contracts of whatever nature for labor, services or work or for the purchase or lease of materials, equipment, supplies or other personal property involving $2,000.00 or more. The said institutions, departments and agencies shall establish and maintain such purchasing facilities as may be necessary to carry out the intent and purpose of this article by complying with the requirements for competitive bidding in the operation and management of each such institution, department or agency.

(c) Contracts entered into in violation of this article shall be void.

(d) Nothing in this section shall be construed as repealing sections 9-2-106 and 9-2-107. (Acts 1957, No. 343, p. 452, § 2; Acts 1961, No. 870, p. 1365; Acts 1969, No. 1053, p. 1973, §§ 1, 2; Acts 1976, No. 751, p. 1032, § 2; Acts 1985, No. 85-689, p. 1106; Acts 1990, No. 90-631, § 1.)

The 1990 amendment, effective April 25, 1990, inserted "or advertising of the state parks by the department of conservation and natural resources" in the first sentence of subsection (a).

Collateral references. — Waiver of competitive bidding requirements for state and local public building and construction contracts. 40 ALR4th 968.

Public contracts: low bidder's monetary relief against state or local agency for nonaward of contract. 65 ALR4th 93.

§ 41-16-21.2. Exemption of certain departments or agencies whose principal business is honorariums from competitive bid laws.

All laws to the contrary notwithstanding, any state department or agency whose principal business is honorariums is hereby exempted from the provisions of the state competitive bid laws on purchases and contracts for services made by such department or agency. (Acts 1982, No. 82-565; Acts 1989, No. 89-963, p. 1930.)

The 1989 amendment, effective May 19, 1989, deleted "and whose annual appropriation, from the legislature is less than $75,000" following "honorariums."

§ 41-16-22. Competitive bidding not required on purchases from federal government.

Collateral references. — Waiver of competitive bidding requirements for state and local public building and construction contracts. 40 ALR4th 968.

§ 41-16-23. Letting of contracts without public advertisement authorized in case of emergencies affecting public health, safety, etc.

Collateral references. — Waiver of competitive bidding requirements for state and local public building and construction contracts. 40 ALR4th 968.

§ 41-16-24. Advertisement for and solicitation of bids; bids to be sealed; opening of bids; bids, etc., to be retained and to be open to public inspection; contracts not to be split to avoid requirements of article; certain partial contracts declared void.

(a) The purchasing agent shall advertise for sealed bids on all purchases in excess of $5,000.00 by posting notice thereof on a bulletin board maintained outside his office door or by publication of notice thereof one time in a newspaper published in Montgomery county, Alabama, or in any other manner and for such lengths of time as he may determine; provided, however, that the purchasing agent shall also solicit sealed bids by sending notice by mail to all Alabama persons, firms or corporations who have filed a request in writing that they be listed for solicitation on bids for such particular items as are set forth in such request and such other persons, firms or corporations the purchasing agent deems necessary to insure competition. If any person, firm or corporation whose name is listed fails to respond to any solicitation for bids after the receipt of three such solicitations, such listing may be cancelled by the purchasing agent, at his discretion.

(b) All bids shall be sealed when received, shall be opened in public at the hour stated in the notice, and all original bids together with all documents pertaining to the award of the contract shall be retained and made a part of a permanent file or records and shall be open to public inspection.

(c) If the purchase or contract will involve an amount of $5,000.00 or less, the purchasing agent may make such purchases or contracts either upon the basis of sealed bids or in the open market, in his discretion.

(d) No purchase or contract involving an amount in excess of $5,000.00 shall be divided into parts involving amounts of $5,000.00 or less for the purpose of avoiding the requirements of this article. All such partial contracts involving $5,000.00 or less shall be void. (Acts 1957, No. 343, p. 452, § 6; Acts 1961, No. 870, p. 1365; Acts 1976, No. 751, p. 1032, § 4; Acts 1983, No. 83-773, p. 1414, § 1; Acts 1989, No. 89-687, p. 1351, § 2.)

The 1989 amendment, effective May 11, 1989, substituted "$5,000.00" for "$2,000.00" throughout the section.

Collateral references. — Waiver of compet-itive bidding requirements for state and local public building and construction contracts. 40 ALR4th 968.

§ 41-16-27. Manner of awarding contracts generally; award of negotiated contracts; records as to awarding of contracts to be open to public inspection; preference to be given to Alabama commodities, firms, etc., in contracts for purchase of personal property or contractual services; maximum duration of contracts for purchase of personal property or contractual services; awarding of medicaid contracts.

(a) When purchases are required to be made through competitive bidding, award shall, except as provided in subsection (e), be made to the lowest responsible bidder taking into consideration the qualities of the commodities proposed to be supplied, their conformity with specifications, the purposes for which required, the terms of delivery, transportation charges and the dates of delivery provided, that the awarding authority may at any time within five days after the bids are opened negotiate and award the contract to anyone, provided he secures a price at least five percent under the low acceptable bid. The award of such a negotiated contract shall be subject to approval by the director of finance and the governor. The awarding authority or requisitioning agency shall have the right to reject any bid if the price is deemed excessive or quality of product inferior.

(b) Each bid, with the name of the bidder, shall be entered on a record. Each record, with the successful bid indicated thereon and with the reasons for the award if not awarded to the lowest bidder shall, after award of the order or contract, be open to public inspection.

(c) The purchasing agent in the purchase of or contract for personal property or contractual services shall give preference, provided there is no sacrifice or loss in price or quality, to commodities produced in Alabama or sold by Alabama persons, firms or corporations.

(d) Contracts for the purchase of personal property or contractual services shall be let for periods not greater than three years.

(e) Contracts for the purchase of services for receiving, processing, and paying claims for services rendered recipients of the Alabama medicaid program authorized under section 22-6-7 which are required to be competitively bid may be awarded to the bidder whose proposal is most advantageous to the state, taking into consideration cost factors, program suitability factors (technical factors) including understanding of program requirements, management plan, excellence of program design, key personnel, corporate or company resources and designated location, and other factors including financial condition and capability of the bidder, corporate experience and past performance and priority of the business to insure the contract awarded is the best for the purposes required. Each of these criteria shall be given relative weight value as designated in the invitation to bid, with price retaining the most significant weight. Responsiveness to the bid shall be scored for each designated criteria. If, for reasons cited above, the bid selected is not from the lowest bidding contractor, the Alabama medicaid agency shall present its reasons for not recommending award to the low bidder to the medicaid interim committee. The committee shall evaluate the findings of the Alabama medicaid agency and must, by resolution, approve the action of the awarding authority before final awarding of any such contract. The committee shall also hear any valid appeals against the recommendation of the Alabama medicaid agency from the low bid contractor(s) whose bid was not selected. (Acts 1957, No. 343, p. 452, § 9; Acts 1961, No. 870, p. 1365; Acts 1976, No. 751, p. 1032, § 5; Acts 1982, No. 82-353; Acts 1990, No. 90-300, § 1.)

The 1990 amendment, effective April 12, 1990, substituted "three years" for "one year" in subsection (d).

§ 41-16-30. Conflicts of interest of purchasing agents, assistants, etc., generally; making of purchases or awarding of contracts in violation of article.

Collateral references.
Public contracts: low bidder's monetary relief against state or local agency for nonaward of contract. 65 ALR4th 93.

§ 41-16-31. Institution of actions to enjoin execution of contracts entered into in violation of article.

Award to other than lowest bidder. — A bidder for public work cannot base a right of action for damages against the public body upon a statutory requirement that contracts for the performance of public work shall be let to the lowest bidder, and cannot recover lost profits in case the contract is, contrary to the statute, awarded to a higher bidder. Urban San. Corp. v. City of Pell City, 662 F. Supp. 1041 (N.D. Ala. 1986).

ARTICLE 3.

COMPETITIVE BIDDING ON CONTRACTS OF CERTAIN STATE AND LOCAL AGENCIES, ETC.

Cross references.
As to nonapplicability of competitive bid laws to a county industrial development authority, and its directors, officers, etc., see § 11-92A-19.

State authorities should have discretion in determining who is the lowest responsible bidder. — This discretion should not be interfered with by any court unless it is exercised arbitrarily or capriciously, or unless it is based upon a misconception of the law or upon ignorance through lack of inquiry or in violation of law or is the result of improper influence. Mobile Dodge, Inc. v. Mobile County, 422 So. 2d 56 (Ala. 1983).

§ 41-16-50. Contracts for which competitive bidding required; manner of awarding contracts generally; award of contracts to resident bidders; negotiation of contracts; joint contracts.

(a) All expenditure of funds of whatever nature for labor, services or work, or for the purchase of materials, equipment, supplies or other personal property involving $5,000.00 or more, and also the lease of materials, equipment, supplies or other personal property where the lessee is or becomes legally and contractually bound under the terms of the lease, to pay a total amount of $5,000.00 or more, made by or on behalf of any state trade school, state junior college, state college or university under the supervision and control of the state board of education, the city and county boards of education, the district boards of education of independent school districts, the county commissions and the governing bodies of the municipalities of the state and the governing boards of instrumentalities of counties and municipalities, including waterworks boards, sewer boards, gas boards and other like utility boards and commissions, except as hereinafter provided, shall be made under contractual agreement entered into by free and open competitive bidding, on sealed bids, to the lowest responsible bidder; provided, that in the event a bid is received for an item of personal property to be purchased or contracted for from a person, firm or corporation deemed to be a responsible bidder, having a place of business within the county, where the awarding authority is the county or instrumentality thereof, or within the municipality, where the municipality or an instrumentality thereof is the awarding authority, which such bid is no more than three percent greater than the bid of the lowest responsible bidder, the awarding authority may award the contract to such resident responsible bidder. In the event only one bidder responds to the invitation to bid, the awarding authority may reject the bid and negotiate the purchase or contract, providing the negotiated price is lower than the bid price.

(b) The governing bodies of two or more contracting agencies, as hereinabove enumerated within the same county or adjoining counties, may provide by joint agreement for the purchase of labor, services or work, or for the purchase or lease of materials, equipment, supplies or other personal property for use by their respective agencies. Such agreement shall be entered into by similar ordinances, in the case of municipalities, or resolutions, in the case of other contracting agencies, adopted by each of the participating governing bodies, which shall set forth the categories of labor, services or work, or for the purchase or lease of materials, equipment, supplies or other personal property to be purchased, the manner of advertising for bids and of awarding of contracts, the method of payment by each participating contracting agency and other matters deemed necessary to carry out the purposes of the agreement. Each contracting agency's share of expenditures for purchases under any such agreement shall be appropriated and paid in the manner set forth in the agreement and in the same manner as for other expenses of the contracting agency. The contracting agencies entering into a joint agreement, as herein permitted, may designate a joint purchasing agent, and such agent shall have the responsibility to comply with the provisions of this article. It is provided further that purchases, contracts or agreements made pursuant to a joint purchasing agreement shall be subject to all of the terms and conditions of this article.

(c) It is further provided that all bidders must furnish a bid bond on any contract exceeding $10,000.00; provided, that bonding is available for such services, equipment or materials. (Acts 1967, Ex. Sess., No. 217, p. 259, § 1; Acts 1975, No. 1136, p. 2234, § 1; Acts 1979, No. 79-452, p. 732; Acts 1979, No. 79-662, p. 1160; Acts 1980, No. 80-429, p. 598; Acts 1981, No. 81-434, p. 679, § 1; Acts 1985, No. 85-281, p. 180, § 1; Acts 1989, No. 89-687, p. 1351, § 3.)

The 1989 amendment, effective May 11, 1989, substituted "$5,000.00" for "$3,000.00" in two places in subsection (a).

Good faith is single most important requirement of the competitive bid law. J.F. Pate Contractors v. Mobile Airport Auth., 484 So. 2d 418 (Ala. 1986).

Failure to substantially comply with section violates "exclusive grants of special privileges" proscription of Alabama Constitution, § 22. — A city's grant of an exclusive contract for wrecker service that does not substantially comply with the bid law necessarily violates the constitutional proscription of Ala. Const., § 22. Primarily this is true because competitive bidding of the contract is a fundamental requirement for compliance with

either law. In order to escape its "exclusive grants of special privileges" proscription, our organic law mandates that governmental grants of exclusive franchises be subjected to a free, open, and competitive market. Kennedy v. City of Prichard, 484 So. 2d 432 (Ala. 1986).

Compliance with section satisfies Alabama constitutional proscription against government's "exclusive grants of special privileges." — Compliance with the competitive bid law will generally satisfy the constitutional proscription against the government's "exclusive grants of special privileges," Ala. Const., § 22. Indeed, not only are these two laws — one organic and one statutory — legally compatible, but the minimum constitutional requisite for upholding the instant franchise consists substantially in its compliance with the statutory requisites. Kennedy v. City of Prichard, 484 So. 2d 432 (Ala. 1986).

A comparison of the Solid Wastes Disposal Act and the Competitive Bid Law prior to the 1982 amendment to § 41-16-51 reveals no repugnancy between the two enactments. The former only grants counties the authority to contract with private agencies for the disposal of solid wastes and the latter, when incorporated therein, prescribes the procedure for awarding these contracts. Maintenance, Inc. v. Houston County, 438 So. 2d 741 (Ala. 1983).

The fact that the legislature expressly enacted an exemption for solid waste disposal contracts from the Competitive Bid Law militates in favor of the view that, prior to the 1982 amendment to § 41-16-51, such contracts were subject to the bid law. Any interpretation to the contrary would render the amendment superfluous, and it cannot be presumed that the legislature used language without meaning or application. Maintenance, Inc. v. Houston County, 438 So. 2d 741 (Ala. 1983).

Contract for providing wrecker service to city violated competitive bidding requirements where: (1) the ordinance authorizing the contract established the fixed price for each towed vehicle (thus eliminating the primary object of the competitive bidding process), and (2) the completed contract, tailored specifically to fit a particular wrecker service's operation, was already executed by that wrecker service before bid offers were tendered by the city to competing wrecker services. Kennedy v. City of Prichard, 484 So. 2d 432 (Ala. 1986).

Exemption under section 4-3-60. — The competitive bid law did not apply to a contract to construct a new terminal building at Bates airport in Mobile because the Mobile airport authority is exempt from that law under § 4-3-60. J.F. Pate Contractors v. Mobile Airport Auth., 484 So. 2d 418 (Ala. 1986).

Successful bidder for carpet replacement not required to be licensed general contractor. — The replacement of worn carpeting cannot be characterized as the construction of an "improvement," the only term in § 34-8-1 under which such work could conceivable fit, so the work is not the type of work performed by a general contractor as defined in § 34-8-1. Therefore, the successful bidder for carpet replacement is not required under this section to be a licensed general contractor. McCord Contract Floors, Inc. v. City of Dothan, 492 So. 2d 996 (Ala. 1986).

State authorities should have discretion in determining who is the lowest responsible bidder. — This discretion should not be interfered with by any court unless it is exercised arbitrarily or capriciously, or unless it is based upon a misconception of the law or upon ignorance through lack of inquiry or in violation of law or is the result of improper influence. Mobile Dodge, Inc. v. Mobile County, 422 So. 2d 56 (Ala. 1983).

Property interest of unsuccessful low bidder. — The provision for letting the contract to the lowest responsible bidder is for the benefit of the public and does not confer on a bidder any right enforceable at law or in equity. Urban San. Corp. v. City of Pell City, 662 F. Supp. 1041 (N.D. Ala. 1986).

Award to other than lowest bidder. — A bidder for public work cannot base a right of action for damages against the public body upon a statutory requirement that contracts for the performance of public work shall be let to the lowest bidder, and cannot recover lost profits in case the contract is, contrary to the statute, awarded to a higher bidder. Urban San. Corp. v. City of Pell City, 662 F. Supp. 1041 (N.D. Ala. 1986).

Hospital acted in good faith in awarding contract to competitor who was not the lowest bidder. — Assuming that contracts entered into by hospital were subject to the requirements of the Competitive Bid Law, evidence did not support unsuccessful bidder's claim that the hospital acted arbitrarily, capriciously, or in bad faith in awarding the contract for the patient headwall systems to competitor who was not the lowest bidder; hospital exercised good faith by awarding the contract to the supplier whose product most closely fit the specification standards developed by the project architect and the quality of product desired by the hospital. Hospital Sys. v. Hill Rom, Inc., 545 So. 2d 1324 (Ala. 1989).

Burden of proof where state agency seeks to escape contract liability. — Where a city or state agency seeks to use the Competitive Bid Law to escape contractual liability, the burden is on the opposing party, in defending against a summary judgment motion, to present evidence of material and detrimental reliance on the contract to support the application of the equitable remedy of estoppel. Layman's Sec. Co. v. Water Works & Sewer Bd., 547 So. 2d 533 (Ala. 1989).

"An item of personal property" within the proviso of subsection (a) is a single specified article of movable, animate or inanimate, property, merchandise, supplies, raw materials, finished goods, or wares, or a group of such articles specified separately. Tin Man Roofing Co. v. Birmingham Bd. of Educ., 536 So. 2d 1383 (Ala. 1988).

"Re-roofing of elementary school" did fit within the definition of "an item of per-

sonal property" under subsection (a). Tin Man Roofing Co. v. Birmingham Bd. of Educ., 536 So. 2d 1383 (Ala. 1988).

Cited in Mobile Wrecker Owners Ass'n v. City of Mobile, 461 So. 2d 1303 (Ala. 1984).

Collateral references. — Waiver of competitive bidding requirements for state and local public building and construction contracts. 40 ALR4th 968.

§ 41-16-51. Contracts for which competitive bidding not required generally; governing bodies or instrumentalities of counties, municipalities and certain state and local institutions to establish and maintain purchasing facilities and procedures for competitive bidding in operation and management of institutions, facilities, etc., under supervision and control thereof; contracts entered into in violation of article void; penalty.

(a) Competitive bids shall not be required for utility services, the rates for which are fixed by law, regulation or ordinance, and the competitive bidding requirements of this article shall not apply to:

(1) The purchase of insurance;

(2) The purchase of ballots and supplies for conducting any primary, general, special or municipal election;

(3) Contracts for the securing of services of attorneys, physicians, architects, teachers, superintendents of construction, artists, appraisers, engineers, consultants, certified public accountants, public accountants or other individuals possessing a high degree of professional skill where the personality of the individual plays a decisive part;

(4) Contracts of employment in the regular civil service;

(5) Contracts for furnishing of fiscal or financial advice or services;

(6) Purchases of products made or manufactured by the blind or visually handicapped under the direction or supervision of the Alabama Institute for Deaf and Blind in accordance with sections 21-2-1 through 21-2-4;

(7) Purchases of maps or photographs from any federal agency;

(8) Purchases of manuscripts, books, maps, pamphlets or periodicals;

(9) The selection of paying agents and trustees for any security issued by a public body;

(10) Existing contracts up for renewal for sanitation or solid waste collection and disposal between municipalities and/or counties, and those providing the service; nor

(11) Contractual services and purchases of commodities for which there is only one vendor or supplier and contractual services and purchases of personal property which by their very nature are impossible of award by competitive bidding.

(b) This article shall not apply to:

(1) Any purchases of products where the price of such products is already regulated and established by state law;

(2) Purchases made by individual schools of the county or municipal public school systems from moneys other than those raised by taxation or received through appropriations from state or county sources;

(3) The purchase, lease, sale, construction, installation, acquisition, improvement, enlargement or expansion of any building or structure or other facility designed or intended for lease or sale by a medical clinic board organized under the provisions of sections 11-58-1 through 11-58-14;

(4) The purchase, lease or other acquisition of machinery, equipment, supplies and other personal property or services by a medical clinic board organized under the provisions of sections 11-58-1 through 11-58-14;

(5) Purchases for public hospitals and nursing homes operated by the governing boards of instrumentalities of the state, counties and municipalities;

(6) Contracts for the purchase, lease, sale, construction, installation, acquisition, improvement, enlargement or extension of any plant, building, structure or other facility or any machinery, equipment, furniture or furnishings therefor designed or intended for lease or sale for industrial development, other than public utilities, under the provisions of sections 11-54-80 through 11-54-99 or sections 11-54-20 through 11-54-28 or any other statute or amendment to the Constitution of Alabama heretofore or hereafter enacted or adopted authorizing the construction of plants or other facilities for industrial development or for the construction and equipment of buildings for public building authorities under the provisions of sections 11-56-1 through 11-56-22;

(7) The purchase of equipment, supplies or materials needed, used and consumed in the normal and routine operation of any waterworks system, sanitary sewer system, gas system or electric system, or any two or more thereof, that are owned by municipalities, counties or public corporations, boards or authorities that are agencies, departments or instrumentalities of municipalities or counties and no part of the operating expenses of which system or systems have, during the then current fiscal year, been paid from revenues derived from taxes or from appropriations of the state, a county or a municipality; nor

(8) Purchases made by local housing authorities, organized and existing under chapter 1, Title 24, from moneys other than those raised by state, county or city taxation or received through appropriations from state, county or city sources.

(c) The said state trade schools, state junior colleges, state colleges and universities under the supervision and control of the state board of education, the city and county boards of education, the district boards of education of independent school districts, the county commissions and the governing bodies of the municipalities of the state shall establish and maintain such purchasing facilities and procedures as may be necessary to carry out the intent and purpose of this article by complying with the requirements for competitive bidding in the operation and management of each such state trade school, state junior college, state college or university under the supervision and control of the state board of education, the city and county boards of education, the district boards of education of independent school districts, the county commissions and the governing bodies of the municipalities of the state and the governing boards of instrumentalities of counties and municipalities, including waterworks boards, sewer boards, gas boards, and other like utility boards and commissions.

(d) Contracts entered into in violation of this article shall be void and anyone who violates the provisions of this article shall be guilty of a Class C felony. (Acts 1967, Ex. Sess., No. 217, p. 259, § 2; Acts 1967, No. 209, p. 573; Acts 1967, No. 769, p. 1625; Acts 1969, No. 763, p. 1352; Acts 1980, No. 80-463, p. 723; Acts 1982, No. 82-425, p. 667, § 1; Acts 1982, No. 82-508, p. 840, § 1; Acts 1983, No. 83-515, p. 778; Acts 1984, No. 84-298, p. 666; Acts 1989, No. 89-665, p. 1319.)

The 1989 amendment, effective May 11, 1989, added "and anyone who violates the provisions of this article shall be guilty of a Class C felony" in subsection (d).

A comparison of the Solid Wastes Disposal Act and the Competitive Bid Law prior to the 1982 amendment to this section reveals no repugnancy between the two enactments. The former only grants counties the authority to contract with private agencies for the disposal of solid wastes and the latter, when incorporated therein, prescribes the procedure for awarding these contracts. Maintenance, Inc. v. Houston County, 438 So. 2d 741 (Ala. 1983).

The fact that the legislature expressly enacted an exemption for solid waste disposal contracts from the Competitive Bid Law militates in favor of the view that, prior to the 1982 amendment to this section, such contracts were subject to the bid law. Any interpretation to the contrary would render the amendment superfluous, and it cannot be presumed that the legislature used language without meaning or application. Maintenance, Inc. v. Houston County, 438 So. 2d 741 (Ala. 1983).

The providing of security does not constitute a service where the individual's personality is a decisive factor, and therefore, the contract did not fall within this exception to the Competitive Bid Law. Layman's Sec. Co. v. Water Works & Sewer Bd., 547 So. 2d 533 (Ala. 1989).

Collateral references. — Waiver of competitive bidding requirements for state and local public building and construction contracts. 40 ALR4th 968.

Public contracts: low bidder's monetary relief against state or local agency for nonaward of contract. 65 ALR4th 93.

§ 41-16-52. Expenditures for repair or lease of heavy duty off-highway construction equipment may be made without regard to provisions of article.

(a) All expenditure of funds of whatever nature for repair parts and repair of heavy duty off-highway construction equipment and of all vehicles with a gross vehicle weight rating of 25,000 pounds or greater, including machinery used for grading, drainage, road construction and compaction for the exclusive use of county and municipal, highway, street and sanitation departments, involving not more than $6,000.00 made by or on behalf of any county commissions and the governing bodies of the municipalities of the state, and the governing boards of instrumentalities, including waterworks boards, sewer boards, gas boards and other like utility boards and commissions, shall be made, at the option of said governing boards, bodies, instrumentalities and commissions, without regard to the provisions of this article. The foregoing exemption from the provisions of this article shall apply to each incident of repair as to any such repair parts, equipment, vehicles or machinery. The amount of such exempted expenditure shall not be construed to be an aggregate of all such expenditures per fiscal year as to any individual vehicle or piece of equipment or machinery.

(b) The option provided by subsection (a) of this section may be exercised by said governing boards, bodies, instrumentalities and commissions by specific reference to this section on any and all purchase orders and purchase commitments executed by said governing boards, bodies, instrumentalities and commissions; provided, however, said option shall not be exercised by any employee, agent or servant unless done so after having received official prior approval of the respective governing board, body, instrumentality or commission or unless exercised pursuant to a formal policy adopted by such governing board, body, instrumentality or commission setting out conditions and restrictions under which such option shall be exercised.

(c) All expenditures of funds of whatever nature for the leasing of heavy duty off-highway construction equipment and all vehicles with a gross vehicle weight rating of 25,000 pounds or greater, including machinery for grading, drainage, road construction and compaction for the exclusive use of county and municipalities, highway, street and sanitation departments, involving a monthly rental of not more than $3,000.00 per month per vehicle or piece of equipment or machinery but not to exceed $8,000.00 per month for all such vehicles and pieces of equipment made by or on behalf of any county commissions and the governing boards of municipalities of the state and the governing bodies of instrumentalities, including waterworks boards, sewer boards, gas boards and other like utility boards and commissions shall be made, at the option of the said governing boards, bodies, instrumentalities and commissions, without regard to the provisions of this article. (Acts 1969, No. 493, p. 952; Acts 1971, No. 2338, p. 3771; Acts 1981, No. 81-626, p. 1042; Acts 1984, 2nd Ex. Sess., No. 85-40, p. 42.)

Collateral references. — Waiver of competitive bidding requirements for state and local public building and construction contracts. 40 ALR4th 968.

§ 41-16-53. Letting of contracts without public advertisement authorized in case of emergencies affecting public health, safety, etc.

Collateral references. — Waiver of competitive bidding requirements for state and local public building and construction contracts. 40 ALR4th 968.

§ 41-16-54. Advertisement for and solicitation of bids; bids to be sealed; opening of bids; bids, etc., to be retained and to be open to public inspection; when purchases or contracts may be made in open market; contracts not to be split to avoid requirements of article; certain partial contracts declared void.

(a) All proposed purchases in excess of $5,000.00 shall be advertised by posting notice thereof on a bulletin board maintained outside the purchasing office and in any other manner and for such lengths of time as may be determined; provided, however, that sealed bids shall also be solicited by sending notice by mail to all persons, firms or corporations who have filed a request in writing that they be listed for solicitation on bids for such particular items as are set forth in such request. If any person, firm or corporation whose name is listed fails to respond to any solicitation for bids after the receipt of three such solicitations, such listing may be cancelled.

(b) All bids shall be sealed when received, shall be opened in public at the hour stated in the notice, and all original bids together with all documents pertaining to the award of the contract shall be retained and made a part of a permanent file or records and shall be open to public inspection.

(c) If the purchase or contract will involve an amount of $5,000.00 or less, the purchases or contracts may be made upon the basis of sealed bids or in the open market.

(d) No purchase or contract involving an amount in excess of $5,000.00 shall be divided into parts involving amounts of $5,000.00 or less for the purpose of avoiding the requirements of this article. All such partial contracts involving $5,000.00 or less shall be void. (Acts 1967, Ex. Sess., No. 217, p. 259, § 6; Acts 1975, No. 1136, § 2; Acts 1988, No. 88-540, p. 838, § 1; Acts 1989, No. 89-687, p. 1351, § 4.)

The 1989 amendment, effective May 11, 1989, substituted "$5,000.00" for "$3,000.00" throughout the section.

§ 41-16-55. Effect of agreements or collusion among bidders in restraint of competition; knowing participation in collusive agreement.

Any agreement or collusion among bidders or prospective bidders in restraint of freedom of competition, by agreement, to bid at a fixed price or to refrain from bidding or otherwise shall render the bids of such bidders void and shall cause such bidders to be disqualified from submitting further bids to the awarding authority on future purchases.

Whoever knowingly participates in a collusive agreement in violation of this section involving a bid or bids of $3,000.00 and under shall be guilty of a Class A misdemeanor and, upon conviction, shall be punished as prescribed by law.

Whoever knowingly and intentionally participates in a collusive agreement in violation of this section involving a bid or bids of over $3,000.00 shall be guilty of a Class C felony, and upon conviction shall be punished as prescribed by law. (Acts 1967, Ex. Sess., No. 217, p. 259, § 4; Acts 1984, No. 84-471, p. 1091; Acts 1988, No. 88-540, p. 838, § 2.)

§ 41-16-57. Awarding of contracts generally; preference to be given to Alabama commodities, firms, etc., in contracts for purchase of personal property or contractual services; when sole source may be specified; rejection of bids; records as to awarding of contract to be open to public inspection; maximum duration of contracts for purchase of personal property or contractual services.

(a) When purchases are required to be made through competitive bidding, awards shall be made to the lowest responsible bidder taking into consideration the qualities of the commodities proposed to be supplied, their conformity with specifications, the purposes for which required, the terms of delivery, transportation charges and the dates of delivery.

(b) The awarding authority in the purchase of or contract for personal property or contractual services shall give preference, provided there is no sacrifice or loss in price or quality, to commodities produced in Alabama or sold by Alabama persons, firms or corporations. Notwithstanding the foregoing, no county official, county commission, school board, city council or city councilmen or other public official, state board, or state agency charged with the letting of contracts or purchase of materials for the construction, modification, alteration or repairer of any publicly owned facility may specify the use of materials or systems by a sole source, unless:

(1) The governmental body can document to the satisfaction of the state of Alabama building commission that the "sole source" product or service is of an "indispensable" nature, that all other viable alternatives have been explored and determined that only this product or service will fulfill the function for which the product is needed. Frivolous features will not be considered.

(2) The sole source specification has been recommended by the architect or engineer of record and also documents that there is no other product available and that the use of the requirement is of an indispensable nature and why.

(3) All information substantiating the use of a sole source specification is documented in writing and is filed into the project file.

(c) The awarding authority or requisitioning agency shall have the right to reject any bid if the price is deemed excessive or quality of product inferior.

(d) Each record, with the successful bid indicated thereon, and with the reasons for the award if not awarded to the lowest bidder, shall, after award of the order or contract, be open to public inspection.

(e) Contracts for the purchase of personal property or contractual services shall be let for periods not greater than three years. "Lease-purchase" contracts shall be let for periods not greater than five years. (Acts 1967, Ex. Sess., No. 217, p. 259, § 9; Acts 1975, No. 1136, § 3; Acts 1985, No. 85-281, p. 180, § 2; Acts 1989, No. 89-665, p. 1319; Acts 1990, No. 90-300, § 2.)

The 1989 amendment, effective May 11, 1989, in subsection (b), added the second sentence of the introductory language and subdivisions (1) through (3).

The 1990 amendment, effective April 12, 1990, rewrote subsection (e).

State authorities should have discretion in determining who is the lowest responsible bidder. — This discretion should not be interfered with by any court unless it is exercised arbitrarily or capriciously, or unless it is based upon a misconception of the law or upon ignorance through lack of inquiry or in violation of law or is the result of improper influence. Mobile Dodge, Inc. v. Mobile County, 422 So. 2d 56 (Ala. 1983).

Cited in Maintenance, Inc. v. Houston County, 438 So. 2d 741 (Ala. 1983); Mobile Wrecker Owners Ass'n v. City of Mobile, 461 So. 2d 1303 (Ala. 1984).

Collateral references.

Public contracts: authority of state or its subdivision to reject all bids. 52 ALR4th 187.

Public contracts: low bidder's monetary relief against state or local agency for nonaward of contract. 65 ALR4th 93.

§ 41-16-60. Conflicts of interest of members or officers of governing bodies or instrumentalities of counties, municipalities and certain state and local institutions generally; making of purchases or awarding of contracts in violation of article.

Collateral references. — Public contracts: low bidder's monetary relief against state or local agency for nonaward of contract. 65 ALR4th 93.

ARTICLE 5.

CONTRACTS FOR SALE OF CERTAIN STATE PROPERTY.

§§ 41-16-100 through 41-16-109. Repealed by Acts 1984, No. 84-249, p. 392, § 9, effective October 1, 1984.

Cross references. — For provisions making the director of the department of economic and community affairs responsible for the distribution, transfer, or disposal of surplus personal property owned by the state, see now § 41-16-120 et seq.

ARTICLE 6.

DISPOSITION OF SURPLUS PERSONAL PROPERTY OWNED BY STATE.

Code commissioner's note. — Acts 1984, No. 84-249, § 6 provides: "All appropriations heretofore made to the finance department for administering the disposal of surplus property under article 5, chapter 16, of Title 41 shall be transferred to the surplus property division of the department of economic and community affairs, along with all personnel, records, accounts, equipment, and such other necessary things connected with the surplus property operation as determined by the finance director."

§ 41-16-120. Director of department of economic and community affairs responsible for distribution, etc., of surplus personal property; definitions.

(a) The director of the department of economic and community affairs shall be responsible for the distribution, transfer, or disposal of all surplus personal property owned by the state and all right, title, interest, and equity in said property shall be transferred to said department for such purpose. The director may delegate to the chief of the surplus property division such supervision and control of the distribution or disposal of the aforementioned state owned surplus personal property.

(b) As used in this article, the following terms shall have the following meanings, respectively, unless the context clearly indicates otherwise:

(1) DIVISION. Surplus property division of the department of economic and community affairs.

(2) SURPLUS PROPERTY. That property declared by the personal property management coordinator of each state department, bureau, board, commission or agency to be surplus and so designated in writing to the chief of the division. All real property owned by any state department, bureau, board, commission, agency or institution, and any subdivision thereof; including, but not limited to, real property owned by any state college, university, two-year college, technical school, or other postsecondary institution of higher learning shall be handled in the manner provided in section 41-4-33, or such other provisions of law as may be appropriate but in no circumstance shall any law regarding real property acquired, owned or disposed of by the state or any subdivision thereof be amended, substituted or in other manner altered by this article.

(3) ELIGIBLE AGENCY. Any city, county, board of education, volunteer fire department, civil defense agency or state department, board, bureau, commission or agency that is not found to be in violation of division rules and regulations during the 12 months immediately preceding the intended purchase.

(4) COORDINATOR. That officer or employee who shall be designated by the head of each department, board, bureau, commission, institution, corporation or agency of the state, in writing, to the division, to be the personal property management coordinator.

(c) The coordinator shall report to the surplus property division of the department of economic and community affairs any personal property declared surplus by his department, board, bureau, commission, institution, corporation, or agency and deliver said property to any place designated by the division to be the proper place for such delivery.

(d) The division shall be authorized to promulgate such administrative rules and regulations as deemed necessary including, but not limited to:

(1) Promotion of surplus property;

(2) Shipment of surplus property;

(3) Storage of surplus property;

(4) Length of retention of surplus property;

(5) Public auction of surplus property;

(6) Such other rules and regulations as, from time to time, may be determined to be necessary.

(e) The division shall have authority to sell surplus property at fair market value, as established by the division and set out in its published rules, to incorporated cities, counties, volunteer fire departments, boards of education, civil defense agencies and state departments, boards, bureaus, commissions, or agencies. Payment for purchases by any of the abovementioned entities shall be made within 30 days after such purchase. If payment is not made within 30 days after a purchase, then such purchase shall be declared void and in default, and the property shall be returned immediately by the defaulting purchaser to the division.

Provided, however, the governing body of any municipality with a population of less than 5,000 shall be given preference on the disposal of all surplus motor vehicles owned by the state of Alabama except those motor vehicles transferred to other state agencies.

Said municipalities shall notify the division, in writing, of type motor vehicle needed. A list shall be maintained by the division of such needs on a first come, first served basis and will be used to notify the municipalities when needed vehicles become available. Any municipality so notified shall have seven work days in which to reply to the notice and accept or refuse the available vehicle.

(f) Any nonprofit corporation which is authorized to purchase federal surplus property shall be authorized to purchase state surplus property under this section provided the corporation complies with all federal laws, regulations and guidelines regarding the purchase of surplus federal property. (Acts 1984, No. 84-249, p. 392, § 1; Acts 1987, No. 87-584, p. 953.)

§ 41-16-121. Availability of surplus property; publication and dissemination of list of property; disposition of hazardous material prohibited.

(a) Surplus property shall be made available at such times and places as determined to be appropriate by the division for inspection and acquisition by those agencies determined to be eligible for such acquisition under criteria developed and published by the division.

(b) The division shall periodically publish a list of all surplus property held by it at the time of such publication.

(c) The published list shall be made available to all state departments, boards, bureaus, commissions, institutions, corporations, or agencies.

(d) The published list shall also be made available to all eligible counties, cities, boards of education, civil defense agencies, and volunteer fire departments.

(e) The division will determine the manner in which the list of surplus personal property shall be published.

(f) The division shall not be authorized to handle or dispose of any regulated hazardous materials. (Acts 1984, No. 84-249, p. 392, § 2.)

§ 41-16-122. Authority of division.

(a) The division shall be authorized to collect fees for transfer, handling, shipping, classification, warehousing, bidding, destruction, scrapping, or other disposal of property and such other fees as may be deemed appropriate in order to insure the continued efficient operation of the surplus property function of the department.

(b) The division shall establish two accounts within the state treasury for the operation of the surplus property function as follows:

(1) The first account shall be known as the federal surplus property account into which all moneys received from the distribution of federally donated surplus property shall be deposited;

(2) The second account shall be known as the state surplus property account into which all moneys received from the distribution of state owned surplus property and any funds appropriated from the state general fund for the operation of the surplus property function shall be deposited.

(c) Any moneys deposited into either of the aforementioned accounts may be expended from time to time by the department for operation of the surplus property function including, but not limited to, repairs, salaries, rent, travel, acquisition of exchange and surplus property, and all other necessary operating expenditures providing, however, that on September 30 any unencumbered moneys remaining in the state surplus property account, up to an amount equal to the operating expenses of the quarter ending on September 30, shall be set aside for use during the quarter beginning October 1 for the purposes heretofore stated and any remainder shall revert to the state general fund. The federal surplus property account shall be a perpetual account, and funds therein shall not revert to the state general fund. (Acts 1984, No. 84-249, p. 392, § 3.)

§ 41-16-123. Provisions relating to property held by division less than 60 days from publication of list of surplus property; penalty.

This section shall apply only to that property that has been held by the division for a period of not less than 60 days from the date said property is first published in the list of surplus property, as set out in subsection (b) of section 41-16-121, and not purchased by any agency as set out in subsection (e) of section 41-16-120.

(1) All contracts made by, or on behalf of, the state of Alabama, or any department, board, bureau, commission, institution, corporation, or agency thereof, of whatever nature for the sale or disposal of tangible personal property owned by the state of Alabama, other than:

a. Alcoholic beverages;

b. Products of the Alabama Institute for Deaf and Blind;

c. Barter arrangements of the state prison system;

d. Books;

e. School supplies;

f. Food;

g. Property used in vocational projects;

h. Livestock;

i. Property owned by any state college or university not under the control of the board of education of the state of Alabama, which has trade-in value which may be credited against the cost of replacement property purchased in accordance with the Alabama competitive bid laws; and

j. Types of property, the disposal of which is otherwise provided or by law or which, by nature, are incapable of sale by auction or bid, shall be let by free and open competitive public auction or sealed bids.

(2) Every proposal to make a sale covered by this section shall be advertised for at least two weeks in advance of the date fixed for receiving bids. Such advertisement shall appear at least once a week for two consecutive weeks in a newspaper of general circulation in the county where the sale is to be made, and a copy of such proposal shall simultaneously be posted on a readily accessible public bulletin board at the main office of the chief of the division. Advertisements for bids shall state the item or items to be sold, by class and description, where the property is located and the dates, time, and place the property may be inspected. The advertisements shall further state the date, time, and place of auction or opening of sealed bids, and no bid shall be received at any time after the time advertised.

(3) The bids shall be publicly taken or opened, in case of sealed bids, by the chief of the division and all bidders shall be entitled to be present in person or by representative.

(4) The award of the contract shall be made to the successful bidder within 72 hours after taking of the bids.

(5) The bid of the successful bidder so marked, as well as the bids of the unsuccessful bidders in the case of sealed bids, shall be placed on file open to public inspection and shall become matters of public record.

(6) If a successful bidder shall fail to accept award of a contract, then he shall be prohibited from bidding at any sale held by the division for a period of 12 months following such failure to accept.

(7) The chief of the division may sell all items by lot or by individual item, whichever method, in his opinion, will bring the highest return for the items so advertised.

(8) In the event all bids received are less than the estimated market value of the property, the chief of the division shall reject all bids and readvertise and rebid.

(9) Nothing herein shall be construed to prevent the chief of the division from contracting with the highest bidder for any type of property to sell to that bidder all of that type of property at his bid price during that fiscal year providing such possible arrangement was included in the initial request for bids.

(10) All property advertised under the provisions of this section shall be available for inspection during the normal state office hours and at whatever place advertised for at least 48 hours prior to sale.

(11) All property sold under the provisions of this section shall be paid for by the purchaser or his representative by cashier's check, bank draft, certified check, U. S. currency, or notarized bank letter stating that the holder may purchase surplus property and also stating a maximum amount, at the time of acceptance of bid and award of contract, and said removal shall be not later than seven days after the awarding of the contract; provided, however, that the time limit of seven days shall not be applicable to sales of standing timber.

(12) All proceeds from sales made under the provisions of this section shall be paid into the state treasury or other legally authorized depositary to be credited to the proper fund as set out in subsection (b) of section 41-16-122 prior to final distribution as set out in subdivision (16) of this section.

(13) No officer or employee of the state of Alabama or any of its departments, boards, bureaus, commissions, institutions, corporations, or agencies shall act as agent for any bidder; provided, however, that such officers or employees shall not be excluded from bidding on or purchasing state property at public sale or sealed bid.

(14) Any sale of tangible personal property or standing timber of the state made in violation of the terms of this article shall be null and void, and the person or persons responsible for the violation shall be subject to liquidated damages of not less than $1,000.00 nor more than $10,000.00, which may be recovered for the state of Alabama by the attorney general by civil action in the circuit court of Montgomery county. Any moneys recovered by the attorney general under this section shall be equally divided between the office of the attorney general and the state general fund.

(15) The provisions of this article shall not apply to the sale of diseased, storm or fire-damaged timber, nor shall it apply to timber cut on rights-of-way or easements. Such timber may be sold or otherwise disposed of in such manner as the commissioner of conservation and natural resources deems in the best interest of the state; provided, that no sale of diseased timber shall be made until the state forester shall certify that such timber is diseased, and such certification shall be in written form and filed with the director of finance.

(16) Whenever any surplus property that was purchased with either earmarked state funds or restricted federal funds is sold by the division, the proceeds from such sale, less administrative expenses, shall be deposited to the credit of the specific fund of the state department, commission, or agency from which the original purchase of such property was made within 30 days from receipt of said proceeds. If the source of the original purchase of the property was a general fund appropriation, then said sale proceeds, less any administrative fee, as set out in the rules authorized to be

promulgated by the division, shall be credited to the account from which it was purchased. In no event shall the said administrative fee, as mentioned above, exceed 25 percent of the gross sale price.

(17) All educational and eleemosynary institutions, not exempted in subdivision (1) of this section, governed by a board of trustees or other similar governing body, the department of mental health, and state docks department shall be governed by the provisions of this article.

(18) Violation of any of the provisions of this article shall constitute a Class B misdemeanor punishable as prescribed by law. (Acts 1984, No. 84-249, p. 392, § 4.)

§ 41-16-124. Effect of article upon status of division employees.

All personnel, including those on personal service contracts, working within the surplus property division of the department of economic and community affairs at the passage of this article shall, by virtue of this section, be considered to meet the requirements of the department in terms of education, training, and experience and shall automatically be placed within the state merit system with permanent status with all the rights and privileges thereof and shall enjoy the same employment and retirement privileges and rights as the legislature may determine from time to time or as may be otherwise determined by law or administrative rule or regulation according to the rules and regulations of the personnel department of the state of Alabama. All new future employees of the surplus property division of the department of economic and community affairs shall be required to meet the requirements of the state merit system.

All present employees of the surplus property division of the department of economic and community affairs shall remain in their respective positions and continue to enjoy employment conditions including, but not limited to, salary range and advancement at a level no less than those enjoyed prior to the enactment of this article. However, nothing herein shall be construed to prevent or preclude the removal of an employee for cause in the manner provided by law. (Acts 1984, No. 84-249, p. 392, § 5.)

§ 41-16-125. State plan of operation for state agency for federal property assistance.

The temporary state plan of operation for the state agency for federal property assistance which was approved by the governor of Alabama on July 14, 1977, and accepted by the general services administration on September 14, 1977, shall become the permanent state plan of operation; provided, however, the division shall have authority, with approval of the governor, to revise said plan from time to time in accordance with regulations as established by the general services administration pursuant to Public Law 94-519 which governs the distribution of federal surplus property. (Acts 1984, No. 84-249, p. 392, § 7.)

CHAPTER 19.

BUDGET MANAGEMENT.

§ 41-19-10. Authority of agencies/departments as to administration of programs and appropriations generally; preparation, review, approval, etc., of annual plans for operation of programs; granting of salary increases, etc., by agencies/departments; transfers or changes of appropriations; quarterly reports by department of finance as to operations of agencies/departments.

Code commissioner's note. — Acts 1984, No. 84-325, § 2, provides: "For the purposes of section 41-19-10, the office of prosecution services is considered within the same program as the offices of district attorneys. Upon approval of the finance director, transfers of any budget excesses from district attorneys objects of expenditures may be made to the office of prose- cution services objects of expenditures. Any such transfers to said office shall not revert to the general fund and may be expended by the office of prosecution services in accordance with applicable law. Any such transfers to the office of prosecution services are limited to two and one half percent of district attorneys annual budget."

CHAPTER 20.

CONTINUATION OR TERMINATION OF STATE AGENCIES.

§ 41-20-3. Specification of termination dates for certain agencies; date and procedure generally for termination of agencies not designated; committee's right to review and make recommendations.

Code commissioner's note. — Acts 1983, No. 83-369 continues the polygraph examiners board, pursuant to the Sunset Act.

Acts 1983, No. 83-370 continues the Alabama board of registration for professional engineers and land surveyors, pursuant to the Sunset Act.

Acts 1983, No. 83-371 continues the Alabama licensing board for general contractors, pursuant to the Sunset Act.

Acts 1983, No. 83-372 continues the board of examiners of landscape architects, pursuant to the Sunset Act.

Acts 1983, No. 83-373 continues the Alabama board of bar examiners, pursuant to the Sunset Act.

Acts 1983, No. 83-374 continues the board of registration of architects, pursuant to the Sunset Act.

Acts 1984, No. 84-93, § 1, continues the board of social work examiners, pursuant to the Sunset Act.

Acts 1984, No. 84-94 continues the Alabama board of examiners in psychology, pursuant to the Sunset Act.

Acts 1984, No. 84-95 continues the Alabama state board of public accountancy, pursuant to the Sunset Act.

Acts 1984, No. 84-96 continues the Alabama board of funeral service, pursuant to the Sunset Act.

Acts 1984, No. 84-97, continues the Alabama real estate commission, pursuant to the Sunset Act.

Acts 1984, No. 84-98, continues the insurance department, pursuant to the Sunset Act.

Acts 1984, No. 84-99, continues the securities commission, pursuant to the Sunset Act.

Acts 1984, No. 84-100, continues the board of pilotage commissioners, pursuant to the Sunset Act.

Acts 1984, No. 84-101, continues the public service commission, pursuant to the Sunset Act.

Acts 1984, No. 84-102, continues the professional entomologists, horticulturists, plant pathologists, floriculturists and tree surgeons examining board, pursuant to the Sunset Act.

Acts 1984, No. 84-103, continues the plumbing examiners board, pursuant to the Sunset Act.

Acts 1984, No. 84-104, continues the liquefied petroleum gas board, pursuant to the Sunset Act.

Acts 1984, No. 84-105, continues the state board of auctioneers, pursuant to the Sunset Act.

Acts 1984, No. 84-106, continues the Alabama board of nursing, pursuant to the Sunset Act.

Acts 1984, No. 84-107, continues the state board of heating and air conditioning contractors, pursuant to the Sunset Act.

Acts 1984, No. 84-177, continues the Alabama board of cosmetology, pursuant to the Sunset Act.

Acts 1984, No. 84-178, continues the Alabama alcoholic beverage control board, pursuant to the Sunset Act.

Acts 1985, No. 85-15, § 2, continues the board of examiners for fire bosses and mine foremen, pursuant to the Sunset Act.

Acts 1985, No. 85-283 continues the board of examiners of nursing home administrators, pursuant to the Sunset Act.

Acts 1985, No. 85-332 continues the board of nursing, pursuant to the Sunset Act.

Acts 1985, No. 85-333 continues the board of optometry, pursuant to the Sunset Act.

Acts 1985, No. 85-334 continues the board of physical therapy, pursuant to the Sunset Act.

Acts 1985, No. 85-335 continues the board of pharmacy, pursuant to the Sunset Act.

Acts 1985, No. 85-336 continues the board of veterinary medical examiners, pursuant to the Sunset Act.

Acts 1985, No. 85-337 continues the board of hearing aid dealers, pursuant to the Sunset Act.

Acts 1985, No. 85-338 continues the board of medical examiners and the medical licensure commission, pursuant to the Sunset Act.

Acts 1985, No. 85-359 continues the board of podiatry, pursuant to the Sunset Act.

Acts 1985, No. 85-360 continues the board of dental examiners, pursuant to the Sunset Act.

Acts 1985, No. 85-361 continues the board of examiners for speech pathology and audiology, pursuant to the Sunset Act.

Acts 1985, No. 85-613 continues the board of chiropractic examiners, pursuant to the Sunset Act.

Acts 1986, No. 86-106, § 2 continues the surface mining commission until October 1, 1987.

Acts 1986, No. 86-114 continues the radiation control agency and its radiation advisory board pursuant to the Sunset Act.

Acts 1986, No. 86-115, § 2 continues the state oil and gas board pursuant to the Sunset Act.

Acts 1986, No. 86-116, § 2 continues the board of dental examiners pursuant to the Sunset Act.

Acts 1986, No. 86-117, continues the board of registration for foresters, pursuant to the Sunset Act.

Acts 1986, No. 86-118, § 2 continues the heating and air conditioning board, pursuant to the Sunset Act.

Acts 1986, No. 86-557 continues the board of general contractors, pursuant to the Sunset Act.

Acts 1987, No. 87-157, continues the board of examiners of landscape architects, pursuant to the Sunset Act.

Acts 1987, No. 87-158, continues the board of bar examiners, pursuant to the Sunset Act.

Acts 1987, No. 87-159, continues the polygraph examiners board, pursuant to the Sunset Act.

Acts 1987, No. 87-160, continues the surface mining commission, pursuant to the Sunset Act.

Acts 1987, No. 87-175, continues the licensing board for general contractors, pursuant to the Sunset Act.

Acts 1987, No. 87-414, continues the board of registration of professional engineers and land surveyors, pursuant to the Sunset Act.

Acts 1987, No. 87-544, continues the board for registration of architects, pursuant to the Sunset Act.

Acts 1988, No. 88-128, § 2, continues the pilotage commission, pursuant to the Sunset Act.

Acts 1988, No. 88-131 and No. 88-132, § 2, continue the plumbing examining board, as renamed the plumbers and gas fitters examining board, pursuant to the Sunset Act.

Acts 1988, No. 88-133, continues the insurance department until October 1, 1989, pursuant to the Sunset Act.

Acts 1988, No. 88-134, continues the public service commission, pursuant to the Sunset Act.

Acts 1988, No. 88-135, § 2, continues the board of examiners of mine personnel, pursuant to the Sunset Act.

Acts 1988, No. 88-136, § 2, continues the state board of public accountancy, pursuant to the Sunset Act.

Acts 1988, No. 88-137, § 2, continues the securities commission, pursuant to the Sunset Act.

Acts 1988, No. 88-138, § 2, continues the board of auctioneers, pursuant to the Sunset Act.

Acts 1988, No. 88-139, § 2, continues the examining board for professional entomologists, horticulturists, plant pathologists, floriculturists and tree surgeons, pursuant to the Sunset Act.

Acts 1988, No. 88-140, § 2, continues the board of cosmetology, pursuant to the Sunset Act.

Acts 1988, No. 88-141, § 2, continues the board of social work examiners, pursuant to the Sunset Act.

Acts 1988, No. 88-142, § 2, continues the liquefied petroleum gas board, pursuant to the Sunset Act.

Acts 1988, No. 88-143, continues the board of funeral service, pursuant to the Sunset Act.

Acts 1988, No. 88-155, continues the alcoholic beverage control board, pursuant to the Sunset Act.

Acts 1988, No. 88-214, § 2, continues the real estate commission, pursuant to the Sunset Act.

Acts 1988, No. 88-216, § 2, continues the board of examiners in psychology, pursuant to the Sunset Act.

Acts 1988, No. 88-217, § 2, continues the board of heating and air conditioning contractors, pursuant to the Sunset Act.

Acts 1988, No. 88-932, continues the board of heating and air conditioning contractors, pursuant to the Sunset Act.

Acts 1989, No. 89-232, continues the board of physical therapy, pursuant to the Sunset Act.

Acts 1989, No. 89-233, continues the board of optometry, pursuant to the Sunset Act.

Acts 1989, No. 89-234, continues the board of examiners in speech pathology and audiology, pursuant to the Sunset Act.

Acts 1989, No. 89-235, continues the board of pharmacy, pursuant to the Sunset Act.

Acts 1989, No. 89-236, § 2, continues the board of veterinary medical examiners, pursuant to the Sunset Act.

Acts 1989, No. 89-238, continues the board of examiners of nursing home administrators, pursuant to the Sunset Act.

Acts 1989, No. 89-242, continues the board of podiatry, pursuant to the Sunset Act.

Acts 1989, No. 89-243, continues the board of nursing, pursuant to the Sunset Act.

Acts 1989, No. 89-244, continues the board of medical examiners and medical licensure commission, pursuant to the Sunset Act.

Acts 1989, No. 89-258, continues the insurance department, pursuant to the Sunset Act.

Acts 1989, No. 89-268, continues the board of hearing aid dealers, pursuant to the Sunset Act.

Acts 1989, No. 89-269, continues the polygraph examiners board, pursuant to the Sunset Act.

Acts 1989, No. 89-284, continues the real estate commission, pursuant to the Sunset Act.

Acts 1989, No. 89-406, continues the plumbers and gas fitters examining board, pursuant to the Sunset Act.

Acts 1989, No. 89-407, continues the board of dental examiners, pursuant to the Sunset Act.

Acts 1990, No. 90-104 continues the oil and gas board, pursuant to the Sunset Act.

Acts 1990, No. 90-105 continues the board of registration for foresters, pursuant to the Sunset Act.

Acts 1990, No. 90-106 continues the academy of honor, pursuant to the Sunset Act.

Acts 1990, No. 90-107 continues the surface mining commission, pursuant to the Sunset Act.

Acts 1990, No. 90-108 continues the general contractors board, pursuant to the Sunset Act.

Acts 1990, No. 90-109 continues the state radiation control agency, pursuant to the Sunset Act.

Acts 1990, No. 90-110 terminates the hall of fame board.

Acts 1990, No. 90-553, § 13, which is codified as § 41-4-292, provides: "The Telecommunications Division of the Finance Department shall be subject to the provisions of the Alabama Sunset Law of 1981, and shall be classified an enumerated agency under § 41-20-3 Code of Alabama 1975, as amended, and shall terminate in 1992 unless continued as therein provided and, if continued, shall be reviewed every two years thereafter and terminated unless then continued as provided by said law."

CHAPTER 22.

ADMINISTRATIVE PROCEDURE.

Cited in West Ala. Remodeling, Inc. v. Ireland, 412 So. 2d 766 (Ala. 1982); Horn v. Alabama Bd. of Exmrs., 437 So. 2d 1047 (Ala. Civ. App. 1983); Humana Medical Corp. v. State Health Planning & Dev. Agency, 460 So. 2d 1295 (Ala. Civ. App. 1984).

§ 41-22-1. Short title.

Cross references. — As to the effective date of this section with regard to the Alabama department of environmental management and as to the validity and adoption of rules of that department, see § 41-22-27 (f).

Section 20-2-53 takes precedence over the provisions of the Administrative Procedure Act, § 41-22-1 et seq. Benton v. Alabama Bd. of Medical Exmrs., 467 So. 2d 234 (Ala. 1985).

Judicial notice of rules issued by state board of health. — Since rules and regulations issued by state board of health were part of Alabama Administrative Code, court of criminal appeals correctly held that trial court could take judicial notice of them. Vizzina v. City of Birmingham, 533 So. 2d 658 (Ala. 1988).

Cited in Albertville Nat'l Bank v. Sand Mt. Bank, 414 So. 2d 928 (Ala. 1982); Personnel Board v. King, 456 So. 2d 80 (Ala. Civ. App. 1984); Childress v. City of Huntsville, 459 So. 2d 1008 (Ala. Crim. App. 1984); Stuart v. Historic Whse., Inc., 505 So. 2d 298 (Ala. 1986).

§ 41-22-2. Legislative intent and purpose; effect on substantive rights; applicability; authority to prescribe rules and regulations required in connection with this chapter.

Code commissioner's note. — Section 15-18-8.1 provides that any and all rules and regulations issued by the department of corrections pursuant to the provisions of § 15-18-8 shall be subject to the Alabama Administrative Procedure Act.

Cross references. — For rule-making procedure under the Alabama Surface Mining Control and Reclamation Act of 1981 and requirement that copies of its rules be filed with the Legislative Reference Service and the regulatory authority's principal office, see § 9-16-75. As to the effective date of this section with regard to the Alabama department of environmental management and as to the validity and adoption of rules of that department, see § 41-22-27 (f).

The Administrative Procedure Act, enacted in 1981, was intended to provide minimal due process procedural requirements for all state agencies when taking actions affecting the rights and duties of the public. Benton v. Alabama Bd. of Medical Exmrs., 467 So. 2d 234 (Ala. 1985).

Nothing in this act relieves agencies of duty to comply with additional procedural requirements otherwise established by law. Benton v. Alabama Bd. of Medical Exmrs., 467 So. 2d 234 (Ala. 1985).

Agencies of the state legislature not subject to Administrative Procedure Act. — The board of adjustment is not subject to the Alabama Administrative Procedure Act (AAPA) because it is an agency of the state legislature and is thus specifically excepted from the definition of an agency to which the AAPA applies. Medical Laundry Serv. v. Board of Adjustment, 486 So. 2d 1305 (Ala. Civ. App. 1986).

Section's applicability to sections 32-5A-191(d) and 32-5A-195(j). — Whether an individual whose driver's license is revoked under §§ 32-5A-191(d) and 32-5A-195(j) is entitled to an administrative hearing is a matter of substantive law. That law is that no such hearing is allowed because revocation under the DUI statutes is mandatory. The Alabama Administrative Procedure Act, which is solely limited to procedural matters, has not altered this substantive law. Bryant v. State Dep't of Pub. Safety, 494 So. 2d 425 (Ala. Civ. App. 1986).

Exhaustion of remedies under § 41-22-11 before proceeding under § 41-22-10. — It is clear, when §§ 41-22-10 and 41-22-11 are construed in pari materia, as they must be, and in light of the express purposes of this section, that a litigant must exhaust his administrative remedies under § 41-22-11 before he may proceed to the circuit court under § 41-22-10. Stuart v. Historic Whse., Inc., 505 S.W.2d 298 (Ala. 1986).

Cited in Mobile Infirmary Ass'n v. Emfinger, 474 So. 2d 731 (Ala. Civ. App. 1985); Potts v. Bennett, 487 So. 2d 919 (Ala. Civ. App. 1985).

§ 41-22-3. Definitions.

The following words and phrases when used in this chapter shall, for the purpose of this chapter, have meanings respectively ascribed to them in this section, except when the context otherwise requires:

(1) AGENCY. Every board, bureau, commission, department, officer, or other administrative office or unit of the state, including the Alabama department of environmental management, other than the legislature and its agencies, Alabama state docks, the courts or the Alabama public service commission or the state banking department, whose administrative procedures are governed by sections 5-2A-8 and 5-2A-9. The term shall not include boards of trustees of postsecondary institutions, counties, municipalities, or any agencies of such local governmental units, unless they are expressly made subject to this act by general or special law.

(2) COMMITTEE. The joint committee on administrative regulation review shall be the members of the legislative council.

(3) CONTESTED CASE. A proceeding, including but not restricted to ratemaking, price fixing, and licensing, in which the legal rights, duties, or privileges of a party are required by law to be determined by an agency after an opportunity for hearing; provided, however, that the term shall not include intra-agency personnel actions; shall not include those hearings or proceedings in which the Alabama board of pardons and paroles considers the granting or denial of pardons, paroles or restoration of civil and political rights or remission of fines and forfeitures; and which are hereby exempted from the provisions of sections 41-22-12 through 41-22-21, relating to contested cases.

(4) LICENSE. The whole or part of any agency franchise, permit, certificate, approval, registration, charter or similar form of permission required by law, but not a license required solely for revenue purposes when issuance of the license is merely a ministerial act.

(5) LICENSING. The agency process respecting the grant, denial, renewal, revocation, suspension, annulment, withdrawal, or amendment of a license or imposition of terms for the exercise of a license.

(6) PARTY. Each person or agency named or admitted as a party or properly seeking and entitled as a matter of right (whether established by constitution, statute or agency regulation or otherwise) to be admitted as a party, or admitted as an intervenor under section 41-22-14. An agency may by rule authorize limited forms of participation in agency proceedings for persons who are not eligible to become parties.

(7) PERSON. Any individual, partnership, corporation, association, governmental subdivision, or public or private organization of any character other than an agency.

(8) QUORUM. No less than a majority of the members of a multimember agency shall constitute a quorum authorized to act in the name of the agency, unless provided otherwise by statute.

(9) RULE. Each agency regulation, standard or statement of general applicability that implements, interprets, or prescribes law or policy, or that describes the organization, procedure, or practice requirements of any agency and includes any form which imposes any requirement or solicits any information not specifically required by statute or by an existing rule or by federal statute or by federal rule or regulation; provided, however, all forms shall be filed with the secretary of the agency and with the legislative reference service and all forms (except intergovernmental, interagency, and intra-agency forms which do not affect the rights of the public and emergency forms adopted pursuant to section 41-22-5) shall be published in the Agency Administrative Code. The term includes the amendment or repeal of all existing rules but does not include the following:

    a. Statements concerning only the internal management of an agency and not affecting private rights or procedures available to the public;

    b. Declaratory rulings issued pursuant to section 41-22-11;

    c. Intergovernmental, interagency, and intra-agency memoranda, directives, manuals or other communications which do not substantially affect the legal rights of, or procedures available to, the public or any segment thereof;

d. Determinations, decisions, orders, statements of policy and interpretations that are made in contested cases;

e. An order which is directed to a specifically named person or to a group of specifically named persons which does not constitute a general class, and the order is served on the person or persons to whom it is directed by the appropriate means applicable thereto. The fact that the named person who is being regulated serves a group of unnamed persons who will be affected does not make such order a rule;

f. An order which applies to a specifically described tract of real estate; or

g. Any rules or actions relating to:

1. The conduct of inmates of public institutions and prisoners on parole;

2. The curriculum of public educational institutions or the admission, conduct, discipline, or graduation of students of such institutions; provided, however, that this exception shall not extend to rules or actions of the state department of education;

3. Opinions issued by the attorney general of the state of Alabama;

4. The conduct of commissioned officers, warrant officers and enlisted persons in the military service;

5. Advisory opinions issued by the Alabama ethics commission; or

6. Hunting and fishing seasons, bag or creel limits promulgated by the commissioner of the department of conservation and natural resources. (Acts 1981, No. 81-855, p. 1534, § 3; Acts 1986, No. 86-472, p. 880, § 1.)

Cross references. — For rule-making procedure under the Alabama Surface Mining Control and Reclamation Act of 1981 and requirement that copies of its rules be filed with the Legislative Reference Service and the regulatory authority's principal office, see § 9-16-75. As to the effective date of this section with regard to the Alabama department of environmental management and as to the validity and adoption of rules of that department, see § 41-22-27 (f).

Agencies of the state legislature not subject to Administrative Procedure Act. — The board of adjustment is not subject to the Alabama Administrative Procedure Act (AAPA) because it is an agency of the state legislature and is thus specifically excepted from the definition of an agency to which the AAPA applies. Medical Laundry Serv. v. Board of Adjustment, 486 So. 2d 1305 (Ala. Civ. App. 1986).

The swing bed amendment adopted by the health council was a "rule" within the definition set forth in subdivision (9) of this section since the amendment resembled legislation, since the state health plan (SHP) prescribed, implemented, and described state policy and procedure, and since there was no distinction between requirements for granting a certificate of need (CON) and a rule for determining who was granted a CON. Traylor Nursing Home, Inc. v. Alabama Statewide Health Coordinating Council, 543 So. 2d 1179 (Ala. 1988).

Health council was an agency within the meaning of subdivision (9) since, although the basic purpose of the health council was to serve in an advisory capacity to the state agency, the health council was not prohibited from promulgating rules and regulations. Traylor Nursing Home, Inc. v. Alabama Statewide Health Coordinating Council, 543 So. 2d 1179 (Ala. 1988).

"Contested case". — An ABC board off-premises beer licensing proceeding is a "contested case" under the definition provided in subsection (3) of this section. Potts v. Bennett, 487 So. 2d 919 (Ala. Civ. App. 1985).

Intra-agency personnel actions not "contested cases". — Judicial review is limited to "contested cases" under § 41-22-20 and intra-agency personnel actions do not fall within the term "contested case" as defined by this section. Heatherly v. Kemsel, 504 So. 2d 285 (Ala. Civ. App. 1986).

Judicial review pursuant to the Alabama Administrative Procedure Act is limited to "contested cases" under this section, and intra-agency personnel actions do not fall within the term "contested case" as defined by subdivision (3). Klein v. State Bd. of Educ., 547 So. 2d 549 (Ala. Civ. App. 1988).

Proceeding to review teacher's contract dispute is not a contested case. — Although the postsecondary education department is an "agency," the proceeding to review a teacher's contract dispute cannot be categorized as a "contested case" within the meaning of subdivision (3). Klein v. State Bd. of Educ., 547 So. 2d 549 (Ala. Civ. App. 1988).

ABC board has power to make determinations, decisions, orders, statements of policy and interpretations. — Subsection (9)(d) of this section gives the ABC board the power to make determinations, decisions, orders, statements of policy and interpretations in off-premises beer licensing proceedings. Potts v. Bennett, 487 So. 2d 919 (Ala. Civ. App. 1985).

§ 41-22-4. Adoption by agencies of rules governing organization, practice, etc.; public access to rules, orders, etc.; effect of rules, orders, etc., not made available to public.

Cross references. — As to the effective date of this section with regard to the Alabama department of environmental management and as to the validity and adoption of rules of that department, see § 41-22-27 (f).

Improper location and surroundings valid basis for denial of off-premises license. — Application of policies upholding improper location and surroundings as a valid basis for denial of off-premises license to the case at bar did not violate this section. Potts v. Bennett, 487 So. 2d 919 (Ala. Civ. App. 1985).

While the notice requirement of § 41-22-5 does not apply in a contested case proceeding, subsection (a)(4) of this section makes it clear that all final orders, decisions, and opinions issued after October 1, 1982, except those expressly made confidential or privileged by statute or order of court, must be made available for public inspection and copying, at cost, and indexed by name and subject. There is no exception for contested case proceedings. Potts v. Bennett, 487 So. 2d 919 (Ala. Civ. App. 1985).

Cited in State Dep't of Revenue v. Estate of Hill, 505 So. 2d 1240 (Ala. Civ. App. 1987).

§ 41-22-5. Notice of intent to adopt, amend, or repeal rules; submission of data, views, etc., by interested persons; procedure for adoption of emergency rules; effect of this section on other procedural requirements; validity of rules in substantial compliance with this section; limitation of proceedings to contest rules.

Cross references. — As to the effective date of this section with regard to the Alabama department of environmental management and as to the validity and adoption of rules of that department, see § 41-22-27 (f).

While the notice requirement of this section does not apply in a contested case proceeding, § 41-22-4(a)(4) makes it clear that all final orders, decisions, and opinions issued after October 1, 1982, except those expressly made confidential or privileged by statute or order of court, must be made available for public inspection and copying, at cost, and indexed by name and subject. There is no exception for contested case proceedings. Potts v. Bennett, 487 So. 2d 919 (Ala. Civ. App. 1985).

§ 41-22-6. Designation of agency secretary; filing of copies of rules with secretary; information as to authorship of rules; filing of copies of rules with legislative reference service; maintenance of and public access to permanent registers of rules; effective dates of rules.

(a) Each agency shall have an officer designated as its secretary and shall file in the office of the secretary of the agency a certified copy of each rule adopted by it, including all rules, as defined in this chapter, existing on the effective date of this act. Each rule or regulation promulgated, whether the original or a revision, and all copies thereof, shall have the name or names of the author or authors, respectively, on its face. The secretary of the agency shall keep a permanent register of the rules open to public inspection.

(b) The secretary of each agency shall file in the office of the legislative reference service, no later than 15 days after the filing with the secretary of the agency and within 90 days after completion of the notice as required by subdivision (1) of subsection (a) of section 41-22-5, in a form and manner prescribed by the legislative reference service, a certified copy of each rule adopted by it, including all rules, as defined in this chapter, existing on the effective date of this act, but excluding any rule under review by the committee. The legislative reference service shall keep a permanent register of the rules open to public inspection.

(c) Each rule hereafter adopted is effective 35 days after filing with the legislative reference service, except that:

(1) If a later date is required by statute or specified in the rule, the later date is the effective date;

(2) Subject to applicable constitutional or statutory provisions, a rule becomes effective immediately upon filing with the legislative reference service, or at a subsequent stated date prior to indexing and publication, or at a stated date less than 35 days after filing, if the agency finds:

a. That a statute so provides; or

b. That this effective date is necessary because of immediate danger to the public health, safety or welfare, or because the action is required by or to comply with a federal statute or regulation which requires adoption of a rule upon fewer than 35 days' notice. In any subsequent action contesting the effective date of a rule promulgated under this paragraph, the burden of proof shall be on the agency to justify its finding. The agency's finding and a brief statement of the reasons therefor shall be filed with and made a part of the rule. Prior to indexing and publication, the agency shall make reasonable efforts to apprise the persons who may be affected by its rules of the adoption of rules made effective under the terms of this paragraph. (Acts 1981, No. 81-855, p. 1534, § 6; Acts 1986, No. 86-472, p. 880, § 1.)

Cross references. — As to the effective date of this section with regard to the Alabama department of environmental management and as to the validity and adoption of rules of that department, see § 41-22-27 (f).

The secretary at any state agency is the officer designated to be the keeper of the written guidelines utilized by the state board of health regarding chemical tests for intoxication. Childress v. City of Huntsville, 459 So. 2d 1008 (Ala. Crim. App. 1984).

Cited in Vizzina v. City of Birmingham, 533 So. 2d 652 (Ala. Crim. App. 1987); State v. Petro-Lewis Corp., 534 So. 2d 302 (Ala. Civ. App. 1988).

§ 41-22-7. Contents, publication, and availability of agency administrative codes, Alabama Administrative Code, and Alabama Administrative Monthly; filing of rules, amendments and repealers with legislative reference service; uniform system for numbering rules; omission from publications of rules which are applicable to only one county; cost to agencies for use of Alabama Administrative Monthly.

Cross references. — As to the effective date of this section with regard to the Alabama department of environmental management and as to the validity and adoption of rules of that department, see § 41-22-27 (f).

§ 41-22-8. Form for petition for adoption, amendment or repeal of rules; procedure upon submission of petition.

Each agency shall prescribe by rule the form for petition requesting the adoption, amendment or repeal of a rule and the procedure for submission, consideration, and disposition thereof. Within 60 days after submission of a petition, the agency either shall deny the petition in writing on the merits, stating its reasons for the denial, or initiate rule-making proceedings in accordance with section 41-22-5; provided, however, an agency which has its next regularly scheduled meeting beyond said 60-day period, may by written notice extend said period for not more than 30 days during which it shall deny or inititate rule-making proceedings. (Acts 1981, No. 81-855, p. 1534, § 8; Acts 1986, No. 86-472, p. 880, § 1.)

Cross references. — As to the effective date of this section with regard to the Alabama department of environmental management and as to the validity and adoption of rules of that department, see § 41-22-27 (f).

§ 41-22-9. Adoption by reference of codes, standards, and regulations of other agencies of this state or the United States or of other approved organizations; form of reference; availability from agency of information as to rules, etc., adopted by reference.

Cross references. — As to the effective date of this section with regard to the Alabama department of environmental management and as to the validity and adoption of rules of that department, see § 41-22-27 (f).

Statutory authority for state hospital planning development agency's incorporation by reference of federal regulations is found in this section. University of Ala. Hosps. v. Alabama Renal Stone Inst., Inc., 518 So. 2d 721 (Ala. Civ. App. 1987).

§ 41-22-10. Action for declaratory judgment as to validity or applicability of rule; stay of enforcement of rule by injunction.

Cross references. — As to the effective date of this section with regard to the Alabama department of environmental management and as to the validity and adoption of rules of that department, see § 41-22-27 (f).

Purpose. — In passing this section, the legislature did not intend to provide a petitioner with an election of remedies whereby he could, if he so chose, circumvent the authority of an agency by filing an initial action for declaratory judgment in the circuit court. Its intent was merely to make it clear that, in those instances where an agency refuses to act on a petition for declaratory or injunctive relief, such declaratory or injunctive relief is available in the circuit court. Stuart v. Historic Whse., Inc., 505 So. 2d 298 (Ala. 1986).

Person is required to request declaratory ruling from an agency pursuant to § 41-22-11 before he may proceed under this section. If the agency issues such a declaratory ruling, a petitioner's only avenue of judicial review is by appeal. However, if the agency fails to issue such a ruling, the petitioner may resort, as provided in this section, to an action for a declaratory judgment in the circuit court. Stuart v. Historic Whse., Inc., 505 So. 2d 298 (Ala. 1986).

Exhaustion of remedies under § 41-22-11 before proceeding under this section. — It is clear, when this section and § 41-22-11 are construed in pari materia, as they must be, and in light of the express purposes of § 41-22-2, that a litigant must exhaust his administrative remedies under § 41-22-11 before he may proceed to the circuit court under this section. Stuart v. Historic Whse., Inc., 505 S.W.2d 298 (Ala. 1986).

Failure of agency to make declaratory ruling. — Under the express language of § 41-22-11(b), a person may resort to the relief provided in this section after the agency involved has failed to make any declaratory ruling on the merits of a petition. Stuart v. Historic Whse., Inc., 505 So. 2d 301 (Ala. 1986).

Review available for failure of agency to issue declaratory ruling. — Although judicial review of "rulings" made by an agency is expressly limited by § 41-22-11(b) to that manner of review used in contested cases, no such qualification is made upon the review available for the failure of the agency to issue a declaratory ruling. In these instances, a person may resort to the declaratory action envisioned by this section. Stuart v. Historic Whse., Inc., 505 So. 2d 298 (Ala. 1986).

Question was properly raised in circuit court. — Where the Court of Civil Appeals reversed the trial court's holding that the actions taken by the state personnel board to discontinue reallocation constituted a rule change under the Alabama Administrative Procedure Act, and where the basis for the Court of Civil Appeals' decision was the finding by the trial court that the state employees association had not exhausted all administrative remedies, the Court of Civil Appeals erred since the question was clearly contemplated in this section and was properly raised in circuit court. Alabama State Personnel Bd. v. Cook, 544 So. 2d 167 (Ala. 1989).

Swing bed amendment was not valid because health council did not "substantially comply" with Alabama Administrative Procedure Act (AAPA) procedures; health council failed to publish proposal or adopted amendment as required by AAPA, and health council gave only 30 days' notice of the public hearing rather than 35 days' notice of the hearing as required by AAPA. Traylor Nursing Home, Inc. v. Alabama Statewide Health Coordinating Council, 543 So. 2d 1179 (Ala. 1988).

§ 41-22-11. Petition for declaratory ruling as to validity of rule, as to applicability of any rule or statute enforceable by an agency, or as to meaning and scope of agency order; form and contents; binding effect of agency ruling; effect of failure to issue ruling; judicial review.

(a) On the petition of any person substantially affected by a rule, an agency may issue a declaratory ruling with respect to the validity of the rule or with respect to the applicability to any person, property or state of facts of any rule or statute enforceable by it or with respect to the meaning and scope of any order of the agency. The petition seeking an administrative determination under this section shall be in writing and shall state with particularity facts sufficient to show the person seeking relief is substantially affected by the rule. Each agency shall prescribe by rule the form of such petitions and the procedure for their submission, consideration and disposition, and shall prescribe in its rules the circumstances in which rulings shall or shall not be issued.

(b) A declaratory ruling is binding on the agency and the person requesting it unless it is altered or set aside by a court in a proper proceeding. Such rulings are subject to review in the circuit court of Montgomery county, unless otherwise specifically provided by the statute, in the manner provided in section 41-22-20 for the review of decisions in contested cases. Failure of the agency to issue a declaratory ruling on the merits within 45 days of the request for such ruling shall constitute a denial of the request as well as a denial of the merits of the request and shall be subject to judicial review. (Acts 1981, No. 81-855, p. 1534, § 11; Acts 1986, No. 86-472, p. 880, § 1.)

Cross references. — As to the effective date of this section with regard to the Alabama department of environmental management and as to the validity and adoption of rules of that department, see § 41-22-27 (f).

Person is required to request declaratory ruling from an agency pursuant to this section before he may proceed under § 41-22-10. If the agency issues such a declaratory ruling, a petitioner's only avenue of judicial review is by appeal. However, if the agency fails to issue such a ruling, the petitioner may resort, as provided in § 41-22-10, to an action for a declaratory judgment in the circuit court. Stuart v. Historic Whse., Inc., 505 So. 2d 298 (Ala. 1986).

Exhaustion of remedies under this section before proceeding under § 41-22-10. — It is clear, when § 41-22-10 and this section are construed in pari materia, as they must be, and in light of the express purposes of § 41-22-2, that a litigant must exhaust his administrative remedies under this section before he may proceed to the circuit court under § 41-22-10. Stuart v. Historic Whse., Inc., 505 S.W.2d 298 (Ala. 1986).

Failure of agency to make declaratory rule. — Under the express language of subsection (b) of this section, a person may resort to the relief provided in § 41-22-10 after the agency involved has failed to make any declaratory ruling on the merits of a petition. Stuart v. Historic Whse., Inc., 505 So. 2d 301 (Ala. 1986).

Review available from failure of agency to issue declaratory ruling. — Although judicial review of "rulings" made by an agency is expressly limited by subsection (b) of this section to that manner of review used in contested cases, no such qualification is made upon the review available for the failure of the agency to issue a declaratory ruling. In these instances, a person may resort to the declaratory action envisioned by § 41-22-10. Stuart v. Historic Whse., Inc., 505 So. 2d 298 (Ala. 1986).

§ 41-22-12. Notice and opportunity for hearing in contested cases; contents of notice; procedure upon failure of notified party to appear; presentation of evidence and argument; right to counsel; disposition by stipulation, settlement, etc.; contents of record; public attendance at oral proceedings; recordings and transcripts of oral proceedings.

(a) In a contested case, all parties shall be afforded an opportunity for hearing after reasonable notice in writing delivered either by personal service as in civil actions or by certified mail, return receipt requested. However, an agency may provide by rule for the delivery of such notice by other means, including, where permitted by existing statute, delivery by first class mail, postage prepaid, to be effective upon the deposit of the notice in the mail. Delivery of the notice referred to in this subsection shall constitute commencement of the contested case proceeding.

(b) The notice shall include:

(1) A statement of the time, place and nature of the hearing;

(2) A statement of the legal authority and jurisdiction under which the hearing is to be held;

(3) A reference to the particular sections of the statutes and rules involved; and

(4) A short and plain statement of the matters asserted. If the agency or other party is unable to state the matters in detail at the time the notice is served, the initial notice may be limited to a statement of the issues involved. Thereafter, upon application, a more definite and detailed statement shall be furnished.

(c) If a party fails to appear in a contested case proceeding after proper service of notice, the presiding officer may, if no adjournment is granted, proceed with the hearing and make a decision in the absence of the party.

(d) Opportunity shall be afforded all parties to respond and present evidence and argument on all material issues involved and to be represented by counsel at their own expense. Provided, where the statutory determinative process is a multi-level or multi-step procedure, the opportunity to present evidence need be afforded the parties at only one level or step in the determination process, unless otherwise provided by statute establishing such determination process.

(e) Unless precluded by statute, informal dispositions may be made of any contested case by stipulation, agreed settlement, consent order or default or by another method agreed upon by the parties in writing.

(f) The record in a contested case shall include:

(1) All pleadings, motions, and intermediate rulings;

(2) All evidence received or considered and all other submissions; provided, in the event that evidence in any proceeding may contain proprietary and confidential information, steps shall be taken to prevent public disclosure of that information;

(3) A statement of all matters officially noticed;

(4) All questions and offers of proof, objections and rulings thereon;

(5) All proposed findings and exceptions;

(6) Any decision, opinion or report by the hearing officer at the hearing; and

(7) All staff memoranda or data submitted to the hearing officer or members of the agency in connection with their consideration of the case unless such memoranda or data is protected as confidential or privileged; provided, if such memoranda or data contains information of a proprietary and confidential nature, it shall be protected by the agency from public disclosure.

(g) Oral proceedings shall be open to the public, unless private hearings are otherwise authorized by law. Oral proceedings shall be recorded either by mechanized means or by qualified shorthand reporters. Oral proceedings or any part thereof shall be transcribed at the request of any party with the expense of the transcription charged to the requesting party. The recording or stenographic notes of oral proceedings or the transcription thereof shall be filed with and maintained by the agency for at least five years from the date of decision and shall be made available for inspection by the public, except in those cases where private hearings are authorized by law, or where the proceedings shall be ordered sealed by order of court, or are required to be sealed by statute.

(h) Findings of fact shall be based solely on the evidence in the record and on matters officially noticed in the record. (Acts 1981, No. 81-855, p. 1534, § 12; Acts 1986, No. 86-472, p. 880, § 1.)

Cross references. — As to the exemption of the Alabama department of environmental management from the provisions of this section, see § 41-22-27 (f).

Agencies are not granted authority to make rules in conflict with sections. — When the legislature established the procedures for appeals delineated in §§ 41-22-12 through 41-22-20, it intended that a uniform procedure be established that would apply to and govern all agencies covered by the Alabama Administrative Procedure Act (AAPA); the legislature did not intend to grant, nor did it grant, to the agency any authority to make rules in conflict with those specific sections; rules of agencies should not be allowed to erode or repeal such intended uniformity; variations should occur only through legislation creating "other law," not through an agency rule or regulation that conflicts with the AAPA provisions. Hand v. State Dep't of Human Resources, 548 So. 2d 176 (Ala. 1988).

Applicant for an off-premises beer license need not be given any more due process than is required by the AAPA and the alcoholic beverage licensing code. Potts v. Bennett, 487 So. 2d 919 (Ala. Civ. App. 1985).

Cited in Stevens v. Blake, 456 So. 2d 795 (Ala. Civ. App. 1984); Bryant v. State Dep't of Pub. Safety, 494 So. 2d 425 (Ala. Civ. App. 1986).

§ 41-22-13. Rules of evidence in contested cases.

In contested cases:

(1) The rules of evidence as applied in nonjury civil cases in the circuit courts of this state shall be followed. When necessary to ascertain facts not reasonably susceptible of proof under those rules, evidence not admissible thereunder may be admitted (except where precluded by statute) if it is of a type commonly relied upon by reasonably prudent persons in the conduct of their affairs. Agencies shall give effect to the rules of privilege recognized by law. Except as hereinafter provided, objections to evidentiary offers may be made and shall be noted in the record. Whenever any evidence is excluded as inadmissible, all such evidence existing in written form shall remain a part of the record as an offer of proof. The party seeking the admission of oral testimony may make an offer of proof by means of a brief statement on the record describing the testimony excluded. All rulings on the admissibility of evidence shall be final and shall appear in the record. Subject to these requirements, when a hearing will be expedited and interests of the parties will not be prejudiced substantially, any part of the

evidence may be received or may be required to be submitted in verified form; provided, the adversary party shall not be denied the right of cross-examination of the witness. The testimony of parties and witnesses shall be made under oath. Provided, however, in the hearing of a contested case where judicial review of the case is by trial de novo, the agency may announce that it shall not be necessary that objections be made during the hearing and upon such announcement, it shall not be required or necessary that objection to be made to any testimony or evidence which may be offered by either party, and on the consideration of such cases the agency shall consider only such testimony and evidence as is relevant, material, competent and legal, and shall not consider any testimony or evidence which is irrelevant, immaterial, incompetent or illegal, whether objection shall have been made thereto or not, and whether such testimony be brought out on direct, cross or re-direct examination, or is hearsay. The agency shall not be required to point out what testimony or evidence should be excluded or not considered. Either party, on submission, shall have the privilege of calling attention to any testimony or evidence which is deemed objectionable. If specific objection be made to any evidence and a ruling made thereon by the agency, this exception shall not apply to such evidence.

(2) Documentary evidence otherwise admissible may be received in the form of copies or excerpts, or by incorporation by reference to material already on file with the agency. Upon request, parties shall be given an opportunity to compare the copy with the original.

(3) A party may conduct cross-examination required for a full and true disclosure of the facts, except as may otherwise be limited by law.

(4) Official notice may be taken of all facts of which judicial notice may be taken and of other scientific and technical facts within the specialized knowledge of the agency. Parties shall be notified at the earliest practicable time, either before or during the hearing, or by reference in preliminary reports, preliminary decisions or otherwise, of the facts proposed to be noticed and their source, including any staff memoranda or data, and the parties shall be afforded an opportunity to contest such facts before the decision is announced unless the agency determines as part of the record or decision that fairness to the parties does not require an opportunity to contest such facts.

(5) The experience, technical competence, and specialized knowledge of the agency may be utilized in the evaluation of the evidence. (Acts 1981, No. 81-855, p. 1534, § 13; Acts 1986, No. 86-472, p. 880, § 1.)

Cross references. — As to the exemption of the Alabama department of environmental management from the provisions of this section, see § 41-22-27 (f).

Cited in Regional Dialysis v. Northeast Ala. Kidney Clinic, Inc., 480 So. 2d 1229 (Ala. Civ. App. 1985).

§ 41-22-14. Intervention in contested cases.

Cross references. — As to the exemption of the Alabama department of environmental management from the provisions of this section, see § 41-22-27 (f).

§ 41-22-15. Majority requirement for adoption of final decision in contested cases; use of proposed orders in cases where any official is unfamiliar with the case; finality of proposed orders.

Cross references. — As to the exemption of the Alabama department of environmental management from the provisions of this section, see § 41-22-27 (f).

No requirement for specific vote designation. — An analysis of this section, as well as § 34-24-366, reveals that no requirement exists calling for a specific vote designation. Evers v. Medical Licensure Comm'n, 523 So. 2d 414 (Ala. Civ. App. 1987).

Board's letter of denial of a beer license met the minimum requirements of this section and § 41-22-16 by apprising the applicant of its findings and conclusions, denying the application for stated permissible reasons, i.e., that the applicant's establishment, for which the beer license was sought, was too close to a school crossing and would be detrimental to the safety of the school children and create a traffic hazard, and further noting the opposition which had been voiced to the application. Spivey v. City of Florence, 480 So. 2d 598 (Ala. Civ. App. 1985).

§ 41-22-16. Form and content of final order; when final order to be rendered; service of notice and copies of final order.

(a) The final order in a proceeding which affects substantial interests shall be in writing and made a part of the record and include findings of fact and conclusions of law separately stated, and it shall be rendered within 30 days:

(1) After the hearing is concluded, if conducted by the agency;

(2) After a recommended order, or findings and conclusions are submitted to the agency and mailed to all parties, if the hearing is conducted by a hearing officer; or

(3) After the agency has received the written and oral material it has authorized to be submitted, if there has been no hearing. The 30 day period may be waived or extended with the consent of all parties and may be extended by law with reference to specific agencies.

(b) Findings of fact, if set forth in a manner which is no more than mere tracking of the statutory language, shall be accompanied by a concise and explicit statement of the underlying facts of record which support the findings. If, in accordance with agency rules, a party submitted proposed findings of fact or filed any written application or other request in connection with the proceeding, the order shall include a ruling upon each proposed finding and a brief statement of the grounds for denying the application or request.

(c) If an agency head finds that an immediate danger to the public health, safety, or welfare requires an immediate final order, it shall recite with particularity the facts underlying such findings in the final order, which shall be appealable or enjoinable from the date rendered.

(d) Parties shall be notified either personally or by certified mail return receipt requested of any order and, unless waived, a copy of the final order shall be so delivered or mailed to each party or to his attorney of record. Provided, however, that, except as hereinafter provided, notification of any order other than a final decision or order subject to judicial review may, where permitted by existing statute, be delivered by first class mail, postage prepaid, and delivery shall be effective upon deposit of the notice and, unless waived, the final order in the mail; provided, the notification of the final order subject to judicial review, together with a copy of the final order, shall be delivered either by personal service as in civil actions or by certified mail, return receipt requested. (Acts 1981, No. 81-855, p. 1534, § 16; Acts 1986, No. 86-472, p. 880, § 1.)

Cross references. — As to the exemption of the Alabama department of environmental management from the provisions of this section, see § 41-22-27 (f).

Minimum requirements of due process were met where the facts which formed the basis of the dental board's decision were cited extensively and its conclusion of guilt merely tracked the language of the statute. Vining v. Board of Dental Exmrs., 492 So. 2d 607 (Ala. Civ. App. 1985).

The purpose of subsection (b) of this section is to provide the unsuccessful applicant for administrative relief with an adequate explanation of the reasons for the denial. Nursing Home of Dothan, Inc. v. Alabama State Health Planning & Dev. Agency, 542 So. 2d 940 (Ala. 1989).

Minimum requirements of subsection (b) were met. — Where an unsuccessful certificate of need applicant was constructively apprised of the reasons for the denial, the minimum requirements of subsection (b) of this section were met. Nursing Home of Dothan, Inc. v. Alabama State Health Planning & Dev. Agency, 542 So. 2d 940 (Ala. 1989).

This section requires an administrative agency to include findings of fact and conclusions of law in its final order. Thompson v. Alabama Dep't of Mental Health, 477 So. 2d 427 (Ala. Civ. App. 1985).

Board's letter of denial of a beer license met the minimum requirements of this section and § 41-22-15 by approving the applicant of its findings and conclusions, denying the application for stated permissible reasons, i.e., that the applicant's establishment, for which the beer license was sought, was too close to a school crossing and would be detrimental to the safety of the school children and create a traffic hazard, and further noting the opposition which had been voiced to the application. Spivey v. City of Florence, 480 So. 2d 598 (Ala. Civ. App. 1985).

Cited in Evers v. Medical Licensure Comm'n, 523 So. 2d 414 (Ala. Civ. App. 1987); Nursing Home of Dothan, Inc. v. Alabama State Health Planning & Dev. Agency, 542 So. 2d 935 (Ala. Civ. App. 1988).

Collateral references. — Doctrine of res judicata or collateral estoppel as barring relitigation in state criminal proceedings of issues previously decided in administrative proceedings. 30 ALR4th 856.

§ 41-22-17. Filing of application for rehearing in contested cases; form and content; effect of application on final order; grounds for rehearing; service of application on parties of record; agency decision on application.

Cross references. — As to the exemption of the Alabama department of environmental management from the provisions of this section, see § 41-22-27 (f).

Agency must enter order within 30 days. — If the agency does not enter an order within 30 days of the filing of the application for rehearing, the application is deemed denied by operation of law at the expiration of the 30-day period and further, the statute is clear that the applicant is required to file the notice of appeal within 30 days after the decision on the application for rehearing. Davis v. Alabama Medicaid Agency, 519 So. 2d 538 (Ala. Civ. App. 1987).

Appeals from agency decisions are

purely statutory, and the time constrictions must be satisfied. Davis v. Alabama Medicaid Agency, 519 So. 2d 538 (Ala. Civ. App. 1987).

§ 41-22-18. Disqualification from participation in proposed order or final decision based upon conflict of interest or personal bias.

Cross references. — As to the exemption of the Alabama department of environmental management from the provisions of this section, see § 41-22-27 (f).

§ 41-22-19. Grant, denial, renewal, etc., of licenses.

Cross references. — As to the exemption of the Alabama department of environmental management from the provisions of this section, see § 41-22-27 (f).

Cited in Bryant v. State Dep't of Pub. Safety, 494 So. 2d 425 (Ala. Civ. App. 1986); Evers v. Medical Licensure Comm'n, 523 So. 2d 414 (Ala. Civ. App. 1987).

§ 41-22-20. Judicial review of preliminary, procedural, etc., actions or rulings and final decisions in contested cases.

(a) A person who has exhausted all administrative remedies available within the agency (other than rehearing) and who is aggrieved by a final decision in a contested case is entitled to judicial review under this chapter. A preliminary, procedural, or intermediate agency action or ruling is immediately reviewable if review of the final agency decision would not provide an adequate remedy.

(b) Except in matters for which judicial review is otherwise provided for by law, all proceedings for review shall be instituted by filing of notice of appeal or review and a cost bond, with the agency. A petition shall be filed either in the circuit court of Montgomery county or in the circuit court of the county in which the agency maintains its headquarters, or unless otherwise specifically provided by statute, in the circuit court of the county where a party (other than an intervenor) resides or if a party (other than an intervenor), is a corporation, domestic or foreign, having a registered office or business office in this state, then in the county of such registered office or principal place of business within this state.

(c) The filing of the notice of appeal or the petition does not itself stay enforcement of the agency decision. If the agency decision has the effect of suspending or revoking a license, a stay or supersedeas shall be granted as a matter of right upon such conditions as are reasonable, unless the reviewing court, upon petition of the agency, determines that a stay or supersedeas would constitute a probable danger to the public health, safety, or welfare. In all other cases, the agency may grant, or the reviewing court may order, a stay upon appropriate terms, but, in any event, the order shall specify the conditions upon which the stay or supersedeas is granted; provided, however, if the appeal or proceedings for review to any reviewing court is from an order of the agency increasing or reducing or refusing to increase rates, fares or charges, or any of them, or any schedule or parts of any schedule of such rates, fares or charges, the reviewing court shall not direct or order a supersedeas or stay of the action or order to be reviewed without requiring, as a condition precedent to the granting of such supersedeas, that the party applying for supersedeas or stay shall execute and file with the clerk of said court a bond as provided for and required by statute or law. If the circuit court shall fail or refuse to grant supersedeas or stay, the party seeking such relief may petition the appropriate court to which the appeal or review lies to order a supersedeas or stay of the action or order of the agency from which review is sought. After the required bond shall have been filed and approved by the clerk, such agency order shall be stayed and superseded, and it shall be lawful to charge the rates, fares or charges which have been reduced, refused or denied by said agency order, until the final disposition of the cause. The provisions of this subsection shall apply when applicable, anything in Rule 60 of the Alabama Rules of Civil Procedure restricting the provisions of this subsection to the contrary notwithstanding.

(d) The notice of appeal or review shall be filed within 30 days after the receipt of the notice of or other service of the final decision of the agency upon the petitioner or, if a rehearing is requested under section 41-22-17, within 30 days after the decision thereon. The petition for judicial review in the circuit court shall be filed within 30 days after the filing of the notice of appeal or review. Copies of the petition shall be served upon the agency and all parties of record after the petition is filed with the court. Any party to the agency proceeding may become a party to the review proceedings by notifying the court within 30 days after receipt of the copy of the petition. Any person aggrieved may petition to become a party by filing a motion to intervene as provided in section 41-22-14. Failure to file such petition within the time stated shall operate as a waiver of the right of such person to review under this chapter, except that for good cause shown, the judge of the reviewing court may extend the time for filing, not to exceed an additional 30 days, or, within four months after the issuance of the agency order, issue an order permitting a review of the agency decision under this chapter notwithstanding such waiver. Any notice required herein which is mailed by the petitioner, certified mail return receipt requested, shall be deemed to have been filed as of the date it is postmarked. This section shall apply to judicial review from the final order or action of all agencies, and amends the judicial review statutes relating to all agencies to provide a period of 30 days within which to appeal or to institute judicial review.

(e) If there has been no hearing prior to agency action and the reviewing court finds that the validity of the action depends upon disputed facts, the court shall order the agency to conduct a prompt fact-finding proceeding under this chapter after having a reasonable opportunity to reconsider its determination on the record of the proceedings.

(f) Unreasonable delay on the part of an agency in reaching a final decision shall be justification for any person whose rights, duties, or privileges are adversely affected by such delay to seek a court order compelling action by the agency.

(g) Within 30 days after receipt of the notice of appeal or within such additional time as the court may allow, the agency shall transmit to the reviewing court the original or a certified copy of the entire record and transcript of the proceedings under review. With the permission of the court, the record of the proceedings under review may be shortened by stipulation of all parties to the review proceedings. Any party found by the reviewing court to have unreasonably refused to stipulate to limit the record may be taxed by the court for such additional costs as may be occasioned by the refusal. The court may require or permit subsequent corrections or additions to the record when deemed desirable.

(h) The petition for review shall name the agency as respondent and shall contain a concise statement of:

(1) The nature of the agency action which is the subject of the petition;

(2) The particular agency action appealed from;

(3) The facts and law on which jurisdiction and venue are based;

(4) The grounds on which relief is sought; and

(5) The relief sought.

(i) In proceedings for judicial review of agency action in a contested case, except where appeal or judicial review is by a trial de novo, a reviewing court shall not itself hear or accept any further evidence with respect to those issues of fact whose determination was entrusted by law to the agency in that contested case proceeding; provided, however, that evidence may be introduced in the reviewing court as to fraud or misconduct of some person engaged in the administration of the agency or procedural irregularities before the agency not shown in the record and the affecting order, ruling or award from which review is sought, and proof thereon may be taken in the reviewing court. If, before the date set for hearing a petition for judicial review of agency action in a contested case, it is shown to the satisfaction of the court that additional evidence is material and that there were good reasons for failure to present it in the contested case proceeding before the agency, the court may remand to the agency and order that the additional evidence be taken before the agency upon conditions determined by the court. The agency may modify its findings and decision in the case by reason of the additional evidence and shall file that evidence and any modification, new findings, or decision with the reviewing court and mail copies of the new findings, or decision to all parties.

(j) The review shall be conducted by the court without a jury and, except as herein provided, shall in the review of contested cases be confined to the record and such additions thereto as may be made under subsection (i) of this section. Judicial review shall be by trial de novo in the circuit court where review is sought from tax assessments, tax determinations or tax redeterminations, rulings of the revenue department granting, denying or revoking licenses, or rulings on petitions for tax refunds, or, unless a subsequent agency statute provides otherwise, where an agency statute existing on the effective date of Act No. 81-855, 1981 Acts of Alabama, or thereafter enacted provides for a trial de novo on appeal to or review by the courts; provided, however, in the review of tax assessments, tax determinations or tax redeterminations, rulings of the revenue department granting, denying or revoking licenses, or rulings on petitions for tax refunds, the administrative record and transcript shall be transmitted to the reviewing court as provided in subsection (g) of this section, and, on motion of either party, shall be admitted into evidence in the trial de novo, subject to the rights of either party to assign errors, objections or motions to exclude calling attention to any testimony or evidence in the administrative record or transcript which is deemed objectionable or inadmissible. Provided further that, with the consent of all parties, judicial review may be on the administrative record and transcript. The court, upon request, shall hear oral argument and receive written briefs.

(k) Except where judicial review is by trial de novo, the agency order shall be taken as prima facie just and reasonable and the court shall not substitute its judgment for that of the agency as to the weight of the evidence on questions of fact, except where otherwise authorized by statute. The court may affirm the agency action or remand the case to the agency for taking additional testimony and evidence or for further proceedings. The court may reverse or modify the decision or grant other appropriate relief from the agency action, equitable or legal, including declaratory relief, if the court finds that the agency action is due to be set aside or modified under standards set forth in appeal or review statutes applicable to that agency, or where no such statutory standards for judicial review are applicable to the agency, if substantial rights of the petitioner have been prejudiced because the agency action is:

(1) In violation of constitutional or statutory provisions;

(2) In excess of the statutory authority of the agency;

(3) In violation of any pertinent agency rule;

(4) Made upon unlawful procedure;

(5) Affected by other error of law;

(6) Clearly erroneous in view of the reliable, probative, and substantial evidence on the whole record; or

(7) Unreasonable, arbitrary or capricious or characterized by an abuse of discretion or a clearly unwarranted exercise of discretion.

(*l*) Unless the court affirms the decision of the agency, the court shall set out in writing, which writing shall become a part of the record, the reasons for its decision. (Acts 1981, No. 81-855, p. 1534, § 20; Acts 1986, No. 86-472, p. 880, § 1.)

Cross references. — As to judicial review of any order of the environmental management commission modifying, approving or disapproving an administrative action of the Alabama department of environmental management, see § 41-22-27 (f).

Section 22-21-275 overrides this section for judicial review of SHPDA. — The method for obtaining judicial review of State Health Planning and Development Agency (SHPDA) rulings on certificate of need applications which is specifically set forth in § 22-21-275(14), must override the general provisions for obtaining judicial review of an agency's adverse actions set forth in subsection (b) of this section. Such a result arises from the language of subsection (b) itself. Mobile Infirmary Ass'n v. Emfinger, 474 So. 2d 731 (Ala. Civ. App. 1985).

Subsection (b) of this section specifically exempts from its judicial review filing provisions those matters for which judicial review is provided by other law. Because judicial review of actions of State Health Planning and Development Agency and the Board on certificate of need applications is specifically governed by § 22-21-275(14), the only logical conclusion is that § 22-21-275(14), and not the Alabama Administrative Procedure Act must govern the filing of a petition or complaint for judicial review in this case. Mobile Infirmary Ass'n v. Emfinger, 474 So. 2d 731 (Ala. Civ. App. 1985).

The initial provision of subsection (b) of this section specifically exempts from the statute those "matters for which judicial review is otherwise provided for by law." In this case judicial review is specifically provided for by § 22-21-275(14). Thus, that statute must govern, and not this section. This interpretation of subsection (b) is in accord with the longstanding rule that where a special statutory provision is provided as an exclusive method of review for a particular type case, no other statutory review is available. Mobile Infirmary Ass'n v. Emfinger, 474 So. 2d 731 (Ala. Civ. App. 1985).

Subsection (k) of this section requires that the commission's decision be taken as prima facie just and reasonable. In other words, the reviewing court must give the commission's decision a presumption of correctness, and it may not substitute its judgment for that of the commission as to the weight of the evidence on questions of fact. Dawson v. Alabama Dep't of Envtl. Mgt., 529 So. 2d 1012 (Ala. Civ. App.), cert. denied, 529 So. 2d 1015 (Ala. Civ. App. 1988).

Under subsection (k) of this section, the circuit court may reverse or modify an agency's decision only if it determines that the agency action is due to be set aside or modified under standards set forth in appeal or review statutes applicable to the agency or if substantial rights of the petitioner have been prejudiced. Alabama Medicaid Agency v. Norred, 497 So. 2d 176 (Ala. Civ. App. 1986).

Under this limited standard of review, the circuit court must give the agency's determination of noneligibility a presumption of correctness. Alabama Medicaid Agency v. Norred, 497 So. 2d 176 (Ala. Civ. App. 1986).

Agencies are not granted authority to make rules in conflict with sections. — When the legislature established the proce-

dures for appeals delineated in §§ 41-22-12 through 41-22-20, it intended that a uniform procedure be established that would apply to and govern all agencies covered by the Alabama Administrative Procedure Act (AAPA); the legislature did not intend to grant, nor did it grant, to the agency any authority to make rules in conflict with those specific sections; rules of agencies should not be allowed to erode or repeal such intended uniformity; variations should occur only through legislation creating "other law," not through an agency rule or regulation that conflicts with the AAPA provisions. Hand v. State Dep't of Human Resources, 548 So. 2d 176 (Ala. 1988).

Review procedure of the act is in two parts. The first part requires that a notice of appeal be filed with the agency within 30 days of its decision. The second part requires that a petition for review be filed in the circuit court within 30 days of the filing of the notice of appeal. This section also authorizes the circuit court to extend the time for filing the review petition for a period not to exceed four months. However, it does not authorize an extension of time for filing the notice of appeal with the agency. Consequently, the trial court was without authority to extend the time for filing the notice of appeal with the agency. State Medicaid Agency v. Anthony, 528 So. 2d 326 (Ala. Civ. App. 1988).

Department's regulation could not legally provide another method of review. — The legislature had not created a method of judicial review of the department's actions different from that promulgated by subsection (b), and the department's regulations could not legally provide another method of judicial review of the department's actions. Hand v. State Dep't of Human Resources, 548 So. 2d 176 (Ala. 1988).

Scope of review. — Judicial review of administrative decisions is limited in scope as to whether the order is supported by substantial evidence, whether the agency's decision is reasonable and not arbitrary, and whether the agency acted within the power conferred upon it by law and the Constitution. Ferlisi v. Alabama Medicaid Agency, 481 So. 2d 400 (Ala. Civ. App. 1985); Alabama Medicaid Agency v. Norred, 497 So. 2d 176 (Ala. Civ. App. 1986).

Judicial review of the agency's determination regarding reimbursement is quite limited under the Alabama Administrative Procedure Act. Alabama Medicaid Agency v. Beverly Enters., 521 So. 2d 1329 (Ala. Civ. App. 1987).

The review obtained under certiorari is essentially the same as that provided for under the Alabama Administrative Procedure Act.

Thompson v. Alabama Dep't of Mental Health, 477 So. 2d 427 (Ala. Civ. App. 1985).

Where personnel dispute arose prior to October 1, 1983, judicial review would be by certiorari rather than under the provisions of the Alabama Administrative Procedure Act. Thompson v. Alabama Dep't of Mental Health, 477 So. 2d 427 (Ala. Civ. App. 1985).

Petition for a writ of mandamus was not the proper vehicle for judicial review of board's denial of beer license. Review in the circuit court is by an appeal from the board's decision. Spivey v. City of Florence, 480 So. 2d 598 (Ala. Civ. App. 1985).

Dismissal of petition for mandamus. — Even if a writ of mandamus was a proper method for obtaining judicial review of board's denial of beer license, the trial court did not err in dismissing the petition for the writ as untimely where the applicant filed the petition more than 60 days after she received the board's letter of denial, and did not file a notice of appeal with the board. Spivey v. City of Florence, 480 So. 2d 598 (Ala. Civ. App. 1985).

Agency rulings reviewed with presumption of correctness. — Unless otherwise authorized by statute, the final rulings of a state agency must be reviewed with an attendant presumption of correctness. Benton v. Alabama Bd. of Medical Exmrs., 467 So. 2d 234 (Ala. 1985).

In an administrative appeal case, when there is ample evidence to support the decision of the administrative agency, it is not the duty of the trial court to substitute its judgment for that of the administrative agency. Alabama Dep't of Pub. Health v. Perkins, 469 So. 2d 651 (Ala. Civ. App. 1985).

Circuit court must attribute to the Alabama Medicaid Agency's decision a presumption of correctness. Alabama Medicaid Agency v. Light, 507 So. 2d 107 (Ala. Civ. App. 1987).

An agency's interpretation of its own regulation must stand if it is reasonable, even though it may not appear as reasonable as some other interpretation. Ferlisi v. Alabama Medicaid Agency, 481 So. 2d 400 (Ala. Civ. App. 1985).

Findings upheld if supported by substantial evidence. — In implementing the standard of review set out in subsection (k) of this section, the circuit court should uphold the findings and conclusions of personnel if those findings and conclusions are supported by substantial evidence. Alabama ABC Bd. v. Tyson, 500 So. 2d 1124 (Ala. Civ. App. 1986).

A decision cannot be said to be "arbitrary" where there is a reasonable justification for the decision or where the determination is founded upon adequate principles or fixed standards. Alabama Dep't of Pub. Health

v. Perkins, 469 So. 2d 651 (Ala. Civ. App. 1985).

Judicial deference to an administrative agency tends to insure uniformity and consistency of decisions in light of the agency's specialized competence in the field of operation entrusted to it by the legislature; because of the specialized competency and the uniformity of decisions, a court frustrates legislative intent and usurps the discretionary role by stepping in when the agency's choice is not clearly unreasonable or arbitrary. Alabama Dep't of Pub. Health v. Perkins, 469 So. 2d 651 (Ala. Civ. App. 1985).

Trial court may not merely recite statutory grounds for reversal. — In view of the judicial deference granted an agency's decision, the trial court cannot merely recite the statutory grounds for reversal or modification set forth in subsection (k) when setting aside an agency's findings, and in addition to the statutory grounds for reversal, the trial court must provide, pursuant to subsection (l), specific reasons in its order to support its conclusions. Alabama Medicaid Agency v. Peoples, 549 So. 2d 504 (Ala. Civ. App. 1989).

Reversal of agency determination. — Absent a showing that an agency decision was unsupported by substantial evidence, that it was unreasonable or arbitrary, or that the agency acted outside its authority, its determination may not be reversed. Nursing Home of Dothan, Inc. v. Alabama State Health Planning & Dev. Agency, 542 So. 2d 935 (Ala. Civ. App. 1988), aff'd, 542 So. 2d 940 (Ala. 1989.)

Failure of circuit court to list reasons for rejecting agency decision is grounds for reversal. — Because the standard of review to be applied to an administrative decision is necessarily a limited one, the appeals court, without a listing by the circuit court of its reasons for rejecting the agency's decision, cannot determine if the circuit court complied with the prescribed review standard. Thus, for the failure to list the reasons for its decision, the judgment of the circuit court must be reversed and the cause remanded. Alabama Medicaid Agency v. Beverly Enters., 504 So. 2d 1211 (Ala. Civ. App. 1987).

Exempting language of subsection (b) applies to all of this section. Such an interpretation is in accord with the rule that, where a statute provides an exclusive method for judicial review, no other statutory review is available. Mays v. Sabel Steel Servs., Inc., 500 So. 2d 467 (Ala. Civ. App. 1986).

Administrative Procedure Act does not limit de novo review in tax appeals to circuit court. — The legislature never had any intent that the Administrative Procedure Act should limit or prohibit a de novo review in tax appeals to the circuit court. State v. Service Engraving Co., 495 So. 2d 695 (Ala. Civ. App. 1986).

Agency must enter order within 30 days. — If the agency does not enter an order within 30 days of the filing of the application for rehearing, the application is deemed denied by operation of law at the expiration of the 30-day period and further, the statute is clear that the applicant is required to file the notice of appeal within 30 days after the decision on the application for rehearing. Davis v. Alabama Medicaid Agency, 519 So. 2d 538 (Ala. Civ. App. 1987).

No judicial review of intra-agency personnel actions. — Judicial review is limited to "contested cases" under this section and intra-agency personnel actions do not fall within the term "contested case" as defined by § 41-22-3(3). Heatherly v. Kemsel, 504 So. 2d 285 (Ala. Civ. App. 1986).

Appeal from agency decision on Medicaid benefits must be filed within 30 days. — The trial court exceeded its jurisdiction when it allowed plaintiff, who had been declared ineligible for Medicaid benefits, to file her notice of appeal with the Medicaid Agency more than 30 days after the agency decision. State Medicaid Agency v. Anthony, 528 So. 2d 326 (Ala. Civ. App. 1988).

Appeals from agency decisions are purely statutory, and the time constrictions must be satisfied. Davis v. Alabama Medicaid Agency, 519 So. 2d 538 (Ala. Civ. App. 1987).

Judicial review of actions before securities commission. — Subsections (a) and (b) of § 8-6-32 provide for the sole method of judicial review of actions before the securities commission. Thus, these provisions, rather than the provisions of the Alabama Administrative Procedure Act, govern the manner of review in cases involving securities commission actions with respect to securities. Doggett v. Alabama Sec. Comm'n, 511 So. 2d 204 (Ala. Civ. App. 1987).

Appeal from action of state health planning and development agency. — There being no statute providing for nonapplicant's appeal of the actions of the state health planning and development agency, the procedures provided by the Alabama Administrative Procedure Act, including venue, were applicable. The circuit court therefore did not abuse its discretion in denying the agency's motion to transfer the appeal to Montgomery county, the official residence of the agency. AMI Brookwood Medical Center v. State Health Planning & Dev. Agency, 500 So. 2d 1149 (Ala. Civ. App. 1986).

Deadline for filing appeal as to unemployment compensation claim. — Since judicial review of unemployment compensation claims is provided for by other law, § 25-4-95, that statute, with its 10-day deadline for filing an appeal, must therefore govern in unemployment compensation cases, rather than the 30-day deadline of the Alabama Administrative Procedure Act. Mays v. Sabel Steel Servs., Inc., 500 So. 2d 467 (Ala. Civ. App. 1986).

For statement by trial judge held insufficient under this section because it did not set forth the reasons for the court's determination that the commissioner was in error, see Alabama Medicaid Agency v. Norred, 497 So. 2d 176 (Ala. Civ. App. 1986).

Court may not substitute its judgment for that of the Alabama Medicaid Agency when weighing evidence. — The court of civil appeals may not substitute its judgment— nor could the circuit court substitute its judgment—for that of the Alabama Medicaid Agency when weighing the evidence. Alabama Medicaid Agency v. Light, 507 So. 2d 107 (Ala. Civ. App. 1987).

Decision against Medicaid applicant upheld. — Where a Medicaid applicant was entitled to recover the benefits under certain tendencies of the evidence, but according to other portions of the evidence, the Medicaid agency could have concluded that the applicant had not proven by convincing evidence that she transferred her home (without consideration one month before she filed her application) to her son exclusively for a purpose other than establishing her eligibility for Medicaid benefits, the agency's decision against the applicant was upheld. State v. Day, 531 So. 2d 1244 (Ala. Civ. App. 1988).

Cited in Personnel Board v. King, 456 So. 2d 80 (Ala. Civ. App. 1984); Coleman v. Alabama ABC Bd., 465 So. 2d 1158 (Ala. Civ. App. 1985); Regional Dialysis v. Northeast Ala. Kidney Clinic, Inc., 480 So. 2d 1226 (Ala. Civ. App. 1985); Alacare, Inc.-North v. Baggiano, 785 F.2d 963 (11th Cir. 1986); Marchetti v. Alabama Bd. of Exmrs. in Psychology, 494 So. 2d 448 (Ala. Civ. App. 1986); Wood v. Baggiano, 509 So. 2d 242 (Ala. Civ. App. 1986); Alabama State Bd. of Pharmacy v. Stewart, 547 So. 2d 562 (Ala. Civ. App. 1989).

§ 41-22-21. Appeal of final judgment of circuit court under section 41-22-20.

An aggrieved party may obtain a review of any final judgment of the circuit court under section 41-22-20 by appeal to the appropriate court to which the appeal or review lies. The appeal shall be taken within 42 days of the date of the entry of the judgment or order appealed from as in other civil cases, although the appeal may be taken regardless of the amount involved. (Acts 1981, No. 81-855, p. 1534, § 21; Acts 1986, No. 86-472, p. 880, § 1.)

Cross references. — As to judicial review of any order of the environmental management commission modifying, approving or disapproving an administrative action of the Alabama department of environmental management, see § 41-22-27 (f).

Cited in Regional Dialysis v. Northeast Ala. Kidney Clinic, Inc., 480 So. 2d 1226 (Ala. Civ. App. 1985).

§ 41-22-22. Creation of joint committee on administrative regulation review; composition, chairman, meetings, compensation and expenses, etc.; functions of the committee.

Cross references. — As to the effective date of this section with regard to the Alabama department of environmental management and as to the validity and adoption of rules of that department, see § 41-22-27 (f).

§ 41-22-23. Submission of proposed rules by agency to the joint committee on administrative regulation review; approval, disapproval, or amendment by committee; criteria for review of rules.

(a) The notice required by subdivision (1) of subsection (a) of section 41-22-5 shall be given, in addition to the persons therein named, to the chairman of the legislative committee. The agency shall furnish the committee with 25 copies of the proposed rule or rules, and no rule, except an emergency rule issued pursuant to subsection (b) of section 41-22-5 shall be effective until these copies are so furnished. Any member of the senate or house of representatives who requests a copy of proposed agency rules from the chairman of the joint committee on administrative regulation review shall be provided a copy and the agency proposing rules shall furnish additional copies of the proposed rule or rules immediately. The form of the proposed rule presented to the committee shall be as follows: New language shall be underlined and language to be deleted shall be typed and lined through.

(b) The committee shall study all proposed rules and, in its discretion, may hold public hearings thereon. In the event the committee fails to give notice to the agency of either its approval or disapproval of the proposed rule within 60 days after publication in the Alabama Administrative Monthly, the committee shall be deemed to have approved the proposed regulation for the purposes of this section. In the event the committee disapproves a proposed rule or any part thereof, it shall give notice of such disapproval to the agency. Any disapproved rule shall be suspended until the adjournment of the next regular session of the legislature following the date of disapproval and suspension of the committee or until the legislature shall, by joint resolution, revoke the suspension of the committee. The rule shall be reinstated on the adjournment of said legislative session in the event the legislature by joint resolution, fails to sustain the disapproval and suspension of the committee.

(c) The committee may propose an amendment to any proposed rule and may disapprove the proposed rule and return it to the agency with the suggested amendment. In the event the agency accepts the rule as amended, the agency may resubmit the rule as amended to the committee. In the event the agency does not accept the amendment, the proposed amended rule shall be submitted to the legislature as disapproved, as provided in section 41-22-24.

(d) An agency may withdraw a proposed rule by leave of the committee. An agency may resubmit a rule so withdrawn or returned under this section with minor modification. Such a rule is a new filing and subject to this section but is not subject to further notice as provided in subsection (a) of section 41-22-5.

(e) The committee is authorized to review and approve or disapprove any rule adopted prior to October 1, 1982.

(f) In determining whether to approve or disapprove proposed rules, the committee shall consider the following criteria:

(1) Would the absence of the rule or rules significantly harm or endanger the public health, safety, or welfare?

(2) Is there a reasonable relationship between the state's police power and the protection of the public health, safety, or welfare?

(3) Is there another, less restrictive method of regulation available that could adequately protect the public?

(4) Does the rule or do the rules have the effect of directly or indirectly increasing the costs of any goods or services involved and, if so, to what degree?

(5) Is the increase in cost, if any, more harmful to the public than the harm that might result from the absence of the rule or rules?

(6) Are all facets of the rulemaking process designed solely for the purpose of, and so they have, as their primary effect, the protection of the public?

(7) Any other criteria the committee may deem appropriate. (Acts 1981, No. 81-855, p. 1534, § 23; Acts 1986, No. 86-472, p. 880, § 1.)

Cross references. — As to the effective date of this section with regard to the Alabama department of environmental management and as to the validity and adoption of rules of that department, see § 41-22-27 (f).

§ 41-22-24. Reconsideration of disapproved rules by the legislature.

On the first day of each regular session of the Alabama legislature the chairman of the committee shall submit a joint resolution sustaining the disapproval under section 41-22-23 by the joint committee of any proposed regulation to each house of the legislature for their study. Such resolution with the disapproved rule attached shall be referred by the speaker of the house or the lieutenant governor or both to an appropriate committee or committees, other than the joint committee on administrative regulation review, for consideration and such committee or committees shall schedule hearings thereon, if requested by an affected party or the submitting agency. The legislature may, by joint resolution, sustain the disapproval of the committee under section 41-22-23. In the event the legislature fails to sustain such committee disapproval by the adjournment of the next regular session of the legislature, the rule shall be reinstated. (Acts 1981, No. 81-855, p. 1534, § 24; Acts 1986, No. 86-472, p. 880, § 1.)

Cross references. — As to the effective date of this section with regard to the Alabama department of environmental management and as to the validity and adoption of rules of that department, see § 41-22-27 (f).

§ 41-22-25. Construction and applicability of chapter.

(a) This chapter shall be construed broadly to effectuate its purposes. Except as expressly provided otherwise by this chapter or by another statute referring to this chapter by name, the rights created and the requirements imposed by this chapter shall be in addition to those created or imposed by every other statute in existence on the date of the passage of this chapter or thereafter enacted. If any other statute in existence on the date of the passage of this chapter or thereafter enacted diminishes any right conferred upon a person by this chapter or diminishes any requirement imposed upon an agency by this chapter, this chapter shall take precedence unless the other statute expressly provides that it shall take precedence over all or some specified portion of this named chapter.

(b) Except as to proceedings in process on October 1, 1982, this chapter shall be construed to apply to all covered agency proceedings and all agency action not expressly exempted by this chapter or by another statute specifically referring to this chapter by name. (Acts 1981, No. 81-855, p. 1534, § 25; Acts 1986, No. 86-472, p. 880, § 1.)

Cross references. — As to the effective date of this section with regard to the Alabama department of environmental management and as to the validity and adoption of rules of that department, see § 41-22-27 (f).

The introductory language "Except as expressly provided otherwise by this chapter . . ." specifically excepts those matters where the Alabama Administrative Procedure Act itself states an exception to its requirements. Mobile Infirmary Ass'n v. Emfinger, 474 So. 2d 731 (Ala. Civ. App. 1985).

Language "Except as expressly provided otherwise by this chapter" in subsection (a) indicates that, where the Alabama Administrative Procedure Act expressly provides otherwise, the rights and requirements provided by the AAPA do not apply, even though they may be more liberal than the rights and requirements provided elsewhere. The AAPA does "expressly provide otherwise" in the case of those procedures governing judicial review of the final decision of an agency. Mays v. Sabel Steel Servs., Inc., 500 So. 2d 467 (Ala. Civ. App. 1986).

Cited in Springhill Hosps. v. Alabama State Health Planning Agency & Mobile Infirmary, 549 So. 2d 1348 (Ala. Civ. App. 1989).

§ 41-22-26. Repeal of inconsistent laws.

Cross references. — As to the effective date of this section with regard to the Alabama department of environmental management and as to the validity and adoption of rules of

that department, see § 41-22-27 (f).
Cited in Lambert v. Alabama Real Estate Comm'n, 490 So. 2d 18 (Ala. Civ. App. 1986).

§ 41-22-27. Effective date of this chapter; validity, review, etc., of existing rules; disposition of adjudicative proceedings commenced prior to October 1, 1983; effective date and applicability as to Alabama department of environmental management.

(a) This chapter shall take effect at 12:01 A.M., October 1, 1982; provided, however, that section 41-22-22 shall take effect October 1, 1981. In order that the legislative reference service may appoint and hire an aide to receive the rules and in order to promulgate the Alabama Administrative Code and the Alabama Administrative Monthly as soon as possible, subsections (a) and (b) of section 41-22-6 and subsections (a) through (e) of section 41-22-7 shall also become effective October 1, 1981. It shall be the duty of all agencies in existence on the passage of this chapter and all agencies created thereafter to cooperate with the office of the legislative reference service in compiling the Alabama Administrative Code and the Alabama Administrative Monthly by submitting to the committee all rules now and hereafter in effect, and all proposed rules.

(b) All existing rules shall be indexed by October 1, 1983, and the administrative code of each agency shall be completed and up-to-date at that time and the Alabama Administrative Code shall be completed and up-to-date by November 15, 1983.

(c) Any rule in effect before 12:01 A.M., October 1, 1983, except those adopted following a public hearing that was required by statute, shall forthwith be reviewed by the agency concerned on the written request of a person substantially affected by the rule involved. The agency concerned shall initiate the rule making procedures provided by this chapter within 90 days after receiving such written request. If the agency concerned fails to initiate the rule making procedures within 90 days, the operation of the rule shall be suspended. The right of review established by this subsection shall be exercisable no earlier than October 1, 1983.

(d) All rules in effect on September 30, 1983, shall be and become invalid on October 1, 1983, unless:

(1) Such rules are properly filed, indexed, and included within the administrative code of the agency in accordance with all the provisions of this chapter; and

(2) Such rules adopted prior to October 1, 1982, were validly adopted under procedures in effect prior to those provided in this chapter, or were readopted pursuant to the requirements of this chapter; or

(3) Such rules adopted on or subsequent to October 1, 1982, were validly adopted pursuant to the requirements of this chapter.

(e) All contested cases and other adjudicative proceedings conducted pursuant to any provision of the statutes of this state that were begun prior to October 1, 1983, shall be continued to a conclusion, including judicial review, under the provisions of such statutes, except that contested cases and other adjudicative proceedings that have not progressed to the stage of a hearing may, with the consent of all parties and the agency conducting the proceedings, be conducted in accordance with the provisions of this chapter as nearly as feasible.

(f) Sections 41-22-1 through 41-22-11 and 41-22-22 through 41-22-27 shall take effect with regard to the Alabama department of environmental management at 12:01 A.M. on October 1, 1986. All rules which were validly adopted by the Alabama department of environmental management prior to October 1, 1986, under procedures in effect at the times such rules were adopted shall be valid, and all such rules adopted by the aforesaid department shall be properly filed, indexed and included within the administrative code of the aforesaid department in accordance with all the provisions of this chapter by October 1, 1987. The Alabama department of environmental management shall be exempt from the provisions of sections 41-22-12 through 41-22-19. Except as provided in subdivision (6) of subsection (c) of section 22-22A-7, judicial review of any order of the environmental management commission modifying, approving or disapproving an administrative action of the Alabama department of environmental management shall be in accordance with the provisions for review of final agency decisions of contested cases in sections 41-22-20 and 41-22-21. (Acts 1981, No. 81-855, p. 1534, § 27; Acts 1986, No. 86-472, p. 880, § 1.)

The review obtained under certiorari is essentially the same as that provided for under the Alabama Administrative Procedure Act. Thompson v. Alabama Dep't of Mental Health, 477 So. 2d 427 (Ala. Civ. App. 1985).

Where personnel dispute arose prior to October 1, 1983, judicial review would be by certiorari rather than under the provisions of the Alabama Administrative Procedure Act. Thompson v. Alabama Dep't of Mental Health, 477 So. 2d 427 (Ala. Civ. App. 1985).

Cited in Alabama Bd. of Nursing v. Herrick, 454 So. 2d 1041 (Ala. Civ. App. 1984); Humana Medical Corp. v. State Health Planning & Dev. Agency, 460 So. 2d 1295 (Ala. Civ. App. 1984); Coleman v. Alabama ABC Bd., 465 So. 2d 1158 (Ala. Civ. App. 1985); Regional Dialysis v. Northeast Ala. Kidney Clinic, Inc., 480 So. 2d 1226 (Ala. Civ. App. 1985).

DEPARTMENT OF ECONOMIC AND COMMUNITY AFFAIRS

CHAPTER 23.

DEPARTMENT OF ECONOMIC AND COMMUNITY AFFAIRS.

Article 1.

General Consideration.

Sec.
41-23-1. Creation; composition; transfer of functions, etc., to department.
41-23-2. Implementation of duties and functions by employees in classified service; salaries.
41-23-3. Transfer of appropriations to department.
41-23-4. Appointment of director; term of office; salary; qualifications; planning and programming by department.
41-23-5. Establishment of divisions; appointment of division chiefs; oath of office; restrictions on employment; directors of merged agencies abolished; purpose of chapter.
41-23-6. Promulgation of rules and regulations.
41-23-7. Legislative oversight commission.

Article 2.

Alabama Enterprise Zone Act.

41-23-20. Short title; legislative findings and purpose.
41-23-21. Definitions.
41-23-22. Criteria for qualifications of enterprise zones; number of enterprise

Sec.
     zones; maximum size and life of enterprise zones.
41-23-23. Applications; selection of zones; enterprise zone advisory council; legislative oversight committee.
41-23-24. Tax incentives; adoption of rules to implement tax credits and incentives; maximum tax credit per new permanent employee; application of tax credits; tax credits are in addition to exemptions and credits under chapter 18 of Title 40; no credit for taxes to other states.
41-23-25. Nontax incentives.
41-23-26. Additional requirements for business, etc., to receive benefits.
41-23-27. Annual report of department.
41-23-28. Required agreement by appropriate governing authority.
41-23-29. Powers and duties of department.
41-23-30. Contracts with eligible businesses to provide for tax exemptions; preference to Alabama manufacturers; endorsement resolution; certification as to employees; wage subsidies.
41-23-31. Rules and regulations; cooperation of agencies.
41-23-32. Federal tax exemptions and enterprise zone legislation.

Cross references. — As to the responsibility of the director of the department of economic and community affairs for the distribution, transfer, or disposal of surplus personal property owned by the state, see article 6, chapter 16, Title 41.

ARTICLE 1.

GENERAL CONSIDERATION.

Code commissioner's note. — Sections 41-23-1 through 41-23-7 have been designated as article 1 of this chapter in view of the enactment of article 2, §§ 41-23-20 through 41-23-32, by Acts 1987, No. 87-573.

253

§ 41-23-1. Creation; composition; transfer of functions, etc., to department.

There is hereby created and established the department of economic and community affairs within the office of the governor and directly under his supervision and control. The department of economic and community affairs shall consist of: the governor, the office of state planning and federal programs, the Alabama department of energy, Alabama law enforcement planning agency, the office of highway and traffic safety, and the office of employment and training as presently created by and provided for in sections 41-9-205 through 41-9-214, sections 41-6A-1 through 41-6A-11, sections 41-8A-1 through 41-8A-4, sections 41-8A-8 through 41-8A-10, and sections 41-8A-12 through 41-8A-13, 32-4-1 through 32-4-7, and Executive Order No. 34, 1980, respectively, and in accordance with the applicable federal laws. All respective functions, duties, responsibilities, obligations, property rights, appropriations, employees, property and supplies as provided by said sections, and whether accruing or vesting, are hereby transferred to and vested in the department of economic and community affairs. (Acts 1983, 2nd Ex. Sess., No. 83-194, p. 363, § 1.)

§ 41-23-2. Implementation of duties and functions by employees in classified service; salaries.

Present employees in the classified service of the state merit system within each agency transferred in section 41-23-1 whose job classifications are not abolished hereinafter, shall continue with the department of economic and community affairs in such functions deemed necessary to carry out the duties and responsibilities of the department of economic and community affairs. Other employees necessary to implement the duties and functions of the department of economic and community affairs may be employed subject to the provisions of the state merit system laws and shall be entitled to the same rights and benefits thereunder. Salaries set for such employees shall not exceed the salary set by law for executive department heads.

Nothing herein shall be construed to prevent or preclude the removal of an employee in a manner provided by this article, or for cause in a manner provided by law. (Acts 1983, 2nd Ex. Sess., No. 83-194, p. 363, § 2.)

§ 41-23-3. Transfer of appropriations to department.

All appropriations heretofore or hereafter made to: the office of state planning and federal programs, the Alabama department of energy, the Alabama law enforcement planning agency, the state manpower planning council (CETA), the office of highway and traffic safety, and the office of employment and training are hereby consolidated and transferred to the department of economic and community affairs. (Acts 1983, 2nd Ex. Sess., No. 83-194, p. 363, § 3.)

§ 41-23-4. Appointment of director; term of office; salary; qualifications; planning and programming by department.

(a) The governor shall appoint a chief administrative officer to be designated as director of the department of economic and community affairs. Such officer shall serve at the pleasure of the governor at a salary to be set in the same manner and with the same limitations as otherwise provided by law for executive department heads. The director of the said department shall be a member of such boards, councils and commissions, as they relate to his authority under the provisions of this article, and as required and currently authorized under the various federal programs and as approved by the governor.

(b) The governor through the department of economic and community affairs shall encourage comprehensive and coordinated planning and programming of economic and community affairs. (Acts 1983, 2nd Ex. Sess., No. 83-194, p. 363, § 4.)

§ 41-23-5. Establishment of divisions; appointment of division chiefs; oath of office; restrictions on employment; directors of merged agencies abolished; purpose of chapter.

(a) The director of the department of economic and community affairs, with the approval of the governor, may establish such division or divisions as may, in his discretion, be reasonably necessary for the administration and enforcement of any law, rule or regulation with which the department is charged or the performance of any of its functions or duties. Each division in the department shall be headed by and be under the direction, supervision and control of an officer who shall be designated as the chief of such division. All chiefs of divisions shall be appointed by the director of said department, with the approval of the governor. Before entering upon the discharge of their duties, such chiefs of divisions shall take the constitutional oath of office. Each of such officers shall devote his full time to his official duties and shall hold no other lucrative position while serving as such. The offices or positions of director of any of the merged departments or agencies are hereby abolished.

(b) It is one of the purposes of this article to coordinate, into one department, the functions of the office of state planning and federal programs, the Alabama department of energy, Alabama law enforcement planning agency, the office of highway and traffic safety, and the office of employment and training or any successor thereto. There is hereby established the following divisions: the office of state planning and federal programs, the Alabama department of energy, Alabama law enforcement planning agency, the office of highway and traffic safety, and the office of employment and training. The functions of each division shall be administered by a division chief who shall be full-time and salaried as now provided by law. Each division chief shall report to and be under the supervision of the director of the department of economic and community affairs. (Acts 1983, 2nd Ex. Sess., No. 83-194, p. 363, § 5.)

§ 41-23-6. Promulgation of rules and regulations.

The director of the department of economic and community affairs may prescribe such reasonable rules and regulations for the conduct of its business and made in accordance with the Alabama Administrative Procedure Act. (Acts 1983, 2nd Ex. Sess., No. 83-194, p. 363, § 6.)

§ 41-23-7. Legislative oversight commission.

(a) There is hereby created the department of economic and community affairs legislative oversight commission to consist of the chairman and deputy chairman of the senate committee on finance and taxation, three members of the senate to be appointed by the lieutenant governor, the chairman and vice-chairman of the house ways and means committee, and three members of the house of representatives to be appointed by the speaker of the house.

(b) The commission shall hold an organizational meeting within 30 days after this bill is enacted, and shall elect a chairman and vice-chairman from among its members. Thereafter, the commission shall meet at least two times annually, and additional meetings shall be held at the call of the chairman or upon the request of six or more members. Such meetings shall be held with the director of the department of economic and community affairs in attendance.

(c) The commission shall adopt its own rules of procedure for the transaction of business, and a majority of the members present shall constitute a quorum for the purpose of transacting business or performing authorized duties.

(d) Each member of the commission shall be entitled to his or her regular legislative compensation and per diem and travel expenses for each day he or she attends a meeting or conducts business of the commission, and such compensation and expenses shall be paid from the funds appropriated for the use of the legislature.

(e) The commission shall monitor and evaluate the management and operations of the department of economic and community affairs, shall recommend to the legislature the enactment of such laws respecting the department of economic and community affairs as the commission shall deem desirable, and shall submit a written report on the operations, finances and grants made by the department of economic and community affairs during each regular session of the Alabama legislature. (Acts 1983, 2nd Ex. Sess., No. 83-194, p. 363, § 7.)

ARTICLE 2.

ALABAMA ENTERPRISE ZONE ACT.

§ 41-23-20. Short title; legislative findings and purpose.

This article shall be cited as the "Alabama Enterprise Zone Act."

The legislature of Alabama hereby finds and declares that the health, safety, and welfare of the people of this state are dependent upon the continued encouragement, development, growth, and expansion of the private sector within the state and that there are certain depressed areas in the state that need the particular attention of government to help attract private sector investment into these areas. Therefore, it is declared to be the purpose of this article to stimulate business and industrial growth in the depressed areas of the state, both in urban and rural areas, by the relaxation of certain governmental controls, by providing assistance to businesses and industries, and by providing state and local tax and nontax incentives in these areas. (Acts 1987, No. 87-573, p. 897, § 1.)

§ 41-23-21. Definitions.

For purposes of this article, the following terms shall have the meaning hereinafter ascribed to them, unless the context clearly indicates otherwise:

(1) COUNCIL. The enterprise zone advisory council.

(2) DEPARTMENT. The Alabama department of economic and community affairs.

(3) GOVERNING AUTHORITY. The governing body of a county or municipality.

(4) ENTERPRISE ZONE. A geographic area which is economically depressed, in need of expansion of business and industry and the creation of jobs and designated to be eligible for the benefits of this article, and is a target by governments for development by providing tax and nontax incentives to private enterprise.

(5) RURAL ENTERPRISE ZONE. An enterprise zone located in a non-MSA county, as such is defined by the United States Bureau of the Census.

(6) URBAN ENTERPRISE ZONE. An enterprise zone located in an MSA county, as such is defined by the United States Bureau of the Census. (Acts 1987, No. 87-573, p. 897, § 2.)

§ 41-23-22. Criteria for qualifications of enterprise zones; number of enterprise zones; maximum size and life of enterprise zones.

(a) The department shall establish criteria for qualifications of enterprise zones. These criteria shall not be in conflict with any provisions of federal enterprise zone legislation that may be enacted for enterprise zones which apply for federal designation. The department shall give consideration to the following:

257

(1) Unemployment.

(2) Poverty rate.

(3) Per capita income.

(4) Migration.

(5) Number of residents receiving public assistance.

(b) There initially shall be 10 enterprise zones within the state of Alabama, excluding any zones established in Birmingham [pursuant to Act No. 83-142, S. 18 of the 1983 Second Special Session (Acts 1983, p. 150)] and Prichard [pursuant to Act No. 83-676, S. 506 of the 1983 Regular Session (Acts 1983, p. 1065)], and Montgomery [pursuant to Act No. 86-201, H. 538 of the 1985 Regular Session (Acts 1986, p. 264)]. Within 18 months after passage of this article, additional geographic areas shall be targeted as enterprise zones. There shall not be more than 27 enterprise zones established in Alabama.

(c) Each zone shall not exceed a maximum of 10,000 acres.

(d) The maximum life of a zone shall not exceed 15 years. (Acts 1987, No. 87-573, p. 897, § 3; Acts 1989, No. 89-659, p. 1310)

The 1989 amendment, effective May 11, 1989, substituted "more than 27 enterprise zones" for "more than 25 enterprise zones" in the last sentence of subsection (b).

§ 41-23-23. Applications; selection of zones; enterprise zone advisory council; legislative oversight committee.

Selection of zones and the general guidelines for implementation of the provisions of this article shall be as follows:

(1) The Alabama department of economic and community affairs shall see that all applications are processed as follows:

a. The state or any governmental entity in the proposed area may submit an application for zone designation.

b. Each application should provide a statement of incentives being offered by the governmental entities, such as:

1. Regulatory relief or waiver;

2. Services provided;

3. Tax incentives;

4. Other nontax incentives.

c. It is contemplated that state, county and/or municipal governments may devise an innovative package of local incentives in their respective jurisdictions and aggressively pursue zone designation.

(2) Zones shall be selected by the department, with input from the advisory council, which shall have the responsibility for the general implementation of the law.

(3) An enterprise zone advisory council consisting of members of the Alabama development office, southern development council, department of industrial relations, department of education, Alabama highway department, department of environmental management, department of agriculture and industries, department of revenue and other qualified individuals or organizations shall be appointed by the governor with provisions to

insure geographic representation of rural and urban areas. This council shall be limited to 11 representatives and shall serve at the pleasure of the governor.

(4) A legislative oversight committee shall be appointed by the lieutenant governor and the speaker. Such committee shall consist of three members from the house of representatives and three members from the senate appointed by the respective officers of each body. (Acts 1987, No. 87-573, p. 897, § 4.)

§ 41-23-24. Tax incentives; adoption of rules to implement tax credits and incentives; maximum tax credit per new permanent employee; application of tax credits; tax credits are in addition to exemptions and credits under chapter 18 of Title 40; no credits for taxes to other states.

(a) Any provisions of Title 40, chapter 18, notwithstanding, and specifically any provisions of sections 40-18-22, 40-18-35, 40-18-35.1, 40-18-37 and 40-18-38, to the contrary notwithstanding, the following tax incentives may be available to any business, industry or manufacturer who complies with the provisions of this article:

(1) INCOME TAX CREDIT. — There may be a five-year credit of varying proportions of taxes due from zone operations: first year, 80 percent; second year, 60 percent; third year, 40 percent; fourth and fifth years, 20 percent. This credit is available for corporations, partnerships, and proprietorships provided that 30 percent of the new permanent employees were formerly unemployed for at least 90 days prior to this employment.

(2) CREDIT FOR EXPENSES OF TRAINING NEW EMPLOYEES. — There may be a tax credit for the expenses of training new employees in new skills. The maximum credit shall be $1,000.00 per employee.

(3) CREDIT FOR NEW INVESTMENTS. — There may be a credit for new investments within the state in the following amounts: 10 percent on first $10,000.00 invested, five percent on next $90,000.00 invested, and two percent on remaining investment. This credit is also available for improvements to existing facilities, provided at least five new permanent employees are hired.

(4) LOCAL TAXES. — A reduction of permit fees, user fees and business, professional and occupational license taxes may be permitted by the local governments. This incentive is optional and shall be stated when the area applies for zone designation.

(b) The commissioner of the department of revenue shall formulate, promulgate, issue and enforce any reasonable and necessary rules to implement any state tax credits or incentives.

(c) It is expressly provided that any tax credit, pursuant to this section, shall not total in excess of $2,500.00 per new permanent employee hired pursuant to this article. This tax credit may be applied in all enterprise zones to any state income tax liability or any state franchise tax liability and shall be used for the taxable year in which the increase in average annual employment occurred to the maximum allowed. However, if the entire credit cannot be used in the year earned, the remainder may be applied against the income tax or franchise tax for the succeeding two years or until the entire credit is used, whichever occurs first.

(d) All tax credits herein prescribed may be in addition to any exemptions and credits authorized in Title 40, chapter 18.

(e) No tax credits for tax incentives shall be authorized for any credit for taxes, fees or funds to other states or territories. (Acts 1987, No. 87-573, p. 897, § 5.)

§ 41-23-25. Nontax incentives.

Nontax incentives shall include:

(1) REGULATION EXEMPTIONS. — The local governments may exempt regulations to the extent they propose in the application for designation; however, no such exemption can adversely affect the health and welfare of the citizens of the state. Such exemption shall be by resolution or ordinance.

(2) EMPLOYEE TRAINING AND TECHNICAL ASSISTANCE.

a. Employee training may be made available to zone business through the department.

b. Technical assistance in business start-ups. A business starting up in the enterprise zone may be afforded technical assistance such as accounting, planning, etc., through a public university or state junior college in the area, which has agreed to accept such responsibility. Assistance may be provided by the small business development centers, technical assistance centers and others.

(3) INCREASED OR SPECIALIZED SERVICES PROVIDED BY LOCAL GOVERNMENTS. — The local governments would state in the application for designation such increased services it would provide, such as fire protection, police protection and utility services. All services are at local option. (Acts 1987, No. 87-573, p. 897, § 6.)

§ 41-23-26. Additional requirements for business, etc., to receive benefits.

Additional requirements for a business, partnership, corporation or individual to receive benefits shall include:

(1) The business must expand its labor force or make new capital investments or prevent a loss of employment to an existing business.

(2) A business may not have closed or reduced employment elsewhere in Alabama in order to expand into the zone. (Acts 1987, No. 87-573, p. 897, § 7.)

§ 41-23-27. Annual report of department.

The department shall report annually to the legislature and the governor, and provide a thorough evaluation of the implementation of the zone law, including: numbers of business activity; actual new income for the state after taxes and benefits pursuant to this article; number of new employees; cost to state for each new employee; and state and local taxes generated. (Acts 1987, No. 87-573, p. 897, § 8.)

§ 41-23-28. Required agreement by appropriate governing authority.

The department shall designate qualified enterprise zones only after receiving notice from the appropriate governing authority that it additionally agrees to:

(1) Devise and implement a program to improve police protection within the zone.

(2) Give priority to the use in the zone of any UDAG, CDBG, JTPA, industrial bonds, or other funds received from the appropriate agencies of the federal government.

(3) Assist the department in certifying employers to be eligible for said benefits.

(4) Authorize the department to supersede certain specified local regulations and ordinances which may serve to discourage economic development within the enterprise zone.

(5) Assist the department in evaluating progress made in any enterprise zone within its jurisdiction. (Acts 1987, No. 87-573, p. 897, § 9.)

§ 41-23-29. Powers and duties of department.

The department shall administer the provisions of this article and shall have the following powers and duties in addition to those mentioned elsewhere in this article and in other laws of this state:

(1) To monitor the implementation and operation of this article and conduct a continuing evaluation of the progress made in the enterprise zones.

(2) To assist the governing authority of an enterprise zone in obtaining assistance from the federal government, including the possible suspension of federal regulations within the enterprise zone.

(3) To assist the governing authority of an enterprise zone in obtaining assistance from any other department of state government, including assistance in providing training, technical assistance, and wage subsidies to new businesses and small businesses within an enterprise zone.

(4) To assist any employer or prospective employer within an enterprise zone in obtaining the benefits of any incentive or inducement program authorized by Alabama law.

(5) To submit an annual written report evaluating the effectiveness of the program and any suggestions for legislation to the governor and the legislature no later than the third day of each regular session.

(6) To promulgate rules and regulations to effectuate this article, in accordance with the Administrative Procedure Act.

(7) To notify each legislator whose district includes any portion of an enterprise zone when the department designates such a zone. (Acts 1987, No. 87-573, p. 897, § 10.)

§ 41-23-30. Contracts with eligible businesses to provide for tax exemptions; preference to Alabama manufacturers; endorsement resolution; certification as to employees; wage subsidies.

(a) The department, after consultation with the council, and with the approval of the governor, may enter into contracts with eligible businesses to provide:

(1) For the exemption from sales and use tax imposed by the state of Alabama or from sales and use tax imposed by its political subdivisions, upon approval of the governing authority thereof, of the purchases of the material used in the construction of a building, or any addition or improvement thereon, for housing any legitimate zone business enterprise, and machinery and equipment used in that enterprise.

(2) For certain exemptions from income taxes levied by the state of Alabama levied on eligible corporations and individuals, for a period of five years.

(3) For certain exemption of corporate franchise taxes levied by the state of Alabama for a period of five years.

(b) The department may enter into the contracts provided in subsection (a) of this section provided that:

(1) The business and its contractors give preference and priority to Alabama manufacturers and, in the absence of Alabama manufacturers, to Alabama suppliers, contractors, and labor, except where not reasonably possible to do so without added expense, substantial inconvenience, or sacrifice in operational efficiency.

(2) The request for such exemption is accompanied by an endorsement resolution approved by the appropriate local governing body, port district, or industrial development board in whose jurisdiction the establishment is to be located.

(3) The business is or shall be located within the boundaries of an urban or rural enterprise zone.

(4) The business located in an urban or rural enterprise zone and receiving the benefits of this article certifies that at least 35 percent of its employees:

a. Are residents of the urban enterprise zone hosting the location of the business at the time of their employment; or are residents of the same county in which a rural enterprise zone is located; and

b. Were receiving some form of public assistance prior to employment; or

c. Were considered unemployable by traditional standards, or lacking in basic skills; or

d. Any combination of the above.

Such certification must be updated annually in order for the business to continue receiving the benefits pursuant to this article.

(c) The department, in cooperation with the council, may enter into agreements with employers located in either urban or rural enterprise zones under which the employers may receive wage subsidies payable from the United States Department of Labor JTPA manpower block grant funds, to the extent that these funds are granted to the state of Alabama by the United States Department of Labor. (Acts 1987, No. 87-573, p. 897, § 11.)

§ 41-23-31. Rules and regulations; cooperation of agencies.

The directors of the Alabama department of economic and community affairs, Alabama development office, department of education, the department of industrial relations and the commissioner of the department of revenue shall be authorized to formulate reasonable rules and regulations necessary to implement the provisions of this article and shall cooperate with each other in the implementation of this article. (Acts 1987, No. 87-573, p. 897, § 12.)

§ 41-23-32. Federal tax exemptions and enterprise zone legislation.

The provisions of this article shall be complementary to and consistent with federal tax exemptions and be superseded when necessary by the passage of federal enterprise zone legislation. (Acts 1987, No. 87-573, p. 897, § 13.)

CHAPTER 24.

ALABAMA COMMUNITY SERVICE
GRANT PROGRAM.

Effective date. — The act which added this chapter became effective April 27, 1989.

§ 41-24-1. Definitions.

The following words and phrases, whenever used in this chapter, shall have the respective meanings unless the context clearly indicates otherwise:

(1) ACT. The Alabama Community Service Grant Program Act of 1989.

(2) GRANT. The award by a state grant-making agency of funds appropriated by the legislature or from funds received as gifts or donations to a

qualifying grant-recipient agency for expenditure according to the provisions of a grant proposal.

(3) GRANT-MAKING AGENCY. A state agency of the state of Alabama, designated by the legislature through an Alabama community service grant program appropriation, having authority to approve grant proposals, direct and coordinate the expenditure of grant funds.

(4) GRANT PROPOSAL. A written plan for the expenditure of grant funds by a grant-recipient agency, which meets one or more of the purposes delineated in section 41-24-3, subject to approval by and to be expended under the direction of the head of the grant-making agency.

(5) GRANT RECIPIENT AGENCY. A local community agency, organization, institution or project within the state of Alabama whose grant proposal has been approved by a grant-making agency. (Acts 1989, No. 89-354, p. 700, § 1.)

§ 41-24-2. Purpose.

The purpose of this chapter is to create the Alabama community service grant program to advance the program objectives of participating state departments and agencies by the awarding of grants to qualified community agencies, institutions, organizations and projects within the state of Alabama. The legislature recognizes that the program objectives of the several departments and agencies of the state of Alabama can be advanced and, in some cases, advanced in a more economical manner by awarding grants to qualified grant recipient agencies, when the expenditure of such grant funds are made under the approval, direction and in coordination with the grant-making agency. The legislature may from time to time appropriate state funds to grant-making agencies in accordance with the provisions of this chapter under the title, "Alabama Community Service Grant Program"; said funds shall be awarded to grant recipient agencies in denominations approved by and the expenditure of same shall be under the control of the heads of grant-making agencies. (Acts 1989, No. 89-354, p. 700, § 2.)

§ 41-24-3. Purposes for which Alabama community service grants shall be made.

Alabama community service grants shall be made only for the following purposes: 1) To enhance the education of the citizenry through activities, expenditures for capital improvements or equipment, that promote literacy, learning, arts appreciation, public health and mental health; 2) to promote activities that provide human and social services which reduce the hardships of old age, poor health or poverty; 3) to promote the marketability, yield or quality of Alabama-produced agricultural commodities; and 4) to promote the preservation, restoration, development and propagation of Alabama's natural resources, recreational facilities, environment, history, culture, transportation lanes, tourism, public safety, historic landmarks and buildings. (Acts 1989, No. 89-354, p. 700, § 3.)

§ 41-24-4. Authority and responsibilities of heads of grant-making agencies.

It will be the responsibility of the heads of grant-making agencies to evaluate grant proposals based on the criteria shown in section 41-24-5; to monitor and insure that the expenditure of grant funds are in accordance with the associated grant proposal, this chapter and relevant state laws; and upon finding that such grant expenditures are not in accordance with the aforementioned conditions, to suspend the release of further grant funds and take action to recover the improperly expended grant funds; to design and distribute its grant proposal instrument; to maintain up-to-date records of all grants that are currently in effect; to maintain records of all completed grants and grant proposals that were denied for a period of three full years; and may promulgate reasonable rules to implement and enforce the provisions of this chapter. (Acts 1989, No. 89-354, p. 700, § 4.)

§ 41-24-5. Criteria used to evaluate grant proposals.

The heads of grant making agencies shall evaluate grant proposals based on the relevance of such proposals to the purposes for which such grants shall be made, as stated in section 41-24-3; the extent to which such grant proposal advances the program objective(s) of the grant-making agency, the ability of the grant recipient to fulfill the objectives of the grant proposal, the extent to which the grant proposal can benefit the greatest number of citizens, without persistently excluding any geographic regions of the state. All of the above information may be ascertained by appropriate measures, which shall include interviews, public hearings and recommendations by members of the legislature. (Acts 1989, No. 89-354, p. 700, § 5.)

TITLE 43.

WILLS AND DECEDENTS' ESTATES.

Chap. 4. Repealed.

CHAPTER 2.

ADMINISTRATION OF ESTATES.

Cross references. — As to authority of fiduciary to make certain elections, etc., in light of the generation-skipping transfer tax, see § 19-5-1 et seq.

ARTICLE 1.

GENERAL PROVISIONS.

Collateral references. — What constitutes rejection of claim against estate to commence running of statute of limitations applicable to rejected claims. 36 ALR4th 684.

ARTICLE 2.

GRANT OF LETTERS TESTAMENTARY AND OF ADMINISTRATION.

Division 1.

Grant of Letters Testamentary.

§ 43-2-20. Generally.

Purpose. — By enacting this section and § 43-2-47, the legislature intended for the probate courts of this state to have the discretionary authority to appoint a special administrator, under certain circumstances, prior to issuing letters testamentary. One of those circumstances is when the validity of a will is contested. This is so even when the executor named in the will is not subject to disqualification under § 43-2-22. Smith v. Snider, 497 So. 2d 484 (Ala. 1986).

Cited in Henderson v. Briarcliff Nursing Home, 451 So. 2d 282 (Ala. 1984).

§ 43-2-22. Disqualification of certain persons to serve as executor or administrator.

Purpose.

By enacting §§ 43-2-20 and 43-2-47, the legislature intended for the probate courts of this state to have the discretionary authority to appoint a special administrator, under certain circumstances, prior to issuing letters testamentary. One of those circumstances is when the validity of a will is contested. This is so even when the executor named in the will is not subject to disqualification under this section. Smith v. Snider, 497 So. 2d 484 (Ala. 1986).

In other jurisdictions, a change of resi-dence for the purpose of acquiring letters of administration requires a union of act and intent. Owens v. Ford, 451 So. 2d 796 (Ala. 1984).

Appointment as coadministrator after nonage disability removed. — A widow who at the time of her husband's death was disqualified from being appointed as administratrix of his estate because of her age could not be appointed a coadministrator after her disability of nonage was removed. Ex parte Holladay, 466 So. 2d 956 (Ala. 1985).

§ 43-2-24. Supplemental letters for minors and married women upon removal of disability.

Section not applicable to supplemental letters of administration. — By expressly providing in this section for supplemental letters only where the would-be recipient of these letters is "named as executor in a will", the legislature clearly expressed its intent that this section should not apply to supplemental letters of administration but should only apply to testate estates and only provide for issuance of supplemental letters testamentary. Ex parte Holladay, 466 So. 2d 956 (Ala. 1985).

Appointment as coadministrator after nonage disability removed. — A widow who at the time of her husband's death was disqualified from being appointed as administratrix of his estate because of her age could not be appointed a coadministrator after her disability of nonage was removed. Ex parte Holladay, 466 So. 2d 956 (Ala. 1985).

§ 43-2-29. Grant of letters testamentary after revocation of letters of administration.

Probate should not be denied solely because the estate has been fully adminis- tered and settled. Guyton v. LaBossiere, 423 So. 2d 841 (Ala. 1982).

Division 2.
Grant of Letters of Administration.

§ 43-2-40. Generally.

In relation to sections 43-2-42 and 43-2-47. — No authority is conferred upon a special administrator in § 43-2-47 to take any action with regard to the decedent's interest in realty. Other than the preliminary duty of collection and preservation, a special administrator has nothing to do with the administration of the estate, as contemplated by this section and § 43-2-42. Nothwithstanding these limitations, it would appear that a special administrator does have sufficient means available to protect the assets of the estate until letters testamentary are issued. Smith v. Snider, 497 So. 2d 484 (Ala. 1986).

Cited in Henderson v. Briarcliff Nursing Home, 451 So. 2d 282 (Ala. 1984).

§ 43-2-42. Order of grant of administration.

I. GENERAL CONSIDERATION.

In relation to this section and § 43-2-47. — No authority is conferred upon a special administrator in § 43-2-47 to take any action with regard to the decedent's interest in realty. Other than the preliminary duty of collection and preservation, a special administrator has nothing to do with the administration of the estate, as contemplated by this section and § 43-2-40. Notwithstanding these limitations, it would appear that a special administrator does have sufficient means available to protect the assets of the estate until letters testamentary are issued. Smith v. Snider, 497 So. 2d 484 (Ala. 1986).

Appointment as coadministrator after nonage disability removed. — A widow who at the time of her husband's death was disqualified from being appointed as administratrix of his estate because of her age could not be appointed a coadministrator after her disability of nonage was removed. Ex parte Holladay, 466 So. 2d 956 (Ala. 1985).

If person unfit to serve, for whatever reason, it would be proper to remove her on that basis; but it is not proper to revoke her letters so as to give effect to a preference when the person holding the preference has waived it. Williams v. Tolbert, 519 So. 2d 500 (Ala. 1988).

After lapse of statutory period no one has right to claim any priority or preferences to such appointment, those entitled being declared by the statute expressly to have relinquished their right to the administration, by having failed to apply for it. Williams v. Tolbert, 519 So. 2d 500 (Ala. 1988).

Common-law marriage. — Where some, but not all, of the criteria generally indicative of public recognition that decedent and plaintiff were living together as man and wife were present, it could not be said that the trial court's judgment finding that decedent was plaintiff's husband by common-law marriage and that plaintiff was entitled to priority in grant of letters of administration was palpably wrong, without supporting evidence, or manifestly unjust. Downs v. Newman, 500 So. 2d 1062 (Ala. 1986).

Cited in Jacobs v. Chandler, 451 So. 2d 295 (Ala. 1984); Gillilan v. Gillilan, 483 So. 2d 401 (Ala. 1986).

§ 43-2-43. Renunciation or relinquishment of right to administration.

If person unfit to serve, for whatever reason, it would be proper to remove her on that basis; but it is not proper to revoke her letters so as to give effect to a preference when the person holding the preference has waived it. Williams v. Tolbert, 519 So. 2d 500 (Ala. 1988).

After lapse of statutory period no one has right to claim priority or preferences to such appointment, those entitled being declared by the statute expressly to have relinquished their right to the administration, by having failed to apply for it. Williams v. Tolbert, 519 So. 2d 500 (Ala. 1988).

§ 43-2-44. Grant of administration when more than one person entitled thereto; preference of whole blood over half blood.

Provision of section for appointment of coadministrators only applies where several persons of same degree of kindred to intestate are equally entitled to share in his estate, and thus are equally entitled to serve as administrator. Ex parte Holladay, 466 So. 2d 956 (Ala. 1985).

Appointment as coadministrator after nonage disability removed. — A widow who at the time of her husband's death was disqualified from being appointed as administratrix of his estate because of her age could not be appointed a coadministrator after her disability of nonage was removed. Ex parte Holladay, 466 So. 2d 956 (Ala. 1985).

§ 43-2-45. Letters not granted until five days after intestate's death; examination of applicants and witnesses.

Although this section allows the probate court to inquire whether the deceased "left any will," it does not provide for a full-blown trial to determine the validity of such a will. Guyton v. LaBossiere, 423 So. 2d 841 (Ala. 1982).

For opinion discussing the ways in which the procedure for granting letters of administration differs from the procedure for probating a will, see Guyton v. LaBossiere, 423 So. 2d 841 (Ala. 1982).

§ 43-2-47. Special administrator ad colligendum.

Purpose. — By enacting this section and § 43-2-20, the legislature intended for the probate courts of this state to have the discretionary authority to appoint a special administrator, under certain circumstances, prior to issuing letters testamentary. One of those circumstances is when the validity of a will is contested. This is so even when the executor named in the will is not subject to disqualification under § 43-2-22. Smith v. Snider, 497 So. 2d 484 (Ala. 1986).

Section clearly states that a special administrator may be appointed in "any contest respecting the validity of a will." No distinction is made between a contest filed in probate court and one filed in circuit court. Smith v. Snider, 497 So. 2d 484 (Ala. 1986).

This section and §§ 43-2-20 and 43-2-22, confer upon a probate court the discretionary authority to appoint a special administrator pending the contest of a will filed prior to the issuance of letters testamentary. Smith v. Snider, 497 So. 2d 484 (Ala. 1986).

In relation to sections 43-2-40 and 43-2-42. — No authority is conferred upon a special administrator in this section to take any action with regard to the decedent's interest in realty. Other than the preliminary duty of collection and preservation, a special administrator has nothing to do with the administration of the estate, as contemplated by §§ 43-2-40 and 43-2-42. Notwithstanding these limitations, it would appear that a special administrator does have sufficient means available to protect the assets of the estate until letters testamentary are issued. Smith v. Snider, 497 So. 2d 484 (Ala. 1986).

Even though the special administrator of a decedent's estate cannot pay the debts of the estate, estate taxes are certainly within the realm of reasonable expenditures, as determined by the probate court, that are necessary for the preservation of the estate. Smith v. Snider, 497 So. 2d 484 (Ala. 1986).

ARTICLE 3.

NOTICE OF APPOINTMENT OF EXECUTORS OR ADMINISTRATORS.

§ 43-2-60. Generally; time of notice.

The personal representative must give notice of the appointment, stating the name of the deceased, the day on which letters were granted, by what court, stating the county and notifying all persons having claims against the estate to present the same within the time allowed by law or that the same will be barred. The notice of appointment,

(1) For actual notice as required in section 43-2-61(1), must be given as soon as practicable after a creditor's identification is known; and

(2) For publication notice as required in section 43-2-61(2), must be given within thirty days from grant of letters. (Code 1852, § 1734; Code 1867, § 2057; Code 1876, § 2426; Code 1886, § 2075; Code 1896, § 122; Code 1907, § 2586; Code 1923, § 5811; Code 1940, T. 61, § 93; Acts 1989, No. 89-811, p. 1618, § 1.)

Comment to 1989 Amendment

The 1989 amendment to this statute was necessitated by *Tulsa Professional Collection Services, Inc. v. Pope,* 485 U.S. 478, 108 S.Ct. 1340, 99 L.Ed.2d 565 (1988), in which the Supreme Court declared that the Oklahoma nonclaim statute violated the due process clause of the United States Constitution's Fourteenth Amendment. Although the Oklahoma statute provided for notice to creditors, the statute provided solely for notice by publication. Due process, however, requires that *actual notice* be given to "known or reasonably ascertainable creditors" of the decedent. In effect, the *Pope* decision clarified an uncertainty that had existed for some time by expressly making *Mullane v. Central Hanover Bank & Trust Co.,* 339 U.S. 306, 70 S.Ct. 652, 94 L.Ed 865 (1950) and *Mennonite Board of Missions v. Adams,* 462 U.S. 791, 103 S.Ct. 2706, 77 L.Ed.2d 108 (1983) applicable in the probate of decedents' estates.

The *Pope* case subsequently has been applied in Alabama. Alabama statutes [Ala. Code (1975) §§ 43-2-60 and 43-2-61] were declared as being violative of the due process clause of the Fourteenth Amendment to the United States Constitution. [*Greyhound Financial Corp. v. Lochwood Investors I, Ltd., __ F. Supp. __ (N.D. Ala. 1988)* CV 87-L-5499-NE (citing the *Pope, Mennonite Board of Missions,* and *Mullane* cases as authority)]. In *Jefferson Federal Savings & Loan Ass'n v. Clark,* 540 So.2d 61 (1989) the Alabama Court stated that *actual notice* is required to a "known or reasonably ascertainable" creditor before applying a nonclaim bar.

The 1989 amendment to this section provides for *actual notice* to "known or reasonably ascertainable" creditors of a decedent's estate to assure that "due process" standards, as declared in the *Pope* case, will be met in Alabama.

The 1989 amendment, effective May 16, 1989, substituted "The personal representative must give notice of the appointment" for "Executors and administrators must, within one month from the grant of letters, give notice of their appointment" in the first sentence of the introductory paragraph, added the second sentence of the introductory paragraph, and subdivisions (1) and (2).

Constructive notice held insufficient. —

Where a nonclaim statute was a nonself-executing provision constituting state action (due to the probate court's involvement in appointing an executor), the constructive notice by publication in a paper was insufficient and actual notice by mail was required where creditors were "known or reasonably ascertainable." Jefferson Fed. Sav. Loan Ass'n v. Clark, 540 So. 2d 61 (Ala. 1989).

§ 43-2-61. Manner of giving notice.

Notice, as prescribed in section 43-2-60, must be given:

(1) By first-class mail addressed to their last known address, or by other mechanism reasonably calculated to provide actual notice, to all persons, firms, and corporations having claims against the decedent, who are known or who are reasonably ascertainable by the personal representative within six months from the grant of letters; and

(2) By publishing a notice once a week for three successive weeks in a newspaper of general circulation published in the county in which the letters were granted or, if none is published in the county, in the one published nearest to the courthouse thereof or in an adjoining county. (Code 1852, § 1735; Code 1867, § 2058; Code 1876, § 2427; Code 1886, § 2076; Code 1896, § 123; Code 1907, § 2587; Code 1923, § 5812; Code 1940, T. 61, § 94; Acts 1989, No. 89-811, p. 1618, § 2.)

The 1989 amendment, effective May 16, 1989, rewrote this section.

Constructive notice held insufficient. — Where a nonclaim statute was a nonself-executing provision constituting state action (due to the probate court's involvement in appointing an executor), the constructive notice by publication in a paper was insufficient and actual notice by mail was required where creditors were "known or reasonably ascertainable." Jefferson Fed. Sav. Loan Ass'n v. Clark, 540 So. 2d 61 (Ala. 1989).

Cited in Mathews Realty Co. v. Dennis, 549 So. 2d 481 (Ala. 1989).

ARTICLE 4.

BONDS OF EXECUTORS AND ADMINISTRATORS.

§ 43-2-80. Persons required to give bond; amount; sureties required; approval by probate judge.

Cited in Ex parte Holladay, 466 So. 2d 956 (Ala. 1985).

§ 43-2-83. Discharge of surety; new bond.

Cited in Ex parte Holladay, 466 So. 2d 956 (Ala. 1985).

ARTICLE 5.

LIABILITY OF EXECUTORS AND ADMINISTRATORS.

§ 43-2-110. Limits of liability generally.

Executors held liable. — Executors' failure to adhere to statutory procedure regarding order of abatement in § 43-8-76, as well as their failure to receive bids or have property appraised prior to its sale, constituted a breach of the trust imposed on them as executors of the estate and justified trial court's order that the executors repay to the estate the difference between the amount received by them for the property and the appraised value thereof. Stone v. Curry, 512 So. 2d 66 (Ala. 1987).

ARTICLE 6.

ACTIONS BY AND AGAINST EXECUTORS AND
ADMINISTRATORS.

Division 1.

General Provisions.

§ 43-2-131. Limitation on actions against executor or administrator.

Manifest purpose, etc.
This section does not go into effect, and
hence is not a defense, where there has been no
administration of the estate. Central Acceptance Corp. v. Colonial Bank, 439 So. 2d 144
(Ala. 1983).

Cited in Edwards v. Vanzant, 492 So. 2d 990
(Ala. 1986).
Collateral references. — Determination of,
and charges against, "augmented estate" upon
which share of spouse electing to take against
will is determined under Uniform Probate
Code § 2-202. 63 ALR4th 1173.

ARTICLE 10.

ADMINISTRATION OF ESTATES OF PERSONS PRESUMED DEAD.

§ 43-2-230. Applications for letters of administration.

Whenever letters of administration on the estate of any person presumed to
be dead on account of absence for five or more years from the place of his last
domicile within this state shall be applied for, it shall be the duty of the judge
of probate to whom the application shall be made to accept and file the same
and to thereupon take the testimony with respect to whether the petitioner is
entitled to such letters; and, if the court is satisfied by the testimony that the
applicant would be entitled thereto were the supposed decedent in fact dead,
the court shall cause to be advertised in a newspaper published in the county,
once a week for four consecutive weeks, the fact of said application, together
with notice that on a day certain which shall be at least two weeks after the
last of said advertisements, the court will hear evidence concerning the
alleged absence of the supposed decedent, and the circumstances and duration
thereof. (Acts 1939, No. 46, p. 53; Code 1940, T. 61, § 157; Acts 1984, No.
84-258, p. 426, § 1.)

§ 43-2-231. Appointment of personal representative.

It shall be lawful for the respective probate courts of this state to appoint a
personal representative of the estates of persons who are presumed to be dead
on account of absence for five or more years from the place of their last
domicile within this state as provided in this article. (Acts 1939, No. 46, p. 53;
Code 1940, T. 61, § 156; Acts 1982, No. 82-399, § 8-102; Acts 1984, No.
84-258, p. 426, § 1.)

ARTICLE 11.

ADMINISTRATORS AD LITEM.

§ 43-2-250. Appointment.

Requiring appointment of administrator ad litem for estate of deceased contenant indicates interests of estate require representation. — In a suit involving a sale for division, the personal representative of a deceased cotenant should be made a party to the suit, or, if there is not a personal representative, then the trial court should appoint an administrator ad litem. Requiring the appointment of an administrator ad litem for the estate of a deceased cotenant indicates that the interests of the estate require representation. Loving v. Wilson, 494 So. 2d 68 (Ala. 1986).

Under this section three things must, etc. In accord with bound volume. See Loving v. Wilson, 494 So. 2d 68 (Ala. 1986).

Error not to appoint administrator ad litem where all elements necessary for appointment are present. — Where all of the elements necessary to require an appointment of an administrator ad litem are present, it is error for the trial court not to appoint one for each of the estates. Loving v. Wilson, 494 So. 2d 68 (Ala. 1986).

Cited in Central Acceptance Corp. v. Colonial Bank, 439 So. 2d 144 (Ala. 1983); Smith v. Tribble, 485 So. 2d 1083 (Ala. 1986); Connors v. Mulvehill, 679 F. Supp. 1071 (N.D. Ala. 1988); McCormick v. Langford, 516 So. 2d 643 (Ala. 1987).

ARTICLE 12.

RESIGNATION, REMOVAL, ETC., OF EXECUTORS OR ADMINISTRATORS.

Division 1.

General Provisions.

§ 43-2-274. Appointment of administrator after final settlement.

Appointment of administrator to distribute personalty. — This section allows an administrator to be appointed, after a final settlement, to distribute personalty. In addition, this provision appears to apply to personalty which is in the estate at the present time but which for some reason was not administered, perhaps due to an error by the administrator. Ex Parte Elliott, 477 So. 2d 358 (Ala. 1985).

Fraudulent conveyance 40 years previously. — There is no Code provision which would allow an administrator to be appointed to trace property that was allegedly fraudulently conveyed approximately 40 years ago and attempt to bring it back into estate for distribution to petitioners. Ex parte Elliott, 477 So. 2d 358 (Ala. 1985).

Division 2.

Removal and Proceedings to Require New or Additional Bond.

§ 43-2-290. Causes of removal generally.

Removal only upon proof one or more grounds. — Alabama law provides for removal of administrator only upon proof of one or more of the grounds for removal stated in this section. Ex parte Holladay, 466 So. 2d 956 (Ala. 1985).

The removal of a trustee is a matter which rests in the discretion of the trial court and on appeal the scope of review is limited to determining whether the court has abused its discretion. Jones v. McGuirt, 416 So. 2d 970 (Ala. 1982).

Appointment as coadministrator after nonage disability removed. — A widow who at the time of her husband's death was disqualified from being appointed as administratrix of his estate because of her age could not be appointed a coadministrator after her disability of nonage was removed. Ex parte Holladay, 466 So. 2d 956 (Ala. 1985).

Cited in Mills v. Neville, 443 So. 2d 935 (Ala. 1983); Galin v. Johnson, 457 So. 2d 359 (Ala. 1984).

§ 43-2-293. Application for removal or additional bond.

The procedure to follow in seeking the removal of an executor is statutory. Galin v. Johnson, 457 So. 2d 359 (Ala. 1984).

Cited in McCormick v. Langford, 516 So. 2d 643 (Ala. 1987).

ARTICLE 13.

COLLECTION, INVENTORY AND APPRAISEMENT OF PERSONAL PROPERTY.

§ 43-2-311. Testator may exempt executor from filing inventory or making report or final settlement.

Cited in Galin v. Johnson, 457 So. 2d 359 (Ala. 1984).

Collateral references.
Wills: effect of gift or specified percentage or share of estate (or residuary estate) to include specific property found to be of a greater value than share bequeathed. 63 ALR4th 1186.

§ 43-2-312. Contents of inventory.

The inventory must set forth the property, enumerating each item separately, all debts or demands due or accruing to the decedent, the time such debts or demands are due, the amount of the same and how evidenced, with the credits, if any, and the name of the debtor and the amount of money. (Code 1852, § 1725; Code 1867, § 2048; Code 1876, § 2417; Code 1886, § 2069; Code 1896, § 116; Code 1907, § 2580; Code 1923, § 5804; Code 1940, T. 61, § 191; Acts 1984, No. 84-258, p. 426, § 1.)

§ 43-2-313. Oath upon return of inventory.

On the return of the inventory, the executor or administrator must take and subscribe an oath, to be administered by the judge of probate, or any justice of the peace or notary public of the county, that such inventory is full and complete, as to the property of the decedent, which has come to his knowledge or possession. (Code 1852, § 1726; Code 1867, § 2049; Code 1876, § 2418; Code 1886, § 2070; Code 1896, § 117; Code 1907, § 2581; Code 1923, § 5805; Code 1940, T. 61, § 192; Acts 1984, No. 84-258, p. 426, § 1.)

§ 43-2-314. Repealed by Acts 1984, No. 84-258, § 2, effective May 7, 1984.

§ 43-2-315. Time for returning inventory.

The inventory must be returned within two months after the grant of letters. (Code 1852, § 1730; Code 1867, § 2053; Code 1876, § 2422; Code 1886, § 2072; Code 1896, § 119; Code 1907, § 2583; Code 1923, § 5807; Code 1940, T. 61, § 194; Acts 1984, No. 84-258, p. 426, § 1.)

§ 43-2-316. Supplemental inventories.

The executor and administrator must make supplemental inventories of the decedent's estate coming to his knowledge or possession after making the first inventory. (Code 1852, §§ 1731, 1732; Code 1867, §§ 2054, 2055; Code 1876, §§ 2423, 2424; Code 1886, § 2073; Code 1896, § 120; Code 1907, § 2584; Code 1923, § 5808; Code 1940, T. 61, § 195; Acts 1984, No. 84-258, p. 426, § 1.)

§ 43-2-317. Repealed by Acts 1984, No. 84-258, p. 426, § 2, effective May 7, 1984.

ARTICLE 14.

KEEPING ESTATES TOGETHER.

§ 43-2-336. Cultivation under direction of executor or administrator.

When the estate of any decedent is kept together the real estate may be cultivated under the direction of the executor or administrator. (Code 1852, § 1903; Code 1867, § 2267; Code 1876, § 2607; Code 1886, § 2216; Code 1896, § 284; Code 1907, § 2749; Code 1923, § 5988; Code 1940, T. 61, § 204; Acts 1984, No. 84-258, p. 426, § 1.)

§ 43-2-338. Annual settlements.

Cited in McCormick v. Langford, 516 So. 2d 643 (Ala. 1987).

ARTICLE 15.

CLAIMS AND DEBTS.

Collateral references. — Testamentary option to purchase estate property as surviving optionee's death. 18 ALR4th 578.

What constitutes rejection of claim against estate to commence running of statute of limitations applicable to rejected claims. 36 ALR4th 684.

Division 1.

Presentation.

§ 43-2-350. Time and manner of filing claims — Generally.

(a) All claims against the estate of a decedent, held by the personal representative of the decedent or by an assignee or transferee of the personal representative, or in which the personal representative has an interest, whether due or to become due, must be presented within six months after the grant of letters, or within five months from the date of the first publication of notice, whichever is the later to occur, provided however, that any creditor entitled to actual notice as prescribed in section 43-2-61 must be allowed thirty days after notice within which to present the claim, by filing the claims, or statement thereof, verified by affidavit, in the office of the judge of probate, in all respects as provided by section 43-2-352. All claims not so presented and filed are forever barred, and the payment or allowance thereof is prohibited. But this subsection shall not apply to claims of personal representatives to compensation for their services as such, nor to sums properly disbursed by them in the course of administration.

(b) All claims against the estate of a decedent, other than the claims referred to in subsection (a) of this section, whether due or to become due, must be presented within six months after the grant of letters, or within five months from the date of the first publication of notice, whichever is the later to occur, provided however, that any creditor entitled to actual notice as prescribed in section 43-2-61 must be allowed 30 days after notice within which to present the claim, and if not presented within that time, they are forever barred and the payment or allowance thereof is prohibited. Presentation must be made by filing a verified claim or verified statement thereof in the office of the judge of probate of the county in which the letters are granted. Claims which have not been filed and which are liens against the property of the decedent may be paid by the personal representative to protect the assets of the estate. The provisions of this subsection do not apply to heirs or devisees claiming as heirs or devisees. (Code 1852, §§ 1883, 1884; Code 1867, §§ 2239, 2240; Code 1876, §§ 2597, 2598; Code 1886, §§ 2081, 2082; Code 1896, §§ 129, 130, 132; Code 1907, §§ 2589, 2590, 2592; Code 1923, §§ 5814, 5815, 5817; Acts 1931, No. 722, p. 839; Acts 1931, No. 723, p. 840; Code 1940, T. 61, §§ 210, 211, 213; Acts 1989, No. 89-811, p. 1618, § 3.)

The 1989 amendment, effective May 16, 1989, rewrote subsection (a); and in subsection (b) substituted "or within five months from the date of the first publication of notice, whichever is the later to occur, provided however, that any creditor entitled to actual notice as prescribed in section 43-2-61 must be allowed thirty days after notice within which to present the claim" for "testamentary or of administrator" in the first sentence, deleted "Such" from the beginning of the second sentence, deleted "real or personal" preceding "property of the decedent" in the next-to-last sentence, and substituted "devisees claiming as heirs or devisees" for "legatees claiming as such" in the last sentence.

I. GENERAL CONSIDERATION.

"All claims against the estate of decedent" includes tort claims. — The statute of nonclaim is clear and unambiguous and must be construed to mean just what the words import, and the words "all claims against the estate of the decedent" should be construed to include all claims not specifically excepted, and thus to include tort claims. Ivory v. Fitzpatrick, 445 So. 2d 262 (Ala. 1984).

Where one party, through own negligence or error, pays to debtor funds that constitute security on the debt owed, he cannot invoke aid of equity. To rule otherwise would violate the policy behind the nonclaim statute, this section and needlessly leave transactions subject to collateral attack on equitable grounds beyond the six-month period. Clark v. Jefferson Fed. Sav. & Loan Ass'n, 519 So. 2d 465 (Ala. 1987).

Constructive notice held insufficient. — Where a nonclaim statute was a nonself-executing provision constituting state action (due to the probate court's involvement in appointing an executor), the constructive notice by publication in a paper was insufficient and actual notice by mail was required where creditors were "known or reasonably ascertainable." Jefferson Fed. Sav. Loan Ass'n v. Clark, 540 So. 2d 61 (Ala. 1989).

Cited in Piel v. Dillard, 414 So. 2d 87 (Ala. Civ. App. 1982); Wadsworth v. Hannah, 431 So. 2d 1186 (Ala. 1983); Williams v. Williams, 438 So. 2d 735 (Ala. 1983); Lamar v. Lamar, 470 So. 2d 1242 (Ala. Civ. App. 1985).

Collateral references.
Claims for expenses of last sickness or for funeral expenses as within contemplation of statute requiring presentation of claims against decedent's estate, or limiting time for bringing action thereon. 17 ALR4th 530.

II. CLAIMS HELD BY PERSONAL REPRESENTATIVE.

General basis of nonclaim statute.
In accord with the bound volume. See Stone v. Curry, 512 So. 2d 66 (Ala. 1987).

III. OTHER CLAIMS.

A. Generally.

Suit against coexecutrix individually. —

While case law may support the argument that a suit for the appropriation of funds by an executor or administrator who has died must be brought against the estate of the executor or administrator within the nonclaim period, there is no authority which would require such a suit against defendant individually to have been brought within six months of the date she was appointed coexecutrix of estate. Kettler v. Fryer, 480 So. 2d 1229 (Ala. Civ. App.), cert. denied, 480 So. 2d 1232 (Ala. 1985).

B. Presentment.

Filing of a suit in circuit court within the six-month limitation period obviates the need of filing in the probate court as required by the nonclaim statute. Ivory v. Fitzpatrick, 445 So. 2d 262 (Ala. 1984).

C. Claims Against the Estate.

Wrongful death. — A wrongful death claim is subject to the provisions of the nonclaim statute. Ivory v. Fitzpatrick, 445 So. 2d 262 (Ala. 1984).

The six-month nonclaim period under this section and the two-year limitation period of the wrongful death statute are conditions precedent to the maintenance of a suit against an estate of an alleged wrongdoer based upon a wrongful death cause of action. Ivory v. Fitzpatrick, 445 So. 2d 262 (Ala. 1984).

A wrongful death claim against an estate, irrespective of the existence of insurance proceeds, is barred by the statute of nonclaim unless the claim is presented within six months after the probate court grants letters testamentary. Ivory v. Fitzpatrick, 445 So. 2d 262 (Ala. 1984).

Statutes of limitation are not applicable to wrongful death actions. However, the nonclaim statute is not simply a statute of limitations in that the whole theory of the statute is to create a defense broader in its operation than the statute of limitations, not only barring remedies, but extinguishing debts and liabilities. Ivory v. Fitzpatrick, 445 So. 2d 262 (Ala. 1984).

§ 43-2-352. Verification of claims.

I. GENERAL CONSIDERATION.

Collateral references. — Claims for expenses of last sickness or for funeral expenses as within contemplation of statute requiring presentation of claims against decedent's estate, or limiting time for bringing action thereon. 17 ALR4th 530.

§ 43-2-354. Notice and hearing; judgment; costs; appeals.

Payment of filing fees not jurisdictional. — Appeals from probate court to circuit court require a filing fee in the circuit court; however, payment of filing fees in the circuit court within the time allowed for appeal is not a jurisdictional requirement for perfecting such an appeal. Finch v. Finch, 468 So. 2d 151 (Ala. 1985).

An action pursuant to section 12-11-60 is not a substitute for an appeal, and the provisions of this section do not apply to it. Jones v. Fairley, 447 So. 2d 709 (Ala. 1984).

Collateral references.

Validity of nonclaim statute or rule provision for notice by publication to claimants against estate—post-1950 cases. 56 ALR4th 458.

Division 2.

Payment and Preference.

§ 43-2-370. Property charged with payment of debts.

Power to have real property sold for payment of debts. — When decedent died intestate, the legal title to a one-half interest in his real property vested eo instante in his son; however, it vested subject to the statutory power of the administratrix to take possession of it and obtain an order to have it sold for payment of the debts of his father's estate. Pennington v. Bigham, 512 So. 2d 1344 (Ala. 1987).

§ 43-2-373. Payment of claims barred by statute of limitations.

Agreement between two partners, that neither of them would contend that claims of other regarding partnership accounting would be barred by statute of limitations, was a promise not to plead the statute of limitations. That promise was made on October 23, 1978, at which time the statute of limitations began to run against the promise. Thus, the promise not to plead the statute of limitations would have precluded one partner from pleading the statute of limitations at least through October 23, 1984. Slayton v. Slayton, 521 So. 2d 928 (Ala. 1988).

ARTICLE 16.

SALE OF PERSONAL PROPERTY.

§ 43-2-412. Contesting application.

Any person interested may appear and contest such application, and show that no sale is required, or that it is more for the interest of the estate that other property should be sold. (Code 1852, § 1745; Code 1867, § 2069; Code 1876, § 2435; Code 1886, § 2094; Code 1896, § 144; Code 1907, § 2608; Code 1923, § 5834; Code 1940, T. 61, § 230; Acts 1984, No. 84-258, p. 426, § 1.)

ARTICLE 17.

RENTING AND SALE OF REAL ESTATE.

Division 1.

For Payment of Debts and for Division.

§ 43-2-440. Renting of lands.

Collateral references.
Landlord-tenant security deposit legislation.
63 ALR4th 901.

§ 43-2-441. Authorization to sell — Where will exists.

Lands may be sold by the executor or by the administrator with the will annexed, for the payment of debts, when the will gives no power to sell the same for that purpose. (Code 1852, § 1754; Code 1867, § 2079; Code 1876, § 2447; Code 1886, § 2103; Code 1896, § 155; Code 1907, § 2619; Code 1923, § 5847; Code 1940, T. 61, § 243; Acts 1984, No. 84-258, p. 426, § 1.)

§ 43-2-442. Same — In case of intestacy.

In case of intestacy, lands may be sold by the administrator for the payment of debts. (Code 1852, § 1755; Code 1867, § 2080; Code 1876, § 2448; Code 1886, § 2104; Code 1896, § 156; Code 1907, § 2620; Code 1923, § 5848; Code 1940, T. 61, § 244; Acts 1984, No. 84-258, p. 426, § 1.)

Realty of persons dying intestate descends to the heirs, etc.
When decedent died intestate, the legal title to a one-half interest in his real property vested eo instante in his son; however, it vested subject to the statutory power of the administratrix to take possession of it and obtain an order to have it sold for payment of the debts of his father's estate. Pennington v. Bigham, 512 So. 2d 1344 (Ala. 1987).

§ 43-2-449. Repealed by Acts 1984, No. 84-258, p. 426, § 2, effective May 7, 1984.

§ 43-2-450. Order of sale for payment of debts.

On the hearing of such application, and when the application is by an executor or administrator with the will annexed, that no power is given by the will for that purpose, the court may direct the sale of all, or such portion of the real estate as may be necessary to pay the debts; and such sale may be had on such credit as the court may direct, not exceeding two years. (Code 1852, § 1760; Code 1867, § 2086; Code 1876, § 2456; Code 1886, § 2112; Code 1896, § 165; Code 1907, § 2629; Code 1923, § 5858; Code 1940, T. 61, § 253; Acts 1984, No. 84-258, p. 426, § 1.)

§ 43-2-452. When depositions required.

Waiver of depositions under local act. — There was no reversible error in trial court's failure to require depositions as specified in this section, where a local act was directly on point and clearly permitted the court to exercise equity jurisdiction and allows the parties to waive the depositions required. Clark ex rel. Caddell v. Clark, 514 So. 2d 1321 (Ala. 1987).

§ 43-2-453. Evidence of title.

Cited in Richardson v. Richardson, 417 So. 2d 158 (Ala. 1982).

§ 43-2-465. Right of purchaser to cite executor or administrator to report sale.

Cited in Richardson v. Richardson, 417 So. 2d 158 (Ala. 1982).

§ 43-2-466. Repealed by Acts 1984, No. 84-258, p. 426, § 2, effective May 7, 1984.

§ 43-2-467. Correction of mistake in description of lands sold.

Cited in Richardson v. Richardson, 417 So. 2d 158 (Ala. 1982).

ARTICLE 18.

SETTLEMENTS AND DISTRIBUTIONS.

Division 1.

General Provisions.

§ 43-2-500. When annual or partial settlement required.

Executor failure to make annual settlement of his administration. — Although an executor is required by this section to make annual settlements of his administration, his failure to do so, in the absence of evidence of some other maladministration prejudicial to the estate, does not mandate his removal. McCormick v. Langford, 516 So. 2d 643 (Ala. 1987).

§ 43-2-501. When final settlement may be made.

Petition for removal held timely. — Where there was no basis for concluding that the trial on petitioner's breach of warranty claim constituted a step toward final settlement, petition for removal in the midst of trial on the claim against the estate was timely. Ex parte Clayton, 514 So. 2d 1013 (Ala. 1987).

§ 43-2-502. Filing of account, etc. — Generally.

In making settlements of an administration, the executor or administrator must proceed as follows:

He must make out an account between himself and the estate he represents, charging himself with all the assets of the deceased which have come into his possession, except the lands, and crediting himself with all the credits he is by law entitled to; which account, verified by his oath, must be filed with the judge of probate of the court having jurisdiction.

With such account he must also file written evidence in his possession, on which he relies to sustain the credit side of such account, which may consist of an affidavit or any other legal evidence, in the discretion of the executor or administrator.

He must, at the same time, file a statement, on oath, of the names of the heirs and legatees of such estate, specifying particularly which are under the age of 19 years; and, if any of them are persons of unsound mind, it must be stated; but if the names, ages or condition of such heirs or legatees are unknown and they reside out of the state, they may be made parties as unknown heirs or legatees.

He must state the sum of funds of the estate which he has used for his own benefit, the time and the profit resulting from such use, if over legal interest, or, if he has not so used any of the funds of the estate for his own benefit, he must expressly deny on oath that he has so used such funds, and any party interested in the the estate may contest the same.

He shall be allowed all reasonable premiums paid on his bond as administrator or executor. (Code 1852, § 1802; Code 1867, § 2137; Code 1876, § 2509; Code 1886, § 2135; Code 1896, § 203; Code 1907, § 2668; Code 1923, § 5901; Code 1940, T. 61, § 295; Acts 1988, 1st Ex. Sess., No. 88-943, p. 565, § 1.)

Petition for removal held timely. — Where there was no basis for concluding that the trial on petitioners' breach of warranty claim constituted a step toward final settlement, petition for removal in the midst of trial on the claim against the estate was timely. Ex parte Clayton, 514 So. 2d 1013 (Ala. 1987).

Executor required under this section to file with probate court those documents supporting his statement of account or to provide a sufficient explanation for his failure to do so. Where he did not do that, the probate court's final settlement order was reversed and the case was remanded to that court for further proceedings. McCormick v. Langford, 516 So. 2d 643 (Ala. 1987).

§ 43-2-503. Filing of account, etc. — Liability for failure to file statement.

Failure to make proper settlement renders executor or administrator and his sureties liable for all damages arising therefrom.

American States Ins. Co. v. Copeland, 534 So. 2d 275 (Ala. 1988).

§ 43-2-507. Auditing of account; proof of credits.

Burden of proof, etc.

Burden of proving credits in settlements of estate falls on administrator, who must adduce satisfactory proof of existence and correctness of each item to be credited. American States Ins. Co. v. Copeland, 534 So. 2d 275 (Ala. 1988).

§ 43-2-510. Credit for expenses of minor distributees.

(a) When the estate of a decedent is solvent, the executor or administrator, out of the assets in his hands, may defray the necessary and reasonable expenses of maintaining and educating minors who are entitled to distribution therein, and who have no legal guardian; and, upon any partial or final settlement by him, the probate court must allow him credit for such expenses. To the extent the expenses are not within the family allowance, the expenses shall be charged against the shares of such minors and deducted therefrom on any distribution of the estate.

(b) An executor or administrator defraying such expenses must file with his account for a settlement a separate account of the amounts paid therefor on account of each of such minors accompanied by proper vouchers, showing the amounts and for what expended. (Code 1876, §§ 2644, 2645; Code 1886, §§ 2159, 2160; Code 1896, §§ 227, 288; Code 1907, §§ 2676, 2677; Code 1923, §§ 5909, 5910; Code 1940, T. 61, §§ 305, 306; Acts 1984, No. 84-258, p. 426, § 1.)

Division 3.

Compelling Settlement of Executor or Administrator Whose Authority Has Ceased.

§ 43-2-550. Final settlement required following death, removal or resignation of executor or administrator.

Cited in McAleer v. Noonan, 454 So. 2d 962 (Ala. 1984).

Division 9.

Compensation, Commissions, Fees, etc.

§ 43-2-680. Executors and administrators may be allowed fair compensation, etc.

I. GENERAL CONSIDERATION.

This section sets the foundation upon which executors and administrators are provided compensation for their services. McCollum v. Towns, 435 So. 2d 17 (Ala. 1983).

The language of this section is permissive, etc.

The setting of executor's fees and commissions is a matter entirely within the judicial discretion of the trial court. The language of this section, which allows for compensation to executors and administrators, is permissive, rather than mandatory. Stone v. Curry, 512 So. 2d 66 (Ala. 1987).

Collateral references.

Authority of probate court to depart from statutory schedule fixing amount of executor's commissions and attorney's fees. 40 ALR4th 1189.

II. WHEN COMMISSIONS ALLOWED ON RECEIPTS AND DISBURSEMENTS.

Alabama does not allow fiduciaries commissions on real property, whether it be on the appraised value of the land, or the proceeds therefrom as a result of a sale in the administration of the estate. McCollum v. Towns, 435 So. 2d 17 (Ala. 1983).

The reason for not allowing real estate to be used to measure the amount of a fiduciary's fee is that real estate vests immediately in the heirs at law, subject only to recapture by the administrator or executor in the event this property is needed for the payment of debts of the decedent. McCollum v. Towns, 435 So. 2d 17 (Ala. 1983).

III. AMOUNT OF COMMISSION.

Section 43-2-681 is a limitation, etc.

Section 43-2-681 is a limitation on the amount of compensation that can be awarded under this section. McCollum v. Towns, 435 So. 2d 17 (Ala. 1983).

Rule as to court's discretion.

Supreme Court has the authority and the duty to correct the decision of the trial court by allowing for an increase in the fee of an executor or administrator or by allowing it to be reduced if there has been an abuse of discretion. McCollum v. Towns, 435 So. 2d 17 (Ala. 1983).

Computation of compensation.

This section means that the maximum that an executor or administrator of an estate in Alabama may receive for ordinary services is two and one-half percent of the receipts and two and one-half percent of the disbursements. McCollum v. Towns, 435 So. 2d 17 (Ala. 1983).

§ 43-2-681. Commissions on money or property sold or distributed.

This section is a limitation on the amount of compensation that can be awarded un- der § 43-2-680. McCollum v. Towns, 435 So. 2d 17 (Ala. 1983).

§ 43-2-682. Court may allow compensation or attorney's fees up to time of settlement.

The complete list of criteria used in the estimation of the value of an attorney's services includes the following: (1) the nature and value of the subject matter of the employment; (2) the learning, skill, and labor requisite to its proper discharge; (3) the time consumed; (4) the professional experience and reputation of the attorney; (5) the weight of his responsibilities; (6) the measure of success achieved; (7) the reasonable expenses incurred; (8) whether a fee is fixed or contingent; (9) the nature and length of a professional relationship; (10) the fee customarily charged in the locality for similar legal services; (11) the likelihood that a particular employment may preclude other employment; and (12) the time limitations imposed by the client or by the circumstances. Of course, there would hardly ever be a case where the determination of attorney's fees brought into play every criterion. Van Schaack v. AmSouth Bank, 530 So. 2d 740 (Ala. 1988).

Cited in Mills v. Neville, 443 So. 2d 935 (Ala. 1983).

Collateral references.

Authority of probate court to depart from statutory schedule fixing amount of executor's commissions and attorney's fees. 40 ALR4th 1189.

§ 43-2-683. Previous fees considered upon final settlement.

Cited in Mills v. Neville, 443 So. 2d 935 (Ala. 1983).

CHAPTER 4.

ADOPTION OF ADULTS FOR PURPOSES OF INHERITANCE.

REPEALED.

§§ 43-4-1 through 43-4-4. Repealed by Acts 1990, No. 90-554, § 38, effective January 1, 1991.

Cross references. — For present provisions pertaining to adoption, see chapter 26-10A.

CHAPTER 7.

UNIFORM SIMULTANEOUS DEATH ACT.

§ 43-7-2. No sufficient evidence of survivorship; disposition of property of decedents.

Construction of the words "children ... entitled to share" that limited the distribution of trust estate to only those children to whom the trustee could apportion a share was a reasonable and consistent construction and one that derived the grantor's intent from the plain usage of the entire phrase in question. It described only those children of the grantor who survived the last to die of the parents. Since the parents and children were killed simultaneously, no children survived the parents, the trust failed for lack of a beneficiary, and the estate descended by intestacy. Gafford v. Kirby, 512 So. 2d 1356 (Ala. 1987).

§ 43-7-4. Joint tenants or tenants by the entirety.

Construction of the words "children ... entitled to share" that limited the distribution of trust estate to only those children to whom the trustee could apportion a share was a reasonable and consistent construction and one that derived the grantor's intent from the plain usage of the entire phrase in question. It described only those children of the grantor who survived the last to die of the parents. Since the parents and children were killed simultaneously, no children survived the parents, the trust failed for lack of a beneficiary, and the estate descended by intestacy. Gafford v. Kirby, 512 So. 2d 1356 (Ala. 1987).

CHAPTER 8.

PROBATE CODE.

Collateral references. — Proper disposition under will providing for allocation of express percentages or proportions amounting to more or less than whole of residuary estate. 35 ALR4th 789.

ARTICLE 1.

GENERAL PROVISIONS.

§ 43-8-1. General definitions.

The new probate code did not change the law by implication so that the widow's share should bear the burden of the estate taxes equally with the children's share. Moss v. Horton, 544 So. 2d 898 (Ala. 1989).

Legislature did not intend to change existing law other than to increase share and treat widow and widower equally. — While it is true that in the new probate code the legislature abolished the estates of dower and curtesy, there is no implication that the legislature intended to change existing law other than to increase the share and to treat widow and widower equally. Moss v. Horton, 544 So. 2d 898 (Ala. 1989).

Child not entitled to share in trust. — Child who had previously been adopted by her mother's second husband was not entitled to a distributive share in a private trust funded by public donations, which had been established for the benefit of the widows and children of two police officers killed in the line of duty, one of whom was the child's natural father, as she had not been intended by the settlors to be included. Barnett ex rel. Barnett v. Beck, 481 So. 2d 348 (Ala. 1985).

Cited in Henderson v. Briarcliff Nursing Home, 451 So. 2d 282 (Ala. 1984); Cater v. Coxwell, 479 So. 2d 1181 (Ala. 1985).

Collateral references.

Word "child" or "children" in will as including grandchild or grandchildren. 30 ALR4th 319.

Payable-on-death savings account or certificate of deposit as will. 50 ALR4th 272.

§ 43-8-2. Construction of chapter; purposes and policies.

Where sole surviving attesting witness denies signing will, other evidence, proving execution, admissible. — Where the sole surviving attesting witness denies that she affixed her signature to the will as an attesting witness, other evidence may be admitted to prove the execution and attestation. To disallow such secondary evidence would be contrary to the underlying purpose of the statute, which is to discover and make effective the intent of a decedent in the distribution of his property. London v. Harris, 507 So. 2d 468 (Ala. 1987).

Cited in Cater v. Coxwell, 479 So. 2d 1181 (Ala. 1985).

§ 43-8-3. Supplementary effect of principles of law and equity.

Cited in Garrard v. Lang, 489 So. 2d 557 (Ala. 1986).

§ 43-8-5. Relief against fraud; limitations.

Cited in Vandegrift v. Lagrone, 477 So. 2d 292 (Ala. 1985).

Collateral references.

Fraud as extending statutory limitations period for contesting will or its probate. 48 ALR4th 1094.

§ 43-8-8. Effective date; transition provisions.

Cited in Wilder v. Mixon, 442 So. 2d 922 (Ala. 1983); Garrard v. Lang, 489 So. 2d 557 (Ala. 1986).

ARTICLE 3.

INTESTATE SUCCESSION.

§ 43-8-40. Intestate estate generally.

I. GENERAL CONSIDERATION.

Construction of the words "children ... entitled to share" that limited the distribution of trust estate to only those children to whom the trustee could apportion a share was a reasonable and consistent construction and one that derived the grantor's intent from the plain usage of the entire phrase in question. It described only those children of the grantor who survived the last to die of the parents.

Since the parents and children were killed simultaneously, no children survived the parents, the trust failed for lack of a beneficiary, and the estate descended by intestacy. Gafford v. Kirby, 512 So. 2d 1356 (Ala. 1987).

Collateral references.

Wills: effect of gift or specified percentage or share of estate (or residuary estate) to include specific property found to be of a greater value than share bequeathed. 63 ALR4th 1186.

§ 43-8-41. Share of the spouse.

For discussion of the constitutionality of Alabama intestacy scheme, see Handley ex rel. Herron v. Schweiker, 697 F.2d 999 (11th Cir. 1983).

Distributions listed in this section and § 43-8-42 mandate who shall inherit, without exceptions. The probate process necessitates such mandates in order to simplify the process and avoid floods of litigation over who the deceased would have intended to inherit. Crosby v. Corley, 528 So. 2d 1141 (Ala. 1988).

Intestate succession not controlled by equitable considerations of worthiness. — The legislature, by mandating that wrongful death proceeds be distributed according to the statute of intestate distribution, necessarily perceived that some beneficiaries would be totally unworthy of inheriting. The statutory law of intestate succession is not controlled by, nor conditioned upon, equitable considerations of worthiness, fitness, and misconduct, etc. On the contrary, it is controlled by a set of rules that attempt to dispose of the deceased's property in a way the deceased would have had a will been executed, by recognizing the natural law of consanguinity, or of blood, and the natural affections of a person toward those nearest him in that relationship. Crosby v. Corley, 528 So. 2d 1141 (Ala. 1988).

Father's misconduct towards daughter did not prevent his sharing proceeds of wrongful death settlement. — Father was entitled to share in the proceeds of the settlement of the action based on the wrongful death of his daughter despite evidence of his gross misconduct during the daughter's life since the father's wrongful conduct did not cause the death of his daughter, and therefore, by receiving his statutorily mandated share of the wrongful death proceeds, he is not profiting from his own wrongful act. Crosby v. Corley, 528 So. 2d 1141 (Ala. 1988).

Mother and daughter not in privity. — Where mother's intestate rights were dependent on continued existence of marital relationship, but daughter's intestate rights arose from a different source — the alleged paternity of the person whose heir she claimed to be — and did not depend on continued existence of the marriage, mother and daughter were not in privity in regard to those interests. Tatum v. Kelley, 481 So. 2d 1132 (Ala. 1985).

§ 43-8-42. Share of heirs other than surviving spouse.

I. GENERAL CONSIDERATION.

Distributions listed in this section and § 43-8-41 mandate who shall inherit, without exceptions. The probate process necessitates such mandates in order to simplify the process and avoid floods of litigation over who the deceased would have intended to inherit. Crosby v. Corley, 528 So. 2d 1141 (Ala. 1988).

Intestate succession not controlled by equitable considerations of worthiness. — The legislature, by mandating that wrongful death proceeds be distributed according to the statute of intestate distribution, necessarily perceived that some beneficiaries would be totally unworthy of inheriting. The statutory law of intestate succession is not controlled by, nor conditioned upon, equitable considerations of worthiness, fitness, and misconduct, etc. On the contrary, it is controlled by a set of rules that attempt to dispose of the deceased's property in a way the deceased would have had a will been executed, by recognizing the natural law of consanguinity, or of blood, and the natural affections of a person toward those nearest him in that relationship. Crosby v. Corley, 528 So. 2d 1141 (Ala. 1988).

Construction of the words "children ... entitled to share" that limited the distribution of trust estate to only those children to whom the trustee could apportion a share was a reasonable and consistent construction and one that derived the grantor's intent from the plain usage of the entire phrase in question. It described only those children of the grantor who survived the last to die of the parents. Since the parents and children were killed simultaneously, no children survived the parents, the trust failed for lack of a beneficiary, and the estate descended by intestacy. Gafford v. Kirby, 512 So. 2d 1356 (Ala. 1987).

Father's misconduct towards daughter did not prevent his sharing proceeds of wrongful death settlement. — Father was entitled to share in the proceeds of the settlement of the action based on the wrongful death of his daughter despite evidence of his gross misconduct during the daughter's life since the father's wrongful conduct did not cause the death of his daughter, and therefore, by receiving his statutorily mandated share of the wrongful death proceeds, he is not profiting from his own wrongful act. Crosby v. Corley, 528 So. 2d 1141 (Ala. 1988).

Mother and daughter not in privity. — Where mother's intestate rights were dependent on continued existence of marital relationship, but daughter's intestate rights arose from a different source — the alleged paternity of the person whose heir she claimed to be — and did not depend on continued existence of the marriage, mother and daughter were not in privity in regard to those interests. Tatum v. Kelley, 481 So. 2d 1132 (Ala. 1985).

Disclaimer by son of decedent constituted a transfer of his interests in the personal property of his father's estate to his son. Pennington v. Bigham, 512 So. 2d 1344 (Ala. 1987).

Cited in Melvin v. Parker, 472 So. 2d 1024 (Ala. 1985).

Collateral references.

Descent and distribution: rights of inheritance as between kindred of whole and half blood. 47 ALR4th 561.

§ 43-8-43. Requirement that heir survive decedent for five days.

Right to claim homestead allowance and exempt property does not survive the death of the second spouse; thus, if a surviving spouse dies without claiming a homestead allowance or exempt property out of the predeceased spouse's estate, the surviving spouse's estate may not make these claims. Cater v. Coxwell, 479 So. 2d 1181 (Ala. 1985).

Cited in Shotts v. American Income Life Ins. Co., 518 So. 2d 1244 (Ala. 1987).

§ 43-8-45. Division of estate where representation is involved.

I. GENERAL CONSIDERATION.

Disclaimer by son of decedent constituted a transfer of his interest in the personal property of his father's estate to his son. Pennington v. Bigham, 512 So. 2d 1344 (Ala. 1987).

§ 43-8-48. Parent and child relationship.

I. GENERAL CONSIDERATION.

Paragraph (2)(b) of this section does two things. It first codifies the holding in Everage v. Gibson, 372 So. 2d 829 (Ala. 1979), that paternity may be established by an adjudication prior to the father's death. It also goes one step further and permits establishment by adjudication after death of the father upon proof by clear and convincing evidence. Free v. Free, 507 So. 2d 930 (Ala. Civ. App. 1986).

Child not entitled to share in trust. — Child who had previously been adopted by her mother's second husband was not entitled to a distributive share in a private trust funded by public donations, which had been established for the benefit of the widows and children of two police officers killed in the line of duty, one of whom was the child's natural father, as she had not been intended by the settlors to be included. Barnett ex rel. Barnett v. Beck, 481 So. 2d 348 (Ala. 1985).

Where paternity of illegitimate child established after death of father, child inherits through intestate succession. — Paternity of an illegitimate child may be established after the death of the father through an adjudication supported by clear and convincing evidence. When so established, such a child may inherit from the father through intestate succession. Cotton v. Terry, 495 So. 2d 1077 (Ala. 1986).

Same statute of limitations in action to establish paternity as in establishing rights of inheritance. — Under paragraph (2)(b) of this section, paternity may be established after the death of the father upon clear and convincing proof. The action to establish paternity may be brought within the time allowed by law to establish rights of inheritance in any case. Free v. Free, 507 So. 2d 930 (Ala. Civ. App. 1986).

Cited in Ragsdale v. Altec Indus., Inc., 456 So. 2d 54 (Ala. 1984); Lewis v. Heckler, 752 F. 2d 555 (11th Cir. 1985); Hart ex rel. Morse v. Bowen, 802 F.2d 1334 (11th Cir. 1986).

II. DECISIONS UNDER PRIOR LAW.

Editor's note. — The decision of Everage v. Gibson, 372 So. 2d 829 (Ala. 1979), annotated in the bound volume, has been modified. See Abrams v. Wheeler, 468 So. 2d 126 (Ala. 1985).

Inheritance from father where child legitimated in paternity decree. — Child legitimated by means of a paternity decree before the death of her father could not be barred from inheriting from her father's estate based upon the application of the invalidated and unconstitutional statute of limitations in former § 26-12-7. Abrams v. Wheeler, 468 So. 2d 126 (Ala. 1985), modifying Everage v. Gibson, 372 So. 2d 829 (Ala. 1979) (decided under law prior to this section).

§ 43-8-49. Advancements.

If a person dies intestate as to all his estate, property which he gave in his lifetime to an heir is treated as an advancement against the latter's share of the estate only if declared in a contemporaneous writing by the decedent or acknowledged in writing by the heir to be an advancement. For this purpose the property advanced is valued as of the time the heir came into possession or enjoyment of the property or as of the time of death of the decedent, whichever first occurs. If the recipient of the property fails to survive the decedent, the property is not taken into account in computing the intestate share to be received by the recipient's issue, unless the declaration or acknowledgment provides otherwise. (Acts 1982, No. 82-399, p. 578, § 2-110.)

Code commissioner's note. — This section has been set out in order to correct an error in the bound volume.

§ 43-8-57. Dower and curtesy abolished.

Cited in Marino v. Smith, 454 So. 2d 1380 (Ala. 1984); Reeb v. Murphy, 481 So. 2d 372 (Ala. 1985).

Collateral references.
Construction, application, and effect of stat-utes which deny or qualify surviving spouse's right to elect against deceased spouse's will. 48 ALR4th 972.

ARTICLE 4.

ELECTIVE SHARE OF SURVIVING SPOUSE; ABATEMENT.

§ 43-8-70. Right of surviving spouse to elective share.

I. GENERAL CONSIDERATION.

Gross estate should be reduced by home-stead and exempt property allowances prior to calculation of the surviving spouse's elective share. Garrard v. Lang, 514 So. 2d 933 (Ala. 1987).

Petition for elective share not signed or filed. — Where the facts that a claim for homestead allowances and exempt property was drafted at the same time as the petition for elective share but was not signed or filed, and the widow lived for approximately three more months without signing or filing the claim, precluded a conclusion that a general prayer for relief in the elective share petition consti-tuted a claim for homestead allowance or exempt property. Nichols v. Barnette, 528 So. 2d 322 (Ala. 1988).

Finding that widow's estate entitled to one-third of husband's estate held errone-ous. — The finding by trial judge that widow's estate was entitled to one-third of the cash amount of husband's estate as an elective share was not clearly erroneous or manifestly unjust, where testimony was presented that the net value of her separate estate was $7,000 at the time of husband's death and the evi-dence also showed that his estate consisted of two life insurance policies totaling $27,341.26 and a 1978 model Ford valued at $1,000. Nichols v. Barnette, 528 So. 2d 322 (Ala. 1988).

Cited in Cater v. Coxwell, 479 So. 2d 1181 (Ala. 1985); Garrard v. Lang, 489 So. 2d 557 (Ala. 1986).

Collateral references.
Construction, application, and effect of stat-utes which deny or qualify surviving spouse's right to elect against deceased spouse's will. 48 ALR4th 972.

Determination of, and charges against, "augmented estate" upon which share of spouse electing to take against will is deter-mined under Uniform Probate Code § 2-202. 63 ALR4th 1173.

§ 43-8-71. Right of election personal to surviving spouse.

I. GENERAL CONSIDERATION.

Cited in Cater v. Coxwell, 479 So. 2d 1181 (Ala. 1985).

Collateral references.
Construction, application, and effect of stat-utes which deny or qualify surviving spouse's right to elect against deceased spouse's will. 48 ALR4th 972.

Determination of, and charges against, "augmented estate" upon which share of spouse electing to take against will is deter-mined under Uniform Probate Code § 2-202. 63 ALR4th 1173.

§ 43-8-72. Waiver of right to elect and of other rights.

Executor has burden of showing that under this section waiver was made after fair disclosure. Garrard v. Lang, 489 So. 2d 557 (Ala. 1986).

Requirements for surviving spouse to waive rights. — A surviving spouse may waive the right of election, homestead allow-ance, exempt property, and family allowances under this section by a valid waiver that meets three requirements: (1) it must be in the form of a written contract or agreement; (2) it must be signed by the party waiving the right; and (3) there must have been a fair disclosure. Ruzic v. Ruzic, 549 So. 2d 72 (Ala. 1989).

Statutory rights not waived where no evidence of disclosure to widow of her

rights. — In light of the lack of evidence of any disclosure to widow of her rights, the trial court plainly and palpably abused its discretion in finding that widow had waived her statutory rights by endorsing a check for $10.00 as provided for her in her husband's will and an additional $1000.00 check which executor claimed was in settlement of her rights. Garrard v. Lang, 489 So. 2d 557 (Ala. 1986).

Cited in Cater v. Coxwell, 479 So. 2d 1181 (Ala. 1985).
Collateral references.
Construction, application, and effect of statutes which deny or qualify surviving spouse's right to elect against deceased spouse's will. 48 ALR4th 972.

§ 43-8-73. Procedure for making election; petition; time limit; notice and hearing; withdrawal of demand; order of court; enforcement of order.

I. GENERAL CONSIDERATION.

Petition for elective share not signed or filed. — Where, the facts that a claim for homestead allowances and exempt property was drafted at the same time as the petition for elective share but was not signed or filed, and the widow lived for approximately three more months without signing or filing the claim, precluded a conclusion that a general prayer for relief in the elective share petition constituted a claim for homestead allowance or exempt property. Nichols v. Barnette, 528 So. 2d 322 (Ala. 1988).

Finding that widow's estate entitled to one-third of husband's estate held erroneous. — The finding by trial judge that widow's estate was entitled to one-third of the cash amount of husband's estate as an elective share was not clearly erroneous or manifestly unjust, where testimony was presented that the net value of her separate estate was $7,000 at the time of husband's death and the evidence also showed that his estate consisted of two life insurance policies totaling $27,341.26 and a 1978 model Ford valued at $1,000. Nichols v. Barnette, 528 So. 2d 322 (Ala. 1988).

§ 43-8-74. Entitlement of surviving spouse to certain benefits regardless of election.

Cited in Cater v. Coxwell, 479 So. 2d 1181 (Ala. 1985); Garrard v. Lang, 514 So. 2d 933 (Ala. 1987).
Collateral references. — Determination of,

and charges against, "augmented estate" upon which share of spouse electing to take against will is determined under Uniform Probate Code § 2-202. 63 ALR4th 1173.

§ 43-8-75. How elective share satisfied; what property applied first; apportionment of others' liability for balance of elective share.

Collateral references.
Determination of, and charges against, "augmented estate" upon which share of

spouse electing to take against will is determined under Uniform Probate Code § 2-202. 63 ALR4th 1173.

§ 43-8-76. Order of abatement.

Executors' failure to adhere to statutory procedure regarding order of abatement in this section, as well as their failure to receive bids or have property appraised prior to its sale, constituted a breach of the trust imposed on them as executors of the estate and justified the trial court's order that the executors repay to the estate the difference between

the amount received by them for the property and the appraised value thereof. Stone v. Curry, 512 So. 2d 66 (Ala. 1987).
Collateral references. — Determination of, and charges against, "augmented estate" upon which share of spouse electing to take against will is determined under Uniform Probate Code § 2-202. 63 ALR4th 1173.

ARTICLE 5.

SPOUSE AND CHILDREN NOT PROVIDED FOR IN WILL.

§ 43-8-90. Omitted spouse.

Purported common law wife's request for jury trial denied. — In a probate proceeding in which the purported common law wife filed a motion for determination of widowhood, the probate court did not err in striking her request for jury trial, where she did not file a contest to the will, which would have carried a right to a jury trial, but had merely filed a claim as an omitted spouse, since there is no common law right to a trial by jury in the probate court. Kemp v. Kroutter, 531 So. 2d 854 (Ala. 1988).

Collateral references.
Sufficiency of provision for, or reference to, prospective spouse to avoid lapse or revocation of will by subsequent marriage. 38 ALR4th 117.

Determination of, and charges against, "augmented estate" upon which share of spouse electing to take against will is determined under Uniform Probate Code § 2-202. 63 ALR4th 1173.

§ 43-8-91. Pretermitted children.

I. GENERAL CONSIDERATION.

Collateral references.
Adopted child as subject to protection of statute regarding rights of children pretermitted by will, or statute preventing disinheritance of child. 43 ALR4th 947.

ARTICLE 6.

EXEMPT PROPERTY AND ALLOWANCES.

§ 43-8-110. Homestead allowance.

Cross references. — For annotations construing similar former provisions see annotations that follow § 6-10-60 through § 6-10-62.

Purpose. — The legislature created the homestead allowance and the exempt property provision to preserve part of the decedent's estate from creditors and to protect the surviving spouse and minor children. This purpose is evident from the priority given to these rights over all other claims against the estate. Cater v. Coxwell, 479 So. 2d 1181 (Ala. 1985).

Right to claim homestead allowance and exempt property does not survive death of second spouse; thus, if a surviving spouse dies without claiming a homestead allowance or exempt property out of the predeceased spouse's estate, the surviving spouse's estate may not make these claims. Cater v. Coxwell, 479 So. 2d 1181 (Ala. 1985).

The homestead allowance may be drawn from personal property or realty under the new Probate Code. Garrard v. Lang, 514 So. 2d 933 (Ala. 1987).

Calculation of surviving spouses's elective share. — The gross estate should be reduced by the homestead and exempt property allowances prior to calculation of the surviving spouse's elective share. Garrard v. Lang, 514 So. 2d 933 (Ala. 1987).

Petition for elective share not signed or filed. — Where, the facts that a claim for homestead allowances and exempt property was drafted at the same time as the petition for elective share but was not signed or filed, and the widow lived for approximately three more months without signing or filing the claim, precluded a conclusion that a general prayer for relief in the elective share petition constituted a claim for homestead allowance or exempt property. Nichols v. Barnette, 528 So. 2d 322 (Ala. 1988).

Cited in Wilder v. Mixon, 442 So. 2d 922 (Ala. 1983); Garrard v. Lang, 489 So. 2d 557 (Ala. 1986); Harville v. Williams, 545 So. 2d 25 (Ala. 1989).

§ 43-8-111. Exempt property.

Cross references. — For annotations construing similar former provisions see annotations that follow § 6-10-63 through § 6-10-65.

Purpose. — The legislature created the homestead allowance and the exempt property provision to preserve part of the decedent's estate from creditors and to protect the surviving spouse and minor children. This purpose is evident from the priority given to these rights over all other claims against the estate. Cater v. Coxwell, 479 So. 2d 1181 (Ala. 1985).

Right to claim homestead allowance and exempt property does not survive death of second spouse; thus, if a surviving spouse dies without claiming a homestead allowance or exempt property out of the predeceased spouse's estate, the surviving spouse's estate may not make these claims. Cater v. Coxwell, 479 So. 2d 1181 (Ala. 1985).

Calculation of surviving spouses's elec- tive share. — The gross estate should be reduced by the homestead and exempt property allowances prior to calculation of the surviving spouse's elective share. Garrard v. Lang, 514 So. 2d 933 (Ala. 1987).

Petition for elective share not signed or filed. — Where, the facts that a claim for homestead allowances and exempt property was drafted at the same time as the petition for elective share but was not signed or filed, and the widow lived for approximately three more months without signing or filing the claim, precluded a conclusion that a general prayer for relief in the elective share petition constituted a claim for homestead allowance or exempt property. Nichols v. Barnette, 528 So. 2d 322 (Ala. 1988).

Cited in Garrard v. Lang, 489 So. 2d 557 (Ala. 1986); Harville v. Williams, 545 So. 2d 25 (Ala. 1989).

§ 43-8-112. Family allowance.

Right to claim homestead allowance and exempt property does not survive death of second spouse; thus, if a surviving spouse dies without claiming a homestead allowance or exempt property out of the predeceased spouse's estate, the surviving spouse's estate may not make these claims. Cater v. Coxwell, 479 So. 2d 1181 (Ala. 1985).

Cited in Garrard v. Lang, 489 So. 2d 557 (Ala. 1986).

§ 43-8-114. Spouse may retain dwelling, etc., until assignment of homestead.

The spouse may retain possession of the dwelling house where the surviving spouse resided with the decedent, with the offices and buildings appurtenant thereto and the plantation connected therewith until homestead is assigned, free from the payment of rent. The obligation to pay rent, if any, on the dwelling shall be an obligation of the decedent's estate. (Code 1852, § 1359; Code 1867, § 1630; Code 1876, § 2238; Code 1886, § 1900; Code 1896, § 1515; Code 1907, § 3824; Code 1923, § 7437; Code 1940, T. 34, § 50; Code 1975, § 43-5-40; Acts 1984, No. 84-258, p. 426, § 1.)

A widow has no right to enter and occupy any part of her deceased husband's estate or to retain possession thereof as against the heirs or those claiming under them until the date of the assignment of dower. Wilder v. Mixon, 442 So. 2d. 922 (Ala. 1983).

The widow does not receive a property interest in her husband's lands automatically upon his death. — She becomes vested of a life estate only upon confirmation of the assignment of dower by the court. Wilder v. Mixon, 442 So. 2d. 922 (Ala. 1983).

The widow's right to dower is only an equity or chose in action until dower is assigned to her by the court. Wilder v. Mixon, 442 So. 2d 922 (Ala. 1983).

The widow is entitled, etc.

In Alabama, the widow does have a statutory right of quarantine. This is strictly limited to the dwelling house where her husband most usually resided next before his death, with the offices and buildings appurtenant thereto and the plantation connected therewith. Wilder v. Mixon, 442 So. 2d 922 (Ala. 1983).

Release of marital rights not established. — While it is true that the payment of taxes and cutting of timber for profit have, under certain circumstances, been considered hostile acts of ownership for the purpose of establishing title by adverse possession, in the facts of this case they are not the equivalent of a release of marital rights. Hayden v. Robinson, 472 So. 2d 606 (Ala. 1985).

Cited in Marino v. Smith, 454 So. 2d 1380 (Ala. 1984).

§ 43-8-115. Discharge of debtor from liability for wages, etc., owed intestate former employee of another; status of funds paid under this section.

(a) Whenever an employee of another shall die intestate and there shall be due him or her any sum as wages or salary the debtor may discharge himself from liability therefor by paying such amount to the surviving spouse of the deceased employee or, if there is no surviving spouse to the person having the legal custody and control of his or her minor child or children, or either as the case may be, who may commence an action for and recover the same as part of the property or allowance exempted to them.

(b) Any sums paid in accordance with the provisions of subsection (a) of this section shall be considered as part of the exempt property, as defined in section 43-8-111; and, if the sums exceed $3,500.00 the excess shall be considered part of the family allowance, as defined in section 43-8-112. (Acts 1984, 1st Ex. Sess., No. 84-788, p. 179.)

ARTICLE 7.

WILLS GENERALLY.

Division 1.

Execution of Will.

§ 43-8-130. Who may make a will.

I. GENERAL CONSIDERATION.

In order to execute a valid will, a testator must understand the business and consequences of making a will; he or she must remember the property to be devised, the persons who are the natural objects of his or her bounty, and the manner in which the disposition of the property is to occur. The law presumes that every person of full age has such testamentary capacity. A person may make a valid will even though he or she is not competent to transact the ordinary business of life. Barnes v. Willis, 497 So. 2d 90 (Ala. 1986).

"Sound mind" test still remains the standard for determining testamentary capacity. This holding merely requires that the factual question of testamentary capacity be determined at the § 26-7A-7 hearing, rather than when the will is contested. It is possible that one who is sufficiently mentally incapacitated to require a curator may still possess mental capacity to make a will because testamentary capacity may be less than the competency to transact the ordinary business of life. A determination to appoint a curator is not an adjudication of testamentary capacity. In regard to situations where the ward is physically incapacitated but mentally competent, the statute may still be applicable and provide a measure of protection. Barnes v. Willis, 497 So. 2d 90 (Ala. 1986).

Ward of court. — The statutory phrase itself—"any instrument in writing" in § 26-7A-7—clearly includes a will, which is a common and traditional instrument for the disposition of property. Furthermore, when an incapacitated individual attempts to make a will, the situation presents a ripe opportunity for designing persons to take advantage of the individual, which the curatorship statutes are generally intended to prevent. The legislature is authorized to treat the act of making a will as one needing the protection of the court. Therefore, a will is an "instrument in writing" within the meaning of § 26-7A-7. If a ward desires to make a legally effective will, then notice and hearing must be provided, and the court's approval must be obtained in accordance with the statute. Barnes v. Willis, 497 So. 2d 90 (Ala. 1986).

Cited in Board of Trustees v. Calhoun, 514 So. 2d 895 (Ala. 1987).

Collateral references.

Electronic tape recording as will. 42 ALR4th 176.

§ 43-8-131. Execution and signature of will; witnesses.

I. GENERAL CONSIDERATION.

Alabama law has rejected the idea of permitting holographic wills in the historic sense (i.e., a will entirely in the handwriting of the testator and valid without witnesses) to be validly executed in Alabama, unless the testator is a nonresident. The rule in Alabama is that an instrument must be subscribed by at least two witnesses to be valid as a will. Thus, a probate court has no jurisdiction to probate an instrument not attested properly. Black v. Seals, 474 So. 2d 696 (Ala. 1985).

Signature required. — Without the signature of the testator, the document fails to satisfy the statutuory requirements and there can be no will. Board of Trustees v. Calhoun, 514 So. 2d 895 (Ala. 1987).

Document with signature of one witness not valid will. — Where nurse witnessed and signed will, and two additional persons, daughter of testatrix and husband of other daughter, witnessed the will but did not sign as witnesses until after the death of the testatrix, the document bearing the signature of one witness was not subject to probate as a valid will pursuant to Alabama's Uniform Probate Code. Pope v. Clark, 551 So. 2d 1053 (Ala. 1988).

Cited in Logan v. Citizens Nat'l Bank, 460 So. 2d 1239 (Ala. 1984); Tyson v. Tyson, 521 So. 2d 956 (Ala. 1988).

Collateral references.

Electronic tape recording as will. 42 ALR4th 176.

§ 43-8-132. Self-proved will — Form and execution; how attested will made self-proved; effect.

(a) Any will may be simultaneously executed, attested, and made self-proved, by acknowledgment thereof by the testator and affidavits of the witnesses, each made before an officer authorized to administer oaths under the laws of the state where execution occurs and evidenced by the officer's certificate, under official seal, in substantially the following form:

"I, _____, the testator, sign my name to this instrument this ____ day of _____, 19___, and being first duly sworn, do hereby declare to the undersigned authority that I sign and execute this instrument as my last will and that I sign it willingly (or willingly direct another to sign for me), that I execute it as my free and voluntary act for the purposes therein expressed, and that I am 18 years of age or older, of sound mind, and under no constraint or undue influence."

_____

Testator

"We, _____, the witnesses, sign our names to this instrument, being first duly sworn, and do hereby declare to the undersigned authority that the testator signs and executes this instrument as his last will and that he signs it willingly (or willingly directs another to sign for him), and that each of us, in the presence and hearing of the testator, hereby signs this will as witness to the testator's signing, and that to the best of our knowledge the testator is 18 years of age or older, of sound mind, and under no constraint or undue influence."

_____
Witness

_____
Witness

State of _____
County of _____
　　Subscribed, sworn to and acknowledged before me by _____, the testator and subscribed and sworn to before me by _____, and _____, witnesses, this _____ day of _____, 19____.

SEAL　　　　　　　　　　　　　(Signed) _____

_____
(Official Capacity of Officer)

　　(b) An attested will may at any time subsequent to its execution be made self-proved by the acknowledgment thereof by the testator and the affidavits of the witnesses, each made before an officer authorized to administer oaths under the laws of the state where the acknowledgment occurs and evidenced by the officer's certificate, under the official seal, attached or annexed to the will in substantially the following form:

"STATE OF _____
"COUNTY OF _____
　　We, _____, _____, and _____, the testator and the witnesses, respectively, whose names are signed to the attached or foregoing instrument, being first duly sworn, do hereby declare to the undersigned authority that the testator signed and executed the instrument as his last will and that he had signed willingly (or willingly directed another to sign for him), and that he executed it as his free and voluntary act for the purposes therein expressed, and that each of the witnesses, in the presence and hearing of the testator, signed the will as witness and that to the best of his knowledge the testator was at that time 18 years of age or older, of sound mind and under no constraint or undue influence."

_____
Testator

_____
Witness

_____
Witness

　　"Subscribed, sworn to and acknowledged before me by _____, the testator, and subscribed and sworn to before me by _____, and _____, witnesses, this _____ day of _____, 19____.
SEAL　　　　　　　　　　　　　(Signed) _____

_____
(Official capacity of officer)

(c) If the will is self-proved, as provided in this section, compliance with signature requirements for execution is conclusively presumed, other requirements of execution are presumed subject to rebuttal without the testimony of any witness, and the will shall be probated without further proof, unless there is proof of fraud or forgery affecting the acknowledgment or affidavit. (Acts 1981, 3rd Ex. Sess., No. 81-1209; Code 1975, § 43-1-30.1; Acts 1984, No. 84-258, p. 426, § 1.)

§ 43-8-136. Revocation by writing or by act; when witnesses required.

I. GENERAL CONSIDERATION.

This section clearly contemplates two essential elements in order to effectuate revocation of a will: There must be performance of one or more of the specified acts to a degree that materially and permanently destroys the efficacy of the document, and the testator must intend for the act to revoke the will; one without the other is insufficient to effectively revoke a will. Board of Trustees v. Calhoun, 514 So. 2d 895 (Ala. 1987).

Removal of signature. — The act of the testator in cutting out, erasing, or otherwise obliterating his or her signature on the instrument, or the removal of the signature page, is sufficient to revoke the entire will, when performed with such intent. Board of Trustees v. Calhoun, 514 So. 2d 895 (Ala. 1987).

The fact that the signature page of the will was detached and missing created a rebuttable presumption of animo revocandi. Board of Trustees v. Calhoun, 514 So. 2d 895 (Ala. 1987).

Where will was in the possession and control of the testator, it was presumed that missing signature page was removed and destroyed with the intention of revoking the will. Board of Trustees v. Calhoun, 514 So. 2d 895 (Ala. 1987).

The fact that the testator had executed previous wills that contained similar bequests did not indicate the testator's intent at the time the signature page of the will was removed, and it was insufficient to overcome the presumption that at the time the signature page was removed the testator intended to revoke her entire will. Board of Trustees v. Calhoun, 514 So. 2d 895 (Ala. 1987).

Collateral references.

Revocation of prior will by revocation clause in lost will or other lost instrument. 31 ALR4th 306.

Sufficiency of evidence of nonrevocation of lost will not shown to have been inaccessible to testator—modern cases. 70 ALR4th 323.

§ 43-8-137. Revocation by divorce or annulment; revival by remarriage; no revocation by other changes or circumstances.

I. GENERAL CONSIDERATION.

Collateral references.

Prior institution of annulment proceedings or other attack on validity of one's marriage as barring or estopping one from entitlement to property rights as surviving spouse. 31 ALR4th 1190.

Sufficiency of provision for, or reference to, prospective spouse to avoid lapse or revocation of will by subsequent marriage. 38 ALR4th 117.

§ 43-8-138. When will revived on revocation of subsequent will.

I. GENERAL CONSIDERATION.

Collateral references.

Revocation of prior will by revocation clause in lost will or other lost instrument. 31 ALR4th 306.

Sufficiency of evidence of nonrevocation of lost will not shown to have been inaccessible to testator—modern cases. 70 ALR4th 323.

§ 43-8-139. Incorporation by reference.

Alabama adheres to doctrine of incorporation by reference. Tierce v. Macadonia United Methodist Church, 519 So. 2d 451 (Ala. 1987).

The document which is to be incorporated must have been in existence at the time the will was executed, it must be referred to in the will, and it must be identified by clear and satisfactory proof as the paper referred to. Tierce v. Macadonia United Methodist Church, 519 So. 2d 451 (Ala. 1987).

Collateral references.

Electronic tape recording as will. 42 ALR4th 176.

§ 43-8-140. Testamentary additions to trusts.

This section provides that revocation of the inter vivos trust underlying testator's pour-over scheme results in lapse of any devise in will to that trust. This is perhaps a legislative determination that a testator, by such a revocation, evidences an intent that the devise is to be distributed according to a residuary clause or by intestacy, rather than by the terms of the trust. Tierce v. Macadonia United Methodist Church, 519 So. 2d 451 (Ala. 1987).

Collateral references.

Validity of voting trust created by will. 77 ALR4th 1194.

§ 43-8-141. Reference to events of independent significance.

"Facts of independent significance." — The chief requirement of the doctrine of "facts of independent significance," is that the document referred to in the will have a separate legal identify and existence, and not be solely for the purpose of supplementing the will. Tierce v. Macadonia United Methodist Church, 519 So. 2d 451 (Ala. 1987).

Division 2.

Probate of Will.

§ 43-8-161. Time limit for probate.

A will is ineffective until duly probated. — No court can take notice of or give effect to a will until probated. Davis v. Townsend, 435 So. 2d 1280 (Ala. 1983).

Merely giving a will to a probate court for recordation in the will book does not constitute "filing for probate" within the meaning of this section. There must be evidence that the person intended to probate the will. Guyton v. LaBossiere, 423 So. 2d 841 (Ala. 1982).

Section is a statute of limitations.

This section is a statute of limitations, which must be pled in order to be enforced. Hollis v. Wallace, 481 So. 2d 875 (Ala. 1985).

And is tolled where fraud is proven.

If the existence of a will is fraudulently concealed from the proponent, he is effectively precluded from filing a petition for probate, whether it is the contestant or some third party who is guilty of concealing the will's existence. The proponent should not be deprived of the opportunity to establish his right to the property by the fraudulent concealment of the will by an heir at law of the deceased who, by concealing the existence of the will, seeks to obtain property rights to which he is not entitled. Vandegrift v. Lagrone, 477 So. 2d 292 (Ala. 1985).

Filing within one year of discovery of fraud. — While as a general rule wills which are not filed for probate within five years after the testator's death are ineffective, if the proponent's failure to file a timely petition to probate the will is occasioned by fraud, the filing of the petition within one year from the time the petitioner discovered, or by reasonable diligence should have discovered, the fraud is effective as a timely filing. Vandegrift v. Lagrone, 477 So. 2d 292 (Ala. 1985).

This section could not be raised as a defense in an interpleader action by one who failed to contest probate of will or to timely remove probate to circuit court, as to do so would be to bring a collateral attack on the probate proceedings, and a judgment or decree of probate may not be collaterally attacked or impeached unless it is plainly void or has been made without jurisdiction. Hollis v. Wallace, 481 So. 2d 875 (Ala. 1985).

Collateral references.
Fraud as extending statutory limitations period for contesting will or its probate. 48 ALR4th 1094.

§ 43-8-167. Mode of proving will generally.

Where sole surviving attesting witness denies signing will, other evidence, proving execution, admissible. — Where the sole surviving attesting witness denies that she affixed her signature to the will as an attesting witness, other evidence may be admitted to prove the execution and attestation. To disallow such secondary evidence would be contrary to the underlying purpose of the statute, which is to discover and make effective the intent of a decedent in the distribution of his property. London v. Harris, 507 So. 2d 468 (Ala. 1987).

§ 43-8-172. Protection of bona fide purchasers, etc.

Cited in Hollis v. Wallace, 481 So. 2d 875 (Ala. 1985).

Division 3.

Contesting Validity of Will.

§ 43-8-190. Who may contest will; filing objections; making up issue; trial by jury.

I. GENERAL CONSIDERATION.

The language of this section is mandatory. Summerhill v. Craft, 425 So. 2d 1055 (Ala. 1982).
Cited in Simpson v. Jones, 460 So. 2d 1282 (Ala. 1984).

II. CONTEST PRIOR TO PROBATE.

No contest under this section after probate, etc.
In providing for the contest of a will before the probate thereof, this section requires the filing of the contest in the probate court before a final judgment, order, or decree is rendered admitting the will to probate. Steele v. Sullivan, 484 So. 2d 422 (Ala. 1986).

III. WHO MAY CONTEST.

Not every interested person need be made a party to a contest conducted before the will has been probated. Hart v. Jackson, 510 So. 2d 202 (Ala. 1987).
Meaning of, etc.
In accord with second paragraph of bound volume. See Guyton v. LaBossiere, 423 So. 2d 841 (Ala. 1982).

V. TRIAL BY JURY.

Purported common law wife's request for jury trial denied. — In a probate proceeding in which the purported common law wife filed a motion for determination of widowhood, the probate court did not err in striking her request for jury trial, where she did not file a contest to the will, which would have carried a right to a jury trial, but had merely filed a claim as an omitted spouse, since there is no common law right to a trial by jury in the probate court. Kemp v. Kroutter, 531 So. 2d 854 (Ala. 1988).

VI. PROCEEDINGS AND JUDGMENT.

The jurisdiction of the probate court to entertain all proceedings contesting a will is a statutory and limited jurisdiction. Summerhill v. Craft, 425 So. 2d 1055 (Ala. 1982).
The probate court is required to transfer a contest after the demand to transfer is made, it retains no further jurisdiction to hold a hearing to probate the will nor to issue an order that the will was duly proved. Summerhill v. Craft, 425 So. 2d 1055 (Ala. 1982).
After probate, court has no jurisdiction, etc.
In accord with bound volume. See Steele v. Sullivan, 484 So. 2d 422 (Ala. 1986).

§ 43-8-195. Admission or rejection of will.

Collateral references.
Sufficiency of evidence to support grant of summary judgment in will probate or contest proceedings. 53 ALR4th 561.

§ 43-8-196. Costs.

Cited in Bleidt v. Kantor, 412 So. 2d 769 (Ala. 1982).

§ 43-8-198. Transfer of contest to circuit court; appeal from judgment of circuit court; certification of judgment, etc., to probate court.

The language of this section is mandatory. Summerhill v. Craft, 425 So. 2d 1055 (Ala. 1982).

Jurisdiction statutory and limited.
In accord with first paragraph in bound volume. See Steele v. Sullivan, 484 So. 2d 422 (Ala. 1986).

The jurisdiction conferred on the circuit court by this section is a statutory and limited jurisdiction. Kaller ex rel. Conway v. Rigdon, 480 So. 2d 536 (Ala. 1985).

It is clear that will contest jurisdiction, being statutorily conferred, must comply with the statutory language strictly in order to quicken jurisdiction of the appropriate court. Bullen v. Brown, 535 So. 2d 76 (Ala. 1988).

Procedure must be complied with exactly. — Because will contest jurisdiction is statutorily conferred, the procedural requirements of the applicable statute must be complied with exactly. Kaller ex rel. Conway v. Rigdon, 480 So. 2d 536 (Ala. 1985).

Transfer must be demanded at time of initial pleading. — This section mandates that, in order to transfer to the circuit court a valid contest of a will not yet admitted to probate, and thereby to confer proper jurisdiction upon the circuit court, a party must demand transfer at the time he files his initial pleading. Kaller ex rel. Conway v. Rigdon, 480 So. 2d 536 (Ala. 1985).

"Initial pleadings" must be first responsive pleading after filing of will contest. — While the proponent of a will files a pleading when he files the petition for probate of the will, this pleading cannot serve as a proponent's "initial pleading" for purposes of this section. Were it to be so regarded, a proponent would never have an opportunity to transfer a will contest, since at the time he files a petition for probate no will contest has yet been filed. Logically then, the "initial pleading" for the proponent of a will must be the first responsive pleading after a will contest has been filed.

Kaller ex rel. Conway v. Rigdon, 480 So. 2d 536 (Ala. 1985).

Thus proponent can only demand transfer when he files answer. — The proponent of a will must file an answer as his responsive pleading to the complaint brought by the contestant. Since this is his initial pleading in the will contest, a proponent can only make a motion to transfer when he files an answer. Kaller ex rel. Conway v. Rigdon, 480 So. 2d 536 (Ala. 1985).

Failure to file pleading at same time as motion to transfer. — Although proponent filed motions and papers with regard to will contest, where proponent did not file a pleading at the same time he filed the motion to transfer, he did not comply with the procedures mandated by this section, and thus the circuit court lacked jurisdiction to try the contest. Kaller ex rel. Conway v. Rigdon, 480 So. 2d 536 (Ala. 1985).

Circuit court's lack of jurisdiction over a will contest can be raised at any time. Kaller ex rel. Conway v. Rigdon, 480 So. 2d 536 (Ala. 1985).

Statute of limitations held to have run prior to will contest. — Where the heirs filed a motion for a continuance in order to have an expert examine the purported signature of the testator but did not attack the validity of the signature in that motion, nor did they in any other manner attack the validity of the will, there was no contest of the will in the probate court when the heirs petitioned the circuit court for the removal of the estate to circuit court on the ground that it could best be administered in that court, and the petition for removal itself was not a complaint. Since neither the motion for a continuance nor the petition for transfer constituted a complaint, and thus, if § 43-8-199 was thought to authorize the heirs' action, nothing had been filed to toll the operation of the six-month limitation under that statute, and it was not until after eight months later that the heirs alleged any grounds for contesting the will, the statute of limitations contained in § 43-8-199 had run before the heirs' complaint was filed. Bullen v. Brown, 535 So. 2d 76 (Ala. 1988).

§ 43-8-199. Contest in circuit court after admission to probate — Generally.

I. GENERAL CONSIDERATION.

Purpose of section.
This section was enacted to provide an additional opportunity for contesting a will already admitted to probate. Simpson v. Jones, 460 So. 2d 1282 (Ala. 1984).

Effect of section.
This section mandates that, in order to commence a valid contest of a will already admitted to probate, a person with an interest in the will file a complaint in circuit court and quicken that court's jurisdiction of the contest. Simpson v. Jones, 460 So. 2d 1282 (Ala. 1984).

This section provides the sole remedy where a person interested in an estate fails to join a will contest in probate court. Hollis v. Wallace, 481 So. 2d 875 (Ala. 1985).

Jurisdiction statutory and limited.
It is clear that will contest jurisdiction, being statutorily conferred, must comply with the statutory language strictly in order to quicken jurisdiction of the appropriate court. Bullen v. Brown, 535 So. 2d 76 (Ala. 1988).

Where more than six months have expired before the petition to remove is filed, application of this section is barred. Hollis v. Wallace, 481 So. 2d 875 (Ala. 1985).

Section 43-8-161 could not be raised as a defense in an interpleader action by one who failed to contest probate of will or to timely remove probate to circuit court, as to do so would be to bring a collateral attack on the probate proceedings, and a judgment or decree of probate may not be collaterally attacked or impeached unless it is plainly void or has been made without jurisdiction. Hollis v. Wallace, 481 So. 2d 875 (Ala. 1985).

Commencement of an action under this section is the commencement of a statutory, adversarial proceeding. Simpson v. Jones, 460 So. 2d 1282 (Ala. 1984).

Jurisdiction of probate courts. — While the plain and clear language of this section, speaks only to the circuit court's jurisdiction in will contests, to say that such nomenclature deprives those probate courts in the appropriately populated counties via Acts 1961, No. 974, from any post-probate jurisdiction would, in the court's view, read such act right out of existence. Acts 1961, No. 974, enacted subsequent to this section, must be given its clear meaning and effect must be given to its obvious purpose. Coleman v. Richardson, 421 So. 2d 113 (Ala. 1982).

Cited in Montgomery v. Burchell, 456 So. 2d 60 (Ala. 1984); Burch v. Burgess, 521 So. 2d 921 (Ala. 1988).

Collateral references.
Fraud as extending statutory limitations period for contesting will or its probate. 48 ALR4th 1094.

Sufficiency of evidence to support grant of summary judgment in will probate or contest proceedings. 53 ALR4th 561.

II. WHO MAY CONTEST.

In order to be considered an "interested person" and have standing to contest a will, an individual must, at the time of probate, have some interest that would be injuriously affected by the establishment of the contested will and to maintain a will contest, it is essential that the contestant have a real, beneficial interest, not simply an expectancy or an inchoate right. Ames ex rel. Parker v. Reeves, 553 So. 2d 570 (Ala. 1989).

III. THE CONTEST AFTER ADMISSION TO PROBATE.

A. Nature.

The jurisdiction of the circuit court, etc.
Where action to contest a will was first filed in the probate court and later transferred to circuit court, contestant did not properly file in circuit court so as to invoke jurisdiction under this section. Kelley v. English, 439 So. 2d 26 (Ala. 1983).

Once the trial court determined that certain persons necessary to the adjudication of the contest were not named as parties in initial complaint, it was incumbent upon the court to order that such persons be made parties to the contest. Hons v. A. Bertolla & Sons, 537 So. 2d 456 (Ala. 1988).

Section 43-8-200 does not require the contestant to include all parties interested in the will in his complaint, and certainly did not require that this be done within the six-month time period set out in this section, since § 43-8-200 is merely a codification of the longstanding rule that certain persons, such as devisees, heirs, etc., of the testator are "indispensable parties" to a will contest, and therefore, after a will contest is properly instituted in circuit court, they must be made parties to the contest. Hons v. A. Bertolla & Sons, 537 So. 2d 456 (Ala. 1988).

Contest filed too late.

Where the heirs filed a motion for a continuance in order to have an expert examine the purported signature of the testator but did not attack the validity of the signature in that motion, nor did they in any other manner attack the validity of the will there was no contest of the will in the probate court when the heirs petitioned the circuit court for the removal of the estate to circuit court on the ground that it could best be administered in that court, and the petition for removal itself was not a complaint. Neither the motion for a continuance nor the petition for transfer constituted a complaint, and thus, if this section

was thought to authorize the heirs' action, nothing had been filed to toll the operation of the six-month limitation under that statute, and it was not until after eight months later that the heirs alleged any grounds for contesting the will; hence, the statute of limitations contained in this section had run before the heirs' complaint was filed. Bullen v. Brown, 535 So. 2d 76 (Ala. 1988).

C. Issues and Judgment.

Summary judgment proper. — Plaintiff's failure to produce any evidence that the property was not purchased with partnership funds or to rebut the presumption in subsection (b) authorized the trial court to grant summary judgment in favor of the personal representatives. Hons v. A. Bertolla & Sons, 537 So. 2d 456 (Ala. 1988).

§ 43-8-200. Same — Parties; conclusiveness of judgment.

Once it is determined that a person, not named as a party to the contest, is within one of the categories of "interested" parties listed in this section and is therefore a necessary or indispensable party under this section, the court must order that he be made a party to the contest. Hons v. A. Bertolla & Sons, 537 So. 2d 456 (Ala. 1988).

This section is analogous to the joinder of persons needed for just adjudication as set out in Rule 19, A.R.Civ.P. Hons v. A. Bertolla & Sons, 537 So. 2d 456 (Ala. 1988).

This section does not require the contestant to include all parties interested in the will in his complaint, and certainly did not require that this be done within the six-month

time period set out in § 43-8-199, since this section is merely a codification of the long-standing rule that certain persons, such as devisees, heirs, etc., of the testator are "indispensable parties" to a will contest, and therefore, after a will contest is properly instituted in circuit court, they must be made parties to the contest. Hons v. A. Bertolla & Sons, 537 So. 2d 456 (Ala. 1988).

Once the trial court determined that certain persons necessary to the adjudication of the contest were not named as parties in the initial complaint, it was incumbent upon the court to order that such persons be made parties to the contest. Hons v. A. Bertolla & Sons, 537 So. 2d 456 (Ala. 1988).

§ 43-8-201. Same — Additional time for contest by infants and persons of unsound mind.

Cited in Garmon v. Moon, 438 So. 2d 299 (Ala. 1983).

ARTICLE 8.

CONSTRUCTION OF WILLS.

§ 43-8-221. Choice of law as to meaning and effect of wills.

Collateral references.
Wills: effect of gift or specified percentage or share of estate (or residuary estate) to include specific property found to be of a greater value than share bequeathed. 63 ALR4th 1186.

§ 43-8-222. Controlling effect of intention of testator.

Will considered as a whole. — In determining the intent of the testator, the court will consider the instrument as a whole and not just a single bequest. Matthews v. Matthews, 477 So. 2d 391 (Ala. 1985).
Collateral references. — Requirement that holographic will, or its material provisions, be entirely in testator's handwriting as affected by appearance of some printed or written matter not in testator's handwriting. 37 ALR4th 528.

Wills: effect of gift or specified percentage or share of estate (or residuary estate) to include specific property found to be of a greater value than share bequeathed. 63 ALR4th 1186.

§ 43-8-223. Construction of will to pass all property, including after-acquired property.

Collateral references.
Determination of, and charges against, "augmented estate" upon which share of spouse electing to take against will is determined under Uniform Probate Code § 2-202. 63 ALR4th 1173.

Wills: effect of gift or specified percentage or share of estate (or residuary estate) to include specific property found to be of a greater value than share bequeathed. 63 ALR4th 1186.

§ 43-8-224. Anti-lapse provision; applicability to deceased devisees and to class gifts.

Collateral references.
Effect of impossibility of performance of condition precedent to testamentary gift. 40 ALR4th 193.

§ 43-8-225. Effect of failure of testamentary provisions.

Redemption of stock subject to specific bequest. — Where, at the time of testator's death, all 150 shares of stock that he had specifically bequeathed to his ex-wife had been redeemed by corporation, and there were no securities of this type in the estate at the time of his death, no other securities of the same entity, no securities of another entity derived from those securities, and no additional securities of the entity owned by the testator in a plan of reinvestment, under § 43-8-226 testator's ex-wife was not entitled to receive any part of that stock, including the proceeds of the redemption, upon the death of the testator. The proceeds of the redemption would be included in the testator's estate as part of the residue under this section. Matthews v. Matthews, 477 So. 2d 391 (Ala. 1985).
Collateral references.
Ademption of bequest of debt or balance on debt. 25 ALR4th 88.
Effect of impossibility of performance of condition precedent to testamentary gift. 40 ALR4th 193.
Wills: effect of gift or specified percentage or share of estate (or residuary estate) to include specific property found to be of a greater value than share bequeathed. 63 ALR4th 1186.

§ 43-8-226. Specific devise of securities; change in securities; accessions; nonademption.

Code commissioner's note. — The reference in the commentary to "§ 19-3-273" should be "§ 19-3-274."

Bequests held specific. — Bequests of stock by the testator, included in the same sentence of the will with the bequest of "One (1) bedroom suite, mahogany, consisting of bedstead, mattress and springs, 6-drawer chest, 4-drawer chest and nite table; and my stereo with the cabinet and all records," were specific bequests. Matthews v. Matthews, 477 So. 2d 391 (Ala. 1985).

Redemption of stock subject to specific bequest. — Where, at the time of testator's death, all 150 shares of stock that he had bequeathed to his ex-wife had been redeemed by corporation, and there were no securities of this type in the estate at the time of his death, no other securities of the same entity, no securities of another entity derived from those securities, and no additional securities of the entity owned by the testator in a plan of reinvestment, under this section, testator's ex-wife was not entitled to receive any part of that stock, including the proceeds of the redemption, upon the death of the testator. The proceeds of the redemption would be included in the testator's estate as part of the residue under § 43-8-225. Matthews v. Matthews, 477 So. 2d 391 (Ala. 1985).

§ 43-8-227. Nonademption of specific devises in certain cases; proceeds of sale, condemnation, insurance or foreclosure; sale by guardian or curator.

Collateral references.
Effect of impossibility of performance of condition precedent to testamentary gift. 40 ALR4th 193.

§ 43-8-230. Construction of generic terms to accord with relationships as defined for intestate succession; when person born out of wedlock treated as child of father.

Collateral references.
Word "child" or "children" in will as including grandchild or grandchildren. 30 ALR4th 319.

§ 43-8-231. Ademption by satisfaction.

I. GENERAL CONSIDERATION.

Collateral references.
Wills: effect of gift or specified percentage or share of estate (or residuary estate) to include specific property found to be of a greater value than share bequeathed. 63 ALR4th 1186.

ARTICLE 9.

MISCELLANEOUS PROVISIONS.

§ 43-8-250. Contracts concerning succession, etc.; no presumption of nonrevocation from joint or mutual wills.

Collateral references.
Antenuptial contracts: parties' behavior during marriage as abandonment, estoppel, or waiver regarding contractual rights. 56 ALR4th 998.

§ 43-8-252. Effect of divorce, annulment, or decree of separation.

I. GENERAL CONSIDERATION.

Cited in Garrard v. Lang, 489 So. 2d 557 (Ala. 1986).

Collateral references.
Prior institution of annulment proceedings or other attack on validity of one's marriage as barring or estopping one from entitlement to property rights as surviving spouse. 31 ALR4th 1190.

§ 43-8-253. Effect of homicide on intestate succession, wills, joint assets, life insurance and beneficiary designations; effect of bona fide purchase by third party or good faith payment by obligor, etc.

Collateral references.
Homicide as precluding taking under will or by intestacy. 25 ALR4th 787.

ARTICLE 10.

CUSTODY OF WILLS.

§ 43-8-270. Duty of custodian of will after death of testator; liability.

Collateral references.
Involuntary disclosure or surrender of will prior to testator's death. 75 ALR4th 1144.

ARTICLE 11.

UNIFORM DISCLAIMER OF PROPERTY INTERESTS.

§ 43-8-291. Right to disclaim interest in property.

Collateral references.
Creditor's right to prevent debtor's renunciation of benefit under will or debtor's election to take under will. 39 ALR4th 633.

§ 43-8-294. Effect of disclaimer.

Disclaimer by son of decedent constituted a transfer of his interests in the personal property of his father's estate to his son. Pennington v. Bigham, 512 So. 2d 1344 (Ala. 1987).

§ 43-8-295. Waiver and bar.

The right to disclaim property or an interest therein is barred if the property is encumbered. Therefore, by virtue of the judgment creditor's lien, the son's disclaimer of interest in the real property that his father owned at the time of his death was of no effect. Pennington v. Bigham, 512 So. 2d 1344 (Ala. 1987).

TITLE 44.

YOUTH SERVICES.

CHAPTER 1.

DEPARTMENT OF YOUTH SERVICES AND YOUTH SERVICES BOARD.

ARTICLE 2.

DEPARTMENT OF YOUTH SERVICES.

§ 44-1-22. Employees of department.

Cited in Parks v. Department of Youth Servs., 439 So. 2d 690 (Ala. 1983).

§ 44-1-27. Standards for programs and youth detention facilities; licensing and inspection of youth detention and foster care facilities.

Cross references. — As to department of public safety providing criminal conviction information on applicants for positions of child care and treatment, including foster parents, see § 26-1-4.

Collateral references. — Foster parent's right to immunity from foster child's negligence claims. 55 ALR4th 778.

§ 44-1-28. Subsidies for youth detention facilities.

Cited in Coosa Valley Youth Servs. Corp. v. Etowah County, 460 So. 2d 1232 (Ala. 1984).

§ 44-1-32. Determination of social service plan.

Negligently released juvenile offender. — The mere fact that the department of youth services may have violated their duties as set out in this section did not mean that it deprived a woman, raped by a negligently released juvenile offender, of her rights without due process of law under federal civil rights statutes. Jones v. Phyfer, 761 F.2d 642 (11th Cir.), rehearing denied, 768 F.2d 1353 (11th Cir. 1985).

§ 44-1-39. Restrictions on release or use of records.

Collateral references. — What constitutes legitimate research justifying inspection of state or local public records not open to inspection by general public. 40 ALR4th 333.

ARTICLE 4.

YOUTH SERVICES DEPARTMENT DISTRICT.

Cross references. — As to advancement of meeting expenses of members and employees of county and city boards of education by the Department of Youth School District and the Alabama Institute for Deaf and Blind, see § 16-13-14.

CHAPTER 2.

INTERSTATE COMPACT ON JUVENILES.

Article 1.

General Provisions.

Sec.
44-2-8. Rendition amendment to Interstate Compact on Juveniles.

ARTICLE 1.

GENERAL PROVISIONS.

§ 44-2-8. Rendition amendment to Interstate Compact on Juveniles.

(a) This section shall be known as "The Rendition Amendment to the Interstate Compact on Juveniles."

(b) This amendment shall provide additional remedies, and shall be binding only as among and between those party states which specifically execute the same.

(c) All provisions and procedures of articles V and VI of the Interstate Compact on Juveniles shall be construed to apply to any juvenile charged with being a delinquent by reason of a violation of any criminal law. Any juvenile, charged with being a delinquent by reason of violating any criminal law, shall be returned to the requesting state upon a requisition to the state where the juvenile may be found. A petition in such case shall be filed in a court of competent jurisdiction in the requesting state where the violation of criminal law is alleged to have been committed. The petition may be filed regardless of whether the juvenile has left the state before or after the filing of the petition. The requisition described in article V of the compact shall be forwarded by the judge of the court in which the petition has been filed. (Acts 1986, No. 86-419, p. 626.)

CHAPTER 3.

REGIONAL CUSTODY AND CARE OF YOUTHS UNDER JURISDICTION OF JUVENILE COURT.

§ 44-3-1. Definitions.

Cited in Coosa Valley Youth Servs. Corp. v. Etowah County, 460 So. 2d 1232 (Ala. 1984).